Wherever Green is Worn

Tim Pat Coogan is one of the best known figures in Ireland. Author, broadcaster and former editor of the *Irish Press*, he has written several books, including two definitive works, *The Troubles* and *The IRA*; the pioneering study, *Ireland Since the Rising*; *On the Blanket*; and a number of others including his bestselling autobiographies *Michael Collins* and *De Valera*.

Praise for Tim Pat Coogan:

Michael Collins
'Superb ... What most impressed me about the book is the author's manifest and passionate desire to discover and tell the truth of a fearsome story still veiled by lies, partisan propaganda and, above all, myth.'
Paul Johnson, *TLS*

De Valera
'Essential reading'
Lord Longford in the *Evening Standard*

The Troubles
'He touches on every issue of significance and enlivens a horrific story with wit ... *The Troubles* will be essential reading for any future scholar of Irish peace-making.'
Observer

Wherever Green is Worn

The Story of the Irish Diaspora

Tim Pat Coogan

arrow books

To the achievements of the Irish,
and may reverence never descend upon us

Published by Arrow Books in 2002

7 9 10 8

Copyright © Tim Pat Coogan 2000

The right of Tim Pat Coogan to be identified as the author of this work has
been asserted by him in accordance with the Copyright, Designs and Patents
Act, 1988

First published in the United Kingdom in 2000 by Hutchinson

Arrow Books
The Random House Group Limited
20 Vauxhall Bridge Road, London SW1V 2SA

www.randomhouse.co.uk

Addresses for companies within The Random House Group Limited can be found at:
www.randomhouse.co.uk/offices.htm

The Random House Group Limited Reg. No. 954009

A CIP catalogue record for this book
is available from the British Library

ISBN 9780099958505

The Random House Group Limited supports The Forest Stewardship
Council® (FSC®), the leading international forest-certification organisation.
Our books carrying the FSC label are printed on FSC®-certified paper.
FSC is the only forest-certification scheme supported by the leading
environmental organisations, including Greenpeace. Our
paper procurement policy can be found at
www.randomhouse.co.uk/environment

Printed and bound in Great Britain by Clays Ltd, St Ives PLC

CONTENTS

THE MUSIC-MAKERS

Arthur O'Shaughnessy

We are the music-makers,
   And we are the dreamers of dreams,
Wandering by lone sea-breakers,
   And sitting by desolate streams:
World-losers and world-forsakers,
   On whom the pale moon gleams:
Yet we are the movers and shakers
   Of the world for ever, it seems.

With wonderful deathless ditties
We build up the world's great cities,
   And out of a fabulous story
   We fashion an empire's glory:
   One man with a dream, at pleasure,
   Shall go forth and conquer a crown;
And three with a new song's measure
   Can trample an empire down.

We, in the ages lying
   In the buried past of the earth,
Built Nineveh with our sighing,
   And Babel itself with our mirth;
And o'erthrew them with prophesying
   To the old of the new world's worth;
For each age is a dream that is dying,
   Or one that is coming to birth.

ILLUSTRATIONS

FIRST SECTION

Cambrai ms., containing the longest surviving passage in Old Irish (*Bibliothèque, Cambrai*)
Carrying the relics, 1789 and 1998 (*E. O'hAnnracháin*)
Irish emigration, as seen in a British cartoon (*Hulton Getty Picture Collection*)
The priest's blessing (*Topham Picturepoint*)
The quay at Cobh (*Topham Picturepoint*)
The coffin ship (*Hulton Getty Picture Collection*)
Emigrants to Canada, 1929 (*Hulton Getty Picture Collection*)
Working on the *Jeanie Johnston* (*PA News*)
Poster for Michael O'Leary VC (*PA News*)
An Irish girl arrives in Britain (*Hulton Getty Picture Collection*)
Pictures from the Paddy Fahey Collection (*Brent Archives*)
Gerald Conlon on release (*PA News*)
The Birmingham Six on release (*PA News*)
Celtic fans parade their colours (*PA News*)
Young drummer on Orange Lodge march in Glasgow (*PA News*)
Rhodri Morgan with Dr J. J. Lynch, Director of FAS (*FAS, Frank Fennell Photography*)

SECOND SECTION

Emigrants arrive in the USA (*Topham Picturepoint*)
Tammany Hall (*Hulton Getty Picture Collection*)
President Kennedy visiting Cork (*Hulton Getty Picture Collection*)
The Kennedy family grieves the death of Michael Kennedy (*PA News*)
Archbishop Spellman (*Hulton Getty Picture Collection*)
Archbishop Cushing (*Hulton Getty Picture Collection*)
Irish Canadian lumberjacks (*Hulton Getty Picture Collection*)
John Mitchel (*Hulton Getty Picture Collection*)
Ned Kelly (*Hulton Getty Picture Collection*)
Paul Keating (*PA News*)
Irish soldiers in Lebanon (*Hulton Getty Picture Collection*)
Commander of UNIFIL decorates Irish soldiers (*PA News*)
Bob Geldof (*Hulton Getty Picture Collection*)
Mgr Desmond Hartford, released by kidnappers (*PA News*)
Tony O'Reilly and his wife (*PA News*)

Michael O'Leary, RyanAir (*PA News*)
EU Finance Minister, Charles McCreevy (*PA News*)
George Best (*PA News*)
Sean Fitzpatrick (*PA News*)
Eddie Irvine (*PA News*)
The Corrs (*PA News*)
Brian Moore (*PA News*)
Seamus Heaney (*PA News*)
Pierce Brosnan (*PA News*)
Liam Neeson (*PA News*)
Michael Flatley (*PA News*)

INTRODUCTION

MY AIM IN THIS WORK has been to try to explain why the Irish left Ireland in such numbers, where they went, what triumphs or disasters befell them and, by interviewing representative members of the contemporary diaspora, to tell in their own words how the Irish are faring now. So far as I know, no book of a similar scale to this has ever been attempted. I have travelled extensively in Africa, America, Argentina, Asia, Australia, Canada, the Caribbean and Europe, and yet there are vast areas of the world still unreported – India, China, Russia . . . I would have attempted these had the publisher's deadlines allowed. They remain for another book or another writer. Any of the countries mentioned, to say nothing of the continents, are more than worthy of a book in their own right.

The canvas is so huge that no one book could attempt to describe fully the great outpouring. I have only been able to paint with broad brushstrokes, but I hope that an authentic picture of an important subject has resulted; that I have managed to give a broad general portrait, enlivened by some human, anecdotal detail, of the astonishing story of how a small island, behind an island far out in the Western Atlantic, beyond Europe's rim, added significant enrichment to the human experience. Some 70 million people on the globe are entitled to call themselves Irish – a remarkable statistic when one considers that there are only five million people on the island of Ireland itself, and of these at least 800,000 living in North-Eastern Ireland say they are not Irish at all and describe themselves as British!

As will become apparent in succeeding pages, the Irish diaspora is the outworking of two forms of colonialism, those of Mother England and Mother Church. I have been interested since boyhood in what was then known not as the diaspora, but as emigration. Like nearly every other Irish person of my generation, some of my closest relatives were forced into unwilling emigration. I have always lived near Dun Laoghaire where 'the mailboat' left for Holyhead, in Wales, and the sight of the shabby, set-faced horde pouring down Marine Road and on to those uncomfortable, vomit-producing ferries for dead-end jobs, punctuated by pub and prejudice, was one of the haunting memories of childhood. Nobody talked about those people, nobody did anything for them. Theirs was a fate that did not speak its name – except, from time to time, when drunkenness or fighting caught the attention of the papers. Then there would be head-shakings and comments along the lines of: 'Isn't it terrible to think of them letting down the country?' Denial was all where the emigrants were concerned. Though a certain degree

of acknowledgement did grow over the years, it was along the lines indicated
by Sean Dunne (1956–97) in his poem 'Letter from Ireland':

> The country wears their going like a scar,
> Today their relatives save to support and
> Send others in planes
> For the new diaspora

As I grew older and travelled, my imagination was seized by the extent of
the Irish population in the world outside Ireland and the variety of conditions
in which it lived. The number of people I have bumped into in different parts
of the globe who either lived near me or went to school with me or my
daughters – and increasingly grand-daughters – brought home to me in simple
fashion the scale of the outpouring. I have never lived more than a couple of
miles from where I was born in County Dublin. Yet if one were to make a sort
of statistical template designed to cover the whole country, based on my own
experience of meeting the Irish abroad, then the scale of the haemorrhage
becomes apparent, the origin of that figure of 70 million understandable. The
idea of writing a book took hold in the 1980s. My circumstances had changed.
I wanted to travel, and I wanted a change from writing about the Northern
'Troubles' and Irish historical topics.

I planned to go after my book on Michael Collins was published in October
1990. However, fortunately or unfortunately it was an instant success, and my
publishers thought that my next work should be a biography of his arch rival,
de Valera, with the diaspora book following. Then, the twenty-fifth
anniversary of the coming of British soldiers to Northern Ireland during the
current phase of Anglo-Irish hostilities loomed in 1995, and the publishers
again persuaded me that my next work should be a book spanning the history
of the Troubles. This appeared in the autumn of 1995. Tours and book
signings occupied me until Christmas. I managed some preliminary reading
and contact-making, and finally took off to circumnavigate the globe in
February 1996, the day after the IRA ended their ceasefire with a bomb in
Canary Wharf, London.

It was a terrible, but in a way, appropriate, backdrop because so much of
the Irish diaspora's view of themselves and of their nationality is coloured by
the happenings in Northern Ireland. So many ideas of Irish identity have been
formed by, with or from Britain. Particularly in England, so much of the good
or bad the Irish do is viewed, often unconsciously, against a horrific historical
backdrop. In America, much of the consciousness of being Irish was
awakened by the Troubles. The same is true, although with less political effect,
of the Irish in other parts of the globe:

Abroad, the history of Irish emigration is one of the success stories of the
world. Dispossessed and ravaged by war, famine and centuries of economic
decline, the Irish nevertheless managed to battle their way to pinnacles of
political and economic success, epitomised by the entry to the White House of

John Fitzgerald Kennedy, the descendant of a Famine emigrant from County Wexford. Success was not achieved without great suffering and loss, both in terms of life and human happiness. For some, the dream was never realised and they died nightmarish deaths: on the battlefields of Europe; in the coffin ships in which they fled the Famine; digging canals in the toxic swamps of New Orleans; or of alcoholism in the lonely doss-houses of the British Midlands. Some, however, not only hung on to the lower rungs of the ladder of achievement, but battled their way to the top in the arts, the churches, finance, politics and the armies and navies of the world.

At home, the performance of the so-called Celtic Tiger has resulted in a situation where there is net immigration into Ireland and Irish officials go abroad seeking to persuade Irish emigrants or the descendants of Irish emigrants, to return to Ireland to take up the increasing number of jobs available. As this is being written an item on RTE news is describing how a jobs fair in St John's, Newfoundland, funded by the Irish jobs agency FAS, attracted 5,000 applicants. The next Census is due in the year 2001, and is expected to show a small but significant increase in the population of the Irish republic – literally, a historic turnaround. Sadly however, economic and political conditions in Northern Ireland have dictated that the troubled six North-Eastern counties of contention are still haemorrhaging their best asset – their young people. Young Protestants in particular are taking the emigrant route. As the statistical profile of the elderly is also high – 35 per cent of the largest Protestant sect, the Presbyterians, are over seventy-five – this is an ominous portent for the once dominant Protestant and Unionist people. It would not be the least of the hoped-for dividends if the Peace Process would enable this young, energetic, hard-working component of the Irish family to stay at home.

Today the results of the great scattering of the centuries are chiefly located in North America and in the United Kingdom. From the 1920s onward, Britain became the prime destination for Irish emigrants. Perhaps as many as eight out of ten Irish who left the country in the immediate post-Second World War years headed for the United Kingdom. However, very sizeable proportions of the Irish or Irish descendants can be found in the populations of Australia, Canada and New Zealand, largely as a result of nineteenth- and twentieth-century emigration. Of course, pockets of Irish can also be found anywhere that man has inhabited the globe – there is still a significant Irish population in Argentina for example.

Wars and famines were not the only reason the Irish arrived in places far from home. The cod fish brought them to Newfoundland; a good priest, Father Fahey, brought them to Argentina. However, in general, the pattern of Irish emigration was laid down in the sixteenth century. The Irish had been emigrating to England from the time of the Norman dislocations, nearly four centuries earlier, since the influence of an English Pope and his English advisers first introduced a military and political aspect to the manner in which the Christian inhabitants of the two islands worshipped the same God.

The British began passing laws to contain Irish 'vagrants' shortly after the · Normans arrived in Ireland in the twelfth century. The irritation of the British with 'the Irish question' had begun. As it began, so it would continue. The larger island never saw the problem of the Irish within its shores as having anything to do with the fact that it had invaded the smaller isle.

When invasion began in earnest under Elizabeth I, and the Anglican Reformation was superimposed on Ireland, Catholic Irish emigration may be said to have begun in a major way. In the sixteenth and seventeenth centuries there were four separate waves of emigration stemming from wars in Ireland. In the 1580s the Munster Chieftains set sail for Spain and Portugal. Because the Navigation Acts and the Penal Laws crippled seafaring enterprise, as they did land-based commerce, Ireland is not generally regarded as a maritime country, but these emigrants made a particular impact on the Spanish Navy. The success of the conquest in 1603 made for a further outpouring from Ireland, again largely to Spain, and, to a degree, to Brittany. Cromwell's wars drove regiments and their camp followers to France and Spain in the years 1652 and 1653, and in addition, Cromwell transported several thousands from Ireland to the West Indies and to Virginia. It may be that as many as 35,000 men were shipped out, some 12,000 including women to the West Indies. Later in the seventeenth century, after the Protestant victory which resulted in the Treaty of Limerick in 1691, the celebrated flight of the 'Wild Geese' took place. In this exodus, well in excess of 20,000 men set sail for the regiments of Catholic France, accompanied by their wives and children.

From this time Irish Brigades operated not only in France but also for the Catholic powers of Spain and Austria. Even the Russians were eager to recruit Irish soldiers. Along with the military emigration, a certain mercantile tradition grew up as the Irish established communities in the ports of Western Europe. The influence of some of these merchants, some of whom became known as 'wine geese', is indicated even today by businesses such as the brandy-producing firm of Hennessy, founded by an Irish emigrant from Cork in the eighteenth century, Richard Hennessy.

The eighteenth century also saw the beginning of the Irish presence in a substantial way in the Canadas and in America. The first waves of emigrants were largely composed of Ulster Presbyterians, who left for a combination of reasons: rising rents, falling trade in the linen industry and discrimination against them by the Anglicans. Presbyterian Ulstermen and their families established the Scots/Irish tradition in America. The ending of the Napoleonic Wars in the early part of the nineteenth century, and the subsequent decline in agricultural prices, quickened the pace of both Catholic and Protestant emigration.

Then the great cataclysm of the Famine befell in the 1840s. A huge shoaling outward of panic-stricken people occurred, and Ireland suffered a physical and psychological shock from which it is probably true to say that the country and its people are only recovering in our time. A million died and probably as many as two-and-a-half million people left Ireland in the decade 1845–1855.

They left their country and they founded an empire – for Mother Church. As Sheridan Gilley declared in admiring tones which might not be universally echoed by today's Irish population:

> Quite the most remarkable achievement of nineteenth-century Ireland was the creation of an international Catholic Church, throughout the Celtic diaspora in the British Empire and North America. A true Irish Empire beyond the seas . . .[1]

The achievement was remarkable, but it would be more accurately described as 'a true Vatican empire beyond the seas'. The Irish built the churches of the world, but they bred and they read what their priests and nuns told them to.

Emigration became the Irish leitmotiv. It is calculated that from 1855 to the outbreak of the Great War in 1914, over and above the Famine departures, a further four million left Ireland. Their impact on the world was so colossal that in America for example, it is estimated that some 38 million of the 43 million who at Census time give their ethnic origin as Irish, are of Catholic origin. This sector, the Green tradition, succeeded in launching the contemporary Irish Peace Process in the teeth of opposition from the Protestant Orange tradition, its supporters in the British Conservative Party, and their powerful allies in the American Departments of Justice and State.

The coming of native government to a part of Ireland in 1921 did little to stem the flow of emigration. Over a million left the country in the years 1951–1961 for example. When modern Ireland gained its independence in the early twenties, the twenty-six counties affected, economically speaking, consisted of little more than Guinness's Brewery and a large farm. The country's heavy industry, and most of its taxable capacity, lay in the six North-Eastern counties, which had been partitioned, under duress from the Protestant and Unionist majority, from the Dublin-ruled twenty-six. To the devastation of the destructive Anglo-Irish War of Independence, which ended in 1921, there had to be added the ruinous cost of the subsequent Civil War of 1922–3. By way of homely illustration, it may be remarked that in the 1920s, when peace had been restored, the Irish Cabinet Minister responsible for the licensing laws, Kevin O'Higgins, introduced the 'Holy Hour' to pubs, between 2.30 and 3.30 p.m. The order, aimed at breaking up 'the long sitting' and getting people back to their offices after lunch, only applied to four cities. Practically speaking, in the rest of the country, there was no significant office population. The consequential lack of commercial activity can well be imagined.

It was paralleled by an equal lack of activity in tackling emigration. As the London Irish community leader, Gearoid O'Meachair, has said, for several decades the official attitude in Ireland could be summarised as: 'diplomatic blind eye – a catalogue of neglect'.[2] In September 1997, Cork University played host to a major seminar on the Irish diaspora organised by Piaras MacEnri, which was addressed by one of Ireland's most distinguished diplomats, Noel Dorr. Dorr was a former Secretary of the Department of

Foreign Affairs, and ex-Ambassador to the Court of St James. He had also
been stationed in London as a junior diplomat. From this earlier stage of his
experience he gave the conference one of the most revealing pieces of
information of the entire Seminar.

It concerned a young Dublin widow with a large family who had written to
the embassy seeking help in finding what state aid might be available to her in
London. Dorr, moved by her plight, spent a considerable time researching the
various avenues open to the woman before penning a reply. However, in those
days letters from the embassy had first to be vetted in Dublin. Dorr's missive
came back from headquarters with a note saying, 'Not to be sent: It is not the
policy of the Government to encourage emigration.' The unacknowledged
reality of the State was that it subsisted largely because the safety valve of
emigration drew off the potential for social upheaval. Few people in
government had any idea how to tackle emigration, and those that had, like
Sean Lemass, were not listened to by conservative figures like Eamon de
Valera, the longest reigning Irish political leader. His 1952 Budget taxed a flat
economy, with a view to encouraging protectionism and the subsidising of
agriculture. Irish agricultural produce was sold on the British food market at
the expense of the Irish tax-payer. De Valera stated that:

> The whole objective of the economical and social policy of the Government and of the
> implementation of that policy through the various departments of State concerned is to
> create such economic and social conditions in this country as will lead to the stopping of
> emigration.[3]

This was hypocritical rubbish. Neither de Valera, nor the Coalitions which
temporarily deprived him of office twice in the 1950s, had the slightest notion
of how to create such 'economic and social conditions'. A Government report
on emigration published in May 1954 found that the Republic had the highest
ratio of dependants, two non-earners to every three producers, of twenty-five
countries examined. However, its proposals for dealing with this state of
affairs consisted of a good deal of inappropriate, canting observations such as
the following:

> In general it may be said that those who remain single through selfishness, or through
> over-anxiety about the future, or for any other such reason – for instance, the woman who
> does not want to give up her independence, or her job, or the man who does not want the
> burden of supporting a home – are failing in their duty to God, themselves, and the race.[4]

The country had been neutral during the Second World War. Neutrality
provided a spur to emigration as the British recruited heavily in Ireland for the
manpower which built the aerodromes, dams and roads on which the war
effort depended. It also meant that Ireland did not receive the post-war
stimulus of Marshall Aid, and remained inward- and back-looking until well
into the sixties. The country operated a stultifying, Church-motivated

censorship that made of the censorship board's list of banned authors an excellent guide to contemporary literature. Eamon de Valera clung on to power, blind, nearing eighty, unable either to lead or leave, preventing any fresh ideas emerging on the economic and social front. Finally, as the decade closed, a great Irish civil servant, Dr T. K. Whitaker, the Secretary of the Department of Finance, produced a report for the Government pointing out that the continued economic viability of the State was seriously in question. He was authorised to draw up a blueprint for economic reform. Shortly afterwards de Valera was prevailed upon by his colleagues to resign as Taoiseach (Prime Minister) and run instead for what was then the largely figurehead post of Irish President.

He was succeeded by a man whom he had excluded from the premiership for far too long, Sean Lemass, who had anticipated Whitaker's thinking. Even during the Second World War he had been urging that when the war ended Ireland too should produce its own Beveridge Plan. In his seven years in office, Lemass revolutionised Irish government. Apart from following the sort of economic policies advocated by Whitaker, he introduced new faces and new departures, two of which are central to our story. Firstly he set Ireland on the path to Europe, being initially frustrated by De Gaulle's veto on European enlargement. Then he tackled the Irish educational system which, at the time, was very much an instrument for the perpetuation of Roman Catholic clerical power.

The key to the change lies in one damning statistic which was published in the year 1965. An OECD-funded commission set up in that year found that half of all Irish schoolchildren left school permanently at the age of twelve. Third-level education was largely a matter for the children of the better-off, and only a tenth of those attending secondary school made it through to university. There were roughly 14,000 university students in the Republic at that time. The greatly increased spending on education which Lemass initiated as a result of the Report made for less clerical power and more empowerment for Ireland's youth. Today there are currently 112,000 students in Irish universities, eight times the number when Lemass took over. The number of pupils in secondary schools has almost tripled to 372,000 compared to the 1965 figure of 142,000.

Then in 1973 Ireland joined the EEC.

The full picture of what this has meant commercially in terms of both imports and exports may be studied in the index under the heading of 'Irish trade with the EU'. Here, a few key statistics will illustrate the immense changes which have come about. In 1973, Ireland exported a total of IR£393 million to Britain, and a total of IR£684 million to the other countries which made up the EU at the time of writing. In 1997, Ireland exported IR£7,487 million to the UK, and a total of IR£23,268 million to the EU. In 1973, Irish imports from Britain were IR£535 million, and only a total of IR£877 million with Europe as a whole. In 1997, the figures were IR£8,001 million for Britain, and IR£14,148 for the rest of Europe.

As so much is heard about the transformation of the once turf-fuelled Irish economy into a 'Celtic Tiger' I might add that these figures should of course be read in terms of scale. They represent a highly creditable improvement, but compared to the larger European economy, one should think less in terms of a Celtic Tiger than of a mouse that roared. However, the changes wrought by education and improved economic planning did provide notable improvements within Ireland: for example, a relaxed censorship and a more open society generally. External influences such as television and improved travel facilities had their effect.

The texture of society began to be influenced by the decision to join the EEC well before entry was achieved. American and Japanese companies started coming to Ireland to use it as a back door into Europe. As Europe took hold and the multi-nationals piled in, the spin-offs began. On a practical level, Irish craftsmen and businesses began supplying the new companies. This meant that they had to develop world standards within Ireland. Irish managers were trained by the multi-nationals and thus built up extensive contacts which they, and the Irish business community as a whole, profited from. The country began modernising and diversifying away from the fixation with the British and the British market. Paradoxically, as it did so, its sons and daughters became better equipped for, and more sought after in, the British economy.

There were hiccups. During the seventies and eighties the public finances were allowed to get out of control. Interest rates soared. So did unemployment and its inevitable concomitant: more emigration. The eighties saw the 'illegals' era in America. As we shall see, the solution to this problem ultimately led to the Peace Process.

Back in Ireland two major changes occurred as the eighties closed. The public finances were brought under control and a new form of social partnership was introduced between government, business, the farming community and the trade unions. The birth of the Celtic Tiger followed and traditional emigration tapered off.

Irish people are now working for Irish companies abroad, and for practically every other organisation one can name in the European Community. Relatively obscure groups such as the administrators of the Lome Pact, or organisations dealing with Eastern Europe or Russia, tend to seek out Irish employees who have a reputation as problem-solvers.

Language training has improved immeasurably. Against a background of such colossal upheaval the stereotype of the Irish emigrant began to change: from that of a young labourer with no skills save the strength of his arm, and weaknesses such as homesickness, the bottle and mental illness, to someone with a university-level qualification, a bent for one of the newer sciences, a knowledge of the American and European job markets, and consequentially increased confidence and psychological strength. The stereotype of the Irish woman emigrant changed also. More and better qualified women now make low-cost air journeys in the wake of the maids and waitresses who once took the mailboat. Emigration has always tended to be an enabling experience for women, more so than men. It offered a better prospect than that of impoverished spinsterhood on a relative's farm, a drab bed-sit, or drudgery as a housewife trying to cater for too many children with too little money. More women than men now emigrate.

I can now report that everywhere I have gone in the world, either for the purposes of this book or for other reasons, there is, as in Ireland itself, a tremendous and ever-growing interest and pride in Irish culture and Irish achievement. For example, some people scornfully refer to St Patrick's Day celebrations as being 'stereotypical' – but stereotypes survive because of the degree of truth in them, not merely for reasons of the hackneyed or the false. As we will see, everywhere I travelled I found Irish communities enthusiastically organising ever-growing St Patrick's Day celebrations of Irishness by methods the saint never dreamed of: throwing vegetables at spectators in New Orleans, organising horse-races in Nairobi. Irish music and Irish writing were all enthusiastically supported in all their manifestations, be they packed houses for *Lord of the Dance* or *Riverdance*; plays like Brian Friel's *Dancing at Lughnasa*; lengthy leases on the *New York Times* best-seller list for Tom Cahill and Frank McCourt; cinematic partnerships like that of Jim Sheridan and Daniel Day Lewis in *My Left Foot*; or concerts by Irish groups such as the Chieftains, the Corrs, Boyzone and U2. Even in my own humble experience, I found from America to Australia to Argentina that any lecture I gave was always packed by people who asked serious questions about what was going on in their native country (or that of their parents or grandparents).

Two things have interacted: one the fact that the Irish have reached a plateau of success in their countries of adoption; the other that Irish success at home, coupled with the progress of the Peace Process, has created a heightened interest both in visiting Ireland and learning about it. Dublin is now the tourist mecca of Europe. One of the major Irish institutions is the *Irish Times* newspaper. Its website on the Internet provides an important focal point for the diaspora and records incredible levels of 'hits'. Other factors have helped also. The election of Mary Robinson in December 1990 both transformed the Irish Presidency from being a figurehead position and demonstrated to the world that Ireland is now a society which produces modern, professional women. In addition, Robinson, more than any other Irish public figure, showed an interest in Ireland's emigrants. One of her first acts in office was to have an electric candle placed in a window of her official residence, both in their memory and to beckon them homewards. The Good Friday Agreement of 1998 explicitly provided for recognition of the diaspora, and there is a movement to secure votes for emigrants in Irish elections.

Compared to the shabby days of emigration and unemployment in my boyhood, the transformation is immense. Of course problems remain. Ireland still needs to have a care for her less fortunate. For some the boom has come too late. To be yesterday's man is one thing. To be yesterday's broken, ageing, unemployed emigrant is tragic. Some of today's new emigrants still fall through the cracks. Not every Sean or Mary has the requisite educational or visa qualifications. Optional emigration by skilled people who have a prospect of returning is an enriching experience both for them and their host society, but enforced emigration is still a wrenching one. And one of the most shaming facts of all is the hostility, and near-racism, which badly conceived immigration policies on the part of the Irish government fuelled towards asylum-seekers and economic migrants to Ireland, all over the Irish Republic in the year 2000. Hopefully the emerging signs of opposition to this sort of prejudice, once only too often directed against Irish emigrants all round the globe, will help to curb this ugliness. However, overall, the description of today's Irish diaspora is a good-news story, which it has been a pleasure to tell. May it get even better during the forthcoming millennium.

Tim Pat Coogan
Eventually, Glenageary, County Dublin

ACKNOWLEDGEMENTS

'OH NO!,' SAID THE LADY from the Arts Council, 'We only give grants for literary projects.' Readers are therefore free to conclude that the members of the Irish diaspora are not the stuff of literature. But, whatever they decide, the Arts Council lady's *pronunciamento* makes all the more heartfelt the thanks I extend to all those who did help me with this project, both at home and abroad. Whatever myths there may be about the Irish character, let it be said that their reputation for hospitality rests on unshakeable foundations. Across five continents, people welcomed me into their homes, made introductions for me, took time off to show me around, placed cars and telephones at my disposal, answered my innumerable requests for further information after I had returned home, and generally made it clear that, whatever the Arts Council's view, the telling of the Irish story was a task worth assisting.

While I would like to award each individual a mark of one hundred and one per cent for co-operation, there is one corps whom I must single out for special mention and that is the men and women of the Irish diplomatic service. On a professional level my experience of Irish diplomats was such that it came as no surprise to find that in Brussels the verdict on the Irish contribution to Europe was universally summed up as: 'The Irish punch above their weight.' But, staying with them in their homes, observing them at the human level, their empathy with and knowledge of the countries to which they were accredited, the commitment with which they served their own state, the erudition, humour and, often, the courage, with which Ireland's representatives performed their roles, added up to what could only adequately be described as a sophisticated definition of patriotism at its best.

Shamefully, but inevitably, I am sure that the names of some individuals will have fallen through the cracks of memory, or disappeared along with the scraps of paper on which they were written, I apologise to all such, but to them as to those whom I can recall, a deep sense of gratitude is extended. Amongst the many members of the Department of Foreign Affairs who helped me I am indebted in particular to:

Ray Bassett, of the Anglo-Irish Division, Eamon O Tuathail, formerly accredited to South Africa, and currently Ambassador to the Holy See, Joe Small, Ambassador to Italy, and his wife Mary, Art Agnew, formerly accredited to Argentina, who has become the first Irish Ambassador to Mexico, and his wife Sylvia, Sile Maguire, now also accredited to Mexico, Richard O'Brien, the Irish Ambassador in Canberra, and his wife Bernadette, Ted Barrington, the Irish Ambassador to The Court of St James, John Swift, Ambassador to the Hague, both the former Ambassadors to America,

Dermot Gallagher and his successor, Sean O'hUiginn, Antoin MacUnfraidh, the former Ambassador to Canada, Maeve Collins, of the Irish Embassy in Ottawa, Declan Smyth in the Madrid Embassy, Denis O'Leary, Ireland's Permanent Representative to the European Community, Eamon Ryan, Ambassador to Belgium, Pat O'Connor, Ambassador to France and his wife, Patricia, Michael Forbes, also of the Paris embassy, Declan O'Donovan, Ambassador to Japan, his predecessor, the late Sean Ronan, Orla Tunney, Rodney Walsh, the Honorary Irish Consul in Auckland, his opposite number in Newfoundland, Craig Dobbin, Conor O'Riordan and Dan Mulhall, in the newly created posts of Consuls General to Wales and Scotland respectively, Jim Hennessey, formerly of the New York Consulate, Sean O'Regan of the press section, Dublin, Joseph O'Brien, Honorary Consul in Nairobi, Pat Curran, formerly Chargé d'Affaires in Uganda, the Irish representative in Lesotho, Fintan Farrelly, and his wife Catherine.

EUROPE

Denis Staunton, Barbara John, Padraig O'Dochartaigh, Sabina Hertz, George Broderick, Catherine Spank, Finbar Morris, Frank McGlynn and Alison Moffat, Noreen Lynch, Fr Thomas Healy, Michael Spillane, Pierre Jonannon, Rosin Dockery, Patricia Black, Brian Loughney, Paul Brennan, Eoghan O'hAnnrachain, Eamon Gallagher, Padraig Flynn, John Downing, Tommy Gorman, Gerry Murphy, Maurice Biggar, Billy O'Hara, Terry McKenna, Ger Barry, Dave Donovan, Liam Jenkins, Dr Mary McLoughlin, David Alford, John Liddy, John Morris, Dessie Flanagan, Anthony Warde, Deirdre McCluskey, Ruari de Burca, Count O'Donnell, Toni Van Marle, Lorraine Twohill, John Clifford, Sean Comaskey, Mark Gilligan, Seamus O. Doherty, Ann Rigney, Msgr John Fleming, Fr Liam McCarthy, Bro Austin Connolly, Fr Michael Breathnach, Dr Charles Dempsey, Joan Fitzgerald, Paddy Agnew, Denis Rafter.

UNITED KINGDOM

Deirdre McGuire, Michael McGuire, Aidan Hennigan, Jon Snow and Madeline Colvin, Mary Hickman, Jonathan Moore, Norah Casey, Donal Mooney, Mary Clancy, Fr Gerry Kivlehan, Sr Sarah, Brendan MacLua, Jim O'Hara, Sean Hutton, Christine Kinealy, Joe McKeever, Pat Sweeney, Bridie McCarron, Gearoid O'Meachair, Eugene Hickey, Patrick Buckland, Tommy Walsh, Mike Ford, Elizabeth Malcolm, Fr Pat Brown, Fr Gerry French, Roy Foster, Sean Farry, Sr Teresa, John McEntee, Tim O'Keefe, Brendan and Perpetua Kilcullen, Marie Murphy, Myles Gray, Jim O'Connell, P.J. Walsh, Bridie McGowan, Marie Anderson Hammet, Bridie Rooney, Fr Gerry McFlynn, Bill and Bernadette Feeney, Tom Cassidy, Mervyn Busteed, Michael Hopkinson, Cardinal Winning, Derry Jeffares, Tom O'Neill, Fr Noel Barry, Arnold Kemp, Tony Meehan, Ian Bell, Angela Graham, Barry Tobin,

ACKNOWLEDGEMENTS

Tom Flaherty, Paul O'Leary, Liz Curtis, Bishop Daniel Mullins, Mike Flynn, Mark Tinney, Joe Moore, John Kane, Deirdre Moylan, Mary Ann Lysaght, Carmel Murphy, Francis Heerey, Thomas Gallagher.

USA

Charles and Wilma Mooney, Eamon McGinn, Bill Kennedy, Ted Kennedy, Gene and Margie Quinn, Danny Coleman, Paul Quinn, Niall O'Dowd, Patricia Harty, Kevin Cullen, Adrian Flannelly, Andrew Greally, Emmet Larkin, Peter Quinn, Joe Jamesion, Pat Doherty, Peter King, Emer Mullins, Fr Colm Campbell, Sr Mary Herminia Muldrey, Bob Scally, Marion Davies, Chuck Feeney, Michael Stack, Pat Hughes, Pete Hamill, Jim Murphy, Clare Grimes, Angela Carter, Ray O'Hanlon, Dick Keane, Tom Farley, Colette O'Brien, Hal Antin, Bruce Morrison, Maeve Mahon, Billy Bulger, Tom English, Joseph O'Leary, Linehan O'Connell, Sr Lena Deavey, Fergal Woods, Adele Dalsimer, Liz Shannon, Rosemary McDonagh, John Ridge, Tom Nolan, Ivan Cuddihy, Mike McCormack, Gene Foley, Jim and Ildi Flannery, Mary Guinan, Jim Fitzgerald, Ray O'Flaherty, Johnny Hannigan, Fionnula Flanagan and Garret O'Connor, Paul Breen, Dan McFadden, Nora Friedman, Martina Ni Dhomhnail, Tom McEnery, Brian Downes, Diane Donovan, Tom Cahill, Terry Moran, Barbara Panter, Warren Rogers, Kate Higgins, Fr Jack Wall, Tom Riley, Brian O'Dwyer.

CANADA

Mary Durkan, Cyril Byrne, David Wilson, Michael Quigley, Mike Greene, Michael Conneally, John Kelly, Robert J. Grace, Gerry and Buzz O'Brien, Joe O'Brien, Jim Baker, Ann Dooley, Marianna Gallagher.

AUSTRALIA/NEW ZEALAND

Conor and Kate Horgan, Val and Mary Noone, Mary Elizabeth Caldwell, Bernie Brophy, Paul Ormonde, Al and Ellnor Grassby, Anne Cross-O'Brien, Phyllis McGrath, Lady Mary Fairfax, Chris Massero, Anne Blackwell, Margaret Hellman, Ron and Harriet Conoplia, Kay Collins, Mick O'Shea, Jarlath Ronayne, Jan and Chris Watson, Joe O'Sullivan, Bob Reece, Walter Thomson, Fr John Brosnan, Jim Stynes, Charlie Smith and Joan Walsh, Peter Brennan, John Monahin, Ann McCutcheon, Aideen McGarrigle, Tom Keneally, Vicki and Steve Lee, Patrick O'Farrell, Fr Edmund Campion, Rod Hall, Irene Stevens, Malcolm Campbell, Rory Sweetman, Bryan Vaughan, Jo Jo Johnson, Sam MacCreedy, Michael Kelly, Anne Marie Whitaker, Frank O'Donoghue, Anne O'Donoghue, Niam McMahon, Shiela McCabe, Liam Cogan, Hughie Greene, Brian Edwards, Fr Thomas Ryder, Peter Gallagher, B.D. Cunningham, Tom MacNamara, Hugh McGuire, Oliver Lee, Aidan Ahern, Kitty O'Brien, Paul Keating, Jim McKiernan.

AFRICA

John O'Shea, Ian Dolan, Shay Byrne, Sr Miriam Duggan, Ian Clarke, Derek Kavanagh, Aisling Stewart, Robert Law, Michael Pike, Sr Kevin, Noreen Prendeville and her husband Goti, Fr Jack Kiggins, Tony Gleeson, Rena Hanrahan, Marcus Schoon, Cleo O'Reilly, Fr Peter Reilly, Philip Curtin, Brian Kavanagh, Fr Eddie Lawlor, Sr Mary Kileen, Ken Killian, Brian O'Sullivan, Sr Columbiere, Sr Nula, Sr Catriona, Geoff Loane, Joe O'Brien, Br Colman, St John Kelliher, Dominic McSorley, Fr Aengus Finucane, Niall Tobin, Donal and Patricia McCracken, Noel Maloney, Fr Sean O'Leary, Sr Deirdre Hannon, Sr Marion Moriarty, Sr Linda Prest, Danny O'Herilihy, Sr Eileen Gallagher, Fr John Cleary, Eoin Hand, Tess Wade, Sr Imelda, Sr Margaret, Jack O'Donovan, Pat O'Halloran, Dr Brenda Corcoran, Joseph O'Brien.

CARIBBEAN

Dennis McClean, Peadar O'Sullivan, Fr Bobby Gilmore, Michael and Helen O'Malley Camps, Deirdre and Aron Camps, Fr Larry Finnegan, Carole and Cedric Osborne, Fr Gerry Mclaughlin, Br de Lellis O'Sullivan, Mike Greene, Barbara Jensen, Fr Anthony de Vertuill, Marion Callaghan, Fr Tiernan, Denis Solomon, Ross Graham, Alan and Kathleeen Walker, Barbara Lalla, Dr Maura Imbert, Sr O'Reilly, Archbishop Anthony Pantin, Pat Osmond.

LATIN AMERICA

John Edmund Rossiter, Hilda Sabato, Guilermo Howlin, Willy Patrick Ford, Louis Maria Flynn, Alex Quinn, Sylvia Cryan, Guillermo McLoughlin, Pat and Fatima Rice, Maureen, Margaret and Kathleen Duggan, Fr Kevin O'Neill, Santiago Brady, Juan Jose Delaney, Paddy Gaynor, Fr Fidelius Byrne, Colette Cullen, John Cleary

JAPAN

Mary Jordan and Kevin Sullivan, Jim Cashman, Fr William Johnston, Fr Donal Doyle, Fr Joe O'Leary, Tom and Rosaleen Hardiman, Harry Sweeney, Arisa Mori, Bob Welch, Mike Grey, Masako Saito, Richard Ryan, Ken' ichi Matsumura.

ONE

EUROPE

One day Professor Ernst Lewy remarked to me in conversation: 'You cannot understand the Middle Ages unless you know something about Ireland.' Ireland might indeed be called a harbinger of the Middle Ages. Not, to be sure, the only one, but one of the most effective. During the centuries between Christian antiquity and the Carolingian revival, when the foundations of medieval Europe were being laid, only the Irish had something to contribute that was new as well as lasting. Ancient Christianity had come to the Irish under conditions that were as extraordinary as they were unique, and its integration into Ireland's national culture is without parallel. Early Christian Ireland, in turn, has for centuries been unrivalled as a spiritual power in continental Europe. All over Western Christendom the traces of Irish monks and teachers bear witness to their country's historic mission. In the fabric of the medieval world the Irish strain is not the most conspicuous one. It is often too subtle to be easily detected, but it could not be missed even where it is latent.

Ludwig Bieler, *Ireland – Harbinger of the Middle Ages*

FRANCE

In a very real sense, I was able to validate the truth of the foregoing quotation during the course of one weekend in the month of June, 1998. The weekend was organised by an Irish bureaucrat Eoghan O'hAnnracháin, Financial Controller of the European Parliament in Luxembourg, who for some twenty years beforehand had organised similar annual outings for people with a shared interest in European sites which had historical connections with Ireland.

I found the experience both enriching and, at times, surprisingly moving. For example, while inspecting the longest continuous manuscript passage in the Irish language which is held at the Bibliothèque Municipale in Cambrai, we were treated to a lecture on the text by O'hAnnracháin. He first addressed himself to his French listeners in French and then turned to his Irish hearers to describe, in Irish, what had been written by an Irish missioner some time prior to the year AD 700. As O'hAnnracháin spoke, it suddenly dawned on me that he was referring to an era before the English language was invented, during which Irish was spoken in Europe's halls of learning and the Irish monks held aloft the torch of enlightenment against the encircling Dark Ages.

1

Perhaps it was a subconscious realisation of how the emerging force of English culture subsequently almost extinguished that torch in the monks' homeland, but, for no reason which I could logically explain, I suddenly discovered tears in my eyes.

The occasion was not the only one during that hectic weekend on which opportunities arose for pondering the poignancy of Irish history. Our travels took us also to scenes of blood and wasteful valour such as the world war battlefield of the Somme and the earlier slaughter at Fontenoy in which the Irish changed European history. However, as the weekend was an Irish affair, not alone was the tear frequently punctuated by the smile; most of the proceedings were conducted to either the sounds of music, the roars of encouragement at sporting encounters or the clinking of glasses. It was in its way a perfect microcosm of the Irish experience in Europe in terms of both history and psychology.

I rendezvoused with O'hAnnracháin's group of over a hundred persons at the Hotel Ibis in Amiens. Here I discovered that the Mayor of Amiens was hosting a reception for the Irish and that we were retaliating by putting on a display of hurling and Gaelic football. Before me at the hotel I found a contingent from the Aer Lingus Hurling Club. They had landed in Brussels at around 6 o'clock that morning, hired a car, called in to various hostelries en route and had timed their arrival in Amiens to coincide with the commencement of the hotel's Happy Hour. A great deal of happiness set in throughout the ensuing weekend. Our group was diverse. It contained harpists, flautists, bowran players, drinkers, thinkers, story-tellers, diplomats, bureaucrats, politicians, and representatives from hurling and Gaelic football clubs located on continental Europe. We even had our own chaplain, Father Pat O'Connor, who normally ministered to the Irish community in Luxembourg. Despite the rigours of the tour he got a surprising turnout for his morning mass.

We also had a piper, supplied courtesy of the Irish Army, Sergeant Christy McCarthy, and a harpist, Nodlaig Brolly, furnished by the Irish Traditional Music Association, Comhaltas Ceoltoiri na Eireann. Nodlaig, who was studying law at Trinity College, Dublin, possessed a voice of such sheer beauty that whenever she began to sing, to her own accompaniment, the audience, be it part of a street carnival, a pub sing-song, or a church attendance, was instantly transfixed into attentive silence. Her physical beauty matched that of her singing, but when a demonstration of Gaelic football was called for, she demonstrated both her musical heritage – her parents are famous Derry musicians and singers – and her sporting background – her brother, like her father before him, was one of the stars of Derry's Gaelic football team. She threw off her shoes to show the good burghers of Amiens how a Gaelic football should be kicked.

The rock-hard rugby football pitch on which the demonstration was staged ensured that Nodlaig spent the rest of the week limping on badly swollen feet. Fortunately her singing was unimpaired. After the Happy Hour, and a convivial dinner, were finished, we took ourselves to an Irish pub, the My

Goodness, via the old town Invalides, where O'hAnnracháin produced from his encyclopaedic memory some of the history of the Irish, generally members of the Irish brigades, who had either served in Amiens or been treated at the Hotel Dieu Hospice. One such soldier was Michael Davern who had lost a leg at the Battle of Fontenoy (11 May 1745). Davern was luckier than most. He at least lived, but his story was a reminder of the horrors of wartime surgery carried out in those days without antibiotics or anaesthetics. Amongst our party was another Michael Davern, the Irish Minister of State for Agriculture.

Any lingering solemnity at the memory of Davern's forebear's vicissitudes died away with the last notes of our piper's lament and we headed for the My Goodness where the Irish influx, greatly enhanced by Nodlaig's presence, was greeted warmly by both staff and patrons. Accordingly the foundations for a morrow of historical research, and the staging of a hurling match, were laid by drinking and singing until 4 o'clock in the morning.

Our appearance at the Amiens Bibliothèque after breakfast resembled that of one of the coloured prints on display. It showed a 'groupe de Irlandais en exile en Flandre (vers 1540)'. The group was a sorrowful-looking quartet consisting of a bare-footed woman whose shabby robe barely concealed her breasts, a boy with pipes, a kern (soldier) with sword and spear and the leader of the group, probably the woman's husband, a minor chieftain dressed in robes that had obviously seen better days. Possibly the chieftain had come, or been driven, to the continent from Ireland, accompanied by a retinue which had been devastated by the ravages of either battle or cholera. Whichever had befallen the unfortunates, our group empathised with their pangs. However, for the benefit of our hosts we maintained a façade of polite interest in the display of Irish military and monkish artefacts. These were plentiful as Irish soldiers had fought and bled in most of the armies which once raged over the area.

In one battle the Spanish captured the city early in 1597 with the aid of three Irish Brigades, only to lose it again in September of that year to the French king, Henry IV, who recaptured it with the aid of other Irish soldiers. The Irish were able to move around Europe, either because they were welcome as mercenaries, or because relatives, friends or refugees had gone before them. Some of the most famous refugees in Irish history had stopped in Amiens before us. These were the 'Great Earls', the Earls of Tyrone and Tyrconnell, who set sail from Rathmullan on the shores of Lough Swilly in County Donegal on 4 September 1607. Effectively speaking, the British had broken the old Gaelic order a few years earlier, at the Battle of Kinsale where a force of Spanish who had landed to assist the Irish were defeated with their allies on Christmas Eve in 1601. The English Commander, Mountjoy, was greatly assisted in this victory by the inevitable divisions amongst the Irish, who had failed to unite in the face of a common enemy. The Flight of the Earls was an acknowledgement that they were no longer safe in their own country. Safer, but impotent, the life of Hugh O'Neill, the Earl of Tyrone, in Rome was one of poverty and unrequited importunings to the Spanish Ambassador for a Spanish army to reinvade Ireland.

However, when they passed through Amiens in October 1607, the Earls were unaware of what lay ahead of them and were still in sufficiently good spirits to do as we were doing, take in some sight-seeing. The account of their stay in Amiens, recorded by the diarist to the party, Tadh O'Cianain, describes their arrival at:

> a famous and important city in France named Amiaunce, a defensive gateway of France, a distance of six short leagues. They were detained for a while at the gate until they obtained the directions from the governor of the place. They then entered immediately.
>
> They went to the beautiful, gorgeous church called Our Lady's. The head of John the Baptist was shown to them. It was in a glass of crystal, evident and visible to everybody present, and many wonders and miracles were attributed to it.

As we shall see, the Irish connection with Catholic Picardy generally, and the Amiens area in particular, was at one time strong and continuous. Ironically, however, most Dubliners today are only aware of the city's name because of the fact that it is in Dublin's Amiens Street that one catches the train to Protestant Belfast. (The Street was named in honour of a treaty between the British and the French signed in Amiens in 1802 which brought a temporary halt to the Napoleonic Wars.) Understandably the spirit of those picked for that afternoon's hurling match was initially more akin to that captured by the artist who portrayed the group of Flanders Irish we saw in the Amiens Bibliothèque than of an All-Ireland hurling final in Dublin. However, once the players took the field, the blood coursed more vigorously and an obvious determination to put on as good a display as possible took hold.

One of the Aer Lingus Happy Hour warriors, whom I had been unable to awaken earlier in the day (for some unknown reason, certainly not a reputation for early rising, I had been given the task of rousing them from the ravages of the My Goodness), was injured and had to limp off the pitch. An Aer Lingus colleague took his place, performing prodigies of goalkeeping until he too fell victim to the hard ground and had to come off. His place was taken by the My Goodness victim, who limped back on the field, despite my expostulations, muttering: 'Fuck it, I can't let down the lads.' The same spirit had prompted two shortfalls in team numbers to be made up by a young diplomat, Derek Dignan, from the Irish Embassy in Paris, and by the Minister's principal civil servant Patrick Burke, who decided that the risk of decapitation, through lack of practice at this most skilful, and dangerous, of stick games, would be outweighed by the shame of failing to put out an adequate team for a display of the national sport on a foreign field.

The subsequent performance of all concerned made me ponder on the embodiment of national characteristics in certain sports. The Irish, for example, have the reputation of being a warlike race. Yet they can safely allow thirty men armed with hurling sticks on to a field with only one referee to separate them. One can score a point by sending the ball over the bar between the goal posts, but the principal objective is penetration, to drive a goal past the goalkeeper into the net which counts for three points.

The English, on the other hand, only allow two stick- or bat-wielding players on to the field at the same time in their national sport, cricket, in which the objective is to knock the bails off. Hence the English game could legitimately be described as being a castration rite, the Irish one symbolising the virtues of (relatively) peaceful penetration. However, to return to our weekend.

That evening there was a reception for the Irish party given by the Mayor of Amiens, in the room in which the Treaty of Amiens was signed, in honour of the Irish monks and scholars whose influence had sustained the Christian traditions in the area which had given rise to the magnificent cathedral of St John the Baptist.

Sadly the cathedral may indeed have another very strong Irish parallel, though not one either welcomed or adverted to by the churches of either France or Ireland. In Amiens, as the account of the Earls' visit indicates, the head of John the Baptist is an object of great veneration. However, there are disturbing *sotto voce* voices which whisper that Walon de Sarton, who brought the head back from the crusades, in 1206, had in fact been duped by an Arab gentleman who had built a profitable trade on the all too ready availability of such heads as a result of the crusaders' endeavours on the battlefields of the day.

The Irish parallel occurred to me as the Irish group was being shown around the cathedral, the largest Gothic building in France, because shortly before visiting Amiens, I had been made aware of a memoir preserved in the family of some successful Mayo emigrants to America. After a relatively short spell, they were able to equip themselves for a holiday in their native village of Knock. They brought with them such new-fangled American gadgets as a machine which could throw pictures on walls and gable ends. Shortly after the young Mayo men's return, the villagers of Knock began to report miraculous sightings of the Blessed Virgin flickering along the exterior walls of Knock parish church. The Mayo men returned discreetly to the US, but, in their wake, reports of an apparition grew so that today there towers over Knock, not a church, but a basilica, which was blessed by Pope John Paul II in the year 1979. Indeed, as will be discussed later, it could well be said that the contemporary Irish Peace Process stemmed from seeds sown by a speech made during his Irish visit. Theologically, therefore, I suppose it could be argued that, whatever the physical causes of the venerations, neither the influence of Saint nor Virgin is wholly absent from either place of worship!

After the Mayor's reception there was a banquet at which I was given a place of honour sitting beside a gentleman who from his appearance I took to be a farmer. He told me that we would be 'visiting his house' the following day. I received this intelligence with what I hoped was due politeness and began making my plans to escape the posse of miscreants who had earlier signified their intention of proving the truth of Tom Moore's dictum that the best of all ways to lengthen our days is to steal a few hours from the night. I failed of course, and found myself back in the My Goodness where I was treated to a typically Irish display of exuberant generosity. Being the only one present not drinking Guinness, I had had to make do with not very palatable white wine. Suddenly one of the young hurlers, who had driven down from Paris to take part in that afternoon's match, reappeared looking somewhat out of breath – and plonked down a bottle of very fine red wine on my table. He had just run a couple of kilometres to and from a wine shop to ensure that having agreed to fall in with their plans for the evening, I would not be condemned to sipping an unwelcome tipple.

Again the morning came cruelly upon us, but most of the party continued on with the tour – the Aer Lingus party headed off to catch a flight, some with a view to honouring a commitment to meet friends at the Coachman's Inn near Dublin Airport at 4 pm, while one went to pick up his family in Dublin to take them on a holiday to Singapore . . . diasporic activity indeed. The rest of us moved on to visit the battlefields along the Somme river, which flows past Amiens. As we drove, we heard lectures on the horrors of tank warfare and the heroism of those who died, not for reasons of imperialism, but, in the words of a man who died in the fighting, the Irish poet Tom Kettle: 'for a dream born in a herdsman's shed and the secret scriptures of the poor'.

Some 600,000 men of the 'armies of Great Britain and Ireland' are commemorated in Amiens Cathedral as having died in three particular engagements: the Battle of the Somme in 1916, and the defence of Amiens and the so-called March of Victory in 1918. For Irish people that area of France is almost unspeakably significant. Here they had fallen in their thousands for a land not theirs, in a war that achieved nothing but to sow the seeds of Nazism and a future war. Here was commemorated the heroism of the men of the Protestant Ulster Volunteer Force (the UVF). The corps was originally founded by anti-democratic forces in the Unionist and Conservative Parties to deny the introduction of Home Rule to Ireland in 1912, despite the fact that the Catholics of Ireland had voted for it by a majority of over three to one. When the First World War broke out, the UVF was subsumed into the 36th Ulster Division.

In July 1916, the Ulstermen fought with tremendous heroism in the Somme battles. At Thiepval the men had climbed out of the trenches even before the supporting barrage had lifted. They charged Thiepval Wood in the teeth of heavy machine-gun fire and in an hour and a half overwhelmed five lines of German trenches, even managing to penetrate the famous Schwabben redoubt. However, they were unsupported on both their right and left flanks – indeed on occasion were shelled by their own artillery – and were constantly raked by machine-gun fire and intermittently subjected to ferocious counter-attacks. The area is dominated by a huge memorial arch. To me its significance lay not in its appearance, but in its symbolism. Unlike similar arches to the fallen, it rises, not above busy haunts of the living, like the Arc de Triomphe in Paris or the much smaller, but still impressive Grafton Street entrance gate to St Stephen's Green in Dublin, but above the deserted acres of the silent dead.

Eventually the Ulstermen had to fall back with a loss of 5,000 men in one day. They were the only soldiers, north of the Albert–Bapaume Road, to pierce the German line. Nationalist Catholic units emulated the heroism of the Ulster Protestants a few months later on 3 September 1916, when Irish troops captured Guillemont, losing almost half of the 2,400 soldiers in the fighting. Again the casualties were worsened by 'friendly fire' falling amidst the Irishmen.

Unlike in England itself, conscription was not introduced in Ireland and these Irish volunteers fought for England alongside the Ulstermen who, at home, had sworn to fight them to deny them their democratic right to Home Rule. The Nationalists joined up believing the Irish Parliamentary Party leader, John Redmond, who felt that the Catholic Irish should join in the liberation of Catholic Belgium and Northern France from the Germans. Moreover he thought, mistakenly, if the Nationalists fought alongside the Unionists, that after the war the bonds of comradeship would result in the Unionists dropping their opposition to Home Rule.

In the First World War, as in most other wars, Irish regiments, or regiments containing a high proportion of Irishmen, already constituted a significant component of the British Army. However, their sacrifices did nothing to change Unionist attitudes. There were two full divisions of what might be termed Nationalist Irish, the 10th and the 16th. Apart from Irishmen living in Britain (there were London Irish, Liverpool Irish and Tyneside Irish battalions), there were huge enrolments from amongst the Irish living in Scotland, Australia, Canada, Newfoundland, New Zealand and South Africa. The nine Irish Infantry Regiments – including the Irish Guards – contained such famous units as the Connaught Rangers, the Dublin Fusiliers, the Munster Fusiliers, the Leinster Regiment and the Royal Irish Regiment.

Amongst the casualties suffered by the Irish during the fighting in the Somme area were 200 Connaught Rangers, shelled at Guillemont by British artillery fire which fell short. Guillemont also saw the award of two Victoria Crosses to Irish soldiers. Private Tom Hughes of the Connacht Rangers, an apprentice jockey, proved once again that it is not the size of the dog that counts, but the fight in the dog. Despite being wounded, Hughes single-handedly destroyed a machine-gun post and captured several prisoners. Lieutenant John Holland of the Leinster Regiment, who back in Ireland had joined the Irish Volunteers to defend Home Rule, and then followed John Redmond's leadership to the trenches, led his battalion's bombers. He was one of only five who survived and was instrumental in capturing several German dug-outs.

As we drove along the Somme battlefields, the thought occurred to me, not for the first time during the period of my research and writing this book – which also happened to coincide with the highest levels of prosperity yet achieved in Ireland's history – that it was no accident that Irish material well-being had increased sharply during a period when the grip of both Christ and Caesar were loosened on the collar of the Celtic Tiger. For once, Irish energies were not being massively drawn off to further the ambitions of foreign based ecclesiastical and temporal rulers.

Nationalist troops also captured Ginchy. A memoir of the Dublin Fusiliers' chaplain, Father Willie Doyle, describes the taking of Ginchy as being due to a phenomenon all too often met with on European battlefields – an Irish infantry charge: 'The wild rush of our Irish lads swept the Germans away like chaff. The first wave went clean through the village and out the other side, and were it not for the officers, acting under orders, would certainly be in Berlin by this time.'

This delirium of the brave resulted in the Nationalists matching the Unionists in horrific loss: almost 40 per cent of the 16th Division of some 11,000 officers and men became casualties at Guillemont and Ginchy. Amongst them was the poet, Tom Kettle, and the ironies of the British and Irish relationship did not end with the extinguishing of the herdsman's dream. A comrade of Kettle's, who saw him fall, was Emmet Dalton who would later fight the British alongside Michael Collins in the vicious Black and Tan War in Ireland, and, of course, as we toured the battlefields, the descendants of the 36th Ulster Division, comprising today's UVF, were still prepared to kill Catholics in Northern Ireland. It was thought by the Germans that Ginchy was impregnable. It and Guillemont have this much in common where contemporary Ireland is concerned, virtually no one ever heard of either village.

Cambrai, the site of the ancient monkish manuscript I described at the outset, is also little known in Ireland, though it has an important place in military history as it was the site of a major experiment in the then new form of warfare – the use of tanks. The British Commander, Haig, made an unsuccessful effort to capture Cambrai using British tanks and Irish infantry. Both the Nationalist and the Unionist regiments were in the thick of the fighting and indeed managed to capture the strategic villages of Moeuvres and Gouzeaucourt. However, the famous Hindenburg Line held and, bereft of reinforcements, the Irish were forced to fall back, relinquishing their costly captures to the Germans.

It proved an interesting experiment in historical perspective to reel back from the bloody images that lay behind the deceptively peaceful sea of white crosses, which we traversed to enter Cambrai and its Bibliothèque, and cast our minds back to the days of the monk whose work had brought us there, and who in his day had advised his followers to: 'weep with the afflicted and rejoice with the joyous'.

The original text was composed sometime in the late seventh century. Apart from the advice given above, the manuscript, a homily, contains quotations from the prophet Daniel, from Hieronymous, and from a number of the epistles. It speaks of the three martyrdoms which the early monks embraced in the service of Christ. These still fuel the caring tradition which we will encounter in more detail in the section on Africa. The martyrdoms were described as being white, red and green: the white is that undergone by the one who separated from all he loved, often to the accompaniment of fasting and hard physical exertion, for the love of God; the green entails separation from desire, often accompanied by laborious works of penance; and the red is the martyrdom which claims the life of Christ's follower. Down through the ages there has been no shortage of volunteers for all three categories amongst the Irish.

The Cambrai manuscript's antiquity, and historical importance, may be gauged from the fact that the earliest continuous passages in the French and German languages, preserved in the Bibliothèque Nationale in Paris, are the oaths taken in 842 by Charles the Bald and Louis the German, at Strasbourg, to end the wars which followed Charlemagne's death in 814. These consist of a total of only seventy words in French and sixty in German. The Irish text, which, from its content, was clearly designed for an Irish audience, consists of three hundred and fifteen words with one hundred and fifty nine words of interpolation in Latin. The identity of the author is not known and the text only survives because about a century after it was written, a bishop of the day (Albericus, Bishop of Cambrai 763–790) directed that the text be copied along with a number of Latin manuscripts which, like it, were deteriorating with age. Even in the copy one can see the characteristic blemishes of cowhide scholarship which helped to give rise to a famous Irish art form. Here and there the circular holes left by warble fly are still visible. Not being able to obtain perfect hides, the early Irish monks overcame these blemishes by filling them up with drawings, sometimes caricatures, of the faces of people known to them, and also by drawing elaborately fashioned capital letters around which serpents and saints, harps and flowers were intertwined in the fashion made internationally famous by discovery of such works as the Books of Kells and Lindisfarne.

Our party was so interested in the work of the unknown Irish scholar of Cambrai that we had to leave to another day the inspection of another early Irish monk's manuscript, also preserved in the Bibliothèque. It is signed Thomas di Hibernia, Thomas the Irishman. Nor, to my regret, did we have time to research the exploits of another monk who took my fancy, Abbé Griffin, Canon of the Cathedral of Cambrai, who is remembered for his hospitality to his exiled brethren. A branch of my mother's family is said to be descended from the Griffins, which may explain certain things!

Apart from their skill as educators, the monks' grasp of writing made them invaluable assistants to figures like Charlemagne, who was himself illiterate, and depended on them to keep his records. Constantly on the move to supervise his vast domain, Charlemagne relied on the Irish monks to keep track of essential matters, such as who had paid taxes, and who had not. The compilation of manuscripts, a feat regarded with greater awe than the accomplishments of computer scientists in our time, sometimes aroused superstitious fears. The Vikings for example had a custom of 'drowning the books', believing that if the books were immersed in water their magical powers would be washed away.

Apart from the fact that time has not been allowed to wash away the Cambrai text, it has another significance, noted by O'hAnnracháin:

> It is a reminder of hundreds of thousands of Irish people who came to the continent as missionaries, as traders, as teachers, as mercenaries and as workmen. Few made the return journey. Their traces on the continent are growing fainter with the passage of time. There is a plaque to Saint Gall in the Swiss town named after him; there is a Celtic cross at Fontenoy; in Berlin, there is an illustration by Dürer of a group of Irish soldiers and workers – and other, alas too few, mementos elsewhere.[1]

Alas indeed, pollution has resulted in a greater degree of fading befalling the Cambrai manuscripts in this century than in the previous nine combined. It would be a service to European cultural history if either the growing French-Irish links (or those between the Irish diaspora generally) were to prompt some group or individual to present Cambrai with a humidifier to help protect the precious text.

The strength of the Irish monkish tradition was dramatically underlined at our next stopping place after Cambrai, the parish of Dompierre sur Helpe, a tiny Avesnes hamlet well away from any of the tourist routes. In the medley of sight-seeing and sleeplessness, I had forgotten why we were visiting Dompierre, and I discovered that the reason lay in the boot of a car driven by the farmer with whom I had shared the banquet at Amiens. The boot contained a reliquary containing the remains of St Etton, thought to have been born in Ireland in 590 and to have died in 654. Etton may be a local translation of the name Aodhagan (Aidan) which would not have been pronounceable in the Avesnes area. (The Irish language has approximately 110 sounds as compared to a more general average of forty-five.)

From what is known of Etton and his career, it is deduced that Pope Martin I sent him to Arras to convert the Belgian Gauls. Having achieved some success in this region he then moved to the district known today as Dompierre on the Helpe River. The village was christened by Etton himself (Dominus Petrus) to commemorate his own visit to Rome, the see of St Peter. By now he had acquired a reputation for effecting near miraculous cures. Stained-glass windows in the church at Bien Villers au Bois record one such, the restoration to life of a young woman, who he apparently aroused out of a deep coma. The cures continued at Dompierre. Apparently Etton had a knowledge of psychology. Dumbness can be caused by shock and reversed by the same means. Etton profoundly impressed the locals by striking a mute with his staff, thereby causing him to cry out and regain his speech.

He became a cult figure in the area. His relics remained objects of veneration at Dompierre for 700 years, but prior to the Treaty of the Pyrenees (7 November 1659), they were sent to Mons, then a walled city, for safe-keeping. A number of attempts were made to have the relics returned, but legal measures proved unsuccessful. Then the French Revolution broke out, in 1789. All over France, churches, monasteries and châteaux were pillaged, but not in Dompierre. It is recorded that some 400 people, barefooted as pilgrims, but nevertheless carrying weapons, went to the Abbey at Liessies, to which Etton's relics had been consigned, and 'asked' the Abbot to return them. Local legend has it that he did so 'willingly'. Apart from the relics, Etton's memory is commemorated in the Dompierre area by a number of objects, a statue in the church, a holy well, and, it now emerged, the reason for our presence, an annual procession.

Four of our party now hoisted the reliquary containing Etton's remains on to their shoulders, and we set off on the ancient pilgrimage route, singing the Cantique à Saint Etton to the air of Ave Maria. The refrain is:

> Amour et Gloire
> A notre Patron!
> Amour et Gloire
> Au grand Saint Etton

We stopped for prayers at a wayside chapel, a statue of St Etton and a holy well. Our path lay through fields, woodland and along a narrow winding road. Local people joined in in sizeable numbers and, preceded by our piper, who blew manfully and continuously throughout a warm French summer's afternoon, we proceeded back to the seventh century.

Dogs barked, cattle lowed and startled cocks crowed as the Irish returned to Dompierre. The thoughtful preparations for our visit included cutting a wide swathe through a meadow, so that we could move through a field of hay. In one isolated forest glade, a statue to St Etton had been bedecked with a huge display of green fern and orange and white lilies. A lady smiled apologetically at me, and explained: 'We did not have no Irish tri-colour.' Nearby, I stumbled over a rock, almost covered by vegetation. It was what we would term a mile-stone, dating from the time when a Roman road passed by. The procession concluded with a mass in the cool marbled parish church, whose resonant walls enhanced Nodlaig's singing and harping.

By now a certain listlessness had begun to descend on even the most indomitable of the Irish present, and we proceeded dutifully, rather than with enthusiasm, to the last port of call of the tour – the home of my farmer dinner companion. The 'house' turned out to be a château and 'the farmer' the local baron, His Excellency the Count Chambure. The château was a famous one at which Hitler apparently stayed during the Occupation (the Baron's grandfather had the bath destroyed when he discovered that Hitler had washed himself in it). Champagne was served, copiously, at tables arranged before the castle alongside a shimmering moat. All the local dignitaries of the area were there, the Mayor, the Prefect of Police, and a host of country folk who from their faces could just as easily have been sitting in the sunshine before an Irish country castle.

The impression of Irishness was heightened when, after a felicitous response to the speeches by the Irish Ambassador to Luxembourg, Ms Geraldine

Skinner, the champagne worked its alchemy, tiredness disappeared and the Irish music and dancing recommenced. When we eventually took our leave of those gracious and hospitable surroundings, we were cheered from every window and doorway for several kilometres around Dompierre. The Irish return had been appreciated.

The Irish for their part have every reason to appreciate their outreach to Europe since joining the EEC in 1973. Gerry Murphy, the head of the Irish Trade Board in Brussels, the heart of the EU, summed up the change for me in one statistic: 'Twenty years ago there were less than ten Irish companies in Europe. Now they're passing the three hundred mark, the Irish people are working for Irish companies in Europe.'[2]

They are also working for practically every other organisation one can name in the European Union. Relatively obscure groups such as the administrators of the Lome Pact or organisations dealing with Eastern Europe, or Russia, tend to seek out Irish employees. EU requirements oblige such organisations to employ Europeans, and the fact that the Irish are universally regarded as punching above their weight gives them an added attraction. Murphy pointed out to me that in the mainstream area of the European Commission itself, the Irish have more staff proportionate to their size than any other country. The limiting factor now is not job availability nor qualifications, but the fact that the Irish economy has improved so much that people want to move home as their children grow. The buoyancy of the Irish economy is such that the Trade Board maintains a job site on the Internet.

However, for those with the wanderlust, Europe generally beckons welcomingly. Murphy made a point that I found echoed all around the world: 'We don't have a colonial attitude. No baggage from the past, no hang-ups. We can get along anywhere. I met the top guy in the Czech Finance Department the other day – he was an Irish man.' The German building boom has meant that Irish students are opting more for German than the traditional French, but languages generally are at the top of contemporary Irish students' curriculum. Murphy mentioned an incident which had occurred shortly before we met – forty students from one Dublin university alone had descended on the office looking for summer jobs. They didn't mind what sort of work they did, so long as it enabled them to learn a language. The European ties, rather than the traditional British and American ones, are strengthened by placement schemes whereby, in co-operation with the Trade Board, Irish workers are placed in various European concerns for a year. They then go back to Ireland, where they are snapped up by European companies which have located in Ireland and need skilled workers with a knowledge of the continent.

Just how many Irish people are employed in European enterprises is hard to tell. The drifting population is large and, apart from the drifters, a high percentage, possibly the biggest one, of Irish citizens, never register with an embassy in any country they live and work in. However, the Trade Board, using as a gauge the 'hits' on the *Irish Times* website, reckons the Irish presence to be 'huge'. The *Irish Times* occupies a unique position in the estimation of Irish society, both at home and abroad. At home it is the paper of record, abroad it is the most favoured method of satisfying the traditional Irish hunger for news at home, and of what is happening in the world generally.

A few key trade statistics will illustrate the immense changes which have come about since Ireland joined Europe as indicated in the Introduction. In 1973, Ireland exported a total of IR£393 million to Britain, and a total of IR£684 million to the other countries which make up the EU at the time of writing. However, by 1997, Ireland was exporting IR£7,487 million to the UK and a total of IR£23,268 million to the EU. In 1973, Irish imports from Britain were IR£535 million, and from Europe, IR£877 million. In 1997, the figures were IR£8,001 million from Britain and IR£14,148 from the rest of Europe.

The increasing human contact which inevitably grew in the wake of this expansion of trade helped to make explicable and smooth over some rather less attractive Irish developments in Europe – the extension to Europe of the IRA's campaign against the British. The British Ambassador to the Hague, Sir Christopher Sykes, was killed in 1979. That year also a British army band in Brussels was subjected to a bomb attack in which seven bandsmen and fourteen civilians were injured. In 1987 thirty people were injured in a car bomb explosion outside the British Army Headquarters in Rheindahlen, West Germany. Over the next three years there were some twenty gun and bomb attacks on British servicemen. Three members of the RAF died in separate attacks at Nieuw Bergin and Roermond in Holland on the same day in May 1988. The campaign, which petered out in 1990, also claimed the lives of some innocent bystanders. In one case, the wife of a British serviceman was shot in her car after being mistaken for her husband. In another, two Australian tourists were taken for off-duty military personnel and shot dead.

The precursors of the IRA, the ancient Celts who exploded into Central Europe during the eighth and sixth centuries BC, were a fearsome warrior race, known as Gauls, who posed a serious threat to the Roman Empire until their power was broken in terrible slaughters conducted by Julius Caesar.[3] The strain of scholarly Celticism, which the excursion to Amiens and Cambrai commemorated, did not begin to make its presence felt until some time after St Patrick's Christianising mission to Ireland in the fifth century AD. The early Celts, possibly impelled into their warlike wanderings by a population explosion like the subsequent Viking eruption from Scandinavia, have left significant archaeological remains in Austria, Germany and Switzerland. Indeed, as we shall see (page 254), some scholars think they were the first Europeans to reach America.

They certainly invaded Greece. It is thanks to Greek chroniclers such as Strabo (64 BC–AD 21) that the Celts became the first trans-Alpine civilisation to be recorded. We knew they invaded modern Turkey, the Iberian Peninsula, and have left strong traces in today's world in Scotland, Wales, Cornwall, and in the Breton regions of France, but above all in Ireland. Today's Republic of

Ireland is the only independent Celtic nation in the world. The Celts who invaded Ireland probably did so in the middle of the fourth century, after they had already invaded Britain. It is thought that these were mainly Iberian Celts. Their language differed from that of the British Celts, being known as Goidelic. In Scotland, the Scots Gaelic tongue evolved and in Wales, Welsh. The Roman custom of referring to the Irish as Scoti was based on the widespread use of Latin for centuries and the fact that the Irish had established monasteries in Scotland.

One Celtic foundation myth is that Hercules had a child by the daughter of a Celtic king, Bretannos, some thirty miles north-west of today's Dijon. Her name was Celtine and their son was named Celtos, from whom the Celts are said to have taken their name. The more popular Greek name for the Celts was the Galateae. It was the Galatians who were to become the first non-Jewish people to become Christians and it was to them that Paul of Tarsus wrote his epistle, in turn one of Christianity's foundation documents. Apart from language, the Celts have left traces of their passing in the Roman roads of England, for example. The Celts were great horsemen and charioteers, and were able to move rapidly across their possessions by means of expertly built wooden roads. The existence of these roads made it possible for the Romans to move even more efficiently by building in stone over the Celtic foundations.

More enduring than roads or Christian texts, however, are the Celtic characteristics, traces of which are still visible, though hardly in the heightened form of the early Celts! These have been described as being remarkable under the headings of appearance, behaviour in war, morality, and skills, not only in warfare but in the gentler arts.[4] The Celts were a big people. An early description, by Diodorus Siculus, tells of them being 'tall of body with rippling muscles, and white of skin, and their hair is blond . . . the women of the Celts are not only like men in their great stature, but they are a match for them in courage as well'.

The Celts had a habit of going into battle naked and of challenging their opponents to individual combat before all-out engagement commenced. Livy records that:

> This fierce people have travelled and fought many races of mankind and have taken almost the whole world as their abode. Their tall stature, their long, flowing red hair, their great oval shields and enormous swords, together with their songs which they sing as they march into battle, their howlings and leapings and their fearful din of their spears and swords as they pound their shields – following their ancestral custom – all are carefully designed to strike terror into their enemies.

These tactics were often successful, the Romans, for example, forbade their officers to engage in pre-battle individual duels, as the casualties mounted in such conflicts. The fearsome Irish infantry charge remained a sometimes decisive element in European warfare down to the twentieth century.

14

However, Celtic methods of warfare also had their limitations. Livy also records that:

> It has been discovered, through our experience in battle with the Celts, that if you sustain their first charge, into which they hurl themselves with blazing passion and blind rage, then their limbs will quickly tire, they grow slack with sweat and weariness, their muscles will not sustain their weapons and they drop from their hands. They are flabby in body and irresolute after their initial passion subsides. They are rendered prostrate by sun, dust and thirst, so much so that you don't even have to kill them to subdue them.

Drink and sex probably played their part in creating the 'slack with sweat and weariness'. Athenaeus of Naucratis records that although the Celts had 'very beautiful women' they 'enjoy boys more; so that some of them often have two lovers to sleep with on their beds of animal skins'.

The Celts were said to be:

> exceedingly addicted to the use of wine . . . and to 'fill themselves with the wine which was brought into their country by merchants, drinking it unmixed, and since they partake of this drink without moderation by easing of their craving for it, when they are drunken they fall into a stupor or a state of madness . . .'[5]

The demon drink therefore, as much as homosexuality, may have caused the Celts to sometimes overlook the attractions of their busty, lusty womenfolk. However, all commentators agree that the Celts set a premium on hospitality, and strangers were always welcome at a feast. Apart from their conviviality, descriptions of Celtic feasts from Graeco-Roman times parallel almost exactly those of Irish chieftains described in the Irish sagas, such as the Red Branch Knights or Cuchulainn Cycle: 'When the meat was served up, the bravest hero took the thigh piece, and if another man claimed it, they stood up and fought in a single combat until their death.'

Hospitality, brawling and a fairly unbridled sexuality continued to be the hallmarks of the Irish during and after the time of St Patrick. As Thomas Cahill has noted:

> Irish sexual arrangements were relatively improvisational. Trial 'marriages' of one year, multiple partners, and homosexual relations among warriors on campaign were all more or less the order of the day. Despite Patrick's great success in changing the warrior mores of the Irish tribes, their sexual mores altered little.[6]

So little in fact that as late as the end of the twelfth century the kings of Clan Connaill traditionally celebrated their inauguration by publicly copulating with a white mare. It took famine and the preoccupation with sex of a guilt-laden, celibate Jansenistic Church to introduce a note of puritanism into the Irish population in the 1850s, and that only lasted for a little over a century.

As we will see, the Aran Islands played a significant role in the history of both early Irish and European Christianity, but there is also a famous root situation anecdote concerning a visit paid by an American priest, witnessed by this writer, to that wild, western outpost. It occurred on a dark autumn day after he had obviously spent a night in a somewhat reckless encounter with the oral Irish tradition (Jameson, Guinness, etc.). When the islands finally hove into sight, over a heavy, Atlantic swell that queasily combined with the smell of diesel to remind the priest of the unwisdom of the previous night, he was horrified. Gazing at the streaming, black wilderness of rock, with sparse grass here and there, tinted orange by sea spray, he exclaimed: 'In the name of God, what do they DO out here?'

Two bystanders volunteered contrasting, but not totally inaccurate, explanations. One, an earnest professional Irishman-type from Dublin, dressed in tweeds and an Aran sweater, replied: 'They have their own, true, pure Gaelic culture.' The second man assimilated this for a moment and then, in respectful tones, opined: 'Father, they have fishing and fucking, and in winter, there's no fishing . . .'

The priest was what the Aran Islanders would call 'a returned Yank', possibly impelled by a promise, or a donation, made in Boston to visit island ancestors, but he was also coming to an island made famous by Irish priests fourteen centuries before his birth. The Aran Islands were one of a set of famous monastic sites 'the Harvards and Stanfords of the early Middle Ages'[7] which began to spring up in the wake of the mission of St Patrick, who probably died around the year AD 461. St Patrick was not the first important cleric to visit Ireland, there are records of bishops who preceded him at least a century earlier, but he is the one who left the most lasting impression, both as missionary and exemplar. The son of a Roman official, he was captured by an Irish war party raiding for slaves and brought to Ireland, where he suffered years of hardship as a herdsman before making his escape. He studied on the islands of Lerins, off the coast of Cannes, in the south of France and spent more than thirty years at Auxerre, before being made a bishop and returning to Ireland.

He came to an island which had largely escaped Roman influences. The Irish branch of the Celts lived much as had their forefathers before Caesar destroyed their power, herding cattle, sheep and swine rather than going in for tillage. This type of agriculture would predominate in Ireland until after the Norman invasions of the twelfth century. Nevertheless the Celts reached a high level of civilisation. Artefacts and archaeological remains, such as the great fort at Newgrange, in County Meath, have established that the Irish Celts had developed advanced skills in mathematics and the working of precious metals, and also that the Celtic bardic tradition had been highly developed. The people evidently set great store by friendship, hospitality and their own reputations. Boastfulness was not regarded as a crime, neither was slavery, nor human sacrifice.

From the time of Patrick, however, the energy of the Celts came to be increasingly diverted towards a preoccupation with learning and Christianity.

As Europe slid into the Dark Ages, great monasteries arose in Ireland: at Armagh, on Inis Mor, the largest of the Aran Islands, and at Kildare where St Brigid founded two monasteries, one for men and the other for women. The sexes were kept strictly segregated even in church, where there were separate entrances for men and women. Nevertheless, it is recorded of Brigid that amongst her many miraculous deeds was the disappearing of a foetus from the womb of a young nun who continued to serve in the convent after the 'miracle'. The individualism of the Irish Church would sow the seeds of much tragedy later, as we shall see, but the teaching of Christianity appeared so attractive to the Irish that the country was soon dotted with monasteries throughout the sixth century: Armagh and Aran were added to by Clonard, Clonmacnoise, Bangor, Clonfert, Durrow, Derry, Glendalough and Lismore, to name but a few.

These monasteries were centres of hospitality and education as well as of piety. The Venerable Bede records that both the nobles and commoners were welcome, some to embrace the monastic life, others to study. Bede describes students 'going about from one master's cell to another'. A major incentive to seeking out a multiplicity of tutors must have been monkish hospitality to the students: 'all these the Irish willingly received,' says Bede, 'and saw to it to supply them with food day by day without cost, and books for their studies, and teaching, free of charge'.

As Europe slipped further and further into barbarism in the wake of the crumbling of the Roman Empire, the monks developed new methods of manuscript illumination, and became in effect the publishers of Europe. They were as welcoming of new ideas as they were of new faces, a fact which caused more puritanical monks elsewhere to condemn Irish education. The Englishman Aldhelm of Malmesbury, who had been taught by the Irish, warned against their system in a letter to a Saxon student: 'What advantage does it bring to the sacrament of the orthodox faith to sweat over reading and studying the polluted lewdness of Prosperpine, or Hermione, the wanton offspring of Menelaus and Helen, or the Lupercalia and the votaries of Priapus?'

Aldhelm might have been one of the Irish censors of my boyhood. However, far from implementing such strictures in their own country, the Irish monks began exporting their form of education to other countries in the latter part of the sixth century. The tradition of Green martyrdom had already taken the Irish monks to barren, inhospitable island sites off the Irish coast: St Enda's monastery on Inis Mor was a holiday home compared to the terrible Scellig Rocks off the Kerry coast, where food had to be passed up by baskets, and even seagulls and puffins have to be careful of down-draughts and tumultuous seas.

Their faith was such that it carried them, in primitive leather currachs, to the Hebrides, the Faroes, and even to Iceland. They went out on the stormy oceans convinced that if God willed it, they would land safely, whatever the weather. Some, therefore, took no oars; others, it is said, dispensed with either

17

food or water. From their wanderings we have legends, such as the Brendan Voyage or that of Bran, which have fascinated scholars to this day, including scholars in Tokyo where Bran's story has been translated into Japanese.[8]

The voyaging monks who set off in the green mode made a particular impact on Iceland, where today they will show you caves with carvings wrought by the Irish Papar, as the monks are known in Iceland. The monkish settlements pre-date the coming of the Vikings, and to this day the Icelanders will tell you that the Irish gene is the most important of their heritage. Iceland's Westman Islands are called after the Irish who followed in the monks' footsteps and, as in the very different climatic region of Argentina, are credited with introducing sheep. As St Brendan who set sail in the sixth century had written about 'Sheep Islands', this probably means that the Irish brought sheep either to parts of Iceland or the Faroes where they had hitherto been unknown, rather than deserve the credit for introducing the animal to the northern latitudes generally.

Ultima Thule as Iceland was called by the Celtic navigator, Pytheas, who sailed to the region from modern day Marseilles, through the Pillars of Hercules, was well known in Ireland. The monk Dicuil, writing of this strange land in 1825, noted that there was no daylight there in winter, but the summer nights were so bright that 'whatever task a man wishes to perform, even picking lice from his shirt, he can manage as well as in clear daylight'.

The first monks seemed to have settled in Iceland and the Faroes somewhere around the year 825, and from then on tales about the strange countries percolated back to Ireland.

Today the Icelanders treasure their Irish heritage and, apart from the almost mandatory interest in Irish music and Guinness which one finds worldwide, one comes across all sorts of examples of Irish influence. The President Olafur Ragnar Grimsson stressed to me how keen he was to see cultural and tourist contacts increased between the Irish and the Icelanders. The Icelanders already come to Ireland in large numbers during the off-peak tourist season, when the availability of seats on the Icelandic airline, coupled with the favourable rate of exchange (for the Icelanders), make Dublin a tourist mecca. Reykjavik's television station was modelled on RTE, and the presenters of the various radio and TV programmes I appeared on were obviously knowledgeable about Irish literature, and very much up to speed with developments on the Peace Process. The interviewer for the major Reykjavik newspaper, *Morgan Bladid*, David Logi Sigurdsson had done his MA at Queens in Belfast on a comparison of the Irish and Icelandic languages.

About a half an hour's drive from Reykjavik, my friend Arnie Gunnarsson, a former journalist, with whom I once reported on the Vietnam War, now runs a clinic at Hveragerdi. The clinic would be remarkable in a large European city, but it appears truly wondrous when encountered amidst the snow and ice of a volcanic island which only supports a population of some 270,000.

18

It features mud baths, massage, an organic food diet, heated outdoor swimming pools, and exercise machines of all sorts. The skill therapists, including an acupuncturist from Beijing, would make the place a mecca for international celebrities (Yoko Ono is but one of many visitors who have slipped quietly in and out of the clinic), were it not for the fact that the Democratic and Republican spirit of the Icelanders decree that the facilities be retained mainly for the Icelanders, particularly the elderly.

I was introduced to one such patient at the clinic by an Irish nurse, Brigid McEvoy, from Co. Kilkenny, who is now a Bahai, living in Hveragerdi with her teacher husband. The patient, an old man, Kristjan Arnasson, who lives alone and who suffers from coronary and other problems, followed the North of Ireland troubles with interest, and had written a poem about the deaths of the three Quinn brothers, after Loyalists threw a petrol bomb into their home. It contained the following:

> Out of the whirlpool of virulent news,
> Hatred, revenge and cruel abuse,
> Three torches emerged, so bright, oh so bright!
> Three little brothers in Ireland one night.
> Three innocent children, they had to die.
> But Almighty God, can you explain me why? ...

> It hit my soul as a fiery blow
> I could not help it, my tears had to flow! ...

> It will not be easy to cease the fight.
> But don't let the boys die for nothing that night! ...

I read the poem on New Year's day, 2000, in one of the comfortable bungalows which dot the grounds of the clinic. Outside it was gusting to Gale Force 9 on the Beaufort scale, and the snowflakes drove into one's face like needles. Yet through the windows one could see the glow from the thermally heated greenhouses in which the Icelanders were defying nature by growing, amongst other things, bananas, roses and flowers and vegetables of all sorts. It didn't seem fanciful to imagine that the early Irish monks had created a glow of interest, which also defied time and impossibly harsh weather conditions to survive in the old man's poem and to the start of a new millennium.

Aided by jet travel, the contemporary Brendan Society sets off from Dublin to take its members to parts of the globe today which it is virtually certain Brendan never saw. Nevertheless, one will encounter legends of Brendan coming ashore in Florida, Newfoundland, and even in Mexico, where in some tales he takes the place of Quezecotal. The contemporary German city Brandenberg was originally named after him. Tim Severin first achieved international fame with his book, *The Brendan Voyage*, in which he chronicles the voyage made by himself and a small group of companions in a leather boat

19

similar to the one Brendan would have used. He retraced the route which Brendan may have taken from Kerry via the Aran Islands to the Hebrides, and on to the Faroes, Iceland, and ultimately to Newfoundland.

However, the two greatest (and best authenticated) names in this outward migration are those of St Columba, also known as St Columcille, to Iona off Scotland, *circa* 563–5, and St Columbanus, to the Frankish and Lombardian kingdoms about twenty-five years later.

The work of Columcille and Columbanus is well documented. The two Green martyrs are credited, in the case of Columcille, with converting the Scots and the Northumbrians, and Columbanus was responsible for the conversion of the Alemanni on the upper Rhine. Columcille, a member of the aristocratic clan Conall, had founded some forty-one monasteries in Ireland by the time of his forty-first birthday. A man who loved poetry, books and beautiful things, he became the subject of one of the most celebrated legal verdicts in Irish history, and embarked upon Green martyrdom as a result.

Columcille, also known as the Dove of Derry, after he founded his first monastery there, many centuries before invaders would change its name to Londonderry, copied under cover of darkness a beautiful psalter owned by his master, but was discovered and brought before King Diarmait. Diarmait's decision went against Columcille: 'To every cow its calf, to every book its copy.'

Columcille found a pretext to avenge this verdict when one of his followers was killed on Diarmait's orders. He mustered his powerful clan (the same one which gave such unusual prominence to a white mare at the King's inauguration) and worsted his judge in a bloody battle which claimed some 3,000 lives. His penance was Green martyrdom, and he sailed from Ireland to Iona with twelve companions. The following stanzas are from a poem allegedly written by him:

> Grey eye there is
> that backward turns and gazes;
> never shall it see again
> Ireland's women, Ireland's men.

> I ever long for the land of Ireland
> where I had power,
> an exile now in midst of strangers,
> sad and tearful.

> I have loved the land of Ireland
> – I cry for parting;
> to sleep at Comgall's, visit Canice,
> this were pleasant.

He did not in fact cut his link with Ireland but continued to govern his monasteries in Ireland from Iona. At a famous assembly at Druim-Cetta *(circa* 580) he is said to have intervened to save the poets of Ireland from suppression. Columcille's life in Iona, which ended in 597, was responsible for some of the great British monasteries, Lindisfarne, Jarrow, York, Melrose and Whitby.

Columbanus is thought to have been born in Leinster *circa* 543. It is said that a conversation with a woman hermit cured him of concupiscence and he decided to become a monk, stepping over the threshold of his home across the prostrate body of his mother, who did not want him to enter a monastery. He landed in France with twelve companions around 591.

The Merovingian kingdom[9] was racked by dynastic quarrels and, to Columbanus's eyes at least, depraved by the activities of a decadent nobility and a hypocritical clergy. To counteract this Columbanus furthered the Irish penitential system in his monasteries and attracted the sons of noble men for education. He enjoyed the patronage and protection of King Childebert II of Burgundy and Austria, and his principal monasteries at Annegray, Fontaine and Luxeuil were important establishments. However, Columbanus was not welcome to the clergy of Gaul, and he also followed a number of Irish practices which were to draw fire at the Synod of Whitby. His principal offence was one which, as we shall see, would later provide a pretext for bringing down great misery on Ireland: unlike the continental monasteries, his foundations were not subject to the jurisdiction of the bishop in whose diocese they were established. In fact, Columbanus had a bishop of his own who conferred holy orders, and exercised other functions, which the continental bishops considered to be their right.

After the death of Childebert, Columbanus was expelled from Burgundy by Childebert's son, Theuderic II, but he returned to Luxeuil where he was arrested and brought under armed guard to Nantes, for forcible repatriation to Ireland. However, a storm forced his ship back to harbour and the captain of the ship, apparently taking the storm as a sign from heaven, released Columbanus who then went on to become involved in controversy with Pope Boniface IV. Eventually he was offered a site at Bobbio in the Apennines where he founded his last monastery. He died in 615. Today Bobbio is the scene of a popular annual festival organised by the Irish community in Italy.

Other Irish saints followed in the footsteps of Columbanus and Columcille. Great European cities arose around monasteries founded by Irish monks: Auxerre, Bobbio, Fiesole, Laon, Liège, Lucca, Lumieges, Regensburg, Reichenau, St Gaul, Salzburg, Trier, Vienna, and Würzburg. In France one may easily trace the Irish influence: through the foundation of a monastery by St Ronan in Brittany; another, near Meaux by St Killian; through St Fiacre's foundation of Breuil Abbey; and in Picardy, by the monastery of St Riquier, called after Richarius, a noble man who abandoned the call of the world, the devil and the flesh in response to the preaching of Irish monks; or in more subtle ways such as in a well-known children's nursery rhyme which commemorates the seventh century Frankish King Dagobert and his Irish adviser St Eloi:

Le bon Roi Dagobert
A mis sa culotte a l'envers,
Le Bon Saint Eloi lui dit,
'O Mon Roi, Votre Majeste est mal cullottee,'
'C'est vrai,' lui dit le Roi,
'Je vais la remettre a l'endroit.'

O, Good King Dagobert
Has put his trousers on inside out,
The Good Saint Eloi has told him,
'O My King, Your Majesty is ill-trousered,'
'It's true,' remarked the King,
'I must set myself aright.'[10]

Dagobert II was forced to become a monk in the dynastic struggles of the time, and was sent to study in Ireland before being allowed to return as a pretender – obviously the reputation of the Irish monks on the continent, and their education facilities in Ireland, were such as to merit them being entrusted with the destiny of an important royal figure. As Bieler notes:

> In the course of the feuds which inevitably broke out again between the rulers of the rival kingdoms, the kings themselves as well as their respective mayors took great interest in the Irish monks who came to their shores, and gave them their protection. Both sides, it would seem, were anxious to enlist the moral support of the Irish peregrini, who by that time often enjoyed a reputation for sanctity and learning by the mere fact that they came from Ireland.[11]

Queen Bathilde, wife of Clovis II of Neustria, invited monks from Luxeuil to found the monastery of Corbie in Picardy, which gave the river Somme a happier Irish tradition than did the First World War. From the time of its foundation *circa* 657, it became renowned as an intellectual centre, which kept alive the traditions from which sprang the great cathedral of St John the Baptist at Amiens. Other famous peregrini include the three brothers, Sts Fursa, Follian, and Ultan. Fursa, the visionary who emerged from a coma to describe in great detail the terrors of the next world, dominated medieval thinking on the after-life until Dante wrote the *Inferno*. Fursa died in 650, but his monastery at Peronne provided both a literary as well as a religious link with Ireland. For, along with providing contact between monks in Ireland and the continent, it also contained important texts such as St Patrick's confession and epistle, from which subsequent lives of the saint were derived.

St Killian, who was martyred in 689 near Würzburg, still provides a link between Germany and Ireland. Apart from the continuing veneration of the saint in the Würzburg area, the German school in Dublin is known as St Killian's, and the name is still a popular one at many Irish christenings. St Killian was apparently slain on the orders of Duke Gozbert of Wircibur (Würzburg) at the behest of his betrothed, a lady called Geilana, whose

22

husband, the Duke's brother, had just met an untimely end, thereby allowing her to marry the Duke. Canon law forbade marriage between in-laws, but Frankish law did not and Geilana apparently took exception to Killian's citing of canon law in the face of her ambitions. Two other Irish monks who are thought to have perished along with Killian are St Colman and St Totnan.

It is said that over one hundred Irish saints are still remembered in Germany and Austria, as are numbers of Schottenkirchen and Schotten-kloster (literally Scottish churches and monasteries) which were in fact founded by Irish monks. Irish monks also founded some of Germany's most famous monasteries, notably in Cologne, and the Irish monkish tradition is particularly strong in Bavaria, where amongst the names of several Irish saints, that of Virgil (in Irish, Fergil) is remembered for being the first Bishop of Salzburg.

Some of the leading minds of the Carolingian Renaissance were Irish, most notably Johannes Scottus or John Scottus Eriugena, as he was known. (Eriugena was his own description of himself, meaning 'scion of Ireland'.) Johannes Scottus was the outstanding philosopher of the Middle Ages and was thought to be one of only two men in Western Europe who could speak Greek. A noted theologian, he preached that everyone, even the devil, would ultimately be saved through God.

His own wit and personality obviously saved him from the consequences of his too ready tongue. Legend has it that during one boozy session, he replied to Charles the Bald's question: 'What separates a fool from an Irishman?' 'Only the table.'

He may have been murdered by his pupils. It is said that they, objecting to his habit of forcing them 'to think', turned their metal styluses on their teacher.

Another Irishman, Sedulius Scottus, is thought by some to be the ancestor of Goliardic poetry. He also wrote extensively on the gospels and regarded himself as a kindred spirit of Horace, whose style he emulated in a verse which has resonances of clerical problems in our day. The poet seeks to harmonise the conflicting calls of his vocation, scholarship and the good life:

> I read and write and teach, philosophy peruse,
> I eat and freely drink, with rhymes invoke the muse,
> I call on heaven's throne both night and day,
> Snoring I sleep, or stay awake and pray.
>
> And sin and fault inform the life I plan:
> Ah! Christ and Mary pity this miserable man.

In a long and damning indictment of neglected Irish scholarship Dr Beresford Ellis reminds us that there is a vast corpus of Irish achievement lying unrecognised in the libraries of Europe.[12] He cites everything from discoveries in medical science made by long-forgotten Irish doctors, to a history of Irish women, to the calendar which St Columbanus relied upon in his argument with the Pope. Dr Beresford Ellis makes the point that Columbanus's calendar (to be accurate a tenth-century copy of it) was discovered by accident in Padua, in the late 1980s. What else still lies undiscovered?

A particularly glaring omission, especially in these days of gender studies, is the *Ban-Shenchus (The History of Women)*, which arguably is Europe's oldest surviving piece of feminist literature. It deals with famous Irish women pre-twelfth century. Seven copies of this survive. They make clear that the women of Ireland were every bit as rumbustious, and as interesting, as were their menfolk. Although no other country has the ability to study the lives of so many of its prominent women of early history, the *Ban-Shenchus* has lain ignored since its only examination several decades ago.[13]

Writing about the contribution of the Irish to the civilisation in the years between the fall of Rome and the rise of medieval Europe, Thomas Cahill has written:

> Wherever they went the Irish brought with them their books, many unseen in Europe for centuries and tied to their waists as signs of triumph, just as Irish heroes had once tied to their waists their enemies' heads. Wherever they went they brought their love of learning and their skills in bookmaking. In the bays and valleys of their exile, they re-established literacy and breathed new life into the exhausted literary culture of Europe. And that is how the Irish saved civilisation.[14]

From the Middle Ages on, however, we enter an era in which Irish civilisation was itself ravaged by invading forces. The first of these were the Vikings who destroyed monasteries such as Lindisfarne, Iona, Inis Murray, Armagh, Glendalough, Bangor, Moville, Clonfert, Clonmacnoise and Kildare. These raids also had the effect of turning Irish clerical students and monks towards Europe to get away from the Norsemen, and so one wave of invasions slowed the pulse beat of Irish monastic contribution to Europe. In order to understand how others would change this contribution into a largely military one – that of the 'Wild Geese', as the members of the Irish Brigades which fought on the continent with the Catholic powers were known – some Irish history has to be understood.

The Norsemen's power was broken at the Battle of Clontarf in the eleventh century. Though they came as bloody pillagers, they did leave cities behind them: modern Irish cities such as Dublin, Waterford, Wexford, Wicklow and other coastal towns owe their origins to the Norsemen. Before they came Ireland was a densely wooded country whose people lived by herding animals, and in which the monasteries took the place of cities, and it was their power, combined with a clash of culture, partly between the Irish Celtic Church and that of Rome, but also between the Irish and the British temperaments.

The Celts versus the Romans dispute came to a head at the Synod of Whitby in AD 664. The Synod decreed that the Celts should follow the Roman custom in two key areas in particular. The Celts tonsured their clerics from ear to ear, which meant shearing the hair only at the front of the head, but the Romans left only a crown of hair around a tonsured cranium. A more serious source of division was the fact that the Irish used a different method for fixing Easter from that of the Romans, commemorating it on the fourteenth day of the lunar month, if it was a Sunday, and making the date of the spring equinox 25 March.

A second conclave, several centuries later, had more serious consequences for the Irish Church. This occurred at Winchester in 1155, where the English bishops and clergy backed a proposal that Ireland be invaded and brought under the English crown, then held by Henry II. Notwithstanding the Irish contribution in spreading Christianity throughout Europe, a view was promulgated that the Irish Church was sunk in barbarity. Evidence to the contrary was overlooked. For example, although the pre-Viking flood of Irish monks had slackened, during the twelfth century, in the period immediately before and during British clerical attempts to gain control of the Irish or 'Celtic' Church, Irish Benedictine monks spread important monasteries throughout Germany and elsewhere in Europe. Foundations arose at Regensburg, Constance, Erfurt, Eichstatt, Nuremberg, Vienna and Würzburg. From Vienna Irish monks spread out to Kiev, so significant a Russian capital at the time that it was known as 'the mother of Russian towns'.

The English clerics' real objective was to place the Irish Church under the control of Canterbury. They had been foiled in this objective three years earlier at the Synod of Kells where Pope Eugenius III had ruled that the Irish Church was well able to look after itself, despite the fact that the major reform proposed by the 'Romans' would have placed the 'Celts' under a new system of control: dioceses and provinces governed by bishops, appointed from Rome. These reforms would have meant bringing about fundamental changes in Gaelic Ireland, altering practices and attitudes which went back to pre-Christian times. These involved matters relating to such fundamentals of the Church as baptism, marriage, clerical celibacy, the sacraments, and, dare one say cynically, above all, control of Church property.

Foundations such as Glendalough, Kildaré, Bangor and Clonmacnoise had become veritable cities in which learning and the arts flourished. So did the amassing of wealth, and, with their eyes on the money, the great ruling clans saw to it that abbots tended to succeed each other by the rules of hereditary succession, rather than the laws of Rome. In these circumstances, the bishops, appointed by Rome, raised their croziers in impotent anger rather than authority. In that point counterpoint of the Irish character, penance and mortification went hand in hand with extreme wealth as some monks had begun to set up more austere monasteries as early as the end of the eighth century – on the lake island of Lough-Cree, at Finglas and at Tallaght, for example. The rule of these monks, known as 'culdees', may be gauged by these extracts from the penitential table. Serious sins were to be punished by:

spending the night in.water on nettles, or with a dead body . . . spending the night in cold churches or remote cells while keeping vigils and praying without respite – as though one were at the very gates of hell – unless a little weariness chance to occur between two cycles of prayer when one may sit.

'Grievous sin' for someone who could not read merited:

three hundred genuflexions and three hundred properly administered blows with a scourge, at the end of each hundred a cross-vigil until the arms are weary. 'I beseech pardon of God', 'May I receive mercy'. 'I believe in the Trinity' – that is what one signs without ceasing until the commutation is completed; further, frequent striking of the breast and perfect contrition to God.

However, these mortifications failed to convince the Roman/Norman axis that Ireland did not need further scourgings, and, as has so often happened in Irish history, it was an Irish hand that proffered the lash when Diarmait MacMurchada, King of Leinster, obtained Norman assistance in his struggles with other Irish chieftains. In theory, Ireland was ruled by one High King and several lesser kings. In fact, the individual chieftains were a law unto themselves, feuding, making and breaking alliances with and against each other as they saw fit. MacMurchada was more politicised, and ruthless, than his peers. He once had his soldiers carry off and rape a Kildare abbess, not because he disliked nuns – he was in fact a noted benefactor of convents and clerical establishments – but because the rule of the order specified that the abbess had to be a virgin, and he wanted the job for a niece of his. He had the foresight to see what an asset the tough, French-speaking Norman knights would be in his own dynastic struggles.

He also had the advantage of having an English pope in Rome. The Englishman Nicholas Breakspear had been inaugurated as Pope Adrian IV in 1154, and gave ear to another English cleric, John of Salisbury, who successfully lobbied him on behalf of Henry II's claims on Ireland. The Pope issued a bull authorising Henry to 'enter Ireland to improve the state of the Church there'. Salisbury described the bull's origins:

In response to my petition the pope granted and donated Ireland to the illustrious king of England, Henry, to be held by him and his successors, as his letters, still extant, testify. He did this in virtue of the long-established right, reputed to derive from the donation of Constantine, whereby all islands are considered to belong to the Roman church. Moreover, through me the pope sent the king a gold ring, set with a magnificent emerald, as a sign that he had invested the king with the right to rule Ireland, it was later directed by the king that this ring be kept in the public treasury.[15]

With Adrian's 'donation' there begins the era of the 'two colonialisms', Mother England and Mother Church. Between them they created and sustained one of the great ironies, and injustices, of recorded history. Because the Irish kept alive the ancient faith, they naturally came strongly under the influence of the papacy. But, through the papal *traison des clercs*, with the British monarchy, Ireland's fidelity to Rome meant that after the Reformation in England, she fell under the sway of a Protestant nation, and was ravaged and put to the sword because of her popery.

MacMurchada's initiative bore tangible fruit in 1169 with the coming to the Wexford coast of a group of mixed Norman and Welsh led by the Norman FitzStephen. Though it is an over-simplification to call this Norman coming the start of '800 years of British oppression', as some Republican apologists would have it, the landing of MacMurchada's allies does mark the point at which a succession of invaders from the British mainland began to ravage parts of Ireland. After some initial slaughterings, the Irish accepted a system whereby their lands were surrendered to Henry II, and then regranted back to them. This resulted in Irish and Normans intermarrying both literally and culturally to a point where it was said that the invaders became 'more Irish than the Irish themselves'. Nevertheless, the sphere of Norman influence did not extend much beyond a strip of land along the east and north-eastern coast adjoining Dublin which was known as 'The Pale'.

The strip got vastly larger under Henry VIII, the Elizabethans, and Cromwell. The Anglo-Normans had at least had the bond of religion in common with the Irish, not so the products of the Reformation. They systematically plundered the country, taking large areas of the land away from its original owners and giving it to planters. One result of the plantations was today's Northern Ireland problems. Another was mass slaughter. As Brendan Bradshaw has observed:

> This combination of mass slaughter *ad terrorem* and blatant disregard for the conventions of the code of honour was to recur with dismaying regularity down to the end of the sixteenth century ... Against this background the notorious Cromwellian massacres at Drogheda and Wexford in 1649 take their place, not as uniquely barbaric episodes, but as part of a pattern of violence which was central to the historical experience of the inhabitants of the island in the early modern period.[16]

Subjected to genocide, denied a legal existence, the Irish became prey to repeated famines and diseases. One of these famines, the Great Famine of the 1840s, which, as we shall see was to have a profound effect on the diaspora, particularly in America, we will treat of later, but for our European purposes, we need to look in particular at two sets of wars, one immediately, that involving the French, the other involving the Spanish. Both helped in the creation of the 'Wild Geese'.

As our journey through the Irish experience in Europe began in France, I will begin the story of the 'Wild Geese' era with the French military intervention in Ireland although chronologically the Spanish had sent fleets, and traded there, before them; and the Wild Geese were not confined to France and Spain; nor did Irish mercenary activities begin with the Wild

Geese. Dürer, the German artist, has left us portraits of Irish mercenaries
dating from the year 1521, which make it clear that these were not gentlemen
whom one would wish to encounter on a dark night. During the Thirty Years
War, Irish mercenaries were responsible for a notable assassination, that of
Count Wallenstein, Duke of Friedland, in 1634. Wallenstein, who was
planning to desert the German emperor who was struggling to assert his
authority over various local princes, attempted to extract an oath of loyalty
from his Irish and Scots troops. The Irish, however, decided to remain loyal
to the emperor, and an Irish Colonel, Devereux, struck the fatal blow. The
Irish also struck a great number of fatal blows on German soil later on in the
century, when, in the service of the French under General Melac, they took
part in the destruction of Heidelberg in 1688. The Irish were so ferocious that
women and children did not feel safe even when claiming the sanctuary of the
cathedral. Because of, rather than despite, their terrible reputation Irish
soldiers were prized by the Soldier King himself, Frederick William I of
Prussia.

However, it is the French-Irish connection which is the principal tributary
of the Wild Geese tradition. It stems from the year 1690. The Irish had thrown
in their lot with the Jacobite cause led by one of history's poltroons, the
Catholic King James II, known to the Irish of the time as Seamas a chaca
(James the Shite). He was one of the first to flee the Boyne battlefield and
arrived in Dublin announcing, 'My cowardly Irish troops have run away.' To
which a gentlewoman is said to have replied: 'And you, my Lord, have won
the race.' The Protestant victory at the Boyne is still commemorated today as
the most important date in the Orangemen's calendar, 'The Glorious Twelfth'
(12 July). In fact, the Pope was on the side of the Orangemen at the time and
ordered a Te Deum to be sung when he heard the result.

The Irish wars were merely bloody side-shows to the overall European
conflict between the Dutch William III, whom the Pope supported, and the
French Louis XIV. Sizeable contingents of Frenchmen fought on both sides
of the Boyne. Because of Louis's persecution of the Huguenots many had
taken refuge in Ireland both before and after the revocation of the Edict of
Nantes in 1685. They established significant settlements in Dublin, Cork,
Lisburn, Portarlington and Waterford. These well-doing people were a
particularly valuable addition to Irish society. One of them, Louis
Crommelin, founded the linen trade in Northern Ireland which was to be a
source of prosperity in the region for more than two centuries after the Battle
of the Boyne. Another descendant of Huguenot stock, Sean Lemass, would
prove himself the most effective Irish Prime Minister of the twentieth century.
The Huguenots also formed a particularly effective component of William's
army at the Boyne. Schomberg, the Williamite commander, himself a former
Marshal of France, who had been born in Heidelberg, gave his men the order
to charge by pointing out Louis's detachments in James's army and
exclaiming: 'Messieurs, voici vos persecuteurs.'

However, the price of those troops' presence is not often acknowledged by

Irish historians, or indeed French ones for that matter. There is a general tendency to see the Wild Geese era in a wholly romantic glow. In fact the romance was suffused by a sometimes cruel tint of pragmatism. To begin with, Louis stipulated that in return for his sending troops to Ireland, the Irish would make up the losses to his armies. Accordingly, in May 1690, 6,000 Irish troops departed for France under the command of Justin McCarthy, Viscount Mount Cashel. In return Louis sent an army of his battle-hardened troops to Ireland under the command of the incompetent General the Marquis de St Ruth. St Ruth, who used his Irish troops as cannon fodder at the disastrous Battle of Aughrim, where some 7,000 Irish were cut down, suffered the poetic justice of losing his own head to a Dutch cannon ball.

Subsequent Irish resistance came to an end following the siege of Limerick in 1691. After he had surrendered, Patrick Sarsfield, Earl of Lucan, remarked to a British officer: 'As low as we are now, change kings with us and we will willingly try our luck with you again.' But the Irish had run out of luck. The Treaty of Limerick guaranteed that the Irish would enjoy the same religious liberty as they had under Charles II. However, the ink was scarcely dry before the victors began seizing the estates of the Irish landowners. The Irish had no means of redress against these confiscations. The English Parliament was militantly Protestant and passed a law decreeing that only Protestants could sit in the British Parliament.

Moreover, a penal code, begun under William and Mary and continued under Queen Anne, also decreed that henceforth the law would not recognise Catholics. They could not sit either on juries or in Parliament. In Ireland this also meant that Irish Catholics could not hold land, nor own a horse, above the value of £5. They were of course excluded from trade and the professions. The Irish cattle trade had already been destroyed under Charles II; now the commercial code was worsened to ruin the Irish woollen trade also. As the British historians Carter and Mears wrote many years later:

> The Treaty of Limerick was shamefully broken ... No Englishman can read without shame this unworthy passage in our history. The broken Treaty of Limerick, the harsh and mean laws, were bad enough. But the complete lack of any sense of responsibility towards the conquered race was worse. Had the policy of the English in Ireland been followed elsewhere, there would have been no British Empire today.[17]

After the Irish defeat, some 20,000 soldiers and civilians were allowed to set sail, in Sarsfield's words, to 'make another Ireland in the armies of the great King of France', but there was little of the high heroic in the manner of their leaving. Macaulay described what happened as follows. The men were lined up and:

> the Roman Catholic clergy were called in ... a sermon was preached, and the duty of adhering to the cause of the church and 'a plentiful allowance of brandy was served out.' It was by no means strange that a superstitious and excitable kearne should be ready to

promise whatever his priest required, neither was it strange that when he had slept off his liquor and when anathemas were no longer ringing in his ears, he should feel painful misgivings.[18]

To heighten these misgivings, in the days after the men had initially overwhelmingly decided to enlist, word came that the first of the Irish troops to land had been 'ungratefully received', being 'scantily fed' and receiving no pay or clothing. They had had to sleep rough. On hearing this, many of the troops still in Limerick either deserted or threw down their arms and refused to board the ship. One of the factors preying on the Irish soldiers' minds was the presence of thousands of their women and children who clogged the fields and roads all around Limerick, and who faced starvation if their menfolk left them. Sarsfield promised the men that he would take the women and children also, and so a large embarkation commenced – too large, there was not enough room aboard for all who wanted to sail. Even after the passage of centuries, Macaulay's description of what happened next is poignant in the extreme:

> After the soldiers had embarked, room was found for the families of many. But still there remained on the waterside a great multitude clamouring piteously to be taken on board. As the last boats put off there was a rush into the surf. Some women caught hold of the ropes, were dragged out of their depth, clung till their fingers were cut through, and perished in the waves. The ships began to move. A wild and terrible wail rose from the shore, and excited unwonted compassion in hearts steeled by hatred of the Irish race and of the Romish faith ... The emaciated and broken-hearted crowd ... dispersed to beg their way home through a wasted land, or to lie down and die by the roadside of grief and hunger.

As Macaulay said after that ghastly embarkation: 'In Ireland there was peace. The domination of the colonist was absolute. The native population was tranquil with the ghastly tranquillity of exhaustion and despair.' Most of those leaving believed and hoped that departure to 'another Ireland', would result some day in their returning to their native country with French support to drive out the British. However, it was not to be. Nevertheless, not only in the seventeenth but throughout most of the eighteenth century, until the era of the French Revolution, tens of thousands of Irishmen left Ireland to die on Europe's battlefields. The generally accepted figure for the death toll amongst the Irish who served the armies of France in the Wild Geese era is between 450,000 and 500,000 men, quite apart from the inevitable deaths amongst women and children dependants, either through hardship or collateral casualties. The Irish regiments were always allocated the most dangerous objectives, the highest ridges, the most fortified town, the gallant rearguard action. Their fatally efficient discharge of their orders meant just that – they suffered terrible casualties.

For a time after Limerick there were in fact two Irish armies in France: one a Jacobite army under the control of King James II, the other the Irish Brigade which served France. The latter's regiments were commanded by members of the former Irish aristocracy in Ireland, men with names such as Berwick, Bulkelly, Clare, Dillon and Walsh. The Irish who served James were regarded as the King's army in exile. They retained the distinctive British Red Coat and English was the language of command, even when the Irish Army served under the command of the King's allies, the Bourbons. As Macaulay wrote, 'scattered over all Europe, were to be found brave Irish generals, dexterous Irish diplomatists . . . These men were the natural chiefs of their race, having been withdrawn, what remained were utterly helpless and passive.' Neither Stuarts nor Bourbons realised Irish aspirations. The Irish fought in most of the campaigns of the period only to see their hopes of a return to Ireland dashed by the Treaty of Ryswick in 1697 by which Louis XIV recognised William of Orange as the King of England. The Jacobite army was disbanded, but the Irish Brigade remained and many of James's army joined up.

However, a combination of the War of the Spanish Succession and the death of James II in 1701 caused Louis XIV to think again about supporting the Stuarts, and a fresh Jacobite army was recruited. The Irish Brigade was also brought up to full strength and the Irish fought and died in a litany of battles: in Italy, Flanders, Bavaria, Spain; at Blenheim, Malplaquet, Oudenarde, Ramillies; and at the Siege of Cremona. The Irish did not confine their pugnacity to the battlefield. One anecdote which survives from the days of the Wild Geese concerns what was intended to be the dressing-down of the Irish commander, Count Dillon. However, when the King of France told Dillon that the Irish troops gave him more trouble than the rest of the French army, Dillon delivered the devastating reply: 'The enemy make the same complaint, your Majesty.'

The principal engagement of the Irish brigade occurred during the War of the Austrian Succession, during which France and Prussia sought to install a Bavarian over the claims of Marie-Therese of Hapsburg, who was supported by the Austrians, the British and the Dutch. This occurred at Fontenoy, a plateau some five miles south-west of Tournai. The stakes were high: had the British won, they would have controlled northern France, the Dutch would have ruled modern Belgium, and Louise XIV's reign would hardly have survived.

The British advance was slowed by the use of four pieces of artillery whose use is variously ascribed to either the Duke de Richelieu, a Captain Isnard, or to Thomas Arthur Lally, a colonel of an Irish regiment. What is certain is that at a crucial juncture, all six regiments of the Irish Brigade were employed with spectacular results. The Brigade charged under the war cry 'Cuimhnigid ar Luimneach' (Remember Limerick), and smashed through the British lines, forcing a retreat. The French historian, Jean-Pierre Bois, has judged that the Irish Brigade's charge was the decisive factor in the battle.[19] Overall the British lost 5,000 dead or wounded, but in percentage terms the Irish losses were heaviest: a total of 656 killed or wounded, out of an enrolment of 3,870 officers and men.

Fontenoy is commemorated in all sorts of ways in Ireland to this day, in the name of a GAA Club, and in a poem by Thomas Davis, which in its day was a rallying cry for the Young Ireland movement, and was still taught in school when I was a boy:

> How fierce the look these exiles wear,
> who're wont to be so gay,
> The treasur'd wrongs of fifty years
> are in their hearts today!
> The treaty broken, ere the ink wherewith 'twas
> writ could dry.
> Their plunder'd homes, their ruin'd shrines,
> their women's parting cry.
> Their priesthood hunted down like wolves,
> their country overthrown.
> Each looks, as if revenge for ALL were stak'd
> on him alone.
> On Fontenoy, on Fontenoy, nor ever yet elsewhere,
> Rush'd on to fight a nobler band,
> than these proud exiles were!

The impact of Fontenoy was such that on the morning of the Battle of Culloden in 1746 Bonnie Prince Charlie exhorted his officers: 'Gentlemen, let us inflict another Fontenoy on Cumberland.' Apart from acknowledging Fontenoy the Young Pretender was also recognising the fact that the Scottish Rising which had begun the year before in 1745 was largely the work of Irishmen:

> It was planned, promoted, financed and directed by Irishmen. The officers of the Irish Brigade contributed generously. Prince Charles obtained 180,000 livres from Irish Bankers in Paris. One Irishman fitted out a privateer with eighteen guns. The expedition was commanded by Col. Sir John O'Sullivan. A detachment drawn from the Irish Brigade, drawn from its six regiments, fought alongside the clansmen.[20]

'Fought and died', would be a more apt description. It was the heroic, but fatal, rearguard stand of the Irish which enabled an Irish officer, Colonel Warren, to escort Bonnie Prince Charlie to safety and a life of ignominy in Paris.

However, Europe has a surfeit of battlefields and when I visited Fontenoy, very little was immediately visible to the eye by way of commemoration of this Irish epic. The most startling manifestation of an Irish, or at least Celtic, influence was a small boy who bounded in front of the car as Eoghan O'hAnnracháin and I drove into the village of Fontenoy. Red-haired, freckled, round-faced and blue-eyed, he could have been met with on the outskirts of any one of a thousand Irish towns. Where did he come from? I don't know, but as Eoin remarked, 'You can't beat nature.'

The topography has been changed by the planting of woods and by agriculture. Buildings, including a large sugar factory, are encroaching on the actual battlefield. In the local tavern, 'the Café des Irlandais', few of the locals knew how the place got its name, although there are pictures on the walls commemorating the battle. One shows a famous incident in which an English officer, standing before his troops, enquires of his French counterpart if he would like the honour of firing first. The Frenchman declined, saying with foolish gallantry: 'Les Anglais tierent les premiers!' It was literally a fatal mistake. The Frenchman did not realise how much English musketry had improved and the first volley created slaughter and panic.

There is also a photograph showing a nearby memorial cross erected by the Irish in 1907. The existence of the cross indicates something of how the Irish diaspora spread through the world as a result of the sort of policies which caused them to be present at Fontenoy in the first place. The cross was erected through the efforts of the American Order of Hibernians, a London committee headed by R. Barry O'Brien, and a Dublin one headed by the Lord Mayor of Dublin, A. J. Hutchinson. The memorial is inscribed to the: 'Soldats de la brigade Irlandaise qui sur le champ de Fontenoi se vengerent de la violation de Trait de Limerick.' Underneath it is an outline of the Limerick Treaty Stone inscribed:

> On this stone was signed the Treaty in which England guaranteed religious liberty to the Irish. She violated the Treaty and the Irish, hunted from their fatherland, entered into the French armies and warfare on the battlefields of Europe.

The memorial is showing signs of wear, and, like many Irish links with European history, should be attended to. It, and a statue of the Blessed Virgin in the nearby church which was presented by Louis XIV to the Irish, may seem inadequate tributes to their gallantry, but these small symbols tell us something of the tradition which even today makes life in France far more welcoming to the average Irish emigrant than does employment in Britain. Several of the younger members of the O'hAnnracháin tour, who had worked in bars or building sites in England, remarked to me how much more at home they felt in France than they had in the UK. The welcome is rooted, not only in the tradition of Columbanus and Columcille, or even of the Irish Brigades, but in the tradition of friendship between the great Irish clans and the French.

Writing to a friend in October 1870, the historian William Lecky observed: 'In Ireland we are passionately French, partly because we think ourselves rather like the French, partly because of the Irish Brigade which served under France, and partly because the English take the other side.' All of Lecky's observations are correct – French visitors to Ireland often remark on the 'Latin' quality of the society – but there is another reason for the French affinity, part of the wider Irish out-reach to Europe. Along with the military tradition a strong artistic and commercial connection also grew up, particularly in France. The Irish kept in touch with their own country and made not a vice but a virtue of the custom of nepotism whereby the Irish ascended the social, military and ecclesiastical ladders of the day. For example, Lecky lists the following:

> Lord Clare became Marshal of France; Browne, who was one of the very ablest Austrian generals, and who took a leading part in the first period of the Seven Years' War, was the son of Irish parents; and Maguire, Lacy, Nugent, and O'Donnell were all prominent generals in the Austrian service during the same war. Another Browne, a cousin of the Austrian commander, was Field Marshal in the Russian service and Governor of Riga. Peter Lacy, who also became a Russian Field Marshal and who earned the reputation of one of the first soldiers of his time, was of Irish birth . . . He sprang from an Irish family which had the rare fortune of counting generals in the services . . . of Austria, Russia and Spain. Of the Dillons, more than one attained high rank in the French army, and one became Archbishop of Toulouse. The brave, the impetuous Lally of Tollendal, who served with such distinction at Dettingen and Fontenoy, and who for a time seriously threatened the English power in Hindustan, was the son of a Galway gentleman. Among Spanish generals, the names of O'Mahony, O'Donnell, O'Gara, O'Reilly and O'Neill sufficiently attest their nationality . . . Wall, who directed the government of Spain with singular ability from 1754 to 1763, was an Irishman . . . By parentage MacGeoghegan, the first considerable historian of Ireland, was chaplain to the Irish Brigade in the service of France. The physician of Sobieski, King of Poland, and the physician of Philip V of Spain were both Irish; an Irish naturalist named Bowles was active in reviving the mining industry of Spain in 1752 . . . In the diplomacy of the Continent Irish names are not unknown. Tyrconnel was French Ambassador at the Court of Berlin. Wall, before he became chief minister of Spain, had represented that country at the Court of London. Lacy was Spanish Ambassador at Stockholm, and O'Mahony at Vienna.

The Wild Geese chapter began to close in the second half of the eighteenth century. A costly piece of gallantry, at Lafelt, in 1747, two years after Fontenoy, played its part. Some 800 officers and men of the Irish Brigade lost their lives in this, the last great battle of the War of the Austrian Succession. The French army was victorious, but some of the fatal gallantry displayed by the French officer at Fontenoy caused Marshal Saxe to adjourn hostilities for lunch after Lafelt was captured. He thus allowed the retreating Austrians to pass through a ravine and the British, Dutch, Austrian and Hanoverian forces were able to regroup around Maastricht – a town around which considerable hostilities still rage in the ranks of British Conservatives, because of its role in the European Union. After the battle, an English officer testified both to the Irish troops' bravery and, *inter alia*, the omnipresent British failure to recognise the concept of nationhood amongst the Irish which was a constant source of regret to Irish nationalists through the centuries. He saw them, not as members of the Celtic nation, but as rebels against a lawfully appointed British king. The officer wrote to a friend:

> It was generally believ'd that the young pretender was a volunteer in that action, which animated these rebellious troops to push so desperately; and as what advantage the French had at Fontenoy as well as now, was owing to the desperate behaviour of this brigade; it

34

may well be said that the king of France is indebted for his successes to the natural-born subjects of the crown of Great Britain.

The Young Pretender was of course nowhere near the scene of the action, though some of the Irish troops who had survived the Irish Brigade's rescue of him at Culloden did fight at Lafelt. One of them, Colonel William Warren, miraculously escaped with his life, despite the fact that seven projectiles, either musket balls or pieces of shrapnel, struck his clothes during the engagement. One hit him in the cod piece. Either this or the Colonel was unusually well formed for in a letter to his brother Richard he speaks of his suffering no ill effects beyond a certain swelling and a soreness in the affected area: '. . . the ball hit ye brass button of my britches and only broke ye flesh at the bottom of my belly just at ye root of my yard and swool greatly but that is all gone.[21]

Now all that remains to remind either the Irish, or the French, of the ferocity of the battle is a Celtic cross, erected incongruously enough by the Cork City Choral Society, in 1964, on the left bank of the river Meuse, near Lafelt and about three miles from Maastricht.

Losses in battle and increasing disillusionment with the aberrant Prince Charles combined to diminish Irish enthusiasm both for the Jacobite cause and enrolment in the Irish Brigades. The manifest injustice of the treatment meted out to the Irish Count Lally (he was beheaded in 1766, falsely accused of having sold Pondicherry, in India, to the English) helped to quell Irish enthusiasm for recruiting into a French regiment. The Brigades continued in both France and Spain, but the Irish connection was increasingly maintained only through the officer cadre as the Irish peasantry developed a reluctance to get themselves killed in foreign wars. The unlikely combination of papal diplomacy and the outbreak of the French Revolution brought this phase of the Irish Brigades to a close.

By 1770 Vatican diplomacy had come to recognise that the policy of attempting to control the Irish Church through Catholic monarchs in England, initiated under Nicholas Breakspear, was ceasing to pay dividends. Accordingly, recognising that the dissolute Stuart line was never going to rule England, the papacy moved in 1770 to rescind the Stuart privilege, that of appointing Irish bishops, which had caused the British to visit much misery on the Irish. In chess terms the Pope may certainly be adjudged to have successfully traded a pawn for not one but several bishops. For, as Westminster suspicions of the Irish hierarchy subsided, the harshness of the penal laws was correspondingly relaxed. The marked drift amongst Irish Catholics towards turning Protestant (in order to hold property or gain advancement) was halted. This had been so pronounced that by the 1780s only 5 per cent of the land of Ireland remained in Catholic hands. However, Catholic Relief Acts were passed in 1778 and 1782 which enabled the Irish both to teach and hold land. Catholic seminaries were set up from 1790 onwards, the great National Seminary of St Patrick's College, Maynooth, being established in 1795. Henceforth, in furtherance of papal policy, the Irish hierarchy would support British imperial policy. Under it, Mother Church would successfully organise her Irish children into a worldwide empire. The siren song of continental influence and 'godless republicanism' would be sternly resisted.

In France, the outbreak of revolution led to the formal suppression of the Irish Brigades in 1791. The fact of being what the revolutionaries saw as an élitist corps that had been officered by men with titles like Count Dillon, Lord Clare or the Duke of Berwick, and closely identified with the Bourbons, inevitably caused many prominent Irish Brigade figures to fall victim to the terror. One officer, Theobold Dillon, did not survive long enough to reach the guillotine; he was murdered by his own troops. Admiral Henry MacNamara was torn apart by a mob. On the other hand, an Irish Augustinian priest, Philip Crane, was the subject of one of the most incredible escapes from the mob recorded during the entire course of the terror.[22]

Crane was en route from Rome to Paris when a fellow Irishman told him that another Irishman, Charles Tottenham, from New Ross in County Wexford, was in prison, condemned to execution on a bogus charge of being an English spy. Crane's instinctive reaction, knowing the role of Tottenham and his family in New Ross in subjugating Catholics, was to exclaim: 'He's no friend of ours.' However, he repented this unchristian utterance almost immediately and decided to rescue Tottenham. He got into the prison, disguised as a baker delivering the daily bread, and then made his way to the condemned cell and exchanged places with Tottenham.

However, although it was indeed a far, far better thing he had done than he had ever done before, Crane managed to evade the fate of Sidney Carton in Dickens's *A Tale of Two Cities*. Somehow he persuaded the authorities that he was a chaplain of the Goddess of Liberty, who had recently been crowned at the Cathedral of Notre Dame, secured his release, and returned to Wexford. Here he became prior of the Augustinian Community who, under the prohibitions of the time, were living in wretched conditions. Tottenham had become the powerful Mayor of New Ross and was still 'no friend' of Catholics generally, but he was an honourable man who acknowledged he owed an immense debt to Crane. Accordingly he returned to Crane the former Catholic parish chapel site, on a hill overlooking the town, for a peppercorn rent of ten shillings a year. The Augustinians still occupy the site at the time of writing.

Another Irish cleric who came even closer to the guillotine was the Abbé Edgeworth from Edgeworthstown in Longford. He had been confessor to King Louis XVI's sister Elizabeth, and attended the King prior to his execution. Just before the blade fell he is said to have exclaimed to the King: 'Fils de Saint Louis, montez au ciel.' Somehow Edgeworth lived through that grisly episode to become chaplain to Louis XVIII.

Inevitably, of course, some Irishmen took the revolutionary side. Two of the seven prisoners who caused the attack on the Bastille were Irish; some of the attackers were Irish: James Blackwell was a student at the Irish College;

another was Joseph Kavanagh, a shoemaker, who later became a feared police officer. Probably less feared was another Irish shoemaker, one Daniel Murphy, whose daughter Marie-Louise had transcended her origins in Rouen to become mistress to Louis XV. Jean Baptiste O'Sullivan is remembered for having brought his own brand of the Terror to Nantes, and the Irishman, Robert Arthur, became such a zealous republican that he was nicknamed 'Little Robespierre'.

In Spain, the situation became equally confused. As revolutionary notions spread, General O'Donoju (O'Donoghue) attempted to stem the flow at the head of the loyalist Ministry of War in Cadiz. His counterpart, under King Joseph Bonaparte in Madrid, was General O'Farril. These divisions represented similar fissurings throughout Spanish society and throughout Italy and the Low Countries. William D. Griffin has judged that the 'earthquake of revolution' shattered 'the Irish nation in exile'.[23] In so far as the Irish Brigades were concerned he is correct. Keenly aware of the loss in manpower occasioned by earlier policies (in 1793), the British relaxed the laws against Catholics holding commissions in the British Army. Many of the Franco-Irish officers thus received commissions from King George III, against whom they had fought in the American War.

Today, as in other parts of Europe, the descendants of the Wild Geese are to be found in the higher reaches of French society. As a historian of the Wild Geese, Renagh Holohan has written that the term is one which carries social cachet:

To this day, in dusty chateaux in rural France, families proudly maintain genealogical tables which, in some cases, date back to 11th Century High King Brian Boru. Although many of Les Oies Sauvages (Wild Geese) send their children to Ireland for some part of their education, they still retain a romantic view of the motherland that is perhaps as out of touch with the Ireland of today as their frequently proclaimed royalist views are out of step with modern France.[24]

Franco-Irish military co-operation did not end with the Wild Geese. Developments in France had caught the imagination of progressive elements in both the Irish Presbyterian and Catholic communities in Ireland, who founded the Society of the United Irishmen. The growth of the United Irishmen, and the persuasive powers of their emissary to France, Theobald Wolfe Tone, persuaded the Directory to send a fleet to Ireland in 1796. However, a Protestant wind blew and the fleet was dispersed harmlessly (for the British). Two years later, in 1798, another French force, a very small one, was despatched to Ireland, landing in County Mayo. However, communications difficulties and vastly superior British forces, aided by Protestant militias, resulted in bloody suppression of the proposed uprising so much so that Napoleon decided against giving any significant assistance to another rebellion, led by a friend of Wolfe Tone's, Robert Emmet, in 1803. However, after Emmet's rising was crushed, Napoleon did create an Irish legion formed from former United Irishmen who hoped to return to fight in Ireland. At his coronation Napoleon presented the legion with a green flag inscribed with his name on one side and a harp without a crown on the other. The motto of the flag was 'L'independence d'Irlande'. The legion did fight the British, but not in Ireland. They fought in Spain, Portugal and at Waterloo before being disbanded in 1815. As Miles Byrne, who had been a United Irishmen general in 1798 wrote: 'The loss of the battle of Waterloo . . . put an end to our career and to all further hopes of aid from France to relieve Ireland from her bondage.'

The Irish sympathised with the French in the Franco-Prussian War of 1870 and sent an ambulance corps to France. The Compagnie Irlandaise, a unit of Irish volunteers commanded by Captain Kirwan, became the second foreign regiment of the French Foreign Legion. The Legion had a bearing on the subsequent course of Irish history inasmuch as one of the principal architects of the 1916 Rising, John Devoy, became a legionnaire in 1863 so that he could study infantry warfare. He decided after two years that he had learned enough and deserted.

One of the most significant contributions of the Irish 'nation in exile' to Europe as a result of conditions in Ireland was the spread throughout the continent of Irish Colleges. These were maintained by donations of kings, bishops, the Irish Catholic nobility in exile and such of their relations as had managed to survive in possession of wealth in Ireland. Apart from training clergy, the colleges educated many of the children of the Wild Geese regiments and of the Irish mercantile class which developed on the continent. The growth of the Irish Colleges was given a further impetus by the decrees of the Council of Trent which laid down that in future all priests should be seminary trained. There was no university in Ireland and the monasteries had been suppressed since the fourteenth century, therefore Irish clerics and scholars had been enrolling in Oxford, Cambridge, Bologna, Salamanca, Alcala de Henares, Valladolid and Cologne. Beginning in 1578 with the Irish College in Paris, eighteen Irish Colleges for secular clergy were established on the continent. This development was accompanied by the setting up of a dozen or so Colleges by religious orders such as the Augustinians, Capuchins, Carmelites, Dominicans, Franciscans and Jesuits.

In Rome, both St Clemente (Dominican) and St Isidore's (Franciscan) are still flourishing, as is the last fully functioning Irish College, which still trains priests for the Irish Church. It is also a centre of hospitality, Irish hierarchical influence, and a popular place for the Irish to get married in. The colleges were normally located near continental universities, and usually formed part of them. The more famous of these colleges were those of Paris, Rome and Salamanca, but there were also important foundations in Prague, Lisbon, Louvain, Nantes, Bordeaux, Douai, Tournai and in Vielun, Poland.

These colleges were a vital element both in educating the 'Irish national in exile' and in the spread of the influence of Roman Catholicism amongst the Irish diaspora. For example, as we shall see, the Irish College in Prague played a part in the story of the Irish in far off Newfoundland (Chapter Four), and products of the Irish College in Rome in that of even further off Australia (Chapter Five). However, like much else the Irish did for their Church, these achievements were bought at a terrible price. Back in Ireland, the best the returned priests could hope for was hunger and poverty, a life on the run; the worst a martyr's fate – but still the recruits came.

It may be said with accuracy that the Irish were to be found in every walk of French life. Along with the Wild Geese there were the Wine Geese. Several famous names in the French wine-growing district, especially in the Bordeaux and Cognac regions, are of Irish origin: Château MacCarthy, Château Lynch-Bages, Château Lynch-Moussas, Château Leoville-Barton, Château Clarke, Château Boyd-Cantenac, Château Kirwan. The Hennessy brandy label stems from Richard Hennessy, a former officer in the Dillon regiment of the Irish Brigade, who set up the famous brandy distillery in 1765. As strong spirits have ruined many an Irish writer, I feel I should acknowledge the assistance and encouragement Hennessy's have given to Irish writing. For some twenty years, during my tenure as editor of the *Irish Press*, Hennessy sponsored a new Irish writing page in which, for two decades, numbers of significant talents were discovered and every poet of consequence in Ireland had their work published.

Only one of the Wine Geese firms is now in Irish hands, those of Anthony Barton, a remarkably youthful-looking seventy-year-old, who was born in Ireland. He is the ninth generation of his Protestant Anglo-Irish family to manage the lucrative Bordeaux label.[25] He owes his inheritance of châteaux, vineyards and other property, partly to the fact that his ancestors avoided the French inheritance laws by keeping their Irish passports and by shunning marriage to French women. Under French law property must be divided equally among direct descendants. To avoid this the Bartons practise primogeniture. Anthony is married to a Danish wife and his children, though born in Copenhagen, have Irish passports. The other reason the Bartons still own their property is because of their friendship with the Guestier family. During the French Revolution Hugh Barton escaped the Terror by returning to Ireland to sit the Revolution out, leaving the business in the hands of his partner, Daniel Guestier. When Hitler's armies invaded France the then controlling Barton, Ronald, again turned the business over to another Daniel Guestier and enlisted in the Royal Iniskilling Fusiliers. His property was safe when he came back, a much-decorated war hero.

The French have retaliated for this intrusion of Irish wine-growers and distillers into their territory by taking over the distilling of Irish whiskey in Dublin. Pernod Ricard bought Irish Distillers and now produces Jameson whiskey.

Apart from the liquor industry, the Irish made names for themselves as bankers. Figures like Robert Dillon in Bordeaux, Walter Rutledge in Dunkirk, and Richard Cantillon in Paris, were all considerable personages in French society in their day.

Some of the Irish, however, had a seamy side to their industry. For example, Anthony Walsh and Walter Rutledge, were like other Irish – the Clarkes and the Shiels for example, also of Nantes – active practitioners of the slave trade. Also, part of the money which men like these devoted to the Jacobite cause came not merely from slavery, but from privateering in the West Indies. The Irish Church condemned slavery, but this was directed at ending the custom whereby Irish raiders, like those who brought Patrick to Ireland, enslaved Britons. The wealthy Irish émigrés of France, however, were as little troubled by the horrors visited on Africans as were many of their fellow countrymen in America in the following century.

French/Irish interest waned somewhat in the nineteenth century, although Daniel O'Connell and his movement were part of the inspiration for the French Catholic Liberal movement as spearheaded by intellectuals such as Lacordaire, Lamennais and Montalembert, and the great diarist, Alexis de Tocqueville, has left us one of the most insightful portraits of Ireland in the famine years. After the Famine, the Paris Revolution of 1848 was a strong motivating force in the abortive Young Ireland rising. Probably foreseeing just how abortive it could be, the French poet-president Lamartine confined his assistance to recollections of the long-standing friendship between the French and the Irish, but the Young Irelanders brought back with them to Dublin a magnificent silk flag of green, white and orange: green for the Catholic and Irish tradition, orange for the Protestant and British tradition, and white for peace between them. It is the flag which flies over today's Dublin Parliament. However, the original hope of the Young Irelanders that both traditions would clasp hands under its fold 'in generous and heroic brotherhood' is still somewhat short of fulfilment.

French authors and journalists were active on the Irish side during the Black and Tan War, and Paris was always a beckoning beacon for Irish revolutionaries, like the Fenian brotherhood, or Irish intellectuals, like Oscar Wilde who died in Paris. He originally wrote *Salome* in French. Great figures of the Irish 'Celtic Revival' such as George Moore, Yeats and Synge were francophiles. Yeats, in fact, died in the south of France. James Joyce owed *Ulysses* to Paris and Sylvia Beach, the bookshop owner who published it. His disciple, Samuel Beckett, also found Paris a mecca. However, apart from the occasional young Irish intellectual going to Paris to 'find' him or herself, a certain amount of tourism, and the annual French rugby international, it would be true to say that by the mid-twentieth century, Irish/French connections had become thin and distant.

Apart from the influx of the new Irish blood, two other factors helped to re-kindle the Franco-Irish relationship (three if one allows for the impact in cycling-besotted France of the Irish cyclists, Stephen Roche and Sean Kelly. Roche actually went so far as to storm the citadel of this most French of sports by winning the Tour de France). One was the visit in 1969 to Ireland of Charles de Gaulle. This helped to stimulate interest between France and

Ireland generally, and in particular to remind both peoples that on his mother's side, de Gaulle's ancestors were MacCartans from County Down. (No Irish grandparents could be provided for President François Mitterrand, but the warm welcome he received in Ireland in 1988 was well publicised in the French media nevertheless.) The visit by the Irish President, Mary Robinson, to France, in May 1992 was an even greater media event and the pace of cultural exchange quickened visibly. An Irish exhibition opened in Paris in 1996 and was later exhibited throughout France. This display of literary and creative artistry greatly heightened awareness of Ireland.

In an article printed in 1988, Piaras McEnri, a former Irish diplomat who at the time of writing works in emigration studies at Cork University, published the results of a survey he had conducted into the Irish in France with the aid of the Université de Paris 111.[26] He found that, in Paris, something had 'changed dramatically' in the previous five years. There had not been a single Irish pub five years earlier, nor an Irish restaurant.[27] The Association Irlandaise, which printed his article, had not been founded. Now it runs a regular radio programme, fields football teams, organises language classes in Irish and French, as well as classes in music and dancing, and looks after the welfare of Irish emigrants. He pointed to the growing attraction of visiting Irish musical performers, and the increasingly favourable image of Ireland.

The reasons for the changes which McEnri identified were both political and economic. Politically, from the time of joining the EEC (on 1 January 1973), the Common Agricultural Policy made France and Ireland close allies in Europe. Increased levels of education and prosperity in Ireland led to the same sort of sharp increase in Irish trade with France as they did to the EU as a whole. In 1973, Irish exports to France totalled only IR£45 million and the French sold the Irish IR£52 million in return. By 1997, Irish exports to France had shot up to IR£2,763 million. In return Ireland imported IR£1,210 million. These increasing volumes of trade led to a corresponding increase in the numbers of Irish people living in France and vice versa. More than thirty French factories have opened in Ireland, as have French banks and insurance companies. There is now a flourishing Franco-Irish Chamber of Commerce in Dublin, and the Dublin branch of the Alliance Français is the largest in Europe.

The St Patrick's Day celebrations are a barometer of the strength of an Irish community anywhere. In France the St Patrick's Day celebration is now a sort of mini-Bastille Day, a remarkable transformation, given that the Saint's festival was unknown up to the mid-eighties. The visibility of Irish culture, in all its forms, is even more remarkable. In a development, not entirely welcomed by old Paris hands such as myself, Irish pubs have supplanted many of the old cafés in and around Paris. Irish whiskeys and stouts are well known, and well consumed by the French, and of course Irish music is to be encountered everywhere. All the bigger names in the Irish musical world, Enya and the Corrs in the traditional forms, and the Pogues building a bridge between the world of the Chieftains and that of U2, have devoted followings in France, as they have anywhere in the world that radio, TV, tapes, or CDs are to be had.

As in every Irish community, there is inevitably a fringe element of 'bicycle Irish' not computed by the Irish Embassy, but probably just as numerous as the section which is accounted for (15,000). In the main, these will be younger people, working at a variety of jobs, bar-tending and so forth, possibly having dropped out for a year or two to see something of the world before continuing their studies. Not all will return to university, though experience shows that a sizeable proportion will, and the others generally either find a French partner or settle into one of the numerous comfortable niches afforded by prosperous Europe.

Pierre Joannon the Honorary Irish Consul to the south of France, does not have either an Irish name or accent, but he is a knowledgeable Hibernophile.[28] His interest stems from a visit he paid to Ireland in 1964 whilst on his honeymoon. He and his wife had planned to visit Scotland, but came to Ireland instead because of a typhoid scare. During a visit to Portrush, in Northern Ireland, Joannon encountered an Orange procession and he was so fascinated by the sight of the bowler-hatted, sash-wearing figures that he began a study of their origins which led him, through Irish history, eventually to become an honorary Irish Consul.

He lives in a pleasant villa in Antibes, in the south of France, which has been twinned, appropriately enough, with Kinsale in Ireland, the town where the breaking of the old Gaelic order led to the strengthening of French/Irish links. Antibes is not the sort of setting that someone like myself would have associated with the Irish diaspora. I was reared at the ferry port of Dun Laoghaire on Dublin's south-east coast from whence I saw tens of thousands of shabby, sad men and women depart to break their dreams against the walls of Coventry and Cricklewood. In Antibes, the rich swim amidst the biggest of bank accounts and the briefest of bikinis. The huge yachts owned by international financiers and Arab princes differ from the ferries which the emigrants boarded at Dun Laoghaire to cross the turbulent Irish Sea in some essential respects. They are larger, far more luxurious, and come equipped with helicopter landing pads. Joannon is something of a Renaissance man. A wealthy businessman, broadcaster and journalist, he is also a respected authority on Irish history, who has an interest in Michael Collins, and has written a book about him.

When the film on Michael Collins, starring Liam Neeson, was shown in France, Joannon gave a brief talk on Collins and Ireland at over half a dozen celebrity charity showings. Normally, he said, such talks would be expected to last about ten minutes, followed by the odd question or two, but in the case of the Collins film the questioning always went on for more than an hour. That indicates something of the interest in Ireland, but it may possibly also indicate something of an underlying layer of anti-British sentiment, which some say is part of the motivation for the growing French interest in Irish history and

Irish studies. Part of the French resentment stems from British policy over Europe in the present day; part is bitterness about some British actions in the past. Apart from the sinking of the Vichy fleet, the French have still not forgotten how the British Air Force reduced to rubble some Normandy towns during the allied landings, even though the Germans had either withdrawn or no longer posed a threat.

I discussed this with Paul Brennan, Professor of Irish Studies at the Sorbonne, and President of the prestigious Société Française d'Études Irlandaises, which co-ordinates Irish studies throughout France. He agreed that one would have to factor in a degree of anti-British sentiment in the current boom in interest in Irish studies at the Sorbonne and elsewhere. Irish studies come under the banner of the English studies programme and Brennan finds that English language students are 'flocking in' to the Irish programme. There is also a stimulus to Irish studies, both at school and tertiary level, in the activities of the Ireland Fund of France. Modelled on the Ireland Funds of other countries, it funds scholarships between Ireland and France.

Joannon made the point that Irish people's impact on French society is sometimes difficult to quantify because they tend to assimilate so well:

> They learn the language, blend into society and their temperament is so similar to that of the French that they get on well together. But the British don't seem to be as keen on learning the language, they keep together and here in the South of France you find they bring over their own foods, newspapers, churches even.

When I travelled to France to research this book, McEnri's findings had been enormously overtaken. The changes he wrote about concerned an era in which Irish people largely came to France, meaning in effect Paris, to work as au pairs, at the OECD, or UNESCO, in a handful of state companies, or, if they had private means, simply to get out of Ireland. McEnri witnessed just the beginning of a process which is now in full flow. A striking feature of this, described by Mme Patricia Black with an enthusiasm which befitted the President of the Association of Irishwomen in France, has been the number of Irish women who have found satisfying careers in France. She supported McEnri's survey:

> Around the 1980s it began to change. Irish women were getting more education at home. They were acquiring linguistic skills. They began to get better jobs. I remember when you'd find very large numbers of Irish girls as secretarial workers in the OECD, or working as nurses, very often without the languages, or as au pairs. In the OECD, the Irish girls would stay four times as long as the British and were very highly educated.[29]

When she mentioned the length of time Irish girls stayed on in Paris, Mme Black touched on the very significant factor in Irish emigration in days gone by: pride. She says frankly:

I had a Victorian father. He taught us pride. Pride in ourselves and in our country. The idea of going to England was not on our horizon. There were nine in our family. I was interested in music and I came to the OECD, intending to study music and live in Paris for a year.

Instead she stayed for a lifetime. Though Patricia was luckier than most, what kept her in Paris was staying power, the same factor that kept the Irish secretaries at their desks. Like Patricia, they were brought up never to admit loneliness, not to cut and run, because the economic background that impelled them outward was not something to return to. It is probably unnecessary to remark the influence of Mother Church in all this. Indifferent to the human suffering caused by such a policy, the Church encouraged Catholics to breed large families, no matter what their education or income levels. This furtherance of the Vatican's geo-political aims impacted harshly on both the Irish economy and Irish individual happiness.

Patricia was one of the lucky ones. She did not have to have recourse to the Irish nuns, who, prior to the watershed 1980s, rescued many Irish girls from economic, psychological and sexual problems. The Order of Poor Servants of God, an Order which once did such work, no longer acts as an agency to place Irish girls in au-pair jobs. At the time of writing, there are probably more foreigners doing such work in Dublin than there are Irish girls abroad. Family sizes have dropped and Irish girls are better educated, and want larger horizons. Inevitably one will still find some young people 'working on the black' or in low-paid areas. Disney World, Paris, has a bad reputation amongst the Irish in this regard. In general, however, even though one will often find them working in bars or relatively lowly paid service industries, contemporary Irish young people tend to be highly educated, well motivated and have the benefit of the traditional Irish system of networking. If, after a few years, one still finds them behind a counter, it may be because they have ideas about buying the business.

There are two famous institutions in Paris which symbolise both the historical links between the French and the Irish, and the contemporary emigrant wave which is strengthening those links both culturally and economically. One is the College des Irlandais, south of the Pantheon, in the Rue des Irlandais in the 5th arrondissement – and the other is likely to be found in several different arrondissements: Brian Loughney, who owns some of the more flourishing Irish pubs in Paris, Dublin and the world. Him we will encounter in his natural habitat a little later, the Irish College beckons first.

The College is lucky to be in a position to beckon anyone. It was closed down at the height of the Terror because of an outburst of that Irish rowdyism that caused Louis to rebuke Dillon. A group of the College students decided to play a football game on the Champs de Mars and in the process knocked the Statue of Liberty off the Altar of the Fatherland. However, Irish diplomacy managed to rescue the situation and the College reopened – but not even the Irish were able to parry a blow struck against the College –

subsequently by the British. The French paid the College authorities compensation for the endowments which disappeared during the Revolution, but Perfidious Albion snaffled the compensation to help in the building of London's Marble Arch and the Brighton Pavilion.

These were but two of the many vicissitudes endured by the College since its foundation as an institute of higher education in 1578 by John Leo Waterford, with a small group of Irish clerical students in what was then the College de Montigu. The College gravitated from the College des Lombards, in the University of Paris in 1677, and over the centuries sent hundreds of priests back to Ireland, and some fifty bishops. The College acted as a refuge for exiled Irish in the Penal days and as a prison during the Revolution, during which its superior, Father Martin Glynn, was guillotined. A student of the college at the time of the Terror, Father Murphy from Wexford, survived only to lose his life for his role in the 1798 rebellion in Ireland which the French Revolution inspired. In 1870, the College became a hospital for French soldiers, which caused the Prussians to shell it, but it survived to become an American refugee centre in 1945 and, later that year, a refuge for Polish clergy who had survived Dachau.

In its heyday the college became the intellectual centre of the Irish in Paris, and some of its habitués produced important work, amongst them Richard Cantillon, the essayist whose writings on the nature of commerce led to his being dubbed 'the father of modern banking'. Apart from being a centre for Irish intellectuals, the College was also a repository for valuable manuscripts. One of these, Leabhar Mor Leachain (The Great Book of Lecan), an important example of early monkish gospel art, was shipped out of the College to the Royal Irish Academy in Dublin, just one step ahead of the outbreak of the Revolution. Although it suffered during the Revolution, the library still holds an immensely valuable collection of old books and manuscripts.

In its day, students at the College included Napoleon's brother Jerome, the future King of Westphalia, and the Empress Josephine's son, Eugene de Beauharnais. However, as the power of the Irish hierarchy waned, and the requirement for the College declined, the Irish Church became less and less concerned with its upkeep. Today the College is administered by a trust, which is controlled by a 14-member board, half Irish, half French. It has taken on a new lease of life as a cultural and recreational centre for the Irish and their French friends, as well as accommodating students and visitors to Paris.

The College is administered by Roisin Dockery, one of the professional women of the type referred to by Mme Black as exemplifying the contemporary Irish woman emigrant to France. She came to Paris intending to stay for a year, and at the time of our meeting had been there ten years and acquired a husband. She bears out the general consensus that the Irish are welcome in France and have similar temperaments to the French. Bord Failte, the efficient Irish Tourist Board capitalises on these similarities in its advertising, and sends increasing numbers of tourists for the stereotypical 'peace and quiet, green, unspoilt Irish holiday', which nevertheless also manages to combine in its appeal noisy nights of drinking and dancing till the small hours in Irish pubs and discos. It all feeds back into the ever-increasing numbers of French visitors who come to the Irish centre. So many, in fact, that during 1998 there were complaints from the neighbours who objected to the late (and loud) Irish music!

Wandering around the tree-shaded quadrangle enclosed by the college buildings, my eyes fell on three symbols that I felt encapsulated not merely the Irish College's history in France, but the entire Irish experience. On one table there stood a pint glass still half full of lager. Obviously, although some contemporary Celt had failed to meet the Homeric standards of his ancestors the previous night, attempts to do so were continuing. Over the row of tables on which the lager reposed were a set of plaques commemorating the Irish Dioceses whose bishops and priests were once educated in these pleasant surroundings: Ossory, Kildare, Ferns, Clogher. Typical of a Church ever conscious of hierarchical ranking, plaques for Dublin and Armagh were placed on either side of the main archway, in a careful balancing act: Armagh is the Archdiocese wherein the red hat traditionally resides, but Dublin is the largest Archdiocese in Ireland. However, perhaps the most significant sight was a set of television cameras, set up to interview, amongst others, myself and Pierre Joannon, on the significance of the Irish diaspora – in particular, the remarkable influence of the Irish in America, in influencing the changes in British (and IRA) policy which had brought about the Peace Process. The manifestations of Ireland's presence had changed from the days of the College's heyday, but who is to say that its heyday as an intellectual centre has yet to come? Certainly its vibrancy remains.

According to Brian Loughney, the vibrancy will increase. Not only does he see inside his pubs an exponential growth in Irish visitors to France; he sees them outside it also. One of his hostelries, the James Joyce in the Boulevard Gouvion-St Cyr, is also the stopping point in Paris for buses from the enormously successful cheap-fare RyanAir Company. I joined him on the day the Irish commemorated James Joyce. No one allowed the fact that the courts had just handed down a ruling which had precluded what was intended to be the centrepiece of the day's proceedings, a reading from *Ulysses*, to interfere with the festivities. (A Mr Sean Sweeney had obtained the injunction in his capacity as 'trustee de la succession littérature de l'écrivain James Joyce'.) The celebration had fulfilled the first rule of any Irish gathering: the split.

More importantly, the James Joyce had just been voted the best pub in France in a competition organised by the Kronenbourg beer company. Bloomsday, 16 June, is the day when Joyceans come out to play. And play they did. That year, 1998, there were James Joyce readings in a global Bloomsday linked up by the Internet, so there were readings in places as far apart as Buenos Aires, Tokyo, Rome, San Francisco, Paris and Dublin. Allowing for the differences in scale and content it is time to say that Bloomsday is rapidly becoming the diaspora's second most important feast day, after St Patrick's Day. Certainly it was a Big Day at Loughney's. The Irish Ambassador and his wife led a phalanx of dignitaries, who sat down to a lunch that began *circa* 12 midday, June 16th, and concluded some time before midday June 17th. The survivors of the Battle of Fontenoy had no more claim to endurance medals than had the small handful of us who kept pace with Loughney throughout the proceedings.

He also owns one of the best known pubs of any nationality in Paris, Kitty O'Shea's. Called after Parnell's mistress, it, and its eponymous sister establishment in Dublin, was being added to by a similar, though larger, hostelry in Boston as this was being written. Loughney began work at the age of eleven, and, after a career in banking, went into the pub business in Dublin. He had already become a legend, before he disregarded the warnings of Dublin's 'are you crazies?' and headed for Paris where he adapted the tradition of the Wild Geese to that of the 'Guinness Geese' by opening Kitty O'Shea's de Paris. Loughney is a classical example of that complex breed, the Mayo Businessman: shrewd, incredibly energetic, hard-working, tough beyond belief, and princely in their hospitality. A Mayo man will break your back in a business deal and then give you the shirt off his own back, or the meat off his plate, in the subsequent drinking session, for which he will insist on paying.

As if we had not absorbed enough punishment already, after the ambassadors and the media had left, Brian gathered around him a hard core which included myself, to go on a tour of Brazilian bars, because Brazil was playing in the World Cup that night. In between visiting packed scenes of Brazilian revelry, Brian talked about the Diaspora. He had worked in London as a young emigrant and taken an interest in emigrant welfare. 'There was nothing for the Irish, nothing,' he said, and then he interjected a remark I had heard echoed all over the globe: 'The Irish over here have it made.' However, he went on in the same breath to indicate how recent a phenomenon this was:

> I remember trying to get politicians interested in doing something to help people like a homeless 16-year-old couple I found on the London streets. She was pregnant. I spoke to a Labour politician about getting help for the Irish Centre in Camden Town, and he turned me down. He said that sort of thing was sectarian! [The Centre, as we shall see, is run by Oblate priests. Author.] I got a Fianna Fail friend, David Andrews, the then Irish Foreign Minister, to let me bring an Irish chaplain to his constituency meeting. The constituency was in Dun Laoghaire, where so many of the emigrants embarked, and the chaplain told the meeting: 'There is no nation that treats its emigrants with such finality.' That's all changed now. They don't have to put up with the shit any more. Education has changed everything.

Not quite everything. The Mayo character remains intact, no matter how far removed from Ireland. As we sat in a hilarious gathering outside a Brazilian haunt, we were joined by a famous Brazilian musician who said he would be honoured to play in one of Brian's pubs. 'Certainly,' said Brian, buying him a large whiskey. 'Certainly. But no money. No money.' 'Certainly,' replied the Brazilian, clinking glasses with him. You can take the man out of Mayo, but you won't take Mayo out of the man.

GERMANY

The contact between Germany and Ireland, while of a different order to that of either France, Spain or Italy was, and is, highly significant and gives every indication of growing more so. As the German diplomat and scholar, Martin Elasser – a former German Ambassador to Ireland, who on retirement continued to live in Ireland – reminds us, in an important work, Ireland and Germany have 1,000 years of shared history.[30] The military association did not end with the Wild Geese era. Wolfe Tone, the founder of Irish Republicanism, had a strong association with Hamburg, where his sister lived, and where he was a welcome guest while escaping the attentions of the British in the 1790s; and in 1899 Irish republicans served under John MacBride (whom the British would later execute after the 1916 Rising) in the joint German-Irish war effort on behalf of the Boers.

Also, in a very real sense, modern Ireland can trace its lineage through Germany, or rather through German armaments. The 'Howth rifles' which the 1916 insurgents used in the bloody labour ward of Dublin's GPO, wherein the modern Irish Republic was born, were sailed into Howth from Germany, in the yacht *Asgard* by Erskine Childers, just as the thunderstorm of the First World War was breaking. Childers in turn was an essential link in a chain of events which had its origins in New York where the old Fenian, John Devoy, who had turned to the French and its Foreign Legion for his military training, now turned to the Germans for his weaponry. He negotiated with von Bernstoff, the German Ambassador to America, and with von Papen, who subsequently became Hitler's puppet Chancellor, for German aid for an Irish uprising. The Germans supported the idea as it would distract British resources during the impending world conflict. One effect of these negotiations was the sending of Roger Casement to Germany in a futile effort to raise an Irish Brigade from the ranks of Irish soldiers captured while serving in the British Army. Only fifty-five of the POWs agreed to change their allegiance.

Disillusioned both with his lack of progress and the realisation that the Germans were not going to send much in the way of armament, and nothing in the way of officers or men to help the Irish, Casement came back to Ireland with pacific intent, though aboard a German arms ship. His aim was not to further the use of the weapons, but to persuade the insurgents to call off the rising which, without the expected German support, was clearly doomed to failure. However, he was captured in Kerry, as was the arms shipment. The ship's captain, Karl Spindler, scuttled his ship, the ·Aud, was captured, and survived the war. Casement was not so lucky. He was hanged in August, 1916. His death, coming long after all threat from the revolutionaries had subsided, was one of the principal causative factors in swinging popular support behind the men of 1916, and the physical force tradition.

Actually, some historians would argue that the Irish situation itself was a causative factor in bringing about the First World War. The Unionists, with their plans for armed resistance to Home Rule, were known as the 'Kaiser's Irish friends'.[31] Carson, the Unionists' leader, said in the House of Commons that he would prefer Kaiser William II to John Redmond, the Irish Nationalist leader, and assured the Kaiser personally that he had many friends in Northern Ireland. The Germans apparently believed the Unionist-Tory bluster about creating civil war, should Home Rule be introduced to Ireland, and over-calculated the degree of British pre-occupation with Ireland.

German-Irish cultural and economic links were also an important factor in the heightening of a consciousness of being Irish which helped to create modern Ireland. Throughout most of the nineteenth century and up to the end of the Second Reich (1918), there were honorary German Consuls at the bigger Irish ports. Spread throughout the country at large there were German sausage-makers, bandsmen, watch-makers and others engaged in a variety of different callings. However, the principal interaction took place in the field of Celtic studies, notably that of the Irish language, through co-operation between the founder of the Gaelic League, Douglas Hyde, who had married into a German family, and Kuno Meyer, the German Celtic scholar, in the early 1900s. Subsequently, particularly under the Nazis, Celtic studies became something of a political football as the Hitler regime used them, and Celtic scholars, as an arm of Nationalist Socialist policy. However, before the Celtic studies question ever arose, there had been substantive contact between Catholic Ireland and Catholic Germany. Daniel O'Connell's portrait hung in many a German home. He was recognised as one of the inspirations for Joseph Gorres's Catholic movement. In turn Goethe, Schiller and other leading German figures were translated by James Clarence Mangan and appeared in the *Dublin University Review*, sparking off a widespread Irish interest in German literature. This was furthered by the work of James Pentland Mahaffy, later Provost of Trinity, who translated Kant's *Critique of Pure Reason*, and at a more popular level by the Young Irelanders' paper *The Nation*. *The Nation* published German poetry in translation by Oscar Wilde's mother, Jane Frances Elgee, who achieved a widespread following under the *nom de plume*, 'Speranza'.

The whole notion of Irish nationhood received a fillip from the philosopher Herder. His publicising of the work of Irish monks in manuscripts such as those at Würzburg helped to revive within Ireland, as well as within Germany, the idea of Ireland as a nation with its own distinctive language. A romantic view of Ireland conveyed by the immensely popular travel diaries of Count Puckler-Muskau, published in 1826 and 1829, the year of Catholic Emancipation, stimulated popular German interest. This was furthered at different times by people as diverse as the poet Heine and by Friedrich Engels who interested Karl Marx in the Irish issue. Engels had a life-long relationship with two Irish sisters, Mary and Lizzy Burns, who had contact with the Manchester Fenians. The Irish women's influence caused Engels to make the visits to Ireland which resulted in his highlighting not only the horrific post-famine conditions, but the slave labour conditions which obtained in the 'dark satanic mills', the shirt factories of Derry. Mary Burns and the Marx children saw to it that Engels's last wishes were respected and, in 1895, consigned his ashes to the Irish Sea.

No doubt quite a number of people in Bavaria would have cheerfully consigned the ashes of a notorious Irish person of the nineteenth century to the sea also, if they could have immolated her. This was the Irish girl Eliza Gilbert who was probably born in Limerick and, after a marital breakdown and a host of scandalous relationships, made her way to Munich. Here, in October 1846, Eliza, now metamorphosed into Lola Montez, infatuated Ludwig I, King of Bavaria, with her freely bestowed charms. She passed herself off as a Spanish noblewoman and persuaded Ludwig to make her a Countess. Alas, her meddling in politics created a student revolt, which ultimately not only brought down Lola but Ludwig as well. The student revolt became a popular uprising and, in 1848, Ludwig was forced out of Bavaria. Lola resumed her career as a dancer and then went on the American lecture circuit. She died in New York in 1861.

A more stable Irish visitor to Germany in the wake of the Montez uprising was Thomas Mulvany who arrived in the Ruhr Valley the year after Ludwig was forced to flee. Mulvany was an engineer who had helped to develop the Irish canal system. He also built canals in Germany – the Rhine-Wesser-Elbe canal and the Dortmund-Ems canal were two of the important waterways he created – but his most famous initiative was the creation of a number of lucrative coal mines in the Ruhr area. He gave his mines Irish names, Shamrock, Hibernia, and Erin, and in between canal building and coal mining found time to build an ironworks in Duisburg and to found the Dusseldorf stock exchange.

However, while the careers of interesting individual Irish people had their impact on Germany, German movements and personalities had a far greater influence on Ireland. Arthur Griffith, the founder of Sinn Fein, was deeply influenced by the German transformation from a rural into a massive industrial economy, and in particular by the theories of the German economist, Friedrich List, on self-sufficiency. These helped him in developing the concept of Sinn Fein, 'Ourselves Alone'.

A great formative influence on the sports-loving Irish in the Celtic Dawn period of renaissance prior to the 1916 Rising was the Gaelic Athletic Association which rediscovered hurling and created Gaelic football. The GAA, which was founded by Michael Cusack in 1884, also followed a German example, that of the Turnvater Jahn movement.

Another formative influence in the heightening of a sense of national identity amongst the Irish, who at the time were enthusiastically encouraged by London to consider themselves British, as good colonials should, was the

German Kuno Meyer. His translation work uncovered much of the Irish cultural heritage which had lain buried in unregarded Irish manuscripts. He also helped to mobilise international support for the retention of Irish in the Irish university system. At the invitation of Douglas Hyde, Meyer became the driving force behind the foundation of the School of Irish Learning in Dublin in 1903 and its influential journal, *Eiru*. The importance which the Sinn Feiners attached to the work of Celtic scholars like Meyer may be judged from the fact that before the country had even got its independence, the Dail voted money to publish the work on the sagas of the Celtic scholar, Rudolph Thurnysen.

Actually had the 1916 leaders developed a theory which some of them favoured, Ireland by then might have had a German king. The idea of installing Kaiser William II's youngest son, Prince Joachim, was discussed by Padraig Pearse and by Joseph Plunkett. Plunkett visited Germany as part of the 1916 planning. Nothing came of the idea, but the German contacts by the Irish nationalists were used by the British as a pretext for a major round-up of all the Irish leaders including de Valera in 1918. One of the men whom Casement had recruited for his Irish Brigade, Joseph Dowling, was put ashore from a German submarine near Crab Island in Galway Bay. It was never quite clear what he was supposed to be doing because his first and only decisive action was to head for a pub where the police picked him up. However, the British propaganda machine cranked out reports of a German plot as a pretext for rounding up as many of the Sinn Fein leaders as they could lay hands on.

During the War of Independence, and subsequent to it, the Irish maintained emissaries in Berlin. The first Sinn Fein emissary was Nancy Wyse-Power. A replacement for her, Charles Bewley, later became a full ambassador to Germany, and embarrassed the Irish by his pro-Nazi sentiments to a point where he had to be recalled in 1938.

After independence German/Irish contact bore fruit both in the cultural and economic spheres. Figures like W. B. Yeats enthusiastically promoted German literature, and German musicians were given official positions in Ireland. Aloys Fleischmann and his son taught at Fleischmann Senior's School of Music, and the Irish Army School of Music was founded under the German Colonel Fritz Brase. One of the most famous transatlantic flights in the early days of aviation was accomplished in 1928 by an Irish pilot, Commandant Fitzmaurice, and two Germans, Baron von Hunefeld and Captain Kohler. They emulated Lindbergh's flight, but in the opposite direction, by flying from Baldonnell Airport outside Dublin to Newfoundland in thirty-six hours.

The principal industrial development within Ireland after independence was the building of a huge hydro-electric power station on the Shannon between 1925 and 1929. Its importance to the Irish economy may be judged from the fact that it cost IR£5 million at a time when the Irish state's annual budget ran at around IR£25 million. It was built by the German Siemens

Company at the instigation of an Irish engineer, Tommy McLaughlin, who had worked for Siemens in Germany. Several other important Irish industrial developments were founded with the help of German expertise. These included the Irish Turf Board, the Irish Glass Bottle Company, an electric light bulb factory, and a meat plant, Roscrea Meats. During the Second World War, the Allies, who were buying meat from the plant, discovered that it was being run by a German, and complained to the Irish Government that they were afraid of being poisoned!

Some Germans resident in Ireland during the thirties, like Helmut Clissmann, who during the Second World War became an intelligence officer, developed links with fellow student radicals which led to contact with the IRA. For example, Frank Ryan, who fought with the Republican Brigade in Spain, was released through Irish diplomacy from a condemned cell in Spain, and eventually fetched up in Berlin where he was put in contact with the right-wing IRA leader, Sean Russell, who had masterminded the pre-war bombing campaign in England. The Nazis arranged for both men to be sent back to Ireland, in a submarine, to foment whatever discord they could, on the principle that if it was bad for England, it had to be good for the Germans. However, Russell died en route and was buried at sea. Not knowing the details of his mission, Ryan returned to Berlin, where he died, lonely and isolated, suffering from deafness brought on by his jail experiences, before the war's end.

Throughout the war, the Germans maintained an Irish radio service. It began with a weekly talk in Irish, extolling the virtues of the Third Reich, as a sort of follow-up to the nightly broadcast delivered by William Joyce, 'Lord Haw Haw', whom the British hanged after the war. The Irish services then expanded into a nightly bi-lingual broadcast in both Irish and English set up by Dr Adolphe Mahr who had formerly been a director of the National Museum in Dublin. Most of Mahr's helpers were German, like Hilde Poepping, a student of Celtic Studies who had been at Galway University. However, a number of Irish-born people were involved. There was the novelist Francis Stuart, whose principal activities consisted of teaching English and lecturing on Irish/German studies. He became of interest to the Nazis because of his marriage into a famous Irish Republican family. His wife Iseult was a half-sister of Sean MacBride and step-daughter of John MacBride, who was executed for his part in the 1916 Rising. Another Irish figure involved with the station was Elizabeth Mulcahy, who married Clissmann, and who later returned to Dublin with him to help in setting up a flourishing pharmaceutical business.

There was also a John O'Reilly, whose father, ironically enough, was the policeman who had arrested Casement. O'Reilly was one of a handful of supremely inefficient spies whom the Germans managed to land in Ireland during the war, with a view to making contact with the IRA. His policeman father handed him over to the authorities for safe-keeping and he survived the war. The spies generally only managed to remain at liberty for a matter of hours, or at best days, before being captured by the Irish police. The legendary German efficiency seems to have deserted the Nazis in their dealings with wartime neutral Ireland. The spies included a former circus strongman, an Indian, and two South Africans. Only one, Dr Herman Goertz, managed to stay at liberty for any length of time (1940–41), through making contact with Francis Stuart's wife – an experience which gave him an insight into, but not an affection for, the workings of the hopelessly disorganised wartime IRA.[32]

Backed by draconian laws and strict wartime censorship, the Irish security forces completely smashed the organisation which never even remotely came near any significant linkage with the Nazis, or mounting any effective operations. There may have been one lapse in Irish security. Hempel, the German Ambassador, hearing from an Irish seaman that the Canadians were massing for a raid on Dieppe, may have been able to use the German Embassy's transmitter to get a warning to Berlin which turned the operation into a disaster for the Allies. Normally, however, although officially neutral, Ireland's policy in effect favoured the Allies. This was not always acknowledged by British leaders. Churchill especially was outraged at the notion of a member of the British Commonwealth remaining neutral while England was at war. Such attitudes were greatly reinforced when, at the war's end in an excess of diplomatic courtesy, de Valera – as he had done a little earlier on the death of Roosevelt, when he called on the American Ambassador, David Gray, to express his condolences – called on the German Ambassador to express his sympathy on the death of Hitler.

In Ireland, popular sympathy was generally anti-German because of the Nazis' anti-Catholic policy. This was subsequently heightened by the revelations of the Holocaust, which were becoming known at the time of de Valera's visit. However, it cannot be claimed that Ireland in any way distinguished itself by its efforts at sheltering the Jews. The number of refugees who were allowed into Ireland was shamefully tiny. As the researches of a distinguished Irish academic, Dermot Keogh, have shown, Ireland's response to the Holocaust can, at best, be described as minimalist and ungenerous, and certainly lacking in any display of empathy on the part of a nation that had itself suffered such persecution.[33]

William Joyce was hanged in Wandsworth prison on 3 January 1946 because of his wartime broadcasts from Berlin. Although born in Galway, wherein he supported the Black and Tans, Joyce, who left Ireland for his own safety when the Anglo-Irish War ended, held a (wrongfully obtained) British passport when he left England for Germany after participating in Sir Oswald Mosley's fascist activities. At his trial the British prosecution argued that he had committed treason in going to Germany, because his British passport conferred on him a protection to which he owed a corresponding allegiance.

The controversy over Joyce's execution has more or less faded from memory – mainly kept alive in the pages of Rebecca West's book, *The Meaning of Treason* – but Francis Stuart, another broadcaster from Berlin in the Mahr/Joyce era, became a centre of controversy as this book was being written. Stuart, now dead but then in his nineties, and living in a nursing home, benefitted under the Irish Government's scheme of assistance to writers and artists. Despite his age, Maire MacEntee, an Irish poet, and her husband, Dr Conor Cruise O'Brien, tried to have the benefit withdrawn. The affair generated much argument and letters to the editor of the *Irish Times*, but the MacEntee/O'Brien proposal failed.

Sitting on a Berlin balcony, sipping wine with the Irish scholar and TV executive, Padraig O'Dochartaigh, I was reminded of how deep-rooted was the Irish language contact between Germany and Ireland. O'Dochartaigh and I knew each other through our contact with the Aran Islands where his father, a distinguished Irish scholar, maintained a holiday home. In the 1890s the islands were a favourite haunt of German academics. One of these, Nikolaus Fink, published a massive work on the Aran dialect, *Die Araner Mundart*, which helped to develop O'Dochartaigh's interest in German studies and, *inter alia*, helped to bring him to Berlin. As a boy O'Dochartaigh, and his brothers, walked in Fink's footsteps. Like him, they collected old phrases and unusual words and brought them back to their father. O'Dochartaigh's six-year-old son, Fionn, spoke both Irish and German but had yet to learn English.

Young Fionn's experience, however, would hardly be typical. The great days of Meyer and Fink are gone in so far as the study of the Irish language is concerned. One finds a boom in Irish pubs, a widespread interest in Irish music, a lesser one in Irish writing, and a still smaller one in Irish studies. There is also a hangover of interest from Heinrich Böll's enormously popular *Irish Diary*, describing the Ireland of the 1950s. However, by contrast with this idyllic account of life as it appeared from a cottage on Achill Island in County Mayo, today's Irish students are increasingly aware of Germany as a potential source of employment in the computer age. In the new millennium, the study of German is a growth industry in Ireland. Irish studies in Germany are far less sturdy. Contemporary Celtic studies in Berlin are under threat through lack of funding.

Sabina Hertz who lectures in the Celtic Department of the Humboldt University of Berlin told me that from one hundred students, attendance at classes had dwindled to eighteen.[34] Sabina attributes the lack of funding to the Germanisation of German society in which Celts don't fit. It's obvious to an outsider that the German economy has its post-unification problems, although these are to be reckoned on the scale of irritation, rather than the desperation which confronted Germany after the ending of the Second World War. Employment is constricting, particularly for students, but even if official support for Celtic studies is dwindling in Germany, Irish students have the luck of the Irish on their side in the competition for jobs. They finish their academic year several weeks ahead of the German one, and have a high percentage of the jobs snapped up before the German students emerge from their examination halls.

The growth of Irish trade with Germany has been particularly spectacular since 1973, rising from IR£54 million of exports to IR£4,354 billion in 1997. When Ireland joined the EEC, Germany was selling the Republic almost twice as much (IR£93 million) as it imported, but, as with the rest of Europe, the energising effect of EU membership has enabled the Irish to alter the relationship so that at the time of writing the Irish have somehow managed to sell their giant trading partner some three times what they buy, IR£1,536 billion. In fact, a German banker who does extensive business with Ireland, spoke to me with a bemused asperity about Irish business practices that is not uncommon in Germany:

> You set up your International Financial Services Centre to help Germans evade tax. You never put anything in writing. Everything's a grey zone, a sort of huge black economy, and you manage to get the EEC to accept a far lower rate of corporation tax than any other country in Europe, and even though your economy is doing so well, it seems you'll be able to hold that rate for several years into the Millennium, still draw EEC subsidies, and, at the same time, have the highest growth rates in Europe.

All this is true, but the scale of the Irish economy is tiny by German standards. The major flaw of the Irish to tidy German minds is the fact that the Irish seem to bend the rules as a matter of course, and, while still staying within the law, regard the word 'no' as a starting point at any negotiation rather than its ending. All the virtues of the Irish which Sean Cumiskey (see pages 106 et seq) extolled for me in Amsterdam are acknowledged in Germany also.

However, in Germany, one can still come across examples of the sort of 'bicycle Irish' culture that is more traditionally associated with life amongst the Irish in the more insecure areas of the British building trade. The huge explosion of building works of all sorts that followed the dismantling of the Berlin Wall attracted hordes of Irish labourers, who were prepared to work long hours and live in deplorable conditions, just one jump ahead of the tax and emigration authorities. Sometimes if their conditions were not deplorable to begin with, they were when the Irish moved on. Sabina Hertz, a passionate supporter of all things Irish and Welsh (she refuses to accept letters from government departments dealing with Welsh matters in English, and returns them for translation into Welsh), had an experience which is unfortunately far from being unique. Even Sabina's faith in and friendship for the Irish wavered after she rented her apartment to two Irish workers. According to her, 'Two paid, ten stayed.' She said that the furniture was covered in mould and could not be used any more. The space under the beds was used as a tip. There was writing on the walls and about the only thing the Irish lads contributed to the flat were some 'quite obvious' pictures of women! Sabina got quite heated as she described how: 'One fellow asked for the photos to be given back. I said yes, give me 1,000 marks, that will pay for part, only part of the damage.' She shook her head sadly as she exclaimed, 'I never experienced anything like that.' No, but one would have to concede, many another landlady did. As

Sabina herself charitably pointed out: 'The boys work under bad conditions and accordingly they act badly.' Irish workers (or Portuguese, or Turks for that matter) frequently encountered bad employers. The young men would be hired initially at 30 marks an hour. Then after a few weeks they would be told, 'the work isn't going too well' – and they were paid less, if they were paid at all. Unscrupulous employers could raise objections to their work, claiming that paint had not been put on properly or some such.

It has to be said that some of the worst offenders against good employment practices are Irish lump contractors. Just as in the bad old days of the British (and sometimes the Irish) building industry, these often do their hiring, and sometimes paying, in pubs. The Oscar Wilde in Berlin was once a favourite venue for those in the building trade. The drink-orientated culture of bad living conditions and general discomfort and insecurity, indicated by Sabina Hertz, has another predictable side-effect – fighting. One hears stories of ferocious fights involving Irish building workers.

There are allegations that young people got into trouble in Berlin whether from the sort of causes outlined above, or through running out of money, or whatever, very little was done for them by the Irish authorities. The Irish Embassy was in far-away Bonn (post-unification plans ordained a move to Berlin) and the response to such situations tended to be to say 'sorry' and advice to the help-seekers to contact the Embassy's offices in Berlin. Naturally, though more forgivably, very often the answer there too would also be 'sorry'! By the late 1990s that phase of brutal labouring work in the construction industry had become less significant, although examples of it could still be found. The German economy slowed down under the strain of both German unification and the world recession. Moreover, as the great muddy trenches were now dug and filled with concrete, the demand was for more skilled, older workers. These enjoy a totally different lifestyle to that of their younger compatriots at the pick and shovel end of the business. They come to Germany on contracts negotiated in Dublin and stay for a fixed period of time in good accommodation.

Irish workers who lie outside these arrangements, or indeed outside arrangements of any sort, are the 'tarmacadam people'. Barbara John, a striking-looking woman in her fifties, is the chief German official in charge of the integration of foreigners in Berlin. (It should be remembered that Germany at the time of writing houses within its borders half of all the refugees settled in Europe outside their own countries.) She told me that she was not aware of any very noticeable legal or social problems affecting the Irish, most of whom work in construction. Her immediate problem concerned a group of Bosnians who were sitting-in in another part of her office building and refusing to be sent back to Bosnia. 'But we tell them – the war is over,' said John, looking puzzled, 'and they still will not go home.'

I was shortly to get a very good insight into reasons why the Bosnians might have reacted as they did, as we shall see (section page 99). On the ground in Bosnia, a cessation of violence was very far from meaning peace. However, for the moment my interest was taken by the one problem Barbara John did cite involving Irish citizens. It concerned 'the tarmacadam people'. These travelling people, whose politically correct term in Ireland is 'travellers', were originally known as 'tinkers'. This is not the place to discuss how much of the travellers' appalling public image is due to prejudice, and how much due to their own anti-social, and often very violent, behaviour. Suffice it to say that, one busy Friday afternoon at peak traffic time, Frau John, a former teacher of German to German teachers, got a distress signal from the Berlin police. The Wall had just come down and foreigners of all sorts were pouring into Berlin, seeking the new opportunities, amongst them the Irish tarmacadam people.

Approximately fifty families with their vehicles, laden with tarmacadam which they proposed to spread before an unsuspecting German public, had halted at a busy roundabout. They were refusing to move, and as no preparations of any sort had been made for them, the police warned that if something were not done speedily they would be forced to take action. Frau John found an Irish solution to an Irish problem. She contacted 'The Good Priest', Father Paul, an Irishman popular amongst the Irish community, to negotiate with the travellers. While he did so she found them another site. She then arranged for a 'festival', or open day, at police headquarters to enable the police and the travellers to explain their respective cultures to one another.

As Frau John spoke, I got a kaleidoscopic vision of a similar scene being enacted at police headquarters in Dublin: I imagined some German traveller explaining to the Irish Garda Commissioner: 'Nein. Das slash hook which you seized at the wedding, along with das lump hammers, and das clubs, is nicht und lethal weapon. Das ist und cultural artefact . . .'

Sad to say my rather cynical reflection was given at least some validity a few days later.[35] I was told of another convoy of travellers which had been stopped by the German police. Many of the vehicles were apparently overloaded, some were uninsured, and some were even stolen. However, if the Barbara John approach is to be continued, such episodes will not interfere with the growth of German-Irish friendship.

In Munich during the late eighties and early nineties Irish workers established a virtual tent city. As in Atlanta, one can trace the contemporary Irish presence to the Olympics – job opportunities created by the Munich Olympics attracted a flood of young Irish. The tent city was not without its problems. An Irish girl was murdered there, and in retaliation hooligans attacked and fatally injured a German camper in Phoenix Park, Dublin. Mercifully these sort of incidents are spoken of as much for their rarity as for their horror. One can get a hint of the conditions which prevail in the advice put out in a newsletter for the benefit of Irish young people by St Killian's parish in Munich, where Father Thomas Healy is the parish priest. The young people are warned that they must acquire some knowledge of German, have a valid passport, a return ticket home and fill in all the registration forms required by the German authorities. It warns that work and accommodation are hard to come by, though both can be had with the application of due diligence. I attended mass at St Killian's. The small church was filled with a largely youthful congregation, who followed the service with great devotion and participated enthusiastically in the singing.

Afterwards, mingling with the congregation, one could see clearly that the mass provided both a cultural and religious rallying point. A feature of St Killian's is the weekly adjournment to a local Italian restaurant, where people catch up on the news and gossip. Noreen Lynch from Dublin was the pastoral assistant, taking a prominent part in the service, the life of the parish, and proving an invaluable source of information about the experience of the younger Irish in Munich, and Germany generally.

Shortly before my visit there had been trouble at Magdeburg, to the north of the country. Protests had erupted against Irish, English and Portuguese workers. Such disturbances give rise to continual fears about the rise of a right-wing movement in Germany, but the Irish finding on the threat of fascism tends to be that while it is 'not absent', and has to be a cause of concern, neither is it present. If any grouping should feel threatened in Germany, it is the Turks. The 'line of blood' provision in German law as a requirement for German citizenship means that even Turkish third, generation, born children do not become German citizens – and there are 1.9 million Turks in Germany, a continuing focal point for racism, particularly in Bavaria. The Irish, however, tend to report friendship and acceptance rather than any form of hostility, or even reserve, once Irish nationality is established. One does find students lining up at 2 o'clock in the morning outside the student employment agencies, but their efforts seem to be rewarded with employment, albeit achieved with a far greater degree of difficulty than those Celtic Tiger products who come to Germany armed with computer and business qualifications which secure jobs for them before they leave Dublin.

'You don't get many sad cases,' said Michael Spillane, a Trinity-born statistician who, along with his day job, was building up a popular business in importing Irish newspapers and magazines. Spillane is a classic example of the young Irish entrepreneur. He had set up his business based on a combination of the latest technology, all imported from Ireland, and traditional Irish networking. He was on first-name terms with every member of the staff likely to be on any one of three shifts at the four airports which serve Munich. His contacts extend to the baggage handlers who physically remove the papers from the planes, and he has the home telephone number of everyone he does business with.

Spillane proved himself to be the archetypal problem-solver in the manner in which he got me out of a jam. At the time of writing, the Irish banking system is going through an unprecedented bout of bad publicity because of greed and poor regulation in the sector of the economy that had fattened most on the Celtic Tiger. Apart from established instances of massive tax evasion and a custom known as 'grazing', whereby customers' accounts had bogus charges deducted from them, or extra interest charged, ordinary customer service has fallen off drastically. Before leaving Ireland, I had called into my bank as I always did before a trip, to warn them to keep an eye on my current account to ensure that if needs be, money should be moved from a savings account to ensure that my credit card was always in balance. However, this was not done, and on a Saturday afternoon in Berlin, with hotel bills to be paid and air tickets to be purchased, I discovered that the ATM rejected my card. Bailed out in Berlin by Denis Staunton of the *Irish Times* (more networking), I made my way to Munich where on the Monday I phoned my bank in a state of mind better imagined than described. It was arranged that money would instantly be telegraphed for me to a bank in Munich, and I was given a freephone number to call to make the necessary pick-up arrangements. Murphy's Law struck again, however. The freephone number was continually busy, and I had no way of finding out what branch had my money, as my Dublin bank apparently didn't know either.

As I fumed and fretted, I couldn't help thinking of Heinrich Böll's famous account of how two young Germans in a similar predicament to mine fared with an Irish bank manager in rural Ireland in pre-Celtic Tiger days, when they attempted to get a cheque cashed. Basically the outcome was a great expenditure of emotional scar tissue on their side, and of traditional Irish courtesy on the part of the bank manager, the whole drama being permeated by 'sorry'. They didn't have Spillane on their side. 'Fuck the freephone number,' he intoned. 'You have to be very clear and direct. Germans expect *you* to know what you're asking. Vagueness or going outside the system leaves you in shit.'

He phoned the head office of the bank whose name I had been given, found out the address of the branch in Munich which dealt with cases such as mine, and we set off at a gallop, arriving just as the porter was closing the front door. Again Spillane's problem-solving skills, and knowledge of German, achieved the desired result. I got my money, and as we prepared to leave, Spillane suggested that I slip the girl we dealt with ten marks. It was a nice touch. We had entered the bank amidst protests, but we left it to the accompaniment of broad smiles. Spillane was examining the possibilities of starting up a business in Albania, to which he travels frequently. I don't know whether Slobodan Milosevic and the Kosovo Liberation Army have rendered this project unsound, but if anyone can start up a profitable business in that unfortunate country, it will be Michael Spillane.

The growth in the attendance at the Munich St Patrick's Day procession is indicative of the growth of the strength of the Irish community as a whole. So many people turned up for the first parade, in 1996, that it moved off ahead of schedule. A cloud of squad cars and motorcycle cops descended on the march, and it appeared for a moment as if the parade was about to be banned. However, it emerged that the organisers had applied for all the necessary permissions in advance. It was the early start which threw the cops, so the parade was allowed to proceed after some diplomatic negotiation by the

Grand Marshall, Frank McGlynn. By 1998, the parade had become a recognised annual feature of Munich life, and attracted some 10,000 participants.

McGlynn and his partner Alison Moffat run a variety of Irish activities, not only in Bavaria but throughout Germany, covering the social, cultural and commercial spectrum. They put Irish people in contact with German business, or social outlets, run the German-Irish Bavarian Friendship Society, and produce Irish tapes and CDs under the label Frozen Ferret Music. The name dates back to a performance by Frank as a colonel in Brian Friel's play *Freedom of the City*. It took him to Northern Ireland, where he saw ferret armoured cars in action, hence the title. Irish-German relationships are far from frozen. Indeed, unless there is a world trade collapse, economic, and hence cultural and social links appear set to increase significantly.

SPAIN

> O my Dark Rosaleen,
> Do not sigh, do not weep!
> The priests are on the ocean green
> They march along the Deep.
> There's wine . . . from the royal Pope
> Upon the ocean green;
> And Spanish ale shall give you hope,
> My Dark Rosaleen!
> My own Rosaleen!

The foregoing poem, a translation by James Clarence Mangan (1803–1849) of a poet whose identity is disputed, but who preceded Mangan centuries earlier, gives an idea both of the antiquity of the Hispano/Irish links, and of the deep-rooted belief in the Irish psyche that one day deliverance would come from Spain.[36] It is taken as given by the Spaniards that the Irish are in fact Spaniards who at some stage wandered northwards. An oft quoted saying used to buttress this view is that of the Spanish writer, Salvador de Madariaga, who said that the Irish are like Spaniards stranded by mistake in the north of Europe. He said that every time he spoke to an Irishman he felt that, in reality, he was talking to somebody from south of the Pyrenees.

My own acquaintance with Spaniards would tend to bear out Madariaga's judgement. They all say that they feel at home in Ireland, and by way of proving it, tens of thousands of Spanish children are sent to Dublin each summer to learn English. The Spanish apparently share the belief of George Bernard Shaw, that the best English in the world is spoken in Dublin. Certainly the numbers arriving grow larger every year and 'the Spanish student' has increasingly become a staple item in many a Dublin household budget.

An important side-effect of this student influx is the fact that increasingly in

Spanish decision-taking echelons, one finds executives who are both knowledgeable about Ireland and keen to further and develop the relationship with Spain. Nor is the flow all one way. One out of three Irish tourists holidaying abroad goes to Spain, and increasing numbers of Irish people are buying holiday villas or retirement homes there.

Many of the Irish foundation legends bear out the contention that the Spanish students' forebears were, in fact, the ancestors of their Irish hosts today. There is the legend of an Iberian Celt called Mil, who set sail for Egypt with his family and fought with the Pharaoh Nectanebus against the Ethiopians. He is said to have married a daughter of the Pharaoh, called Scota, and had two very Irish-sounding sons by her in Egypt, Eber (or Hiber) and Amergin (or Amheirgin), allegedly the first Irish poet. Mil is said subsequently to have returned to Iberia with his wife and sons and set out for Ireland, dying en route. His wife is said to have been killed fighting the magical tribe, the De Danaan, in what is now County Kerry.

One of the De Danaan's attributes is said to have been their ability to bring down magic mists on their foes. Certainly, as anyone who has spent a holiday in Kerry will acknowledge, thick heavy mist is a feature of that beautiful, mountainous, but very rainy area. At all events some say that it is from Mil that the Gaels of Ireland are descended. Undoubtedly the terms Iberia and Hibernia suggest a common ancestry, perhaps that of Hiber.

In Spain, however, they like to tell you that today's Irish are Milesians, or sons of Mile, who set sail from under the Tower of Hercules, also known as Breogan's Tower, in La Coruña, Galicia. Unquestionably, today's Galicia has an extraordinarily Irish feel to it. The accent is very similar to the lilting tones of County Cork, which once had close ties with Spain. In Cork one can still find examples of a type of small wooden sailing boat remaining from the days when these boats brought Irish produce to Spain and sailed home loaded with Spanish onions. In Galicia itself one will encounter such obvious Celtic indicators as red hair, stone dolmens similar to the burial stones found in Ireland, and a sort of bagpipe which resembles the Irish uilleann pipe.

These mythological tales are of course folkloric. However, it is a fact of history that from the beginning of the 1590s, when the Irish chieftains rose against the English, they looked to the King of Spain on the grounds of common ancestry. Red Hugh O'Donnell sought help from Philip II, saying that following the defeat of England, Ireland would give allegiance to the crown of Spain. Hugh O'Neill wrote in similar terms telling the Spanish king that he based his plea on the fact that his lineage had its origins in Cantabria.

The fact that both the Spanish and the Irish believed these links to exist certainly helped to forge other strong links. One can still see the remnant of a once famous Spanish trading district at Spanish Arch in Galway. Off the Galway coast, at the approach to the island of Inisboffin, there are ruins which show where the Spanish were once well enough established to build fortifications and a church. Unfortunately another Galway landmark, recalling a more dionysian and possibly a more dangerous aspect of these links, disappeared somewhere in the last twenty years or so – a pub in Galway's central Eyre Square called Josephine Poinard. A more sombre relic of the Spanish is Lynch's Castle in Galway's main street. From a window in this castle, Mayor Lynch of Galway hanged his own son for the murder of a Spanish merchant, having failed to find an executioner to do the deed for him.

It is said that Columbus used a Galway man, then living in Spain, as the pilot for the first part of his westward voyage, because the Irish seafarers had a good knowledge of the western routes from Spain. Some also argue that part of Columbus's inspiration for his voyage lay in the stories about St Brendan. Certainly the reputation of Irish sailors and navigators dictated that several were included aboard the Armada. Irish trade with Spain was such that there were Irish consuls in many Spanish ports during medieval times. There was considerable commercial traffic with the coastal ports of Ireland, extending from Waterford around the Cork and Kerry coast, and up to Sligo. The Irish chieftains of the period, Desmond, MacCarthy, O'Driscoll, O'Flaherty, O'Malley and O'Sullivan, maintained contact with Spain both through the traders and the monks, although in the case of the latter, to a lesser degree than with either France or Italy.

The Irish exported hides, leather goods, woollen articles and salted fish, principally herrings. In return, the Spanish sent back weapons, steel implements and wine, none of which could be created in Ireland because of the geographical and political climates. It is recorded that Irish-made cloaks and saddle cushions were prized in Spain. The Sayos, a flowing Irish tunic, was particularly popular in Catalonia. The story of the herring's impact on the Irish economy and on trade with Spain during the fifteenth and sixteenth centuries deserves to be better known than it is, particularly in view of the sorry state of Irish fisheries today. The herrings migrated from the Baltic to the Irish coast around the middle of the fifteenth century, thereby contributing to the decline of the Hanseatic League. For the Irish the herrings' arrival was akin to the discovery of an oilfield in our day. The value of the herring soared, through a combination of circumstances: the prevailing Catholic laws of abstinence, which prohibited meat on so many occasions, and the need for a nourishing food that would sustain the crews of the ships that multiplied so rapidly in those days of the expansion of sail. The fish greatly increased trade in the Pale area and brought marked prosperity to the south and south-west of Ireland.

Here a great boom took place in castle and monastery building, part of it based on Spanish trade. Fleets of over 600 Spanish fishing vessels were recorded off the Cork and Kerry coasts by the third quarter of the sixteenth century. Records of the period show that, for the right to fish in Kenmare Bay alone the Spaniards paid one chieftain, MacFineen Duff, £300 a year, a sizeable sum in those days.[37]

Thus, trade, a shared religion, and the widespread perception of a common Iberian Celtic ancestry, all served to deepen Hispanic-Irish relations when the trade issue interacted with the political one to make the Irish turn to Spain as a haven. The British can be said to have begun seriously attempting to limit Irish trade in favour of their own under Edward II. In 1339, he directed that a fleet of naval ships prevent commerce between Ireland and European ports. However, the Irish and the Spanish, and in particular the Basques, managed to circumvent the blockade by using Basque fishing boats. In 1465 the fishing boats were carrying so much valuable cargo to and from Ireland and Spain that Edward IV passed another, much flouted, law forbidding any boat to fish in Irish waters unless it had English permission.

The screw was further turned in 1477 by a directive that Irish-minted money would not be acceptable in England. This was a serious blow to the Spanish/Irish trade as hitherto the Irish coinage had been prized in Spain. Further blows fell. The British introduced a devalued currency to Ireland. This allowed English merchants and administrators on the one hand to obtain goods in Ireland for export at a 25 per cent discount, and on the other, to pay their occupying armies in cheap money. Then, in 1494, Irish merchants were forbidden to export anything without a special permit, granted only if the shipment took place through an English port after the payment of a tax to the crown.

When it was discovered that this trade was continuing in clandestine fashion from ports distant from English authority, the British hired privateers to sink unauthorised ships. Yet somehow the trade link with Spain survived until the Navigation Act of 1637 inaugurated an era whereby no vessel could trade abroad unless it had been built in England, sailed out of an English port, and had a crew which was 75 per cent English. Finally, in 1670, Charles II killed off the already seriously declining Irish shipbuilding industry by forbidding any Irish trade with the colonies save in horses, servants and provisions.

The political and military involvement of the Spanish with the Irish followed Henry VIII's rupture with Rome (and *ipso facto* Catholic Ireland), and, more importantly, that with Spain under his daughter, Elizabeth I. Both interacted with papal diplomacy so that Italian troops also became involved in the Irish wars. The idea of Spanish aid began its entry into Irish affairs in the reign of King Philip II of Spain and it continued in those of King Philip III, and IV. The intensely pragmatic Philip II was not moved merely by the various myths and legends concerning Irish and Spanish relationships. His Most Catholic Majesty had a theocratic objection to listening to the complaints of subjects against their liege lord, but a combination of Elizabeth's policy tilt against Spain and the murder of the Irish chieftain Shane O'Neill, who had been interceding for Spanish assistance through the Spanish Ambassador in London, Count Feria, caused him to change his mind. He sent two military expeditions to assist the Irish in rebellions against Elizabeth I.

The Irish leader, James FitzMaurice FitzGerald arrived at Smerwick Harbour, Kerry, at the head of a Spanish-Italian force on 18 July 1578. He brought with him a papal legate, Nicholas Sanders, and letters from the Pope addressed to the Irish chieftains, calling on them to rise in defence of the Catholic religion and absolving them from allegiance to Elizabeth. This force took up an ill-fated defensive position at Dun an Oir (the fort of gold) where it was joined by Irish troops and by a further 600-hundred strong papal contingent on 12 September 1580.

. To understand subsequent Elizabethan, and indeed English, policy generally, towards Ireland, it should be borne in mind that, apart from the fact that papal and Spanish intervention in what the Queen regarded as part of her kingdom was highly unwelcome, there were other factors at work. There had been a Catholic uprising earlier in her reign in the north of England, which Elizabeth put down with great cruelty. As a result the Pope (Pius V) issued a papal bull excommunicating her and declaring that English Catholics need no longer owe allegiance to the heretic queen. In addition Ridolfi, the agent of her cousin Mary (Queen of Scots), and the Spanish Council discussed a proposal to assassinate Elizabeth. Elizabeth retaliated by making it high treason for an English subject to implement a papal bull.

It was the era of the St Bartholomew Massacre during which Catherine de Medici of France had thousands of Huguenots massacred in the streets of Paris. English anti-Catholic feeling was further inflamed when the Irish, whom Elizabeth and her decision-takers regarded as savages anyhow, began to give ear to Jesuit missionaries from the French college of Douai. The fervour engendered by the Jesuits was a contributory factor in the rebellion, led by the Earl of Desmond, which brought the papal force to Smerwick. After a siege the defenders ultimately surrendered on 10 November, expecting to be accorded the status of belligerents. However, the British, under Sir Walter Raleigh and 'Black Tom' Butler, the Anglo-Irish Earl of Ormond, massacred the Spanish-Italian-Irish force in a manner that would set the tone both for the wars of extermination which the English were to wage, and for the series of tit for tat massacres of Protestant and Catholic that would continue for centuries. To give but one example: after the surrender, three of the prisoners, Father Lawrence Moore, Oliver Plunkett and William Walsh, a servant of the papal legate's, had their legs broken on a forge and, after a night of agony, were hanged, drawn and quartered the following day.

Not surprisingly all these efforts either to enforce or resist the Book of Common Prayer did nothing to further the cause of ecumenism in Irish history. Brendan Behan once created a sensation on American television by quoting the English translation of an Irish verse which survives from those days of Tudor warfare:

> Don't talk of your Protestant Minister
> Nor his church without temple or state
> For the foundation stones of his religion
> Were the ballocks of Henry the Eight!

Spanish aid was central to the major uprising which Hugh O'Neill conducted against Elizabeth between 1595 and 1603. This too was defeated, at Kinsale, partly because of quarrelling between the Irish leaders. As we have seen, the Great Earl went into exile. However, from those days onwards, friendship between the Irish and the Spanish was based not on legend, but on foundations of religion and considerations of *raison d'état* which had been sealed in blood. The Irish who enlisted in the service of Spain were recognised as Spanish citizens. The Spanish grandees were amongst the most aristocratic – and defensive of their élite status – cadres in Europe, but the Irish émigrés of noble birth were accorded not merely citizenship but had their nobility status conferred in Spain also.

Both Spain and Spanish Flanders opened their ports and their purses to Irish exiles. The generosity of the Spanish towards the Irish is certainly one of the marvels of history. The Irish alone amongst non-nationals were automatically given all the rights of Spanish citizenship once they entered Spanish territory. These privileges were confirmed by various monarchs down to the point of specifying that the Irish were not to be regarded as foreigners. For example, a decree on 3 February 1792 stipulates that:

> The Irish established in these dominions shall keep and maintain the privileges which they have, by which they are made equal to native Spaniards; and that the formalities of the oath, to which all other nations have been forced to submit, shall not be exacted from the Irish, seeing that by the mere fact of their settling in Spain the Irish are accounted Spaniards and enjoy the same rights.

Under lobbying from the Irish these privileges were renewed under successive monarchs and, in return, the Irish served the Spanish loyally.

There were some exceptions to this harmonious record. Responding to English diplomatic activity the then ruler of the Spanish lowlands, Don Francesco De Melo, to the sound of drums, had a proclamation published at Dunkirk, declaring it unlawful to render any succour to the Irish under pain of the most severe penalties.[38] Fear of similar penalties, this time promised by the English, caused the Irish to act in an even harsher fashion during the Armada saga. Popular legend has it that the Irish succoured the Spanish sailors who survived the wreck of the Armada all along the Irish coast, from Kerry in the south to Antrim in the north. In fact, the Irish handed over many of these unfortunates for execution. At Doonbeg, County Clare, the O'Briens slit the throats of sixty of the exhausted Spaniards whose ship had been driven on the rocks. The remainder were executed by the High Sheriff, one Clancy, an Irishman.

Nevertheless, the honours accorded to the Irish in Spain by successive Spanish rulers were extraordinary. So, in return, were the services that the recipients accorded to the Spanish. In the space of 100 years, reaching a peak towards the middle of the eighteenth century, more than 150 Irishmen rose to become generals in the Spanish Army. Irishmen served Spain as ambassadors

to Austria, France, Italy, Denmark, Russia, Sweden, Prussia, the Netherlands, and, remarkably, even to England. At one time or another the Irish held
all the more important ministerial posts: Ministers of Finance, War, External
Affairs, and even Prime Minister. In seeking to give examples of distinguished
Irishmen in Spanish service, the difficulty is who to leave out, not who to put
in.

Obviously basic ability was a major factor in these men's advance, but the
respect accorded the Irish from the King downward in Spanish society was
equally important. For example, one of the great sagas and tragedies of the
Nine Years War was the two-week-long retreat of O'Sullivan Beare from
Glengarriff in County Cork to Leitrim in the north, during the December and
January of 1602–3. By the time he reached Leitrim, only thirty-five of the
some one thousand men, women and children who had set off with him had
survived the merciless onslaughts of both winter and hostile native chieftains
supporting the British. Philip III ordered a ship to Ireland in 1604 to rescue
him, and granted him a pension and a knighthood. O'Sullivan Beare was
about to return to Ireland in 1618 when he was killed by the English spy, John
Bathe, in Madrid.

The first Irishman to become Prime Minister of Spain was Richard Wall
(1694–1778). His parents had settled in France after the Treaty of Limerick,
and he served in the Spanish navy in the Sicilian Campaign of 1718. He
subsequently became Spanish Ambassador to the Republic of Genoa and to
England (in 1747). After serving as Lieutenant General and Minister for
Foreign Affairs, he became Prime Minister in 1754 and served under two
kings, Fernando IV and Carlos III, before retiring in 1763. James Francis
FitzJames Stuart (1696–1738) was Spain's first Ambassador to Russia. His
father was the Duke of Berwick, and, like Wall, he was born in Spain. He
became Duke of Lima and Colonel of the Irish Regiment of Limerick in the
Spanish army. He later became Ambassador to both Vienna and Naples. The
present Duchess of Alva is his descendant.

Felix O'Neill (1702–1796) was captured after the Battle of Culloden. On his
release, he turned down high military rank from both Frederick the Great of
Prussia and Maria-Theresa of Austria, becoming instead Colonel of the
Spanish Regiment of Hibernia. He rose to the post of Lieutenant General, and
became a member of the Spanish Supreme Council of War. Another O'Neill,
Arturo O'Neill (1736–1814), was born in Ireland in Mayo, whence his family
had been transplanted by Cromwell. He too served in the Regiment of
Hibernia in his youth, fighting for Spain in Algiers. His Commander-in-Chief
was also an Irish General, Count Alexander O'Reilly of County Meath.

One of Spain's most respected military figures of modern times was
Lieutenant General Don Alfredo Kindelan y Dunay, a direct descendant of
the Kindelans, of the ancient chieftains of Cinel Laoghaire, in County Meath.
This family claims descent from Niall of the Nine Hostages, the Irish king who
enslaved St Patrick. Deprived of their ancestral holdings, the Kindelans found
refuge in Spain and rose to become generals and governors of Spanish

possessions. General Alfredo Kindelan, who died not long before I began this book, was an aviator, a scholar, a distinguished author, a former Minister for Air and a Commander-in-Chief of the Spanish Air Force. He is popularly known as 'the first pilot of Spain'. Other figures of Irish descent who held high posts in the Spanish armed forces in recent years include a Rear Admiral McCarthy, an Admiral O'Dogherty, and a Lieutenant Commander Trayner.

One of the most heroic episodes of the Hispanic/Irish connection involved the defence of Gerona against the French by the much weakened Hispano-Irish Regiment, Ultonia (Ulster). The Regiment consisted of only 422 officers and men at the commencement of the siege in June 1808. They held out until December 1809 under the leadership of men whose surnames tell their own story: Colonel Antonio O'Kelly, Major O'Donnell, Commandant O'Donovan, Captains Fitzgerald and Sarsfield. The first French onslaught by an army of about 6,000 men was repulsed. Gerona, a small but key town, was then surrounded by a much larger army, 33,000 strong, which included almost 3,000 artillery gunners, but O'Kelly refused a call to surrender. The entire male population of the town was organised to resist by Major O'Donnell, and Donna Lucia de Fitzgerald (a lady of the Wild Geese) organised the women into the Company of Santa Barbara, becoming its first Commandant.

On 10 August 1809, the French army made an all-out attack on Montjuich Fort, which guarded the city walls. By the end of the attack, every member of the Ulster Regiment was either dead or wounded. Lucia Fitzgerald's group of women succeeded in bringing to safety the wounded who could not walk. A diarist of the time has left a description of the scene:

> In the square of San Pedro were the women of the Company of Santa Barbara, noblest of their sex, who only moments before were filing under a rain of shells, bombs and grenades to administer to the needs of the defenders; with the silent eloquence of example, more persuasive than any words, they communicated their spirit and courage to the soldiers of Montjuich; in their arms they carried the wounded to the blood-covered floors of the hospital. Certainly Gerona was that day the abode of heroines.

As in France, the list of Wild Geese is both lengthy and prominent at the highest level of Spanish society. One of the most distinguished titles in Spain is that of Duke of Tetuan. The present Duke, Don Leopoldo O'Donnell, is a direct descendant of the last O'Donnell inaugurated as a chieftain in Ireland. The O'Donnells were one of the great chiefly families of Ireland. It was Hugh Roe O'Donnell who, with Hugh O'Neill, led the last fight for Gaelic independence which ended at Kinsale. After Kinsale, Hugh Roe sought refuge in Spain, anticipating the Flight of the Earls by a few years. He was subsequently poisoned by a British spy. The O'Donnells became one of Spain's first families, their most colourful figure being Don Leopoldo O'Donnell (1809–1867), the first Duke of Tetuan. A brilliant soldier, his defence of the lines of San Sebastian against the Carlists in 1838, before he was thirty, made him famous, and he became a general within a decade. He survived being sentenced to death to serve as Prime Minister of Spain on three separate occasions between 1856 and 1866. One of the busiest streets in Madrid, La Calle O'Donnell, is called after the former Prime Minister.

Count Lucena Hugo O'Donnell, heir to the present Duke of Tetuan, is a wine-grower, a former naval officer, and a respected military historian. He maintains a lively interest in the Irish born in Ireland and Spain, and was quick to point out to me that Mary Robinson is an O'Donnell on her mother's side. The Count was also proud to tell me that his wife is from that most Irish of Spanish districts, Galicia, and that his children (he has four, three sons and a daughter) have learned some Irish and visit Ireland regularly. When I met him in Madrid, he was planning that year's quintennial Wild Geese visit to Donegal and the places associated with the O'Neills and O'Donnells.[39]

Had an idea of de Valera's come to fruition, the Count's interest in Ireland might have been even more direct. Not long after becoming Prime Minister in the 1930s, at a time when he was pondering his new constitution, de Valera raised with the Count's great-grandfather, the then Duke of Tetuan, the idea of restoring a monarchy in Ireland. A descendant of one of the Great Earls would have been an obvious candidate for the post, but de Valera did not pursue the idea.

As with most nationalities, the obvious place to find the Irish in Spain today, apart from in the ever-growing number of Irish pubs, is in the costas, the mecca of both tourists and transient workers. As befitted a wine-grower, however, the Count drew attention to an older scene of Irish involvement, the wine trade. The Irish links are most obvious around the sherry and wine-growing district of Jerez de la Frontera. Here one encounters prominent producers with names like Garvey, Terry, Morphy and O'Neale. Jerez's annual sherry festival is often dedicated to Ireland, as one of the principal importing countries.

Commercially, although Ireland's trade with Spain is not the largest of the EU countries, it is one of the fastest growing. Irish exports to Spain which were only IR£8 million in 1973 had risen to IR£892 million in 1997. Imports which were also only worth IR£8 million in 1973 had gone up to IR£276 million. The Irish import road vehicles, vegetables, fruit, wine, iron and steel, and, apart from tourists, send out electronic and consumer goods and fish.

No pun intended, but fish has proved a bone of contention. The Spanish still fish in Irish waters but, in place of the British, they now have to contend with EU regulations. They get around these by ploys such as building boats with concealed storage space, using illegal nets, and generally over-fishing. The only break in the pattern of Spanish/Irish friendship occurred in 1996, when the Canadian Government, led by a Minister of Irish descent, Brian Tobin, began cracking down on the Spaniards. Ireland's trawlers immediately blossomed with maple leaf flags. However, this glitch was overcome and, not only does trade with Spain continue to flourish, plans are also afoot in Dublin to build on the old Irish presence within the Spanish imperial network – Latin American markets.

Culturally, you can find traces of the Irish on the streets of Madrid. The Calle de Los Irlandes, a quiet vein rather than an artery of Madrid traffic, marks the area where the first church, hospital and college of St Patrick were founded by the Irish in 1629. Shortly afterwards, two of Spain's greatest literary figures, Lope de Vega and Pedro Calderon de la Barca, showed themselves subject to Patrick's influence. Until recent times purgatory was an important feature of Spain's penitential faith. It was the general importance attached to Catholic Europe to such purgatorial exercises and the contemplation of The Last Things, which gave importance to the writings of St Fursa mentioned earlier. The phrase 'to endure the pains of St Patrick' still survives in Spanish. Lope de Vega (1562–1635) and Pedero Calderon de la Barca (1600–1681) both wrote works based on St Patrick's purgatory. De Vega's play was *El Mayor Prodigio*; Calderon's was *El Purgatorio de San Patricio*. This purgatory, based on a retreat Patrick made to Lough Derg, still Ireland's most important pilgrimage site, was made famous in Spain by an Irish writer called O'Sullivan, whose work was known to the two Spanish writers.

A more contemporary Irish literary connection is the work of Kate O'Brien (1897–1974), who first came to Spain in 1922 as a governess. O'Brien got under the skin of Spain in more ways than one. Her love and empathy for the subject was balanced by a candour which caused Franco to ban her for twenty years in 1937. Amongst Kate O'Brien's enormous literary output of plays, novels, travel books, diaries and newspaper articles, her Spanish writings stand out. These include *Mary Lavelle* (1936), *That Lady* (1946), her monograph of *Teresa la Villa* (1951), and the work that got her banned – a fate which also befell her under the Irish censors of the period – *Farewell Spain* (1937), a travel book in which she describes not merely the attractions of Spain, but the demerits of Franco and the fascists.

Although Ireland was officially neutral in the conflict, the Spanish Civil War exercised a powerful influence on Irish intellectuals. Irish contingents fought on opposite sides. The International Brigade, which had an Irish unit 200 strong, claimed the poets, writers and left-wing IRA men. The more traditional and conservative Irish Catholics were to be found in General Eoin O'Duffy's unit, which fought for Franco, with 800 men. The best known of the International Brigade poets is Charlie Donnelly who died at the Battle of Jarama, defending Madrid, at the age of twenty-three. He left some trace of his passing, and that of his comrades, in his poem, entitled with sad appropriateness, 'Last Poem'.

> Between rebellion as a private study and the public
> Defiance is simple action only which will flicker
> Catlike, for spring. Whether nerve-roots is secret
> Iron, there's no diviner can tell, only the moment can show.
> Simple and unclear moment, on a morning utterly different.
> And under circumstances different from what you'd expect.

Your flag is public over granite. Gulls fly above it.
Whatever the issue of the battle is, your memory
Is public, for them to pull awry with crooked hands,
Moist eyes. And villages' reputations will be built on
Inaccurate accounts of your campaign. You're names for orators,
Figure stone-struck beneath damp Dublin sky.

The contemporary Irish singer Christy Moore helped to rescue from oblivion the names of a number of other young Irish idealists whom he listed in his popular song, 'Viva la Quinta Brigada'. Also, a television series called *The Olives are Bleeding*, by Cathal O'Shannon, a distinguished Irish TV journalist, evoked a deep and sympathetic response when it was shown in Ireland.[40] Another figure of interest was Walter Starkie, Professor of Spanish Literature at Trinity College Dublin (1926–1948). As a young man he fell in love with Spanish gypsy culture and music. He stayed with the gypsies, learning their music, which yielded a popular book, *Adventures in Spain with the Violin*. This was followed by other works based on gypsy culture that earned Starkie membership of the Real Academia Espanola de la Lengua. He died in Madrid in 1976.

As this book was being written, a number of Irish artists were maintaining the links forged by O'Brien and Starkie. The Irish scholar Ian Gibson is greatly respected for his work on Lorca. Gibson, a Trinity College graduate, had taught in Queens University, Belfast, for a time before setting out to Grenada in 1964 where he wrote *The Assassination of Garcia Lorca* which became the cornerstone of a Spanish biography of Lorca (also translated into English), which many Spanish critics regard as definitive. John Liddy, a poet from Limerick, who runs the British Council's Library in Madrid, has also translated Spanish literature into English, and runs a bilingual journal, *The Stony Thursday Book/Cudarno de Madrid*, which he edits, along with Liam Liddy and Miguel Artega.

Over a pleasant dinner with one of Madrid's top translators, Deirdre McCluskey, from Northern Ireland, the Secretary of the Irish/Hispanic Cultural Society, who works as a translator in Spanish television, and Dublin-born Denis Rafter and his wife Judy, an Australian, whom he married in Rome, I was left in no doubt of the enthusiasm with which Irish culture is received in Spain. Irish films are increasingly popular there. The black comedy *I Went Down*, starring Brendan Gleeson, attained near cult status, and the sale of Irish CDs and tapes is prodigious. If one checks a display of Celtic music in a store it almost inevitably turns out to be mainly Irish. There is also an eager and growing audience for readings of Irish poetry and fiction and for lectures by visiting Irish figures. There are Irish language classes to be had in Madrid and, needless to say, the Wild Geese Society is flourishing.

This society, which is composed of Spanish people of Irish descent, includes the majority of Spanish families with Irish names. These include O'Neills, O'Donnells, O'Sullivan Beares, O'Connors, MacCrochans, Treanors,

Kindelans and Kirkpatricks. As an indication of their standing in Spanish society, it might be pointed out that, apart from O'Donnell, the Duke of Tetuan, whom we have already encountered, these names include the Marques del Norte (O'Neill), and the Marques de Valdeiglesias (Kirkpatrick).

Denis Rafter has produced and acted in works by Synge, O'Casey, Stoppard, Chekov, Wilde and Shakespeare. He took me to a Spanish production he was directing at the Teatro de la Comedia, which was a bit like being invited by an Irishman to see a production which he was directing with the Royal Shakespeare Company. Rafter, in fact, first came to Spain as an Aer Lingus executive, and maintains his business contacts by ventures such as directing the Irlanda EXPO '92 for the Irish Government. He had trained as an actor in the Abbey Theatre in Dublin. At the time of writing, three of his productions were touring Spain. Nothing if not versatile, Rafter developed a panto dame role that brought him royal favour. King Juan Carlos's sons were brought to see the show by their nanny, fell in love with it and came back repeatedly, bringing their mother, the Infanta, with them.

Modern Spain obviously owes King Juan Carlos a great deal more than his family's encouragement of Denis Rafter. Following his successful defence of democracy against the military in 1981, Madrid, despite its thundering traffic, is one of the most relaxed cities in Europe. It only comes to life late at night, and one can walk the streets with complete safety, far more so, unfortunately, than one can in Dublin. Although the old Spain of the Church omnipresent is gone, churches are still respectably full at mass time, but in the streets, one sees neither clerical nor military uniform. The consensus is that neither would be appropriate in the present easy-going climate. After hearing so much about the benignity of this climate towards the Irish, I decided to test popular opinion for myself in a homely way, by visiting one of Madrid's ever-growing total of Irish pubs, Finbar's owned by John Morris from Dublin.

As soon as I walked in the bar, young Dessie Flanagan from Newry, County Down, stuck out his hand and said: 'How're ya – we met in Stirling.' Indeed we had. I had visited the Scottish university as part of my research over a year earlier, and had met Dessie, his mother and sister. I remarked at the time how involved in the life of Ireland the lad was, even though he lived in Scotland. Unlike his young Protestant counterparts at the university, most of whom were not planning to return to Northern Ireland, he was so interested in what was happening that he left our table to phone home to find out what were the results in that day's hurling and Gaelic football matches.

He was still interested, even though he had taken a year off study to come to Spain; he had just had a call from his mother in Newry with the day's scores. He and John Morris were emphatic that the Spanish like the Irish, and treat them well. As a young man, Morris and his father had been forced to emigrate to England to find work, and he remembered seeing signs in guest houses: 'No blacks, dogs or Irish need apply'. Of course, like Deirdre McCluskey, who once found that she lost a flat in London because of her Irish accent, he subsequently made many English friends; nevertheless either experience would have been unthinkable in Madrid.

Morris's business partner, also an Irishman, is teaching English in his own school. The Spanish student tradition means that the Spaniards come more easily to an Irishman than to an English-run school. As Spain, like Ireland, goes further down the EU road, it's ironic that the language the Spanish most want to be taught is that of the anti-EU English. As with my interviewing worldwide, I adopted a sort of focus group approach, seeking the views of different people from different backgrounds. This was particularly easy to do in Finbar's because John Morris runs an Irish musical group which attracts a wide cross-section of people. He deprecatingly described their playing as 'a cross between Irish music and yahoo music'.

Actually, as I would discover later in the evening, the group was very good. One of its members was Anthony Warde, one of Ireland's best banjo players. He was enjoying himself in Spain where, like the other ex-pats, he found that the possession of an Irish passport, allied to some degree of skill or talent, was a veritable guarantee of success. This view was shared by all the musical group, which, apart from Anthony and John Morris, included a German and two other Irishmen. The only complaint they had was the difficulty of adjusting to the terrible Madrid heat.

They took me with them to their gig for the night. It was held in a square on the outskirts of Madrid which was a combination of settled, leafy suburbia and high-rise buildings. Here we rendezvoused at yet another Irish pub, where there was a lively crowd, mostly of Spaniards, happily drinking Guinness amid scenes of Ireland and notices advising of forthcoming Irish gigs and lectures. Prior to the Irish group going on, the stage was occupied by a heavy metal group which attracted, if not an ecstatic, at least a reasonable round of applause. However, when the Irish group started to play, bars and cafés began to empty, windows went up in the surrounding tower blocks, and the square began to fill up. The group played a combination of Irish rock and traditional music, changing the words of such familiar Irish songs as 'The Waxy's Dargle' to 'The Waxy's Fiestas'.[41]

I'm sure they meant it kindly, but accounted it a dubious compliment when, in my honour, they changed the traditional Dublin ballad, 'Tim Finnegan's Wake', to 'Tim Pat Finnegan's Wake', with a flamenco background (the song commemorates a wake at which the supposed corpse came back to life when whiskey was spilled on it). However, the crowd obviously loved any and all versions. Young and old danced in the square and simply refused to let the group off the stage, demanding and getting something like 45-minutes' worth of encores. Very obviously there is some Celtic affinity between the Spaniards and the Irish, where Irish music is concerned, but for the Irish too, music has a bonding attraction at a deep subconscious level.

John Morris illustrated this in a story concerning his 21-year-old son, whom he had brought home with him to Ireland the previous year. The young man had spent most of his time in England, and after a day of sight-seeing in the city, John brought him to one of Dublin's most popular venues, Johnny Fox's pub in the Dublin mountains. There was a lively session to the accompaniment of bodhrans, fiddles, flutes, spoons and guitar. As the music crescendoed, John's son unexpectedly put his arm around his father's shoulders and hugged him, saying simply: 'Thanks, da.' The young man had discovered a door into his own culture – one he had hardly been aware of until then. As both the Irish and the Spanish increasingly rediscover, and redefine, a nearly forgotten heritage, many a young Irish person in contemporary Spain has reason to echo the young man's impulsive comment and say: 'Thanks, Spain.'

ITALY

If one wished to pick out a point at which began the close friendly relationships which currently exist between the Irish and the Italians, one need go no further than the 1990 World Cup, Italia 90. This is where the contemporary boom in Italian tourism to Ireland began. Italian TV showed pictures of unspoilt Irish scenery and Alitalia, the Italian national airline, began playing Irish muzak. Suddenly Ireland was the in place – for reasons of the personality of the people as much as the scenery. The first match in which Ireland was involved was played in Sardinia. The Italian authorities, expecting to have to deal with English-type soccer fans, penned up the Irish contingent in a series of barred enclosures. One Irish fan, struck by the resemblance to sheep pens, started baaing. The baaing was taken up by those on either side of him, and soon the entire stadium rang to the sound of sheep bleating. The gesture caught the imagination of the Italian public.

The Irish proceeded to win further good opinions by proving themselves able to consume prodigious quantities of alcohol with no adverse effect other than a tendency to generate a belief amongst Irish fans that Patrick Murphy could out-sing any Italian tenor. Popular goodwill towards the Irish was heightened by an outburst of U2 mania in Italy, and by the exploits of the Irish racing driver Eddie Irvine with Ferrari. The bonds of friendship proved so durable that when the Irish defeated Italy in the 1994 World Cup, the result was not fisticuffs but the biggest street party in recent New York history.

One of the most knowledgeable commentators on Italian perceptions of Ireland is Paddy Agnew, in Rome for the *Irish Times* and for RTE. He remarked that ten years earlier, when he phoned up people and mentioned Ireland they were apt to reply: 'Where? Iceland?'[42] Since then, apart from rock music, soccer and tourism, a very good press for the Celtic Tiger has also created a favourable image of Ireland. The Italians admired the way the Irish went about securing structural funds from the European Community, and then actually spending the monies on the purposes for which they were intended. This is not universally the custom in Italy. The Italians comment favourably on Irish infrastructure, roads, phones, education and the way the

Irish built up their economy. While I was visiting Rome, the Italians by contrast were uneasily beginning to face up to the problems of overhauling their industrial base to meet EU criteria. They were starting to acknowledge the magnitude of the problems involved in doing so in a country in which 53 per cent of industry was state controlled, and which has little or no social security programmes. The safety net for the old and the disadvantaged still tends to consist of the extended family. No family means no net. The results are visible in the numbers of shuffling derelicts one sees in the streets.

However, to get a more in-depth picture of the nature of Irish/Italian relationships, one has to go back a lot earlier than either U2 or EU. Rome has had a very special position in the Irish consciousness for centuries. The papacy, as we have seen, played an important role in Irish affairs as far back as the early monks. Subsequently, despite the very dubious role played by the Pope in the Norman invasion, the papacy was looked to as a source of deliverance in the dark days of the 1640s. Through the intercession of the Irish Franciscan Luke Wadding, Pope Urban VIII did send some money and armaments to the Irish – but the papacy's overriding concern at all times was with what was happening in the centre stage theatre of Europe, rather than in the little theatre in the Atlantic, however devout its cast and audience.

Nevertheless, as a source of both refugee and pilgrimage, Rome exercised a kind of magic hold over the Irish mind. The sword of Hugh O'Neill, The Great O'Neill, who for a time worsted Elizabeth's armies before being forced into exile, is still preserved in St Isidore's Franciscan Monastery. The heart of Daniel O'Connell, who died in Genoa in 1847 at the height of the Great Famine, was lodged in a silver casket in the Irish College in the Street of the Irish, near St John of Lateran. By the time of the Irish independence movement of the twentieth century, Rome, apart from the Irish in America, was the only centre to which the Irish could look for meaningful political and moral support. When I was writing my book on Michael Collins, I found that one of the most interesting sets of documents I encountered was that dealing with the efforts of the Irish, through the sympathetic rector of the Irish College, Dr Hagan, to counter the effects of British diplomacy which sought in vain to persuade the Vatican to condemn the Irish uprising.

After the Irish achieved a degree of independence, the Vatican was the first state to which an ambassador was appointed, and for several decades Rome figured so largely in the affections of the Irish Department of External Affairs that when, after the Second World War, Joseph Walshe, one of the Department's most notable figures, retired as Secretary of the Department, his request to be posted to the Vatican was agreed to as a special favour. In the post-war period also, the Irish Minister for External Affairs, Sean McBride, a former Chief of Staff of the IRA, who was later awarded both the Nobel and Lenin Peace Prizes, joined hands with the Roman Catholic Archbishop of Dublin, Dr John Charles McQuaid, to collect money for a fund set up to combat Communism in Italy.

Today, a posting to the state of Italy itself, rather than to the Vatican, would be regarded by the Department as the more prestigious post, but the Vatican Embassy, apart from being a sumptuous building, with its own swimming pool, is still a significant listening post for the Irish Government. Much useful information finds its way to Dublin because the Church has representatives in every corner of the globe, but the change in emphasis in the Rome postings reflects both the increasing secularisation of Irish society and the effects of Ireland's membership of the European Community. Irish trade with Italy has increased dramatically. Exports went up from a mere IR£18 million in 1973 to IR£1,149 million in 1997. Nowadays the Irish business community, and many of the staff of Irish state institutions, focus on the industrial centre of Milan, rather than on Rome. However, it is to Rome that the Irish turn for holidays, to visit St Peter's and, perhaps, see the Pope, and an increasing trend in recent decades, as the cost of Irish weddings soars, is to get married in the Irish College.

The Vatican pays great lip service to the contribution of the Irish Church, as well it might. The contribution of religious Irishmen and women to Roman Catholicism is one which, whatever one's personal faith, or lack of it, entitles the Irish Church to be regarded as the Emerald in the Crown. Nevertheless, behind the scenes one detects a faint air of displeasure emanating from the Vatican concerning the contemporary Irish Church. The various Irish clerical paedophile scandals, and the well-publicised fathering of children by two notable Irish clerics, Bishop Eamon Casey and Father Michael Cleary, played a part in dulling the sheen on the Emerald. So too did the Irish hierarchy's inability to deal with the growth and influence of a schismatic sect within the Irish Church, one of whose adherents, Father Patrick Buckley, demonstrated an ability to wield two powers highly displeasing in Curial circles. First, he showed that he could not be prevented, as a properly ordained priest, from celebrating marriages – including marriages of an ever-growing class of Irish persons, divorcees. This puts a breach in Rome's fortifications against divorce. Second, his sect ordained him a bishop, which meant that he could ordain other priests in his own mould. Episcopal powers, it will be remembered, are a contentious issue with Rome, going back to the days of St Columbanus.

Part of the Vatican's attitude is based on the conservatism of Pope John Paul II. Shortly before I visited the Eternal City, a particularly popular member of the Irish hierarchy had led a pilgrimage to St Peter's, during which it was observed that he was wearing a short-sleeved shirt. This fact was duly conveyed to His Holiness and his consequent displeasure transmitted to the offending bishop. However, part of the fall off in respect for the Irish hierarchy lies in the Church's geo-politics. At the time of writing, the papacy is concerned about the North/South relationship, proselytising Protestantism in Latin-America and Africa, the growth of Islam in the world and the fact that North American Catholicism verges on a state of near schism with Rome over its stance on abortion, married clergy, the ordination of women, contraception and divorce.

Pope John Paul II, though abhorred by theological liberals, politically speaking, is a world statesman of the highest rank and nothing if not a realist. He is best assessed not in terms of theology but of the days when the papacy was a temporal power. As a celibate and a Pole, his approach to those issues which are grounded in sexual relations or gender is completely out of tune with Western values, but his alliance with the Americans in the ending of the Cold War was the contemporary version of the Holy Alliance. It was he more than anyone else who brought down Communism by setting in train in his native Poland the domino effect that eventually toppled the Berlin Wall and the ruling Communist Party in Russia. From his perspective, and that of the Curia, in the numbers game, the ever-filling churches and seminaries of Africa and Eastern Europe outrank the Irish Church's contribution of yesteryear.

In the scholastic year in which I visited Rome (1998) the great Irish seminary of Maynooth had opened its doors to a total of only twelve students when term began. In Dublin, Clonliffe seminary supplies priests to the Dublin Archdiocese. It used to be estimated (*circa* 1988) that, with natural wastage, Dublin required around twenty-five priests each year to maintain parochial manning levels. Taking the normal drop-out ratio into account, securing the twenty-five ordinations at the end of seminary training was generally reckoned to require 125 student enrolments at the commencement of the first year's training. In 1998, when the Clonliffe term began there were no students for enrolment, and, Dublin apart, already some rural parishes have run short of priests.

An indication of the consequential weakening status of the Irish Church in Rome is the failure to find a red hat for the former rector of the Irish College, Sean Brady, currently the Archbishop of Armagh. His predecessor, like those for a century before him, was not only Archbishop, but a cardinal. However, in January 2001, one was found for the deeply conservative Desmond Connell, Archbishop of Dublin, a friend of Cardinal Ratzinger, the leader of the Vatican Right. The choice, coming at a critical time in the peace process, annoyed many Irish nationalists affronted at the undermining of the unstated message that, though partitioned, Ireland was one. The transfer southward of the red hat was seen as a consequence of Rome's desire to keep control of the church in right wing hands.

As with the Spanish, various legends ascribe a common origin to the Italians and the Irish. One of the early tribes whom mythology credits with establishing a pre-history civilisation in Ireland are the Partholonians, who are said to be descended from Noah's brother. Their existence is recalled by the name Partholon, which is often given to boys as a Christian name, and in the passage graves and mounds which survive from the New Stone Age. Some Italian writers, like Enzo Farinella, draw attention to the great Irish passage graves of Dowth, Knowth and Newgrange, which predate the pyramids by a millennium, and cite their close similarity to similar architectural wonders in Sicily in order to establish links between the Partholonians, who came from Sicily, and the Irish.[43] Certainly a cynic, viewing the spreading political, banking, and industrial scandals in Ireland at the time of writing, would be inclined to concede the presence of a marked affinity with the Sicilian Mafia.

Another shared foundation myth concerns King Arthur, the Celtic hero of the court of Camelot, who is said to have been buried in Mount Etna. A version of the Arthurian return legend involves two powerful Italian and Irish families, the Fitzgeralds, or Geraldines, of Munster, and the Gherandini family of Florence, who viewed each other as cousins, and remained in close contact from the early fifteenth century onwards. From this cousinly connection, there was extrapolated out of the Arthurian legend, the prophecy that the Emperor Frederick II, supported by the Florentines, would unite with the cousins of Munster to one day free not only Ireland, but Italy. Such legends, combined with the fact that many Italian families were educated by some version of the Irish Church, be it nuns, monks or Christian Brothers, helped to provide a substratum of shared identity between the two peoples.

This substratum was given particularly tangible form by the great Irish Franciscan, Luke Wadding. Wadding founded St Isidore's in Rome, and a few years later the Irish College in 1625. From this period there date also the origins of two other Irish foundations, those of the Dominicans in San Clemente, and of the Augustinians' Irish National Church, St Patrick's, which, with St Isidore's and the Irish College, make up the four cornerstones of the contemporary Irish presence in Rome.

To the religious dimension was added various Irish military and political activities. A contingent of Wild Geese, making up the Irish Bodyguard, as it was known, of the Duchy of Parma earned a lasting reputation for valour at Cremona in 1702. The Bodyguard was retained by the Duchy for thirty years after the engagement. In 1860, another contingent of Irish troops, some 1,400 strong, fought in the defence of Spoleto, for the Vatican against the forces of unity who had invaded the papal states. During the Risorgimento, Irish nationalists and Italian liberals formed a common bond. O'Connell, who did all he could to curb rebellion at home, applauded the Italian insurrection of 1830. Mazzini was one of the exemplars who inspired the Young Ireland revolutionaries of 1848. Interestingly, given the fact that the institutions involved had been created in the first place because of religious persecution by the English, Rome's Irish Colleges escaped confiscation when the Piedmontese captured the city in 1870, because the Colleges successfully claimed that they were under the protection of the British Government!

The English heritage also resulted in the ironic fact of the Irish legation being the only English-speaking one to remain open in Rome during the Second World War. Delia Murphy, in her day a famous ballad singer, was the wife of the Irish Minister to the Vatican, T. J. Kiernan. She was thus able to help the legendary Irish Scarlet Pimpernel, Monsignor Hugh O'Flaherty, in his work of assisting fugitives from the Gestapo all through the German occupation. O'Flaherty's network, which included members of the Italian carabinieri, or police force, saved countless Jews and escaped prisoners of war from the firing squad and the gas chamber.

In Ireland, the Italian connection has created some of the most important portions of the Irish architectural heritage. Castletown House designed by Alexandra Galilei and Dublin still shows the influence of the famous Italian renaissance architect, Andrea Palladio. Several great Irish houses which survive from the Georgian era were embellished by stuccadori whose names are still remembered in Ireland. The Cypriani, Castrucci, Geminiani and the La Franchinis have left stucco angels dispensing baskets of flowers across the ceilings of grand homes throughout Dublin and the countryside. Also remembered with respect are figures like Carlo Bianconi, who bought up horses and carts cheaply at the end of the Napoleonic Wars, and gave Ireland a mail and coach service. By 1837 Bianconi owned almost 1,000 horses. During the 1980s, Dublin took great pride in the fact that it could install a direct access rapid transit system (DART) powered by electricity. This was able to make the journey from Bray in County Wicklow to Dublin some twelve miles away in thirty-six minutes – the same time taken by a Bianconi coach in the 1800s!

Another Irish Italian who achieved enduring fame outside Ireland as well as in, was Guglielmo Marconi. His mother was Annie Jameson, daughter of John Jameson, who founded the famous Dublin whiskey distillery in 1780. Marconi developed his revolutionary radio transmission system at Clifden, County Galway, and he sent the world's first radio signal back to Ireland from that most Irish of outposts, Newfoundland. Other small but telling references to Irish/Italian links dating from the days of Bianconi, Marconi, and the Grand Tour can be seen all over Dublin. For example, close to where I live, there lies a beautiful, Naples-recalling bay, spanned by a road named after the Italian philosopher, Vico. It in turn is accessed by traversing Sorrento Road. Contemporary Irish/Italian links are maintained by the flourishing Italian Culture Institute in Dublin and by a network of Italian fish and chip shops and restaurants all over the country.

I referred earlier to the four cornerstones of the Irish presence in Rome being St Isidore's, San Clemente, St Patrick's and the Irish college. This is not to overlook other very deep-rooted religious links such as the work of the Irish Christian Brothers. In fact, Brother Austin Connolly was one of a group of key figures in the Irish community which the Irish Ambassador to Rome, Joseph Small, one of the stalwarts of the Irish diplomatic service, and his wife Mary brought together at a dinner which Small graciously hosted in my honour at his residence. Around the table there sat representatives of the Irish business community, academia, and international institutions such as the European Commission Office, and the FAO. Between them, under Small's shrewd interlocutorship, they gave me an unforgettable *tour de l'horizon* of what Italy and Ireland meant, and mean, to each other. Obviously the men who control the four Irish cornerstones of the enduring Irish presence in Rome had their own importance, but in a sense the entire Irish diaspora was exemplified in the person of another guest, said to be the leading dentist in Rome, Dr Charles Kennedy.

I say this because when I began my travels for the purposes of this book, I had sometimes heard people in Dublin query Mary Robinson's frequent assertion that there were 70 million people on the globe entitled to call themselves Irish. I had travelled fairly extensively, even before beginning my researches, but, in so far as living is concerned, I have never moved more than three miles from the point on the east coast of Ireland in Monkstown, County Dublin, where I was born. I went to school, married and raised a family, all within a sliver of the Irish coastline a few miles long. Yet everywhere I went in the world I constantly bumped into someone whom I had either gone to school with, grew up with, worked with, or who had gone to school with one of my children, or, increasingly, grandchildren! It was a small but useful illustration of how colossal must have been the outpouring from the country as a whole. Dr Kennedy and his family constituted a prime example of the scattering. His father was a County Offaly-born doctor who had served in both the British Army and Navy. His mother was of English and Scots origin and he was born in Shropshire. One of his brothers was a parish priest in New Orleans. Another became a doctor and reared nine children in Newfoundland – he retired and died in County Cork, but a son still carries on his practice in Canada. A sister served as a Wren in the Royal Navy, married a Fleet Air Arm pilot and also lives in Canada. Another brother, who spent the Second World War as a wireless operator on a ship ferrying ammunition to the East, now lives with his family in Australia. Yet another brother who had served with the British Army in Gibraltar during the war, also did dentistry and lived for a time in Australia before settling in England. All the family, including Charles himself, keep in regular contact with Ireland, both by phone, letter, and visits. Charles became a dentist in Nova Scotia, and practised in California where he was already feeling too European and out of place when the Watts riots occurred. He found a man with a shotgun on his landing, as he came down the stairs after viewing the fires from his roof. He moved to Harley Street in London where his US doctorate was a passport to considerable professional success. Eventually, however, he tired of London and moved to Rome, where he and the ambience were clearly suited to each other.

Of what might be termed the Cornerstone Custodians, Father Luke Dempsey, a magnificent Dominican of Aquinas-like proportions, wearing a green T-shirt, was the coolest figure (in more ways than one) amongst our suited, collar-and-tied gathering. Next day, when he showed me around San Clemente in his full Dominican robes, the superior of San Clemente looked like a Spanish galleon under full sail. Another monk, Father Liam MacCarthy, superior of St Isidore's, was shy and deceptively unobtrusive, his classical Franciscan humility masking an equally classical Franciscan intellect. Before coming to Rome, Father MacCarthy had served for many years in Belfast, of whose Protestant people he spoke lovingly and perceptively. His presence in Rome, like the divisions in Belfast, goes back to the great Protestant/Catholic dissensions of the past, which led to St Isidore's being created in the first place. The burly cheerful figure of Father Michael Breathnach, lately returned from working in America, belied the problems he faces in running St Patrick's. This unique part of Ireland's heritage faces equally unique challenges posed by falling vocations and changing mores – changes which go to the heart of the question of Irish identity. Symbolically, in order to meet them, part of St Patrick's has been turned into a management institute.

Alongside these men sat Monsignor John Fleming, President of the Irish College. Slight, alert, affable, diplomatic, Fleming literally walks in the footsteps of some of the greatest names not only in the Irish Church, but in Irish history. His predecessor is now the Archbishop and will possibly become the Cardinal of Armagh. Once one would have safely prophesied a similar role for Fleming, but as indicated earlier, the Emerald in the Crown does not glisten as of yore. Fleming himself says that all he wants to do is: 'retire to a quiet parish somewhere and catch up on my reading'.

In his introductory remarks to our post-dinner discussion, Ambassador Small had remarked that in his view the most significant Irish figure to come to Rome was Luke Wadding. Touring the college with Fleming, it was easy to understand why Small made this assertion. Wadding was born in Waterford in 1588 to the son of a wealthy merchant. Both of his parents dated from the Norman coming, and while devoutly Catholic, by ancestry were loyal not to Ireland but to the King of England. Luke Wadding, however, would prove himself loyal both to his native country and the old religion. The atmosphere he grew up in was heavily Catholic, a matrix which altered in degree rather than in kind right up to the time of my boyhood when for example in Lent, the 'Black Fast', which included both prayer and abstinence, was still widely practised.

The fourteen Wadding children were expected to recite The Office of the Blessed Virgin every day; twice a week, the penitential psalms with the accompanying litanies of the saints; then, once a month, the Officium Defunctorum (Office of the Dead); morning and evening prayers; and the nightly rosary with all the 'trimmings' which pious people traditionally put in: special prayers for the dead, indulgence prayers and so on. Not surprisingly, after this conditioning, Luke joined the Franciscan Order in Portugal whence he had journeyed on a family business trip. One of his close friends in the seminary, Richard Synnott, would subsequently be martyred by Cromwell. Wadding's reputation for brilliance caught the attention of Philip III, who sent him to Rome as part of an effort to have the doctrine of the Immaculate Conception defined. At that time, Spain was riven by theological argument on the issue.

In Rome, Wadding built up a formidable corpus of published work. He was the epitome of the scholarly monk. Unless one has seen the widespread fervour for archaic, dense, theological scholarship displayed by some Irish clergy, it is difficult to comprehend the phenomenon. My uncle, Martin Toal, who produced, amongst other works, a twelve-volume collection of *Patristic Homilies from the Fathers* (of the Church) had passed the half-century mark when he came to Rome, from Australia, to commence this undertaking.

Discovering that he would require German to study the sources properly, he promptly set about learning the language, and duly produced his books.

For his part, Wadding produced a sixteen-volume edition of the writings of John Duns Scotus, which alone would have established his reputation, to which, amongst a vast corpus of other work, he added an awesome 24-volume history of the Franciscan Order, the original of which can be inspected in the library of St Isidore's. Much of his popular reputation in Ireland, however, rests on the fact that he was the central international figure during the nine years of warfare which began in Ireland in 1641. The Thirty Years War was reaching its climax during much of this period, and from his vantage point in Rome, Wadding was engaged in diplomatic initiatives involving the Pope, the Dutch, the French and the Spanish, in an effort to engage the Catholic powers on the side of the Irish.

Apart from the efforts of British diplomacy, Wadding was continually hampered, not merely by the conflicting claims on the papacy, but by the ultimately ruinous divisions between the Irish chieftains, and between the Anglo-Irish Catholics, who were loyal to England, and the native Irish Catholics. Moreover, the Pope was preoccupied with what amounted to a European Protestant alliance with the British Parliament. Apart from the ineffectual Smerwick landings, Spain, the chief source of hope, had largely failed to come to Ireland's assistance. Nevertheless, Wadding succeeded in obtaining a brief for the Irish Generals, Owen Roe O'Neill and Thomas Preston, commending their enterprise and granting them a 'plenary indulgence in the hour of death'.[44]

More tangibly, Wadding succeeded in having sent to Ireland two papal emissaries, firstly Father Pier Francesco Scarampi, and subsequently, two years after Scarampi, Archbishop Rinucinni, in 1645. Both men brought with them substantial amounts of money and weaponry. However, the Catholic Confederation of Kilkenny, to whom Rinucinni in particular was formally appointed Nuncio, was disunited. The Confederates recorded one notable success, under Owen Roe O'Neill, the Battle of Benburb (5 June 1646). This caused a Te Deum to be sung in the Basilica of St Mary Major, and the standards captured by the Irish were hung in triumph in the Cupola of St Peter's. Alas, papal Te Deums tend to have an unlucky echo in Ireland, and the Confederates subsequently suffered a series of defeats, which culminated in the crowning disaster, the arrival of Oliver Cromwell in Ireland. The sword of the Lord Protector soon cut through the shoots of Catholic Irish liberty, and in Rome intrigue and the setbacks in Ireland turned the tide of Vatican diplomacy against Wadding. After 1648, the Pope refused to receive any further appeals concerning Ireland.

Wadding, however, continued to be an influential figure in other spheres and his hand may be seen today behind two of Rome's four Irish cornerstones, St Isidore's and the Irish College. Wadding, who had earlier founded a Franciscan convent, set up St Isidore's as a missionary training college in 1625. Around the same time, the Pope, Urban VIII, appointed Ludovico

Ludovisi as Cardinal Protector of Ireland. Wadding convinced the new protector that the best way to assist the Irish Church would be to found a College to train priests for Irish dioceses. Thus an Irish College was created, close by St Isidore's. Wadding effectively ran both institutions until 1635 when the Vatican found in favour of a proviso in Ludovici's will which placed the Irish College under the control of the Jesuits. Wadding thereupon cut the painter, and set up a new Irish College.

The rule of the College was tough. The standards of the time did not include much in the way of provision for either recreation or holidays. Not only were students not allowed to return to Ireland during their studies, they had to sign an agreement undertaking not to apply to the College for the eventual fare home! This may have accounted for the relatively disappointing performance of the College in the first century of its existence. Of the 200 or so students who passed through its doors between 1628 and 1798 – a period which included the worst days of the penal laws – not many returned to Ireland. Because of the rigours of the time, some died in their student days, and some dropped out. Others were ordained for religious orders and assigned to continental houses. Nevertheless, some of the most important figures of the Irish Church date from those days. Oliver Plunkett, who became Archbishop of Armagh and was martyred in 1681, was canonised a saint in 1975. Another student, Philip Clery of Raphoe, is currently being considered at the Vatican for canonisation.

Less noble additions to the tradition of the Irish Church may have had their origins in the Irish College also. A prefect of studies, Pietro Tamborini, was fired in 1778 when it was discovered that some of the students who passed through his hands were spreading the teachings of Cornelius Jansen in Ireland. Jansen (1585–1638) was a Dutch theologian who preached a St Augustine-style doctrine of predetermination. In other words salvation was predetermined and everyone not so pre-ordained was doomed to perdition. One would have thought that this doctrine might have encouraged people to believe either, that as predestination existed nothing one did in the way of transgression could affect salvation, or, that as they were probably doomed in the next life they might as well enjoy themselves in this.

However, possibly because St Augustine believed that ejaculation was arrived at through a temporary loss of one's will, Jansenism became bound up with a Tartuffe-like hypocrisy and a life-denying prudery where sex was concerned. Apparently, predestination or no, sexuality could get one taken off the saved list. Unfortunately the excision of Tamborini did not remove Jansen from the Irish body politic. In fact, his hold on Irish clerical teaching was strengthened after the foundation of Maynooth College in 1795. Many of the professors had become imbued with Jansenistic doctrines during their training in France and not only spread them through Ireland, but all over the world, via Irish priests and nuns.

As the Irish church grew in strength throughout the nineteenth century, so the Irish College moved centre stage in the world church. Some of the most powerful clerics in Australia, Canada and New Zealand were all products of the Irish College in Rome. The two most important college figures of the nineteenth century were the Rectors Paul Cullen (1832–49) and Tobias Kirby, who succeeded him in 1850. Kirby ruled the College until 1891, and Cullen, in effect, became the Irish Church, after being consecrated Archbishop of Armagh in February 1850. He then transferred to Dublin and was made a Cardinal.

The latter part of the nineteenth century was the era of 'the prisoner in the Vatican', during which the Pope made very few public announcements or forays outside the papal enclave. The era also marked the ending of the papacy as a political power, and in the disturbed conditions of the time, during which the Irish Church was producing a seemingly inexhaustible supply of nuns and priests, the Irish College became one of the most powerful institutions in the world church.

Amongst the important figures produced by the College were some of Kirby's vice-rectors: the Benedictine Bernard Smith, Australia's first cardinal; another Australian cardinal, Cullen's nephew, Patrick Moran; and a second Cullen nephew, Michael Verdun, who became Bishop of Dunedin (New Zealand). Some of these names will cross our pages later as we tell the story of the Irish in the Antipodes. With them will be conjoined the names of Archbishop Croke, Archbishop Sir James Duhig of Brisbane, and Archbishop Liston of Auckland. Apart from producing figures like these, the significance of the College lay in the fact that under Cullen and Kirby, it became in effect the Irish hierarchy's embassy in Rome, and the centre to which Irish bishops and priests, many of them ex-Irish College students, turned when they wished to have a cause pleaded with the Vatican.

The political influence of the College was such that it is said that de Valera consulted with the then Rector of the College, Monsignor Hagan, before founding the Fianna Fail Party in 1926. In fact de Valera had independently come to the conclusion that he would never fulfil his dreams of securing power if he continued in his role as leader of Sinn Fein, with its para-military wing and its policy of not recognising the institutions of state. He did visit Hagan surreptitiously before the foundation, but it was more likely that this had to do with attempting to secure a fair wind from the Vatican for the new venture (de Valera would have been regarded as having been excommunicated by a hierarchical decree during the Irish Civil War), than with Hagan's urgings to follow the path of peace.

The College, however, may have played a role in the securing of peace in Ireland as this book was being researched. The origins of this go back to a speech delivered by the Pope at Drogheda during his visit to Ireland in September 1979. A sentence in this speech, which castigated violence, adverted to the fact of there being other ways to pursue political objectives, and drew attention to the responsibility of constitutional politicians to show leadership in this regard. Gerry Adams publicly challenged Church or political leaders to state what these methods were. A sort of public dialogue ensued between himself and Archbishop Daly, the Irish primate. Observing this, an Irish Redemptorist monk, Father Alex Reid, began a series of contacts between Adams and various other Irish political and church leaders which ultimately led to the IRA ceasefire of 31 August 1994, and to its resumption in 1996, after a breakdown in February of that year.

Father Reid showed not only rare initiative, but great courage and endurance in his dealings with the tough and turbulent actors in this drama, on both sides of the religious divide; loyalist paramilitaries as well as Republicans came to trust him. In his endeavours he received equally rare latitude and support from Church authorities. In Rome, I learned that there may have been a supervening reason for this encouragement, and indeed to the entire Peace Process, which no one suspected at the time. The Pope's speech was in fact written in the Irish College by the then Bishop Cathal Daly. Daly, who later became a Cardinal, shuttled between the College and the Pope's summer residence at Castelgandolfo, preparing several drafts of the speech, before the Pope finally delivered it in Ireland. Although I would be greatly at odds with John Paul's stance on many issues, when I visited Castelgandolfo I felt that I owed him a toast over Ireland. Accordingly, as the moon came up over the lake, which the Pope's residence overlooks, Dr MacCarthy and I raised our glasses in the direction of the papal residence from a nearby restaurant terrace.

Today's Irish College is still a nerve centre for the Irish, albeit on a restricted scale. It still fulfils its function of preparing priests for Irish dioceses and is a key social gathering place for the Irish community in Rome. Lectures, recitals, receptions keep its spacious corridors and impressive reception rooms buzzing. The increasing trend amongst Irish couples of opting for a Rome wedding means that, though vocations are dropping like a stone, in the College one can see the paradoxical sight of young people literally queuing to receive pre-marriage instruction.

The College is redolent of both the sadness and the fierce piety of Irish history: here a tapestry depicting the martyrdom of St Oliver Plunkett, there the crucifix he brought to his execution; yonder the inscription to the two Earls, O'Neill and O'Donnell, who took part in the great Flight. O'Neill died in the College; a plaque tells you: 'Here are the bones of Hugh O'Neill.' A decent discretion omits the fact that the lonely, embittered, exiled Earl died alone. No wife came to the College. Luke Wadding's driven countenance is depicted in marble and on canvas. Mighty-engined though his brain was, he was clearly a man with much on his mind. Set into a wall, there is an impressive marbled memorial to O'Connell who, in his will, decreed that his heart be interred in the College. The purse of Bianconi, the transport magnate, ensured that his wishes were carried out and marked by an unusually beautiful marbled fresco.

The memorial to Kirby, the great Rector of the College, not only commemorates a man, it encapsulates a style now not only out of vogue, but mocked by the sophisticates of contemporary Dublin. Kirby's marbled countenance is framed by round towers, wolfhounds, harps, a sunrise over the hills of Erin and the inscription 'Eireann go bragh'. Fashions change.

A remnant of the Claudian aqueduct dating from the year AD 47 is built into the College wall. What will Ireland and the Irish be like by the year AD 3,047? Will they still be predominantly Catholic? Will there be a Roman Catholic Church? In such a setting, such speculations are not merely fanciful but inevitable.

There are some who would say that it is entirely appropriate that the most impressive Irish conerstone is set atop a pagan temple! Whatever division of opinion there may be about this it is certain that the chapels, frescoes, sculptures and paintings San Clemente contains make it one of the great attractions of Rome. I particularly like the medieval layout of a chamber where, from a central carved high chair, students still defend their theses. The Basilica, which is built on a site that makes Claudius's aqueduct seem modern, came into the possession of the Irish Dominicans in 1677. Prior to this, San Clemente had been in the hands of the Ambrosian Order, whose condition in the year 1625 may be gauged from a bishop's letter which indicates that the travails of the contemporary church are not without precedent:

> The congregation of S.Ambrogio al Nemo in this diocese of Milan is on the brink of ruin. Of the fifty religious of the Order in the diocese, about five are worthy of the name. Of the others, two are in prison, two are apostates and assassins, the rest are dishonest and a scandal.[45]

The foregoing is taken from a work by one of the great scholars of the Dominican Order, the late Father Leonard E. Boyle. In appearance he was a frail aesthete, but with an output that rivals Wadding's, albeit with a Donegal twinkle in the eye which depictions of the great Franciscan do not record. Boyle with his manuscripts and his doctorates provided a marked contrast to Father Luke Dempsey. Whether scudding massively from hospitable table to kitchen, or parting the crowds who daily throng the Basilica, Dempsey seems the archetypical Jolly Friar, appreciating equally the merits of a vintage manuscript or a vintage wine. In his disquisition of San Clemente's history, he showed himself in equal parts knowledgeable, human and discreet. Deftly traversing one rather lurid patch, he remarked airly: 'One gather there was some difficulty about bed-warmers and that sort of thing . . . !'

The Basilica is situated a few hundred yards from the Colosseum, and is called after Pope St Clement, who died *circa* AD 100. Excavations have shown that it contains four levels: the present Basilica, the original fourth-century Basilica, an earlier first-century building and, below it, buildings which were destroyed in the Neronic fire of AD 64. Excavations also revealed one of Rome's more remarkable sites, a second-century Mithraic temple. Accordingly, as today's Roman Catholic worshippers throng the Basilica, or pick over the souvenirs and guide books available in the Repository, they do so standing above a pagan temple. At the temple level, one can examine rooms and artefacts uncovered through the benefactions of one of the more famous characters of the Irish/American Church, Cardinal O'Connell of Boston. O'Connell was known as 'Gang plank Bill' because of his propensity for taking off on voyages. Perhaps it was his fondness for water which led him to make a donation to San Clemente which, in 1912–14, allowed a 700-yard tunnel to be built from the Cloaca Maxima at the Colosseum to drain a lake which had filled San Clemente's lower rooms with water.

Cardinal O'Connell apart, one of the figures most responsible for the preservation of San Clemente was Father Joseph Mullooly (1812–1880). In a sense, Mullooly exemplified the policy which Cullen and Kirby put into operation through the nearby Irish College, namely the expansion of the Irish Church under the protection of the flag of the British Empire.

Mullooly was Bursar of San Clemente when a republic was proclaimed in Rome in 1849, after Pope Pius IX had fled the city the previous November. He got a nun to make two English flags for him, and hoisted one over San Clemente itself, ignoring threats from national guards that the Basilica would be burnt to the ground if the flag were not taken down. Intrepid Mullooly then went in person to protect another piece of Irish Dominican property, possibly more dear to the heart of a true Irishman than even San Clemente itself, the Order's vineyard. By the time he got there, what Mullooly termed the 'brigands of the insane Roman Republic' had made off with some 200 barrels of wine. Despite being fired at, arrested, and told that he was to be taken to S. Callisto to be shot, Mullooly managed to save the vineyard. Somehow he sent off a note to the British Ambassador, seeking help, and hoisted his second British flag. The Torrione vineyard episode might be taken as a parable for the Irish Church over the next century or so. Subsequently, Mullooly's spirited lobbying also paved the way for the exemption of San Clemente from the Law of Suppression of 1873. Henceforth, the 'insane Roman Republic' recognised the foreign national identity of 'Collegium Hiberniae Dominicanae'.

San Clemente afforded sanctuary to Jews during the Second World War. When we came to a fine painting of Tobias rubbing his eyes with a fish, to cure the blindness caused by the bird droppings, Father Dempsey told me it had a deeper significance than its biblical connotation. The Jews used to conduct their religious services under the painting, Tobias being an Old Testament figure with whom they could identify.

St Isidore's is a paradigm of the Irish Church. The place breathes antiquity, but, out of sight, there has been a coming to terms with modern life. What appears to be nothing more than a normal well-tended garden in fact conceals a three-storey car park under the monastery. The value of St Isidore's in real-estate terms would be stratospheric, but within its walls, one is only conscious of two characteristics, humility, on the part of the monks, and hospitality.

I was struck by the combination of the antiquity of the place and its relevance to the Troubles in Northern Ireland. The young man who let me in had come to religion via the Troubles in Belfast and, amongst the community generally, Northern accents fell frequently on the ear. The tragedies of the

Troubles were obviously a source of concern to the community, many of whom were either from the North or had served there. One didn't have to be unduly imaginative to cast one's mind back to the troubled times which led to the foundation of places like St Isidore's. In the main hall a principal feature is a large mural depicting a ruined Irish monastery, roofless and empty, the loving craft which created it visible only in the few surviving arches and a Celtic cross. The monastery's records begin in 1668, and contain the name of the members of the community from that date. I held an Irish grammar (O'Molloys) in my hand dating from 1677. This paled in antiquity compared to a printed Bible dated from 1446 which could be taken as marking the crossroads between manuscript and print. The coloured initials were hand-painted. Another of the monastery's valuable possessions is the sword of the great O'Neill which he had brought with him to Rome after leaving Ireland in 1607. Sitting on the roof of the monastery, looking across the city from the Via Veneto, enjoying one of the great views of Rome, I dared to hope that perhaps the ceasefires meant that at last the sword has been sheathed.

St Patrick's (just around the corner from St Isidore's), with its school of management, also provides an excellent example of the adaptability of Mother Church. The Irish National Church idea seemed a good one at the time it was first mooted. St Patrick's College had been in existence on the Via Piemonte since 1892 as an Augustinian Training College (the Irish Augustinians first came to Rome to escape persecution at home in 1656). The church was built on the Via Boncompagni in 1911. However, neither foundation was easily created. Archbishop Croke wrote to the Prior of St Patrick's when the project was first mooted, in 1886, saying that 'money will come pouring in on you from all quarters in golden showers'.[46] Unfortunately it didn't, and though the College was built, there wasn't enough money for the church. Various strategems, including leasing part of the College to the Italian Government, had to be resorted to before the church was finally built.

Today the Church is the scene of 180 weddings on average each year. Irish people from all around the world come to Rome to get married economically, granted, but to get married nevertheless. Father Breathnach had performed a wedding not long before my visit in which the groom's mother acted as the best man. That wedding, like many of the others in St Patrick's, is an interesting commentary on what the Celtic Tiger's overheated economy is doing to the cost of marriage. It's interesting that though vocations are dropping, couples do want to make the commitment of marriage in a religious setting. Could one speculate that a combination of the old Irish fidelity to the faith, coupled with a new approach by the Vatican to the issues of married priests and women priests, might yet turn the vocational tide?

The turn around, if it comes, will be a big one. At lunch at St Patrick's, I met Bishop Sheehan, who had been a student in the College himself, and was passing through Rome en route to his African diocese. When he went, Father Breathnach would be alone in the house. He too had been a student at St Patrick's, at a time when there were sixty students under its roof. It was a place

87

of rigorous regime, but it was always a house of hospitality. Even today, this is its most obvious characteristic. Less obvious is the source from whence will come the money required to keep St Patrick's going, but the Augustinians are a resourceful bunch, and they're Celts.

One of the more famous Roman monuments is the statue of the Dying Gaul, at the Capitoline Museum, said to be a marble copy of the original bronze work of the sculptor Epigonus, who created a new style of Hellenic art to commemorate the victory of the Pergamum armies over the Celts in 228 BC. It shows the dying warrior, on his shield, with his sword, spear and trumpet, still supporting himself upright on one hand – literally not taking it lying down. This, and other works by Epigonus, such as the Celtic warrior putting himself to the sword, having first slain his woman, may be taken as having, on the one hand, immortalised the Celts, and, on the other, having marked what appeared to be the moment of their destruction as a force. History, however, teaches us that the Celts were still displaying new life and energies long after the year 228 was forgotten. One of the more vigorous Celtic voices to be heard in contemporary Rome, or indeed Italy, is that of the Irish poet Desmond O'Grady, who has lived in Italy for several years. His poem, 'The Dying Gaul', is a classic example of how in the Irish imagination the high heroic and the earthy combine:

> The hour at last come round
> the stroke that scores the kill
> taken, there follows a painless,
> partly nostalgic withdrawal –
> a drag to the sideline – to a clean piece
> of this world's dying ground.
>
> Lean legs nerve like an athlete's,
> Raised kneecaps gleam altar marble.
> Thigh shanks knot. The curled
> weighty balls bag low and the gentle
> penis limps childless. Tousled,
> his head's like a young brown bull's
> Reclining, at repose upon
> one unwound nude haunch,
> pelvis and dragged-out legs draining, his belly's bunch
> about the navel's wrinkles.
> Life strains on his taut right arm.
>
> The blood clots, the nerve
> sings and all his joints
> jamb stuck. His grounded gaze,
> like the madman's private smile, confronts
> the process' revelation – the ways
> death consummates, like love.

In Rome, as elsewhere, new battles await the Irish, but one feels that, as in the past, they will confront 'the process' revelations'.

HOLLAND

As the contemporary Dutch rank fourth in terms of buying Irish exports to Europe, they would arguably merit a visit for trade reasons alone. For an Irish historian, however, the reasons become irresistible when one recalls that Holland, that industrious little polder, only the size of Munster, which manages to sustain a population of 15 million around the plug hole through which Europe's great rivers empty into the North Sea, is above and beyond all this, the birthplace of 'King Billy of Pious and immortal memory'. Dutch William, while he failed to uphold the Treaty of Limerick, nevertheless still keeps aloft the hopes of Protestant Ulstermen that they too will somehow reclaim their territory from the papish tide. Possibly it was the prayers of the Orangemen which decreed that my visit to Holland would contain the most embarrassing moment of my European trip.

This was brought about by a combination of uncharacteristic Dutch inefficiency and Murphy's Law (if it can go wrong, it will go wrong). I was en route from Amsterdam to The Hague to attend a reception which the Irish Ambassador, John Swift, was kind enough to host for me at his residence, when literally my train was stopped in its tracks. An electrical fault had caused a bridge in front of us to shoot up in the air and stay there, a circumstance which of course created widespread havoc to rush-hour transport schedules. On top of this Murphy's Law proceeded to kick in. As I was seeking directions from a friendly Dutch fellow-passenger, his alternative train was announced unexpectedly and he shot off – taking with him the piece of paper on which I had written down the Ambassador's address and telephone number.

There was nothing for it but to return to my hotel, check my address book and phone Ambassador Swift, to assure him that I had not fallen by the wayside in the red-light district. This intelligence, to judge from the sudden increase in decibels from those in the background, was received with equal measures of dubiety and ribaldry. Actually, there was, and unfortunately still is, a good reason, apart from the obvious, why I might have visited the red-light district, and made contact with Amsterdam's underworld. In recent years, some of Ireland's nastiest criminals have taken to hiding out in Amsterdam. In the summer of 2000 there were four Irish deaths in two separate incidents. Fortunately, the Dutch system is like the Japanese one. It ensures that the underworld does whatever it does only to its own. Thus, as it exists well out of sight of the tourists and the law-abiding citizenry, this invisible export remains invisible.

The visible exports resemble those met with elsewhere in Europe: Irish bars, Irish records and CDs and, in the excellent Dutch/English language bookshops, very often the works of Irish authors. On the trade front, Irish business with the Netherlands has followed the general European pattern of rapid growth subsequent to joining the EEC. In 1973, Irish exports to the Netherlands were IR£38 million. By 1997, they had reached a total of IR£2,386 million. As with every other European trading partner, the Irish have also somehow managed to induce the canny Dutch to buy more from them than they sell to them. Imports rose from IR£37 million in 1973 to IR£831 million in 1997, roughly a third of exports.

John Swift found that at least a third of his time was devoted to trade matters. There are some thirty Dutch factories in Ireland and some of the bigger Irish companies like Smurfits and Cement Roadstone have expanded into the Netherlands. Agri-business is also expanding, partly because of the traditional Dutch expertise in this area, but also because of the openness of the Dutch system to outside investment. Where regulations are concerned, Irish businessmen find it easier to operate in Holland than in either France or Germany, for example. There are now five flights a day between Amsterdam and Dublin.

Generally speaking, the Irish find it easy to obtain employment in the Dutch multi-nationals or, in the summer, in the tourist service industries. In one universally popular service industry, however, it is alleged that the Irish boys do not do as well as their more polished Dutch counterparts: Dutch girls as a class are said to be unresponsive to the mating call of the Celtic Tiger. This can be heard ringing through the bars and discos of Amsterdam, but it loses some of its resonance when filtered through the mists of that traditional Irish courtship aid, a minimum of fourteen pints of Guinness. By contrast, the Irish girls are correspondingly highly successful in the mating game where Dutch men are concerned.

In the business world, the deceptively easy-going Irish personality is a byword for success in ascending the corporate ladder. A good example is Peter Casey, senior vice-president of ABN Amro, the fourth largest bank in the world. Amro has had a presence in Ireland since Ireland joined the EEC, and its business has grown steadily.

The Casey-like figures have the additional importance that they are a potential plus for Irish Industrial Authority executives approaching corporate Europe with a view to attracting investment in Ireland. Sean Comaskey, the Industrial Development Authority's (IDA) man in Amsterdam, also covered the Benelux countries, Scandinavia and Spain, and his findings were a mirror image of those of Gerry Murphy in Brussels.[47] In a word, the qualities of personality which helped to create a good image of the Irish – either at the time the monks were spreading Christianity in Europe, or when the races of the Earth were digging for wealth during the great gold rushes of the pioneering days in Australia and California – are still extant and still paying dividends. Comaskey said he found that the Irish were universally well liked throughout his entire area of operation. As Gerry Murphy had observed also, the Irish were regarded as being confident, hard-working, flexible and 'can do' in their approach to problem-solving. The Irish educational system, and the manner in which the Irish have used EU funds, were also generally admired. The rising tide of EEC membership which lifted all Irish boats has left behind the days when the disparity between Holland and Ireland was such that a common observation was: 'If the Dutch had Ireland they'd feed the world, but if the Irish had Holland, they'd drown.'

The principal negative Comaskey had encountered was the effects of the Northern Ireland troubles. After an atrocity phones tended to go dead, either in the tourist trade or the investment business. Otherwise, Ireland is seen as a nice place to have an office. From a position wherein the only European languages to be taught in Irish schools were a little French, less German and, because of the Church, a lot of Latin, the Government is now concentrating on developing linguistic skills. Irish representatives abroad, like Comaskey, go to big companies and ask them what languages they expect to need in future. The answers then feed into Irish educational policy. One result of this which he cited is the ever-increasing growth in the call service business. One can make a call in Amsterdam which will be booked through Dublin, and connected with, say, Venezuela. Unconsciously Comiskey also bore out one of Murphy's major findings concerning the Irish job market. He was returning to Ireland to ensure an Irish education for his children. In Holland, as elsewhere in the world, return rivals exile, as a concept in the Irish diaspora.

Where the average Dutchman or woman is concerned, in the words of Toni van Marle, who studied in University College Dublin and at Trinity College, before returning to the Celtic Studies Department at Utrecht University: 'The awareness spectrum stretches from total ignorance to deep involvement. Questions range from, "Is Ireland dangerous?" to a knowledge of the literature.' A favourite bicycle sticker in Amsterdam of recent years was 'I've read *Ulysses*.' People tend to have a mythological romantic notion of Ireland: 'Peat, Celtic poetry, a yearning for the past vision, a green perception,' said van Marle. The green perception was deepened by the Eurovision Song Contest, which Ireland has won several times in recent decades, resulting in the competition being repeatedly screened from the Republic. This generated miles of TV coverage of what came across as a tourist paradise.

The Northern Irish situation was of course considerably less alluring. The Dutch regard the divisions as dinosauric. Alas for the illusions of the bowler-hatted brigade who hold aloft the banners of William of Orange in Ireland: religion-inspired controversy in Ireland simply baffles the Dutch, and not merely that involving violence between Protestant and Catholic. For example, a case which much exercised the consciences of the pious in Ireland – that of a traveller child, made pregnant against her will, who wanted an abortion – aroused astonishment amongst the Dutch. Getting the abortion involved a Supreme Court hearing and, subsequently, an amendment to the Irish Constitution. Abortion, like divorce which also required an amendment to the Irish Constitution, is regarded as a basic human right in Holland. Yet I found that even the hard-headed Dutch spoke wonderingly and admiringly of the widespread Irish love of country. This characteristic seems both archaic and endearing to them, but their hard-headedness means that the interest in Ireland has not translated into a surge towards Irish studies along French lines. Dublin-born Ann Rigney, who teaches Celtic Studies at Utrecht University, says that though Celtic Studies are, under the Dutch educational system, protected by law, nevertheless funding is continually in crisis.

The Dutch are interested in the English language and they buy Irish writers more in furtherance of their English than out of a widespread love of Irish culture. However, I did find that wherever this did exist it was deep-rooted. A Dutchman, the financial controller of an important corporation, was described to me as 'eating and drinking Irish literature, Irish music, everything Irish'. Against this, Ann Rigney could point out that an important book on Ireland and the Irish by her husband Joseph Leerson, a distinguished Dutch scholar whom she met at the Yeats' summer school, was not widely known in Holland, though it had made quite an impact in Canada.[48]

As in Europe generally, if one asked a Dutch person to say what they knew about Ireland, they would produce a cultural template that included Mary Robinson, literature, and *Riverdance*. A lot of the time they like Irish music without realising that it is Irish music. Seamus O'Doherty, who runs O'Donnell's, an Irish bar in a fashionable location which he chose after 'very systematic research', tells a story about a visit to his bar one day by a man from the Performing Rights Society.[49] O'Doherty, a staunch Irish Republican, who has 'every Irish traditional record there ever was' was astounded to discover that the inspector did not know that Clannad, U2 and Van Morrison were Irish. Nor do most Dutch people realise that one of the most-often heard voices on Dutch radio is that of the Irish singer and songwriter, Johnny Logan, who has won the Eurovision Song Contest twice.

O'Doherty was inclined to downplay talk of a widespread Irish network in Amsterdam: 'If you compare the Irish to the Yanks, they are not well organised. They don't have Wives' Clubs and so forth.' I forbore from pointing out to him that such clubs are not much met with in Ireland either, although the First Wives' Club is growing. However, he did touch on one important point concerning the Irish community which now applies to Europe generally, with the possible exception of Germany: 'You never see Irish labourers in the bars any more.' One reason you don't is because the boom in Ireland has meant they can get better wages at home.

Sean Lynch, who was an important figure in the Dutch construction industry, gave up his extensive Dutch interests to return to Ireland and set up an agency to attract Irish construction workers back to Ireland. Yet, though the usual debate rages over the exact numbers of Irish in Holland – from official estimates of 4,500 registered with the Embassy and probably some 2,000 floaters, to possibly three times that number unofficially – there is obviously some significant Irish presence in Amsterdam.

Mark Gilligan, himself a musician, and the impresario who brings most Irish musicians to Holland, finds that St Patrick's Day is his busiest of the year. On that day in 1998 he had forty-seven bands at various venues. He is married to a Dutch wife and, apart from occasional encounters with Irish begrudgery, describes himself as being very happy: 'The Irish are settling down here now. They are not just moving through on the craic. I remember years ago I'd have friends ringing me up to ask could you get us a few drugs. That's all over.'

The Irish have an unsuspected Dutch market for their wares. Cold statistics reveal that one of the fastest selling Irish products in Holland is the Slendertone massage machine. More-detailed research reveals, in the words of my informant, an Irish governmental employee, that: 'They're brought by the gays. They use them to massage their bums.' Which I suppose goes to prove that Irish success depends, to a large extent, in Holland as elsewhere, on an ability to rub people up the right way.

BELGIUM AND BRUSSELS

And what of the Irish in the capital where so much of Ireland's current prosperity was generated? How fare they in Brussels, home to the most cumbersome, most complex, most consensus bedevilled, and at the same time most effective experiment in trans-national government which man has yet devised, the European Community? 'Excellently' is the short but incomplete answer – incomplete because it must be explained that even though since joining the EU, relations between the Republic and the EU have been excellent (although there could be storm clouds ahead as will be indicated later), the Irish had a cordial and significant association with Belgium itself long before the EU was even dreamt of. Even when trade figures hardly warranted it (Irish exports to Belgium and Luxembourg combined were only IR£28 million in 1973), Dublin maintained an Irish embassy in Brussels. Nowadays trade has caught up with tradition. The Republic sells almost twice as much to Belgium and Luxembourg (IR£1,754 million) as it does to Spain (IR£892 million). The Irish in Belgium itself are highly regarded. A good rule of thumb for an embassy is the number of its nationals who do or do not end up in trouble, and Eamonn Ryan, the Irish Ambassador to Belgium, told me that he found that the Embassy had 'an amazingly low consular problem to deal with'. The image of the Irish is good, they are well educated, have good incomes, and there are very few points of friction between them and the host community.

The foundations of the Irish image were laid at Louvain, where in 1607 the Franciscans established an Irish College in the capital of the Brabant province in Flemish-speaking Belgium. This, as has been noted, was the year of the Flight of the Earls, and the Flight helped to give rise to one of Belgium's most famous fishing stories. The two Earls had set up their respective households on either side of the river Dyle which runs through Louvain. One winter's day a manservant crossing over the frozen river between the O'Neills and the

O'Donnells speared a salmon he saw trapped in a pool under the ice. The unfortunate fish found posthumous renown through becoming known as 'the biggest salmon ever seen in either Brussels or Louvain . . .'

Louvain was completed in 1617 with the help of King Philip III of Spain, and was destined to become one of the most illustrious of the Irish Colleges. Apart from providing an important continuous link with Ireland, it was one of the greatest, if not *the* greatest, centres of publishing in the seventeenth-century Church. It did not limit itself to pious publishing, psalters and so on. The College's output had an important role in sustaining the Irish language and a knowledge of Irish history. Apart from publishing some of the earliest Irish dictionaries and grammars, Louvain produced an edition of one of the great books of Ireland: *The Annals of the Four Masters*, a mammoth compilation of Irish history by four scholarly monks. It was paid for by an Irish chieftain, O'Gara of Sligo, who feared that the swelling tide of invasion from the larger, neighbouring isle was about to wash away Irish civilisation, and he wanted a record made before all was lost.

It was the existence of Louvain which gave the cry of 'plucky little Begium' whatever resonance it had in Ireland during the British recruiting drive of the First World War. Subsequently, a Belgian battlefield witnessed the only instance of orange and green fighting alongside each other in the war (as opposed to merely fighting on the same side). The 16th Irish Division and the 36th Ulster Division fought together at Messines Ridge. To commemorate this unique event, and boost the Peace Process, a Peace Tower was erected by the British and Irish Governments at the Peace Park in Mesen (Messines) in 1998. The tower was the brainchild of a Fine Gael politician from the Republic, Paddy Harte, and a former Protestant para-military from Derry, Glen Barr, who ran an organisation called 'A Journey of Reconciliation Trust' aimed at bringing together people from both the orange and green traditions. Symbolically the pair subsequently had a public falling-out. The tower was built by workers, mainly young people, drawn from both sides of the border. It was inaugurated by the President of Ireland, Mary McAleese on 11 November 1998 in the presence of King Albert and Queen Paola of the Belgians and Queen Elizabeth of England.

Louvain itself has also become a symbol, both of North-South co-operation and of the Republic's successful move into Europe. In 1984, it was handed over to the Irish Government by the Franciscans, and under the chairmanship of an outstanding Irish public servant, Dr Tom Hardiman, a former Director General of Radio Telefis Eireann (RTE) turned banker, Louvain once more became a vibrant Irish centre of learning – but in a new guise. Taking advantage of its strategic location, just twenty minutes from Brussels, the College became a European Institute dedicated to: 'establishing and organising an international centre for education, training and research in the broadest sense, in the fields of economics, science, social provisions, philanthropy, art, etc'.[50] It has fulfilled this role with considerable success, while at the same time involving North of Ireland personnel and educational institutes, both in policy-making and the operations of the college – the head of the North of Ireland Civil Service, Mr J. Semple, was a member of its board at the time of writing. It is a good example of the monastic tradition both of learning and sanctuary at work in a secular setting.

How are the Irish viewed in the Brussels of the bureaucrats, in the European institutions? Denis O'Leary, the Irish Permanent Representative to Brussels, answered the question in homely but telling fashion:

> In many ways the Irish are regarded as the good boys of the class. You only have to visit Ireland to see where the money went, the new roads and other infra-structural projects. The Irish educational system, the manner in which the Irish got its public finances in order, have all contributed to an impression here of Ireland being the success story of the EU. And of course that success is carried over into the cultural field. Nowadays, the Irish don't need any introduction to Brussels. We've had 25 years of involvement with the Commission, the Erasmus Project, the economic development, everything. On top of that some of the Irish civil servants and Foreign Ministers made lasting reputations here.

I found for myself that this view of Irish public representatives was widely shared. Irish politicians of all parties received high marks: Fianna Fail's Commissioners Ray McSharry and Padraig Flynn, Fine Gael's Foreign Minister, James Dooge, or Peter Sutherland, as the Commissioner who handled the negotiations that led to the opening of markets; the Labour Leader, Ruairi Quinn; Prime Ministers Garret FitzGerald, John Bruton and Charles Haughey, were all mentioned to me as having done well in their European dealings. Ireland maintains a permanent representation of fifteen Government departments, including the Attorney General's office, in Brussels, a very tangible evidence of the will of the Irish people to make Europe work. Alongside these considerations, there is the fact that any Irish Government in power when the European presidency came around made sure that all the stops were pulled out. All five Irish presidencies are regarded in Brussels as having been well managed by the political élite – well-taken opportunities to show what Ireland can do.

So much for the bureaucrat. What was the view of the recently retired senior Irish political figure in Brussels, Commissioner Padraig Flynn? He summed it up in a phrase one hears over and over again in Brussels amongst the Irish community: 'We have punched above our weight.' Flynn (the interview occurred before the mass resignation of the Commission in 1999) was the EU's Social Commissioner, a former Fianna Fáil Minister for the Environment who has had occasion to deny vigorously allegations of receiving money from building interests during his term in office in Dublin. The other names on the doors on his corridor were internationally known, Jacques Santer, Neil Kinnock, Leon Brittan and Emma Bonino, but, behind his old style folksy Bostonian pol façade, Flynn proved himself a shrewd and effective politician, of that peculiarly Irish type, a conservative with a social conscience. His conservatism involved him in controversy in the early stages of his European career: a group of Nordic feminist members of the European Parliament objected to his being placed in charge of a portfolio dealing with women's interests, and those duties were removed from him.

An archetypical smoke-filled back-room figure, Flynn's forte is working the system, wheeling and dealing behind the scenes until consensus is achieved. His native County Mayo is legendary for producing politicians of this type. I have already mentioned the Basilica at Knock in the context of the papal visit and the somewhat less assured visitation by the Mother of Jesus. However, it should also be known that, not content with the building of the Basilica, the parish priest, Monsignor Horan, decided that the area merited an international airport. He duly organised the building of one, in the teeth of opposition from every aviation expert, civil servant and economist in the country. It is sited in one of the most beautiful, boggy and benighted districts of Ireland, but it has taken the hardship out of emigration, or return, for the people of Mayo and boosted the tourist trade into the bargain. The road that takes you past a signpost describing this monument to belief over statistics as 'Knock International Airport' would compare favourably with any German autobahn. The difference is that very often the only traffic on it is that which I encountered passing the signpost on my last drive in the area, a donkey and cart. This was followed a little later by a small herd of cattle with a large EU subsidy. The road has been nicknamed, after the politician who got it built, the 'P. Flynn boreen'.

I felt it worthwhile to remind myself of this background when I analysed not so much the man himself as the fact that he was now sitting in a Commissioner's chair, literally at the top level in Brussels. It was still a live memory in his family that relations of his had gone ashore at Grosse Ile (see page 388), at the mouth of Canada's St Lawrence River, amidst the floating corpses of famine cholera victims. The Flynns survived to make their way down the Canadian coast to Boston, where they became long-shore men. Whatever their degree of sensitivity to political correctness and the feminist lobby, when the P. Flynns of this world go to battle in Brussels for disadvantaged areas, be they in the west of Ireland or the north of Italy, they do so with a deep sense of the justice of their cause.

Flynn summed up the advantages of Europe for the Republic of Ireland:

When we joined the EEC, we were 80 per cent dependent on the UK and that's now down to 30 per cent, but apart from our benefit, the Irish experience has been valuable to the whole community. We have de-bunked the myths of the periphery, that the small countries on the edge of Europe will always be the poor relations. Irish people are highly respected. They're seen as creative, Irish civil servants are regarded as co-operative, hard-working. We're recognised as the best manager of European funds. Our example is studied by the Czechs, the Slovenians, Poland, Hungary. They've seen how we've been able to assert ourselves economically and politically, to get economic independence in fact. Our style of negotiation is studied also. We're a small nation, but a world-stage people.

Flynn was certainly correct here, in so far as the Republic's own perception of the country's standing was concerned. As we spoke, the Irish Ambassador in Spain was packing to take up a new post in New York. His task was to get Ireland a seat on the UN Security Council!

There will be problems ahead for Ireland in the EU, and Flynn touched on some of them. The object of the cohesion fund was to bring the poorer European states up to the threshold of 75 per cent of the European average income. At the time of writing, the wealthier parts of Ireland, the east coast and the cities, had achieved 104 per cent of the European average. Thus the Republic's entitlement to claim Objective One status, to obtain EU funding for being disadvantaged, is threatened. At the time of writing the Republic was attempting to fend off the threat by having the country divided into rich and poor areas. In some of the disadvantaged areas – for example, border areas where partition has inhibited economic growth or, in particular, the west of Ireland – some 45 per cent of farmers' income still came from Brussels. However, under pressure from independent deputies on which a coalition government depended, Dublin included in its list of disadvantaged areas two counties which could not reasonably be termed poverty stricken (Kerry and Clare), thereby jeopardising the entire application.

Many people feel that Ireland has already done well enough out of the EU. In 1998 Brussels's annual subsidy to Irish agriculture was running at IR£1.5 billion. The Irish taxpayer only contributed IR£200 million to farming, which is responsible for approximately a third of Ireland's foreign earnings and some 340,000 jobs. On top of all this, the reforms of the Common Agricultural Policy, now in train – which decoded, mean the slashing of the farm budget, which currently eats up two-thirds of the EU's budget – coupled with the loss of Objective 1 status means that certainly, by the year 2006, a good deal of the European transfers to Ireland will have diverted to the newer East European members of the EU. In addition, the Europeans, particularly the Germans, are resentful of the fact that the Irish negotiators managed to secure tax concessions for Ireland which enable the Republic to go on attracting inward investment because of more favourable corporation tax rates than apply anywhere else in the EU.

The foregoing is certainly threatening. However, while in the Irish context, the subventions from Brussels have been huge, they have to be kept in perspective. Money alone is not what makes a society prosper. The British annually spend more than their Exchequer receives in tobacco receipts on the Six County Statelet of Northern Ireland, some £10 to £14 billion – but all that that has achieved is the creation of a political slum. So it is reasonable to be optimistic that what has been invested in infrastructure and, above all, education, will carry Ireland past the station where the Brussels gravy train ends.

One station which Ireland will find it difficult to pass lies in the hitherto sacrosanct area of Irish neutrality. It is unlikely that Ireland will ever join NATO, but Flynn articulated the Brussels (and Dublin) party line by saying that he envisaged Ireland becoming part of a Common European Defence Policy as opposed to a Common Foreign Policy. 'Why would people not want to defend Europe?' he asked rhetorically. 'We're not talking about invasions, we're talking about defence.' Flynn reckons that neutrality will not be a crisis issue, merely one which can be dealt with by a protocol added to Ireland's Deeds of European Membership. *Peut-être*, as the French say, but as the Bosnian situation and the Balkans generally show, these distinctions between defence and invasion may not be so easy to sustain in reality – particularly as the fudge over joining a 'common foreign policy' in real terms comes down to Ireland's joining the NATO-backed Partnership for Peace, which at the time of writing the Government managed to slide into without allowing a referendum on the subject.

Defence issues apart, before my Brussels visit was half over, my ears were showing a tendency to ring from the sound of all the praise heaped on my countrymen. While, even allowing for the statutory upbeat official attitude of both, it was cheering to have figures like Flynn and O'Leary corroborate the general good impression which I had gained of my countrymen in Europe, nevertheless the sustained litany of praise gave me a sudden insight into an action of Brendan Behan's on a famous occasion. During one of the last great public spasms of Roman Catholic piety and self-assertion, the Marian Year of 1955, a high mass was celebrated at Croke Park in the presence of a huge congregation of cardinals, a bevy of bishops and a multitude of monsignori and lesser clergy, to say nothing of a hosting of the Plain People of Ireland. Why Behan was there, or more importantly, who let him in, I don't know, but, as what the catechism of the day termed The Awful Moment of the Consecration approached, Behan lurched to his feet and bellowed: 'Come on the Druids!'

Was there a Druidic point of view which was being concealed from me? I approached some journalistic colleagues in Brussels to find out. There wasn't, it seems. Ireland was entitled to bask in a European glow of popularity. John Downing, the European correspondent of the *Irish Independent*, said, 'These days you can't pick up a continental paper without reading terms like vibrant, youthful, friendly, boom, Celtic Tiger, and so on.' He said, 'The Irish are extraordinarily visible. They are far outnumbered by the Portuguese, for example, but the Irish seem to be everywhere. You get the impression that there are tens of thousands of them.'

This is not surprising, perhaps, given the Irish penchant for drawing attention to themselves. While I was visiting, an Irish bar in the centre of Brussels brazenly put a huge banner across the front of the premises, claiming to be the 'World Cup HQ'. Certainly it could have passed for such, to judge from the buzz in the place while the matches were being played. Moroccans, Norwegians, whatever, seemed to feel it was the place to be on the night of the big game. Apart from self-promotion, the Irish impact was heightened by the success of individual Irish people in key sectors. Because of the general belief that the Irish seem to be able to work the system better than most, Irish consultants are very much in demand for specialised tasks. For example, making Objective One status claims!

One seems to bump into the Irish at every hand's turn. The head of the Consumer Lobby Association is an Irishman, Jim Murray. If one needs electrical work, the big firm is Finnegans, just as the corresponding building company is Kellehers. Britain's perverse attitude to the European Community also helps the Irish, in the same way that a certain residual anti-British feeling helps Irish studies in France. Sometimes it appears that being English-speaking, but not British, is a qualification in itself. The Europeans are exasperated by official British attitudes to Europe. On the one hand, it is a demonstrable fact that the senior executives of major United Kingdom companies working in Europe say openly: 'Of course we're going to go into the single currency.' On the other hand, it is a mantra with the Conservatives in particular, that Britain will stay out – a mantra moreover in which they were joined by a majority of the British electorate in the 1999 European elections. The Irish attitude of unaffected enthusiasm for Europe thus contrasts very favourably with the British one. My visit to the European Headquarters coincided with another factor that was also redounding to Irish credit, the Peace Process. There was a tremendous welcome for the Good Friday Agreement in Brussels, and figures connected with the Agreement, like John Hume and Mo Mowlam, were hailed in both Brussels and at the European Parliament in Strasbourg.

Tommy Gorman, the long-term RTE correspondent in Brussels, who is one of the most knowledgeable European commentators, echoed the general chorus of approval for the Irish performance in Brussels, and itemised some of the factors which are taking the sense of loneliness and loss out of the emigrants' life: cheaper flights and phone calls, the Internet and, a very important factor for the sports-mad Irish, Setanta, the television company which screens the Irish hurling and football matches. 'Emigration is not a big deal nowadays,' he says, but thoughtfully he pointed to one area of sadness, which he called the Oisin complex. Oisin was an Irish mythological character who returned from the land of eternal youth on a visit to his native land, only to age immeasurably when he disobeyed the instruction not to take his foot from the stirrup to touch the ground. Said Gorman: 'People are sometimes afraid to go home. They might have money and be doing well, but they are afraid that they will grow old suddenly. How do you judge when you go back? At what point in the scale do you turn for home? People who have made a career in Europe both love and dread going home.' This is true of the Irish in other parts of the world as well, of course, one of the inescapable penalties of emigration. Return to the old country, re-immigration, can often be as traumatic as emigration itself.

BOSNIA AND CROATIA

Let us conclude our European journey by visiting Bosnia, an area where both the debate over neutrality and the future of the Irish Church become very real.

At the end of one of the best books about the Irish written anywhere, *The Irish in Australia*, by Patrick Farrell, the author raises the question: Can one imagine Ireland and the Irish without the Church? In the years since Farrell wrote his book, the answer 'yes' has come to seem less and less unlikely. However, as this fact became more obvious, and in large measure more welcome – in so far as the growth in the 'yes' response represented a fall-off in the once preposterous levels of authoritarianism in Rome's formerly lucrative Emerald mine – a less attractive obverse side of the coin also became clearer: there were correspondingly increased levels of selfishness and materialism culminating in an appalling outburst of Nimbyism (not in my back-yard) throughout Ireland over the government's admittedly ham-fisted and badly thought out plans for housing asylum-seekers. For Ireland of all nations this was an act of historical ingratitude for what the world had done down through the centuries for her asylum seekers. Does this mean that we should leave Ireland's contribution to European civilisation saying that by the end of the second millennium the call of the monks, and the call to arms, has been replaced by the call of Mammon? 'Not quite' is the answer.

Granted the ravages of the skin-deep culture have struck contemporary Ireland. One can immediately trace its spoor in the crisp empty universality of: 'No problem'; 'Hello. Hotel Rip Off here. Angela speaking. How may I help you?' – or (sometimes even delivered in mid-evening): 'Have a nice day!' Nevertheless, the caring tradition of the monks, albeit in contemporary guise, is still extant, and its manifestations are to be found in Europe, in war-torn Bosnia – as, more traditionally, they are still to be met with in the third world, to exemplify which, as we shall see in Chapter Seven, I have taken Africa.

In Bosnia the light once borne by the monks still flickers in secular hands. The most obvious sign of an Irish presence when I visited Sarajevo was a hundred and fifty military personnel, both men and women, serving, not as Wild Geese this time, but as members of the European Community Monitor Mission (ECMM). Cheerful, jokey, and casually efficient, they were part of the belated international effort to respond to a carnage that should have been halted long before it was. The international community's failure to do so led to the additional horrors of Kosovo.

You can meet the Irish off duty, as you can meet most of the other expatriates serving with international missions in Bosnia Herzegovina, in David Alford's Irish pub, The Harp, Sarajevo's liveliest meeting place. Alford had served with the Irish Army and decided to settle down in Sarajevo rather than return to Ireland when his tour finished. Appropriately enough, he opened his bar on Independence Day, 4 July 1997, and word of mouth had ensured that by the time the first pint was pulled, the place was a success. Everyone goes there. There is no closing time. When I spoke to him he was planning his next project, a golf driving range.

Just the normal sort of commercial success story one could find anywhere, you might think. Except that not far from the bar there is a huge graveyard where some of those killed in the fighting are buried. I say 'some' because

Sarajevo itself is one huge graveyard. The roofless houses ringing its airport are like rotting teeth in a fractured skull. Similar sights extend right across Bosnia Herzegovina. There are no angels, and few nice guys, in the story of what befell old Yugoslavia, but it is not an over-simplified desire to blame one 'baddie' that makes Slobodan Milosevic a supremely evil man. What he did both in Bosnia and in Kosovo was sheer unadulterated butchery – and in both cases, the internal community let him get away with it. It was only after NATO became directly engaged on the ground in Kosovo that the West began to highlight the torture chambers and so on. Up to then the memory of Vietnam so paralysed American decision that one State Department official told me that in the early days of the Bosnian conflict she was censured for using an 'emotive term' in her reports. The offending phrase was 'ethnic cleansing'. The people who have been brought to The Hague, or even the drunken mountebank Radovan Karadzic, who to the time of writing has managed to evade arrest, were only puppets. Milosevic pulled the strings and masterminded the Hitlerian strategy of ethnic cleansing – cruel, premeditated and efficient. One can see the outcome in the gutted buildings appearing across Bosnia, like monstrous Stations of the Cross. Mementoes to ferocity can be seen everywhere, in writhing girders, smashed buildings and incongruous flashes of red. These are the red tiles on the pavements to show where people fell.

Standing in Sarajevo, at the spot where the Archduke Ferdinand and his wife, Sophia, were assassinated by a Serb, thereby triggering off the First World War, one does not need to be unduly fanciful to imagine how very easily a similar worldwide conflagration could be rekindled in the former Yugoslavia. Bankrupt as they are, on more than one occasion the Kremlin's rulers nearly succumbed to the temptation of taking Russians' minds off their troubles by joining in the war on the side of their fellow Slavs, the Serbs, and the Chinese were similarly enraged by the NATO bombing of their embassy.

It was still not safe to step off the road around Alford's. There could be a mine in the roadside grass. This is an area in which a children's school and a maternity hospital were deliberately shelled. Not far away is the scene of the incident which finally brought in the international community, the market place which was mortar-bombed, killing one hundred and sixty people. Close to the pub, one can see huge bunkers, only a few metres apart from each other. From these, Serbs and Muslims shelled each other. They were so close that in lulls between bombardments the combatants spoke to each other, generally to enquire for news of friends and relatives.

The pub, like the better Irish pubs, is a social centre. Nearby there is a school which has 890 children. They have to attend in shifts. Alford's had recently arranged to send 100 of them on a skiing holiday; eighty-nine of them had no parents. The pub sponsors 'the hardest working kids, not the best or brightest, the hardest workers', and has organised a computer course for the children.

The spirit of the Sarajevans is remarkable. During my visit there was a local

101

derby between Sarajevo's two leading soccer teams. The atmosphere in the streets was electric. There were young people everywhere wearing the rival colours, drinking quite heavily, and the police were omnipresent. Yet no riot or violence erupted. An air of good humour prevailed in the huge stadium, the site of Torville and Dean's great figure-skating victory. The stadium was destroyed in the war, and then rebuilt by the Italian Government. As Alford's customers streamed into the bar after the match, one Irish GAA fan paid it the highest compliment he knew: 'Jaysus, the atmosphere was terrific. It was like a game between Dublin and Kildare.'

Unemployment is one of the many threats to the fragile peace. The vast pool of young people, who don't remember the war, are now bored and resentful. Most of the work in the area consists of jobs provided by the international community's presence. Then there are the hidden problems. Apart from the war itself, the biggest killer amongst women is the high incidence of breast and cervical cancer. There was no screening during the fighting, and now there is very little equipment to carry it out either. Understandably, mental illness levels are high too, but, within easy reach of Alford's, Brother Tom of the Irish Saint John of God Brothers opened a psychiatric hospital with the help of the Irish NGO Refugee Trust. Brother Tom is one of the legends of Bosnia. He was the longest-serving humanitarian worker there and, not surprisingly, shortly before I arrived had had a triple bypass.

The religious tradition of the Irish has also reasserted itself in somewhat incongruous fashion both in Sarajevo and in Croatia. In pre-war Sarajevo very few people went to mass. Now the numbers of Irish – it is said that proportionately they outnumber everyone else in the caring agencies – means that the main Roman Catholic church is packed on a Sunday. As in Munich, most of the mass-goers would not attend church regularly in Ireland, but do so abroad out of a sense of belonging, as much as for spiritual reasons.

In Croatia, the opening of Mostar Airport has meant that pilgrimages to yet another shrine to Our Lady, that at Medjigore, have resumed. Direct flights from Dublin mean that hundreds of bridge-playing Irish widows, and members of their families brought along with varying degrees of willingness or reluctance, are now once again basking in a flow composed of equal parts Marian piety and duty-free alcohol. During the war an uncomputed number of Irish mercenaries fought on the side of the Catholic Croatians. It is known that several were killed in fighting around the Kupres region, but details of their fate, or the whereabouts of their graves, are scanty. However, the fate of one famous Irish mercenary, Tom Crowley, is well known. He was a celebrated instructor with the Croatian Army, the original tough Sergeant Major. When he did what he had so often warned his men not to do, stepped on a land-mine, Croatian papers devoted several pages of obituary to him.

Croatia appears so smiling and unscathed by war that it might be part of another continent, rather than a part of the former Yugoslavia. From the moment one steps out of Zagreb's modern airport, run with a noticeably friendly efficiency, one escapes from Europe's contemporary variant of the Thirty Years War. You re-enter the world of credit cards, post office facilities and car hire. There are no shell marks and prosperous-looking traffic surges by welcoming cafés. The sidewalks are filled with relaxed, friendly people. The atmosphere reminded me of Ireland a couple of decades earlier. People seem to have an instinctive friendliness and signs of Roman Catholicism were everywhere. Priests dressed in the old style black would offer no cause for displeasure to Pope John Paul II. The attitude of some rather frumpy-looking women I noticed in the company of a couple of pilgrimage groups I ran into was that of old Ireland too: deferential to the priest. The holiday resort, Split, with its white soil, islands and sandy beaches, seemed such a paradise that one could be forgiven for thinking that the wartime horror stories were exaggerated, media hype perhaps.

No exaggeration. No hype. The reality of what happened in the Balkans if anything has been understated. One woman who can certainly be said to have both upheld the Irish caring tradition, and at the same time bound up some of the wounds of the ethnic cleansing process, is Mary McLoughlin, a Cork-born doctor in her early forties, who when I met her was the Bosnian Field Director of the Irish NGO, GOAL. She operated in Gorajde, an hour and half's drive from Sarajevo. In fact she probably saved Gorajde from going the way of the other UN enclaves from which the UN pulled out, leaving the populations to the throat-slitters. Mary managed to get out dispatches and generate such media attention in Gorajde that the international community, additionally jolted by the dispatches of another courageous Irishwoman, Maggie O'Kane of the *Guardian*, eventually moved to save the enclave.

Gorajde is set in a valley through which runs the river Drina. Surrounded by high wooded hills, it seems at first glance to be a gem of a town. During the war, however, it was a hell hole whose successful defence defies all military logic. The Serbs held the mountain peaks and thus the place became a giant bowl in which Muslims clustered at the bottom and the Serbs commanded the rim, raining down mortar and artillery fire at will. I asked one man how the townspeople had survived. He replied simply: 'We were fighting for our families and our homes.' Heart and hearth were the motivating factors, not Islam. In fact, the people of Bosnia were very often Muslim in name only. Sarajevo, for example, was one of the most secular cities in Europe. However, as a by-product of the war, one can now see veiled women in the streets, apparently because the Iranians are offering financial aid to the heads of families on condition that people return to the old ways. In Gorajde, one of the principal features of the shattered town is the shining gold spire of a new mosque, built by the Saudis. Liberal Muslims are uneasy at these developments.

Mary told me her story over dinner on the balcony of a restaurant beside the Drina.[51] As usual the Bosnians had the muzak turned up so loud that, until we managed to convince the manager of the near-impossibility of conversation, that we actually wanted it turned off, conversation was difficult. In a way, however, the incongruous clashing of the blaring music with the peace of the scene was an appropriate introduction for the story Mary recounted. Appropriately enough also, there had been a minor earthquake in Gorajde as I arrived. Up-river, not far from where we sat, enjoying a cooling breeze, as swallows skimmed the river, and sparrows flew in and out of bullet holes, there is a place called Foca. Here, on an evening like ours, Karadzic's men systematically knifed to death 3,500 men, women and children. Their bodies were then thrown into the Drina at night, so that they flowed past our balcony. The war criminals who organised this massacre are still living in the area and fomenting trouble. Foca was once 60 per cent Muslim, but at the time of my visit no Muslims dared live there.

Mary had worked in Ethiopia, the Sudan, Vietnam and in Iraq, where she was rounded up by Saddam's men as a hostage during one of his jousts with the West. When she felt she had discharged her debt to the less-fortunate countries, she returned to Ireland and got married. However, her doctor husband was killed in a car crash in 1987 and she came to Bosnia, intending to stay for a year only, but, during the Gorajde siege, she said: 'I developed an affiliation with the local population that will last all my life.'

The people went out at night in the woods to collect firewood, knowing that the forests were infested with land-mines and Serbian troops. It was either that or freeze to death. There was no electricity, no running water, but flour, oil and beans were available from a depot run by the United Nations High Command for Refugees (UNHCR), to which people crawled under cover of darkness. Probably as many people died from pneumonia, hypothermia and lack of drugs for heart conditions as were killed in the bombardment. Yet, somehow, the human spirit triumphed. For example, Ennis, a Muslim whose grandparents were murdered by Chetniks, is now Mary's driver, employed by GOAL. He forsook dentistry to organise a team of mechanics who managed to keep the occasional generator going, and find parts and petrol to keep the semblance of a transport fleet in being.

Incredibly, when the siege was lifted after all these vicissitudes, Mary's work in Gorajde was interrupted by a blow struck, not from within Bosnia Herzegovina, but from Dublin. Bad blood had built up between certain officials in the Department of Foreign Affairs and the abrasive director of GOAL, John O'Shea, of which we will hear more on. Unfounded allegations of misuse of funds were raised and suddenly both European Community Humanitarian Office (ECHO) finance and that from the Department of Foreign Affairs were shut off. Mary was at the time engaged in a multiplicity of projects which she had somehow managed to get off the ground in the face of huge odds: for example, apartments for people who once lived in good homes, but who had not seen running water for seven years. The apartments have two rooms and a bathroom. Each can house ten people (provision always has to be made for the extended family). A two-room apartment may not seem much, but it is a paradise to people who have been sharing one room with from two to four families, and sharing one latrine between twenty families.

Another of Mary's projects is an imaginative one which attempted to rehouse both Muslims and Serbs in the nearby Serb-controlled town of Kopaci. This posed all sorts of difficulties – for example, both sides have lists of what to one are war heroes, and to the other war criminals. Anyone on a list was not eligible for a house. The principal difficulty, however, was and is that the Serbs simply don't want any Muslims resettled. Meetings with the Serb authorities tend to take the form of listening to monologues about the treachery of the Croats and the Muslims and the lack of understanding by the international community. If one disregarded the accents one could imagine oneself back in Belfast, listening to a Unionist explain why the Catholics should not be given houses. Like the Unionists, the Serbs will, if enough pressure is exerted, agree publicly to projects, and even sign up to them (as with the Good Friday Agreement in Belfast), but when the cameras switch off they seek to interpret them so that they will gain in the implementation what they lost in the negotiation. If they can manage it, only their side will get the jobs or the houses. To get anything at all built, Mary first somehow had to arrange for a cement factory to be set up. One of the first things one notices as one drives into this most mundane looking of undertakings is a plaque commemorating the GOAL contribution. Another Irish-aided project is the local pharmacy, where the Pill is much in demand. 'They're big into contraception here since the war,' Mary says. She had to defer some of her plans for apartment building, because the local decision-takers decreed that a bus station should take precedence. The elders reckoned that returning Muslims would be more prepared to face the dangers and the hardships involved in trying to rebuild Gorajde if they could at least step out of a bus into something approaching modern surroundings.

And dangers there certainly are. For example, the route to Sarajevo itself takes one up vertiginous mountain roads and down equally precipitous valleys, once traversed by the old Turkish merchant caravans and now much frequented by bandits. Local warlords are in collusion with the police. Cars are stopped and tribute exacted. Mary's car was fired upon when her driver refused to stop for three gunmen who later turned out to be off-duty Serbian police. Night driving is dangerous, and people travel in mini-convoys. When I suggested we pick up a mother and child standing on a deserted country road Ennis shook his head and exclaimed: 'No way. You don't know what might be hiding behind them.'

I thought of Belfast again when Mary brought me to another project she is involved with, a primary school funded by the Irish Government, and now filled with healthy-looking, happy children, all of whom had lost several relations in the fighting. I asked if there were any Serb children in the school and the teacher looked at me as though I had two heads.

Yet, to one used to the North of Ireland situation, I found surprisingly little bitterness. Ennis, for example, told me that when he began to read about the war period he saw it as history repeating itself. 'Believe me,' he said, 'I do not hate. I know ordinary Serbs did not mean anything, but had orders.' The war has ruined his hopes of a professional career – like his wife, his immediate future is one of working for an international aid agency, which is how he learned his excellent English – but he is a rooted man, living in his own community, a man of respect. Mary too was obviously deeply respected. Everywhere we went people waved and called out: 'Hello Mary.' She worked a punishing routine. She slept in her office and lived in one room to keep warm in the brutal Bosnian winters. Up at six am to face a diet which, when I was with her, was slowly improving, but still mostly consisted of fried bread or fried potatoes; cheese or eggs occasionally; rubbery salami frequently. Even apart from the war the legacy of Communist shortages still had to be overcome.

She made light of her problems saying: 'The trick is to remember that the Serbs pour the whiskey after 10 am and the Muslims won't produce the bottle, if they do at all, until after twelve! It's easy to push yourself when you're working with local officials who push themselves too and who really want things done. Or when things happen like the other day, when the oldest man in Gorajde came in to sign a contract for an apartment. He used to live in a lovely house, but now he and his family live like animals. However, now he'll probably live to see them all rehoused. You just have to make sure your project gets done, no matter what.'

But one day in 1997, as mentioned earlier, it became impossible to get the job done. Suddenly, without warning, the Department of Foreign Affairs in Dublin cut off funding. Brussels, that is to say ECHO, followed suit. Across the globe, GOAL projects ground to a halt. In Gorajde, Mary found that the waving also stopped and that recriminations began. Apart from coping with her own disappointment, she found herself assailed on all sides. Everyone, from heart-broken mothers of large families who saw their chances of a home disappear, to unpaid tradesmen, to angry local government officials, vented their frustrations on what was to them the only manifestation of the Irish Department of Foreign Affairs' policy in Gorajde – Mary McLoughlin. On top of this understandable reaction, she also found that she had to cope with an unexpected source of hostility. Several expatriates chose to regard the GOAL affair as a slur on them and were rude towards her.

She was isolated and under severe stress, and her situation was compounded by the then poor state of communications which made it impossible for her to find out what was going on. In an attempt to get the funds flowing again, she decided to go back to Dublin. There she found the GOAL headquarters virtually under siege from people who had contributed money to the charity in good faith. Rumours were circulating throughout the country that funds had been misappropriated. Stories had appeared in the media that Brussels had become concerned and had initiated an investigation into GOAL's finances. Disgruntled ex-GOAL employees, and civil servants in the DFA, all of whom had suffered in the past from John O'Shea's tongue, were giving briefings which helped to keep the rumour machine running at full throttle. The idea that Brussels had become alarmed and, of its own volition, had launched an investigation was firmly established and widely accepted.

Mary spent the first weeks of her return answering the phone and trying to reassure angry callers. However, the crisis could not have come at a worse point in Irish public opinion. There had been scandals involving malpractice in the beef industry, in banking, and at the highest political level. Priests were being accused of widespread buggery. The state blood services had been discovered to have been infecting women with hepatitis. Ireland's neutral army, which has never taken part in a war, was threatening to bankrupt the exchequer because so many soldiers were bringing lucrative proceedings against the state for deafness allegedly caused by gunfire! The idea that GOAL, which had a special place in the public's affection, was also joining the ranks of the scumbags was just too much. Too much for Mary McLoughlin also; she had a nervous breakdown.

While she was recovering, GOAL weathered the storm. In Brussels, an audit established that though some procedural irregularities might have occurred, money had not been misappropriated and ECHO funding was restored in July 1997. However, even though there had been governmental changes in the meantime, DFA refused to untie its purse strings until October 1998. Nevertheless the public were reassured by the announcement from Brussels and GOAL slowly swung back into favour. It might have swung faster if people could have been made aware of circumstances revealed privately in a letter which the ECHO Head of Unit in Brussels, Sabato Della Monica, sent to Jose Pinto-Teixeira, in charge of ECHO, Bosnia. The letter officially informed Pinto-Teixeira that GOAL was eligible for ECHO funding and that he could proceed with paying what was outstanding on previously signed GOAL contracts. However, even more significantly, the letter also made it clear that the audit which had cleared GOAL had been initiated not by Brussels, as had been alleged, but because of: 'Irish Government officials' suspicions of misuse of funds'.[52]

It was a nasty episode, neatly encapsulating the point counterpoint of the Irish character – on the one hand the pugnacious, undiplomatic but caring spirit that carried the monks across the oceans in currachs and the missionaries into fever-laden, uncomprehending Africa; on the other, the begrudgery and mean-spiritedness of the Men Who Live by Files. However, Mary recovered and returned to Gorajde and the uphill, demanding work I found her immersed in during June 1998.

She and Ennis drove me to Sarajevo and bade me a hasty farewell as they charged off to a crucial meeting which would decide whether or not ECHO would agree to put up new funding. A few months later I received a progress report from her.[53] There was good news and bad news. She wrote as follows:

To backtrack to June. ECHO Sarajevo were pleased with the GOAL project proposal and Brussels approved the funding for it within a week. We started constructing 20 of the 50 houses included in the project (9 Muslim and 11 Serb units) and were working on the water and electricity projects when the Serb Mayor of Kopaci, Slavko Topajovic, withdrew his support and declared in writing that the activities were breaking the laws of repatriation and reconstruction and were to stop immediately.

GOAL got legal advice and after many meetings the mayor allowed us to complete the 20 houses just before the Bosnian elections on 12–13 September. Now he has backtracked again and says the first part of the project still has no legal basis and this must be resolved before we can start with the remaining construction.

Our lawyers say otherwise. With winter just beginning this is very bad news for us and the unfortunate families living in bad conditions while waiting for their houses. I cannot say what the final outcome will be as the recent elections brought many hard-line nationalists into the Serb and Croat Bosnian National Assemblies. We will continue the legal fight to complete this project and ECHO are supporting GOAL all the way.

Otherwise the remaining projects are going very well and GOAL has completed repairs to 97 of the 108 houses and the full 31 apartments ongoing when you were in Gorajde. A few other projects have been started and will be completed this year.

And all so calmly said and understated ... not a word about the monumental frustrations involved. For, although Mary accurately set out her problems in all their bleakness, she did not touch on the fundamental reality that permeates everything in Bosnia – you can bring a horse to the water but you cannot make him drink. The Serbs were brought to Dayton under pressure from the Americans, but back in Bosnia they are frustrating the accords by every means in their power. The Kopaci obstructions are only the tip of an iceberg. The tragedy of the Kopaci policy is that it feeds on itself: the other side begins putting up barriers to the resettlement of Serbs, and so it goes. Whether or not the peace settlement will hold together, only the future will tell, but as I conclude my chapter on the Irish in Europe I find it beguiling to think how appropriate it was, in these gender-conscious days, that a woman should be maintaining the spirit of the monks. Perhaps, as feminist Catholics assert, the Holy Spirit is a woman after all. Indeed, She may even be Irish.

Two

The United Kingdom

Wild Irish: the less civilized Irish; formerly those not subjected to British rule, also called 'mere Irish'.

Oxford English Dictionary, Vol. 3, Clarendon, Oxford, 1989

Overall the Survey suggests that whatever historical and contemporary problems there have been, or are, the British are favourably disposed towards the Irish. They hold positive images of Ireland, and of the characteristics of the Irish. They reject ideas of the Irish born in Britain as foreigners; and instead they see them much as they see one another. There is also a sizeable group of British-born people with Irish connections who claim an Irish dimension to their identity. For all these – and other – reasons, the Irish have much good will to draw on in Britain.

ICM – Bradford University Survey, 1994

The Troubles of the last 30 years, particularly when they have spilled over into English towns and cities, have had a most damaging effect on the Irish community in this country. We have paid a heavy price in police harassment, press and popular prejudice and a series of massive miscarriages of justice. Thankfully, this dismal period is at an end and a new mood has been marked by the now routine visits of Irish Presidents and politicians to Irish communities around Britain.

Irish Post, 2 January 1999

'PERSECUTED! PERSECUTED!' A schoolmate of mine heard these words beating through the alcoholic fog shrouding his consciousness one 1950s' morning, and woke up to find that his companion in the bare doss-house room was sitting up in bed, screaming at the heavens, 'Persecuted! Persecuted! I am sick, sore and fed up, shitting on newspapers, rolling it up and throwing it in corners! Persecuted . . . !' I don't know what became of the persecuted one, but my schoolfriend succumbed to alcoholism in his early thirties. We heard that he had died one night, vainly trying to stagger back to a psychiatric institution from which he had been discharged some time earlier. David was one of those who fell through the yawning cracks·in the Anglo-Irish relationship which are accurately illustrated, though not fully depicted, by the quotations given above.

At the time of writing one could say, with some confidence, both that those cracks are in the process of being filled in, and that the hopeful auguries for the future contained in the last two quotations appear to be on their way to removing from British society the sort of attitudes which gave rise to the first, and to others like it. Certainly, if one proceeds on the principle that the bottle is always better viewed as half-full rather than half-empty, one can find increasing evidence to support this view. Yet one must also acknowledge that the healing process still confronts a considerable task in dealing with the detritus of history and the threat to relationships which a breakdown in the Peace Process would pose. A very striking difference between the Irish community in the UK and that in the US was the extent to which the American Irish were prepared to put their heads over the parapet on the Northern Ireland issue, compared to their counterparts in Great Britain. Writing in *Irish Studies*, in 1985, Steifoin O'Brennian accurately defined the position as follows:

> For eight hundred years Irish people have taken up arms to rid Ireland of English domination. To the British state these people have been rebels, traitors and latterly criminals . . . the IRA have attacked British soldiers and bombed British cities. This has caused successive waves of hysteria in the media. The average Irish person in the workplace is usually asked an opinion on whatever has taken place. This is a problem. Most Irish people want a united Ireland and a sizeable number support the IRA. However, to say this can have adverse results, imprisonment without trial or deportation under the PTA [Prevention of Terrorism Act]. That apart, the Irish person is aware of English ignorance of Anglo-Irish history and is unlikely to antagonise colleagues or jeopardise promotion prospects by pointing that ignorance out. The result is nothing said, no discussion, no progress and until the question of Ireland is taken out into the open it will remain that way.[1]

Ten years after O'Brennian wrote the foregoing, the survey carried out by ICM Research and the Department of Peace Studies at Bradford University in 1994 found that there had been some progress. As many as 82 per cent of Britons expected to find in Ireland a beautiful countryside and 67 per cent expected to meet with friendliness towards British visitors; 83 per cent disregarded 'Irish jokes' and regarded the Irish as being just as intelligent as the British themselves. In fact 4 per cent considered them more intelligent! The traits which the British most attributed to the Irish were: a good sense of humour (67 per cent), patriotism (58 per cent), fun-loving (45 per cent), fluency with words (36 per cent).

Perhaps the most important finding of the survey was the implicit impact of the Irish on British society. Of those surveyed, roughly one person in four in Britain had Irish relatives, including in-laws, and three out of five had Irish friends, acquaintances or fellow workers.

Surveys of course are open to the charge that they can prove whatever those who pay for them wish them to prove; and in this case, before commissioning the survey, the Peace Studies Department said, in a statement accompanying the findings' release, that it 'suspected that the British are well disposed towards their Irish neighbours'. Moreover, the survey did not include those most vulnerable to anti-Irish prejudices, Irish emigrants themselves. Persons born in Ireland were excluded. In the year that it was published, another poll, carried out under the auspices of the leading Irish community service agencies[2], found that of those who had approached the agencies in the preceding twelve months: '. . . one in eight clients had experienced racial harassment; adding police harassment and arrests under the PTA, the proportion of clients who experienced racial harassment increased to one in five'.

A 'key recommendation' of the survey was 'a link with community organisations through a network which collates evidence on racial harassment and discrimination and develops a strategy to challenge anti-Irish racism'.

ENGLAND

I was reminded of this one day in London while talking to two of my old friends and colleagues from the *Irish Press* about this book.[3] Both of them had worked in the paper's London office. Aidan Hennigan, the former London editor, is the doyen of Irish correspondents in London. A Mayo man, with the enviable distinction of owning his own island in a lake, he will not return to Ireland because, even though well past the retirement age for lesser mortals, he refuses to leave 'the best club in Europe', the House of Commons. The other is John McEntee, who is now the editor of the *Daily Express* diary column.

There was a certain gradation of emphasis in how they saw the Irish/English relationship from the perspective of their respective ages, Hennigan being almost thirty years older than McEntee. However, while citing certain undeniable difficulties encountered by the Irish in England, both men were at pains to stress the level of friendship they had themselves encountered. Hennigan recalled an incident while he was studying law at Gray's Inn, as a mature student.[4] Some of the most High Tory of his fellow would-be lawyers came up to him after particularly bad bombing atrocities in London, those of Hyde Park and Regent's Park, and insisted on taking him out to dinner that evening to cheer him up. Here I might add that my own experience in England amongst professional colleagues has been one of unfailing courtesy and friendliness.

However, this widespread friendly attitude did not prevent the Hyde Park atrocity forming the basis for one of the worst miscarriages of justice cases of the entire Troubles, that of Danny McNamee. Just before Christmas of 1998, the Appeals Court conceded that the verdict of the original jury was unsafe and he was released after being in prison since 1987. Some of McNamee's pleasure at this finding was dissipated, however, by an accompanying statement which most Irish people would regard as typical British judicial anti-Irish prejudice, put in purely to damage McNamee's chances of compensation. The court said that the fact that the original verdict was unsafe did not mean that he was innocent, or that he had spent years in jail for a crime that he did not commit. Yet, during the appeal it emerged that, as in the Guildford Four case, there were several factors which would have proved his innocence at the time, had the evidence not been deliberately disregarded.

The relationship works on two levels. There is the official world of courts, police and Crown Prosecution Service, all weighted in time-honoured (or dishonoured) fashion so as to convict an Irish person, any Irish person, in the wake of an atrocity. Then there is the ordinary human friendliness of the people.

John McEntee described how the official approach affected his work psychologically. After a bombing incident, he attended a press conference given by the police chief Sir Robert Mark, and found that he had to nerve himself to ask questions in the prevailing atmosphere. Sir Robert, all steely charm and joviality, greeted his question with: 'Ah! Do I detect a hint of an Irish accent?' And when McEntee pursued his questioning, Sir Robert counterpunched with: 'You'd know more than I about these things . . .'

Encountering that sort of approach at a top-level police press conference might be regarded as a legitimate professional hazard for a journalist, but attitudes within the police force also have a bearing on the fact that in the 1990s four separate reports concluded that the Irish had the highest percentage of incidents of 'stop and search' by police, and that the Irish were disproportionately represented in statistics for the victims of crime.[5] In the borough of Islington, Irishwomen were 80 per cent more likely to be the victims of crime than other ethnic groups. Overall, whereas the Irish comprised 14 per cent of the population of North London, they experienced 19.3 per cent of the crime.

These facts are the product of long-term difficulties stemming from the historical relationship between Ireland and England, complicated in recent decades by the ugly manifestations of the failure to find a solution to the last festering sore left by this relationship, Northern Ireland. Both my journalist friends stressed the effects of bombing on ordinary day-to-day relationships. McEntee instanced the case of the office phone cleaner, an Irishwoman, who had been working in London for decades, doing her daily rounds of offices. After a bombing, one customer with whom she had been dealing for twenty years, turned his back on her.

He also found that his own hackles rose at some of the jokes occasioned by the Troubles. For example, he told one English colleague that he found such a joke 'both upsetting and offensive'. His colleague had asked him had he heard that the IRA man Frank Stagg, who had died on hunger strike, had been awarded 'the slimmer of the year' award. Given the Irish sense of humour, I am quite certain that McEntee would have heard similar tasteless jokes in the *Irish Press* newsroom in Dublin. The rasp came however from hearing them told in an English accent in London.

The Prevention of Terrorism Act was identified by both journalists as a prime source of the problems faced by the Irish community. McEntee cited a story involving a son of the former Nationalist political leader in Derry, Eddie McAteer, who was pursuing a career in the London art world and had no contact with politics of any kind. McEntee had arranged to visit Shane Paul O'Doherty, also from Derry, in jail. (O'Doherty, a former IRA bomber, subsequently renounced violence and became a peace campaigner after his release and return to Ireland). McEntee's principal reason for visiting him was the fact that a colleague on the newsdesk had known O'Doherty as a boy in Derry, and asked John to call on him during his London stint. He brought McAteer along on the visit, because he too was from Derry. Duty discharged, McEntee thought no more of the visit and returned to Dublin shortly afterwards. However, the roof fell in on McAteer. He was held for five days under the PTA [Prevention of Terrorism Act], and questioned as to 'why he had taken a journalist along with him to visit O'Doherty?' He became an object of suspicion at his work, lost his accommodation and, finding English life increasingly threatening, gave up his career and returned to Derry.

Hennigan's career in journalism at every level of Irish and English society had provided him with unrivalled insights into the attitudes that form some English decision-taking. He recalled meeting Margaret Thatcher at a Newspaper Society Conference which he attended with Conor O'Clery of the *Irish Times*. She came up to the two Irish journalists and, linking arms with them in the friendliest way possible, asked them for their views on Irish opinion, North and South, concerning both British policy and the IRA. Having listened long, and apparently attentively, she paused for a moment after the two journalists had given their opinions, and then asked in a puzzled way: 'But why don't you get these people to *inform*?'

Thatcher apart, Hennigan listed a number of factors which he felt contributed to difficulties in Anglo-Irish relationships:

> You've got this yeomanry tradition, the Tory backbenchers, the old ladies who put on the hats and their best clothes, and sit in front of the television, waving the Union Jack for the Queen's Christmas address. People mock these things and try to say they don't exist, but then look at the Falklands. Where did that spirit come from? Then of course you've got to allow for the effect of the bombings, Deal, Birmingham, Guildford, Mountbatten, Brighton and Airey Neave. Those two were aimed straight at Maggie. That's where you get the blue lights flashing outside the Irish digs, and the kid losing his job in the wrong. I was in the House of Commons when Woy (Roy Jenkins) introduced the PTA. The atmosphere was terrible here sometimes. That's how you got your Birmingham Sixes and Guildford Fours. The Judith Ward case was the worst of all. She was a hundred miles away from the crime they sent her down for.

Both journalists stressed that there was a marked improvement in attitudes towards the Irish since the coming of the Peace Process and the departure of the Tories. McEntee joked, 'Nowadays if they hear you're Irish, people want to rub up against you.' Apart from the Peace Process, they attributed the improving attitude to the general buzz about Ireland being the 'in' place to spend a holiday, the growth of the Irish economy and the type of emigrant it was turning out. Hennigan's summing up was:

> The broad mass of the British people are a decent, tolerant lot. You get the odd exception, the backbencher, or the old boy drooling away in the House of Lords, and sometimes the occasional docker type talking about 'those Oirish coming over here to take our jobs'. But overall the thing is improving. Of course, if the Peace Process breaks down and the bombs start going off, people have little or no grasp of the historical background and we'll all be back to square one . . .

Taken together, the foregoing and the contrasting findings of the two surveys indicate both the existence of a large corpus of British goodwill towards the Irish and some strong countervailing attitudes which help to explain both the feelings of superiority contained in the dictionary definition, and how intelligent, educated Irish persons could find themselves so alienated as to end up in the conditions indicated by the 'shitting in newspapers' anecdote. All the foregoing have their place in the mosaic of the Irish experience in England. There is friendliness, there is tolerance, there is prejudice and there is alienation and exploitation, sometimes visited upon their own by the Irish themselves.

The early Anglo-Irish relationship

Before going into individual cases, it is important to remind ourselves that these malfunctions of justice did not occur overnight. They are part of the detritus of the long and troubled history of the Anglo-Irish relationship. During the so called 'Dark Ages' following the fall of Rome, there were strong Irish connections with both the north and west of Britain. The northern Irish tribe the Scotti, brought their name and Gaelic culture from Ulster to what is now Scotland, and there was an Irish kingdom in Wales for hundreds of years before Norman times. Irish pirates commonly raided the British coast and were in fact apparently responsible for kidnapping Patrick, the Irish patron saint, from his affluent Roman family. Ironically, the first Irish emigrants to Britain were Irish people uprooted from Ireland by the Norman invasions. By 1243 they had become so numerous that a statute was passed aimed at driving the Irish beggars out of England. It was to be the precursor of many such ukases. In 1413, for example, another law ordered that: 'All Irishmen and Irish clerks, beggars, called chamber dekyns, be voided out of the realm.' One effect of this type of law was that, instead of driving the Irish out of 'the realm', it helped to create the tradition of Irish recruitment into Britain's armies. The numbers of Irish joining the British Army and Navy again shot up subsequently, because of the dispossessions caused by the sixteenth- and seventeenth-century invasions of Ireland. By the early nineteenth century the Irish probably formed as much as 40 per cent of the membership of the army alone.

Generally speaking, the early Irish pirates and the contemporary Republican incursions notwithstanding, the Irish did not invade Britain, except in the service of an English ruler, or would-be ruler. For example, Lambert Simnel was crowned King of England in Dublin and, after the last battle of the Wars of the Roses (Stoke in 1487), fetched up not on the throne of England but working in the kitchens of King Henry VII. Bonnie Prince Charlie was another unsuccessful aspirant to the English throne whose cause was supported by Irish regiments. Mainly, however, it was the British who invaded Ireland, to further imperial objectives. From the time of Henry II in the twelfth century a succession of British monarchs found themselves engaged in 'putting down rebellions in Ireland'.

An Irish apologist might argue that these 'rebellions' were merely Irish attempts to take back their own property, which the English rulers systematically confiscated from the native Catholics and parcelled out to 'loyal' Protestant planters, from whom, for example, the present North of Ireland Unionists derive. However, as we have seen in the European chapter, the existence of this font of rebellion on its western flank meant that the decision-takers of England frequently faced the spectre of domestic invasion by continental Catholic powers using Ireland as a stepping stone. Imperial ambition, fear of the continental threat and anti-Catholicism combined to generate policies for dealing with the Irish, particularly on the part of the Elizabethans and Cromwell, indicated by this description of the methods of the Elizabethan Governor of Munster, Sir Humphrey Gilbert:

> ... that the heads of all those (of what sort soever they were) which were killed in the day, should be cut off from their bodies and brought to the place where he encamped at night, and should there be laid on the ground each side of the way leading out into his own tent so that none could come into his tent for any cause but commonly he must pass through a lane of heads which he used *ad terrorem*, the dead feeling nothing the more pains thereby; and yet it did bring a great terror to the people when they saw the heads of their dead fathers, brothers, children, kinsfolk and friends, lie on the ground before their faces, as they came to speak with the same colonel.[6]

Early Irish settlements were recorded in Bristol around the eleventh century, and by the fourteenth century, there were settlements in Liverpool, London, Norwich and York, but for the purposes of this book, the term 'the Irish in Britain' may be taken as relating to three principal waves of emigration. The first occurred in the 1840s as a result of the Great Famine, when the failure of the potato crop was allowed to develop from a crisis into a catastrophe.

THE GREAT FAMINE

In round numbers the Great Famine cut the Irish population from some 8 to 6 million. Perhaps a million people died in Ireland itself, and another million emigrated, thereby initiating a period of population decline that continued almost to the time of writing. In fact only one crop failed, the potato, and the British Government allowed food to be exported from Ireland all through the crisis of the mid-1840s which culminated in 'Black '47'. During this period, apart from huge quantities of food such as meat and butter, or crops like millable wheat, more cattle than people were shipped out of the country. The dimensions of the Famine were such that it may be that, even if this food had been kept in the country, it would not have been sufficient to feed all the starving anyway. Most of the victims, like those of Africa today, were used to a specific type of food, in this case, the potato, but in the circumstances, even the sight of a sandwich passing under armed guard before people dying from hunger would have been a revolutionary symbol.

The Famine was no more the only source of Irish emigration than it was the only famine. In fact, the nineteenth century saw some dozen famines in different parts of the country before what is known as the Great Famine occurred, from 1845 onward. However, the Great Famine both epitomises the symptoms and the causes of misrule in Ireland.

By the 1830s, more than two million people lived on the edge of starvation for two-thirds of the year, receiving enough to eat only in the four months after harvest. Countless thousands of people had become dependent on a piece of land just about big enough to hold a hovel and a garden of potatoes. Those lucky enough to have a job from a landowner were probably given no pay, save what they could grow or perhaps rear in the form of a pig.

A commission on 'The state of the poor in Ireland' recorded a number of reasons for the disastrous state of the huge Irish underclass: religious differences; political extremism, absentee landlords, lack of investment, the prevalence of alcoholism, the 1800 Act of Union.[7] The novelist, Canon Sheehan, famously blamed: ' . . . the whole ghastly genealogy of Irish history, and particularly the Act of Union . . . the Union begat outlawry, and outlawry begat Whiteboyism; and the Whiteboyism begat informers and judicial murders, and judicial murders begat revenge'.[8]

Canon Sheehan rightly indicts the Act of Union for exercising a baneful influence, but what he does not state is how the Act deprived Ireland of what I may call 'The Initiative Factor', the power of creating any system of helping itself. The Act suppressed the Irish Parliament and transferred the seat of government to Westminster. The professional classes, the artisans, the publishers, the people with the ambition and the means to achieve successful careers, and in so doing generate prosperity for others, left for London in droves. At Westminster itself, the Irish representatives were powerless to affect the course of events in Ireland. With some 100 members in an assembly of over 650, they were easily outvoted throughout the nineteenth century, if they chose to object to an imperial measure. At the time of the Famine most of them would not have wished to so object, being drawn from that section of the Irish population which upheld the empire: the Protestant Ascendancy class. When the Great Famine struck, the situation might be likened to that which occurred after the *Titanic* had hit the iceberg. Certainly the collision created great damage, but what created the loss of life, the impact or the scarcity of lifeboats?

One incident serves to illustrate the vulnerability of the Irish in dealing with the crisis through having no government or effective decision-taking machinery of their own.[9] In November 1845, when the dimensions of the looming catastrophe were becoming clear, Daniel O'Connell and a large deputation, which included figures like the Duke of Leinster, called on the Lord Lieutenant, Lord Heytesbury, to urge on him a relief plan, drawn up by O'Connell. Had it been adopted it would have greatly alleviated the Famine's effects. It proposed not only stopping the export of food from Ireland, but advocated the importation of food from abroad for free distribution. The deputation also proposed that relief work be provided out of the public purse, that loans for famine relief be raised and that the whole scheme, which had been drawn up by O'Connell, be paid for by increasing taxes on landlords, particularly absentee landlords.

As most of the men backing O'Connell in urging these courses were themselves landlords, neither their practicality nor their sincerity can be doubted. However, the Lord Lieutenant received the proposals 'very coldly', read a prepared reply which in effect rejected the proposals, and ushered the delegation out immediately he had finished reading. O'Connell's subsequent pleas in the House of Commons fell on deaf ears, and he died in Genoa in 1847, a broken man, as the Famine reached its peak.

The English liberal, Sydney Smith, once declared:

> The moment the very name of Ireland is mentioned, the English seem to bid adieu to common feeling, common prudence and common sense, and to act with the barbarity of tyrants and the fatuity of idiots.[10]

Few fair-minded people familiar with the course of Irish history could disagree with his verdict. However, I feel that here one should enter, not so much a caveat, as an extra dimension to the tragedy – Church teaching and the human frailty factor. The teaching issue raises the questions: to what extent was the death toll exacerbated by the Catholic Church's teaching on birth control? And: to what extent does Irish fertility differ from other nations, because of factors other than Church teaching? Pure wretchedness for example indicates that sex may have been one of the only pleasures available to the poor, but the Irish have displayed higher fertility levels than other races. Cecil Woodham-Smith, for example, quotes statistics for the Famine era which suggest that:

> in the Irish quarter of Boston ... one birth a year occurred for every 15 persons of population, whereas in England the rate was 1 to 31, in France 1 to 35, and in some non-Irish parts of Boston, 1 to 50.[11]

There is a very old Irish toast which helps to explain Cecil Woodham-Smith's observations about Irish birth rates: 'Slainte go saol agat, paiste gac blian agat, agus bas in Eireann.' It means: Health and life to you, a child every year to you, and death in Ireland. 'Health' and 'life' need no explanation; a child every year was insurance in sickness and old age; and death in Ireland meant one did not have to emigrate involuntarily. Though when famine, or pestilence or slaughter struck the result was both emigration and death, the Irish toast explains the fight-back from near extirpation at several points in the history of the race. Yet fertility reached the peak it did in Ireland at the onset of the Great Famine, and continued amongst the Irish outside the country after it.

The 'pleasure factor' is not one which surfaces much in discussions of the Famine amongst Irish people, and nor, as with other awful topics – the Holocaust or slavery, for example – do certain other complicating side issues. Just as some Jews collaborated with the Nazis, and slavery could not have existed were it not for the co-operation of the African chiefs who sold their people into bondage, so did some Catholic Irish profit from the Famine. Unwillingly, but none the less efficiently, Irish Catholic soldiers escorted the consignments of food which passed through the ranks of the starving to be exported. Irish Catholic members of the Irish Constabulary kept themselves and their families from joining these ranks by assisting in the wholesale evictions which accompanied the Famine. Irish Catholic farmers rented the land from which the starving were driven. Many a contemporary Irish Catholic 'strong' farming family owes its prosperity to land acquired because of the misery of their co-religionists in those terrible times. Such factors – apart from the overriding one of not wishing to give aid and comfort to the IRA's historically anti-British ideological underpinning – help to explain the unease with which the Irish Government commemorated the Famine in the 150th Anniversary period of 1995–8.

Overriding all the foregoing, a major contributory factor to the disaster was the cold inhumanity of Malthusian-minded, *laissez-faire* preaching, English politicians like the Chancellor of the Exchequer, Charles Wood, and administrators like Charles Trevelyan, the Assistant Secretary at the Treasury, effectively the man most responsible for dealing with the Famine. He, and others like him, appear to have treated the Famine as an opportunity to engage in social engineering. Sir Robert Peel, the British Conservative Prime Minister, had arranged for cargoes of grain to be shipped to Ireland and distributed surreptitiously, so as not to arouse Tory wrath at breaches of the Corn Laws. At the time these laws were the subject of the most acrimonious debate to convulse the Conservative Party until the European issue in our day, and the results were calamitous for Ireland.

Peel wanted to lower the tariffs on corn, not merely to feed the starving Irish, but in order to provide cheap food for the new proletarian populations then flooding into the cities of industrial England. The Conservatives, however, were riven on the issue because of the opposition of powerful Tory landlords who were using the protectionist laws to profit by growing high-cost corn. Peel ultimately fell in June 1846, ironically over a trumped-up Irish issue. A successful parliamentary ambush over an Irish coercion measure had been prepared by Disraeli with the aid of dissident Tories, and the unsuspecting Peel did not have his votes marshalled when a sudden division was called.

Lord John Russell succeeded him and he appointed Wood who gave Trevelyan his head over Ireland. Trevelyan slashed relief spending on the starving, one of his first acts on Peel's departure being to cancel the grain shipments. Trevelyan's approach greatly worsened the shambolic situation then prevailing in Ireland. Years of neglect, brutal repression, and hence maddened responses in the form of agrarian outrage, had created a land-holding system of inefficient, mind-boggling complexity.

For example, Lord Monteagle, a landlord whom we will again encounter in an Australian context (see page 451), wrote to a friend in 1846, detailing a typical situation on his estate.[12] In 1781, 125 acres had been leased to a farmer at an annual rent of £10. Sixty-five years later, the lease was still in force, but now there were 236 people living in thirty-five homes on that holding. 'Even if the farm were given to them,' Monteagle said, 'it would not help their situation,' and he reasoned that evicting some of them would bring 'untold trouble'. His solution was to help those willing to emigrate to do so, and a number of Monteagle's tenants subsequently found themselves beginning a new life in Australia as a result. However, the tenants of other landlords frequently found themselves on the side of the roads, a prey to starvation. There were wholesale evictions aimed at creating larger, more profitable holdings, and the scenes which accompanied the Famine are branded into the Irish folk memory:

> Surrounded by weeping women, frightened children and sullen men, the bailiff would read the [eviction] notice, empty the house and set the wreckers to work. A gang of half a dozen 'destructives', many themselves victims of eviction doing this dirty work to feed their families, could pull down a dozen houses in a day, for the simple cabins were pathetically easy to destroy. They tied a rope to the roof beam, and led it down through the house and out the door. When the beam was broken with a few blows, a strong pull on the rope brought the roof crashing into the house and all that remained was to level the walls with crowbars.[13]

Needless to say, such action begat reaction, and the various agrarian societies struck back. Known by different names such as Captain Rocks and Whiteboys, they used the common weapons of darkness and terror. Livestock were crippled, houses burnt, intimidation and murder were commonplace, and the Irish countryside was in a state of semi-insurrection which caused a Lord Lieutenant under Wellington, Lord Anglesey, to write: 'There exists to the most frightful extent a mutual and violent hatred between the proprietors and the peasantry.'[14]

Not only were the Catholic peasantry fighting evictions and the exactions of landlords, they were also resisting the payment of tithes to the Protestant Church. The tithes system, whereby the Catholic Irish laity were levied to pay for the support of the Protestant clergy, led to fierce pitched battles all over the country. Frequently lives were lost when police attempted to enforce the collections.

All these antipathies of course also helped to provide a stimulus to emigration for small farmers and tradespeople who could afford to get away from the hatreds. The bulk of these were Protestants who, as we shall see, mainly emigrated to Canada (see Chapter Four).

To add to the woes of the population, a cholera epidemic broke out. Life was literally nasty, brutish and short; a quarter of the population died without reaching the age of forty. Diary entries from the period, like those of Humphrey O'Sullivan, a schoolmaster, shopkeeper and botanist who lived in Callan, County Kilkenny, give an indication of the quality of life:

> Livid famine is all over the countryside . . . poor people without any kind of work to buy any kind of food. There are not even alms for the paupers . . . We saw a pretty girl kneading peat. Her foot was slender, her calves and knees as white as bog cotton, her thigh round and beautiful, naked almost to her stout buttocks. She was the daughter of a farmer once rich; but the struggle of life went against him. He became bankrupt, the landlord took his crops, the minister his corn and horses, and the church tithe collector took his table, pot and blankets. Between them they pushed him down in life, along with his wife and handsome children. These are the circumstances that drove him to a small hovel beside the mountain and set his beautiful daughter to kneading peat.[15]

> July 10th:

> The devilish peelers beat a lot of innocent people. They beat up two merchants in their own houses. They can't be tolerated.

Obviously the overall situation could not be 'tolerated' either. The British decided to extend the Poor Law to Ireland, not to alleviate the situation there, but to stem the tide of starving destitute Irish flowing into British cities where the Poor Laws were already in force. As if to validate Sydney Smith's judgement on English attitudes to Ireland, the laws were so framed as to make a miserable situation worse still. Relief could only be offered to those who went to workhouses, but in order to prevent the workhouses being overrun by paupers, the regime in these institutions was made deliberately harsh. Consequently, many preferred to commit minor crimes so that they could be sent to prison instead.

As the landlords had to pay for the workhouses, via the rates, the increasing cost of the Poor Law scheme made them look to emigration as a means both of dealing with the congestion of the land and the soaring cost of Poor Law relief. If anything, this measure served to increase the pressure on the English cities and, as we shall see later – particularly in the cases of Australia, America, and Canada – it quickened the tide of human misery that poured out of Ireland across the oceans of the world.

THE SECOND AND THIRD WAVES OF EMIGRATION

When one considers that the population of Ireland fell by some 25 per cent, two million people between 1841 and 1861, one gets some indication of the dislocation, deprivation, and sheer loss of energy suffered by Irish society. One result of course was to make the Irish heavily dependent on the United Kingdom as a source of employment. Another was to greatly increase the strength of the Roman Catholic Church in Great Britain. John Henry Newman acknowledged this fact in 1852, saying: 'The English Church was not, and the English Church is once again . . . it is the coming of the Second Spring.'

By 1861, 7 per cent of Scotland's population, and 3 per cent of England's was of Irish origin. Wars and depressions had encouraged a second major flow of the Irish to England in the first half of the nineteenth century, and emigration to the UK increased again after America imposed immigration restrictions in the early twentieth century. The Second World War provided a further catalyst which continued throughout the fifties. Britain badly needed Irish man- and womanpower. Without the huge amount of Irish male and female labour which poured into England during the war years, Great Britain would have found it difficult to maintain the war effort.

A third wave of emigrants broke on Britain's shores during the 1980s. The Action Group for Irish Youth estimates that in the decade between 1981 and 1991, roughly half a million people, most of them single and under twenty-five, settled in the south of England.[16] The majority settled in the South East, some 32 per cent of them in the Greater London area. The 1991 census showed that 850,000 Irish-born people lived in England, and observers of the Irish community place the number who can claim Irish descent at something approaching two million. Thus, at roughly 1.5 per cent of the British population, the Irish are the largest ethnic group in England.

Obviously, with such a large group involved, in a situation in which at times bombs go off, and coffins travel back and forth across the Irish Sea, unpleasant side effects will develop in the host community. One of the survivors of the IRA bombing campaign which marked the outbreak of the Second World War resigned from the IRA when he learned: 'That they were going to put bombs in public toilets and post-boxes, and also pollute reservoirs. It did not occur to them that members of the Irish population in England posted letters, used toilets and drank water.'[17]

THE ANGLO-IRISH RELATIONSHIP IN MORE RECENT TIMES

The IRA apart, the Irish in Britain also suffered from a lack of leadership. In his book, *The Irish in Britain*, Kevin O'Connor has described the Irish workers in Britain in the thirties as suffering from:

a profound absence of social leadership, rendering them as mere factory and building-site fodder, totally at the whim of economic forces. Only in the traditional immigrant areas of Scotland and the North-East was there in existence the semblance of a receiving community structure into which they could absorb with confidence, being the continuum of previous generations' activity in community and trade union affairs.[18]

For reasons which will be more fully examined later, this situation was not to be seriously addressed for some fifty years. The sector which might have provided a community leadership, the Irish professionals, tended to hive itself off into a ghetto of its own. Following the 1916 Rising, and the Black and Tan War, some Irish professionals coming to London were received with hostility in the average London clubs, so they formed a club of their own, the National University of Ireland Club, near Westminster Cathedral. Members of this establishment neither had, nor sought, contact with their less affluent compatriots in places like Camden Town's Rowton House. Here the Irish were more tolerated than accepted. Individual priests did what they could to help the less fortunate Irish, and the socialist Connolly Association, which took its name and policies from the executed 1916 leader James Connolly, tried to raise the political consciousness of the Irish workers, but with very little effect.

The consciousness of the British public was only too well raised by the IRA bombing campaign of 1938, with serious consequences for the popularity of the Irish in Britain. The influx of Irish workers during the war, while valuable to the war effort, also aroused some animosities amongst those who had relations fighting abroad: 'Our lads are fighting and you Irish are coming over here to take our jobs,' was a frequent taunt encountered by Irish workers and their children in London's East End, for example. However, the war's end helped to bring about an improvement as friendships forged during the fighting spilled over into business and professional relationships.

The 1944 Education Acts benefited the building of Catholic schools, and the spread of education, growth of the welfare state, and the post-war building boom all helped to create a feel-good factor amongst the Irish. One prominent Irishman who did not share this feeling, however, was George Bernard Shaw. When the Irish Club was founded in Eaton Square, London, in 1948, he was invited to join, but wrote back as follows:

> I can imagine nothing less desirable than an Irish Club. Irish people in England should join English clubs, and avoid each other like the plague. If they flock together like geese, they might as well have never left Ireland. They don't admire, nor even like one another. In English clubs they are always welcome. More fools the English perhaps; but the two are so foreign that they have much to learn from their association and co-operation.[19]

At the time of writing, the Irish Club has lost cachet amongst the burgeoning Irish emigrant middle class, but for several decades after its founding, it was an important focal point in Irish social life in Britain. Other focal points of a different kind were provided by the Behan brothers, Brendan, Brian and Dominic. Brendan brought the London stage to life with plays like *The Quare Fellow* and *The Hostage*; Brian, also a playwright, brought the building of London's South Bank complex to a halt with a strike in 1958; and Dominic wrote a famous song containing the lines:

> The Sea oh the Sea
> It's gradh geal, mo croidhe[20]
> Long may it roll between
> England and me.

Between the three of them the Behans served to keep alive the tradition of the Irish as literati, drinkers and trade union activists. As well as trade union involvement along Brian Behan lines, the Irish increasingly became involved in Labour Party politics. Of 363 Labour MPs in the 1966–70 Parliament, thirty-five were of Irish descent. In the 1970 General Election, an *Irish Post* survey calculated that 84 per cent of the Irish vote went to the Labour Party. Harold Wilson's administration concluded an Anglo-Irish Free Trade agreement with Dublin and returned the remains of Roger Casement, executed in 1916, to his native country. In a by-election held in 1969, Michael O'Halloran, an Irish emigrant, was elected to Westminster for Islington. It appeared that at last Anglo-Irish relationships were on a good footing both in England itself and between the two islands. Even in the ranks of the Conservatives, the hand of friendship was extended to the Irish, or rather to the Irish vote, with the formation of the Irish Conservative Association by an Irish Tory, Paul Dwyer. Alas, the shadow of Northern Ireland was to have a blighting effect, for the Conservatives were allied to the Ulster Unionist Party.

Although much of Jim Callaghan's policy in Ireland had been to talk Green and act Orange, Labour nevertheless had reined in both the army and the Unionists in their efforts to curb the growingly unstable situation in the Six Counties. However, within a few days of winning the 20 June General Election, (on 3–5 July 1970) the Tories unwittingly launched a recruiting drive for the Provisional IRA. A section of the Lower Falls Road in Belfast was cordoned off and the area was ransacked for arms. Several deaths were caused both by army vehicles and in savage hand-to-hand fighting, carried out amidst choking clouds of CS gas. No searches at all took place on the Loyalist side, even though by then the Loyalists had caused several deaths and explosions, and the Nationalists had still to kill anyone.

The first British soldier did not die until February 1971, and, according to Hansard at the time, the Loyalists had 112,000 licensed weapons. (Unionist-appointed Justices of the Peace gave out licences with such gay abandon that one gentleman was empowered to purchase two machine-guns which, according to his application form, he required 'to kill otters' – a prohibited species.) Internment followed, directed solely at Catholics, and Nationalist feelings of injustice were expressed through the mushrooming ranks of the

IRA. They were also expressed on the British mainland. A canister of CS gas was hurled into the House of Commons in July 1970, and tons of masonry on to the streets of London in October 1971 when the Post Office Tower was bombed. The IRA bombing campaign was under way and ancient anti-Irish prejudices in England were about to be both rekindled and grievously added to during the ensuing twenty-five years of 'the Troubles'.

The Irish became the targets of hostility, derived not merely from the fall-out of individual contemporary atrocities, but from historical animosities, myths and prejudices. The Commission for Racial Equality reported in 1997: 'The main features of this hostility were: its virulence; lack of connection with any understanding of the political background; blanket application to all Irish people; triggered solely by hearing Irish accents.'[21]

The report went on to give a number of specific cases of people who had suffered, particularly from the fall-out of the Birmingham pub bombings. The effects of such cases will be dealt with later. However, at this stage, I think I can say with some confidence that during my researches I witnessed some important turning points for the better in rectifying the situation highlighted by the CRE report. The most obvious one occurred at the General Election of 1 May 1997. Britain voted for change and Ireland was part of that change in two intertwined ways, one involving a personality, the other the political process. Politically, prior to the election, the Federation of Irish Societies – a very broad-based, and representative grouping – and the *Irish Post* newspaper had targeted forty constituencies in which the Irish population outweighed the Conservative majority. Whether they responded directly to the Irish organisations' call or simply reacted out of distaste for a sleazy and faltering Government, the Irish certainly voted against the Tories.

The personality point came home to me forcibly at an election party given by Helena Kennedy, QC, the daughter of a Donegal emigrant to Glasgow. When the news of Michael Portillo's defeat was announced, an animal passion of delight suffused the hitherto restrained gathering which included people like Salman Rushdie, Jonathan Miller, Claire Rayner and Gail Rebuck. Not only were the glitterati cheering the fall of the Tory icon, they were also, though most of them would not have realised it at the time, signifying the fact that it was the son of another Donegal emigrant who had just taken a significant step towards power – Tony Blair.

Irish roots apart – although these are clearly of importance to him, unlike Margaret Thatcher, who is not known for references to her Kerry ancestry – Blair's huge majority made him independent of the Ulster Unionists. Hitherto, they had been able to hold up the Peace Process because, due to the divisions in the Conservatives over Europe, the Tory leader, John Major, had depended on their support to remain in power. One of Blair's first steps on being elected was to brief Dublin on New Labour's new and constructive approach to the Northern Ireland problem, and the Irish reaction to the initiative was summed up for me privately by an Irish Government spokesman who commented that: 'If they deliver on what they say they're going to deliver, the results will be historic.'

The final outcome of the Irish Peace Process is unclear, dangerously so, at the time of writing, but it has to be said that the early performance of the New Labour team, led by Blair himself and in particular Mo Mowlam, bore out the spokesman's assessment (although the influence of Peter Mandelson, who succeeded Mowlam, was less well thought of in Dublin). Blair bluntly told the Unionists' leader, David Trimble, that the British taxpayers expected people who, in Northern Ireland, claimed to be British, to behave like British citizens when it came to living with their neighbours. The result was the Good Friday Agreement of April, 1998. Later that year, on 26 November, Blair again made history, this time in Dublin, by becoming the first British Prime Minister ever to address the joint Houses of the Oireachtas (Parliament). He said:

> Ireland, as you may know, is in my blood. My mother was born in the flat above her grandmother's hardware shop in the main street of Ballyshannon in Donegal. She lived there as a child, started school there and only moved when her father died, her mother remarried and they crossed the water to Glasgow. We spent virtually every childhood summer holiday up to when the Troubles really took hold in Ireland . . . it was in the sea off the Irish coast that I learned to swim, that my father took me to my first pub . . . for a Guinness, a taste I've never forgotten . . . Even now in my constituency of Sedgefield which at one time had 30 pits . . . virtually every community remembers that its roots lie in Irish migration to the mines of Britain . . . we, the British and the Irish are irredeemably linked.

They are indeed. Another less public indication of changing Anglo-Irish attitudes, this time in London, came at the banquet which marked the ending of the annual general meeting of the Federation of Irish Societies which was also held around the time of the election. The banquet was addressed by the popular Irish Ambassador, Ted Barrington. In a pithy phrase he told his audience, drawn from all parts of the UK: 'Integrate, but don't assimilate.' He advised his hearers to work with their host community as good citizens should, but to stand up for their entitlements, to be conscious of their Irish background and culture; and to maintain and develop their Irish identity as a contribution both to British society and to other minority cultures. On the one hand, the Irish were being given a clear incentive to come out of the closet and put their heads over the parapet. On the other, the Ambassador was simply acknowledging the reality of the fact that the 'RyanAir generation', named after the low-cost airline on which so many young Irish emigrants came to Britain in the eighties and nineties, were, on average, far better educated than their predecessors and hence more confident and less inclined to suppress their own culture in order to avoid drawing attention to themselves. In the same week that the ambassador spoke, Donal Mooney, the then editor of the *Irish Post* had observed to me that the proper concept for the contemporary Irish emigrant was that of expatriate. The word 'emigrant' should be banished.

Here, at the risk of digression, I might observe that some of the complexities involved in the process of reassessment involved in coming over to England – or perhaps more accurately, coming out in England – were underlined later in the evening of the banquet. The speeches were followed by a dance, during which my partner was a psychotherapist, an extremely good-looking, intelligent, blonde: Sister Theresa of the Loreto Order. After we returned to our table following a particularly energetic Irish dance, The Siege of Ennis, which involves swinging people about in a manner never envisaged by the inventor of the law of gravity, someone remarked that at a meeting earlier Irish gay and lesbian representatives had been affiliated to the FIS. It then emerged that a man in his fifties sitting beside me, wearing a collar and tie, was a) a priest and b) that two of the four people he had just been doing the 'spin' with (two men link hands to swing the two women off their feet) were gay and lesbian representatives. Startled, the priest reacted instinctively: 'God, if I'd known that, I wouldn't have asked them to dance!' A devoted worker for the Irish community, he was in no way homophobic, but for someone of his generation, for whom participation in a dance was already something of an adventure, gays and lesbians were a bridge too far.

HEADS ABOVE THE PARAPET

There are sections of the Irish community who on first sight would appear never to have their heads under any parapet, and indeed some of them will tell you that there is no parapet. To an extent they are correct. For them there is none. Yet another survey (I promise readers that after this I will not inflict further surveys on them for some time), carried out at around the same time as the FIS AGM, showed that, compared to one in nine amongst the host community, one in six of the Irish community earn over £30,000 a year.[22] (In evaluating this statistic it should be borne in mind that a head teacher, for example, earns around £25,000.) Certainly, if one attended a paean to Irish yuppiedom like the Irish Wild Geese Ball in the Hilton Hotel, one would be conscious of bank accounts, not parapets. Deprivation, prejudice or the shadow of the Prevention of Terrorism Act do not touch the lives of most of those who attend. Of the roughly two and half million either Irish-born or second generation Irish, quite clearly some have achieved enormous success and made an equally enormous contribution in several fields. That of heroism in the ranks of 'the old enemy's' armed services may be gauged from the book by Richard Doherty and David Truesdale, *Irish Winners of the Victoria Cross* (published in Ireland by Four Courts Press in 2000), which indicates both the extent of Irish courage and the tangled relationship between the two islands. Since the VC was inaugurated in 1856 more than 200 Irishmen have been awarded the decoration. These included three members of Wanderers Rugby Club, Dublin, two Black and Tans, two B-Specials and a member of the IRA who fought against the Black and Tans. The Irish of course also literally made a contribution on the sporting fields and in the construction industry, but also in the arts, medicine including nursing, teaching, the armed services, the caring professions and the financial sector. Their presence in this last area is so marked that the distinguished American journalist, Dick Rapporter, of

Forbes Magazine, remarked to me as this was being written: 'If you took the Irish out of the City of London, the financial services world would collapse.'

Charles Lamb once said that there were two races of men: those who borrow and those who lend. What strikes one forcibly, looking at the Irish community in England, is that there are two markedly contrasting groups of Irish: those indicated by the 'shitting in the newspaper' anecdote and those who do well, extremely well. In 1997, the *Irish Post* began producing an annual magazine profiling some of the latter. As the then Chief Executive of the *Post*, Douglas Baxter, wrote, it was 'a near impossible task to produce a definitive list'. Nevertheless, the journal, *Business '97, the influential Irish in Britain*, ran to eighty-eight pages which in terms of gloss, gush and colour photography, rivalled *Hello* magazine. But it contained a well-documented story of Irish success. Movers and shakers from the Irish community occupied the driving seats in every sector one could think of.

The *Post*'s listings apart, the average Englishman or woman in the street would, depending on their age bracket, immediately recognise figures such as, in entertainment, the late Eamonn Andrews, or Terry Wogan, Des Lynam, Frank Delaney and the great TV racing commentator, Peter O'Sullevan, now retired. In sport, soccer legends like Pat Jennings, Roy Keane, Dave O'Leary, Martin O'Neill, Denis Irwin and Joe Kinnear would be household names. In politics, Kevin McNamara and Clare Short, or in rock 'n' roll, which some might see as a branch of politics, Shane McGowan of the Pogues[23] or Liam and Noel Gallagher of Oasis. In fact, the really extraordinary thing about the *Post*'s thick, well-researched pantheon is that the paper had so many names to choose from in the world of business alone that none of the foregoing personalities is included (except Lynam, in an advertisement for Jameson whiskey. The caption reads: 'the ultimate smoothy'!).

Nor was the publication a once-off. By the year 2000, its successor was using smaller type but had increased to 200 pages. Those pictured included Brendan O'Neill, Chief Executive of ICI, Peter Sutherland, Chairman of Goldman Sachs International, who grew up two doors from where I was born, Gerry Robinson, Chairman of Granada, Baroness O'Cathain of the Barbican, President of the Chartered Institute of Marketing, and Matthew Barrett, Chief Executive of Barclays Bank, who as we shall see (Chapter 4) already had a spectacular career in Canada behind him before being head-hunted by Barclays. One of the success stories profiled was that of Hugh Murphy, Chairman of the Charles Street Group. Speaking of his South Armagh ancestry he said: 'I do believe that, to understand where we are, we must acknowledge where we came from.'

Any Londoner going to work, on any given day, can expect to see evidence of Irish industry as they pass by construction sites or observe cranes dotting the London skyline. Names like Brophy, Clancy, Durkan, Gallagher, McKenna, McNicholas, Murphy, O'Halloran, O'Brien, O'Rourke, are all major players in the British construction industry. Some, like Tommy McNicholas or the Clancys, Kevin, Dermot and Mary, work in firms which grew big under their fathers, and then, under them, grew bigger still. Others, like John Murphy, did it the hard way, emigrating from unemployment-ravaged Kerry as a young man and building up one of the most visible companies in all England. Who has not seen one of Murphy's green trucks at one end of the country or the other? Murphy not only built the mile-long railway tunnel at London's Stansted Airport in 1991, he also built a financial portfolio which includes interests in hotels, property and shipping. Today John Murphy, once a penniless emigrant from County Kerry, is a fixture in the *Sunday Times* annual list of Britain's richest 500.

One doesn't need the *Sunday Times* to know that one of Britain's richest corporations is Unilever. This corporate giant was valued at £35 billion at the time of writing – thirteen billion more than the combined worth of Ireland's total exports to the EU, including England. The chairman of this Anglo-Dutch colossus is Niall Fitzgerald, who began his accountancy career in a Dublin animal feeds company. From the time, 1974, that he turned his back on his native Sligo to join Unilever, Fitzgerald's career moved in only one direction – upwards. Unilever is a quintessential international conglomerate. The world is its market place, but while Fitzgerald has shown himself supremely well able to perform in that market place, he has maintained a sense of where he came from: 'I have a strong sense of Irishness, even though I probably won't live in Ireland again. That does not mean that I'm not very committed to it, and everything I think about has an Irish sense to it.'[24] Fitzgerald has demonstrated this sense of commitment by adding to his hectic schedule the responsibility of joining committees set up by the Irish Government when called upon to do so. He thinks that it is his sense of Irishness which makes him more direct in his approach than is the British norm, and this has been a particular advantage to him in dealing with the Dutch: 'I've never been afraid to express my views, even if they're wrong, and that tends to get you heard.' It does indeed.

If one seeks the flamboyant, there is Eddie Jordan, the Formula One racing mogul, who founded Jordan Racing, and who lives by the belief that: 'If you get it right, you get a fortune. If you get it wrong, you go bankrupt.' Jordan, who was instrumental in giving Ayrton Senna his first drive, and in bringing fellow Irishman Eddie Irvine on to the world stage, owes his position in Formula One racing to a bank strike in 1970. Thrown out of work, he fetched up in Jersey, and discovered the delights of 100cc kart-racing. When the strike ended, he resumed his job while at the same time continuing as a kart-racer. He had several successes at the sport and took a sabbatical from the bank to give himself time to decide whether or not to put the kart before his career. The kart won. Jordan then moved from karts to motor racing. In 1980, in a lock-up garage in Silverstone, he founded Jordan Racing with the aid of his wife Marie, who helped with the finances by taking a £40-a-week job as a packer in a local factory. Jordan again changed gear, moving upwards from Formula Three to Formula One in 1991, and again Marie helped with the financing, this time by acquiescing in the mortgaging of their home to raise funds. A subsequent comment of hers conveys something both of her own dedication and that of her (literally) driven husband:

> I never really thought I was the nervous type, but my hands broke out in a rash, you know, thinking about selling the house, where to school the kids, things like that. But that was what Eddie really wanted to do. It was driving him on. I knew there was no way it would be anything other than this.[25]

At the time of writing, Jordan has successfully fought his way through the Formula One world's unique blend of mega money, champagne, angst, nerve, skill and vitriol, to rank amongst the world's top three or four teams, winning his first Grand Prix in Belgium in 1998. He employs the shamrock logo in most of his merchandising, his teams are dressed in green outfits and he makes a point of employing several Irish people – not, he says, simply because they are Irish, but because they are good at what they do.

Irish people have made a particular impact on the media. As Avril MacRory, from County Waterford, both epitomises and points out, there has been a growing Irish media presence in England in recent decades. One tends to meet the Irish, and particularly Irish women, at every level of journalism, television and the Internet. The Managing Director of Yahoo! UK and Ireland is Martina King; and Caroline Marland may have the looks of a top model, but she is Managing Director of Guardian News Ltd. MacRory herself was head of music programmes for BBC television until she took over as head of the Millennium project. Her finding is that her countrymen and women have a particular feeling for the media world, and that they are able to realise their talents in the media sphere because of the Irish educational system: 'They don't have that inferiority complex, they know they are as good as anyone else ... It is a tribute to what has happened in Ireland over the last thirty years.'[26] This really is the central point of modern awareness of Ireland and the Irish, be it in England or anywhere else. Appreciation of Irish qualities has gone up in direct ratio to the manner in which the Irish themselves have improved their own society and enabled more and more of their own people to realise their potential, both at home and abroad.

Irishwomen in particular have become increasingly well aware of their potential. In April 1999, a group of influential Irishwomen got together to launch Women's Irish Network (WIN) to enable businesswomen in England to develop business relationships and professional contacts and to raise funds for worthy Irish causes. Its founders included Polly Devlin, the novelist, Mary Clancy, Hazel Hutchinson, a banker, and Norah Casey, the editor-in-chief of the *Irish Post*. WIN was an instant success. Its regular attendees include Cherie Blair and the partner of the Irish Taoiseach, Celia Larkin.

However, that X-factor of Irish talent, the original who makes it without a background in formal education, is to be plentifully met with in England also. For example, Vince Power, the owner of the Mean Fiddler organisation, has become – as was said of the archetypical Kerry farmer – outstanding in his own field. That is to say, he runs most of Britain's major outdoor festivals. Apart from his famous Mean Fiddler establishment itself, Power, who came to London from Waterford at the age of sixteen, runs several other musical venues in London and elsewhere, and has trained up his children to help him manage his multi-million-pound empire by beginning the same way he did, picking up empty beer glasses in the Mean Fiddler.

Power is one of that rare breed who proved himself both a jack of all trades and a master of them. While he worked in the demolition business in the mid-sixties, he spent his spare time restoring and dealing in second-hand furniture, and ended up with ten furniture shops. Furniture and demolition would not at first sight appear to go hand in hand as business ventures, but Power discovered that the people who moved out of the houses he was demolishing tended to leave old furniture behind them. From repairing and selling this, he traded up to running a string of outlets for the sale of new furniture. Then, in 1980, his interest in country music led him to open the Mean Fiddler. From country he branched out to putting on Irish acts like Christy Moore, Moving Hearts, and the Pogues, and country rock acts like Jason and the Scorchers and Los Lobos. He became involved in the Reading Festival, and, indeed, all his other outdoor venues, because of his philosophy of 'keeping on, pushing out, and taking a risk'. In January 2001 Power launched a reverse takeover bid of his parent company which reportedly earned him £26 million. Power describes himself as single-minded, stubborn and disciplined, and even though he has reared his family in England and lived there for thirty-three years, he still regards Ireland as his home and among other acquisitions has bought Tramore racecourse. However, he acknowledges that it's not realistic for him to go back, given his British-based business interests.

Such indications of achievement by the Irish in England tend to make the idea that the Irish community could also suffer from serious discrimination seem far-fetched. Yet, if one decodes the conversation of one of the achievers, the outlines of difficulties soon appear. For example, Mary Clancy is one of the most prominent women in the Irish community. A director of the family building firm that now employs 1,400 people, she is stylish and also one of the wealthiest, and the most involved in helping out with the 'problem business'. Her father was in his twenties when he came over during the 1950s and got a job in British Oxygen. He took sub-contracting work after his day job was over, and finally expanded so that he could give up British Oxygen. Says Clancy:

> He was a man of great zest, 'very into the Irish music'. He played golf and was interested in everything. I remember a lot of Irish resented that sort of thing. In fact I wasn't that involved with the Irish or their charities, or their problems. But one day a neighbour of my mother's, in Lahinch, County Clare, where we have a house, rang me up and started talking about the problems of young kids over here, drugs, prostitution, etc. He asked me to go to dinner that night in Paul McGuinness's house.[27]

Mary didn't know who Paul McGuinness was, and her caller, Des Fitzgerald, had to tell her that he was the manager of U2. Fitzgerald had been to a dinner in Dublin a little earlier, at which the prominent Dublin socialite and charitable fund-raiser Norma Smurfit had lectured him on what was befalling young Irish people in London. Like a snooker ball impacting on the other balls on the table, the energy of the Smurfit lecture began to take effect and McGuinness had drawn a selection of the beautiful people to his Notting Hill Gate home. For most of the evening, Mary wondered what she was doing in such company. Speaking of the evening, and of another similar occasion, she made a very significant point which goes to the root of Irish insecurities in Britain.

Mary had also had an invitation from Tony O'Reilly, the world's best known Irish businessman, to a fund-raising dinner at the Dorchester Hotel for his Ireland Fund. A former Irish rugby international, and a British and Irish Lion, O'Reilly admires Britain and the British, describing them to me once as 'the soundest people on earth'. His advice to those who would emulate his success is 'dress British, talk Irish – and think Jewish.' His meteoric rise to the very top of corporate America, and his subsequent development of private worldwide business interests, began when, as General Manager of the Irish Dairy Board, his London reputation caused him to be head-hunted by the Heinz Corporation of America. He both made a success of the post and built up a personal media empire. O'Reilly's company owns newspapers, Internet, broadcasting, magazine, telephony, multi-channel TV, and commercial printing interests, as well as newspapers and magazines in a variety of countries: Australia, the United Kingdom, Ireland, New Zealand, South Africa, Portugal and Mexico. In London, he controls the *Independent* Newspaper, in New Zealand, the Wilson Hartnell Group, and in South Africa, the Argus papers. In Australia he controls the APN. His group has assets of 1.8 billion and a turnover of IR£900,000 million. O'Reilly is viewed with a degree of reserve by Irish Nationalists and by people involved in the Peace Process, because of his ownership of the *Sunday Independent*, which has constantly denigrated the Nationalist position, and has consistently attacked architects of the Peace Process like John Hume (to a degree that as a result of Irish/American pressures, O'Reilly finally oversaw the holding of a lunch in the *Independent* offices to which Hume was invited, and a truce declared). Moreover, he has been criticised for not taking a more upfront position in the Irish/American lobby, which finally helped to broker the Peace Process, as Irish American tycoons like Chuck Feeney or Bill Flynn have done. His Ireland Funds have been scornfully described as nothing more than gigantic worldwide PR operations for O'Reilly. On the credit side, however, it must be recognised that O'Reilly's activities, both through his personal success and his fund-raising, have raised the profile of the Irish throughout the world. I have encountered young businessmen from Dublin to Sydney and Sydney to San Francisco who look to him for inspiration when founding their various charities and dining clubs.

However, despite this clear evidence of Anglophile inclination on O'Reilly's part, Mary Clancy was extremely 'iffy' about his Ireland Fund Project. As she told me, she is on record as saying at that stage:

> and it has always been thus, England has always been viewed as the enemy. You can go out to America and fund-raise. Everyone there wants to be Irish for a day. Over here, people are making their living getting by on a day-to-day basis, to a certain extent only with the full consent of the British public. You don't actually go around biting the hand that feeds you, which was always the problem about setting up something as 'shouting about yourself' as the Ireland Fund.
>
> I was very unsure about getting involved, about the political ramifications, where the money was going to go. But five years on, I have grown up to the fact that what Tony O'Reilly has done is raise the profile of the Irish abroad, whether it be in England or America. And it's not the stage Irish, it's the committed, intelligent, business Irish, the cultured Irish, the Irish people didn't know about. It also happened on a historical basis – suddenly it's good to be Irish and it's fashionable to be young and Irish. So, in one way you can look at £150.00 a head and say 'they'd be better off staying at home and giving the money away', but the reality is it's about profile. At that dinner, there were a lot of people who were not Irish, and Tony had been attempting to network with those people so that they have a perception of the Irish as not holding meetings in pubs, but meeting people of other nations at the same level, moving across barriers.[28]

And that is the significant point Mary made about Irish insecurity. Those comments speak volumes for the difference in the attitudes between the Irish in Britain and in America. No Irishwoman in America at Mary Clancy's level would think of the American public as 'allowing them to get by on a daily basis'. This approach is buried with the memory of American nativist hostility to the Irish. In America, being Irish is now something to be unambiguously proud of.

In England Mary Clancy has achieved the supreme accolade amongst the Irish. People tell you that 'Mary is sound.' To be deemed a 'sound' man or woman is the ultimate Irish character reference. She has presence; classical wide-cheekboned Irish features, topped by red hair, create a Maureen O'Hara-style image. Moreover, as indicated, she is the epitome of the modern successful Irish businesswoman. However, if her experience of British society led her to the kind of reservations indicated about getting involved publicly in Irish affairs, even with someone of Tony O'Reilly's impeccable Anglophile credentials (he received a knighthood in 2001), the pressures to keep one's head under the parapet on a building site or factory floor, where one's British co-workers take their opinions from the *Mirror* and the *Sun*, can well be imagined.

Mary overcame her reservations and went on to invest her fund-raising activities with an energy and professionalism modelled on Jewish lines. She became Chair of the Irish Youth Foundation, and has helped to raise badly needed money for Irish charities such as Safe Start, the Irish Chaplaincy, the Piccadilly Advice Centre and other meritorious groups. The Irish Youth Foundation has become almost as important as the official Government welfare organisation DION, and routinely runs enormously successful gala fund-raising occasions, at which individual donors, like Michael Smurfit, have given sums of £250,000.

Nevertheless, unlike in America, an attitude towards Irish emigrants in the UK persists whereby they are regarded as being in Britain only on sufferance and they are lucky to be allowed to have jobs. This patronising attitude overlooks the fact that Irish workers, be it at pick and shovel or professional level, have made an invaluable contribution to the British economy, not because of kind-heartedness on the part of the great British public, but because they either did what the British did not want to do, or performed necessary tasks better than their competitors.

On the other hand, their own leaders often told them that they should not organise, except in the service of Mother Church. To do so for other purposes could, and probably would, be displeasing to Mother England. Indeed, as late as the early stages of the compilation of this book, it was official Irish governmental policy that the Irish in Britain should not be encouraged to organise a lobby on Northern Ireland, on the grounds that it would make bipartisanship impossible in the House of Commons.

This of course is nonsense. A powerful Irish lobby, as American experience has shown, attracts bipartisan respect. Both Democrats and Republicans – even Republicans as ardently pro-Thatcher as Ronald Reagan – have shown themselves mindful of Irish American wishes. However, as we shall see, by the end of the century there were significant developments amongst the Irish community, both at parliamentary and grass-roots level, aimed at tackling some of the disabilities the Irish suffer from. One involved MPs who set up the All-Party Irish in Britain Parliamentary Group at Westminster. Another was the holding of the Community Futures Conference in London, which, for the first time ever, brought together representatives of black, Irish and minority ethnic communities in Britain to tackle inequality on a national basis. A third was the emergence, on the initiative of a dynamic young Irishwoman, Norah Casey of the *Irish Post*, of the Irish faction in the London Mayoral Election of May 2000 (see below).

Another significant Irish influence in Britain, as readers will have deduced from the frequent references to the publication in these pages, is the *Irish Post* newspaper, founded in February, 1970 by Brendan MacLua. The paper was one of the Irish community's portals to empowerment. It played a vital role in giving the Irish not alone a voice but a centre to group around in the bad years which followed the Tories coming to power. The Clare-born MacLua who, like most of the best Irish journalists of the era, once wrote for the *Irish Press* group, when dealing with the Irish community in Britain, spoke with a compassion, knowledge, and a passion, which made him one of the best after-dinner speakers I have ever heard. Once, at a dinner organised by some friends in his honour in Dublin, I heard him lecture a fashionable audience on the significance of the fact that that year's top Irish dancing competition in Dublin had been won by a black girl of Irish ancestry from London.

In those pre-*Riverdance* days most of those present would have considered it almost as unfashionable to be associated with Irish dancing as with the IRA, but MacLua held them in thrall as he developed his theme of the reservoir of Irish talent and accomplishment, deserving of respect, but lying unsuccoured and unrecognised across the Irish Sea. He dismissed his, and the paper's role, with a self-deprecating understatement: 'We lived with the issues.' But the Irish tycoon Michael Smurfit, son of an English father and an Irish mother, paid the *Post* the supreme accolade by taking it over, as he did also its sister publication in New York, Niall O'Dowd's *Irish Voice*. In both cases, while retaining a healthy interest in the bottom line, Smurfit guaranteed the publications' continued success by recognising that, as with a motor car, certain competing elements are essential. Commercial and editorial inputs, like oil and water, are both needed, but have to be kept separate.

The Chief Executive of Smurfit Media UK, whose activity in the London Mayoral Election has been mentioned above, and Editor-in-Chief of the *Irish Post*, is Norah Casey, a 40-year-old, former nurse who emigrated from Ireland when she was seventeen. She left nursing for a career first in the nurses union, then in medical journalism with the *Nursing Standard*, moving on through both executive and broadcasting activities to become one of the best known figures in the London Irish Community before being headhunted by the Smurfit organisation. She built on the paper's existing readership by a highly successful re-vamp, in March 2000, aimed at a younger audience which nowadays is apt to be as concerned with opportunities for buying property in Dublin as with GAA or Irish dancing results. Casey brought both journalistic and political clout together during the London mayoral election campaign won by Ken Livingstone. On its front page the paper's headline proclaimed 'The Irish can decide mayoral election'. But, in addition, in a ground-breaking, Irish-American style, demonstration of heads above the parapet, she chaired a meeting between representatives of the Irish community and the candidates in the Camden Irish Centre to assess their commitment to Irish issues across a broad range, health, education, housing, the encouragement of Irish culture, as well as problems stemming from Northern Ireland. Predictably Livingstone's mastery of detail in all these areas made him the star of the night. Some of the other candidates did not even know what the stop-and-search issue involved, for example.

To the Irish community, Livingstone's differences with Margaret Thatcher and Tony Blair, are almost an irrelevancy. He stands in that line of Labour representatives – Bernie Grant, the MP who died not long before Livingstone was elected, was another – who went far beyond the line of duty in aiding their Irish constitutents. Brendan MacLua assessed Livingstone's contribution to me as follows:

> Ken Livingstone (between 1981 and 86) did more for the Irish in London, including giving dignity and financial aid, than did all *Dublin governments combined for the Irish worldwide during sixty five years* (The reference is to the years between the founding of the Irish State and Mrs Thatcher's destruction of the Greater London Council in 1986, author).

He cared more than did any Taoiseach for the Irish abroad and he was ahead of all in the Peace Process. Thatcher downed him because of Ireland and like the Phoenix he has risen again.

Livingstone's critics would dismiss that tribute as hyperbole. But, as should by now have emerged from these pages, the 'catalogue of neglect' of Irish emigrants by their own country and the amazing swing in the fortunes of the Irish both at home and abroad in a period of some fifteen years, are symbolised by the need for Livingstone's contribution, the impact it made, and the fact that today's London Irish have become powerful enough to invite him, and his rival candidates, to a pre-election meeting to give an account of himself.

THE IRISH CHAPLAINCY GROUP IN LONDON

I have been visiting the United Kingdom and writing about Anglo-Irish affairs for over forty years. Most of my books have been published by London publishers, including one that reviewers have been kind enough to describe as 'the definitive work on the IRA', which I dedicated to an Englishman! However, the only thing that my visits and researches have taught me with certainty is that the more one learns the more there is still to learn. Taking a broad canvas like 'the Irish in Britain', one must be aware a) just how broad it is, and b) how many shades of light and darkness, how many brushstrokes one will encounter: for every view there is a counter-view, for every failure a success, for every heartbreak a triumph. All make up something of the mosaic. All are authentic. Individually, all of them can be misleading.

No writer can hope to escape entirely from the charge of giving either a selective or an unrepresentative view. For the purposes of this book, however, I was fortunate to have the benefit of speaking not only to a great variety of individuals, but to a number of groups representative of age, gender, and class, brought together in what the market researchers rather grandly term 'focus groups' by organisations such as the Irish Chaplaincy in London. The existence of the Chaplaincy, incidentally, relates to a major difficulty once encountered by the Irish: the culture clash between English-born and ordained priests, and first-generation Irish emigrants. The tensions between the two led to the Irish hierarchy setting up the Chaplaincy which has flourished in the UK, and elsewhere in the world, since the 1950s. It is one of the better manifestations of the Irish Church, and a real contribution to the diaspora.

The London Chaplaincy group included two teachers, one of them a former business executive; a woman who ran a big haulage operation, and whose sons were Oxford graduates; a man who worked with the mentally handicapped; a father and son who ran a big construction business; a number of women who had become active in the caring field after rearing families; a psychotherapist; a chaplain who dealt with Irish prisoners; a woman professional photographer; a young man who had fallen victim to the Prevention of Terrorism

Act; and a senior activist with the Federation of Irish Societies.[29] A property developer and a consultant surgeon sat in on the second session.

I subsequently found that, like the observations of the two journalists, McEntee and Hennigan, the points they made were very largely applicable to the country as a whole. Such differences as I encountered were, generally speaking, those of degree rather than kind. One point which struck me forcibly, albeit in the manner of the Sherlock Holmes story wherein the point was that the dog did *not* bark, was how infrequently the Church was mentioned, save as something whose influence had to be shaken off. I found this particularly intriguing because our discussions took place on Church property in the presence of clerics and nuns who were obviously popular and well respected. The regard, however, had been earned on an individual basis. I came across this phenomenon several times subsequently. Individual priests and nuns – like the legendary Father Bobby Gilmore, whose work for emigrants I also encountered in New York and in Jamaica; or Sister Sarah who was once stigmatised by the Home Office as a 'subversive' because of her work for Irish prisoners – were mentioned spontaneously and with great affection, but awe towards Mother Church had ebbed at almost the same rate as for the other colonial power which once shaped Irish experience, Mother England.

What follows is a cross-section of the Chaplaincy groups' observations and experiences.

Brendan, who had done well in the building industry, had left a small town, Balla in County Mayo in the west of Ireland, with his mother, in 1954 at the age of sixteen: 'It was the last resort, coming to the land of the enemy.' They were initially the only two passengers aboard the train, but by the time it had crossed the county boundary it was packed. It was Brendan's first train journey, and the first time that he had seen the sea, or been on a boat. He remembered that everyone was sick and that his mother looked 'years older' when they arrived from Holyhead at Euston, which he found 'the biggest anti-climax of my life'. The station appeared broken down, the people shabby and ghostly. Emissaries from the Legion of Mary were meeting the train to save the girls from pimps. Brendan was lucky: he had a sister in London who gave him his first English breakfast, a fried egg on toast, and brought him to an apprenticeship with an electrician. That was when one saw signs everywhere reading either 'No Irish need apply' or 'No dogs, Irish or blacks', but Brendan remembered the early days with some affection. He had left a thatched house with no sanitation, but 'the maligned English landlady shared her bathroom, let you watch telly and gave you a good Sunday dinner. It was better than many an Irish landlord.' Brendan was to do well in the building industry.

After he had spoken, a general discussion took place which reminded me of peeling onion skins. As fresh layers were revealed, these were sometimes accompanied by tears. Loneliness was cited as a big factor amongst the older generation. Everyone agreed with the woman who remarked: 'The only place to go was the pub. I don't know how people came through what they did. The squalor, the drinking.'

The other place to go, particularly for women, was the Church. One woman told how she landed in London late one evening in 1952 to begin training as a nurse. She had no idea where the hospital was located, so she made for a church. It was locked and there was a thick fog. She could see nothing and she sat on the steps, weeping from tiredness and uncertainty. A man loomed up out of the fog and offered to help: 'I told him to hop off. But he said, "No dear – I'm blind", and he did help me.'

The men were inclined to talk about the advantages which 'the building' offered, especially to young unskilled men. It gave them a start, kept them on the straight and narrow. However, very marked differences in perceptions began to appear, particularly as between men and women. A Mayo woman began talking about her early days in London: she had run away from home, initially with her boyfriend, but after a year came home with him to family forgiveness and a big wedding in her native Claremorris. Back in England, and seven children later, she faced the fact that her husband was alcoholic, and put the children in a convent. The shock therapy worked for a time: her husband gave up drink and an eighth child arrived. She worked as a cleaner to support the children, and her husband reverted to drink. She joined Al-Anon and worked at a variety of jobs, during which a ninth child arrived. Her husband died at the age of fifty-one. Though she is married now and is seemingly happy, her experiences left her with a feeling of deprivation. 'Al-Anon helped me to cope, to put up with things like people mimicking my accent, but I never had a chance of immersing myself in my own culture. I love Ireland, but I have lost something.'

The women agreed that, apart from the honed down nature of an existence devoted to supporting children with either a dysfunctional husband or no partner at all, another shared difficulty was the necessity they found to drop their Irish identity. 'When we came over, it was "No Irish. No Blacks. No dogs." When they heard your accent . . . So you soon got an English accent.'

Mention of drink also provided a trigger. We talked about characters who drank themselves into the gutter. 'They used to earn £600 a week as labourers during the Thatcher boom years. There was a great deal of drinking and domestic violence. A lot of marriages broke up. Fellows ended up on their own with nothing.' The psychotherapist remarked on the high incidence of repressed sexuality she encountered amongst her Irish patients. This characteristic, as we shall see, had a horrific impact on the AIDS issue.

Practices in the building industry contributed to both the drinking and the ending up with nothing. One of the women observed: 'In the fifties and the early sixties, there weren't that many Irish pubs, but now most of the landlords are Irish. They keep the young fellows up until two or three in the morning drinking. Then they can't get up for their work and they lose their jobs, and start going on the skids. The Irish landlords sometimes won't cash their cheques until late at night, when the young fellows will have rung up a big slate. Then on top of that, they'll stop 4 per cent out of the cheque for cashing it.' Loneliness was continuously cited as a cause of drink: 'The only place they had to go was the pub, I don't know how the men came through it.' Many of them didn't, of course.

The women were particularly bitter about 'the lump' system, whereby subcontractors took pieces of large construction projects and then hired workers on a cash-in-hand basis. Most of these 'subbies' were Irish, and the women stigmatised them as being 'the ruination of the Irish'. The money-in-hand system meant no tax was paid, and the men didn't 'put up any stamps'. When one woman told me that her husband was left without entitlement to a pension after a lifetime in the building industry, there was a general agreement that 'not one man in fifty lived to draw the pension' because of the lump. Those were the 'warm Paddy' days, when the joke, and custom, on building sites was that the best way to keep out the cold was to ensure that the Irish labourer sweated. It was a time of 'long distance men', a legendary breed of Irish construction worker who travelled all over the United Kingdom, generally living on not much more than a pub diet of alcohol and Scotch eggs, in equally unappetising digs, performing prodigies of skill and effort – until their strength gave out. In their early days in England, the women recalled, some Irish builders went out of their way to employ Connemara men because, coming from Irish-speaking districts, they had no English and were easier to bamboozle.

This sort of anecdote obviously threw up as many complaints against bad Irish employers as it did against examples of anti-Irish prejudice on the part of English people – but what about an obvious source of redress against both sets of evils, in which the Irish have traditionally played an important role, the trade union movement? There seemed to be very mixed feelings about unions. Some criticised them for their authoritarian character: 'I remember the union organisers coming on the site saying "Join or else." If you didn't join, you'd be out of a job all over the borough.'

Another version of job loss came from the building contractor who gave chapter and verse of how he lost contracts through Orangeism: 'When my tender went in the brethren gave a copy to a rival company, run by an Orangeman. He hadn't even sent in a tender originally. We were expected to get the job, but he was able to study our bid and undercut it just that tiny little bit to make it look good, and he got the job. That sort of thing happened a good deal, particularly under Major.' That 'sort of thing' would have been the standard pattern in Northern Ireland at one time, but I was surprised to find it a factor in London. However, I was assured that, despite all the very evident strengths of the Irish in the construction industry, such influences could not be overlooked.

Everyone agreed that political Irish prisoners got a very bad time. Subject to abuse from warders and inmates, they were generally denied the prison jobs, scrubbing, working in kitchens, etc. They were kept isolated within the prison system, and their families were subject to the practice of 'ghosting', whereby they would turn up to visit a prisoner, only to find that he had been moved to some other jail. This effectively meant that a family which had come from Ireland for the visit to, say, Brixton, would not have the resources to travel on to Durham or some such place.

A frequently voiced suggestion was that the Irish should get organised 'the way they were in America'. Various reasons were given as to why this had not happened. The predominant one was that in America there was no difficulty about being both Irish and American, but that in England, given latent prejudice and the actively malign effect of the Troubles, this was very often impossible. 'In your heart, you're Irish. You can't be English as well,' I was told. The authoritarianism of Irish society was cited, as was the rigorousness of figures such as the Irish ganger or the Irish matron. The support system for the Irish was the family and the Church. Neither encouraged political activity. There was a tendency to look back: money was sent back to Ireland, visits were made back to Ireland; but nothing seemed to have come over by way of support or leadership from Dublin. Several times I was told that the Jewish diaspora was far better organised.

What about the British Labour Party, to whose tradition Irishmen like the Chartist, Fergus O'Connor, contributed so much? After our Chaplaincy sessions concluded, I put this question to a former Labour MP, Michael Maguire. Maguire worked in the mines at St Helens, outside Manchester, in the late 1940s. His parents had come over from Ireland in 1928 when he was a baby of four or five months old. He represented Macclesfield as an MP from 1964 to 1987 when he was de-selected, a victim of the divisions in the Labour movement over Arthur Scargill and the miners' strike. He had been in favour of a ballot. On the general question of the Irish issue in British politics where Labour was concerned, Maguire's verdict was:

> You didn't question the Irish issue. Even though we were Labour, you have to remember that Labour was never elected by England. It got the votes in Wales and Scotland and the Party contained just as many bigoted Orangemen as did the Tories. There was always an anti-Catholic vein, particularly in Scotland. [The system of trade union bloc voting in the Labour Party meant that the Scottish trade unions, which tended to be Presbyterian and to identify with their co-religionists in Northern Ireland, gave this element particular 'clout' in the Labour Party]. Then the Irish declared a Republic and the whole anti-partition campaign of the 1949-early 50s period helped to heighten Irish consciousness. But there was a bit of backlash to the Declaration of the Republic [in 1949]. The Declaration of the Republic was seen as anti-British, and anti-Monarchical. People were keen to point out to you that the Irish had free entry to England. We should have been more grateful for these sort of privileges. People just generally didn't know very much about Ireland. Remember there was this convention whereby Northern Ireland wasn't discussed at Westminster because the issue was supposed to be dealt with solely by Stormont. Bernadette [Devlin] upset that apple cart.

One of the more interesting points brought up at the group was the observation by the psychologist who remarked that she found that shame was a major cause in people's failure to become articulate politically. 'People felt that they had failed in having to go to England. They told themselves they were only going to stay for two years at most. They didn't want to mix with the ghetto Irish, who were perceived as being working class, heavily Roman Catholic and into the GAA [Gaelic Athletic Association – see page 179]. The more up-market Irish Club had a good reputation around the sixties, but it's not much respected now. A fine building was turned into nothing but a drinking club. There wasn't much leadership anywhere. I know an Irish Cabinet Minister who was approached to take an interest in the emigrants, and all he said was, "Let them go, they'll come back with money."'

One spin-off of this attitude is that the Irish tended not to go home 'unless you were a big success, and had money'. There was a lot of false pride. One woman told me that when she went home, her husband warned her 'not to let the neighbours know that she was going out to work'. Another difficulty in getting home was the level of airfares. There was a good deal of criticism of the Irish national airline, Aer Lingus, which over the years was regarded as having overcharged the Irish community: 'They'd put the fares up whenever there was a big holiday. British Midland was far better, and then Ryanair came along and really put manners on them.'

There was a big gap between those who wanted 'political activity' and those who wished to get involved in Irish cultural and social affairs. On top of this there was a degree of class barrier. The tendency of the middle class and the grass-roots not to mix was accentuated by virtue of the fact that the Irish in England, and particularly in London, did not have a great tradition of uniting on political issues, as in America. Several times, I was given anecdotes of what happened 'the morning after a bomb'. (As we will see later, part of this reaction depended on which city the bomb went off in.) 'My husband was picked up in a pub. He wasn't connected with anything. Nor my son, but he was picked up too. They got out eventually, but the neighbours said, "There's no smoke without fire."'

Although she was not a member of the London focus group, I feel I should digress here to give the experiences of one 65-year-old woman who gave me a stark account of what the 'no smoke without fire' syndrome had meant to her life. Ironically, this occurred in Manchester, where the Irish have one of the best relationships with the host community of any English city. The woman was working in a sewing factory when the Troubles broke out, and 'Bernadette was going well' (Bernadette Devlin). One day, the manager sent for her, and said: 'You're a good worker, but I feel it's my duty to make life as unpleasant for you as possible.' There followed 'five years of hell'. She got obscene phone calls and letters 'from all over', including the National Front, threatening to 'burn her out'. One day, a 'red-haired Orangeman' came to where she was working and spat on the floor. On another occasion, she was called into the manager's office. She said: 'He had everything on display, and he said, "Do something with that. It's all the Irish are good for."' Her children were young and her husband had disappeared; her wages were £70 a month;

the manager told her that she'd have a good rise if she came to work on Sunday for sex. 'I was very isolated. The pressures were mighty.' But she did not succumb to them. She kept her pride, her job, and, without 'going to the works on Sunday', reared her family successfully.

The indiscriminate use of the Prevention of Terrorism Act was constantly mentioned by the group: 'The police come to your place of work, or they cordon off your digs with yellow tape while they search the place. People ask what's going on, and you find yourself changing the digs, or losing the job, or both.' As McEntee's experience of bringing a friend to visit a jailed IRA man illustrated, the police had a certain psychological template in mind when they seized people for interrogation. One priest, who affected a beard and civilian clothing, told me after I had spoken to the group that he found himself stopped almost every time he got off the plane from Dublin, but 'I carried my passport and I was a priest. Generally they respect the calling. But what happens if you are a working-class young fellow who is not a priest ... I remember being scared shitless one night when I was put up against a wall by twenty-four cops with Uzis. It was scary.'

A ten-year study published in 1994[30] drew up a picture of the sort of person most likely to fall foul of the Act:

- A person who carries political books with papers
- A student
- A person whose family lives in a nationalist area of Northern Ireland
- A person who has a criminal record
- A person who has had contact with Sinn Fein
- Anyone who questions the authority of the examining officer

Persons of this profile, and some others, made up a total of almost 7,000 people detained under the Act, but of these, only three or four persons a year on average 'received a significant custodial sentence'.[31]

During our talks there was criticism of the Irish for being racist in their attitude towards blacks, but then the discussion led on to another frequently met complaint: the enforced 'invisibility' of the Irish. 'The thing about the poor blacks is they can't change their skin. They stand out. But we're white, and we can change our accent. And that's why you get people changing their names, or, if they don't change, they'll deny their Irishness.' It was reckoned that only one Irishman in ten did not assimilate in the first generation. By way of reaction, it was pointed out, some Irish go 'over the top', everything Irish is best. They won't come out of the ghetto.

EMPOWERMENT

The underlying issue which came up time and time again was empowerment, giving the Irish some method of bringing home their grievances to the governments of both Dublin and London. The specific issues most cited were: discrimination, particularly in the operation of the Prevention of Terrorism Act; and the question of including 'Irish' as an ethnic category in the census as a method of addressing discrimination in all its forms and tackling the AIDS menace. At the time of writing, it was almost impossible to quantify accurately the incidence of AIDS amongst the Irish community because 'Irish' was not included as a category in the census. However, this will not be the case in future census-taking because, as in other areas of Irish grievance, the Blair Government has shown itself willing to act. And why not? The Home Office Minister responsible for making the change, Michael O'Brien, is a second-generation Irishman.

The issue of empowerment involves not merely creating mechanisms in their host community to improve the lot of Irish emigrants, it also involves seeking the vote for Irish emigrants abroad. Although it is not the most burning issue, nor the one most likely to come speedily to fruition, it is a slow burner which may yet prove to be of the greatest long-term significance. For, as part of the Good Friday Agreement – and partially in recognition of the Irish American contribution to bringing it about – the importance of the diaspora was specifically acknowledged. Subsequently, the Irish Constitution was amended by referendum in 1998 to include the wording of the Agreement on Irish citizenship:

> It is the entitlement and birthright of every person born in the island of Ireland which includes its islands and seas, to be part of the Irish nation. This is also the entitlement of all persons otherwise qualified in accordance with law to be citizens of Ireland. Furthermore, the Irish nation cherishes its special affinity with people of Irish ancestry living abroad who share its cultural identity and heritage.[32]

Thus the sort of assertive activity which the 'votes for emigrants' betokens, though it closely parallels the rise of the Irish community in Britain, cannot be judged merely in UK terms alone. It has implications for the Irish in America, Canada, Australia and the Argentine, and for the Irish in Ireland. It arises because of increasing Irish prosperity and self-confidence, forces which in the Irish case would, one imagines, make for political conservatism. However, there is a view in decision-taking Dublin that an extension of the franchise to emigrants, of which there are such a huge number, could carry with it the danger of an injection of unstable radicalism into the Irish body politic. Hence, at a political level, the attitude towards conceding votes to emigrants has tended to be: 'Oh Lord, make me good – but not yet!'

However, in response to sustained lobbying efforts which will be described in more detail below, the 1997 General Election Manifesto of Fianna Fail, the largest Irish political party, included the following:

> Fianna Fail are committed to working out the necessary arrangements to give emigrants the right to vote in Dail, Presidential and European Parliamentary elections, and in

referendums. This can be done without amending the Constitution. Initially, those who have lived abroad for up to 10 years will be eligible. Our target is to have a voting system in place by the year 2000.

However, by February 2001, when this was revised, Fianna Fail had done nothing to implement the pledge. Nevertheless, the manifesto commitment is an indication of how far up the priority list the issue has moved in little more than a decade. It owes its rise to sport, the greatest single bonding issue between the Irish and the English, as anyone who has attended annual English racing festivals like Aintree or Cheltenham will readily agree. If sport does prove to be of lasting political significance to the Irish diaspora and the 'votes for emigrants' issue, in a very Irish paradox, it will have been partly due to an Englishman. In my lifetime, one of the two or three most popular figures in Ireland has been the Englishman Jack Charlton, who brought the hitherto largely unregarded Irish soccer team to the second stage of the knock-out competition of the 1990 World Cup, Italia 90.

One of the great features of the competition was the Irish encounter with Italian culture, and for one young man it served to crystallise all his thoughts on the nature of being Irish, its opportunities and its obligations to the emigrants. David Reynolds grew up a stone's throw from where I live in a well-respected middle-class surrounding. His father Michael, and his mother Nilah, were respectively Director of the Irish Confederation of Building Industries and an art connoisseur. David for a time went into the booming property business of the 1980s but by 1990 he had tired of its crassness and the miseries it brought in its wake, and was ready for a fresh enthusiasm. It dawned on him in Rome, in St Peter's Square:

there were all these Irish people from all over the world. I remember groups of Irish from obscure American states, from every continent. There was this enormous groundswell of support and well-being. It occurred to me that no Irish government present or past ever really tapped into it or has ever, in my mind, really made an effort to maintain the bond, or to strengthen the bond. It's hard to put into words what I felt. There I was in St Peter's Square in the Vatican, the centre of the Catholic Church, with all these Irish people that have had to emigrate. And here they are coming back to this, to their Irishness, to support the national football team.

Also in '89/90 I remember this couple and they were getting on the Dublin/London flight and they were in their thirties. They weren't eighteen or nineteen, they were in their early thirties, and they were both bawling their eyes out. It was really strange, very emotional. I wanted to go up to them and say: 'You don't have to go, here's your job, your money.' People in their thirties were being forced to emigrate, it was just wrong.[33]

David decided that the best way of doing something about righting this wrong was to join Glor na Deorai, the Irish votes for emigrants group which had been in existence for some two years previously and was particularly active in both England and America. He seeks the right to vote for a fixed amount of years after leaving Ireland, preferably for a period of about twenty years. He points out, correctly, that the majority of the world's democratic states extend their voting rights to the emigrants. Though there is sharp division on the issue, the surveys commissioned by Glor na Deorai show that, as one would expect with a politically conservative race like the Irish, that the emigrants would tend to vote along traditional lines, very much as their families did. Helped in large measure by the dynamism which David Reynolds brought to the movement, Glor na Deorai succeeded in getting a private member's bill introduced in the Dail in 1991, which was defeated by only 66 votes to 62. This would have given votes to Irish emigrants for fifteen years after becoming non-residents. So far, the most concrete offer the movement has secured is an official governmental proposal to give the emigrants representation in the Senate. As this body, effectively speaking, is about one-tenth as useful as the House of Lords, Reynolds and his friends turned it down – but they intend to keep campaigning. Reynolds says:

> Governments are made up of Irish people – so it is not wanting to have a voice against the Government. It is wanting a voice in the Government and within the democratic process. The movement is not anti-government because the Government is Irish, and we are Irish. If half the country stays on, so the other half will have to emigrate, they can't expect for themselves to get away with it . . . We have a way of not facing up to reality . . . Abortion, divorce, contraception, homosexuality . . . Irish failure to face up to emigration is worse than any of these things. We are all colluding in this together, whether we like it or, not . . . Sexual issues have had their share of attention. Now it's time to focus on the economy and emigration . . .

Reynolds did focus on the economy and ironically it may yet shift his focus from emigration. For the success of the Celtic Tiger has attracted him and some of his activist friends back to Ireland. But whether the Irish economy continues to boom or bust, the Irish will always be a travelling people with an interest in their homeland. The voting issue will not go away.

THE COMMUNITY FUTURES CONFERENCE AND THE ALL-PARTY IRISH PARLIAMENTARY GROUP

The Community Futures Conference and the All-Party Irish Parliamentary Group referred to earlier are specifically aimed at achieving a precise picture of the nature and extent of discrimination, with a view to eradicating both. These sorts of groups tend to have an overlap of membership, a problem identified by someone prominent in both groups: John McDonnell, the Labour MP for Hayes and Harlington, a second-generation Irishman. While admitting that they were in a sense 'preaching to the converted', he stressed the importance of 'getting a programme of action and approaching government with it – and by "approach" I mean hound them'. The Conference, in November 1998, was attended by over a hundred delegates from a variety of different groups and agencies. Addressing it, Rabbi Julia Neuberger, Chief Executive of the King's Fund, a charity which researches health problems, described the similarities in patterns of deprivation between the Irish and the blacks: 'Like the black community, Irish people had worse health and accident rates than the general white population. Like the black community, they were more likely to be wrongly diagnosed by a doctor.' Elaborating on this point, Baroness Helena Kennedy QC, who has acted on behalf of many of the wrongly convicted Irish prisoners, made a significant point. The Home Office statistics on conviction rates showed little difference in sentencing between blacks and whites: 'But when Irish defendants were taken out of the white group, it made an incredible difference.' The Irish were much more likely to be imprisoned than other white people.

Obviously the people whom McDonnell wanted to hound are the MPs at Westminster, and he was one of a group of MPs elected to office in a small but potentially highly significant grouping, which came together on 2 December 1998. Its significance lay in the fact that it was an all-party grouping. Even Conservative MPs pledged support, and a vice-chairman position was left vacant for Sir Patrick Cormack, Conservative. The Chairman was Kevin McNamara, and McDonnell was appointed Secretary. The group also made a leap of faith which not every political observer might be inclined to share, in that its treasurership was allocated to the House of Lords! While judgement on performance must await the verdict of time, the group certainly began with an agenda which went to the root of the difficulties between the Irish and the host community. It agreed that the Commission for Racial Equality Report, *Discrimination against the Irish Community in Britain*, which has already been quoted from, would be its primary source material in an effort to tackle the Report's 'most striking finding', namely:

> the high levels of anti-Irish hostility routinely encountered by Irish people in Britain . . . experiences during the past 50 years recounted by interviewees reinforce the idea that anti-Irish racism is endemic in British society . . . all aspects of Irish people's lives are affected by racism, which carries the potential for discrimination. Particularly serious consequences may arise when state institutions are involved. For example, 25% of those interviewed reported negative responses from the police.

As indicated, the Group's first action was successfully to lobby the ministries responsible on the census question. The group has also pledged itself to further the interests of the Irish in areas such as housing, employment, training, social care, health and education. Housing is a particularly pressing concern. The 1991 census revealed the Irish have the lowest levels of home ownership compared to any of the main minority groups. The overall proportion of ownership is still well below the indigenous white population: 44 per cent Irish-born compared to 59 per cent. It further showed that the Irish were still more likely than any other minority community to live in privately rented, run-down accommodation, lacking in basic amenities:[34]

QUALITY OF HOUSING: LONDON 1991

	Irish-born	Other white	Black Caribbean
Lack/share baths W/C	3.6%	2.4%	1.6%
No central heating	22.2%	20.1%	14.2%
Not self-contained	5.2%	2.7%	2.4%
Source: OPCA 1991			

Not surprisingly in view of these statistics, a survey carried out the following year by Cara, the Irish Housing Association, amongst a number of emergency hostels, revealed the fact that the Irish comprised the largest percentage of the minority groups using the service. However, perhaps the most disturbing fact thrown up by these investigations was the statistic that although the Irish comprised between 25 and 50 per cent of those living in hostels, only 4 per cent of the housing accommodation allocated to such groups went to Irish people. In the housing area, as in many others, the 'invisibility' factor affecting the Irish created a large part of the problem.

One of the most respected activists in the housing field is Angela Birtell, born in Liverpool of an Irish mother, a former Labour councillor, and Housing and Welfare Officer at the London Irish Women's Centre. Her work in Camden confirmed her belief that Irish people suffered racism in the allocation of housing: 'It was a combination of ignorance and deliberate cost-cutting. But at the root, there was racism and discriminatory treatment of Irish people. I think that made me aware at the time of the need for Irish people to be pushing demands for Irish ethnicity to be recognised, to be more visible.'[35]

The increased visibility, and 'clout', signified by the foundation of the Irish lobby amongst Westminster parliamentarians, is one tangible sign that Birtell's ambitions may be approaching fruition. At the time of writing, some sixty MPs had expressed an interest in joining. Behind these signs of solidarity lies the electoral reality that, as we have seen, in the London mayoral elections in the year 2000 the Irish constituted a highly significant voting block.

AIDS, HOMOSEXUALITY AND DRUGS

Now let us turn to some of the other issues with which the new groupings and approaches will have to concern themselves. Literally, the most virulent one is that of AIDS and the interaction of the problem with the census ethnicity question. Where the Aids issue is concerned, it is, literally: ' . . . so easy to get fucked, in every sense of the word'. The speaker was Tim O'Keeffe, a former Roman Catholic priest, who had left the priesthood because he could not reconcile the call of celibacy with living with his male partner, and is now working as an AIDS counsellor amongst the Irish community in London.[36] O'Keeffe's work is highly spoken of, as is that of another Irish AIDS worker, the bearer of a famous name, Michael Collins, a grand-nephew of the Irish revolutionary hero Michael Collins, who gave up the opportunity of working in his father's lucrative Cork law practice to work amongst his stricken compatriots in London. Statistics were hard to come by, but there was a general awareness, as the AIDS scourge began to bite, that more Irish people were dying of AIDS in London than the official Irish statistics for all of the Republic. Accordingly, in 1988 O'Keeffe and Collins got together with a number of other Irish people, most of whom had lost a gay lover, to found Positively Irish Action on AIDS.

As one might expect, they found that the principal sources of AIDS were the drug users and gay men. Much of the Irish gay community lived chaotic, vulnerable lifestyles. Perhaps their original impulse to emigration was sexual exile, to get away from the stigma attached to coming out in a local rural community. This is a very real hazard. In his excellent memoir of working as a labourer in Scotland, *Farewell to Mayo*, Sean O'Ciarain, an intelligent, sensitive man, describes how he and a group of his fellow Irish workers behaved towards a young homosexual in post-war Scotland:

> I had never heard of the likes, neither had some of the others. One girl from Faulmore knew what he was, 'He is a nancy boy, that's what he is,' she said, 'a good thrashing that's what he needs.' 'What's a nancy boy?' someone asked. 'A nancy boy is a man that does be going after other men. Can't be bothered with the women at all.'
>
> The long and the short of it was we decided to give the man a lesson. That evening when he came up, five or six of us set about him. He did not fight back, but ran. We chased after him. We were not able to catch up with him, so we let the stones fly. They were hopping off his back as he went down the lane and us after him. After that he did not come back near the place again.[37]

Today, nearly fifty years later, one would not find such attitudes in urban centres, or amongst middle-class Irish. However, in rural Ireland attitudes have not changed very greatly. While I was writing this book a formerly well-liked figure in a Connemara village announced on local radio that he was gay. Local people, fearing that their children might contract AIDS, ostracised him and his windows were broken.

Another very widespread problem exists amongst drug users. The sufferer might have resorted to crime to feed a habit, and wound up on the run from the law in both Irish and English jurisdictions.

The sheer culture shock generated by AIDS is one of the most difficult side-effects of the disease to deal with amongst the Irish. Tim O'Keeffe found that one of the most harrowing circumstances he had to cope with was that of dealing with middle-aged or elderly Irish parents, of conservative Roman Catholic outlook, who suddenly had to cope with the reality of AIDS:

All they would have known was that their son would have been sharing a house with someone else. They'd think this was an economic arrangement, and wouldn't have a clue either that it was a gay relationship or that the son was HIV positive. The next thing you know, they'd have to confront the reality that their loved one was both dying and had AIDS. Maybe they'd come into the bedroom, or the hospital ward, and find the lover comforting their son, holding his hand. The older people were distraught at the idea of the neighbours finding out. There they were, worried about the neighbours and sin, and a gay man dying in the bed, needing comfort. So they were completely isolated, there was no sharing of grief, no one to tell them that it's all right to be angry.

He talked of one such case in which a young man from a Kerry village had died. Three years later, another boy from an address in the same village, only a few streets away, also died. Because of the curtain of silence, neither family knew of the other's existence. They could have helped each other, but there was no communication: 'If they went to their parish priest, he'd have talked in terms of sin.' Tim still writes to people whose sons have been dead nine or ten years, he find it gives him some hope and comfort, but he didn't hold out a great deal of comfort concerning the contemporary AIDS picture amongst the young, working-class Irish. He finds that 'the present-day scene' is about the same as when he first came to it: 'Still young people coming on line. The problem about gay pubs and drink is that it lessens the sense of danger. You go in and meet someone and bang.' By way of illustrating 'the bang' he told me the following story:

This young Irish lad had never had sex – until he went to this gay pub. At first he chickened out. Then he went back in and had a drink. He met a fellow in the pub who told him he had just had a test and that he was okay. He had no condom. They had sex and the lad developed a monumental flu within a few weeks. He tested positive and he was dead a year later.

The lack of condoms is not confined to the gay community. Tim also told the story of a student nurse who too was a virgin, lonely and uninitiated, when she was picked up in a pub after a few drinks. She had sex without a condom in her first few days of training – and had an abortion a couple of months later.

O'Keeffe would calculate the Irish gay and lesbian population in London as 'huge'. He says:

The biggest group amongst the gays is Irish, most of them sexual exiles. You get this picture of the Irish working on the buildings. But it's much more complex than that. It's very complex for the Irish themselves. They have to deal not alone with the AIDS and the drugs, but sin. Guilt can be helpful, it's a combination of truth sometimes, and a load of shite. But remorse and penance are good compared to paralysis. They're certainly better than the Tory absence of either, and better of course than cruelty or greed.

However, it means that there is very little one can offer to terminally ill people, apart from being with them. Though you find that the sacraments are very useful in dealing with those who are left. I'd carry a Mass kit, and I'd say Mass after a person had died, sometimes using stale bread. But it helped the parents to say that it was all right to be hurt and annoyed, and at the same time, to be thankful for life. The trouble is that the traditional Irish cultural tradition where sexuality is concerned makes kids very vulnerable. They come over here completely unaware of loneliness, of what enablement means. Unfamiliar with the idea of comfort, and, of course, completely unaware of the need to say: 'yes, I'm going to have sex,' and to take a condom with them. But girls feel that having a condom with them would stigmatise them as 'slappers', you know, a slut, 'the local bike'.

Irish culture has very good things about it, the need for consideration for other people, for example, but the facing up to sexuality was not one of their strengths. Like everything else concerning the Irish diaspora, one has to point out this attitude is changing.

Tim found that in his service, which is based in a South London drug centre (anonymity is observed, so that nobody living in the pleasant street, or patronising its bars and shops, is aware of the nature of the service provided by the 'Health Care Centre'), that half of the staff were Irish. So too, however, were half of the patients. Change has come too late for many.

THE PREVENTION OF TERRORISM ACT

One of the most perceptive, and experienced, observers of the Irish scene in Britain is the trade unionist, Gearoid O'Meachair, a guiding spirit in the Federation of Irish Societies. In February of 1996 he prepared a report on the Irish community which had this to say of the operation of the Prevention of Terrorism Act:

> Leaving aside such issues as raised by the cases of the Guildford Four and Birmingham Six, Home Office figures for sentenced foreign nationals for all criminal cases demonstrate that under English law 57.2% of Irish men under 30 are presented for sentencing, compared to 38.15% in Ireland . . . The Irish Community would not wish to stand in the way of any reasonable legislation which, within the bounds of European Rights would be of assistance in preventing terrorism. But the bombing of Canary Wharf shows again that the PTA [this bombing occurred during February, 1996, the month in which the report was written] does not prevent terrorism acts. Since its inception approximately 6,500 people in England, Scotland and Wales have been arrested and many, many thousands of others have been questioned and detained.[38]

However, as O'Meachair pointed out, the most telling point about the PTA is the manner in which it was clearly designed to intimidate the Irish community. Of all those arrested, 97 per cent were Irish, yet despite all the arrests only 3 per cent were finally charged: 'We are all under suspicion by virtue of our Irishness,' concluded O'Meachair.

In order to put a human face on statistics, let us examine the case of one of those who 'by virtue of his Irishness', found himself under suspicion. Sean Farry was thirty years of age when I interviewed him.[39] I was able to verify the truth of what he said, both through the Irish Chaplaincy service and because, over the years, his case had become known and had been taken up by a number of journalists and media figures, including Tara Holmes of the *Catholic Times*, Martin Collins of the *Irish Post*, the TV comedian Jeremy Hardy, and Billy Power of the Birmingham Six. As the *Catholic Times* said: 'It's no great gamble to protest Sean's innocence ... his case is well documented and few journalists now bother to employ carefully couched language.'[40]

His ordeal began in 1991, probably by accident – the PTA template which I mentioned earlier fits him. Farry was emigrating to find work in England, having completed his secondary school education in County Sligo. He had bought his ticket in advance but misjudged his arrival at Dun Laoghaire, so that he found the mailboat gates closing just as he got there. He still has that ticket as a souvenir of the event that changed his life. He returned to Dun Laoghaire the following day and bought another ticket for Holyhead. He thought vaguely that he would be starting 'a new life' and that he'd probably get a job with the help of his fiancée's brother, who lived in Nottingham. Despite being slightly apprehensive about the idea of emigration, he was on the whole exhilarated at the prospect that the streets of England might after all be paved with gold, and that he would strike it lucky. 'I didn't realise,' he said, 'that for every wonderful success, there are a hundred broken men.'

He was extremely lucky not to become one of the 'broken men' himself. When he landed at Holyhead, he was one of a group of passengers who were selected at random and asked by an official to fill out a disembarkation document. As he was filling it out, the official beckoned over 'two men in suits'. They asked him questions similar to those on the card, where he was going, what he worked at, etc. Then one of the men asked him would he mind coming with them while they checked out whether or not he was a 'wanted terrorist'. Sean dumurred, pointing out that his train was leaving, but he was told that if he did not come willingly, the Prevention of Terrorism Act would be invoked. He was placed in a room which he described as 'a high-tech cell. It was full of cameras and things.'

After about fifteen minutes, the two detectives returned and began questioning him. Like many immigrants, or people who have had a brush with the law, every detail of the first few hours in the new environment remained fresh in Sean's mind, even when more dramatic incidents which occurred later had blurred. The only difference between his initial interrogation and that of other interviewees to whom I have spoken was that, at points when he objected to the questioning, his interrogators would talk to each other in Welsh. They asked him about his religion, the Irish cause, terrorism and subversion. With his visions of a new life before him, Sean replied that he gave no thought to any of these matters. He didn't believe in women and children being murdered, but beyond that, he'd never given much though to Northern Ireland.

The men asked him if he had any Irish contacts, or friends in the Irish community in England. If he did come across anything bearing on the

Northern situation, would he ring them? He replied no, that he didn't want to get involved. He was told that it would be 'in his interests' to co-operate, that funds were available. Then the questioning switched to enquire: 'Would you do your citizen's duty?' He protested that of course he would, but the questioning grew more menacing, and he was warned that, 'Things could be made very difficult for you, Paddy. You're not at home now, Paddy. You'd be better off staying at home, Paddy.' Despite the menace, he was ultimately allowed to go, albeit with a warning that he'd be better off staying at home. Sean was to have considerable opportunities for testing the truth of that observation over the next five years or so.

He of course missed his first train, but was sitting in a subsequent one when one of his interrogators appeared, took his ticket from him and wrote a telephone number on it, saying, 'There you are Paddy, that could be in your interest.' Sean had given his sister's address in Cricklewood as his English home, but carried out his plan to go to Nottingham.

The day before St Patrick's Day, 16 March 1991, his nightmare began in earnest. It was afternoon, he was in a pub. 'Suddenly,' he said, 'there was this *Miami Vice* scene. There was a heli-spotter, cops, police cars, men with blackened faces.' The customers' IDs were checked. After his was examined, a policeman went to the phone, came back to him and said, 'Something's wrong. What are you doing for St Patrick's Day?' He was arrested and taken to a police station, separated from a number of others who had been rounded up also, strip searched, his belt and laces removed, and charged under the Prevention of Terrorism Act. He was told he could not contact anyone, and subjected to much the same type of questioning he'd encountered at Holyhead originally, except that this time he was told that there had been three men with a gun in the pub, and that he was going to stay in custody until the police found out who they were.

The fact that he had given his sister's address on the landing document, but had instead gone to Nottingham, was brought up, and it was put to him that 'life could be made easy for him' in England. Again he was asked did he agree with women and children being blown up, and told that there were funds available, if he knew anyone or anything. Ultimately, he was released without charge. This was the start of a Kafkaesque routine for him. Over a period of six months he moved three times, but there was no escape from the police, nor from the effects of the harassment: 'I lost a job after two days. Once the cops came around, I was a leper.'

Farry's experience, and that of thousands like him, sent a see page of fear, amounting almost to paranoia, throughout the Irish community. In part, this is what it was designed to do, to make people either disinclined to support militant republicanism, or willing to give information. In part, it was just bad and wastefully expensive police work, furthered by the IRA bombing campaign, the influence of a Tory Government and a vicious internecine 'turf war' between Scotland Yard and MI5. Scotland Yard has traditionally handled Irish politically motivated crime and, equally traditionally, has shown itself to be imbued with an 'ends justify the means' philosophy when it comes to securing convictions. This mind set was worsened with the ending of the Cold War when hundreds of now unemployed MI5 operatives were given something to do by being set to work on the IRA.

In my book *The Troubles*, I have described how, in Northern Ireland, the redeployment heightened tensions between MI5 and MI6, which traditionally handled overseas espionage and counter-insurgency.[41] The feuding greatly benefited the IRA as the two agencies' rivalry resulted in information not being pooled and energies being wastefully diverted. In the UK itself, where MI5 was traditionally the dominant domestic counter-insurgency force, the fight against IRA terrorism became one of the agency's principal justifications for existence. In the battle with Scotland Yard neither side was too scrupulous about the methods used. Thus, in the quest for IRA scalps, the PTA became an invaluable instrument for 'fitting up' suspects and making the figures for arrests look good.

Farry discovered, as did others in his situation, that strange Irishmen began joining their company in bars or at Irish occasions. There would be questions to him and his fiancée about political matters, terrorism, the IRA. Psychologically, the surreal atmosphere, the fear and paranoia gnawed at him. Economically, the harassment and lack of jobs began to tell in areas such as housing, relationships with the DHSS, and even with the Post Office. Then, a little over a year after the *Miami Vice* incident, he was arrested on a trumped-up criminal charge.

Earlier in 1992, in February, he had been arrested in the company of one of the strange Irishmen, a Cork man, with a taste for asking questions about matters political. He had been using a credit card given to him by his prospective brother-in-law. It was alleged that the card was stolen. By now, he had become used to being held in custody overnight. However, the nights suddenly got longer after a hold-up took place at a garage some quarter of a mile away from where he was sitting in a car, in the company of the inquisitive Cork man. The first that Farry knew about the hold-up was when he heard a bang at the back of the car, which he thinks was caused by someone bumping into it. The next thing he knew was that a man with a gun ran past him. He and the Cork man were arrested. The Cork man was released, but Farry was ultimately charged with two robberies: a burglary earlier in the year and that involving the running man. A bag with the takings from the robbery, some £900, had apparently been found near the car.

It ultimately turned out that Sean had been in hospital on the night of the first burglary. Nevertheless, Murphy's Law took its course, as it tended to do in such cases involving Irish people. He was remanded in custody until November 1992. During this period, he was found with a box of matches, which were deemed to be 'incendiary devices'. From then on, he was treated as a Special Security prisoner, strip searched, forced to sleep with the light on every night, and accompanied by armed police and dog patrols when going to court. He had to wear yellow fluorescent patches on his clothes. Warders would bang on his doors and shout obscenities at him. All his possessions were taken from him each night. Nevertheless, one day, a gun was 'found' in the prison. A story was put around that he was going to be 'sprung', and he was regarded as a 'Provo' before his case ever came to trial.

It would take too long to detail all the discrepancies in the evidence and statements brought against Farry. Suffice it to say that he felt his was a mini-Birmingham Six/Guildford Four trial. The atmosphere in the court was hostile and the judge would not allow Sean's medical evidence to go before the jury. Sean did not go in the witness box, but he remembers the prosecution's case taking 'a very long time. Mine seemed to take about three minutes.' The man with the gun whom he had seen run past him had outrun a pursuer who was a Territorial Army PE instructor. Sean had had spinal fusion in the Adelaide Hospital in Dublin, and could not have outrun anyone. The judge initially ordered that Sean's medical records be produced, but then said that in his professional opinion they would not aid the defence and they were not used. The pursued thief had short, black hair and a Nottingham accent. Sean had long, fair hair and an Irish accent. A picture of the running suspect went missing, and all that was produced in court was a blurred photocopy. A starting pistol found in Sean's flat was held to be the one used in the robbery, but this pistol was defective and could only be fired if one used two hands, one to move the chamber, the other to pull the trigger. The running man had been able to fire his gun with one hand. The fingerprints on a bag picked up near the scene of the robbery were not checked, and so on, and so on.

It all added up to a seven-year sentence for Sean. He was found guilty of two robberies and 'resisting arrest'. There followed a litany of jails: Lincoln, Nottingham, Long Lartin, Birmingham. He was attacked by prisoners and warders as 'an IRA man'. On one occasion, an Irishman serving a life sentence saved his life, when a posse of loyalist-minded prisoners came for him with knives. The 'lifer', a one-handed man, managed to slam a cell door in their faces, with his one hand. The 'lifer' also saved him from rape, and from drug pushers. At one prison, a warder shouted at him: 'Are you not dead yet Paddy? Do you want us to do it for you?' and pushed razor blades into the cell. He told Sean how to cut himself 'across for attention – long for out'. The warder then told other prisoners that Sean was a child killer and a rapist.

On top of these incidents he was constantly fined extra days or sometimes weeks for alleged breaches of prison regulations, which meant that his stay in jail was lengthened. Sean's mother died two weeks after he was released, but he wasn't allowed to leave the country to attend her funeral under the terms of his eventual release. Had it not been for the time penalties, he would have been free to go to Ireland. Initially, he was devastated psychologically, but when I met him, he was recovering with the help of counselling provided by the Irish Chaplaincy. He said: 'I didn't let them break me. I didn't give in and say I was guilty. You have to stick up for what you believe in. If I didn't do that I'd have gone under.' He kept writing letters to the papers until eventually his case was taken up by the *Irish Post* and the *Catholic Times*.

In 1998 he got married. A sympathetic Irish businessman who read about his case in the *Catholic Times* gave him a job in an information technology consultancy firm. At the time of writing he had become the father of a baby girl and was studying for an MBA degree. Friends have backed him in making a compensation claim which is currently winding its way through the courts. So he was one of the lucky ones – ultimately. He reckons, to judge from the people he met with in jail, that some two-thirds of the Irish PTA-type prisoners were 'fitted up'.

THE IRISH MIND SET

Sean's case is part of the fall-out from ancestral legacies which in our day include the PTA. The historian Nicholas Mansergh has described how the past lives on in the Irish mind in an impressionist form very different from the concrete perception of the English.[42] He wrote about a Tipperary farming neighbour of his who described to him in accurate detail how the Danes had built their intricate burial mounds. Impressed, Mansergh asked the farmer how he had come by such arcane lore. The farmer replied 'quite casually' that his grandfather had told him how the Danes built their mounds, having seen them build one nearby. In fact, the mound that the farmer described would have been built a thousand years before the grandfather was born.

Mansergh points out rightly that these contrasting, imaginative qualities of the Celt, coupled with history, have:

> Far-reaching implications ... responsible for much misunderstanding. If Anglo-Irish relations are to be viewed, as they must, in the light of those psychological differences which have accentuated so greatly their unhappy phases, then it is necessary to retrace one's steps to those early days when the Irish Saints first came over to convert the inhabitants of the sister isle to Christianity.

He points to the fact that through geographical isolation, Ireland had developed 'a distinctive, though brittle, civilisation, which equalled, and probably surpassed anything that contemporary Europe produced'. Divesting this civilisation of the Golden Age myths, concerning a land of saints and scholars, Mansergh reminds us, however, that there remains: 'a hard core of reality which has been the decisive influence in moulding the Irish outlook'.

Mansergh is absolutely correct in his assessment of the Irish outlook, as a famous incident in one of my local pubs illustrates. As the Awful Moment of closing time approached, one of the customers attempted a stratagem which had hitherto achieved a fair degree of success in permitting 'after hours' drinking. He struck up a conversation on a topic designed to catch the landlord's interest. It did, and on cue the pub divided evenly (and knowledgeably!) on the question of: were the Danes defeated at the Battle of

Clontarf because the tide came in, or because the tide went out? Unfortunately, as the pints flowed, one of the 'tide-in' school allowed himself to get carried away. He heatedly demolished a 'tide-out' exponent with a thunderous broadside beginning: 'My grandfather was there . . . !' Realising his error, he continued gamely but lamely: 'was der relation on my mother's side to a man whose grandfather's great grandfather, was at . . .' etc. However, the spell was broken, the publican realised that he'd been had, and cleared the bar.

It is not quite so easy to clear the slate of the costs of the Anglo-Irish relationship borne by many Irish emigrants. Reputable Irish societies such as the Action Group for Irish Youth, the Bourne Trust, the Federation of Irish Societies, the Irish Commission for Prisoners Overseas and the National Association for Probation Officers have collected statistics which paint a bleak picture of many areas of Irish experience.

I always think of a fairly disgusting incident which symbolised the reality of emigration for so many shabby, downtrodden, and very often ultimately clinically depressed, Irishmen and women who make up the reality of that period. My exemplar had obviously comforted himself not wisely but too well before the mailboat sailed from Dun Laoghaire for Holyhead. He found himself getting seasick and, knowing nothing about boats, staggered to the bow of the ship, not the stern, to vomit. The strong headwind meant that there was a resultant sharing of the riches on the crowded foredeck. I can still hear the rattle of peas and carrots off the superstructure as the unfortunate prepared himself for the rest of the sea voyage. This of course was followed by a gruelling train trip to Euston, if not further, and then a sick, grey facing into a dead-end job the next day, probably followed by a return to an even more deadening digs in the grey streets of Cricklewood or Camberwell.

The pea and carrot man's routine was the norm for too many. A survey carried out in Camberwell, South London, around the time of the mailboat incident found that: 'For the Camberwell psychiatric population as a whole, 3.1 per cent had primary diagnosis of alcoholism . . . the figures for the 134 Irishmen located were 13.4 per cent alcoholism.'[43] Some survived through cultivating the arts of the downtrodden, a forelock-touching, fawning false friendliness. Some managed to wrap their pain in a silent, tattered dignity as they plodded on from digs to dole to death. Others, the bawling, brawling drinkers, tried to repel reality and eternity with the booze and their fists. They caused police Black Marias to be called 'Paddy wagons', earned a 'no Irish need apply' reputation amongst some landladies, and inspired Christy Moore's ballad, 'From Clare to here':

> Oh! There's four who share the room
> As we work hard for the crack
> And getting up late on Sunday
> I never get to Mass
>
> It's a long long way from Clare to here . . .
> It gets further day by day . . .

When Friday night comes around and he's only into fighting
My ma would like a letter home but I'm too tired for writing

And the only time I feel alright is when I'm into drinking
It eases off the pain a bit and levels out my thinking.

HEALTH AND THE ALCOHOL PROBLEM

Improvement came in both Ireland and England but, inevitably, it came too slowly and too selectively for some. Writing in 1996, Gearoid O'Meachair could still point out that census figures showed that the Irish were developing unusually high levels of substance abuse *after* arriving in England. In fact O'Meachair wrote that:

> The mental and physical health of the Irish in Britain is near-alarming. Psychiatric admission rates amongst the Irish are double that of the English and Welsh. Irish men are three times more likely to suffer from depression and neurosis; Irish women are twice as likely. The extent of alcohol abuse, and to a lesser degree drug abuse is of chronic concern. The evidence would suggest that most Irish people with an alcohol dependency developed it *after* arriving in Britain.

Lest it be thought that O'Meachair was putting a partisan slant on the figures, it should be noted that independent studies, printed in the *British Medical Journal* in 1996, also gave an alarming picture of Irish health.[44] The studies showed that the overall mortality of first-generation Irish people – born both north and south of the border – exceeded that of all residents of England and Wales by some 30 per cent for men and 20 per cent for women. For cancers there was a 'significant excess'. The conclusions state that: 'While socioeconomic factors remain important, cultural and lifestyle factors are likely to contribute to this adverse mortality.'

The following tables given an indication of Irish mental health levels in 1981:

	Republic of Ireland		Northern Ireland		England		Caribbean	
	M	F	M	F	M	F	M	F
Schizophrenia	158	176	103	111	61	58	259	235
Other Psychosis	36	50	28	52	16	27	28	40
Depression	197	410	143	266	79	166	65	152
Neuroses	62	111	44	80	28	56	6	2
Personality Disorder	62	80	50	52	30	35	22	42
Alcohol Abuse	332	133	261	90	38	18	27	9
Drug Abuse	13	8	17	8	5	3	13	0

It has been suggested that the high levels of alcoholism recorded mask what are in fact symptoms of schizophrenia amongst the Irish, and that is why the Caribbean peoples appear to have more schizophrenics than the Irish.

There is no way of arguing about suicide totals, however. A person is either dead or alive, and in this melancholy field there are clearly more Irish dead.

Comparative figures showing mortality from suicide by selected places of birth – England and Wales 1979–1983

	Age 20–49 (SMR = 100)		Age 20–69 (SMR = 100)	
	M	F	M	F
Place of birth				
All Ireland	143	165	126	130
Indian Sub-continent	74	121	71	103
Caribbean Commonwealth	80	67	80	59
African Commonwealth	125	132	122	126

As the Irish suffer the worst physical and mental health of all ethnic groups and the host population, these levels of stress, to say nothing of downright anguish, also reflect themselves in other indicators – for example, Irish divorce rates were higher than average – but statistics, no matter how shocking, are only numbers. What the numbers refer to are people: Irish people who cry and drink and fight and sometimes, like the Jews, use humour in an effort to overcome their miseries. There is a well-known Irish joke, which is unusual in the sense that it is told, albeit defensively, by the Irish themselves. It concerns an English cockney foreman who asked a young Irishman looking for a job as a labourer: 'What is the difference between a girder and a joist?' The young Irishman replied: 'Goethe wrote *Faust*, and Joyce wrote *Ulysses*.'

The reality behind this sort of humour was well summed up in 1991 by the report of an Irish welfare service, The Irish Support and Advice Centre, Hammersmith, which noted:

> Younger immigrants are generally better educated and today many young men on the building sites can talk about Goethe and Joyce as well as girders and joists. They may have three to six years of post secondary education, and to find yourself working in an unskilled job and at the receiving end of all the cruel little jibes about the ignorant Irish can be a sort of torture in itself. Nevertheless, casual work in construction is the most readily available work for many young school leavers and graduates who have come here looking for wider horizons and a chance to practise their skills. While they look for that first break (it may take months or years to find something related to their studies, especially in a recessionary climate), they often have no choice but to pick up a shovel.[45]

The report, which was published in the same year as the figures on suicide given above, then went on to list some of those for whom the break never came. I feel that at least two cases are worth reproducing. The first one is significant, not only for its general application, but because it shows also how Irish attitudes in Ireland can add to the emigrants' woes in England. It tells the story of 'Jim', a classical example, albeit an unusually lucky one, an Irish labourer who had no choice 'but to pick up a shovel':

Jim has just reached retirement age. He is neatly dressed, gentle, well-spoken and loves company. Today with the help of the Irish Support and Advice Centre he lives in a nursing home but the last twenty years of his life were spent living rough. Shuttling from bed and breakfast to squats to derelict buildings to skips to prison to hospital and back again on to the street. For twenty years food was a problem. Staying warm was a problem: at least if you are drunk you can get to sleep. Washing was a problem. Clothes were a problem: clothes that are lived in and slept in week after week get loused up. Work was out of the question. Friends were a problem: the only people who would accept you were other street people and they are locked into the camaraderie of alcoholism. It's against the rules not to drink, not to binge when you have a little money, not to be one of the gang.

But Jim comes from a good family. His father and grandfather had trades and they provided money for Jim to buy into the trade in the late thirties when he left school, but it was a recessionary time in Ireland and there was nothing for him. He took unskilled work with farmers, butchers or in the abattoir. Sometimes he was unemployed and finally he left Ireland in the early fifties, hoping for better luck in Britain. Those were the days of the 'No blacks, no Irish, no dogs' signs in the boarding houses and the Irish immigrant had a lot of negative stereotyping working against him. Jim worked in construction and in the oil industry, again unskilled temporary work. Despite the record-breaking affluence of this country in the fifties and sixties, the golden opportunities never came his way. He lived in B and B, rented rooms and sometimes derelict buildings. He returned to Ireland at one point in the sixties but after a disagreement with his family brought on by the tensions of unemployment, he left again. Marriage was never an option, something which he regrets because two is company and these are lonely days. But he never had a steady job and didn't feel he could provide for a family: 'I never looked at tomorrow because the way I was going I couldn't.'

Year by year his drinking became worse. If you work on building sites, the pub is the focal point of social life: many people then (and now) kept to the pubs as a relief from the mistrust and dislike they found elsewhere. It was a place to hear about the next job in the construction trade and where you met the foreman on Friday for your pay. The tradition is to treat everyone lavishly when you are in the money, and then when you are down on your luck they treat you. But Jim's problems were closing in on him. He had an accident and broke his hip. He was now about forty-five and when you are unskilled all you have to sell is your youth and your health. Both were running out and the next twenty years must have been hell. Work became more and more sporadic as his health worsened. Jim doesn't shout or protest or complain, which is probably one reason why he has lived to the ripe age of sixty-five. The wild ones, the angry ones, burn out quicker and many die in their early fifties or even younger – a third of world life expectancy.

From the early seventies on, Jim was a regular visitor at the Centre. We helped him with clothes, advice and referrals to drying-out centres. We also put him back in touch with his family in Ireland. Like many people on the street, he had become estranged from them because the distance between their relative comfort and his seemingly endless bad luck was too great, and when you live a transient life you don't have a fixed address. The years slipped away, and he is not really welcome home. There is no welcome mat for the Irishman who hasn't mined the streets of London for immigrants' gold. Now he has found some security in his old age, but he is cut off from his old friends because if you won't take part in the endless rounds of drinking, you are somehow ostracised, you have offended group morale.

The second case history, reported by Father Jim Kiely, tells the story of someone who did 'offend group morale'. It concerns a woman, 'Maura', who came from Kerry:

She took to drink because she had a sense that she had lost a dream. Married at seventeen to a local showband musician, she had three beautiful children and a lovely home of which she was very proud. Her husband was away a lot on tours, and he found lots of female attractions in the dance halls. Maura didn't like this and she raised hell. Her husband was violent and abusive and refused to change his ways. Maura wouldn't accept his behaviour, but she had nowhere to go. Her relationship with her own father had always been bad, and it was never an option to go home. Maura decided: 'If I can't beat him I'll join him', and turned to the bottle as a remedy for her broken heart and her broken home. She went to live with another man and took her children. It was the dole, the pub, and begging in the streets. Sometimes she sent her children begging for her and the oldest one still remembers it. Aged twenty now, the girl is very disturbed by her past, embarrassed when she meets people she used to beg from when she was six years old. She is traumatised too by the fights between her parents – she still has the scar on her face from one family marathon in which she was hit by a flying plate meant for her father. Eventually Maura left the children in the care of her mother and came to London with her common-law husband Sean.

They had two more children, both taken into care, and contact was broken with the family in Ireland. Maura and Sean lived rough and both were alcoholics by this time. Sean also beat her and she was obsessed with the idea that she would be dead by the time she was thirty-seven, like one of her uncles. Indeed she was. She died last Christmas following a drinking bout. She didn't look that much older than her thirty-seven years, she still had some of her good looks, although her skin was roughened by the winters out on the street. At the Irish Support and Advice Centre we will miss her visits – she loved to talk and could be charming although when drunk she was a holy terror. We'll also long remember our sense of loss that this young woman's life was wasted. Whatever little help we could give her was just a Band-Aid over the huge fallout area of family breakdown that destroyed her confidence.

But we could do one last kindness: we arranged for her remains to be shipped back to Ireland, where her parents buried her. Alive she was too much of a problem for anyone to cope with, but dead she was welcome. Dead women don't shout and don't drink.

THE INFLUENCE OF CHURCH AND PUB

Mother Church, because of her policies on contraception, and her sometimes stultifying effect on Irish society, has to take some of the blame for the consequences for Irish emigrants. Irish women in particular were condemned to lives of penile servitude because of the Church's attitude to abortion, contraception and divorce. Nevertheless, for several decades, the Church, as an institution, did more to alleviate hardships than successive Irish governments. However, this said, one must take note of some substantial governmental improvements. At the time of writing, the Irish Government was spending some £750,000 a year on various schemes aimed at improving the lot of the emigrant community, largely through the Dion organisation, the official Irish governmental channel for such aid. However, given the new-found strength of the Irish economy, it is not a lot, and 'the good priest', that legendary icon to which most Irish people turned (or clung) in times of difficulty, will play a central role in the Irish community for many years to come. Inevitably, a researcher will find him or herself being told: 'You should see Father X, or Sister Y about that. He/she is great.' I encountered the work of so many of these figures in my travels that it is impossible to list them all.

In parts of the country where the Irish experienced particular difficulties, someone like Father Joe Taaffe in Birmingham provided a rare beacon of comfort. In London, Father Gerry French of the Irish Chaplaincy, Sister Sarah and Sister Joan Kane, along with Father Gerry McFlynn, of the Irish Commission for Prisoners Overseas,[46] constantly cropped up in conversation. So too did the names of Father Bobby Gilmore of Kilburn, Father Paddy Smith of Acton and Father Denis Cormican of Camden. Of course community leaders were not exclusively priests or nuns. Any list of such leaders in Britain in the decade 1988 to 1998 would have to include the Labour MP, Kevin McNamara; Michael Forde of Manchester; Jack Griffin and Bill Halley in Portsmouth; Gearoid O'Meachair, Joan Flynn and Lisa Murphy in London; and the dedicated Tommy Walshe in Liverpool. In nearby Manchester, the philanthropy of the Kennedy brothers, John and Joe, who made multi-million-pound fortunes through their construction and tunnelling activities, are inevitably mentioned in flattering terms in any conversation concerning the Irish.

Also, although in some quarters the ancestral antipathy between English clergy and their looked-down-upon Irish confrères still exists, at the very highest level the late Cardinal Basil Hume was a notable supporter of the Irish and of Irish causes. My friend the late Cardinal Tom O'Fiaich, an ardent Gaelic scholar and a strong nationalist, told me that when he was being considered for the Red Hat, the Foreign Office lobbied the Vatican to prevent his being appointed. One of those approached to lend weight to the Government's exhortations was Cardinal Basil Hume. However, he turned down the advances and told O'Fiaich that he would neither say nor do anything to prevent his elevation.

Hume played a pivotal role in the release of the Guildford Four. One day he received a courtesy call from the then Home Secretary, Douglas Hurd, who wanted to inform the Cardinal that that afternoon he would be announcing that he was turning down an application by the Four to appeal against their sentences. He explained the grounds on which he would be doing this to the Cardinal. However, His Eminence, who was noted for his retentive memory, reeled off a string of counter points and additional facts of which the Home Secretary had not been aware. To his credit, Hurd replied frankly: 'Obviously, my civil servants have not briefed me properly,' brought himself up to speed, and subsequently allowed the Appeal which ultimately freed the Four.

The important role of the pub in Irish life has already been adverted too. Steve Hennessey researched the subject in Bristol, which has a long-standing relationship with Ireland and the Irish. He works in the mental health field, an area which, as he says himself, has caused him to reflect on 'the preponderance of Irish users of drug, alcohol and mental health services'. He discovered that: '. . . whereas 7 per cent of adult male Bristolians considered themselves to belong to a 'public house group', for the Bristol Irish community's adult males the figure was 25 per cent'.[47]

Understandably, he remarked of the finding that he did not know whether it ought to make him 'laugh or cry'. Whichever way one reacts, the statistic serves to underline the importance of a pub owner in the Irish community. Along with the 'good priest', one can also meet the 'good publican', albeit not so frequently! However, they do exist. By accident I encountered one while in pursuit of a member of the former category, Father Pat Browne of Kilburn. I had been told to enquire where he lived at The Gloucester, which sported a sign on the outside saying, 'A Warm Friendly Welcome Always Assured'. However, inside, the first person I encountered was a man from South Armagh delivering a loud monologue in praise of the IRA! No one paid any attention to him. The publican was helping an old lady to choose from a pile of baps, humouring her with remarks as, 'Yes, that's a nice one,' or 'what about this nice big one?' In fact the baps were of identical size, but that incident constituted both her mainstay meal and principal human contact of the day. The lady was the daughter of one of Dublin's most famous Lord Mayors, Alfie Byrne. Mary had been notably charitable in her earlier days, renowned for taking in beggars. Now she was losing her memory. Lonely but proud, she would die with dignity in London rather than go back 'in defeat' to her native place. I later found that the publican, Liam Tarrant from Kerry, was not kind merely to her. Father Browne told me that Tarrant was 'to some what the church is to others'.[48] Amongst his benefactions was an annual Christmas party for the old folk of the district. The role of the good publican is so well recognised that one Irish publican, Joe Reilly, who runs the Waggon and Horses at Surbiton with his wife Brighid, was awarded an MBE in the New Year Honours list. I was told that the couple have raised 'vast sums' for charity over the years.

Father Browne had himself just come from the funeral of an old person, another 'Jim'. The funeral was one which could have been replicated anywhere the Irish gathered in England:

There were only four at it. The corpse lay in the morgue while relatives were sought. It was a typical end for one of the single Irish of the fifties. He had the Irish disease of inferiority. They didn't mix unless they had to. They shrank from doffing their hats to the Brits, and they lived in their ghettos: Mayo men in Camden Town, Kerry men in Kilburn. They had no friends except the Irish, and these were very often superficial contacts in the world of the pub. Their friends wouldn't know much about them, and at the end, there'd be no friends.

What were Father Browne's observations about the Irish of the decades after the fifties? A medley of contrasting findings is the answer:

The Irish are very racist. Is it inferiority? 'We'll do to others what was done to us?' A lack of confidence in their own culture? Lack of education, whatever, but somehow they seem overawed by the Muslims' wealth. I find the younger people are doing better, moving to the suburbs and so on. They're more proud of being Irish. The music has a lot to do with that. They take a pride in learning Irish music and dancing. Yet they're great royalists too. There was a great pride in Mary Robinson going to the palace to see the Queen. Twelve o'clock mass now is like the United Nations, but the Irish are still the backbone of the parishes – they have a tremendous sense of compassion, particularly the nurses.

THE IRISH CENTRE

After talking to Father Browne, I visited the Mayo men's mecca, the Irish Centre in Camden.[49] Important as it is to the immigrants from Mayo, this Centre has a far wider significance in the overall history of Irish emigration to the United Kingdom. Its history and activities epitomise all that is best and worst in the story of both Ireland's treatment of her own people, and by the host community. Its origins go back to the early fifties and the work of a dedicated community leader, Maurice Foley, a young Irish social worker in Birmingham. Foley produced a scarifying report on the conditions of Irish workers both in that city and the Midlands generally. On 23 July 1951, the Irish Ambassador of the period, F. H. Boland, told Dublin that Foley's findings were accurate.[50]

The Irish at that period were pouring into Birmingham, Coventry, and Wolverhampton in the wake of the rearmament boom. As Boland pointed out, British citizens were themselves, as a result of the war, living in 'sub-human conditions'. Foley's report spoke of what this meant in turn for the accommodation available for Irish manual workers. It was grossly over-crowded, ill-kept, dirty, and the cost was 'exorbitant'. He cited the example of a house in which fifty young Irishmen lived, paying a rent of £2 a week each for the privilege of sleeping fifteen to a room, and supplying and cooking their own food. It was commonplace in such accommodation for male shift workers to occupy the beds by day, and girls to do so by night. The sanitary conditions were often 'appalling', and the diet of these unfortunates, most of whom had no idea of how to cook, consisted of little more than tea and buns. Needless to say, there was a high incidence of alcoholism, TB and gastroenteritis amongst the Irish population.

De Valera's response to this report was to post a copy to the Irish Church hierarchy because it had 'moral and religious aspects', and to instruct his Ambassador at the Court of St James to make 'suitable representations to the British Government'. Then, with groundwork now ready against the unfavourable publicity which the report's publication might be expected to generate about his government's responsibility for emigration problems, de Valera launched a counter-publicity drive. He made a speech to a Fianna Fail gathering in Galway (on 28 August 1951), the day after Boland made his representations to the Secretary of State for Commonwealth Relations in London. This, and the fact that he had written to the bishops, enabled de Valera to make the fraudulent claim that he had taken 'definite action'. He went on to assert brazenly that many of those who emigrated could have found plenty of work at better pay and in far better conditions than those obtaining in England, and he concluded by feeding his audience a part of his staple political diet, an attack on Perfidious Albion: 'avaricious landlords' were operating a policy of 'anything is good enough for the Irish'.

In fact, many of the landlords involved were themselves Irish. However, the ensuing press controversy throughout England, but particularly in the Midlands, directed attentions away from de Valera's culpability in the matter of emigration and away from an important factor concerning the Church's responsibility for some of the accommodation problems. Irish clergy in England often used their influence to prevent Irish workers taking English digs, where they would have been far better off, so that they could in effect create ghettos in which the Church could control them, almost as if they were still at home. Boland gave an example of one such case in Southwark, London, where the local parish priest thought it was a good idea to have 150 Irishmen living in 'three smallish houses' where 'the men were kept together in accommodation run by a man of good character'. Undoubtedly that landlord's 'good character' also ran to seeing that a percentage of his profits went to the support of Mother Church, i.e. the parish priest.

However, concerned members of the Irish community in Britain of the calibre of Maurice Foley continued to lobby the Irish Government to do something about the plight of the emigrants. In December 1953, 20,000 emigrants signed a petition urging the Government to help in the setting up of an Emigrant Information Centre in Birmingham, but de Valera refused a grant for this project. The Department of Foreign Affairs subsequently drew up a memorandum which, while it washed its hands of any financial responsibility for providing hostel or welfare centres for Irish boys and girls in Britain, nevertheless proposed that a trust fund be set up. This would not be the Government's responsibility, but would rely on voluntary subscription in Ireland and England, amongst 'the Irish in Britain with the help and co-operation of their English friends'. De Valera had 'their English' deleted, and while disclaiming all responsibility for finance, nevertheless indicated that 'he would consider what might be done towards assisting in the collection of money in this country'.

The report envisaged that the Fund would have the support of the Catholic clergy, and so it did – the English Catholic clergy: Cardinal Griffin (of Irish origin) launched the Fund to build an Irish Centre in Camden Town, London, on 20 January 1955 with a £1,000 cheque. He said of the Irish: 'We should always be grateful for what they have done to help us . . . Tragedy has under God's providence led to an immense strengthening of the Church in this country . . . the contribution which the Irish emigrants have made to the development of the Church in this country is incalculable.'[51] His Irish counterpart in Armagh, Cardinal Dalton, a schoolmate of de Valera's, subscribed only £200, although the Archbishop of Dublin, Dr McQuaid, was more generous with £500. With the help of the British hierarchy – and the pennies of the poor Irish emigrants – the Irish Centre was finally opened in Camden town on 27 September 1955.

How had things changed for the patrons of the Centre in the more than four decades which had elapsed between de Valera's evasion of responsibility for its birth and the time of my visit? In some ways 'very greatly' was the answer, in others 'not at all'. I couldn't help feeling that there was something symbolic in the spectacle of an old man I saw standing on the stairs, looking wistfully into the Centre's capacious ballroom as the singer sang 'Farewell to dear old Dublin through my tears'. When I mentioned the old man to Father Gerry Kivelehan, the jolly oblate friar who runs the Centre, he shook his head and replied: 'Once you're in the problem business, you'll have no shortage of them.'

Father Kivelehan had been in the 'problem business' for most of his life. He'd worked in Birkenhead, where he saw the catastrophe of the Cammell Laird shipyard closure, and that of other shipyards, on the employment situation. He'd also been in welfare work in Liverpool. Over the years, he'd seen at first hand the impact both of the de Valera years and the improvements brought by the Sean Lemass era. He expected that the Centre's share of problems in the coming year would amount to some 10 to 15 per cent of the 30,000 Irish emigrants expected in London.

They won't have documentation, birth certs, anything like that. They'll be on welfare. Of course they won't have any National Insurance. The Job Seekers Allowance has replaced the dole, so landlords know tenants may not have rent. Accommodation is a big problem. There is no hostel accommodation . . . We have just fixed up five from Slattery's in shelter in Kilburn. [Slattery's provides much availed of cheap bus and boat journeys from Irish cities to London] We'll get them freshened up with a course of some sort that'll look good on their CV.

He repeated what I had heard at the Chaplaincy seminar, that there were plenty of service jobs available, but that they paid so badly that it was almost impossible to subsist on them, unless there was some form of family back-up. The inevitable consequence of course is debt, drink, drugs and, equally inevitably, 'lots of mental health problems'.

A good deal of the Centre's work goes into dealing with the elderly Irish of the fifties building booms, but nowadays the Centre also has a big cultural facet to its activities: dancing, music, lessons on the fiddle, Irish language classes, drama. There is also something which I have spoken at myself, a book fair, which is becoming an increasingly important event on the Centre's annual calendar, as it is accompanied by lectures and seminars on aspects of Irish life both in England and Ireland. The younger Irish tend to focus on justice and peace issues, the older ones on welfare, visitation of the elderly, seeking entitlements for the needy, and so on. The operation of the Prevention of Terrorism Act has created a fertile breeding ground for Sinn Fein. Many of the young justice and peace activists are strong Sinn Fein supporters and Gerry Adams is a folk hero amongst the younger Irish.

As indicated, under the Tories, distinctions between supporting Sinn Fein and being active in the IRA did not mean a great deal to the police. Under the shadow of the PTA, gatherings of Irish, or the organisers of such gatherings, were equally suspect. Even Father Kivelehan himself was not exempt. When he arrived at the Centre, he brought with him in his briefcase his basic documents: birth certificate, passport, his degrees, and his National Insurance cards. The police broke into his flat there and took the briefcase. After he reported it missing, he found it mysteriously reappeared 'in a strategic place', but the contents of the case had obviously been gone through and, presumably, checked and copied. This is the background to the 'problem business', Camden Town Irish Centre style. The good part of the story is that Father Kivelehan found that once the Centre or its associated agencies got involved in a case involving an Irish person in trouble with the police, the police ceased to be dismissive.

Then other authorities followed suit. This he judged to be 'an incredibly important dimension to our work'. Because of the role played by the Centre in cases such as those of the Bridgewater Three (a miscarriage of justice case involving British defendants) or the Birmingham Six, the Centre's work is appreciated and people involved in the Bridgewater and Birmingham cases regularly visit the premises.

Even with the Celtic Tiger roaring away to the West, the Centre's bedrock activity is still welfare, either helping the newly arrived, younger emigrants, or catering for the older relics of the boom days. It looks faintly shabby, homely and old-fashioned. A principal adornment on Father Kivelehan's wall is the famous Colman Doyle photograph of the young Jacqueline Kennedy with JFK, taken for their visit to Ireland in 1963. Once it hung in every Irish farmhouse kitchen; now the farms are emptying as Brussels turns a chilly eye on the Common Agricultural Policy. So the young still leave the country, many of them passing through the doors of the Centre. The corporate Irish sector is generous in its support of annual big events run for charity, but still places like the Centre depend very much on the hands-on approach of whoever is in charge. Father Kivelehan's 'nine to nine' routine involves a very literal approach to being 'hands-on'. During our talk we were interrupted from time to time by people coming to him with problems, the last of which was to ask him to change a barrel of beer!

REVISING HISTORY

Few people in the world have had to so strongly define their identity by, with, or from another country as have the Irish. Other examples, like the Canadians *vis-à-vis* the Americans, or the Koreans compared to the Japanese, may be given. Nevertheless, the question of how the Irish and the English see, teach and read about each other, is the stuff of centuries-old controversy, exacerbated in our time by the North of Ireland situation. The controversy has centred on different areas: how the past was interpreted; how emigration was explained away, by attempting to conflate it with the question of nationalist identity; how the contemporary troubles were reported.

Where Ireland is concerned the term 'revisionist history' came to mean not a matter of revising opinions in the light of new research or insights, but of contemporary politics. To shore up the Tory/Unionist approach to the Troubles, history teaching became a tool in the counter-insurgency war against the Provisional IRA, an attempt to cut the guerrillas off from their ideological hinterland. This approach began to gain ground in both Ireland and England during the 1970s as the British sought to introduce a policy of 'criminalisation' towards the IRA. No more were the paramilitary prisoners to be regarded as *de facto* prisoners of war. They were to be treated, in the words of Merlyn Rees, the Secretary of State for Northern Ireland, under whom the policy was introduced, 'like ODCs' (Ordinary Decent Criminals).[52] Two other policies were introduced at the same time: 'Normalisation' and 'Ulsterisation.' Ulsterisation need not concern us here, it was modelled on the American exit strategy in Vietnam which involved trying to get the natives to do the fighting against the Viet Cong. Decoded, the Belfast version of Vietnamisation was intended to be RUC *v* IRA, thus lessening the burden on the British Army. Normalisation, a word with significant resonances for students of Irish history, we will come to later. Let us first look at the impact of criminalisation.

The British hunger strikes of 1980/81 broke out in protest against the criminalisation policy. In terms of support for Sinn Fein, the strikes were the contemporary equivalent of 1916. The Republicans were strengthened, not crushed. However that well-known academic species, Conference-Going Man, and his alter ego, Chair-Seeking Personage, realising how the wind was blowing, joined in the airbrushing of Irish history. On the one hand, it was held that Nationalism, like God, was dead – something connected only to Belfast and bombs; on the other, that anything nationalistic was an impediment to the inward flow of investment, and the upward surge of Irish yuppiedom. This had a convenient and direct bearing on the question of Irish governmental attitudes towards emigrants, for, as the Irish geographer, Jim McLoughlin, has written:

> In stressing the inevitability of emigration, historical revisionists and modernisation theorists have also de-politicised the causes of Irish emigration. Thus, unlike their Scottish, Welsh, and English counterparts, Irish historians have been poor defenders of the 'moral economy' of rural and working-class communities which have regularly been devastated by emigration. Indeed contemporary attitudes to Irish emigration reflect a serious devaluation of nationalism as a philosophy informing social and economic policy in Ireland. Today nationalism has been so seriously 'narrowed' that it has been almost

exclusively associated with Republicanism and political violence in Northern Ireland . . . we are more concerned about attracting high-tech industry and tourists to Ireland than thinking about ways of blocking the haemorrhage of young adults from the country.[53]

This attitude neatly complemented long-standing English propagandist approaches. As Liz Curtis has pointed out, British colonists, be they Norman, Elizabethan, or Victorian, argued in justification of their campaigns that the Irish were a culturally inferior race, in need of English civilisation.[54] So sunk in barbarism were they that they could not even practise their own religion properly and had to have reform imposed on them by an English pope aided by Norman knights.

Ironically, periods of anti-Catholic xenophobia in England, like the Gordon riots for example, also had a negative effect on the Irish population. The Gordon riots occurred in London in 1780, and resulted in the destruction of Catholic churches and property. Their proximate cause, the introduction of a Catholic Relief Bill, also helped to stir Protestant fears which interacted with the French Revolution and the subsequent Napoleonic Wars to give British Nationalism its conservative, hierarchical and monarchical characteristics. Not only did the vicar enjoin his listeners to thank God for the squire and his relations who showed everyone their proper stations, that proper station was directly opposed to the Rome-dominated, superstitious Catholicism of the Irish.

As the geographers Busteed and Hodgson have noted:

For the English the Irish provided 'the richest, and most enduring, source of nationalist demonology' (Daniels, 1993:6). This was multi-layered demonology. In the first place, it cast Ireland as a place of almost incomprehensible endemic political instability, warfare and violence. Thus, a sixteenth-century English civil servant, quoting a proverb that 'the war of Ireland shall never have end' remarked: 'Which proverb, touching the war of Ireland, is always likely to continue, without God set it in men's breasts to find some new remedy that never was found before.'[55]

The *laissez-faire* theorists thought for a time that the Great Famine might provide a 'new remedy'. Instead, as its victims flooded into England, new problems were created. The Irish put an intolerable strain on the fairly primitive relief systems of the time. They also competed for jobs against English navvies who regarded themselves as having superior skills to the Irish who worked for lesser wages, as a ballad of the period commemorates:

> When work grew scarce and bread was dear
> and wages lessened too,
> and Irish hordes were bidders here
> our half-paid work to do.

In addition, in 1850, with the arrival of the Famine hordes still a very live memory, the restoration of the Catholic hierarchies triggered off all the old anti-Catholic emotions. The ensuing fights and riots between the Irish and the British, or the Scotch Presbyterians, kept the fires of prejudice well stoked. The Irish, whether in Belfast or Glasgow, Liverpool or Manchester, used similar tactics to protect themselves. Contemporary TV viewers will be familiar with scenes of Belfast Catholic women protesting by banging bin lids on the ground. Their mothers, during the pogroms of the early twenties, used the same tactics when Loyalist assassination squads invaded their districts. The murder yell is part of the folklore of working-class Catholic Belfast: a long-drawn-out keening cry of m-u-r-d-e-r.

This tactic was used in England also. In Manchester, for example, where the Irish clustered together in low-rent accommodation, it was remarked how an Irish crowd thousands strong could be assembled, within seconds it seemed, when there was some incursion by hostile forces, such as police intent on seizing illicit stills. The *Manchester Guardian* of 2 January 1830 describes one such riot. Apparently the owner of the still broke into: 'a loud Irish cry, which immediately brought to the spot a great number of people who . . . attacked the officers with sticks, stones and brick-bats. A Battle Royal ensued.'

Similar scenes could have been witnessed throughout the latter part of the nineteenth century in any of the big urban centres. However, as Mervyn Busteed has pointed out, the work of a well-meaning social reformer, Dr James Philips Kay, meant that: 'The Manchester Irish were destined to play a key role in the popular attitudes towards the Irish migrant in urban Britain.'[56] Kay, who had been horrified by his experiences in the 1832 cholera epidemic, wrote a pamphlet seeking to heighten awareness of the conditions in which the urban working class lived. However, the pamphlet was to have the unlooked-for side-effect of causing the Irish to be blamed for giving good patriotic native Britons a bad example in the matter of being able to subsist while spending very little on non-essentials such as accommodation, food, furniture or clothing, and a very great deal on the staff of Irish life – alcohol.

The stereotypical image created was that the Irish sought out these kind of conditions because of their own inherent slovenliness and inadequacy. These stereotypes were then added to by the outrage of cartoonists and British politicians at nineteenth-century Irish efforts to undo the Act of Union, which snuffed out the Irish Parliament after the 1798 rebellion. The researches of figures such as Liz Curtis, or the three distinguished historians who produced the book, *Drawing Conclusions*, have demonstrated the unlovely results.[57] Whether they were Constitutionalists like Charles Stewart Parnell, or Revolutionaries like the dynamiting Fenians, the Irish were lumped together by *Punch* cartoonists as murderous simian creatures, made up in equal portions of cruelty, depravity and untrustworthiness.

THE MEDIA APPROACH

Such images, so necessary for justifying the imperialistic project in Ireland, can be traced in a straight line from Giraldus Cambrensis, Gerald of Wales, who accompanied the first Norman invaders of Ireland, through Thomas Carlisle. Carlisle described Ireland as a 'huge suppuration', a 'human swinery', whose inhabitants were 'a black howling Babel of superstitious savages'. British press coverage of contemporary Troubles continued the Carlisle tradition. A typical comment amongst those polled for the purposes of the CRE Report was: 'You get a certain amount of anti-Irish feeling about, stirred up by gutter rags like the *Sun*. Wonder how Irish people can read the *Sun*.' The Report concluded that the: 'widespread acceptability of anti-Irish attitudes in Britain is reinforced and legitimised by the media'.

The *Guardian* newspaper, the 'Insight' team on the *Sunday Times* during the early days of the Troubles (before Rupert Murdoch took over), and the continued work of individual journalists and broadcasters such as Robert Fisk, Jon Snow, Peter Taylor and Robert Kee should be exempted from this stricture. Indeed they should be praised all the more highly because of operating in such a climate. Overall, however, it is true that there was little or no attempt to explain the problem in historical terms. The officially propagated view was that the army had been sent in to keep the Irish from slaughtering each other. The related facts, that the British Government had turned a blind eye to the injustices perpetuated by the Unionists' majority rule, while at the same time using British taxpayers' money to uphold that rule, were generally ignored. On 18 August 1969, just after the troops were sent in, the *Mirror*, then generally regarded as the soldiers' newspaper, carried a 'historical teach-in on Ireland' whose slant may be judged from the following: 'The Irish agree on one thing only. That is to go on arguing and fighting about a peace that has not existed in their history.'

This approach was not confined to the 'other ranks'. On 28 August, a paper more attuned to the views of the officers and gentlemen class, the *Sunday Times*, propagated a different version of the same view, after Ken Livingstone, then leader of the Greater London Council, had drawn a parallel between British treatment of the Irish and Nazi treatment of the Jews:

Talk of this kind is worth answering only because it can otherwise gain ground among the gullible. Over several centuries Britain did behave callously towards Ireland, considering it as an outpost to be secured, not as a people to be reconciled. But the great reducer of the Irish population was emigration, and the principal reasons for it were ones which would have beset any offshore agricultural economy.

Since 1969 (to look no further back) the main note of British policy in Northern Ireland has been altruism. Successive British governments have committed British lives and money on a large scale, seeing – rightly or wrongly – no other way to keep some sort of peace and prosperity in a place they would just as soon be out of. To count that wicked, or to regard even the accompanying military heavy-handedness as on all fours with the systematic murderousness of the IRA, is to turn morality upside down.

Irish readers of that in England might have been inclined to write to the editor, suggesting that the late Oliver Cromwell or perhaps the Famine might have been included amongst the 'great reducers of the Irish population', but the 'invisibility' factor generated by the sort of incidents detailed earlier paralysed pens. No paralysis affected the pens of cartoonists however: Cummings and JAK cheerfully resurrected murderous ape-like images of the *Punch* cartoon era to make their points. Michael Cummings told the *Irish Times* (on 29 May 1982) that he had a cartoonist's licence to depict the Irish as being 'extremely violent, bloody-minded, always fighting, drinking enormous amounts, getting roaring drunk'. Further, he argued that the IRA's violence did tend to 'make them look rather like apes, though that's rather hard luck on the apes'. Cummings also said that there was: 'a rather curious convention . . . the Irish tend as a nation to have rather long upper lips. The cartoonist JAK (of the *Standard*) had all his Irish people with sideburns to the middle of their cheeks; that was his way of putting over the Irish'.

JAK had other ways of 'putting over the Irish'. On 29 October 1982, his most controversial cartoon appeared in the *Standard*. It showed a cinema hoarding displaying a poster for 'the ultimate in psychopathic horror movies: THE IRISH'. A group of ghouls appeared under these words, armed with drills, dynamite, knives and guns, disporting themselves in a graveyard. The film, which was attributed to 'Emerald Isle snuff movies', featured 'the IRA, INLA, UDF, PFF, UDA, etc., etc.'.

The GLC withdrew its advertising in the *Standard*, then worth some £100,000 a year, but the *Standard* did not apologise, and was not censored by the Press Council. In fact, the Press Council said that the banning of advertising was 'a blatant attempt by a local authority to use the power of its purse to influence the contents of a newspaper article and coerce the editor'. While I was researching this book, considerable annoyance was caused to the Irish community by articles appearing on successive days in the *Daily Mail*. One was by Paul Johnson, the other by Ian Wooldridge. Johnson wrote after a bomb scare had caused chaos in London, to the effect that the Irish, as a race, were closet IRA supporters, who not only rejoiced when British soldiers were killed, but supported governments and a judiciary which showed 'emotional sympathy for the gunmen'. Therefore, Johnson proposed to fine the Irish community. He proposed a financial punishment for any Irish person entering Britain, and further financial sanctions against anyone found trading with Irish companies. This suggestion was illegal under European law.

The following day, the same paper published an article from Ian Wooldridge in the sports section, headed 'Let's ban every Irish horse, Irish jockey and Irish trainer from the Cheltenham Festival'. Wooldridge also made some what were no doubt intended as jocose comments, about bombing Dublin and Cork. However, as Dublin figured in what was the greatest single loss of life in the entire course of the Troubles – the Dublin and Monaghan bombings (worse even than Omagh) – the jocosity was lost on the Irish.

In addition to political stereotyping, some of Britain's most popular TV soaps, *Brookside*, *Coronation Street* and *EastEnders*, depicted Irish characters as drunks, morons and wife-beaters. After an episode of *EastEnders* portrayed Ireland as being more or less populated by such types, Ambassador Barrington complained to the BBC and received an apology. On hearing this, Peter Mandelson is said to have remarked that he wished Barrington would explain his secret to him, because he had been trying throughout his career, without success, to get the BBC to apologise for anything!

Obviously most of what has been said so far derives to a greater or lesser extent from history. Therefore, if history is part of the problem, it would appear to be self-evident that learning from it is, by definition, part of the solution. However, that is not how the matter was universally perceived. For many decades, the answer to the problem was simply not to teach the other side's history. This policy applied right across the board. In the UK children grew up learning virtually nothing about Irish history. What little the schoolchild did glean was largely a matter of the history of the British in Ireland. Every so often some British ruler, be it Queen Elizabeth I or Oliver Cromwell, would be portrayed as being distracted from their illustrious labours by having to put down yet another rebellion amongst the disloyal, chronically turbulent Irish. In the Republic of Ireland, because of the Civil War, Irish history ended with the 1916 Rebellion. My book, *Ireland Since the Rising*, published on the fiftieth anniversary of the rising, gave my generation their first insight into the formation of the Irish state, and what created the political parties they voted for. In the Six Counties, Protestant children were taught English history and Catholic children were taught Irish history, along the lines of that taught in the Republic.

However, as the Northern Troubles intensified, and the IRA grew stronger, the teaching of history in some quarters began to be looked upon as an arm of the counter-insurgency process. The mid 1970s saw Dublin and London introduce complementary information policies. In Dublin, Dr Conor Cruise O'Brien, the then Minister for Posts and Telegraphs, attempted without success to extend the prohibitions of the Broadcasting Act concerning Sinn Fein to the newspapers. In Northern Ireland, the British attempted to 'criminalise' the IRA, so as to cut them off from their ideological hinterland in Irish history. Suddenly 'revisionism' began to mean not the revision of historical opinions based on new research or fresh insights, but the re-interpretation of the past with an eye to contemporary politics.

TWO CONTROVERSIES OF IRISH IDENTITY

The revisionists, however, were dealt two crippling blows in two separate controversies. One of these, dealing with interpretations of Irish history, was conducted publicly in academic journals; the other was somewhat more private and centred on the issue of who should control a body set up to improve Anglo/Irish cultural relations and further the spread of Irish studies.

The first blow to the revisionists came in a famous article by Brendan

171

Bradshaw of Queens' College Cambridge, in *Irish Historical Studies*, November, 1989. His arguments were at first confined to a small circle, but ultimately spread through the academic body politic to find a widespread acceptance. The 'normalisation' policy referred to earlier was intended for physical application to the Six Counties. In other words, an attempt was made to make the area appear normal in the midst of turmoil by devices such as immediately repairing bomb damage, and by pumping money into the arts and into leisure facilities.

Although he made no direct reference to this policy, Bradshaw's article served to draw attention to the fact that historians were engaged in the same process – 'filtering out the trauma', as he put it, from Irish history. In a telling passage he illuminated the fact that the strategy involved in presenting the plantation of Ulster and other parts of Ireland, with all their attendant butcheries of men, women and children, was one of 'normalisation':[58]

> the crown's brutal repression of eighteenth century violence . . . is one of normalisation: the abnormality is analysed in terms of a more normal historical process. Thus as treated in recent monographs . . . the colonisation of east Ulster and Munster respectively becomes a mere matter of internal British migration, part of a vaguely suggested larger pattern of continuing settlement.

As Bradshaw pointed out, some historians were at the time attempting, by the use of euphemism and a clinical tone, to extend the 'filter out the trauma' approach even to the Famine, the 150th anniversary of which was approaching. In some quarters a belief appeared to exist that the Irish had got it wrong somehow.

Graham Davis wrote:

> The popular success of Woodham-Smith's *The Great Hunger*, published in 1962, derived from its portrayal of the shortcomings in the administration of famine relief by the Treasury official, Sir Charles Trevelyan. Although the tone was politer than the emotive rhetoric employed by Mitchel, Woodham-Smith's narrative of the unfolding drama was equally forthright in condemnation of the ideological blindness demonstrated by the British Government.
>
> Despite an interval of a hundred years the Mitchel thesis was largely accepted and indeed developed in *The Great Hunger*, a book that ran to six impressions between 1962 and 1980. What had been common currency among poor Irish emigrants in the New World was now the established view among a popular readership in Britain.[59]

The first thing to be said about the foregoing is that *The Great Hunger* did not owe its success to the portrayal of Charles Trevelyan. It was due to the fact that it was a gripping read, which burst on a new generation of Irish readers in the 1960s like a thunderbolt. Dr Conor Cruise O'Brien, who could not be accused of over-indulgence towards the Nationalist viewpoint, said of Woodham-Smith: 'Her just and penetrating mind, her lucid and easy style, and her assured command of the sources have produced one of the great works not only of Irish nineteenth-century history, but of nineteenth-century history in general.'[60]

The second point concerns Davis's condescending reference towards the 'poor Irish emigrants in the New World'. This reflects an élitist view, commonly met with amongst Conservatives and Unionists, that there is an inner core of truth about their position on Ireland which the dullards in Dublin and London cannot comprehend. The Americans, of course, are completely out of touch, romantics at best, IRA fund-raisers at worst. To this school of thought, for Cecil Woodham-Smith to suggest, not merely to the unenlightened Americans, but to the sophisticates of the 'popular readership in Britain' that Britain's role in the Famine was in any way culpable, was just too much; particularly, Davis noted in pained tones, as Robert Kee gained 'an even wider audience' for the Woodham-Smith view in his books and television series on Ireland. The fact that Robert Kee might have a better, or perfectly defensible, insight appears to have eluded him.

However, at the risk of stating the obvious, may I point out that most people in the 1990s, apart from a few students, would not have turned to the hard-to-come-by writings of a nineteenth-century figure like John Mitchel for their knowledge of the Famine. (Mitchel's career will be encountered in the Australian chapter.) Their knowledge of the Famine is derived, not even from Cecil Woodham-Smith (who based her researches on state papers, quite independently of Mitchel's tractarianism), but from the huge corpus of new research which was generated by the anniversary of the Famine in this decade. As a result, few fair-minded people would any longer attempt to deny the judgement of Christine Kineally in her major work published in 1994:

> the response of the British Government to the famine was inadequate in terms of humanitarian criteria, and increasingly after 1847, systematically and deliberately so. The localised shortages that followed the blight of 1845 were adequately dealt with but, as the shortages became more widespread, the government retrenched. With the short-lived exception of the soup kitchens, access to relief – or even more importantly, access to food – became more restricted. That the response illustrated a view of Ireland and its people as distant and marginal is hard to deny. What, perhaps, is more surprising is that a group of officials and their non-elected advisers were able to dominate government policy to such a great extent.
>
> This relatively small group of people, taking advantage of a passive establishment, and public opinion which was opposed to further financial aid for Ireland, were able to manipulate a theory of free enterprise, thus allowing a massive social injustice to be perpetrated within a part of the United Kingdom. There was no shortage of resources to avoid the tragedy of a famine. Within Ireland itself, there were substantial resources of food which, had the political will existed, could have been diverted, even as a short-term measure, to supply a starving people. Instead, the government pursued the objective of economic, social and agrarian reform as a long-term aim, although the price paid for this ultimately elusive goal was privation, disease, emigration, mortality and an enduring legacy of disenchantment.[61]

One person who had no difficulty in identifying with the foregoing assessment was the British Prime Minister, Tony Blair, who set the tone for the current improvement in Anglo-Irish relationships, at the start of his premiership, by apologising for the Famine. His comments, circulated from Downing Street, made a particular impact in Ireland when conveyed to the Irish public by the British Ambassador, Veronica Sutherland, at The Great Famine Commemoration at Millstreet, County Cork, and read by the actor Gabriel Byrne:

> That one million people should have died in what was then part of the richest and most powerful nation in the world is something that still causes pain as we reflect on it today. Those who governed in London at the time failed their people through standing by while crop failure turned into a massive human tragedy. We must not forget such a dreadful event.[62]

Apart from the Orange element, Blair's gesture was widely welcomed by the Irish community – with some few exceptions. Obviously, if Irish, and British, history had been properly taught, such widely polarised views would not have existed. However, Irish history remains such a contentious issue that until very recently, the early eighties at best, one would generally, if not inevitably, look in vain to academia for any signs of polarisation being rectified. The quarterly journal, *Irish Studies in Britain*, was in its seventh edition, that for the Spring/Summer of 1985, before one could read an article, by Mary FitzGerald, detailing a submission to the Department of Education to set up the first BA in Irish Studies in England – and the editor of the journal thought it prudent to put a question mark after the headline: 'First BA in Irish Studies?'[63]

Fortunately, despite Margaret Thatcher, caution proved unnecessary. As in America and elsewhere, something of an explosion of Irish studies took place. As Mervyn Busteed told me:

> the appeal of Irish studies was immediate and widespread, not merely amongst students. All the social classes from the retired surgeon, to the unemployed labourer, to the housewife who wanted to stretch her mind after rearing the kids. They all took courses. Most of these people had more experience of life than I had, when as a 21-year-old student I turned to Irish studies.[64]

There are now several degree courses in Irish studies at various centres: at Strawberry Hill, Middlesex; the Institute of Irish Studies in Liverpool University; at the University of Manchester and the University of Luton; at Bath College of Higher Education; at Bradford University; and interest is growing in several other centres. Moreover, as a result of lobbying by the Gaelic League and by groups such as the Irish in Britain Representation Group, the Irish language appeared on the British National Curriculum in September 1999. In London, the University of North London became a centre for Irish Studies courses, the collection of archival material, and for a valuable series of papers, edited by Dr Mary Hickman, which were published from

1990 onwards. Independently of these developments, a donor funded a Chair of Irish History at Oxford, the Carroll Chair of Irish History. This, which was envisaged originally as concentrating on late medieval and early modern history, went to one of Bradshaw's prime targets, the leading revisionist Roy Foster who, whatever his viewpoint, is a fine scholar and writer. At Magdalene College, Cambridge, there is the Charles Stewart Parnell Fellowship originated by a former Irish rugby international, the late Andy Mulligan, and the Anglo-Irish philanthropist, Billy Bourne Vincent, which attracts distinguished visiting fellows from Ireland and the diaspora.

Nevertheless, all the contentions of both the Northern Irish issue and the related question of defining the place of the Irish in British society came to the surface in the second serious controversy affecting the issues of Irish studies and Irish identity. The sequence of events was as follows.

The Anglo-Irish Agreement of 1985 had a cultural as well as a political dimension to it and both Governments were committed to encouraging cultural links. The first steps were taken by a group called Anglo-Irish Encounter. This was headed by Kenneth Whittaker – the former Secretary of the Irish Department of Finance, who promoted the first coming together of a Northern and Southern Prime Minister, the Lemass/O'Neill meetings of 1965 – and Sir David Orr, former Chief Executive of Unilever, captain of London Irish Rugby Club and, at the time of writing, Chancellor of Queen's University. The group organised a meeting in London, attended by the English and Irish Ministers of Education, Sir Keith Joseph and Gemma Hussey, after which it was agreed to set up what became formally known as the British Association for Irish Studies (BAIS). The BAIS received support from both Governments and received a grant of some £150,000 from Allied Irish Banks. The bank's Chairman, Niall Crowley became one of the BAIS's patrons. Others included Seamus Heaney, Tony O'Reilly, Sir David Orr and Kenneth Whittaker. Much good work was done, and the committee continued in being, more or less controversy-free, until circa 1990 when there developed that occupational hazard of all Irish committees and organisations, 'The Split'.

The row has been ascribed to various causes and clashes; those who subscribed to the Bradshaw viewpoint versus those who sought to 'filter out the trauma' and to a disagreement as to what funding should be provided for the Irish Studies Department at Liverpool. But wherever the real truth of the matter lies, the undeniable fact is that the divisions grew so heated that the Irish ambassador, Joseph Small, felt it necessary to take the unusual step of intervening. He managed to broker an agreement on 28 January 1993, which he sweetened by securing a grant from the Soldiers and Sailors Fund to help the BAIS finances. Relationships improved so much that by the end of the year, when an election was held to provide officers for the Association, there was only one contested position, that of Chairman, for which Sean Hutton defeated Graham Davis.

Despite splits, spin doctors and the Murdoch press, the Irish had validated a judgement made in Brendan Bradshaw's celebrated article:

Invited to adopt a perspective on Irish history which would depopulate it of heroic figures, struggling in the cause of national liberation; a perspective which would depopulate it of an immemorial native race, the cumulative record of whose achievements and sufferings constitutes such a rich treasury of culture and human experience; a perspective, indeed, from which the modern Irish community would seem as aliens in their own land – for 'the past is a foreign country – in face of such an invitation the Irish have clung tenaciously to their nationalist heritage. Who could blame them?

However, as Bradshaw also pointed out, this is not a plea for green history. The Northern Irish Protestant tradition is also as much 'in need of imaginative and emphatic elucidation as that of its southern neighbours'. The requirement is for a sympathetic exposition of both Irish traditions and – in so far as this is possible – of their English next-door neighbour.

And beyond all these contentious issues there lies yet another vitally important, but largely untapped, lode to be mined for its immensely valuable contribution to the riches of Irish history. For, as Clare Barrington, the author of the bibliography, *Irish Women in England*, (Cork University, 1997) points out in the introduction to that work:

Until recently, readers of the history of Irish emigration could be forgiven for believing that the typical emigrant was male, possibly accompanied by a wife or other dependant females. In truth, Irish emigration is a remarkable story of female self-determination. During most decades since the 1880s, more women than men have emigrated from Ireland. The vast majority of these women were single, younger than their male counterparts and travelled alone. This large, sustained emigration of single females is an anomaly in the history of European emigration, as women from other countries did, generally, emigrate with husbands and fathers.

This 'anomaly' was a marked feature of emigration to America also and is discussed in Chapter 3. In the British context one of the principal figures involved in the raising of a consciousness of being Irish, both men and women, in British society, Bronwen Walter, Reader in Social and Cultural Geography at Anglia Polytechnic University, corroborated Barrington's judgement saying:

One of the most extraordinary aspects of Irish Studies in Britain has been the silence about the lives and experiences of women. Not until the very end of the twentieth century have Irish women in the diaspora finally made it onto the research agenda. No major conference or publication can now exclude women, although many established academics still manage to ignore or sideline gender in their analysis.

Walter would pinpoint the breakthrough for recognition of the fact that 'the lives and the experiences of Irish navvies was not the whole story' as coming in 1988 with the publication of *Across the Water: Irish Women in Britain*.[65] She points out that this collection of first-hand experiences of Irish women was also 'far ahead of its time in its inclusiveness – of the second generation, travellers, black Irish and lesbian women and acknowledgement of the devastating effects of the Prevention of Terrorism Act on families.' Of course, as she ruefully indicates, 'Many of these topics remain to be pursued.'

For, as if to underline the validity of Walter's judgements, two major controversies broke out as we were corresponding, in December of 2000.

One broke out after it was discovered that, the previous October, the Humberside Police Force had been issued with a policy directive instructing police officers to report all dealings with Irish people to the Special Branch. Irish associations erupted in fury at what was perceived as an attempt to return the Irish to the status of a 'suspect community'

The Irish Ambassador, Ted Barrington, raised the matter with the Home Office Minister, Mike O'Brien, who distanced himself from the memo, pointing out that it was not official Home Office policy to target whole groups of people (*Irish Post*, 16 December 2000). Not surprisingly, subsequent to the Barrington meeting, the memo was withdrawn 'with immediate effect' on the instruction of Humberside Police Chief Constable, David Westwood. But the incident had a jolting effect on the Irish community, creating a feeling aptly summed up in Kevin McNamara's comment: 'I thought the days of snooping were over. This is taking us back to the 1970s.'

As this row was boiling up, David Trimble, the Ulster Unionist Party leader, was also unsuccessfully attempting to recall the BBC's attitudes of the seventies towards Irish coverage. He wrote to the BBC's Chairman, Christopher Bland, seeking to prevent the screening of Ronan Bennett's £6 million pound drama series *Rebel Heart*, based on the events of 1916 and the Anglo-Irish war, saying that Bennett was:

> an active IRA apologist whose forays into writing have been hopelessly one-sided . . . I believe that the BBC as a public service broadcaster must examine whether funding and broadcasting such a film by such a writer really is a service to the public in Northern Ireland at such a sensitive time.

In the course of the letter, Trimble also said that the fact that Bennett had served a year in jail in 1975 for the murder of an RUC man made him 'a most unsuitable person to be commissioned to write a screen play dealing with a controversial aspect of Irish history for transmission in Northern Ireland.'

Bland rejected Trimble's criticism, telling him that if he watched the series he would find it 'honest and thoughtful', a judgement with which, whatever one's dramaturgical reservations about the production might be, it is difficult to disagree. But, as Bennett's conviction had been overturned by the Court of Appeal, Trimble's letter, which was leaked to the *Sunday Times*, became the subject of controversy in both Ireland and England and perhaps ensured a larger viewing audience for the four-part drama when it was shown by both RTE and BBC at the end of December 2000 and early January 2001.

Symbolically enough however, in terms of both women's role in the Irish diaspora and the relationship of Ireland and England outside the Six Counties arena, another distinguished Irish woman commentator, Norah Casey, summed up the millennium year state of the Irish, in both Ireland and

England, by pointing out that, as she was writing to me[66]: 'Marie Jones' wonderful play *Stones in His Pockets* has taken the West End by storm' and that she herself, and her paper, were 'busy (or stupidly some might say) encouraging our readers to return to Ireland.' At the same time she expressed the hope that, because of the Anglo-Irish relationship, the thirty year old *Post* would 'be alive and strong in another thirty years' time.'

The indications are that it will be. The *Women in Britain* volume cited by Walter was followed by another milestone publication, the inclusion – after debate – of the volume *Irish Women and Irish Migration* in Paddy O'Sullivan's massive series, *The Irish World Wide*. This work brought together for the first time a range of historical and present-day analyses, which suggested possibilities for changing the established male-centred view of the Irish diaspora. As Walter commented: 'A late but challenging start has been made on transforming the map of Irish Studies. The world looks very different when women are also located at the centre.'

Walter was too modest to claim credit for her own important part in this gender re-location. She, with Mary Hickman, was co-author of the 1997 Commission for Racial Equality Report which as we have seen was adopted by the Irish Parliamentary Group at Westminster. The Report was also a significant factor in the inclusion of an Irish category in the 2001 British Census, a vital break-through in the battle by Irish welfare groups to be given access to resources available to minority ethnic groups. A second benefit of the Census inclusion had already become apparent at the time of writing. Students applying for a university place can now tick an 'Irish' box to record their ethnic identity rather than in the all-embracing but divisive 'white' category.

But, as with most facets of the Anglo-Irish relationship, this indication of increasing harmonies is accompanied by continuing discordancies. Walter says that:

> The way the 'Irish' box has been placed in the census question is very unfortunate. The ethnic question is primarily a chance for second and later generations to identify themselves, since birthplace is recorded elsewhere. But people of Irish descent are forced to choose between 'British' or 'Irish', when many would probably prefer a hyphenated identity of some kind. Moreover there are no other subdivisions of 'White', so that the Irish stand out as oppositional to the British and the only population who would like to claim cultural difference. A more positive attitude to white difference would have been shown by subdividing the British themselves into English, Scottish and Welsh as well as by naming the other large minorities such as Greek Cypriots. Such an acknowledgement of 'white' diversity in Britain could play an important part in challenging the taken-for-granted rigidity of the black/white divide.

Walter made a further important contribution towards breaking down such divides in 2000 with the publication of her book *Outsiders Inside*, which explains why many Irish women in Britain question whether they are in fact 'white' and why Irish women are 'visible' in the U.S. and 'invisible' in Britain. Such explorations and the growing interest in Irish studies and the pursuit of identity are now increasingly common, signs of an increasing awareness of the strength, and diversity of that identity. In 2000 also Paddy Logan edited a book, *Being Irish*, which included interviews with one hundred people. Reviewing it favourably, as it deserved, Ted Barrington commented that:

> Many who see themselves as Irish have never been to Ireland. It [Irishness] is not to be found in exclusivist definitions of race. There are Black Irish, Asian Irish. It is not religion. The Irish world-wide speak many languages and English with many accents . . . it is not geography, nor law, nor genetics, nor a brogue . . . it is to be found in a cultural space that both embraces and transcends these categories.

This is really another way of saying that Irishness carries a particularist imprint of the Celtic personality, but it is no bad concept with which to conclude an examination of the study of Ireland and the Irish.

THE GAELIC ATHLETIC ASSOCIATION

Sport is a particularly passionate focus of identity for the Irish, and one of its most passionate areas is that of Gaelic games. The Gaelic Athletic Association was founded in 1884 by Michael Cusack as part of the general upsurge of a consciousness of being Irish which accompanied the Celtic dawn of the foundation of the Gaelic League, and when the Yeats, Synge, Lady Gregory renaissance led to the foundation of the Abbey Theatre. In many ways that era paralleled the spirit of the Ireland of our time. The GAA, often referred to by the irreverent as the Grab All Association, is the largest Irish sporting organisation and, though it does not play international competitions, it nowadays provides links with the Irish in the countries of the diaspora. Gaelic teams travel back and forth to America and Australia, and, in an interesting development, Australian rules football – which some see (and I think, rightly) as a derivative of Gaelic football – is increasingly being played in Ireland by teams brought from Australia, or in Australia by teams from Ireland. This is a significant development for the GAA because, for decades after the achievement of Irish independence, the organisation encapsulated all the fierce inwardness and 'Ourselves Aloneism' of Irish Catholic identity. Until the 1970s the GAA forbade its members to play or attend 'foreign games' – that is, the 'Garrison games' traditionally played by the British Army in Ireland: rugby, hockey, cricket or soccer. Nor could its clubs raise money by staging 'foreign dances' – rock and roll. The dances favoured by officialdom were the pre-*Riverdance*, pre-sexual revolution, staid versions of the no-lifting-of-the-leg-above-the-knee kind of Irish dancing.

At the time of writing, the GAA will not admit members of either the British security force or of the Royal Ulster Constabulary to the organisation. In some ways, the GAA resembled the Church, because the organisation exercised both a form of control and, for some, conferred a comforting form of distinctive identity on its members. For rural emigrants in particular,

Gaelic games and the GAA were a valuable method of finding their feet in British society. The GAA's network provided friendships, jobs and digs. Membership was an essential rite of passage for many an Irishman who later emerged on the national and then international stage. Michael Collins, for example, was the treasurer of, and one of the foremost players for, the London GAA club, the Geraldines.

The hurley stick, sometimes referred to as the 'Tipperary rifle' during the recent Troubles, was once a symbol of national defiance. Young IRA volunteers of the post–1916 era, prevented from drilling openly with guns, would march in processions with their hurling sticks on their shoulders. Hurling and the GAA also provided both a source of, and a feed into, the oral Irish tradition of heroic storytelling. The deeds of great hurlers and footballers of the past are told and retold, until they assume mythical proportions akin to figures from Irish legend, such as the Fianna, or Cuchulain. As a boy, I attended an All-Ireland Hurling Final at Croke Park in Dublin with my father, and for years treasured the programme as a souvenir. Amongst the pen pictures it gave was one of a famous goalkeeper who trained 'by standing in a barn door on a summer's evening stopping swallows . . .'.

In Ireland the GAA is so flourishing and powerful that, in the 1996 budget, the Government made an outrageous attempt to curry favour with its membership by donating some IR£20 million of taxpayers' money towards the cost of re-constructing Croke Park. Nevertheless, one of the stalwarts of the GAA in England, Eugene Hickey, told me that he finds that soccer is causing a decline in membership.[67]

There are reasons for this decline other than soccer, however, which have to do with the changing nature of Irish identity. Sport, like news and the more popular Irish TV chat shows and soaps, are now generally available via the Tara Television Company. Of particular relevance to the GAA is the fact that sports programmes are screened in pubs with Sunday opening licences. Sunday is traditionally the day on which most GAA games are held – an unstated, but potent, indication of how the Catholics undermined 'the Lord's Day Observance' of Sunday sport in Ireland. Also, the quarrelsome internal politics of the GAA tend to be a turn-off for young people; being a quintessentially Irish association, the GAA is notoriously prone to that most Irish of failings, 'the Split'.

Hickey did have hopes that the growth of youthful teams, under 8s, under 14s and so on, largely composed of children born in England to Irish parents, would help to restore the GAA's fortunes, but as we spoke, he felt that the organisation had entered upon a period of decline. His own son was playing rugby, although he was a GAA medallist, and he felt that Jackie Charlton had unwittingly proved himself to be the GAA's greatest enemy. Hurling, the *Riverdance* of sport, still attracted big crowds, particularly amongst women, who were also showing a growing interest in camogie, the female version of hurling. Traditionally, priests took a prominent part in the organisation and training of hurling and football games, but Hickey stroked his chin reflectively as we talked, and remarked: 'That's a funny thing you know, but you don't see many priests training the camogie teams.' Perhaps under another Pope . . .

Hickey made another observation which indicates something of the time warp of GAA: 'London Irish put GAA to shame for facilities.' This was a perennially heard comment during my football- and hurling-playing days – the GAA recorded huge attendances, but deplorable conditions for its players compared to rugby clubs. I turned up at a Gaelic football pitch once and innocently enquired of one of the organisers: 'Where are the showers?' To which the organiser replied, pointing upwards at some approaching black clouds: 'You'll get plenty of showers when those come over.'

LONDON IRISH RUGBY CLUB

As indicated elsewhere, most new Irish emigrants to Britain now head south. There has been a significant shift away from the northern areas and as the historian Jim O'Hara points out, the continuation of a vigorous, dynamic Irish presence in Britain is increasingly dependent on the second- and third-generation Irish. O'Hara points to three areas to indicate the grounds for his optimism that this dependency will be fruitful, first hand knowledge of the growing enthusiasm involved, from his own involvement in Irish studies, sport, and in music – he takes part each year in the annual Celtic music festival in L'Orient. He points out that: 'Some of the finest exponents of traditional Irish music in Britain are young second-generation either carrying on a family tradition, or pupils of some of the great emigrant musicians, such as Brendan Mulkere, whose teaching has inspired so many young musicians.

As the success of the Irish soccer team illustrates, sport is the most popular arena for the second-generation Irish. One of the Irish community's oldest sporting organizations is London Irish Rugby Football Club, founded in 1898 and since then a focal point wherein both Orange and Green have worn the emerald jersey in harmony.

Professionalism and the changing patterns of emigration have changed the nature of the club. As O'Hara, a star player in his day, explained to me, it is no longer owned by its members but has become a company with directors and shareholders. The current squad of some thirty players contains only a half-dozen with Irish connections, and in order to find a bigger ground with greater facilities, first team matches were played at the Harlequins' ground at Twickenham. In 1990 the venue was moved from its West London base to Reading football team's ground some forty miles down the M4 motorway. Like Glasgow Celtic, the club's sense of Irishness now rests with its Irish directors and supporters rather than its professional players.

I attended a match on what was both a critical and a gala day in the club's history. It afforded me an opportunity of seeing both the best, and the worst, aspects of Irish sport and professionalism in operation. It was the last match of the 1997 season, which it was essential for London Irish to win, because defeat would have brought relegation and a huge drop in sponsorship.

Many of the people at the ground were either visitors to London, or Irish-born emigrants who had done well in England. I met several people I knew, and I would have to say that in many ways the occasion presented the best side of Irish friendliness and hospitality – corporate sponsorship ensured that the refreshments marquee was large and well filled in every sense of the word. Happily, London Irish duly retained this sponsorship by winning the match convincingly, helped, let it be said, by the exertions of their mighty Samoan lock forward. But herein lay the problem. London Irish, like other leading rugby clubs, was coming to terms with commercialism.

Both at the game and in the nearby bars afterwards, the discussion was not about the play. The *leitmotif* of the afternoon was summed up by an overheard comment that 'That fucking wanker isn't worth £75,000 a year.'

Somewhat depressed at the all-pervasive note of commercialism, I brightened up when I saw one of the afternoon's gladiators in a corner, a huge figure of a man, listening very intently to his mother. 'Now that,' I thought, 'is a more traditional Irish sight: Respect For The Mother.' Subsequently I learned that the mother was also the player's agent.

Jim O'Hara put the afternoon in context: 'to cope with the demands of the modern game, the first XV has to be composed of first class professional players of whatever nationality. But the character of the club is maintained through the membership, through the fact that at weekends, hundreds of small boys, second-generation Irish like my son Ruairí, tog out in junior teams. They are the membership of the future of this great Irish institution.'

Most of what has been written so far concerns London. Let us make a necessarily brief and incomplete examination of some other cities associated with the Irish in England. One can encounter tangible evidence of the influences of the past in different ways and in different places.

LIVERPOOL

In Liverpool, during a visit to the Irish Centre in Mount Pleasant Street, I found that the large gold letters proclaiming the Centre's identity, on the outside wall, were in some cases twisted, or, in others, missing altogether. The vandalisation had occurred in 1996, during a riot, when Loyalist sympathisers attacked a St Patrick's Day procession. Inside, the Centre itself was seedy and run down, a paradigm of the way in which the Irish community in Liverpool has disintegrated, either through death, movement to other parts of the country, or evolution into the middle classes and a transfer to the suburbs.

However, the Irish Centre vandalisation has to be understood in terms of Liverpool's Labour politics rather than the straightforward ancient animosities of Orange and Green. In the early sixties, the Centre, once the vibrant hub of Irish activities in the city, had fallen on evil days, and gone into liquidation. It was taken over by new management, a man and woman who had been members of the Militant Tendency group in Labour. Following Neil

Kinnock's purging of that element from Labour, the couple espoused a Wearing of the Green position. The holding of the 1996 St Patrick's Day procession was prefaced by media interviews which contained unflattering references to Orangeism, and a confrontational atmosphere reappeared once more in Orange/Green relationships. There is a strong pro-Ulster Loyalist element in Liverpool: the Netherfields district, for example, is referred to as 'the Shankill of Liverpool', and UDA graffiti, and fund-raising, are common in certain strongly Orange areas. In the event, the procession became the target of Orange rioters – hence the twisted signs etc. That particular management also went into liquidation and, at the time of writing, the prospective purchaser of the Centre was said to be a Chinese businessman.

However, the various activities associated with the Centre go on in other parts of the city. For example, Irish music, games and so on flourish amongst the 17,000 first-generation Irish who are reckoned to live in Liverpool, together with a far greater number of Irish descent. Some of the most distinguished scholars in the field of Irish Studies were to be found teaching at Liverpool University, at the Irish Studies Centre founded by Patrick Buckland – figures like Marianna Elliott, Christine Kineally and Elizabeth Malcolm. The Irish in Liverpool still display a marked empathy with their native country when the opportunity arises. As this book was being written, for example, during November 1998, the venue for the speaking engagement by the Irish President, Mary McAleese, had to be moved three times in order to secure a hall large enough to accommodate the ever-rising demand for tickets.[69] In the end, the President spoke to an audience of 900 at the St George's Hall.

Liverpool in its day was not only the major port of the British Empire, but a hotbed of Orangeism and a magnet that drew tens of thousands of Irish, particularly after the Great Famine. This volatile mixture led inevitably to strife, and as early as 1819, Liverpool recorded its first Orange/Catholic riot. Reports of the time could well have been written about the contemporary Garvaghy Road situation in Portadown, County Armagh. As in the contemporary situation, the Orangemen wanted to walk through a Catholic area, that of Dale Street, and were attacked by a Catholic mob.

THE ORANGE AND THE GREEN

Here, at the risk of digression, I feel that it would be helpful to the reader to give some indication as to why the terms 'Orange' and 'Green', which figure large in this book, generally occur against a backdrop of riot. The terms serve to encapsulate complex and deeply embedded traditions, stretching back into Irish history. However, an image made up of two houses, a disastrous IRA raid, and a five-pound note will, I hope, shed light on the complexity.

One of the houses is a neat, single-storey building with a corrugated roof, small porch and some severely clipped shrubbery. The house is that of Dan

Winter at The Diamond, Loughgall, County Armagh, where the Orange Order was born in 1795. It followed a bloody pitched battle over land between Protestant 'Peep O Day Boys' and Catholic Defenders, near what was then Dan Winter's Tavern. The IRA raid took place on 8 March 1986, also at Loughgall, when one of the IRA's most feared Active Service Units (ASUs), led by a top commander, Jim Lynagh, was wiped out in an ambush set by the SAS. Some of the unit were captured alive, but were apparently put lying face downwards and shot dead. In its way, the destruction of Lynagh's unit was as big a reverse for the Republicans as had been the Battle of the Diamond for their predecessors in 1795. Both defeats were due to the same cause: in that district, the forces of Protestanism were strong and could rely on local information and support to fructify the roots of the Orange Lily in blood.

The other house, a fine, basemented, two-storey building with a large garden, stands at the corner of Baggot Street and Herbert Street, in a busy section of commercial Dublin wherein one finds professional services ranging from those provided by architects and restaurateurs to those available at the nearby headquarters of the Bank of Ireland. Other services are provided along the even nearer banks of the Grand Canal. It was once proposed in the early days of pious nationalism which followed the setting up of the Irish Free State that the handsome trees lining this attractive waterway should be cut down, because of the habitat they provided for prostitutes. However, the trees were saved on the grounds of the argument proposed by a Senator, the surgeon and writer Oliver St John Gogarty, that they were more sinned against than sinning. So, one can still find on a morning after a busy weekend, before the corporation sweepers have gone to work, a sizeable deposit of used condoms, indicating that the trees' services are still being availed of as the century draws to a close.

Very likely the condoms were purchased with a five-pound note which bears on it a likeness of the woman who made the house on the corner of Baggot Street world-famous: Mother Catherine Mary McAuley, founder of the Congregation of the Sisters of Mercy, established by her in Baggot Street in 1831. The Mercy Order owes its foundation to the conditions of the time: poverty, the exploitation of the poor, especially women, and in particular the abuse, both sexual and otherwise, to which servant girls were commonly subjected. A legacy of £25,000, a huge sum for the time, enabled Catherine to launch a movement which not only made a significant contribution to alleviating the conditions of the poor at that time, but which for nearly two centuries afterwards educated generations of Catholic women around the world. In so doing, convents often became the targets of anti-Catholic rioters, and of 'convent disclosures': lurid tales about the alleged goings-on within their walls such as 'The Story of Maria Monk, The Awful Disclosures of A Young And Beautiful Nun', which were widely used at moments of excitation such as the Know-Nothing agitation in America, or during the anti-popery crusades of preachers in Orange centres like Belfast or Glasgow.

The year 1829 was a time of Catholic emancipation; Irish Catholics had won religious liberty thanks to Daniel O'Connell's sustained campaign. However, it was to be a year of subjugation, not emancipation, for Catherine McAuley. Catherine had not intended to found a convent. She had seen herself and her helpers as engaged in social work and the provision of a refuge for abused women. However, one day, a priest called to Baggot Street to say that it was the decision of Archbishop Murray that the house be given to another order of nuns, the Sisters of Charity, but that a few rooms would be provided for McAuley and her followers.

It is said that 'Catherine replied quietly without any sign of distress, "The house already belongs to the Archbishop. He is free to do with it whatever he wishes."'[70]

After the priest left 'Catherine went to her room and did not appear again for some hours'.[71] Her withdrawal was understandable. Firstly, she had invested everything she owned in Baggot Street, intending it to be not merely a house of refuge but a centre from which she and her associates could go out to minister to the poor. This facility was denied to cloistered nuns. Secondly, she herself had established a trust fund which effectively placed the Archbishop in control of Baggot Street. However, she sent a note to the Archbishop, telling him that she had received his message, and was ready to do whatever he asked.

The next day, the Archbishop called on her claiming on one hand that he had not authorised the priest's visit, but stating on the other that he could see the advantages of her community becoming a religious organisation. Catherine knew she was being made an offer she could not refuse. The idea of independent-minded women running their own affairs, free of the control of a male-dominated episcopacy, was not something the Vatican would tolerate. However, in return for Catherine's acceptance of the idea, the Archbishop successfully interceded with Rome for permission to found a new congregation for women without cloister. After training by the Presentation Order, the new Order opened on 12 December 1831. There was no centralised control other than the overall formation based on Catherine's teaching and example. They operated under the jurisdiction of whichever bishop was in control of any area in which they were working. Paradoxically this circumstance led to the Order's influence being greatly strengthened throughout the world, because bishops were keen to invite them into their dioceses as much for their absence of troublesome head offices as for their charitable works.

However, the Murray diktat meant that the Order of Mercy (like many other congregations of Irish nuns) would be permeated by the warring spirits of Catherine's warm outgoing compassion and the juridical, dehumanising 'numbers count' rule of Rome. A distinguished Irish doctor, working in America on the treatment of sexually transmitted disease, Mary Guinan, a pioneer of AIDS research, remarked to me truly that: 'The Black Muslims and the Catholics push numbers at the expense of individuals.'[72] Perhaps not surprisingly, Dr Guinan was planning to return to Ireland at the time to open a family planning clinic. The rigidity of control, the Jansenistic attitude towards sex and the numbers factor were to become a principal reason for many of the criticisms subsequently levelled at Irish nuns around the world. The attitude to sex outside marriage tended to produce a frigidity inside marriage, partly in response to the distress caused by over-breeding, that was responsible for a great deal of trauma.

There were other side-effects. For example, at the time of writing, the Sisters of Mercy, despite their manifold good works, are the subject of considerable criticism in Ireland for the manner in which they ran huge 'industrial' schools (the Irish Christian Brothers ran similar, more draconian schools for boys). These schools ran on a capitation basis – the Government paid so much per head, thus putting a premium on numbers: the more pupils, the more income. As a result of a *trahison des clercs* on the part of the Church, the politicians, the Department of Education and even the courts, tens of thousands of children were funnelled into harshly regimented boarding schools run by nuns. Joyce once gave a bitter but accurate description of Ireland as being a place where Christ and Caesar were hand in glove. Undoubtedly, some of the children reared in these schools were in need of shelter and training, albeit of a more humane type, but equally, some of the children who ended up in such schools did so because the local parish priest, often acting on very dubious information, appeared before a compliant district justice to say that a child should be taken from 'a bad mother'. In the thirties, forties and fifties Ireland had the highest percentage of children in 'industrial' schools of any country in Europe. Now, as revelations[73] mount about the poor food and harsh treatment meted out to children, the baby of Catherine McAuley's reputation is in danger of being thrown out with the bath water of Rome's additives. Some of the sexual revelations are making people wonder whether the traditional anti-Catholic rhetoric about nuns was altogether unfounded.

The Orange Order and the members of Mary McAuley's Order rarely came into direct conflict. The significance of the two movements to their respective traditions lies more in the differing world views which they symbolise.

Catherine was described as being 'remarkably well made, round but not in the least heavy', with 'a good carriage', and eyes which had a 'strange expression of reading your thoughts'. The thoughts of this pious, but attractive and energetic woman must have been a tumult of conflicting emotions. One of her last acts on the day she died was to wrap up her shoes and the 'instruments of penance', instructing one of her nuns to burn the parcel without looking at its contents.

The 'instruments' used by the Orange Order, however, were not intended for voluntary self-flagellation, but for infliction on their Papist adversaries. Guns, swords and cudgels, rather than tongs were the implements used, particularly in the brutal suppression of the 1798 rebellion.

THE ORANGE ORDER

The fundamental precept of the Orange Order as proclaimed in 1795, and subsequently, was 'loyalty': that is, loyalty to the throne of England and the British connection. In fact, in practice, Orange loyalty has always been highly conditional – the Orangeman would be loyal to the leader who was loyal to him, in the old Scottish 'banding' tradition. Members of the order have always reserved the right to withhold loyalty when they see fit. This is why there are pictures on TV of Union Jack-waving crowds hurling petrol bombs at British soldiers in Northern Ireland who seek to prevent them marching into areas where they are not wanted. However, because of their 'loyalty' Orangemen traditionally expected to be preferred for any jobs or council houses which might be available.

The reality of Orangeism, and much of traditional Unionism, is three-fold: the British heritage, the Protestant religion and supremacy. Most upholders of the Green tradition have no difficulty with the first two characteristics. It is the third which creates the clashes.

A combination of Presbyterianism and an anti-intellectual, anti-artistic, canny type of persona which pervades the so called 'Scotch Irish' of Northern Ireland has led most commentators to judge that the Orangemen are exhibiting traditional Lowland Scottish traits. In fact, it could equally well be argued that the Orangemen's attitude to their Catholic neighbours derives from the wide area lying on both sides of the English-Scottish border. The constant warfare, raiding and 'reiving', that is, cattle rustling, and the near total instability of the border area for centuries, were certainly well calculated to impart 'our' law and 'our' order – in other words, ruthlessness and hostility to either a native population or the practitioners of another creed. These traits served the Scotch/Irish planters well, not only in dealing with the native population in Ireland, but, as we will see, in that of America as well.

By 1963, when the Order uncharacteristically dropped its veil of secrecy, its purposes were expressed in the more decorous terms whereby every aspirant Orangeman was asked:

> do you promise, before this Lodge, to give no countenance, by your presence or otherwise, to the unscriptural, superstitious, and idolatrous worship of the Church of Rome? And do you also promise never to marry a Roman Catholic, never to stand sponsor for a child when receiving baptism from a priest of Rome, nor allow a Roman Catholic to stand sponsor for your child at baptism? And do you further promise to resist, by all lawful means, the ascendancy, extension and encroachments of that Church; at the same time being careful always to abstain from all unkind words and actions towards its members, yea, even prayerfully and diligently, as opportunity occurs, to use your best efforts to deliver them from error and false doctrine, and lead them to the truth of that Holy Word, which is able to make them wise unto salvation?

After 1798, during which the Orange Order played a vigorous, and often brutal, role in crushing the Rebellion, the Order spread to England where it exhibited certain of the characteristics of Mother Catherine McAuley's Foundation, in as much as it was fraternal, exhibited a genuine concern for the welfare of its members, and spread throughout the British Empire. There, however, the similarities end. In Ireland, the Orange Order's tradition of the maintenance of both property and identity by armed force was (for a time) useful both to the forces of the Crown and the landlord in dealing with the natives; in England, the Order was a tool used by the Tories to combat the Liberals; but as times changed the Order became something of an embarrassment to the British, both in England and Ireland. However, in Ireland, as this was being written, it still served as a vehicle for those to whom change meant economic and political frustration. Steve Bruce has encapsulated these frustrations in a memorable observation by a disgruntled Loyalist:

> What chance did we have? With us, you got bucked out of school at fifteen and into the shipyards and that was you. They used to walk past our house every day in their nice uniforms going to their good school up the Antrim Road and getting a better education than us and suddenly they are going on about civil rights.[74]

Today the shipyards of Belfast offer something like a twelfth of the employment opportunity they once held out to a Protestant-only work force, but the neatly uniformed convent schoolgirls trot along to their schools and their post-smoke-stack opportunities in ever-increasing numbers, part of an ever-rising tide of Catholic demography which, in part, derives its power from the work of the followers of Catherine McAuley and others like her. The Orange Order's response is to vent its frustrations on God and Government by attempting to march through areas which were once Protestant strongholds but are now Catholic estates, like the Garvaghy Road in Portadown, County Armagh, not far from Loughall.

The first Grand Lodge of the English Orange Institution came into being in Manchester in 1807, with a peculiar class element which would surface later in Northern Ireland and in America, both in the Know Nothing Movement and in the anti-Catholic Ku-Klux-Klan. The employers used the Lodges to keep their Protestant workers divided from their Catholic fellows so as to keep down wages. The shared membership of the Lodge gave the ordinary Protestant worker delusions of grandeur when he was invited, once a year or so, to the landlord's hall for a social occasion; but the landlord, or the industrialist, took care, when the really significant gathering, the policy meeting, took place, that it would be held mid week, in the afternoon, when the workers were at their jobs. They also used ex-soldiers whose inculcated loyalty to 'law and order', 'king and country' was easily manipulated into a force for countering socialism.

From the early 1800s, the Orange movement became intertwined as much with putting down the spread of Labour organisations in the cotton and mining areas as with anti-Catholic policies and a virulent type of fundamentalist Protestanism, continued in our day by the Reverend Ian Kyle Paisley. The Paisley of the combustible early period of Orangeism in Liverpool was a North of Ireland preacher, Hugh McNeile. His doctrine was described thus:

> They were asked why they would not keep quiet and allow Protestants and Catholics to live quietly together; his answer was that the Roman Catholic system was opposed to the perfect law of God and the gospel of his Saviour . . . That was a system with which they would not and ought not live in peace.[75]

'THE DREGS OF SOCIETY'

McNeileism, which like Paisleyism, paid off in political as well as in theological terms, was exacerbated by the numbers who fled to escape the Famine. The following quotation gives an indication of the scale of this exodus to Liverpool:

> that between the 13th day of January and the 13th day of December 1847, both days inclusive, 296,231 persons landed in this port from Ireland: that of this vast number, about 130,000 emigrated to the United States; that some 50,000 were passengers on business and the remainder were paupers, half naked and starving, landed for the most part during the winter, and becoming immediately on landing, applicants for parochial relief . . .[76]

The emigrants crowded into cellars and basements. People of both sexes crammed fifteen and sixteen at a time into single rooms. Conditions in which the RSPCA would not allow a dog to be kept nowadays were the normal lot of the poor, not merely of the Irish, but the typhus which these conditions helped to spread became known as 'the Irish fever', and the Famine-fleeing Irish were described in a select vestry report of the time as being 'so disgustingly filthy, that little can be done as yet to stay the great mortality among them'.

The British public were conditioned to evaluate the Irish catastrophe in terms of its impact on British society, rather than in terms of its causes. *The Times* in a leader of 2 April 1847 said:

> Ireland is pouring into the cities, and even into the villages of this island, a fetid mass of famine, nakedness and dirt and fever. Liverpool, whose proximity to Ireland has already procured for it the unhappy distinction of being the most unhealthy town in this island, seems destined to become one mass of disease.

That was, of course, the year of the Famine's peak, but official England took the view that the calamity was somehow the fault of the Irish rather than of a government which allowed a fertile island to slide into starvation. The Irish population was half that of England at the Famine's outset, and two and a half times that of Scotland's, but it reduced by 2 million through death and emigration in the Famine's immediate aftermath and, through emigration, by a further 2 million over the next decade. Liverpool, together with that other most Irish and most sectarian of British cities, Glasgow, felt much of the impact of the dislocated population. The results were a heightening of both sectarian and anti-Irish sentiment. The *Liverpool Herald* of 17 November 1855 summed up the Orange viewpoint:

> Let a stranger to Liverpool be taken through the streets that branch off from the Vauxhall Road, Marylebone, Whitechapel and the north end of the docks, and he will witness such a scene of filth and vice, as we defy any person to parallel in any part of the world. The numberless whiskey shops crowded with drunken half-clad women, some with infants in their arms, from early dawn till midnight – thousands of children in rags, with their features scarcely to be distinguished in consequence of the cakes of dirt upon them, the stench of filth in every direction – men and women fighting, the most horrible execrations and obscenity, with oaths and curses that make the heart shudder; all these things would lead the spectator to suppose he was in a land of savages where God was unknown and man was uncared for. And who are these wretches? Not English but Irish papists. It is remarkable and no less remarkable than true, that the lower order of Irish papists are the filthiest beings in the habitable globe, they abound in dirt and vermin and have no care for anything but self-gratification that would degrade the brute creation . . . Look at our police reports, three-fourths of the crime perpetrated in this large town is by Irish papists. They are the very dregs of society, steeped to the very lips in all manner of vice, from murder to pocket picking and yet the citizens of Liverpool are taxed to maintain the band of ruffians and their families in time of national distress . . .

LARKIN'S WAY

Here it might be remarked that these terrible conditions were to have a lasting effect on Ireland itself, which for a brief period offered the prospect of an end to Orange bitterness, for a lion of the Irish labour movement, James Larkin, roared out of the slums of Liverpool where he was born in Comberemere Street to Irish emigrant parents in 1876. Larkin, who with James Connolly founded the Irish Transport and General Workers Union, had well honed the sense of savage indignation at the excesses of capitalism, which he was to turn on the employers of Ireland with tumultuous effect, before he came to Dublin to organise the dock workers of Belfast and Dublin in 1907. His experiences in Liverpool had convinced him of the folly of sectarianism, and for a brief period after his arrival he managed to unite both Orange and Green in the interests of the workers. The lodges and the employers ultimately drove them apart again. However, Larkin and Connolly, who had been born in Edinburgh, like Larkin the son of impoverished Irish emigrants, helped to transform Ireland. Connolly founded The Irish Citizen Army to defend workers from police brutality, and led this tiny corps into the 1916 Rising, dying before a firing squad after the rebellion. Larkin lived to become the most dynamic force of the century in the Irish trade union movement. Throughout his life his love of beauty, his hatred of the life-denying squalor and constricted horizons occasioned by poverty remained rooted in his early experiences of Liverpool life. His memory is preserved in Liverpool today by a plaque marking his birthplace, and by a street called after him: Larkin's Way.

RIOTS AND RABBLE ROUSERS

Larkin grew up against a backdrop in which, apart from poverty, issues such as the restoration of the Roman Catholic hierarchy had intertwined with anti-Irish sentiment to the detriment of working-class Catholics and Protestants, causing very savage rioting in Birkenhead and Liverpool. On top of these specific *casus belli*, McNeile's activities ensured that the cry of 'no popery' resounded at election times, generally to the benefit of the Tories, with consequential inevitable violence. The growth of the movement for Home Rule for Ireland, and the rise of Fenianism, in the 1860s, also provoked violence. To the Irish stew was added the crisis in the Anglican Church between the fundamentalists and the ritualists, so that one riot blurred into another. Older Catholic Liverpudlians of Irish descent, at the time of writing, could still remember their Protestant fellow citizens being referred to as 'George Wisers'. George Wise, another Paisleyite-type Evangelical and rabble rouser, exercised a literally disturbing influence on the streets of Liverpool leading up to the First World War. Wise professed to love individual Catholics while hating the power of Rome. As in our time, in Belfast and throughout Northern Ireland, such protestations inevitably resulted in the heads of individual Catholics and Protestants being broken.

Notable examples of such happenings were the Wise-inflamed riots of 1909. Disturbances broke out in the parish of Holy Cross in Vauxhall during Catholic celebration of the sixtieth anniversary of the founding of the Catholic mission to the area. The Orange element objected to the fact that statues of the Virgin were carried in procession, and that members of a religious order (the Benedictines) wore habits. These riots were a mirror image of events that subsequently befell in Belfast. Protestants afterwards expressed strong feelings of betrayal because the police attacked them. 'Their law' and 'their order' had been directed against *them* instead of at the idolatrous papists! As in Northern Ireland, the police, with good reason, were often regarded by the Irish Catholics as the legal arm of Orangeism, but, as in Ireland, when conscientious officers attempted to administer the law impartially the meat in the sandwich syndrome took over.

The onset of the First World War no more brought a spirit of harmony between the Liverpudlian Protestants and Catholics than it did between those representatives of the Orange and Green traditions from Northern Ireland who served together at the Somme. The widespread nature of the rioting diminished, almost disappeared, but the sectarian feeling continued throughout the Troubles. Other Protestant rabble rousers came forward to offer themselves as successors to Wise; for example, the Reverend H.

Longbottom, like Ian Paisley after him, ran a 'memorial church' in which little good was said of the Catholics. Even without the Troubles, relics from the past could be seen on the streets of Liverpool during the sixties. For example, Frank Neal has recorded that it was not unusual to find a piece of bacon hanging in places like Netherfield with a sign on it reading 'cured at Lourdes'.[77] The tensions of the early Troubles' era were brilliantly captured by Alan Bleasdale in his hilarious, though often horrific television drama which tells the story of what happened when a Green and an Orange outing were maliciously booked into a club on the same night.

LATTER DAY LIVERPOOL

Urban renewal, unemployment, and education cut into the Orange/Tory dominance. One of the last really major intrusions of an Irish political issue into Liverpool affairs occurred during the Irish Treaty negotiations when Lord Birkenhead had to leave the Irish Treaty negotiation table in Downing Street to pay a surreptitious visit to the sick-bed of A. T. Salvidge, in Liverpool, to reassure him that the Treaty would not in any way cut across the interests of the Ulster Orangemen. Salvidge was a power both in the Tory Party in Liverpool and in militant Protestantism. Had he used his influence, as chairman of the forthcoming Conservative Party Conference in Liverpool, against the Treaty, the Conservative Party might not have ratified it.

By the 1960s, the most prominent (and inaccurate) symptoms of the ancient antagonisms were the 'Catholic soccer clubs'. The presence of prominent Irish soccer players from Dublin like Peter Farrell in Everton, or Ronnie Whelan and Steve Heighway in Liverpool gave rise to this mistaken description. It was popularly said that every Irish priest in Liverpool had a season ticket for Liverpool FC, and that candles burned in every convent for the welfare of the Irish soccer stars. Both may well have occurred – nevertheless, the membership and ownership of these clubs remained predominantly Protestant. However, the resumption of strife in Northern Ireland meant that, as in previous years, trouble in Ireland was replicated in Liverpool, albeit to a lesser extent than of yore. Stones came through the windows of Kevin McNamara's home, and his children had to contend with some of the same uglinesses that were common in his youth. A Labour MP for Hull, McNamara grew up in a strongly Irish background. Irish songs, Irish music, Irish games were the recreations of his childhood. The Irish were a politically aware community. A joke of McNamara's boyhood was that the Irish in Liverpool grew up trained to do three things: go to Mass on a Sunday, vote Labour and join the Transport and General Workers Union.

The joke contains an interesting omission: it does not refer to Protestants of Irish descent, be they Irish Anglicans or militant Orangemen. Although these express a strong sense of Irishness – which the great British public would be the first to acknowledge, deeming them as much Paddies as any Republican – to the 'Irish', that is the Irish of Catholic descent, they are regarded as part of

192

the British fabric of society. An even more interesting, and certainly more significant, omission was that of Kevin McNamara himself from the Labour front bench, at Orange insistence. I am indebted to, of all people, the Unionist leader David Trimble for an insight as to how this came about. Trimble and I had been taking part in a fairly abrasive television debate, under the chairmanship of Jon Snow, in a Midlands television studio, and a production assistant obviously made as little distinction between two kinds of Irishmen as is commonly made between the Orange and Green traditions by the wider British public. Accordingly, as the two Irishmen were going to the same airport, and the same country, it was arranged that they should share the same taxi! Fortunately, off camera, Trimble and I got on well (sadly, on that occasion only) and, warmed by a little post-programme hospitality, he confided in me that he did not expect Kevin McNamara to remain as Labour spokesperson for long.

Our taxi journey took place not long after the Unionists had been instrumental in voting through the Maastricht Treaty in the House of Commons, where Tory divisions had left John Major dependent on the Ulstermen's vote. Watching the outcome of the vote, John Smith, the then leader of Labour, arranged to meet with a Unionist delegation to enquire whether, if Labour were in power and in a similar type of situation, the Unionists might consider supporting Labour. The Unionists replied that they would, but that their price would include the replacement of Kevin McNamara as spokesperson on Northern Ireland. With a smile like moonlight on a tombstone, Trimble said to me as our taxi drew up at the airport, 'Don't be surprised if Kevin ceases to be the Labour spokesperson shortly.' He did. John Smith died suddenly and prematurely, but Mo Mowlam duly succeeded Kevin McNamara. However, let it be said that, while the dropping of McNamara was clearly a poor return for his years of devoted service to the Labour Party and the Irish community, Mo Mowlam subsequently made a historic success of the position of Secretary of State for Northern Ireland.

BIRMINGHAM

I have already given an indication of the situation of the Irish community in Birmingham in the brief sketch outlining de Valera's attitude to emigration in the immediate aftermath of the Second World War. One of Birmingham's, and indeed, England's, best-known Irish figures, who grew up in those years, is the courageously outspoken Clare Short, Secretary of State for International Development in the 1997 Labour Cabinet, and one of the last representatives of the gritty, ruggedly individualistic old Labour tradition of Keir Hardie. Short defines her Irishness as being an integral part of her, which defines her sense of identity, knowledge of history and world view. Her great-grandfather on her mother's side was Irish, and her father was born in Crossmaglen, County Armagh. He was a teacher and head of a primary school, and Short remembers him as having had 'a proud dignified life, and carried on working for the cause of Ireland'. It was a political family. Her father was secretary of the Birmingham branch of the Anti-Partition League, so Clare and her four sisters and two brothers grew up in a house wherein Irish history and the partition issue were familiar topics of conversation.

Having studied political science at university, Short went to work in the Home Office, which was then (in the early sixties) responsible for Northern Ireland. She described how in those days 'Northern Ireland was just two little rooms in the Home Office in Whitehall'. The 'two little rooms' phrase in fact says all that needs to be known about why Northern Ireland was allowed to turn into the political slum which it became under the Unionists, before the British stepped in after the Troubles broke out and began trying to encourage democratic reform. The whole thrust of British policy in those days was to let sleeping dogs lie, and pay as little attention as possible to Northern Ireland. Unfortunately, sleeping dogs have a way of waking up.

Clare Short too began waking up to a political impulse. After working in the Home Office, meeting politicians and ministers, she thought, 'I could do that. If I'd never met them, I'd never have formulated the thought that someone like me could do it.' So she stood for, and won, the seat of Birmingham Ladywood in 1983. In general, though she has had a turbulent career in politics, Short finds that she has 'a very warm, very nice relationship with my constituency'.

One institution with which she did not have a nice relationship was Rupert Murdoch's *News of the World* newspaper. After she had attacked the exploitation of women as Page Three girls, the Murdoch press attempted a smear campaign against her. Representatives of the *News of the World* contacted everyone she had known for the previous twenty years, trying to dig up nonexistent dirt on her by methods such as offering money to anyone who could produce a compromising photograph of her. In characteristic fashion, Short reacted by announcing to the Commons what was afoot and complaining to the Press Commission before the *News of the World* could get anything into print. She received front-page retractions, but it was a pretty trying time.

Worse was to come over her defence of the innocent men accused of the Birmingham bombings. She got death threats, a big postbag and a bad press. In those days, to speak out against partition or miscarriages of justice was a recipe for being labelled a member of the IRA. Short says that she was able to deal with the pressures because of her Irish roots, and 'the family thing'. 'I had a very secure, not wealthy but loved, childhood in a house full of people and full of children, and that sort of love and security stays with you. My mum was with me in Birmingham, I'm in touch with all my brothers and sisters, I go to Ireland at least once a year to see relatives. So I think the most important thing you can give a person when they are a child is security. It goes with you all your life . . . the other thing I was given was a deep sense of who we were and where we came from, of our Irishness and of the injustices historically that have been done to Ireland, and to our people . . . so it followed logically that we were for those who were badly treated.'[78]

These days amongst the relatives whom Short is in touch with is a son born of an earlier relationship. He is now a solicitor in the financial district of London, and he and Clare only rediscovered each other's existence as this book was being written. He was born when Clare was a student. The reunion helped to balance the tragedy of the death of her husband Alex Lyon, who, like Clare, was a Labour MP, but who ironically lost his York seat the year in which Clare won hers. He died in 1995, suffering from Alzheimer's disease.

THE AFTERMATH OF THE BIRMINGHAM BOMBS

The reasons that Clare Short was targeted as an IRA spokesperson and that Birmingham became notorious for anti-Irish prejudice were the infamous explosions on the night of 21 November 1974. IRA bombs killed twenty-one innocent civilians and injured some 180 more. At this remove, it's difficult to recapture the atmosphere of fear and hatred that affected the Irish community in the wake of this atrocity. Birmingham had already been experiencing marked anti-Irish prejudice for a decade before. The large influx of Irish emigrants during the 1950s had led to tensions, and sociologists had commented on the bad impression created in some English minds by the Irish as early as 1967.[79] Even then, the Irish were identified as 'the main problem group among newcomers'.[80]

Already having my own anecdotal evidence of people changing their Irish accents, adopting a low profile, being discriminated against in housing, I had no difficulty in accepting the veracity of these cases cited by the CRE report:

My husband was thrown off the bus. It's not like we did it. It wasn't our fault. In the car factory they were working with spanners and hammers. He was frightened. The police sent coaches to bring them home. He had his mouth busted – stitches.

I was working at Rover and the director rang to enquire if I was being harassed, that I should be allowed to go home. I was the only Irish person and they couldn't have been nicer. The Rover workers in the factories marched out to campaign to send the Irish back home.

Dead silence when I went to work – the silence spoke enough.

I felt dreadful – there weren't any Irish at work in the hospital. I was the only one not called in – although I only lived up the road from the hospital – to do the emergency packs, but I went in to volunteer. I got the cold shoulder and abuse.

They treated us horribly and treated us like dirt. Our children could just as likely be in the bomb. They were bad to us in the shops. Englishmen did not treat us the same as the day before. You could not blame them for that.

This was a terrible time. All the Irish community was in shock and people reacted to them. I took my children to school and an Englishwoman gave us verbal abuse. She said, 'Why

don't you fucking go back?' I asked her to think that people in the bomb were Irish. The
doctors and nurses trying to save them were Irish.

Two reliable witnesses who were present in Birmingham in those days
recalled the scene for me. One was Tommy Walsh, a leading community
activist from Liverpool, whose calibre may be judged by his response to my
question, 'How should I describe you?' He replied, after a lifetime – he is now
sixty-eight – spent spearheading practically every worthwhile social or
cultural initiative undertaken by the Irish community in Liverpool: 'Ah, say
I'm a GAA man.' Typically, when he heard of the bombings, Walsh went to
Birmingham to render any assistance he could. He found the Irish Centre in
'a state of siege'. He had to be smuggled in in an ambulance. Apart from the
angry crowds outside, almost equally angry phone calls were pouring into the
Centre, many from the media. In addition, distraught relatives were phoning
the Centre in an effort to find out anything they could about loved ones who
might have been caught up in the bombing.

The other witness to the hysteria was a Columban priest, Father Gerry
French, who subsequently became Director of the Irish Chaplaincy in Britain.
Prior to the Birmingham pub bombings, another explosion was exercising the
public mind. An IRA man, James McDaid, had been atomised in a blast, out
of which only his thumb could be recovered. In the wake of this explosion,
Birmingham's Roman Catholic Bishop, George Patrick Dwyer, who had
earlier issued a strong condemnation of the introduction of internment to
Northern Ireland, being heavily criticised as a result, seized the opportunity
not only to issue a justifiably strong condemnation of violence, but to declare
in addition that the bomber would not get a Catholic funeral. This presented
a crisis of conscience for Irish priests, particularly for men like French, who
tried to live by the principle of loving the sinner while hating the sin. One of
his colleagues, the republican-inclined Father Desmond Gill, decided for the
sake of the family, if nothing else, that what was left of McDaid should get a
Christian blessing. McDaid was to be buried in Ireland but, although fearful
of the consequences, Father Gerry decided to go along to the removal of the
remains ceremony to give his confrère moral support.

The atmosphere there was a mixture of tension, the bizarre and the
macabre. Hostile crowds ringed the church, and there was a huge police
presence. French remembers that his thoughts were a medley of wishing that
he were anywhere else in the world, and worries as to what were his duties as
a good priest and at the same time a good Irishman. This was the
psychological deposit of centuries of such conflicts between the dictates of
Christ and Caesar for Irish priests. Above all, however, he was moved by
feelings of pity for the bewildered and grief-stricken figures of McDaid's
widow and three-year-old child. Father Gill actually broke down and wept
when they both took their places behind the coffin. As if this were not enough,
the emotionalism of the service was heightened by the fact that the family and
some neighbours of Frank Stagg – who was later to die on a subsequent

hunger strike – also came to the service. Naturally, they too were confused, apprehensive and grief-stricken.

The bizarre touch was provided by 'this rather aristocratic sort of woman, wearing a red wig, whom I took at first to be a Rose Dugdale type of figure. [Rose Dugdale was the daughter of a prominent British aviation tycoon, who had espoused the Republican cause and had just been sentenced to prison because of the attempted bombing of a barracks in Northern Ireland, by dropping milk churns filled with explosives from a helicopter.] She said that she was a mature student from Cheltenham. She'd come to show solidarity. And she was giving out all sorts of republican sentiments about British rule in Ireland and about how appalling it was that the bishop had banned services. "Would they treat Christ like that?" she said. The next day she rang me up and started going on about the bombings. But I said that nothing whatever could possibly justify such an atrocity, and gave them no support whatever. I didn't think about my response. It was simply my spontaneous reaction as a Christian priest. But, as I began to see more of her, I realised that she wasn't a Rose Dugdale type, she might even have been a plant. God knows what would have happened if I had given the slightest sign of approval for the bombings.'

God knows indeed, because the bombings which Father French was referring to were the Birmingham pub explosions which went off as the plane taking McDaid's remains back to Ireland was still in the air. It had been held up for hours because the airport workers refused to handle the coffin.

This whole sequence of events provided some of the most heated controversy, both in Ireland and England, in the entire history of the Troubles. Although what subsequently befell the men wrongly sentenced for the bombings was completely unjust and inexcusable, the atmosphere of the time makes their case explicable, if not forgivable. Knowledgeable members of the Irish community who were in Birmingham at the time will still say that the fact that speedy arrests were made prevented nineteenth-century Liverpool-type riots making their reappearance.

Over the years, during visits to Birmingham, I was given dozens of verifiable incidents ranging from midnight phone calls to physical violence and verbal abuse that became the commonplace of Irish existence in the wake of the atrocities. Pubs were petrol-bombed, the windows of Irish premises smashed. One simple incident which has stayed with me occurred during a taxi journey twenty years after the bombings, in 1994. I remarked to the driver that I thought I could detect a hint of an Irish accent. He replied, 'That's because you're in the taxi, mate. If English people got in, I'd make sure to cover up the accent.' The Irish community in Birmingham has spent the intervening years 'covering up' from the fallout from the Birmingham incidents.

The irony is that one doesn't encounter any visible sign of this tension at its source. The bombs went off within a few yards of each other, at New Street and in the Bull Ring, but there are no twisted letters to indicate the existence of dark passions. In fact, when I went along to visit the pubs, I found that no one in the streets around could tell me where the bombs had been. The only person who knew was a man selling a Socialist newspaper. The whole area has been developed, and time has flowed over the carnage, but I fancied I could still hear Madame Roland's famous cry echo around the Bull Ring. As they took her to the guillotine she exclaimed: 'Oh liberty, what crimes are committed in thy name.'

THE DULL TIDE OF GREY

A report for Birmingham City Council published in 1996 highlighted the impact of the PTA coupled with the aftermath of the bombings as key problems for the Irish community.[81] The bombings created: '. . . an immediate local media backlash against the Irish'. The Irish community were found to feel they were under 'public surveillance' by both the police and the indigenous population. I was left in no doubt that many Irish people in Birmingham felt that this distrust was still a factor in their daily lives. One consequence of this distrust is the fact that limiting long-term illness rates amongst the first-generation Irish people are roughly double those for the rest of Birmingham's populations as the following table shows:

Limiting long-term illness in the total and Irish-born population

	Total Population %	Irish-born population %
Birmingham	14	23
Aston	16	28
Nechells	14	27
Sparkbrook	15	29
Sparkhill	13	19
Source: 1991 Census		

The report found that this sense of oppression was not confined to working-class people:

First- and second-generation Irish interviewees occupying professional occupations felt that their Irishness presented an impediment to their career development and work conditions. One woman was told that she had no future in management while her accent remained, others were subjected to derogatory Irish jokes. First- and second-generation interviewees said that they felt under pressure to underplay their Irish identity. This suppression of Irish identity has implications for younger generations of Irish people for whom explicitly Irish role models in these areas often do not exist.

This deprived background tends to have a self-perpetuating effect. Teachers talk about pupils seeing no purpose in study or the acquisition of academic qualifications. The Birmingham report listed a number of reasons for this attitude, ranging from bullying, to prejudice, to a belief that they are going to be unemployed no matter what exams they pass. Young second-generation Irish women as a category tended to be hardest hit by this syndrome. The lower-scale, lower-paid jobs tended to be the parameters of most young women's lives. Talk of upward social mobility in these cases is often seen as not merely irrelevant, but downright mocking. Yet, as in ghettos anywhere, social mobility is repeatedly achieved by young people lucky enough to run across a good teacher or career guidance officer. When they did study, and discovered the opportunities available to them, some young Irish people's horizons expanded enormously and their expectations soared. But, the 'being down so long it feels like up' syndrome means that social workers in Birmingham report that, in their experience, they find that Irish people don't believe that the services on offer are available to them.

One of the problems specifically highlighted in the Birmingham report comes back to the census ethnicity question – the difficulty a shared language and colour poses for Irish people seeking the benefit of statutory social services: 'Their familiarity with the English language obscures their often cultural and vernacular difficulties.' Communicating with service providers often turns out to be an ordeal in which the Irish person literally finds himself talking through a glass partition, without achieving communication.

The report made a number of recommendations on employment counselling, advice on small businesses, a programme of encouragement for Irish people to access welfare and benefits advice, and so on. These things take time of course, and the gap between 'the influential Irish in Britain' and the dull tide of grey, rather than green, which is emblematic of so much of the Irish community in Birmingham, will not readily evaporate. Nevertheless, it seemed to me that a significant part of the general 'lifting of the heads over the parapet' process which has been accelerating since the Labour victory in 1997, occurred with the launching of a Birmingham Irish Business Forum in 1998. Also, the Birmingham St Patrick's Day parade is growing in size annually, to a point where it ranks not far below those of London and Manchester. Perhaps therefore the fact that there are that many Irish, or Irish descended, willing to step forward can be taken as a sign that the Irish, and the English, in Birmingham are putting their bad days behind them.

MANCHESTER

The contrast between the flourishing Irish Centre in Manchester and the seedy one in Liverpool aptly symbolises the different sense one gets of their respective Irish communities. As I have never ceased to marvel, one of the remarkable features of the Irish diaspora is the number of people who voluntarily give of their time to help their community and who make a real difference, not merely locally, but over a wide area. Obviously proactive ambassadors, like Joe Small or Ted Barrington, can provide leadership and make an impact, but, as indicated earlier, there are private individuals who also make a valuable contribution.

In Manchester, one of the names at the top of everyone's list where involvement in the Irish community is concerned is that of the businessman Michael Forde, both through his work nationally for the Federation of Irish Societies, and in his capacity as Chairman of the Irish World Heritage Centre at Cheetham Hill, in Manchester. Here I might add that it is not only his activities on behalf of the Irish which cause wonderment. When I first met him, he was training for an epic feat of endurance which he subsequently completed successfully. In seven days, twelve hours and thirty-nine minutes, he completed a 3,000-mile cycle race from California to Savannah, Georgia. The route took him over the Rocky Mountains, through Las Vegas and the state of Nevada, across Utah, New Mexico, East Texas and Oklahoma. Forde and his team only slept two hours in every twenty-four. They were one of only seven teams to finish, and were the first team from either Britain or Ireland to complete the course. Whoever said life begins at forty must have had Forde in his mind. He was fifty-five when he completed the race.

The Heritage Centre acts as a social and cultural centre, a distribution agency for the sale of Irish produce, a folk museum (with a thatched Irish cottage), and its dining hall makes a point of stocking wines grown in Irish-owned vineyards around the world. The place varies between being full and packed. People go there for their socials, their parties, their meetings. If Ireland are playing at anything from tiddlywinks to the World Cup, the Centre's widescreen TVs are the places which attract the buzz. The energy and cross-section of people one meets at the Centre are representative of the sort of vibrancy one can expect to encounter amongst the Irish in clubs, pubs and meeting houses throughout the city.

None of this was easily achieved; even in the fairly immediate past things were difficult. As Forde tells it, 1981–2 was the defining time for the Irish:

> The Irish community were really under pressure. The Troubles were awful. You had hunger strikes, Birmingham, Guildford. You had newspaper headlines screaming about 'murdering Irish bastards'. You had a famous Irish priest, like Father Taaffe, being described in a tabloid as 'an IRA priest'. Father Joe was just the opposite. He had condemned the Birmingham bombings as unjust, and he spent his life working for the underprivileged. That meant of course that he was known for standing up for his own people. So he drew fire.

Such experiences were viewed as something to be put up with, rather than combated, but Forde and a group of friends and fellow-workers at the centre decided to take their response a step further:

> We said, hang on. We built this place [Manchester]. We did some research. We talked to the Irish Government, and we went around the country looking at Irish clubs and Irish Centres of all sorts. We found that they all shared one characteristic. They tended to keep people out, or at least they only seemed to attract the Irish. We decided we'd invite everyone in. Manchester is part of our heritage. We said we'd get the city involved. We'd

invite representatives of the police, the fire services. We went around hospitals where you'd find as a matter of course that the Irish nurses would be fund-raising for various charities. So we made the Centre available for that sort of activity. We placed a great emphasis on cultural activities, and we got in people that way that would never have come here.

If you've got some non-Irish charitable group which raises, say, £3,000 or £4,000 in the Irish Centre, you create a benign impression. One thing you do for sure is show them that the place isn't full of IRA people. So we made a point of inviting other ethnic groups. The first fund-raiser for the Vietnamese Boat People, for example, was held in the Irish Centre. We started off ethnic associations for Nigerians, Italians, Hungarians, Filipinos, Ukranians. The councillors started using the Irish example as a headline for such groups. The council have given us fourteen acres of prime land to build an Irish Heritage Centre. They see that as having a major part to play in the regeneration of the city.

Needless to say, being an Irish project, at the time of writing one group which had still not come up with any funding was the Irish Government, though Forde was hopeful that Dublin might make a donation as a millennium project.

The Centre has a worldwide database of Irish history and culture and houses artefacts from eighty-six different countries. In a nutshell, what Forde and his friends have helped to do in Manchester is to prove, if the concept needs proving, that the famous American melting-pot concept no more works in Britain than it does in America. Cultural diversity, preserving one's own ethnicity, while co-operating with one's neighbours, enriches the host community as much as it does the emigrant one. This seems self-evident, but confidence amongst the Irish community in Manchester, as elsewhere, is a plant of fairly recent origin. Figures like Mo Mowlam and Tony Blair were pleased to attend Irish award ceremonies at the time of writing, but an Irish festival did not get off the ground in Manchester until 1996. It was an instant success and immediately became an annual event.

THE 'MANCHESTER MARTYRS' AND THE 'STALKER AFFAIR'

Manchester was once the scene of one of the most embittering incidents of the nineteenth century, the public execution of three Irishmen, 'the Manchester martyrs', at Salford gaol, on 23 November 1867. This arose out of the accidental shooting of a policeman, Sergeant Brett, during the rescue of the Fenian leader Colonel Kelly and his companion, Captain Deasy. The description of the trial and its aftermath reads like a nineteenth-century version of the Birmingham Six case. Some of those originally sentenced were pardoned because the journalists who covered the hearing sent a memorandum to the Home Office outlining its deficiencies. Following the journalists' action, public opinion began to change. In the words of the man who organised the escape, F. L. Crilly:

> Friends of humanity and justice among the English people now took courage and spoke out. They said that on evidence and a verdict thus confessed to be tainted and untenable, it would be monstrous to take human life.[82]

However, the Orange and Tory element wanted blood and the exercise of clemency was decried as an attack on England's life and property. Accordingly, three of the men involved in the conspiracy to free Kelly and Deasy were hanged. After their deaths, huge funeral processions were held throughout Ireland; hundreds of thousands of mourners followed empty coffins inscribed with the men's names, Allen, Larkin and O'Brien, thus also inscribing them indelibly in the pantheon of Irish martyrs. After a speaking engagement in Manchester I repaired with some friends to an Irish pub. On the way home our driver detoured, as he does regularly, so the car would pass the spot where the men were executed.

During the recent Troubles in 1987, Manchester was also the scene of the disgraceful John Stalker affair. Not only was this good and sincere police officer hounded out of the police force to prevent him continuing his inquiries into the 'shoot-to-kill' activities of the RUC, but his friend, the businessman Kevin Taylor, who had stood by him in his difficulties, was, as was later admitted in the courts, also subjected to gross injustices by the Manchester police. The police are also suspected by the Irish community of being responsible for the desecration of the Irish memorial in Moston Cemetery, a National Front area.

THE SHOCK OF THE CITY

However, members of the Irish community will also tell you that Manchester today is remarkably prejudice-free. This is doubly remarkable when one considers that the city was once synonymous with Irish poverty, and was also the area where the Orange Order took some of its most significant founding steps in Britain, before spreading to Liverpool with the results outlined earlier. Manchester, the city of the Peterloo[83] massacre, was the 'shock city' of the nineteenth century: what Chicago became and Los Angeles is now. The largely rural Irish emigrants, some of whose individual stories will be told later, must have been hit by tremendous culture shock. As Mervyn Busteed pointed out to me, this grappling with the Mancunian ethos was a feature of Irish life in Manchester until the fifties: 'All they had to offer was their sweat and their shovels. They used to walk from the little Ireland ghettos in the heart of Manchester city itself away out to the fields and farms around the city every morning, and then walk back in the evening.'[84]

Obviously the Catholic Church played an essential role in creating a bulwark for the Irish against the shock of the city. Mother Church was a source of identity, a uniform, and an army which fought on the Irish side – but in certain ways the Irish were borne down by what bore them up. Michael Maguire gave me an account of what growing up in Manchester was like for someone who was brought from Ireland to Manchester as an infant by his parents in 1928.[85] In his boyhood and young manhood, Maguire was not conscious of much anti-Irish propaganda: 'It was like now, a lot depends on the paper you read. But St Helens was a citadel of the Irish. There were seventeen churches with a presbytery attached to every church, holding possibly as many as five or six curates and the parish priest. The Irish were integrated in the area since the Famine times. But our history was English, and sanitised at that, so as to cause the least offence to the host nation. The idea was to make us proud to be English Catholics.'

Maguire was the classical Irish trade union, Labour-oriented type of Irish worker. His career began in the mines which once flourished around St Helens and played a part in the Black and Tan War. Michael Collins used to get explosives ferried over to Dublin from the Irish miners who worked the pits. As we have seen, Maguire ultimately became a Labour MP, so he would have been one of the few whose head was consistently over the parapet, despite the efforts of sanitisation. He remembers an occasional figure from the days of his youth amidst the ranks of Irish professionals, who would have been similarly inclined. For example, the family doctor: 'Dr Paddy was so nationalistic that when his Irish red setter died, he wouldn't allow it to be buried in England.' However, most Irish professionals dropped their Irish identity to get ahead.

Education is what changed things. Maguire's own family are a paradigm of what education has meant to the Irish.

> In my day, a majority of Irish went for the heavy industry labouring type job. Remember that out of seventeen schools in the area, there were only about thirty boys who qualified for higher education. There should have been 25 per cent at least of the school-going population. There were huge Irish populations in Wigan, Warrington, Widnes, and so on. Those are towns the size of Cork. The Protestant kids went ahead on simple merit to the grammar school system, but we had sort of a ghetto. We had our own hospital and seminary in St Helens. We had our own groceries, our own shops, and industries had been established. It was an acceptant kind of society. You respected authority, didn't question the Church.

MANCHESTER NOW, AND MANCHESTER THEN

By chance I happened to visit Manchester in the wake of the Manchester bombing of June 1996, and I naturally expected to find considerable bitterness over the outrage. But I genuinely did not find any. Amazingly, the general reaction of ordinary people seemed to be that the shopping centre had been an eyesore, and that its departure was a good riddance. The fact that no one was killed in the explosion probably helped to create this reaction. Apart from British outrage at England's second city being bombed, I had also expected to find Irish outrage at the fact of such an Irish city being chosen as a target. As Pat Sweeney, famous throughout the Irish community in England for his work for Comhaltas Ceolteori Eireann (the Irish traditional music association), pointed out to me the following year:

> The Irish built it, the Irish blew it up, and then the Irish demolished the wreckage. The morning after the blast, I went along, and there was a Durkan from County Sligo working the demolition ball for Pat McGuinness from Donegal. There were hundreds of Irish employed, working twelve hours a day, from all over the country.[86]

For on a weekend in May 2000 Pat achieved the distinction of becoming the first non-Irish resident to be elected President of the Comhaltas world-wide network of 400 branches, 31 of them based in Britain. He himself worked as a labourer, and later as a foreman, in the construction industry for most of his life:

> Like most Donegal men, I started in the camps, in tunnel construction. We built airfields, dumps, motorways, reconstruction after the war. The Irish built Manchester. I wish I could have done as much for Ireland.
>
> I'd never allow any animosity in the men under me, and I never had any trouble with anti-Irish prejudice. We had a show at Comhaltas, Irish music, song, and dance, a week after the bombing, and it was sponsored by the local traders. I remember an old lady giving me five pounds, and saying: 'It's not your fault. The Irish are decent, hard-working people.' The night after the Birmingham bombing, we were supposed to take part in a parade. We had a float organised. I asked a local sergeant what he thought. He said, 'You go ahead, you do tremendous work for the youth' – the float collected the most money in the parade.

I talked to Pat at a well-attended social for old folks in the Grove Club, where he was demonstrating his prowess as the self-proclaimed 'worst bingo caller in Manchester'. People of different walks of life had gathered either for the bingo or to help me with my researches. The club, situated in a pleasant leafy suburb, was once a run-down basement billiard hall. Now it's as fine a premises of its type as one would find anywhere in the world. Della Costello, the wife of the owner Michael, talked about the older club regulars in what will by now be familiar terms to readers:

> They'd come in for a bit of warmth as much as the pint. They were great men once, but now they'd be living on their own. 'Della,' they'd say, 'if you don't see me for three days, come looking for me.' In the past while, my husband has found at least four of them. I remember an old soldier, he was a classical example of the neglect of the aged under the Tories. We managed to get him buried after a struggle, but it was in a pauper's grave with no service. So I said there's going to be no more lonely graves and we have a group now that will make up a funeral, so that no one goes to the grave alone.

The Irish reverence for death and its rituals was strong in Della. She recalled how her mother would go on to the building sites and ask for help to bury someone: 'She'd get the money no trouble. There was great camaraderie. People used to help each other. When my mother and father died, their funerals were like film stars'.' As the group talked, not only did a picture of the value of the community's shared ethic emerge, so did that of individual philanthropists, like the Kennedys. One got an insight into why such figures were held in affectionate respect.

Both Della and Pat made a point which I had heard from both Tommy Walsh and Michael Forde: 'You never step back, you have to be strong.' While they would stress that Manchester was an easier place to live for the Irish than elsewhere, they were conscious of pressures from the National

Front, and even from MI5. Comhaltas was infiltrated by 'a tall Cockney' who turned out to be from MI5, and disappeared after his cover was blown: 'But we know that he was replaced by somebody else. The phones of all the leaders of Irish societies are tapped, and they know they're watched, but we go ahead, and organise our Fleadhs [Musical Festivals] and dancing competitions. It's one way of professing your Irishness, through the culture.' It's also one way of assessing the growth of the Irish emigrant economy; an Irish harp for example would leave little change out of a thousand pounds, and the gorgeously colourful brocaded Irish dancing costumes, some for children not yet in their teens, can cost several hundreds, but Comhaltas and its competitions are mushrooming.

Comhaltas organises about 2,500 functions a year. Pat founded the first branch in 1972 and there are now thirty-eight branches in Britain. Pat has been given civic receptions in Bolton, Stoke and Bedford, but back in the early days of Comhaltas the money just was not there. 'In those days,' he said, 'a lot of Irish children went to school in winter only. Once the fine weather came, their parents would be away working in England while the children ran the farm.'

Della gave examples of how she encountered prejudice:

> When I was at work I remember after a man found out that I was Irish, he wouldn't sit with me at lunch. I remember after a bombing, my sixteen-year-old, he goes to a Catholic paid school, saying, 'Oh mum, you don't know the jibing I get.' They'd be saying things like, 'Has your father been at it again?' So I told him, either you speak to the Sister, or I'll go in. So he told the Sister and she called a meeting and threatened expulsions if there were any more remarks like that. That stopped it. But that's a common sort of thing for Irish kids. And some of the police had done terrible things, and you'd get a lot of anonymous calls, if there's an Irish wedding in the club, that sort of thing. But you don't get the kind of PTA harassment that you get in London, or the kind of thing they get in Birmingham.

John Kane, a former builder, is now a widower, and particularly proud of his computer scientist son who is also a university lecturer, though he hastens to add that his three girls got degrees also! He stressed the tolerance of Manchester: 'Manchester is far better than Liverpool for tolerance. I wouldn't wear my pioneer pin in Liverpool, but in Manchester they gave me the key! I found them lovely people. I loved the life. I had a great family.' Listening to Pat and John talking about the experiences of the Irish in their youth, which, as readers will see, echo those described by Brendan at the London Chaplaincy seminar, I got a vivid picture of the culture shock that coming to England must have entailed for their generation. Pat said:

> I remember the Canon in the centre of the hall with a big blackthorn stick, waving it once the music stopped, to make sure that the boys and the girls got back to their own sides of the floor. We used to have house dances, but the clergy ended them. They got money for running the hall. Of course once the music started again, there'd be a rush of boys over to the girls. Then after the dance, I remember the curate, he used to have a big white mac and a cap. And a big stick. And he'd be beating the boys and girls who'd go together.

Amongst the people taking part in the discussion were a husband and wife who had emigrated later than John, in the early sixties, but the wife recalled that in Dublin before getting married, she was told that she'd have to wear black 'because she wasn't pure'. She said, 'I thought if I got married in white, and the priest found out that I wasn't a virgin, he'd have to burn his stole.'

John continued:

> When it came to our time to go [to emigrate], we didn't know where we were going. We'd be medically examined in Dublin, and labelled. [Although Ireland was allegedly neutral, de Valera facilitated recruiting for their work camps by agents of big British builders such as McAlpine. The Irish workers were not subject to conscription and were exempt from income tax for their first six months in the UK.] I remember coming out from the fields and the hedges on my first train. Every 104 miles I think it was, we had to stop and get turfed up. And then we came to urban England for the first time. The camps had about fifty beds in the dormitory, but we didn't mind that. We built the aerodromes, the dams, the roads. Without the Irish the British couldn't have fought the war. Holyhead was the great leveller. I remember going to a dance and thinking to myself, imagine if they could see me at home – dancing with a teacher. Or a nurse coming up to me at the ladies' excuse me! In fact I married a nurse.

There was another side to the emancipation provided by the shovel. Pat Sweeney described the routine after a trench collapsed: 'The foreman would call out, "Count the shovels." That's how you knew if someone was missing.'

Dominic Behan's famous ballad commemorates many an Irish navvy's death:

> I stripped to the skin with darkie Finn;
> Way down upon the Isle of Grain
> With Horse-Face O'Toole, we knew the rule;
> No money if you stopped for rain.
> McAlpine's God was a well-filled hod;
> Your shoulders cut to bits and seared
> And woe to he who looked for tea,
> With McAlpine's Fusiliers.
>
> I remember the day that the Bear, O'Shea,
> Fell into concrete stairs,
> What Horse-Face said when he saw him dead;
> It wasn't what the rich call prayers,
> I'm a navvy short was the one retort,
> That reached upon my ears,
> When the going's rough;
> Then you must be tough,
> With McAlpine's Fusiliers.

The industrial accident rate amongst what another famous song termed the 'Paddys on the Railway' (or the aerodrome, canal, or hydro-electric dam for that matter) must have been appalling. Recording this aspect of the Irish experience in Britain alone would be a valuable task for some contemporary researcher. The men worked seven days a week, three weekends on, one off. An average day was twelve hours at £1.50 an hour. The camp life had a bearing on the creation of a ghetto mentality, helping to cut the Irish off from the mainstream of British society. As Pat said, 'We were a race apart. We were mad, shouting, singing on our nights off. It wasn't our war. We didn't give a shit. We were young.' Even apart from the camps, this 'in but not of' attitude to British tribulations was an Irish trait. An old neighbour of mine, who worked as a labourer in Coventry to support his wife and children back in Dublin, used to reminisce about the Coventry bombings, and he remarked on how the sense of apartness conveyed a feeling of invulnerability. When the sirens blew, he and his mates would automatically head for a welcoming pub or club, where they would drink through the air raids. However, even years afterwards, having vividly described the corpses in the streets, the buses filled with seemingly unmarked passengers all dead from blast, he would always remark, 'Ah, we were well out of that. That's one thing I agreed with Dev on. He kept us out of the war.' What he meant was, his wife and children were kept out of the war. Once they were safe, he didn't worry.

After the war, in Manchester and throughout the Midlands, life was hard for the Irish. The group in the Grove reminisced about stories of fighting and hard drinking in places like the steel town of Corby. This led to reserve on the part of landladies: 'the Irish are all the same' attitude meant that, as was common at the time, Pat walked around all day with another lad looking for digs, before he eventually got them from a Scots woman. However, through all the dislocation and the hardship, there ran, as there did with the Irish in most place of the world, a sense of community and of obligation. A Della Costello in Manchester could have been a Catherine Shannon in Boston talking about her memories of her mother's hospitality while she was growing up in New York: 'You'd wake up with bodies everywhere. My brother would have come over to the house and brought lads with no home or job. On a Sunday, the place was decked out like Lyons Cafe. Mother would be stuffing everybody with bacon and cabbage.'

Pat had a similar memory: 'The mother of the house would be asked by some other woman, "Do me a favour", and you'd have lads being fed for miles around. The Irish worked together and played together.' He recalled a local park, where on a Sunday afternoon: 'There'd be about a thousand boys and girls, all in their best suits. Nobody drinking, just having the crack. If you bought an ice cream, you couldn't go wrong for a date that night. And the Irish looked after each other. I remember Mick Murray. He hired for Wimpey's – Mick never turned an Irishman away.'

Della entered a pessimistic note: 'The young people don't seem to have the same nature. When you think of the way we worked. Look at the nurses. Where would you get the equal of Irish nurses? Now you find the young ones looking at their watch.' A vein of sadness ran through our discussion.

Pat summed up a rewarding career in England by saying, 'My heart's in

Ireland, but the English are very fine people.' Della agreed with his view of the English, but she said, 'I feel robbed of my culture. I mean, I'm doing very well, but I often feel resentful and I say, "Why couldn't my parents make a living in Ireland?" I feel robbed of my Irish childhood.'

Sarah Allan had worked in England for over fifty years. She also touched on the sense of resentment at men's 'having to go' at vulnerable Irish girls. She thought that girls had a tougher time than men:

> When I was fifteen, my father took me to Dublin. I remember him buying the tickets, one return and one one way. We walked around Dublin all day. We had a one and threepenny lunch in Woolworths. Then he brought me to Westland Row to get the train to Dun Laoghaire to catch the Holyhead boat, and then get the night train to Euston. I couldn't afford a night in a hotel in London. He told me, 'You'll see the train with Dun Laoghaire written on it.' I was exhausted when I got to London. Someone from the home place was on the train and they recognised me, and I slept on the floor going to Euston. The neighbour looked after me. When I got to London, I stayed with an aunt for one night. She was a housemaid in a hotel. She got me a job as a chambermaid. I got twenty-three shillings a week, and I sent a pound home.

Her jobs gradually improved to the point where she could send two pounds a week home. Then, her work took her to Manchester:

> I loved it, and I never left it, but even though I did get on, the resentment would well up when I'd go home. I'd see my brother, and I'd feel angry, because he didn't have to go – even though I love him to bits. But I left not with high hopes. I was frightened and broken-hearted and bloated with tears, but you had to tell them you were all right, even though the loneliness was terrible. I still go back four times a year, even though my father was buried last April. If I lived in Ireland I'd fight tooth and nail to keep my kids at home.

When the question of addressing community needs came up, an Irish nun at the seminar shrewdly indicated the untapped political potential of the numbers of Irish in public life: 'All the councillors seemed to be of Irish descent, but, in places like Whittington or South Manchester, you'd find huge majorities for Conservatives, anything from 8,000 to 27,000.' Deirdre Carroll, a care worker engaged on visitation, found that there was some 'subtle discrimination', but that Manchester was one of the most acceptant places in England for the Irish. Hazel and Pat Craig, who put on a country and western act, and have six grown-up children, used to be well-known entertainers in Dublin before coming to Manchester some twenty years earlier. They both said they never had any problem and, like everyone else in the group, considered it a part of their normal routine to donate some of their free time to the community.

As with the group I had spoken to in London, it was from the women that criticism of the practices in the building trade originated. Whereas Pat would unconsciously recall the camaraderie and the Wimpey executive who never turned an Irishman away, when the nun was talking about the different categories of Irish she encountered, she talked not merely of problems such as loneliness and old age but she pointed out that some of the older men are victims of their own people, subcontractors and the lump system. 'How do you fight your own?' she asked.

Perhaps the answer to that question may yet prove to be: 'Because contemporary Ireland is creating conditions in which fighting will no longer be necessary'. On a brilliantly sunny afternoon in May 2000. I stood on the railway bridge leading to London's Olympia exhibition centre and watched people pour past me in football-crowd dimensions. They were mainly young and heading for a job fair, sponsored by the *Irish Post* and the Irish Government jobs agency, FAS, aimed at attracting Irish emigrants back to Ireland. Some 14,000 attended the fair, the first in a series across Britain. Thinking of the pea and carrot man, of the once strong and hopeful Irish workers now living out their twilight years in places like London's Arlington House men's hostel, I found the occasion a deeply moving experience.

The Irish Tanaiste, Deputy Prime Minister, Mary Harney, told the gathering that in order to sustain and develop the flourishing Irish economy, the government had pledged itself to bring in 200,000 people from abroad over the next five years. It was hoped, and anticipated, that a major portion of that inward flow would be returning Irish emigrants. Obviously the emigrants in question will be the skilled, 'the job ready', in recruitment agency parlance. But Fr Kivlehan's 'problem business' will not go out of business. As many young people as ever continue to drop out of school. The alcohol or drug addicted, people fleeing abusive relationships, or those going into sexual exile, still present themselves to the Irish Centres seeking help in proportions similar to those obtaining in the bad days. One in eleven of the people sleeping rough on the streets of London are Irish. But the migratory trend from Ireland to Britain has reversed. FAS calculates that there is now a net migration of some 20,000 people per annum. Remarkably, the *Economist* has calculated (28 August 1999) that in 1999 19 per cent of these were British. Therefore, given a successful outcome to the Peace Process, and a continuation, albeit at a slower rate, of Irish economic growth, it is not unduly fanciful to envisage future Anglo-Irish relationships taking place along the lines of two interdependent and increasingly prosperous neighbours, rather than between opponents forever doomed to re-enact roles written for them by their ancestors.

I will conclude with an anecdote from Aidan Hennigan which perfectly sums up the dichotomy often commented on by Irish journalists, between the friendly attitude of most British journalists as contrasted with the official attitudes of some policy formulators in both politics and the media. On the day of the signing of the Good Friday Agreement he took a visiting niece to dinner in the House of Commons. He said that: 'At least seven of my colleagues came up to me and put their arms around me, saying "well done." As he says ruefully: 'It's hard to reconcile that sort of thing with the attitudes of the *Daily Telegraph* and the *Daily Mail*.'

WALES

On the face of it, Wales should have been a cockpit of interest from which to study the evolving nature of the Anglo-Irish relationship and the position of the Irish within the United Kingdom, because of two related happenings. The first, the Good Friday Agreement of 1998, had led to Consulates General being appointed in Edinburgh and Cardiff, and as a result, the Irish became the first country in the world to appoint a Consulate General to Wales, the experienced Conor O'Riordan, who had previously been a part of the Anglo-Irish team in the Irish Department of Foreign Affairs, and Irish Consul in Boston. The second was of course the establishment of the new Welsh Assembly, the elections for which, as in Scotland, were held in May 1999.

However, I must confess that a cynic might well have regarded both departures as being akin to the curse of *Hello* magazine – famously, portrayal of a happy marriage in that journal tends to be followed by a visit to the divorce court. I got distinct *Hello* resonances during the first of a number of trips researching Welsh/Irish relationships – calamity tended to be visited on those most responsible for said relationships. First, Mr Ron Davies – the man nominated as Labour's leader for the proposed Welsh statelet – resigned after proceedings on London's Clapham Common which, while they may have been gay, were certainly not joyful in their outcome. Next, I proposed to interview the principal Irish figure in the Welsh Catholic Church, the Most Reverend John Ward, Archbishop of Cardiff, but the day before[87] I hoped to speak to His Grace, he was released on bail after charges were brought against him by a woman who claimed that the Archbishop had sexually assaulted her while he was a young priest and she a child. But after the arrest and charges, which must have had a traumatic effect on the Archbishop, the charges were dropped. It was a bad time for the Catholics of Wales, whether of Irish descent or not: the month before I sought the interview with the Archbishop, his former press spokesperson, Father John Lloyd, a well-known parish priest, was sentenced to eight years' imprisonment at Chester Crown Court for eleven indecent assaults, one rape and a serious sexual offence.

These vicissitudes aside, it has to be said that compared to the prosperity of the Home Counties, or the confidence of Scotland, Wales is a depressed area. Nowhere in the United Kingdom did the sword of Attila the Hen (Mrs Thatcher) fall more grievously than on the Welsh mining industry. The combination of the decline of the smoke-stack industries and Wales's sparse population (2.8 million) hit the emigration-prone, industry-starved region hard. In Cardiff I encountered more interest in the building of the new rugby stadium than in the opening of the new Welsh Assembly, and I got the impression that the city would have been more excited at the advent of a new tenor, or rugby outside-half, than a new Secretary of State for Wales. Part of this lack of interest was caused by the feuding in the Labour Party over Davies's successor. The Welsh wanted Rhodri Morgan. They got Alun Michael, Tony Blair's nominee, thereby fuelling fears that the new Assembly was going to be nothing more than a rubber stamp for New Labour decisions taken in London.

Eventually, however, the Welsh got Morgan. In the process, New Labour discovered that it is no more feasible to concede half independence than it is to create a half pregnancy, a point which, aided by the Irish, Ken Livingstone was to make later in the year, in London. I had the pleasure of sitting in the Welsh Assembly, with Conor O'Riordan, on the day in February 2000, when Alun Michael conceded his unpopularity and resigned, following a vote of no confidence. Significantly this drama occurred on the same day that that paragon of New Labour virtue, Peter Mandelson, brought down the Belfast Assembly with a stroke of his pro-consular pen, thereby dashing many of the hopes for the Good Friday Agreement, which had led to O'Riordan's and my presence. But the hopes for stronger Irish/Welsh links remained justified.

The following night O'Riordan gave a party for me. The first guests were Rhodri Morgan and the hero of the Alun Michael resignation saga, Lord Dafydd Elis-Thomas, the Chairman of the Assembly. Had Thomas done as the New Labour members present had wished and postponed the no confidence vote and delayed acceptance of the resignation, Millbank, Labour's London HQ, would have had time to get the Heavy Gang down to Cardiff, arms would have been twisted and Alun Michael might well have been saved. However Thomas insisted that democratic procedures be observed. A sort of Welsh version of the Prague spring ensued, the prestige of the Assembly soared, and one of the first places that Morgan and a team of Welsh experts in trade, the EU and tourism visited was Dublin. Here they were received with friendship and respect by everyone from the Taoiseach down and given valuable briefings on how, in all those fields, the Irish had managed to metamorphosis their state into prosperity from depression.

Prior to the Alun Michael departure the only person I met who was bullish about the Welsh economy was an Irishman, Martin Tinney, who runs a successful art gallery in Cardiff dedicated to showing Welsh art. He found that he was experiencing a boom, and that there was increasing interest in his exhibitions in Dublin.

Certainly there is a great deal of government-generated building activity in the Cardiff Bay area, where a hotel room can cost as much as £500 per night, but in the rows of comfortable little family hotels which flank fashionable Cathedral Street a room can be had for as little as £12. (Similar hotels in London would cost approximately £60 and upwards.) A commonly met with comment was that the average Welsh national income was some 25 per cent lower than that of the rest of the UK. Obviously, against that economic backdrop, neither a new Consulate General, however significant, nor the presence of some 20,000 first-generation Irish could be expected to make a very dramatic impact.

Nevertheless the value of the Irish connection in Welsh circumstances was not lost on Rhodri Morgan. I have already alluded to the economic turnaround and opportunities indicated by the Irish government sponsored job fair at Olympia. Before coming to London, FAS staged a similar fair at Holyhead, where countless thousands of worried Irish emigrants once first set foot in the United Kingdom. Morgan addressed the gathering and exhorted his hearers that life in Dublin at work was better than unemployment at home.

In Wales, as anywhere else in the world, one finds one's share of Irish entrepreneurs. For example, Larry Ryan harnessed those traditional Irish implements of upward mobility, the pick and shovel, to the old adage that dirty hands make clean money, to such good effect that he became a millionaire. Even though conventional Tory wisdom closed the Welsh mining industry – often sealing in millions of pounds' worth of brand new machinery – he went into rivers and slag heaps to recover waste coal in such profitable quantities that he now winters in the Spanish sun, free of any necessity for coal's heat.

Appropriately enough, also at the time of writing, the other figure cited in Wales for his ability to make money from coal was also an Irishman, Tyrone O'Sullivan. O'Sullivan is a sort of Welsh Lech Walesa. As a miner he helped to pull his dead father out of rubble after a collapse, and subsequently became Chairman of the Tower Mine Project, run on a co-operative basis by miners who had sufficient faith in him to listen to his suggestion that they should put their redundancy money into the enterprise. It is now the only deep mine in Wales, selling coal both at home and abroad to power stations. O'Sullivan employed the best consultants available to advise on marketing and so found a profitable niche. Obviously, the fiercely proud Welsh mining tradition which Thatcher destroyed has prompted a chorus of 'I told you so' from supporters of coal. The fact that O'Sullivan had recently hired a small number of apprentices was also being hailed as a major sign of hope at the time of my visit. The success of the two Irishmen in making money out of coal has prompted speculation that, like the railways, the policy of wholesale closures may have to be reassessed. Assessment of the role of the Irish diaspora in Wales must also be somewhat speculative, and in terms of overall impact could probably be fairly described as being something of the order of that of the two mining entrepreneurs: significant, but not very visible in overall terms.

As there was very little IRA activity in Wales during the Troubles, there was correspondingly little anti-Irish sentiment. However, despite the higher levels of acceptance than in other parts of the United Kingdom, the decline of the Welsh economy has resulted in today's Irish community becoming less organised than that in either Scotland or England. Yet, a very sizeable proportion of today's Welsh population has some Irish blood in it. A generally accepted estimate is that of Cardiff's total population, some 50 to 60 per cent have at least one Irish forebear. This admixture is due to a number of factors: past emigration, Irish fecundity and intermarriage, based on wholehearted Irish male acceptance of the old Welsh ideal that a perfect woman conforms to the 'Three Fs': fervent in church, frugal in the market place, and frantic in bed. The prosaic contemporary reality, however, is that the 1991 census shows that the first-generation Irish population is only 19,494. The Irish are to be found in areas of North Wales like Clwyd, and in South Wales in Cardiff, Newport, Port Talbot and Swansea, where there is a flourishing Irish Club run by Jim O'Rourke. This is also a large Irish student population in Welsh universities, particularly in Glamorgan.

Older Irish residents will tell you that the Irish community has become diffuse and scattered, and that the sense of community is not what it once was. Mike Flynn, the proprietor of the Royal Oak, a Cardiff landmark, told me wistfully: 'In the fifties and sixties this was a boom town. Plenty of work. The pubs stayed open all night. There was a great sense of community amongst the Irish. They'd get off the train at Tudor Street [a guest house area]. No trouble finding a room. No trouble getting a job. Everyone helped each other. Then after a couple of years they'd be able to move out of Tudor Street and get their own place. It's not the same now.' It was the Welsh version of the story of the Irish and the boom years in the UK generally.

Today the Irish are represented, inevitably, by the Roman Catholic clergy and nuns. It is doubtful if any Welsh parish is without an Irish priest, and Catholic schools run by nuns and priests are an integral part of the community. Equally inevitably, one will find the Irish working in construction, in nursing and, to a lesser degree, in the professions, but Irish organisations such as the GAA or Comhaltas Ceoltoiri Eireann appear to be in decline.

The GAA is a barometer of Irish emigration. If local teams in, say, Mayo or County Louth, are finding it difficult to field a full team, then the chances are one will find plenty of players turning out in San Francisco or Sydney. In Wales today, the GAA sometimes finds it hard to field full teams. The shortage of players is in large part a reflection of the fact that Irish workers are staying home. The student body is transient, and permanent workers are very often employed in work gangs or involved in shift work which does not lend itself to training.

The year 1999 was the first year in living memory that Tommy Flaherty, the father of the GAA in Cardiff, could remember the St Patrick's Day parade not being run by the GAA. Flaherty is the archetypal figure of an Irish construction worker. He is also a prime example of the type of unpaid, dedicated community worker one encounters in every Irish community. Greying now, with arms the size of an average man's thigh and a merry open face, his dedication to the game is legendary. Year after year, after days spent in fiercesome physical work that would, and did, kill lesser men, he would drive around the estates in a battered van, picking up young lads to drive them to training sessions. An even more arduous chore was the Sunday morning drive around the same addresses to get the Saturday night warriors out of bed for the Sunday game.

He remembered the days when a committee meeting would be attended by as many as fifty members; now it frequently proves impossible to field a full team, never mind introduce new blood to committees. There is more support for Gaelic pastimes in the valleys, but these are unemployment-stricken areas, not assured reservoirs for the future. A great deal depends on community

WHEREVER GREEN IS WORN

leadership. Tommy cited the case of a wealthy Irish businessman in Southampton who kept students employed during the summer so that they were available to play Gaelic football. As a result the game flourishes in that city.

Curiously, one organisation which thrives against this trend is the Rose of Tralee competition which holds a series of competitions throughout Wales to find an Irish-descended Welsh Rose of Tralee, who will then be sent to take part in the finals in Tralee in County Kerry. The Rose of Tralee is a worldwide phenomenon, to be found wherever the Irish cluster, but in Wales it owes much of its strength to a handful of dedicated enthusiasts, Frank and Theresa Sheridan and Joe Moore. Joe, an Antrim-born male nurse, was involved in a myriad of worthwhile Irish group activities ranging from the Rose of Tralee competition, to the GAA, to sending in reports to the *Irish Post*: anything to keep the kids out of trouble and the flag flying.

Irish dancing is also in a flourishing condition. Two of Cardiff's young Irish dancing champions, Gweno Saunders and Peter Harding were in America dancing with the *Lord of the Dance* and *Riverdance* troupes respectively. Saunders, however, is Cornish, not Irish. Her father has no Irish connections, but he speaks Irish, Cornish and Welsh.

INTERACTION

Although the Irish community's contemporary presence is diffuse and uncoordinated, the tradition of the Irish in Wales is a strong one. Partly it goes back to the early Irish monks who spread the Celtic Church from Ireland to the Celtic regions of what is now the United Kingdom, and partly it is due to more recent influences: Irish emigration, notably after the 1798 Rebellion and, in the nineteenth century, the Great Famine; and the development of mining, quarrying and railways throughout Wales. Part also goes back to the root of today's Anglo-Irish relationship.

The proximity of the Irish and Welsh coastlines inevitably resulted in an interaction between the two. There are Ogham inscriptions in south-west Wales which indicate a lengthy Irish presence. The Irish clans, the Desi and the Ui Liathain, from what is now the Cork-Waterford area of Southern Ireland, settled south-west Wales in the fourth and fifth centuries. As Roger Price has pointed out: '... for perhaps 400 years there was an Irish kingdom in Wales'.[88] Northern Wales too was settled by the Irish, but some ethnic cleansing which took place in the sixth century seems to have concentrated the Irish more to the south and western areas. The Irish resonances in many Welsh place names derive from such settlements. In their turn Welsh refugees from the English traditionally found asylum in the Norse kingdoms in Ireland during the tenth and eleventh centuries.

It was from Wales that the Norman knights first invaded Ireland. When Robert Fitzstephen landed at Bannow Bay, County Wexford in 1169, he was accompanied, according to Giraldus Cambrensis, by 'the flower of the youth

214

of Wales'. Strongbow, the most important Norman leader of the early arrivals, was the Earl of Pembroke. To this day, the roads (and hence subsequently the railways) of Wales run not north/south but east/west, because of their original purpose: the ferrying of troops to Ireland to put down hostilities. The manner in which Wales and Ireland were viewed strategically during the reign of Elizabeth I may be gauged from the fact that the Lord Deputy of Ireland, Sir Philip Sidney, was also President of Wales.

The Royal Regiment of Wales first saw service at the Battle of the Boyne in 1690, and two other Welsh regiments – the 24th Foot and the Royal Welch Fusiliers – also first went into combat during the Williamite campaign which preceded and followed the battle. The history of Welsh military involvement in Ireland was underlined at the start of the current Troubles with the arrival of the first British soldiers on the streets of Belfast – a Welsh regiment. During the contemporary IRA campaign I had an encounter with a Welsh officer which encompassed much of the frustration and bafflement experienced by the more cerebral members of the British Army in trying to cope with the political vacuum in Northern Ireland. I was being interviewed by an American TV company in Crossmaglen, County Armagh, which at the time was occupied by a Welsh regiment. A tall, fine-looking officer came over to see what was going on, and our local interlocutor, a Crossmaglen man, asked him would he like to go before the cameras and 'tell the American people what he was doing there'. The officer declined, shaking his head wearily and saying: 'I often ask myself the same question.'

The cock-eyed British/Irish relationship is equally well symbolised by the fact that just as the British saw Wales as a place to go through en route to Ireland, the Irish saw Wales as a place to go through to get to a job in the south-east of England. Most of the hundreds of thousands of Irish who landed at Holyhead had no intention of staying in Wales. Most of the Welsh who come to Ireland would do so via Fishguard, which links with Rosslare in Co. Wexford, rather than via Holyhead, a far-away pimple on the backside of the Anglesea coast.

THE CHANGING FORTUNES OF RELIGION

The early Celtic Churches had close links. The patron saint of Ireland may have come from Wales and that of Wales from Ireland: Irish tradition has it that St Patrick was seized by Irish pirates from his Welsh home (although in Scotland one would want to tread warily in disputing the Scots' claim to owning Patrick's birthplace); St David is said to have had an Irish mother, Sant None, and the Welsh claim that he had many Irish disciples amongst the students who studied at Menevia.[89] Which arm of the Celtic Church inspired the other is a matter of debate. Although Irish monks generally get the lion's share of historical credit for spreading the gospel, defenders of the Welsh tradition argue that Saint David's rule was copied in Ireland by the Irish who borrowed other practices from him. For example, one of the Irish monks who studied under David was Saint Damnoc, who is said to have brought bee-keeping to the Irish monasteries. Legend has it that every time he returned to Ireland, the bees he cared for at Menevia followed him across the Irish Sea. Each time Saint Damnoc returned the bees to Saint David, but finally David allowed him to keep them. I'm afraid that my efforts to sort out which set of Celts influenced the other only elicited from a Dublin expert the verdict on the Saint Damnoc tale that it sounded authentic because there were 'plenty of Bs in Wales!'

Wales's pre-Reformation Catholic past can be traced in all sorts of ways: as Angela Graham has pointed out in her film *Plant Mari* (Children of Mary), there are 149 Marian place names, 9 Marian shrines and 50 flowers called after the virgin. At the time of writing, Catholicism is the largest Christian sect. As in Ireland, the Church had its martyrs in penal days, and established a college in Rome to train priests to return to Wales to preach the forbidden religion at the risk of their lives. However, in Wales the Reformation worked. The assault upon the power and property of the Roman Catholic Church initiated by Henry VIII so that he could marry Anne Boleyn was carried on by his daughter Elizabeth I to such good effect that the Welsh Catholic Church was all but extirpated. It clung on in parts of Wales, principally Monmouthshire, because some of the Welsh aristocracy managed to remain Catholic themselves and to protect their Catholic tenantry. The position in 1813 was such that Bishop Collingridge reported that Monmouthshire apart, there were only two missions in the whole of Wales, Brecon and Holywell. However, the flood of Irish emigration in the nineteenth century reinvigorated the Church and within a very short time, the Irish outnumbered the Welsh Catholics. Today's relatively powerful position of the Roman Catholics in Wales is largely attributable to the Irish input.

Initially priests were few and far between, but the feeling of the immigrants for their clergy may be gauged from the action of the Irish workers of Bridgend: as soon as they got themselves established into some sort of a community they commissioned an itinerant pedlar to find them a priest and warned him, under severe penalty, not to come back without one. Nevertheless, the Welsh Church moved cautiously in meeting the new demand. Mass was said in cottages and in lodging houses before the building of churches was even contemplated. The Irish Bishop of Menevia, Dr Daniel Mullins, has described both the inhibitions of the time and how a handful of Irish clergy helped to overcome them:

... the experience of the centuries of persecution made them very cautious about starting new centres lest the ancient and deep-rooted prejudices should again be aroused to the detriment of the Catholic people. It was only with the arrival of men like Father Portal in Merthyr, Father Millea in Cardiff, Father Kavanagh in Swansea and Father Tobin among the railway workers in North Wales, that the building of a renewed people could begin. In Cardiff itself, the arrival of the Rosminian Fathers was to begin a new vision and a new hope.[90]

In other words, in the eyes of the Church, Wales was viewed as missionary territory at the time of the early Irish influxes. The poverty of the Irish was such that, despite their affection for their priests, it is recorded that a Father Carroll of Merthyr Tydfil kept body and soul together by selling salt fish. Yet the power of the clergy, even in the midst of poverty, is illustrated by stories of the great days of Newtown, when even the toughest brawlers ceased fighting when the priest approached. A story of the fish-selling Father Carroll illustrates how this power could be exercised in less peaceful fashion. One day he was spat upon in Merthyr and is said to have remarked to a passing Irishman that by the next day the man would never spit again. Nor did he. He was killed in the ironworks.

In the latter part of the nineteenth century, the type of Catholicism which the Irish brought to Wales was that which the ultramontane Cardinal Paul Cullen, Archbishop of Dublin, spread throughout the world. Wherever the Irish went, Cullen's influence saw to it that a strong emphasis was laid upon the authority of the Church, going to mass, church building, and the curbing of traditional Irish religious practices such as the celebrations of wakes, which were often much better fun than a wedding. Indeed, to this day, a good Irish funeral generally offers more conviviality and less rancour than the average wedding celebration. However, the wakes which Cullen deployed his influence against involved drinking and playing sometimes quite erotic games. The eroticism needs no explanation, but the drinking, particularly in Wales, was used as a method of defraying funeral expenses. The bereaved family would install a barrel in the house, obtained on 'tick'. The mourners would be given a few glasses and in return place some money on the coffin lid, and so the passage to the next world was eased both economically and emotionally.

As with the Irish throughout the world, the Irish clergy and nuns who came to Wales extended their influence through their charitable work for the poor and their labours in education, and inevitably the name of a 'good priest' cropped up during many researches. In this case it was Canon Sean Carney who had been a Sinn Feiner in Ireland, before the death of his friend, Sean South, in the Brookborough raid of 1956 turned him towards the priesthood. He was cited as one of the few priests to demonstrate an interest in Irish culture and history: 'Father Sean would help the Famine commemoration committee, for example, but from the other priests you get a deafening silence.' This comment contained a hidden commentary on the history of the Irish clergy in Wales. In most Welsh parishes, there is an Irish priest. Of Wales's three bishops, two are Irish-born and one is of Irish descent. Up to the early sixties, an Irish prelate, Archbishop McGrath, ensured a dominant position for Irish priests in the Cardiff diocese to such an extent that Welsh priests were virtually banished to the periphery. His successor, Archbishop Murphy, a typical 'bricks and mortar' Irish bishop, built schools and church buildings of all sorts with such gay abandon that the Royal Bank of Scotland was relieved to see the diocesan overdraft taken over by an Irish bank. Despite all this, although religious duties were conscientiously discharged, the diocesan priests generally constituted a curiously apathetic force in the Irish community. They were not prominent in the GAA for example, and when their holidays came around, tended to take a plane to Ireland.

As elsewhere in the United Kingdom, the Irish priests vigorously sought local funding and local control of schools and hospitals, instituted and upheld Cullen-style, ultramontane Roman Catholicism, but did not, in the main, seek to inculcate a tradition of Irishness. In Cardiff, for example, men now in their sixties were taught how to play rugby or to box, but learned no Irish history. They were prepared for assimilation into an English-dominated society. One can evaluate this cultural gear change if one considers that back in the twenties Conradh na Gaelige, the Gaelic League, was a force in the life of Irish people in Cardiff.

LANDLORDS

As indicated earlier, the Normans set out on their conquest of Ireland through Wales and they were rewarded for their efforts by being given some of the fertile Irish land around the Kildare town of Naas. There is a chapel in Naas still dedicated to Saint David, and the towns of Menevia and Naas have been twinned. Giraldus Cambrensis also came to Ireland in the wake of the Normans, with harmful effects on the reputation of the Irish, honed his hate creation techniques on the Irish to such good effect that he was chosen to preach the Third Crusade. There is a statue to him in the shadow of Llandaff Cathedral, commemorating his preaching of the Crusade from that site. Contemporary Arabia has as little reason to honour Cambrensis's memory as have the Irish. After being interviewed for the Cardiff *Mail* I therefore took particular delight in stipulating that I be photographed sitting on Giraldus's memorial.

His efforts helped to inaugurate a system whereby some of the great landlords of Wales also acquired vast estates in Ireland. Landlordism was as unpopular in Wales as it was in Ireland: the respected historian, Dr John Davies, has noted that there was 'a deep awareness that the landlords had no organic link with the culture of the mass of the people'.[91] He quotes the judgement of another scholar, Professor David Williams, that the landlords of Wales were 'a parasitic class', 'arrogant, extravagant, and shiftless, spending their useless lives in the preservation of game and its wholesale slaughter'. Not only might this description have equally well applied to Irish landlords, Welsh landlords very often *were* Irish landowners also: the south-east of Ireland where the Normans first landed is still known as the baronies of Forth and Bargy, and names in the districts such as Codd, Devereux and Strafford date from the days of the first landings. The Barons Harlech, who have given their name to Welsh TV, owned 21,000 acres in Sligo; the Earl of Dunraven had 14,000 in Limerick; the Earls of Pembroke are reckoned to have drawn some £35,000 a year in rents from Ireland at a time when this sum would be worth almost one hundred times what it is today. The writer

Above: Extract from the Cambrai ms., copied *c.* 790, which contains the longest passage in Old Irish to survive anywhere. A passage refers to 'white martyrdom and green martyrdom and red martyrdom'.

Right: Carrying the relics, 1789: the relics of St Etton are brought back to Dompierre: from the window of the church at Dompierre.

Right: Carrying the relics, 1998. From left to right, Claran Mulhern, Patrick Mulhern and Robert Galvin.

Above: How emigration was presented in British cartoons.

Below: Emigrants receive the priest's blessing, 1851.

Above: A scene of the quay at Cobh, 1851.

Left: The coffin ships: a journey to the New World.

Above: Emigrants to Canada embark from the tender Robina to the C.P.R. Liner Duchess of York, 1929.

Left: A replica of the emigrant ship Jeanie Johnson is worked on by shipwright Peter O'Regan near Tralee. It is hoped it will make a voyage across the Atlantic early in the new millennium.

Right: This British poster, produced in 1915, showed the Irish Guard Michael O'Leary VC with the aim of boosting enlistment in Ireland during the First World War.

Below: A young girl arrives in England from Ireland in the 1950s, one of some 20,000 a year who emigrated at this time. The Catholic Women's League and the Legion of Mary, amongst other organizations, offered help to new arrivals.

Cumann lúit cleas ʒaeveal —
C.C. lonnvain
(Gaelic Athletic Association—London County Board)

HURLING AND FOOTBALL Matches

EVERY SUNDAY AFTERNOON
Football 3.30. Hurling 4.45

at

G.A.A. SPORTS GROUNDS
Avery Hill Road, Eltham, S.E.9
Southern Railway from Charing Cross, Waterloo & London
Bridge to New Eltham Station.

ST. COLMCILLE GROUNDS,
London Colony, St. Albans
(Adjoining London Colony Hospital)

DAGENHAM PARK,
Dagenham, Essex
(5 minutes walk from Princess Cinema)

ADDRESS YOUR ENQUIRIES TO CO. BOARD SECRETARY—
P. CASEY,
1 Monks Crescent, Walton-on-Thames, Surrey.

Woodgrange Press Ltd., London. E.7

After Mitcham, New Eltham was the most popular sports ground in the London area in the 1950s.

Pictures from the
Paddy Fahey
Collection
showing Irish life
in London in the
1950s and 1960s.

Right: Gerard Conlon, the first of the Guildford Four to be freed, outside the Old Bailey in London (1989).

Below: The Birmingham Six, also photographed outside the Old Bailey in London after their convictions were quashed (1991).

Above: Celtic fans display their team colours during a Scottish Premier League match against Rangers at Parkhead. The match was marred by crowd disturbances.

Above: A young drummer boy marches through Glasgow on a procession organized by the Orange Lodge of Scotland in 1999.

Right: Rhodri Morgan, First Secretary of the Welsh Assembly, makes a point to Dr J. J. Lynch, the Director General of FAS, during the Irish careers exhibition at Holyhead.

Elizabeth Bowen is a descendant of the Welsh squire Henry Bowen, who founded the dynasty which for centuries lived at Bowen's Court, near Mallow, Co. Cork.

As late as 1923, hostility against one of these Welsh/Irish landlord families, that of Sir Charles Phibbs of Sligo, was such that he left Ireland for good, and built up a successful estate at Plas Gwynfryn. One of the inducements prompting Sir Charles's return to Wales was the digging of a grave on his front lawn to the accompaniment of slogans on the walls of his house and anonymous letters telling him that he would soon be the grave's occupant.

The power of this class was deployed against nationalism in both countries. The Welsh and Irish landlords voted against Home Rule for Ireland, and the system of education they favoured for the peasantry was that which Padraig Pearse termed the 'murder machine' – in other words, a system deliberately modelled upon that of England, which aimed at turning out pupils who thought of themselves as English. As we shall see, the system found favour in British colonies as far away from Wales and Ireland as the Caribbean. Both in Ireland and Wales, children subject to this system carried a tally stick on which a notch was cut each time they were caught speaking either Irish or Welsh. At the end of the day, the notches were counted up and beatings meted out accordingly.

Some Welsh parliamentarians, like Thomas Ellis, advocated the bringing together of both Celtic reformers and Celtic peoples, because 'their present oppressors are the same and their immediate wants are the same'. In the year Ellis wrote this, 1886, one of the names put forward for nomination in his constituency of Meirionydd was Charles Stewart Parnell. However, this brotherhood of the Celts, as perceived by intellectuals like Ellis, was not seen in the same light by the Welsh working class.

ANTAGONISM AND RIOTS

One of the results of the 1798 rebellion was an influx of Irish refugees to Wales, but the spirit of Giraldius Cambrensis awaited them. An observer of the time noted that 'a powerful and rancorous enmity possesses the bosoms of the Welsh against the Irish'. Not surprisingly, the following century saw a succession of anti-Irish riots in Wales as the Irish poured in in search of the jobs available in the mines, copper and iron works in Cardiff, Dowlais and Merthyr Tydfil, Nantyglo, Newport, Swansea and Tredegar. Then the Famine emigration increased Irish numbers and Welsh hostility.

The Irish encountered antagonism, not so much from the Orange and Green tensions of Glasgow and Liverpool, as from economic and ethnic antipathies. It could be argued that the character of Welsh hostility towards the Irish was gentler than that of the average Orange mob, in the sense that when Welsh gangs descended on an Irish township they generally contented themselves with driving out the menfolk, leaving the women and children unharmed. Traumatic though this form of attempted ethnic cleansing was, it did afford the possibility of the men sneaking back to their homes when things quietened down. Nevertheless, there were as many, if not more, anti-Irish riots in Wales as in any other part of the United Kingdom. The tendency for some writers to wax lyrical over Celtic affinities bears the same deceptive patina of romance as does the story-telling approach to the history of the Irish regiments in Europe, the Wild Geese, which we have encountered in the chapter on the Irish in Europe.

In fact, as the historian of the Irish in Wales, Paul O'Leary, has noted, there were nineteen major anti-Irish riots between 1826 and 1882, beginning with the conflicts at the Bute Ironworks in the Rhymni valley in 1826, where some sixty or seventy Irish had been brought in to work on the building of a number of blast furnaces. The Irish were taking the brunt of Welsh fears that an impending depression would mean cuts in wages. The Bute disturbances set the pattern of succeeding decades. The lives of steel workers were indeed nasty, brutish and short: if a twelve-year-old 'puddler' fell into a blast furnace, the death was scarcely noticed; certainly it merited neither inquest nor compensation. The deaths of adults attracted only marginally more attention. A descendant of Irish steel workers, now a University College of Wales, Cardiff, professor of architecture, has recalled how part of his grandfather's job was to tell women that their husbands had been killed in the steelworks.[92] His notification of his task consisted of nothing more than a cold piece of paper pushed through his front door bearing only a name and an address. The rest was up to him.

The understandable anger and turbulence of Welsh working-class society was vented on the heads of 'strangers', of whom the loud, unruly Irish were the most visible examples. The Irish in Wales were subject to attacks by the 'Scotch cattle', a Welsh variant of the Irish agrarian societies who attempted to intimidate unpopular landlords, or tenants who had moved on to an evicted person's land. The 'cattle' would surround homes at night, blowing horns and bellowing. The 'cattle' also made copious use of the tactic of sending anonymous threatening letters.

Yet, despite all this, and despite the fact that they were vastly outnumbered by English immigrants in search of Welsh-provided jobs, the Irish also took a significant part in events directed at improving the lot of the Welsh working class, including the Merthyr Rising of 1831, and the Chartist Rising at Newport in 1839. Historians of the Welsh labour and trade union movement point to the formation by the Irish of the National Amalgamated Union of Great Britain and Ireland as the starting point for organised labour in Wales.

However, radical appreciation of the Irish contribution to Chartism was considerably offset by the role which other members of the Irish community played in combating the growth of socialism. The urgings of the conservative Roman Catholic clergy resulted in Irish militia units being formed to assist the authorities in crushing the Chartists – so much for the appeal of the Chartists' founder, the Irishman Fergus O'Connor, to the 'blistered hands, and fustian jackets of the genuine working man'.[93]

HORROR AND DETESTATION

On 1 February 1847, the first ship to carry refugees from the Famine to Wales arrived in Newport, which for decades before Cardiff was developed formed the main entry point for Irish emigrants to Wales. The *Wanderer* had taken an incredible forty-one days to get from Baltimore in County Cork to Newport as bad weather had beaten the vessel back several times. She carried 113 destitute starving passengers, men, women and children. On 6 February, the *Monmouthshire Merlin* described the condition of these unfortunates when they arrived in Newport: 'Men, women and children, to the number of twenty-six, were found in a dying state, stretched upon a scanty portion of straw which but partially protected them from the hard and damp ballast on which they were lying in the hold.' However, the paper records that 'prompt and efficacious assistance' was rendered in the way of proper nourishment by the Misses Homfray and Lewis. These humanitarian ladies, assisted by a number of gentlemen from the Newport area, restored the refugees to health to such an extent that the *Merlin* noted that 'but one death is likely to ensue'.

This admirable pattern of assistance was swamped by the sheer weight of numbers which succeeding Famine ships brought to the Welsh shore. As Paul O'Leary has noted:

> Welsh hostility increased proportionately. Anti-Irish riots occurred sporadically throughout Wales in these decades, culminating in the vicious riots at Tredegar in 1882. Integration into Welsh society after the famine was not easy. The occupational profile of the Irish differed in important aspects from that of the host society, the Irish being over-represented in the unskilled category, and they tended to live apart from society at large. The Irish in Swansea became more, not less segregated between 1851 and 1871, and Martin Daunton has pointed out that in 1871 the Irish in Cardiff experienced a similar degree of segregation as black Americans in Philadelphia in 1860 – a comparison which suggests a high degree of isolation indeed.[94]

The populations of southern Welsh towns shot up steeply. For example, from a point in the mid 1820s when it was recorded that there were only two Irishmen in Cardiff, the 1841 census, taken after the building of Cardiff's first dock (1836–39) and the Taff Vale railway (completed 1841), recorded that there were 1,206 Irish-born, or children of Irish-born parents living in Cardiff, out of a total of 10,077. By the time of the next census, ten years later, there were at least 16,259 people living in Cardiff (a further 2,086 persons aboard vessels in the port on the night of the Census were excluded, but it is safe to assume a high proportion of Irish amongst them) and of these almost 3,000 were Irish, constituting 18.3 per cent of Cardiff's residents.

'Little Irelands' made their appearance in the slums of the city and the huge numbers of starving, pestilence-ridden Famine victims aroused the same sort of horror and detestation as they did elsewhere. A public meeting held in Exeter Hall in Cardiff, to organise aid for the starving Irish, broke up in disorder when a Protestant clergyman said that the Famine 'was a visitation by the Almighty for their apostasy' and that the Roman Catholic religion was that of apostasy. Pub brawls, often resulting in deaths, added to the overall attrition levels. One such fatal stabbing in 1848 led to the burning of the Catholic church in Cardiff and a prolonged period of rioting in which neither army nor police were used to protect the Irish.

The official attitude of the authorities towards the Irish at this time may be gleaned from the following 1847 governmental report on education in Wales (generally known as the 'Blue book'):

> From the tradespeople upwards English is spoken . . . but Welsh is still prevalent amongst the adult labouring class . . . There is little poverty except amongst the Irish . . . The (beer) trade was said to be thrown into the hands of any idle vagabond . . . the beerhouses were generally brothels as well as beerhouses: trade unions, chartism and every mischievous association had its origins in them.

Another report at the time, the Rammell Report on Health and Sanitation in Cardiff in 1850, paints a horrific picture of what conditions were like for the Irish. Over half of those born in the 1840s died before the age of five. This startling statistic appears less surprising if one considers the conditions in Stanley Street, which contained over 400 Irish. It was approximately ten feet wide, unlit, only partly paved, and had an open and often overflowing sewer running down the middle. There was only one well, filled with contaminated water, and living conditions were such that a lodging house run by a man called Harrington was said to contain fifty occupants, all sleeping in the one room. Not surprisingly, epidemics of cholera, dysentry, smallpox and typhus were common.

As elsewhere in the United Kingdom, these afflictions were regarded as being the fault of the Irish. Living conditions were linked to the question of wages. In August 1853, the Welsh language journal, *Y Diwygiwr* (the *Reformer*), reported:

> It is certain that the Irish are to be greatly blamed for many things. They undermine wages in many areas through working below price. They can well afford that; because some dozen of them live helter-skelter in some hole of a house, and they send their wives and children about begging, and they will live on the worst fare, and if someone dares say a word to them it is not surprising if they do not stab a knife between his ribs.

A *Punch* cartoon of this period showed a crowded street, peopled with simian-visaged beings underneath a sign reading 'Logins Fur Thravelers'. The caption read: 'A Court for King Cholera'.[95] Press reports certainly helped to keep anti-Irish sentiment alive, despite the contradictory effect of Gladstonian liberalism and the strong support for Welsh radicalism amongst the Irish. For example, after the five-day riot at Tredegar in 1882, which resulted in the Irish quarter being destroyed and the people being expelled, the Welsh newspaper *Tarian y Gweithiwr* (The Workman's Shield) commented:

> There is a limit to the toleration and patience of the Welsh as with any other nation, and
> if strangers insist on quarrelling with them without cause, they should be forced to take the
> inevitable consequences.

There was great uncertainty about employment, because iron production was losing out to that of steel. The Irish bore the brunt of this uncertainty and the riots that broke out in Tredegar were particularly vicious, lasting for almost a week. By then the Irish-born population of Wales had grown to some 28,000 or 2.18 per cent of the total population.

ACCEPTING THE LINK

Yet, by the end of the nineteenth century, the Irish were more popular in Wales than in either England or Scotland. In the same way in which the present-day growth of multi-national firms in Scotland is helping to diminish sectarian employment practices, the huge influx of English emigrants into Wales, in pursuit of the jobs created by the coal-fuelled Welsh Industrial Revolution, helped to create a mass culture in which the Irish were more easily incorporated. Moreover, the Irish predilection for education meant that the rising tide of the Industrial Revolution lifted their boats higher up the economic shore than those of newer emigrants.

There were other factors at work. The Irish had become closely involved with the new Welsh Labour movements, and the Welsh with the Irish demand for Home Rule. This latter involvement was not based on affection for the Irish but on the deep-rooted, long-running, nonconformist support for Gladstone and the Liberal Party. Gladstonian Liberalism, with its support for Home Rule in Ireland, brought the Welsh to the Irish side to the extent that in 1897, at the Ireland v. Wales match at Llanelli, the crowd chanted 'Home Rule for Ireland'. There were also some cultural linkages between the Welsh language and Irish language movements. Padraig Pearse, the 1916 leader, was an honoured visitor to Welsh Eisteddfods.

A Welsh-born Prime Minister, David Lloyd George, had a more hotly debated, long-term effect on Ireland than any British leader of the twentieth century. Lloyd George, though deified in Wales, was for decades a hate figure to Irish Republicans because of his role in the Irish Treaty negotiations. Yet, without him today's Republic of Ireland would not exist.

Lloyd George's great Irish adversary was Michael Collins, who he first tried to hang and then sat down with to do the Treaty deal. Collins's career reminds us that three features of Irish life meshed in Wales: whiskey, revolutionaries and prison.

Near Bala in North Wales is the small village of Frongoch, once the site of a whiskey distillery which went bankrupt in 1910. (This last is not surprising as it is said that nonconformist sentiment against strong liquor was such that the whiskey could only be moved out of the distillery at night.) After the outbreak of the First World War, the premises were used as a German prison camp. Then, after the 1916 Rising, a large number of those who had taken part, together with an even larger group who had not but who were rounded up anyhow, were interned in Frongoch. Frongoch was the classic 'Republican University'. Men of all walks of life, from every part of Ireland, were brought together and as a result the seeds, not only of revolution but often of education, were sown amongst men who might otherwise never have met each other. It was in Frongoch that Michael Collins began to reorganise the Irish Republican Brotherhood and to plot the next round against England. Looking out at the barren beauty of Bala's lakes and mountains, Collins evolved the theories of guerrilla warfare and intelligence gathering which ensured that the IRA would never again be caught holding a series of fortified buildings from which they could be blasted out by superior fire and manpower. Not surprisingly, during the ensuing Anglo-Irish war, South Wales became an active centre of IRA gun-running, so active in fact that the British Cabinet used to get weekly reports on IRA activity in Wales. Many of the Frongoch men were to become ministers in Irish Governments, like General Richard Mulcahy or Dr Jim Ryan. Some, like Terence MacSwiney, were to gain world attention through dying on hunger strike during the Black and Tan War.

The contribution of Welsh politicians to Ireland, however, has tended to be controversial to say the least. It was a Welsh Secretary of State, Merlyn Rees, who caved in to the Loyalist strikes which destroyed the Sunningdale Agreement of 1973 and so continued the Six Counties on the bloody road which may, or may not, have ended with the conclusion of the Good Friday Agreement in 1997. It was also a Labour administration under Jim Callaghan, whose name indicates his Irish ancestry, which self-destructed itself over Ireland by a particularly disreputable piece of pandering to the Unionists. In order to secure Unionist support for his wafer-thin majority, Callaghan's Government increased the number of Westminster constituencies so that the Unionists could secure a greater number of seats. The manoeuvre backfired when the Belfast MP Gerry Fitt, who normally voted with Labour, abstained in protest and Labour were defeated by one vote, thereby paving the way for the Thatcher Years. Had Fitt voted with Labour as was his wont, the vote would have been tied, the Speaker would have voted with the Government, and Labour would have remained in power. However, in fairness, let me conclude by saying that the office of another Welsh politician at Stormont (albeit one of Irish descent), Paul Murphy, the Minister for Finance during Mo Mowlam's tenure, was a happier and better remembered interlude.

SPORT

Within limits, sport, particularly rugby and boxing, provided a unifying bond between the Welsh and the Irish. A famous Irish rugby player, William O'Neill, won the first of many international caps for Wales, against the Springboks in 1906, while working as a Cardiff docker. The son of famine emigrants, he would have been highly unlikely to have been chosen for such a distinction in his more caste-laden native country. However, even in egalitarian Wales, the prejudices of the time were strong enough to cause him to change his name to Billy Neale.

The tradition of rugby-induced friendship endured, both between the Irish and the Welsh within Wales and between the two countries. Before the Celtic Tiger took off in the 1990s, the biennial Welsh rugby international in Dublin was one of the brightest spots in the tourist year. To judge from the amount of money they spent, the hordes of red-and-white scarfed, singing Welshmen must have begun saving for the occasion soon after the final whistle blew for the previous year's international. I remember one year in which the match was cancelled. As a result the publicans on the east coast of Ireland declared what amounted to a week of national mourning. The matching descents of the Irish on Cardiff Arms Park have also had a markedly beneficial effect on the Welsh brewing industry.

Arguably the greatest sporting figure whom Wales has produced was the Irishman 'Peerless' Jim Driscoll. He was Featherweight Champion of the British Empire and in his lifetime embodied the ideal of the working-class hero: the man who fought his way out of the slums with iron fists and a golden heart. His Lonsdale Belt, a magnificent piece of enamelled metalwork, is preserved in the Royal Oak in Cardiff. The walls of the pub are adorned with pictures of great fighters and singers of the past and present, either on their own or talking to the contemporary landlord, Mike Flynn, whose wife is a member of Driscoll's family. The pub is a museum of Welsh-Hibernian memorabilia, both in its decor and its customers. Here come Plaid Cymru, socialists, Irish language enthusiasts, GAA players and everyone who wants to both partake of a sense of Irishness and the pub speciality, Brain's Strong Ale, better known as SA or Skull Attack. This lethal beer is poured on draught from kegs 'horsed' into the pub on trollies. The beer is poured flat and is guaranteed to do more for your head than the late Jim Driscoll's fists. It conferred on me the mistaken impression that I could sing. After a rendition of 'Foggy Foggy Dew', which did not lead to my picture being hung alongside Pavarotti's, Mike Flynn clapped me on the back and said: 'Never mind. You're a good writer!' With friends like these who needs enemies? Upstairs there is a gym where the would-be Driscolls of today are trained.

The history of the Irish in Wales over the last 150 years is bound up in the story of Driscoll, his family and his birthplace. He was born in the Newtown district of Cardiff to Cork emigrant parents, and his story reminds us yet again that Irish emigration was not confined to men. Women probably outnumbered men, but because the men were more visible, working on huge public construction works, down the mines, or up at the bar, oral history and newsreel footage convey an impression of a predominantly male society. In fact, apart from their heroic endeavours in keeping homes together, women worked not merely in traditionally female occupations – 'in service', sewing, scrubbing and so forth – but often at harsh manual labour. Driscoll's mother, like many another turn-of-the-century Irish emigrant, performed what we would regard today as slave labour to feed her family. Her first husband was killed in a railway accident, leaving her with four children. In between rearing her huge family, she worked at what were then common jobs for women, unloading potatoes on the docks, or selling fish.

In the Newtown district, where the Irish congregated, chest and breathing diseases afflicted every family. The undertaker's hearse was the only, and most frequent, touch of grandeur in the district. The children ran barefoot and Driscoll himself died in his forties from a pulmonary ailment.

Newtown was the name given to the warren of little streets built to house the Irish workers who built Cardiff's docks. This vibrant area, dominated by St Paul's Church, was destroyed in 1966 to make way for development. In its century-long existence, it could have been used as a microcosm for an Irish ghetto anywhere in the world. Julia Burns has drawn a vivid portrait of life in Newtown.[96] There was a strong sense of Irishness furthered by the scrimping and saving necessary to pay for Irish lessons. As Burns said of her grandmother, it was 'little short of amazing that she felt she should send her children for lessons at that time [1922], when money was so short. She must have felt a great sense of loyalty and "belonging" to her Irish past.'

The people of Newtown also felt 'a great loyalty' to each other. Burns writes:

When my Uncle Davey (died 1993) was working in London and my father, Tommy, was away in Birmingham, each one would send most of his pay packet back home to Newtown. This money would arrive early Monday and the postman would be followed immediately by a visit from a neighbour. All the front doors were open and you simply walked into your neighbour's hallway or room if you needed to find them. This neighbour would walk in and ask "ave the postman been, Mary?' My Nana would then lend her neighbour the money sent by her two sons. This neighbour would pay back the money every Friday so that Nana could do her own shopping and pay her bills and then, according to Aunty Mary, the neighbour would be seen 'like a ship in full sail' going 'over the bridge' – i.e. leaving Newtown in the direction of 'town' – a huge, well padded woman. On her return journey every Friday she looked 'like a wraith' (I quote) because, of course, she had disposed of all the extra items of clothing in the pawnshop where they presumably spent every weekend. Thus my grandmother kept another family from trouble whilst carefully maintaining her own fragile economy.[97]

The end of Newtown may also be taken as a microcosm of the subsequent history of the Irish in Cardiff. Burns has described how her grandmother left before the demolition:

They carried her out with her eyes tight shut because she said she could not bear the parting. This little community had survived all the poverty and hardships of the adjustment to a new life as immigrants in a strange land, two world wars, a general strike and the depression period, only to be deliberately dismantled and scattered once more throughout the city, never quite to regain the closeness and support of 'Little Ireland'. The

Irish communities are gone, but names like Burns, Murphy, Kane, Flynn, Tobin, O'Neill and Doyle abound in Cardiff, Swansea and throughout Wales.

Driscoll began his pugilistic career to help out with the family finances. He started in fairground booths, often fighting ten or fifteen bouts in a day against men many years older and far heavier than himself. When he moved into the professional arena, Driscoll won almost all of his forty bouts. He finally retired from the ring after being defeated by a Frenchman eleven years younger than himself, whose manager insisted that the fight go for twenty rounds. Short of money, Driscoll agreed. He led for fourteen rounds, but in the fifteenth his lungs gave out and his seconds threw in the towel. He is remembered in Cardiff for his charity. Asked why he habitually shelled out to an old boxer who begged on street corners, he replied: 'I gave him more money than he ever earned in the ring.'

Above all, Driscoll is remembered for his Nazareth House bout. Nazareth House was and is a famous Cardiff orphanage, and Driscoll had promised the nuns who ran it that he would stage an exhibition bout for the home. At the time of the promised bout, he was offered a world championship fight in New York. He had already beaten the champion on points, but in those days the title transferred only on a knock-out, and Driscoll was the clear favourite to win the return bout. However, the fight clashed with a scheduled charity appearance on behalf of the Nazareth home – so he turned down the world championship fight and returned to Cardiff to give a free performance which earned the nuns £6,000.

His funeral in 1925 was followed by a crowd of over 100,000 people, the largest ever seen in Cardiff. In 1995, a statue to his memory was erected by subscription which included donations from contemporary boxing idols such as Prince Nasseim. The affection in which Driscoll was held served to bring together both Catholic and Protestant, Welsh and Irish, and Driscoll's career may legitimately be regarded as one of the turning points in Welsh/Irish relationships.

To sum up then, though the history of the Irish in Wales has been turbulent, its present and recent past has been mercifully tranquil. Its future will be determined by the future of the Welsh economy and by the working out of the Good Friday Agreement, the success or failure of which will determine whether Dublin maintains an Irish Consulate General in Cardiff both as a symbol of growing Anglo-Irish friendship, and a rallying point for the Irish community. Perhaps a pointer for the future is the fact that one of the first representatives elected to the new Welsh Assembly in the 1999 election was the Irish-born Dr Brian Gibbon.

But given the Irish and Welsh fondness for singing perhaps the best way to leave the story of their relationship is with a song. As the other common interest of the Celts is disputation, the song I have chosen is 'The Holy Ground'. Cork men regard this as one of their anthems, because its title is also the name of a district in the town of Cobh, but, in Wales they will tell you that, like bee-keeping, the Holy Ground originated in Wales, in Swansea:

> Adieu, my fair young maidens, ten thousand times adieu
> We must goodbye to the Holy Ground, and the girls that we love true
> We will sail the salt sea over, and return again for sure, to seek the girls
> Who wait for us—in the Holy Ground once more.
> Fine Girl you are!
> You're the girl I do adore, and still I live in hope to see, The Holy Ground once more: Fine girl you are!

SCOTLAND

The Irish in Scotland, especially the Glasgow Irish, are viewed as the 'Cinderellas' of the Irish diaspora, at the bottom of a league headed by the Boston and New York Irish. But historians are rediscovering the central role played by the Irish in Scotland in the horrendous post-Famine period through their support of Daniel O'Connell, Isaac Butt and Charles Stewart Parnell. You cannot tell the story of Michael Davitt, the founder of the movement which led to a resolution of the Irish land problem, without reference to his links with Glasgow Celtic Football Club and the West Highland co-operative movement.

Closer links between Scotland and the Republic of Ireland had been growing in the years preceding the conclusion of the Good Friday Agreement in 1998. In Scotland the quickening of the devolution debate, combined with the resurgence of the Scottish National Party, had led to a renewal of interest in the Irish experience in self-government, which in turn was heightened by the increasingly impressive performance of the Irish economy. Significantly, a few weeks before the Agreement was signed, the *Glasgow Herald* (2 March 1998) carried a report of a conference organised in Dublin for the benefit of Scottish tourist operators who wanted to study how the Irish had make a success of their tourist industry. Back in Scotland the Scottish Development Board was only too well aware of how the Irish Industrial Development Authority inveigled to the Republic industries which the SDA had hoped to bring to Scotland. On a less competitive level Scottish universities had also shown their awareness of Irish political developments by conferring honorary doctorates on figures like the former Taoiseach, Albert Reynolds, and on Mary Robinson.

Even before the country had presidents and prime ministers, Irish nationalism had a tradition of impacting on Scottish politics. As Richard J. Finlay had pointed out: 'Those who were concerned with devolution, either for it or against it, tended to look to Ireland for evidence to back their particular case.'[98] In the nineteenth century the Liberals promoted Home Rule for Scotland as a means of making the idea of Home Rule for Ireland more acceptable in the UK. As John Cooney has observed, the leading contemporary devolutionist, Alex Salmond, the leader of the Scottish National Party (SNP), recognised the importance of Ireland in the wooing of the Scoto-Irish vote away from its traditional allegiance to Labour.

Cooney is a Glaswegian Irishman, who apart from being the political correspondent of *Ireland on Sunday* is also the Dublin correspondent of the *Glasgow Herald*. The annual Humbert Summer School which he organises in Co. Mayo, is the principal meeting point between the Scots and the Irish. He told me: 'Labour's hold over the descendants of the Irish in Scotland is slipping as a result of the 'greening' of the Scottish Nationalist Party under Alex Salmond, [its leader until the autumn of 2000, *author*], who wanted Scotland to emulate Ireland's 'Celtic Tiger' performance in the European Union.'

'SCOTLAND HAS MUCH TO LEARN FROM IRELAND'

Salmond had grasped a significant fact, which had apparently eluded the Ulster Unionists, namely that the numbers of Catholics in Scotland (roughly 825,000) balanced those of Protestants in the Six Counties. In August 1998, he chose the Humbert Summer School to deliver a speech lauding the Celtic Tiger which aroused much favourable comment amongst Scots of Irish-Catholic descent who provide the overwhelming bulk of the Scottish Catholics. Salmond said that 'Scotland has much to learn from Ireland', and advocated practical cultural co-operation, such as exchanging television programming, particularly programmes in the Irish language, to help Scotland's 'under-achieving Gaelic language television sector'. However, it was Ireland's European experience which he felt had most resonance for Scotland:

> One has only to look around Ireland to see that whole-hearted membership of the European Union is good for small nations. It not only brings economic benefits, but it also increases the reach and influence of such nations.[99]

Salmond's emphasis on a larger, European view helped in his development of friendly relationships with the leader of Scotland's Roman Catholic hierarchy, Cardinal Thomas Winning. Though Salmond is not a Catholic, one of his initiatives involved writing a regular column for the Catholic diocesan newspaper, *Flourish*. This would have been unthinkable for his fundamentalist Presbyterian, anti-Catholic predecessors who founded the SNP. One of the theoreticians of Scottish nationalism, Andrew Dewar Gibb, Professor of Scots Law at Glasgow University, in 1930 had published a book, *Scotland in Eclipse*, which contained sentiments that found a resonance with many Presbyterians:

> In the heart of a dwindling, though virile and intelligent, race, there is growing up another people, immeasurably inferior in every way, but cohesive and solid, refusing obstinately,

at the behest of obscurantist magic-men, to mingle with the people whose land they are usurping.

Dewar, and those who thought like him, wanted the Irish sent back to Ireland. In our day, Salmond's wider view has paid off. Cardinal Winning's fears that an accession to power by the SNP might lead to a revival of the old Presbyterian campaign against state aid to Catholic schools were allayed, and in October 1998, the Cardinal told the Bishops' Conference of the European Union that Scottish Nationalism was now: 'mature, respectful of democracy and international in outlook'.[100]

The Cardinal forecasts an independent Scotland in about a decade's time. This prediction took something of a knock during the election campaign for the new Scottish Assembly when Alex Salmond came out against the NATO action in Kosovo. Because of their military traditions and their naval and submarine bases, the Scots are emotionally drawn towards support for NATO and Salmond's stance told against him at the polls, reflecting the fact that many Scots had begun to think again as to what independence might bring in the way of future policy shifts. However, for our purposes, what counts is that the hatchets of the old sectarian Irish-Scottish antagonisms have largely been buried in Scotland – never mind what one may hear from time to time during and after Rangers-Celtic encounters.

DEVOLUTION

A visitor to Scotland is struck by the heads up, spring-in-the-stride air of contemporary Scots. A few days after Labour's victory in May 1997, I witnessed an interesting debate on what the outcome portended for Scotland, in the Dumbarton home of Bill and Bernadette Heaney. The Heaney family are a perfect example of the upwardly mobile trend of the Catholic Scoto-Irish. Heaney is a prominent journalist, the editor of the *Lennox Herald*, and correspondent for most of the bigger London newspapers. Bernadette is a social worker, and their son Brian, who was present at the dinner, took his call to the bar two years later. If one were to design a family motif for the family it would be in the form of a shamrock embodying Labour, Ireland and St Patrick's Church, Dumbarton.

The other guests were old family friends, the Labour whip and subsequently Minister for State at Stormont with Mo Mowlam, Tom McFaul and his wife. During the discussion there was a very marked division of opinion between McFaul and Brian Heaney as to what a new assembly would mean; McFaul averred that the people would never risk the extra taxation involved in moving towards independence. Politely and respectfully, in a fashion which indicated a bright future in the law, young Heaney countered every argument. Neither statistics nor the possession of political insights overawed him. He, and his girlfriend, were confident that an assembly was only a beginning. Independence lay around the corner. It certainly seemed so at the time. London's interference in, and indifference to, Scotland's affairs had just been rejected at the polls. The Conservatives, the Unionists' traditional allies, had failed to win a single seat north of the border.

Once in Downing Street, Tony Blair acted within a few days of the debate in the Heaney home to fulfil his pre-election promises on devolution. The first Bill introduced by the new Government (on 15 May 1997) was the Referendum Bill which paved the way for the setting up in Scotland of a 129-member Parliament, elected under the additional member system, and with the power to vary taxation. In Dublin, the Government, anxious to be seen both to co-operate with Blair and further the spread of devolution to the Six Counties as well as to Scotland and Wales – while at the same time putting a brake on Unionist ambitions to use the British Council as the principal channel for matters concerning Belfast and the UK – established the Consulates General in Scotland and Wales. This decision to improve both Dublin–London and Dublin–Cardiff–Edinburgh relationships meant that plans for other important expansions of Dublin's diplomatic activity had to be put on the back-burner, and the opening of embassies in both Brazil and Mexico were shelved.

In making its choice, Dublin was also acknowledging the fact that, if independence does come to Scotland through factors such as Salmond's leadership and the growth of Scottish Nationalism, it will also owe much to a switch of ancient allegiances, from Labour to the SNP, on the part of the Catholic Scoto-Irish. This was not what Labour envisaged when opting for devolution of course, and it was most certainly not what the Ulster Unionists foresaw either when they pressed for closer links with Scotland in the form of a British-Irish Council! Some Unionists had fondly believed that the old anti-Catholic hard-line Unionism of Protestant Scotland, with its Ulster affinities, was still a powerful political force. As we shall see, there was a substantial historical background to this belief, but it was no longer valid in the 1990s.

THE EARLY DAYS

Today's Scottish establishment is embarrassed by the history which gave rise to the Irish gibe: 'If you scratch a Scotsman, he'll bleed orange.' When it became known, in January 1999, that Ian Paisley's DUP Party was planning to field candidates in the Scottish Assembly elections the following May, the Orange Order bluntly told Paisley:[101] 'There's no place for you in Scottish politics', and the Grand Master of the Orange Order in Scotland, Ian Wilson, said the DUP intervention would be 'distinctly unhelpful'.[102] The *Scotsman* summed up the mood of contemporary Scotland in an editorial which said of Paisley that he was:

> ... more than capable of poisoning the debate over the Union with his 19th Century theology and his 18th Century politics. Even the Orange Order would rather this particular

man of the cloth steered clear . . . let the voters of Scotland make their opinion of religious intolerance abundantly clear. Scotland says NO, as it were.[103]

It may be remarked that the *Scotsman*'s editorial call for religious tolerance was consistent with a similarly enlightened attitude on the part of the paper, during the upheavals over the '19th Century theology' which were at the base of the Unionists' misplaced optimism in the British-Irish Council. In fact the story of Irish emigration to Scotland, and Scots emigration to Ireland, goes back to the earliest days of Christianity and beyond. During the contemporary Troubles in the Six Counties of Northern Ireland that once formed part of the ancient nine-county province of Ulster, the Scots' Argyll regiments were prominent in the fray. There was both an aptness and an irony in this because it was the Scoti of Ulster who settled Argyll after the fall of the Roman empire, bringing with them ancient Gaelic culture and the name by which that part of Britain lying above the border is known: Scotland. The subsequent significant Irish contribution to Scots monastic development has already been outlined, but the Irish also made a significant contribution to the survival of the Catholic religion in Scotland after the Reformation. The Irish Franciscan mission to Scotland in the seventeenth century was conducted at a level of hardship which may be gauged from the fact that, in 1636, a Father Cathaldus Ward is recorded as having travelled on foot from the Isles to Edinburgh to obtain flour and wine.

Other more well-known contributions of the Irish to Scottish history include the fatal devotion of the Irish Catholics to the Stuart cause. Culloden was an Irish as well as a Scottish disaster. However, for our purposes, it is fair to say that the foundations of the considerable Irish presence in Scotland today, and much of the rancour which Paisley hoped to take advantage of, was laid down by the Famine. The horrific descriptions of thousands of starving, fever-ridden Irish emigrants pouring into dock areas, often to collapse and die as soon as they touched dry land, were as true of Glasgow as they were of Liverpool or Manchester. The figure in the 1851 census for Irish-born in Scotland was 207,367. This represented, according to official statistics, an increase of 81,046 in the Irish population in the ten-year period, but the historian James Handley has estimated that this last figure should be at least 30 per cent higher.[104]

At all events, the numbers were unquestionably large and the impact of the emigration to Scotland was disagreeable both for the Irish and the Scots. The authorities began shipping Irish 'vagrants' and beggars back to Ireland, but this was not enough for the *Glasgow Herald*, which commented:

These repressive measures may be good so far as they go; but as yet there is nothing done to prevent these same Irish vagrants coming back, and bringing thousands of others along with them. We fear they are induced to leave Ireland under the most disillusive notions of the comfort and abundance that awaits them there, and there is too much reason to believe that they are coaxed or driven out of the sister kingdom by those who should succour

them, and who only desire the absence of these wretched unfortunates in order that the
burden of caring for them may be shifted from their own shoulders upon ours.[105]

The *Herald* was correct, insofar as part of its observations were concerned.
There was a move afoot by landlords to clear tenants off their estates, either
for reasons of rent arrears, or out of a desire to rid their estates of small,
uneconomic holdings to concentrate on pasture. Townlands were denuded of
their tenantry. So rigorous were the clearances that not only were those who
had fallen foul of landlords evicted, people who encouraged the evictees to
stay in their native districts, by offering them shelter, were also evicted.
Attempts to adapt nineteenth-century agricultural practices to changing
economic patterns fell harshly on both the Scots and the Irish.

If one goes to the Broomielaw district of Glasgow, on the Firth of Clyde,
they will show you where the starving Irish shoaled ashore. Sometimes the
starvelings were met by miners' agents who offered them the jobs – at lower
wages – and the homes taken from evicted Scottish Protestants. Thus were the
flames of sectarianism fanned. A short distance from the Broomielaw, further
up the Clyde, at Greenock, they will point out the spot where tens of
thousands of Scots emigrants took ship for the New World. They too were
cleared off the estates by their landlords, partly to get them off their small
uneconomic holdings, and partly because famine had also broken out in parts
of the Highlands and on the islands, albeit with far less grievous results than
were allowed to develop in Ireland. Nevertheless this Scottish famine had both
a long-term and a long-distance bearing on Scots/Irish relationships. As John
MacLeod observed:

The scale of the famine disaster was so great that the Government decided that the powers
which were decreed to deal with the Irish famine should be extended to Scotland . . . but it
soon decided that the only real solution for the problem was a wholesale emigration of
people. Today then as a result, we have a Canadian Province called 'New Scotland' [Nova
Scotia] having more Gaelic speakers than Scotland and boasting an all-Gaelic University,
whereas in Scotland we have only some universities with Gaelic departments.[106]

ORANGE/GREEN HOSTILITY

One result of the Scottish exodus to the Canadas was that Orange/Green
hostilities crossed the Atlantic, and another that they intensified in Scotland.
Hunger is a great force in keeping down wages, and the Irish were hungry
enough to take any work, no matter how arduous, at lower rates than the
Scots. Over the half-century, from 1850 to 1900, the Irish were the largest
component of the unskilled labour force but earned the lowest wages and were
the principal victims of the 'truck system', the Scots version of the American
'company store' which was as much a feature of the Irish emigrants' daily life
as was the pawn shop. Mines and other heavy industry concerns made a
practice of paying their workers at irregular intervals, so that necessity for

credit mounted up. Advances against pay due were then made, but on the stipulation that the money had to be spent only in the company store. The margins of profit and the quality of the goods sold can well be imagined, but the system was defended on the grounds that the Irish, if left to the free control of their own money, would probably spend it on drink or otherwise fritter it, not being used to the handling of money in their native country.

These sorts of prejudices helped both to create and fuel a particular fury amongst Scots Protestants against the Maynooth Grant and the restoration of the Catholic hierarchy. Various anti-papal societies came into being throughout the 1850s, amongst which the Scottish Reformation Society was a particularly active lobby. Apart from holding public meetings and issuing tracts, the SRS funded bursaries for those who excelled in examinations on topics such as the abominations of 'papal aggression'. The clout of the SRS may be gauged from the fact that one candidate who had voted in favour of the Maynooth Grant, Lord Melgund, polled only 353 votes out of a total of 8,385. All these anti-Catholic activities had a direct bearing on the Irish, whose ever-increasing numbers were both revivifying the Catholic Church in Scotland, and providing tangible targets for Protestant wrath.

Two of the more spectacular preachers of the sort of extreme anti-Catholic doctrines associated with Ian Paisley in our day were the so-called 'Angel Gabriel' and Alessandro Gavazzi, who later continued his anti-Catholic crusade in Canada. The Angel Gabriel's real name was John Sayers Orr and his crowd-pulling gimmick was to emulate his angelic namesake by sounding loud blasts on a trumpet. But the walls which came tumbling down were not those of Jericho but quite often those of Catholic homes. Amongst the various disturbances which he created, Sayers incited riots in Greenock on 12 July 1851, vandalising a church in Barehope Street and making such a bear garden of the town that Irish workers were dismissed from their employment and had to take to the hills with their families for safety.

. 'Gabriel' was supported in his activities by the connivance of the authorities who dismissed a Catholic policemen, John Bradley, who had arrested Protestant hooligans for spattering filth on a parish priest's house. Magistrates handed down derisory fines on those found guilty of wrecking Catholic shops. Armed attacks on Catholic police who attempted to stem these attacks were also treated lightly by the courts. To us, there is a certain degree of symbolism in the fact that in 1855 the Angel Gabriel was placed in Paisley jail as his followers rioted, destroying Catholic schools and property. Ironically, in what should have been his natural stamping ground of Belfast, the Angel found no audience whatever – the authorities placed him in jail until the 12th of July celebrations were over. He died in jail in his native Demerara, in 1856; British Guiana had given him a three-year sentence for insults to the bishop and nuns of the colony which had passed unpunished in Scotland.

Gavazzi had been a Catholic priest, but threw in his lot with the opponents of the Pope and the papal states. He subsequently came from Italy to Britain and was made particularly welcome in Scotland, the *Glasgow Herald* judging his attraction to be on a par with that of Jenny Lind, the Swedish Nightingale. However, this judgement was not shared by the Irish in Canada, who had more freedom to express their displeasure at his anti-popery. The agitations of the Angel Gabriel and of Gavazzi helped to give rise to two anti-Catholic journals, the *Bulwark* and the *Scottish Protestant*, both of which appeared in 1851. The editor of the *Scottish Protestant*, the Reverend James Gibson, said he had no wish to affront Catholics, nor to 'stir up feelings of strife or hatred against them', but he balanced this amiable sentiment by remarking of the Irish in Scotland:

> If the hopes of the Popery to regain her dominion of darkness in this kingdom of Bible light are beginning to revive, it is because she is colonising our soil, from another land, with the degraded hordes of barbarized and enslaved victims, which she proudly styles her subjects.[107]

Apart from such purely sectarian publications, the ordinary newspapers of the time, for example the *Scottish Guardian*, published in Glasgow from 1832 to 1861, also added their measure of hemlock to the haggis. The *Guardian* slogan was 'No compromise with Popery'. It campaigned against Irish occasions such as Daniel O'Connell's visit to Scotland in 1835, and told its readers on 8 March 1849 that the Great Famine was caused by Irish 'barbarous spiritual destitution, its moral and intellectual poverty'.

The Reform Church of Scotland had grown directly out of its opposition to Rome in the sixteenth century. Now Rome was counter-attacking by sending its illiterate hordes into the country from Ireland, and a belief took hold amongst the Scottish Presbyterian churches that the descendants of Calvin and Knox had a duty to seek the conversion of Roman Catholics. One of the more bizarre choices to propagate this mission was the Irish-speaking Reverend Patrick MacMenemy, an Irish Presbyterian from the Glens of Antrim. MacMenemy's mission hall in Edinburgh added a new dimension to the term 'muscular Christianity' as Catholics tried to break up his meetings and Presbyterians and Papists belaboured each other for the love of God. Like the Reverend Ian Paisley in our day, he acquired a doctorate from an obscure American university but, unlike the Reverend Ian, he fell foul of the lure of the flesh. In 1885 a Liverpool court was told that not only had the Reverend MacMenemy assaulted a policeman, the assault had taken place in a brothel.

However, while MacMenemy's particular crusade collapsed, the general hostility to Irish Catholic emigrants continued. Promotion was denied to Catholics in the public service, the police, and even, in a celebrated case of 1858, in a Dumfries lunatic asylum. Greenock and Port Glasgow were noted for Protestant/Catholic tension, as was Dumbarton. Here, in 1855, the shipyards of Denny's and Rankine's solved the problem posed by the attempts of Protestant shipwrights to throw Catholic workers into the furnaces by sacking the Catholics. The Dumbarton troubles were attributed to the fact that the Angel Gabriel had been blowing his trumpet in the town a few days earlier. The following year also saw Catholic property, including a church, burned by a Protestant mob in Kelso. A jury returned a verdict of 'not proven' on those charged with the offence. The Orange and Green rioting became so dangerous throughout the mid-1850s that Ayrshire, Dumbartonshire, Lanarkshire, Renfrewshire and Stirlingshire banned 12th of July processions. However, despite the bans, trouble flared repeatedly. In 1859, a march from Paisley was led by off-duty policemen who joined in an attack on Catholics. Similar police complicity in Orange violence occurred at the riots in the Glasgow suburb of Partick in 1875 when the Home Rulers who had organised a commemoration of Daniel O'Connell's centenary were attacked by Orangemen, and several days of savage hand-to-hand fighting took place before order was restored. Orange and Green clashes also occurred at Coatbridge and Motherwell. In both places the tradition of the Orangemen holding a celebration on 12th July and the Catholics holding one in mid-August – either to celebrate Our Lady's Day or fly the Home Rule flag – resulted in fearsome riots in 1883, despite the attempts by Catholic clergy to prevent the Home Rulers marching. However, as the century wore to a close, Protestant/Catholic tensions eased. As we shall see, they were to flare up again in the 1920s but, before examining the twentieth-century sectarianism it should be noted that Scottish-Irish tensions in the nineteenth century did not exist only between Catholics and Protestants.

CATHOLIC DIVISIONS

Very deep divisions also opened up between the Catholic Irish and the Scots Catholics. The explosion in Irish Catholic emigration to Scotland was part of the problem. It was estimated that in 1779, Glasgow had only thirty Catholics, no priests and no Catholic churches. Thereafter, two forms of Catholicism flowed into the city, the native Scottish Highlander variety and the Irish sort. By 1893, a fifth of Glasgow's population was Catholic. The Irish were exuberant, given to devotional activities such as the rosary, public processions and wakes, and a very public demonstration of their faith. The Scots were less demonstrative, tight-fisted where money was concerned and, above all, constantly fearful of provoking a Protestant backlash, or industrial clearances, similar to the ones that had driven them out of the Highlands. The Irish, however, came from a tradition of outspokenness: a background where someone was constantly either fighting for what they believed in or encouraging others to do so. Consequently they had a more 'in your face' approach to politics than the deferential Scots Catholics to whom revolution was something in the past that had died with Bonnie Prince Charlie.

For the Irish, no sooner had the bloodshed of the 1798 Rebellion ceased than that of Robert Emmet's began, and then there followed throughout the entire nineteenth century a succession of other upheavals: the agitation for Catholic emancipation, repeal of the Union, the Famine, the continuing simmering war over land, the anti-tithe campaign directed against the paying of tithes for the support of a Protestant clergy. No sooner had these convulsions died away than Fenianism took over, followed by Parnellism and the Home Rule movement. The Scots Catholics looked on aghast as decade after decade each convulsion sent over a wave of prospective revolutionaries bent on taking over their jobs, their peace of mind and their religion. There was a huge growth and then a huge haemorrhaging of population as emigrants from Ireland came in at one port and, after a short stay, went out from another.

There was equally huge poverty. For a very long time in the nineteenth century the education of Catholic girls lagged behind that of boys because of poverty. [108] The girls were even more likely than the boys to be kept at home to help with the chores, or to be at work as half-timers in factories – a head-mistress of a Catholic girls' school in Dundee recorded a strike amongst half-timers against their miserable wages in 1874. Children of both sexes were irregular in school attendance. The boys did a variety of jobs including fruit picking, planting, turnip growing, potato picking, carrying golf clubs and working as scarecrows.

The way out of this poverty trap was of course education, but who was to pay for it? The Irish Catholics began to complain that no sooner had they and their clergy built up a parish than the Scottish bishop would direct that a Scots priest take over the parish, and the Irish priest be sent off to some other poor area to build up a new Catholic nucleus. In 1864 there were only three Irish priests serving the 130,000 Catholics of Glasgow. It was an early version of the 'native clergy' policy which the Vatican would implement in the following century in other parts of the world, chiefly in Australia.

TEMPORALITIES AND SPIRITUALISTS

At the root of the hostility between the Scots and the Irish lay not merely a culture clash and questions of accountability, but Vatican geo-politics. The Church at the time was regaining its footing after the stresses of the French Revolution and the Napoleonic era. Whereas the Irish generally subscribed to Daniel O'Connell's philosophy of Catholic liberty, Rome pursued an anti-democratic, anti-liberal policy symbolised by the 'papal shamrock' of altar, castle and throne. In the case of Scotland, as elsewhere, this came down to an alliance between the two colonialisms, Mother Church and Mother England against the Irish vision.

The Irish priests were mainly drawn from All Hallows College in Dublin, set up to provide priests for the Irish Mission expanding in the wake of the ever-increasing diaspora. The Scottish priests largely came from a closely knit Highland community in Banffshire and were used to running small parishes which consisted of interlocking families. There was no tradition of the priest rendering financial accounts to the parishioners. There was, however, a tradition of appointing members of these families whenever a Church vacancy occurred. Neither psychologically, nor administratively did this background

237

prepare the Scottish clergy for a sudden explosion of generous, but raucous, demanding Irish parishioners.

In Glasgow in the 1860s the parishes of St John's and St Mary's were allowed to grow to 18,000 and 15,000 respectively, but still the Scottish bishop would not subdivide them into smaller units run by Irish clergy who could relate to the concerns of their often traumatised emigrant flocks. For their part, the near-starving Irish who contributed their pennies to the church considered, with some justice, that they were literally being used as Canon fodder. They were not given a fair return in terms of either priests or the provision of expenses for church buildings. A famous row which erupted in Glasgow between a prominent parish priest, Father Scott, and his Irish parishioners, encapsulated the issues.

Like most Scottish clergy, Father Scott feared that the outcome of Daniel O'Connell's agitation for Catholic emancipation in Ireland was likely not only to cause a Protestant backlash in Scotland but also to lead to the growth of militant secret societies in Scotland on Irish lines. He also feared that O'Connell's Catholic Association would take money from his parish which he needed for the church debt. Overarching Father Scott's personal antipathies there arose the more important factor of Vatican policy. His opposition to the Catholic Association's collections led to his parishioners demanding that he furnish accounts showing the parish's earnings and outgoings. Some servant of history preserved a marvellous account of Father Scott's response from the pulpit delivered in a broad, Banffshire accent:

If yer nae pleas't wi' the way I dae for her gude, what for dinna'ye tak' a sail to Rome, and see hoo ye come on at the Vatican, if ye ken whar that is; or, maybe, a lot o' ye that's camstreery and bully-rag me here wad like to try the way that they dae in McLean's Kirk ower the water there. The males and females, they tell me, a' get in a word in eleckin' their ministers and layin' oot the siller; and that's what a pack o' ye wad want to hae hereh – to meet, and spyke, and jw, and instruc' mee hoo to ae we' this, and hoo to dae we' that. But I'll tak' care o' ye. Ye first meddle wi' Temporalities, and if ye wad get yer ain way ye'd nae be lang o'tryin' yer han' at the Spiritualities. Ye little ken that the Temporalities cost me a hunnerfold mair bother than the Spiritualities. This is a Catholic Church, and I sall ever keep it sae, for nai ane o' ye I'll alloo to cheep. That's my deceeshin for yes disestia' a' nicht.[115]

Father Scott's dialect was symbolic of the difficulties of a shared language which have traditionally existed between the Irish and the inhabitants of the sister isle. His attitude to the Irish demands for the democratisation of their Church was shared by his Scottish confrères, though, to be fair, back at home the Irish would have received the same rebuff to any attempts to seek an accounting from an Irish parish priest. 'The temporalities' would always be denied on the ground that concession on them would lead to a demand for a say in 'the spiritualities'. Infallibility was a dogma upheld by Irish parish priests long before the Pope got around to arrogating it to himself at the First Vatican Council in 1870.

For the Irish emigrants in Scotland, an Irish parish priest was one of their own. Those like Father Scott manifestly were not. It is not overstating matters to say that near civil war broke out between the Irish and the Scots. In 1864 twenty-two leading Irish clergy sent a memorial to Rome which contained a massive indictment of Scottish control. Not only were the laity not informed of debts incurred in their name, but the Scottish clergy controlled: 'all ecclesiastical property, lands, churches, chapels, houses, schools, colleges, orphanages, reformatories and cemeteries'.[109] When the Scots counter-attacked the All Hallows men on every ground from liquor to lechery, the Irish replied in kind. For instance, Bishop John MacLachan was all set to take over the diocese of Edinburgh in 1884, but was ambushed at the Vatican by another memorial prepared by Irish clergy and laity. The memorial contained detailed allegations of a lengthy sexual relationship between the Bishop and a Catholic woman teacher.

Much of the hostilities centred around the *Glasgow Free Press*, a Catholic newspaper edited by a layman, A. H. Keane. This published the allegations of the Irish clergy against their Scottish superiors and campaigned for the appointment of an Irish bishop and for a separate Scottish hierarchy. The Vatican became involved in the dispute, and in October 1867, the English Archbishop Manning was appointed to inquire into the controversy. His reports bore fruit in the form of an instruction from Cardinal Barnabo, Prefect of Propaganda, to the three Scottish bishops to act against the *Free Press*. On 9 February 1868, the paper was killed by a denunciation from the altar of every church in Scotland:

> to read or support publications such as the one in question . . . is a grievous fault . . . and one which . . . will subject whoever is guilty of it to the gravest ecclesiastical censures.

Freedom of the press thus taken care of, Cardinal Manning then moved to put a stop to the feuding. He got two bishops to resign, Bishop Gray (Scottish) and Bishop Lynch (Irish), and the western district, the scene of the worst bitterness, was placed under an Englishman, Charles Eyre, who became Archbishop when the hierarchy was restored in 1878. Thus the Vatican's geo-political view prevailed. As Bernard Aspinwall has observed:

> ultramontane unity prevailed in an efficient, bureaucratised, professionalised church. A deferential, subordinate, more conservative and settled laity built the new churches, schools and institutions. An Anglo-Scottish, English, landed Catholic élite provided further reinforcements. Nationalisms were contained within ultramontanism.[110]

Aspinwall summed up the Church which emerged as 'British, businesslike and bureaucratic', an accurate enough description, but within it a distinctive type of ghettoised Irish Catholicism emerged. The parish became a way of life, controlling every area: education, economic, political, even recreational. As W. M. Walker observed:

Within their substitute society the immigrants were exhorted to the virtues of docility and resignation while, institutionally, the structure of parochial organisations compelled precisely this acquiescence . . . the most obvious feature of Irish Catholic parochial life was the power exercised by priests – power which did not stop short of physical violence.[111]

The two Mother Colonialisms were getting along nicely.

TATIE HOKING

By 1906, Irish emigration to Scotland had declined to 1,818 annually, from 8,807 thirty years earlier. The bulk of these emigrants came from Ulster, chiefly from Antrim, though the frequency of sailings from Derry meant that that county was well represented also, as was Donegal. Appropriately enough, given the impact which the failure of the potato crop had on the Irish, one of the great sources of contact and employment for the Irish in Scotland was 'Tatie Hoking', potato picking. Migrant workers from Ireland, notably from Achill and Donegal, had travelled to Scotland to pick potatoes since the nineteenth century. Whole families migrated each season to the potato-growing districts of Ayrshire, Stirlingshire, Fife and the Lothians. They were paid so much per each acre harvested, and though the system was attended by considerable hardships, in general it worked well enough to last until the 1950s. The Donegal workers tended to have the better of things insofar as living conditions were concerned, because they came over singly or in small numbers and so were relatively easy to accommodate. In some districts, the Lothians for example, there was a tradition of providing reasonable accommodation. However, the Achill people moved in large groups, comprising both men and women, and presented more of an accommodation problem than the Donegal folk who were generally from the same family.

The housing of the Irish potato pickers became a scandal in Scotland following an outbreak of gastroenteritis on a Stirlingshire farm. A doctor who examined the farm said afterwards: 'I had never myself seen human beings lodged so utterly indefensible as regards both health and decency.'[119] He described finding twenty-one men and women living in a one-roomed seventeen-foot-square 'bothy', without either running water or sanitary facilities. The average bothy was simply a large, open shed. These conditions led to an examination of the accommodation in the rest of Stirlingshire and in Dumbartonshire, and it was discovered that in less than half of the farms surveyed was there segregation of the sexes. In one case, a cow byre housed 17 men, 5 women, 6 calves, a pile of manure and a heap of chaff. The stories of such workers have been immortalised by two writers in particular. Patrick MacGill's *Children of the Dead End* is one of the classic pieces of literature of the early twentieth century and MacGill's memory is still commemorated in Donegal by the holding of the annual MacGill Summer School. Another Donegal writer, an ex Tatie Hoker, 'Paddy the Cope' Gallagher, has also left a priceless sociological record of those days in *My Story*.

Their writings, and a stirring social conscience, prompted improvements in the conditions of the 'Tatie Hokers', but these came slowly. Various inquiries culminated in a Royal Commission report in 1912 which made various recommendations about the provision of beds, sanitation, ventilation and so on, but consciences were stirred as to how much remained to be done when a fire in a barn in Ayrshire in 1924 claimed the lives of nine potato pickers, five men and four women. Bye-laws were tightened up. Nevertheless, conditions continued to be such that another fire in Kirkintilloch, in September 1937, claimed ten lives. The attitude of de Valera's Government to this tragedy was a report which stated that the only effective method of improving conditions of migratory workers was to prevent them migrating, which was not feasible. Therefore, the report stated:

> We are unable to suggest any effective means by which the government of this country could bring about change for the better in the conditions under which migrants are recruited. While recognising that the ideal to be aimed at is the creation at home of economic conditions which will render migration unnecessary, we do not recommend any state interference with existing methods of recruitment of migratory workers while they continue to migrate.

Given this sort of indifference at governmental level, and the fact that most potato pickers were uneducated men and women, it is not surprising very little improvement had occurred a decade later – no that Irish exploiters joined Scottish exploiters in abusing the system. One reason that the Tatie Hokers continued to work was that they had a family support system, and had built up good relationships with individual farmers. However, by the close of the 1950s, because of the construction boom, traditional potato pickers became something of an endangered species. As a result, an Irish mafia began to form groups whose work they then sold to farmers. It was the potato-picking version of the 'lump' system, and many of the workers recruited were from the most vulnerable sections of society, with no families behind them. For a time the mafia bosses were able to brutalise them into accepting low wages, long hours and conditions of near serfdom. Objectors were beaten up, girls were suborned into prostitution, and children who wished to continue their education at the end of the summer were physically prevented from returning to Ireland.

Eventually, newspaper reports forced reforms on the system, but as late as the 1970s, some Irish people were still ensuring that their fellow countrymen and women would become Children of the Dead End. Not surprisingly, harsh working conditions and the alienation from society caused by sectarianism induced the same sort of social problems we encountered south of the border. A survey conducted by James Daragh in 1977 showed that Catholic marriages ended in divorce 'much sooner' than did those of other denominations.[112] Moreover 'cruelty by husband' was the most frequently cited ground for divorce. As Daragh commented: 'It requires no great perception to guess that this is another of the consequences of the Scottish Catholic drink problem.'[113]

THE FRANCHISE

The First World War did something to damp down sectarian tensions. On its outbreak the Archbishops of Edinburgh and Glasgow had appealed to Catholics to join up and thousands answered the call, six of them winning Victoria Crosses. The wartime sacrifices brought returns for the Church in the shape of the Education Act of 1918, which brought Roman Catholic schools into the State-supported system.

As in the rest of the UK, the reform of the franchise helped to democratise Scotland. The Scottish electorate increased by 183 per cent between 1918 and 1919, from 779,000 to 2,205,000. The male electorate doubled and women received the vote for the first time. From a position of disenfranchisement a majority of Scoto-Irish Roman Catholics (forming the overwhelming majority of Scotland's approximately 600,000 Roman Catholics) now had both the vote and a tendency to vote Labour.

Two men in particular influenced this tendency, David Lloyd George, the Liberal Prime Minister, and John Wheatley, an Irish miner who was elected to Glasgow Town Council in 1910. Lloyd George alienated the Irish from the Liberals by unleashing the Black and Tans on Ireland. Wheatley, however, wooed his fellow-countrymen into the ranks of labour. He was placed in charge of housing policy in Ramsay MacDonald's first government and is regarded both as the architect of municipally owned housing schemes and the 'client system' in local government which they gave rise to.

However, the moves towards toleration also concealed within themselves the seeds of a backlash. The Labour Party and the trade unions were increasing in numbers, and in Russia, the star of socialism was in ascendant. The Presbyterian Church leaders were worried about their loss of control over the working classes. The rosy dawn of social reconstruction, which had grown in popularity during the war years, soon clouded over. Conservatives held a majority in Parliament after the 1918 election, and were unsympathetic to the fulfilment of promises about industrial and housing reform. In Scotland, the Presbyterian Church leaders switched from criticism of the excesses of capitalism to those of working-class self-indulgence. Drinking, gambling, sexual activity, paralleled by laziness in the work place, became the targets.

SUPPORT FOR THE IRA

To the spectre of fears about labour unrest were added the prospect that the growing Anglo-Irish War might cross the Irish Sea to Scotland. There was some substance to this last. John Cooney says: 'During the War of Independence (1919–21), the Irish in Scotland, secretly but at great risk, provided more money, guns and explosives for Irish freedom than any other segment of the Irish diaspora, as was recognised by Eamon de Valera.' While de Valera's estimate of the importance of the Scottish contribution to the War of Independence was deliberately inflated – because he and his faction used accusations concerning Scottish Republican funds to smear Michael Collins – Scoto-Irish and Irish emigrant support for the War of Independence in Ireland was of significance to the struggle. Apart from the money, guns and explosives for the IRA in Ireland, the Catholics provided safe houses in Scotland for men on the run from the fighting. There was a Fenian tradition in Scotland – the republicans had tried to blow up Tradeston Gasworks in 1883 – and, apart from Glasgow and Edinburgh, the IRA found it relatively easy to organise a network of dumps and safe houses and companies of volunteers right across Scotland. Dundee, Dumbarton, Stirling, Leith, Dumfries, Blantyre, Hamilton, Bothwell and Carfin all had IRA units. Much of the explosive came from Irish miners; a substantial quantity of the arms came from that perennial source of IRA weaponry, the British Army. Most of the material was shipped to Ireland via Liverpool and the success, and strength, of the IRA's Scottish connection may be gauged from the fact that, throughout the war, the authorities were only able to intercept microscopic quantities of 'gear'.

There had been a small number of really public, temperature-raising incidents, such as shooting policemen, when, on 4 May 1921, there occurred the Glasgow version of the incident which gave rise to the 'Manchester Martyrs'. One of the most prominent IRA commanders, Frank Carty of Sligo, was captured in Glasgow while recovering from wounds sustained in Ireland. In an attempt to rescue him from a police van en route to Glasgow's Duke Street prison, police Inspector Johnston was shot dead, and Sergeant Stirton wounded. Some twenty participants and non-participants in the attempted rescue, including a Catholic priest, Father McRory, were charged. The trial, and in particular Father McRory's arrest, fanned sectarian tensions to white heat. However, the Anglo-Irish Truce of July 1921 helped to defuse the situation. Subsequently, all the accused were acquitted, even though Ellis the hangman had already measured the accused for the drop, in anticipation of a guilty verdict. Michael Collins had also taken the precaution of sending his élite squad of assassins, 'The Twelve Apostles', to Edinburgh to attempt a last-ditch rescue. Ironically, the only accused IRA man to die was Sean Adair who went to Ireland to fight on Michael Collins's side in the Irish Civil War. He was shot in Sligo by a unit commanded by Frank Carty who had sided with de Valera.

THE EDUCATION ACT

All the fears generated by the foregoing crystallised around the 1918 Education Act. The Act transferred schools to local authorities, while at the same time guaranteeing their religious freedom, the right of access to pupils by priests, and the right to employ Catholic teachers. These provisions had the effect of pouring petrol on the dying embers of the previous century's bigotry.

The slogan 'Rome on the rates' became loud in the land. Anti-Catholic groupings multiplied and, at the same time, Catholic energies became reinvigorated. It is said that a grotto in the village of Carfin in Lanarkshire attracted a quarter of a million pilgrims in the summer of 1923. Catholic groupings such as the Catholic Young Men's Society and the Legion of Mary spearheaded a growth in Scoto-Irish Catholic identity. Unfortunately, as Stewart Brown has detailed in a memorable essay, it also served to provoke a corresponding Protestant hostility.[114]

In May 1922, two motions were brought before the General Assembly of the established Church of Scotland calling for repeal of the Education Act and a restriction on Irish Catholic emigration. It was argued that the Irish Catholics were responsible for crime and were a drain on the State's purse. In support of the motion, the Reverend John MacLagan said that the Irish emigrants 'had most abominably abused the privileges which the Scottish people had given them'. Other speakers described the Education Act as part of a conspiracy by the Roman Catholic hierarchy to bring Scotland under the sway of Rome. From the introduction of the two motions, there flowed a campaign against the Scoto-Irish Catholics which continued until the outbreak of the Second World War. The Protestant population of Northern Ireland was exempted from the campaign against the alien Irish Roman Catholics because the Orangemen were seen as being 'of the same race as ourselves and of the same faith'.

By 19 July 1928, the campaign had reached such a pitch that Government Ministers met leaders of the Presbyterian Churches in London. The Church leaders told the Ministers that Scotland faced a murderous racial and religious war if Catholic Irish were not banned from the shores of Scotland. Not only was emigration to be halted forthwith, all the Irish in Scotland who had been born in the new Irish Free State and were at the time receiving either hospital treatment, poor relief or had been found guilty of a criminal charge, should immediately be deported. In addition, native-born Scots should be preferred over the Irish in every form of Government service. The Church lobby was so powerful that the Cabinet actually discussed the question of emigration controls after the July meeting, but decided against attempting to implement curbs. The Government's policy at the time was that Ireland was not a foreign country and that the restriction of movement of people within the British Isles was undesirable.

This did not deter the anti-Irish lobby. As Tom Devine has pointed out, two anti-Catholic movements of the time, the Scottish Protestant League led by Alexander Ratcliffe, and the Protestant Action group led by John Cormack, did far better at the polls than did Oswald Mosley in the 1930s.[115] The Presbyterian campaign did have links with Fascism, sending delegates to the 1932 conference in Stockholm of the 'International League for the Defence and Furtherance of Protestantism', an anti-Catholic grouping based in Berlin. In its July 1933 edition, ILDFP's journal, *Protestantische Rundschau* (*Protestant Review*), approved of the attitude of the Scottish General

Assembly. The Assembly had decided that the Church of Scotland should not condemn anti-Semitism in Germany because the 'Judenfrage' in Germany was akin to Scotland's 'Irischenfrage'. In July 1935, Protestant Action supporters attacked the Eucharist Congress held in Edinburgh. Coaches carrying women and children were stoned, and for weeks after the Congress, Catholics were intimidated out of their work places. The approach of the World War, however, forced a reappraisal of Presbyterian policies. Independent-minded Presbyterians pointed out that a time was coming when Protestant and Catholic would have to stand together against the evils of Nazism.

Nevertheless, the effects of the campaign outlived the war in the form of discrimination in employment. One of Scotland's contemporary heroes is the Scoto-Irish Catholic comedian Billy Connolly. He tells a story from his teenage days of applying to become an engineer in the shipyards.[116] His rival for the job 'was a posh guy who couldn't point to an engineer'. Connolly had two engineering certificates but the other boy had 'a Boys Brigade badge on his blazer' and 'he was swept in to be an engineer'. Connolly was sent back to the 'black squad', the welders. Years later when he had become a world star, he said the injustice 'instilled a kind of darkness' in him, a sense that 'you've no chance no matter what you do'. In the end of course ship-building's loss proved to be the world's gain, but not every young Catholic apprentice had Connolly's stellar talent, and the 'darkness' he experienced fell over many a career. It was the coming of multi-national companies to Scotland, with a 'hire on merit' policy which weakened discrimination throughout the 1980s, but even at the time of writing, the inclusion of 'Irish' and 'Catholic' on a CV containing otherwise impeccable credentials, would not necessarily endear a job applicant to some older-established Scottish firms.

SANITY REASSERTS ITSELF

Part of the reason for the virulence of the inter-war anti-Irish anti-Catholic campaign lay in the employment situation. Shipping and mining both declined drastically in the twenties and thirties. Some 30 per cent of the insured work force was out of work. Emigration reached new levels in this climate. In one short period, from 1919 to 1926, some 300,000 Scots emigrated, a terrible drain coming on top of the carnage of the First World War. Then, in March 1929, the *Glasgow Herald* published a series of articles showing that not only was Irish emigration just a fraction of what the Presbyterian campaign claimed, but, because of the recession, the Irish were in fact emigrating in droves to America, Canada and Australia. The effect of the *Herald* series was a classic example of what good journalism can do in bad times. The articles banished fears of Scotland being engulfed in a Green tide and sanity reasserted itself as, on the Protestant side, some divines took the opportunity to show that not every Presbyterian cleric was a ranting bigot. On the Catholic side the hierarchy also played a steadying role in damping down controversy and avoiding confrontation, though this approach carried the inevitable drawback of encouraging the Scoto-Irish tradition of keeping the head down.

There were other forces at work in Scottish society to encourage this tendency. Throughout the late nineteenth and early twentieth century, the children of Irish emigrants had a tradition of leaving school and going into unskilled occupations to eke out the family income. Apprenticeships to the craft trades were thus denied them. They helped to perpetuate these conditions by putting their political energies into the Home Rule movement, rather than Scottish Labour politics. A great deal of political and financial energy was also drawn off by involvement in building up the Catholic Church. It is a matter of pride, preserved in oral history by Scoto-Irish Catholics in Dumbarton, for example, that St Patrick's Church is adorned by a tabernacle manufactured out of the wedding rings of the faithful.

Even for those who had an education, the all-pervasive atmosphere of religious discrimination ensured that emigration, rather than advancement, was the lot of many. In 1947, James Handley noted:

> Discrimination permeates all ranks of national life from the humblest manual labourer to the professions. To take but one example: in the last fifty years Scoto-Irish have attended the universities of Scotland in increasing numbers. Since the Education Act of 1918 the same qualifications for the teaching profession are demanded from them as from their Protestant colleagues. Yet in the high administrative posts of the profession – the inspectorate, the directorates of education, supervisorships and so on – one will search in vain for a Catholic occupant. Catholic doctors and dentists have a similar tale to tell.[117]

Such blatant discrimination, however, was perceived by a section of Scottish Presbyterianism as part of God's law, rather than as an outrage to Christian principles. It is recorded that after a meeting of the Glasgow Presbytery of the Free Church of Scotland shortly after the fall of Hong Kong, the loss was attributed not to Japanese military prowess, but to the fact that a Christmas high mass had been broadcast from a Scottish Benedictine monastery.

POST-WAR IMPROVEMENT

The post-war boom, and a certain amount of hangover from the camaraderie engendered by war, did something for the Scoto-Irish community. The building of dams, roads, railways, in raising prosperity levels also raised those of toleration. The Irish benefited too from the extension of local government and the power that it brought to the Labour Party. The Irish Catholic instinct for education began to bring its inevitable return as a sizeable Catholic middle class emerged. In addition, the calibre of the Irish emigration to Scotland also changed. The *Irish Post* Business '98 survey showed that the 48,500 Irish-born living in Scotland had higher incomes than their British counterparts. Some 12 per cent earned more than £30,000 a year compared to 7 per cent of

Britons. Moreover, Irish incomes had increased steeply: 50 per cent more Irish people had incomes of over £20,000 compared to five years earlier.

The post-war transition was not immediate. Tony Meehan, a Scoto-Irishman who runs one of Scotland's biggest PR firms, TMA (Tony Meehan Associates), was once both the All England and the All Ireland Irish dancing champion. He feels that the reason this background did not tell against him in certain quarters is because some people in Scotland think that he has an English accent (he has worked in America and England):

> Even now there are some firms who might not employ you if they thought you were a Catholic. But there have been tremendous gains in the last ten years with Rangers hiring Mo Johnston [Johnston was the first Catholic to be publicly hired by Glasgow Rangers] and Kennedy becoming President helped to make Catholics seem more respectable to the Scots.[118]

Despite Kennedy's election however, Catholics of Irish origin were not welcome 'for security reasons' as workers on the Polaris nuclear submarine project, and in 1981, Arnold Kemp, the editor of the *Glasgow Herald*, was officially informed that the employment of Catholics on the paper was frowned upon. However, little more than ten years afterwards, the Managing Director was a Catholic of Glaswegian/Irish stock. Similar oral evidence could be produced for many other firms. The prejudice broke down as multinational companies began increasingly to operate in Scotland and as Catholics who had been reared in Glasgow or Edinburgh came back from London from Head Office to manage Scottish subsidiaries and thus influence employment policies. Irish names began to surface in the judiciary, and in the ranks of executivedom.

RAPPROCHEMENT

The presence of figures like Cardinal Thomas J. Winning at the helm of the Catholic Church, and of the Reverend McLellan at that of the Presbyterians, both of them pronounced ecumenists, has helped to further and deepen this process. The overall political scene is also conducive to rapprochement. I had the honour of being invited to lunch by the Cardinal at Chesters College to meet the Scottish hierarchy, and found no sense of any cloud hanging over the gathering.[119] The bishops were at ease in their country and community. The talk was of politics, the growth of the devolution movement, hopes for the Peace Process and a growth in Scottish/Irish ties. There was a slight residual fear that the SNP might revert to its old ways over education, some discussion on Labour's attitude towards abortion and a little dissertation on the history of the Irish community in Scotland. The only slightly vehement note was struck when I dared to raise the question of whether or not St Patrick had actually been born in Dumbarton. He was – the Cardinal said so!

I was left with a picture of a conservative, but charitably minded group, which took an understandable pride in the achievement of Catholic schools, graduates from which were increasingly out-performing their counterparts from State schools. At the time of writing, the Church controlled 16 per cent of Scotland's school-going population, with 352 primary schools and 64 secondary schools, chiefly in the western area. The gathering's stated main concern was about furthering the work of Vatican II and the ecumenical movement. Obviously the various problems of the Church to do with paedophilia and other scandals were a worry, but 'anti-popery' was not a pressing concern. In fact, Father Noel Barry, the PRO to the Archdiocese, chuckled, rather than frowned, over the contemporary variant of the Angel Gabriel/MacMenemy/Paisley-type preacher, the colourful Jack Glass. Cardinal Winning had preached at an ecumenical pilgrimage against which Glass demonstrated, and when the Cardinal offered to shake hands with Glass, he refused. Later, however, when the cameras were removed, Glass came back, extended his hand to the Cardinal, and, after a warm handshake, said to him: 'I've got to watch my back!'[120]

The Cardinal may have to watch his front on the educational issue. For while the virulent anti-Catholic strain of Scottish life has gone underground, except where the Celtic-Rangers football clashes are concerned, tensions may lie ahead at a more cerebral level. Lindsay Patterson, a Scottish educationalist, acknowledges the role that the Church has played in lifting the Catholics out of the ghettos into the mainstream, and thus combating sectarianism. However, he argues that that work is now completed and that the Church should now pay for 'the privilege of having an influence on educational policy which no other religious organisation has'.[121] Patterson's view was shared by the Aberdeen branch of the EIS, the largest teaching union in Scotland, which put down a motion opposing denominational schooling. Whether this debate grows only the future will tell, but it seems clear that the result will be determined not so much by denominational attitudes as educational excellence. If the Catholic schools can maintain their levels of achievement they will get support, including some Protestant support.

COMING TOGETHER

The coming together of the Protestant and Catholic traditions can be observed at all sorts of levels. At the Robbie Burns night in Edinburgh in 1998, a black-tie affair in a fashionable hotel, the attendance included a large number of Labour councillors of Catholic and Irish extraction, and a representative section of the growing Scoto-Irish professional and middle class. One of these, a prosperous businessman in his late thirties, looked around him wonderingly and remarked to a friend: 'You know, I never thought I'd set foot in a gathering like this. Burns was for the Orangemen only. He was completely foreign to my tradition.' So Billy and Dan (the Protestant workers referred to as 'Billies' after King William of Orange, the Catholics 'Dans' after Daniel O'Connell) can mingle in tuxedoes in contemporary Scotland, in a manner unknown in the days when dungarees were more commonly worn. Apart from simmering tensions in places like the Gorbals district of Glasgow, the social and religious apartheid of the days when the young businessman's parents were his age, would have made it almost impossible for him to meet Billy and discuss Burns in a pub in, say, Dumbarton, before he went to college. The granting of pub licences to Catholics was frowned upon, and the Protestants tended to socialise either in a bowling club or a masonic club with their own community.

THE EUROPE CONNECTION

Like everything else in the relationship of the Irish in the United Kingdom with their host communities, the future depends on the success of the Peace Process, but certain organic growths within Scotland seem to point towards closer Irish/Scottish links. The whole movement towards a Europe of the Regions, making for increased local autonomy, slots into Scottish developments. At the same time, the contemporary success of the independent Republic of Ireland is making Dublin something of a role model in Glasgow and Edinburgh. It may be said that goads, rather than incentives, towards seeing Dublin in this light are provided by unwise utterances by English decision-takers in London.

While I was researching this book, Robin Cook, the Foreign Secretary; Gordon Brown, the Chancellor of the Exchequer; and Eddie George, the Director of the Bank of England, all made statements which visibly rankled with the Scots, even though Brown and Cook are themselves Scottish. The two politicians poured scorn on the idea of Scotland's ability to go it alone, saying that Scotland was too small for such an experiment. I heard observations to the effect that the Republic of Ireland was smaller than Scotland, and look at what the Irish had done. And what about the Danes? The Finns? Eddie George made an observation which was seemingly completely acceptable to Britain's heavily London-based media, but was anything but well received in Scotland. He defended Britain's over-valued pound and the Bank of England's interest rate policy, saying that the price of high interest rates, essential for Britain's economic well-being, was job losses in the northern part of the country. As one Scot said to me: 'Decoded that means bugger the Scots. It doesn't matter what jobs are lost in the Border regions, so long as the fat cats in the Home Counties stay prosperous.' At a time when traditional industries, particularly knitwear, were closing in the Borders, through Asian competition, my Scottish friend was particularly nervous about the impact of the high pound on the exports of the Japanese-owned factories located in Scotland: 'These boys have their problems with Asian flu without the Bank of England making things worse, staying out of the Euro and so on. We'd be better off getting into Europe, and getting the Brussels lolly like you boys did.' This canny Scottish pragmatism is only one facet of the developing relationship between the Irish diaspora in Scotland

and the mother country. The Ulster Unionists, it would appear, will find as time evolves that their insistence on strengthening east/west links may do more to benefit the Green than the Orange tradition.

GLASGOW CELTIC

I can't leave Scotland without touching upon that great symbol of the Irish presence in Scotland – and of Orange and Green divisions through its clashes with Glasgow Rangers – Glasgow Celtic Football Club. The club owes both the inspiration for its founding and its name to an Irish Marist, Brother Walfrid from Sligo, who announced the formation of 'The Celtic Football and Athletic Club' on 6 November 1887. The reasons behind the club's formation were explained by Brother Walfrid and a Committee of fellow Catholics in a circular issued the following January:

> The main object of the club is to supply the East End conferences of the St Vincent de Paul Society with funds for the maintenance of the 'Dinner Tables' of our needy children in the missions of St Mary's, St Michael's and Sacred Heart. Many cases of sheer poverty are left unaided through lack of means. It is therefore with this object that we have set afloat the 'Celtic'.[122]

Brother Walfrid and his collaborators would have been thunderstruck if they could have looked into the future to see how the good ship Celtic altered course from those early charitable objectives to achieve a commercial reputation worth nearly £200 million at the time of writing – and a cultural reputation of being one of the two principal lightning rods of Scottish sectarianism, the other being the Protestant club, Glasgow Rangers. The teams' legendary encounters, known as the Old Firm games, diffuse and distil all the ancient rancours of the Orange and Green traditions.

The atmosphere for an Old Firm game is unlike any other in Europe. The Celtic fans are liable to be singing Nationalists' ballads, like 'A Nation Once Again', and either wearing Celtic's green and white colours or sporting tricolours. Amongst the Rangers fans one can find members of the British National Front and Loyalist supporters wearing UVF tattoos, singing Orange songs, chanting anti-Irish slogans and making suggestions to the Pope which would be both morally wrong and physically impossible. Obviously given the historical background I have sketched in the previous pages, the all-pervasive sectarianism of Scottish society was such that sport could hardly have escaped its blighting influence, but students of the game say that the real bite in the Celtic/Rangers relationship commenced with the extension of operations by the Harland & Wolfe shipbuilding company from Belfast to Glasgow in 1912. Harland & Wolfe brought not only its workers but the legendary bigotry of the Belfast yard.

When Celtic moved to a spacious new ground in 1892, Michael Davitt, the founder of the Irish Land League and a moving spirit in the West Scotland co-operative movement, laid a shamrock-sprouting sod from Donegal in the middle of the pitch. Some versifier of the period commemorated the occasion as follows:

> On alien soil like yourself I am here;
> I'll take root and flourish, of that never fear;
> And though I'll be crossed sore and oft by the foes
> You'll find me as hardy as Thistle or Rose.
> If model is needed on your own pitch you'll have it.

However the symbolism of the sod proved not to be what the author hoped. It was stolen and the poet maladicted the thief as follows:

> The curse of Cromwell blast the hand that stole the sod that Michael cut;
> May his praties turn to sand – the crawling thieving scut.

There were times in the club's subsequent turbulent history of clashes with Rangers when the 'Curse of Cromwell' did indeed appear to fall on Celtic supporters. Even as I visited Scotland, one Glasgow Rangers supporter, Jason Campbell, was in jail for slitting the throat of a 16-year-old youth whose offence was to pass him in the street wearing a Celtic scarf. A move by Ulster Loyalists to have Campbell transferred to Belfast, so that he could benefit from the Peace Process early release scheme, was abandoned in the face of a storm of outrage.

There were other murderous attacks on the day of the 1999 Celtic-Rangers final. In one a Catholic teenager was stabbed to death 200 yards from his home. In another attack a Catholic celebrating his twentieth birthday was shot in the chest with a crossbow. The crime of both victims was to wear Celtic shirts.

On the night of the attacks the Vice-chairman of Rangers, Donald Findlay, QC, was videoed during the celebrations for Rangers' win singing anti-Irish, anti-Catholic songs. He had to resign. The depth of Findlay's feeling may be gauged from the fact that although he was born on St Patrick's Day, he refuses to acknowledge his birthday on that date and instead celebrates it on the Orangeman's festival, July the 12th, the anniversary of the Protestant victory at the Boyne. One of his party pieces was: 'We're up to our knees in Fenian blood. Surrender or you die.'[132] It has to be said that Findlay's rabble-rousing attitude was not that of the club's boss, David Murray, who had gone on television the night before the final to appeal for calm.

Celtic has a better record than Rangers for crossing the sectarian divide in its hiring policies. A ballad still sung with fervour in Glasgow commemorates the Protestant John Thompson, the Celtic goalkeeper who was accidentally killed during a game against Rangers in 1931:

Play up, you Glasgow Celtic, and keep up the old brigade.
No more you see John Thompson for his last game he has played.
Farewell to you John Thompson, for the best of friends must part
No more we will stand and cheer you from the slopes of Celtic Park.

Apart from the ballad, after his tragic death, Celtic fans paid Thompson the tribute of hanging his portrait in their homes alongside that of the Pope.

One of Celtic's all-time greats was Jock Stein, a Protestant who became a legendary manager of the club when his playing days were over, and Kenny Dalglish, another former Celtic star in his playing days, is also a Protestant. He was initially hailed by the Celtic fans as 'King Kenny', when he returned to the club as football director after the 1999 Cup Final, although the appointment of Martin O'Neill as the club's manager in 2000 indicated that his crown may not be too secure.

In 1989, Rangers decided that commercial imperatives dictated that they should begin to emulate Celtic's more ecumenical hiring policies and sign Catholic players. Unfortunately they began by enticing a Celtic player, Mo Johnston, to Ibrox Park! The vitriolic reaction of the Celtic fans was such that the unfortunate Johnston had to leave Scotland for a team in Kansas City.

The Celtic club may be taken as a symbol both of the increasingly close links between the Republic and Scotland, and of the upward mobility of the Scoto-Irish community. The Chairman of Celtic until 1999 was the Scoto-Irish Catholic businessman, Fergus McCann, who built up the club from a valuation of £6 million to one of £180 million. One of the key directors on the board is the Dublin financier, Dermot Desmond. It can also be taken as a symbol that old attitudes die hard. Frank Roy, Parliamentary Secretary to the Secretary of State for Scotland, had to resign, after he objected to the Irish Taoiseach coming to Scotland to open a famine memorial on the night of an Old Firm game, because he said the visit could inflame sectarian tension. It is alleged that his remarks were prompted by Ulster Unionist contacts. Certainly they caused an embarrassing cancellation of Ahern's visit – the memorial was already inscribed with the date he was supposed to have unveiled it, February 11, 2001 – and the Scottish Executive issued Ahern with an apologetic official invitation for a later date.

POINTERS TO THE FUTURE

By way of a hopeful footnote to the Celtic/Rangers saga, and perhaps as a pointer for the future, it might be observed that in 1999 the captain of St Patrick's GAA team in Dumbarton, Scott Proctor, was a Protestant who sometimes turned up to training sessions wearing a Glasgow Rangers jersey. Another hopeful indicator is the fact that, at the time of writing, Scottish youngsters are pouring into Dublin to take up jobs in bars, restaurants and hotels as the Celtic Tiger purrs on.

THREE

AMERICA

The young men of Ireland who wished to be free and happy and come here as quick as possible. There is no place in the world where a man meets so rich an award for good conduct and industry as in America.

In the foulest stench that can be conceived of, so soon as the eyes had become accustomed to the darkness prevailing everywhere but under the open hatch, a mass of humanity, men, women and children would be seen lying over each other above the deck, often half naked, many covered with sores and all with filth and vermin to an incredible degree; the greater portion stupefied or in a delirious condition from typhus or putrid fever, cholera and smallpox; all were helpless and among them were often found bodies of the dead in more or less advanced stages of decomposition.

Such a sight would surely prompt any being, above the brute, to call aloud to the Great God for vengeance upon those who rendered possible in any country a condition so destructive of life, that the people in their flight would prefer even such an alternative as this!

Adams was asked to the White House, and Sinn Fein were given leave to solicit funds in the States. The Brits went ape-shit. Major refused to return Clinton's calls for over a week. When Adams visited the White House Clinton told him: 'You fucking Irish – I'm catching shit.' Adams replied: 'Now you know what I'm up against, and how I feel!' They both laughed and Clinton said: 'We'll make it work.' And he did.

THE FOREGOING QUOTATIONS encapsulate some of the major reasons why the Irish have been going to America since significant emigration began in the eighteenth century; the differing perspective on the New World afforded to Orange and Green; and how something of a revolutionary pulse continued to beat amongst the followers of the Green with such increasing strength that it was ultimately responded to by the White House as the twentieth century was ending.

The first comment was made in a letter written in 1785 by an Irish Protestant emigrant from Strabane, County Tyrone, John Dunlap, the printer of the American Declaration of Independence, founder of the first American daily newspaper, the *Pennsylvania Packet*, and at the time of writing the letter to his brother-in-law in Ireland, the proud owner of 100,000 acres of Kentucky land.

The second is a contemporary doctor's description of the conditions in which Irish Catholic famine emigrants arrived in New York aboard the 'coffin ships'.[1] The doctor was a nephew of Robert Emmet who was hanged, drawn and quartered for leading a rebellion in protest at the administration which ultimately gave rise to the famine. His father, Thomas Addis Emmet, had escaped his brother's fate to become one of New York's most distinguished lawyers.

The third is from a description of an encounter between the Sinn Fein President, Gerry Adams and President Bill Clinton at the White House in 1995, taken from an interview with Congressman Peter King.

The story of the Irish in America is a chronicle of the triumph of the human spirit over adversity. It is literally true to say that the Catholic Irish worked their way upwards from the slime. In New Orleans, the port of entry to the ante-bellum South, there is a Celtic cross, erected to the perhaps 25,000 Irish who died in conditions of muddy horror while digging the New Basin Canal. In contrast, while the Presbyterians had to struggle against discrimination in Ireland, in general the Protestant Irish, particularly the Anglicans, started their careers in the New World with certain economic and political advantages, through the British connection.

However, it is possible that the Irish got there before there was a British connection. For, while it is generally accepted that the Irish began coming to America in significant numbers in the late sixteenth and early seventeenth centuries, they may have got there several centuries before that and – according to Mike McCormack, historian of the Ancient Order of Hibernians – invented the Christmas card in the process![2]

The 'card', bearing an inscription in the early Celtic writing, Ogham, was discovered carved in stone in Wyoming County, West Virginia. The inscription was translated by Dr Barry Fell of Oxford, President of the Epigraphic Society. Fell first translated the petroglyph inscription, which took the form of a ten-foot inscription cut into the recessed portion of a cliff underneath a rocky overhang, from Ogham into Old Irish, then into modern Irish, and from thence into English, as follows:

> At the time of sunrise, a ray grazes the notch on the left side on Christmas Day, the first season of the year; the season of the Blessed Advent of the Saviour Lord Christ. Behold He is born of Mary, a woman.

A ray of 'sunrise' did indeed appear as promised. On 22 December 1982, it was first authenticated, appearing exactly as does a similar shaft of light, at the same time of year, at Newgrange in County Meath, Ireland, striking into the heart of the huge prehistoric burial mound there. The identity of the person or people who left the petroglyph is not known, but in 1985, its authenticity was validated by the Celtic scholar, Professor Robert T. Meyer. He stated:

Nobody could have faked this sort of thing unless they had a very deep knowledge of Celtic philosophy, for this is very archaic, and probably from the 6th or 7th centuries. This, for Celtic scholars, is probably at least as important as the discovery of the Dead Sea scrolls . . . because it shows that Irish monks, I suppose, came here I would say, about 1500 years ago.

Following the Wyoming County discovery, other Ogham inscriptions were found in West Virginia at Bears Fork in Fayette County and Horse Creek in Boone's in Kentucky, in Shell Rock Canyon, Colorado, and in Newfoundland. At various times all these inscriptions have been credited to the ubiquitous St Brendan, which is obviously impossible. However, it is not impossible that these markings are the work of early Irish monks, who were known to be incredible voyagers.

Edward Nugent, who is sometimes credited with being the first Irishman in America, certainly appears to have been a throwback to his Celtic ancestors who had a fondness for head hunting. In 1586 he was a soldier in an English regiment engaged against the Indians in the vicinity of what is now Edenton, North Carolina and he volunteered for a mission which could only have commended itself to an Irish guerrilla. As his senior officer, Captain Ralph Lane, noted in his diary:[3]

An Irishman serving me, one Edward Nugent, volunteered to kill Pemisapan, King of the Indians. We met him returning out of the woods with Pemisapan's head in his hands, and the Indians ceased their raids against the British camp.

It could be said that the real foundations of modern emigration to America lay in an 'Act to prevent the further growth of Popery', passed by the British Parliament in the year 1704. The Act enjoined a Sacramental Test on all citizens of the realm, forcing them to take an oath of loyalty to the Established Church. By this Act the Presbyterians were as much discriminated against as were the Catholics, but they had an edge over their Catholic counterparts inasmuch as they had a little money and, very often, a trade. This gave them an independence of action and a certain rudimentary support system which, along with a sturdy independence of spirit, made them successful colonists. There wasn't all that much difference in fending off hostile Indians while at the same time building up a ranch or a farm, and carrying out the same type of operation in Ireland under threat from dispossessed Catholics.

As the scale of American opportunities came to be understood in Ireland, more and more emigrants, Protestant and Catholic, made their way to the New World. By the end of the Napoleonic War era, perhaps as many as 350,000 Protestant and 35,000 Catholic Irish had emigrated to America, concentrating first in Philadelphia and then spreading out through the thirteen American colonies. Decline in Ireland and land in America provided irresistible compulsions for emigration.

The would-be settlers were promised free land for the first five years and after that a peppercorn rent of a shilling an acre. The early Catholic emigrants, however, did not have the money to take up this sort of opportunity, and initially generally travelled to America as indentured servants. The cost of a passage to the States at this period was approximately £4.50, roughly equivalent to half a year's wages for a labourer, so a ship's captain would give the emigrants a free passage to America, and on arrival sell their labour to a farmer or merchant for a period of approximately five years. Some employers grossly ill-used their employees, treating their slaves far better on the principle that they would still be their property after five years. The system did have its advantages, however. Many a poor Irish emigrant used the period of indenture to acquire skills which rapidly set him on the road to fortune once the period of indenture was over.

The pace of emigration from Ireland began to accelerate as a result of the fall in agricultural prices which followed the ending of the Napoleonic Wars in 1815, so that by the time the Famine burst on the country in 1845, over a million Irish had come to America. By then, Catholic numbers were catching up with those of Protestants, and the Famine caused the Catholic numbers to swamp those of the Protestants. Between 1846 and 1851, well over a million people left Ireland, and the after-shock of the Famine continued to impel people out of the country up to the time I began researching this book.

Even before the Famine, the Catholic Irish came to America in greater numbers than were recorded. The burgeoning timber trade with Europe meant that the trade across the Atlantic was largely a matter of wood to Europe, particularly England, and then ballast back to America – and ballast is what a significant proportion of the poor Irish Catholics became. Their conditions were far worse than those of African slaves. The slaves were valuable property, but it was a matter of indifference to skipper and ship-owner as to whether ballast arrived dead or alive, or did not arrive at all. Obviously in a time of such erratic statistic-gathering, the numbers of Irish Catholics arriving in the growing port cities of America during the late eighteenth and early nineteenth centuries were not accurately computed. There was the added factor that in a largely Protestant Anglo-Saxon-dominated environment, it became commonplace for the Irish to change their names to give them an Anglicised ring, actively espouse a new religion, or simply abandon the old one. Either way, Irish Catholic numbers are difficult to compute.

Irish emigration differed from that of the rest of Europe in that, while some whole families did emigrate, nevertheless the bulk of Irish emigrants were single persons. They were generally youthful and unskilled, the children of small farmers or labourers, and amongst them there were usually as many women as men. It's no accident that the identical statues of the first emigrant to enter the Ellis Island clearing station – one at Cobh in County Cork, the major port of embarkation, and the other at Ellis Island itself, off New York – commemorate a woman, fifteen-year-old Annie Moore.[4]

Ellis Island was opened in 1856. It replaced Castle Gardens which was originally a fort, then it was a concert hall, before being opened as an emigration reception centre. For many emigrants the hardest part of the trans-Atlantic crossing was the ferry trip from nearby Staten Island, where they disembarked, to Ellis Island where their health was checked. Would they get in? Many did not and were sent back, when some ailment or disability was discovered at the last hurdle. I visited the Ellis centre, now a tourist attraction, with my old friend, Hal Antin, a New York businessman of French-Russian-Jewish origin. We found his parents' names and those of his Uncle Benjamin's family. The family were detained on the island for a whole month before Benjamin managed to use influence to get them off.

Benjamin Antin was of that great tradition of liberal Jewishness that helped to change American society, campaigning for the abolition of child labour and the introduction of free education. The Irish were also leaders in the fight against child labour. Like the Jews, and the Germans, the Italians, the Poles, the Armenians and the Greeks, and all the other immigrants, they were not merely part of the story of America's development, they were the reason for it. In this chapter, for reasons of space not parochialism, I can tell of only a fragment of the Irish experience, and nothing of the great pageant of the other races' contribution to the mighty tide of immigration to the land of opportunity. It must be remembered, however, that at every step of the way the Irish and the other emigrants interacted. Sometimes they intermarried. More often they competed. Attitudes of clannishness, of competitiveness, of prejudice, were honed in a clash of cultures and their shared struggle for survival.

While few would challenge the fact that that struggle was an intrinsic part of the Irish experience, considerable controversy has raged over the nature of Irish emigration to the US. One, once widespread, generalisation is that the Irish were almost exclusively to be found in the cities, scarcely venturing out to the wide open spaces, because of poverty, lack of energy and a recoil from the notion of working land after the horrors of the Famine. Another, espoused by the eminent Irish-American historian, Kerby Miller, is that the Irish did not consider themselves emigrants at all, but exiles unjustly torn from their beloved native land, to which they continuously yearned to return. This view is vigorously opposed by another distinguished Irish-American scholar, Lawrence McCaffrey, who sees this concept as casting the Irish in the role of dysfunctional dreamers, rather than in their true role as pragmatic, hard-working people who bettered themselves and their families by coming to America. McCaffrey writes:

> Very few immigrants, even if they experienced discrimination in America and had to work hard to maintain marginal levels of comfort, ever expressed a desire to return to Ireland. For them, the United States was the land of promise. Although it might have fallen short of original expectations, it offered much more freedom and opportunity than did Ireland . . . It took time, but in large part they realised their dreams.[5]

A fourth theory, espoused by another prominent historian, one of Unionist inclination, Donald Harman Atkinson, is that the bulk of Irish emigration to America is of Protestant origin.

In fact, all these views have some basis in truth. Taking the last one first. It is true that the Protestant Irish, of both Anglo and Scottish descent, were initially the predominant grouping to emigrate to America. However, as James Leyburn has pointed out, in each of the seven years after the Famine's worst phase (1847–54), the combined total of Catholic emigration was equal to that of the total of the so-called Scotch Irish emigration before it.[6] Should the Scotch Irish be regarded as Irish?

If the criteria of being 'Irish' is that one feels Irish, then certainly 'very doubtfully' is the answer. The reason that the Scots were 'planted' in Ireland by the English Crown in the first place was that they were Lowland Presbyterians, with a detestation of Catholicism, who could be relied upon to hold the plantation lands seized from the Irish. What about 'Scotch'? In Scotland they tell you that there are no such people as the Scotch. That is the name of a drink. In Glasgow or Edinburgh they like to be described as either Scots or Scottish. The debate about the nature of the Scotch Irish intensified as the Catholic Irish established themselves in America, and the activities of an organisation called the American Protective Association, dedicated to proving the Green tradition was hostile to the American way of life, led to riots in Boston in 1895.

Subsequent dispute about the contribution of the Irish Catholics to America led to the founding of the American Irish Historical Society in 1897, and to a vast literary output from the historian Michael O'Brien, seeking to extol the merits of the Irish Americans, at the expense of the Scotch Irish. The satirist Calvin K. Brannigan summed up the controversy in a poem, 'The gathering of the Scotch-Irish Clans', as follows:

> We'll sit upon the pint-stoup and we'll talk of auld lang syne
> As we'll quaff the flowing haggis to our lasses' bonnie eyne.
> And we'll join in jubilation for the thing that we are not;
> For we say we aren't Irish, and God knows we aren't Scot![7]

By 1963 the increasing assimilation of the Irish Americans into the American mainstream had virtually quelled the polemics, but John Fitzgerald Kennedy unwittingly stirred them up again by deciding to visit the land of his ancestors. The Ulster Unionist element attempted to counter the publicity generated by this symbol of Catholic Irish American achievement by inviting a prominent member of the Scotch Irish tradition, a member of the famous Mellon family, to open the refurbished family home in Ulster.

The Mellon family had emigrated to Pennsylvania from Tyrone in 1818. One of the children was Thomas Mellon who grew up to become a lawyer, banker and one of the architects of Pittsburgh's subsequent prosperity. His son Andrew became Secretary of the Treasury for both Presidents Harding and Coolidge, and was one of the founders of Gulf Oil, Alcoa and the Union

Steel Company which later joined with the United States Steel Corporation. Andrew also donated his world-famous art collection to America's National Gallery of Art. Andrew's son Paul and other members of the Mellon family were amongst America's leading business figures and philanthropists. Sadly he died as this book was being written. However, despite their achievements, it is unlikely that the Mellons would have been honoured in Belfast, had the Unionists not felt the need to counter Kennedy's visit.

As it was, the record for the summer of 1963 in Ireland's six north-eastern counties show pictures of Captain Terence O'Neill, the Six County Prime Minister, and his Mellon trophy, competing for attention in Irish newspapers (particularly North of Ireland newspapers) with those of John Fitzgerald Kennedy and Jackie in the South. Ironically, many years later, when the North of Ireland troubles had again prompted the Unionists into an uneasy quest for public recognition of their ancestry, it was to Senator Edward Kennedy that they ultimately turned to achieve it. The Unionists had been seeking some American politician of stature, and Scotch Irish ancestry, to read into the Congressional Record a list of their more distinguished forebears. They finally turned to the man who bears the name most associated with their rival tradition's achievement and, on 5 March 1997, Kennedy duly read the names into the Senate record.

The factual position concerning the Scotch Irish is that they are descendants of some 200,000 Scottish Presbyterians who were planted in Ireland during the early seventeenth century. It is from them that today's Protestant majority in north-eastern Ireland descends. Those who left Ulster in the late 1600s settled largely in the Chesapeake Bay area, and one of them, Francis MacEmie, is today regarded as the father of American Presbyterianism. It is estimated that a further 250,000 emigrated to America in the pre-Revolutionary War period of the eighteenth century. They settled mainly in New England initially, but, having fallen out with New England's Congregationalists, shifted, after 1725, towards Pennsylvania, settling first in and around Philadelphia, then spreading to the Carolinas and Georgia.

Hard-working, Calvinist, grim and stern, more moved by the concept of being Children of Wrath than of Love, they made a very significant impact on American society. It was one of these men, the Reverend William Tennant, who established the famous Log College to train Presbyterian ministers near Philadelphia, *circa* 1726. The Log College became closely intertwined with the College of New Jersey, founded some twenty years later, which developed into Princeton University. Other early settlers who left their mark were Arthur Dobbs, Governor of Carolina in 1753, John Dunlap, already adverted to above (page 253), and five signatories of the Declaration of Independence: Thomas McKean, Edward Rutledge, James Smith, George Taylor and Matthew Thornton. The services of the Irish Volunteers, including a large number of Scotch Irish volunteers, in the revolutionary army were such that Lord Mountjoy complained to the British Parliament, 'We have lost America through the Irish.'[8]

259

It would be impossible to attempt to list all the achievements of Americans of Scotch Irish ancestry, but it is worth noting that several of them became presidents of the US. The fathers of Andrew Jackson, James Buchanan and Chester Alan Arthur were each born in Northern Ireland. Presidents James Polk, Andrew Johnson, Ulysses Grant, Grover Cleveland, Benjamin Harrison, William McKinley and Woodrow Wilson were all of Scotch Irish ancestry; so were American icons like Sam Houston, first President of the Republic of Texas, who led Texas into the Union, and the folk hero, Davy Crockett, who died at the Alamo. In the arts, Edgar Allan Poe, Stephen Foster, Horace Greeley, who founded the *New York Tribune*, and the founder of the *New Yorker*, Harold Ross, could all have traced their ancestry back to Scotland via Ulster.

Though they may have imbibed one half of their heritage through sipping Scotch whisky occasionally, it is difficult if not impossible to discern amongst the Scotch Irish anything of the affinity with Ireland that one encounters amongst Irish American Catholics. Indeed the Protestant-Catholic cleavage, the Know Nothingism of their tradition, has generated an attitude that reminds one of the Anglo-Irish Duke of Wellington's remark concerning his Irish ancestry: that being born in a stable did not make one a horse.

Woodrow Wilson railed against the sense of Irishness retained by Irish Catholic Americans, which at the time of the First World War manifested itself in opposition to joining 'England's war'. He condemned the 'Irish-Americans' as being unpatriotic 'hyphenates'. Leaving Woodrow Wilson's war aims to one side, his epithet may be taken as reflecting the way most members of the Scotch Irish tradition saw themselves: they were not amongst the hyphenates, they were Protestant Americans. However, where America is concerned the so-called Scotch Irish tradition put down deep roots and made a valuable contribution which deserves to be recognised in its own right, untarnished by attempts to involve it in Unionist propaganda.

To return to the other questions concerning the nature of Irish emigration, I believe that a fairly full answer as to whether the Irish should be thought of as exiles or pragmatists will emerge as we follow their story through these pages (or at least it should do so!). For the moment therefore a short response will suffice: the answer is 'both'. To turn to the more practical issue of whether the Irish emigrants should be thought of as urban or rural dwellers, the short answer is again – 'both'. The Irish are indeed accurately thought of in terms of sustained progress from stinking slums in eastern America to the scents of the White House Rose Garden. In 1870 over half the Irish-born population of America still lived in New York, Pennsylvania and Massachusetts. These emigrants were responsible for substantial Irish presences in New York, Boston, Brooklyn, Philadelphia, Pittsburgh, Albany, Buffalo, Scranton and Fall River. However, America is such a mobile, rapidly changing society, that a mere ten years later, on the opposite, western coast, the Irish also formed a third of San Francisco's population of some 250,000 people, and enjoyed in that city and in California a far healthier and more welcoming physical, economic and political climate than they did amongst the nativists to the east. The overall reality of Irish emigration is that the Irish were heavily involved in American development at every conceivable level.

To give but one example, the entire expansion west owed a considerable debt to one Joseph Murphy, a wagon-maker who came from County Louth at the age of twelve. By 1839, he had established himself as a wagon-maker in St Louis, but then the Mexican Government put a tax of $500 on each wagon entering its territory via the Santa Fe trail. Murphy reacted by inventing a wagon which held four or five times the normal load of 1,000 pounds. This minimised the tax bite considerably, and the trade which the Mexicans had hoped to kill flourished instead. Murphy also developed a new type of wagon for the Oregon trail. This had to be commodious enough to take both the families and the provisions for the lengthy journey. Accordingly Murphy developed 'the Prairie schooners', which sailed through hostile Indians and the empty vastnesses of the West, bearing the legend 'J. Murphy, St. Louis' painted on their sides.

In the frontier lands as in the cities, the Irish were engaged in everything from law enforcement to what might be termed the realms of the sacred and profane. Leander McNelly was both a founder and the most famous member of the Texas Rangers. He has been described as: 'the quiet one, the exemplar of all Irish law and order men, [who] gained a deserved fame and became a legend in which all the forgotten sheriffs and patrol men of his race can share'.[9]

In contrast to McNelly, at the profane level, we have the legendary Irish outlaw, Billy the Kid, who fought for the McSween/Chisholm faction in the Lincoln County (New Mexico) Range War of 1878, with ultimately fatal results for himself. His opponents were also Irish: the Murphy/Dolan gang, led by Lawrence G. Murphy from Wexford and James J. Dolan from Galway, who murdered Billy the Kid's benefactor, an Englishman called John Tunstall. The Kid, known as William Bonney, was in fact originally named McCarthy, after his mother Catherine, an Irish emigrant who married a William Antrim, thus creating the name Kid Antrim, which later metamorphosed into legend as Billy the Kid.

At the sacred level, while it is true that some Irish clerical leaders, notably Archbishop Hughes of New York, used their influence to keep the Irish in the urban ghettoes – where they were more easily looked after, marshalled and controlled – a number of other bishops attempted to get them out and settled on the land. These efforts were not universally successful but nevertheless, around the time of Billy the Kid's premature demise, Bishop John Ireland, for example, was earning recognition for being responsible for what one historian has described as: 'The largest and most successful Catholic colonisation programme ever undertaken in the United States.'[10]

Ireland had his setbacks, but between 1876 and 1881 he managed to establish villages and farming communities throughout western Minnesota, some of them with Irish names like Clontarf and Avoca, which are still flourishing today. In Ireland's time the railroad companies controlled land stretching for up to five miles on either side of their tracks. At the outset of his project the bishop contracted with the Saint Paul and Pacific Railroad to become the agent for some seventy-five thousand acres of this land in Swift County, and over the next five years added hugely to it by negotiating similar contracts with five different Minnesota railroad companies.

A simple gesture on the part of Gene Foley, a former member of John Fitzgerald Kennedy's cabinet, brought home to me just how deep and widespread is the Irish penetration of areas outside the north-eastern cities. Foley began our discussion by placing a map of America on the table and saying, 'This is the best way to show you where we settled, where my family went, and where they are now.'[11] Then, moving his finger, he took me on a *tour de l'horizon* of the Midwest. For Gene, the prairies of Kansas, Illinois, Iowa and Minnesota, or the mountains of Montana, were as much a part of his mental landscape of his heritage as were suburbs of the Bronx, Boston or Chicago. Gene's grandparents had originally come to Minnesota as part of one of Bishop Ireland's schemes.

The Foley landscape, and that of countless thousands like him, is why today in America, right through the alphabet, from Antrims in Michigan, to Wexfords in Iowa, Irish place names abound, with the names of the bigger cities, like Cork, Dublin and Derry, replicated several times.

The Irish made a notable impact on the West Coast during the early days of the California Gold Rush which began in 1848, but they had in fact been in the San Francisco area for decades before that. In the days when California belonged to Mexico, a gentleman called Timothy Murphy altered his title to Dom Timoteo Murphy and, by what were reportedly dubious methods, acquired a huge tract of land in the San Rafael area. Another all-time great practitioner of said dubious methods was Sam Brannan, the son of a Waterford man. Brannan, who converted from Catholicism to Mormonism, loved drink and women so much that he consumed a great quantity of both. There was no reason to question his business ethics however, because he didn't have any.

In many ways he could be regarded as the builder of San Francisco. He founded California's first newspaper, built some of the first houses in San Francisco's Happy Valley, and created an exodus to the goldfields by striding down Montgomery Street one bright May day in 1848, holding up a bottle filled with gold nuggets shouting 'Gold, gold, in the American river.' He was also responsible for the establishment of the California Land Commission which, in effect, gave Americans a licence to steal Spanish and Mexican land. By 1856 he was the richest man in California. Then, debauchery and a costly divorce settlement almost consigned him to a pauper's grave, but the year before he died, appropriately enough, a cemetery which he had invested in was sold at a huge profit, and he was able to pay off his debts and die in comfort.

Two other Irishmen who discovered vast riches in the West, this time in Nevada, were not so lucky and died penniless. These were Patrick

McLoughlin and Peter O'Reilly, who discovered the Comstock Lode, one of the richest deposits of gold and silver found during the entire Gold Rush era.[12] The mine had been worked profitably for some years, but it was assumed that its best days were long over when, in 1864, John Mackey, James C. Flood and William O'Brien formed a partnership which eventually resulted in them becoming known as 'the Silver Kings'. Mackey had an instinctive genius for mining, and sinking a new shaft he hit a fresh lode which eventually yielded the Silver Kings 100 million dollars in silver, a mind-boggling figure in the year 1873.

The elevation of the Irish to the highest pinnacles of political and economic success in the US occurred, like bankruptcy, in three ways, gradually, suddenly and – traumatically. Two episodes which occurred during my researches into this book make the point. They involved astrophysics and cannibalism. The cannibalism led me to a friendly, witty cocktail hour with Paul Breen, a relaxed, prosperous, forty-something Californian lawyer.[13] We talked about a camping expedition from his boyhood. He and his brother Patrick signed in for a lake-side stay at Donner State Park. 'When the Rangers saw my brother's name they couldn't believe it at first. Then, when we got bigger, people used to make jokes: Throw a Donner party – we'll have ribs! The Irish sense of humour.'

It was probably the Irish sense of humour that played a part in keeping alive Paul's ancestor, Patrick Breen and his family during one of the most horrific episodes in the history of America. He had been en route to California when an unlucky decision to turn left instead of right at a place called Little Sandy, Wyoming, led to the party of eighty-seven pioneers, led by George Donner, being trapped by snowdrifts in the Sierra Nevada Mountains between November 1846 and March 1847. Of the eighty-seven only forty-eight survived. Patrick Breen's family were amongst the lucky ones but, as with the others, survival was only achieved at hideous cost, described as follows by the authority on the tragedy, Joseph King:

At four in the afternoon on 12 March 1847, seven men on a rescue mission from Sutter's Fort reached the head of the Yuba River in California's High Sierra. At an altitude of seven thousand feet, they found a pit twenty-four feet deep. It had been created by a campfire, kept burning for about seven days, descending as it melted the snow. At the bottom of the pit around the fire were huddled eleven miserable human beings. At the surface were the mutilated bodies of three other human beings, their flesh stripped from their arms and legs, their hearts and livers and brains removed. A pot was boiling on the fire. It was one of the most pitiful sights in the history of the old West.

The eleven survivors numbered two adults and nine children, ages one to fifteen. The adults were two immigrants from County Carlow, Ireland. Patrick Breen, fifty-one, and his spouse Margaret, whom he called Peggy, forty-one. They were members of the tragic Donner Party. Patrick Breen was the author of one of the most remarkable documents of the American West. Entrapped with his large family in the snows for over four months near what came to be known as Donner Lake, Patrick Breen kept a diary of the ordeal, now a prized possession of the Bancroft Library at Berkeley, California.

The story of the Breens, from Ireland to that horrible pit in the snow and their eventual escape, has never been told completely or accurately. The entire Breen family not only survived the ordeal at the high camp by Donner Lake, but they were also largely responsible for the survival of a mother and four children whom they took into their crude shanty, and for another four children not their own who came out alive from the pit in the snow which came to be known as Starved Camp.[14]

The Gold Rush, and the coming of the railroad, which ironically followed the route of the Donner trek, brought prosperity to the Breens who, when they arrived in San Benito County, were the first English speakers in the area. The family subsequently became wealthy ranchers whose descendants were, and are, prominent in the artistic, professional and political life of California. However, Paul's father, a grandson of Patrick Breen, never spoke of the Donner incident. 'I wonder,' asked Paul, in temporarily pensive mood, 'was the trauma passed on . . . ?'

A similar question could be asked of many a prosperous Irish family in America, but the astrophysics incident is more typical of the ease with which today's Irish emigrants get to California, and how they live when they get there. It occurred at a prestigious dinner in honour of the Irish Consul General in San Francisco, Declan Kelly, attended by a number of dignitaries who included my old *Irish Press* colleague, the Lord Mayor of Dublin, Brendan Lynch. Brendan was presented, on behalf of the citizens of Dublin, with a sprig of shamrock by a young astrophysicist Gerrard Hyanga from Termonfeckin in County Louth who had studied at Trinity College, Dublin. He had been responsible for growing the shamrock (*infallium dubium*) – aboard a spacecraft, during a journey of 4.1 million miles in which it circled the earth 161 times.

In political terms the Irish made a journey of similar length before the shamrock began to be handed round in the White House, and the better-off Irish were generally to be found voting Republican – of the Ronald Reagan, rather than the Gerry Adams variety. The years from the Famine to the presidential candidacy of Al Smith in 1928 appeared, on the surface, to be a steady, if bruising, climb to success; but Smith's heavy defeat shook the growing confidence of many Irish Americans. Then, the Wall Street crash the following year ushered in the depression years of struggle and uncertainty, during which the Irish were sometimes tempted to follow false prophets like Father Coughlin (see page 299). However, the Irish contribution to the war effort and in particular the huge growth in educational opportunity offered by the GI Bill of Rights gave the Irish a new and improved status, on which the election of Kennedy set a seal.

The intense interest in Ireland which grew up in the wake of the explosion of the troubles in Northern Ireland lay in the future. Neither amongst the Irish Americans, nor the decision-takers in Dublin, was there any vision of building a relationship even remotely resembling that of the Jews with Israel. Irish Americans might be improving their lot in America, but the hard work involved in rearing their large families meant there wasn't much time for ethnic concerns beyond the annual St Patrick's Day re-immersion in the old traditions. The Irish Government's interest in the American segment of the diaspora was not much different from the level of indifference shown towards that of the UK.

During the fifties some faltering steps were taken in attracting investment and tourists to Ireland. Tourism was an infant industry, very largely dependent on the Grimes family of New York, who owned both the *Irish Echo* and a travel agency. Paddy Grimes was popular in GAA circles and his agency was as much a social club as a ticket agency. As Clare Grimes, his widow, who after his death became the Katherine Graham of Irish American journalism, recalled, in the fifties and sixties buying a ticket to Ireland was an occasion in itself.[15] People would come into the agency to buy their ticket, and 'have a little nip' in the kitchen behind the shop in Columbus Circle. Purchasing a ticket could take half a day. The charter flights were like flying parties and fleets of buses used to depart from Columbus Circle to the airport, very often with Irish motorcycle cops acting as outriders. Paddy used to organise the seating so that people sat in sections apportioned by county, and unorthodox arrangements for the supply for drinks ensured that the term 'getting high' took on an application beyond that of altitude.

Paddy only booked Aer Lingus, and, apart from individual bookings, was responsible for some thirteen charter flights every summer – a major factor in the survival of Aer Lingus on the Atlantic route. This was a significant era in Irish tourism and aviation but, to put it in scale, it should be born in mind that as this is being written, nine flights a *day*, on bigger planes, leave New York for Dublin and Shannon. As the years passed, the Irish Government's policy could be summed up initially as: 'Come to Ireland by Aer Lingus, the Friendly Irish Airline, and buy plenty of Irish whiskey, Waterford Glass, and Irish tweed.' Then, as a certain amount of industrial development occurred and the Irish Industrial Development Authority was set up, to the tweed and the whiskey was added: 'Support the IDA.' Finally, as the troubles worsened, the message was extended to read: 'And don't support the IRA.'

The second and third generation Irish were moving up the corporate ladder to such an extent that by the mid-eighties it was commonly said that approximately 30 per cent of the CEOs on *Fortune* magazine's list of the Top Five Hundred American Companies were Irish. However, there was no effort either to canalise this clout into helping to solve the Northern problem, or to take any worthwhile initiative on behalf of the tens of thousands of illegal Irish emigrants living twilight zone existences in America. The type of attitude which gave rise to the anecdote Noel Dorr told concerning the instruction he received regarding the emigrant woman's application for information to the London Embassy had its impact in America also. Tip O'Neill, Speaker of the House, used to tell a story about the 1965 Kennedy immigration bill which set new criteria for emigration to the United States, and had the effect of creating hundreds of thousands of Irish illegals in the successive decades. O'Neill said: 'I could have walked out on the floor of the House, and got an exemption for

Ireland in five minutes flat. All I needed was a phone call from the Irish Embassy. But the call never came.'[16]

A vacuum now developed in Irish American policy. The Provisionals' support group, NORAID, attracted blue-collar and a limited amount of middle-class support, but overall had the effect of repelling the mainstream.

A significant development in Irish American political interest in Northern Ireland had come about through a meeting in Bonn between Ted Kennedy and John Hume in 1972. Previously, Jack Kennedy had let it be known that he intended to take some initiatives on partition and on US investment in Ireland.[17] His visit to Ireland in 1963 had made a deep impression on him. As a boy, like all the Kennedy children, his interest in Ireland was maintained by his mother. The Fitzgeralds' ancestor, Patrick Fitzgerald had emigrated from Wexford in Famine times and it was from this side of the family that JFK learned his favourite song 'The Boys of Wexford':

> We are the boys of Wexford
> who fought with heart and hand
> to break in twain
> our galling chains
> and free our native land

Dallas intervened before aspiration could be translated into action. However, Ted Kennedy, who had also visited Ireland, was impressed with Hume and his vision of the problem as a civil rights issue rather than a United Ireland one. As a result, the Four Horsemen Group was set up, consisting of Ted Kennedy; Tip O'Neill, the Speaker of the House; Governor Carey of New York; and Senator Patrick Moynihan, also of New York. This group issued statements on St Patrick's Day, supported the Dublin Government's policy, and condemned American fund-raising for the IRA. It played an important role in influencing President Carter to speak out on the Irish issue, and also helped to get President Reagan to influence Margaret Thatcher into concluding the Anglo-Irish Agreement of 1985. This in effect was an effort by both Dublin and London to stem the tide of growing Sinn Fein support, in the wake of the hunger strikes which claimed the life of Bobby Sands, by conceding a consultative role to Dublin in Six County affairs.

However, apart from the containment of Sinn Fein, there was no coherent policy proffered to Irish Americans as to what cause they might rally around. Being Irish, according to the signals emanating from Dublin, under pressure from London, could mean being a terrorist. I got an insight into the discordances and dissipation of effort this created through a lunch in a Chinese restaurant in San Francisco in the spring of 1981. A group[18] of us, under the baton of Bob Callahan, met and decided, as one does in Chinese restaurants in beautiful down-town Berkeley, that what the world needed was an Irish journal of quality. One was duly produced, *Callahan's Irish Quarterly*. Bob was, and is, a gifted writer and editor, with the essential prophetic vision.

His magazine featured both Catholic and Protestant revolutionaries; Bernadette Devlin appeared alongside Andy Tyrie of the Protestant Ulster Defence Association. The *Quarterly* had a fine literary and current affairs content, was well researched and laid out – and had a short life.

One of the two essential reasons for this, we will encounter again in these pages, racism. A cover of the *Quarterly* showed a stereotypical *Punch* cartoon figure which represented the sort of bigotry which Callahan (and we) urged should be fought – a simian, nineteenth-century Irishman doing an Irish jig. Right on, we're all against that, said Irish America. But, and when the penny dropped it was a very big but, the green caricature had a black face . . .

The second reason was emblazoned on the magazine's back cover:[19]

Q: Why an Irish Quarterly now?
A: There's a war going on in the North. There's a social and cultural revolution going on in the South. And in America, the Irish no longer know just who the hell they are. It's time my friend. It's more than time.

Callahan was correct in stating that the Irish did not know who the hell they were (or, more accurately, were worried about what they were being told) but he was wrong about the time, not morally but politically. In 1981, there was no consensus. But there shortly would be. A new issue was approaching, into which that of Northern Ireland's Six Counties of contention would shortly be subsumed.

By the 1980s, a quiet revolution was occurring. The level of education among the emigrants was far higher than in previous decades, but most of them were 'illegals'. They did not qualify for visas and lived in hourly dread of being arrested and deported. Behind his patina of Hollywood Irish charm, Ronald Reagan's presidency took a hard line. Part of his strategy was to deny that there was an illegals problem. I interviewed him at the White House on the eve of his Irish visit in June 1984, and he told me that his information was that the Irish were not taking up the visas available to them.

Under Reagan, legislation prescribed huge penalties for employers who took on illegals. The Immigration and Naturalisation Services had 900 armed employees visiting work places, checking papers. Even without this threat the illegals already lived in a twilight zone, taking jobs which were generally well below their intellectual and educational qualifications. They moved, however, in a world in which *The Quiet Man* image of John Ford's Ireland was fading. Audiences had flocked to see Brian Friel's play about contemporary emigration: *Philadelphia, here I come*, and emigration proved to be the issue which transformed the Irish American scene.

Early in May 1987, two young men, Sean Minihan and Pat Hurley, both of them from Cork, both of them graduates, one of them, Hurley, an illegal, went to a meeting of the Cork County Association in New York. The main item on the agenda dealt with the entertainment for the following year's St Patrick's Day. 'Jasus,' enquired Hurley, in a stage whisper, 'what are we doing here?'

'Would you like to say something?' responded the Chairman, handing him the microphone. Initially traumatised into silent embarrassment, Hurley managed to collect his thoughts and launched into a passionate exposition of the problems he, and a hundred thousand like him, faced in their daily lives. He spoke for half an hour and by the time he was finished, the audience were on their feet demanding action.[20] They got it. A few days later Hurley summarised his speech in a Viewpoint article in the *Irish Echo*.[21] After pointing out that the contemporary emigrants had performed a patriotic act in emigrating, so sparing Ireland the burden of maintaining them on a grossly overburdened welfare system, he went on:

> if we are prevented from prospering and realising our potential in this country, then Ireland too will stagnate and decline. For though we are thousands of miles from Ireland, we are still her hope and future. If we fail, Ireland will fail.
> We are no different in nature to you immigrants who came before us. We cherish the same hopes and dreams that you once cherished . . . Immigrants of the past do not forget us. Do what you can to help us in our plight.

The plea was answered four days later at a public meeting in the Cork Hall when the Cork County Association sponsored a new grouping, The Irish Immigration Reform Movement (IIRM). Almost overnight Hurley and Minihan found themselves the spearhead of what the *Irish Echo* columnist Mike Devlin described as 'an alternative government, a government in exile'.[22] On the one hand this was the Dublin politicians' worst nightmare, but on the other the votes of the emigrants' families were too important to be overlooked. This potential was harnessed when, with that instinct for the authentic that subsequently made him Ireland's leading broadcaster, a young Irish radio show host, Pat Kenny, decided to do a full programme on the issue – from Cork Hall, on the first of June. Its impact helped to ensure that the Irish Government put its weight behind the lobby effort.

In America itself, a significant influence was Niall O'Dowd, one of the Chinese restaurant warriors who had helped to launch *Callahan's Irish Quarterly*. O'Dowd, a former teacher, is the contemporary standard bearer of a distinguished tradition of Irish American journalism: that of emigrants, like John Boyle O'Reilly of the *Boston Pilot*, or Patrick Ford of the *Irish World*, who came to America with very little money, and who either founded, or took over, small newspapers and built them up into organs of real political and social influence.

In 1985, O'Dowd had transferred to New York to launch a successful new Irish American newspaper the *Irish Voice*. With his help, and the continuing support of the *Irish Echo* and the leading New York Irish radio personality, Adrian Flannelly, the illegals themselves organised one of the most effective lobbying groups ever to descend on Washington. The IIRM modelled its structures on the Irish governmental system; its national council was akin to a Cabinet; its steering committees, finance, ethnic contact, welfare, etc. were similar to ministries. Chapters of the movement, organised on Irish local government lines, mushroomed in New York, Boston, Chicago, San Francisco, Fort Lauderdale, Kansas, San Antonio and Los Angeles.

Leading Irish political figures like the Kennedys (Senator Ted and Congressman Joe) and Ray Flynn, Mayor of Boston, supported the new departure, as did Congressman Brian Donnelly. Donnelly's name would ultimately be appended to one of the laws passed as a result of the agitation, which provided the 'Donnelly visas'. However, one of the most effective politicians of all was Bruce Morrison of Connecticut, the son of a German Lutheran mother and the grandson of a Scotch Irishman. Morrison was a member of the important Congressional sub-committee on immigration and he effectively shepherded through the legislation, signed into law in 1990 by President Bush, which created the 'Morrison visa'. The new laws had the effect of granting an increased number of visas to a number of favoured countries, thus more or less mopping up the illegals.

The campaign was a learning experience for the young Irish campaigners. At the time the immigration issue was a thorny one which generated a good deal of hostility, particularly between the Hispanic community and organised labour. The Irish too had their traditional 'them' and 'us' attitude, but Morrison played an important role in getting this dropped in favour of what he termed an 'added value' approach: in other words, the necessity of making the visa pool bigger, trading a Murphy for a Gonzales.

Initially, Morrison, who went to Yale Law School with Bill Clinton and Hillary Rodham, had been more interested in civil rights than Irish issues, but the IIRM campaign brought him into contact with the North of Ireland problem and with Irish American community leaders, particularly with O'Dowd, whose generalship and journalism during the campaign had impressed him.

O'Dowd had not forgotten the message on the cover of *Callahan's Irish Quarterly*, and the manner in which the young IIRM campaigners had adapted to the new politics of America suggested a means of translating it into action. He began having conversations with Morrison and a number of leading Irish Americans, in particular the billionaire philanthropist, Chuck Feeney, one of the pioneers of the duty-free shops idea, and Bill Flynn, Chairman of the once tiny Mutual Assurance Company of America which he had built into one of the giants of the insurance industry. They agreed with him that the IIRM momentum should not be lost. Contact was established with Sinn Fein and an agenda was worked out. It included an IRA ceasefire; a visa for Gerry Adams to enter the US; recognition of Sinn Fein as a political party by the US authorities; reform of the RUC; and the appointment of a peace envoy to Ireland by the American administration.

The agenda attracted bi-partisan support. On the Republican side, Congressman Pete King would co-operate with Democratic stalwarts like the Kennedys, Chris Dodd, National Chairman of the Democratic Party, and the respected figure of veteran civil rights lawyer and Irish issues campaigner,

Paul O'Dwyer of New York. From the ranks of labour, Joe Jamison of the AFL/CIO had no difficulty in working with capitalists like Feeney and Flynn, who were particularly enlightened examples of their genre. Feeney eventually put up the money which enabled Sinn Fein to open an office in Washington. He had given away more than $600 million to deserving causes without anyone knowing it because, in order to preserve his anonymity, he did not claim tax relief on his donations, and it was only the sale of his interest in the duty-free shops chain DFS and his involvement in the Peace Process that brought his philanthropy to light.

Flynn created the context for an Adams visit by inviting him to address the prestigious National Committee on American Foreign Policy, and then lobbied Clinton to grant him a visa. Flynn also dug into his pockets to ensure that loyalists too could come to America, to be reassured that they had nothing to fear from an American-brokered peace. The new lobby was helped at this time by the fact that there was a particularly good Irish diplomatic pairing in Washington: the Ambassador Dermot Gallagher, who had previously been Ambassador to England, and Brendan Scannell, the Counsellor, a former Consul General in Boston. They proved to be a notably sure-footed and effective duo around Capitol Hill as a new climate developed and the chorus of 'don'ts' directed at Irish America was replaced by one of 'Call your Congressman.'

Back in Ireland, John Hume's initial doubts at the wisdom of the new agenda were quelled and he entered into crucial secret negotiations with Gerry Adams which ultimately paved the way to an IRA ceasefire. On top of all these developments, a new Taoiseach assumed power in Dublin in 1992. Albert Reynolds, a former dance-band impresario and a manufacturer of dog food, demonstrated a hitherto unsuspected passion for the Northern issue. This led to a breakthrough with John Major, the British Prime Minister, in the form of the Downing Street Declaration of 1993, which raised the possibility of Sinn Fein entering talks on the future of Northern Ireland if hostilities ceased.

However, the greatest single unlooked-for energising influence was that of one William Jefferson Clinton. Niall O'Dowd was one of a group of Irish Americans headed by the veteran civil rights lawyer Paul O'Dwyer, who, during the presidential primaries of 1992, met with the Arkansas hopeful in a New York hotel to hear what the candidate proposed on Ireland. They came away impressed to a point of near amazement by his grasp of the subject. O'Dowd recalls that as they left the hotel, Paul O'Dwyer remarked to him wonderingly: 'If this guy does half what he promises, he's going to knock their socks off.'[23] It was decided to support Clinton in the presidential race and a new grouping called Irish Americans for Clinton/Gore was set up under the chairmanship of Clinton's student friend, Bruce Morrison.

Clinton, like Morrison, had an interest in civil rights issues, and felt that the lesson of the American civil rights movement was that the ultimate authority and responsibility of the Federal Government had been demonstrated at

Little Rock in a way which the London Government manifestly had not done over Northern Ireland. There was also the small matter that in the previous election a majority of white professionals had voted for Bush. The one segment of this vote which Clinton could hope for was the Irish Catholics.

When Clinton began talking initiatives over Ireland, he initially ran into determined opposition from the State Department and the Department of Justice, both traditionally strongly pro-London in their approaches to any issue involving the Irish and the British. Eventually, he decided to by-pass State and Justice and entrusted Irish policy to the National Security Council headed by Tony Lake. In Washington a top Lake aide, a former Kennedy staffer, Nancy Soderberg, became a key figure in the Peace Process. In Dublin an even more central figure was Clinton's new Ambassador to Ireland, Jean Kennedy Smith, a sister of JFK and Ted. Her sustained and successful efforts on behalf of the Peace Process eventually led to her being made an honorary Irish citizen.

During this time the Conservative Party, which was historically and temperamentally opposed to the Irish lobby's demands, depended for its continuance in office on the votes of the Ulster Unionists in the House of Commons. They angrily resented the Irish American intervention, and brought pressure to bear on John Major to resist the American suggestions, particularly that of a Peace Envoy to Belfast. However, the activities of the O'Dowd group and the influence of the Kennedy family ensured that the objections of the Unionists and the British to the granting of the Adams visa were overcome, even though there was an unprecedented freeze in London-Washington relationships for some time as a result.

Finally the Irish American group ended up becoming their own peace envoys. It was to them, at a historic meeting in Belfast at the end of August 1994, that Gerry Adams announced in confidence that there would be an IRA ceasefire announcement forty-eight hours later, on 31 August 1994. Senator George Mitchell ultimately became an actual peace envoy through his chairmanship of the Belfast talks which, with the aid of former Finnish Prime Minister, Hari Holkeri, and the former Canadian Chief of Staff, General de Chastelain, eventually led to the signing of the Good Friday Agreement in Belfast in 1998.

And so the White House acquired a patina of green. The relationship turned out to be 22-carat shamrock. When Clinton was at the nadir of his fortunes during the Lewinsky affair, it was the Irish Americans who rallied to his support. Brian O'Dwyer, Paul's son, made a highly publicised presentation to Clinton (the Paul O'Dwyer Peace and Justice Award, in memory of his father who had died a year earlier) on the White House lawn, just as Kenneth Starr was sending his report to Congress. The presentation generated the only favourable publicity Clinton had received in a long while.

After Clinton had finally shrugged off the Starr challenge, the St Patrick's Day party in the White House the following year (1999) was the biggest ever; over a thousand people attended. At the annual Ireland Fund dinner held in

271

Washington the same week, the 1,300 strong attendance included not only predictable figures such as the Irish Taoiseach, Bertie Ahern, Mo Mowlam, the Secretary of State for Northern Ireland, John Hume, Gerry Adams, and the British and Irish Ambassadors, but more than a hundred members of Congress and the Senate, drawn from both Republicans and Democrats. Orrin Hatch (Republican, Utah) remarked truly: 'We fight each other most of the time, but when we get together, people get out of the way.' In his after-dinner speech, Ted Kennedy, who was the guest of honour, brought down the house by rewording an old Irish toast: 'May the road rise up to meet you, may the wind be at your back, and may you be in Heaven a half-hour before the Special Prosecutor knows you're dead.' Heads were definitely over the parapet. Ted Kennedy told me his assessment of the importance of the Irish issue in contemporary Washington: 'This Irish issue is a world issue. It's up there with the Middle East or Bosnia. It merits that kind of attention here in Capitol Hill now.'

Such is the surface outline of how the final climb to that pinnacle of attention was achieved. Let us turn now for a brief examination of how the slow, painful groundwork for the ascent was laid down.

BLACK AND GREEN AND BOSSES

Boston's Bayside Club was packed to suffocation. Television lights beamed down and beads of sweat gathered on the black trade unionist's face as he stood at the microphone telling an Irish joke, one with literally black humour: 'My members get on great with the Irish. The only thing is they have this problem with their eyesight. They see all these guys marching by on St Patrick's Day, but you keep hearing them saying: The mothers! The mothers . . . !'

The audience roared with knowing laughter and beside the trade union leader the host of the television programme, Billy Bulger, President of the Massachusetts State Senate, clapped and smiled. We were attending what, until near the end of the millennium, was one of America's classic St Patrick's Day rites, Billy Bulger's annual 'roast'. Everyone was in good humour, and no outsider would have realised that we were watching scar tissue heal over one of Irish America's longest running sores: the overall Irish relationship with Afro-Americans and the immediate legacy of the long-running bussing controversy which first erupted in 1974.

The atmosphere was a tribute to Bulger himself, one of the prime opponents of bussing and the figure who could legitimately be thought of as the last of the old style Irish-American bosses. An examination of Bulger's career provides an excellent starting point from which to begin a short journey through the histories of Afro-Irish relationships and Democratic Party machines run by Irish political chieftains, particularly in the Irish bastions of New York and Boston.

At a roast Bulger was always in sparkling form. In between interviewing celebrities, linking up with the White House for his annual televised chat with the incumbent president, or singing a duet with the State Governor, he sang, did tap dances and told jokes in an unending stream. His patter was a combination of ascerbic contemporary observation and homage to the traditional totems of Irish America: religion, family, politics and his personal icon, James Michael Curley, the legendary boss of all bosses in Boston politics.

James Michael Curley, known popularly as 'the purple Shamrock', and as 'the rascal King' by a biographer, was a professional politician, who lived by running for a variety of public offices. The orphaned child of Irish emigrants, he used to say of his childhood surroundings: 'Life was grim on this corned beef and cabbage riviera.' To prove his point he told a story of how one day, while he was walking with his uncle, he saw some coins on the ground and bent to pick them up. His uncle kneed him in the groin, and pocketed the money. Certainly, to judge from his subsequent career, that incident coloured a good deal of Curley's political thinking. He became Lord Mayor of Boston in 1915 after persuading his opponent, John F. Fitzgerald, the legendary 'Honey Fitz', father of Rose Kennedy, grandfather of John Fitzgerald Kennedy, not to seek re-election. The persuasion took the form of a threat to explain to the Bostonian electorate that Fitzgerald was having an affair with a Miss 'Toodles' Ryan.

However, Curley became vastly popular because of the lavish amount of public money he spent on public works in the course of the various offices he held during his career. His dispensation of jobs on the city payroll, and expenditure on projects such as Boston City Hospital, parks and swimming pools benefited the poor. He liked to be known as the Mayor of the Poor. One of his methods of ensuring this was to attack the rich. In the course of a typical Curley diatribe he once said that the term 'codfish aristocracy' was 'a reflection upon the fish'. Curley raised chuckles and blood pressures in equal measure. His continual attacks on the Protestant Brahmins drove a wedge between them and the Catholic Irish, which, instead of becoming dulled by time, was sharpened by his tactics. However, his roguery earned him affection rather than opprobrium from the Boston Irish. He went to jail for two months once because he sat an exam for a poor (and stupid) supporter. That jail term was to be worth many votes to him subsequently.

When he backed Roosevelt against Al Smith in 1932, he was debarred from joining the Massachusetts delegation to the Democratic National Convention. However, Curley got around this problem by appearing at the Convention as the leader of the Puerto Rican delegation, Senor 'Jaime Miguel Curleo'. There was a serious downside to Curley's 'them' and 'us' politics. Apart from the fact that the Mayor of the Poor lived in a 21-room mansion (emblazoned with shamrocks) he drove both people and capital out of the city. He taxed the Brahmin property owners heavily and sold tax breaks in exchange for campaign contributions. The general turmoil which his confrontational style engendered helped to leave Boston worse off after him than it had been before. He was broken politically by a jail sentence for fraud in 1947, even though he received a presidential pardon from President Truman, and died a poor man at the age of eighty-four in 1958. However, the image of James Curley which remains in the affectionate memory of many less well-off Boston Irish is the one he would have wanted: 'Mayor of the Poor'.

Thus, Bulger struck a chord when he mentioned his name. The roast was always packed to the doors. In fact, my first impression on seeing the Bayview Club at 8 am on a St Patrick's Day morning in 1988, was that somebody somewhere knew someone in whatever Department enforced fire regulations. Over the years, on subsequent visits to the roast, it became evident that everybody knew, and nobody mentioned, who that somebody was. Everyone who was anybody in Boston's Irish community wanted an invitation. Guests and audience crowded at trestle tables to eat corned beef and cabbage, drink flowed freely, the sound of Irish music competed with the music from the tills. On stage, Billy produced his astonishing patter. During the last roast performance which I attended, the State Governor, William Weld, a Republican, had composed a song especially for the occasion entitled 'He'll never come back, no he'll never come back'. An outsider would have been forgiven for thinking that the song was about a local ice hockey star or some such, who had been sent to the sin bin. In fact he was talking about Billy's brother 'Whitey', one of America's most notorious gangsters.

The only people who escaped being roasted by Bulger that day were Boston's Cardinal, Wacko Hurley, and myself. The Cardinal for obvious reasons, me because fortunately Billy likes my books, and Wacko because South Boston likes Wacko. He successfully fought a two-year legal battle to convince the US Supreme Court that the organisers of the St Patrick's Day Parade could not only decide who they wanted in their parade, but who they did not want. Wacko, who with his green shirt and prominent jaw looked for all the world as if he had stepped out of a contemporary variant of a *Punch* cartoon, didn't want gays in the parade – and he made it clear from the platform that he and his friends would remember at the polls those who had not supported him in the fight. Wacko might look funny to outsiders, but he was no joke in South Boston.

Bulger's energy was astonishing. After a non-stop performance of over four hours in near-suffocating heat, he would then lead the St Patrick's Day procession, subsequently returning to South Boston to preside over open house at his home. Approaching the house, one could hear the Irish music from the end of the street. Music runs in the family: Bulger's son, Brendan, won an All-Ireland fiddle championship at the Oireachtas Festival in Dublin. Inside the house Bulger's astonishingly good-looking children handed around beer. A hogshead filled with ice and tins of Budweiser, standing in the corner of one of the rooms, served as the South Boston variant of the miracle of the loaves and fishes – the Bulger children kept it filled. The music, the dancing and the drinking flowed all day, but not a drop ever passed Billy's lips nor did one hear a word said that would have been out of place in the city's most exclusive salon.

He is a font of paternal advice. On a visit to his home I witnessed a young man tell him that he was thinking of applying to become a policeman, 'That's a fine career,' replied Bulger, 'but before you apply, write down everything you can think of for and against the job – and then make your mind up.' As we set off on a tour of South Boston he checked the time with his chauffeur. 'Remember,' he said, 'you have a class to go to at six thirty. We can take a cab.'

One St Patrick's Day fell during a controversy over the siting of an incinerator to destroy the city's rubbish. Ted Kennedy showed up at the roast with a huge mock sack of refuse. 'Where are we going to put the incinerator, Billy?' he asked to roars of approval from those who wanted it sited on Billy's turf. 'Hyannisport,' (where the Kennedy summer home is located) replied Billy, to even louder roars from those in the audience who didn't see why the rich should dump their rubbish on them. Billy had the last laugh. The incinerator was eventually sited in Weston, one of Boston's most up-scale (and most outraged) suburbs.

The exchange was straight out of the Curley heritage, defending the Irish, the underdogs, against the Brahmins. Times had changed. Kennedy, and even Bulger himself, could be regarded as Brahmins nowadays – but the memory of the past cuts deep. That memory is centred on the explanation of the emergence of the Irish in Democratic Party machine politics, the boss syndrome and Irish hostility to the blacks: poverty.

Describing the phenomena of the Irish Democratic machines run by Irish bosses in the big cities, Chris McNickle succinctly told how these machines became powerful and how they achieved their distinctive character. In a word, the Irish turned their disadvantaged status to advantage. In the north-eastern cities, their numbers were both high and concentrated in Irish areas which made organisation easy. As McNickle points out:

> The hierarchical nature of the Catholic Church and its demand for discipline offered an effective model for a political party to follow. And when they arrived in the United States, the Irish already had a long, if perverse acquaintance with an Anglo-Saxon political system. They had learned from the English about electoral fraud, judicial chicanery, and manipulation of the rules for partisan advantage. They understood politics as the means one group used to secure power for itself, to hold on to it and to exploit it. Morality had nothing to do with it, nor did any grand ideology. For the Irish, politics differed from other professions only in detail. It was a way to earn a living.[24]

As the Irish swarmed into the stews of America after the Famine, one of the first lessons they learned was: Look After Your Own. In the implementation of this gospel the machines threw up some of the most charismatic, caring and corrupt figures in American political history. The late nineteenth century yielded in New York, 'honest' John Kelly, and 'Boss' Richard Croker; in Chicago, Mike McDonald; in Boston, Pat Maguire; in San Francisco, Christopher Buckley. As the twentieth century wore on, the Irish tradition produced new faces and names: Frank Hague in Jersey City; the enduring Daley dynasty in Chicago; James Michael Curley, Martin Lomasney and 'Honey' Fitzgerald in Boston; Dan O'Connell in Albany; and Tom and Jim Prendergast in Kansas City.

Mayor Frank Hague, who took over Jersey City in 1917, used to tell about an incident that occurred in 1937 in which he overruled a bureaucrat who denied the request of two Irish boys to change from day to night school so that they could work, on the grounds that this was 'the law'. Hague told him, 'I am the law. These boys go to work.' He was and they did. Those were the years when a foreman would ask a job-seeker: 'Protestant or Catholic?' As a memoir of the time recalls: 'If you said Protestant, even though the map of Ireland was on your face, you got a job. If you said Catholic, the clerk said: "No work today."'[25] Hague retaliated against WASP power with a liberal use of the 'Lazarus franchise' and methods which led to a famous medical centre he built being said to contain '100% steal'![26]

I remember myself listening to stories from my late friend Frank Riley, who sold insurance. When he first came to New Jersey, big employers like Colgate used to exhibit signs saying: 'No Irish, no Catholics'. One of Frank Riley's sons, Frank Jnr, became the youngest ever Vice President of the Chase Manhattan Bank. Another joined the FBI and a daughter became a Reverend Mother. Hague was not directly responsible for these classically Irish careers, but he, and others like him, helped to create the conditions in which the Frank Rileys could rise. Hague himself ultimately fell in a cloud of that odour which all too often emanated from Democratic Party machines, corruption. He died, discredited, in 1956.

Apart from corruption, one thing which the Irish bosses had in common was that they worked hard. The following could have been taken from any of their diaries. In fact, it is from that of George Washington Plunkitt, an Irish butcher who, as a Tammany chieftain in the 1870s, became renowned for 'looking after his own'. In turn, they looked after him. He made a fortune out of harbour transport and general contracting. Alastair Cooke called him 'the model of the Samaritan politician'. Plunkitt himself described Tammany Hall, as 'the only lasting democracy'. What he meant was that when the tumult and the shouting of elections died away, only Tammany Hall could be depended on to look after the poor. Here is an account of his typical day:

2.00 am. Aroused from sleep by a bartender who asked me to go to the police station and bail out a saloon keeper who had been arrested for violating the excise law. Furnished bail and returned to bed at three o'clock.

6.00 am. Awakened by fire engines. Hastened to the scene of the fire ... found several tenants who had been burned out, took them to a hotel, supplied them with clothes, fed them and arranged temporary quarters for them.

8.30 am. Went to the police court to secure the discharge of six 'drunks', my constituents, by a timely word to the judge. Paid the fines of two.

9.00 am. Appeared in the municipal district court to direct one of my district captains to act as counsel for a widow about to be dispossessed . . . Paid the rent of a poor family and gave them a dollar for food.

11.00 am. At home again. 'Fixed' the troubles of four men waiting for me: one discharged by the Metropolitan Railway for neglect of duty: another wanted a job on the road, the third on the subway, and the fourth was looking for work with a gas company.

3.00 pm. Attended the funeral of an Italian. Hurried back for the funeral of a Hebrew constituent. Went conspicuously to the front both in the Catholic church and the synagogue.

7.00 pm. Went to district headquarters to preside over a meeting of election district captains, who submitted lists of all the voters in their districts and told who were in need, who were in trouble, who might be won over (to Tammany) and how.

8.00 pm. Went to a church fair. Took chances on everything, bought ice cream for the young girls and the children, kissed the little ones, flattered their mothers and took the fathers out for something down at the corner.

9.00 pm. At the clubhouse again. Spent $10 for a church excursion. Bought tickets for a baseball game. Listened to the complaints of a dozen pushcart peddlers who said they were being persecuted by the police. Promised to go to police headquarters in the morning and see about it.

10.30 pm. Attended a Hebrew wedding reception and dance. Had previously sent a handsome wedding present to the bride.

12.00 pm. In bed.[27]

The Irish did not easily manipulate Tammany to their own advantage. Like most powerful institutions in America the Irish had to break into it. Called after a Delaware Indian chief, its head was known as the Grand Sachem (Chief) and its members paraded on Festival days carrying bows and arrows and tomahawks, hence one of its nicknames, the Wigwam. The Irish literally broke into Tammany on the night of 24 April 1817. They wished to make a protest against the way the Tammany Society, then the city's most powerful political machine, discriminated against the Irish. This they did by breaking up both the furniture and those Tammany members present who proved recalcitrant. Despite the uproar, the Irish failed to get Tammany to nominate an Irishman for Congress, but after 1821, when New York State abolished the property vote and conceded universal franchise, the Irish became a valuable commodity to Tammany's leadership. (By way of illustration of the background reasons for the Irish troubles, in the Six Counties this property vote was not abolished until the Protestants of Northern Ireland were forced to concede the franchise after the troubles had broken out in the mid-sixties.) An Irish vote was as good as any other and the Famine emigration ensured that

277

there were plenty of them. Thus Tammany swung from being a bastion of nativism to becoming the most important citadel of Irish power in America.

Plunkitt's 'Samaritan tradition' lived on amongst the 'Celtic bosses'. For example, the legendary Thomas 'T. J.' Prendergast of Kansas City is still remembered, not for being prosecuted for graft but for his princely generosity. When the ferocious winter storms ravaged Kansas City, he would habitually send trucks to the neighbourhoods, filled with anything his people might need, coal, clothing, food. During the deadly influenza epidemic of 1918–19, 'T. J.' risked his life going around tenements, checking personally to see who needed help. Like Plunkitt, all Prendergast sought in return was the vote of those he cared for. Like Plunkitt, he made a fortune out of construction.

There was another side to Bossism, however. Tammany itself fended off the challenge of the Reformist Henry George and his United Labour Party, in New York's 1886 mayoral election, through blatant chicanery. Tammany Hall controlled the police, most of them Irish, and the police saw to it that the votes of a burgeoning new urban electorate did not count. As Steven P. Erie has recorded: 'Uncounted ballots, nearly all for George, were seen floating down the Hudson for days after the election'[28] – just as in Northern Ireland, machine politics saw to it that votes were recorded from 'the dead, the departed, and even the unborn'.[29] The ward bosses undermined labour and socialist parties through their patronage and by using corrupt officials and judges to halt parades and prevent meetings; they impeded the growth of Italian and Jewish businesses by denying permits and rigorously enforcing Sunday closing hours. Opponents were often arrested on trumped-up charges. Knuckle-duster-wielding thugs broke up peaceful gatherings. Even though they had made it through the 'golden door' of opportunity by landing in America, emigrants, particularly poor emigrants, still had to contend for scarce resources.

The basis for some Irish American attitudes towards blacks were sown in that scarcity. In Ireland, the Irish once had a proud record of anti-slavery. The Council of Armagh as far back as 1177 outlawed Irish trade in English slaves. In 1830, the greatest Irish leader of the nineteenth century, Daniel O'Connell, had only one other Irish member to support him in the House of Commons. He was approached on behalf of the West Indian slavery lobby and offered the support of the lobby's twenty-seven members if he would agree not to speak out against slavery. O'Connell answered nobly: 'Gentlemen, God knows I speak for the saddest people the sun sees, but may my right hand forget its cunning, and my tongue cleave to the roof of my mouth, if to save Ireland, even Ireland, I forget the negro one single hour!'[30]

However, the liberator's sentiments did not find universal acceptance amongst his countrymen in the land of liberty. Some leading Irish Americans, like John Boyle O'Reilly – the former Fenian who escaped from penal servitude in Western Australia to become editor of the *Boston Pilot*, a best-selling author and one of Boston's most respected citizens – were confirmed abolitionists. But, there was also a more influential core of conservative opinion which did not want to see the Irish mixed up in the abolition campaign. As far back as 1842, Bishop John J. Hughes of New York condemned an address from the people of Ireland, sponsored by O'Connell, attacking slavery. Hughes claimed that he was no friend of slavery but that it was 'the duty of every naturalised Irishman' to repudiate the address 'with indignation', because it had 'emanated from a foreign source' and was interfering with domestic American policy. Whether Hughes was in reality expressing the familiar authoritarian attitude of Irish bishops towards anything that either was, or could be interpreted as, interference with domestic Church policy is a moot point. What is certain is that, as indicated by the experiences of the Irish in New Orleans, the Famine influx created a nationwide competition for jobs at the bottom of the skills ladder: jobs which no one else would do except the Irish – and the blacks.

There were several riots directed against blacks in Philadelphia between 1834 and 1849 in which the Irish took part. In one of the worst of these, in 1842, the Irish were almost solely responsible. The riot began when the Irish attacked a procession organised by blacks to celebrate both the virtues of temperance and the emancipation, by the British, of West Indian slaves. It lasted for days and was characterised by great brutality and the destruction of black property, including churches. The Irish believed that if they could drive the blacks from the City of Brotherly Love, they could take over jobs vacated by the blacks. Thus, in an era when the Irish had their own churches burned, and were subject to racialist attack right across the English-speaking world, the Irish themselves were sometimes guilty of an equally gross racialism. Sometimes a fellow feeling doth make us wondrously unkind.

Dock labouring, both in northern and southern ports, was a particular source of conflict between the blacks and the Irish until the 1860s but earlier in the nineteenth century, the brawling Irish had fought each other for jobs. For example, there was a Homeric encounter during the building of the Chesapeake and Ohio Canal in 1834, between over a thousand Cork and Longford workers, which was only subdued with the aid of a strong force of militia and troops. As the century wore on, however, the Irish learned a basic, brutal lesson about nativist-dominated American society in which the employers' associations deliberately fostered racial and ethnic tension as a means of both controlling the workforce and keeping wages low. The Irish could make their way upwards, by uniting amongst themselves, but as whites not as Irish. The Longshoremen's United Benevolent Society, formed in 1852, and exclusively Irish, marched in the St Patrick's Day procession and maintained a rigorous 'whites only' policy towards blacks.[31]

This attitude led to ferocious battles along the docks whenever strikes occurred and black workers were brought in to replace the striking Irishmen – but the Irish saw nothing incongruous in fighting these fights and then, on St Patrick's Day, marching behind a banner inscribed not only with the flags of Europe and America, but the words: 'We know no distinction but that of merit.' The merit lay in the power of Irish labour to organise in the face of job competition from all quarters. In the 1830s, New York, the centre of the American trade union movement, was largely controlled by either native-born or British Protestants, but by the 1860s almost half the city's trade union leaders were Irish Catholic.

For much of this period the Irish were under sustained attack from nativist American sentiment, manifesting itself in the Native American Party of the 1840s, and the Know Nothings of the 1850s. The Know Nothings took their name from the fact that members of a secret nativist organisation, the Order of the Star Spangled Banner, had a practice, when asked about their activities, of replying: 'I Know Nothing.' Nativist onslaughts were such that there was an outbreak of Catholic church burning in Philadelphia, in the run up to the 1844 election. On election night in New York it became known that some 1,000 nativists intended to burn down the old St Patrick Cathedral, at Mulberry Street and Princes Street. Archbishop Hughes stationed 3,000 armed members of the Ancient Order of Hibernians around the church and sent a letter to the Mayor, James Harper, saying that he would turn New York into 'a second Moscow' should any harm befall the church. No churches were harmed there. However, in Philadelphia, along with the churches, whole blocks of Irish homes were destroyed. The nativists were incensed at the influence of a 'foreign prelate', Bishop Kenrick. Kenrick had succeeded in persuading the school board to allow Catholic children to read the Douai version of the Bible rather than that of King James in the public schools.

Nativist hostility towards the Irish was a complex thing: a combination of politics, the slavery issue, traditional Protestant and Anglo-Saxon prejudice against Catholics, particularly Irish Catholics, and severely practical economic considerations. As a contemporary observer wrote:

> The Yankee hod-carrier, or Yankee wood-sawyer, looks down with ineffable contempt upon his brother Irish hod-carrier or Irish wood-sawyer. In his estimation, 'Paddy' hardly belongs to the human family. Add to this that the influx of foreign labourers, chiefly Irish, increases the supply of labour, and therefore apparently lessens relatively the demand, and consequently the wages of labour, and you have the elements of a wide, deep, and inveterate hostility on the part of your Yankee labourer against your Irish labourer, which manifests itself naturally in your Native American Party.[32]

Unfortunately, one must also acknowledge that, as with nativist attitudes towards the Irish, a sizeable proportion of Irish labourers also developed an 'inveterate hostility' towards their black competitors. Sometimes enlightened Irish trade unionists like Peter Maguire, who founded the Brotherhood of Carpenters, deliberately set out to cater for blacks, even though in the circumstances of the time, this had to be done on an apartheid basis. In the South for example, at one stage eleven of the sixty-eight branches of the union were black. However, in New Orleans from 1870 onwards, as unionisation spread, Irish dock leaders co-operated with blacks, both in work-sharing and, throughout a number of hard-fought strikes, in work stoppage. In 1907, the

Irish – and black-led Dock and Cotton Council fought against majority white opinion in New Orleans to establish the right of whites and blacks to work together. The Irish and black union leaders realised that in an ethnically diversified society union was strength.

Politically, as had been indicated, the Irish were generally machine-marshalled, vote-early-vote-often Democrats. The more aristocratic Know Nothings could be thought of as Whig-inclined and revolted by the vulgar excesses of the foreign, and in particular the Irish, rabble pouring into America by the hour. Within the political antagonism there was also the Yankee doubt as to whether the Catholic Church would ever allow its followers to become proper Republicans.

Some historians argue that the Irish sacrifices in the American Civil War dulled antagonisms and made the Irish more acceptable to WASP society, but long after the Civil War had ended the *New York Herald* could still attack the Irish Catholic leader of Tammany Hall, 'Honest' John Kelly, in the following terms:

> the people have an opportunity to see just what sort of an institution the Catholic Church is in politics and to understand what a farce it would be to pretend that free government can continue where it is permitted to touch its hand to politics, or, indeed, to exist, for where it exits, it will not leave politics alone. This is a Protestant country and the American people are a Protestant people.[33]

It has to be conceded that, from the four corners of the world, evidence of the Church's attitude towards 'Godless republicanism' could have been garnered in support of this thesis. Also, as we have seen, on top of all these factors the Irish were opposed to President Lincoln and the Republican Party, in their desire to see slavery retained. Nevertheless, the defensive reaction amongst the Catholic Irish towards a protective shield like Tammany Hall, in the face of attitudes like those of the *New York Herald*, can well be imagined.

The outbreak of the Mexican War yielded a prime example of the clash in outlook between Irish soldiers and nativist officers in the San Patricio Brigade episode, but the war also put a temporary damper on the fires of nativism. However, the fires flared up again as emigration soared in the 1850s. In his marvellous book *How the Irish Became White*, Noel Ignatiev made the shrewd observation that: 'The Irish cop is more than a quaint symbol.'[34] As he pointed out, the appearance of Irish cops on the streets of Philadelphia marked a turning point in the Irish struggle for a place in the American sun. The cops owed their appearance to the fact that a Democrat had become Mayor of the city. He in turn owed his victory to one William McMullen who, by today's standards, would be described as a thug.

McMullen was the leader of one of the main firehouse gangs of the city, 'the killers'. In those days, whoever controlled the count won the election, and as McMullen recorded in his diary, 'the best fighters would get possession'. McMullen took care of his own, they took care of him, and so a Quaker and a Liberal, Richard Vaux, who had a tradition of supporting the Irish, routed the Know Nothings and McMullen was appointed to the board of inspectors of Moyanesing prison. He used the position not merely for inspection purposes, but to release a number of his friends. Released also from nativist shackles, Irish cops strolled the streets of Philadelphia, as they would do in the great cities of America, becoming part of the Irish and American legend. And so law and order followed the fists, knives and knuckle-dusters of figures like McMullen. The Irish were not blind to the shortcomings of the McMullens and the ward heelers, but they knew that without them, law and order, as they experienced it, would be nativist law and order.

In Boston, that citadel of the Irish, the Irish viewed nativist abolitionists as hypocrites. As Thomas H. O'Connor has pointed out, the attitude of the Irish emigrants in Boston was that of the rest of America: whites believed that the blacks were inferior, 'ignorant, savage, brutish, given to emotional pulses and animal passions', fit only to be ruled by the superior white race.[35] If blacks were freed from slavery, bloody revolution would follow. O'Connor observed:

> Boston Irishmen regarded most of the liberal, upper-middle-class, native American Protestants who made up the membership of the local abolition movement as bigots and hypocrites who pretended to be concerned with human rights and the plight of poor black people (whom they cared no more about than the 'fifth wheel of an omnibus,' the Pilot scoffed), but who joined the anti-Catholic forces of the Know-Nothing movement and campaigned against the interest of poor white immigrants.[36]

Those attitudes gave rise to two episodes in particular which linger in the history of American racism, and which still have powerful resonances in Boston. In 1854, white Liberals secured the passage of a law in Massachusetts which stated that no child should be debarred for reasons of 'race, colour or religious opinions' from a public school within the borders of the Commonwealth. The law resulted in boys in a white school being walked across the town to a black one from whom an equivalent number of pupils were walked to the white school. Objectors to the scheme in the Irish community pointed out then, as they would over a hundred years later during the 'bussing' crisis of the 1970s, that the Protestant abolitionists who had advocated this measure were not affected by it – they sent their children to private schools.

As the Civil War toll mounted, Lincoln introduced conscription on the Union side. This was resented to a degree on racial grounds by the Irish, and by other emigrant workers, but above all, objections centred on the unfairness of the draft system. It fell on the poor. Those with $300 could be exempt. To many an Irish labourer, three never mind $300 would have been difficult to raise. Anti-draft riots broke out all over the country, but those of New York live longest in folk memory. Fighting was particularly savage, the death toll may have been around the 500 mark, as troops armed with cannon quelled the rioters. The fearsome Irish women – descendants of the Celtic viragos who accompanied their menfolk into battle, and precursors of the Belfast warrior women who came out in our day rattling their bin-lids on kerbsides to warn of British soldiers' incursions – were a particular factor in the struggle. They urged their men to die fighting for their homes, rather than be taken off to the battlefields as cannon fodder to die so that blacks might take their jobs while the rich escaped scot free. (Blacks had been used to break a particularly bitter New York dock strike shortly beforehand.)

During the rioting, blacks were lynched and the Irish added a sexual dimension to the racism by burning down black brothels. The riots tarnished the image of the Irish as reliable supporters of the Union for which, nevertheless, as we shall see, they would fight valiantly – but they fought for their rights as citizens in a nativist white Republic, not for black emancipation. Their principal foe was not the Confederate States, but poverty. So it was in the American Civil War; so it would be during Boston's 'bussing' crisis.

It is necessary to remember the appalling conditions of New York in the 1850s. These were created not only by the Famine influx but by a series of depressions which hit the city. A committee appointed by the State legislature in 1856 reported on tenements which were: 'dim, undrained courts, oozing with pollution, dark, narrow stairways, decayed with age, reeking with filth, overrun with vermin, rotted floors, ceilings begrimed and windows stuffed with rags, inhabited by gaunt shivering forms and wild ghastly faces'.[37] In 1858, not surprisingly, 64 per cent of the admissions to the city's alms house were Irish. The Irish also had a higher percentage than any other group in the lunatic asylums, the charity hospitals and the prisons. They had the highest rates of cholera, typhoid and typhus.

Along with this terrible deprivation, however, there went a vibrancy and a clannishness which is summed up by the Irish term Sinn Fein. Its literal meaning is We Ourselves. During the mid nineteenth century there was much to fuel this sentiment. In the four years after the worst year of the Famine, 1847, 1.8 million emigrants landed in New York. Of these, 848,000 were Irish. (The next largest group were Germans.) Work opportunities exploded. America was in the throes of a canal and railroad building boom, and there was a great demand for Irish girls in service. It is reckoned that by 1851 New York played host to some 12 per cent of all America's Irish population, and had become the country's major port of entry for the Irish. By 1880, according to the US census, one-third of New York's population was Irish. By now, they were breaking out of the ghettos. It is true that in what is now Central Park, some 20,000 Irish lived in a shanty town raising goats and pigs, and 20 per cent of the Irish worked as labourers, compared to only 4 per cent of native-born Americans, but there were increasing numbers of Irish cops on the streets and Irish women working as domestics in homes, hotels, the needle trade, running boarding houses and selling groceries and liquor. The earlier migrants' descendants were beginning to produce a business and professional class. Lawyers, teachers, doctors and journalists emerged.

Archbishop Hughes presided over the growth of a variety of religious-run charities, hospitals and schools. He invited the Irish Sisters of Mercy to New York in 1846, a development which, as we shall see, would have a lasting and beneficial impact on the upward mobility of Irish American Catholic women. Hughes might be thought of as the leading progenitor of that type of assertive Irish American Catholicism which becomes so visible on St Patrick's Day each year as it passes by Hughes's St Patrick's Cathedral on 5th Avenue: a distinctly Irish combination of ultramontane pietas and patriotism. He was notably unsympathetic to both German and Italian clergy and worshippers who wanted to set up their own parishes or institutions. On one occasion, when the Germans tried to establish a cemetery of their own, he threatened to interdict the church and lock its doors. He was following the Vatican line that there should be one ultramontane church for all. Some of his initiatives, however, were both lasting and benign. Out of a plethora of organisations which he encouraged, a number did noble work, including benevolent societies such as the St Vincent de Paul Society, the Friendly Sons of St Patrick and the Irish Emigrant Society. This last had a remarkable impact.[37]

Marion Casey has described the pitfalls which lay in wait for the emigrant before he or she ever set foot in New York:

> 'Ticket raids' and 'dollaring' were rife in Liverpool, the busiest port in the transatlantic immigration business, where aggressive brokers averaged a twelve and a half percent commission on each fare. Emigrants were sold tickets for ships that simply didn't exist or for departure dates which left them stranded for months in the port city. They exchanged British coins for American 'bank notes' that were often worthless in New York. Remittances from relatives in America, especially in the form of pre-paid tickets, helped the Irish emigrant avoid some of these pitfalls. Tickets marked 'Paid in America' are a testament to the limited experience Irish men and women had with cash or travel beyond their home places, as well as a widespread inability to read English.[38]

Having somehow surmounted these snares and made it across the Atlantic, the emigrant then faced a variety of other dangers: 'improper lodging houses', 'illusive advertisements', 'crooked contractors', 'dishonest prospectuses' and 'remittent sharpers'.[39] The Irish Emigrant Society, founded in 1841 by a group of New York Irish, combated these and other abuses. If a servant girl received bad treatment from an employer, the Society intervened. It provided advice to new immigrants as to where employment might be found, and also provided redress from immigrants who had been conned into buying bogus drafts when sending home money to relations in Ireland to help them to emigrate.

As numbers rocketed, the Emigrant Society expanded its activities to found the Emigrant Industrial Savings Bank in 1850. Thus was aided the birth of that enduring Irish testament to race, place and pietas, 'the American letter'. During the Famine decade (1845–54) the Irish sent back some $19 million in 'The American letter' to their families in Ireland, much of it in the form of pre-paid tickets so that families could be reunited. Thus chain migration was born. Inhabitants of parishes in Ireland followed their parents, brothers, sisters, uncles and aunts across the Atlantic.

The historian Arnold Schrier calculated that during the latter part of the nineteenth century the Irish in America sent over $260 million back to Ireland. Taking into account the conditions of the time, Dennis Clarke reckoned that this generosity amounted to 'the greatest transatlantic philanthropy of the nineteenth century'. The following is a typical letter, written in a clear, educated hand, by one dutiful daughter to her parents in Cork in the aftermath of the Famine:

New York, September 22, 1850

My dear Father and Mother,

I remit to you in this letter 20 dollars, that is four pounds, thinking it might be some acquisition to you until you might be clearing away from that place altogether and the sooner the better, for believe me I could not express how great would be my joy at our seeing you all here together where you would never want to be at a loss for a good breakfast and dinner.

Your ever dear and loving child,
Margaret McCarthy.[40]

Charles Dickens wrote of one particular Irish slum, the notorious Five Points in New York, as being the home of everything 'loathsome, drooping and decayed'.[41] In truth, the Five Points was a noisome place, but as Marion Casey has demonstrated, when the records of the Emigrant Savings Bank were examined, it was found that even in these awful conditions, Irish people made regular savings and at the same time continued to send money home. A Mary O'Connor borrowed $2,000 in 1855 to buy a three-storey brick house. She paid $120 in interest each year and paid off the mortgage on 8 December 1880. By then, her house had appreciated in value to $12,000. The Emigrant Savings Bank supported many Mary O'Connors and Margaret McCarthys.

In Hughes's day, the Catholics frequently had to defend themselves, both physically and politically, from nativist attack. The 1844 election-night dangers which threatened to turn New York into another Moscow flared up repeatedly. The Orange Riots of 1870 and 1871 caused seventy-six deaths and widespread injuries, after the largely Protestant 84th Militia Regiment fired on a Catholic crowd who were protesting against an Orange march. Nativist sentiment was encouraged by rabble-rousing preachers of 'The Angel Gabriel' type.

The Irish response was to organise under the banner of their disciplined authoritarian, hierarchical Church and the equally authoritarian Democratic Party machine controlled from Tammany Hall. Both paid off. As the spires of St Patrick's Cathedral dominated 5th Avenue, so did Tammany Hall control the patronage of the city's government. The *New York Times* of 17 September 1869 claimed that out of a total of 800 jobs, Tammany gave forty-six to Germans and the rest to Irish. In ante-bellum New York, the Irish moved up to such a position that the London *Times* wrote that: 'In New York there is scarcely a situation of honour or distinction from the chief magistrate down to the police, that is not filled by the descendant of some Irish man who lived in savage hatred of England beyond the Pale.'[42]

Tammany continued to be a powerful, even dominant, force in New York politics until the 1920s, under one of the most famous Irish bosses, Charles Francis Murphy, who took over 'the Wigwam' in 1902. Murphy proved adept at wooing the city's growing Jewish population, and Tammany saw to it that the Democrats repeatedly became mayors and controlled the leading State spending boards. Murphy was responsible for the emergence of the reformer Robert Wagner, who later became a senator, and for the election of Al Smith as Governor of New York in 1918. Ironically, it was probably the fact that Smith emerged as a powerful figure in his own right that spelled the beginning of the end for Tammany.

Smith was one of the most progressive figures in American history. A devout Catholic, he nevertheless defended the rights of Socialists to hold seats in the New York Assembly during the first American 'red scare' years of the 1920s. He also pardoned Jim Larkin, the Irish labour leader who had been sentenced for advocating syndicalism. He refused to support the censorship of books or material advocating contraception, although as a Catholic he opposed birth control. Equally courageously, he fought a losing battle in sponsoring an amendment to the US Constitution in 1924 banning the use of child labour, in the teeth of the Catholic hierarchy's objections.

Above all Smith reformed New York State government and brought in some landmark legislation. He had taken part in a factory inspection commission, set up after fire claimed the lives of 146 women in a New York sweat shop in 1911, and had encountered: 'whole families, mothers with their children, little boys and girls, working all the daylight hours and seven days a week in the canneries and the fields'.[43] In office he set about introducing legislation which abolished the worst of these abuses. Night work for women was banned. Workers were given one day a week off. He introduced a 48-hour week for working women, improved workmen's compensation, vastly increased spending on education and saw to it that women teachers were paid the same as men. He also put through a law which encouraged private enterprise to take part in slum clearance and housing development.

The flamboyant song-writing Jimmy Walker was also both a Tammany man and a reformer supporting Smith-style legislation, allowing Sunday baseball, and restricting boxing matches to a duration of fifteen rounds. Under him, major New York development projects were begun. These included the building of the Queens-Midtown Tunnel, the West Side Highway and the Triborough Bridge. He was elected Mayor of New York in 1925 and re-elected in 1929, defeating Fiorello La Guardia. However, he was forced to resign three years later, taking flight for Europe amidst increasing rumours about links to crime, and his affair with millionairess Betty Compton. The growth of the Italian and Jewish groups, combined with his own native genius, then installed Fiorello La Guardia as Mayor of New York in 1933.

La Guardia, the 'little flower', ruled until 1945, when another Irishman, William O'Dwyer, brother of Paul, supplanted him – it was to prove a transient success. O'Dwyer had barely had time to appoint a peace commissioner here, a fire chief there, when storm clouds of allegations of corruption and links to organised crime broke over his regime, causing him to resign in 1950, and become American Ambassador to Mexico. Robert Wagner, who became Mayor in 1953 was to prove the last Irish Mayor of New York, and, *horresco referens*, by that time Tammany Hall itself was being run by an Italian, Carmine de Sapio!

The early fifties were also the years of an Irish-American political figure whom many of today's Irish would be glad to see as part of any tradition rather than their own: Joseph McCarthy, whose name has passed into history as a synonym for some of the worst vices in politics. William V. Shannon summed up McCarthy's impact on Irish Americans as follows:

McCarthyism was a major crisis in the coming of age of the Irish Catholic community in the United States. It derived strength from the worst, the weakest and the most outdated parts of the Irish experience in this country. But it also evoked and tested the best in that experience. It was fed by old parochialisms, old prejudices, old misunderstandings. But it was also combated by growing sophistication and deepening moral and political maturity.[44]

McCarthy was born to the son of an Irish father and a German mother in an Irish enclave of Grand Chute, Wisconsin, in 1908. His own mother was born in Ireland. He was a complete charlatan. Having worked his way through College and becoming a judge (of dubious repute), he became a Republican senator in 1946 after an election campaign in which he campaigned, sometimes in his marine corps uniform, as 'Tail Gunner Joe', despite the fact that he had spent the war in the South Pacific as an intelligence officer, a role in which he probably never heard a shot fired. After an undistinguished first term, he bounded on to the national stage in 1952 by making anti-communism his re-election platform. At Wheeling, West Virginia, he made his infamous claim that: 'I have in my hand a list of 205. A list of names that were made known to the Secretary of State as being members of the Communist Party and who nevertheless are still working and shaping policy in the State Department.'

The Democrats made the mistake of setting up a Senate investigation into his farrago of lies, offering McCarthy an opportunity, which he gleefully seized, of blustering and lying his way across the recently installed TV screens of America. His charges made him a feared national figure. It was the time of the Alger Hiss affair in which similar charges in the Senate had uncovered a case of genuinely un-American activity. Blue-collar America, especially blue-collar Irish America, had few relatives or friends in the State Department. McCarthy found Communists everywhere, in the State Department, in Hollywood, the media. He wrecked the careers of outstanding Americans like the former Secretary of State, Dean Acheson, and caused the leading American political columnist, Drew Pearson, one of his critics, to lose the sponsors of his radio broadcasts. Several other lesser figures had suffered damage to their careers and reputation before he overreached himself by finding Communists in the army, an institution which did have considerable blue-collar associations. The Senate finally passed a resolution condemning McCarthy on 2 December 1954. The censure motion broke the spell of fear which McCarthy had been able to weave in those days of both the Cold War, and the Hot War of the Korean conflict.

McCarthy was a kind of political low-water mark for the Irish experience. The Kennedy years followed and by the eighties the *New York Times* could point out that: 'If there are fewer policemen in New York who have Irish names, there are more stockbrokers that do.'[45] In fact the police tradition is far from ended. Some would still refer to the New York Police Department as 'NYPD Green', and there are figures like the Dublin-born John Timoney to prove it. Timoney joined the NYPD at the age of nineteen and became the youngest ever four-star chief at the age of forty-four. At the time of writing, he is the head of the 9,000-strong Philadelphia police force. Interestingly enough, he revamped the NYPD's training methods by basing the system on that employed by the Irish police force, the Gardai. 'The Gardai, in my estimation, are probably the best-trained police department in the world,' he says.[46] His New York results were so good that he also introduced the Irish system to Philadelphia.

Philadelphia is a special case with the Irish. It was one of the earliest focal points of emigration, the scene of a protracted and bitter struggle with nativists and the source of one of the classic works of Irish American literature, Denis Clark's *The Irish in Philadelphia*. The home of the legendary film star, Grace Kelly, and her even more remarkable father, the champion rower and business tycoon, Jack Kelly (and of her brother Jack, also an Olympic oarsman), Philadelphia was also the home of Joe McGarrity, a prime example of the Irish Revolutionary tradition in America. McGarrity evolved from being a close friend and generous host to de Valera when he first came to America in 1919, to being one of his most bitter critics and the principal Irish American sponsor of the IRA. When de Valera founded his own newspaper in Ireland, he called it after the publication founded by McGarrity in Philadelphia, the *Irish Press*. McGarrity supported the IRA bombing campaign in England, and prior to the Second World War and up to the time that the IRA split into 'provisional' and 'official' wings in 1970, all statements issued by the IRA Publicity Bureau appeared over the pseudonym 'Joseph McGarrity'.

Philadelphia's particularism notwithstanding, however, I feel that I should point out that in my experience the hospitality and the interest of the Philadelphia Irish is to be found replicated all over the US – in Albany, Boston, Atlanta, Minnesota, Chicago, Washington or San Francisco.

The people I went to see were mainly Catholics. I had made contact with a lawyer, Michael Stack, and visited the city of brotherly love as I had visited cities all over the world, expecting to take soundings on the Irish experience in a significant setting. However, when I arrived at Stack's offices, I found that he had arranged a gathering of friends and colleagues to meet me. Instead of my interviewing them, the gathering took the form of a question and answer session on Northern Ireland. It wasn't a manifestation of the legendary 'trickiness' of Philadelphia lawyers. It was a demonstration of unaffected interest in their country of origin. Both during the lengthy exchange, which went on for the best part of three hours, and at a hospitable lunch afterwards, I would estimate that questions to me about the Irish situation outweighed those from me about the American one by a ratio of some 10 to 1. Some of Philadelphia's most prominent citizens had gathered for the occasion and from the impression conveyed by the level of interest and knowledge displayed in their questioning, they could easily have passed as a group of Belfast professionals, were it not for their accents.

Back in Ireland there was an election campaign in progress, and they bemoaned the lack of an electoral pact between Sinn Fein and the SDLP which was resulting in a splitting of the Nationalist vote. Another cause of concern echoed a common theme amongst the Irish American community right across the States, the 'insulting attitude' of the Dublin Government. Shortly beforehand, an Irish Cabinet member had spoken about people in America being out of touch and having a romantic view of Sinn Fein. I marvelled, not for the first time, despite the evident involvement of the Irish Americans in the Northern issue, their frequent use of fax, telephone and e-mail to say nothing of constant visiting, at how persistent this sort of attitude is in Dublin.

Philadelphia is a stronghold of the Democrats, but this is not the norm nowadays for the Irish. For, as the numbers of Irish lawyers, bankers, and doctors increased, so did the numbers voting Republican, particularly under Ronald Reagan. The knowledgeable Adrian Flannelly painted me a cynical-sounding but accurate picture of how some emigrants can switch from the traditional Irish political allegiances, while at the same time developing an increased consciousness of being Irish:

> He gets a job, a green card, and then a wife and kids. Ten years down the road, since he emigrated, he rediscovers Ireland, through the music, a play perhaps, whatever. So he started out as a bus driver. Now he cashes in his entitlements. He buys a bar. Now he doesn't feel too happy about Donnelly visas and Morrison visas, and so forth, making his staff dearer. He was better off giving out about 'Terrorists' and employing illegals that couldn't talk back to him.[47]

Upward mobility has taken its toll. By the time the *New York Times* made its comment about the increasing number of Irish stockbrokers, New York had lost much of its Irish population, either to the suburbs or to other parts of America. Famous New York districts such as the Bronx, Inwood, Western Manhattan, or the legendary Hell's Kitchen, which once housed the infamous Irish 'Westies' gang, had lost much of their Irish population to Asians, Hispanics and blacks. By the 1990s, one looked for the Irish mainly in pockets like Woodside in Queen's, Bay Ridge in Brooklyn and Norwood in the Bronx.

Despite the flood of undocumented illegals who poured into New York from Ireland during the 1980s, the number of people claiming Irish ancestry in New York fell between 1980 and 1990 by 111,000, and most observers believe that it is still falling.

The flight to the suburbs was in part responsible for the Boston bussing crisis. In part this was also due to the tide of civil rights legislation flowing through America's cities and states, generated to no small degree by the support of Catholic Irish Americans, some with impeccable Bostonian credentials, like the Kennedys. The National Association for the Advancement of Coloured People (NAACP) demanded that the *de facto* segregation of Boston public schools be addressed. The Boston Irish, particularly in the South Boston district, resented the imputation of racism and pointed out that, as the Chairwoman of the Boston School Committee, Louise Day Hicks constantly argued, blacks lived in black districts, whites in white, and therefore each race sent its children to the nearest school. However, under the Racial Imbalance Act of August 1965, passed by the Massachusetts State Legislator, Boston schools failed the test that any school with more than 50 per cent black was imbalanced.

In Boston's inner city, the bulk of black students attended schools that were at least 70 per cent black, and over 80 per cent of the children in white schools were white. In the affluent suburbs and in rural parts of the State, where only small numbers of blacks lived, no such difficulties arose, and blue-collar Irish American neighbourhoods, like South Boston, felt that they were being used as laboratories for experiments carried out by wealthy professional legislators who did not have to confront the problems of unemployment, or lack of promotion in public service jobs such as the police and the fire service, because of affirmative action. The inhabitants of the poor white ghettos wanted to know why they did not get the same attention that the blacks were receiving. In a nutshell the attitudes of the mid-1970s were very much those of the mid-1850s.

Under pressure from the NAACP, it was finally decided to bus students from white to black schools and vice versa. The flashpoint court ruling came on 21 June 1974, from Judge Arthur Garrity who, as embittered 'Southies' were fond of pointing out, sent his own children to expensive private schools. The resultant troubles were to last for over a dozen years. Amongst the many lasting images of violence and racial hatred are the TV pictures of a mob attacking Senator Ted Kennedy as he pleaded outside City Hall for an end to segregation. During the crisis, as Lawrence McCaffrey has observed:

> ... television viewers all over the United States and in Europe saw angry Irish faces and heard hate-filled Irish voices shouting obscenities and racial insults at frightened African American teenagers exiting buses that had transported them from the South End and Roxbury to schools in Charleston and South Boston. They also observed Irish gangs assaulting blacks and lines of Irish women marching with religious banners, praying the rosary, and beseeching the Blessed Virgin to protect their neighbourhoods from African Americans.[48]

The Irish, however, saw themselves caught in a struggle for basic survival in which they were opposed by outside experts of all sorts, who knew nothing about their tightly knit community history. Worse, they had no friends in the media, and their clergy and political representatives had turned against them in a universal portrayal of the South Boston Irish as the thugs and harridans who shouted insults and threw stones at black children as they entered school to commence their own battle for survival.

One of the Irish leaders who spoke of the 'despair' and the disillusionment which afflicted the South Bostonians because they could no longer 'control' their own lives or make their own decisions was State Senator William Bulger. Bulger said of South Boston:

> The strength that we had in that place was the stability of the family and the community. And the community can't exist very long if its institutions, especially the schools, are being dismantled. As a parent, I felt it was the natural right of the parent to make these decisions.[49]

Bulger went on to become one of the most successful State Senate Presidents in Massachusetts' history. In 1990, it was thought that he faced his strongest challenge to date for the office, but South Boston gave him a 2 to 1 majority over his Republican opponent. That result was rooted in the bussing crisis, Bulger's strong Irish identity, and his equally strong tradition of doing as his hero, James Michael Curley, had done, looking after his own. His first act on the night of his victory was to go to the Bayside Club and sing 'The Bold O'Donoghue', about a legendary Irish outlaw in the Australian outback.

As indicated earlier, Bulger himself has connections to another legendary outlaw, his brother Whitey for whose arrest the FBI offered a reward of $1 million in 2000. Like Billy Bulger himself, the Bayside Club and the annual St Patrick's Day Roast, Whitey Bulger forms part of an Irish American tradition which both exemplifies and explains how the Irish both defended and climbed out of their ghettos with the help of figures like William McMullen and James Michael Curley.

Billy Bulger is one of the most intelligent, likeable, literate and compassionate people I have encountered in American public life. Yet, a critic of his once wrote the following:

> I love a good fight. And in the 27 years since I moved from Brooklyn, New York, to Cambridge, I've had more than my share of them. I've argued cases and causes in the Soviet Union, in Poland, in China, in the Middle East, in the deep South . . . Wishing to oppose mediocre, reactionary, and nepotistic judicial nominations by both Democratic and Republican presidents, most recently that of George Bush's first cousin, whom the President put on the United States Court of Appeals in New York.
>
> But until last December, I had never ventured into my own State House to battle with local barons, dukes, and tribal leaders. What I learned is that the Massachusetts State House Patronage Game can be more underhanded, more *ad hominem*, more tribal, and more dangerous than taking on the KGB. Nothing in my experience prepared me for the rough-and-tumble of Billy Bulger's feudal turf protection.[50]

Praise indeed! However, if one drives around South Boston with Billy Bulger, a different image appears. He is hailed in the street. In a restaurant it takes him thirty minutes to drink a cup of coffee because of the number of people who come up to him. Even though he had left politics to become President of Massachusetts State University, it was obvious that in South Boston, in the year of our Lord 1998, Billy Bulger was still a cult figure. As a boy, Bulger had two heroes, Demosthenes and James Michael Curley. From the one he studied oratory, the other politics. He is in part borne down by what bears him up: his family, his South Boston support, his entire tradition. Bulger had the ability to make an impact on national politics, but with Whitey in the family, there could be no question of his even attempting a run for the White House. Whitey apart, bussing turned Bulger into one of the liberals' resident hate figures on the American political landscape. Bulger himself says that his darkest moment came when bussing began in 1974, and he stood outside the school that he had himself attended as a boy, watching federal authorities coming and going:

> I was standing there with all these people I knew, watching helplessly as these federal people ran in and out of the school I went to, wearing war helmets. It was quite over-whelming. 'Gosh, what are we ever going to do about this?' I just had no answer for anyone, including myself. It was a black day. There were worse days, but none affected me so personally as that. It was my school as a kid.[51]

But for those who supported bussing, the abiding image of Bulger is of him standing face to face with Police Commissioner Robert di Grazia outside South Boston High School, telling the Commissioner to 'Go fuck yourself.'

That's not how The Beam normally reacts to pressure. Bulger was nick-name 'The Beam' because as a boy he studied so hard that his bedroom light bulb shone late into the night. He was a perfect son, one of nine children, to his parents James Joseph and Jane. His father lost an arm in a railway accident and the family were reared in a housing project. His parents were still remembered with respect in the district. Both were classical Irish types, the father, humorous, literate, a supporter of the New Deal, Mayor Curley and 'the books'; the mother, devout, cheerful, totally devoted to her family and community. Billy funded his school career through scholarships. His speech is peppered with quotations from everyone from Demosthenes to Pericles, to Seneca, to Francis Bacon, to James Michael Curley.

Bulger first indicated to his teacher, Father Karl Thayer, during a Greek class in 1952 that, as the Jesuit would say later, he was to become 'a leader of men'. Thayer had set his class the task of delivering a five-minute oration in the style of Demosthenes who, having been accused of wrong-doing, drove his accuser into exile with a famous defence which drew on the tenets of Athenian democracy. Bulger instead took fifty minutes to deliver a Demosthenic defence of Curley, who had recently served a prison sentence for using his position to line his pockets. Despite the length of his oration, Bulger's classmates, most of them like Bulger himself from working-class districts of Boston which regarded Curley as a hero with a cornucopia, rose to their feet to give him a standing ovation.

Bulger subsequently used the GI Bill of Rights to study the Greek language, English literature, and to become a lawyer at Boston College. His study of Curley was probably his most valuable political course. Despite a hostile media which increasingly turned on him after the bussing crisis, his membership of the Senate was crowned by becoming Senate President in 1978. He was classically Irish Conservative on social issues, but the purse strings were opened automatically where the poor were concerned. If asked about his social policy he is apt to smile and quote from John Boyle O'Reilly's 'In Bohemia', in condemnation of 'organised charity':

> The vulgar sham of the pompous feast
> Where the heaviest purse is the highest priest;
> The organised charity, scrimped and iced,
> In the name of a cautious, statistical Christ.

A quiet, private man, Bulger undergoes a Curleyesque sea change when he stands before a microphone. His critics describe him as an urban populist, a past master of the black arts of the smoke-filled back room, whom one crosses at one's peril. His defenders point to his championship of the arts and education, to his compassion for elderly constituents.

While Bulger was preparing himself for the State Presidency, his brother James, nicknamed 'Whitey' because of his blond hair, was launching himself into a career of violence and crime that eventually led him to Alcatraz prison. In jail, he too studied. His reading generally consisted of military strategy and the history of wars and battles. Whitey had a habit of not merely reading about a war from one side, but of seeing what the opposing generals had to say. He used this knowledge in a number of ways: partly to become one of America's most wanted criminals; partly to stay out of jail – he never served a day in prison after leaving Alcatraz in the mid-1960s – and partly to play one law enforcement agency off against another.

The history of the FBI's attempts to trap Whitey Bulger is one long story of mortification. Bugs in his car and his home were mysteriously discovered. Raids on a known Bulger hideout would net prominent associates, but never Whitey. Eventually, the *Boston Globe* established that Whitey was a long-time FBI informant. But no one has ever satisfactorily established whether or not the FBI were also informing him of efforts to trap him.

His career is the direct antithesis of his brother's. Billy married his childhood sweetheart Mary and became a model husband and father to their nine children. Whitey developed a reputation as a mean street fighter, a womaniser and an enforcer for Boston's powerful Killeen gang. He shot up through the ranks of the organisation after Donnie Killeen left his four-year-old son's birthday party in answer to a mysterious phone call, only to die at the hands of an unknown assassin as he started up his car. Whitey subsequently came to be regarded as one of the crime lords of Boston.

A devoted family man, Billy is known to have been deeply saddened by his brother's activities, but blood is thicker than water and Whitey was a regular visitor to his home, and a well-loved uncle in the eyes of his children.

The muscle, or 'McMullen', part of the Bulger myth interacted with the Samaritan side of Billy Bulger's public life to create a political reality. Even if Billy did not have superlative political skills, the fact that his brother might, just might, be lying somewhere in the long grass, served to create a certain, shall we say, circumspection in the minds of opponents. In fact, the only time that Whitey seems to have used his muscle politically was during the bussing crisis, and he used it benignly. He passed the word to his associates that he wanted trouble kept to a minimum. It is said that the reason that Southie was safe from street crime, rape or muggings, although drugs proliferated, was because of Whitey's influence. Federal state and local authorities vainly tried to arrest him on suspicion of various crimes, but Whitey Bulger is remembered in South Boston for things like giving a puppy to a little boy whose dog had been run over.

In the project where Whitey grew up, the Mary Ellen McCormack Development, there is a Veterans' Park. The park fell into disrepair and in order to raise funds to renovate it, a committee offered commemorative bricks at $50 each. The $50 entitled people to inscribe a loved one's name on the brick. A group of elderly women got together and contributed $5 each to etch Whitey Bulger's name. One old lady explained that as a boy, Whitey was always polite, particularly to the elderly, and he kept hooliganism in check. 'If he saw you with your groceries, he'd take them and carry them in the house for you.' By that time, 12 October 1996, Whitey had already been on the run for two years. His famous intelligence service had warned him just before he was indicted for racketeering.

The old lady would have wholeheartedly agreed with the central point which Billy made about his brother in an interview:

A: He was always a very good brother, and cared very much for his brothers and sisters. He was always very devoted to his mother, and generally, whatever the rockiness was . . . occurred outside.
Q: Outside the family, outside the neighbourhood?
A: When he'd be in any kind of difficulty, it would be outside.[52]

In South Boston, as elsewhere in the Irish diaspora, what one does outside one's community is outweighed by how one performs within it. The Irish look after their own.

Billy Bulger retired in 1996 to become President of Massachusetts State University. Some say that Whitey is now in the Federal Witness Protection

Programme. The roast is no more, and the city is the poorer for its passing. It was the real last hurrah, a slice of Irish American political, religious and sociological experience that will not be seen again – neither, it seems will bussing controversies. At the time of writing the practice has generally been abandoned throughout the United States, including South Boston.

THE CHURCH

'No nation contributed as much as Ireland to the vast expansion of the Catholic Church in the United States of America in the nineteenth century.'[53] This is a factual statement not intended to detract in any way from the contribution of the French, who preceded the Irish immigrants, the Germans who arrived concurrently, nor of the French Canadians and Italians who arrived later in the century.

The first Irish priest was Father Richard Arthur, pastor of St Augustine, Florida, who landed in 1597 from a Spanish ship. The first Federal census of America was conducted in 1790 and the growth of the Church in the years which had intervened from the time of Father Arthur's arrival were calculated from the census by America's first Catholic bishop, John Carroll. Carroll reckoned that there were some 150,000 people of Irish ancestry, 44,000 of whom had been born in Ireland. Amongst these were some 35,000 Catholics out of a total population of 3 million.

Carroll was a member of the leading Irish Catholic family of the colonial period. The Carrolls had come to Maryland in 1688 and, despite the anti-Catholic temper of the times, held great estates and took a leading part in public life. Charles Carroll, of Carrolltown (the Carrolls named their properties after their estates in Ireland) was the only Catholic signatory to the Declaration of Independence. Had George Washington not decided to run for a second term, Charles would have achieved far greater fame. He would have anticipated John Fitzgerald Kennedy by 169 years in becoming the first Catholic President of the United States, for in 1792 there was an expectation that Washington, who was not in good health, did not intend to run again. Had he not done so, the Federalists had selected Carroll as his replacement.

A cousin, Daniel Carroll, became a delegate to the Constitutional Convention, and it was another cousin, John, who became the first Catholic bishop of the United States. In 1785, he became Prefect Apostolic to the American Church. His influence laid the foundations for the emergence of Baltimore as the intellectual, and indeed political, centre of the Roman Catholic Church in America under Cardinal John Gibbons and his ally, Archbishop John Ireland of St Paul, Minnesota. Between the time of Carroll and Gibbons, the Catholic population of America went up to over 6 million, led by a largely Irish hierarchy.

The Church had performed prodigies in the building of churches, schools, hospitals, the organisation of new parishes and the training of priests and nuns. In the cities, particularly in New York, the Church was very much what it was back in Ireland, albeit richer. In the enclosed Catholic ghettos, a bishop or a parish priest had all the power. The bishop was the boss to a degree not easily understood in these more secular times. Someone who today, let us say, had the American franchise for Toyota cars coupled with the political power of a State governor, counted for little alongside someone who had the agency which controlled sexual relationships, morality, education and entry to the next world.

The cement which bound all these activities together was the inculcation of a sense of guilt and sin. Catholics were taught according to a primer of the time that by sinning one gave:

> the death-blow to your immortal soul; you have drawn down upon yourself the anger and punishment of the living God, a God who in his just vengeance is awful and terrible; that he it is who cast forever into hell the holy angels when they first rebelled against him; that, alas! many of the damned who are now groaning in the eternal pains of hell, have not committed so great and so many sins as you.[54]

Such doctrines were earnestly promulgated by Archbishop John Hughes of New York, Cardinal McCluskey, who succeeded him, Archbishop Corrigan who came after McCluskey and Bishop Bernard McQuaid of Rochester. These men could well be thought of as bosses in very much the same sense as were the chieftains of Tammany. Hughes in fact described himself as being both Bishop and Chief, and he applied his chieftainship with an equally heavy hand to all the Catholics under his control, be they French, German or Italian. He said openly that he had made war, and successful war at that, on lay trustees within the Church: 'Episcopal authority came from above, and not from below, and Catholics did their duty when they obeyed their bishop.'[55]

This spirit had not entirely died out at the time of writing. I was taking part in an interview with Adrian Flannelly on his popular Saturday morning radio programme in New York when he was called away to an urgent telephone call. He whispered to me to keep talking, and then came back looking somewhat stressed. The call had been from what he described as 'a legal eagle' on behalf of the Archdiocese of New York, threatening fire and sword because Adrian had been adjudged not to have given sufficient publicity to the candidate supported by the Archdiocese in a contemporary election.

During Hughes's episcopacy (1838–64) there was some concern amongst Catholic intellectuals about how the Church should relate to American society. Orestes Brownson, a Protestant intellectual who had converted to Catholicism before the Civil War, had anticipated the problems which would be created for American society and the Church if an Irish-driven hierarchy insisted on regarding Boston and New York as the next parishes to the Aran Islands. However, the ante-bellum New York archepiscopacy saw such ideas not as topics of legitimate debate, but as a *casus belli*. When the Catholic intellectual, Thomas D'Arcy McGee, tried to develop Brownson-type arguments with a view to bringing Irish Catholics into the American mainstream, he was run out of town. The persistent view was that expressed by Hughes when his priests sought more freedoms: '. . . he would teach them Monaghan canon law; he would send them back to the bogs whence they came'.[56]

As went the Church in New York, so to a large extent did the Church of America. Conservatism struck deep roots. In Boston for example, Cardinal William 'Gang plank Bill' O'Connell ruled for almost forty years from 1906. During those formative decades he lived an opulent life, cut off from the concerns of ordinary workers, consorting only with the rich and powerful. O'Connell once worked for a brief interlude in a factory and fled within hours from the slave conditions of child labour. Unlike the other 12-year-old wage slaves, the future cardinal was able to return to a wealthy family. However, despite the fact that he often spoke of the horror of his brief brush with child exploitation, O'Connell's ties with the rich became such that, in 1924, he joined with the rest of the hierarchy in condemning a proposed amendment to the US Constitution banning child labour. O'Connell said the proposal was: 'Socialistic, as it puts the state above the parents'. Like many such misdirected broadsides, the real target of the Church was the spectre that State intervention in any field might somehow diminish Church control. His narrow interpretation of the censorship laws meant that the term 'Banned in Boston' became affixed to nearly every work of worthwhile literature produced during his era.

His successor, Richard Cushing (1895–1970), a more attractive character personally, was destined to become one of the legendary figures of the contemporary Irish American Church. According to an oft-told anecdote of his, he was standing in a wagon haranguing a crowd to vote for a friend when his parish priest suddenly hauled him down and, kicking him hard in the backside, roared: 'Make up your mind; either you're going to be a priest or a politician.' Cushing said that he decided to become a priest so that he could be both!

He was as good as his word. Hubert Humphrey also frequently told an anecdote about a courtesy call he paid to Cushing in which he learned how he came to be defeated by John F. Kennedy in the crucial 1960 West Virginia primary. Cushing said: 'I'll tell you who elected Jack Kennedy. It was his father Joe and me, right here in this room.' Cushing had advised Joe Kennedy which Virginian Protestant ministers (Virginia is overwhelmingly Protestant) were to receive 'contributions' which sometimes amounted to $500. Cushing explained his rationale to Humphrey: 'It's good for the Lord. It's good for the Church. It's good for the preacher – and it's good for the candidate!'

Cushing, the son of a County Cork blacksmith, became famous as a mega-buck fund-raiser who moved from a youthful position of extreme Con-servatism to one of an unprecedented ecumenism. He preached in Jewish synagogues and Masonic temples, and once instructed his flock: 'When a Catholic fails to take a stand against racial prejudice or intolerance, he is a slacker in the army of the Church militant.' He made his most profound impact on the American public through his association with the Kennedy family, with whom he maintained cordial relations all his working life – it was he who saved Ted Kennedy from excommunication after he divorced – officiating both at their marriages and funerals. Many people forgave him the overly long invocation he delivered at Kennedy's inauguration as President when, just under three years later, he broke down during the President's funeral mass, in the midst of entreating the angels to carry Jack to heaven.

Irish American Catholicism should not be thought of as unrelentingly conservative. Cardinal Gibbons of Baltimore, the first Irish cardinal, a skilled diplomat and an approachable human sort of man who enjoyed a game of cards or a good cigar, was in favour of the Brownson-McGee approach. He and his close friend Archbishop Ireland of Minnesota operated almost literally on the frontiers of America, and in a situation in which Catholics were in a minority. Even had they wished to, they could not have swung their croziers with the ruthless abandon of their New York colleagues. Gibbons and Ireland wanted to develop a type of Catholicism suited to the evolving American society. They saw no merit in trying to replicate the structures, and strictures, of the old world in the new. However, the New York school tried to keep Catholics from mixing with non-Catholics, and were not comfortable with the laity starting up organisations of their own, even fraternal ones like the Ancient Order of Hibernians.

The Gibbons-Ireland school of thought was clearly seen in contra-distinction to that of the conservative New York faction of Corrigan and McQuaid in the Father Edward McGlynn case. Gibbons was a supporter of the workers' right to organise unions, he condemned child labour and observed once that 'one sanctimonious miserly millionaire' did more harm to Christianity than a dozen cases of burglary or drunkenness. Gibbons was a champion of the working man throughout his life. His New York colleague, Archbishop Corrigan, however, excommunicated Father McGlynn for the socialist tendency displayed in supporting the single tax plan of the reformer, Henry George. McGlynn was later reinstated after Pope Leo XIII had published his encyclical *Rerum Novarum*. The controversy was not only dramatic in itself but it marked a point at which the Church did make a perceptible shift towards the concept of improving society through social reform rather than by charitable works and alms giving – but only a shift.

Gibbons was again to the fore in a major controversy involving the Knights of Labour which was America's first coast to coast trade union movement. The fact that it was led by an Irish Catholic, Terence Powderly, did not endear it to the conservative wing of the Church. The Canadian Archbishop of Quebec, Dr Taschereau, obtained a ruling from Rome condemning the union in Canada, and Archbishop Corrigan sought to have the ban replicated in America. However, Gibbons opposed him, pointing out that there were half a million Catholics in the Knights and that labour had rights as well as capital. He commented: 'To lose the heart of the people would be a misfortune, for which the friendship of the few rich and powerful would be no compensation.'[57] Backed by his friend Ireland and Bishop Keane of Richmond, Gibbons lobbied his contacts throughout the world church to enlist the support of the Vatican to prevent the condemnation.

Eventually Pope Leo who, as *Rerum Novarum* indicated, was sympathetic to the working man, supported Gibbon's contention that a condemnation would cause the American working class to look upon their hierarchy 'with as much hatred and suspicion as they do in the Church of France'. So, through the leadership of Cardinal James Gibbons, and the example of the individual nuns and clergy who went down into the stinking tenements of the new world, the old Irish identity between the priest and the people was preserved.

Nationalism and an affinity with Labour combined in the person of Father Peter Yorke, who was famous for his campaigns against the American Protective Association, and in favour of organised labour in the San Francisco area. He became Vice-president of Sinn Fein in the United States, and was one of the principal figures in the struggle for the recognition of an Irish Republic in 1921. A contemporary Labour priest is Monsignor Charles Rice, a veteran civil rights activist who marched alongside Luther King and Dr Spock on the Pentagon in the major anti-Vietnam incident of 1967. Rice, inspired by the ideas of Dorothy Day of the Catholic Worker Movement, first appeared on a picket line supporting workers at Heinz Foods in 1930, and was one of the moving spirits behind the formation of the CIO, at whose first National Convention in 1938 he gave the invocation. At the time of writing, Charles Rice was still turning out a column for the *Pittsburgh Catholic* that he first began writing sixty years ago. The only time he missed a column was when a hostile bishop transferred him to a remote parish for his activities on a picket line, and dropped the column – but Rice outlived the bishop, and a successor, Bishop, later Cardinal, John Wright, brought him back.

In his lifetime Father Rice has seen the Church grow in strength. The visible signs are everywhere: the convent school girls in their neat uniforms marching under the banners of St Theresa's or St Brigid's in the St Patrick's Day processions across the nation; the Irish graduates moving up the social scale because of the Catholic school network; the multiplying church spires which proclaim not only here be Catholics but here be Irish.

However, behind the façade of power, there were deep uncertainties. The candidacy of the Catholic Al Smith had gone down in flames in the presidential election of 1928. To Irish American eyes, nativism appeared to have bared its teeth once more. The great crash of 1929 followed, leading to the bleak years of depression. All these forces ushered Father Charles Coughlin on stage. Coughlin, the 'radio priest', was the first great 'shock jock' of the century. At the height of his popularity in the mid thirties, his audience is estimated as having been some 40 million listeners. His impact in this pre-television age was colossal. When he preached, his church, the Shrine of the

Little Flower on Woodward Avenue, Detroit, was filled to overflowing to such a degree that crowds of up to 25,000 people were recorded standing outside. As the Depression bit, Coughlin's talks, which had commenced in 1926, switched to embrace political themes. He attacked Communism, and capitalism with equal facility.

As hubris took hold, Coughlin switched from being a supporter of Roosevelt and the New Deal to being one of the President's most bitter critics. His populism, which in its own way could be seen as a forerunner of McCarthyism twenty years later, took on an increasingly disturbing tone as the sky darkened over Europe. Coughlin developed a nasty strain of anti-Semitism and became loud in his praise of both Hitler and Mussolini. As an Irish Catholic priest, Coughlin was listened to with respect by Irish American Catholics, many of whom were suffering from the effects of the Depression. Encouraged by their clergy to keep their distance from non-Catholics at the best of times, in these for many the worst of times, attacks on Jewish control of Wall Street had a widespread appeal. Caught up in the perennial struggle within the Irish soul of seeking respectability, while at the same time leaning towards the radical and the rebellious, Irish American Catholics felt drawn to a figure who had attained that pinnacle of respectability, the Catholic priesthood, and was at the same time an outspoken rebel.

Coughlin's Ordinary, Bishop Gallagher, who had supported him, died in 1937. His successor, Archbishop (and subsequently Cardinal) Mooney, was not a supporter, but, mindful of Coughlin's following and the hornets' nest stirred up by the hierarchy's silencing of Father McGlynn, Mooney hesitated to confront Coughlin until America entered the Second World War. By then Coughlin's popularity had ebbed. He had founded a political party, the Union Party, which had been decimated in the 1936 presidential election and his radio audiences dwindled. Nevertheless, he managed to resist Archbishop Mooney's efforts to get control of his considerable wealth and of his journal, *Social Justice*, by putting frontmen in positions of nominal control. When America entered the war, however, the Justice Department complained to the Archbishop that *Social Justice* was reprinting Nazi propaganda. Mooney finally moved to silence Coughlin, but he was allowed to continue in charge of the Little Flower parish until his retirement in 1964. He died largely a forgotten man in 1979.

One Irish Catholic cleric who did not hesitate to confront Coughlin was a protégé of Archbishops Ireland and Gibbons, Monsignor John Ryan. Ryan's writings and his belief in social reform by legislation brought him to Roosevelt's attention. The President invited Ryan to pronounce the benediction at his inauguration, the first time that a Catholic priest had participated in the ceremony. Ryan, a professor at Catholic University, Washington, confronted Coughlin at every turn. He pointed out the fallacies of his economic doctrines, attacked his anti-Semitism, and bluntly accused him of lying in a famous radio address which he made on behalf of the Democratic National Committee during the 1936 presidential campaign.

Ryan was subsequently appointed a member of Roosevelt's three-man Board of Appeals for the National Recovery Administration.

Coughlinism surfaced again in the brief but ugly emergence of Senator Joe McCarthy with his witch-hunting campaigns of the early 1950s. Irish American Catholics' support for McCarthy stemmed in part from the cultural and intellectual isolation which their Church had furthered, and in part from memories of past discrimination which left many in the Irish community with a conviction that the Irish had a unique role to play through their religion in the struggle against Communism, a struggle in which Jews, liberals and Protestants could not be trusted. During the year in which he was ultimately to be destroyed by the Senate, McCarthy received endorsements from a number of leading Irish Americans and Irish American organisations. He was the featured speaker at the Emerald Society communion breakfast attended by 6,000 Catholic members of the New York City Police Force, at which Cardinal Spellman openly applauded him and shook hands with him, to the accompaniment of loud cheering from the assembled police. At a dinner in Chicago on St Patrick's Day, he was introduced as the man who typified the spirit of the American Irish.

However, other Irish Church leaders took a more honourable position. Bishop Bernard Shiel drove some of the most damaging nails into the coffin of McCarthy's reputation, countering Spellman's support in the same week as the communion breakfast, by pointing out that:

the Church does take a position on lies, calumny, the absence of charity, and calculated deceit. These things are wrong – even if they are mistakenly thought of as means to a good end. They are morally evil and to call them good or to act as if they were permissible under certain circumstances is itself a monstrous perversion of morality. They are not justified by any cause – least of all by the cause of anti-Communism which should unite rather than divide all of us in these difficult times.[58]

The Gibbons-Ireland tradition was still alive. However, two cardinals of Irish background did what they could to kill it off. These were Cody of Chicago and Spellman of New York. Cardinal John Patrick Cody of Chicago (1907–1982) was one of the most controversial members of the American hierarchy. Yet, in the early 1960s, he became the darling of the liberals, when he enforced integration in parochial schools in New Orleans in his capacity as coadjutor bishop to the ailing Joseph Frances Rummell. He succeeded Rummell as Archbishop in 1964 and continued on a liberal path, launching an inter-faith organisation, Operation Understanding, which invited non-Catholics into Roman Catholic churches.

He was appointed Archbishop of Chicago in 1966, and was literally welcomed by a fanfare of trumpets at Holy Name Cathedral, after arriving in Chicago aboard his own special train of seven coaches and accompanied by a retinue that included ninety-six priests. However, the trumpets began falling silent within a year of his installation. Both blacks and liberals found him cold and autocratic, and a $250 million fund-raising campaign which he launched soon ran into trouble. Worshippers walked out of Holy Name Cathedral on Christmas Eve 1969, as Cody, who had not long been appointed a cardinal, was celebrating midnight mass, in protest at 'pompous spending'.

The noted author and sociologist, Father Andrew Greeley, became one of his most prominent critics, charging that only the early deaths of both Popes Paul VI and John Paul I had prevented their removing him from Chicago. Cody and his diocesan supporters dismissed Greeley's charges and it appeared that the Cardinal was in fact favoured in the eyes of the Vatican when Pope John Paul II stood beside him in Chicago's Grant Park, co-celebrating mass with him during the Pope's tour of America in 1980.

It proved less easy to turn a deaf ear to Greeley's charges when, in September 1981 the *Chicago Sun Times* ran a series of articles alleging that Cody had diverted a million dollars in tax exempt church funds to Helen Dolan Wilson, a lifelong woman friend, a married woman who was seventy-four at the time of the disclosures. The newspaper also reported that a Federal Grand Jury in Chicago, having investigated these allegations, had issued subpoenas both for the Cardinal's personal banking records and the accounts of the Chicago Archdiocese. However, before the matter could be thrashed out in court, Cody, who during his last twenty years had been plagued by diabetes and heart problems, died on 25 April 1982.

There had been seven coaches in the train which first brought him to Chicago as Archbishop, and ninety-six priests. Now, at his funeral mass, the changing times for Chicago and the American Church were reflected in the fact that the entire graduating class of the St Mary of the Lake Seminary acted as the Cardinal's pall-bearers. There were only seven young deacons, the smallest graduating class in Chicago's Archdiocesan history.

Cardinal Spellman, who ruled New York from 1939 to 1968, was a noted fund-raiser, and one of the most political figures in Irish American Church history. He sought to extend Catholic censorship to films and campaigned for more money for Catholic schools. Continuing the Hughes tradition, he closely identified himself with the police and the Army. The Pope, it was noted, was known as the 'vicar of Christ', but Spellman was described as 'the military vicar'. He had considerable clout in Washington, where he won particular favour from Lyndon Johnson because of his support for the Vietnam War. Apart from his support for McCarthy, Spellman demonstrated the familiar illiberal attitude of many Irish American clerics by criticising the reforms of Vatican II. Part of Spellman's antipathy towards Roman policies may have been generated by the fact that in 1957 the Vatican split the New York Archdiocese in two; Brooklyn and Long Island became a new diocese in its own right. Born to Irish parents, he made no particular point about his Irishness. Power, not the Irish, was what interested him most. However, under him, the Irish continued to have a dominant role in the Brooklyn Archdiocese. But after Spellman died, the Vatican pointedly appointed an Italian to head the new diocese, the first time an Italian

American had intruded on turf hitherto sacrosanct to the Irish.

Spellman's successor, Terence Cooke, found himself at odds with sections of the Irish American community in 1983 when he refused to meet the St Patrick's Day Parade Grand Marshal, Michael Flannery, on the steps of St Patrick's Cathedral. Flannery was a life-long Republican, a supporter of the IRA, and a founder member of NORAID. Cooke was supported in his attitude by the Dublin Government, who instructed the Irish Ambassador, Sean Donlon, to step down from the podium whenever a NORAID contingent passed. Prominent New York politicians, Governor Hugh Carey and Senator Patrick Moynihan, also boycotted the parade.

Cooke died the following year and was succeeded by the late Archbishop John O'Connor (his funeral took place on May 8th 2000). O'Connor took a less confrontational attitude towards Flannery, a highly popular and respected member of the New York Irish American community. O'Connor acknowledged Flannery as he proceeded up the aisle to say mass on St Patrick's Day, and he later visited the IRA prisoner, Joe Doherty, in jail. O'Connor's more inclusive public attitude was mirrored by his private interest in the Irish situation. He kept close personal contact both north and south of the border, sending representatives to Ireland on fact-finding missions at regular intervals each year, and was a close personal friend of Bill Flynn, one of the principal Irish American architects of the Peace Process.

However, under O'Connor the Irish American grip on the Church was loosened. O'Connor himself, an ex-Marine, was a strong figure in the Conservative mould, but demographic changes and an influx of Hispanics (some 40 per cent of New York's Catholics are said to be Hispanic at the time of writing) reduced the Cardinal's clout. He lost a celebrated battle against the New York City Board of Education after the Board decided against his wishes to distribute condoms to students as part of the war against AIDS – in which, let it be said, O'Connor saw to it that the Archdiocese plays an important role through its health and counselling programmes.

Although incredibly wealthy, and still powerful, in some ways the contemporary Irish American Church reminds me of Bennett Cerf's famous definition of 'conflicting emotions'. It was, he said, 'like watching your mother-in-law back your new Cadillac over a cliff'. Falling vocations, and changing attitudes amongst the laity on issues like abortion, contraception, married clergy, and women priests, have all contributed to a decline in clerical authority. As Dr Mary Guinan, an Irishwoman who, significantly, was one of the team that first identified Aids in 1981, remarked to me in Atlanta one day her experience was that: 'Catholics have abortions, divorces and practise birth control in the same proportions as do Protestants.'[59]

They also have to contend with other human problems such as paedophilia. I got a disturbing perspective on this scourge talking to Father Colm Campbell from Belfast, one of the best-known Irish priests in New York. At the time Father Campbell ran a series of programmes for the Irish Apostolate, an offshoot of the Irish Episcopal Chaplaincy. 'Programmes' is a denatured way of saying that Father Campbell was the man most emigrants turned to when troubles befell them, but on top of these multiple duties he also ran a counselling programme for paedophile priests in the Archdioceses of Brooklyn and New York. I had heard it said that recidivism amongst paedophiles was far higher than people wished to acknowledge, or believe. When I asked him what he thought the percentage of reoffence was, he shook his head gloomily. 'It's high, very high. Some say that it can go as high as 100 per cent.' He paused for a moment and went on: 'They say, you know, that the urge is nine times that of the alcoholic . . .'

As Father Campbell and I chewed our hamburgers in the mundane setting of an Irish bar in Lexington Avenue, I felt for a moment that a curtain had been drawn back on a vista of lives lived in a welter of hell and hypocrisy because of some ghastly genetic implant.

The 1960s emigrants were very much in the old straight-arrow Irish mould, conservative and hard-working. However, the 1980s crop tended to sport long hair, smoke marijuana, drink, get into fights and generally behave like the 1980s generation in Ireland. This resulted in a culture shock for the 1960s group who initially stretched out a welcoming, networking hand to their younger fellow emigrants. The hand was speedily withdrawn when the new generation was perceived to be 'letting down the Irish'. Many an anonymous phone call to the FBI or the Emigration Services followed. As a result of the social problems thrown up, the Irish Apostolate followed also. When I met Father Campbell, forty or fifty calls a day for his assistance were not unusual. From his parish, St Theresa's in Sunnyside, Queens, he ran everything from welfare services to mother and baby groups, to Irish masses, to Irish dancing and language classes. The *Irish Voice* described his activities as an 'irreplaceable part of life for many immigrants'.[60]

The reasons for emigration are varied. Some come simply to better themselves, and with the increasing levels of education in Ireland before they leave, do just that quite easily. Others take the traditional labouring route. In New York for example, the equivalent of McAlpine is the Breslin Company which provides opportunities in construction. At the time of talking to Father Campbell, there was a huge project under way in restoring the subways and one got the impression that every second young Irish labourer was employed on it. Andy Breslin himself was a legendary figure who came to New York as an emigrant at the age of nineteen. A sizeable proportion of young people simply came 'for the craic'. Many of these were inner-city dwellers, or travellers, who had taken advantage of the increased availability of tourist visas to step on a plane with no pre-planning whatever. A third group, which was not quantifiable but was sizeable, consisted of the 'getaway' group who would come to America to get away from abuse in a relationship, or to explore a sexual preference.

Such exploration could be dangerous in New York. Shortly before our talk, a young Irish barman who had taken up with the wife of an imprisoned mafiosa was savagely murdered. His face had been nailed to the floor of a warehouse, and his testicles cut off and placed in his mouth before he was finally killed by a shotgun blast through the head. This obviously was an extreme case, but coping with unexpected death was a familiar ritual for Father Campbell and for the Irish. He found that the traditional 'we're here for each other' syndrome was as strong as ever; it was standard practice to take up a collection in the Irish bars for the widow and family of those bereaved by an accident. By way of illustrating the amounts involved, Father Campbell cited a current case involving a child on a life-support system for whose family $10,000 had been collected without difficulty. Money is also collected without much difficulty when emigrants find themselves facing legal expenses arising from either political or visa problems.

New York is an ever-changing landscape. The once famous Irish ghettos of Jamaica, the Bronx, had emptied of their Irish populations during the sixties and seventies, but the huge wave of renewed emigration in the eighties provided new Irish tenants who now had to move into a largely black or Hispanic neighbourhood, where young men cruised the streets in cars with 'boom boxes' blaring. Rent control meant that accommodation was cheap in these districts, but the environment could be quite hostile – and not merely as between various ethnic groups, but between the Irish themselves. In the Bainbridge and Woodlawn areas, which are heavily Irish districts, there were increasing reports of trouble between the newer illegals and the older established Irish Americans. Ironically, relationships in these districts between the young Irish and the police were so bad as to be a source of concern, a reversal of the times when most of the police would have been Irish.

Father Campbell's own work fell victim to the changing times. It is said that the Brooklyn Archdiocesan Catholic Migration Office took exception to his high profile, and the fact that he had set up Irish Services Inc., a non-profit-making organisation that intended to become a latter-day variant of the Emigrant Savings Bank by setting up a credit union. In the event, having shortly beforehand sponsored him for a green card so that he could continue his work, he was told by the Church authorities that his time was up in St Theresa's, because he had come to the end of his five-year term. Ironically, he transferred (in March 1999) to the old St Patrick's Cathedral in an area which, since Archbishop Hughes's time, has become an Italian and Chinese district. A sign on the local school says it all. It is inscribed in Chinese with an English translation underneath saying: 'St Patrick's School Chinese Enrichment Programme'. New York is in little danger of becoming 'another Moscow' these days, but though Hughes has passed on, his 'Monaghan theology' still lives apparently.

Homosexuality has also brought highly publicised reverses for Church policies, particularly in New York. In 1987, O'Connor ordered that masses for homosexuals be ended. These were being conducted by Jesuits at the Church of St Francis Xavier in Manhattan. Obviously acting in accordance with the Cardinal's wishes, the St Patrick's Day Parade Organising Committee banned the Irish Lesbian and Gay Organisation (ILGO) from marching in the parade in 1991. However, the Cardinal's wishes were flouted when the Manhattan AOH invited the ILGO to march under their banner. Mayor Dinkins, a black, whom Paul O'Dwyer had supported, marched with this section instead of taking the Mayor's normal position at the head of the parade. In a marked departure from the Spellman era, Dinkens also showed himself notably unresponsive to telephone calls from the Archdiocesan office.

The atmosphere which the Gays Shall not March campaign generated on the day was described to me by a leading Irish psychiatrist, Deirdre Mahon. She went to Fifth Avenue, intending to cheer the gay contingent as it passed her vantage point, but, she says, 'I was afraid to open my mouth. The hostility in the crowd was frightening. People were genuinely angry, and they booed and hissed when the gays came by. Most of them weren't New Yorkers at all. They came in from out of town for the protest.'

Some of the least attractive images ever recorded at any St Patrick's Parade anywhere were those of parade stalwarts, in their vaguely comic-opera outfits of top hat and swallow tail, pointing their ponderous posteriors towards the gays, as the ILGO passed the reviewing stand. Their view was summed up by the parade's organiser, Frank Beirne, who said: 'No group that has a position contrary to the teachings of the Catholic faith has a place in our parade.'[61] Beirne told Irish America: 'This is an AOH parade. It is our parade. It is up to us to preserve it, protect it, and turn it over to the next generation, the way it was turned over to us since 1762 – big strong, Irish, Catholic, beautiful and united, all marching to one tune of unity, honouring St Patrick, the glorious apostle of Ireland . . .'

At one stage in 1992, it appeared that the gay issue might result in City Hall banning the Parade altogether, but a Federal Court ruling denied the ILGO's right to march. Though Mayor Dinkins and his officials refused to march in the Parade, his successor, Rudolph Giuliani, took his place in the Parade in 1994. Curiously however, like bussing, once a touchstone for liberals, the issue of gays' right to march is also losing its appeal for Irish liberals. A feeling had taken hold at the time of writing that the issue had been forced by people who had no interest in the Irish or the abstract right to protest, but who were pursuing a political agenda of their own.

One of New York's leading Catholic intellectuals, Peter Quinn, author of *Banished Children of Eve*, one of the epic novels of Irish America, summed up the Church's contribution as follows: 'The Church succeeded. It kept hope and it kept discipline. Now faith and nationality can be separate. The Irish American Church was a historical institution formed by the Famine. It's only now people are coming out of the "crouch"'. Quinn, who went to Irish Catholic schools from primary stage right up to university, made a number of important points about the Church and the lasting economic and political effects of its educational legacy: firstly, that the well-educated Irish have developed and will retain their interest in Ireland; and secondly that the number of highly placed Catholic executives who have been created by that educational system are now well placed to further that interest. He made a point about the number of Irish Americans in CEO positions in the communications industry: 'When you go in to see them, it's not Mr Smith from Princeton. The British political information people don't have it all their own way any more. It's amazing the level of knowledge, how well informed Irish Americans are on Northern Irish issues.' Quinn's point about Irish executives in high places is well taken, the men who control huge investment portfolios are very often Irish – and they haven't hesitated to indicate to the Northern Ireland authorities that any investment of their funds in the Six Countries is contingent on fair employment practices being implemented. Says Quinn, 'They understand affirmative action and that sort of concept. The only thing they find difficult to comprehend is the "not an inch" mentality. The arms of New York City should be inscribed "Let's make a deal." That's the culture here.' Over the centuries the deals cut by the Irish to make the American Catholic Church what it is today have helped to shape that culture.

WOMEN

The contribution of Irish women to American society is so vast as to merit not one but several books in its own right.

America's contribution to Irish women is equally valuable. One woman, with her finger on the pulse of Irish American life to a greater degree than most is Patricia Harty, who edits the glossy and influential bi-monthly *Irish American* magazine. The magazine's annual Top 100 Irish American awards are a roll call of Who's Who in America. Over the years the awards have grown in stature to a point where, at the time of writing, they are regarded as one of the most prized accolades an Irish American can receive.

Like generations of Irish women before her Harty found emigration a liberating experience. It was only when she came to America and began to read Irish literature that she became aware of figures like James Joyce, Frank O'Connor or W. B. Yeats. She had been reared on a Tipperary farm with twelve brothers and sisters, but although Ireland had been limiting, her pride in being Irish is almost a tangible thing. It goes hand in hand with a deep appreciation of the benefits America conferred on her and thousands like her: 'I loved America from the moment I landed, even though I was an illegal. As you can see, I'm tall, and at home people used to say that I'd make a fine Ban Garda (policewoman). But over here, everyone's tall. When I started to work, all the girls did waitressing and the boys headed off to construction, laying pipelines and so on. Everyone helped each other. There was great networking. There still is.' She came first to San Francisco and, after a period studying the theatre and literature, founded the *Irish American* newspaper with Niall O'Dowd.

The couple married and moved to New York, where in 1985 they founded first the *Irish Voice* newspaper, then the *Irish American* magazine and threw themselves into the IIRM fray. Although the marriage failed, the publications prospered, and Harty and O'Dowd maintain a harmonious professional relationship, which in itself could probably be regarded as a prime example of the new Irish American approach to political co-operation set in train by the IIRM campaign. She regards the magazine's subscribers almost as part of her family, and is passionately *engagé* about issues concerning the Irish.

Harty's fruitful career lay mainly in the east and west coasts, but for generations Irish women have done well for themselves all over the US. If we focus, however briefly, on a city, a movement and an order of nuns from a fragment of that history, some sense of the scale of the mosaic will appear. The city is Chicago, the movement that of organised labour, and the nuns those who followed Catherine McAuley, late of Baggot Street, Dublin. Let us remind ourselves that in post-Famine Ireland the devastation of the economy dictated that women came bottom on the totem pole. Lack of marital opportunity, and a stigma deliberately attached to illegitimacy – inculcated by an increasingly doctrinaire Church, determined under the leadership of Paul Cullen to tame the Irish in accordance with Rome's wishes – led to a situation wherein a study of fifteen countries conducted in the 1890s showed Ireland to have the lowest percentage of illegitimate births, 2.46 per cent of the total birth rate. This indication of a low incidence of extra-marital sex becomes even more remarkable when one remembers that Ireland was a society in which people married little and late. It was a time of the arranged marriage, the dowry, and almost total subjugation of the wife by the husband. For those without a dowry, America beckoned.

In Chicago between 1870 and 1900, the Irish-born population increased to 73,912 or 12.6 per cent of the foreign-born population. The parameters of most of their lives were bounded by the parish. The Irish were the poorest of the poor. They lived in shanty homes without electricity, plumbing, water or heat. Yet at the behest of Mother Church, they built churches in excess of $100,000. The church was followed by schools and hospitals, all the essentials around which a community could group.

Where they did group, property values went up, industries moved in, and small businesses sprouted. However, though commerce increased, poverty remained endemic. This bore particularly heavily on women, particularly married women who had to rear huge Irish families on small American wages. One of the horrific results was child labour, the sending out of twelve-year-olds, not to play with dolls but to have their fingers sliced off and their hair entangled by dangerous machinery. Sometimes, as they did in every other part of America, Irish wives and mothers responded to the economic challenge by taking in boarders. Working outside the home was discouraged, not merely on cultural or religious grounds but because of the problem of looking after the children. Sometimes tragedies ensued when mothers locked their children in the house and went to work. Unmarried women worked in domestic service, in factories, in meat-packing.

The volatility of the labour market meant that many families underwent the trauma of either desertion or being split up as the male bread-winner moved to another State to look for work. Catholic charities such as the Society of St Vincent de Paul helped out in such circumstances, but alleviation, rather than cure, was the best that could be hoped for. Wages for married women working outside the home averaged only seven or eight dollars a week. If they did not work, they and their children faced possible starvation and certain eviction. If the children were well, the mother could take the risk of leaving them at home, albeit running the risk of tragedy, but sickness posed a cruel dilemma.

Generally, at the start of the century single women were domestic servants and waitresses; widows and deserted wives were in industry, although in Chicago, as elsewhere, the bulk of jobs available in teaching, textiles, clerking, and shop sales were held by women of all nationalities. By 1900, although the Irish only comprised an eighth of the total foreign-born population of Chicago, they had the greatest number employed as servants and waitresses. The domestics were required to live in and not to have children. 'Gentlemen callers' were firmly discouraged. Brigid generally did not have the culinary skills or domestic sciences sought by the better-off American employers, but generally she was hard-working, intelligent, willing to learn and to save her money. Living in meant that she could save for a dowry or to bring a younger member of the family over from Ireland.

The ladder to a better way of life for poor immigrant women was education, and it was the nuns who held that ladder. The Irish nuns were particularly valuable in carrying out the Vatican's policy of advancing the Church by means of either the British Empire, the English language, or both. As in the United Kingdom itself, the Irish nuns were generally not allowed to become vehicles of specifically Irish culture, but of a Catholic one. As Deirdre Mageean points out:

> Irish religious were not transmitters of ethnic identity, indeed, [they] accelerated the assimilation of Irish emigrants into American life . . . Nuns, the main educators in the parish, were vital to the success of Irish American women. They concentrated on their own gender, and encouraged them to enter the professions. They also provided resources for many Irish women who were unable to cope with the exigencies of urban life.[62]

For, as Mageean has further indicated, not only did Irish girls receive a first-class education, they received more education than either their brothers or the children of foreign-born fathers.[63] The national school attendance figures for 1900 show that attendance for girls with Irish fathers exceeded that of the daughters of all foreign-born fathers. Mageean says:

> American Catholic nuns inherited a tradition of female education that was centuries old. Although they did not neglect the teaching of boys, they invested disproportionate effort in educating their own sex . . . the nuns encouraged females to continue education . . . The promotion of female education does not appear to have been specific to the Chicago Irish, although it was in Chicago that the first girls' Catholic high school was founded.[64]

The nuns acted as role models for their pupils, many of whom would later join the convents and become teachers themselves. For the turn-of-the-century Irish woman in Chicago, life in the convent appeared to offer not servitude but independence, when set against the example of so many marriages either continuing in abuse, or ending in desertion or widowhood, to say nothing of the agonies of childbirth and the drudgery of housework. This is not to say that life in the convent was a bed of roses either; the nuns often worked for no more return than food and lodgings and subsidised the education of the poorer pupils from the fees charged to the children of non-Catholic parents attracted by the good results achieved by the Catholic institutes. For those who neither married nor entered the convent, Sister Brigid was a symbol of upward mobility who propelled them into the professions, teaching, nursing and the trade unions.

The feminists will be glad to hear that nuns still take a dim view of housework. 'A button will never be sewn at McAuley', is the proud boast of an educational establishment which encapsulates both the impact and the teaching of Irish religious women in America in general and in Chicago in particular. Mary Catherine McAuley had a profound influence on Chicago, as she had elsewhere in America. A group of her nuns were invited to Chicago in 1846 and immediately commenced a variety of good works. They catered for the sick, the destitute, the deserted, and acted as social workers visiting the poor in their homes and the prisoners in their jails. They also opened schools. Along with building Chicago's first permanent hospital, they opened the first parochial schools, the first night schools for Catholic adults and the first orphanage.

I visited Mother Mary McAuley High School on 99th Street in the company of the sort of ex-pupil with whom Mary McAuley's name is associated, Mary Kate Higgins, Vice-president of a major Chicago-based insurance corporation.[65] In her final year at the school, Mary Kate was seventeen and the present President of the school, Mother Corinne Raven, was twenty. Her only instrument of authority was a white veil, but talking to Mother Corinne, an attractive, dark-haired woman with a white coif and flashing eyes, I very speedily discovered an even more potent instrument, her powerful personality. She is the archetypal figure of the nun who could have been either a Wall Street tycoon or a corporate CEO had she not become a Reverend Mother.

The school is the largest all-girls high school in the United States, with an enrolment of 1,960 pupils. Educationally, the school has been recognised as an exemplary secondary school by the US Department of Education, and on the sporting field has acquired a similar reputation. In volleyball, for example, the 'Mighty Macs' are regarded as the best team in the country. The mission statement of the school is:

Mother McAuley Liberal Arts High School is a Catholic educational community committed to providing a quality secondary education for young women. In the tradition of the Sisters of Mercy and their foundress, Catherine McAuley, we prepare students to live in a complex, dynamic society by teaching them to think critically, communicate effectively, respond compassionately to the needs of their community and assume roles of Christian leadership. In partnership with parents, we empower young women to acknowledge their own giftedness and to make decisions with a well-developed moral conscience. We foster an appreciation of the diversity of the global community and a quest for knowledge and excellence as life-long goals.

Mother Corinne puts it more succinctly: 'Part of the mission is to turn out strong Catholic women with beliefs. A lay person could head this school with respect. Most administrators are religious now, but that won't be so in the future. A lot of things are possible for lay leaders of the church.' Mother Corinne doesn't see her ex-pupils operating like Opus Dei, the secretive élite Catholic action group operating in the professions and in the decision-taking branches of government, but openly in the life of the community. At a time of falling vocations, she spoke confidently of 'a revitalisation of the parishes'. Her assistant, Michelle Whitehead, was a Moran before marriage, so obviously the Irish revitalisation is already under way. I'd be inclined to bet also that the flow of 'strong Catholic women' is going to continue.

Corinne suggested that the best way for me to sample the ambience of the school would be to wander around with Mary Kate, under the guidance of two contemporary pupils, Devin Cahil and Paddy Arvesen, both of Irish grandparentage. Both girls were active in student politics. Paddy visualised a career in urban planning, and Devin had her sights set on the State Department, hoping to become an ambassador some day. They were interested in their Irish heritage, and looking forward to the day when the school would go on-line with a similar establishment in Ireland. They hastened to assure me that there was 'nothing dirty on the Internet . . . it's all monitored'.

They reckoned that Catherine McAuley was stricter than other schools, but both of them agreed that they were 'the better for it', and opined that their teacher was 'the best in the whole world'. There was a liturgical ceremony in progress as we visited the church. It had a very McAuley-esque air to it. There was a lot of dancing and singing to the accompaniment of a musical group and the ceremony's emphasis was on participation as opposed to authority. There was no communion and no priest. In the 900-strong auditorium, a better-appointed venue than many professional theatres, *Fiddler on the Roof* was in production. There may have been some symbolism in the juxtaposition of two posters on display: one showed Edmund Ignatius Rice, the founder of the Irish Christian Brothers, the other Michael Flatley, the founder of *Riverdance*.

In the library, another poster proclaimed: 'Free knowledge. Bring your own container.' As a susurration of whispering indicated that some of the 'containers' might be filling with gossip rather than knowledge, a firm McAuley-esque voice from the librarian's desk brought immediate silence with a crisp: 'Ladies, p-l-e-a-s-e.' The school shone; corridors, classrooms, the smiles of the students all gleamed the same message: 'Here is constant effort' – a message that came across even more loudly watching the seriousness with which a group of girls in the huge gym worked out during a class break. The school canteen and leisure facility contained both a T-shirt shop and a Pizza Hut. Paddy and Devin both praised the quality of the food, but they had no plaudits to spare for the concept of co-education. 'Never,' they chimed firmly. 'Here you can be what you want. You can develop character. Girls wouldn't talk in class with boys present. Volleyball would become subject to football. We'd be like girls in other schools who are up early to do their hair and their nails before they come to class.' They spoke about their school and their friends in terms of developing 'a loving, nurturing relationship'. They agreed with Mary Kate when she remarked that Catherine McAuley's was 'a cool place to be smart'.

Afterwards, as I mentally sorted out the images of Mary McAuley's, it occurred to me that one of the areas which offered scope for the development of a 'nurturing relationship' was the racial one. I had seen very few black 'Mighty Macs', but undeniably the influence of Catherine McAuley had travelled a long way from Baggot Street, Dublin.

Summing up the contribution of the nuns Deirdre Mageean judged that:

> Given the forces that drove so many Irish women out of Ireland and their fierce pursuit of economic independence, it is not surprising to find them over-represented in the professions and in trade unions. Their entry into these worlds was facilitated by the fact that they were highly literate and English-speaking.[66]

'Fierce pursuit' is an apt term. The most famous woman in American trade union history was Irish-born Mary Harris better known as 'Mother' Jones, the sobriquet she adopted to avoid police harassment. Harris came to live in Chicago after her husband and four children died in a yellow fever epidemic in Memphis. Just as she was getting on her feet, she lost everything she owned in the great Chicago fire of 1871. She then joined the fledgling Knights of Labour, and became a mine-workers' organiser. On one occasion, she was convicted of conspiracy to commit murder, at a kangaroo trial organised by the copper bosses in Colorado, but she was cleared after a Senate investigation. She took a leading role in most of the tumultuous turning-point trade union battles of her time, including the Haymarket riot in Chicago in 1886 and the American Railway Union Strike in 1894 in Birmingham.

Describing a strike in the Irish district of Kensington, Philadelphia, in 1903 Harris wrote:

> 75,000 textile workers were on strike. Of this number at least ten thousand were little children. The workers were striking for more pay and shorter hours. Every day little children came into Union headquarters, some with their hands off, some with the thumb missing, some with their fingers off at the knuckle. They were stooped little things, round-shouldered and skinny.[67]

She organised the children into a march that went from Philadelphia to Oyster Bay, New York, to the home of President Theodore Roosevelt whom she hoped would use his influence to end child labour, but the President refused to meet with the children.

There were many more Irish trade unionists whose influence spread beyond Chicago. Not content with bearing ten children, Elisabeth Flynn Rogers also gave birth to the Working Women's Union in September 1878. In addition, she helped to found the Women's Catholic Order of Foresters, a fraternal life insurance company. Margaret Haley, known as 'The Lady Labour Slugger' combined with another teacher, Catherine Goggin, to form the Chicago Teachers' Federation, which not only improved the lot of teachers, but became an instrument for social reform. At the turn of the century, 97 per cent of elementary teachers in Chicago were women. Under the tutelage of Haley and Goggin, these women introduced the concept of female white-collar trade unionism to America. Agnes Nestor, Mary Kenny O'Sullivan and Hannah O'Dea organised their sisters into trade unions in the glove-making, bookbinding and meat-packing industries of Chicago, and the waitresses were organised by Elisabeth Moloney, whose approach to trade unionism was a combination of hard-nosed bargaining and nun-like purity. She didn't merely want more money for waitresses, she demanded they be given respect as well.

One of the most prominent women trade unionists of all was Elisabeth Gourley Flynn, born to Irish emigrant parents in Concord, Massachusetts. She joined the Industrial Workers of the World (IWW), the Wobblies, in 1906, a year after the movement was founded in Chicago. Flynn became one of America's most famous advocates of women's rights. Dressed as a schoolgirl in white blouse and long skirt, she first appeared on a platform in New York at the age of sixteen, and, according to the novelist Theodore Dreiser: 'electrified her audience with her eloquence, her youth and her loveliness'.[68] Dreiser termed her 'an East Side Joan of Arc', and one of America's leading theatrical producers, David Belasco, tried unsuccessfully to get her to take up acting. However, she opted for the barricades instead, becoming a lifelong Communist, and taking part in some of the most dangerous mining and logging confrontations in American labour history. Another famous Wobbly, the martyred Joe Hill, enshrined her memory in the song, 'The Rebel Girl'. Her revolutionary well-springs came from Irish soil. She said in her autobiography:

> My ancestors were immigrants and revolutionaries from the Emerald Isle . . . There was an uprising in each generation in Ireland, and forefathers of mine were in every one of them. The awareness of being Irish came to us as small children, through plaintive songs and heroic story . . . As children, we drew in a burning hatred of British rule with our mother's milk. Until my father died, at over eighty, he never said 'England' without adding 'God damn her'! Before I was ten, I knew of the great heroes, Robert Emmet, Wolfe Tone, Michael Davitt, Parnell, and Jeremiah O'Donovan Rossa.

The Irish socialist leader, James Connolly, whom the British had to shoot sitting in a chair as he could not stand before the firing squad because of his wounds, was a frequent visitor to the Flynn home in the Bronx during his time in New York, and Connolly's associate, Jim Larkin, was another friend of the family. After a mayor of New York City remarked: 'There are Russian socialists, and Jewish socialists, and German socialists ... but thank God there are no Irish socialists!', visitors to the Flynn home formed the Irish Socialist Federation. These people were Irish, socialist and revolutionary. A neighbour, a German blacksmith, made them a portable speaking platform, with specially designed detachable iron legs, which could be used as shillelaghs when required. Annie Flynn, Elisabeth's mother, made a green and white banner adorned with harps and shamrocks and the inscription 'fag-a-balach' (clear the way).

Trade Unions

The Irish contribution to the trade union movement was not of course confined to women only. For, as John J. Sweeney, the contemporary President of the American AFL/CIO, has pointed out, most trade union leaders at the turn of the century were Irish.[69] In his speech, Sweeney gave a roll call of some of the outstanding names in the development of the movement, beginning with Terence Powderly, the motivating spirit behind the first major Labour movement, the Knights of Labour. Another Irishman, Peter Maguire, was with the great Samuel Gompers, of Dutch-Jewish extraction, the founder of the American Federation of Labour. He was also the man who originated the concept of that American institution, the Labour Day holiday. In mining, steel and transport, Irish names like John Mitchell, Peter Murray and Mike Quill were but some of those taken from a list which, if given in full, would fill this page. These men helped to revolutionise conditions in one-time horrific industries.

As the working conditions visited on children resulted in the kind of injuries described earlier, the horrors visited on adults can well be imagined. The late nineteenth-century and early twentieth-century America was an emerging industrial colossus. It was the time of the Robber Barons, the then venerated pioneers of American capitalism who terrified Wall Street and drove men to early deaths, as railways and canals cut across a virgin landscape and miners clawed riches for others from the bowels of the earth.

A survey of the Steward coppermine in Butte carried out in 1921 found the water temperature at the lowest level – 3,800 feet – was 113°F, and the rock temperature only five degrees lower.[70] Mules were used underground but toilet facilities were not, and the 'smells of human and animal excrement mingled with those of sweat, blasting powder, rotting food and tobacco'. More serious was the killer rock dust which affected as many as 40 per cent of all miners, adding to the deaths caused by rock falls and fires. Conditions in canal and railroad building were also both brutal and brutalising. The canal building era, *circa* 1815–1860, yielded some 4,000 miles of canals, most of them dug by Irishmen equipped with little more than pick and shovel and a frequently lethally applied charge of black powder. 'Safety precautions' often took the form of covering as much of the head and face as could be shielded by a shovel. The era also roughly coincided with that of the railroads.

Both forms of development had a number of factors in common. They employed Irish people, had horrendous working conditions and, being under-funded, frequently delayed or even defaulted on the payment of the pitiable wages of the time – roughly $10 to $12 a month. The canals, like the railroads, brought immense economic benefit in their wake. They opened up new territories and helped to develop existing cities. As William Kennedy remarked to me, 'If there hadn't been an Albany, there wouldn't have been a Chicago.' The famous 'big ditch' dug from Albany to Buffalo could be taken as a principal factor in New York's economic boom from 1825 onwards. The implications of this were understood and acted on in Chicago and elsewhere. Canals also brought prosperity to cities like Philadelphia, Pittsburgh and Baltimore, as they did to the States of the Midwest, Ohio, Indiana and Illinois, all of which were linked up with the Great Lakes via the Mississippi and Ohio river systems.

The 'lump' system of the time permitted even worse abuses than those encountered in Britain's building industry. Subcontractors on the canals were often unable to meet their pay rolls in the summer; in the winter when frost struck there was no work at all. Even when there was work, the workers lived in the most miserable of shanty accommodation, beset by the dangers of cave-ins, flooding, malaria and cholera. Cholera was not confined to the canals. Twenty-five miles west of Philadelphia, near the Amtrak line, there is a mass grave filled with the bones of Irishmen who died of the disease. They received no help of any sort from anyone in their death throes until a party of Sisters of Charity nuns made their way to the site.

No one really knows how many Irish died in the digging of New Orleans' New Basin Canal in the 1830s, but a figure of 20,000 to 30,000 is generally accepted. The canal, linking Lake Pontchartrain with the city, lay through a swamp and men died like flies from cholera, malaria and yellow fever. Their memory is commemorated by a Celtic cross and by a ballad:

> Ten thousand Micks
> They swung their picks
> To dig the New Canal.
> But the choleray was
> Stronger 'n they
> And twice it killed them out.

The Canal was six miles long, six feet deep and sixty feet wide. The Irish were paid a dollar a day for battling with black slime, mosquitoes, snakes and alligators. They lived in huts along the canal banks, shopped in the company store and used community lavatories. Slave owners would not allow slaves to work on the canal project because of the conditions and the disease. Cholera and malaria are fearsome killers in their own right. Cholera causes acute cramping, diarrhoea and dehydration; malaria sends its victims oscillating between bouts of chill and fevers in which the body temperature rises as high as 107 degrees.

Yellow fever is worse than either. Known as the strangers' disease, because it preys on newcomers, it creates internal haemorrhaging and progresses through delirium to convulsions and coma. The appalling symptoms included bleeding from the nose, mouth or rectum. Victims' tongues sometimes turned red, others might develop purple faces and yellow eyes. Either way, people died spitting up partially digested blood, which led to the disease being given the name 'the black vomit'.

Here it might be noted that New Orleans, not a city generally associated with the Irish, in fact played an important role in their history in America, quite apart from the canals. Possibly as many as 250,000 Irish entered America via New Orleans, then America's second busiest port of entry in the wave of immigration following the Famine, and by 1860 there were some 38,000 Irish – a sixth of the population – living in the city.

Initially the Irish were at the bottom of the New Orleans social pile. The city created particular difficulties for them. It was divided not only along colour lines, but by rivalry between the Americans and the Creoles. Like the Americans who despised them for their poverty and their religion, the Irish spoke English, but like the Creoles, who spoke French, they were Catholic. There was considerable competition with the black population over work, and the Irish earned the reputation of being prepared to work for the lowest wages, thereby adding to the hostilities.

The Irish Channel, the Irish quarter, was noisy, overcrowded, violent and insanitary, but over the years the Irish literally dragged themselves up from the slime, entered the trades and the professions, and in 1892 had prospered to such a degree that a John Fitzpatrick became the first Irish American Mayor of New Orleans.

According to New Orleans folklore, an Irish police chief had unwittingly played a part in another notable 'first' two years earlier. Chief David Hennessy, who was fatally shot on 15 October 1890, is alleged to have been the first victim of the Mafia. Nine years earlier Hennessy had become a particular hate figure for the Sicilian community by arresting a famous Sicilian bandit, Esposito, and sending him to New York for trial. Esposito was sentenced to death for, amongst other crimes, eighteen murders, but his sentence was later commuted. A vendetta commenced against not only Hennessy, but everyone who gave evidence against him.

After Hennessy's murder, nineteen or twenty Sicilians and Italians were arrested and charged. However, on 13 March 1891, a jury acquitted some of the defendants, and declared a mistrial for the rest. It was to prove a very unlucky 13th indeed. Concurrent with the verdict, two ships arrived from Sicily with 1,800 emigrants aboard. In other ethnic circles, including Irish ones, anger and fear mounted at both the verdict and the prospect of an Italian takeover of the city. The day after the acquittals, newspaper advertisements announced that all 'good citizens' were invited to a meeting later in the day to do something about the failure of justice. After listening to fiery speeches, a large crowd bore down on the prison.

A group of Irish Mercy nuns went to the jail in an effort to head off the lynching, and their leader, Mother Austin Carroll, persuaded the Sheriff to unlock the cells of the Sicilians to give them a chance of escaping. The Sisters were then locked in for their own safety. However, the Sicilians failed to make it outside the prison walls, and were shot or hanged. The lynching resulted in the United States Government paying an indemnity of $25,000 to the Italian Government.

Eamon de Valera paid a memorable visit to the city in April 1920 during his American fund-raising tour. En route to New Orleans, his train was involved in a head-on collision with another locomotive in a blinding rain and electrical storm. His visit was a controversial one; the Irish contingent gave him a warm welcome, but the British Consul General protested at his being received as 'President of the Irish Republic'. A compromise was worked out by the Acting Mayor, A. G. Ricks, in the absence of the Mayor, who had extended the original invitation to de Valera, but had left the city before the visit. Under Ricks's compromise, de Valera was given the freedom of the city, although he was received not as President but as 'a distinguished guest', and the Acting Mayor made it clear that he was acting on behalf of a de Valera welcoming committee which included 'some of our best citizens', rather than conferring the freedom of his own volition. De Valera subsequently received an Honorary Doctorate of Laws at New Orleans Jesuit University, Loyola. An Irish Jesuit, Father O'Brien, pointedly inscribed the guest register in a manner which explains how the term 'Jesuitry' got into the dictionaries: 'N.B. The first autograph on this page is that of His Excellency, the Hon. Eamon de Valera, President, the Republic of Ireland.'[71]

There is some dispute as to the origins of the current Irish Channel St Patrick's Day Parade. It is said that the parade began not so much to honour the Saint as in response to the banning of the Irish from the official Mardi Gras celebrations. It is also said that the reason the contemporary Parades begin with Mass at Alphonsus's, is to ask for forgiveness for sins which the marchers intend to commit. At all events, the Irish retaliated on the French by developing their own version of the Krewes, the organisation which supervises the marching clubs which are the backbone of the Mardi Gras Parades. After the Second World War, the Irish Krewes were organised into one big parade by Ronald Burke, whose grandson Richard was still organising St Patrick's Day Parades as this was being written. The Irish have their own version of the French tradition of throwing trinkets from the Mardi Gras floats: they hurl

317

the makings of an Irish Stew at the onlookers. It has become a tradition for spectators to come armed with bags to gather up the vegetables which hurtle, sometimes, especially in the case of potatoes, quite painfully from the floats. What is the origin of this strange custom? A hubristic tempting of the Gods in time of plenty, or a propitiation so that famine will not strike again? Certainly, whatever the reason, the potato is still playing a role in Irish culture. However, for those who fear that the potato is all that Irish cooking has to offer I should point out that the famous Brennan Restaurants of New Orleans are regarded as providing what is probably America's finest cuisine and form the hub of much New Orleans social life.

As with the canals, rail contractors frequently failed to pay wages on time and the conflicts generated by such failures and the terrible conditions often brought the Irish workers into conflict with the militia. The Irish retaliated by founding crude trade unions of their own, bands which were in effect transplanted variants on the agrarian secret societies of the old country. In addition to the violence generated by the conditions, and the whiskey with which the labourers were sometimes paid, there was often faction fighting between the Irish themselves. Faction fighting was common in nineteenth-century Ireland, with groups from one parish, or a family, testing the thickness of each other's skulls on fair days and religious holidays. The custom became even more violent and more bloody on the canals. Stories of epic conflicts between various county groupings have passed into legend.

In battling with mine owners to alleviate the conditions of the workers, Terence Powderly also had to contend with the onslaughts of the Church, who condemned him for leading a secretive, quasi-Masonic labour organisation. (The secrecy was introduced to combat company spies.) When, to satisfy the Church, Powderly (whose father emigrated to America after being jailed for three weeks for shooting a rabbit on his landlord's estate in County Meath) got rid of the secrecy surrounding the Knights, he was attacked by his Protestant members for giving in to the Church. However, with the aid of Cardinal Gibbons, Powderly managed to negotiate both the rocks of the Scylla of Church condemnation and the Charybdis of his nativist membership, and henceforth Catholic trade unionists did not have to fear contradiction between their association and their Church.

Peter Maguire, the son of Famine emigrants, who was raised in the horrific slums of New York, founded America's first Carpenters' Union and was the central figure in founding the American Federation of Labour (AFL), in Pittsburgh in 1881, which represented Craft Unions. Eventually the AFL would merge with the Committee for Industrial Organisation (CIO), founded by John L. Lewis in 1935. Its first director was John Brophy who, like his Irish emigrant father before him, was a coal miner. Brophy had both organising ability and courage – in those days addressing a Labour rally one ran the risk of being either beaten or shot to death. Brophy and his colleague, Philip Murray, Vice-president of the CIO, another graduate of the Irish Miners' College of Hard Knocks, managed to convince the CIO membership that strikes could be fought and won by non-violent methods. It was Murray who, more than any other single individual, unionised the steel industry.

One of the most colourful of all the twentieth century's Irish Labour figures was 'Red Mike' Quill. Quill came from a Republican family in County Kerry which, having fought the British, then took arms against the Irish over the Treaty of 1921. The combination of being on the losing side and the economic conditions at the time impelled the Quills towards America. He and his brother John became travelling salesmen for religious goods throughout the Pennsylvania region. One of the most ordered items by Catholic mining homes of the area was a framed print of The Crucifixion. However, the popularity was of short duration, for when the prints were unpacked it was discovered that Jesus Christ was depicted with the heart on the right side of his body. Not altogether surprisingly Quill subsequently became a Communist! He also became a subway worker, like so many unskilled young Irish men before and after him. Unlike the bulk of his colleagues however, Quill was not prepared to put up with the low wages which the unskilled commanded. He set out to improve conditions by organising the Transport Workers' Union.

In taking on hostile and very powerful employers, Quill put his IRA training to good effect, demonstrating the conspiratorial skills, the courage and the discipline to organise a trade union in the conditions of the time. He needed the same attributes in even greater measure to combine membership of the Communist Party and the Catholic Church. He eventually broke with the Communists in 1948, joined the Democratic Party and became a supporter of Truman. Quill might be thought of as an exemplar of the revolutionary Irish strain in the trade union movement; many of the men around him had been through British prisons and courts, and sometimes to preserve secrecy used the Irish language for their communications. The IRA campaign of the1950s owed something to the arms, money and explosives which came to Ireland from the Transport Workers' Union.

The trade union leader who managed to harmonise the revolutionary fire of the Mike Quills and the Mother Joneses with the more conciliatory approach of the Philip Murrays was George Meany, a plumber by trade, of Westmeath ancestry. Meany was partly responsible for several major developments in American society. Amongst the many successful campaigns which he helped to sponsor were those to introduce social security, Medicare and Medicaid. He fought racism and insisted on merging the hitherto separate black and white Union Locals (branches) around the country into single units. He also courageously took on the Mob in expelling the gangster-infiltrated Teamsters Union from the AFL/CIO, even though they were major contributors. Meany died in 1980.

A successor was John J. Sweeney whose parents were born in Leitrim. Speaking to the Irish American Labour Coalition, President Sweeney summed up the Irish contribution as follows:

There is scarcely an important event in American Labour history in which the Irish did not play a significant part . . . The Irish were amongst the great overthrowers, they were also amongst the great reformers. They at once swelled the ranks of the hot-headed, the radical, the cautious, and the conciliatory.[72]

He concluded by urging his listeners to 'draw inspiration' from 'Mother' Mary Jones's words: 'My address is wherever there is a fight against oppression. My address is like my shoes; it travels with me. I abide wherever there is a fight against wrong.'

THE MOLLY MAGUIRES

By coincidence I witnessed a remarkable stage enactment of the dilemmas of securing justice and apportioning guilt while I was researching the Molly Maguire story, itself one of the classic stories of questionable justice affecting the Irish, not only in the history of the trade union movement but of American folklore. The production, if that is the correct term, was called, *The Trial of Hamlet for the Murder of Polonius*. It takes the form of having distinguished lawyers and psychiatrists debate Hamlet's mental state at the time of the killing, backing up their arguments with quotations from *Hamlet*. Only Hamlet appears in period costume, and he does not speak. The play is the work of Anthony Kennedy, a judge of the US Supreme Court. I saw it in Chicago where, as is customary, the audience listens to the arguments, adjourns for dinner, and returns to hear the verdict of the jury. In Chicago, as generally occurs, the prosecution failed to prove their case, although the women on the jury, as was also usual, found Hamlet guilty because of his treatment of Ophelia.

It was entirely appropriate that Tony Kennedy should have produced such a work. He is descended from a family who took part in the real-life Molly Maguire drama, set in the Pennsylvania coal mines of the late nineteenth century. Unlike Kennedy's play, a unanimous verdict was returned: guilty. The twenty Irish defendants were hanged. While Kennedy's present eminence may be taken as an indication of how far the Irish have come from the brawling, brutal days in Lacakawanna County and elsewhere in Pennsylvania, nevertheless the Irish will always be inextricably bound up with the history of American mining. Irishmen were involved in innumerable legendary tales like the finding of the Comstock lode, or Tom Walsh's gold strike at Ouray, Colorado, which led to his purchasing the ill-fated Hope Diamond. This blue 44½-carat jewel brought misfortune to all who owned it, including Walsh and his family.

However, nothing in American mining history rivals the mythic stature of the Molly Maguires. The story encapsulates the exiles' sense of ancestral injustices; the hardships and injustices of the mining industry itself; the struggles of the Irish everywhere in America to form unions in order to earn a decent living for themselves and their families; and the hostility of the forces of nativism and big business which were ranged against them. Some say the Molly Maguires never existed at all. They were merely the creation of coal barons who wanted an excuse to crack down on the unions and the Irish, which were practically the same thing. Others say that they were a band like one of the traditional Irish secret societies which fought landlordism in Ireland. What is undeniable is that twenty alleged members of the Molly Maguires were executed in Pennsylvania after trials which would hardly be countenanced today. A priest, Father McDermott, who had heard the confessions of two of the executed men, said publicly that he believed they were innocent.

Mention has been made earlier of the Irish seeing themselves as exiles, not emigrants. The Pennsylvanian coal fields are no bad location in which to observe this sense at work. As we have seen, the principal exponent of the theory, Kerby Miller, has argued that the whole business of being in America was to many Irish emigrants an act of injustice in itself.[73] Most of them dreamed of going back to Ireland at some point. On top of the sense of exile, in the Pennsylvania coal fields of the 1870s the Irish were only too keenly aware that physically they were doing one of the most dangerous and dirtiest of jobs. Moreover, they were again working for absentee English stock holders whose WASP cousins had brought in Welsh and English miners to work the coal fields as contract miners being paid so much a ton. To worsen the sense of injustice, the Irish were being paid wages which only amounted to a fraction of the monies received by the English and Welsh.

The genesis of the conflict lay in a meeting in New York in 1873. A group of mine owners and railroad tycoons – Franklin Gowen, Charles Parish, Asa Packer and a number of others – had come together to set up the first price-fixing cartel in American history. They controlled both the mines and the railroads which shipped the coal out of them, but they didn't control the Mine Workers' Union, the Workers' Benevolent Association, and in particular the strong Irish element of the Union. During the draft controversy of 1863, General Charles Albright led a force into Schuylkill County in a futile bid to enforce conscription. He was driven off by thousands of armed Irish labourers led, amongst others, by one Jack Kehoe. Albright took his revenge fifteen years later. Having become a State prosecutor in the meantime, he helped to send Kehoe to the gallows, for a murder committed ten years earlier, claiming that he was a Molly Maguire. In a tradition of always seizing the opportunity of making a bad situation worse, only too well established by some clerics, the Catholic Archbishop of Philadelphia, Archbishop Woods, wrote to the mine owners congratulating them on the verdict, and subsequently several parish priests in the area refused Catholic burial to suspected Mollies or members of the AOH. The organisation had been excommunicated by both Woods and Bishop O'Hara of Scranton. In the circumstances the two priests who gave spiritual comfort to the condemned men acted with great courage, particularly Father McDermott. The families of the executed men suffered ostracism as a result of such attitudes.

Many years later, however, the executed men were granted posthumous pardons. At a ceremony held in January 1979 to mark the signing of the pardon for Kehoe, Governor Sharp of Pennsylvania, after adverting to the anti-Irish and anti-Labour sentiment which had prevailed at the time of their trial, commented:

> We can be proud of these men known as the Molly Maguires, because they defiantly faced allegations to make trade unionism a criminal conspiracy. These men gave their lives on behalf of the Labour struggle.[74]

That struggle intensified in places like Lackawanna and Schuylkill counties as the cartel forced down prices by dumping, thus driving the smaller operators out of business, so that they could take over their mines. Wages fell so low that, even after a sixty-hour week, the Irish miners could not feed their families. The Irish responded by wildcat strikes, and by exercising political clout through the Ancient Order of Hibernians. The AOH switched from supporting Democrats to Republicans, and the Republicans won many state appointments including the governorship as a result. The cartel retaliated with a campaign spearheaded by the *Miners' Journal*, owned by a Welsh American fundamentalist Protestant, Benjamin Bannan, who portrayed the Irish Catholics as drunken violent thugs. In fact, there was a great deal of violence in the Pennsylvanian fields, in places like the Lackawanna, Carbon and Schuylkill districts. For example, in Schuylkill alone, between 1862 and 1875 there were 142 unsolved murders and hundreds of cases of assault. However, it was subsequently proved that the crime rate before the Molly Maguire phenomenon occurred was as high as it was during it, and no higher than elsewhere in American coal mining areas during the 1860s and 1870s.[75] However, Bannan continually raised the spectre of a secret society, known as the Molly Maguires, operating from within the ranks of the AOH, to murder unpopular company agents.

Gowen, the cartel leader, took the campaign a stage further. He enlisted the services of that archetypical figure of Irish detestation, The Informer – in this case an Armagh man, James McParland, a member of the Pinkerton Detective Agency – to infiltrate the AOH and secure evidence against supposed members of the 'Mollies'. He made it clear he wanted death sentences. McParland succeeded so well that, as indicated earlier, twenty members of the Mollies were hanged between 1877 and 1879 – ten of them on the morning of 21 June 1877, before an audience which included 200 invited guests. The sort of justice the men received may be gauged from the fact that two of them were executed one morning while the telegraph operator banged unavailingly on the front door of the prison, with a telegram from the Governor ordering a stay of execution. The execution warrant had merely stipulated that they be hanged on that day. Any time up to midnight would have sufficed. It was said -

that the hand-print of one of those executed, Alex Campbell, who like the others died protesting his innocence, could not be erased from the wall of Carton County Jail, and the place became a tourist attraction.

Certainly the imprint of the Molly Maguire story never left Irish American consciousness. The Irish actor Richard Harris starred with the Scotch Irish Sean Connery in the film *Lament for the Molly Maguires*. There are several books about the affair, one of them, *A Molly Maguire Story*,[76] written by a grand-nephew of Alex Campbell to exorcise the ghosts conjured up by the stories he heard from his father as a boy. Some saw the divine hand of retribution in the subsequent fates of those responsible for the Maguires' hangings. After the Irish were put down, a wave of strikes involving Germans, Welsh and Swedes hit the cartel. Gowen's company went bankrupt and he shot himself in 1889. Parish also went bankrupt. Packer, his wife and two sons all died in the space of a year, and then the Packer Company went bankrupt. The sheriff who arrested Campbell dropped dead before Campbell was executed, General Albright, the prosecutor, who both secured the death verdict and argued with the Board of Pardons that it was imperative that it should not be commuted, choked to death while eating. Pinkerton suffered a stroke after Campbell's execution and never recovered. McParland lapsed into alcoholism and paranoia and died alone. This followed another mining trial, which his side lost, largely because the great American lawyer, Clarence Darrow, used the Molly Maguire episode to eviscerate him in court. It seems reasonable to speculate that, had Darrow been representing the Maguires before a less biased court, they would not have been found guilty.

Today's Pennsylvania Ancient Order of Hibernians could serve as a paradigm for the Irish in the US. In 1995 I addressed the annual St Patrick's Day AOH dinner in Lackawanna County. Had I not been there I would have been in the White House to witness the historic party given by President Clinton both to celebrate the day, and encourage the Peace Process by welcoming Gerry Adams to the festivities, but the Lackawanna dinner was an impressive affair in its own right. I was escorted to and from my hotel by a large police motorcycle escort, and 1,200 tuxedoed gentlemen, many of them sober, turned up for the dinner, which was attended by every politician of consequence in the State.

Were there really Molly Maguires in the ranks of the 1870 AOH? Were the hanged men innocent? Was Hamlet guilty of the murder of Polonius . . . ? Like Hamlet the Maguires cannot speak, but it is possible to judge the difference between the manner in which the status of deorai, or virtual outlaws, was enforced on the Irish coal miners of Pennsylvania, with what befell them in the copper fields of Montana. Copper mining is just as dangerous and unhealthy as coal mining, and the copper barons could be just as ruthless as their coal counterparts. The difference lay in the identity of the principal copper baron. He was Marcus Daly, an Irish Catholic, who came to Butte, Montana in 1876. Daly was born in Ballyjamesduff, County Cavan, in 1841. He had worked on the Comstock lode, and had been sent to Butte to investigate the commercial potential of a silver mine. He reported that the mine looked promising, invested in it himself and became the mine's manager. With the profits he went on to buy the Anaconda mine, which he converted to copper production.

By the end of the 1920s, after Daly had won the 'War of the Copper Kings', one of the legendary corporate battles of American business history, his Anaconda Copper Mining Company had become the eighth largest industrial company in the US. However, Daly's lasting importance to the story of the Irish American is not the colossal riches that he unearthed, but the massive Irish emigration that he encouraged both into Butte, and the nearby town of Anaconda which he founded. He also supported Irish societies, like the Order of Hibernians and the Clan na Gael. The Irish flocked to him from the mining camps of California, Nevada and Utah. By the end of the 1890s, the Anaconda Company paid more wages 'than Kansas pays those who reap its wheat or Louisiana those who pick its cotton'.[77]

The Butte Irish earned so much money that it was estimated that 40 per cent of those who worked there between 1880 and 1890 were able to go back to Ireland, buy a farm, marry and settle down. For them at least the deorai question was settled. An even greater number sent back money to Ireland, either to alleviate the lot of those who remained at home, or encourage them to come to America.

THE IRISH IN FLEET, FIELD AND CIVIL WAR

The steel of American nationhood was tempered in the forge of battle by a liberal admixture of Irish blood. As might have been expected, given the Celtic military tradition, the Irish fought with distinction in many of America's turning-point battles from the revolutionary wars down to the present time. What is often overlooked, however, is the fact that these battles took place on sea as well as on land. Because the British Navigation Acts, described earlier, destroyed the Irish shipping industry, a belief arose that the Irish have no maritime or naval tradition. This of course overlooks the contributions of Irish sailors to the navies of the world – particularly that of Great Britain, and of Argentina whose navy, as we shall see, was founded by an Irishman, Admiral William Brown. In the case of America, the misconception that the Irish did not have a maritime history is particularly wide of the mark. The Irish left their imprint both on naval architecture and on the annals of combat.

Experts disagree as to who should be regarded as the father of the American Navy, John Paul Jones or the Wexford-born John Barry, but none deny that Barry gave homeric service to the fledgling American Navy. Having established a reputation as a sailor and a trader out of Philadelphia, he was given command of the brig *Lexington*, and on 17 April 1776 captured the British vessel *Edward*. This was the first capture of a British warship by a commissioned American vessel. For the rest of the war, he continued to harry a British fleet and afterwards was placed in charge of the US naval effort to put down the Algerian pirates. He died in 1803, still on active service, the highest ranking officer in the navy.

Another Irishman who made naval history was John Philip Holland, who persuaded the Fenians to fund him in developing a submarine, the *Fenian Ram*, in 1878. The Fenians had visualised the new invention as being a devastating way of striking at the British, but they disintegrated before Holland could develop the submarine's potential. However, his work laid the groundwork (or sea bed) for submarine design thereafter. His Holland SSI, commissioned on 30 March 1890, was the first submarine of the US Navy, and his work as we shall see (Chapter 10) had a profound effect on the Japanese Navy also.

Alfred Thayer Mahan, President of the Naval War College, and the grandson of a 1798 revolutionary who escaped to America after the rebellion, changed naval thinking throughout the world with his classic work *The Influence of Sea Power upon History*.

Thomas F. McManus was one of the few emigrants of his time, during the worst days of the Famine, to land in Boston with a highly developed skill. Before emigrating he had been a prosperous sail maker in the fishing port of Skerries in north County Dublin. He, and more particularly his son Thomas, were responsible for changing the face of the New England fishing fleet. The McManus design changed the Grand Bank Schooners from fast but very dangerous boats into even faster, and much safer vessels. For the latter quarter of the nineteenth century, McManus was the outstanding name in fishing fleet architecture.

The Perry brothers, Oliver and Matthew, whose mother was born in Ireland, each made their own kind of history. Oliver defeated a British fleet on Lake Erie in 1813 and Matthew 'opened Japan to the West' in 1852. Thomas MacDonough built on Oliver Perry's victory a year later on Lake Champlain by defeating another British fleet. Between them, the two victories saved New York and Vermont and drove the British to the negotiating table, thus ending the second Anglo-American War.

In the American Civil War, Irish commanders faced each other on opposite sides. The Confederacy's principal naval organiser was Matthew Maury, an Irish Huguenot, and one of the pioneers of oceanography. Dublin-born Stephen Rowan, a veteran of the Mexican War, was a leading Union commander, who inflicted a decisive defeat on a Confederate fleet, under another Irish commander, W. F. Lynch, off North Carolina in 1862.

Admiral William Leahy was the first American five-star Admiral. He served with distinction in both the Spanish-American War, and the First World War, before being appointed Chief of Staff during the Second World War by President Roosevelt, a post which he also held under Truman.

The tragedy of the Sullivan brothers during the Second World War is one of the sagas of the American Navy. Having survived a childhood rafting accident by sticking together, the brothers believed that they should stay together in the war also. They successfully lobbied the navy to break its rules about members of the same family serving on the same ship and consequently all five of the brothers were aboard the *Juneau* when a Japanese torpedo ripped into the ship during the Battle of Guadalcanal, in the Pacific, on a November night in 1942. One, George, was among the 140 who survived. However, he perished in the lifeboats, along with 129 of the other survivors who succumbed to sharks, thirst and starvation because of delays in mounting a rescue operation.

The story of the Sullivans was made into a Hollywood movie of the same name and it formed part of the inspiration for Steven Spielberg's film *Saving Private Ryan*. This fictional tale tells the story of a mission into occupied France to rescue a Private James Francis Ryan whose three brothers were killed in action a week earlier.[78] Ironically, Spielberg shot the film not on Omaha Beach, but in County Wexford in neutral Ireland. Had America decided to invade Ireland during the Second World War the County Wexford beaches would have been the chosen landing places.

As indicated already, the Irish, both Protestant and Catholic, played such a prominent role in the American revolutionary wars that the British blamed them for the loss of America. What is not so generally realised is the fact that, along with the blame, the British tried to fob off the shame of defeat on the Irish also! The Irish were of course heavily engaged on both sides of the war. One Charles O'Hara was second-in-command to Lord Cornwallis, the British Commander. O'Hara, a colourful, dashing figure, was the son (probably illegitimate) of the Irish peer, Lord Tyrawley. The formal surrender by Cornwallis to the Franco-American force led by Generals Rochambeau and Washington, at Yorktown, was arranged for noon on 20 October 1781. However, Cornwallis said that he was too ill to attend and sent O'Hara in his stead. O'Hara tried to avoid the humiliation of surrendering to the mere colonials and offered his submission to Rochambeau, but Rochambeau pointed him towards Washington who, seeing that Cornwallis had not turned up, directed him to his own second-in-command, General Lincoln. O'Hara made the best of a bad job, surrendered, received a parole, and dined bonhomously with both Washington and Rochambeau on successive nights.

The term 'Irish Brigade' gained a new resonance in military history with the coming of the American Civil War. The Irish fought on both sides of that appalling conflict, suffering terribly, but when people talk of the 'Irish Brigade', they are, generally speaking, referring to troops who fought for the Union.

The original Irish Brigade included the 63rd, 69th and 88th New York infantry regiments. The 69th was soon involved in controversy. It was largely officered by Irish nationalists who had come together in Republican clubs inspired by the Young Irelanders' rebellion of 1848, and its colonel, Michael Corcoran, refused to muster the regiment to honour the Prince of Wales on a visit to New York in 1860. Corcoran was held for court martial, but was released on the outbreak of the Civil War in April 1861. Subsequently the Irish Brigade was enlarged to include the 28th Massachusetts and the 116th Pennsylvania, remnants of the 7th New York Brigade. The 29th Massachusetts Brigade also fought in the Irish Brigade during hard service in the Peninsular campaign and at the Battle of Antietam at which the Irish Brigade suffered 540 casualties.

There is a famous description by a survivor of an even worse slaughter, under Marye's Heights at Fredericksburg, describing how the Irish Brigade were cut down. Thomas F. Galley wrote:

> The Irish Brigade . . . comes out from the city in glorious file, their green sunbursts waving . . . every man has a sprig of green in his cap and a half-laughing, half-murderous look in their eyes. They passed just to our left, poor fellows, poor, glorious fellows, shaking goodbye to us with their hats! They reach a point within a stone's throw of the stone wall. No further. They try to go beyond, but are slaughtered.[79]

That should be read in conjunction with a glance at Albrecht Dürer's sketch of a group of Irish soldiers whom he encountered during the European Wars of 1521. As he shoulders his battleaxe, one young lad has the same look in his eye that Galley spoke of. But it's not murderous. The lad is lonely, uprooted, but defiant and determined to sell his life dearly. Put him alongside some hundreds or thousands like him and you get the charge which swept away the British at the Battle of Fontenoy. But Fredericksburg was no Fontenoy. It was a major modern war fought with weapons of mass destruction. As the boxwood was out, the men wore sprigs of green in their caps. Unfortunately they could not replace the sprigs with armour, and when Meagher (of whom more later) gave the order to charge, they stepped forward to certain death. Some of them, as the hail of lead and shrapnel burst upon them, instinctively and uselessly turned up the lapels of their coats, as they would have against real hail.

On the Confederate side, the Irish did not join up because they wished to maintain slavery, but because they had adapted to Southern life. From Pennsylvania southwards, the population was predominantly Celtic, a fact which, one would have thought, should have lessened the force of the argument that the Irish stayed only in the slums. Unlike the disdainful WASPS, the Celts, largely Irish albeit with some Scottish mixture, were associated with dancing, drinking, fighting, gambling and allied pastimes. Bishop Berkeley once observed that: '. . . while in England many gentlemen with a thousand a year never drank wine in their houses, in Ireland, this could hardly be said of any who had but a hundred a year'. The bishop queried 'whether any kingdom in Europe be so good a customer at Bordeaux as Ireland'.[80]

A good question indeed. The Celtic migrants to America, unlike those to New England, felt free to carry on in the Old South just as they had done in Ireland, and as Grady McWhiney noted: 'The lazy Celtic ways that so infuriated the English, infuriated the Yankees as well, neither could understand people, who as one critic charged, spent as much time as they could "in idleness and drinking, to the great injury of . . . both . . . morals and industry".'[81]

McWhiney also commented that 'the Southerners propensity to fight surprised and disturbed many observers'. He cites a contemporary commentator who could have been writing at the time of the Romans: 'The whole race was warlike and fierce, and ready to fight with the greatest ardour . . . but accompanied with a rashness and temerity, not very compatible with military discipline.' One of the most famous generals on the Confederate side, Pat Cleborne, a Cork Protestant who was killed in the war, wrote to his brother summing up what might be termed a fairly typical Celtic attitude: 'I am with the South in life or death, victory or defeat.' He said that the slavery issue did not concern him but the Southerners 'have been my friends and have stood by me on all occasions'.[82]

A further motivation for joining the Civil War armies was the fact that many Irishmen saw the war as a useful opportunity for getting the training needed to drive the British out of Ireland. Had death not put an end to their dreams, most of the officers of the Irish Brigades fully intended to carry on the old fight when the Civil War ended. Peter Dunne, in his novel about the New York draft riots, encapsulated this sense of exile from the Garden of Eden by taking the title of his book from a famous old Irish Catholic prayer: *Banished Children of Eve*.

The tragedy of the Irish during the Civil War fighting could be said to have been epitomised by the experiences of two men in particular, John Mitchel and Thomas Francis Meagher. Both were Young Irelanders who had been transported to the Antipodes after the failed rebellion of the Young Ireland Movement in 1848. Having escaped and made their way to America, Meagher became Commander of the Irish Brigade slaughtered on behalf of the Union and John Mitchel became a leading publicist on behalf of the Confederates. He lost two of his sons, Willie and John, at Fort Sumter and Gettysburg respectively. A third son, James, would probably have been killed also if Mitchel senior had not used his influence to secure him a post of relative safety away from the front.

The Irish Brigades fought in some of the most famous battles of the Civil War. At Antietam, the Brigade Chaplain, Father Corby, who later became President of Notre Dame, gave the men a general absolution before battle commenced. When it did, two Irish Brigades, the 63rd and the 69th, lost 60 per cent of their men within a few minutes. Meagher's horse was shot from under him. Prior to the engagement, he had listened to the entreaties of a unit of 120 newly enrolled recruits who objected to being given Provost duties out of the line of fire, and had allowed them to take part in the fighting. Seventy-five were either killed or wounded. After the battle, Meagher wrote to his wife, Libby: 'The poor little Brigade was woefully cut up – I have not more than 750 in camp today – the best of my officers too, killed.'

Worse was to follow. Of Fredericksburg, Meagher would subsequently write: 'Of the 2,200 men I led into action the day before, 218 now appeared on the ground that morning.' The Irish fought with such bravery that the Confederate officer whose troops cut them down, General George Edward Pickett, wrote to his wife afterwards: 'Your soldier's heart almost stood still as he watched those sons of Erin. My darling, we forgot they were fighting us, and cheer after cheer at their fearlessness went up all along their lines.'[83] Mitchel's two sons served under Pickett.

Later the feelings of the Irish, struggling to make sense of the slaughter, while at the same time contending with nativist mistrust, were expressed in John Boyle O'Reilly's dubiously romantic poem, 'At Fredericksburg, December 13th, 1862':

> With Meagher at their head, they have dashed at the hill!
> Their foemen are proud of the country that born them;
> But, Irish in love, they are enemies still.
> Out rings the fierce word, 'Let them have it!' the rifles,
> Are emptied point-blank in the hearts of the foe:
> It is green against green but a principle strifes
> The Irishman's love in the Georgian's blow.
> The column has reeled, but it is not defeated;
> In front of the guns they reform and attack;
> Six times they have done it, and six times retreated;
> Twelve hundred they came, and two hundred go back.

On the night of 13 December, some of the survivors of the day's butchery began singing the ballad: 'Ireland boys hurrah'. It is recorded that the chorus was taken up for some six miles along the Union lines, and was then echoed by the Irish on the Confederate side. In truth, however, the Irish had little to hurrah about, and Meagher acknowledged this by resigning his commission after the Battle of Chancellorsville, which followed six weeks later and reduced the Irish Brigade to 500 men. Meagher had wanted to take his Brigade out of the line and rest it while re-enforcements were organised. However, his request was refused. He subsequently withdrew the resignation, but in the meantime the New York draft riots occurred and he was not offered another command.

The bloody saga of the Irish Brigades continued at what some have described as the bloodiest and certainly one of the most decisive battles of the Civil War, that of Gettysburg, in which, on the Confederate side, one of the principal commanders was Major General Robert Emmet Rhodes. On the Union side, Father Corby again blessed the 500-strong remnant of the Irish Brigade. The image of the priest standing on a rock blessing the troops has become one of the most enduring in the annals of Irish America. One of the many memorials dotting the Gettysburg battlefield today is the statue of Corby, which allegedly stands on the actual boulder. There is a replica of this statue at Notre Dame. The fact of his hand being raised in benediction led students of that citadel of American football to christen the statue 'fair catch Corby'. However, whatever Corby's blessing did for the Irish in the next world, it has to be said that it did little to prevent them departing this one. The Brigade was almost wiped out. One of the principal sources of its devastation was a battery of Confederate guns, commanded by the Westmeath-born Captain James Reilly.

The 69th fought with great gallantry in the First World War, albeit again having difficulty over the British connection. An attempt was made in France to issue the 69th with British uniforms which the Irish refused to wear. By the war's end, the Irish regiment had suffered 3,501 casualties. The famous Colonel William 'Wild Bill' Donovan led the survivors in a victory parade through a tumultuously welcoming New York.

In the Second World War, the members of the 69th fought in most theatres of the Pacific War. The 69th was the first combat unit to leave the US for the Pacific, as part of the 27th New York Division, and took part in several fierce engagements, including the famous 'Sake' night on Makin Atoll. The regiment charged ashore under Colonel Gerard Kelly, calling out the traditional battle cry 'Fag a bealagh' – 'Clear the Way'. On the night of the Japanese last stand, the Japanese put on their dress uniforms and got drunk on sake. The last great battle involving the 69th was the taking of Okinawa, in which the Irish took Machinato airfield, renaming it Conroy airfield after one of their officers who had been killed in the fighting on Makin. The regiment was officially named 'The Fighting 69th' by army decree in 1963, and St Patrick's Day was recognised as its official regimental day. That year also, President Kennedy visited Ireland and he presented the Irish people with the original colours of The Fighting 69th which are now on public display in the Dail.

The 69th played a role in the foundation of the contemporary CIA. By the outbreak of the Second World War, Wild Bill Donovan had become both a general and an Anglophile. He was Roosevelt's agent in London when war began and decided that America needed a British-style intelligence service. Roosevelt agreed and the result was the Office of Strategic Services (OSS), which Donovan ran throughout the war. The OSS was legendary for its 'dirty tricks' and undercover operations which formed a model for the Central Intelligence Agency (CIA) into which it evolved. One of the many Irish Americans whom Donovan recruited into the OSS was a future director of the CIA, William Casey.

The list of Irish Americans who gave distinguished service to the American Armed Services during the Second World War was not of course confined either to the members of the 69th Brigade or to the Sullivan brothers. Some of the outstanding air aces of the war were Irish. Captain Colin Kelly bombed and destroyed a Japanese warship in the Philippines and, though ordering his crew to bail out, continued to operate his machine until it crashed. Another air ace, Thomas B. Maguire, had shot down a total of thirty-eight Japanese planes before being downed himself while attempting to save another American plane which had come under Japanese fire.

O'Hare International Airport, in Chicago, is called after Edward O'Hare, a pilot aboard the aircraft carrier *Lexington* which was attacked by nine Japanese bombers while its squadron, with the exception of O'Hare, was airborne and operating away from the ship. O'Hare took off single-handedly and shot down five of the bombers and drove the rest into retreat. He too was killed in action. In similar fashion, Audie Murphy, an infantryman, won the medal of honour for single-handedly pinning down a German unit which comprised 200 men and six tanks.

Though much of the glamour has, rightly, been stripped from war, the Irish continue to take to the colours whenever American troops are engaged in hostilities. I once encountered a 'shamrock squadron' consisting of some twenty-two Irish-American-piloted helicopters in Vietnam, and as this is being written, in a new era of warfare, the old tradition is continued in a thoroughly politically correct fashion. One of America's leading astronauts is Airforce Colonel Eileen Marie Collins, the first woman to pilot a NASA spacecraft. She was the first woman pilot of a space shuttle, and participated in space walks and in the historic American inter-planetary rendezvous with the Russian space station, Mir. Appropriately enough her paternal grandfather came from Cork where another Collins also made military history, Michael Collins.

REVOLUTIONARY INFLUENCES

Even though I have been visiting America well nigh continuously since the early 1960s, sometimes repeatedly in the one year, I still find myself surprised at the extent of the influence of Ireland's revolutionary tradition on aspects of American life. One can see how that tradition works in our day by glancing at that quintessentially Irish organisation, The Ancient Order of Hibernians, and at the complementary experiences of three men who might at first glance be thought of as politically at the opposite ends of the ideological spectrum. On the right is Peter King, a New York Republican Congressman; on the left, Joe Jamesion, Research Director for New York State of the American trade union colossus the AFL/CIO and Director of the Irish-American Labor Coalition which mobilises trade union support for the Irish issue. In the centre is Tom McEnery, a former Mayor of San Jose who lent a helping hand in the generation of Ireland's current economic boom.

King is one of the leading American architects of the Peace Process, and one of the few Republicans who consistently supported President Clinton all through the Lewinsky affair. His support for Clinton was based on Clinton's support for the Irish Peace Process. King's grandparents on his father's side were Irish speakers on Inisbofin island off the Galway coast. His mother's family were Republicans (in the Irish sense) from Limerick. He remembered his grandmother speaking about 'that damned Lloyd George', but he had no involvement with the Irish issue. He thought that the Irish problem had ended with the signing of the Treaty in 1921. Then, as a student working at a summer job, he met a man from Northern Ireland, Henry McNamee from County Tyrone, who told him about his experiences: raids by police, IRA activities in the area, and so on.

He began reading everything he could lay his hands on and followed the course of the civil rights movement, in particular Bernadette Devlin's activities. Bloody Sunday happened, then later he met some of the hunger strikers' families when they came to America. All the resonances of his childhood came back. On a visit to Ireland during the blanket protest of 1980, which preceded the Bobby-Sands-led hunger strike, he experienced something which many Irish Americans found difficult to come to terms with – the hostility of people in the Republic towards the Republicans. His cousins referred to the blanket protesters as thugs and murderers. However, he continued to take an interest in the Six Counties and was in the home of the mother of one of the hunger strikers, Sean McKenna, on the day on which she was informed that her son had gone blind.

When he approached the State Department, he found that he got 'more of a pro-Brit line from the State Department than from the Brits'. He came to the conclusion that the IRA was a legitimate force, that there would be no progress over the North without the IRA. He was invited to Belfast, to sit on a tribunal investigating the use of plastic bullets by the RUC, and during his visit one of the hunger strikers died. This was Ciaran Doherty, who was elected to the Dail as a TD for County Cavan in 1981. At Doherty's home he met the hunger striker's parents, an impressive couple. I know both of them and can understand the impact they made. It was at the Doherty funeral also that he saw Gerry Adams for the first time. Talking to King, one gets a sense of the impact which Adams has had on a wide swathe of Irish American opinion. A devout Catholic himself, King was impressed by Adams's evident piety during the funeral mass, and by the fact that he took Communion.

It was also at the Doherty home on the day of the funeral that he met his first group of IRA people, three girls. As he went to the toilet, he came across them tying handkerchiefs across their faces. Outside the house they then formed the firing party, wearing black berets, responding to commands in Gaelic, while helicopters hovered overhead. It all only took a minute, but it seemed a long time.

Throughout this time King was engaged in local politics in the US. He was invited back to Belfast in 1983 to act as an observer in a supergrass trial, and began meeting the husbands and wives, brothers and sisters of IRA and INLA activists. He marvelled at the resilience of the families who had someone in jail. The harassment visited on them by the security forces meant that their role was more difficult than that of those in jail. The fact of getting to know so many people eventually led to his exclusion from the supergrass trial. One day a prisoner's wife, recognising him in the body of the court, waved at him.

When he waved back, he was asked to leave the court. However, although it was possible to remove him from the court, the authorities were not able to remove his subsequent report from the congressional record. In 1984, he made one of the ground-breaking TV programmes which for the first time brought Unionists, IRA and British spokespersons together. Even though the British spokesman, Michael Mates, 'stared straight ahead' and didn't engage, it was none the less 'a step along the way'.

In 1985, he was contacted by Loyalist paramilitaries and asked would he speak out on their behalf. He met a group of Loyalist leaders: George Seawright, John Bingham, John McMichael and Andy Tyrie. Tyrie is the only one alive today, the others were all killed by the IRA. King was struck by how confused and how anti-British they were. The people they saw themselves as fighting for were locking them up, and he could see that they were groping towards some sort of reappraisal of the situation. They were interested in finding out how the IRA lived.

By now he was convinced that the only solution to the Irish problem would be one based on dialogue involving the paramilitaries on both sides. He was elected to Congress in 1992 and was one of the Irish American leaders who took part in the crucial meeting in New York, during the presidential primaries, at which Clinton met leading members of the Irish American community and agreed to do something about the North of Ireland situation. Clinton did not find it easy to translate his views on Ireland into action. After his election, the State Department and the Justice Department, geared to the old special relationship with England, and completely out of sympathy with the Clinton/Gore group's policies, actively resisted the President. He was told: 'Mr President, campaign promises or no, you can't get Gerry Adams into the US. It would be against our anti-terrorist policies.'[84]

As indicated earlier, Clinton reacted to this resistance by appointing the National Security Council under Tony Lake as the vehicle for his Irish policy. Shortly after being appointed, Lake held a meeting with a bi-partisan group interested in the Irish situation. It included Joe Kennedy, Hamilton Fish, Ben Gillman, and King. Lake wasted no time on the usual mantras denouncing terrorism. Says King:

His question was: 'How do people get to the table?' He was using political language. He could have been talking about Russia or Bosnia. At that meeting, the question of the visa for Adams came up. Clinton was looking at the thing in conflict resolution terms. He's the first post-war President and he understands all the forces. He doesn't panic and he rolls with the punches. Possibly also there was some little residual resentment at what Major's people had done during the Election Campaign [the Tories supplied details of Clinton's student days in England to the Bush camp, and also sent personnel to America to assist the Republicans].

Clinton felt that granting a visa to Gerry Adams to visit the States would upset everything and everyone, but that nevertheless it would break the log jam. He obviously has an emotional affinity with Ireland. In the end the visa thing was decided over a round of golf with Chris Dodds. [Senator Dodds, who has a holiday home in the west of Ireland,

333

was Chairman of the National Democratic party.] Dodds told the President he thought the visa was a good idea. It was. It showed the IRA that they could get places with politics. So we got the '94 Ceasefire.

Then in '95, when the second Adams visa was granted, and Adams was asked to the White House, and Sinn Fein were given leave to solicit funds in the States, the Brits went ape-shit. Major refused to return Clinton's calls for over a week.

When Adams visited the White House, Clinton told him 'You fucking Irish – I'm catching shit'. Adams replied: 'Now you know what I'm up against, and how I feel!' They both laughed, and Clinton said, 'We'll make it work.' And he did. He went against Moynihan [a powerful Democratic Senator for New York, and one of the Four Horsemen] when he came out against giving Adams the visa. After Canary Wharf, [an IRA bomb in London created huge damage and ended the first IRA Ceasefire in February 1996], everyone ran for cover. But not Clinton. He understood what the IRA had done [stepped up the pressure so that Unionist opposition to holding talks with the Republicans would be overcome]. The administration panicked. But Clinton didn't. After the bomb he was still talking about 'Gerry', and saying 'we've got to put it back again'. After the Manchester bomb, there was more panic. But Clinton's reaction was: 'That's bad, but we've got to stay with it.'

The importance of the visa is that it brought in everyone, the Corporate types, the Hume types, Conservatives. People united in a way they never did before over an Irish issue, like say, the H-Blocks. That just appealed to the hard-core support. Now the President was involved. Ireland became respectable, up there with the whales and Africa! Gerry Adams took the whole thing out of the time warp, the bog Irish image. You had the White House putting out pictures of Adams with the President, identifying with Public Enemy no. 1. This locked in the President with Adams. Gerry was a partner.

They even made me respectable. I'd been getting pressure from the Irish Government and the Brits because I went on the reviewing stand for the 1985 St Patrick's Day Parade, when the Brits and the Irish Government were boycotting it because of the NORAID element.

All the Irish Americans rested a good deal of their hopes on Gerry Adams. They reasoned that he was too intelligent to attempt to take a revolutionary movement into peaceful politics with the intention of returning to revolution when it suited him. He was personally popular with all who met him on Irish visits, displaying leadership qualities that they felt would make him a credible personality in America, if he could get in. To give people a chance of evaluating his policies, O'Dowd offered him a weekly column in the *Irish Voice*.

When Adams finally did get permission to visit the US, King described the result in colourful terms: 'We were 10 years trying to get this guy into the country. Suppose he'd fucked up . . . ! But he was world class. All parties took to him – even Jessie Helms loved him.'

Apart from Adams there are innumerable instances of Irish revolutionaries who were accepted as pillars of society in America. After the 1798 rebellion there came figures like Dr William MacNevin, who built up a huge practice in New York; or Thomas Addis Emmet, Robert Emmet's brother, who became Attorney General for the State, and whose son I quoted at the start of this chapter. As we have seen, the Young Irelanders produced some of the outstanding soldiers of the American Civil Wars. The 1919–21 War of Independence and the Civil War which followed, contributed leaders to the American trade union movement.

Rebellion also forms part of the heritage of the largest, and certainly the most visible, Irish American organisation, the Ancient Order of Hibernians. This now largely middle-class organisation traces its direct lineage to:

> A legacy of some 271 years of struggle behind it in Ireland. Its origins were linked with a long line of secret Agrarian societies whose main aims were twofold. Firstly to serve as a bodyguard for priest and congregation during a celebration of the mass, then prohibited by the British Government, and secondly, to bring about the destruction of the grossly unjust system of landownership in Ireland that had established a small number of largely alien landlords as owners of practically all the property in the country.[85]

The American branch of the Ancient Order of Hibernians was founded in 1836, but it was not until 1851 that the Society went public and started placing ads in newspapers announcing meetings and so on. The Society was formally incorporated on 15 March 1853 as the Ancient Order of Hibernians, and took part in that year's St Patrick's Day Parade as the AOH. The Orangemen conferred the accolade of serious recognition on the AOH later in the summer by attacking its Fourth of July Parade in Abingdon Square, thereby generating a particularly savage riot. The AOH was closely associated with the Fenians and there was a good deal of cross membership between the AOH and members of Clan na nGael, the support organisation set up by the Fenians. Clan na nGael continued in existence until it became superseded by NORAID as the principal Republican support organisation during the recent Troubles. Again a degree of cross-membership occurred.

The late Judge James Comerford, who ran the St Patrick's Day Parade in New York for decades, caused a sensation at a very lace-curtain AOH function in Dublin Castle in the 1970s, when he told his audience, which included the then Taoiseach Jack Lynch, that as far as AOH was concerned, the Provisional IRA were following in the tradition of the men of 1916. It would not be true to say that every member of the organisation would support the Judge's sentiments, but the organisation does take a more forward position on Northern Ireland than middle-class Dublin would be comfortable with, and does devote much of its energies to ensuring that Irish history is not forgotten. Memorials to fallen Irish heroes, Famine victims, and support for Irish causes are a feature of the Order's existence.

The significance of the AOH and the Irish revolutionary tradition has to do with the ethos of America itself, a curious amalgam of detestation for 'terrorists' and respect for freedom fighters. Joe Jamison, the Director of Communication in the AFL/CIO, who was also one of the Irish American group which helped to broker the IRA ceasefire between Sinn Fein and the White House, is a good example of how the Irish Americans influence the Northern Irish situation and vice versa. He says that 'the effect of twenty-five years of conflict reversed the Irish in the assimilation process'. Some ancestral drum transmitted the message on *Callahan's Irish Quarterly*'s cover to him. He became aware that there was a war going on, and said to himself:

'What's happening – that's where I come from.' America works on an ethnic basis in which you celebrate your ethnicity. That's where you get the Parade syndrome. Here in New York there are over 150 parades in the year. Everyone marches, from Pakistanis, to Greeks, to the Irish, whatever. The Mayor must attend every one of those. You have a culture in which the idea of ethnicity is taken for granted. That's the difference with Britain. Supposing you are in a bar in London, say, and you give a toast: 'To a United Ireland.' Somebody is sure to say something like 'Don't say that. There could be an SAS man at the bar.'

When they say 'Paddies' they mean it as an epithet. But they think you are weird if you refer to them as 'Anglos'. That's the effect of the PTA Act.

Jamison is certainly correct in his differentiating between the way the law as it affects the Irish is interpreted in London and New York. I've had first-hand experience of this through appearing as an expert witness in various IRA trials, and I can testify that the atmosphere in an English court, where IRA activity is concerned, reaches permafrost level compared to either America or France. In a case in the Old Bailey, the evidence against a defendant centred around the fact that he had taken a son by a former marriage back to Belfast with members of his local Warrington pub's social club, and had been photographed with a group under a piece of craftwork made by prisoners in Long Kesh. The defendant, 'Dublin John' Kinsella, had no involvement whatever with the IRA.

However, a nephew of his persuaded him to allow two men to stay in his home for a few nights, and he agreed to bury what he thought was 'swag' for the two after a bribe changed hands. The fact that Kinsella buried the swag under the incinerator in the local allotment would appear to bear out his contention that he thought the holdall contained candlesticks or some such. In fact it contained Semtex. The two lodgers had been involved in a bombing at Warrington, which also involved a high-speed chase and the death of a policeman. Even though Kinsella had not known about any of this, the fact that such serious crimes had occurred obviously indicated the likelihood of a ten-year sentence as an accessory. Accordingly, I accepted the suggestion by his counsel, Helena Kennedy, that I appear as an expert witness, to testify that in Belfast the presence of Long Kesh artefacts in either Nationalist or Loyalist areas could very easily mean no more than that a neighbour had bought something to provide comforts for a friend's son or husband. They were certainly no indication of IRA membership. In fact a real IRA man would be careful not to draw attention to himself by displaying such items.

Moreover, it was abundantly clear that Kinsella had no connection with the IRA because he had instantly yielded up the Semtex when he learned to his horror of the holdall's true contents, and realised what a dangerous hiding place he had chosen. As a result of this, his life was threatened, and he had such a miserable time in prison prior to the trial that he attempted suicide by cutting his throat with the lid of a tomato can. He lived because the weather was so cold that his blood coagulated. I attempted to explain to the court that in West Belfast, as on the West Bank, local tribal and family associations were such that IRA or PLO symbols could be found everywhere, without indicating either membership or even support of either organisation. However, the judge refused to allow any comparison with any place outside Belfast and generally made it difficult for me to explain the psychology of that divided city. He sentenced Kinsella to twenty years in jail.[86]

By contrast, I spent a week in 1998 in a New York courtroom before Judge Kimber Wood, whose many unusual attributes included the insights gained working as a 'bunny girl' in a London Playboy Club. I had been asked to give evidence in a case in which Charles Caulfield had been charged with transgressing US emigration law by entering 'none' as an answer to a query concerning previous criminal convictions. Caulfield had served three years for Republican activities in Portlaoise jail before emigrating to the States. However, his lawyer, Mike Dowd, mounted a stirring defence on the premise that no young Irishman, finding himself standing in the dock in the same courthouse in which Robert Emmett was unjustly condemned to death, could possibly accept that his activities were 'criminal'. To say that they were, by answering 'yes' to the emigration question, would have been a betrayal of his principles and his cause.

In the event, having listened to similarities being drawn between the civil rights movement in America and that in Northern Ireland, from which the contemporary IRA sprang, the jury found that Caulfield had not committed an offence. Activities conducted on behalf of the IRA (his commanding officer was Jim Lynagh, the leader of the ASU wiped out by the SAS at Loughgall) were not regarded as criminal by a New York Federal Court.

One of the most celebrated cases involving the issue of whether IRA membership indicated criminal or political activity was that involving Joe Doherty in New York. During his time in jail, Doherty became a hero, was visited by Cardinal O'Connor and had a New York street named after him. He had escaped from the Long Kesh prison complex outside Belfast, having been found guilty of the murder of a captain of the SAS, and made his way to America. However, the British sought his extradition and he was arrested and brought to trial. After a lengthy hearing, in which trial Judge Sprizzo listened patiently to hours of exposition on Irish history from myself and the former Chief of Staff of the IRA, a Nobel Peace Prize Winner, Sean MacBride, Doherty was adjudged to have committed a political, not a criminal, offence. However, he was subsequently charged with visa offences, and spent nine years in various American jails, before being sent back to the Six Counties, where he was condemned to serve his full sentence, the time in New York prisons not being taken into account. He was ultimately released under the terms of the Good Friday Agreement.

The remarkable feature of the revolutionary legacy for the bulk of Irish

Americans – excepting the relatively tiny percentage who hold the physical force tradition sacred – is how constructive its resonances can be, despite their frequently horrific background. For example, Tom McEnery's grandfather, Patrick McEnery, was on the platform with Parnell when he delivered his famous 'no man has a right to fix the boundary of the march of a nation' speech. The Sinn Fein priest, Father Yorke, was responsible for bringing Patrick to San Francisco, so that he could marry his childhood sweetheart, Catherine Costello, who had emigrated from their native Kerry in 1898. Amongst the letters preserved in the McEnery family are the following:

> Dear Fr Tom,
> I will be going before my God in a few hours. Cheer up and console my wife and child and poor mother. Will you grant me one request and this is to look after Hannah's welfare and bring up my darling son for the Church. It breaks my heart to think of my poor wife and child, but I depend on you to look after them, but for them I never would feel it, because I know I'm going to a better place – to my dear father and brothers who are in heaven. Say masses for my Soul and give money to Fr Ferris, he gave us confession and communion, so cheer up my dear brother. I gave my life as a Soldier of the Republic, but I never expected this would be my fate, but welcome the will of God.

> My dear Mother,
> I am going the long road tomorrow morning, to meet father and my brothers. Be good to Hannah and take care. Sonny – bring him up for the priesthood and don't let anyone interfere with them. Don't be downhearted, you can be proud of me. I am dying a Soldier of the Irish Republic. Goodbye now Mother darling, and we will all meet in Heaven.
> > Goodbye from your darling son, Jim.

The letters, which probably say as much about a Church-inculcated resignation and an emotion-suppressing culture as they do about the intrinsic tragedy involved, were written by Tom's Uncle James. He was executed by the Free State authorities in 1923 after being captured with a group of IRA companions in Clashmalcolm Cave, high above a savage Kerry sea. Two of his companions were drowned before his eyes in a futile attempt to swim through smashing waves. The rest only surrendered, following days without food or water, when bales of burning hay were dropped into the cave mouth. The leader of the group, Aero Lyons, fell to his death as he was being hauled up the cliff when the rope either broke, or was severed.

However, growing up in California, Tom McEnery never heard a word of bitterness about the affair from his father, John Patrick McEnery. John Patrick became Superintendent of the Mint under Truman, State Chairman of the Democratic Party and a successful businessman. One of his employees, who was particularly well loved by the McEnery household while Tom was growing up in San Jose, was an old Irishman called Mick McDonnell. The McEnerys never associated Mick with any revolutionary activity until one day in the 1950s – during which another IRA campaign had sputtered into life in

Ireland – when the FBI came calling and suggested that Mick might be engaged in illegalities. They were politely shown the door. What the McEnerys didn't know, until I told Tom nearly forty years later, was that Mick was also the head of Michael Collins's fearsome assassination team, 'The Twelve Apostles', which he set up to shoot spies and informers. Collins had smuggled McDonnell out of Ireland for his own good during the War of Independence. Later, his brother was killed by James McEnery's comrades during the Civil War. My father's comrades shot James.

Curiously, although Tom McEnery never heard McDonnell speak of Collins, for some reason which he cannot fully explain, when Tom came to do his MA thesis he chose Michael Collins, not knowing that the Mick McDonnell whose activities he was researching for it was the kindly old Irishman of his boyhood, at whose funeral mass he had been an altar boy. However, when he first visited Ireland, he felt as though 'a light switch had been thrown'. He only really began to research the details of his uncle's death after a visit to a bar in Kerry in 1967, during which someone asked him, 'Are you related to the McEnery that was killed in the caves?' Someone else told him: 'Your uncle was shot by the British.' So far as the physical force tradition was concerned, there was no differentiation between the British and the Free State forces. The politics of the sixties were still influenced by the passions of the twenties.

Tom McEnery also went into politics and became the Mayor of San Jose. During his terms in office, the city grew to become the eleventh largest in the US. As it is the gateway to Silicon Valley, McEnery decided that it would be a good idea to twin San Jose with Dublin. However, in the early 1980s, very few people in Irish political circles had heard of Silicon Valley and his proposal fell on deaf ears. Then one day he phoned me from California. I brought the matter to the attention of Charles Haughey, the then Taoiseach, who, whatever his other failings, had a capacity for quick decision-taking, and the cities were duly twinned. McEnery set up the Irish Industrial Development Authority in an office in San Jose and introduced the IDA to the CEOs of some of the world's top computer companies. Subsequently, whoever merits the credits, Intel, Seagate and Amdahl all located in Ireland.

The twinning process has also meant that a great number of Irish public representatives and visiting firemen have fetched up in one of the Silicon Valley area's more important websites on the information super-highway – Hannigan's Bar in Los Gatos. The difference between Hannigan's and the electronic sites is that once enmeshed in Hannigan's web you're trapped, a cyber liver is no use to you.

Another interface of Irish American culture with the Irish Revolutionary tradition of which I obtained first-hand knowledge involved a touch of the macabre to which full justice could only be done by means of a novel, the stage or the movie screen. It embodied all the schmaltzy, but none the less sincere, characteristics of mid-1960s Boston. A legendary Bostonian undertaker called Gene Sheehan – who had left Ireland, rapidly, after an IRA shooting, in the

1920s – subsequently built up a thriving undertaking business in Boston, with an unusual sales pitch. I first became aware of it, sitting in a radio studio in Boston with Tommy Shiels, who in those days ran a celebrated radio programme which included ballads, interviews, sports reports and commercials. He interrupted an interview he was conducting with me to read out a commercial on behalf of Sheehan: 'You all know Gene. The friendly Irish undertaker. Now Gene has introduced a new service. He will take you or your loved ones back to be buried in the old sod by Aer Lingus, "the friendly Irish airline".'

Here it should be remarked that far from being 'friendly' Aer Lingus could rip off its largely captive market to the same extent as even the most voracious of its competitors. Fares shot up at holiday time, and sending one's loved one back to the 'old sod' for burial was made a particularly expensive business. However, about two years after the commercial, my path was to cross that of Gene's once more.

The crossing occurred because, unknown to me, Gene had decided to extend the range of his aeronautical morticianship, and had involved the demise of a well-known figure in the Boston Irish community, a Miss Folen, in his plans. She was a remarkable woman who had left the Aran Islands in her teens under the influence of a vocations-questing nun to travel to Salamanca in Spain to become a nun. Deciding that a career in the convent was not for her, Miss Folen somehow made her way to Boston, went into service, saved her money, and eventually paid her way through nursing school. On her deathbed, after a life of prudently investing her savings, she presented a tempting target for Gene. However, although *in articulo mortis*, the old lady resisted the blandishments of both the friendly Irish airline and 'the old sod' on the very reasonable grounds that there was no way in which the friendly Irish airline could land on her rocky native isle, which was very short in the 'old sod' department.

Gene suddenly found the answer to overcoming her resistance one night as he watched the television news from Vietnam. Helicopters! On the understanding that she would be borne on the last leg of her journey from Shannon Airport to the island by helicopter, Miss Folen gave Sheehan charge of her funeral arrangements and proceeded to breathe her last. Alas, it is said poor Miss Folen's remains never left Boston. After being waked in traditional style, and being inspected reposing in her handsome coffin by the unsuspecting Irish Consul General, Paddy McKiernan,[87] who signed the necessary papers to allow the body to be flown home aboard the friendly Irish airline, it is alleged that plan B went into operation without McKiernan's knowledge.

Legend has it that Miss Folen's remains did not leave Boston, but as has happened before, and since, were either interred in the foundations of a skyscraper under construction or, after the corpse was reduced in bulk by the extraction of the bodily fluids, placed in a coffin under another body and buried under someone else's tombstone. Someone it seems, had other purposes and other contents in mind for the coffin.

True or false, however, man proposeth and God disposeth. The coffin arrived safely at Shannon, but Things Began To Go Wrong. Someone pointed out that on Aran, the wake custom was still very strong, and the burden of probability was that those present would open the coffin on arrival.

Plan C went into operation – with disastrous consequences. Over an isolated patch of countryside, between Shannon Airport and the Cliffs of Moher, the coffin fell from the sling attaching it to the helicopter, and crashed to earth. A new coffin and a new cover story were thus provided: to spare the distress of the relations, the coffin would have to be kept closed, so as to conceal the grisly aftermath of the fall.

Unfortunately, however, in Shannon at the time (1967), there was a very active freelance journalist, Tommy Brown. Tommy realised that the coffin had not simply fallen into any ordinary piece of deserted countryside. It had hurtled on to the townland of Paradise! Accordingly, Tommy circulated the newspapers of the world with an item headed 'Coffin falls into Paradise'. Gene nearly had a heart attack. Press publicity was the last thing he had expected. His nerve began to fail him, and it broke entirely when someone, on whom he practised his cover story, remarked: 'Ah, sure, they won't mind a bit of a fall over on Aran. Sure they're used to taking bodies out of the sea after the crabs and other yokes have been at them. They'll open the coffin, no bother . . .'

Plan D went into operation.

Once more the coffin took off from Shannon, slung underneath the helicopter. This time it got past Paradise safely but, having flown over the Cliffs of Moher, complications set in. The coffin, journalists were informed, developed a swing in the sling and was dropped once more – this time into the western Atlantic. However, possibly not surprisingly, in view of the fact it was now empty, it failed to sink. This circumstance may or may not have had a bearing on the fact that one of the helicopter's two-man crew, described as the navigator, also dropped into the sea. He said afterwards that he did so in order 'to identify the spot where the coffin fell'. History does not record whether he proposed to do this by carving an X on a passing wave, but in any event, the coffin sank. No coffin meant no wake. Gene's worries were over.

Or were they? The Department of Transport and Power was ordered by the punctilious minister responsible, Erskine Childers (a very fine Protestant gentleman who later became President of Ireland, despite being known to his colleagues behind his back as Foreskin Childers) to hold an enquiry into how the coffin apparently developed a pronounced case of falling sickness.

I was only very dimly aware of the general outline of these events and on a day in October 1967 stepped off the train from Dublin to Cork in cheerful frame of mind, having secured an interview with the legendary General Tom Barry, one of the great IRA figures of the Black and Tan War, for my book on the IRA. Barry never spoke to reporters, and the fact that he would talk to me was an Event.

Alas, the General met me at the station to tell me that he could not do the interview. 'Gene has a problem,' he informed me, 'and I have to go with him to Shannon.' I had no idea that Sheehan was in Cork, though I knew him slightly. He was almost as well known in Dublin as in Boston, through having some mysterious connection with the importation and sale of slot machines. To his credit, when he learned of my presence in Cork he raised no objection to my accompanying Barry, himself and their driver, Michael Fitzpatrick, also a well-known Republican, on the journey from Cork to Shannon Airport.

It was a fascinating experience. Barry was a Seanacai, a gifted natural story-teller. As we drove, he told tales of ambushes he had conducted and pointed out places where comrades of his had fallen in the war against the Black and Tans. When we came to such a spot, the car would slow and Barry would solemnly salute the fallen. Judging by the number of salutes, the road between Cork and Shannon must have been a sanguinary place in its day. Certainly one such episode was. Barry recounted with relish how he had chased a Black and Tan across a road and into a pub which we were passing. 'He ran in there,' said Barry, pointing, 'and I followed him in. I didn't see him at first. He'd got down behind the counter.'

'What happened then?' I somewhat naïvely enquired. Came the reply: 'I leaned over the counter and I gave it to the bastard between the two eyes . . .'

At Shannon, Michael Fitzpatrick, a graduate *summa cum laude* of the Tell Them Nothing School, who said he knew no more than I about what was going on, chatted pleasantly for forty-five minutes or so. Then, a pleased-looking Barry and Sheehan reappeared, accompanied by a third man, a low-sized, respectable figure in his sixties, wearing a Pioneer Pin, the emblem of the Total Abstinence Association. He was introduced to me as: a) an ex-member of Barry's old flying column, and b) the head of Shannon Airport security. As I was to discover, the second was like unto the first. After we'd all shaken hands, Barry said: 'Now, the business is out of the way. We can have a few halves.'

Sheehan saw to it that not only did we not have 'halves', we had large ones, and a very great number of them. On the way back to Cork, the mood was far lighter than on the way out. There was a full moon and some of the trees appeared to be moving in a high wind. However, we saluted them whether they moved or not. For all we knew, there could have been an ambush at the base of each one of them at an earlier stage in Irish history. When we had returned to Cork, Barry and I had a final drink over which he confided to me what the purpose of our trip to Shannon had been: 'That oul inquiry over the business of the coffin and the helicopter. I just wanted to make sure that the lads would look after Gene.'

Apparently, whoever the lads were, they did the business. The following July on the Adjournment Debate (a classical time for potentially awkward issues to be dealt with before the Dail goes into summer recess, thereby preventing any nonsense like supplementary questions or protracted debate), reading somewhat uncomprehendingly (as was his wont) from his prepared brief, Erskine Childers announced the results of his Department's inquiry into the lamentable affair of the coffin falling first into Paradise and then disappearing into the Atlantic. The matter, he said, had arisen because of a defective shackle. This circumstance had been drawn to the attention of the company and he could assure the House that there would be no repetition. Whatever the fault with the shackle, the old flying column bonds had obviously held across the Atlantic.

Those bonds were strengthened by the troubles which were beginning to erupt in Northern Ireland at the time of Nurse Folen's obsequies. Here in the words of Joe Jamison is how they helped to enmesh with an emerging consciousness of being Irish in America. He feels that:

observers from Ireland underestimate the extent to which Irish identity in modern America has been decisively shaped by the Northern conflict. It's gone on so long that it seems to have suspended – or maybe reversed – the normal process of assimilation. TV images led to curiosity, to reading, to visits. Visits were not about a search for roots, they confirmed political impressions. Often enough they led, on return, to activist political commitment. Ethnic assertion is easy in this patchwork nation. Unlike in Britain where, for various reasons, the Irish keep their heads down, in America assimilation exists side-by-side with a democratic ideology which celebrates immigrant roots.

I was of the third generation, and a child of the baby boom and the TV age. My grandparents wanted to forget the poverty of Ireland, and rarely spoke of it to their children. My parents, working-class people, were too busy struggling to raise eight children in post-World-War II America to pay any heed to roots. It fell to the next generation to seek reconnection. But, reconnection took place amidst a new conflict. The same is true of hundreds of thousands of Irish Americans, above all in the big US cities, which were now and again refertilised by new waves of Irish immigration.

By 1977, my wife and I and our year-old daughter set foot in Ireland, searching and finding the first, second and third cousins in Tipperary, Longford, Cavan, Antrim and Dublin. Our adventure pushed the older generation into making a first visit to Ireland, the next year.

I have spent much of my adult life in Irish American activist organisations filled with people with stories like mine. Since the late 1960s we have all been seeing TV images of the conflict. The images, the voices stimulated ethnic awareness, then indignation, then sympathy, and often activity. It need not have been so. In the 1950s there was a lingering sense of defensiveness about Irishness. In my parochial school we described ourselves as 'Irish Catholics'. The JFK presidency was the first factor eroding that defensiveness, Thirty years of media imagery of Six County conflict was the second factor. Those children – now adults – usually call themselves 'Irish Americans' and have a robust sense of ethnic identity.

Opinion in Irish America has often been in advance of opinion in the Twenty-Six Counties. For example, Irish America always believed in the possibility of resolving the conflict, even if it lacked the political formula for doing so. For decades, Irish Americans, having visited their relatives in the 26 Counties, have been appalled at the South's apathy about the North. It was an apathy that – one hopes – may be overcome, by the demise of Section 31 [the prohibition in the Broadcasting Act which prevented Sinn Fein spokespersons from appearing on RTE] and an advancing peace process. But grassroots Irish America never accepted Southern apathy as the final word. It was an obstacle to be worked around.[88]

And worked around it was. It was Irish America that involved Clinton in the Peace Process, Irish America which voted for him when a majority of the other white-collar male ethnic groups voted for George Bush, and Irish America which is the political motor force behind the elevation of the Irish issue. It's still a hard-fought field at times. Even though Blair and New Labour have a different approach to Ireland than that of the Conservatives, the traditional institutional forces interface with each other: British intelligence services with the Justice Department; the Foreign Office with the State Department. The Pentagon, because of military alliances around the world, particularly in the former Yugoslavia and in the Middle East, is sympathetic to the British position also.

At times of excitation, membership of the IRA, or even of Sinn Fein, could and did lead to deportations and prosecutions. Cases ranging from denials of visas because of IRA membership to jail sentences, generally for arms trafficking, were common all through the thirty-year conflict and still occur, though less frequently.

The cumulative effect of these cases worsened a widespread uncertainty amongst some emigrants as to whether their future lies back in Ireland or in the States, and this made them hesitate over 'swearing sole allegiance to the US'. This meant that several thousand illegal emigrants did not apply for visas either under the Morrison or Donnelly programmes. Therefore, at the time of writing, an uncomputed but sizeable percentage of elderly immigrants were facing lonely twilight years without social welfare entitlements, afraid to go back to the Ireland they had clung on to in their imaginations for fear of being refused readmission to the America which had employed them.

However, despite such cases and the occasional hiccup (like the fatigue factor that temporarily set in in Washington political circles over the bickering in Belfast which delayed the setting up of the power-sharing Assembly agreed to in the Good Friday Agreement of 1998) the over-arching relationship between America and Ireland is one of growing and deepening friendship and interest. President Clinton tested this friendship when he famously remarked, after one breakdown in negotiations that the protagonists were like two drunks who had been fighting in a pub. They came out, made peace – and went back in and started fighting again. 'What?! Us fight! It's the Unionists!', howled the *Irish Voice*. However in March 2000, less than a year later, Clinton purged his contempt, when he declared not merely St Patrick's Day, but the whole month of March, Irish-American heritage month. A little later, on May 13th, one of the most important demonstrations of the depth and range of the Irish cultural heritage ever mounted in the US was opened in the Kennedy Center for the Performing Arts in Washington, by President Mary McAleese.

The two-week Festival, Island Arts from Ireland, was organised (and part-funded) by Jean Kennedy Smith. The Festival's concerts illustrated the links between Irish music and its American descendant, country music. Its Art exhibitions included works from the Burns collection by Irish artists of the calibre of Jack B. Yeats, Roderic O'Connor, Walter Osborne, and William

344

Orpen. Its readings were from the work of writers like William Kennedy, Frank McCourt and Jennifer Johnson and poets Seamus Heaney, Paul Durcan and Eavan Boland. Musicians such as Mick Moloney, and the *Riverdance* composer Bill Whelan performed their work. Theatrical companies like Druid Theatre and Red Kettle staged the work of Irish playwrights who included Marina Carr and Donal O'Kelly. O'Kelly's play *Catalpa* had a particular resonance, as we will see in our Australian exploration (Chapter 5) it dealt with the John Boyle O'Reilly-sponsored rescue of Irish political prisoners from Australia.

The interest generated by these events and much else in the Festival, which also embraced Irish dance and film-making, was a clear indication, if indication were needed, that it was not alone in the arena of politics that Ireland was 'up there with the whales'.

IRISH STUDIES

St Paul's Minnesota is the home, some would say 'shrine' is a more appropriate term, of Eoin McKiernan who spent his life trying both to popularise and to introduce a note of authenticity into Irish Studies. Along with his duties as Professor at St Thomas University, and raising ten children, Eoin founded the Irish American Cultural Institute and the scholarly review, *Eire Ireland*. Beginning in the 1950s and continuing until the 1980s, McKiernan, like a cultural version of Bishop John Ireland, colonised Irish American society. Each year he brought troops of Irish academics, poets and writers from Ireland on month-long tours of the entire United States. He kept down expenses through using a network of friends to accommodate the visitors, who in turn found large and enthusiastic audiences wherever they went.

The importance of this endeavour may be gauged from a story told by Andrew M. Greeley. Greeley began his acclaimed study of the Irish in America, *That Most Distressful Nation* (significantly sub-titled *The Taming of the Irish*), published in 1972, with an anecdote about a friend who had tried unsuccessfully for several years to obtain Governmental funding for an Irish project in his university. The friend finally went to Washington and brought his proposal to a senior official of the Department of Education. Getting nowhere, he finally lost his temper, and pounding the desk exclaimed: 'There are programmes in Mexican Studies, Scandinavian Studies, Jewish Studies, and of course Black Studies that the Office of Education is financing. Why not a programme in Irish Studies?'

The official also lost his cool and, pounding in return, retorted: 'The Irish don't count!'

That finished the funding application. Such was the climate of the time that Greeley judged: 'We know practically nothing about the American Irish . . . There is little serious history and practically no sociology about the Irish . . .

345

The best one has on the subject of the Irish is a number of stereotypes, frequently superficial at that.'[89]

However, by the time I started to research this book, almost a quarter of a century later, all, in the words of the poet Yeats, was 'changed, changed utterly'. Inevitably a cynic will continue the quotation to observe that, as with the 1916 Revolution, 'a terrible beauty was born'. And obviously, amidst the plethora of publications, seminars, semesters, summer schools, and general odd-ballsism that the massive gear shift which has occurred in American studies has thrown up, some dross was created, but some very fine work was done also.

At a dinner one evening in the home of Chris Kennedy, a son of the murdered Robert Kennedy, I was astounded by the knowledge of the poet Yeats which Chris displayed. Apart from a grasp of the details of the poet's life, he appeared to be able to recite the poetry both effortlessly and faultlessly. When I remarked on his facility, he replied simply: 'I took Adele's course.' The late Adele Dalsimer was one of the most important figures in Irish American scholarship. A founder member of the American Committee for Irish Studies (ACIS), she is responsible for the Boston College Programme of Irish Studies, which is arguably the most prestigious in the US. (That statement probably takes care of my welcome at quite a number of educational establishments!).

Had I not had a witness[90] to her account of how it all began, with whom I was able to check afterwards that I had really heard what I thought I heard, I would not have believed that such a far-reaching, influential academic initiative could have begun as it did. In 1972, Adele and her husband Jim, a prominent Boston psychiatrist, found themselves on a bus in Dublin on their first visit to Ireland. They asked the bus conductor some questions about places of cultural interest, James Joyce homes and so forth, and got off the bus. As they did so, they were hailed by a James Joyce look-alike, complete with boater, bow tie and moustache, who introduced himself, told them he had heard their conversation with the bus conductor, and offered to show them around Dublin.

The man was Terry Flanagan, father of the film actress, Fionnuala Flanagan, and a member of the *Irish Press* advertising department, whom I knew well – and I could understand how Adele and Jim's attitude of initial caution changed to one of being completely bowled over by Terry's personality and encyclopaedic knowledge of literary and historical Dublin. He took them all over the city, announcing airily, 'It's no trouble at all. I'll take the day off.' Not for the first time, nor the last, in his career, Terry was as good as his word, but rarely can a stolen day have yielded such fruitful results. 'There was a story behind every door we passed, a story under every stone.' After the encounter with Terry Flanagan, Adele and Jim wafted through Ireland on a magic carpet of similar experiences: 'People were so anxious to help. The dumbest question, it didn't matter how ignorant we were, people were always patient and helpful.'

At this stage, Adele, who came from a completely Jewish background, had not taught a course in Irish studies. Her knowledge of the subject was confined to an acquaintance with Yeats, but she rapidly became more interested. She attended the first ACIS conference in 1974, and was impressed by meeting Irish American academics like John Kelleher, Emmet Larkin, Larry McCaffrey and Bob Rhodes. On the recommendation of Larry McCaffrey, she secured the appointment of Kevin O'Sullivan to her department and between them they turned a desert green. Adele had been teaching English literature at Boston since 1969, specialising in post-Romantic poetry, but when she looked at her class list she discovered that Yeats was taught as a major British writer, and, even though most of her students had Irish names, when she suggested that Irish literature be taught, she was told, 'You'll get no students.' The reality in most American colleges at that time was that the teaching of things Irish was not considered kosher.

Irish studies were in part tinged with a brush of supposed Anglophobia, in part viewed with the remnants of WASP disdain, and regarded as an impediment to the then prevalent 'melting pot' theory. However, coming from a Jewish background, in which inter-disciplinary studies were regarded as normal, Adele refused to allow herself to be put off by suggestions that Irish studies would be 'navel gazing'. Not only did she lobby the university authorities to make an investment in an Irish programme, she twisted the arm of a wealthy relation to secure an annual endowment of $1,000 which she used to attract lecturers of the calibre of Richard Ellman, Sean MacBride and Seamus Heaney.

Her researches convinced her of the importance of interaction of the forces which influenced Irish literature, history, the Church, the economy, and she came to the decision that it was 'totally opprobrious' that the Irish language should be regarded as something separate from the study of what some see as 'Anglo-Irish literature', and others regard as being merely the result of Irish people writing in English. Accordingly, she enforced a knowledge of the Irish language in her MA course, with the result that, at the time of writing, Irish can be heard spoken in the corridors of Boston College. And it all started with Terry Flanagan overhearing a conversation in a Dublin bus, and taking a day off from the *Irish Press*.

Apart from the numbers of students taking Irish courses, right across America, the health of Irish studies may be adduced from the number of distinguished academics now working in the field: at Bridgewater State College, one of the great literary historians of our time, Charles Fanning; in Chicago, Emmet Larkin, the doyen of Irish Church history, and his friend Laurence McCaffrey; in Missouri, Kerby A. Miller; in Wisconsin, James Donnelly; at NYU Bob Scally, and so on. Nowadays the problem is not who to put in but who to leave out.

Not only does the list of scholars grow, so too does that of pioneers like Adele Dalsimer. In New York the partnership of Loretta Brennan Glucksman resulted in Lew, a former chairman of Lehman Brothers, and at the time of writing Vice-chairman of Smith and Barney, founding Ireland House as a centre of Irish studies at NYU.

However, while this massive transformation has occurred and continued to grow, the shadow of the Northern Ireland situation and the tensions of the Anglo-Irish relationship can still obtrude into the classroom. The extreme sensitivity, some might call it guilt complex, of the British Foreign Office, concerning Britain's record in Ireland, and how it is portrayed in study programmes, was encapsulated in a controversy stemming from an attack on the Governor of New York, George A. Pataki by the British Ambassador to Washington, John Kerr, between October 1996 and January 1997, over the inclusion of the Famine as a school subject in the New York State school system. The Conservatives were still in power in London at the time, and in essence this controversy was a rerun of the issues which had lain at the heart of the Irish Studies controversy in London a few years earlier. Unlike the London issue, however, the debate was widely reported in the press, both in America and Ireland, and was keenly followed by Irish Americans. Predictably, the Murdoch press in both New York and London supported Kerr. The London *Times* said that he was attempting to 'grub ethnic votes'.[91] The *New York Post* said the legislation was part of the Irish Americans' 'quest for victimhood'. [92]

Pataki's crime lay in the fact that he had signed into law a Bill sponsored by Assemblyman Joseph Crowley, to allow (along with existing courses on 'the inhumanity of genocide, slavery . . . the Holocaust') instruction on 'the mass starvation in Ireland from 1845 to 1850'.[93]

In approving the Bill, Pataki said he did so because:

> It is my sincere hope that our State's pupils – a great many of whom descended from Irish immigrants – will develop a respect and universal concern for human rights, the sanctity of human life and a tolerance of other races, religions and points of view. To instill these moral and ethical values in New York State's youth, it is imperative they receive a full appreciation of the lessons of history, however troubling they may be.[94]

In fact, Pataki himself was of Irish emigrant descent. His maternal grandmother was Agnes Lynch from County Louth, and he supported the MacBride principles which are aimed at preventing US investment in Six County companies which practise discrimination. Kerr was seemingly also unaware of the fact that several of his most trusted aides were Irish Americans. Playing on the fact that Pataki was a Republican – which Kerr apparently imagined meant that he was cast in the mould of the Ronald Reagan-Margaret Thatcher relationship – the Ambassador wrote to Pataki eight days after the Bill became law, using the familiar 'Dublin Four', revisionist approach of sonorous language and pitying condescension to upbraid the Governor.[95] The Famine, said Kerr, was a 'natural disaster', not analogous to the Holocaust. Neither the Governor nor the Crowley Bill had said it was. However, the Ambassador continued that the Governor should be aware 'of well meaning and earnest Britons' who had provided relief. The Ambassador's authorities for this assertion were not based on the fact that inevitably some, a minority obviously, decent people in England, and an even smaller minority of the landlord class in Ireland, did try to stem the tide of horror, but on the evidence of 'revisionist historians' whom the Ambassador opined 'now probably dominate' Irish Universities.' On this point only, as Brendan Bradshaw indicated in his famous article, the Ambassador certainly had a weight of evidence on his side.

However, in terms of which Gerald Cambrensis would not have disapproved, His Excellency went on to draw attention to the fact that the British and Irish governments were intent on reconciliation and pointedly declared: 'I hope New York schools will teach that too.'[96] As someone who was close to the subterranean negotiations of those days, I can testify to the fact that if the views of senior Dublin politicians and diplomats involved in the Irish Peace Process at that time had been made known, the classrooms of New York would have resonated to a view of a London toad under the harrow of a Unionist plough which would have occupied the letter writing efforts not only of Ambassador Kerr, but of the entire embassy staff for considerably longer than did the Pataki affair. In the course of the correspondence, which allededly of course dealt with matters arising from *circa* 1845–7, Kerr attempted to tar Pataki with a contemporary IRA brush:

> The IRA's apparent preference for murder rather than negotiations means that Sinn Fein, alone of all parties successful in last year's election, are absent [from the then on-going formal talks in which the Conservatives under Unionist pressure were colluding to keep Sin Kein out of talks on the stated grounds that the IRA must decommission their arms in advance of talks]. I hope that you will add your voice to those of the great majority of the Irish people, and their many American friends, who – with the administration of the two Governments – call on the IRA too to pursue the path of peace.[97]

Kerr resorted to the IRA tactic after Pataki had blown him out of the water with a letter which pointed out the irrefutable fact that nothing in the New York Legislation had equated the Famine with the Holocaust, and defended the Famine as a 'worthy subject of instruction'.[98] He went on to point out that Kerr's description of the Famine as 'a natural disaster' was an insult to the dead which: 'Ignores at least two important issues: how the Irish became so utterly dependent on the potato, and the adequacy of British relief efforts.' Pataki also drew attention to the 'underlying racism' which had suffused British approaches to the Irish during the Famine, and assured Kerr that: 'the children of New York will learn that the Great Irish Hunger was no mere "natural disaster".'

Alas for Kerr, for MI5 and for the Foreign Office, a majority of 'well meaning Britons' then proceeded to install one Anthony Blair in Downing Street the following May, and the new British Prime Minister had so little regard for Ambassador Kerr's protestations, or their Conservative and

Unionist background, that he subsequently validated Pataki's position by apologising for Britain's role in the Famine. However, the Pataki–Kerr correspondence remains as a 'must read' exchange for anyone interested not merely in Irish scholarship, or the Anglo-Irish relationship, but in the background to how Ireland is frequently portrayed in American newspapers, Hollywood or TV.

FILM STARS

The Hollywood film star, Aidan Quinn, has commented that the reason why so many Irish people take to acting is because:

> There are so many people in Ireland with this incredibly strong conservative strain to them – they never do this, and never do that, and never say a bad word – and then there's this wildness, this love of life, this love of dance and laughter . . . And both sides of the character are revered, and held up as an ideal of what you're supposed to be. It's slightly schizophrenic; we're crazy. But that does particularly lend itself to the dramatic arts . . .[99]

If he wishes to do so, Quinn can test out his theories on a number of Irish-born actors who at the time of writing were top Hollywood stars. However, before launching into a litany of such stars, however distinguished, it should be said that the important point about Hollywood and the Irish was the conflict between the way Hollywood wanted Ireland portrayed and the reality. Until practically the time of writing, with the emergence of such gritty stories of the Troubles as *In the Name of the Father* and *Some Mothers' Sons*, Irish topics were subject to relentless censorship and distortion. The distortion probably reached a high point, or a low, in 1992 with *Patriot Games* starring Harrison Ford. This travesty of a portrayal of Irish nationalism was rightly criticised by Joseph McBride of the influential *Variety* magazine. However, Paramount withdrew its advertising from the paper and, in the welter of controversy, McBride departed *Variety*.

The Hollywood distorting mirror has been held up to Ireland for a long time. One of the early directors, Sydney Olcott, was fired for making films such as *The Bold Emmet, Ireland's Patriot*. The British Board of Film Censors (BBFC) had a code which did not welcome depictions of British soldiers in conflict with the lesser breeds without the law. John Ford fell particularly foul of this code. The American censor, Joseph Breen, drew the script to the attention of the BBFC, and as a result, even the word Ireland was cut out of the script before it was released for screening in United Kingdom cinemas and throughout the empire. The Irish also censored the film heavily. It was banned for two years in Ireland, and in Chicago it was condemned by Irish Catholics.

In fact, the attitude of Hollywood to depictions of Ireland could be taken as a classical outcome of the twin pressures of the two colonialisms. Broadly speaking, Mother Church did not want anything shown which did not

350

conform to an idealised, Catholic-hued view of the country. Ultra Irish nationalism also played a part. Would-be film makers of Irish topics in Hollywood, where possible reaction in Ireland was an important barometer, were aware of a view in Dublin which said that Anglicisation was in some ways preferable to Los Angelisation. For their part the British, whose effect on American taste is still far from negligible, wanted nothing which cast a shadow on their record in Ireland. One of the most ludicrous examples of the collaboration between the two was the savaging of John Ford's *The Plough and the Stars*. Apart from censoring chunks of O'Casey's dialogue, the studio (RKO) turned a great playwright's tragedy into a happy ending. The Clitheroes walked into a sunset as though they were the heroes of a cowboy film. Ford was so sickened by what befell his picture that he refused ever to view the final cut.

Similar disasters befell Samuel Goldwyn's film about the life of Michael Collins, *Beloved Enemy*, starring Merle Oberon. No shots (literally) of the IRA shooting at British soldiers were allowed, nor any reference to the Black and Tans. While it wasn't possible to bring the Collins character back to life at the end of the film, the censorship did succeed in turning the Collins story into a romance set against an Irish backdrop. The post Second World War era saw a relaxation in the censorship curbs based on moral or religious codes, but Hollywood remained extremely 'iffy' about IRA themes untl the ceasefire period dawned.

Despite problems such as these, a galaxy of Irish film stars now twinkle in the Hollywood firmament. The list includes Liam Neeson, Pierce Brosnan, Patrick Bergin, Gabriel Byrne, Kenneth Branagh and Stephen Rea. The number of world stars who can claim either Irish parents or grandparents is remarkable: Tom Cruise, Sharon Stone, Harrison Ford, Roma Downey, John Travolta, Meg Ryan, Daniel Day Lewis (whose father was an English poet laureate), Mel Gibson, Dana Delaney, Jack Nicholson, Mia Farrow, Sean Penn, Helen Hayes, Brian Dennehy, Geraldine Fitzgerald and Marlon Brando, who applied for Irish citizenship after coming to Ireland in 1995 to make a film called *Divine Rapture*. The film can hardly have been a rapturous experience for Brando because filming was suspended through lack of funds. Nevertheless, from the moment he stepped off the plane Brando said he felt at home: 'Ireland is like a steel dart going through my heart.'[100]

All of the stars listed above have one thing in common: they follow in a long line of famous Irishmen and women who have dominated the American stage and screen, including James Cagney; George M. Cohan; Bing Crosby; John Ford; Jackie Gleason; Buster Keaton; Grace Kelly; Victor MacLaglen; Audie Murphy, who before becoming an actor was America's most decorated soldier; Pat O'Brien; Maureen O'Hara; and Ronald Reagan, whose acting career, some aver, only really got into its stride when he entered the White House and began to reap the benefit of scripts prepared for him by the right.

Cagney's career was inextricably linked with that of Cohan whose grandfather, Michael Keohane, changed the family name on arrival in

America in 1840. George Michael Cohan's father, Gerry, and his mother, Nelly, used the talents of their children – George had a sister Josephine – to form one of the most famous family acts in the history of American vaudeville. Cohan then graduated to writing and directing and his partnership with Sam Harris yielded two of America's favourite songs: 'Give my regards to Broadway' and 'Yankee Doodle Boy'. Cohan personified a type of image which Irish Americans were keen to see portrayed, someone who was 100 per cent Irish, another 100 per cent American patriot, and at the same time a friendly outgoing type proficient in the arts of song, dance and the stand-up comic. The abiding image of Cohan is a piece of American iconography: a uniformed James Cagney salutes, as he struts his stuff before a chorus line holding American flags, behind an also saluting Uncle Sam who stands beside Liberty holding her torch aloft.

The symbolism of this portrayal is more apt than the wholesome salute the flagism image suggests, as Cagney achieved lasting fame, not through *Yankee Doodle Dandy* (1942) but because of his portrayal of brutal criminals in gangster films like *Public Enemy* (1931) and *Angels with Dirty Faces* (1938). The Whitey Bulgers and the McMullens are never too far beneath the Irish façade of respectability. Nor is the radicalism. The fact that in politics Cagney was a liberal also forced on him the necessity to defend himself from the flag-wavers on a charge of being Communist.

Bing Crosby also achieved a special place in Irish American hearts because of his ability to portray a Cohan-like image of being quintessentially Irish, and at the same time solidly American, particularly for his Oscar-winning performance as the young priest in *Going My Way*. Crosby's crooning abilities were such that, according to the *Guinness Book of Records*, his 'White Christmas' was the best selling 'single' of all time, achieving a sale of some 200 million copies after its release in 1942. Crosby died in 1977, so his success obviously occurred at a time when the great waves of Irish emigration were over, and he only visited the place shortly before he died. Significantly, however, in view of the debate over whether the Irish saw themselves as exiles or emigrants, another of his smash hit songs was 'Galway Bay', which contains the lines:

> Some people say that I'm a dreamer . . .
> But precious dreams are dreamt unto an exile,
> When all the things he loves are far away . . .
> So 'tis maybe some day I'll go back to Ireland
> If it's only at the closing of my day . . .
> To see the sun go down again on Galway Bay.

Jackie Gleason's television show, *The Honeymooners*, ran for only a year (1955–56), but it achieved cult status. Working-class Irish Americans could identify with the scantily furnished flat in which lived Ralph Kramden, a bus driver, and his wife Alice, in not unreasonable strife. Gleason became the most popular figure in American television (other notable Irish names in television during the period, like Ed Murrow and Ed Sullivan, were respectively a news commentator and a talent and chat show host). Gleason was a comic who invented a set of famous characters including Joe the bartender, Charlie the loudmouth, and Rudy the repair-man, but he was also a Hollywood star, returning memorable performances in films such as *Gigot*, *The Hustler* and *Requiem for a Heavyweight*. Gleason was always conscious of his Irish heritage. He once said:

> Both my parents were Irish. Sometimes I feel guilty about living it up. The fleshpots! Delightful hedonism and all that . . . At one time I studied the other religions thinking the answer might lie there. But every time I came back to Catholicism, the religion I was born into. At least with Catholicism, I know where I stand – among the sinners. Faith is to be placed in God.[101]

John Ford claimed he was born Sean Aloysius O'Feeney, but there was no 'O' in the name of his parents, Sean and Barbara Feeney, to whom the young John was born shortly after they had left their native Galway for the US in 1894; and they would appear to have given him a Martin rather than an Aloysius as a middle name. However, either they or the gods also gave him a unique talent. Ford won five Academy Awards for his work as a director. Amongst the stars he developed was a young man who had been christened Marian Morrisson by his Irish-descended parents. Hollywood decided, however, that this was no name for a would-be he-man star, and he was rechristened John Wayne. Ford made him a star in his 1939 classic, *Western Stage Coach*, and he later brought him together, after the Second World War had ended, with a group of other Irish stars, Maureen O'Hara, Barry Fitzgerald, and Victor McLaglen, to make the film which, shot in the beauties of the west of Ireland, launched the post-war Irish tourist trade, *The Quiet Man*.

John Ford's family were committed Irish Nationalists. His father contributed to the IRA during the Irish War of Independence, and Ford himself actually visited Ireland during 'the Troubles', in 1921. The British shipped him out and warned him not to come back, after it was discovered that he had visited a wanted IRA relative of his in Spiddal, County Galway, and brought the fugitive those twin staples of revolution: money and whiskey. For the rest of his life, John Ford remained a contributor to the IRA. Lack of money and his empathy with the IRA combined with his artistic genius to make *The Informer* into the classic it became. Critics assumed that the setting of dark, mist-filled Irish streets showed Ford's passion for realism. In fact, Ford had been forced to use the mist to hide the fact that all he could afford was a set of shoddy broken-down 'flats'. Ford made other Irish American film classics, including *The Last Hurrah*, based on Edwin O'Connor's novel about James Curley, but his other speciality was the West. The Navajo Indians of Monument Valley, Utah, figured not only in *Stagecoach*, but *Fort Apache*, *She Wore a Yellow Ribbon*, *Rio Grande* and *The Searchers*. In his famous *The*

Man Who Shot Liberty Valance, Ford has a newspaper reporter deliver to James Stewart an epigram which could have been applied not only to Ford's own career, but that of a million Irishmen and women: 'This is the West. When the truth becomes legend, print the legend.'

In no area of Irish artistic expression did legend become fact more than in what might be termed the Tin-Pan Alley world. In the late nineteenth century, Tin-Pan Alley began as the area around New York's Union Square, home to both theatres and song publishers. The centre of gravity of American popular music publishing then moved to West 42nd Street in the early 1900s, and by the 1920s, the Alley could be found between 42nd and 56th Street.

The Tin-Pan Alley type of songs had been popular with the Irish long before Tin-Pan Alley was born. Songs like 'Killarney', composed in 1861 by Edmond Falconer and Michael William Balfe, expressed nostalgia for the beauties of a land left behind, the sadness of exile, an idealised vision of motherhood, and of romantic love. In 'Killarney', the singer recalled:

> Killarney's lakes and fells
> Em'rald isles and winding bays;
> Mountain paths and woodland dells
> Mem'ry ever fondly strays.

Mem'ry could also recall 'The emigrants' farewell' (1852) which shows the pangs of forced emigration:

> Then Erin mavourneen, how sad is the parting.
> Old home of our childhood, forever from thee.

Of all the memories, none was so deeply etched as that of 'Mother McCree':

> There's a spot in my heart which no colleen may own,
> There's a depth in my soul never sounded or known,
> There's a place in my memory, my life that you fill,
> No other can take it, no one ever will.

By comparison, the courtship of a would-be Irish mother, who would one day grow into a 'Mother McCree' is positively rollicking, albeit a little contradictory, as the would-be groom apparently wants to change his name as well as the bride's on tying the knot:

> Molly – my Irish Molly – My sweet achushla dear,
> I'm fairly off my trolley – my Irish Molly, when you are near,
> Spring time, you know is ring time,
> Come dear, don't be so slow,
> Change your name g'wan, be game,
> Begorra and I'll do the same,
> My Irish Molly O.

All these songs and a thousand more like them helped to give life to what
H. A. Williams has termed the 'Paddy Actor' tradition. These were literally
stage Irishmen who helped to make the caricature a respectable image. Tyrone
Power, one of the outstanding examples of this genre, first attained stardom
in Samuel Lovers's 1836 play, *Rory O'Moore*. Power, who was born in
Kilmacthomas in County Waterford, founded the theatrical dynasty which
later yielded the Hollywood star, Tyrone Power, and the theatrical director,
Sir Tyrone Guthrie, who gave his home in County Monaghan to the Irish
state. It now serves as a cultural retreat for writers.

A notable successor of Power's in the Paddy Arena was John Chancellor,
the grandson of Irish emigrants who worked on the Erie Canal. Chancellor
changed his name to Chauncey Alcott, and after a one-week visit to Ireland
acquired sufficient of an Irish accent to become an authentic 'Paddy'. He
starred in a series of successful turn-of-the-century Irish musicals:
Mavourneen, *Macushla*, *The Isle of Dreams*. Alcott wrote one of the most
famous Irish songs of all time, 'My Wild Irish Rose', because of a visit to
Killarney. He apparently didn't like the singing of a local and to distract him
from any further renditions, asked him the name of a flower. To this the yokel
replied that the flower was nothing but 'a wild Irish rose'. Alcott's songs, when
rendered by an Irish tenor of the calibre of John McCormack, helped to
spread the scent of the wild Irish rose from theatres packed by Irish Americans
to the salons of America and the world.

Along with 'the Paddy tradition', another font of music flowed. Much of
what is known as Appalachian rhythm is of Irish derivation. From Tennessee
to the Carolinas, Irish music intermingled with English, Scottish and African
rhythms. From this intermingling – which lies at the heart of the success of the
Riverdance musical – there grew blue grass, country, hillbilly and old-time
mountain music. The early settlers, like their fellow countrymen at home in
Ireland, had little money for musical instruments. They often improvised with
items such as spoons, bones, the bodhran (a tamborine-like instrument of
goats' skin stretched over a frame), a washing board or a tin whistle. To own
a fiddle was quite a feat, but with these things, and the traditional Irish love of
song and dance, the Irish settlers created their own ballads and mountain
music style melodies. Irish music also became a vehicle for that traditional
Irish mode of expression, the protest song.

The composer Victor Herbert, who became conductor of the Pittsburgh
Symphony in 1898, also helped to popularise Irish melodies by including them
in his operettas. As the nineteenth century wore on, instruments such as the
flute and the tin whistle and the accordion could be and were purchased by
Irish groups. The work of the musicologist and performer, Mick Moloney of
Philadelphia, has resulted in hundreds of both Irish songs and American-
influenced Irish songs being recorded. Moloney's work, and that of other Irish
musicologists in America, has helped to contribute to the continuing success
of major annual musical occasions such as the Philadelphia Folk Festival, the
Pittsburgh Three Rivers Festival, and the Milwaulkee 'Irish Fest'.

In turn, of course, this success has been enhanced by the enormous success of Irish music originating in Ireland. From the time of the big show bands of the 1950s like the Clipper Carltons, American audiences, and by no means exclusively Irish-American audiences, have been growing for groups as diverse as the Clancy Brothers, the Chieftains, U2, the Corrs, the Cranberries and Westlife, or individual performers like Enya and Christy Moore. Shortly after the film about the effort to set up a Dublin soul group, the Commitments, was released, I visited one of New York's musical megastores. The sales staff told me that the Commitments tape was their best seller. There were banks of it on display, all over the store. It was but one of many indicators of the popularity of Irish music in the US.

WRITERS

Not unexpectedly, where writing is concerned, the race which produced Joyce, Beckett, Synge, Yeats, Shaw and O'Casey did not allow the Atlantic crossing to interrupt the Irish literary tradition. Certainly one Dublin literary institution which has successfully made the transition across the ocean is the 'liquid lunch'. I observed this interesting phenomenon at close quarters at Picino, an Italian restaurant in the Village, to which I was kindly invited by Thomas Cahill. Those present included Frank McCourt and his brothers, including Malachy (whom New Yorkers are frequently misguided enough to mistake for me!), Denis Smith, and the novelist Mary Brestead and Terry Moran – who, presumably because he runs the Department of Communication in NYU, was reckoned to be the right man to put in charge of the finances.

The theory behind the lunch was that it was organised by the Friday Circle to honour Frank's success with *Angela's Ashes*. This seemed such a good idea that some forty-seven people turned up, including certain citizens who turned the lunch into a brunch by arriving early, opening a tab, and breakfasting (hugely) on Scotch. As a veteran of a similar literary group in Dublin, my immediate worry was how much should each person contribute, but nobody else troubled themselves with such peasant concerns, and both the wine consumption and decibel levels soared. The speeches were in the main both witty and short, but I have to confess that a little of their impact was lost on me as guests began to leave with no effort being made to gather money. The few, I feared, would have to carry the many.

So it proved. When the forty-seven had shrunk to twenty-five, a collection was taken up – a very reasonable $40 a head. At around the twelve to fifteen mark, the hat came around again for a further $20 or so. Still very reasonable. But when we had come down to seven, I suddenly noticed Terry Moran standing at the end of the bar with his jacket off and his hands thrust deep into his trouser pockets, gazing blankly before him into the middle distance, like someone who had been expecting to see Man Friday, and found that instead

Ian Paisley had hove into view. 'What's the damage Terry?' I enquired, a good deal of the bonhomie ebbing away at the sight of his obviously stricken countenance. In a weak whisper he replied: '$700 dollars and tip.' Fortunately, one of the guests, the happy possessor of an expense account, came to the rescue – tangible proof that the Irish respect for literature had survived the Atlantic crossing.

In fact, it nourished itself in the crossing's aftermath. In the twentieth century alone, major distinctively Irish voices arose in an attempt to either laugh, rage or sing the stresses of the emigrant experience. To attempt a discussion of the history of nineteenth- and twentieth-century Irish American writing would be far beyond the compass of this work. However, it may be noted that history has produced at least one major historical novelist, Thomas Flanagan, whose trilogy, *The Year of the French*, *Tenants of Time*, and *The End of the Hunt* bridge both ocean and centuries with an insight and an artistry that conceal the stone-masonry of his research with the skill of a stuccadore.

The first major Irish American voice to be heard was that of a fictional character in a newspaper column created by Finley Peter Quinn. This was 'Mr Dooley', a bartender in Bridgefort, Chicago. 'Mr Dooley' made Quinn the most popular journalist of the late nineteenth and early twentieth century. 'Mr Dooley' was born in the *Evening Post* on 7 October 1893. He carried on a monologue in a broad Irish American brogue, that is to say one in which American slang and resonances overlaid the accent Dooley brought over on the boat from Ireland, on all the topics of the day. Everything from the Spanish American War to City Hall politics, the St Patrick's Day Parade and the problems of Irish marriage were discussed and dissected, both by Dooley and a series of other characters invented, or rather translated, by Quinn. For the politician Joyce, the parish priest Father Kelly and the police sergeant John Shea were all modelled on real-life characters. These were but a tiny segment of the parade of Quinn's characters: workers, landlords, firemen, lace-curtain Irish, and would-be entrants to the parlour. In short, 'Mr Dooley' charted the emigrant experience. He came to American thinking that:

> All ye had to do was to hold ye'er hat an' te' goold guineas'd drop into it . . . But faith, whin I'd been here a week I seen that there was nawthin' but mud undher th' pavement – I larnend that be means iv a pick-axe at tin shillin's th' day.

That exploration of the clash between the Irish emigrants' expectation of life in America, and the reality of what American society was like for them and their children, was responsible for James T. Farrell's seminal work of Irish American fiction, the Studs Lonigan trilogy, set in the dream-crushing world of working-class Chicago. Farrell's impact has been attested to by several famous writers. Norman Mailer, for example, told the *New York Times Book Review:*

I read Studs Lonigan in my freshman year at Harvard, and it changed my life . . . I realised
that you could write books about people who were something like the people you'd grown
up with. I couldn't get over the discovery. I wanted to write. When I think of how bad I
might have been at other occupations, I bless the memory of James T. Farrell.[102]

One of the notable features of the major Irish American writers from
Farrell to William Kennedy is how freely they acknowledge their Irishness.
Farrell himself said of his literary origins, 'I generally feel that I'm an Irishman
rather than an American', and on another occasion said he wrote as:

a second generation Irish American. The effects and scars of emigration are upon my life.
The past was dragging through my boyhood and adolescence . . . For an Irish boy born in
Chicago in 1904, the past was a tragedy of his people . . .

The word tragedy takes on a new dimension when handled by one of the
greatest of all Irish American writers, Eugene O'Neill. *Long Day's Journey
into Night, The Iceman Cometh, Desire under the Elms, Anna Christie, The
Emperor Jones* and *A Moon for the Misbegotten* are plays that take their
audiences through the hells of love and hatred in family relationships,
marriage, alcoholism, and murder, under the tutelage of a tour guide of
genius. O'Neill, who was awarded the Nobel Prize for Literature in 1936, also
wrote about the strain imposed on the Irish Catholic emigrant adapting him
or herself to become an American: religion, the difficulties imposed in relating
to Yankee neighbours, of coping with alcoholism or that other disease of the
Irish, tuberculosis. Well did one of the great Irish American actresses, Lorette
Taylor, observe: 'Give the Irish a miserable thought and they created an Ibsen
drama.' O'Neill himself said that the most important thing about himself and
his work was the fact that he was Irish. That ancestry, and the misery, not of
thought but of much Irish experience in America, set O'Neill off on his long
day's journey into immortality. In fact, while trembling on the brink of
mortality himself, during the production of his last play, *A Moon for the
Misbegotten*, O'Neill stipulated that every member of the cast had to be Irish.

Another immortal of Irish American letters was Scott Fitzgerald, of whom
a delightful story was told after he had first won fame with *This Side of
Paradise*, published in 1920. A wealthy lady who was also a great admirer of
Archbishop John Ireland had been looking for someone to write a biography
of her hero, when she heard about Fitzgerald's novel. The lady immediately
went to her local bookstore looking for a copy, announcing: 'I have been
looking for someone to write the life of Archbishop Ireland, and now I think
I have found him. They tell me there is a fine young Catholic writer who has
just published a religious book, *This Side of Paradise*.'

In fact, Fitzgerald, throughout his career, sought to put as much distance
between himself and his Catholic lace-curtain Irish St Paul's origins as he
could. However, his youthful sense of being an outsider from the world of the
shanty-town Irish, yet not a member of the Ivy League world to which the

lace-curtain dwellers aspire, stood him in good stead when he turned his hand to *The Great Gatsby*, that monument to the outsider. *Tender is the Night* is also a heart-broken paean to the attractions and the fallacies of success American style through the eyes of an Irish observer. It could be argued that the use which Scott Fitzgerald was able to make of his Irish Catholic background, however painful the experience, is what separates him from another Irish American writer of Catholic origin, John O'Hara. O'Hara regarded the Catholic Church as a peasant institution, and swiftly left behind him boyhood memories of being an altar boy. There is an Irish sense to his writing, but his characters talk in the tones of WASPS. Unlike Farrell, the people he writes about are not the ones he grew up with.

One man who did write about people he grew up with or, rather, under their shadow, was Edwin O'Connor, whose *Last Hurrah*, the 1956 *roman-à-clef* was about Frank Skeffington, in real life James Michael Curley, Mayor of Boston. O'Connor's intention was to portray how the Irish had advanced in America through politics. The result was a spectacular publishing success and a movie starring Spencer Tracy and directed by John Ford. Through Skeffington, O'Connor makes a fundamentally Irish observation about life and politics: 'Democracy is the art of knowing what people want – and what they'll settle for.' O'Connor's other famous work, *The Edge of Sadness*, dealt with what in its day was a taboo subject, a memorable description of an alcoholic priest and his Irish American background.

It would be surprising if such classical Irish occupations as that of fireman or policeman did not figure in the work of Irish writers, and sure enough, pens as varied and writing at such different levels as those of Mickey Spillane, George V. Higgins, Vincent Patrick, Jimmy Breslin, Joe Flaherty and Denis Smith have given us memorable portraits of the Irish as they fight fire or fraud, or labour in the dangerous world of the 'sand hogs', the tunnel diggers. Presiding over the literary landscape of the urban jungle, and indeed over the contemporary Irish American literary landscape, an outstanding and impressive figure is William Kennedy, creator of the Albany novels. Kennedy's remarkable collection of characters, gangsters, pan-handlers, journalists, gamblers, politicians, play out their roles in New York's underbelly. Like Jimmy Breslin, George V. Higgins and Tom English, Kennedy explores the role of the gangster. To him, Legs Diamond, the hero of *Legs* in the Albany cycle, is an authentic figure on the Irish landscape, and rightly so. As far away as Australia, the outlaw Ned Kelly embodies the Irish vision of the hero who can literally shoot his way to the top.

While the phenomena of the Crime Family and the Mafia are not part of Irish American culture in the sense that they have become associated, fairly or unfairly, with Italian Americans, the gangster, the obverse side of the Irish yearning for lace-curtain respectability, is an important, though not always acknowledged part of the Irish experience. It should be remembered that Al Capone took over Chicago's underworld by eliminating his Irish rivals, notably Dion O'Banion and 'Bugs' Moran. After having Dion O'Banion murdered, Capone carried out what became known as the Valentine's Day Massacre (14 February 1929), eliminating seven of Moran's henchmen at one fell swoop, thus destroying his power. In New York, two of the most notorious gangsters were both Irish, 'Mad Dog' Coll and Owney Madden, who was a member of Lucky Luciano's Jewish-Italian crime syndicate, the 'Commission'.

Even if there had not been Irish gangsters, the Irish would inevitably have become embroiled in or with crime through so many Irishmen becoming policemen. As we saw in New Orleans, folklore has it that an Irish police chief was the first victim of the newly formed Mafia.

The gangster's nemesis, the Informer, is also a familiar figure in Irish writing. An informer, 'Mickey' Featherstone, was as central to Tom English's book, *The Westies*, about the Irish gang that terrorised New York's Hell's Kitchen area in the 1980s, as was Gyppo Nolan in Liam O'Flaherty's novel of the Anglo-Irish War in the 1920s, *The Informer*, which John Ford also made into an award-winning film, with Victor McLaglen in the title role.

Obviously emigration is a theme which continues to hold a fascination for Irish writers, though less in the sense of writing about the difficulties of adjusting to a new way of life, than in the complex exploration of what happens when a writer tries to go back to the old country. Pete Hamill, author, poet, former newspaper editor and columnist, is one of the best-known figures amongst the Irish American community in New York. His parents came from Belfast, and for him, as for tens of thousands of Irish Americans, they 'carried the narrative'. His father's mental horizons were signposted by things like soccer, music halls, and stories about 800 years of British oppression. For Hamill and his generation, the narrative began with America. Hamill's signposts were baseball, Jackie Robinson, frankfurters and the American way. We spoke in a busy newsroom and, gesturing about him, he said: 'It's the same story for young reporters on the paper. Koreans, Italians, Russians have the same gap between their parents and themselves.'

The difference lay in the degree of interest which the Irish took in their native land. For instance, while I was interviewing Hamill, Peter having made the declaration of disassociation from his father's preoccupation with the old country, then proceeded to reel off a lengthy suggested reading list for me which indicated an encyclopaedic knowledge of the Irish and Irish Americans, based obviously on a serious study of the subject. One result of this study of families united by blood and heritage, but divided by the reality of the different experiences of upbringing, is Hamill's novel *The Gift*. This tells the story of how a Belfast-born father and his New York-born son relate to each other in Brooklyn. If possible it should be read in conjunction with another Hamill novel, *Loving Women: A Novel of the Fifties*, written sixteen years later (published in 1989), which traces the loves and losses in the career of a Brooklyn teenager as he grows up during a voyage towards self-realisation, away from the constraints and supports of his background.

One also finds a variation in the emigration motif in the work of Elisabeth

Cullinan, who speaks of the experiences of contemporary Irishwomen on both sides of the Atlantic. The Irish mother and her effects are powerfully portrayed in her *House of Gold*. A more liberated Irish American career woman bestrides the battlefields of Manhattan in *Yellow Roses* and, in *A Change of Scene*, Cullinan tells a story of the difficulty of attempting to go back. The return in this case is of a New York woman, Anne Clark, who studied in Trinity, and finds, like Ossian of old, that it is dangerous to revisit the past.[103] This theme, less applicable to the Cullinan character, who was not born in Ireland to begin with, than to many emigrants, highlights an important problem which, although part of the emigrant experience, is not often addressed: how to adjust to the reality when the dream comes true and it does prove possible 'some day' to go back again to Ireland. Only the landscape remains unchanged, the people have moved on, and the emigrants are now out of place in two cultures. Their roots, their children, are now on the other side of the horizon, and the people they have returned to live with know them not.

These are the uprooted men, the antithesis of 'that rooted man', John Millington Synge, who unblinkingly stayed true to his view of the Irish peasantry, and so touched off 'Playboy riots' against his earthy depictions of their lives and loves on both sides of the Atlantic, amongst audiences who felt that he was portraying an unflattering and unfair picture of the Irish, thus 'lettin' down the country'. In every generation, in every Irish gathering, there will always be claques or experts who will tell you that the Irish are not like that. Their reality is something else. Those who would say that the Cullinans and the Kennedys concern themselves only with the dysfunctional and the misfit, not 'typical' of the Irish Americans, cannot deny, however, that these writers and their other contemporaries are authentically Irish American. As William Kennedy himself puts it:

> I believe that I can't be anything other than Irish American. I know there's a division here, and a good many Irish Americans believe they are merely American. They've lost touch with anything that smacks of Irishness as we used to know it. That's all right. But I think if they set out to discover themselves, to wonder about why they are what they are, then they'll run into a psychological inheritance that's even more than psychological. That may also be genetic, or biopsychogenetic, who the hell knows what you call it? But there's just something in us that survives and that's the result of being Irish, whether from North or South, whether Catholic or Protestant, some element of life, or consciousness, that is different from being Hispanic, or Oriental, or WASP. These traits endure. I'm just exploring what's survived in my time and place.[104]

SPORT

It is perhaps inevitable that a sports-mad but poverty-ridden immigrant group should have thrown up heroes who literally relied on their bare hands for success. The sporting idol of Irish Americans during the late nineteenth century and the early part of the twentieth century was John L. Sullivan, born in Boston to Irish emigrants. Sullivan symbolised the fighting Irish spirit of one stage of the Irish American experience. He said:

> I believe in having a little fight in most everything except funerals . . . We have got to do more or less fighting, or you're simply talking in your sleep. And if you're satisfied to talk in your sleep all your life, you might as well call in the undertaker now and save time.

Sullivan was both the bare-knuckle and gloved heavyweight champion of America. He first won the bare-knuckle title at Mississippi in 1882, successfully defended it in the last bare-knuckle heavyweight title fight in 1889, and finally lost his gloved title in 1892 to 'Gentleman' Jim Corbett in New Orleans. Sullivan had trained the night before by getting drunk, as was his wont. Nevertheless, he had been the five-to-one favourite to win the bout, and not only the crowd but all Irish America was stunned. They had shared Sullivan's oft-repeated belief that he could 'lick any son of a bitch alive'. The fact that 'Gentleman' Jim was also Irish did not atone for his crime in defeating one of America's folk heroes. Sullivan ended his career as a temperance lecturer. His undoubted expertise on the subject made him a success on the lecture circuit, and he ended his days (he died on 6 February 1918) in some comfort.

For decades after Sullivan's death, the Irish dominated the boxing ring, so much so that, in order to get a look in, one unfortunate Italian had to call himself 'Philadelphia Jack O'Brien'. One of the twentieth century's greatest heavyweight champions was Jack Dempsey, the 'Manassa Mauler', until he was defeated after a controversial 'long count' by another Irishman, Gene Tunney, whose son went on to become a congressman. However, Joe Louis effectively both ended Irish dominance in the ring by defeating not one but two Irish champions, Jimmy Braddock (1937) and Billy Conn (1941), and ushered in the era of black supremacy. 'Respectable' Irish American opinion was not sorry to see the era go. Prize fighting symbolised the type of brawling, fighting Irish image they wanted to get away from. Yet 'The fightin' Irish' was the official nickname which the authorities of Notre Dame University adopted in a statement issued in the 1920s:

> The University authorities are in no way averse to the name 'fightin' Irish' as applied to our athletic teams. It seems to embody the kind of spirit that we like to see carried into effect by the various organisations that represent us on the athletic field.[105]

The university was responding in part to the fact that at the time there were several other nicknames floating around Notre Dame's football team – 'Damn Micks', 'Hoosiers', 'Papists', 'Catholics', and even 'Dirty Irish' found their way into sports writers' columns – and in part to the qualitative shift which had occurred in Irish American society through upward mobility, making attendance at Notre Dame possible. Irish emigration had led to the originally French institution – it was founded in 1842 as a mission centre for the Potawatomi Indians as much as a school – being taken over by Irish priests. The Golden Dome on the main building symbolises the height of the Irish climb up the ladder of prosperity. Now, in the words of the university statement, there were 'various organisations' representing the Irish in the sporting world. The brawling days were coming to an end.

When Warner Brothers made the famous film, *Knute Rockne: All American*, about the legendary Notre Dame football coach, they intended to cast James Cagney in the role of Rockne. However, Cagney had taken the wrong side in a recent fight so far as Notre Dame was concerned. He had signed a petition supporting the Republicans against the Fascists in the Spanish Civil War, and the College authorities vetoed him for the part, which went to Pat O'Brien. Another Irishman who made a name for himself in the film was the up and coming Ronald Reagan. A more enduring Irish American contribution to football however centers on the Rooney family of Pittsburgh. Dan Rooney, who co-founded the Ireland Fund of America with Tony O'Reilly, took over the ownership of the famous Pittsburgh Steelers from his father Art.

As the twentieth century wore on, the Irish began picking up increasing numbers of Olympic gold medals for running, jumping, throwing the hammer and the discus. Jack Kelly, father of the actress Grace Kelly, won a gold medal for sculling in the 1920 Olympics, having earlier been debarred, through anti-Irish prejudice, from sculling in the prestigious British event at Henley. Irish names began to show up in the championship lists of golf and tennis. One of the greatest American golfers ever was Ben Hogan, who won the US Open four times between 1948 and 1953. The more contemporary tennis star, John McEnroe, won the US Open singles championship three times, adding the Wimbledon title for good measure in 1981. McEnroe's fiery temperament, like that of his fellow tennis star, Jimmy Conors, left those who witnessed it in no doubt that the term 'fightin' Irish' still had validity.

However, the sport which the Irish dominated above all was baseball. Baseball was America's most popular sport, at least until television gave American football a position it did not deserve, *circa* 1950–60. At the time of writing, America's most popular sporting hero is the Irish American Mark McGwire. McGwire made baseball history during the remarkable 1999 season when he hit 70 home runs, the first man to do so in major league baseball. He thus broke both Babe Ruth's record of 60 home runs and that of the man who surpassed him, Roger Maris, with 61. More important, for the sport and for the great American public that dearly loves a hero, was the manner in which he won it. Throughout the season, he was dogged by Sammy Sosa, who astonishingly hit 66 homers for the Chicago Cubs – McGwire plays for the St Louis Cardinals – the only time in history anything remotely resembling such a dual feat occurred. However, throughout the tense season the two men remained on the friendliest terms, and when McGwire broke Maris's record, he left the diamond to go into the stands to embrace Maris's sons 'for the longest time . . . it was emotional, unscripted and pure'.[106]

It has been argued that the Irish adoption of baseball was a measure of their adjustment to America, aimed in part at contradicting the nativists' view that they were a benighted race from the bogs. It could also equally be true that baseball provided the Irish with an outlet for that co-ordination of eye, strength and timing which they had traditionally displayed in their national game of hurling. It is true that 'the grand old man' of American baseball was Cornelius McGillicuddy (1862–1956), one of the all-time great baseball managers who took the Philadelphia Athletics to immortality. McGillicuddy was best known by his adopted nickname of 'Connie Mack', which he assumed when he found as a player that his real name was too long to fit into a score box: a microcosm of the process of change undergone by millions of Irish emigrants who changed their names, and sometimes their religion, along the road to prosperity. Connie Mack's great rival was another Irish American, the New York Giants' Manager, John McGraw. Between them, these two managers dominated the game.

The ancestral Irish rivalries of Orange and Green replicated a Rangers and Celtic situation in Chicago, where the Catholic team was the Southside White Sox, founded by the Irish American, Charles Comisky, and the Protestant one was the Northside Cubs, owned by Philip K. Wrigley. The White Sox supporters put it about that Wrigley was a member of the Ku Klux Klan. Hence if one entered Wrigley Field, one might as well enter a Protestant church!

To sum up

One of the most informed commentators on Irish America is Andrew Greeley, Professor of Social Science at the University of Chicago, whose National Opinion Research Centre continuously monitors opinion shifts and changes in society of all sorts. In his landmark book, *That Most Distressful Nation* back in 1972, Greeley dealt with the effects of character formation in the Irish home and school. He accepted that the Jewish graduate students who came to the NORC were 'supremely self-confident and assertive, and the Irish Catholics are quiet, timid, and diffident'. The Irish students were every bit as talented as their Jewish counterparts but they tended to be 'paralysed by self-doubt and self-hatred'. Why this should be so is not entirely clear. As Greeley said at the time, there were not many Irish psychiatrists – or young Irish Americans for that matter, who would be caught dead in the office of one.

One Irish psychiatrist who has been studying the Irish since Greeley made his observation is Maeve Mahon, who emigrated to New York in 1974. At that time, there was no Irish doctor in the hospital at which she did her internship. After she joined the Celtic Medical Society, a highly conservative but prestigious New York grouping, she found that for two years she was the only woman in the room, apart from the waitress. By the late nineties, however, things had changed substantially, both in her immediate circle – the Society now has a number of other women doctors – and in Irish attitudes to issues like homosexuality.

Mahon's findings, both amongst her patients and the Irish community at large, are that:

> They are very honest and hard-working. They like drink. They seem to be able to hold their booze more than most. The pubs are social meeting places, places to network, find out about jobs, make contacts.
>
> They're an Irish mechanism for dealing with the challenges of life. The wake is another one. It's a wonderful catharsis. The crying, the telling the little stories about the dead person. It's very healthy. Denial of grief can result in depression, panic attacks, anxiety, sleeplessness, all kinds of aberrant behaviour. But when you come across sexual repression, you find it's attributable to specifically Irish causes, the church, family. People don't need authoritarian structures in their lives. But they sure get them. The Irish are naturally deeply sensual. But we used to have this background of not talking about things. When I came to New York first, I had never heard about things like incest or homosexuality. Like any other race, what counts is the family. If you find a background of good parental stability, you'll find a good stable character.

Greeley had speculated that the differences between the Jewish and Irish students was due to family training. In a Jewish home, affection was lavishly, and overtly, bestowed on the children, whereas in an Irish home, affection was 'implicit'. As Greeley pointed out, the withholding of affection and praise is not merely an attempt to prepare children for the harsh life outside the home, but a method of control – one moreover that was 'widely used in Catholic seminaries, convents and noviciates'. The 'subject' was first reduced to a state of childlike dependence on the 'superior', and then the superior would give or withhold affection in arbitrary and capricious fashion, thus reinforcing a dependency relationship. As a result, the Irish were generally perceived as not being entrepreneurs; they had limited their efforts upwards to business, the professions and politics, but had only done well in the last.

As even a cursory glance at the annual awards in Irish America will show, this position no longer obtains. The Irish either have scaled, or are scaling, the heights of every conceivable sphere of achievement in America, including that of the astronauts, where the appropriately named [Michael] Collins has walked amidst the stars. Greeley's contemporary summation of Irish Americans, a quarter of a century on from his book's publication is:

> The Irish came to America as the poorest of the poor and the most despised of the despised. Nonetheless, by the beginning of the present century, they had already passed the American national average in the proportion of young people at university age who were, in fact, attending universities. They are the most successful of American gentile ethnic groups in education, occupational achievement, and in annual income. They have accomplished this transformation while still managing to be Irish – as my own research has shown conclusively – in their imaginations, in their loyalty to Catholicism, in their occupational choices, and in their family structures. Moreover, their Irish self-

consciousness is in the process of being transformed from noisy St Patrick's Day celebrations to an appreciation of their own cultural heritage, or as this Irish scholar said to me after a long evening session, 'Sure, you Yanks will be Irish long after we become indistinguishable from the Belgians!'[107]

As we come towards the end of our Irish journey through an American landscape, let us remember that the journey began in an Irish one, in Irish homes. The distance travelled, psychologically as well as physically, lay outside the frontal consciousness of many emigrant children, even that of a sophisticate such as Pete Hamill, like a vast unknown prairie. Hamill wrote:

> In Mexico, I often found myself thinking about my mother and father in Ireland and New York. When I came home, I often questioned them, trying to pry from them the life they had lived before they had come to America. Later, I travelled to Ireland, lived there for long periods trying to piece together the frayed ends of the narrative. Of course I failed. There were too many blank places in the story, too many names that meant nothing to me, too many people who had fled. I could never hope to grasp the dailiness of my parents' lives they'd left behind, because Belfast itself had changed . . .[108]

However, the gnawing effort to enter that territory of their parents, and their parents' minds, remains in the minds of many. Here is an account by another intellectual, who like Hamill grew up in Brooklyn, and who like him made the pilgrimage back through the emotional peaks and valleys that stretched between the American and the Irish landscapes. Unlike Hamill, Professor Jim Murphy of the Irish Studies programme at Villanova University feels that he did succeed. As Jim says, he went home with his father, Patrick, and found himself, not so much by grasping the 'dailiness' of his parents' lives but by achieving an empathy with it:

> In the Brooklyn world of my childhood, Ireland was always there on my mental horizon – in the rhythms of speech and turns of phrase of Irish people about the house; in the ballads about the old country and a moonlight in Mayo that could bring my mother to tears; in the Friday night card games in which a priest visiting from Ireland might occasionally loosen his collar and mutter a sort of curse when the Lord failed to fill his inside straight.
>
> Ours was a world of aunts, uncles, cousins; the calendar had its comforting rhythm of gatherings for holidays, baptisms, communions, graduations. And the funerals . . . always uncles . . . John, Michael, Frank. Each death strange in its own way, each one driving my father deeper into himself. I was eight when Uncle John fell over the banister . . . dropped three stories . . . and broke his neck. I didn't really know him but I can still see him falling . . .
>
> I was nine when Uncle Michael fell under the wheels of the IRT subway . . . the family said it was the heart that gave way . . . others whispered that he had jumped . . . My father said his brothers had bad luck. Mikey must have had the old heart attack. John, another story, let him be . . . my godfather, Uncle Frank, the bachelor . . . drank himself to death. I was thirteen when he died, my father was fifty, and was burying his third brother in America. Years later I would begin to understand his loss and the pain which he kept inside as the funerals kept coming.

Uncle Frank is in my parents' wedding picture . . . A lovely picture, taken in New York in a studio, light years away from Leitrim and Mayo. The whole picture speaks of Ireland, of emigration, and of change, especially the poses of the four men – my dad, Uncle Frank, Mark Cummings, and John Foley, my dad's best friend and himself off the boat like the rest of them. There they are in their rented tuxedos, probably for the first time in their lives, looking stiff, awkward, proud of themselves.

Why this formal studio photo session? I now realise that it was to send their word home that all was well, that they were prospering in the new world. The photo sent home says, 'not to worry, all's well'.

What could my grandparents possibly have thought when this picture arrived . . . two of their sons long gone from home and not likely to return; dressed in tuxedos for a marriage, one of their sons marrying a woman they would never meet, a formal occasion at which parents should be honoured and basking in the glow of the moment. But there were no parents in these wedding photos . . . these parents . . . will know many of their grandchildren only in the stream of photographs that will try to shrink the distance.

My dad went home for the first and only time in 1969 . . . my mum had died the year before and my sisters and I . . . gave the trip home as a Christmas present. I was more than willing to be his partner . . . After the deaths of his brothers, all his links to Ireland closed down . . . My dad was a warm, loving man, full of sharp humour, always humming tunes he composed as he went along, but at the same time, he was a man of few words, at least in terms of his personal feelings and experiences. I suspect that is, at least in part, an Irish trait, especially on the male side of the fence.

I don't think I fully understood his emotions at the time . . . there he would be, for five long weeks, 'at home' but in a world of strangers. So again, the distance that was so much a part of the lives of all the Murphys in America came to the fore . . . as it turned out, there was no need to worry. Ireland fitted him like a glove. He settled immediately into its rhythm, his brogue increasing ever so slightly.[109]

When Patrick met his brother Eddie, in Aughakiltubred, in the parish of Cloone, in County Leitrim, there was:

A handshake, no hugs: 'You're welcome home . . . a fine day . . . Here, sit by the fire . . .' Whiskey all around – the only public acknowledgement of a special occasion. I count myself lucky to have been with my dad when he finally went home. Little did I know on that special day, but in two years he would be dead. Eddie is now gone as well. I like to remember the two of them, slowly and a bit awkwardly coming to know each other again. Aunt Maggie giving us a bit of tea, Daddy gradually settling into a rhythm of memory and laughter as old friends came by and nostalgia filled this small, warm, secure place. He was home, a circle had been closed.

I had thought I was taking my dad home. Now, I know he was showing me my own starting place. He took me home.

The importance of photographs . . . In that prose picture of Jim Murphy's lies the answer to the debate as to whether Irish emigrants should be considered exiles or pragmatists. The answer is they were, and are, both.

I will leave the last word on the Irish experience in America to a distinguished Irish American, Jane Byrne, who herself made history by becoming the first woman Mayor of Chicago: 'I remember so well when Jack Kennedy went back to Boston for the first time after his election. He walked to the water's edge and said, "To think my grandfather came here from Ireland with nothing more than the pack upon his back." That was a proud moment for him. It was a proud moment for all Irish Americans. What a stirring time.'[110]

To paraphrase Dylan, for the Irish in America the times, they are still a-stirring.

One of the first letters George W. Bush wrote to any foreign political leader – Sinn Fein claim it was in fact *the* first – after being confirmed as President was to Gerry Adams, assuring Adams of the White House's continuing support for the peace process. And within a few days of Bush's being sworn in, a high-level Republican delegation, which included Peter King, showed up at Government Buildings in Dublin. Ireland was still 'up there with the whales'.

FOUR

CANADA

If we are spectators then we will choose the view that there are inevitable human victims and inevitable survivors. And from that view I believe comes a distancing which is unacceptable and immoral. If we are participants then we realise there are no inevitable victims. We refuse the temptation to distance ourselves from the suffering around us – whether it comes through history books or contemporary television images. And then, although we cannot turn the clock back and change the deaths that happened here, at least we do justice to the reality of the people who died here, taking the meaning of their suffering and connecting it to the present day challenges to our compassion and involvement. If we are participants we engage with the past in terms of the present. If we are spectators then we close these people into a prison of statistics and memories from which they can never escape to challenge our conscience and compassion.

Mary Robinson, President of Ireland,
at Grosse Ile, 21 August 1994

DESPITE THE melody's Irish associations, no one thought it appropriate to sing Tom Moore's *Canadian Boat Song* as we headed out of Quebec, and down the St Lawrence. For we were on our way to visit Grosse Ile, which, outside of Ireland itself, is probably *the* single most sacred famine site in the world. Significantly, in 1994 President Mary Robinson made a visit to Grosse Ile her first official engagement in Canada. Now, three years later, on a misty August morning two large ferries were bearing some 1,800 members of the Ancient Order of Hibernians – scholars, clergy, people interested in the Irish Famine from all walks of life and all parts of the North American continent – towards one of the black holes of Irish folk memory. We were commemorating the 150th anniversary of the 'Irish Summer' in which thousands of the starving terrified victims of the potato blight made it across the Atlantic, only to die of 'famine fever' (typhus) in their own excrement on Grosse Ile, a quarantine island, at the gateway to the New World.

BEFORE 'BLACK 47'

There are other horrific reasons why the Irish commemorate this place, for the island came into use as a quarantine station even before 'black 47'. In 1832, the 'coffin ships', – designed not as passenger vessels but as timber carriers from North America – were filled with Irish people as fare-paying ballast for the return journey. These ships were instrumental in bringing cholera to Canada from Ireland and the flop houses of Liverpool. Some 25,000 people had died in an epidemic which devastated Ireland in that year, and in trying to get away from the outbreak many people contracted cholera in the appallingly insanitary conditions of the filthy, overcrowded vessels.

It is thought that about 1,000 victims were buried in mass graves in Grosse Ile's so called 'Valley of Death', the only place where the soil was deep enough, but the death toll is an estimated one. Many people are known to have drowned in the shallows, too weak to struggle ashore from the boats. In fact, Grosse Ile may have greatly contributed to the spread of the epidemic because it brought the sick and the well into close proximity, and thus thousands of seemingly healthy emigrants left the island carrying the infection, and spread the disease further up the St Lawrence into Quebec, Montreal and the smaller towns and villages.

The 1832 epidemic reached hundreds of miles up the Ottawa River, so ravaging Ontario as to cause the prisoners at Hamilton jail to be freed (except those condemned to death) because 'any other course would be downright murder'.[1] Awful tales of the cholera's spread still persist – some of those consigned to mass graves are said to have been buried while still alive. These inland deaths are said to have been in the region of 6,000: Montreal had close to 2,000 victims, Quebec, 1,500.

Thus, through no fault of their own, the unfortunate Irish brought disaster to their host country. The miracle is that somehow this afflicted race – speaking a strange language and practising a religion which until recently had been outlawed – either seized or were afforded, however grudgingly, sufficient opportunities to wrestle themselves up the ladder of success to the pinnacles they ultimately achieved. Canada occasionally behaved harshly towards the Irish of the green tradition, but it also extended a tolerance which was not always encountered elsewhere in the diaspora.

COMMEMORATING THE DEAD

In view of the nature of the terrible events we were commemorating, the organisers of the AOH pilgrimage had decided that there was only one way to solemnise the moment adequately – the bars were closed. However, it being an Irish commemoration, solemnity was but temporarily achieved. A number of large, beer-bellied men with T-shirts inscribed An Gorta Mor, the Great Hunger, roamed the decks edgily and thirstily. People made cracks about the Great Thirst, and opined that the T-shirt-wearers at least stood in no danger of emulating the starving victims of the past. The raillery became more difficult to sustain as Grosse Ile loomed out of the mist and a colour party formed at the gangway. This party was led by Monsignor Andre Gaumond, Catholic Archbishop of Sherbrooke and the Reverend Bruce Stavert, Anglican Bishop of Quebec, dignitaries from the AOH, representatives from the Irish Embassy and, by courtesy of the organisers, my unworthy self. To the skirl of pipers we stepped ashore and were transported in small buses to an island vantage point marked by a Celtic cross. It was erected by a heroic doctor, George Mellis Douglas, who, had he been listened to, would have greatly alleviated the catastrophe.

In February 1847, months before any of the 'coffin ships' arrived, Dr Douglas warned the Legislative Assembly that the summer would bring greatly increased numbers of immigrants to Canadian shores, because the American ports were closed to the plague-ridden Irish. Knowing something of Irish conditions, he forecast that the closures would: 'augment the number of poor and destitute who will flock to our shores', thereby bringing with them: 'a greater amount of sickness and mortality'. He asked for £3,000 to increase the quarantine facilities. The Assembly gave him £300 – enough to buy fifty extra beds.

In the event the doctor was to use his own money to commemorate the dead. These included four doctors, four priests, two Anglican ministers and more than thirty nurses, orderlies and other helpers. Douglas himself only partially survived the horrors of Grosse Ile. He lived through 'the Irish Summer', healthy in body, but fell prey to depression and, having saved the lives of thousands of emigrants, took his own life at the age of fifty-five. The plaque on the cross he erected reads:

> In this secluded spot lie the mortal remains of five thousand, four hundred and twenty-five persons who, flying from pestilence and famine in the year 1847, found in North America but a grave.

It must be acknowledged that the speeches at the memorial were not polemical. The speakers attempted to create a sense of empathy with the sufferings of the under-privileged of the present through acknowledging the sufferings of those who had gone ahead. As we listened, I discovered that the man standing to my left strongly represented the caring tradition of the Irish which the memory of the Famine helps to nurture. It was Don Mullan, who had survived horrors like seeing bodies being shovelled into mass graves in Zaire by saying to himself: 'This is what we came through.'[2] He was one of those involved in the remarkable campaign which ultimately forced the Canadian Government to recognise Grosse Ile as being particularly important to the Irish (see page 398). He is also a co-founder, with a Choctaw Indian, White Deer, of the organisation Celts and Indians Together (CAIT). During the Famine, the Choctaws – themselves harried and nearly destitute – had taken up a collection to assist the starving Irish.

To my right was an AOH leader whom I had met on the boat. At first sight I had been a little wary of him. He was low-sized and wearing an AOH green blazer and ornate silver-chased sunglasses with black visors; it had been all too easy to categorise him instantly as being a leprechauny, stage Irishman. During the journey, however, I had come to have a high opinion of him. He was obviously a person of both scholarship and political acuity. Now, as we stood looking over the great river, and the islands dotted around us, on our deceptively pleasant wooded island site, an incident occurred which made me ashamed of doubting his sincerity. Standing to attention, as we all did while the speeches were in progress, I sensed a movement. His shoulders were shaking. As I observed him from the corner of my eye without him noticing, I saw him turn his head quickly from side to side to ensure that no one was looking, and then remove his shades and shake free the tears that had been trapped by the visors. Mary Robinson had been correct when she observed:

> Grosse Ile, Oilean na nGael – Île des irlandais – is special. I believe that even those coming to this beautiful island knowing nothing of the tragedy which occurred here, would sense its difference. I am certain that no one knowing the story could remain unaffected. This is a hallowed place.

It is. As we turned down the hill from the memorial to the site where an ecumenical service for the repose of the souls of the dead was being conducted by the two bishops, we saw lying before us what appeared to be a series of lazy beds, the wide drills in which potatoes used to be planted at the time of the Famine. These lazy beds had not been dug for potatoes, but as mass graves in which Famine victims had been buried eight deep. Appropriately enough, as we arrived at the service, the loudspeakers were relaying the *De Profundis*.

THE IMPACT OF THE FAMINE

I had come to Grosse Ile, partly because of the significance of the place of sorrow in Irish history, but also because it lies in the area of Canada in which the Irish diaspora first began putting down roots in North America. After Newfoundland, and the other Atlantic provinces, the St Lawrence was the main artery through which the Irish flowed into the towns of Quebec, Montreal, Kingston, Toronto, the Ottawa Valley and the rest of Canada. Many subsequently made their way into the US.

Every page turned in the story of the Irish diaspora after the 1840s is to some extent, with the possible exception of the very recent past, affected by the Famine. One could take up the melancholy tale of the Great Hunger in America, Australia, Argentina or the United Kingdom, but it seemed to me particularly appropriate in the Famine commemorative year of 1997 to attempt to experience the Famine story in the context of Grosse Ile. This tiny speck of land, a world away from Ireland, at the mouth of one of the world's great rivers, both symbolises the impact of the Famine on the Irish generally and in particular helps to explain their North American experience.

During the Famine period, a million people fled across the Atlantic in conditions which sometimes fell below the miserable standards of the African slave ships. Some 300,000 of the Atlantic emigrants came to British North America and, in so far as records were kept, it is estimated that around 17,000 died aboard the coffin ships and were buried at sea. About twenty thousand died in Canada during 1847, either in the quarantine stations of Grosse Ile, Quebec, Partridge Island and New Brunswick, or in the towns and ditches of Quebec and Montreal.

Prior to the Famine, the bulk of Irish emigrants to North America between 1825 and 1845 had gone to Canada, possibly as many as 450,000 in that period. Of these a third or more are reckoned to have travelled on to the States at a later date. Some of the pre-1845 emigrants received Government assistance to emigrate, but in general most paid their own way. These emigrants were small farmers who were able to buy, on easy credit terms, the 150-acre lots which were available at five shillings an acre from the Government. There was also plenty of work to be found as farm labourers, lumberjacks, dockers or canal-diggers. In turn, Newfoundland, Nova Scotia, Prince Edward Island, New Brunswick, Quebec and Ontario all attracted Irish emigrants.

In the 1830s a combination of assisted passages to Australia and colonial wars helped to turn the tide of emigration elsewhere, notably towards Republican America. However, throughout 1847 the Americans tightened their landing laws so that the Famine ships were not allowed to disembark their desperate, dying cargoes.

A number of landlords in Ireland did make an effort to provide for their tenants so that they would not arrive in such conditions. For example, Colonel Wyndham, who had extensive estates in the Clare Limerick area, saw to it that impoverished tenants were not simply evicted, but received assisted passages to Canada on well-founded ships, arriving healthy and finding work relatively easily. But good ships were so rare that one of the more imaginative millenium projects of the Irish diaspora was the building of a replica of the most famous of the emigrant barques, the 408 ton, three masted sailing ship *Jeanie Johnston*. The *Jeanie Johnston* plied between Tralee in Co. Kerry and Quebec (where it was built), Baltimore and New York, bringing emigrants out and timber back between 1847 and 1858, without ever losing a passenger either through disease or to the sea. Unlike most such ships there was a doctor aboard and the captain, James Attridge, was a humane, skilful mariner.[3] Its owner, Nicholas Donovan and his friend Sir Edward Denny, were representatives of the better type of landlord, who provided assisted passage for their tenants. But overall benevolent landlords were few and made little impression on the total numbers who had left Ireland. As one authority has noted: 'All told, less than 40,000 emigrants are known to have received subsidies from either landlords or the state, between 1846 and 1850.'[3] The overwhelming source of money to pay for the emigrants' passage came from their own relatives or friends who had managed to scrape up enough to leave Ireland themselves, and when settled, sent part of their wages home. The 'American letter', not the landlord or the British Government, was the Irish emigrant's lifeline.

Before the Famine

Traditionally Canada had been a benign and welcoming place for the Irish emigrant. Ironically, one of the most enthusiastic chroniclers of its attractions was Lord Edward Fitzgerald, a leader of the 1798 rebellion which was to give rise to the fatal Act of Union that would have such a direct bearing on the Famine. Writing to his mother from Saint John in New Brunswick in 1773, he said the people of the town were 'all Irish' with a brogue 'not in higher perfection in Kilkenny'.[4] He subsequently found: 'a tract of land peopled by Irish, who came out not worth a shilling and have all now farms worth (according to the value of money in this country) from £1,000 to £3,000.' Fitzgerald liked the quality of Canadian life:[5]

> There were no gentlemen; everybody is on a footing, provided he works, and wants nothing; every man is exactly what he can make himself, or has made himself by his industry. The more children a man has the better: his wife being brought to bed is as joyful news as his cow calving; the father has no uneasiness about providing for them as this is done by the profit of their work. By the time they are fit to settle he can always afford two oxen, a cow, a gun and an axe, and in a few years if they work, they can thrive.

This assessment of the benefits of Canadian life tended to be corroborated by the results of the Peter Robinson experiment carried out in 1823–5. The idea of alleviating the land war then raging in parts of Cork, by sending families to Canada was sold to Robert Horton, the Deputy Secretary of State for War and the Colonies, by Robinson's brother John,[6] who had a scheme for colonising the part of the Ottawa Valley which now includes the counties of Carleton, Lanark and Renfrew. Peter Robinson managed to arrange for shipping in 1823 and 1825 of two consignments of emigrants, numbering approximately 500 and 2,000 persons respectively. The second consignment was located around the Peterborough district of Lake Ontario, radiating out from the Otonabee Valley.

Inevitably some of the emigrants died from the fevers of the time, but in general the settlement worked. Robinson was a diligent and conscientious man who personally scouted the land on which the emigrants were to settle and oversaw the arrangements for their food, transport and medical health. His efforts on their behalf were appreciated by the emigrants, the bulk of whom fared well. The scheme could have provided a model both for settling Canada's vast unpopulated areas and alleviating Irish miseries, but it was not proceeded with on grounds of expense.

Witnesses to the horror

As we have seen, no kindly Peter Robinson figure oversaw the panic-stricken Famine exodus. Ship owners and captains cheated on the emigrants' rations, the ships were plague-infested and the human cargoes were frequently landed in a far worse condition than the slaves that were being imported at the time. A consideration obtained which one finds again and again in the history of the Irish diaspora, whether it be during the building of fever-laden canals in New Orleans, or working the sugar cane fields of the Caribbean: slaves were worth money to their sellers and buyers; Irish immigrants were only valuable at the time of paying their fares or beginning their indentures. Subsequently (if they lived) they could be discarded and replaced.

One scion of a landlord family, Stephen De Vere White, a County Limerick magistrate, was so outraged by the reports of conditions aboard the coffin ships that he went to Canada as an emigrant to study conditions at first hand. He found that frequently:

> Before the emigrant has been a week at sea, he is an altered man. How can it be otherwise? Hundreds of poor people, men, women and children of all ages, from the drivelling idiot to the babe just born, huddled together without light, without air, wallowing in filth, and breathing a foetid atmosphere, sick in body, dispirited in heart, and fevered patients lying between the sound, in sleeping places so narrow as almost to deny them the power of indulging, by a change of position, the natural restlessness of the disease, by their agonizing ravings disturbing those around.[7]

Food was 'generally ill selected and seldom sufficiently cooked'. The 'water supply was insufficient to allow for washing', never mind cater for plague victims suffering from raging thirsts and racked by dysentery. 'The filthy beds, teeming with all abominations' were never aired. De Vere described how the fever outbreak meant that 'the dead and the living huddled together', and how the emigrant agent coming aboard to inspect the ship on arrival staggered back 'like one struck, at meeting the current of foetid infection exhaled from between her decks'. Not surprisingly, it has been said that if it had been possible to place a slab to commemorate every Irish person who died at sea during the Famine period, one could walk dryshod to America.

Another diarist, Robert Whyte of Dublin, has left an account of a Grosse Ile tragedy which sums up the opprobrium which the Famine attached to the word 'landlord' in Irish nomenclature. Whyte noticed a man coming aboard from the island: 'the very picture of desperation and misery, that increased the ugliness of his countenance, for he was sadly disfigured by smallpox and was blinded in one eye'. The man, one of a group sent to Canada by a County Meath landlord, snatched his child from a woman's arms and went below without speaking. A sailor told Whyte what had happened. The man had just buried his wife. The sailor said: 'The man stood at the grave until it was covered, whereupon he snatched two shovels, laid them on the grave in the form of a cross and cried: "By that cross Mary I will go back and shoot the man who murdered you, and that is the landlord."'

THE PLAGUE ARRIVES

The plague actually first arrived in Canada, not at Grosse Ile, but at the quarantine station on Partridge Island, off Saint John New Brunswick, on 5 May 1847 aboard the brig *Midas*. Other ships followed soon after and Partridge Island was soon overwhelmed by the epidemic. As on Grosse Ile, a Celtic cross was erected on Partridge Island, this time on 10 October 1927. Its inscription says:

> This monument was erected in memory of more than 2,000 Irish emigrants, who died of typhus fever, contracted on shipboard during the voyage from Ireland, in the famine year 1847, and of whom 600 were buried on this island. This cross also commemorates the devotion and sacrifice of Dr Patrick Collins, who after administering to the victims of the disease, himself contracted it and died.[8]

It is estimated that some 17,000 emigrants (and that is a conservative estimate) were: 'Shipped from different Irish ports and from Liverpool, worn out with poverty and disease, and labouring under fever of a most infectious and malignant description.'[6] And so memories of mass graves, overworked doctors, heroism and horror, hang in the island's twilight.

Some of the unfortunates became involved in a ghastly game of shuttlecock. After a summer in which the resources of the island's quarantine station had been strained beyond breaking point, the station closed for the year on 1 November. However, on that very day, there arrived from Ireland a coffin ship, the *Aeolus* bearing 428 passengers who had been cleared off Lord Palmerston's Irish estates. They were in such wretched condition that the Health Officer reported:

> There are many superannuated people, and others of broken-down constitutions, and subjects of chronic disease, lame, widows with very helpless families, feeble men, (through chronic disease etc.) with large helpless families . . . nearly 400 or so glaring paupers are thus sent out. Who so tame as would not feel indignant at that outrage.[9]

The authorities attempted to bribe them into going back to Ireland by attempting to pay their passage, but, terrified of re-undergoing the horrors of the voyage and those undergone on Palmerston's estates, the wretched people preferred to cram into grossly overcrowded accommodation available in St John's.

The first ship to arrive at Grosse Ile with plague aboard was the *Syria* which dropped anchor on 17 May 1847 carrying 84 cases of typhus. The first victim to die was Ellen Kane, a four-year-old girl who had contracted the disease in a Liverpool lodging house. Four days after the *Syria* eight more ships arrived, all carrying plague-infected passengers. By the end of the month there was a total of forty ships, stretching down river for almost two miles. All of them had already buried some passengers at sea. On arrival, Grosse Ile was frequently found to be so over-crowded that it could take no more patients, and both on and off shore the living and the dead slept in a ghastly, excrement-smeared mélange. The Canadian authorities were taken completely unaware by the scale of the disaster. No precautions had been taken either to receive the sick or to prevent the spread of the disease.

Suffering agonies of thirst, the sick lay in their own excrement for days on end. Even 'healthy' patients who passed through Grosse Ile contracted typhus and spread the disease once they landed. There was neither sufficient staff to check the ship properly nor, if fever were discovered, to tend to the victims when they were brought ashore. Even soil to bury the dead was in such short supply that rats began swimming from the other islands to feed on the lightly covered cadavers.

RE-AWAKENING INTEREST

The first AOH pilgrimage to Grosse Ile occurred on the fiftieth anniversary of 'the Summer of Sorrow' in 1897. And in 1909 the Ancient Order of Hibernians erected a 46-foot high granite Celtic cross on a vantage point near today's landing stage. The cross bears inscriptions in Irish, English and French, one of which when translated into English, reads as follows:

> Children of the Gael died in their thousands on this island having fled from the laws of foreign tyrants and an artificial famine in the years 1847–48. God's blessing on them. Let this monument be a token to their name, an honour from the Gaels of America. God save Ireland.

Another illustrates the influence of Mother Church on the attitudes of those who sometimes inflicted, but mostly endured, the blows of Irish history:

> Sacred to the memory of thousands of Irish immigrants who to preserve the faith suffered hunger and exile in 1847–8, and stricken with fever ended here their sorrowful pilgrimage.

The unveiling of the cross is recorded in AOH history as 'the grandest and most impressive ceremony that ever took place in connection with Irish affairs in America'. Some 8,000 people from all over the continent made their way to the island to attend an open-air mass celebrated, as was the one I attended, alongside the pits where the uncounted dead were buried.

However, between 1909 and the early 1990s Grosse Ile hardly served as a fitting memorial to the tragedy that had sought it out. The island was used for a time as an experimental laboratory for what is alleged to have been everything from research into cattle diseases to germ warfare. The buildings on the island dating from 1847 fell prey to the elements; only one hospital building called the Lazaretto remained.

Then, in 1992, an event occurred which helped to ignite a growing consciousness of being Irish amongst the Irish Canadian (and American) community, and to re-awaken interest in the Famine. The Canadian Parks Service published a Development Concept which referred to the Irish refugees from the Great Hunger as 'British immigrants' and went on to say that 'the tragic events of 1832 and 1847 had been over-emphasised in the past'.

To digress for a moment, it may be remarked that this attitude closely mirrored that of an Irish Government, led by the right-wing Fine Gael party, some years later: in an episode which represented a significant degree of unease as to its sense of history and contemporary identity, Dublin protested against proposals to have the Famine taught alongside the Holocaust in some American schools. A sort of historical travelling circus was arranged whereby an Irish minister, Avril Doyle, was charged with spreading the official view on the Famine throughout the world. She toured the globe, seeking to ensure that 'the tragic events' would not be 'over-emphasised' – code, in other words, for trying to ensure that Sinn Fein would not derive ideological sustenance from the story of the Famine. In pursuit of this aim, Ms Doyle told a heckler in Melbourne that the Famine should not be regarded as a cause of discord between the British and the Irish, but should be looked upon as 'a shared experience'. Irish Australians were not impressed. Touring the country in her wake, I encountered comments to the effect that rape was also a shared experience, as was that of the encounter between victim and executioner.

However, no such sentiments were allowed to prevail in North America. A group of Irish Canadians, headed by the historian Dr Michael Quigley and a banker Denis Leyne and a community worker Greth Dillon, decided to form Action Grosse Ile. The most remarkable thing about Grosse Ile is that there was agreement amongst the Irish that there should be action.

The population of Irish in Canada had declined from 24.3 per cent in post-Federation Canada in 1871 to 9.6 per cent at the time of the 1961 Census, when the method of census taking changed. However, at the time of writing, it was calculated [10] that 13.2 per cent of Canadians included Irish as one of their ethnic origins. Aculturation, the fact that the Irish tended to opt for America rather than Canada, and the introduction of a points system by the Canadian Emigration Authorities, all served to cut the flow of Irish emigrants to Canada to a matter of a few hundred per year by the time this was being written. Chinese is now the third-largest spoken language in Toronto after English and French and waves of emigration from Vietnam and Hong Kong have been facilitated by the points system which basically favours the emigrant who already has relations in Canada: the hard-working Chinese extended families of the Chinese rapidly earned the money to bring in yet another relative.

The head over the parapet attitude of the Irish in America had already seeped across the Canadian border to such an extent that the mid-1980s had witnessed a remarkable affirmation of Irish identity: the St Patrick's Day parade committee was able to generate sufficient enthusiasm for the idea of reconstituting the parade to induce the Police Chief, William J. McCormack, to allow it to be restaged after a lapse of over one hundred years. The fact that McCormack, an Irishman, had made a major breakthrough in becoming Chief of Police in Toronto was in itself an indication of growing Irish influence.

BLENDING

However, the Grosse Ile commemoration was a much more fraught project. Firstly there is the overriding Canadian attitude towards ethnic or religious differences – people don't want to hear about them. They've had enough trouble between the French and English, the Orange and the Green in the past. The Canadian formula for ensuring that these remain in the past is not so much blending as blanding. At the time of writing, for instance, one hears considerable unease about the Yugoslavian emigrants which the upheaval has thrown up. The emigrants are welcomed as individuals, but the Canadians do not want to know whether they are Croats or Serbs, Muslims or Albanians. All they want to be assured of is that Kosovo troubles will not be translated to their shores.

Similarly, the old Protestant/Catholic tensions still cast historical shadows. As Mary Durkan put it to me: 'I worked in New York before coming to Toronto, and it was as different as night and day. In New York, most of the people you meet or socialise with are southern Irish Catholic. In Toronto they're just as likely to be of North of Ireland Protestant or of British descent as Southern Catholic. Everyone's very polite and friendly, but there are sensitivities which have to be respected. 'When the Grosse Ile agitation began, everyone was petrified in case it would become tainted with an IRA brush. It seemed that this was about to happen when Denis Leyne, one of the principal moving spirits behind the Grosse Ile commemoration project, was picked up in New York with money which the FBI claimed was to have been used in attempted arms dealing. He was eventually acquitted, but died of a heart attack probably brought on by the strain of his experiences with the law, and was therefore absent from the commemoration he had done so much to bring about. His supporters claimed that the popular banker had been set up as part of a dirty tricks operation.

The fallout from the Leyne affair was contained through a combination of skilful diplomacy on the part of the Irish Ambassador at the time, Antoin Mac Umfraidh, and the fact that the Peace Process began. The committee managed to bridge the cultural and political divide between the varying Irish groups. These might be taken as being symbolised by two Irish institutions in Toronto, the Irish Centre and the Ireland Fund. The Irish Centre was located at Dupont Street, an industrial area synonymous with industrial pollution. The Ireland Fund is overseen by Ted McConnell, the Irish Consul General in Toronto, one of the city's most prominent financial consultants. The blend of the grass roots and the boardroom is notoriously difficult to achieve without having issues of the IRA involved, but the facts of Mary Robinson coming to the 1994 Grosse Ile commemoration and Bill Clinton's espousal of the Peace Process, combined with the hard work and political dexterity of the Action Committee, somehow brought off the miracle.

ACTION GROSSE ILE

The group was established at a meeting in Toronto in June 1992. Its mandate was:

> To ensure that the mass graves of the Irish Famine victims of 1847 are perpetuated as the main theme of the National Historic Park on Grosse Ile and is a permanent monument to the Irish role in the building of Canada.[11]

A remarkable lobbying campaign then began. Public representatives, including local government officials, members of school boards, churches and trade unions, were all approached. Television documentaries were aired, articles written, petitions got up, signatures collected, celebrity concerts held. The campaign reached back to Ireland and all around the world, as the Irish diaspora came to see Grosse Ile as a focal point in its heritage. The Action Grosse Ile Committee was included in *Irish America*[12] magazine's Top 100 *Irish America* Award Ceremony in New York in March 1994.

The pressure resulted in the Parks Service agreeing to withdraw its reference to overemphasis and to the holding of public hearings, but otherwise the Irish community demands were not met. The Parks Service pressed ahead with plans to use Grosse Ile as a focal point for the overall story of emigration to Canada but with the Irish experience very much a subsidiary theme. Even after the visit of Mary Robinson in 1994, the Parks Service was still digging in its heels. However, in 1996, a new Minister of Canadian Heritage was appointed, Sheila Copps. She looked on the controversy with a fresh eye, and on St Patrick's Day, 1996, the Chairman of Action Grosse Ile itself, John Masterson, William J. McCormack, and Padraig O'Laighin, chair of the General Assembly of Irish Organisations in Montreal, were able to issue a statement praising the Minister's acceptance of the Irish proposals and saying that the victory was: 'in large part, the result of the impressive unity of purpose shown by the Irish community, not only here in Canada but across the diaspora and in Ireland'.[13]

The Famine played a notable part in recovering the consciousness of being Irish throughout Canada. Apart from the Grosse Ile commemoration, another Famine memorial was erected in Kingston, a monument in a small park, a plaque was placed on Metro Hall, Toronto, and a monument erected on Pigeon Island, New Brunswick. The Toronto plaque was the result of the efforts of a group who had broken away from the main Grosse Ile Committee after the arrest of Denis Leyne.

THE BLACK STONE OF MONTREAL

Controversies erupted on a number of occasions over the 'Black Stone of Montreal' which commemorates Famine deaths in that city. Being the first major port on the St Lawrence after Quebec, Montreal attracted an enormous influx of Famine victims and a quarantine centre was built to the west of the city at a place called Goose Village at Point St Charles. Like Grosse Ile, the scale of the tragedy soon engulfed the facilities available and the situation which resulted was described by Sister McMullen, Superior of the Grey Nuns, in an address to the community in which she described what she had witnessed:

> Sisters, I have seen a sight today that I shall never forget. I went to Point St Charles and found hundreds of sick and dying people huddled together. The stench emanating from them is too great for even the strongest of constitutions. The air is filled with the groans of suffering. Death is there in its most appalling aspect. Those who cry out loud in their agony are strangers, and their hands are outstretched for relief. Sisters, the plague is contagious.

At this stage in her account, Sister McMullen broke down in tears. When she recovered she told the assembled nuns: 'In sending you there, I am signing a death warrant, but you are free to accept or refuse.'

The entire community volunteered to serve. It was as Don Pigeon wrote:

> As happened elsewhere in Canada, generosity outweighed fear and charity overcame xenophobia, at great cost. Several nursing sisters, three priests and a score of layworkers died of diseases contracted by the Irish refugees.

One notable martyr was John Easton Mills, the Mayor of Montreal, whose energy and altruism helped ensure relatively safe and healthy conditions for the Irish. He fell victim in November. He had been predeceased the previous month by another prominent member of Canadian society; the builder of St Michael's Cathedral in Toronto, Bishop Michael Power. Power contracted typhus during his frequent visits to the fever sheds built to house the Irish near today's Queen's Street. He was forty-two when he died. Perhaps the best explanation of the sacrifices made by so many was offered by Father Joseph Connolly, pastor at the new Irish parish of St Patrick's, who explained: 'If I prepared for death and consigned to the silent grave for a period of six weeks or more, some fifty adult persons every day, I was but doing what every priest would be bound to do under similar circumstances.'

The controversy over commemorating the terrible events at Point St Charles began twelve years after 'the Irish Summer'. The site was cleared for the building of the Victoria Railway Bridge, but the Irish labourers refused to work until the location of so much suffering(which sometimes had included the sufferings and deaths of their own relatives) was suitably acknowledged.

They dredged a huge boulder of black stone from the river, placed it on the site of the mass graves and inscribed it:

> To preserve from desecration the remains of 6,000 emigrants who died from ship fever AD 1847–48, this stone is erected by the workmen of Messrs. Peto, Brassey, and Betts, employed in the construction of the Victoria Bridge AD 1859.

The monument was blessed and dedicated by the Anglican Bishop of Montreal on 1 December 1859, and remained as a landmark in the Irish district for some forty years. Then the Grand Truck railway proposed to move the stone to make way for new tracks. Enormous controversy ensued, but the Irish objections were overcome on the grounds that they had no title to the land. However, ten years later, the Anglican Bishop, John Farthing, came across a deed in the diocesan files in which the contractor, Thomas Brassey, to guard against precisely such a controversy, had deeded the grave site in perpetuity to the Anglican Bishop of Montreal and his successors. The railway company was forced to replace the monument.

Then, in 1966, fresh controversy erupted when the city fathers decided to remove the stone once more to enable new roads to be built for Expo '67. Again the Irish community protested and the city fathers gave in – the road was moved, not the stone.

In 1995, after further dispute, the Irish successfully overcame resistance and erected a commemorative plaque in Irish, English and French, facing the stone. Now, each year the Summer of Sorrow is commemorated by the AOH by a memorial mass and a march to the Black Stone.

ASSESSING OUR IRISHNESS

The Grosse Ile commemoration I attended was part religious ceremony, part picnic. As we went about the island inspecting relics of the Famine or attending another commemoration ceremony at the AOH cross, it was possible to talk to people and assess what their sense of being Irish meant. Most of the people on the island appeared to have visited Ireland at least once, and sometimes many times. Occupations ranged from secretaries, police, trade unionists and teachers to bankers, insurance brokers, lawyers and pub owners. Everyone appeared to be politically aware and, with the exception of the trade unionists, to be conservative in their attitudes. The terms 'Liberal' on the disapprobation scale occurred not far below 'PLO' or 'Communist'.

The level of prosperity appeared to be comfortable rather than wealthy, and everyone displayed an interest in history and in seeing a peaceful united Ireland. There was a general hope that Tony Blair's new (at that stage) Labour Government had such a large majority that it would be independent of the Unionist block, unlike his predecessor John Major. I heard no anti-British sentiments, or anti-Unionist sentiments for that matter.

Most people taking part in the pilgrimage were involved in either subscribing to, or collecting for, some nationalist cause: an Irish language class, a historical project, even a programme aimed at bringing Protestants and Catholic children together. A general shared aspiration appeared to be recognition for the Irish contribution to the countries they now lived in. At the various ceremonies of the day, three anthems were played, those of America, Canada, and Ireland. So far as Ireland was concerned, political discussion indicated that only two parties were of interest, Sinn Fein in the North and Fianna Fail in the Republic. Most people there were Catholics, though many would be more accurately described as 'cultural Catholics' rather than practising ones, and it struck me that I saw no black faces and only a handful of priests.

The journey back to Quebec was a jolly affair, with nothing like the forced humour of the morning trip. The fact that the bars were open helped enormously and within minutes of casting off, the Irish wake syndrome set in. We had paid our respects to the dead, and now was the time to buy rounds of drink for each other, and get the music going. The two best dancers at an impromptu hooley which broke out on the after-deck were a Catholic priest and the Protestant bishop's buxom blonde wife. The atmosphere had that air of 'craic' and good-old-boyism that is peculiarly Irish and American.

The only discordant note of the entire day came from a CNN reporter who went around with his camera enquiring if the day had in reality only been a fine opportunity for 'Brit-bashing'? That night a Ceili Mor[14] was held, where the participants in the day's events, many of them in their sixties and seventies, honoured Irish music, dance and song. The particularly Irish oral tradition of Guinness, Jameson, etc was afforded due respect until the small hours of the morning.

A JOYOUS, GOOD-HEARTED OCCASION

Our pilgrimage to Grosse Ile formed part of a tableau of events to commemorate both the Famine and the Irish contribution to Quebec and North America generally. The day after the Grosse Ile ceremonies, a Sunday, there was a gathering at Old St Patrick's Church which is claimed to be the oldest church in North America. It was built by the Irish in Quebec in 1832 in McMahon Street which is called after an Irish priest who was cast in the mould of men like Father Thiery in Australia or of Father Fahey in Argentina, whose contributions to their countrymen's ability to establish themselves in those countries we have encountered in the relevant chapters.

The historian of the Irish in Quebec, Marianna Gallagher[15] – a granddaughter of Jeremiah Gallagher, the AOH leader in Quebec who designed the Grosse Ile Cross – gave a speech in which she recalled the horrors encountered by the Irish on arrival in Canada, but also the great kindness they often experienced. Children orphaned by the Grosse Ile tragedy were not only readily adopted into Montreal and Quebec homes so that they grew up to become prosperous citizens but, with rare sensitivity, their adoptive parents saw to it that they retained their own names, so that the disaster which cost them their families did not cost them their identities. Local politicians speaking in English and French took up this theme. The Mayor said that: 'The Irish are Quebec's best-rooted citizens. The Irish were part of our history, our present, and will be part of our future.' The Mayor was literally correct in his statements, but there are some disagreeable cross-currents which will be adverted to later (page 423).

However, the commemoration services were entirely pleasant and relaxed, conjuring up a friendly spirit not only amongst the participants, but amongst the onlookers. It was a bright breezy morning, banners waved and a police motor-cycle escort preceded us as a parade formed to march to the Basilica of Notre Dame de Quebec for high mass. The only indication of the sombre backdrop to the march was the presence in our midst of a group wearing black Famine-period clothes and carrying a coffin. The people of Quebec waved and clapped as we passed and it was a joyous, good-hearted occasion. Beside me Don Mullan, who had been with me on the Grosse Ile pilgrimage, remarked: 'It's strange to feel everyone's your friend on a march. Imagine all these tricolours in some places back home. I keep waiting for the Orangemen to ambush us.'

For some reason, both Don and I had arrived in Quebec without our luggage. In my case the airline said that it had been held up because I had not checked it through customs at Boston. In fact an airline official had actually carried the bags for me and in my presence handed them over to a Canadian airport official, who assured me that they would be checked through as a matter of routine without any difficulty. I followed the same checking procedure on re-entry to the States without the slightest hitch. In the event, I suffered no greater inconvenience than having to wear the same clothes for forty-eight hours (which admittedly could have been a problem for my friends, had we not spent so much time out of doors), and my bags were waiting for me at my hotel when I returned from Grosse Ile. However, in Don's case the problem was more serious, because the authorities impounded several copies of his book *Eye-witness, Bloody Sunday*, which contained much of the new evidence that later caused Tony Blair to announce a new inquiry into the shooting of thirteen unarmed civilians by British paratroopers, on Sunday, 30 January 1972. Don was put to considerable inconvenience, driving out to the airport, form-filling and arguing before he recovered his property. As the incident cost him the opportunity of distributing his book during the weekend ceremonies, he felt that that could have been the real point of the hold up. It was yet another small example of the little poisons which con-tinually seep through both the Orange and Green components of the diaspora from the North of Ireland situation. It may not be a coincidence that a feature of the Royal Canadian Mounted Police and of the Canadian Special Branch is the large number of ex-Royal Ulster Constabulary who join the forces after serving for a few years in Ulster. It was not until the mid-1980s that a Catholic, William McCormack, managed to rise through the ranks to a senior position in the police force.

In view of the solemnity of the occasion, even the most irreligious of the marchers, myself included, actually entered the sumptuously baroque cathedral, which was ablaze with huge displays of soaring gold leaf. However, good resolutions faltered and eventually withered as the celebrant, an ageing former Archbishop, droned on. It was like being back in Ireland at an old-fashioned high mass, except that the celebrant spoke in French and in more splendid surroundings than those of any Irish church. One by one, the faint-hearted at the back began making their way to a nearby hostelry, run by an Irishman. By the time the service concluded approximately an hour and a half later, the bar was crowded with thirsty worshippers.

As well as the high mass, there was a thanksgiving ceremony and reception in the courtyard of the Petit Seminaire de Quebec beside the Basilica, to express appreciation to the people of Quebec for their kindness to the Famine refugees.

ACCEPTING THE SYSTEM

One of the greatest chroniclers of the history of the Irish in Canada was Nicholas Flood Davin (1843–1901), a County Limerick man who turned from the bar to journalism, and founded a newspaper in Saskatchewan. Davin concluded his major work, *The Irishman in Canada*, as follows:

> The history of the Irishman in Canada closes as it opened with the name of an Irish Governor General on my pen. I have shown what part the Irishman has played in clearing the forest, in building up the structure of our civic life, in defending the country, in battling for our liberties, in developing our resources, in spreading enlightenment, in the culture of literature and art, in tending the sacred fires of religion, in sweeting the cares of life, and I trust I have done this without giving offence in any quarter, or forgetting for a single instance that my paramount duty, as a paramount duty of us all, belongs to Canada.[16]

Davin, who took his own life, some would say a virtually unavoidable outcome for someone who spent his life trying to see good in his fellow countrymen, touches a *leitmotif* that was to be struck with vigour by Irish colonials the world over. They placed the country of their adoption first and in general did not join in rebellions against the imperial power of England, despite the awful relationship of their country of origin with that power. Indeed, a feature of Louis Riel's two rebellions in 1869 and 1885, and of the colonial uprising earlier in the century (1830), was the conservatism shown by the Irish Catholics. When Riel declared a provisional government in the Red River region of Manitoba, with the full support of its mixed-blood Roman Catholic peoples (both Anglophone and Francophone), Irish Orangemen flocked to fight against him. However, Irish Catholics stayed aloof from the independence-minded aspirations of their co-religionists.

There are a number of ironies in this Irish caution. Firstly, Riel's ancestors were Reels from Limerick. Louis Riel was a direct descendant of Jean-

Baptiste Reel who is known to have been married at Boucherville in 1704.[13] Secondly, the Irish had got their first footing in Canada under the French regime: the 'Wild Geese' who had left Ireland for France after the Williamite Wars served in New France, as the colony was then known by the French regiments. Irish surnames were common in New France by the end of the seventeenth century: O'Brennans, Moores, Hamiltons, McCarthys, O'Neills, O'Dwyers and O'Sullivans were all to be met with. Whether one would have wished to meet one particular member of the O'Sullivan clan is a moot point. Timothy O'Sullivan was born in Cork and practised as a surgeon in Montreal from about 1718. He is remembered partly for being a successful doctor who affected 'remedies with which nobody was familiar', and partly for not only beating his wife but his clients into the bargain. As a biographer of his noted: if 'one of Ireland's earliest gifts to Quebec ... failed to achieve immortal greatness, at least he escaped immortal dullness'.[17]

However, despite the legacies of Wild Geese, Reels and O'Sullivans, even the Fenian incursions described later on (pages 408–10) elicited only enthusiasm, not military assistance, from the Irish. They had emigrated to Canada to make a new life and to get away from rebellions and their slaughterous aftermaths. That meant accepting the system and working within it, not seeking to overthrow it by military means.

Another true point Davin makes in his book is that the Irish made a massive contribution to North America (both the US and Canada), out of all proportion to the size of Ireland.

The paternity of modern Canada could be attributed to Guy Carleton from County Tyrone. Under the terms of the Treaty of Paris, England took control of Canada from the French on 10 February 1763. It was Carleton, the Lieutenant Governor of Quebec, who united both French Canadians and British under his command to ensure that England kept its control, after the cessation of the thirteen colonies following which the Americans thought to add a fourteenth, Canada, to the list. Carleton was knighted for his leadership in the successful defence of Quebec in 1775. His most formidable adversary in the war to that point was another Irishman, Richard Montgomery, who was born not far from Carleton in County Donegal. Montgomery was killed in the fighting and Carleton saw to it that he was buried with full military honours.

Another Irish victim of the American War of Independence was the 12-year-old son of Luke Carscallian. Carscallian was part of a movement which had a marked effect on the character of the Canadian population – the emigration of loyalists from America to Canada. These included Catholic Irish loyalists, like the members of the Royal New York Irish Regiment who defended Boston against Washington in 1775, but the bulk of them were of course Protestant Irishmen. They founded the town of Saint John on the Saint John's River and left a lasting imprint on Nova Scotia, Ontario, New Brunswick and the upper St Lawrence.

Carscallian was a well-doing man who, having served in the British Army, had emigrated to America where he had built up a 12,000-acre holding at the outbreak of the rebellion. He was pressed to join the rebels, or be regarded as an enemy, but replied that: 'I have fought for the king, and I will do so again.'[18] A warrant was issued for his arrest, but he escaped to Canada, leaving behind him his fortune and, more importantly, his family. The rebels threatened to hang his son unless he told where his father was hiding. The boy replied 'Hang away', and he was subsequently half-hanged three times. Each time he recovered his breath, he was again asked for his father's whereabouts, and each time he replied 'No'. After the third hanging, the rebels killed him.

NEW BRUNSWICK

The bulk of Irish emigration to Canada occurred before the Famine, chiefly to New Brunswick, Quebec and Ontario, and derived mainly from Ulster and the northern counties of what is now the Republic of Ireland. This area was one of the most densely populated in Western Europe and farm holdings were generally small. In the Northern counties, chiefly Antrim, Armagh and Down, little farms, usually less than ten acres in size, were nevertheless reasonably prosperous because of the linen trade for which they grew flax. However, after the Napoleonic Wars there was a fall-off in trade and in the economy of the country in general, and the estimate of reliable authorities is that between 1825 and 1845 some 475,000 Irish landed in British North America, some 60 per cent of all emigrant arrivals in that twenty-year period.

There was heavy emigration from the ports of Belfast and Derry, to a lesser extent from Sligo, and in the South from Dublin, Limerick, Cork and Waterford. As we will see, the southern ports like Waterford, New Ross and Youghal established links with the maritime states which even to this day have left a noticeable imprint, particularly in Newfoundland. However, as the geographers Cecil J. Houston and William J. Smith have pointed out:

> Ulster remained the core region from which the emigrants were drawn and by the end of the century it had consolidated its position. By the end of the century also, emigration was down to a fraction of what took place after the end of the Napoleonic Wars and the Famine. In the final five years of the nineteenth century, only 3,000 Irish people emigrated to Canada. The strong Ulster presence, in the Irish emigration pattern, probably something more than one half, meant that Ulster Protestantism, and Irish Catholicism also transferred their rancours across the Atlantic. Orange/Green tensions became a feature of the Canadian landscape.[19]

Normally, when the Irish refer to the 'Black North' they mean Northern Ireland, an area where one treads warily, but in Canada it refers to the Miramichi watershed area, a huge expanse of darkly forested flatland, very different from the Irish countryside. It attracted both Protestants and Catholics, particularly Catholics from Schull in West Cork. In the years following the post-Napoleonic Wars depression, the Irish poured in to New Brunswick, and an emigrant song of the period records the fact that they appeared to have headed there joyfully:[20]

Off we go to Miramichi,
Off we go for sugar and tea.
The quicker we get there,
The better for we.

Practically any place was better than nineteenth-century Ireland, but there were severe problems. The profitable lumber trade attracted the Irish, and they competed for work with the Maine lumberjacks with such ferocity that the army had to be sent down from Fredericton, the New Brunswick capital, to separate the warring factions. Natural disasters also befell. The great Miramichi fire of 1825 destroyed the towns of Newcastle and Douglastown, killing 160 people and causing survivors to think that the Day of Judgement had dawned: in rainy treeless Ireland, forest fires were a thing unknown. Survivors had to uproot by the hundred and seek to re-establish themselves elsewhere in Canada. One such, Francis M.C. Phelan of Donegal later became the first Catholic in the Executive Council of the New Brunswick Assembly. Another, Timothy Lane, led a group of survivors to a spot on the Nova Scotia border where he established the Catholic settlement of Melrose.

Apart from natural disasters, the Irish also had to contend with the Canadian equivalent of the 'No Irish Need Apply' policy. The United Empire Loyalist who controlled New Brunswick objected to inundation by 'the scum of the population at home', which the abolition of passenger laws by New Brunswick greatly facilitated.[21] A Lieutenant Governor, Sir Archibald Campbell, also wanted the Irish kept out. He voiced a commonly met with prejudice, that the Irish had many excellent qualities but they were not suitable for frontier life, and went on: 'It cannot be too often or too strongly repeated that the facility which this Province affords them of indulging a naturally wandering disposition, added to the ties, associations and inducements which led them to the States – have hither rendered the great body of Irish emigration to this quarter not only useless, but extremely burdensome to the Province, and worse than a dead loss to the British Empire.'[17]

A CELEBRATED COUP

When American/Canadian hostilities broke out anew in the 1812–14 war, Irishmen were again prominent on both sides. One of the most celebrated coups of this war was carried out by a romantic Irishman, James FitzGibbon. He was in command of a force of thirty men threatened by a force of 700 men under Lieutenant Colonel Baerstler. However, FitzGibbon was alerted by a courageous woman, Laura Secord, the widow of a Royalist, who walked all day and night through wooded Indian territory to warn the Irishman that he was about to be surrounded. The Indians in the area of Beaver Dam, some twelve miles from Niagara, were allies of FitzGibbon, and attacked Baerstler. When FitzGibbon came to the aid of the Indians, Baerstler, fearing an ambush, retreated towards a place which an Orangeman would have told him was ominously well named, Lundy's Lane. (Lundy was the Governor of Derry, who wanted to surrender to King James. Instead the Apprentice Boys closed the gates in the face of the Catholic besiegers, thereby initiating an epic siege, whose commemoration still causes bloodshed in Derry, even as this is being written.)

While Baerstler waited at Lundy's Lane for reinforcements, FitzGibbon scouted his position and realised that he had no hope of attacking the Americans' immensely superior force of horse, foot and artillery. Instead he dotted his men around Baerstler's encampment to give the impression that he had many men under his command, and then audaciously called on the Americans to surrender. Baerstler was deceived and duly gave in. FitzGibbon had captured 500 infantry, fifty dragoons, two field pieces, and several wagons of supplies, to say nothing of the colours of the 16th United States Regiment, and was appointed a captain on the spot. However, to the astonishment of his General, he immediately asked for three days leave of absence although further battles with the Americans were obviously imminent. The General at first refused, but relented when he heard why FitzGibbon sought leave. He wanted to marry his sweetheart so that if he was killed she'd have a captain's pension. FitzGibbon duly rode over 150 miles to Bath, married Mary Shea, and was back in the field before the three days were up. He went on to command an élite unit of his own, 'FitzGibbon's Green 'Uns'.

SETTLING

After the American Wars ended, the Irish were to the forefront of the settlement process – 'taming the wilderness', as the popular phrase had it. A Catholic Anglo-Irish soldier surveyor, Lieutenant General William Butler (1838–1910) described western Canada in 1870 more lyrically as a Great Lone Land, an ocean of grass whose shores were:

the crests of mountain ranges, and the dark pine forests of sub-arctic regions . . . The great ocean itself does not present more infinite variety than does this prairie ocean of which we speak. In winter, a dazzling surface of purest snow; in early summer, a vast expanse of grass and pale pink roses; in autumn too often a wild sea of raging fire. No ocean in the world can vie with its gorgeous sunsets; no solitude can equal the loneliness of a night-shadowed prairie: one feels the stillness and hears the silence, the wail of the prowling wolf makes the voice of solitude audible, the stars look down through infinite silence upon a silence almost as intense . . . men have come and gone, leaving behind them no track, no vestige of their presence.[22]

One settler who most emphatically did leave vestiges of his presence was the remarkable Colonel Talbot de Malahide, a member of the famous Malahide family of north County Dublin. Talbot is remembered for being irascible and unsympathetic to the Catholic Irish, but he was responsible for settlements in the Ontario region, and in all oversaw the founding of twenty-nine townships containing some 180,000 people. He worked out an ingenious arrangement with the Government whereby he was given a grant of 5,000 acres which benefited both him and the settlers. For every settler he placed on a fifty-acre holding, Talbot received 200 acres, until the 5,000-acre target was achieved, but he also ensured that any settler who had made a success of his fifty acres was able to obtain a further 100 acres. Many of these pioneers landed in what was then a vast forest with nothing more than an axe on their shoulders, and could not pay even the reasonable rents of the period. Talbot dipped into his own pocket to assist the needy and is reckoned to have spent over $100,000, which in today's money values would amount to an astronomical sum. Having nearly bankrupted himself, he was eventually given a pension of $2,000 by the Government.

THE FENIAN RAIDS

Probably the three letters most associated with Ireland as this is written are not GOD, but IRA. What they symbolise – a shared impulse towards religion, but a contrasting tradition of physical force – impacted on Canada in marked fashion. It is a demonstrable fact that the invasion of Canada by Catholic Irish Fenians led to the Federation of the Provinces in the Dominion of Canada on 1 July 1867. The Fenian incursions had the effect of overcoming the opposition of the French Canadians in Lower Canada and of the maritime provisions to the idea of confederation.

The Fenian raids into Canada from across the American border are often represented as being nothing more than a piece of hare-brained, dangerous nonsense. However, the basic theory of the incursions was not all that ill-conceived. The object of the exercise was to do something along the lines of what the Americans themselves had already done when they set up the Republic of Texas on Mexican soil for example, or installed a President in Nicaragua, William Walker, on the bayonets of an American militia. The Fenians did not want to seize Canadian territory for reasons of aggrandisement or of profit. Their intention was to secure a bargaining counter in exchange for which they could force the British to concede independence to Ireland.

The Fenians were called after the Na Fianna who acted as praetorian guards to the High Kings of Ireland. They were formed in 1858 from the survivors of the Young Ireland Rebellion of 1848, and, like today's Provisional IRA, employed a cell system, modelled on French Revolutionary societies. Influenced by French Republicanism, the Fenians officially styled themselves The Irish Republican Brotherhood (IRB).

They were led by James Stephens who escaped to Paris after the failed 1848 Rebellion, and John O'Mahony, another '48 survivor who ran the American arm of the IRB from New York. The first major objective of the Fenians was to stage an invasion of Ireland, making use of the Irish soldiers who had fought on both sides of the American Civil War. Consequently in 1865, scores of Civil War veterans made their way to Ireland to organise an uprising. Initially the IRB men achieved considerable success in infiltrating Irish units into British regiments, and on the face of it certainly had the numbers to stage an effective uprising. However, the movement was riddled with informers, and the British scotched the plans for rebellion with a wave of arrests.

It was after the failure in Ireland that the Fenians' attention turned to Canada, and a Senate of fifteen elected IRB delegates, representing both the US and British North America, was set up in New York to act as a Government in exile. The Senate decided to launch an attack against British North America where there were divisions between the two Canadas (the upper, Ontario, and the lower, Quebec) stemming from their British and French origins. The Atlantic colonies of Newfoundland, Nova Scotia, Prince Edward Island and New Brunswick also disliked the idea of a Canadian Confederation.

To the west of the Great Lakes, British North America, as it was known, was owned by the Hudson's Bay Company, the giant fur trading corporation. This vast wilderness was largely peopled by Indians and there were very few white men. Below this area, and bordering on the Pacific, lay the territories now known as British Columbia, but which were then in reality two separate British colonies. Accordingly, it appeared to the Fenians that there was plenty of fertile ground where an Irish flag could be planted across the American border.

There was also a good deal of anti-British sentiment in America in the wake of the Civil War, and the Fenians hoped to take advantage of it. The British had helped the Confederacy, supplying ships, armaments and provisions through the rebels. President Andrew Johnson himself gave the IRB a very broad hint that they could expect little opposition, and indeed there could be covert support for an invasion of British North America: the Fenians were told that Washington 'would recognise accomplished facts'. However, the Fenians, for all their daring and ingenuity, were a prey to the old Irish adage that the first item on the agenda must always be the Split. In the IRB case this developed between the followers of John O'Mahony and those of Major General Sweeney, the distinguished soldier who had fought on the American side at the Battle of Churubusco (after which, ironically, Irish survivors of the pro-Mexican San Patricio brigade were hanged, as we will see later).

O'Mahony reacted by attempting to invade New Brunswick. He intended to seize the island of Campo Bello – which had been the subject of dispute between the British and the Americans – but, as in Ireland, the Fenians were again riddled by informers and the British were forewarned. Troops and warships were sent to the scene and O'Mahony and his men were prevented from crossing the border. O'Mahony's opponents in the Senate were able to persuade Washington to support their side of the argument and his stores and armaments were confiscated by the American Army.

The British mistakenly believed that that was the end of the Fenian threat, as O'Mahony, being the best known of the Fenian leaders, had been the main target of their intelligence activities. However, Sweeney pressed ahead to such good effect that he raised an army of 25,000 heavily armed men supported by ships and field artillery. An invasion was fixed for 31 May 1866.

By now, Sweeney's forces were generally referred to as the Irish Republican Army (IRA) – the first time the title 'IRA' appeared in history – and the contemporary Irish flag, the green, white and orange tricolour, was also flown for the first time during the Fenian invasion. Colonel Owen Starr hoisted it over the captured Fort Erie.

Hundreds of Mohawk Indians joined the Fenians, as did a black company of Union Army veterans. However, general confusion and, in particular, cowardice on the part of a Fenian general, Charles Trevis, who failed to move his troops at the appointed date, doomed the invasion. Some significant engagements did occur. A section of the Fenians, under the command of Monaghan-born John O'Neill, routed the British at Ridgeway. A couple of thousand British troops prudently took the advice of O'Neill's men who charged, bayonets at the ready, shouting the Irish war cry, 'Faugh a balach' (clear the way). The Irish also fought bravely at Fort Erie, recapturing it from the British a second time and retiring in good order under the victor of Ridgeway, Colonel John O'Neill.

After the excitements of the raids died down, President Johnson, who on 6 June finished off any prospect the Fenians had of victory by making a proclamation enforcing the neutrality laws, was revealed to have played a dark hand. Seemingly, he had allowed the Fenians to be armed and had encouraged them to believe that he would tacitly support them only in order to force the British Government into negotiating compensation for their activities during the American Civil War. In fact, on 9 June the US Third Artillery Regiment under Lieutenant Colonel Livingstone stood idly by while the British crossed the border at Huntingdon and proceeded to capture and slaughter Fenians. As a result of this Janus-faced policy, the US Government ultimately obtained a payment of 15 million dollars from the British.

Colonel O'Neill made another attempt to invade Canada in 1870 which failed, as did an attempt he made to aid Louis Riel during the latter's ill-fated uprising. The Riel fiasco ended Fenian incursions into Canada but their effect lingered on. The *Toronto Globe* said in June 1886 that:

> The Fenians have unwittingly done an essential service to the Canadian people by inspiring them with a degree of confidence in their defensive strength which they did not before possess.

A few days later, that 'degree of confidence' was demonstrated. The Dominion of Canada was born.

INFLUENCES

From this period British statesmen such as Gladstone began to consider the

Canadian model as they searched for a solution to the Irish problem. Ultimately, when the Irish Free State came to birth, after the signing of the Anglo-Irish Treaty of 1921, it was modelled on the Dominion status of Canada. An opponent of that Treaty, the former Chief of Staff of the IRA and Nobel Prize winner, Sean MacBride, acknowledged that 'it was Canada who extended the hand of friendship to Ireland in the Council of the then British Empire'.[23] Later, in 1931, Irish and Canadian statesmen co-operated in devising the famous Statute of Westminster from which much Irish and Commonwealth constitutional development subsequently flowed.

In September 1948 came one of the most significant developments in contemporary Irish history. At a press conference in Ottawa the Irish Prime Minister of the day, John Costello, announced the repeal of the External Relations Act. This effectively led to the Declaration of today's Irish Republic the following year, and the departure of Ireland from the Commonwealth.

Although it was claimed that the declaration of the Republic had been agreed before Costello left Ireland for Canada, as a result of the influence of Sean MacBride in Cabinet (and MacBride assured me of this himself), there is a body of evidence to indicate that the decision may also have been influenced by some specifically Canadian influences, of a rather distasteful kind. At this stage memories of Ireland's neutrality during the Second World War still aroused controversy in Canada, and the old Orange/Green, Anglo-Irish discordances were not far below the surface. It was said at the time that the Governor, General Alexander, and his wife had snubbed the Irish during a garden party at McGill University in Montreal. On top of this, it is a demonstrable fact that Alexander, a North of Ireland Protestant, did not include a toast to the President of Ireland after that to the King at a dinner he gave for Costello. There was a particular reason why, apart from the customary niceties of protocol that this should have been done, because the first President of Ireland (1938–45) Douglas Hyde, had strong ties with Canada. Hyde, a South of Ireland Protestant, was also the first President of the Gaelic League which was founded in 1893 to restore the Irish language. Prior to this Hyde had been Professor of Modern Languages at the University of New Brunswick, at Fredericton in 1891.

To cap it all, not only was there no toast to either Hyde or his successor, Sean T. O. Ceallaigh, but the centrepiece decoration of the official dinner table was a replica of the famous cannon 'Roaring Meg', which the Protestants had used to repel the Catholics during the Siege of Derry. The cannon was inscribed 'The Walls of Derry and no surrender'. Not altogether surprisingly therefore, the cannon's symbolic grapeshot is held to have carried away the Irish links with the Commonwealth.

However, when the declaration of a Republic did come, the Canadians were mindful of the long Irish connection with Canada and the Canadian Citizenship Act of 1950 was worded so as to treat Irish citizens in the same way as British subjects. The Irish might have a wayward inclination towards independence of the Crown, but that did not make them 'foreigners'!

393

Thomas D'Arcy Magee

If the history of Fenianism in Canada was to provide a major stimulus to a Canadian consciousness of nationhood, paradoxically it was also responsible for striking down one of the Confederation's major architects, an Irishman, Thomas D'Arcy Magee.[24] A brilliant journalist and poet, he was born at Carlingford, near where today the border separates Louth in the Republic of Ireland from Down in the disputed Six Counties. After working for a time as a journalist in Boston, he returned to Ireland and took part in the Young Ireland Revolution. This caused him to leave Ireland rapidly and return to America with a price on his head. He spent a further spell there as a journalist, and also working for a number of enlightened causes to aid his fellow countrymen. He tried to encourage the Irish out of the slums and on to land in both America and Canada, and popularised night-schools as a method of improving the lot of Irish workers. His criticism of the Church's stranglehold on education aroused the hostility of Archbishop Hughes, and in 1857 he decided to accept the invitation of a group of Irish Catholics to move to Montreal and found a newspaper.

Those who had invited him were caught between various forms of conflict. One was between the French and the English (and – although to a far lesser degree – sometimes between the Irish and the French). The British were in the majority in Ontario, the French in Quebec. There was also conflict within the English-speaking ranks between Protestants and Catholics. The Irish in Montreal were the audience for Magee's paper, the *New Era*, although from the start he addressed himself to a wider constituency. He sought to arouse a sense of Canadian nationhood, to abolish racial and religious dissensions, and to unite the various colonies. His views and his journalism soon led him to politics and by the end of the year of his arrival, he was sitting in the Montreal Parliament.

However, as Magee's career was to so tragically illustrate, there was intolerance on both sides of the Orange/Green divide. Anti-Catholic and Irish sentiment was so strong amongst the Orangemen that they could not countenance the idea of an Irish Catholic speaking in public. A St Patrick's Day lecture which he delivered in 1858 was attacked, and the Orangemen escalated the row into one of Toronto's worst-ever riots. Two years later, the citizens of Bradford met him at the railway station at gunpoint, and forced him back whence he had come, thereby preventing their ears being sullied by a lecture on 'the historical relationships between Ireland and Scotland'.

Inspired in part by Magee's influence, Ontario eventually introduced a system which was later adopted in other English-speaking provinces and for the Protestant minority in Quebec. Catholics elect a school board which collects their taxes and is responsible for Catholic schools in the district concerned. The curriculum does not differ markedly from that of state schools, though religious teaching is added.

On education, as with the other great issue of the day, Magee spent much of his political life at odds with his constituents. The conservatism with which they viewed military adventures also spilled over into constitutional politics. They opposed government by representation, because they feared being drowned politically in a Protestant sea, but Magee saw proportional representation as organic and right, and said so, to their horror and anger. Nevertheless, his oratory and his vision of a new nation of Canada were so spellbinding that his critics were scattered.

Magee gained further support for the idea of confederation when the American Civil War erupted in 1861. Several border clashes between the British and the United States brought the spectre of an American invasion of Canada. Magee joined a coalition which embodied Orange and Green, Liberal and Conservative, and became one of the principal Canadian negotiators, both with the various provinces and the British Government. When confederation came, it showed the evidences of his thinking, particularly in those clauses which dealt with the rights of religious minorities.

Two quotations of his sum up both his political philosophy and the reasons why his own countrymen turned on him. In the first, writing about the education controversy in a letter to a friend, he said that his ambition was to make Parliament a place where it would be impossible for 'unfit and insincere men to find their way into the house with the certificate of a Catholic bishop or the card of an Orange Lodge.'[25] Unfortunately both Catholic pulpit and Orange drum throbbed against Magee in the 1861 election, because of his ecumenical approach to the perennial vexed question of separate schools, and he was defeated.

The second quotation indicates something of both the depth of his opposition to Fenianism and the corresponding reaction which this provoked. Magee was asked by a priest to intervene on behalf of a Fenian prisoner but he refused and chose to make his refusal widely known by way of a public letter: 'The thing you ask cannot be done . . . to whatever punishment the law hands him over, no word of mine can ever be spoke in mitigation; not even under these circumstances, [possible execution] if he were my own brother.'[21]

To him, the Fenian invasions were a disaster. Personally, he disliked secret societies as a result of his Irish experiences. Politically, he was horrified at the potential for destruction that Fenianism might bring upon the heads of the Irish in Canada who hitherto had been successfully fighting their way up the social ladder. With the same reckless courage with which he had espoused government by proportion, Magee attacked the Fenians and their sympathisers.

His formidable oratory, allied to the influence of the Catholic Church, was certainly a factor in halting the spread of Fenianism, although as we have seen, the invasions when they came foundered on obstacles other than those of Magee's creation. His stand cost him dearly, however. He had been promised a Cabinet post in the Government which was to be formed in the new Dominion of Canada, but the Conservative leader, John A. MacDonald, deciding that Magee had become such a figure of division that the Irish vote would be split, withdrew the Cabinet offer and gave no support to Magee in the Dominion election of 1867.

Magee, however, won against the odds, even though his victory triggered off a riot in Montreal. He attended the Dominion Parliament in Ottawa as a private member, but only for a tragically brief period. On the night of 6 April 1868, he was shot dead on the steps of his lodgings, murdered, it is said, by a Fenian. Whether the man who was actually hanged was in fact the assassin, is the subject of argument to this day. What is not disputed is that Magee was one of the founding fathers of modern Canada.

THE ENDEAVOURS OF ALEXANDER McNUTT

While it would be impossible in this compass to do full justice to the intricate story of the Orange and Green traditions in Canada, some general indication of the impact of Orangeism, not only on D'Arcy Magee and his contempories, but on Canada generally, is called for.

As in America, anti-Catholic and Irish sentiment was strong in Canada, pre-dating the arrival of Orange societies. Indeed, in this context, it is beguiling to speculate whether Orange/Green tensions in Ulster itself might have been dissipated before our day if the endeavours of one Protestant Ulsterman, Alexander McNutt, had been allowed to progress. During the 1760s and after, McNutt placed a series of advertisements in Protestant newspapers across Ulster, seeking Protestant emigrants for Canada. One, in the *Belfast Newsletter* in May 1771, addressed his co-religionists as follows:

> Whereas the province of Nova Scotia, the ancient right of Britain is now settling, which will be a grand outlet and relief for all such industrious farmers and useful mechanics as may find themselves under difficulties in their mother country; and Colonel Alexander McNutt . . . is now arrived here with a view to procure settlers and invite all such of his countrymen who it may suit to embrace the present opportunity of removing to this fertile country.

The inducements were generous. Each head of a family was to be given 200 acres and fifty for each child and servant 'free of all rent for ten years'. Importantly, the settlers were to have 'their civil and religious liberties fully secured'.

He succeeded in placing several hundred well-doing, hard-working co-religionists in townships such as Londonderry, Truro, Windsor, Onslow and Horton. Given these emigrants' relative success in their new surroundings, it is legitimate to speculate that chain migration might have led to a very substantial draw-off of Ulster Protestants to Canada. So reasonable in fact was this prospect that the British became alarmed at the thought of losing from Ireland the core element of their power base. A government committee found that: 'However desirable an object the settling of Nova Scotia may be, yet the migration from Ireland of such great numbers of His Majesty's

subjects must be attended with dangerous consequences to that kingdom.'
McNutt's experiment was discontinued. Who knows, had it not been, the
Reverend Ian Kyle Paisley, for example, might have been born to spread his
sweetness on the Londonderry air of Canada rather than of Ireland. He does
as it happens have a branch of his free Presbyterian Church in Canada, but it
does not make a national impact, its support being largely restricted to an
ethnic base of Ulster Protestant heritage. In any event, McNutt's initiative
had the lasting significance of marking the beginning of the strong Ulster
connection with Canada which continues to this day. It is reckoned that 55 per
cent of the Irish who settled in Canada were Protestant, mainly Anglicans,
from the North of Ireland.

THE LODGES

At all events, from the post-Napoleonic Wars era, the emigration of many
Irish Orangemen to Canada meant that the Protestant and British tradition
gained an excession of strength with a particularly anti-Catholic and anti-Irish
patina. The emigrating Orangemen brought with them their memories of
strife over land and of sectarian violence, particularly during the 1798
rebellion. As they gained a foothold in the New World, they began setting up
Orange Lodges, just as they had in the old; and by New Year's Day 1830 the
lodges had grown so numerous that a Grand Orange Lodge of British
America was formed. Its Grand Master was a County Wexford man, Ogle
Gowan. While he appears to have been a sagacious and moderate man, his
surname was associated in Catholic minds with some of the worst excesses of
the '98 rebellion.[26] However Gowan was informed with a more large-minded
vision than his croppie-torturing namesake. He saw that both Irish Protestant
and Catholic traditions were threatened in Canada by being annexed under
American imperialism and Republicanism. He argued therefore that it was
obvious: 'to every philosophical mind that a civil union between Protestant
and Roman Catholic against the gloomy Yankee faction . . . is called for alike
by the dictates of politics, justice and mutual security.'

Despite the misgivings with which Catholics viewed Gowan, the lodges
proved to be a cohesive force for indigenous Protestants, not all of them Irish.
In fact, not all of them were Protestant originally. With their zeal for joining
Irish movements which seemed to offer the prospect of military action, many
Mohawks also joined the Orange Order – less, we may assume, to balance the
effects of those who joined the Fenians than under the influence of some
proselytising clergymen.

THE FIRST CANADIAN ORANGE MARTYR

After Louis Riel executed an Orangeman, Thomas Scott, the Orangeman of
Canada became as convinced as his brother in Ireland that the only good
papist was a dead one. Scott, who has been described as an 'egregious and

violent opponent' of Riel's Provisional Government, may be thought of as the first Canadian Orange Martyr.[27] He was shot on 4 March 1870. Born a Presbyterian in Down, Ireland, he would probably have escaped the firing squad had he not been deliberately defiant to Riel and his mixed-blood Catholic supporters. Riel himself was to lose his life fifteen years later, partly as a result of the presence of Orangemen in the Ontario militia which served alongside the British forces opposed to him under Garnet Wolsey.

SUSTAINED ANTAGONISM

As in Ireland, the lodges were not merely used for fraternal and religious purposes, but were also the foci for violent attacks on their Catholic neighbours, particularly at election times and on the Green and Orange festivals of St Patrick's Day and July 12th. The lodges had a paramilitary character and marriage to a Catholic automatically involved expulsion from the lodge. Orange employers saw to it where they could that Irish Catholics were not hired.

In wide areas of Canada, for example throughout the Ottawa valley in the 1850s and 1860s, burnings and counter-burnings destroyed schools, lodges and churches. Cecil Houston and William Smith recall that Toronto was so strongly Orange that it became known as the Belfast of Canada. They aver however that to 'stress the open physical violence would be to focus on the unusual. One third of all Protestant Canadian neighbours were not on the streets annually fighting with Catholic neighbours.'[28] In fact such large-scale fighting would not be the annual norm anywhere, even in Belfast. The fighting was only the symptom of the deep-rooted disease of sectarianism, and that disease was so virulent in Canada that another historian of Orange and Green relationships found that 'nowhere else, save in Orange Canada did the Irish abroad meet with such sustained antagonism as in Britain'.[29] Two of the clashes which survive in the Orange/Green folk memory from this period were the Gavazzi (1853) and Corrigan (1855) affairs.

In the former, Alessandro Gavazzi, whose path we have already crossed in Scotland (page 251), was attacked by Quebec Catholics when making a speech on the education issue, in which he criticised the Pope and his followers. A riot ensued which was subsequently blamed on the police, most of whom were Irish Catholics belonging to a secret society set up to counter Orange influence, known as the Ribbon Men. A more serious affray occurred when Gavazzi addressed an audience of armed Montreal Protestants. Initially, two Catholics were killed in the mandatory riot elicited by his presence. Then the troops were called in and in subsequent firing, six more people were killed, mainly Protestants. After this, the Benevolent Society, the St Patrick's Society which continues to do good work to this day, became exclusively Catholic as Protestants departed in the wake of the riot.

The second sectarian outburst also involved a Catholic who, like Gavazzi, had converted to Protestantism. In this incident, Robert Corrigan, an

Irishman, was beaten to death by Irish Catholics from St Sylvestre, a strong-hold of Ribbon Men. The adjoining towns were Orange and when an all-Catholic jury freed those accused of Corrigan's murder, the affair became a *cause célèbre*, with the Catholic French-Canadians lining up against the Irish. The hostility which the Irish encountered at this period helped to strengthen the strong feeling of Irish identity which, to a degree, still exists in the Beaurivage region today.

Apart from such episodes, relationships between Protestant and Catholic could be quite good,[30] but varied from place to place. In Quebec, Protestants and Catholics lived in reasonable harmony, and Protestants subscribed money for an organ when the Catholics were building St Patrick's Church. Montreal was also relatively liberal.

Ontario was a different matter. The heaviest concentration of Irish emigrants was in the Ottawa Valley area. These were largely Protestants from Southern Ireland and they discriminated against the employment of Catholics. However, Protestant clergy as a body consistently condemned sectarian violence, and individual Protestants sometimes left the Lodges and campaigned on behalf of Irish issues. One of the most famous of these was Robert Lindsay Crawford, a County Antrim Protestant and an Orangeman, who emigrated to Canada in 1910, having both lost his job and been expelled from the Independent Orange Order which he had helped to found, because of his Home Rule predilections.

In July 1918, Crawford started an opinion journal, the *Statesman*, founded on the London *Nation*, which was of some political influence, and was active in both America and Canada in the cause of Irish self-determination. Another Irish Canadian, this time a Catholic, Miss Catherine Hughes, born on Prince Edward Island, who resigned her position as Assistant to the Alberta Agent General in London after the 1916 Rebellion to become a Sinn Fein organiser, travelled throughout Canada, the US, New Zealand and Australia in the same cause. Crawford became one of her principal supporters and a motor force in the foundation of the Canadian Self-Determination for Ireland League. This drew together such bodies as the Ancient Order of Hibernians, the Gaelic League, the Independent Labour Party and – with another Protestant clergyman, Dr J.A.H. Irwin, a County Antrim presbyterian minister – trumpeted the cause of Irish nationalism in the face of terrific Orange hostility.

Interestingly, Crawford and Irwin mirrored the policy of the Catholic Archbishop Daniel Mannix in Australia where Mannix supported a policy of Australia First. They stood for 'Oh Canada' instead of 'God Save the King', and they supported de Valera's tour of North America. Another prominent Irish Protestant supporter of Crawford and Irwin's activities was Samuel Jordan, a prominent Manitoba businessman who had worked in New Zealand and returned to Ireland to take part in the land agitation on behalf of the Catholic tenantry. Jordan was a strong advocate of Home Rule, and pointed out that many Ulster Protestants shared this view.

The difficulties in reconciling Protestant and Catholic did not all lie on the

Protestant side. While Protestant leaders such as Wolfe Tone and Thomas Davis took an inclusive, republican view of Ireland – seeking to attract adherents under the 'common name of Irishmen' – there were, and are, a not inconsiderable percentage of Catholics to whom the slogan 'Ireland for the Irish', meant 'Ireland for the Irish Catholics'. The Ancient Order of Hibernians, that most Catholic and Nationalist of North American Associations, epitomised the difficulty in a celebrated rewriting of one of Thomas Davis's most notable couplets. This occurred in strongly pro-British and Orange Winnipeg in 1913, when the National President of the Canadian AOH, James J. Ryan, set up a branch there and urged his listeners to be mindful of Thomas Davis's poetic exhortation to Orange and Green:

> It surely is a noble deed
> To show before mankind
> How every race and every creed
> May be by love combined.

However Davis's gospel, as translated in terms suitable for Canadian AOH in the climate of the time, became;:

> How every race of *our* creed
> May be by life combined.

'There is but one True Church and no one can be saved out of it', taught the Irish catechism, and in trying to throw off the colonial yoke of Mother England, Irish Nationalists had always to be mindful of that of Mother Church. However, as Richard Davis notes in a perceptive essay on Orange and Green developments in Western Canada, not all members of the AOH took the sectarian line. Also in Winnipeg, the AOH leader, P. J. Murphy quoted a John Frazer poem which enjoyed wide popularity in Irish Nationalist circles:

> Then let the Orange Lily be thy badge, my patriot brother;
> The Orange for you, a Green for me and we for one another.

However, such appeals failed to match Orange resentment at the fact that the appeals for Orange and Green unity were directed at gaining Orange support for a cause they abhorred – the breaking of the link with the Crown and thus, as they saw it, elevating the cause of Popery. One would be more likely to gain subscriptions from a contemporary Likud supporter to build Arab settlements on the West Bank than to win support for this proposition either from a Winnipeg Orangeman in 1918, or his Belfast counterpart in 1998.

METHODISM

To end this necessarily brief outline of Orange and Green abrasion on a more positive note, it might be remarked that Irish Protestantism gave to Canada, and America, what is today one of the largest groupings in the Protestant penumbra – the Methodists. This group owes its origins to the establishment of the Palatine community around Rathkeale in County Limerick, in the year 1709. The Palatines came from the Palatinate area of Germany, which included the town of Worms, where Martin Luther emerged, and that of Spire, which gave the world the term 'Protestant'. They were driven by the French into emigration to England. From there 500 families eventually went to Ireland and settled on the Limerick estate of Sir Thomas Southwell who required skilled agriculturists to work his holdings to replace the Catholics who had been driven off. There they became so loyal to the Crown that their militia, the German Fusiliers, gave rise to the term 'true blues'. John Wesley frequently addressed the community.

One of Wesley's converts, Philip Embury, became a Methodist preacher, and embarked in June 1760 with a group of German/Irish emigrants from the Southwell estate to New York. Another passenger was the famous Barbara Heck who is said to have induced Embury to preach the first Methodist sermon in America. The ultimate result was the John Street chapel, which Embury built and is now known as 'the cradle of American Methodism'. After Embury's death, some of his community moved to Canada where they settled in the St Lawrence Valley, and fought with the British in the Revolutionary War. The 'true blue' tradition continued with contemporary support for the United Empire Loyalists, and the former Limerick Palatinate settlement has grown into the largest Protestant Church in Canada.

The Orange Order by contrast is in decline; and, as in other parts of the world where there is still a significant Orange presence, for example New Zealand, its membership co-operates with Catholics and is at pains to disassociate from the excesses associated with the order in Ireland. A leading historian of the Irish in Canada, David Wilson, summed up the present position of the Orange Order for me in humorous but accurate terms:

The Orange Order used to be the central institution of Protestant English Canada, and the July 12th parades were major events in cities and towns from the maritimes to the prairies. Now while the St Patrick's Day parades are going from strength to strength, the Orange parades appear as bizarre anachronisms in a multicultural society.

Toronto, for example, was so 'Orange' in complexion that it used to be called the 'Belfast of Canada'; now the July 12th parade has perhaps two or three hundred participants who march past bemused, perplexed or indifferent shoppers.

In rural areas Orangeism has experienced some strange metamorphoses. A few years ago I visited a parade in the Ottawa Valley, in which King Billy rode a brown horse, the music consisted of Irish Rovers recordings and the marchers were addressed by a Catholic priest – something that the folks back home might just have found a shade heretical. Not only that, but the priest's speech pointed out that Protestants and Catholics could indeed co-exist peacefully; their own presence together was living proof of that. Why then was there so much conflict in Northern Ireland? It was those pesky communists who were behind it all, stirring up trouble as part of their general conspiracy to destabilise the west . . . !³¹

THE SHINERS

It should not be thought that the race which gave the word 'Donnybrook' to the English language was entirely dependent upon either the English or the Protestant religion for the creation of strife. Throughout Canadian history the 'brawling Irish outlaw' syndrome has been literally alive and kicking. This was particularly well demonstrated by the 'Shiners' who disrupted the peace of the Ottawa Valley in the late 1820s and early 1830s.

The gang's really violent phase of activity appears to have been caused by the unemployment which followed the completion of the Rideau Canal in 1832. Prior to that, the name Shiners had attached to a group of Irish lumberjacks who frequently fought with the French Canadians over logging jobs. Although there were a few prosperous Catholic timber merchants, in general, Irish Catholics left the timber trade to the Protestants. The principal timber baron of the mid-eighties was John Egan, a Protestant from Galway, who founded the town of Eganville and was known as the King of the Ottowa. His control extended over 2,000 square miles of timber and he employed men by the thousand. The Shiners were not of the Egan type.

As we have seen in the American chapter, employment in canal building was a brutalising business. The work was hard and dangerous and the type of men it produced were often equally so. After the canal digging ceased, Bytown, which had been a canal construction camp, switched to timber and became known as one of the worst townships in Canada. The Catholics lived in the poor east end, surrounded by a sea of Protestant-owned farms. The Shiners' presence turned the St Patrick's Day parade of 1828 into a riot, and from then on the Shiners became a force in the area: a wealthy lumberman, Peter Aylen, converted them into a private army which he used to enforce his logging claims.

Initially the Shiners attacked French loggers, throwing them into the rapids along the Ottawa River, or gashing them with 'Limerick whips', willow branches with a sharpened chisel attached. Weak policing meant that, for a time, the Shiners did as they pleased, and the period from 1835 to 1837 was afterwards known as that of 'the Shiner wars'. Some forty murders were attributed to them. One riot began when a Shiner rode his horse into a French Canadian tavern and he was beaten so badly that he lost an eye. In retaliation the Shiners blew up the owner's house, killing a dynamitard in the process. The Shiners also came into conflict with the Orangemen because Aylen used them to support him in local politicking. The Orange/Shiners conflict worsened after the Shiners beat up the wife and other womenfolk of a Protestant farmer called Hobbs. To add insult to injury, the Shiners also cut the ears and tails off Hobbs's horses. A large posse of Orangemen descended on Bytown to avenge Hobbs's treatment, and only the arrest of one of Mrs Hobbs's attackers prevented a bloody conflict breaking out.

A number of factors broke the Shiners' power. The citizens of Bytown combined against them to organise nightly patrols that kept the streets clear of violence. Also the timber baron, John Egan, set up the Ottawa Lumber Association to regulate the timber industry. Ironically, the events which drove Orange and Catholic elements together, thereby swamping the Shiners, were the 1837 rebellions of French Canadians in Quebec and in Upper Canada. Orange and Green joined together with the British to put them down.

THE DONNELLYS

The other great Irish outlaw saga of nineteenth-century Canada was that of the Donnelly family, which in some respects might be thought of as the Canadian version of the Australian Ned Kelly story. The Donnellys[32] were regarded as pariahs by the Orangemen, by some of their Catholic neighbours who coveted their land, and by the police. The story came to a horrific climax in 1880 with the murder of several members of the family in their beds.

At the time of the murders Bidulph township, Ontario, was fairly evenly divided between Irish Protestant Orangemen and Irish Catholics who painted their front doors green. The Donnellys were Catholics who became involved in a number of feuds with their neighbours. These heated up after the head of the family, James Donnelly from Tipperary, was sent to jail for killing a neighbour in a drunken brawl. Many of the people in the district were also from Tipperary – in fact the Donnelly feud is often referred to as a 'Tipperary vendetta'. Like Ned Kelly, James Donnelly was able to hide amongst his supporters more or less indefinitely, but eventually gave himself up after a year, was sentenced to hang, and then had his sentence commuted to seven years in prison.

However, along with his supporters, James Donnelly also had his enemies. Part of his land was acquired by another Tipperary family, the Mahers, and also the Donnelly boys were often involved in fights because of being taunted about their father's sentence. The Donnellys were finally evicted from their holding after a period of hostilities in which their barn was burned down. The family subsequently started a stage line. Wheels began falling off their rival's stage coaches and, not surprisingly, so did the passengers, sometimes to the accompaniment of serious injury. Various factions formed around the Donnellys and their principal enemies, the Maher family, with the police and the Orange element largely on the side of the latter.

In the years prior to the Donnelly feud a great deal of the hatreds, and the tactics, of the land and tithe wars which were especially hard fought in Tipperary crossed the Atlantic to Bidulph Township. Stables, barns, hotels and shops all developed a remarkable tendency towards spontaneous combustion. William Donnelly fell in love with a Maggie Thompson, whom he tried to kidnap – at her request. However her father thwarted the lovers by forcing her to marry another man. William had a club foot but nevertheless was also a noted dancer, horseman and an accomplished fiddle player. Once when a mob descended on his house he picked up his fiddle, not his gun, and treated the would be incendiarists to a tune 'Bony over the Alps' which he is said to have accompanied by an extempore song, satirising the contemporary Bonaparte invasion.

The Donnellys were blamed for atrocities such as cutting the tongues out of horses, but, like Ned Kelly, they are also remembered for Robin Hood-like traits such as assisting homeless delinquents. For a long time after their murders children were frightened into obedience by being told that the Black Donnellys would get them. The anniversary of their deaths became an annual ghost-hunters night out, celebrated with beer and bonfire as crowds gathered in the churchyard where the Donnellys were buried in the hopes of seeing their ghosts appear.

In the actual atrocity, five members of the Donnelly family, four men and their mother, were done to death on 4 February 1880, through treachery on the part of a friend of the Donnellys who persuaded one of them, Tom, to leave the kitchen door unlocked, so that later in the night he could pick up a coat. Instead Tom's hands were handcuffed while he slept, and he became one of the murder victims. The man who handcuffed him, James Carroll, was subsequently unsuccessfully brought to trial. His trial, and that of another prime suspect, Ellen Maher, was hampered by the fact that the murderers had formed themselves into a secret society both to carry out the murders and escape their consequences.

The saga of the Donnellys also resembles that of Ned Kelly in the part played by the mother, Julia Donnelly, both in rearing her children and in defying hostile authorities and would-be land-grabbers while her husband was in prison. Her daughter Jenny encapsulated Julia's defiant but caring spirit in a grisly, but poignant, letter to her brother William who had preserved 'one of the bones of my mother's arms'. Jenny entreated William to bring the bone with him on his next visit so that: 'I may kiss the loving arm that never failed to throw protection around, and provide for all of us in the darkest day of our need.'[27] One meets with many Julia Donnelly-type women all through the history of the Irish diaspora: termagents who could be tender-hearted. It was indeed their loving arms that threw protection around many an embattled Irish family.

The Donnelly legend was so potent and aroused such interest and controversy that as late as 1964 Julia's descendants were forced by the Church to take down the tombstone erected in 1880. It had described the family as having been 'murdered'. On the new stone, the term was sanitised into 'died'.

THE CULTURAL CONTRIBUTION

Lest the Donnelly and Shiner sagas suggest otherwise, let me hasten to state that culturally, the Irish have made a significant contribution to Canada. Though one of the contributors, Thomas Moore, only struck Canada a glancing blow, during a fourteen-month tour (in 1803–4), that included America and Bermuda the visit yielded *A Canadian Boat Song*. This became Canada's favourite poem for over a century. It owed its origins to five days Moore spent rowing up the St Lawrence. D'Arcy Magee, apart from his political legacy, has left a large collection of poetry. He manages to address politics, without destroying his poetic vision, in a manner that anticipated Yeats. Emile Nelligan, whose father David was an Irish emigrant, was rated 'the only first rate Canadian poet, French or English', by Edmund Wilson. Here it may be remarked that the Irish dimension of not only Nelligan and Magee but a number of other Irish writers, and indeed Irish contributions generally, have tended to be rather ignored in Canada, being bracketed under 'English-speaking peoples.' In fact, this term very often means Irish descended people from either the Catholic or Protestant traditions.

Substantial figures in Irish literary history such as Charles Lever or Douglas Hyde have not insignificant Canadian connections, as indeed have some contemporary writers, the outstanding one being the late Brian Moore.

One of Charles Lever's best-known works, the *Confessions of Con Creegan: the Irish Gil Blas*, has a notable Canadian section. Lever devotes several chapters to Creegan's adventures in nineteenth-century Quebec, particularly in the Irish controlled Lower Town. Moore's hero, Ginger Coffey, is part of an Irish emigrant family who settle in Montreal after World War II. Moore also shows an empathy with Canadian life in his Revolution script. This work deals with the FLQ kidnapping and murder of the Quebec Cabinet Minister Pierre Laporte in 1970. Where Irish American writers are concerned, Mary Anne Sadlier's contribution to nineteenth-century Irish cultural life in Montreal cannot be overlooked. In her day, Sadlier was one of the most influential Irish American writers.

THE IRISH-FRENCH RELATIONSHIP

As Robert J. Grace puts it in his admirable historiographic work *The Irish in Quebec*:

> The Irish-French relationship in Quebec has been appropriately termed 'Aigre-Douce'. Sour in each group's respective struggle to control the affairs of a mixed parish or to secure limited economic opportunities; sweet in the not infrequent instances of co-operation, building projects and especially in the unity which resulted from inter-marriage of the two groups.[33]

Grace details the history of the row between the French and the Irish ecclesiastical authorities which occurred in the latter half of the nineteenth century. Prior to 1840 most of the settlements along the Ottawa River were Irish, and these were under the ecclesiastical control of Quebec. However, as

French colonisation of the area grew, there was conflict between the Irish and the French, particularly in Bytown. The stated *casus belli* was the usual problem arising from the appointment of a priest to a parish who did not speak the parishioners' language. The unstated source of strife was the attempt of a French Canadian hierarchy to extend its hegemony over the Irish. The conflict came to a head when the Archbishop of Toronto, John Lynch, tried to bring the Ottawan diocese under his control. He was opposed by the French Bishop of Ottawa, Duhamel, who succeeded in having Ottawa declared an ecclesiastical province in its own right in 1886.

. The French/Irish rivalry also became involved in the education issue. In 1913 the Canadian Government introduced Regulation XVII prohibiting the use of French as a language of instruction – or indeed of communication – in Ontario schools, and the French and the Irish lined up along linguistic lines in the ensuing debate. These conflicts died down with the abrogation of '17' in 1927 and they could not be compared either in duration or intensity to the Orange/Green hostilities.

A BLURRING

However, the French/Irish rivalry is important in that it has helped to blur Irish identity. I got a sudden insight into this phenomenon aboard a tour bus as we passed one of the great landmarks of the Irish presence on the North American continent, the Basilica of St Patrick's in Montreal. Any Irish visitor to Montreal is told: 'You must see St Patrick's' – and indeed the scale and the workmanship of the magnificently wood-panelled edifice justifies the advice – but I noticed that the tour guide described the Basilica as the 'oldest English-speaking church in Montreal'. I soon found out why. There was a large banner outside the church bearing green lettering which announced that this was the 150th anniversary of the church. The banner was adorned with what only the initiated would identify as *fleur de lys* and shamrocks. But these last were only a slight indication of the origins of the basilica. Inside, a leaflet was available entitled *A Short History of St Patrick's*. One paragraph (out of a total of 27) contained the following:

> St Patrick's Basilica is one of the purest and grandest specimens of the 14th and 15th
> centuries Gothic style in Canada. The soft mellow colours of the walls in the naive [sic] are
> relieved by symbolic emblems, such as the shamrocks of Ireland and the fleur de lys of
> France, reminding us of St Patrick's close association with the Sulpicians, who furnished
> the spiritual leaders for the Irish of Montreal for 138 years.

One cannot blame people for not realising that in fact, the Basilica's furnishing was subscribed by the Irish, and they also built the church, the workmen giving their services free and either sleeping on the floor of the basilica at night or in tents in the grounds which incidentally today lie in the heart of Montreal's financial district. The first mass was celebrated in the Church on

St Patrick's Day in the fateful year of 1847. D'Arcy Magee's funeral took place from St Patrick's and Emile Nelligan was baptizsed there. Magee's pew, in which he customarily heard mass, is marked by a small maple leaf flag.

There is neither pamphlet nor plaque to do justice to this monument to faith and race. The Irish connection has to be deduced from the names of the donors engraved under the stained-glass windows, or from plaques commemorating D'Arcy Magee and Emile Nelligan. For the rest, one might as well be in a French cathedral. St Patrick's stands today as a huge coded memorial to ancient tensions between the Irish and the French clergy. Yet, as a nice old man I met who was arranging flowers on the altar reminded me: 'St Patrick's was built by love. The Irish people gave their money and their work out of love. They only stopped working when it got dark, and they fell down tired and went to sleep in the Basilica.' After talking to the old sacristan, I have to admit that I left St Patrick's thinking that a little activity along the lines of the Action Grosse Ile Committee would not be out of place.

French nationalism, and the passage of years, has created a situation whereby in their book published in 1990, Houston and Smith could write of the Irish:

> They are rarely discussed now except as people who were around in the past. In Canada, the Irish have disappeared and people can no longer point to an Irish township or an Irish block. It is curious that the Irish have become so unknown, so forgotten. Maps of Canada are not short of Irish placenames, Derry, Moira, Maynooth, Inistioge, Dublin, Boyne. Nor is the countryside short of symbols of Irishness – Catholic churches, Celtic crosses as grave markers, and Orange Halls. Although the latter are disappearing fast. Even the folklore surrounding Timothy Eaton, the Ballymena emigrant, who rose to become Canada's pre-eminent merchant, has faded. Timothy's bronze statue in the Eaton Company's main department store in downtown Toronto has been moved from a ground-floor entrance to a nook on the 4th floor, and the right foot is again tarnished, no longer rubbed in reverence by grateful Irish emigrants.[34]

When briefing me before I set out for Canada, Smith, by now President of Maynooth College, told me: 'Have a few bradors [Canadian beer] and read our book. That way you'll find out all there's to know about Canada.' I found it a pleasant but incomplete prescription.

COMING BACK INTO FOCUS

My experiences in Canada completely bore out the authoritative David Wilson's assessment:

> During the 1980s there was a significant increase in Irish migration to Canada, partly as a result of economic difficulties throughout the island, and partly because of the continuing conflict in the north. One of the most striking results of this has been the increased visibility of Irish Catholics in Canada; their presence was registered in the rejuvenated St Patrick's Day parades in a thriving cultural and musical scene, and in the Canadian universities. There has been a veritable Irish Celtic renaissance in Canada.

> ... there has been a significant change in the concept of 'Irishness' in Canada since the
> Second World War. From an Orange culture with an overlay of Hollywood shamrockery
> and leprechaunism we have moved to the world of Guinness at $6 a pint, Irish music
> everywhere you go, and long queues for *Riverdance* and *Lord of the Dance*. To be Irish is
> to be cool.[35]

The reality of Wilson's judgement is twofold. One, had it been otherwise, it would have been totally out of synch with Irish development elsewhere in the globe over the past couple of decades, especially North America. Secondly, the surge in emigration to Canada (as to America, England and elsewhere) during the 1980s notwithstanding, the overall Irish contribution to Canada, Protestant and Catholic, is simply too wide and far-ranging to vanish as easily as Houston and Smith suggest. A glance at the Irish contribution, in politics, the arts, education, law enforcement, religion, trade unions or the foundation of benevolent societies, from the early days of settlement to today indicates that the Irish relationship with Canada is not to be measured simply by the totals of contemporary residence visas.

On 14 May 1998, the Ontario legislature unanimously passed an Act proclaiming March 17th Irish Heritage Day in Ontario. St Patrick had finally triumphed over William of Orange. The subsequent proceedings say all that needs to be said about the present status of the Irish in Canada. The Bill was proposed by John O'Toole who was interrupted by Rick Bartolucci, who sought from the house 'unanimous consent to have O'Toole wear a pin inscribed "very Irish but hardly Green"'. A Mr Patrick Gillen of Irish Traditions Ltd had heard about the proposal and offered to supply pins for the entire house. 'Do we,' inquired Mr Bartolucci, 'have unanimous consent?' They had.

After O'Toole had finished outlining the reasons why he felt the Irish contribution to Canada merited a Heritage Day, Bartolucci arose to second a motion in the following terms:

> The top of the morning to you, Speaker, and the best of the rest of the day to you all. You might wonder, what is an Italian doing standing up with an Irish brogue? Let me tell you that it's been said that imitation is the greatest form of flattery. Today we want to ensure that we flatter the Irish, not only in Ontario and in Canada but in the entire world.[36]

The record of the entire proceedings took up eleven closely typed pages in Hansard[31] as members vied with each other to say how proud they were of their Irish heritage and invoked Irish writers, emigrants and traditions. They told stories, and in the case of Alex Cullen informed the house that he was a descendant of Cuchullain. Old Irish toasts were recalled and finally the Bill was passed unanimously in an atmosphere which caused the speaker, Gilles E. Morrin, to exclaim, 'You better knock all this lovin' off, this is making me sick.' The legislature then arose and sang:

When Irish eyes are smiling
Sure it's like a morn in spring,
In the lilt of Irish laughter
You can hear the angels sing.
When Irish hearts are happy
And the world seems bright and gay,
And when Irish eyes are smiling
Sure they steal your heart away.

The proceedings could easily be derided as sentimental schmaltz, but those men are professional, hardbitten politicians. Their sentimentalism had solid underpinnings. Apart from contributions already recorded, such as those of D'Arcy Magee, consider those of :

Francis Hinks, born in Cork, entered journalism, became a politician, and was Prime Minister of the province of Canada (upper and lower Canada) from 1851 to 1854. John Costigan, member of the New Brunswick assembly from 1861 to 1866, elected to first dominion House of Commons in 1867, who led the Irish Home Rule Movement in Canada and secured a Declaration in favour of Home Rule from the Canadian Parliament in 1882. Edward Blake, leader of the Liberal Party, and a formative influence on the road to an autonomous Canada, Minister for Justice in 1875, who founded the Canadian Supreme Court. Charles Murphy who served under Sir Wilfred Laurier and MacKenzie King in their respective parliaments, became a member of the Senate in 1925. Brian Mulrooney, the former leader of the Conservative Party, was Prime Minister from 1984-1993. Brian Tobin, the Prime Minister of Newfoundland, is also of Irish descent, as is Jean J. Charest, the leader of the Progressive Conservative Party of Canada.

William Roland Fleming, the President of the Toronto Stock Exchange, was born in Dublin, as was Hilary Weston, the Lieutenant-Governor of Ontario. Hilary, a former model and a noted worker for charity, is married to the supermarket magnate, Galen Weston. John Dunne the Chairman of another giant Canadian supermarket company, the Great Atlantic & Pacific Company of Canada (A&P), was born in Tipperary. One of eleven children, he left Ireland in 1954 for Australia at the age of sixteen, where he sustained serious injury working on overhead transmission lines. Memories of an earlier spell in Canada with A&P led him back there. The struggle he must have had to work his way up to his present position can well be imagined. He has the reputation amongst the Irish of being a self-effacing philantrophist who 'actually writes the cheque himself'. At the time of writing the two best known figures in banking and law enforcement were Irish men. Matthew Barrett, the CEO of the Bank of Montreal, who during 1999 moved to become CEO of Barclays Bank, is the son of a well-known Irish bandleader of the fifties, Jack Barrett. He emigrated to Canada and rose in the ranks of the Bank of Montreal to a point where he was sent on the famous Harvard School of Business six weeks' course for top executives, recognised to be one of the world's toughest, and most successful experiences in higher (or at least high pressure) education. Barrett was afterwards described (at a dinner in his honour in Toronto in 1999 by a Harvard representative) as the most brilliant student ever to pass through the course. But for all his accomplishments in the banking world Torontonians chiefly remember Barrett for his short-lived marriage to one of the city's most beautiful daughters, Anne-Marie Sten, who had had several well-known lovers. Two years after marrying, the couple, described in *Toronto Life* magazine, February, 2000, as 'the buttoned-down banker with the pin-up wife', were separated. But, in marrying the younger Sten, the ever-quotable Barrett had at least achieved his ambition of being able to 'smell the roses before I fertilise them'.

William J. McCormack was born to Irish parents on Mauritius, in the Indian Ocean. He was educated in France, England and Ireland and, after a spell in the navy became a policeman in Bermuda, where he met his Torontonian wife Jean, whom he followed back to Toronto becoming first a motor-cycle cop, and ultimately Chief of Police.

Individuals such as McCormack apart, one of the best known Canadian Institutions is the Royal Canadian Mounted Police, 'the Mounties'. These were largely the creation of Sir George French, a member of a distinguished Anglo-Irish family in Co. Roscommon. French was appointed as Commissioner of the North-West Mounted Police in 1873, and led it on a famous march to the Rockies the following year. The march both had the effect of establishing law and order in the West and for stalling the annexation of the area by the United States. The RCMP has employed thousands of Irishmen in its ranks since its inception, mainly those of the Protestant tradition. To this day, RUC men and members of now disbanded organisations in the six county area such as B specials and the Ulster Defence Regiment find a home in the RCMP, if the going gets too much for them in Northern Ireland. This is why, as noted earlier, McCormack's emergence through such ranks was regarded in Irish Catholic circles as something of a watershed. The St Patrick's Day Parade which he was instrumental in restoring in 1988, had lapsed since the 1870s.

The novelist, Brian Moore, who was born in Belfast, emigrated to Montreal in 1948, and became a Canadian citizen. Even though he moved to the United States in 1959 to work as a scriptwriter with Alfred Hitchcock, Canadian themes continued to influence him. He produced a script for example on the kidnapping of La Porte by French separatists, and a novel set in the earliest days of European settlement, *The Black Robe*, the story of a Jesuit missionary, Fr Laforgue, the Black Robed one, whom we see in 1634 attempting to Christianise the Algonquin Indians of New France.

The contribution of Emile Neligan to French-Canadian poetry has already been mentioned, but theatre music and song had their Irish contributions also. One of the most famous artistic directors and teachers in all Canada is the stage, film and TV actor, the Cork-born Sean Mulcahy. Like Mulcahy, two other notable Irish contributors to Canadian theatre are septuagenarians, Joyce Campion and Gerard Parkes. As this is written, all three are working in theatre, film and radio. La Bolduc, Mary Travers, was Quebec's first *chansonnière* and the city's most famous fiddler, Ti-Jean Carigan, incorporated Irish techniques and traditions into his work and is acknowleged to have been a formative influence in the creation of the distinctive Quebecoise music. In the Atlantic region the music is equally distinctively Irisrh and Scottish. The songs, and airs are those of Ireland, the Scottish Highlands and the Islands. The calibre of some of the performers may be judged from the fact that figures like 'Scotty' Fitzgerald and Natalie Macmaster both play with the Chieftains and make international tours in their own right.

A contemporary Irish musician of interest is Darina Ni Mheabhra, a former cellist with the RTE Symphony Orchestra. She has founded her own musical company, Queen of Puddings, and at the time of writing had a triumph in Toronto with her musical 'Beatrice Chancey' which deals with black slavery in Nova Scotia.

In a different genre, John Brady has attracted a sizeable readership for a series of detective stories set in Dublin, and in journalism, the iconoclastic John Doyle of the *Toronto Globe and Mail* has a large following.

As in other parts of the world, Bloomsday is increasingly forming a focal point for the Irish. In June 1999, for example, Mary Durkan, formerly of Dublin, now teaching English at Humbert College and working as a theatre director in Toronto, with her own company Anna Livia, staged a week long Bloomsday festival. Stephen Daedalus walked, followed by an enthusiastic throng, not along Sandymount Strand, but by the shores of Lake Ontario. 'You could see the tower of the waterworks on the horizon, and you'd swear you were looking at Ringsend,' Durkan told me.[37] As one who has taken part in my local Bloomsday commemoration – I live near the Martello Tower where Ulysses begins – I have no doubt that you could soon find yourself imagining that you were looking at Ringsend. In fact as the day progressed I would not be surprised to discover that Ringsend was looking at you! But that is not the point, the significant fact surely is the vast amount of voluntary effort which people like Mary Durkan – and not merely in Canada – annually put into lining up the artists, local authorities, restaurateurs, publicans, theatre owners, costumiers, vintage car owners and so on, who contribute to these celebrations' growing success world-wide. There is some X factor celebration of identity in these occasions which goes beyond the commemoration of a great writer.

Obviously the current renaissance in Irish cultural life in Canada owes its strength to many forces, but if one had to single out a single personality who did most to herald the Celtic dawn in the predominantly orange tinted skies of the 1970s the one chosen would be Robert O'Driscoll. He was originally from Newfoundland, where his name was Driscoll. He added the 'O' in the process of reinventing himself as an Irishman. The cultural climate of the time may be gauged from the fact that in 1971, 60 per cent of Toronto's population identified itself as being either British, or of British background. This had fallen to 12 per cent by the time the 1996 census was taken and is generally agreed to be still falling. O'Driscoll launched the prestigious Celtic Studies Programme at St Michael's College, Toronto in 1975. And he was responsible for the publication, in 1988, of a two-volume work of major importance on the Irish in Canada, which he edited with Lorna Reynolds: *The Untold Story: the Irish in Canada*.[38] This book, and another work of his, *The Celtic Consciousness*, proved so popular that it was announced (in the Spring/Summer 2000 Canadian Celtic Arts Newsletter) that over $100,000 dollars raised through his writings had been distributed to students and to Irish causes throughout Canada. To commemorate O'Driscoll's work for Irish studies a fund was set up in the Spring of 2000 to erect a memorial to him at his grave in Ireland.

O'Driscoll first became famous for the mega-conferences which he organised, such as that on Canada and the Celtic Consciousness in 1978. He persuaded the Federal Government to pump vast amounts of money into the conference. The result, as David Wilson saw it, was:[39] 'A mind-bending mixture of erudition, Old Age sentimentalism and New Age nonsense; I'm still reeling from it to this day!' However Ann Dooley, who replaced O'Driscoll at Celtic Studies assesses the Conference differently:[40] 'Perhaps it needs to be done all over again. You had the "serious" scholars alongside the newer dreamers and believers, of whom Bob was very definitely one . . .' O'Driscoll's last days were tragic: his reason failed him and he lived in a world of paranoia and imagined CIA plots. But as Ann Dooley says:[41]

> The Irish community has grown and matured and found its own leaders, and I don't think in some ways Bob would have been a player now. The Irish community in Toronto has never been better. We support each other. We come out to every event. We make a great crowd. We are now on the circuit of all significant people, political, artistic and otherwise, visiting Canada, perhaps some of that is Bob's legacy . . .

IRISH CONTRIBUTIONS

The contribution of the Irish to religious life was of course immense. The Irish were significant as Canadian missionaries, working both in the isolated frontier settlements and in the cities. The accession of Joseph Lynch from County Fermanagh to the archepiscopate of Toronto marked the beginning of an era during which, for some fifty years, Ontario's leading clergy were all Irish-born or Irish-descended. Father Bernard Lonergan, after whom Lonergan College at Concordia University was named, was one of the major theologians of the twentieth century. The influence of the Irish clergy was particularly strong in the educational field. St Mary's University of Halifax was run by the Irish Christian Brothers and, until recent times most of the university's presidents were Irish or Irish-descended. A Kilkenny man, Benjamin Cronin, the first Anglican Bishop of Huron, founded Huron College in 1863, from which developed the present University of Western Ontario, and St Michael's College, Toronto, founded in 1852 by the Basilian

Fathers, has a long Irish association. Many of its superiors have been Irish. The Irish are also prominent in the development of Loyola College in Montreal, and it was an Irishman, Denis Finnegan, who founded St Patrick's College, Ottawa, in 1929.

As indicated elsewhere, Ireland was the colonial laboratory in which Britain first conducted many of its imperial administrative, military, economic and educational experiments, and its efforts to convince the Irish schoolchildren that they were English bore fruit in Canada. The Irish National Readers, which formed the basis of Ontario's school system, were imported into the curriculum by the educational reformer, Egerton Ryerson, in an effort to inculcate Canadian children with British political and cultural values. This proved somewhat more successful in Canada than it had done in Ireland.

The St Patrick's Society was founded in Montreal in 1834 as a benevolent society to cater for the growing Irish population. It soon established a prominent role for itself in Canadian society, particularly during the Famine era. The society has traditionally been a springboard to high political office: Sir Francis Hinks was a former President, as were four of Montreal's six Irish Mayors. The society currently concerns itself with securing recognition for the Irish contribution to Canadian public life and with Irish studies. One of the many projects it was assisting as this was being written[42] was Dr Michael Kenneally's scheme to establish an Irish Studies Foundation at Concordia University, Montreal. When I met Michael, who had emigrated to Canada from Cork in 1964, he was well on his way to establishing his funding target. The fact that several of Canada's leading financial corporations and individuals had gladly donated large sums of money – not infrequently one hundred thousand dollars each – to the teaching of the Irish language, Irish writing, political science, history, music and drama may fairly be taken as indications of awakening levels of interest in such subjects, refuting any ideas of decline amongst the Irish community.

In fact the very strength of the links between Canada and Ireland sometimes lead to their being taken for granted and overlooked. For example, the largest zinc mine in Western Europe, now under Finnish management, is the Tara mine in County Meath. This, and another zinc and silver mine at Tynagh in County Galway, was discovered through the efforts of a group of young Irishmen who emigrated to Canada in the 1950s. Their leader Patrick Hughes from County Armagh was a 'brickie' by trade. Hughes and his friends, who were working on the construction of a smelter, above the tundra line, decided that the real money in mining lay under the ground. The group which, apart from Hughes, included Michael McCarthy from Cork and Hughes's fellow northerners Joe McParland and Matt Gilroy, began prospecting and eventually discovered the Northgate uranium mine.

Hughes was influenced by the teaching of an old Christian Brother who always told his classes that Ireland was once rich in gold and silver mines and that they were still there – somewhere! The teaching predisposed him to listen to the Irish head of the Irish Geological Survey Service, Morough O'Brien, whom he met on a return visit to Ireland. For years O'Brien had been a voice crying in the wilderness about Ireland's potential mineral wealth. Hughes was impressed and convinced McParland and the others to join him in prospecting in Ireland. The valuable discoveries at Galway and Meath were the result, leading to unprecedented, if not always wisely directed, activity by Irish investors, not only on the Irish stock exchange, but in Canadian mining ventures also.

PRINCE EDWARD'S ISLAND

There are some links with Canada which can be seen without ever leaving Ireland – driving on the winding narrow roads of County Monaghan one will come upon signs saying that such and such a town or village has been twinned with Prince Edward Island.

The twinnings are the result of the initiative of Brendan O'Grady, a former Professor of English at Prince Edward Island University who was born to Irish parents in New York. They were in part a recognition of Monaghan's association with Prince Edward Isle, Canada's Atlantic possession for which the original Indian name was 'the cradle in the waves'. O'Grady helped to pioneer the reopening of contacts with Monaghan which resulted in the growth of what is now a thriving relationship. Irish emigration to Prince Edward Isle had not, of course, been only from that county, emigrants came from every part of Ireland, but there was particularly heavy chain migration from Monaghan. In fact, if the Monaghan people had had their way, Prince Edward Island would today be known as New Ireland, just as its neighbouring Nova Scotia was called after Scottish settlers. However, the British Privy Council rejected the proposal, and the island was called after the Prince Royal in 1798.

In a way, the story of Prince Edward Island is a microcosm of the worldwide growth of Irish consciousness from the 1980s onwards. Against a background of earlier Irish emigration and a history of involvement in the Church and in politics, an interest in things Irish grew steadily there – firstly through the great Irish writers of the twentieth century, then through the music, and then, as the economy improved, through travel back and forth to the old country. The twinnings began in 1990.

The Island is approximately 140 miles long, widening to 35 miles and narrowing to ten. Its population is approximately 140,000, but this swells hugely in the summer. The Irish only form some 25 per cent of the contemporary population (the largest percentage is Scottish) with British and Acadians (French-descended) forming approximately 20 per cent each. Nevertheless, the strength of the Irish heritage became evident when the issue of creating a memorial to the Irish settlers arose. It took a protracted series of meetings, 127 in all O'Grady reckons, but, after holding an international competition, a handsome memorial was begun at Charlottetown Harbour and is under construction as this book is being written. It takes the form of a large circular stone seat facing out to the harbour in the shadow of a Celtic cross and surrounded by thirty-two stones, one from each county in Ireland.

NEWFOUNDLAND'S LINK WITH THE BLACK AND TANS

Nowhere in Canada, or indeed in the world, outside Ireland itself, is the Irish presence so strongly felt as in Newfoundland. In St John's one is aware of Irish resonances on all sides, resonances of music, personality, physiognomy and history.

I stood in the Anglican cemetery at Forest Road, St John's, at the grave of one of the great hate figures of Irish history. Apart from the word Famine, or the name Cromwell, few terms aroused such horror and hatred amongst the Irish as did 'the Black and Tans'. This notorious corps, recruited from ex-servicemen and dressed in khaki tunics with black trousers, were called after a famous Irish hunting pack. During the Anglo-Irish War, they lived up to this analogy, ravaging the countryside and firing at will at anything that moved in field or street. The philosophy behind this counter-insurgency force was that their excesses and reprisals for IRA actions would make the community willing to yield up the guerrillas. It proved to be as ineffective in 1920 as the use of loyalist murder gangs did against the contemporary IRA. The initiation of deniable atrocities and the use of 'pseudo gangs' impacts guerrillas on a civilian population rather than excising them. The people turn towards, not against, the guerrillas for protection and counter-reprisal.

Outside Ireland itself, there is probably no more Irish place in the world than Newfoundland, so it is ironic that this island should have been chosen as his last resting place by the Commander of the Black and Tans, Major General Sir Hugh Tudor. Appropriately enough, Sir Hugh's other claim to fame in military history is as the inventor of the smokescreen, during the trench warfare of the First World War, when he was the Commander of the Ninth Scottish Division. He died, blind and alone, at St Johns' on 26 September 1963, in the Veterans' Pavilion of St John's General Hospital, at the age of ninety-five. Few people in Newfoundland realised that the old gentleman was the notorious Black and Tan commander. In Ireland, Tudor had kept a low profile. Pictures of him did not appear in the press.

It is said of him that he believed that he had been given a dirty job to do and, unlike some of the other regular army generals, such as Crozier and Strickland, he pushed dirty war tactics to the limit. When his subordinate, General Crozier, suspended twenty-six members of the Black and Tans' sister force, the Auxiliary Cadets, for their part in sacking the town of Trim in February 1921, Tudor reinstated them and Crozier resigned in a blaze of publicity that greatly harmed the British pretence that the Government was merely conducting a 'police war' in Ireland, directed against criminal gangs.

After being relieved of his Irish command, Tudor apparently picked on Newfoundland as being a place where the long arm of the IRA would not reach. He worked first for the Templeman's fish company in Bonavista and then transferred to the firm of George M. Barr who is said to have founded Newfoundland's commercial lobster fishery. Tudor subsequently went to live with Barr until the latter's death, when he moved to an apartment in the appositely named, Churchill Square. His wife, two daughters and son never joined him from England, nor did he ever talk about his Irish experiences. He lived quietly by himself, working in the fish business unmolested by anyone, although it is recorded in his obituary that: 'there were times when proceeding to supervise the loading of a fish cargo, he was compelled to run a gauntlet of biting commentary', apparently from Irish crewmen.[43]

However, from sources of my own, I have heard that despite his low profile, his presence in Newfoundland became known to the IRA and that two men were sent to assassinate him. Being good Catholics, they went to confession first. When one of them asked the priest for absolution for the killing which he intended to carry out, the confessor, not unnaturally, sought a few details. Having weighed up the situation theologically, he decided on a practical course and gave the penitent two pieces of information. First was the good news: a) that he would give him absolution, and b) that there was no doubt that he and his companion would be able to carry out their mission successfully. Then came the bad news: the priest enquired innocently whether the would-be assassins had given much thought to their getaway? They had realised of course that Newfoundland was an island? Crestfallen, the would-be killers admitted that the answer to both questions was no. The men had assumed that Newfoundland formed part of the Canadian land-mass. The priest gently pointed out that, in the circumstances, the execution, as they termed it, of Sir Hugh, would inevitably be followed by two further executions, their own. Sir Hugh lived to a ripe old age.

Irish historians have often speculated that Churchill was the real inspiration behind the creation of the Black and Tans. On Newfoundland, I felt I found a clue that indicated that he was. The grand old imperialist came to the icy waters of Newfoundland in the bleak days of the Second World War before America had entered the war against Germany, to sign the Atlantic Charter with Franklin Delano Roosevelt aboard a warship in a storm-tossed fjord. It was one of the turning-point moments of history. During the proceedings Churchill enquired: 'Where's my old friend Hugh Tudor?' Puzzled equerries were despatched to St John's to bring the reclusive old General out of his retirement to meet the two most important men in the Western world.

A man like Churchill, at such a time, in such a place, did not send for any ordinary old comrade unless tied by particular bonds of friendship. Some historians have suggested that Tudor was given command of the Black and Tans because he happened to be in charge of a unit on the Western Front, during the First World War, which mounted a spectacular artillery barrage that made a profound impression on Churchill. Others suggest that the fact that Tudor is said to have invented the smokescreen qualified him to conduct so-called 'police' operations in Ireland. In fact, however, I discovered that the two men's associations went back further – to South Africa and the Boer War.

When Tudor was wounded there, in December 1899, one of the telegrams he received was from Churchill saying: 'Best wishes for a happy Christmas, swift recovery and all the luck of the war.' This was the first war of the century in which guerrilla tactics, and corresponding counter-insurgency measures, were first implemented. It was by studying those tactics that Michael Collins defeated Tudor's efforts and consigned him to a lonely grave in Newfoundland.

The only other occasion on which Tudor's cover was blown was during a visit by King George VI and Queen Elizabeth to Newfoundland in 1938. The old solider attended a reception at Government House, trusting that his Black and Tan record would neither be known to the monarch nor mentioned by anyone else, but as he was introduced, the King, in his high stuttering voice, silenced all conversation momentarily by enquiring loudly: 'Oh, are you the man who commanded in Ireland . . . ?' Whatever mark Sir Hugh made in Irish history, all that marks his presence in Newfoundland now is an orange/pink marble stone in Forest Road Anglican cemetery, St John's. It is not much more than two-foot square, inscribed only with his rank, dates of birth and death. Sic transit the inglorious!

AN UNMISTAKABLE IRISH INFLUENCE

Why General Tudor should have chosen to come to Newfoundland as a safe haven is difficult to explain. Certainly the ruling classes were English, there was a Protestant ascendancy, a reliable Protestant, Orange and Masonic-influenced police force, but few places in the globe can boast of a greater Irish and Catholic influence. Today, one is immediately struck by the Irish-sounding accents of the Newfoundlanders. You meet people who look and sound as though they had just arrived from County Waterford. In fact, that's where most of today's Newfoundland Irish population are descended from, either Waterford itself or the adjoining counties of Kilkenny, Wexford and parts of Tipperary. 'Newfoundland music' is unmistakably Irish in influence and Irish music sessions are a feature of the Newfoundland pub scene.

The relentless Newfoundland zeal to ensure that the brewing and distilling industries do not fall into decline is another demonstrably Irish characteristic. Any tourist driving the Irish route along the Avalon peninsula will find traces of Irish heritage on all sides – the very road signs are inscribed with a shamrock and proclaim that one is on 'The Irish route'. I was more fortunate than most visitors to Newfoundland. I was guided along the peninsula by two of Newfoundland's most prominent residents, the O'Brien brothers. Buzz is a leading figure in the fish business, and Gerry, a distinguished lawyer. (Buzz's son Con, plays and sings with the popular St John's group, The Irish Descendants.) The rocky landscape has the harsh beauty of parts of the Western Irish seaboard: stony beaches, breath-taking seascapes, tall cliffs, a maritime economy in perpetual decay and yet, as in Connemara, there are spotlessly clean homes that reveal an unusual degree of both prosperity and hospitality to the initiated. Our journey also provided one of the greatest single funds of history and local anecdotes that I encountered in a story-telling life. All were entertaining and some bordered on the repeatable.

FISHING

Newfoundland shares other characteristics with the west of Ireland. It has little industry and suffers from heavy emigration: tourism and emigration are the conflicting *leitmotif* of the district. The harsh climate and light soil does not provide much incentive for either cattle or sheep-rearing and one sees little of livestock. The area was particularly hard hit at the time of my visit because of the bans on cod fishing imposed as conservation measures, though these were relaxed a few months later. Reduced cod quotas have been reintroduced on the south coast and the fishermen have also diversified into crabbing and catching capon, a small whitebait-like fish on which the cod feeds. One would be apprehensive, however, about the level of sustainability which either the cod or capon species can offer after decades of over-fishing. The resumption of fishing may prove both premature and dangerous for the continuance of fish stocks.

I had an experience after which I felt I understood the meaning of the word 'primordial'. There was an unusually fine spell of weather and the sea was calm. Gerry O'Brien arranged for his nephew Joe to take us, with his wife, Pat, in an aluminium boat which with an attachment at the bow, was able to make a brief landing at the base of a cliff, just as twilight was falling. When we climbed up we met a glacial geyser and a rocky glen filled with wild flowers, completely unspoiled by any sign of human detritus. The only other way to reach the spot would have been to make a lengthy and exhausting overland trip, feasible only for the fittest. Probably since man first came to Newfoundland, no more than a handful of sailors had ever been able to come ashore where we did.

I could understand the feelings of Tom Moore who, almost two hundred years earlier, in the language of his time, had imagined a Spirit sitting on the edge of Niagara in wintertime:

> Light above the rocks I play,
> Where Niagara's starry spray,
> Frozen on the cliff appears,
> Like a giant's starting tears!
> There, amid the island's sedge,
> Just upon the cataract's edge,
> Where the foot of living man
> Never trod since time began

Around us seabirds dived on sprat and sometimes one could see the black-backed gulls teaching their young how to hunt by slowly pecking and ducking young sheerwaters to death. The cruel ritual of the gulls is a paradigm of the difficulties of survival in iceberg-girded Newfoundland. Another obstacle in the path of survival is the homeric Newfoundland Irish hospitality, a factor which one may encounter in many guises. In my case it was the 'Caribou factor' which I discovered as follows: In an effort to make up the livestock deficit the Canadian Government has introduced Caribou deer to the region and, on the outward leg of an earlier sight-seeing journey, a series of white specks on a distant mountain were pointed out to me, with the aid of field glasses. This sight was described to me as being one of the few examples I would encounter of the government doing something right: a Caribou herd.

On the return trip, after encountering a torrent of 'newfie' hospitality on route, we stopped again to commend the Canadian Government and view the Caribou. The specks appeared to have grown more numerous, and to move up and down. My friends commented on their number, and their movements. Definitely, the government had got it right this time. Eventually however, when it came to my turn with the field glasses I resorted to the unsporting expedient of steadying the binoculars on the roof of the car with one hand, while I held the landscape steady with the other. Thus I found that the great 'Caribou herd' was in fact a series of boulders . . .

Newfoundland was once so rich in marine life that it was known in Ireland as Talamh An Eisc, the land of the fish. They will tell you in Newfoundland that as far back as Tudor times, there was profitable trade in fish between Ireland and Newfoundland. It is said that while Elizabeth I's armies were ravaging Ireland with fire and sword, her soldiers were fed on salted cod caught off Newfoundland by Catholic fishermen, and shipped back to Ireland by Irish Catholic merchants.

The bulk of the fishing trade was in British hands, but a combination of fish and the prevailing winds helped to establish an Irish presence on Newfoundland. A common saying in the Waterford area was: 'They think no more about crossing to fisheries in Newfoundland than crossing the Barrow.' In early summer the fishermen had fair winds at their backs as they sailed to the great fishing grounds, and by the time winter came the prevailing winds would have shifted so that they bowled the fishermen back home again.

At the time of my visit, one could be fined heavily for casting a fishing line off a boat. Rigorous quota systems were in operation for all species of fish, particularly cod, and crustaceans. Bird watching and whale watching had replaced fishing as a tourist attraction. Conservation mania had reached such a pitch that when a plastic cup fell overboard during a boat trip I was on, the skipper cut his several-hundred-horsepower engines and turned back to pick up the offending styrofoam. The O'Brien brothers were able to recount anecdotes from their youth, when slaughters of whales took place in shallow bays with the aid of nets and rifles; lobsters were so plentiful that they were sometimes used as fertiliser, and the general attitude towards nature's bounty was 'if it moves, kill it'. A combination of this attitude and the depredations of Japanese, Dutch, Spanish and Norwegian trawlers inevitably led to the present serious decline in stocks.

A CULTURAL TRANSPLANT

The O'Briens took me to an old house that was being renovated. Under the plaster, wattle showed and the walls had been padded with straw for insulation. The house could have been transported from the County Kilkenny of my boyhood. Pictures of the Sacred Heart and the Pope, framed papal blessings, and the rosary beads of the present owners' parents, all betokened a cultural transplant. The Avalon Peninsula house is by no means unique: in St John's itself one can see a similar home, occupied by two brothers, Mike and Ali O'Brien, aged eighty-seven and eighty-four respectively. The pair farm a 35-acre holding right in the suburbs of the city, and Ali conducts classes in the Irish language which he learned from his father.

A transplant of Irish attitudes has obviously occurred also. During my tour with Buzz and Gerry we were treated in one home to lavish helpings of liquor and fresh crab, and gin, scotch, rum and beer bottles soon adorned the kitchen table. Eventually the talk turned to the decline in fishing. The man of the house explained that the crab had formed part of his quota and now, for the rest of the month, he might as well lay up his boat because at that season most other fish were forbidden to him. Cod, of course, were completely out of the question. As we talked, his vivacious and very good-looking wife was preparing a meal before – another Irish characteristic – she and a friend went to evening mass. The smell was particularly delicious and, on enquiring what she was using in the pan, I was told 'fat back'. Fat back is Newfoundland's contribution to the world's blood-pressure industry. It consists of nothing more or less than the fatty back of a pig. Newfoundlanders appear to have fat back with everything, sex even, I was assured. In this instance the lady of the house was frying cod. I have rarely tasted anything more delicious or more illegal, except perhaps on the Aran Islands during the salmon poaching season. In ambience, accent and attitude, nothing, apart from the Atlantic Ocean, separated that kitchen from those I encountered when I owned a house on the Aran Islands. There were the same head-shakings over neighbours' doings, the same hilarious and libellous commentaries, as it was brought home to me – yet again! – that one reason the Irish sit together so long at table is that people are afraid to leave because of what those who are left behind will say about them when they are gone.

GROWING NUMBERS

Life for the Irish in Newfoundland was not always so pleasant.[44] It is generally assumed that they first came there at the end of the fifteenth century, following the Cabot's voyages. However, well-founded theories also exist that the Irish were coming to Newfoundland and to the other Atlantic provinces before Viking times. The story of St Brendan the Navigator is well known, and in 1977 the writer, Tim Severin, proved that St Brendan, or some of the other Irish monks, could have made it from the west coast of Ireland in a hand-

stitched, leather-skinned boat, to Newfoundland. He called into the Aran
Islands en route where, he records in his book, *The Brendan Voyage*, he and
his comrades were given huge amounts of crabs by a 'red-haired giant'. The
giant was a friend of mine, Michael McDonagh. Ironically, he and another
friend Brian O'Flaherty, were subsequently drowned in a modern fishing
boat, *The Lively Lady*, but Severin and his colleagues in their primitive craft
sagely navigated 'the Stepping Stone Route' to Newfoundland from Ireland:
the Hebrides, Faroes, Iceland, Northern Labrador. To this day, Newfoundlanders will point out for you the spot on the coast where markings on
a rock, said to be in ogham, the early Celtic script, indicate what is claimed to
be St Brendan's landing place.

A less-debated Irish presence is acknowledged to have been in St John's
during the last part of the seventeenth century, chiefly as a result of the fishing,
but also because Irish merchants from the south-east of Ireland had begun
extending their provision trade via French connections with 'New France'.
Irish emigration to other parts of the Atlantic Canadian and New England
seaboards were in full swing at the time, but lightly populated Newfoundland
was most noticeably affected by the Irish influx: 'By 1753, all the major
communities on the Avalon peninsula had Irish majorities; neither the English
settlers nor the English Government anticipated this.'

The growth in Irish numbers alarmed the authorities, and by 1755
Governor Dorrill was attempting to restrict the growth of Irish influence by a
series of discriminatory measures. The celebration of mass became punishable
by heavy fines; religious property was destroyed, and Catholics were
forbidden to own public houses. Irish workers brought out as fishermen were
ordered back at the end of the fishing season. The bringing out of Irish women
was discouraged, and the number of Irish allowed to live in any one household
was curtailed.

UPHOLDING THE AUTHORITY OF BRITAIN AND THE CHURCH

An old Irish priest trying to think of something good to say about his flock is
said to have consoled himself with the fact that 'they murdered and robbed,
but they kept the faith'. In Newfoundland, as in other parts of the diaspora,
the Irish Catholics have shown a distinctively Irish ability to keep the faith,
while at the same time flouting the commandments of the Church. This
dichotomy was in part responsible for the Catholic Church's break-out from
Dorrill-type strictures, and the establishment of its power in Newfoundland in
the first place. This occurred during the era of the 1798 rebellion which
aroused strong emotions amongst the Irish community in Newfoundland, as
it did elsewhere throughout the British Empire. At the time the Prefect
Apostolic to Newfoundland was Bishop James Louis O'Donnel from
Tipperary. With O'Donnel – a Franciscan who came from an aristocratic Irish
family and had been ordained in Prague – Christ and Caesar were most firmly
hand in glove. He was an archetypal figure of the two colonialisms school,

upholding the authority of both Britain and the Church. To him, the path to the advancement of the latter lay through the valley of respect for the former.

He described Newfoundland as 'a howling wilderness' when he got there, and his chapel was the first Catholic church on the island since the days of the French, 170 years earlier. Faction fighting, drunkenness and an earthy regard for the urgings of the flesh rather than of Mother Church were prominent characteristics of the impoverished Irish. During this period, Irish was so widely spoken that when O'Donnel was writing to his colleague, Archbishop Troy of Dublin, asking for a priest, he stipulated that: 'It is absolutely necessary that he should speak Irish.'

In common with many Irish bishops of the time, O'Donnel strongly opposed the doctrines flowing from the French Revolution. His diocesan statutes of 1801 demanded: 'A willing obedience to the salutary laws of England'. These, he said, were preferable to the laws of 'any other country in Europe', particularly those of the 'plotters, conspirators, and favourers of the infidel French'. At the time, the Royal Newfoundland Fencibles, which later evolved into the Royal Newfoundland Regiment, was largely composed of volunteer Catholic and Irish troops led by Protestant officers. In 1799, O'Donnel discovered that the men were taking the United Irishmen's oath, and that a rerun of the 1798 Rising was a distinct possibility. O'Donnel informed the Fencibles' commander of what was afoot and the planned rising was scotched. The only active rebellion which did occur (on 24 April 1800) was cut down as easily as was the Castle Hill revolt in far away Australia. A handful of deserters turned up at a pre-arranged rendezvous at Fort Townsend, but were not joined by the numbers expected. Five of the would-be mutineers were hanged on a gallows erected at the rendezvous point and seven more were sent in irons to Halifax under sentence of death by firing squad.

As a result of his effort during these alarms and excursions, O'Donnel was given a pension of £75 a year by the Crown. In a petition to the King to have his pension continued, O'Donnel urged generosity on the basis that he had been: 'fortunate enough to bring the maddened scum of the people to cool reflection, and dispersed the dangerous cloud that was ready to burst upon the heads of the principal inhabitants of this town, and even of the whole island'.

Because of his services in helping to quell 'the maddened scum', O'Donnel was a popular figure with both the island's Protestants and the British administrators. He was given considerable latitude, as the bonds of the penal laws unravelled, to build up the Church. Prior to his arrival, priests had only been able to operate on the island disguised as fishermen. They were forbidden to celebrate mass, and instead moved amongst their people saying the rosary. Bearing these people up via their faith, O'Donnel set a pattern, familiar to Irish Catholics worldwide, whereby they were borne down instead by a Church authority which, in part, owed its strength to denying them their nationality. As in Ireland, Newfoundland children learned a catechism that changed little between 1800 and the coming of the Second Vatican Council in the latter half of the twentieth century. In Church schools, the questions and answers which a child learned by rote included: 'Are immodest songs, discourses, novels, comedies and plays, especially at wakes, forbidden by the sixth commandment?' Or: 'Is it sinful to have unchaste thoughts?' The answer to the former was a simple 'yes', but the second went into more detail: 'They are always very dangerous, and when entertained deliberately and with pleasure, they defile the soul like criminal actions.'

The overall Irish Catholic ethos explains why a child who learned that catechism in an Irish Catholic school in Newfoundland did not learn any Irish geography, history or literature. Not only did they not learn about Irish leaders in Ireland like Daniel O'Connell or Parnell, they also did not learn about Irish leaders in Newfoundland: men like John Kent, John Valentine Nugent and Patrick Morris who led the fight for self-government. Instead they were taught English geography and studied English history and English literature.

ST JOHN'S BASILICA

O'Donnel was followed by a line of Irish bishops, one of whom, Bishop Michael Fleming, took advantage of O'Donnel's work to make two notable assertions of Catholic power. In the first he marked the coming of Catholic emancipation in 1829, the year of his ordination, by refusing to pay tithes for the support of the Anglican clergy. As Catholics generally followed the bishops' lead, this was the end of the tithe system in Newfoundland. The second was his most lasting memorial, the enormous Basilica of St John the Baptist.

Apart from the Basilica's location, on a plateau on the side of a very steep hill, which must have presented huge logistical and architectural problems when the work began, on 27 May 1839, the economics of the huge structure must have seemed mind-boggling, considering that the Catholic population of St John's at the time amounted to only 14,000 people. However, the huge building symbolises the contrasting qualities of Irish docility and violence even more emphatically than did O'Donnel's successful harnessing of the energies discharged between faith and rebellion. The site was a military preserve which the authorities did not want Bishop Fleming to get his hands on. He only did so after a long fight, involving five separate voyages to England, when the newly enthroned Queen Victoria granted him a nine-acre plot. To compound the symbolism, the site was also the place favoured by the Irish to hold their frequent faction fights.

Men and women turned out in their hundreds to help in the construction of the Basilica with their bare hands. The official guide notes:

Women even used their aprons to carry away the gravel, 8,800 cubic yards were excavated, a task which had been estimated to take two months was completed in two days ... Men proceeded to the woods some twelve miles distant to obtain the timber needed for the scaffolding. Between the hours of 10 a.m. and 1 p.m. in one day, they brought to the site some 4,000 pieces of timber, each of some 30 ft. in length . . .[45]

Despite this Homeric labour, the basilica took eleven years to build. Work was delayed and set back by the great fire that afflicted Newfoundland in 1846, and by the failure of Wright's Bank in London, which swallowed the building fund. The first mass was celebrated in the Basilica on 6 January 1850 by Bishop Fleming himself. The strain of the building had taken its toll and he was 'visibly a dying man'. He retired and died six months later, but the Basilica's spires were destined to throw long shadows. One of the guests at its opening was Archbishop John Hughes of New York. After the ceremonies, he returned to tell his flock that they were 'challenged': if a handful of poor fishermen in Newfoundland could build such a magnificent Cathedral, then wealthy New Yorkers could do even better. St Patrick's Cathedral on 5th Avenue was the result.

St John's Basilica is filled with Irish artefacts – one of the most striking being John Hogan's marble 'The Dead Christ', one of three such statues executed by Hogan; the other two are in Dublin and Rome. The amount of gold finishing in the building is staggering. How the people of those days accumulated such wealth has less to do with thrift and industry than psychology. A simple verse in the official guide book says of the basilica:

> The fishermen who built me here,
> Have long ago hauled in their nets,
> But in this vast cathedral
> Not a solitary stone forgets
>
> The eager hearts, the willing hands
> Of those who laboured and were glad,
> Unstintingly to give to God,
> Not part, but all of what they had.[46]

Recalling his days as a boy in Newfoundland, Patrick O'Flaherty says of his own church (Corpus Christi in Northern Bay) that it too was built largely by free labour and was 'on too grand a scale for the neighbourhood'.[47] So too were 'the priest's beautiful house. His expensive car and coiffured gardens'. O'Flaherty is writing not merely of Newfoundland but of a type of diocesan priest once commonly met with amongst the Irish everywhere. Be it Frank McCourt in Limerick or Vincent Ball in Australia, the Catholic Irish Artist as a Young Man had a common bête noire. Writing about the same period as do McCourt and O'Flaherty (the 1940s and early 50s), Ball describes a wartime visit to Dublin:

Now, my conscience can handle the fact that there are beggars in the street and I'm eating steak and peach melba in the dining room of the Gresham Hotel because I've been in a bloody war and haven't seen a bloody steak for years. But how do all these priests handle it? Doesn't it bother them, as they tuck into their steaks, peach melbas and Irish coffees, that there's all that poverty outside in the streets? Do they, as they walk along O'Connell Street, contribute to all those appeals for help?[48]

O'Flaherty recalls an incident from his boyhood which could have happened anywhere in the Irish diaspora. A newly ordained priest who had been born and raised in O'Flaherty's community, though in a higher social circle than that of the O'Flahertys, paid a visit. It was 'quite an event':

The young priest conversed with us for a while, and then, when he was about to depart, mother and children fell to their knees on the kitchen floor to receive his blessing. Following this, he expected to receive, and was duly given, the sum of $5. This was quite a large amount of money in an era when the truck or barter system between fisherman and merchant was still in effect; and my parents had many mouths to feed. But he pocketed the money with no apparent misgiving. Many years later, he left the priesthood and became a provincial politician. It is hard to tell what is more Hibernian, his eagerness to take the cash, or ours to hand it over.

The nuns played a significant role in Newfoundland as they did elsewhere, and their invisible handiwork can still be recognised by the initiated in the attitudes of the women they inculcated. In the cathedral buildings, one can see other, tangible, evidences of their legacy. There is a huge harp, made in Chicago, and used to instruct girls in music from a world away. The airs of blind Carolan, the harpist, Tom Moore, once sounded through those rooms, as they did in convents throughout the world wherever the disciples of Mother Mary McAuley set up a foundation.

One of Mother Mary's edicts was that no one visiting a convent 'was ever to be let out without a cup of tea', and a huge tapestry commemorates this dictum in St John's. It takes the form of a myriad squares containing tea cups and saucers, each inscribed with the name of a country or city where the sisters have convents. There were tea cups for every corner of the world, from Australia to Washington, Argentina to Arkansas, South Africa to the Philippines. These foundations, like that of Newfoundland, grew on the endeavours of Irish girls who would have left their homes in Ireland at the age of sixteen or seventeen, never to return. Llama rugs, vivid charcoal drawings, evidences of long-forgotten activities taking place a world away from maritime North America hang on the walls, a testimony to faith, industry, talent and the fact that the sea can unite as much as it divides.

BLURRING THE DIFFERENCES

Shipping records show that British ships carried some 45,000 passengers to Newfoundland in the first three decades of the 1800s. Some 75 per cent of these were recorded as Irish, 23 per cent were British and 2 per cent were from Jersey of all places. For a time in the 1830s the Irish were in a majority in Newfoundland, especially around St John's. However, a combination of discrimination and unemployment, combined with the Irish tendency to move on, either to Canada or America, ensured that for most of the nineteenth century the population ratio was 53:47 in favour of the British and Protestant element over the Irish and Catholic one.[49]

Conditions were as appalling for the Irish in Newfoundland as they were elsewhere in the diaspora. One historian records thousands of 'poor and ignorant Irish' drawn by the unsubstantiated hopes of high wages (presumably the British emigrants of the same period were poor, but enlightened) living in typhus-ridden slums around St John's.[43] The slump in cod prices after the ending of the Napoleonic Wars created unemployment, the effects of which were worsened by the continuing emigration, with the effect that: 'the debauched and idle floating population' aggravated the recurrent famine conditions and food riots, and worsened conditions of lawlessness and insubordination.[44] In some of the outports only the presence of a naval or military detachment kept the populace in order through the long winters.

However, the early Irish settlers were not all fishermen or servants. Some owned property, others were artisans, farmers, boat owners or shopkeepers. They were strong enough to resist the discriminatory laws, and the lawlessness, by various strategems and to continue in their ownership of their property and religion. In Newfoundland, as in Ireland itself, penal laws were gradually relaxed and are generally regarded as having ceased by 1832. So to a large extent did the emigration to Newfoundland.

Over the next forty years or so, the Irish population of Newfoundland declined. The days when it was recorded that 400 ships a year arrived from Waterford were over, and the decline showed itself in the 1869 election. The great issue was that of Confederation, which the Irish Catholics opposed, fearing domination by a Protestant-controlled Canada, and the Protestants supported. Newfoundland stayed separate, but did not become as Catholic as the Irish voters had hoped. The 1885 election returned twenty-one Protestant representatives of the Reform Party and only fourteen of the Liberal Catholic. As a result, a Protestant Cabinet was formed.

The election occurred against a background of growing Orange and Green tension. The Orange predilection for marching produced a parade on St Stephen's Day 1883 at Harbour Grace that ended in riot causing five deaths. However, an adroit Catholic prelate, Bishop Power, engaged in some skilful diplomacy which led the Orangemen to adopt a more conciliatory attitude to the Catholics in 1886. The Grand Lodge of the Orange Order voted in September of that year to allow Catholic participation in Government. It may be remarked that Bishop Power probably found it relatively easy to deal with the Orangemen compared to the challenges he encountered with his own flock, particularly with his clergy. Some of the stories surviving from this period indicate strong similarities to that other craggy island made famous by the cult TV series *Father Ted*. Drunkenness amongst the clergy gave the bishop much trouble. The allegation conveyed to Rome was that Power's successor had allowed the episcopal palace to be 'converted into a drinking club'.

The bishop's dining room is preserved as it was in the heydays of the nineteenth century. Visiting it today gives one a glimpse of a silvered and decantered, mahoganied magnificence that must indeed have created a convivial setting for lonely, celibate men to shelter from the chill of icebergs and the fevers of concupiscence. It is a nice question as to whether the prayers of the bishop or of the priests proved more efficacious in resolving the problem. The Pope, Pius IX, instructed the papal Legate to Quebec, George Conroy, the former Bishop of Armagh, to deal with the problem. Conroy's friend and mentor, the formidable Cardinal Paul Cullen, Archbishop of Dublin, whose influence, as we have seen, touched most of the Irish diaspora of his day, advised Conroy that the only way to bring the turbulent and tipsy priests of Newfoundland into line was to make them all undergo a strict retreat. Conroy had a generally successful legatine visit to Canada and North America generally, and planned to make the Newfoundland clergy his last task before returning to Ireland in 1878. He had prepared a lengthy and rigorous retreat schedule involving lectures, prayer, fasting and abstinence – particularly alcoholic abstinence.

However, the demon drink literally got the better of him – before he could curb the devotion of the Newfoundland clergy to the Unholy Spirit, the unfortunate man suffered a heart attack and died at the early age of forty-six.[50] Despite this regrettable incident, Catholic power steadily grew to a point where from 1909 to 1919 the Government was led by an Irish Catholic, E. P. Morris. The war years helped to blur the differences still further as both Protestant and Catholic Irish and English fought together, particularly in the Royal Newfoundland Regiment which had a large Irish contingent and displayed remarkable heroism.

Neither the dawning ecumenism nor the heroism showed much of a return in the form of prosperity. The British, as part of a move to alleviate the problems caused by the depression years,[51] took over Newfoundland's administration by means of a Commission Government which in effect resulted in a suspension of Responsible Government. The question of its restoration became a live issue after 1946, when a national convention was set up to discuss Newfoundland's future. A referendum followed in 1948 in which the Irish voted heavily for Responsible Government, outpolling those in favour of Confederation by some 5,000. A continuation of Commission Government ran a bad third. The result was 69,400 as against 64,066 for Confederation, with 22,311 voting for a continuation of Commission Government.) A second referendum had to be held before the issue was decided in favour of Confederation.

This referendum carried a distinctly sectarian hue. The Catholic Archbishop advised his people to vote against Confederation and the Grand Master of the Orange Lodge circulated a denunciation of the Archbishop's urgings throughout the lodges. However, by the time I visited Newfoundland, sectarian divisions were largely a matter of history. Catholics were not taking their tone from their clergy and a vote on education proposals opposed by the

427

Church was carried with the support of Catholics while I was on the island. Again, as elsewhere in the diaspora, part of the reason for the turning against the Church was a paedophile scandal centring on a famous Newfoundland boys' school, Mount Cashel. This was one of the first such scandals to come to light anywhere in the world and the Newfoundlanders were doubly shocked, not merely at what was revealed but at the notion that they were somehow uniquely perverted.

This is not to say that a movement for Responsible Government – which decoded means independence from Canada – does not exist, despite vast funds from Ottawa which hitherto have helped to keep the island viable. In fact, the discovery of the huge Hibernian oil fields, and the consequent prospect of economic well-being which they hold out, has helped to strengthen this lobby. However, the debate is conducted more along the lines of that on Scottish independence *vis-à-vis* London than of the blind position-taking of the old Protestant/Catholic divide.

Contemporary Newfoundland Irish relationships are on a good footing. Brian Tobin, the present Prime Minister of Newfoundland, told me that John Bruton, the former Irish Prime Minister, was 'the most popular Irish man in Newfoundland'.[52] Unfortunately it cannot be said that the Irish reciprocated Tobin's sentiments. While Bruton was visiting Newfoundland in March of 1996, the balance of parliamentary power shifted in Dublin and Bruton had to scurry home quickly to face a General Election, which he lost. However Tobin's popularity, at least among Irish fishermen, is still high, because of his crackdown on Spanish fishing. A more enduring foundation for Irish Newfoundland links is the Craig Dobbin Foundation. Dobbin is a newfie of Irish descent who is the CEO of Canadian Helicopter Corporations, the largest helicopter leasing company in the world. He is also the honorary Irish Consul General in St Johns.

In May 1993 Dobbin and Elaine Parsons, whom he later married, were guests of the Canadian Ambassador, Michael Wadsworth, and his wife Berni at a dinner in the Ambassador's home in Killiney, Co. Dublin. The guests included the former President of Ireland, Dr Patrick Hillery, the Registrar of University College Dublin, Professor John Kelly, and a colleague of Kelly's, the Professor of Psychiatry in UCD, Noel Walsh. Everyone enjoyed themselves and the following morning Dobbin, who does things on a grand scale, phoned the Ambassador, the Hillerys, the Kellys and the Walshes to join him at a return dinner. This dinner was held at the opposite side of the country that evening at Dromoland Castle, Co. Clare. The small matter of the distance involved was solved by Dobbin's private jet which took off from Dublin Airport at midday. Paddy Hillery, a Clare man, was particularly pleased to take advantage of the lift because he had agreed to throw in the ball to start the Munster Gaelic Football semi-final in Ennis, the capital of Clare, that afternoon.

As John Kelly tells the story,[53] 'it was a great day, a sort of continuation of the dinner party the night before'. The party adjourned to a pub, and Dobbin told Kelly that he'd like to endow some appropriate academic project in UCD. Kelly suggested a chair in Canadian studies, as UCD already had visiting chairs of Australian history and American studies. Dobbin immediately agreed to the £1 million which Kelly reckoned would be required. Then Hillery and Walsh got in on the act. Both are psychiatrists and they proposed that Dobbin should help fund research in Walsh's department. Kelly says, 'with some horse trading over pints of Guinness and glasses of champagne in Dromoland Castle, it was agreed that £750,000 would go for the Chair and £250,000 would fund a perpetual Newman Scholar in psychiatry in UCD.

Over the ensuing 'splendid dinner' Dobbin sealed the bargain by inviting the entire party to be his guests in Newfoundland for a week a few months later, and sent his private plane to fly them over and bring them back. When he asked Kelly did he want the cheque in punts or sterling – sterling was at the time considerably more valuable – Kelly replied that he was never anti-British in matters of business, and Dobbin duly made the cheque out in sterling.

Since those convivial events, there have been two holders of the Chair, Denis Duffy (1995–97), and John Moss (1997-98). In addition Dobbin's endowment has helped the Ireland Canada University Foundation to provide scholarships to further the study of the Irish roots of Cape Breton music, the pre-Famine migration links between Tralee in Co. Kerry and Quebec city, and into subjects such as Newfoundland folklore, and the music and dance of the Ottowa Valley. Were ever one inclined to question the wisdom of the Irish propensity for wining and dining the saga of the Craig Dobbin fellowship should encourage doubters to think again.

Although, this said, I feel that in the interest of the ever-growing Irish-Newfoundland friendship there is one aspect of the wining which might give slight pause for thought. As indicated earlier it is Irish government policy to attempt to induce workers of Irish descent from Newfoundland, as from elsewhere in the diaspora, to come to Ireland to help deepen the roar of the Celtic Tiger. In particular there is talk of attracting some 3,000 workers to the hotel trade in the west of Ireland. A noble objective in every way, one might say, in light of the unemployment which has followed in the wake of the destruction of the Newfoundland fisheries (even the crab is now in danger of being fished out). Well, almost every way. For, like the Newfoundlanders, the men of the west are built on a large scale, and do not come supplied with much in the way of a reverse gear. Moreover, the west of Ireland is also the home of the illegal brewing of poitin, the Irish version of Mountain Dew. But the Newfies themselves are partial to a version of rum known as Screech. One has heard of what happens when Greek meets Greek. But there may be a new chapter to be written about what transpires when Poitin meets Screech . . .

FIVE

AUSTRALIA

Australia was the official Siberia for Irish dissidents at the turn of the century. Their presence there caused the system acute strain and insecurity. Rebellious Irishmen, known as 'United Irish' and 'Defenders' had been sent out in dribs and drabs during the 1790s. But between 1800 and 1805 their influx began in earnest, swollen by political exiles, transported for their role in the rebellion of 1798 . . . The Irish on arriving in Australia were treated as a special class. As bearers of Jacobin contagion, as ideologically and physically dangerous traitors, they were oppressed with special vigilance and unusually hard punishments. They formed Australia's first white minority. From the outset, the Irish in Australia saw themselves as a doubly colonised people.[1]

. . . in Australia, the great nightmare of the defenders of Protestant (British) ascendancy was that the Protestant (British) dyke against poverty, superstition, and a priest-ridden society might be pierced by waves of immigration both bond and free from Catholic Ireland.

The Irish thing was a liability in the sixties. It was very bad news to be identified with Ireland.

The Irish have this place sewn up.

The foregoing quotations might be taken as spanning the gamut of Irish experience in Australia. The colony or continent was first developed by Britain in the same spirit that caused the American humorist on first seeing the Grand Canyon to exclaim: 'That's a good place to dump old razor blades.' Britain saw Australia as a good place to dump unwanted convicts, and as Robert Hughes, from whom this chapter's opening quotation was taken, observed: 'No one was more unwanted than the Irish.'

The transformation occurred much as it did in America, in the teeth of the detritus of the British imperial and Protestant project, but at a different pace, as the recollection given above about Irishness still being a liability in the sixties illustrates. The memory was that of the historian Patrick O'Farrell,[2] one of the giants of Irish scholarship. Yet in the sixties he used to sign himself 'P. O'Farrell'. He told me: 'That hid all the shit, or most of it because I still got a bad time, or at least, a semi-hostile, wondering reception when I announced I was going to study in Dublin. "You're going to University College Dublin! Why?" was the reaction I got.'

The picture today has completely changed. Chairs of Irish Studies have been established, or are being set up, in a number of Australian universities. Student exchanges between Australian and Irish universities are multiplying, as are tourist numbers. Apart from ordinary tourists, an average of 10,000 young backpackers from Ireland come to Australia under the Working Holiday Scheme and make their presence felt on Australian society. Where Australian tourism to Ireland is concerned, the Irish Tourist Board projections visualise some 200,000 visiting Ireland in the year 2000. Two-way trade between Ireland and Australia grew at the rate of 60 per cent per year between 1968 and 1999, to a current total of more than one billion Australian dollars.

The Irish, with their distinctive form of Catholic education, their involvement in politics and trade unions, have always been recognised as having had an impact on Australian culture, but at the time of writing Irish culture in Australia has reached unprecedented heights of popularity. *Riverdance* attracted over 600,000 visitors and the appetite for Irish writing, music and Irish dancing classes is seemingly insatiable.

The attraction is bound up partly with the success of the Celtic Tiger economy, which is closely studied as a model by Australian economists and politicians, partly with the Peace Process, and partly with Australia's own adjustment from having a strong sense of British heritage to a realisation that, as a Pacific nation, it must forge a new, multi-stranded identity for itself with Asia. Within that identity the Irish component is strong.

Al Grassby, the first Australian Commissioner for Community Relations, has estimated that: 'Australia is the most Irish country outside Ireland with one-quarter of all Australians having an Irish connection, just pipping the United States by a half-percent.'[3] The only quibble with this assessment I encountered amongst representatives of the Irish community was that it was too low. It should have been at least a third, possibly even 40 per cent. Either way, no one disputed the concluding claim at the start of this chapter, that the Irish had Australia 'sewn up'.

This judgement was made at a lunch given for me in Sydney by the Irish Ambassador, Richard O'Brien, with two prominent members of the New South Wales Parliament, Brian Vaughan[4] and Johno Johnson. They had witnessed the evolution in attitudes towards the Irish indicated by Patrick O'Farrell's comment at first hand: when they entered politics in the fifties, newspapers commonly carried employment ads ending with the initials NINA: No Irish Need Apply.

It was Vaughan who said that 'the Irish have this place sewn up'; Johnson replied: 'The Irish! The fights, the splits, they do nothing right. They do everything right.' A little later, he unconsciously validated his comment by telling me an anecdote about his fellow legislator while Vaughan was out of earshot. Vaughan, an elegant figure who dresses well and has read everything ever published about Ireland, surprised his parliamentary colleagues one morning by turning up for a meeting in what is now his habitual uniform, a light white or cream safari suit, blue shirt and silk cravat. According to

431

Johnson he was promptly dubbed 'Somerset Vaughan'. In the Antipodes, as elsewhere, the Irish validate Dr Johnson's judgement that 'the Irish are a fair people – they never speak well of one another'.

THE DOOMED CONVICT

A link with the Australia of the days when Johnson and Vaughan began their political careers existed in Melbourne in the presence of Father John Brosnan, Australia's legendary 'knock-about priest', who looked and talked like an Australian version of Spencer Tracy playing an Irish priest in a Hollywood movie. His career was set against a backdrop that gives us a glimpse of a segment of working-class Irish experience in Australia. Father Brosnan was born in western Victoria in 1919, one of the four children of a Kerry railway worker named Joseph Brosnan and his wife, Mary Jane, and acquired something of a status of the old heroes of the Wild West through his association with one of Australia's folk heroes – the Doomed Convict.

Brosnan first became involved with convicts in January 1945 when Archbishop Mannix sent him to Victoria's notorious Pentridge prison as a full-time prison chaplain. His reaction, and that of his family, to this unexpected and very demanding appointment says much about Irish Australian Catholicism and its concepts of loyalty and obedience in those years:

> Members of my family were surprised when they heard of my new parish. However, my parents agreed that it was not their place to question the move. Archbishop Mannix was sending me to Pentridge, and if anyone knew what was best for all of us, it was His Grace.[5]

The Ned Kelly figure who emblazoned Brosnan's name on to Australian public consciousness was Ronald Ryan, who on 3 February 1966 became the last man to be hanged in Australia, executed for his part in the shooting of a prison warder during a prison break. The case became a *cause célèbre*. Though a hard man, Ryan was also a man of great character and presence. As the drama of his trial and sentence unfolded, details of his earlier life emerged and these, along with the efforts of a sizeable anti-hanging lobby, built up a considerable reputation for him.

His father was an alcoholic ex-miner who died of silicosis. After his death Ryan was the mainstay of the family: his mother and brother and three sisters. He wrote to a nun some six weeks before he was hanged telling her that he had been an altar boy and had watched his father waste away:

> Dad's struggle to sustain the family in anything approaching reasonable conditions progressively became more heartbreaking. I can now well imagine the mental anguish and frustration of both mum and dad. This possibly was a contributing factor to my anti-social behaviour of recent years, though it does not excuse it.

Apparently Ryan's troubles began in 1948 when, at the age of twenty-three, he married a girl from a far wealthier background than his. Up to this, Ryan had been known as a good worker who, like many a young Irishman of his type, turned his hand to many things: trapping rabbits, shooting kangaroos, fishing, growing vegetables, working in factories and, with a fair degree of success, to athletics. None of these occupations however yielded the kind of money which his new wife had been accustomed to. Ryan took to gambling, lost money, and began 'short story writing' – prison parlance for forging cheques. The 'stories' led him to jail, where he took part in a prison drama in which he played the part of a warder who escorted a condemned man to the scaffold. On the eve of his own execution he recalled for Father Brosnan a line, the Wildean: 'the coward dies a thousand deaths, the brave man dies but one'. Having recited this paraphrase for the priest, Ryan added, 'I won't be crying when my turn comes.' Nor was he.

Father Brosnan always seems to have got on well with tough men. Even when I talked to him in his presbytery in Melbourne, our tea was served by an amiable giant who once had a reputation as a dockland 'heavy'.[6] Brosnan was known to have a philosophy of not condemning anyone. When someone was described to him as a killer, he would reply, 'So they say, but I don't know for sure, and I'm not going to say it. Even if I did know it, I would not say it. I am a priest, not a police reporter. It is God's job to judge people, not mine.'

When he first met Ryan, a campaign to reprieve the prisoner was building up. Ryan, an expert shot, had aimed to wound the warder, but apparently the fatal bullet was deflected off a bone into the man's heart. However, the bullet either could not, or would not, be found, and it was thought by some that the fatal shot could have been fired by another warder aiming at the escapees. There were several reprieves, and these might have succeeded but for the determination of the Victoria Premier, Sir Henry Bolte, to have a hanging. He told Graham Parkin, the editor of the *Melbourne Age*: 'You bastards beat me on Tate, but I'll beat you over Ryan. He who laughs last laughs best.' Bolte later told his successor that if he wanted to make a mark, he should 'have a hanging'.

Ryan was not a practising Catholic but he agreed to see Father Brosnan on the suggestion of the prison governor – an enlightened man who had come to like Ryan and suffered a crack-up after the execution and retired from the Prison Service – and because he thought it would please his widowed mother, not out of a desire to purchase a little sacramental fire insurance. However, once he began to engage with Brosnan, the priest found 'the guy was a theologian'. Father Brosnan said: 'I'm no stranger to dying. I'd worked in hospitals and in old folks' homes. But I never saw anyone die as well as Ryan.' As the men grew closer, and reprieve after reprieve was turned down, Ryan discovered that some of his associates were planning to break into the jail and rescue him at the point of a gun. Some of the toughest criminals in Australia were involved, and there was a strong likelihood that the attempt could have succeeded, though probably at the cost of warders' lives, and hostage-taking. After word of the escape plans were smuggled into Ryan in code, he arranged for the priest to go on a dangerous mission to his associates which succeeded in having the escape attempt called off, thus condemning Ryan to certain execution.

I interviewed Father Brosnan thirty years after the hanging, and he could remember every detail of it: 'It was probably the best hour of my life. He was a stoic really. He wouldn't allow them to give him a sedative, and only wanted a light breakfast. He said to me, "You'll have done your work by a quarter to eight, this thing isn't a debs ball, who stands where. Come down to be with me." ' In those days the condemned man dropped through a trapdoor and all that remained visible to the audience was the rope. The man died out of sight behind a screen. Brosnan attended to Ryan just before the hanging, and stood below the trapdoor so that Ryan fell directly in front of him. He lifted the cowl from the dying man's head and annointed him as he swung from the rope. It was a quick death. The spinal cord was snapped. The hangman had obeyed Ryan's final instruction: 'God bless you. Whatever you do, do it quickly.' And so Ryan and Brosnan passed into history. Bolte's advice to his successor was not followed up. Ryan was the last man to die by hanging.

With the passing of Ryan, another era was ending. The character of the Church in Australia was altering also and with it, much of Australian society. The 'no Irish need apply' ads were vanishing too, and the Irish were not merely climbing the ladder of success – the young Paul Keating was preparing to go to the very top by becoming Prime Minister.

THE FIRST ARRIVALS

Before analysing that climb let us examine how the Irish got to Australia in the first place, and take a brief look at what befell them from the days of the original Irish settlements to contemporary times.

As elsewhere in the diaspora, or indeed in Ireland itself, developments may be examined under the headings of the sacred and the profane.

The militant element of the sacred we will find best exemplified in the career of Daniel Mannix, (described below). What made him militant was a combination of the prison tradition amongst the Irish, which stretching as it did from the arrival of the 1798 transportees, through those of the Young Ireland and Fenian arrivals, the Ned Kelly episode contributed to a portrait of an embattled church and people ranged against unjust British and Protestant power. The profane, embedded both in the concept of the injustice which led to the prison tradition, and a view that the Protestant pedigree is flawed, is encapsulated in an old Irish poem which was translated by a former Maynooth Professor and President of University College Galway, Monsignor Padraig de Brun. It contains the following:

> Don't talk of your Protestant Minister.
> Or his Church without Temple or State,
> For the foundation stone of his religion
> Was the bollocks of Henry V111.

This pre-ecumenical rhyme catches the earthy disdain that lay behind Irish resistance to those NINA advertisements, the urge to maintain Catholic schools, even at great cost and the veneration of the prisoners whose crime was to resist the unjust depredations of Henry's inheritors, both in Ireland and Australia. Putting it more temperately than the de Brun translation, one of the best minds amongst the antipodean Irish, Patrick O'Farrell,[7] accurately observed:

> The climate of continuing hostility to the Irish in Australia induced conformity, but also generated, as a reaction, an Irish determination to assert a separate but distinctive identity.

The search for that 'distinctive identity' may be said to have begun with the arrival in Australia.

The first convicts to be sent direct from Ireland arrived aboard the *Queen* in Sydney Harbour on 26 September 1791. Australia had been in existence as a convict settlement for some three years before this, and many of those involved in the transportation of convicts were Irish. Some were in the Navy, some were in chains, but all were regarded as English. As Robert Hughes has pointed out in his classic work *The Fatal Shore*:

> To the British there was no such thing as 'Australian' history or culture. For its first 40 years everything that happened in the thief-colony was English . . . it was the largest forced exile of citizens at the behest of a European Government in pre-modern history. Nothing in earlier penology compares with it. In Australia, England drew the sketch for our own century's vaster and more terrible fresco of oppression, the gulag. No other country had such a birth.[8]

As Hughes also says, 'English law makers wish not only to get rid of the "criminal class" but if possible to forget about it.' The Irish prisoners, however, proved to be one of the many compelling reasons why it did not prove possible to forget about Australia. The 'typically Irish' contingent aboard the *Queen* established a 'Paddy the Irishman' reputation almost as soon as they landed. Just as African slaves in Latin America made a desperate, and doomed, effort to regain their freedom by trying to walk to Dahomy, some of the *Queen*'s convicts broke free with the intention of 'walking to China'. Of course these unfortunates knew no more of China than they did of Australia. The derision which they aroused became tinged with fear and loathing, however, as the number of Irish prisoners went up and came to include men who had been sentenced for revolutionary activities. What they had begun in Ireland, it was feared they might continue in Australia.

As Edward Campion says:

> The conquest of Ireland had made them landless people. In 1641 Catholics owned 59% of the land; in 1688 22%; in 1703 14%; by 1788 about 5%. The Protestant proprietors of Ireland maintained their hold on land through the Penal Laws, which kept the Catholic Irish as helots in their own country. When they came to Australia they carried this history with them and passed it on to their children. In time their sense of grievance made Irish Australians one of the primary sources of Australian nationalism.[9]

It was not merely the fact of being deprived of their land which gave the Irish cause for complaint. Bad as this was, the experiences of 1798 itself greatly honed and sharpened their edge of grief and grievance.

THE MEMORIES OF 1798

The Irish are often condemned for having an unwarranted sense of grievance, but however justified this accusation may be in some cases, in post-1798 Australia, the miracle is that they did not have more of a grievance. For as Thomas Pakenham commented:

> The Rebellion of 1798 is the most violent and tragic event in Irish history between the Jacobite Wars and the Great Famine. In the space of a few weeks, 30,000 people – peasants armed with pikes and pitchforks, defenceless women and children – were cut down or shot or blown like chaff as they charged up to the mouth of the cannon.[10]

But the deaths in actual fighting were only part of the story. The Rebellion was in very great part fomented by the excesses of the Protestant landlords and their yeomanry. Maddened by the rumours of an impending revolution led by the United Irishmen with help from France, the Irish Army had developed a condition which its commander-in-chief, General Abercromby, described as 'a state of licentiousness which must render it formidable to everyone but the enemy'. The expression of these and similar views caused Abercromby to be replaced by General Lake, where command was characterised by 'various tortures . . . widely used':

> . . . flogging, rape, picketing (in which the victim was fastened, back to the ground, his wrists and ankles drawn to full stretch and tied to pegs), half hanging, pitch-capping (crowning the victim with a linen cap filled with hot pitch and then setting it alight) and roasting the soles of the victim's feet at a turf fire.[11]

Writing on the subject of pitch-capping, the rebel General, Miles Byrne, in his memoirs, described how the daughters of one notorious sadist, Hunter Gowan, of Wexford:

seemed to take delight and to be amused preparing the poor 'croppies' heads for receiving the pitch-caps, cutting the hair, and making what they called asses crosses on them, previous to the application of this infernal blistering invention of torture, which was introduced into the county of Wexford by the Colonel of the North Cork Militia, Lord Kingsboro, and his vile Orange associates.[12]

Amongst the counter-atrocities which the foregoing 'pacification' methods elicited amongst the maddened peasantry was the burning of a barn full of Protestant prisoners, including women and children, at Scullabogue, County Wexford. Thus, the importance of 1798 memories to the population of both transportees and their jailers can hardly be over-stressed. When a small-scale rebellion broke out at Castle Hill outside Sydney, in 1804, for instance, the site became known as 'Vinegar Hill' after the knoll in County Wexford on which the croppies were cut down by cannon in 1798. The rebels at Castle Hill were easily tricked into capture and surrender. Their leaders were hanged and their bodies exhibited in chains at different vantage points as an example to other would-be rebels, and one of the leaders, Philip Cunningham, was strung up from the stairs of the Government store in Paramatta. In general, however, the target of the Irish in Australia was not successful rebellion, but successful escape.

FROM REBELS TO RESPECTABILITY

A combination of what had happened in Ireland, fear of an uprising, and Protestant/Catholic animosities kept the authorities in a state of semi-terrified hatred of the Irish prisoners. The most famous '98 convict was Michael Dwyer who had held out in the Wicklow mountains for some years after the 1798 Rebellion ended. Eventually he surrendered on terms under which he was to be sent to America, but instead he was despatched to Australia aboard the convict transport *Tellicherry* in 1805.

Dwyer never gave any trouble once he landed but his reputation was such that the Governor, the infamous Bligh of the *Bounty*, jailed him. Dwyer's crime was said to have been the singing of an Irish rebel ballad, which at the time could have cost him a 1,000 lashes and a long term of imprisonment. However, Dwyer and a group of his friends were acquitted. Bligh, nevertheless had the acquittal overturned and banished Dwyer to Norfolk Island. Somehow Dwyer managed to secure his return to the Australian mainland and went on to become a policeman. He developed a drink problem which caused him to be removed from his position of Chief Constable of Liverpool (New South Wales) in 1820. The majority of the transported rebels, however, became: 'the most prominent and prosperous Irishmen in Sydney town'.[13] Dwyer's own descendants are said to have grown to something in excess of a thousand persons, by the time of the 1798 centenary.

THE FLOGGING PARSON

By 1828 the population of New South Wales had grown to some 40,000.
Catholics formed about a quarter of this, with about 8,000 being born in Ireland.
By that time most of the Irish were progressing on the land with much the same
degree of success soon to be enjoyed by their fellow-countrymen in Argentina. In
Australia, however, the Irish had to contend along the way with a very
considerable anti-Catholic and anti-Irish sentiment, illustrated in the celebrated
broadside from the 'flogging parson', the Reverend Samuel Marsden.

> The number of Catholic convicts is very great in the settlement; and these in general composed
> of the lowest class of the Irish nation, who are the most wild, ignorant and savage race . . . men
> that have been familiar with robberies, murders and every horrid crime from their infancy . .
> . governed entirely by the impulse of passion and always alive to rebellion and mischief they
> are very dangerous members of society . . . They are extremely superstitious, artful and
> treacherous . . . They have no true concern whatever for any religion nor fear of the Supreme
> Being: but are fond of riot, drunkenness, and cabals; and was the catholic religion tolerated
> they would assemble together from every quarter not so much from a desire of celebrating
> mass, as to recite the miseries and injustice of their punishment, the hardships they suffer, and
> to enflame one another's minds with some wild scheme of revenge.

Along with becoming the chief Anglican clergyman in New South Wales,
Marsden was also appointed a magistrate. In this latter capacity, Marsden set
out to uncover evidence of a suspected rising in 1800 through the use of the
lash. He forced a Catholic priest, Father James Harold, to place his hand on
the flogging tree and stand so close to the victims that he was bespattered with
the flesh and blood of the tortured. The following graphic description of
Marsden's handiwork by one of the principal '98 leaders, the Protestant
United Irishman Joseph Holt, has become one of the classic passages of
Australian convict literature.[14] Anne Maree Whitaker has recorded one of the
'typical incidents' which originally drove Holt, and many like him, into
rebellion in Ireland:

> . . . on Easter Tuesday, 10 April, in Newtownmountkennedy in County Wicklow a
> Protestant farmer and United Irishman named Joseph Holt, attending the town fair, was
> sickened to witness Ancient Britons cutting the haunches and thighs off of the young
> women for wearing green stuff peticoats.'

However what drunken soldiers wrought in Wicklow was equalled, if not
surpassed, in Australia by the sober clergyman. Holt has left a famous
account of Marsden's handiwork:

> The place they flogged them their arms pulled around a large tree and their breasts
> squeezed against the trunk so the men has no power to cringe . . . There were two floggers,
> Richard Rice and John Johnson the Hangman from Sydney. Rice was a left-handed man
> and Johnson was right-handed, so they stood at each side, and I never saw two threshers
> in a barn move their strokes more handier than these two man-killers did.

The moment they began I turned my face round to the other side and one of the constables came and desire'd me to turn and look on. I put my right hand in my pocket and pulled out my pen-knife, and swore I [would] rip him from the navel to the chin. They all gathered round me and would have ill-used me . . . [but] they were obliged to walk off. I could compare them to a pack of hounds at the death of a hare, yelping.

I was to leeward of the floggers . . . I was two perches from them. The flesh and skin blew in my face as it shook off the cats. Fitzgerald received his 300 lashes. Doctor Mason – I will never forget him – he used go feel his pulse and he smiled and said: 'This man will tire you before he will fail – go on.' During the time Fitzgerald was getting his punishment he never gave so much as a word – only one, and that was saying 'Don't strike me on the neck, flog me fair.'

When he was let loose, two of the constables went and took hold of him by the arms to keep him in the cart. I was standing by. [He] said to them 'Let me go'. He struck both of them with his elbows in the pit of the stomach and knocked them both down, and then stepped on the cart. I heard Dr Mason say that man had strength enough to bear 200 more.

Next was tied up Paddy Galvin, a young boy of about 20 years of age. He was ordered to get 300 lashes. He got one hundred on the back, and you could see his backbone between his shoulder blades. Then the Doctor ordered him to get another hundred on his bottom. He got it, and then his haunches were in such a jelly that the doctor ordered him to be flogged on the calves of his legs. He got one hundred there and as much as a whimper he never gave. They asked him if he would tell where the pikes were hid. He said he did not know, and would not tell. 'You may as well hang me now,' he said, 'but there will be no music out of my mouth to make others dance upon nothing.' They put him in the cart and took him to hospital.[15]

Early Australian society was brutal. Like rugby out-halves there were two kinds of people, the quick and the dead. Apart from the harshness of the climate and the landscape, the dominant British culture feared the influx of the Irish:·

Given the white population of 4,500 in 1800, the influx of 872 English and 722 Irish male convicts in 1800 to 1802, dramatically changed the proportion of Irish from around 20% to 33%.[16]

Given also that, as Winston Churchill accurately pointed out, the British Navy achieved greatness on the three pillars of rum, sodomy and the lash, it is hardly surprising that the lash was the favourite implement of Government against the potentially rebellious Irish.

The harshness of the relationship between the British and the Irish had other repercussions. As we shall see, later in the century, in an effort to combat the conditions created by imperial colonialism, the administrators of the religious variety would enthusiastically use leather in the classrooms, as an aid to the character formation of those educated into mounting successful challenges to the established colonial order.

Yet it was education that led to the first stirrings of friendship between the two cultures. The calibre of many of the early Irish political convicts was such that they inevitably made friends with their jailers who needed their services to run the fledgling settlement. The Irish could read and write and had a knowledge of agriculture, as well as many other skills, so they soon became an intrinsic part of the administration of the antipodean adventure.

THE INFLUENCE OF THE CLERGY

Initially the Irish were priestless, apart from a handful of clerics unjustly swept up in the transportation mania generated by the 1798 Rising. These managed to get back to Ireland after a few years, but in 1820 two, more durable, figures appeared on the Australian clerical scene. These were Fathers Philip Connolly and John Joseph Therry. The latter in particular would establish an enormous personal influence akin to that which we will encounter Father Fahy wielding in Argentina.

As the population of Catholics grew, the influence of the clergy grew with it. A Vicar General, the Englishman Bernard Ullathorne, was appointed in 1833, and Sydney acquired a bishop, another Benedictine, two years later, the saintly John Bede Polding. However, although the Benedictines had a head start in the control of the burgeoning Australian Roman Catholic Church, it was the Irish clergy who gained the ascendancy throughout the nineteenth century. Psychologically and historically they were better placed to empathise with their flocks than any English Benedictines, no matter how dedicated and sincere. As in America, the Irish looked after their own. One exception to this was an English Catholic woman, Caroline Chisiom who, from the time she arrived in Sydney in 1838, performed prodigies in helping Irish colonists, particularly the women, to settle in Australia. Her work improved both the conditions in the ships which brought the emigrants to Australia and their living conditions when they got there.

The Irish curates in Australia, as elsewhere, had an enormous influence over their flocks. The sectarianism of the 'No Popery' movements we have touched on in places like Glasgow or Liverpool was replicated in the growing Australian towns. In Melbourne, for example, Dunmore Lang won an election in 1843 by declaring that his opponent, a Catholic, should not be supported because Melbourne was a Protestant town which could not be represented by someone whose religion stipulated that he had to be a bigot! In such circumstances Father Therry in particular anticipated the approach of Archbishop Mannix in the next century by encouraging his followers in protest against the unjust Protestant and British order. As Edward Campion commented, 'In Australian history sectarianism was to last longer than the rabbit plague.'

However, it would be unfair to regard a Therry or a Mannix as mere Catholic polemicists. Therry's influence on the exiled political journalist, Patrick O'Donohoe, encouraged Donohoe, during his period as editor of the *Irish Exile*, to support the causes of both the Irish convicts and the Aborigines, and they could be seen as laying the foundations for the widely acknowledged involvement of contemporary Irish figures in the struggle for Aborigine rights.

As the number of Catholics increased, the Irish moved under the tutelage of Therry and others like him, from seeking what nowadays, in Northern Ireland, is referred to as parity of esteem, to supporting Irish nationalist causes. When Therry and Connolly arrived in Sydney in 1820 there were some 6,000 Catholics scattered throughout Australia. This number mushroomed throughout the century as the Government introduced assisted immigration schemes which, in the fifty years from 1836 brought some 200,000 settlers to the new continent. 'New' of course is a figurative term. As the Irish writer and academic, Val Noone, writing of what is now the Melbourne district, reminds us:[17]

> The first Catholics in Melbourne, though mostly poor and dispossessed Irish, came in 1834 as part of a British invasion which dispossessed the Koori people of land that had been their home for tens of thousands of years. By 1860, in the area which the British later named Victoria, some nine thousand Aboriginal people died from disease, alcohol, poisoning, shooting and the disruption of their lives, which contrasts with only fifty-nine Europeans killed.

However, emigrants either fleeing from the Irish Famine or towards the Australian gold rushes, impelled by the imperatives of their own survival, did not tarry very long over this appalling record.

Another factor which entered the soul of the Irish in Australia, as it did in Ireland, was ultramontane Catholicism. Rome appointed the bishops and the bishops saw to it that the Roman line was faithfully followed. One of the most successful was James Quinn, the first Bishop of Brisbane (1861). He utilised the assisted immigration scheme to such advantage that for a time Queensland became known as Quinnsland. As well as being a classical bricks-and-mortar bishop, expanding the kingdom of God on earth through a plethora of fund-raising activities, new schools and new churches, he was also a bully and a nit-picking autocrat of the 'Monaghan theology' school who once told members of his flock that: 'I have been ordained and received the Holy Ghost; anyone attacking my character commits a most gross and sacrilegious act.'

The Sisters of Mercy arrived there in 1861 and established the first secondary school in Queensland, All Hallows in Brisbane. As elsewhere, they provided such good education that Protestants sent their children to the school. In particular the nuns were famous for teaching music. Quinn battened on them mercilessly, seizing the monies they raised for his own diocesan purposes and intervening in the nuns' daily lives to the extent of ruling on how their laundry should be done. Quinn was the archetypal anti-feminist Irish cleric. He would not even allow the nuns to go for a drive in the fresh air when they fell ill, generally through overwork.

He was far from being alone in his tyrannical approach. The impact of authoritarian figures like Quinn on an uneducated laity can well be imagined, but their harmful influence on their subordinates (which in turn of course inevitably impacted on the laity) was also immense. In Western Australia,

Bishop John Brady of Perth brought out Irish Sisters of Mercy under false pretences by telling them that 4,000 Catholic children needed a school. Many of these nuns were destined never to see Ireland again. They must have felt the first day's enrolment a poor return for their sacrifice: only six pupils turned up. The Bishop continually interfered in the day to day running of their affairs. When one of the sisters fell ill the Bishop's permission had to be sought before calling a doctor. The nun in charge of the Convent described what happened following the doctor's visit:

> A week after, I thought it necessary to send for him again, which I did without having the permission renewed, and this for two reasons. Firstly, I did not think it necessary in the same illness; secondly, I was sick myself in bed at the same time, and unable to go to the church, and I had been commanded not to write to the Bishop. But what was the consequence of this most unthought of act of disobedience? Your poor children and their convent were placed under an interdict which the Bishop was obliged to come in soutane, rochet and stole to remove!![18]

Interdict! For calling a doctor. But not only nuns suffered from Church discipline. In the early days of the Irish Christian brothers coming to Australia (between 1874 and 1881), out of a total of twenty-nine brothers, only nine were still active in 1883. A report of the period draws a dreadful picture:

> At Emerald Hill they have one far gone in consumption. In Geelong Brother B. Lynch is all but perfectly blind, whilst Brother P. Hennessy is also there trying to recover from a severe attack he had a few months since in Ballarat and which brought him to the point of death. In Ballarat Brother J. Mullen is trying to act as Director and to conduct a school at the same time without an audible voice. In fact it is cruel to have that poor man in school. Then to render things worse B S. Kennedy has to be moved from Ballarat to replace Brother Joseph Barrett who has been very ill for some months. Indeed you may any time get an account of his decease, or what is sadder of his mind completely going, for the doctor says if things go much further with him he will lose his reason. His staff in Brisbane consists of three poor novices, only one of whom could write a passable notice of a boy's absence from school . . .
> P.S. I did not mention Adelaide, as I suppose you are aware two Brothers there are dying of bloodspitting.[19]

Brother Barrett in fact pulled through and ran a school in Brisbane characterised by poverty and strictness for the children coupled with an unworldliness that related directly to the lives the brothers themselves led. Campion notes:

> There were no newspapers or games for the Brothers; food was plain and badly cooked; clothing was old and patched . . . Brothers found little time for personal development or reading. Pitted against university-trained men in the other schools, the Brothers put their energies in cramming pupils after hours.[20]

Although educational training for the brothers increased over the years, the forcing house, leather-in-hand method of cramming continued to be enjoined on brothers all over the world.

In his affectionate memoir of an Irish Australian Catholic teenager attending a Christian Brothers' school in the year 1952, Thomas Keneally describes life under the Irish nuns and sisters. A central instrument in character formation was:

> The quintessential Christian Brother weapon, a number of strips of leather sewn together but with – according to an unreliable legend amongst schoolboys – a hacksaw blade included between the middle layers. Mythologizing about the strap occupied a great part of the time of younger Christian Brother boys. Some Brothers were rumoured to practise giving it in the secrecy of their cells. Some – we believed – stiffened the thing, others made it more flexible. (We were not of course aware of any Freudian imagery in our legend making.) The Brothers had frequently enough told us that we boys and their own community were the totality of their world. We imagined therefore that they spent all their time thinking of us, whether it be in terms of charity or punishment.[21]

The incredible thing about these religious men and women is not so much that they resorted to methods such as the strap and teachings of a fetid, almost lunatic, anti-sexual nature, but that they retained sufficient enlightenment to illuminate the lives of their pupils. Thomas Keneally recalls one of these teachers, nicknamed Dinny:

> Dinny was remarkable because he would appear at the elbow of this boy or that and present them with some special task they had not thought of themselves, a task which related them to the larger universe. In that spirit he came to me one autumn morning and said, 'Young Keneally, ah . . . ah . . . I want you to enter the Newman's Society Essay Prize and win something for the school. I suggest that since you're so crazy about Gerard Manley Hopkins, you should write about him.' He had a slim grey book in his hands. 'Here is a Kenyon Critics essay on Gerard Manley Hopkins.'[22]

The Brothers were not all Dinnys, however. Peter Collins stated that in his day, at Waverley:

> Science and maths ruled. My stirring passion for English and History would have relegated me to the second-rung class had these irresponsible urges been allowed to develop. One did not contemplate more reckless humanities options such as art. Removal from the top class, to which I clung by my fingernails, ran a real risk of being taught English by Thomas Keneally! Mercifully, today's Waverley boasts a strong arts presence . . .[23]

Collins likened the Brothers' regime to that of the American Marine Corps. The Brothers used corporal punishment to help them 'disassemble students and rebuild them in a more efficient, purposeful way'. He reckoned that his five years at Waverley were responsible for his later successes at the Bar and in politics, but Collins did cite the experience of an American acquaintance who had also been taught by the Brothers and subsequently served in the Marine Corps: he reckoned that the Brothers were much tougher than the Marines!

Collins's experience, and that of myriads like him, illustrates the ruthless far-sightedness of the early Irish Church leaders. As we shall see, they had two basic formulae for improving the status of Catholics and, *ipso facto*, that of their largely working-class flock: they controlled their education and directed them into the Labour Party. Methodology to one side, the two policies paid off in terms of Irish political and social advancement. Collins is a member of the Liberal Party, something unexceptional nowadays, but unthinkable not so long ago. Even in the sixties, when Prime Minister Menzies put the seal on the Church's educational policy and recognised the power of the Catholic vote by conceding the principle of state aid for Catholic schools, there was only one Catholic in the Liberal Cabinet.

As it did everywhere, the power of the Catholic Church rested on the twin pillars of awe and guilt. Again Thomas Keneally cannot be bettered for practical insights into how the Australian version of the inculcation process worked. Like tens of thousands of boys of his type, he had entered the Brothers' domain after passing through a junior school run by Irish nuns. One day he took part in a pissing competition in St Martha's boys' toilet, and the contest came to the ears of Mother Concordia: 'Divine thunder was compacted into her eyes and the strip of brow we could see below her celluloid browpiece.' Mother Concordia drew a chalk line some two feet above the ground all around the urinals, then turned to address the trembling piddlers:

> I know what you have been doing to your shame. Think of what your dear mothers would say. You have disgraced them. More importantly, you have wounded our Saviour, and appalled His Blessed Mother. I tell you this: see that mark on the wall. Any boy who piddles above that mark will attract the anger of dear God and cause His Blessed Mother to shed tears of shame.[24]

That took care of the pissing competitions, but it was far from the end of Mother Concordia's influence. Like many another of these extraordinary women, she endured the petty tyrannies of bishops, the deprivation of sex, the denaturing, pin-pricking routine of narrow convent life, because of the X-factor, the inexplicable, driving, controlling Faith. As she lay dying, Keneally relates how the fate of this tremendous woman permeated the school. She had of course no daughters of her own, but she (and they) considered all the girls of the school to be her children. She was the last survivor of the Irish nuns who had originally built the schools of his childhood. One of the star pupils of the school, a girl on whom Keneally had an adolescent crush, as much for the attractions of her mind as her body, was called out from class to say farewell to the old nun. Two nuns took her by the elbows and led her to the deathbed. The dying woman looked up: 'Bernadette, I call upon you to become a Dominican Nun and take my name, Concordia. I will pray for you and support you in the Presence of God.'[25]

The girl duly joined the Order. As Keneally acknowledges, there may have been other reasons why she did so, but that deathbed scene must have had its impact on a sensitive Catholic teenager. It was an extreme version of the vocation retreat in Catholic schools in Ireland during which teenagers were urged to become missionaries. In the days of Mother Concordia's girlhood, and indeed until the Vatican II era, vocation questing in many an Irish convent school often centred around a nun 'back from the missions' giving a religious pep talk to a classroom filled with inexperienced teenaged girls from a rural background. This would be followed by the nun asking: 'Hands up the girl who wants to save pagan New Zealand,' or some such. It could equally well have been pagan England, Africa or Australia. Whatever the mission field, some little Bridget from Ballyragget or Castlecomer or wherever, was sure to put up her hand. Thus began a process of indoctrination which ended with the girl departing from home and family for anything up to thirty-five years without seeing Ireland again – but very often spending those years attempting to replicate the attitudes and values of the Ireland she had left behind.

The first nuns to come to Australia were the Sisters of Charity. It was they who opened Australia's first professional hospital in 1857, St Vincent's in Sydney, having had nineteen years of first-hand experience of the need for a hospital acquired through tending the sick in their homes – often slum dwellings. They accepted patients from any denomination and their first surgeons were all Protestant. When a Catholic priest removed Protestant Bibles from the church, the nuns defied the bishop and insisted that the Bibles be restored, even though their resistance resulted in the return to Ireland of the head nun, Mother de Lacy. A successor of hers managed to keep both her post and her prerogative of appointment when she also successfully defied archdiocesan attempts to instal a doctor of the Archbishop's choice.

The most powerful Irish clerical influence on Australia, however, resided in Ireland, not Australia. This was Cardinal Paul Cullen, whom we first encountered as a towering rector of the Irish College in Rome. In fact he was such a Romanist, and so able, that it was widely said that had Pius IX died a decade or so earlier, Cullen would have become Pope. From the time he was sent back to Ireland as papal legate in 1850, until his death in 1878, the shadow of Paul Cullen stretched from Maynooth to Australia.

This powerful ultramontane prelate, a friend and confidant of Popes and influential Vatican prelates, organised the Irish Church in Rome's image in the mid-nineteenth century. His career prompts the speculation as to what would have happened had the British not imposed the Act of Union of 1800. Suppose there had been an Irish parliament, nurtured by figures like Daniel O'Connell, growing through the decades before Cullen's birth? Would such a figure have opted for the Church or for politics? Had he become an Irish Prime Minister what would that mighty energy have done for Mother Ireland rather than Mother Church? As it was, the type of church, priest and nun whom Cullen created in Ireland was the kind sent to the Antipodes and the empire. In fact the most powerful of them were literally his kind: the Bishops of Brisbane, Bathurst and Maitland were his cousins and the Archbishop of Sydney was his nephew.

Edward Campion has described the Irish Church prior to Cullen as being:

> A bewildering mixture of formal Catholicism, debased Catholic practices, family piety, superstition, magic and Celtic mythology. Catholic convicts brought this with them. Consequently, even without the administration of priests, the Catholic faith survived in colonial Australia as a poem that gave life, meaning or respite. It was a view of the world enabling one to sustain the present and hope for the future. It was also a folk culture, a bond of loyalty to one's fellows.[26]

In the phrase of the great Irish American historian, Emmet Larkin, Cullen sparked off a 'devotional revolution'. In other words, he did away with a good deal of the poetry, strengthened discipline, heightened the standardisation of worship to Roman specifications, and elevated the usage of devotional practices such as novenas, pilgrimages, rosaries, and confession-going. Cullen's nephew, Patrick Francis Moran, was appointed to Sydney in 1884, becoming Cardinal and the most powerful single influence in the Australian Church. Moran had much of the ordinary juice of humanity squeezed out of him before he ever got to Sydney. He commenced his studies for the priesthood, in Rome, at the age of twelve, and heightened this experience by years at his uncle's side in the capacity of secretary.

THE EFFECTS OF THE MORAN COUNCIL

It was Moran who was responsible for two decisions which affected both the Irish in Australia and their Protestant neighbours. In 1885 he called a Council which in effect extended the stipulations of Irish Catholicism to Australia. Firstly, he had it ordained that Catholic parents were to be denied forgiveness in the confessional if they sent their children to a state school without permission. This edict was ruthlessly enforced. When a bishop – Cullen and Moran's relation, James Murray of the Maitland diocese – heard that a Catholic woman had sent her children to a local state school, he descended on her in person. She explained that she was too poor to buy shoes for her children and if they were to go to the nearest Catholic school, five kilometres away, they would have to walk barefooted. An emotional scene developed with the woman pleading poverty and bare feet through her tears. However, the Bishop triumphed by telling the woman that, if the children continued in the state school, he would not allow her baby to be baptised.

A side-effect of the system of separated education was the different world-view it engendered. As Geoffrey Sherington has pointed out:

For colonial children the split between the Catholics and the rest of the community over the question of education was profound. In the Government schools children were taught the glories and virtues of the British Empire; Catholic children learnt that British tyranny was oppressing Irish freedom. Such contrasting views of the world would influence those who came of age, not only in the nineteenth century but also well into the twentieth.[27]

They would indeed – just as they did, and still do, in Belfast. Nevertheless, although a largely working-class, poor population, the Irish Australians somehow managed to keep their own separate school system going without state funding until 1963. Then the Liberal Party Prime Minister, Robert Menzies, introduced funding for science teaching and a battery of scholarships which floated the Catholic system off the rocks. Menzies was not acting out of sympathy for the Catholics so much as recognising that the Labour Party leader, the Catholic Arthur Calwell, was planning to introduce such assistances if Labour won a pending election. By acting as he did, Menzies trumped Calwell's electoral ace, attracted the Catholic vote and won the election.

The other great bone of contention introduced by the Moran Council of 1885, one which also continued to have disturbing effects on Catholic/Protestant relationships virtually up to the time of writing, concerned the marriage of Catholics before a civil authority or a Protestant minister. Either automatically caused Catholics to be excommunicated. Moreover, marriage with a non-Catholic was forbidden, unless the non-Catholic promised to bring up the children of the marriage as Catholics and not to interfere with the Catholics' religious practice. The actual marriage of the Catholic with someone outside the Church was to be conducted without mass, without candles and without flowers – in the sacristy.

Moran promoted the classical Irish 'in your face' style of Church architecture. Anyone familiar with the sight of Irish churches crowning the steepest slopes, be they in Ireland itself, or far-flung Australia or Newfoundland, will recognise both style and motive immediately. 'We are out of the penal era' is the message of those buildings. Nowhere in Australia is it said louder than by the huge Manly College which Moran had built across from Sydney Harbour. Under Moran, a note was sounded within the ranks of Irish Australian Catholics, which was to be echoed in an even louder key under Daniel Mannix: 'Australia First'. The concerns of Australians (and *ipso facto* the Irish Catholic component therein) should take precedence over those of empire. Moran also established another *leitmotif* for Irish Australian Catholicism – sympathy for the workers. He supported some strikes and encouraged the emerging Labour Party which he, and succeeding Church strategists, saw as a vehicle for challenging the established, Protestant order.

St Patrick's Day grew in significance as an indication of Irish energy and increasing power. Again, as elsewhere in the world both before and since, one had to be powerful to survive the celebrations: an account from Bathurst, on 27 March 1833, said, 'They have been keeping St Patrick's Day since the 12th inst. and not ended it yet.'²⁸ Apart from the boozing and brawling, St Patrick's Day became an expression both of Church influence and Irish economic progress.

THE CRIMINAL PATINA

The progress was not unspotted. Robbery with violence was a crime particularly associated with the Irish and with good reason. Governor Brisbane reported in 1824 that: 'It is a remarkable fact that every murder or diabolical crime which has been committed in the colony since my arrival has been perpetrated by Roman Catholics.'

Obviously amongst the transportees there was a high percentage of criminals who ended up in Australia because of poverty rather than politics. By 1837, it was reckoned that a third of the entire population of New South Wales were Irish Catholic convicts. Both criminal and political offenders were soon to be subsumed into a greatly enlarged Irish population. The Famine resulted in the introduction of migration schemes which brought out thousands of displaced persons. Emigration thus combined with transportation to etch indelibly on to the Australian consciousness the equation: Irish + Catholic = Agitation.

The criminal patina hung over the Irish image for decades. Not everyone would go out of their way to proclaim Irish heritage as did one of Australia's favourite sons, Andrew Barton 'Barton' Paterson, the author of 'Waltzing Matilda', who was born in Namable, New South Wales in 1864. Apart from his personal popularity 'Banjo's commitment had been made somewhat easier by a raising of the Irish profile which had taken place following the arrival in Van Diemen's Land (later renamed Tasmania) of a group of unusually gifted prisoners. These were the Young Ireland leaders transported after the 1848 Rebellion. Unlike 1798, this was no sectarian debauch of blood, but a small-scale and gentlemanly affair, conducted with civility and due regard to the rights of private property. The '48 men were generally a well-educated group who would not have become involved in even the most gentlemanly of revolutions were it not for the appalling maladministration of their country. Some, like John Mitchel and Thomas Francis Meagher, we have met already in the account of the American Civil War.

At his trial Meagher had enraged the judge by telling him: 'My lord this is our first offence, but not our last. If you will go easy with us this once, we promise on our word as gentlemen, to do better next time – we won't get caught.' The group were sentenced to be hanged, drawn and quartered, but a wave of protest led to the sentence being commuted to transportation. Amongst the group were William Smith O'Brien, who produced a draft constitution for Tasmania and for an Australian federation; Charles Gavan Duffy, who became a Premier of Victoria; Morris Leyne who became an Attorney General; and Michael Ireland, who succeeded Leyne in the post. Richard O'Gorman became Governor of Newfoundland and Thomas Darcy

McGee became an outstanding political figure in Canada. Daniel Deniehy, a contemporary of the others though not himself a convict, was the son of two Cork convicts who had done well in Australia. He became a solicitor, journalist, university lecturer and, sharing the democratic views of the Young Irelanders, one of the founding fathers of Australian republicanism.

Hard on the heels of the Young Irelanders, in January 1868, a group of Fenian prisoners were set ashore at Freemantle, Western Australia, from the brig *Hougoumont*. One of them, John Boyle O'Reilly, escaped to America a year after being imprisoned. It was he who, seven years later, in 1876, organised the dramatic rescue of six leading Fenian prisoners from Western Australia aboard the *Catalpa*, using money subscribed by Irish sympathisers in the Irish diaspora from Boston to New Zealand. To this day one of the biggest pubs in Perth is called The Fenian Bar, and visitors to the old jail at Fremantle are regaled by the story of how the *Catalpa*, an American whaling ship, got away from the *Georgette*, a pursuing English warship, because the *Georgette*'s captain hesitated to fire on the American flag.

The idea of a prosperous pub being named after them was beyond the realms of possibility in the year that the Fenians first landed, for, apart from the fear which they had engendered by their activities in Ireland and Canada, they were mistakenly implicated by public opinion in an attempt on the life of the visiting Duke of Edinburgh, Prince Alfred. A demented lawyer named O'Farrell shot the Prince in the back on 12 March 1868. O'Farrell, who was in fact drunk at the time, had nothing to do with the Fenians but did have a proven history of insanity. His brother died in a lunatic asylum, but O'Farrell died on the gallows because the premier of the day, Henry Parkes, was an unscrupulous practitioner of the brutal doctrine enunciated years later by Bolte in the Ryan case: a hanging generates much valuable political capital. Even though the Prince's life was saved, at the risk of their own, by two Irish bystanders, the O'Farrell incident generated huge anti-Irish feeling in both Australia and New Zealand.

THE CASUALTY AREAS

Both the prisoner-type and the ordinary immigrant have left very unflattering accounts of Australia in those days. The Fenian John Casey wrote in 1870:

> The population of Western Australia may be divided into two classes – those actually in prison, and those who more richly deserve to be there . . . all are equally dishonest. What more can be expected from a nation of felons. Murder and murderous assaults are manly sports to the colonists . . . they live and die like dogs . . . More real depravity, more shocking wickedness, more undisguised vice and immorality is to be witnessed at midday in the most public thoroughfares of Perth, with its population of 1,500, than in any other city of fifty times its population, either in Europe or America.[29]

Whether Casey was speaking with the benefit of research or of hyperbole, it is interesting to note that, as they did in America and still do in contemporary Britain, the Irish contributed more than their fair share to the statistics of human misery. Statistics of destitution show that after the Famine, for the greater part of the remainder of the century, in what Patrick O'Farrell calls the 'casualty areas of Australian society' the Irish were:

> prominent to the extent of at least double their proportion of the total population. In a
> society whose tendency was to regard poverty itself as a crime, and which was ill disposed
> towards state expenditure and the taxation necessary to sustain it, the negative image of
> the Irish was constantly reinforced by the continuing presence in those areas.[30]

Although only a relatively small proportion of the total number of Irish who came to Australia in the nineteenth century were convicts, whether criminal or political, the Irish as a class were constantly under the tutelage of the police, the prisons and the lunatic asylums, just as they were in New York, Glasgow or Liverpool.

ASSISTED PASSAGE

The Irish who arrived because of chain migration usually had someone to turn to on arrival, but a great number arrived because of assisted passage schemes which aimed at either removing tenants from overcrowded estates or orphaned children and young women from workhouses under the guise of providing settlers with wives. The suitability, or otherwise, of the emigrants to take up a pioneering life was seldom the criterion of such experiments. In Ireland the power of the landlords was such that Lord Lorton had the entire population of Ballinamuck evicted, following which the village was razed. The Lortons of the day 'were law-abiding, according to the law' in the words of T. J. Kiernan, whose father was born in Ballinamuck and who later became Ireland's first Ambassador to Australia.[31]

Even with such draconian powers at their disposal, the landlords were still faced with the problem of disposing of 'these human incumbrances', as they were described at a meeting of landlords in Loughrea, County Galway, in 1839. The chairman of the meeting 'with playful sarcasm' envisaged a new Loughrea in Australia, suggesting that:

> we may select that quantity of land in the best situation and call it Loughrea; and there
> may be a handsome lake, too, attached to it [Loughrea is built around a lake]; and thus
> these settlers may fancy themselves still in their dear Loughrea, with their associations and
> friends about them.[32]

And so, many an Irish cottier, with or without 'friends about them', ended up in the Australian bush.

The assisted passage schemes, of their nature, attracted a type of applicant who did have the physical and psychological aptitudes for survival, and they sometimes carried the additional benefit of conferring a plot of land on the emigrant. Lord Monteagle, who had large holdings in the north and west of Limerick and in parts of Kerry, assisted his tenants to leave the land, around the same time as the Loughrea meeting, but did so humanely. He stepped up his efforts after the Famine which rendered even efficient tenant farmers unable to pay their rents. When rent arrears reached accumulations of some three years, Monteagle made his tenants an offer which most of them felt unable to refuse. He had their assets valued, at their estimate, forgave the difference between the total and the rent owing, and then assisted the tenants to emigrate. As the number of Monteagle emigrants built up, money sent home by those who had gone before added to the flow. As we shall see later, the gold discoveries added to the attractions of Australia, and Monteagle, 'his wife and household' were kept busy, 'coping with the demand for passages, sometimes accompanied by requests for the loan of the deposit'.[33]

THE PIONEERS

Some of these Irish emigrants, arriving with little more than a strong back, an equally strong faith in their God, a farming background, and a plentiful supply of those two great human qualities, courage and durability, succeeded in using the system of land grants to build up legendary holdings. Names such as those of the intermarried Duracks, Costellos and Tullys are still associated with large, flourishing estates at the time of writing. In her celebrated work on her ancestors, *Kings in Grass Castles*, Mary Durack describes how her grandfather Patsy Durack and John Costello, 'rode about throwing open thousands of square miles of country in Queensland'. They gave the various blocks they surveyed Irish names: 'Clare, Scariff, Galway, Lough Derg, Lough Isle, Lough Neagh, Shannon View.' Only when they had used up Irish titles did they resort to Australian nomenclature, 'Yass, Wheeo, Grabbengullen, Goulburn' and so on.

Their methods of marking boundaries were ingenious. These included lighting a fire on a dark night at each end of an intended boundary, then two men carrying lanterns would walk towards each other, pegging the ground as they went. In the morning they would run their lines from peg to peg, between the ashes of the fires. These men carried out their pioneering work in constant fear of death from thirst or from Aborigines, but they succeeded in carving out vast empires in areas where no white man had ever been seen before, and where no stock had grazed previously. Patsy Durack, for example, divided some 2.5 million acres into holdings of 100,000 acres, and John Costello established an incredible holding in excess of eight and a half million acres. Tragically, those who came after did not treat the blacks as the Duracks, the Costellos and the other Irish pioneers had done, and a native population of some 1 million Aborigines was butchered down to less than 50,000.

The O'Brien brothers, Henry and Cornelius, emigrated with their uncles from County Mayo in 1814. Initially, they farmed in the Irish-settled areas around Appin and the Illawarra, later crossing the Blue Mountains into the Yaas area, where they built up large settlements. Two Cork brothers, Clement and Paul Lawless who came after them in 1840, had even greater success. It was reckoned that by the 1850s they had acquired some 725 square kilometres in Queensland. They became so wealthy that they were able to move easily between holdings in Ireland and Australia and both died in Ireland.

THE WORKHOUSE EXPERIMENT

Both the Lawlesses and the O'Briens might be termed gentlemen immigrants in that they had a little capital, thus setting them apart from the struggling convict Irish who gave rise to legendary bush-ranging figures like 'bold Jack Donahoe' and Ned Kelly. They were also very different from those who were sent to Australia in the workhouse orphans experiment of 1848.

The idea behind this scheme was both to rid the workhouses of paupers and to provide women for the colonies. Charles Trevelyan, Assistant Secretary at the Treasury – a man who did more than most to swell the ranks of Irish pauperdom, by the manner in which he helped to transform a potato shortage into a famine – wrote a memo which illustrates the attitude of decision-taking England to the problems of Ireland and Australia at the time:

> The Australians, although not quite so fond of a grievance as the excitable and imaginative Irish, will, nevertheless see that the idea of the Irish workhouses being cleared at their expense is too good not to be made the most of for their own benefit.[34]

In order to minimise protest, Trevelyan proposed that Protestant orphans should be sent initially:

> The perfect thing would be to send 2 shiploads, of Protestant Female Orphans (you must keep this a great secret from Bishop Murray, and everybody except Reddington – and after that they could not complain at our having our own way).'

However, the scheme drew complaints of all sorts. The girls were criticised for 'the use of low and vile language in their intercourse with each other and within hearing of respectable married women.'[35]

There were, as Trevelyan had anticipated, racial and religious prejudices.[36] In the course of a series of newspaper articles, the Presbyterian leader, the Reverend J. D. Lang wrote:

> These young women, who are almost exclusively Roman Catholics . . . have been selected as free emigrants for Australia, expressly with a view to their becoming the wives of the English and Scottish Protestant shepherds and stockmen of New South Wales, and thereby silently subverting the Protestantism and extending the Romanism of the colony through the vile, Jesuitical, diabolical, system of 'mixed marriages' . . . [37]

The scheme was eventually dropped after some two years in operation. The girls were of course largely untrained and employed mainly in domestic service. They were often swindled out of their wages or seduced by their employers and fellow-workers. Some awful stories of exploitation survive from the days of the orphan experiment. For example, amongst other horrific cases, Trevor McLaughlin lists the following:

> 16-year-old Alice Ball from Fermanagh, made pregnant by her married master and alone in a new country, committed suicide by drowning herself in the River Yarra. As one witness at the inquest deposed, 'Even though reins were thrown to her from the bank of the river, she would not, she refused to lay hold of them'.[38]

In all, some 4,175 orphan girls were sent to Australia under the scheme. The majority of them were good workers and, after they married, proved to be equally good mothers and wives. The miracle is not that the children – hurled into the strange environment of Australia after years of harsh and literally ignorant workhouse discipline – sometimes came to grief in their new environment, but that so many of them went on to make far happier and more rewarding careers for themselves than they could have dreamt of in the Ireland of the day.

THE GOLD FIELDS

Gold was one of the great factors in improving conditions. Gold changed Australia and the Irish. It created new prosperity and a new political environment wherein democracy received a powerful impetus. In 1851, the newly declared state of Victoria was the scene of a gold strike. Some 95,000 people crowded into the state. Overseas emigration also went up as gold diggers, many of them Irish, arrived from the far-off Californian fields, in much the same way as today's mobile Irish professionals follow the lure of computer gold from Tokyo to Silicon Valley. In the twenty-five years following the Victoria find the non-Aboriginal population of Australia increased by some 400,000 to nearly 1.1 million.

The Irish were popular in the gold fields. Apart from being hard-working, they generated an atmosphere of good fellowship with their singing and dancing, and their ability to lighten the strain of back-breaking labour with a joke. Their standing gave them a political dimension as the saga of the gold fields evolved. The gold rushes were characterised by all the colourful excesses of gold finds anywhere. Descriptions survive of skittles being played with bottles of champagne and of butter being spread between pound notes and fed to dogs.

The excesses were not confined to the miners. The state Governor was so draconian in his pursuit of minding licence fees that those who did not produce licences on demand were hunted like animals, and often when captured chained to logs. The licences cost £3 a month and not only was their cost a source of resentment to the miners generally but to the Irish in particular, for of course the enforcement of the licensing system against the largely Catholic Irish miners was entrusted to Protestant police. Consequently, the familiar tactic of the Irish yell, warning of the approach of police, frequently sounded across the gold fields. In this case the cry was 'Joe, Joe, Joe'. Eventually, after various provocations, including it is said the insulting of a priest, the miners at the Ballarat diggings decided to rebel. Of the 863 diggers involved, it is estimated that at least half were Irish, mostly from Tipperary. They hoisted the Southern Cross and under the leadership of Peter Lalor, an Irish engineer, brother of the great Irish nationalist writer James Fintan Lalor, threw up a stockade at Eureka in the first week of December 1854. Significantly, the password for entry to the stockade was 'Vinegar Hill'. Another Irish link with 1798 was the employment of pikes – useless in modern warfare, but potent in symbolism.

Underlying the general Irishness of the revolt lay a feeling of Australian nationalism, a revolt against the hierarchy of empire. Mindful of the potential threat to their rule, the authorities put down the uprising with some ruthlessness. Twenty-two of the miners were killed as opposed to six soldiers. Thirteen of the miners were tried for treason, and half of these were Irish, including Peter Lalor, who had lost an arm in the fighting. However, he gained immeasurably in reputation. After a jury trial presided over by an Irish Protestant judge, Redmond Barry, at which the thirteen were acquitted, he went on to become a minister and Speaker of the Victorian Parliament. Lalor was a conservative figure who said later that he despised the diggers. He said that the object of the revolt was 'independence' – and it is as a milestone in the growth of democratic and republican feeling that Eureka is commemorated in Australia.

On 5 December, 1999, the 145th anniversary of Eureka, a statue to the Pikeman's Dog, was unveiled at Ballarat Cemetery. The statue was the work of sculptors Charles Smith and Joan Walsh Smith originally from Co. Waterford, who now live outside Perth, surrounded by the bush in one of the most imaginatively designed studios and homes in Western Australia. The dog, who stayed beside his dead master long after the fighting, was posthumously honoured by the RSPCA with a purple cross.

Speaking at the unveiling, the Irish Ambassador to Australia, Richard O'Brien, placed the importance of Eureka to Australia, the Irish and the world in context by quoting Mark Twain:

> I think it may be called the finest thing in Australian history. It was a revolution – small in size, but great politically; it was a strike for liberty, a struggle for a principle, a stand against injustice and oppression. It was the Barons and John all over again; it was Hampden and Shipmoney; it was Concord and Lexington; small beginnings all of them great in political thinking, all of them epoch-making. It is another instance of a victory won by a lost battle. It adds an honourable page to history; the people know it and are proud of it. They keep green the memory of the men who fell at the Eureka Stockade.

In Western Australia today the Lalor family are still prominent figures in the gold mining industry, which in that area owes much to another Irishman, Paddy Hannan. Hannan, a native of Clare, with two Irish companions, Thomas Flanagan and Dan O'Shea, found gold near Coolgardie in 1893. The site of the discovery was originally called after Hannan, but was later changed to Kalgoorlie. These Western Australian finds not only helped to transform the region but, combined with those at Victoria, meant that at the turn of the century Australia was producing approximately 40 per cent of the world's gold. Hannan's contribution to this wealth was recognised by the Western Australian Government which gave him a pension – of £100 a year! Hannan's dictum was: 'If you're searching for gold, first find water'. The effort to provide the precious fluid in parched Western Australia gave rise to one of the most famous, and most tragic of stories of the history of the Irish in Australia. Charles Yelverton O'Connor from Co. Meath, still referred to as 'C.Y.', or 'The Chief became famous as the engineer who designed Freemantle Harbour, opened in 1897. As a result this imaginative scheme to provide water for the Calgardie and Kalgoorlie goldfields by building a huge dam, east of Perth, from which would run a 525 kilometer pipeline, was begun the following year. However progress was slow. No water flowed and 'The Chief' was subjected to a good deal of unmerited, lout wounding criticism. On the tenth of March, 1902, a deeply depressed O'Connor went for his usual morning ride along Freemantle beach. Unusually he went alone, because his youngest daughter fell ill and did not accompany him as she normally did. O'Connor shot himself on the shore. A month after his body was found water began pumping through the pipeline.

NED KELLY

It is not entirely fanciful to claim for Eureka another continuing influence in Australian folklore. In the week of the uprising, a child was born who would later be sentenced to death by Redmond Barry, the judge who presided over the trial of Lalor and the other Eureka defendants. The child was Ned Kelly, said to be a cousin of the American Wild West hero, Buffalo Bill Cody, and undoubtedly the first boy child born to John Kelly, an ex-convict from Tipperary, and Ellen Quinn, daughter of Catholic emigrants from Antrim. In his short life, Ned Kelly came to embody practically all the characteristics of Irish rebelliousness one can think of: he was courageous, a doomed hero to the Irish, a murderous bush-ranger to the authorities, and he robbed banks and gave money to the needy. One biographer, Ian Jones, to whose work I am heavily indebted,has described him as a combination of Dick Turpin and Robin Hood.

In fact, he was more like one of the Irish 'Raparees' of old: Catholic gentry dispossessed of their land, who had turned to crime and highway robbery, surviving because of close-knit clan loyalties and a shared antipathy to the authorities. By the time Kelly was captured, fighting against enormous odds at Glenrowan in 1880, his mythological status was underpinned not only by his courage, but by the two forces which have traditionally borne up, and borne down, the Irish – land and the police. To the poorer Catholic Irish, the police occupied the position they had always held in popular imagination back in Ireland, they were the oppressors. In Kelly's case, this stereotype was vindicated by the harassments and provocations which the police visited on him and his widowed mother, even to the extent of stealing a horse belonging to him while he was in jail.

The land situation is more complex. A Land Act brought in by the Irish-born Premier of Victoria, Charles Gavin Duffy, was intended to give the smallholders, 'the selectors', both security of tenure and prosperity. In practice however, a combination of factors ensured that the Act had the opposite effect to that intended. Often the Irish emigrants did not select their plots of land wisely, and crops either failed to grow or succumbed to drought. Gradually the bigger land owners, 'the squatocracy', who laid their economic foundations by simply seizing crown land and squatting on it, took over the smaller holdings. Duffy was hurled from office and the Kellys, the Quinns, and several more like them, found themselves condemned to a life of hardship, insecurity, and police harassment.

Against the background of Irish experience, both in Ireland and Australia, these pressures helped to turn Kelly to a life of crime. Inevitably guns went off, police were killed and Kelly and his gang went on the run to become the greatest of the Australian bush-rangers. However, he was not simply a bush-ranger. Apart from the fact that he took care to ensure that he and his comrades acted with courtesy to those they robbed, he toyed with notions of republicanism and gave his activities a patina of ideology. His appeal was such that, although the inevitable Irish informers were present in his saga, he was nevertheless able to sustain himself safely, in the Irish saying, 'on his keeping', that is, on the run, despite the fact that there was a reward on his head which in contemporary terms would be worth 2 million Australian dollars. He was held in such awe that with a gang totalling only four men, he could take over whole towns for a period of days, enabling him to rob banks at his leisure.

Part of his appeal lay in his appearance – he was a man of considerable physical beauty, a great boxer and horseman – and part in the way in which he faced his foes, clad in armour fashioned from plough shares, in the last fatal shoot out. To this day a prized Australian compliment is to be judged 'as game as Ned Kelly'. Part also lay in the extraordinary circumstances surrounding his sentencing and death. Kelly told the judge, Redmond Barry, that he would see him where he was going, and Barry duly died a few days after Kelly's execution. On the threshold of eternity Kelly showed no fear, and said as the rope was fastened around his neck: 'Such is life.'

Overriding these factors, or interlarding with them, is the manner in which Kelly encapsulated Irish resentments. It is said that had his last foray at Glenrowan succeeded, he would have declared a republic. However, a police-carrying train which he hoped to derail was alerted, and thus avoided an ambush which he had laid at Glenrowan. After the failure of the ambush, he would not allow the bulk of his followers to engage the well-armed police, taking them on himself with only three companions in a hopeless stand.

His republican sentiments and the reasoning which led to them were contained in his *apologia pro vita sua,* the so-called Jerildie letter. He had intended the letter to be published in Jerildie's local newspaper, but the editor took flight on his arrival in the town, and a bank clerk to whom he entrusted the document turned it over to the authorities. Kelly's influence was so feared by the authorities that they suppressed publication for decades. The letter castigated the policeman as:

> A traitor to his country, ancestors and religion, as they are all Catholics before the Saxons and Cranmore Yoke held sway. Since then they were persecuted, massacred, thrown into martyrdom, and tortured beyond the ideas of the present generation.

The police force, said Kelly, was composed of: 'big, ugly, fat-necked, wombat-headed, big-bellied, magpie-legged, narrow-hipped, splay-footed sons of Irish bailiffs or English landlords . . .'

This is straight out of the tradition of Irish poetic invective in which the bard castigates his enemies or those of his patron in a stinging hail of hurtful adjectives. Not for nothing did Irish rulers of old fear the poet's wrath. The letter went on to give angry expression to the torments suffered by the Irish in the prison settlements at the hands of the floggers, the hangers and their hirelings:

> What would people say if they saw a strapping big lump of an Irishman shepherding sheep for fifteen bob a week or tailing turkeys in Tallarook ranges for a smile from Julia, or even begging his tucker? They would say he ought to be ashamed of himself and tar and feather him. But he would be a king to a policeman who for a lazy loafing cowardly bilit left the ash corner, deserted the shamrock, the emblem of true wit and beauty to serve under a flag and nation that has destroyed massacred and murdered their forefathers by the greatest of tortures as rolling them down a hill in spiked barrels pulling their toe and finger nails and on the wheel and every torture imaginable.
>
> More was transported to Van Diemens Land to pine their young lives away in starvation and misery among tyrants worse than the promised hell itself. All of true blood, bone and beauty, not murdered on their own soil, or had fled to America or other countries to bloom again another day were doomed to Port McQuarie, Toweringabbie, Norfolk Island, or Emu plains, and in those places of tyranny and condemnation many a blooming Irishman rather than subdue to the Saxon yoke were flogged to death and bravely died in servile chains but true to the shamrock and a credit to Paddy Land.

Kelly was so feared that his body was mutilated, his head removed and the skull used as an ashtray by a Government official. Relations who sought to make money by putting on a play about his life and death were prosecuted, and the Jerildie letter was suppressed until the 1950s when it was reproduced by Max Brown in his book, *Australia's Sons.* Since then it has entered the soul of Australia and the consciousness of its Irish population.

A PSYCHOLOGICAL PROFILE

Though belaboured by their bishops, and bedevilled by prejudice on grounds of both race and religion, the Irish nevertheless continued to come to Australia and to grow in both prosperity and political strength as the white man extended his boundaries across Australia. The ships first dropped emigrants off in New South Wales, around Sydney, then further north, at points like Brisbane, along the coast of what became Queensland, or in the west, at Fremantle, in what today is Perth. By the end of the century the Irish presence in Australia could be calculated as follows:

Irish Born in Australia, 1891

Colony	Irish %
New South Wales	26.3
Victoria	26.5
Queensland	26.1
South Australia	18.5
Western Australia (1901)	21.0
Tasmania	20.0

The centenary of the 1798 Rebellion was marked by the Irish community in every part of Australia in a manner which illustrated both the hold exerted on popular imagination by the Irish Revolutionary prisoners, and the community's growth in economic and political strength. Michael Dwyer's remains were re-interred in Waverly Cemetery, Sydney, under a huge Celtic cross. The ceremony drew enormous crowds and the Waverly memorial subsequently became one of the principal Australian shrines of Irish nationalism. The names of the executed 1916 leaders and, later, those of the ten IRA hunger strikers who died in Long Kesh prison in 1981 were emblazoned in marble at the base of the cross.

Did the foregoing history have an effect on the character and identity of Irish Australians? Psychologically and politically two people unusually well placed to answer that question are Anne Cross O'Brien,[39] a psychotherapist, and Paul Keating, the former Australian Prime Minister. Cross O'Brien's experience in dealing with Irish clients, in particular those who had emigrated to Australia from the 1960s onwards, led her to form a set of conclusions as to how history had left its deposits in contemporary psyches. She took as her starting point the fact that Ireland itself had been occupied by the British for some 800 years and that this period 'as an unreconciled subject people' had radically influenced every aspect of Irish life. As Peter Overlack observed, in an essay comparing Irish and German political romanticism:

The effects of invasion and occupation are parallel themes in German and Irish history. Although the Napoleonic domination of Germany lasted little more than a decade, its effects on intellectual and political development were extraordinarily far-reaching. It was only under the repression of occupation that national consciousness first developed in Germany. The 1813 War of Liberation, which led to Napoleon's defeat, overshadowed the failed revolution of 1848 and even the later Prussian unification of Germany in 1871, and symbolised the unfulfilled promise of a real unity forged in the crucible war against the invader.[40]

Mighty outcomes indeed for a mere ten-year period, so what detritus must 800 years have left behind? Cross O'Brien accepts that a combination of a 'crippling colonial past' and 'the additional phenomenon of Irish emigration' has created a sense in people she has dealt with of being 'perpetual' emigrants, never completely present, or at home, in the here and now. Amongst Irish clients she discovered 'an acute sense of powerlessness' in which Irish people 'consistently under-estimate their own initiatory and decisive capacities'. She sketches a composite client portrait which would probably include the following:

1. Avoidance of overt conflict
2. Problems, for men in particular, with authority figures
3. Difficulties in acknowledging and expressing painful feelings
4. Difficulties with intimacy
5. Unresolved effects of separation

While some of these points, particularly the avoidance of overt conflict, might at first strike an observer as strange, particularly given the history of conflict with authority in Ireland, the composite portrait, to my eyes at least, is recognisable. The state known to analysis as 'cumulative trauma' can sometimes result in the sort of profile Anne Cross O'Brien draws. It is, of course, one not unique to the Irish. Many emigrants would show some or all of the same characteristics, but the Cross O'Brien model certainly contains the kind of symptoms one would expect to find in a displaced people who came from a society which for centuries was based on the exclusion of the many for the benefit of the few.

On the issue of the effect of the second colonialism, Dr O'Brien said of the Church: 'Its influence was, in many ways, positive. The Church, amid misery, was almost the only institution which confirmed the identity of the Catholic Irish, and in a very real sense assured them of their worth.' However, she then goes on to say:

But the Church's influence was also negative, and heavily so. I give three reasons:

1. Irish Catholicism after the Famine adopted a rigid, Roman, highly authoritarian form
2. Its local representatives, the parish priests, being as they were the only local leaders with much education, enjoyed a disproportionate power

459

3. For reasons too complex to detail, Irish seminary training was much imbued with French Jansenism, with its fostering of abnormal guilt, and its consequent dependence on external guidelines

Jansenism has already been described, but it might be remarked here that the particular gloss imparted by Maynooth was two-fold. One was a particularly censorious, holier-than-thou attitude; the second a Tartuffe-like justification for the practitioner's actions by virtue of he or she having a special devotion for, and insight into, the mind of God. This aspect of Jansenism was highlighted by the revelation of several notable cases of contemporary Irish Church figures secretly maintaining mistresses, and fathering children on them, while at the same time publicly upholding such Catholic virtues as the sanctity of marriage and opposition to contraception and abortion. At all events Jansen's shadow came to hang over Australian Irish Catholicism as markedly as did that of Cardinal Cullen. Dr Cross O'Brien wound up her assessment by saying:

> The dysfunctional behaviour of some people of Irish background is linked to the traumatic past of their nation. Under a brutal and prolonged colonial tyranny, the Irish were, in fact, almost powerless. This generated an internal state, a psychological attitude of dependency, an undervaluation of self which lived on even when the historical circumstances changed. Both through the conscious process of inheriting attitudes, customs, and institutions, and by unconscious transmission through the process of 'cumulative trauma', the patterns of the past live on in the present.

At the end of her summary the therapist expressed the opinion that, just as contemporary Ireland has emerged from its awful past, with a triumphant burst of achievement on the economic and artistic fronts, so too would emigrants emerge from the thraldom of the past. That this transformation is occurring, and likely to continue to do so is immediately demonstrable.

A POLITICAL PROFILE

Thus Australia benefited the Irish – but how did the Irish benefit Australia? The former Australian Prime Minister, Paul Keating, is better placed than most to answer that question. He came to embody both the image of the Irish in Australian politics and the controversy surrounding the idea of Australia becoming a republic.

His move towards a republic was depicted as part of an ancestral Irish anti-British sentiment, and he became a lightning rod for pro-British monarchist sentiment, a figure who stirred some of the strongest emotions met with in Australia since the days of the great Labour Party split (for an account of his personal impact see the facing page).

Keating lost power to a coalition of the Liberal and National Parties in the 1996 Federal election, in which there was a devastating five percentage points swing against Labour. For some time after, his successor as leader of the Australian Labour Party, Kim Beazley, sedulously avoided Keating policies, as he tried to heal the factionalism created in the party in the Keating years. However, as the November 1999 referendum on the republic neared, Keating's international vision of politics began to regain favour. As Australia shifted its gaze from England towards 'big picture' policies such as nuclear disarmament and increasing links with Asia, his legacy appeared in a more favourable light, despite some controversies over business dealings and his relationship with President Suharto of Indonesia.

At the time of writing there was very considerable controversy and uncertainty about the outcome of the referendum. The Constitutional Convention, set up in February 1998 to decide on the wording of the referendum and the method of electing a president, decided that this should be done without a popular vote. It was envisaged that the President would be chosen by the Prime Minister from a committee-chosen short list, and then decided on by a two-thirds majority vote in Parliament. This decision divided republicans, as its advocate, the monarchist Prime Minister John Howard, intended it should. Many felt that the Presidency would in fact become either a hack political appointment, or else concentrate too much power in the hands of the incumbent, along the American model. In the event the referendum, held in November 1999, was defeated and the link with the monarchy remained. This did not betoken residual monarchist strength so much as the fact that some republicans voted with monarchists in their strongholds of Queensland, Tasmania and Western Australia – to defeat the referendum proposals temporarily, for most commentators agree that the republican tide cannot be kept out indefinitely.

Paul Kelly, a former editor of *The Australian* newspaper, and a respected author of a number of books about Australia, has summed up Keating's contribution to the republican debate as follows:

> The republican issue will not go away. Paul Keating has put it on the agenda and it will stay on the agenda until the issue is resolved. When Mr Keating met the Queen at Balmoral, he entered that meeting as the first Australian Prime Minister formally committed to the republic and to advancing the cause of the republic. He briefed the Queen on his intentions and his plans. For the first time the head of state was put on notice by an Australian Prime Minister. That meeting was a milestone in our evolution towards the republic.[41]

The nearest Australia came to producing an American-style Celtic Boss was in the person of tall, slim, elegant, Paul Keating, the most impressive man I met in the southern hemisphere. Talking to him privately about a range of topics – Ireland and its impact on Australia, music, French culture, his love of China and of the Napoleonic era – one had to make something of a leap of the imagination to visualise him as one of the most feared parliamentary brawlers in Australian history. Occasionally he assisted the leap: a flash of fire would enter the eyes as he described a performance at the despatch box. This was the arena in which Keating so often employed his own formula for displaying what he defined as: 'The most important qualities of leadership: memory and imagination, both deployed in the broadest sense.'[42] Keating found these two qualities invaluable in answering parliamentary questions: 'In the Australian system you don't get notice of questions. You have to think on your feet, and try and read from your notes at the same time while some bastard is needling you. You got to be able to put them down, so you got to be able to break his back and keep the cool, hold on to your train of thought at the same time.'

What the broken-backed bastard would not realise was that after giving a terrifying performance in the chamber, Prime Minister Keating, the Brawler, would normally sit for hours in his office drinking innumerable cups of tea, listening to Mahler recordings as his drained physical and psychic batteries were recharged. Keating's musings on the Irish in Australia included the following:

> The contribution of the Irish to Australia was to bring a sense of history, culture and sentiment as devices of enlightenment, imagination and belief. A sense of belonging and where they had come from, and a belief in a celebratory quality of the human condition, while at the same time being passionate about the disadvantaged. You'll find that the same guy who will find joy in ambition, enlargement and the triumph of humanity will have a militant commitment to the disadvantaged. The measure of discrimination and of the tolerant was with the Irish. They are the enlargers and the strengtheners of imagination and memory. The Irish have a sense of enlargement. We push the boundaries out. Every so often the enlargers have everything turned over to them because the corporate imperialist does not have much inner life.
>
> The Irish are one of the reasons why there is less snobbery here, why we go in for the pricking of balloons. The Protestant ethic is to know your place, the Irish: 'We'll do better.' They have an irrepressible optimism.

Keating reckons that the Church in Australia 'lost most of its constituency', because it was authoritarian, didn't listen, and was bowled over by the bricks-and-mortar syndrome of measuring success by the 'house on the hill'. In this Keating was unconsciously mirroring a frequently met with judgement in Ireland. Just when the Church succeeded in populating the hills and vantage points of Ireland with spires, the people began cutting off the flow of students to provide the priests to say mass in these lofty churches. Keating rated the Church's contribution, and particularly the Irish component of it to Australia, as being:

> Something genetic, humanist in a paradoxical way, because it was also very Catholic. One discovers as one learns that one has all the sentiments of this heritage without being aware of it. It's when you get the sociological and historical being brought together that you understand the importance of this lineage. One has a cultural affinity with prestige. You want to belong. Your pattern fits. You grow into the role. You adopt values, or rather reactivate them. Then an awareness of mortality comes, and you realise that it is only what goes to the heart and the soul that is worth doing, that informs your political life.

Politics and Keating found each other at an early age. In 1959, at the age of fifteen, he was working for the Australian Electrical Authority. On his first day someone remarked to him, 'You're the one who was dragged up in a Catholic School?' He explained:

> In those days the main stations were run by Catholics and the sub-stations by Masons. The sectarian conflict was still visible in the job ads. In the *Sydney Morning Herald* these warned: 'Catholics need not apply'. That kind of thing was weakening in the sixties but it was still subterranean. The Irish and the Catholics were battlers.[43] That's why they did so well. They ran the Taxation Office from the forties onwards. They got in to the law. They were good at that kind of thing. Whereas the cops were still Presbyterian and Mason. This of course perpetuated the 'them and us' syndrome, the British/Irish tension. It meant inevitably that the agents of the Crown, 'the Poms' or British descendants, were arresting and locking up the Irish and Catholics, when need arose, just as they had been doing back in Ireland for centuries. Then of course they got into politics. Their values really created the Labour Party. The Irish were never in big numbers in banking, for example, until now. So you see, everything brings you back to genetics. History sucks you in.

Keating has a classical Irish and Catholic fatalism: 'We all come and go the same way. A notion that one is inherently superior is inherently and intellectually unsound.' He uses words like 'love' and 'beautiful' unabashedly. He is obviously moved by beauty, in architecture, music, paintings, women. Keating's feeling for the abstract, for beauty, and the same combination of iron-clad discipline with which the Irish blended aestheticism with *realpolitik* to produce the traditions of American machine politics and the monasticism which produced the Book of Kells, is summed up in Keating's advocacy of the republic: 'I tell people that they'll only understand its worth when they have it.'

THOMAS KENEALLY

Another famous Irish Australian who came just below Keating on the monarchists' hate list because of his energetic espousal of the republic is Thomas Keneally, the novelist. The author of *Schindler's Ark* (filmed as *Schindler's List*) wears his international laurels lightly. I took a ferry trip across Sydney Harbour to visit his magnificent hilltop home overlooking the bay, to find a man with whom I had a swim and could have just as easily adjourned to the bar of my local rugby club.[44] Keneally would talk literature if called on to do so but, in a classical Irish way, seemed more enthused by the prowess of his local rugby league team than by his own achievements. The pictures of Hollywood triumphs could be produced on demand, but the ones on display were of him in a Manly jersey with the lads from the dressing room, sinking beers after a recent triumph.

Keneally's attitude reminded me of two other famous Irishmen's description of the importance of the local. One was the former US Senate Majority Leader, Tip O'Neill, who said: 'All politics are local.' The other was the poet, Patrick Kavanagh, who said: 'Out of such a local row, was the Iliad made.' We discussed his book *The Great Shame*, which itself dealt with the diaspora. It centred on the Young Irelanders (chiefly Meagher, O'Brien and Mitchel) and Hugh Larkin, a transportee from whom Keneally's wife, and two daughters are descended. The world launch of the book occurred in the Irish Embassy in Canberra (November 1998). Keneally said afterwards that it was: 'the best book launch of my career – Richard O'Brien knows how to throw a party'. *D'accord!*

Keneally's Irishness could certainly be defined in terms of the enlargement of the memory. It is memory and its 'devices' which clearly inform him. He visits Ireland frequently and is concerned about the Peace Process, but he is obviously concerned with 'enlargement'. His republicanism is an abstract thing, unconcerned with any anti-British quotient, it is simply that this is the best thing for Australia. A product of the Christian Brothers, he felt the paedophile scandals which were affecting the Brothers in Australia, as in every other country I visited, were 'a deep wound on the Irish consciousness'. His old school had a reunion during my visit, but he refused to attend, saying:

> This is no time for a celebratory dinner, congratulatory speeches and so on. That is not to say that the brothers have not made an enormous contribution to the Irish and to Australia. In many ways it was they who shaped today's popular culture. But it's a time for reflecting and putting things right, not celebrating.

THE SPLIT

In the process of reflection indicated by Keneally one has to take into account not merely the impact of the Christian Brothers but that of the Church itself and that other great Irish institution, the Split. The manner in which the former dealt with the latter is exemplified in the contrasting approaches to the challenges of Australian life by two famous Irish Australian princes of the Church, James Duhig and Daniel Mannix. Both were involved in a controversy which exploded in the 1950s, leaving a lasting imprint on political life generally, the Irish community in particular, and *inter alia,* the Church itself.

One of the more popular plays in the latter part of twentieth-century Australia was the farce *The Feet of Daniel Mannix*, put on in the Archbishop's very own Melbourne in 1971. The playwright, Barry Oakley, explained why he chose Mannix as a subject:

> Because he is a central figure, not just of Catholicism, but of Australia itself. For too long he dominated the antipodean scene in a way that was bad for him and bad for Australia. He's the father figure of Irish-Australia and the embodiment of all that's good and bad in that combination, authoritarian – yet an incorrigible meddler in politics. I grew up in that stimulating, monolithic, controversial atmosphere, and the play is an attempt to slough it off, and shed a skin through the convention of comedy.

JAMES DUHIG

Archbishop James Duhig was as important to Irish Australian development and to the Church as Mannix, but he chose a different way of accomplishing his goals from the confrontational Corkman. Duhig (1871–1965), like Mannix, was born in Ireland, in Broadfort, County Limerick, but as his parents emigrated while he was a small boy, he grew up in Australia, and throughout his life sought to play down the divisions aroused by the state of Ireland and the continuing relationship with England. By the time he died, Duhig had become the doyen not only of the Australian Church, but of the world body. He was Australia's senior Archbishop and the world's senior prelate. His doctor, Harry Windsor, forbade him to go to the Vatican Council to take up his honoured place there at the age of ninety-two. A quarrel ensued, the doctor took his leave and Duhig was found sitting in his armchair, exclaiming, 'Poor Windsor! I wonder who will look after me when he is gone.' That sense of humour carried him through the storm stirred up by issues such as conscription, the education issue and the simmering sectarianism which frequently lay close to the surface of Australian life.

One of his notable points of divergence, demanding all his humour and legendary diplomacy, was from Mannix's idolatry of de Valera. Duhig's view was very different. In 1922, he condemned de Valera outrightly saying: 'People say that pride and madness have taken possession of him.'[45] Whereas Mannix welcomed two republican emissaries who came to Australia on behalf of de Valera in 1923 – Father Michael O'Flanagan and J. J. O'Kelly, pen-named Sceilig, the editor of the *Catholic Bulletin* – Duhig denounced them in a statement which summed up all the bitterness and dissension caused in Australia by the Irish Civil War:

> Our people will be divided, dissensions will be caused among friends, bitter things will be said about England, and the old fight – Protestant against Catholic – will be renewed with grave damage to the cause of religion. As far as we here in Queensland are concerned, and I speak particularly for this Archdiocese, there was never a better feeling between all sections of the people than there is at present. That being so, I am not going to jeopardise the peace and harmony by submitting to the advent into Queensland of so undesirable a delegation as that which made its first public appearance in Melbourne on St Patrick's Day.

Duhig was one of the world's greatest bricks-and-mortar men. His biographer said of him that:

> In a series of raids on the hills and river cliffs of Brisbane, from August 1917 to August 1918, he bought large estates in Toowong, Coorparoo, Ashgrove and Dutton Park. Most of these ran to hectares of ground and many carried substantial mansions, the nuclei of the great schools he saw built on them . . . Duhig had entered on a lifetime of scanning the mail for cheques, like a drought-stricken farmer searching the skies for rain. He was constantly whistling up the wind and praying for a storm. At times, his manoeuvrings looked like the dance of a rain maker.[46]

In his own way Duhig could be autocratic and the foregoing quotations make it clear that his accounting practices would not find favour in contemporary times, but he did stand for unity rather than division. He accepted a knighthood as a mark of integration with both British and Australian society. The acceptance of the knighthood was not welcomed by Mannix. His response on hearing of it was to enquire sweetly of his informant: 'And how is Lady Duhig?'

Duhig did not go so far as to accept an invitation to be present at a service to be attended by the Queen in the Anglican Cathedral of St John's. In his reply he stated that he did not wish to 'intrude when the Queen's own Church people were doing her honour'. However, he pursued the cause of Church unity in a very public way:

> Brisbane saw the meaning of unity in the friendship of the two archbishops, Sir James Duhig and Sir Reginald Halse. They were growing old together, and the city became accustomed to seeing the two faces side by side – dignified, kindly, fraternal.[47]

Decoded, that passage may be taken as inferring that as Brisbane was to unity so was Melbourne to disunity – in the person of Daniel Mannix. The story of the split has its roots in Ireland as much as in Australia and, like the divisions over the Civil War, had severe repercussions within the Irish community.

DANIEL MANNIX

Daniel Mannix, was born on 4 March 1854 – appropriately enough, the year of the Syllabus of Errors – at Charleville, County Cork. He entered the Church under the tutelage of his 'domineering mother'.[48] He became a controversial president of Maynooth Seminary where he imposed a combination of strict discipline and an element of refinement. He introduced an etiquette manual, removed books on the index from the college library, and from the student body those who committed infractions of discipline such as smoking. Ironically, he also became embroiled in controversy over the Union Jack emblazoned welcomes which he extended to both King Edward VII and King George V when they visited Maynooth in 1903 and 1911 respectively.

Ironically too, it was his opposition to the compulsory teaching of Irish and the dismissal of the Irish teacher, Professor Michael Hickey, from Maynooth that led to Mannix being translated from the presidency of Maynooth to the see of Melbourne. He was so heavy-handed in his opposition to Hickey's supporters that he sent down six students for the priesthood not long before their ordination. In those days Mother Church could afford to be profligate with her human resources. Vocations poured into Irish seminaries, for reasons not dissimilar to those for which they now fill African religious institutes: the priesthood offers education, status and a degree of security. Mannix had all these when he arrived in Melbourne on Easter Sunday 1913. A tall, striking figure, Mannix, in his early years in Melbourne, laid the foundations of the

1950s explosion. He campaigned for state aid for Church schools, which was one of the great objectives of the Australian Church. In so doing, he had no hesitation in alluding to such things as Cromwell's depredations in Ireland and the fact that in Australia Irish Catholic convicts had been flogged for not attending Anglican services.

Those were the days when Irish Catholics sought education for their children, joined unions and voted Labour as the basic handrails of advancement. Of significance to what happened later was the fact that in those early years in Australia, Mannix, like Moran before him, encouraged Catholics to infiltrate the Labour Party and to use balance of power tactics in achieving his ends. These were also the years of particular conflict over mixed marriages. The code of Canon Law was revised in 1917 to read as follows:

> Canon 1061. The Church does not dispense from the impediment of mixed religion unless (1) There are just and grave reasons therefore. (2) The non-Catholic party shall have given a guarantee to remove all danger of perversion from the Catholic party, and both parties shall have given guarantees to baptise and educate all the children in the Catholic faith; (3) There exists moral certainty that the guarantee to be fulfilled ... the guarantees as a rule to be required in writing ...[49]

This, as can be imagined, led to a good deal of sectarian tension, as did Mannix's other activities. He became identified with the anti-conscription campaign, and when Catholics were alleged (wrongly) not to be doing their share, he replied, 'Apparently not enough nuns are joining.' The 1916 revolution seems to have been the final bridge between his royalty-welcoming days at Maynooth and the marked anti-British sentiment of the rest of his life. Even New Zealand felt the shock waves to such an extent that another Irish bishop, James Liston, as we shall see, wound up in the dock facing a charge of sedition, in part because New Zealand's Protestant establishment wanted it made clear that: 'Mannix outbursts will not be tolerated in New Zealand.'[50]

One of the most famous 'outbursts' was his statement: 'Australia first. The Empire second.' This struck a vein of approval in Irish and nationalist circles and one of execration amongst empire loyalists. Mannix's stance on conscription led to mass demonstrations in favour of his deportation. He particularly enraged extreme Protestant loyalist opinion during the 1918 St Patrick's Day parade: as the band played 'God Save the King' he kept his biretta firmly on his head, but when a float passed recalling the men of 1916 he uncovered. He became a folk hero to the Irish despite the fact that the rise in sectarian temperature resulted in Catholics being denied jobs and lodgings. In his hearers he awoke deep resonances of the days of the floggers and the Fenians and all that lay around them. By 1920, Mannix had become 'arguably the most revered and reviled figure in Australian history'.

In that year, the controversial Catholic businessman John Wren paid for a demonstration in favour of Mannix's position by arranging that fourteen Irish Victoria Cross winners led the St Patrick's Day parade mounted on white chargers. Wren also organised a £50,000 testimonial, which the aesthetic Mannix turned down as he did all personal gifts, and was also behind a huge demonstration on Mannix's departure to Rome for his *ad liminia* visit the following May. The friendship of Wren was to prove a double-edged sword for Mannix when a novel by the communist Frank Hardy appeared, giving not only a thinly veiled, unflattering portrait of Mannix but an even more unflattering account of Wren's dubious business ventures. Mannix's *ad liminia* route to Rome was to have lain via the USA and then Ireland. However, his pro-Irish speeches during the American leg of his journey ensured that he did not achieve the second part. As his liner neared Ireland in August 1920, at the height of the Black and Tan War, a British warship took him off and landed him in Cornwall instead of Cobh. It was, he said, the greatest British naval victory since the Battle of Jutland.

Before Mannix arrived, a number of other Irish bishops from America and Australia, most notably Archbishop Joseph Clune of Perth, had been giving the Vatican the benefit of their insights into what was happening in Ireland. As a result, Mannix received not the papal condemnation he expected, but a furtherance of his policy. The Pope, at his urging, donated some 20,000 lire to Irish relief, and later published a letter of sympathy for the Irish which Mannix had drafted.

The Civil War affected Mannix as it did most other Irishmen of the time. He found himself the only internationally acclaimed bishop who supported de Valera with whom, in America, he had commenced a lifelong friendship. When he visited Ireland in 1925, he was boycotted by the Irish hierarchy with the exception of the Bishop of Cloyne, Dr Michael Browne, who had been Vice-President of Maynooth when Mannix was President. Browne had opposed Mannix over his pro de Valera stance in the Civil War, and only came to see Mannix late in the evening, with the greeting: 'So you've come too, like Nicodemus.' After that visit, Mannix told some of his clergy: 'I will never give my country a second opportunity to insult me.'[51]

An erect six-footer who, amongst other nicknames, was termed a 'consecrated ramrod', Mannix kept fit by walking every day three miles from his residence Raheen to the cathedral. Along the way, he dispensed alms to everyone who accosted him. Once when he gave money to a man who was obviously drunk, saying, 'Don't spend it at the next hotel', the beggar replied, 'Which hotel would you advise, your Grace?'

Mannix had a life-long interest in the lay organisation Catholic Action and supported Catholic journals such as the *Catholic Worker* and some Catholic radio programmes. He made a sizeable contribution to the Australian Church. In fifty years he built some 240 churches and an array of hospitals, seminaries, orphanages and charitable homes of all kinds. Catholic numbers in his diocese went up from 150,000 to 600,000 with a consequential increase in nuns, brothers and priests.

THE MOVEMENT

It was Catholic Action which led to the interaction of the career of this towering figure with that of one of the most extraordinary men produced by Australia, B. A. Santamaria. Santamaria, a lawyer by training, entered on the Australian intellectual/political stage during his student days in 1931 when, at the age of sixteen, he joined the Melbourne Campion Society. The society was founded by an Irish Australian lawyer, Frank Maher, who chose the name Campion, after the English Jesuit martyr, Edmund Campion, 'to denote a break from the Irish monopoly over Australian Catholic life'.[52] The Campionists read Belloc, Chesterton, Maritain, and were influenced by the example of the young Christian Workers Society which had been founded in Belgium some years earlier to bring Christianity into the work place. Santamaria thus became more like a European intellectual than a bright Australian Catholic. In 1935 he wrote *Orders of the Day* which, if one brackets Communism alongside Protestantism under the 'heresy' label in 2 below, fairly well describes his action plan for the rest of his life:

1. To co-ordinate Catholic action through the Commonwealth
2. To hammer Catholicism into an impenetrable fortress on which heresy will shatter itself
3. To mould the 1.5 million Catholics of Australia into an organic unity ready to resume the Catholic offensive

It was not so much Santamaria's objectives as his methods which led to controversy. Basically his strategy depended on gaining an ascendancy over Mannix, and on building up what was in effect a powerful Catholic Secret Society. He succeeded so well that a leading Catholic intellectual and former Santamaria supporter has written: 'Due to the sponsorship of Mannix Santamaria became a quasi or substitute bishop . . . In Victoria in the 1950s and 1960s Bob Santamaria had the aura of a lay bishop.'

Campion judged him the 'most famous Catholic layman in Australian history, except for Ned Kelly'.[53] Santamaria acquired this status largely because of his success in combating Communist influence on the trade unions. Santamaria could write with accuracy: 'We have a National Organisation which is as strongly disciplined as the Communist Party, which possesses the loyalty of its members, and which has succeeded in capturing the imagination of those that participate in it.' As a distinguished Australian historian and Jesuit, appropriately enough another Edmund Campion, has written:

> This was not an inflated assertion, for by September 1945 there were some 300,000 active members of the organisation who would already point to noticeable victories against their Communist opponents. They were organised in parish booths – 72 in Sydney, 52 in Melbourne, 12 in Newcastle with an inter-locking network of factory groups and union groups.[54]

He also pointed out that these members were incredibly dedicated and hard-working.

The Communist threat to Australia appeared a reality and the zealotry and energy of their fundamentalist drive had a mushrooming effect on the Catholic Social Studies Movement, or the Movement as Santamaria's organisation came to be known after its 1945 breakthrough, when the Australian hierarchy, steered by Mannix, who had already given Santamaria some funding, agreed to provide the Movement with a budget of £10,000 a year. Once the bishops gave the Movement a *de jure* and financial status, practically speaking, *de facto* control passed into Santamaria's hands.

Amongst the corps of enthusiastic helpers few would have been more enthusiastic than my two clerical uncles Martin and Timothy Toal. Aboard the liner which first took them to Australia in the late twenties an incident occurred which speaks volumes for both their formation as priests and their own basic simplicity. They were accompanied on the liner by their future bishop, an old man of whom they were greatly in awe. They had been ordained in Genoa, and seen little of the world, apart from an Italian seminary and what they glimpsed from their home in Ireland before answering the call to save souls on the other side of the globe. The voyage was the first time they had ever been in such close proximity to a liner, never mind an Olympian figure like a bishop.

Much to their astonishment the bishop turned out to be a very down-to-earth figure. As they took their late night walk on the deck one evening, after a good dinner, the old man told them about difficulties he was having with another member of the hierarchy. By way of illustrating these he remarked vehemently: 'I don't mind him shoving the umbrella up my arse – but pulling it down open is tearing it altogether!' The shock and wonderment, both on their part and that of my mother's family, at the fact of a bishop being capable of making so human an observation tells us much about the nature of the people and their time. The amazing statement was carefully written down, and included in the first of the letters that arrived dutifully at fortnightly intervals thereafter. Once that letter arrived in Ireland, the bishop's remark entered into the family folklore to be passed on to myself, my brother and sister when we were judged old enough to hear such a thing.

At different times I heard my uncles mention Bob Santamaria and Dan Mannix in terms of respect and affection, but I never fully realised what they were talking about until after they were dead. My uncles were two very different types of men. Martin was a theoretician and a theologian and Santamaria recalled him with obvious regard, when we met in Melbourne.[55] Tim, who stood six-foot three in his socks, and could have been a rugby international had not the Irish Church frowned on the thought of its young men engaging in such activities, was a parish priest in the iron-mining district of Whyalla, South Australia. A kindly man who, with the assistance of Uncle Martin, supported my mother after my father died, leaving her with three young children, Tim used to chortle when he recalled victories over 'the Comms' which he and his co-workers had engineered in the union movement.

However, he never associated these with Bob Santamaria, whom he regarded simply as an admired Catholic activist, speaker and writer. Uncle Tim and many like him were acting against Communism because of what Communists were doing in the world, and, before their eyes, in the Australian Unions. He had built churches and schools, supported hospitals, and by God no Commies were going to take them over or shut them down; and of course, above all, he was doing the Bishop's bidding. The attitude of Father Brosnan in unquestioningly accepting his prison chaplaincy because Mannix knew best was the attitude which prevailed in the Australian Church.

Activities at Whyalla were a microcosm of what happened across Australia. Priests like Uncle Tim gave hands-on encouragement and parish leadership. In other places men of the calibre of Uncle Martin wrote articles and pamphlets, gave talks and preached sermons. The Movement used the tactics of the Communist Party, secrecy, 'the enemy surrounding us', to achieve loyalty, and they didn't hesitate to draw the long bow.

Paul Ormond tells how an uncle of his, like my Uncle Tim a parish priest in South Australia, received an instruction to prepare for the visit of a well-known Jesuit, Harold Lalor, who had been relieved of normal priestly duties to devote himself to Movement work. Father Ormond described to his nephew how Lalor went to work, in classical Movement fashion: 'The meeting was held in the atmosphere of a conspiratorial gathering rather than the gathering of the saviours of the commonweal.' His letter went on:

> The secrecy at this distance seemed so ridiculous, Fr. Lalor's thesis was the danger of imminent takeover of Australia by the Communists. He had possession of the plans and he was aware of the location of Communist arsenals, machine guns and ammunition. The immediate aim of the meeting was to raise finance for the Movement. These poor sheep cockies [country farmers], whose fear was not the loss of faith but the loss of farms and fleeces, took out their cheque books and gave the Movement £800. A neighbouring parish, where a similar meeting was held, raised £1,300.[56]

The lurid 'arsenals' claims were repeated all over Australia, but these happenings were kept from the public at large by the invocation of the Church's power. Ormond's uncle described how Lalor operated:

> Fr. Lalor knew I was not a supporter of the Movement and he was very embarrassed by my presence. He began his lecture by saying that all he was going to say was a 'committed secret', that is, to repeat anything he said would be a mortal sin – it meant nothing to the sheep farmers present, and was obviously intended only for me, presumably I have committed a mortal sin by telling you.

SANTAMARIA'S VISION

The Movement, which was really a portmanteau title for a host of Santamaria-founded organisations, certainly played a large part in checking

471

the growth of Communism in the unions. So, too, did a publicly acknowledged movement, the 'Groupers', which also began in 1945, but within the ranks of Labour not the Church. The Australian Labour Party Conference held in New South Wales voted to set up groups who would challenge the Communists within the union movement by supporting ALP candidates in union elections. The groups proved highly successful, not least because they were heavily infiltrated by the Movement.

However, as the Movement expanded so did Santamaria's vision of what it might achieve. He had goals far beyond the mere combating of Communism and in 1952 outlined these goals to Archbishop Mannix.[57] They included using the Movement to effect a transformation of the Labour movement so as to set up 'a Christian social order in Australia'. The Australian Labour Party was to be the 'puppet's glove' and Santamaria's the hand that manipulated it.

Santamaria told Mannix that he planned 'to introduce into the Federal and State's spheres large numbers of members who possess a clear realisation of what Australia demands of them and the will to carry it out'. Santamaria added a sentence in his letter which must have gladdened Mannix's heart. Not only did he point out that this was the first time in Australia's history that such a programme had become possible, he said that he thought it was the first time 'in the Anglo-Saxon world since the advent of Protestantism'.

Santamaria aimed at: 'settling Catholic emigrants in small agricultural blocks'. Thus the Church would be able to 'gain great excessions of strength because of the religious composition of the migrant groups who would thus be absorbed into Australian life'. In other words: keep them down on the farm, out of the cities, raising their children as Catholics, voting Catholic, and taking their intellectual and moral tone from their pastors. These objectives of Santamaria's were not known to the public when he wrote the letter, or for several years afterwards. Ironically, however, the Communist influence, or rather the fear of it, which Santamaria had done so much to both counter and propagate, resulted in the Movement's growing strength being severely curtailed and a very damaging split developing in the Labour Party.

The 'Outing'

The Prime Minister of the day, Robert Menzies, trumped Labour leader Herbert Evatt's chances of becoming Prime Minister in the election of 29 May 1954 by setting up a Royal Commission into events surrounding the activities of a Russian defector, Vladimir Petrov. It became known that the inquiry was expected to locate spies operating close to certain unnamed politicians, also that certain documents which Petrov had turned over to the authorities would be particularly illuminating. The Menzies smear campaign worked. Although neither Evatt nor any Labour figure was linked to Petrov before the election, the Red Scare turned the tide against Labour in a number of key marginals.

Evatt was naturally disturbed by this, but worse was to come. It turned out that one of the much-discussed documents had been written by Evatt's own

Press Secretary, Fergal O'Sullivan, and the names of several of Evatt's staff were mentioned by O'Sullivan at the inquiry. Evatt decided to represent them before the Royal Commission but his statement led to further divisions within the Labour movement and on 5 October 1954, he decided to counter his critics by in effect 'outing' the Movement. He said that the Labour Party was being undermined by:

A small minority group of members, located particularly in the state of Victoria, which has since 1949 become increasingly disloyal to the Labour movement and the Labour leadership. Adopting methods which strikingly resemble both Communist and fascist infiltration of larger groups, some of these groups have created an almost intolerable situation – calculated to deflect the Labour movement from the pursuit of established Labour objectives and ideals.[58]

Everyone knew he was talking about the Movement and controversy exploded. As Campion says, 'That weekend all Australia was talking about the secret political machine run by the Catholic Church.[59] Both Groupers and Movement figures left the Labour Party to form the Democratic Labour Party, and the war of words attending their departure became a physical one at times, so bitter were the divisions:

In Victoria where the ferment was most pronounced, some Catholics who stayed with the ALP endured abuse and ostracism at the church they had attended all their lives. Other ugly manifestations of the conflict included brutal violence by enforcers, despatch of dead rats to rivals through the mail, and calculated haranguing and harassment of the children of detested opponents.[60]

The difference between what happened in Victoria and the rest of Australia was a matter of degree rather than kind. Suffice it to say that the Mannix-backed Movement left its imprint on Australian politics for decades – until 2 December 1972, in fact, when Gough Whitlam led Labour back to power. However, although it had profound implications for the ALP and the Church, the Split in a sense was the result of an external force where the Church was concerned. Internally, Mother Church had already taken steps to alter the title deeds of her Australian possessions before it ever began – as far back as 1945.

AUSTRALISATION OF THE CHURCH

A famous photograph, reproduced in many Irish and Irish Australian journals, also appears in the memoirs of Arthur Calwell, but with a sting in the tail of its caption. The picture shows Eamon de Valera and Frank Aiken in the company of the singer, Father Sidney MacEwan, standing with Calwell, who arranged the visit, at the Eureka Stockade Monument at Ballarat in 1948. The caption points out that on the evening of the day the picture was taken Calwell was excluded from a dinner to which the others were invited.

The reason for the exclusion occurred on 24 December 1945, when Arthur Calwell claims to have become 'the first Catholic layman in the English-speaking world to challenge a papal appointment'.[61] Calwell, a minister in Prime Minister Ben Chifley's Cabinet, issued a statement to the press denouncing the fact that the Vatican had appointed Norman Gilroy, Archbishop of Sydney, as a cardinal, over the head of Daniel Mannix. Calwell blamed the snub to Mannix on the Papal Nuncio, Dr Panico, an unattractive figure disliked by the Irish generally. One of Panico's practices, when visiting a convent, was to instruct the nuns to wrap up any dinner service, or *objet d'art* that took his fancy, and place it in the boot of his car. The Holy Father, he would assure the unfortunate nuns on such occasions, would be delighted to learn of their contribution to furnishing the Nunciature in a Manner Appropriate to the Office of the Nuncio. Nuncios, like bishops, always insisted that they sought tribute and respect for their office, never for themselves.

However, Calwell, who generated a storm of publicity through his action, was aware that there were deeper forces at work than the influence of one papal nuncio, and he forecast that henceforth only Roman-trained, native Australian bishops would be appointed to Australian dioceses. As he wrote in his memoirs: '. . . it was obvious from the appointment of Cardinal Gilroy that the days of the Irish bishops in Australia were over, to all intents and purposes'.[62]

A process of Australisation of the Church was under way; the sun was beginning to set on Irish influence within the Australian Church.

Significantly, Gilroy was one of the leaders of the charge against Santamaria. To him a basic issue of the crisis was not so much the question of the Church in politics as the fundamental principle that the bishops should rule, not the laity. Not surprisingly, a majority within the hierarchy supported him in this. In New South Wales the split was fought out less in terms of for or against the Movement than in those of Gilroy v. Santamaria.

Not surprising also is the fact that Santamaria told me: 'I was never so much at home as I was when Australian Catholicism was Irish Catholicism.'[63] A wonderfully bright and active little walnut of a man, Bob Santamaria was carrying on his activities as enthusiastically as ever at the time of our talk. What they were was not immediately clear to me, but he operated out of a well-appointed office block in Melbourne. In the words of one of his helpers, who drove me to my next appointment, he was: 'Carrying on the same sort of thing the Movement did.' A sort of joyous pessimism informed Santamaria's conversation. He regarded contemporary Australia as 'bleak and hopeless' for its materialism, high interest rates and unemployment. To him the Split was the 'last big effusion of Irishness.' Indeed it was – but only of the Santamaria era of the Irish Unquestioning of Their Church. Two events in particular may be pointed to as both symbolising and accelerating the process of questioning and change that came upon the Australian Church, and hence upon the Irish, in the 1960s: the Vietnam War and the Second Vatican Council.

OPPOSING WAR

In his book *Disturbing the War*,[64] Val Noone describes how the spirit of independence, released by Vatican II, impacted on Melbourne Catholicism, once the bastion of Mannix and Santamaria. In their opposition to the war in general, and specifically to the involvement of Australian troops in it, Irish Australian Catholics like Noone himself, although he understates his own role, displayed extraordinary courage. Of the many examples which could be given, I will mention only two, those of Denis O'Donnell and Michael Costigan.

O'Donnell, an Australian army cook, was court-martialled and sentenced to a term in a military prison after he had become a conscientious objector in 1968. Apart from pressures exerted by the Army, he also had to withstand those of family, friends and the Catholic Church. While in captivity his chaplain told him it was wrong to oppose the war. However, his stand provoked much sympathetic opposition throughout Australia. Costigan, the acting editor of the *Melbourne Advocate*, owned by the Melbourne diocese, used the paper to oppose the war in the teeth of episcopal opposition. His stance, first articulated appropriately enough on St Patrick's Day 1966, became a national *cause célèbre* during which he said: 'My Irish blood kept me going.'

Unquestionably the Irish (the world over) will continue to demonstrate their fidelity to the Split as an essential badge of Irishness but, as the contemporary flourishing of Irish culture in Australia amply demonstrates, it was far from being the last 'effusion' of the Irish in Australia.

SPORT

In few areas will one find the Irish more effusively enthusiastic than in the world of sport and the Australian Irish sporting heroes have a special niche of their own, the greats occupying a pedestal somewhere near Daniel Mannix and Ned Kelly. In boxing Les Darcy's (1895–1917) pedestal stands alongside those of John L. Sullivan in America or 'Peerless Jim' Driscoll in Wales. He was the original cool clean hero for Irish Australians. He had already won the Australian middleweight and heavyweight titles when he went to America in search of the world middleweight title, but he died there unexpectedly, following a dental operation in Memphis. As Darcy said the rosary daily, went to mass and took care of his mother, the devout believed that the power in his fists had come from God. When his body was brought back to Australia, he had one of the greatest funerals in Australian history, and many Irish Australians hoped to see him canonised as Australia's first saint.

Darcy had had to be virtually smuggled into America, because passports were being refused to men eligible for military service, so his death became intertwined with the great conscription debate of the time. Legends proliferated that he had been poisoned by anti-Irish, pro-war elements. The fact that he had defied the authorities to go to America was seen both as a continuation of the Ned Kelly legend and proof of his desire to earn money to care for his mother.

Curiously, 1917 also saw the death of Australia's other great boxing icon, Larry Foley. Born in 1851, he is regarded as the father of Australian boxing, and passed into legend as an Irish Catholic hero because of his fights with Sandy Ross, Protestantism's champion. Foley, a bare-knuckled brawler, totally unlike Darcy in character or lifestyle, had some Homeric encounters with Ross. They first fought to a draw over seventy-one rounds and then, a year later, Foley knocked out Ross in the rematch.

Irish names appear at the top of the tree in most of the great Australian sports. Swimming is not only a sport but a way of life for Aussies living in the maritime states. The first female Olympic gold medalist (at Stockholm in 1912) was Sarah (Fanny) Durack, a member of the great cattle-droving family who won the 100 metres, and a contemporary swimming heroine is Suzy Moroney, an Irish descendant long-distance swimmer who was taken to Australian hearts after she had swum between Florida and Cuba. In cricket at the time of writing it is a matter of debate as to whether Bill (Tiger) O'Reilly (1905–1992) is the greatest right-arm leg-spin bowler in Australian history, or has the contemporary Shane Warne taken the palm. In racing, Australians concede, with unusual alacrity for Australians, that Bart Cummings is the greatest horse trainer in Australian thoroughbred history. His horse, Saintly, carried off the 1996 Melbourne Cup, making an incredible total of ten Melbourne Cup winners for Cummings. At the time of Saintly's victory, another Irishman, Michael Doohan, had been at the top of the world motorcycle Grand Prix list in the 500cc class. If the talk turns to either tennis or surfing, Irish names are automatically mentioned. In tennis, Pat Cash was a popular figure, both for his Wimbledon win (in 1987) and for the fact that he so strongly identifies himself as being Irish. Cash also, to a degree, fits the victim's stereotype because his international career was seriously inhibited by chronic back problems. In surfing, Bernard (Midge) Farrelly is renowned not only for being the world's surfing champion of 1964, but also for being one of the founders of surfing as an international sport.

In rugby league, the two greatest players are acknowledged to have been Irish: Dally Messenger (1883–1959) is still known as The Master, with Dave Brown (1913–1974) being regarded as the inheritor of his mantle of greatness. In the oval ball code, rugby is regarded in much the same light as that depicted in Ireland by the saying: Rugby is a bowsie game played by gentlemen, soccer is a gentlemen's game played by bowsies, and Gaelic football (or hurling in some versions) is a bowsie game played by bowsies! This slur on the Gaelic Athletic Association code stems from the fierce, partisan, exclusivist affection for the native code on the part of its aficionados.

In Australia, something of that ferocity of partisanship, both on and off the field, can be found in a game largely developed by Irish immigrants, and said by some to have derived from Gaelic football. This is Australian rules football, popularly known as 'footy'. It is said that:

Australia is divided by a deep cultural rift known as the Barassi Line. It runs between Canberra, Broken Hill, Birdsville and Maningrida (Arnhem Land) and it divides Australia between rugby and rules. To the east of this line drawn through Australian imagination, rugby union and rugby league predominate. To the west, Australian Rules is king.[65]

In a nutshell, Sydney plays rugby, Melbourne plays Australian rules. Whether this latter titanic sport was in fact derived from the Gaelic code is a matter of debate amongst sporting historians, a debate, needless to say, which is carried on with the same intensity which covers every other aspect of 'footy'.

An Irishman could be said to epitomise Australia's most famous football club. James Frances (Jock) MacHale (1881–1953) played 262 games for Collingwood Football Club, Melbourne, in the years 1903–18. He then coached the club for a record thirty-seven years in which Collingwood took eighteen Grand Finals. In contemporary footy, MacHale's tradition is carried on by a number of Irish-descended figures with names like Carey, Kelly and Murphy, all of whom are household names. One famous player, Dermot Brereton, demonstrated his Irishness by wearing green football boots.

Support for Gaelic football has grown in Australia in recent years, and 1999 marked the twenty-first anniversary of the foundation of the Australasian Gaelic Athletic Association. The state of the game is such that Australia and New Zealand now stage international fixtures against each other.

Another significant development is the growth of a game with modified rules, based on both Gaelic and Australian rules football. There had been sporadic games played in Australia and Ireland before 1998, but in that year a full-blown combined AFL/GAA series was launched in Dublin, with a replay scheduled for Australia in 1999. One of the hopes of the AFL authorities is that the new game will help to attract to Australia more figures like the legendary Jim Stynes, who played in the 1998 Dublin game before retiring from Australian football.

The Irish-born Stynes is a remarkable man, both on and off the field. In sports-mad Australia, to be a star in Australia's very own brand of football, played with an oval ball and a ferocious disregard for the limits of the human body, is to twinkle very brightly indeed in the fermament of Aussie society. Jimmy Stynes is such a figure.

He was a star Gaelic football player with the Dublin team when he was recruited by a 'footy' team of talent spotters, and brought to Melbourne. He went on to win Australia's most coveted football prize, the Brownlow Medal, in 1991. Off the field, he devoted himself practically full-time to youth work. His 'Reach for the Stars' programme holds workshops in schools and wherever young people congregate, trying to motivate young men, not simply towards achievement but away from the grave. Australia has the highest male suicide rate amongst young adults in the world and Stynes deliberately uses his football fame as a method of getting support for young people: 'I need a high profile to get private sector support for the kids. My value in football is coming to an end. I must find some other way of getting publicity.'

He broke a 53-year-old record of not missing a match through injury by playing 205 matches in a row. Sometimes he took the field with injuries which included broken ribs and torn cartilages, even though his position as ruck man meant that it was a mathematical certainty that his body would be hit hard by other players twenty or thirty times in a game (apart from hitting the ground equally hard). In Australian rules, there is no such thing as a soft game. 'They're all tough,' he smiled. Stynes attributes his own physical toughness to both his father and his mother. His father, a GAA player of note himself, was his most enthusiastic, and demanding, coach, and his mother specialised in natural medicine and prayer.

> She'd be rubbing a cabbage leaf on you when you'd have a temperature of 104 or something. Or she'd give you garlic for a cold. The room stank, but you'd get better. These remedies get you through injuries. That's how my body is so resilient. I recover. My dad used to say that unless you are in hospital, you can play. The ma keeps me going. She is at home praying for me. Her name's Teresa. I call her Mother Teresa.

Stynes is one of the biggest men I have ever met. He was a little late for our interview, so I foolishly began checking nearby tables whenever I noticed anyone athletic, in case he might have come into the restaurant unknown to me. As soon as he entered the room, I realised my mistake. It was as if some Irish hero, hewn from the antique, had suddenly appeared. Not only did he dwarf everyone in the place, a susurration went around: 'That's Jim STYNES.'

Stynes, clearly a highly intelligent, self-controlled person, mastered himself before he mastered football.

> I got a great deal of attention in the media because I was new to the game. It was a great thing for the Irish. But I realised that I had to be careful. Ten years ago you had that Protestant/Catholic thing. But leaving Ireland was the best thing I ever did. My ma and da said the rosary. They were strict Catholics and agreed with the priests. I believe in heightening awareness. As it were, I would try to look down at Croke Park and see what my role was, not merely on the field. It helps you to get away from that victim culture.
>
> Workers tend to be under-valued people, running from one problem to another. They drink to drown their sorrows. You'll find them drinking hard at half-time. After the match, they're stuck in cans. But the funny thing is that they have this great reputation for being hard-working and reliable and well educated. They are all that. They use their imagination more than other people.

Stynes comes from a strongly nationalistic family. He was concerned and knowledgeable about the Peace Process, obviously in close and continuous touch with home. In conversation he showed himself to be well read, not only about Irish history, but about behavioural psychology. He is very conscious of the fact that he has a reputation to live up to in the public eye, and behaves accordingly. He also tries to use his position not only to help Australian youth, but children in difficulty in Ireland. One of his projects is a huge annual Irish ball, the funds from which have helped to run an integrated school for both Protestants and Catholics in Belfast.

Perhaps the most striking aspect of this remarkable young man was the depth of his consciousness of being Irish. I met him with a friend, the talented Melbourne writer and publicist, Paul Ormonde, and we both remarked afterwards on how much of his motivation appeared to stem from the necessity to live up to the expectations of his fellow-countrymen and his family. It was no surprise to pick up his book, *Whatever it Takes*[66] and find it dedicated to his family on page 1, saying 'Without you, there is no me'. The book itself began with a quotation from Buckminster Fuller: 'Integrity is the essence of everything.' In Styne's case, that appeared to be an appropriate sentiment.

A GROWING IRISH AWARENESS

From the 1970s, when I first visited Australia, it seemed to me that Oz was engaged on a journey of self-discovery. In the seventies, republicanism was little heard of, but there were questionings about the validity of regarding Gallipoli, a gallant, but disastrous, engagement, fought on behalf of another power, as being the labour ward of Australian nationhood, which was the establishment view. This quickened in pace, reaching a particular intensity in 1998, when the bi-centennial celebrations occurred. The examination of roots made the Irish heritage in particular become extremely fashionable. Awareness of Irishness was furthered by cultural exchanges and visits from Irish theatre companies such as the Abbey, the Gate, the Druid and the Dublin Opera company. Irish writers became the vogue, particularly those who visited Australia such as John Banville and Colm Toibin. Frank McCourt's *Angela's Ashes* had a tremendous success, as had tours by leading Irish singers like Mary Black and Christy Moore. Visits by people of this calibre had a spin off effect as new Irish groups were formed throughout Australia in their wake.

Riverdance helped to quicken an already widespread interest in Irish dancing, classes in which are mushrooming across the continent. There was also an enormous explosion in the number of Irish pubs in all the large Australian cities. At the time of writing, two of the most popular TV shows in Australia are the Irish-based *Father Ted*, and *Ballykissangel*, and a series on the Irish diaspora *The Irish Empire*, made in co-operation between the Irish television station, RTE, and the Australian SBS, was screened in July of 1999.

The consciousness of the diaspora's importance was greatly furthered by the events of the year 1998, when not only was the Australian bicentenary commemorated, but it was intertwined with both the anniversary of 1798 and the marking of the period of the Great Famine by the inauguration of a major memorial in Sydney. A rash of seminars and conferences focused not just on the events of the past, but on their relevance to contemporary Irish and Australian society. At the same time, the pace of exchange visits between the two countries quickened. The Irish President, Mary McAleese, visited Australia and New Zealand at a time when Australia was in the middle of a hard-fought election campaign, but the election did not detract from the interest in her visit. As the Australian Prime Minister, John Howard, remarked on 8 September 1998, during a bipartisan lunch for the President in Canberra: 'Only the visit of an Irish Head of State could have silenced the guns of battle in the middle of an Australian election campaign.'

Another very successful visit to Australia and to East Timor by an Irish leader, the Taoiseach, Bertie Ahern, in March 2000 may also have done something to silence the 'guns of battle'. The East Timor Ireland Solidarity Campaign (ETISC) has been described by the East Timorese leaders Bishop Carlo Belo and Jose Ramos-Horta as the most successful in the world. The ETISC was founded by an unemployed Dublin bus driver, Tom Hyland, after seeing a TV programme in 1992, made by the Australian journalist, John Pilger. Its first international headline-making operation was a candle-lit vigil outside a banquet in Dublin for Paul Keating in 1993, to protest at Australia's support for the military regime in Indonesia, which both then and subsequently is attributed by his critics to Keating's influence. Ahern continued the Irish support for the Timorese by raising the issue of renewed militarism on the part of the Indonesians with both the European Union and Washington on his return from Australia.

TOING AND FROING

Apart from state receptions by Governors General, and meetings with Irish groupings of all sorts, the President unveiled a statue to Daniel O'Connell at Melbourne's Catholic Cathedral, and addressed a joint sitting of the Parliament of New South Wales. The ancillary toing and froing between Ireland and Australia included a number of visits from Ireland by Irish political leaders and two particularly significant visits to Ireland by Australian dignitaries. One was the first ever official visit by a serving Australian Governor General to Ireland, that of Sir William Deane in April 1999. The other was an earlier visit (in 1997) by the Prime Minister of Victoria, Jeff Kennett. Unlike Paul Keating, who paid what might be termed a sentimental visit to the land of his ancestors during his tenure as Prime Minister, Kennett has no Irish connections. He wanted to see how the Irish industrial miracle had been achieved, and to establish links between Victorian and Irish software and multi-media sectors.

While the republican issue obviously had considerable Irish resonances, another important debate resulted in 'an Irish model' being adopted into the Australian tax code. This was a Goods and Services Tax (GST), based on the Irish Value Added Tax (VAT) which exempts basic items of food from the tax.

Visible Scars

A number of notable Irish individuals occupy important positions in Australian society. Tony O'Reilly is of course revered as is his son Cameron, who for a time ran his father's Australian newspaper interests; an Irishman, Dr Brian Kennedy, has been appointed Director of the Australian National Gallery; Sean Doran from Belfast is Director of the Perth Arts Festival and Paul McGeough from Carrickmacross, County Monaghan, is the editor of the *Sydney Morning Herald*. In a nutshell, in virtually every walk of Australian life, there are Irish people with their feet planted on the ladder of success, very often on the topmost rungs.

However, the past has left still-visible scars. These can be seen all too clearly by visiting the Irish Welfare Centre in Melbourne. On the wall are a series of hats, caps, berets and sun-hats. These are all mementoes of people who relied on the centre's services. Like their counterparts in England, they would have emigrated to Australia in the late fifties and throughout the sixties, but they died in Australia before the birth of the Celtic Tiger. One shabby checked cap bore a particularly poignant adornment, an Easter Lily. The wearer kept the lily, commemorating the Easter Rising, fresh in his thoughts to the end, but prosperity eluded him.

The centre patrons are the sort of people who caused Joseph O'Donoghue, an Irish emigrant who first came to Australia in 1973, to write a poem 'Emigrants', which contains the following:

> The price of Independence – the cost of a job
> To own their own home – and to have a few bob
> Liberation was coming or so they believed
> Equality and justice for each to receive.
>
> . . . The mountains and rivers still look the same
> Some people inherit them – they take the plane.
>
> . . . Not a trace of them left, their words yet untold
> The cost of their freedom – the price of their souls.

Prosperity also eludes a percentage of the Irish who emigrate to Australia today: young people who have overstayed their visas, or who for some reason fall through the cracks in the emigration laws. I wanted to speak to some of them, but they were scared to talk to a journalist. The calibre of the lives of some of them may be gauged from the fact that they sometimes relied on food brought to them in the boot of a car by a Melbourne Centre helper. A centre worker told me that often the food could not be delivered because emigration officials developed a tactic of following the cars from the centre, and as a result the drivers were sometimes forced to drive past the point of assignation, where the would-be recipients were waiting hopefully.

It's difficult to quantify the number of illegal immigrants; the Embassy network regards it as quite a small affair, but welfare sources – for example, a lawyer specialising in immigration cases, Anne O'Donoghue – told me that it was a very serious problem indeed. In issues like this, where the researcher cannot hope to have access to all the facts, I think the best rule of thumb is that of a friend of mine who specialises in the treatment of alcoholism. He told me that he assessed his patients' alcoholic intake by accepting half what their wives' said it was, and doubling the patients' own estimate. The number of 'illegals' is probably in the 10,000–14,000 area, nothing approaching the scale of the American problem, but still serious enough for those concerned.

THE 'LITTLE BLACK COSH'

Anti-Irish prejudice is considerably less in the 1990s than it was in the 1950s. Back then it sometimes took very direct action to secure jobs for people with a Catholic Irish background. For instance, during the fifties, banks in Hobart, Tasmania, would not hire such people. A new Catholic archbishop, changed the picture, however. Archbishop Young organised people of Irish or Catholic origin who had bank deposits to threaten to withdraw their money unless the job discrimination ceased. It did!

Even in the seventies, traces of discrimination lingered: Joseph O'Donoghue, who moved to Perth in 1978, told me that he found it 'very hard to get settled and organised with a wife and two small children, but what made it harder was the anti-Irish paranoia that existed here until about 1983'. He went on:

> I attribute this to the Troubles in Northern Ireland and the fact that W. A. Premier Sir Charles Court was an old guard imperialist plus the fact that, as he later revealed, he was a great admirer of the late Lord Louis Mountbatten who was killed by the IRA.
>
> It's hard, less than two decades later, to imagine the feeling of alienation that was perpetrated on anyone with an Irish accent. The 'Irish Joke', the cartoons, and the letters in the daily newspapers all made you feel that to be Irish was inferior. It got to the stage that kids were being picked on at school.[67]

In the 1980s the Irish Embassy, led by the then Ambassador, Joseph Small, conducted an active campaign against Irish jokes, in response to complaints to the Embassy from people of Irish descent. In a typical letter, on 30 August 1983, Small complained to the *Australian* newspaper:

> Sir, you reported some of my views about the so-called Irish Joke in the *Weekend Australian* of August 20. Unfortunately, the headline and accompanying cartoon chosen to highlight the piece were symptomatic of the very syndrome I sought to explain to your reporter when she contacted me. Such is the all-pervasive conditioning of omnipresent jokes of this kind.
>
> I am not, as reported, advocating the introduction of legislation to outlaw Irish jokes – there is already in Australia official machinery to administer the Racial Discrimination Act of 1975.

Rather I would wish to see the spirit of the relevant legislation observed both by the media and the individual who may feel tempted from time to time to indulge in 'humor' which is in reality denigratory and bears no resemblance to the genuine wit and humor for which the Irish are so justly famous. I find it surprising that the Irish, who have made such an outstanding contribution to the development of this great country should be so widely portrayed in this negative and stereotyped fashion.

The offence which this causes to so many in the Irish community is constantly conveyed to me, and my embassy colleagues, both in Canberra and in the course of our regular travels throughout the country.

Although the Small campaign had a beneficial effect, traces of the controversy can still be found, often unexpectedly. I was being driven to a broadcasting studio one morning, and was jolted out of a reverie about what I was going to say by my English taxi driver, who insisted on delivering a monologue on Irish jokes. He remarked on the fact of: 'All them jokes about the Irish being so thick and all. There can't be no smoke without fire. Must be because they don't get the proper education loike.' One can still encounter pockets of anger at such attitudes. I was interviewed for the *Irish Australian Review* by two talented women journalists, Barbara Walsh and Lisa Killick.[68] They were both highly intelligent. Walsh, the more experienced of the two, who was born in Ireland, had worked in England as a journalist before coming to Australia. She was in her late thirties. Killick, who was nineteen, had Irish ancestors, but was born in Australia, and had no immediate Irish family. Yet she had learnt Irish to a degree of fluency which would obviously have enabled her to conduct the interview in that language had she so wished.

Both expressed passionate anger at the level of anti-Irish sentiment, and cited a number of radio shows and newspaper columnists whom they said not only perpetuated Irish jokes but 'insist on rubbishing Irish authors and film makers'. As Walsh put it, 'There seems to be a little black box in the Anglo-mind with a little black cosh, and the owners feel obliged to wield it against the Irish again and again.'

Vulnerable people, like the sort who benefit from the Melbourne Welfare Centre, would obviously be more affected by the 'little black cosh' than, say, those in Tony O'Reilly's circle. In the course of a paper which she had compiled on the subject,[69] Walsh included a number of disturbing examples of anti-Irish prejudice, including the following by Michael Fitzjames which appeared in the *Independent Monthly* in June 1993 under the heading 'When Irish eyes need punching':

Everything loathsome, meretricious and jejune in current Australian affairs can be traced to its poisonous source in the Irish-Catholic culture which sits like a horse-collar around the long-suffering neck of the Australian people . . . [In 1950s Melbourne] we were almost at the bottom of the social pile but not quite. Certain persons could be distinguished and pointed out as 'Catholic' or, more pointedly, 'Irish', both expressions so freighted with distaste that even now I find myself uncomfortable with acquaintances who bang on about their ghastly upbringing or voodoo religion and hope I'm not wearing that 'who farted?' look my relations had no trouble assuming whenever a tyke staggered into view.

Letters of complaint from the Irish Embassy and community groups about this offering were dismissed by the editor of the paper as 'mere blarney'. This is not how it was seen by the crusading Al Grassby, Australia's Commissioner for Race Relations. He fired off a letter to the editor, in which he said:

> I have received and conciliated upon more than 50,000 formal and informal complaints of racial discrimination and deformation, but I do not believe in my experience that I have read a more bigoted and malicious attack on any ethnic or religious group than that by your writer, Michael Fitzjames, whose article on the Irish in Australia seems to me to be a plea for ethnic cleansing.

Grassby was appointed Australia's first Commissioner for Community Relations in October 1975. He worked with the then Attorney General, Lionel Murphy, later Mr Justice Murphy of the High Court, in the drafting of a Bill to outlaw racial discrimination and show the world that Australia had turned its back on the racist White Australia policy. Interestingly, both Grassby and Murphy had to fight long, costly, but ultimately successful actions brought against them by successive Governments. Their opponents accused them of corruption and attempts to subvert the course of justice, but their supporters claim that their republicanism and hostility to racialism had antagonised the Australian Secret Service.

Grassby, who taught himself Irish after he discovered his ancestry, is recognised as being a lifelong battler for racial equality. His hatred for prejudice began when he discovered that his mother had disguised her accent and changed her name as a young woman, because she was a Catholic living in a Protestant area of Glasgow.

New life was breathed into the anti-Irish stereotype controversy, and into ancestral British/Irish hostilities by the issue of whether or not to concede an Australian visa to Gerry Adams. Al Grassby was one of those who led the, ultimately, successful charge to grant Adams the permission. After much media controversy, Adams finally visited Australia in February of 1999, and was generally well received, although Prime Minister Howard refused to meet him. However, Adams did meet other leading Australian political figures and created a favourable impression even with some of the previously antagonistic Australian media, many sections of which conveyed during the controversy an impression of taking their tone from that of the London *Daily Telegraph* or, more likely, from the desk of Rupert Murdoch.

STRENGTHENING IRISH AND AUSTRALIAN LINKS

The Adams case apart, any Irish visitor to Australia these days is apt to be given a hospitable welcome: when I visited Brisbane, the Queensland Irish Association decided to make up for the shortness of my stay by insisting on holding both a lunch and a dinner for me on the same day! I also attended another prestigious and hospitable lunch in Parliament buildings in Canberra,

AUSTRALIA

this time given by the Irish Parliamentary Friendship Group which has 120 members, making it the largest of such groupings in the Federal Parliament.

Following some intensive diplomatic initiatives by Ambassador Joe Small, the group held its first meeting on May 9th, 1985 in Parliament House. One of the nineteen founding MPs present was Jim McKiernan from Co. Cavan who had left school at fourteen and Ireland at sixteen to make a notable contribution to the already huge Irish presence in Western Australia.

Prior to January 1994 the Oath of allegiance made by new Australian citizens was:

> I swear by Almighty God that I will be faithful and bear true allegiance to Her Majesty Queen Elizabeth the Second, Queen of Australia, Her heirs and successors according to law, and that I will faithfully observe the laws of Australia and fulfil my duties as an Australian.

McKiernan found it opprobrious that in committing himself to Australia, he had to do so through the Head of a foreign nation. Both in the Labour Party and in the Parliament he marshalled a, stoutly resisted but ultimately successful, campaign to have the Oath replaced by the following Citizenship Pledge:

> From this time forward under God [the words 'under God' are discretionary, author] I pledge my loyalty to Australia and its people, whose democratic beliefs I share, whose rights and liberties I respect, and whose laws I will uphold and obey.

The group has visited Ireland to learn about the economy and the Peace Process at first hand. On returning to Australia, it voted for a strengthening of Irish and Australian links, which included the adaptation of some elements of Irish economic and industrial policy; contributions to the International Fund for Ireland; and support for the Peace Process. The Secretary of the group is Jim McKiernan, and a Belfast man, Senator George Campbell, is also an active member. Both Campbell and McKiernan are members of the ALP, but the growing political strength of the Irish has helped to bring Irish people to the fore in the Liberal Party also. The example of Peter Collins has already been noted, but two other members of the current Federal Cabinet are also Irish, John Fahey and Jackie Kelly.

THE LAST WORD

On St Patrick's Day, 1999, the three most senior members of the Federal Party all graced Irish community events with their presence. Prime Minister Howard was a guest of honour at the Irish Australian Chamber of Commerce breakfast in Sydney. The Deputy Prime Minister, Tim Fisher, was similarly honoured at the Lansdowne Club's lunch, also in Sydney, and the Treasurer, Peter Costello, attended P. J. O'Reilly's pub breakfast in Canberra. The Prime

Minister made such a passionate rediscovery of his Irish heritage that a number of reports of the Sydney breakfast referred to him as 'Sean O'Howard'!

I leave the last word on the Irish in Australia to a former Australian Prime Minister, Bill Hayden, who wrote in his autobiography:

> Australian culture too, resonates with the unmistakable Irish influences, a rebelliousness, a suspicion of authority, a touchy cockiness, a testy combativeness, a self-deprecating humour . . . we take from the Irish their penchant for admiring noble heroes who sacrifice themselves to lost causes . . . This is central to the Irish psyche. Think of Ned Kelly, Les Darcy, Phar Lap . . . the heroic legend making from Gallipoli, Anzac Day, we commemorate a heroic defeat as our national apotheosis.[70]

The truth of Hayden's analysis is carved in stone, the names on the Waverley memorial in that Sydney cemetery overlooking the sea. Today's Irish, not least of them those 10,000 backpackers, will see to it that they are not forgotten.

SIX

NEW ZEALAND

'THE DOGS' BOLLOCKS please.'

'Certainly sir,' replied my Peloponnesian taxi driver, and he drove me to one of New Zealand's most popular Irish pubs. Inside the bar, a large wooden effigy of a dog, with its appurtenances delineated in red, remove any ambiguity which might exist as to the provenance of the pub's name. Students of linguistics divide on the subject of the spelling of the dogs' anatomy. There are those who think that an 'a' should be included instead of an 'o'. Others favour the American usage, which replaces the 'ocks' with a rather wimpish sounding 'ix'. However, where drinkers are concerned there is no argument: intending patrons were well advised to come early to be sure of a seat.

The Auckland pub is owned by a group of young Irish musicians who hit upon a great truth: 'Musicians bring wealth to pubs, but very little of it ever attaches to the musicians' – so the group bought their own pub, an old gay lesbian meeting hall. The pub bans television, but not much else, and I found it one of the livelier places I visited on my world tour. It helps to illustrate both the growing interest worldwide in Irish music and dancing, and that 'x' quotient of the outrageous that the Irish brought with them wherever they went, a particularly noticeable factor in staid New Zealand.

One of the features of the premises was the Irish music and dancing classes which were held in the afternoons for children. The prizes given out for the best performers were T-shirts which the little dears proudly wear – thus innocently promulgating the fame of The Dogs' Bollocks, to the frequent discomfort of their elders.

The cheerful vulgarity of the pub's name probably conveys all that needs to be said about the contribution of the Irish to New Zealand popular culture. I have often been puzzled how New Zealand could produce the controlled ferocity of the All Blacks rugby team, given the, as it were, antimacassared background of the country's social life. One could of course argue that the presence of so many Irishmen in All Blacks teams down through the years accounts for the ferocity. One of the most famous All Blacks forwards ever, Sean Fitzpatrick, the hooker and captain of the team, retired as this book was being written. His father, Brian, was also an All Black. Or, one could equally argue that the fire is attributable to the presence of so many Maoris, with whom the Irish traditionally show an affinity.

Amongst New Zealand senior school pupils, the 1999 winner of a scholarship trip, sponsored by Rodney Walshe, to a much sought-after Irish summer school, was Kiane Worsley, of Irish-Maori origin, who sought to apply Irish precedents to solving a Maori problem. (The school itself, run by a Protestant headmistress, Eileen Jackson, is an example of the diaspora at work. Its students, attracted either by ancestral links or interest in the culture are drawn from all over the world.) Her prize-winning essay dealt with the efforts of the Irish government to revive the Irish language based on the *Gaeltachts*, gaelic-speaking districts. Her interest in the subject was stimulated by her Derry-born teacher and her essay called for grants and initiatives similar to those provided by the Irish to help restore the Maori language in New Zealand. It may have sparked further Irish links. My daughter Olwen, who lives with her teacher husband and their family on the Aran Islands, hearing of the Maori respect for the Irish language, has added to Rodney Walshe's existing prize a stay at her home on Inis Mor.

MODERATION

Overall however, New Zealand political culture is tame compared to that of Ireland. I happened to visit the country during a General Election campaign in which the object of the exercise was to defeat the Government of the then Prime Minister, the Irish Jim Bolger. After a close result, and much post-election haggling, Bolger was ultimately ousted – and is now New Zealand's Ambassador to Washington – but the temperature of the election was quite unlike that of either Ireland or Australia. During the television programmes, a kind of a graph, known jocularly as 'the worm', was employed to show viewer approval (determined by phone calls to a pre-selected target audience) of any given speaker. It went up according to the moderation of the speaker's tone and appearance, and dipped whenever they became passionate or aggressive. Even the Irish were affected by the climate of moderation. At a very pleasant election party given by the Irish Honorary Consul, Rodney Walshe, one guest elicited considerable admiration for the amount of Guinness he managed to put away over the course of as many hours: six cans in all. Back in Ireland, a similar party-goer would have had six cans on his way to the party in order to lubricate himself for the real drinking!

The 'worm', the moderation, and the eminence achieved by Jim Bolger, between them sum up the Irish experience in New Zealand. The emigrants did not arrive as convicts, although a sizeable number of Irish convicts who had served their sentences did make their way to New Zealand in the transportation era, and they did not face the same antagonisms and apprehensions as in Australia. Also, the beautiful country that they came to was more like their native Ireland (or the Scottish Highlands). There were undeniably bitter Orange and Green conflicts and sectarian tension over familiar issues such as Fenianism or state aid for Catholic schools, but the flogging, the arrival in chains, the bloodshed of Castle Hill, were happily absent from the New Zealand experience.

THE MAORIS

When the first British Governor landed in 1840 in 'The Bay of Islands' – at what is today known as the settlement of Russell – Kororarek, as it was then, was the 'hell hole of the Pacific'. Every second building was either a grog shop, a brothel, or both.[1]

The New Zealand of the time has been described as consisting of: 'Two distinct islands which were then the preserves of Maoris, Missionaries, and a few groups of traders, whalers and settlers, many of whom were a distinctly poor advertisement for British culture and morality.'[1] Prior to the coming of the white men, the Maoris had no tradition of fermented spirits, but a combination of the generous sexuality of the attractive Maori women and the freely available 'grog' soon spread both syphilis and prostitution.

Prior to the seventeenth-century arrival of the Dutch seaman, Tasman, who christened the place Nieuw Zeeland, white men scarcely knew of the country's existence. The Maoris had their own highly developed civilisation, but this is not to say that, like the Celts in Ireland, they did not fight incessantly with each other. Unlike the Celts, the Maoris sometimes practised cannibalism, but, like the Celts, they also had a slave culture. Their wars, prior to the coming of the white man, might have come straight out of some of the early Irish sagas, with disputes over women or honour leading to bloody or prolonged conflicts.

War took on a different character, however, after Captain Cook literally put New Zealand on the map. The two islands, about 1,000 miles long, divided by a narrow strait, lying some 1,300 miles to the west of Australia, gradually came to be a theatre of conflict between the Maoris and the Pakeha (whites).

The basic cause of the wars was land. Under the Treaty of Waitingi in 1840, the Crown took possession of the islands, but the Maoris were regranted their land, fishing rights and so on. Freedom of religion was also guaranteed, though more for the benefit of the incoming Christian sects than the Maoris. 'Surrender and regrant' was exactly the same formula that had been used by the British colonists in Ireland. In New Zealand – as happened in Ireland with the Treaty of Limerick – what the Crown seemingly proposed, the settlers disposed. The argument, familiar to Irish ears, was that faraway London did not understand the situation, and that on the ground a strong hand was needed. Accordingly, the settlers began encroaching on the land which the Treaty of Waitingi had supposedly guaranteed.

Guerrilla warfare broke out in 1860 and continued until 1872 when British armament finally triumphed. These wars helped to lay the basis for subsequent Irish attitudes to the Maoris because Irish soldiers of all denominations took part in the wars under the British flag. One of the combatants, a Catholic, is quoted as saying:

Begorra it's murder to shoot them. Sure they are our own people, with their potatoes, and fish, and with children. Who knows but they are Irishmen, with faces a little darkened by the sun, who escaped under the persecutions of Cromwell.

Some of the once proud Maoris gradually degenerated to the condition described in Alan Duff's brutally sad novel *Once Were Warriors*,[2] which was also made into an internationally successful film of the same name. The Irish connection with the Maoris is continued by Sir Tipene O'Regan, the leader of the Ngai Tahu tribe on South Island, who is of mixed Irish/Maori descent. He represented the Maoris before the Waitingi Tribunal and succeeded in winning back extensive land and fishing rights for them.

MARTIN CASH

The long and dangerous journey to New Zealand provided a disincentive to Irish emigration for most of the first half of the nineteenth century. The major Irish descent on New Zealand began later than did that on Australia, and was principally post-Famine, although the Irish had been making their mark on New Zealand prior to that era. In fact, the founder of Auckland, and New Zealand's first Governor, William Hobson, was an Anglo-Irishman from County Waterford.

Today people of Irish descent delight in telling anecdotes about Irish 'characters' of the Hobson era, like Martin Cash, a sort of mini Ned Kelly figure, who managed to escape death for killing a policeman, but served a lengthy sentence on Norfolk Island before becoming a policeman himself on his release in 1854. Like a number of other Irish ex-convicts, he made his way from Australia to New Zealand, and in Christchurch he adopted what some might consider to be the complementary careers of policeman and brothel-keeper. Despite becoming a policeman, Cash's memory, like that of Kelly and bold Jack Donohoe, is both remembered and mythologised in ballad form. According to the song, Martin Cash, Gentleman Bush-ranger, was said to be:

> . . . of a good old valiant race, there is no one can his name disgrace,
> he is a noble son of Erin, where the sprig of shamrock grows.

THE GOLD, THE GREEN AND THE ORANGE

Famine apart, there was another great incentive for the Irish to make the perilous journey from Ireland. They swarmed into New Zealand after gold was discovered in May 1861, and so began the identification of the Irish with the west coast in particular which exists to this day. An Irishman, Christopher Reilly, was responsible for important discoveries in the south also, notably the Dunstan gold field. His discoveries were added to by another Irishman, William Fox, who found the Charleston field in the course of a flamboyant prospecting career, punctuated by spells in jail occasioned by his fighting temperament.

It is estimated that the gold finds brought some 25,000 Irish to New Zealand between 1858 and 1867.[3] As in Australia or California, the Irish got on well in the gold fields. These hard-working, hard-drinking men were of above average physical strength, and brought with them a sense of humour and their native customs and pastimes such as card playing and Irish dancing. They also brought with them their politics, and these provided a major source of controversy during the Fenian era. For every wearer of the Green whom the gold attracted to Australia, there was also someone adorned in Orange, and gold-field rivalry between the two broke out in Hokita in 1868 after the execution of the 'Manchester Martyrs'.

A survivor of the Eureka affray, John Manning, had made his way across the Tasman Sea and founded the *New Zealand Celt*. He also became friendly with an Irish priest, Father W. J. Larkin. Larkin agreed to participate in a ceremony which involved parading an empty coffin to the Hokita cemetery and erecting a Celtic cross in memory of the executed men in the graveyard. Manning and the *New Zealand Celt* enthusiastically supported the idea. However, it was equally vigorously opposed by the Protestant press. The Town Council bowed to Orange influence and had the cemetery gates locked. The demonstrators riposted by removing the gates and, as the nominated speaker had failed to appear, Father Larkin gave the oration, despite the fact that his French bishop had telegraphed him, ordering him not to take part in the ceremony.

A war of words then broke out between Manning's paper and the pro-Orange *West Coast Times* which, in the words of one historian, 'did its best to maintain the atmosphere of crisis.'[4]

The war might have been confined to words, were it not for O'Farrell's attack on the Duke of Edinburgh. Tensions soared and the Duke's proposed visit to New Zealand was cancelled. Larkin, Manning and some others were arrested and charged with treason, and a street row, which passed into New Zealand history as 'the Fenian Riots', broke out in the town of Addison's Flat when a group of Irish nationalists attacked an Orange parade. A level-headed Chief Warden of the Nelson South-West gold fields, T.A.S. Kinnersley, had no difficulty in breaking up the rival factions, but the smell of sulphur emanating from the word 'Fenianism' at the time polluted the political and judicial atmosphere. Manning and Larkin went to jail for a month. On his emergence, Larkin was suspended by his bishop and left for America, as did Manning.

SECTARIAN FEELING

The question of Ireland continued to have significant repercussions for New Zealand right up to the time of the Irish Civil War, and was inevitably intertwined with the Roman Catholic Church-led agitation for state aid for

Catholic schools. The Nationalists' support for Home Rule, whilst it did have some advocates in New Zealand political circles, which also wanted a measure of independence, also provoked sectarian feeling. There was always a body of New Zealand political feeling, whether Catholic or Protestant, which supported Irish Home Rule as being a sort of forerunner for Imperial Federation in which New Zealand would enjoy greater autonomy, trading advantages and an expansion of her power in Pacific islands like Fiji. The Orange element, however, argued that if Home Rule were conceded to Ireland, the Empire would inevitably disintegrate along domino theory lines. This would leave New Zealand vulnerable to the Asian Hordes, the Russian Bear and/or the Pope of Rome.

Irish leaders such as Parnell, Michael Davitt and, subsequent to the Parnellite split, John Dillon, all received support from New Zealand's Catholic Irish. In general, the Church was sympathetic to Irish Independence movements. It has to be said, however, practically speaking, that this sympathy consisted of speech making and so on, rather than movement. The Church in New Zealand, as in Ireland, was positively antipathetic to the physical force and oath-bound nature of Fenianism. Godless republicanism had no appeal to the ultramontane Irish Church leaders who dominated the New Zealand Church as much as they did that of Australia. Cardinal Cullen's fine Italian hand stretched into Auckland every bit as much as it did into Sydney or Melbourne.

IRISH BISHOPS

At Cullen's instigation, T. W. Croke was appointed Bishop of Auckland, but Cullen later clashed with his protégé. Croke's nationalist stance has earned him an honoured place in contemporary Ireland – the GAA, of which he was a patron, christened its principal stadium Croke Park in Dublin after him – but it won him less favour in the eyes of Cullen who arranged for him to be called to Rome to be rebuked. However, Croke's ability and standing were such that he was allowed to remain on in his see. His influence on New Zealand Church history was so great that with his arrival, the historian Richard Davis has judged: '. . . the history of the Irish Catholic Church in New Zealand properly commences'.[5] Croke served in Auckland for four years before being translated back to Ireland in 1874 to become Archbishop of Cashel.

Irish priests and bishops began imparting a markedly Irish tone to New Zealand Catholicism from the 1870s onwards. The advent of the able and energetic Bishop Patrick Moran, in 1871, was a significant event. He too was a Cullen protégé. He launched a successful Catholic paper, *The New Zealand Tablet*, which sought to advance the cause of Catholic education by harnessing it to Irish Nationalist sentiment, and his activities, allied to the Maori and Home Rule movements, led to a corresponding rise in Protestant hostility.

However, while the bishops could generally count on their followers' support in these struggles, attempts to replicate Irish political movements in New Zealand had an opposite effect to that intended by Moran and those who succeeded him. The radical Sir George Gray, for example, wanted to break up the great New Zealand estates along lines favoured in Ireland by Michael Davitt's Land League. This struck a chord of response with Irish immigrants, but the bishops were repelled by the fact that Gray was an ardent secularist in the education field, as was John Balance who was born near Belfast and became the first Irish Prime Minister of New Zealand, following a Liberal/Labour Coalition election victory. Balance, a Protestant, was in favour of Home Rule for Ireland; his opponent, William Massey, also an Irishman, was an Orangeman, opposed to Home Rule. Along with Massey's opposition, Balance had to contend with that of the bishops who mistrusted the Liberal leader's stance on education.

A LACK OF BENEVOLENCE

Education, Home Rule, the conscription issue, the 1916 Rebellion, the rise of Sinn Fein and the subsequent Anglo-Irish war all combined to keep the sectarian pot steaming if not always boiling, although it did on occasion boil over. As with the Roman Catholic Church, which was influenced from Ireland by figures like Cullen and his successors, so with the Protestant Orangemen. By 1874 the Dublin Grand Lodge had authorised the foundation of several lodges throughout New Zealand, and the movement gained further strength when Lord Randolph Churchill decided in 1886 that to trump Home Rule 'the Orange card was the one to play'.

The Green counterpart to the Orange order, the Hibernian Australasian Catholic Benefit Society to give it its full sonorous title, was largely a benevolent society which the bishops favoured as a means of drawing off pro-Fenian sentiment. However, the presence of the Orangemen frequently led to a lack of benevolence, the 'in your face' Orange marches often provoking trouble with the Catholics. Two of the most notable clashes occurred in 1879, appropriately enough, on Boxing Day, at Christ Church and Timaru. In both cases the Catholics, inflamed by reports of the anti-Catholic lectures of a renegade Catholic priest, Charles Chiniquy, attacked the Orangemen, and mild prison sentences were subsequently handed down after trials which attracted widespread publicity and generated further sectarian feeling.

Protestant political influence came to be exerted more through the Protestant Political Association, founded in 1917, than through the Order. As its bitter opposition to state aid for Catholic schools showed, it was as staunchly Protestant as the Order, but its confrontations were conducted through newspaper and pressure group campaigns rather than by means of roadside battles.

THE LISTON AFFAIR

The Sinn Fein insurrection in Ireland, as we saw, caused Mannix to be hijacked on the high seas by a British warship in order to prevent him spreading his contagions in Ireland, but the New Zealand hierarchy were cautious about Mannixism. Only one of its members, Francis Redwood, came out in support of the rerouted Archbishop. Amongst those who did not speak out was the cautious James Liston. However, two years after the Mannix affair, Liston found himself at the epicentre of a New Zealand turmoil as great as any provoked by Mannix in Australia. At a St Patrick's Day dinner in Auckland, in 1922, he made a generally unremarkable speech in which, however, he referred to Irish citizens having been 'murdered' by foreign troops. The affair mushroomed out of all proportion because, as already indicated, Liston's remarks were taken by his opponents as an attempt to introduce Mannixism to New Zealand, and by his supporters as being nothing more than the literal truth. Liston was not referring to regular British troops, as was alleged, but to Black and Tans, the counter-insurgency force, who not only had committed murders but had been sent to Ireland for the specific purpose of so doing.[6]

The affair escalated absurdly until finally Liston was charged with sedition. However, a jury decided that hostility to British Government activity in Ireland did not constitute sedition in New Zealand, and Liston was acquitted. The affair had an impact on the subsequent General Election in which Catholics swung to Labour to such an extent that the party's representation increased from eight to seventeen seats. It was a remarkable indication of balance of power tactics because the Catholic vote probably comprised no more than 14 per cent of the electorate.

IRISH MAIDS

One other curious cause of dissension existed in New Zealand. The 'No Irish need apply' syndrome had of course crossed the Tasman Sea from Australia, but one continuing exception to this prejudice was Irish maids, an important segment of the work force in lace-curtain New Zealand. These girls were hired because 'proper English servants' could not be induced to travel to New Zealand. In Canterbury in 1874, it was reckoned that 56 per cent of all foreign-born emigrants were English. Of the rest, the majority were Irish, and – worse! – female. From these women, largely of rural background, the English miladies attempted to fashion maidservants sculpted from a model of snobbish, white-aproned, British respectability a world away from the comprehension of the emigrants.

As in Australia, the girls had to contend with the attentions of the male members of the family they worked for. Unwanted pregnancies, abortion, and social stigmas helped to compound anti-Irish prejudices. The Canterbury emigration agent in London wrote in 1864 that the maids sent to Canterbury must contain 'no Irish'. The words were underscored so strongly that the pen broke, splattering the page with ink.[7]

A New Zealand authority, Anna Rogers, has written:

> The prevailing view of the time [was] that Irish female servants were, at best, sources of entertainment – slightly foolish but well-meaning – but, at worst, stupid, sullen, unfit for any meaningful work. Contemporary cartoons in Australia and New Zealand abounded in depictions of black-visaged servants, generally labelled as 'Biddy', demonstrating extreme stupidity.[8]

In her book she reproduces one of the anecdotes of the time which led her to make this judgement. It concerns a typical 'Mary the Maid':

> On going into the sitting room, I saw three visiting cards on the table, and asked where the lady was. She said, 'Sure I don't know mam. She asked me was you in, an' I said, "She is", so she gave me thim tickets, an' I took them, and shut the door.'

THE SWAGGERS

Such anecdotes of course had a basis in reality, as did the proliferation of stories about Irish 'characters' like Ned Slattery, one of the most famous Irish 'swaggers', the New Zealand equivalent of the more contemporary 'long distance men' of the English building trade. These itinerant workers walked from one job to another. Their worldly possessions were contained in the 'swag' on their back, and as they walked they weeded, or hoed, or hewed, in return for a meal and a place to sleep. The 'swaggers' occupy a place in New Zealand folklore somewhat analogous to that of the Australian bush-rangers, the stories about them generally combining a dash of humour and a demonstration of an ability to buck the system.

Ned Slattery from County Clare, one of the most famous 'swaggers', was known as 'the Shiner'. After the gold ran out, he lived on his wits and it is recorded that in the shanty town of Macraes Flat, he found himself penniless and gasping for a drink.[9] Accordingly, he told a publican, before he was served, that he had no money, only stamps, plenty of stamps – 'enough for a barrel of whiskey'. The publican gave him a bottle and a glass, and the Shiner rapidly used the latter to lower the level of the former. Eventually the publican interrupted his drinking: 'The stamps please.'

The Shiner began to stamp his foot, counting at the same time. The publican grew near apoplectic with combined rage and embarrassment in front of the other customers, 'Postage stamps!' he spluttered.

'Did I say postage stamps?' enquired the still-stamping Shiner.

Eventually the publican had to concede that he had been had, but in typically Irish fashion, he agreed to forgive the Shiner – on condition that he crossed the road and replicate the trick on his arch-rival, a fellow publican and Irishman.

ADJUSTMENT

Poor Biddy and Mary and Sean, and all the toilers and moilers like them, somehow made their way and passed into New Zealand history. With them passed much of the tension and antagonism of the Catholic/Protestant, Anglo-Irish abrasion, chiefly because of the partial settlement of the Irish problem achieved by the Anglo-Irish Treaty of 1921. Subsequently, the problems of the Irish in New Zealand became those of emigrants anywhere: adjustment to a new environment, economic pre-occupations, the struggle up the ladder of economic success, rather than the problems of the land they had left.

Patrick O'Farrell, one of that very rare breed who could have turned his hand to literature equally as well as history, has captured the sense of Irish life in Australia and New Zealand in memorable prose in his *Vanished Kingdoms*.[10] His is an astringent, but affectionate view, seen through his family's eyes, and through the lens of his son Richard's camera. One vignette describes how a potato farming family achieved success: sometimes 'rocks and rubbish' mysteriously found their way into stitched bags. The family had struggled up from the ranks of the 'Biddys' to what was known 'in their reverential and resentful Irish manner' as 'The Big House'. O'Farrell writes:

> This was partly an absurd and pretentious misnomer, in that the family was not Anglo-Irish (the traditional occupants of 'Big Houses' in Ireland) and the house was by no means large. Yet, apart from what the label had to say about the importation into the colonies of slavish imitations of the Irish class system, the House did have some of the classic features of the genre, on a scrawny miniature scale. It hid behind a dense, high hedge, harboured formidably unmarried daughters, was dominated by an irascible old patriarch and (characteristic of a sub-group of such Irish edifices) appeared to radiate an atmosphere of gloom and stand-offishness into its surrounding districts. It constituted a significant local presence, but one neither approachable nor happy.

However, as O'Farrell indicates, not all Irish brought this 'penny-looking-down-on-a-halfpenny' type of provincialism with them. By venturing across the vastnesses of the oceans that separated them from their upbringing, they also enlarged their mental horizons, albeit at the cost of physical and mental exertions that took their toll. Again, in *Vanished Kingdoms*, O'Farrell memorably encapsulates this cost to one emigrant: 'He had lifted his vision from the demarcations and boundaries of Irish ditches and bogs, to the horizons of infinity, and the stretch marks showed in his eyes.' Those stretch marks are to be found in the eyes of Irish emigrants around the world.

THE CASE

It should be stressed that though sectarianism and prejudice have played their part in Australia and New Zealand, both countries are world leaders in the fields of multi-culturalism, social legislation and general fair play (off the rugby field that is!). This manifests itself to a stranger in simple but telling ways. Australian 'mateship' is legendary. If one stands at a lift in an office, for instance, passers-by will inevitably react with a friendly 'Good dy mate'. In New Zealand, however, people tend to be that little bit nicer. The passer-by is apt to accompany his greeting with a 'Can I do anything to help you?'

The blending together of the Protestant and Catholic communities was assisted by this pleasantness and by the diminution of the Irish issue in world affairs generally after the 1921 Treaty settlement. No winds, or at least only very faint ones, blew from Ireland to fan the embers of sectarianism amongst the Irish diaspora. Generally speaking, the Liston affair may be taken as writing *finis* to a long and acrimonious chapter of development. However, there was one outburst of sectarian feeling in the 1950s which should be noted.

Just as Australia had 'the Split' over the efforts to extend the Catholic Church's power into the political arena, so did New Zealand have 'the Case'. This is the nickname for the controversy which erupted over the Catholic Church's campaign to secure Government funding for Catholic schools. No monies were forthcoming at the time but, as in Australia, the issue was ultimately diffused by the Private Schools Conditional Integration Act, which allowed all forms of private schools to enter the state system and its benefits.

At the time of 'the Case', the idea that New Zealand would have a Catholic Prime Minister drawn from the ranks of the National Party seemed remote indeed, but Jim Bolger became Prime Minister in 1990. In a very rare interview, in which he discussed his religion, he paid tribute to the state school system:

> One of the great advantages of going to a state school, a school with a non-religious base, was that we weren't divided. We actually all grew up together, and I would imagine the other children of the school gained as much from it as I did because we didn't see ourselves as different. Sure, we went to different churches, and, from time to time, the Catholic kids attended this or that service which the others didn't attend, and they probably wondered why we did. The natural curiosity of youth.
>
> The experience has served me enormously well over the years, so that I don't in any shape or form judge people on their religious beliefs. I was never segregated out because of mine, and I don't segregate others because of theirs. I work with and meet people of every religious belief, with no difficulty at all, so I think that has proved to be a plus. I never suffered from any vilification.[11]

Whilst his words are obviously carefully chosen, Bolger's description of education and political life in contemporary New Zealand gives a fair enough impression of the quality of life for the Irish there.

BRINGING DOWN THE BARRIERS

Along with the roaring redemptorist preachers of the old-fashioned retreats, Bolger's memory, like that of other New Zealand Catholics, would be of missionary priests who went to places like the Solomon Islands, and died very shortly thereafter, as a result of the hardships encountered. These men formed part of the fabric of the New Zealand inheritance. As Bolger says: 'Those sorts of heroic figures of Catholic missionaries, men and women, who had gone out from the older Catholic countries, and now more latterly some out from New Zealand . . . were in the deep recesses of my mind.' Part of that 'deep recess' can be found in cheerful colloquial slang. For example, a decade or so ago it was not unusual to record, in the report of a score in a rugby match involving a Marist school, that the try was greeted with 'the rattle of the rosary beads', which decodes as Catholic applause. Rugby has tended to be a useful instrument in bringing down barriers of prejudice, as so many leading All Blacks were Catholic educated.

The recollections of childhood and of the brothers tend to be gentler than those of Australians, as reflected in a poem to a dead brother by Sam Hunt:

> I leave you, Brother Lynch,
> bifocalled bright-eyed man;
> can only wish that others
> see you as I do –
> nothing celibate or sorry,
> nothing sad about you
>
> Meantime, warm cheers, cold beers
> good Brother Lynch,
> you have your Heaven yet –
> green shirt open to the neck –
> an old man
> blinking at the sunset.[12]

Brother Lynch was a Marist, one of the main educators of Catholics in New Zealand. He produced, or helped to produce, many of the outstanding Catholic laymen of contemporary New Zealand and his influence was tangible, his presence obvious.

The less tangible evidences of Church divisions like the Orange Order or the Catholic Knights of Southern Cross or the Secret of Opus Dei Society are apparently declining on both sides of the religious divide. Some organisers of the St Patrick's Day parade have achieved an ecumenical rapport with their Orange brethren (the two sides invite each other to their respective parades). Talking to them, I have found them almost sympathetic to the decline in the Orange demonstration strength: 'We had a banquet, but all they had was sandwiches, drinks out of plastic cups, and a video of Orange marches in the Six Counties.'

The St Patrick's Day parade is gaining in strength, and by 1996 attracted some 30,000 participants or onlookers. The Northern Irish problems did have their resonances as one float featured a caricature of John Major, because of his failure to advance the Irish Peace Process, and the police stepped in; but this was an exception. The parades are generally good-humoured and celebratory and would give 'the worm' no cause to wriggle.

However, in 1997 republicanism still wafted onto the New Zealand air from the columns of Vincent Burke's monthly *Saoirse*, and the New Zealand *Irish Post* was also staunchly nationalistic. As Hugh Maguire, a thirty-something Cavan-born art historian, who lectures in Auckland University, put it to me in a memorable phrase: 'We don't have to put up with any of that "grovelling apologetics" for opposing a sense of Irishness that you get in Dublin.' Interestingly, he relates New Zealand's growing acceptance of the Irish community's consciousness of being Irish to the country's increasing recognition of the justice of the Maoris' claims for compensation.

Because of their confiscations, dislocations and problems of adjustments with contemporary society, the Maoris certainly have one experience in common with the Irish. They are taking over from them in the prisons. I spoke to one of the most famous priests in New Zealand, Father Thomas Ryan, who originally came to New Zealand on loan for a five-year period but stayed on when war came, working in education and as a Church representative in the education debate, and he told me that when he first came to New Zealand, a common saying was: 'You'll never be short of an altar boy in prison.' This is changing rapidly. The upward mobility of the Irish, and changing attitudes, particularly amongst Catholic Irish women, are broadening and enriching a society in which, as a young priest, he had found the formation which nuns were expected to give Catholic girls to be 'almost primitive'. Coming from a different tradition from that of Brian Edwards, described below, he nevertheless completely shares his assessment of New Zealand as a 'fair-minded society'.

A WARM POSITIVE FEELING

In Ireland, New Zealand is often spoken of as being one of the last hold-outs of imperial England and of Orangeism, but the prominent New Zealand broadcaster, Brian Edwards, who is of the Northern Ireland Protestant tradition, disagrees. He describes New Zealand people as being:

> Like their climate. They have the open refreshing qualities of sea and sand. The people are transparent and friendly. When I went home, the darkness, the coldness, combined with the devastation of the war, made me immediately yearn for a warm climate with a tolerant people.

When Edwards was a boy, he was taught 'Never turn your back on a Catholic. Never marry a Catholic', and his mother tried to commit suicide when he became engaged to one. He found that coming to New Zealand dissipated all these burdens of bigotry. Edwards strikes a common grace note amongst some members of the Irish community when he says that he couldn't live in Ireland, a plague on both sets of extremists, but, nevertheless, it's nice to be Irish! In New Zealand he finds 'there is a very warm positive feeling for the

Irish'. Any latent sectarianism is related to the educational issue, and he himself never encountered any form of prejudice. In fact he said, 'I use my Irishness shamelessly on the air, and I find people are tremendously affectionate.'

This affection is furthered of course by the achievements of several distinguished people of Irish descent within the community, like Peter Temm, New Zealand's leading High Court judge, or Sir Michael Faye, a merchant banker.

Sport in New Zealand as elsewhere is another reason the Irish generate affection, particularly through the Irish bloodstock industry. Sir Tristam, the highest earning sire in Australasian history, is owned by Patrick Hogan, the proprietor of the hugely successful Hogan stud. New Zealand show-jumping, bloodstock and horse-racing are all helped by Irish stock. In other sports the leading yachtsman is Chris Dixson, whose father is Irish and the coach of the New Zealand soccer team is Joe McGrath from Dublin.

Rodney Walshe, a Dublin Protestant and now the generally liked and respected Honorary Irish Consul, was himself a distinguished rugby player. He, Tony O'Reilly and Nial Brophy, the latter both becoming legendary try-scoring British Lions, all played on the most famous Leinster provincial schoolboys team in history, that of 1953–54. Their particularly Homeric winning encounter · with Ulster was referred by the famous · Dublin headmaster, Kevin Kelliher, who almost caused New Zealand to leave the Commonwealth by sending off one of its sporting icons, Colin Meads, during a sanguinary All-Blacks occasion. However Walshe kept the Kelliher connection to himself and built up a flourishing tourist business in Auckland, and has been responsible for arranging monthly flights bringing large parties of Kiwis to Dublin. On average about 2,500 New Zealanders visit Ireland each month but only about 3,000 Irish a year visit N.Z. For its part Dublin has stepped up the tempo of official visits to New Zealand and figures like President Mary McAlese or the Tanaiste (deputy Prime Minister) include New Zealand in their itinerary when they visit Australia.

Amongst the newer arrivals, who also further Irish networking, is Oliver Lee, a publisher and entrepreneur, with Niamh O'Connor, who, with Shiela McCabe from Northern Ireland, formed the first all-woman legal partnership in New Zealand, runs a popular Irish radio programme. One of their contemporaries is Chris Bourke, then lit. ed. of the influential *Leader* magazine, who told me an interesting story concerning one of the most famous figures in the entire history of the Irish diaspora. Chris had just taken delivery of an interesting family heirloom, a piano once owned by an uncle, Gerard Clarke. When Clarke, who later became a judge, was a student living in the family home in Stephen's Green, Dublin, a fellow student visited him and urged him to approach his mother for a 'loan' of sixpence so that the pair could buy a drink. While Gerard discussed the 'loan' upstairs with his mother, downstairs his friend Jimmy occupied himself playing the Clarke's treasured Bechstein piano. Hearing the music, Mrs Clarke asked who the pianist was, and being told 'Jimmy', remarked, 'He's good', and gave her son twice what he asked for, a shilling. 'Jimmy' was James Joyce.

Everyone I spoke to concerning the older Irish emigrants – that is, those who had come out during the 1950s – told me I had to speak to Hughie Green and his friend and partner Barney McCahill, whose son Bernie played for the All Blacks. Another son, Sean, was a member of the Irish international Rugby Squad. Both are Donegal men. One woman told me, 'I remember them on the trams with their big hands and the shovels.' Nowadays Green and McCahill are regarded as being the archetypically rich Irish. They went from millionaires to billionaires in one anecdote after another but unusually for an Irish community, there was unanimous agreement on one thing: they were wealthy.

Hughie, still a huge, craggy, shaggy, bushy-browed figure, described how their wealth began. 'We got a job to lay twenty-seven miles of cable into the inner city [of Auckland]. We had to do so much per day. The normal pay was £10 a week. We got £27. We had seven workers, six from Donegal and one from Kerry. It was all done by hand. We had an axe to take up the tarmacadam. It was called the Irish compressor. I had £13,000 in the bank at the end of it.' He now has interests in cattle, piggeries and property, as well as construction, and his five children are carrying on the dynasty in various branches of the business. He attributes his success to his training in attending fairs in Ireland between the ages of ten and fifteen. By the age of fourteen, the end of a fair often saw him in charge of eighty-five to one hundred cattle, and he knew every beast, who owned it, where it had to be delivered, and whether or not the beast was paid for. Understandably these skills stood him in good stead later, when he came to New Zealand and had to deal with Chinese, Peloponnesians, Free Masons, British, and Irish New Zealanders. He is strongly nationalistic, ensuring that estates and streets which he builds have Irish names, and takes pleasure in the advances made by the Irish since he landed in New Zealand:

We have gained a lot of ground in forty years. The Irish were very ground-down when I came here first. The place was very British. The Irish got jobs in the cops, the public service, or labouring. We were at the bottom of the heap. We helped each other. You knew every recent arrival. But now you find the Irish at the top everywhere. Tony O'Reilly helped a lot. I like him. He's a good advertisement for the Irish. He shows what can be done.

Hughie, who encourages the spread of Irish dancing and the Irish language, is strongly republican in outlook. He has no particular fondness for money, but gets his kicks out of taking on a difficult job or making a shrewd purchase of cattle. He attributes much of his successful philosophy to an Englishman whom he worked for. He told me: 'If you get any knowledge, the best thing you can do is pass it on; he educated me.'

THE LAST PEBBLE IN THE SHOE

The last pebble in the shoe for the Irish in New Zealand is the Northern Ireland situation. As we have seen, discord in Ireland, be it over Home Rule, or Rome Rule, inevitably spreads throughout the diaspora, to a greater or lesser degree. All over the world I found the Northern Ireland situation obtruding unexpectedly in conversations, at dinner tables, on yachts, in airplanes, but never so surprisingly as in the conversation of Sam McCready, the internationally famous rose-grower from Armagh, who made his home in New Zealand in 1972. A friend of his who owned a pub was shot by the IRA and died after lingering for eight months in a coma. He was a Protestant. Another friend of his, also a pub owner, was chosen in the making of a point by Loyalist gunmen, who shot him on the Orangemen's Feast Day, July 12th. He was a Catholic. McCready talked of these deaths and of much more during our pleasant waterfront restaurant meal. The vista was as peaceful as it was beautiful. Auckland is aptly named 'the city of sails', and the setting made his recollections of Ireland seem all the more horrific. The year he left was a terrible one. Bloody Sunday and Bloody Friday occurred. In the former British paratroopers shot down unarmed civilians during a peaceful protest march in Derry. The latter created indelible images of bits of bodies being shovelled into plastic sacks, after bungled IRA warnings led to civilians being blasted into eternity all over Belfast on a warm, July afternoon.

McCready was in Paris with a charter flight from Northern Ireland, attending a rugby international, when the news of Bloody Sunday was relayed over the loud-speaker system at the airport. Sitting in our restaurant, a world away in time and space, he shook his head sadly as he recalled how the charter members divided when the news came. 'We were all chatting together, Protestants and Catholics. There had been powerful craic over the weekend, and then we heard the loud-speakers. Protestants and Catholics broke up into separate groups and never spoke to each other again for the rest of the trip home.' These were evil memories indeed, but McCready said he had put them behind him: 'Now I just say, a plague on both your houses.' Then, I happened to mention Drumcree.

Drumcree, as readers will recall, is the cemetery and townland outside the strongly Protestant town of Portadown in County Armagh. Linking the town to the cemetery is the Garvaghy Road. Alongside it there stand new housing estates, now largely occupied by Catholics. In the year we spoke, the previous year, and subsequently, the road has been the cause of some of the potentially most dangerous street violence ever experienced in the entire thirty years of the Troubles.

As Drumcree and the Garvaghy Road were mentioned, I noticed that McCready, a strikingly tall, handsome man with white hair and a physique that clearly betokens a lifetime of athleticism and the open air, was reddening under his sun tan and beginning to exude an air of tension. The he burst out: 'Those buggers were walking on my father's grave.' The defiant Orangemen, during the days of stand-off with the police had camped in and around Drumcree cemetery. It turned out that not only McCready's father but his ancestors for several hundred years were buried in that cemetery and the land around it had been his family's. Where conflict and violence were now enshrined, Sam McCready and his people before him had once erected a rose-growing shrine to peaceful husbandry.

I found it eerie to witness the tensions of Northern Ireland suddenly manifest themselves before me while the gentle, rose-growing giant visibly struggled to contain emotions he had obviously hoped to leave behind him in Ireland. As my plane took off from peaceful, beautiful Auckland, I found myself thinking of Sam: just one more reason why, a world away, conditions should be created for his countrymen wherein the equally beautiful Belfast Lough could become a setting of equal tranquillity.

SEVEN

AFRICA

Ex Africa semper aliquid novum. (There is always something new out of Africa.)

Irish fighting units had operated in South Africa for nearly a hundred years and on 25th June 1900, the Irish Transvaal Brigade was vividly reminded of this. As they passed through the small settlement of Bronkhorstspruit, they found the welcome shade of peach trees which had grown up over the previous twenty years. In the first Anglo-Boer war the Connaught Rangers had been ambushed here. Many of the men had had their pockets filled with ripe peaches picked from a nearby orchard. They were buried in their uniforms and the peach grove which soon grew up marked the spot.

> Donal P. McCracken, *MacBride's Brigade Irish Commandos in the Anglo-Boer War*,
> Four Courts Press, Dublin, 1999.

After a week in which 500 civilians were hacked or shot to death in the Congo, Catholic priests were being subjected to sexual torture by prostitutes in Chinese prisons and Ireland's oldest person – a Dominican missionary sister – celebrated her 109th birthday, missionaries are back in the news . . .

> *Ireland on Sunday*, 10 January 1999

IN FACT MISSIONARIES are rarely out of the news in Ireland. What might be termed the caring tradition, or Brendan factor, is still alive and well, even if not in the numbers of other years. In 1998 there were 4,087 missionaries working outside Ireland, compared to 7,120 working in the Third World alone in 1970. According to the Irish Missionary Union, the bulk of those who work in the Third World are in Africa, where in 1996 there were 2,294 Irish Catholic Brothers, Nuns and priests. Irish Protestant missionaries had a total of eighty-five (including Church of Ireland, Methodist and Presbyterian). However, even as religious vocations fall, the Brendan tradition is being added to by lay people who may be either agnostics or believers. Whether men or women, whether of the Catholic or Protestant tradition, they continue to feel that they have an obligation to devote at least part of their lives to the service of other creeds and colours in the Third World. Throughout Oceania, India, the Philippines, and many other places including, as we have seen, Latin America, the Irish have made a significant humanitarian contribution.

The Irish record is not unblemished. In Africa the Irish missionaries were often criticised by their French counterparts for not learning the local languages, and for living like Europeans in brick houses, rather than as the French did in huts, eating local food and drinking unfiltered water in the same way as the Africans.[1] However the French paid a terrible price for adopting this lifestyle. The average French missioner, in the years 1848–1900 was twenty-six on arrival in Africa; he was thirty-two when he died. In turn, the Irish found the French ultra-conservative, patronising and rubric bound.

However, without attempting to adjudicate on issues of missionary technique, or enter debate on religious beliefs, the self-sacrificial quotient of the Irish clearly survived from the era of St Brendan to that of our own. As a leading authority has pointed out:

> In relative terms (per capita of Catholic populations, the Irish were to outstrip all the European missionary countries by the early 1960s; and in absolute terms, by the 1970s Irish totals were amongst the highest in Europe.[2]

This is not the place to pursue the speculation as to what might have been the impact on Ireland, had the Church not siphoned off these selfless energies and high levels of education at a time when third-level education was nothing like as widespread as it is today. However, apart from factors such as EU aid and increased education, the change in vocation patterns from service in the ranks of Mother Church to employment by Mother Ireland must be reckoned to have some impact.

Of course, not all the Irish contribution to the Third World was either noble or selfless. Service in imperial armies, or as administrators, or traders involved in a process of colonial exploitation, is not designed to produce knights in shining armour. None the less, much was done by Irish missionaries – all around the world and often at the cost of their lives – of which any nation could feel proud on humanitarian terms alone, whatever the religious beliefs. For example, merely taking the period during which I was researching and writing this book, half a dozen Irish missionaries have been murdered.

Africa claimed most lives. In Sierra Leone, Father Felim McAllister and Brother Senan Kerrigan were shot during 1994. In that year also Sister Eileen Connell was attacked in a pastoral centre in Warri, Nigeria and died as a result of her injuries. In South Africa, in 1997, Father Malachy Skelton, was shot in Kwa Zulu, Natal, during a car-hijacking. A hijacking may also have cost the life of Father Martin Boyle in Eldoret, Kenya in 1994, but it was continuing denunciation of the growing corruption and human rights abuses in that country by Father Larry Timmons which led to his murder in Lare, in 1997. Before their deaths all these people had performed prodigies in the building not only of churches, but of clinics and schools; in the provision of clean water and housing; in the defence of human rights; in the promotion of women's issues; and in several other fields of human betterment.

Many more are continuing to risk their lives in different parts of the world:

Africa, the Philippines, Pakistan, the Caribbean. For example, as this is being written, in Pakistan, Fathers Paul MacMahon and Denis Carter are confronting landlords who are trying to wrest from the sanctuary the priests have extended, scores of Haris, or bonded labourers, men women, and children. The priests have survived a number of major life threatening situations. Including one in 1998 in which a large force of armed men descended on the parish of Malti, in the Sindh region, during the night, beat up the Haris and loaded them on to trucks. In the darkness, amidst the screams and the shouting, the blows and the bullets, the priests stopped the lorries and managed to get a hundred or so to escape. Amongst these there were deaths and miscarriages as a result of the beatings the Haris had suffered. The priests escaped without serious injury and persisted in their campaign against the landlords. They created an outcry, as a result of which some scores more were returned to their protection. At the time of writing the whereabouts of the rest of the kidnapped Haris is uncertain. But McMahon and Carter are still in Malti, and the landlords know where to find them.

In the Philippines the Irish Columban Fathers have a magnificent record of opposing injustice. I remember on one occasion during the eighties, being on the phone to Fr Niall O'Brien who was at the time in prison. It should be explained that the Philippines is a cock-eyed amalgam of the values of the American Way and ruthless colonial exploitation: 'Sure we built a road – didn't we build a road to the Coca Cola plant?' Combined with allowing prisoners the right to make and receive telephone calls from prison.

As we spoke, (I was then a newspaper editor) armed men appeared on the roof opposite his cell. Niall did not know whether or not they were coming to kill him. Under the American puppet, Marcos, such happenings were common at the time. The line went dead. For what it was worth, I organised a lead story. In any event Niall survived. At the time his case was receiving massive attention in Ireland. He was the parish priest of Inapoy on Negros Island in the Philippines. After years of unfavourable attention from the regime, because of his activities on behalf of his parishioners, he was arrested and charged with the murder of Mayor Sola. In 1983 he was subjected to a mockery of a trial, following a long period of brutalisation, and imprisoned. A combination of student protest which crystallised around his case, coupled with international publicity, eventually secured his release, and the agitation was a major factor in Marcos's fall. Fr O'Brien returned to Ireland to thank the people who had helped him. I met him on Kilronan Pier on the Aran Islands, which had subscribed generously to his campaign, and took him to a pub. The sensation which his ordeal had aroused was as nothing to the frisson in Katie Joe Mac's bar, when Steve Kilmartin, the barman asked him what would he have and Niall replied: 'A glass of milk please.' It was a first, but he got the milk. Steve was always a gentleman. Niall got his vindication too. Apart from the fact that he had helped to bring down the regime in 1997, the principal witness against him confessed that. he hai lied.

In 1997 also Msgr Des Hartford had a grenade thrown into his home on

Above: Emigrants arrive in the USA.

Below: Tammany Hall, where the Democrats are meeting to select their Presidential candidate.

Above: A triumphant President Kennedy returns to Ireland in June 1963. He is shown leaving Cork City Hall, thronged by admirers.

Right: The Kennedy family grieves once more. After the death of Michael Kennedy in a skiing accident in 1997, Senator Ted Kennedy is escorted by Cardinal Bernard Law.

Above: Archbishop Spellman plays ball in the New York Foundling Hospital, 1945.

Right: Irish Canadian lumberjacks in Newfoundland, 1936.

Below: Archbishop Cushing spins a yarn at the Archbishop Cushing Central High School, Boston, 1948.

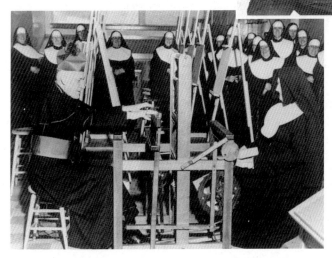

Left: John Mitchel (1815-75), who in his dramatic career was first transported to Australia but later escaped to the United States, where he became a Confederate publicist. His grandson became the youngest ever Mayor of New York.

Below left: Ned Kelly (1854-80), depicted wearing his famous bucket in a shoot-out.

Below right: Paul Keating, former Prime Minister of Australia, advocate of a republic and brilliant despatch-box brawler.

THE IRISH TRADITIONS IN CARING AND WORLD POLICING:

Left: Irish soldiers on duty for the UN in Lebanon, 1987.

Below: The Ghanaian Commander of Unifil hands out service decorations to Irish soldiers on St Patrick's Day, 2000.

Below left: Bob Geldof travels to help combat drought and famine in Africa on behalf of Band-Aid (1985).

Below right: The Roman Catholic priest Mgr Desmond Hartford on his release from kidnappers in the Philippines (1997).

IRISH BUSINESS SUCCESS:

Above: The former rugby international and present international tycoon, Tony O'Reilly, with his wife Chryss Goulandris.

Right above: Michael O'Leary, Chief Executive of Ryan Air, is joined by stewardesses as he announces the low-cost airline's new European routes for 2000.

Right: The Celtic Tiger purrs on in Europe. The Irish EU Finance Minister, Charles McCreevy, shares a joke with the EU Central Bank Governor, Maurice O'Connell (1998).

Right: George
Best in action for
Manchester
United (1968).

Above: All Black Sean
Fitzpatrick lifts the 125th
Anniversary Save and
Prosper Cup after beating
England at Twickenham
(1996).

Middle right: Eddie Irvine
prepares for action in the
British Grand Prix, 2000.

Right: The Corrs
performing in Hyde Park,
London (1999).

Right: Brian Moore, the distinguished novelist and screenwriter, who died in 1999.

Below: Pierce Brosnan as James Bond (1994).

Above: The Nobel Prizewinner Seamus Heaney wins the Whitbread Book of the Year Award for his reworking of Beowulf.

Left: Liam Neeson (1998).

Michael Flatley, the Lord of the Dance (1996).

Mindanao, the southern island of the Philippines. He escaped but a woman was killed. Subsequently he was kidnapped by members of the Moro Liberation Army. Hartford had been caught up in the war between the MLA and the Government which the MLA say has defaulted on its promises to distribute land. The area is a cauldron of tension between the Muslim population which once owned 75% of the land, and now only hold 25%, and the Christians. On being released Hartford commented that the situation was:[3] '. . . a bit like the Northern Ireland situation. There has been a negative history and yet the only way forward is together and peace.'

Another Irish Columban in the Philippines has dealt Manila's sex industry a mighty blow. Fr Shay Cullen has waged for several years a one-man war against the sale of children and teenage girls into prostitution. As a result of his efforts European paedophiles have been successfully prosecuted in their own countries. As this book was being written he caused a sensation by climbing on top of a tall electricity pylon to protest agaiost its'erection near a children's home Olongapo, fifty miles from Manila. He has been beaten up, accused of being a paedophile himself, arrested and jalled. But predations on Manila's swarming street children population, and child abuse of all kinds, have dropped dramatically. Cullen's own estimate[4] is that his campaign has cut the number of prostitutes in Manila from 16,000 to an incredibly low 200.

IGNORANT AWARENESS

When I was a boy, Cullen-type involvement would have been unthinkable for missionaries. My own state of ignorant awareness would have been typical of much Irish public opinion. Missionary activity was concerned with the 'dark continent'. The majority of Irish missionaries still go to Africa, where 56 per cent of them are women, unlike in the rest of the missionary sphere – Asia/Oceania, the Caribbean and Latin America, where the bulk of Irish missionaries are men. I was taught by a missionary order, The Holy Ghosts, which had a particular connection with Africa, but I never remember any of the priests discussing African culture or politics. Certainly we received no insights into how Africans lived their daily lives. Yet, we could easily have been given lectures. Several of our teachers were 'back from Africa'. Of what they did there, all we knew was that they had been 'on the missions', an activity about which we had only the haziest notion, although there were always some African students in the college whose presence we dimly understood had something to do with 'the missions'.

That's the way it was in Ireland, and to a degree still is. One of the contemporary Kiltegan Fathers whose name is spoken of with respect in Kenya is Father Eddie Lawlor. When we talked during my visit to Africa he recalled conversations with his father on his periodic returns to Ireland: 'Have ye bread out there? Have ye butter . . .?'[5]

Above all, the 'black baby' box was widespread. The collections for black babies meant that one's pennies went 'to the missions' to save a black baby from heathenism. Increasingly in recent years, such collections have been directed at alleviating hunger or disease – the word 'famine' has resonances for Ireland which always guarantee a generous response – but in my school-days it never occurred to anyone that there could be anything even remotely patronising in the philosophy that lay behind those collections. We were brought up believing that Africans as a class were as much in need of the civilising influences of the Irish religions as parched earth was of water. It was an image propagated by the missionary magazines with their pictures of a big, beaming Irish priest, generally robed in white, surrounded by a group of adoring, chubby little black children.

AN ASSAULT ON AFRICAN CUSTOMS

The idea that we were supporting an assault on African customs which had evolved over centuries and worked well for the Africans would have seemed bizarre. However, as we shivered in the fogs and rains of Ireland, over there in the heat, Irish nuns in their starched white uniforms and Irish priests in their soutanes were sawing away at the roots of African communal life. Customs such as arranged marriages, polygamy, the bride-price, in the Western world appear feudal. So they are – but in Africa, in the economy of the day, such practices provided children to cater for old age. Each wife had her own hut where she lived with her children in the family compound, with her own respect, rights and privileges. The women tilled and created the huts, and the men looked after the animals, which could include protecting them from predators like lions. Such a system would not survive in an educated, industrialised society. The missionaries, however, were not operating in such a society. With the best will in the world, they were seeking to impose a philosophy derived from the advanced economies of an industrialised world, on one that was in many ways still in the Stone Age. And here, at the risk of digression, may I observe that one wonders whether the idea of paying for a wife is any worse than the concept that a daughter is such a liability that a father must pay a dowry for the privilege of having her taken off his hands.

One of South Africa's best-known Irish priests has prepared a paper in which he says:

the word mission itself is fast becoming a negative connotation. Throughout the world, and particularly in Africa, there is a growing resentment with the concept of foreigners arriving and imposing a foreign lifestyle, all in the name of religion . . . a paradigm shift is taking place where mission is going through a real conversion of sorts . . . the past has shown that in general no one will interfere in [charitable] attempts so long as they merely deal with the symptoms of the problem. The conflict arises when those in ministry turn to the source of the problem and begin to identify it . . . Our task is to bring to the surface the voices from below, from the subconscious – voices that are rooted in the daily experiences of people, experiences of landlessness, squatter camps, migrant labour hostels and poor people who are discovering their sense of human dignity.[6]

IRELAND'S CONTRIBUTION

Some of the complexity, difficulty and scale of the African continent occurred to me during a conversation in Nairobi. An old Africa hand pointed out that the East African region is the area of most continuous conflict in the world, more so even than the Middle East.[7] In the previous ten years, there had been major wars in Ethiopia, Somalia, Uganda, the Sudan and Rwanda. While this was being written there was serious trouble in Kenya itself, in the Turkana region, and political unrest was growing in the rest of the country. Parts of Uganda and the Sudan were still experiencing serious military conflict. During my researches, further very serious troubles broke out elsewhere in Africa: in Burundi, Zaire, Liberia, Sierra Leone; and warfare resumed again between Eritrea and Ethiopia.

Some indication of Ireland's contribution to this troubled continent may be achieved by adapting the following comment of the historian Frances Bernard Doyle who said:

> During the second half of the last century, Catholic education in South Africa was almost entirely in the hands of Irish religious or religions brought from Europe by Irish Bishops. Today these congregations have spread from their original foundations to almost every diocese in the Republic.[8]

Doyle's judgement about Irish congregations spreading 'from their original foundations' could be fairly interpreted by changing the word 'Republic' to 'Africa'. Not having an empire of their own, the Irish escaped some, if not all, of the fallout from Europe's huge interventions in Africa in the latter part of the nineteenth century, so memorably summed up in the despairing utterance of an Ethiopian Emperor, Tewodros II:[9] 'I know their game. First the traders and the missionaries: then the ambassadors; then the cannon. It's better to go straight to the cannon.' He was actually speaking shortly before unsuccessfully engaging an invading British army in 1868 and losing his life.

Given the shared opprobrium for what the Europeans did to Africa, it has to be said that, generally speaking, the Irish are not blamed for having helped to wheel up the cannon.

Obviously, given the vastness of Africa and the multiplicity of languages and tribes, it would be folly to pretend that most Africans even know where Ireland is – but a high percentage of decision-takers do. Irish Catholic religious were responsible for educating a crop of independence leaders which included Tom Mboya, Hastings Banda, Robert Mugabe and Julius Nyerere. Protestant educators did valuable work also. When Carey Francis, headmaster of the Alliance High School in Kenya, died, his coffin was borne by old boys of the school who included six cabinet ministers.

It's probably true to say that neither Catholic nor Protestant educators envisaged the creation of revolutionaries. They saw themselves as performing within the existing political framework, generally in the anglophone countries of sub-Saharan Africa. In colonial days this meant obtaining a work permit at the grace and favour of the colonial governors. Indeed, one of the rituals taught to Holy Ghost seminarians in the 1950s was the correct behaviour On Being Introduced to The Governor and His Lady. Today's realities involve getting similar permissions from African rulers. As we will see, many Irish religious do not let this prevent them speaking out against injustice.

The Irish are seen as not having any ideological baggage.[10] They are liked for having a sense of humour, close to that of the Africans themselves, and for being more easy-going than many other European races. They empathise with the Africans in their unorthodox approach to problem-solving. For example, one still hears stories of how Irish aid workers drove across Sudan's borders without permission in order to bring famine relief to Ethiopia.

The Irish are recognised as not having any imperial superiority complexes, which is very important in the African context. It is recognised that a good deal of the motivation which set Idi Amin on the course which led to the British-supported Kabaka of Uganda being overthrown, and his own bloody regime being installed, stemmed from British condescension. Amin was an NCO in the British army and an excellent athlete, outstanding at boxing, cricket and rugby. His talents were gladly made use of on the field, but when it came to the celebrations afterwards the officer and gentleman class excluded him from their clubhouses and messes.

Apart from the personality factor, the educational legacy of the missionaries and the contribution to health care by Irish nuns are well recognised.

IRISH AID

An Irish White Paper on foreign policy sums up the Irish situation in suitably restrained, but accurate terms:

It will be a mistake to present Irish people as having a concern for the Third World which marks us out from others. In terms of official development assistance, we have only recently begun to bring the level of our official assistance up to that of many of our European partners. However, there is an especially strong non-governmental tradition in Ireland of citizens working in the Third World and contributing to the funding of that work; the high number of people involved, relative to the population, has meant that there is an informed public interest in Ireland in Third World issues. This is reflected in the level of support for the activities of the non-governmental aid agencies, and has a significant impact on the focus of our Foreign Policy . . . Ireland's foreign policy is about much more than self-interest. For many of us it is a statement of the kind of people we are.[11]

One saw an expression of that statement in the Irish response to Bob Geldof's Live Aid Concert, greater in percentage terms than that of any other country.

The formation of a 1992 coalition between the Fianna Fail and Labour Parties resulted in a step being taken towards giving statutory expression to that 'statement of the kind of people we are'. Ireland's contribution to aid was doubled as part of Labour's price for entering Government. It has steadily increased since. The current expenditure is some IR£175 million. Ireland has not managed to achieve the target set by the UN of 0.7% of GDP as the contribution of developed countries to the Third World. In fact, apart from Scandinavian countries, very few parts of the world have. However, the present Government's goal is to increase the current 0.35% to 0.45%, which, given the way the Irish economy is performing, should mean the achievement of a goodly, if not an astronomical, sum. It also gives Ireland the distinction of being the only European country which is consistently increasing its aid budget. All the other countries are cutting back. As a European authority has noted, Ireland, though a small player in absolute money terms, nevertheless in terms of:[12]

> substance and approach it now compares favourably with the other small EU donors; compared with New Zealand, a country identical in size and income per head, it stands up very well under both measures. Ireland's aid programme now forms a significant as well as an integral part of its overall foreign policy. t reflects well on the country. Looking back over 25 years of Irish Aid, people can take justifiable pride in it.

Ireland has six 'priority countries' in Africa – Lesotho, Zambia, Tanzania, Ethiopia, Uganda and Mozambique – which are the principal focus of the Government's Irish Aid Programme. The extra money gives shrewd ambassadors and aid workers greatly enhanced opportunities for helping worthy projects, run by both missionaries and NGOs. Aid is not rigorously confined to the 'priority countries', however. In South Africa, for example, it was good to see a particularly fine representative, Eamon O Tuathail, being in a position to initiate projects, telling meritorious persons: 'You should approach the Embassy for help with so and so . . .', rather than shunning them. It is not so long ago, in pre-Celtic Tiger days, than an Irish Ambassador – and not one accredited to a Third World country either – turned up at a ceremony with a bottle of sherry in his briefcase for the drinks afterwards.

Another fillip to both African interest in Ireland and Irish interest in Africa came during the presidency of Mary Robinson. She visited Somalia on 2 November 1992 during the height of the famine. She was the only head of state to come while the famine was raging and a state of war prevailed. She travelled with only Somalian security, which was taking a risk: the Secretary General of the UN, Boutros Boutros Ghali, was met by mortar and machine-gun fire at the airport. Robinson was photographed by accompanying TV reporters, being reduced to tears by the horrors she met with. Instead of returning directly to Dublin, as she had been expected to do, she went instead to New York, to kindle UN and TV interest in the famine, with great success. Such intervention is invaluable in opening relief bottlenecks. The Red Cross Director, Geoff Loane, told me he was 'plugging away' during the Ethiopian famine when, suddenly, the situation was transformed through a visit by the CNN crew.[13]

THE SCRAMBLE FOR AFRICA

The Irish got to Africa as they did every other place in the world under the British Empire: as soldiers, administrators, traders, professionals and, in particular, as missionaries. More latterly there is a tendency for these to be succeeded by their lay successors the non-governmental organisations (NGOs), but the missionaries still out-number lay volunteers by some ten to one. In conversation after conversation, people mentioned to me how the Kiltegan Fathers, in particular, were working away largely unheard of and unknown outside the districts involved, trying to provide education and health facilities in the slums. Outside the country, such work rarely makes headlines. Inside, it is not always appreciated by the authorities, who are often riled by the Kiltegans' habit of encouraging people to stand up for their human rights. Nevertheless it continues. I decided to follow in the footsteps of both the missionaries and the NGOs.

In his person and philosophy John O'Shea poses all the questions raised by the activities of the aid community. Are they simply, as one old Africa hand, a GOAL field director, asked me rhetorically, merely:

> delaying the approach of the fellows with the machetes. A lot of what we do disappears like a spot of water on a hot rock. Looking at this fellow Moi [the Kenyan President], I feel sometimes that I should be out in the forest with a machete myself.

The more theoretical speak of the need for education and a development-orientated approach. O'Shea does not favour theoretical approaches. He is not the sort of man of whom it could be said: 'I was hungry and ye founded a study group.' Famously, he once startled a Civil Service Committee with a sudden interjection: 'Do you fuckers realise that I have been sitting here for the last hour and I never heard one of you mention the word love? Do you realise that the most important thing you can do for a leper sometimes is to give him a fucking hug?'

In the Aid v. Development debate proponents, roughly speaking, argue as to whether it is better to attend to humanitarian needs or to invest in long-term projects which will help the world to help itself. Like debate over whether the missionaries were bringers of enlightenment or destroyers of local culture, arises from the involvement of the European empires in Africa. These empires, and the great trading companies that followed in their wake, certainly had a pernicious effect. However, Europe and Africa had had a long and often brutal interest in each other well before the period known as 'the scramble for Africa' began. As Basil Davidson has noted, Africa had a trading relationship with the capitalist system of Europe and America which began before 1500, and was of great influence 'before the new Imperialism sent in its armies'. Davidson says:

> What was started by the old coastal partnership, in terms of mercantile and political influence, the Atlantic slave trade continuously enlarged; and what the slave trade

achieved, dreary though these sombre years, these slave trade of the nineteenth century again enlarged in terms of that mercantile and political influence.[14]

This enlargement may be taken as reaching its high point in 1885 at the Berlin Congress, which parcelled out Africa amongst the European nations. William Morris thundered accurately but in vain against the Congress and its objectives:

Populations to rob and ensnare; markets to shoot bad wares into; lands to invest capital upon: to obtain these is the be all and end all of modern statesmanship. For this has the stock jobber's Republic of France waged war successively on Tunis, Madagascar, Tonquin, and China; for this does the Congress sit in Berlin, partitioning the plunder.[15]

The scramble for Africa arose out of a medley of motives. Alongside naked greed there went a concept of a civilising mission, a desire to spread commerce and Christianity, to put down slavery.[16] The depredations of slavery and the poverty and disease encountered in Africa induced the great missionary explorer, David Livingstone, to cry out on his death bed: 'All I can add in my solitude, is, may Heaven's rich blessing come down on everyone, American, English, or Turk, who will help to heal this open sore of the World.'[17]

Between trying to heal this 'open sore', find new markets, prevent their rivals getting in ahead of them, and bring the teachings of Christianity to what were perceived as ignorant races living in the darkness of heathenry, the European powers between them created many new sores, some of which still cause pain today. The story is well told in Thomas Pakenham's magisterial *The Scramble for Africa*, and can be followed through his fascinating pages.[18] However, for our purposes it is sufficient to know three things about the Africa which resulted from the scramble.

Firstly, the scramble created a myriad of states, governed by the Europeans with varying degrees of indolence, inefficiency, rapacity and brutality. These continued when colonialism fell in the late 1960s. Brutality continued between the Europeans and the Africans in some areas, for example in the Portuguese territories of Angola, Mozambique and Guinea, and in the British possession of Rhodesia, now Zimbabwe, which finally gained independence in 1980.

Secondly, the Cold War affected Africa as it did Latin America. In order to keep out Communism, the West propped up a series of repressive regimes which made a mockery of the term democracy; and the Russians in the name of Socialism supported a series of equally exploitive and odious thugs. The ending of the Cold War meant that from then on, circa 1988, a move towards some sort of natural organic development was furthered across the African continent.

Thirdly, in order to have some hope of realising their countries' potential, the members of the Organisation of African Unity had taken the decision in 1963 to respect existing state boundaries. So the straight lines on the map of Africa remained. These lines cut through traditional boundaries, ancestral tribal lands, across areas of mineral wealth, deserts, lakes, with no rationale other than that of the European Scramblers who in the 1870s took what they could get.

Thus, this colonial inheritance, along with two additional damnations – the Third World debt, and the burden of arms expenditure – add to indigenous African difficulties such as tribalism and rampant corruption. Not only are countries crippled by debt and armament repayments so that their peoples often do not have a reliable water supply, the women and children of these countries are literally crippled by having their legs blown off by land mines, supplied by the 'enlightened' democracies of the West, as they go with their buckets to fetch was water there is.

IT IS BETTER TO LIGHT A CANDLE . . .

These factors add to the complexities confronting those who wish to continue upholding the Irish caring tradition in Africa.

The Irish aid agencies are caught up in this debate, exacerbated by falling United Nations financing for aid projects and a general feeling that a more sophisticated approach is required on the part of aid workers. The Africans are glad of assistance, but they would naturally prefer to help themselves, if the resources and training were given to them. In theory this is the correct approach, but in practice it is not always possible. The endemic corruption of Africa often deflects money from worthy causes into undeserving pockets – and not all these pockets belong to Africans. Apart from authenticated instances of corruption which were told to me, it was quite obvious that many aid agencies pay very good salaries to their employees. Sometimes this is inevitable because to obtain expertise, consultants are expensive; but there is also tremendous waste and overlapping. I counted aid vehicles from Canada, the International Red Cross, the UN, Oxfam, UNICEF, Japan, Ireland and Germany, parked outside the Sheraton hotel in Kampala one evening at dinner time.

There is a sort of league table in the aid world. One finds idealistic young Irish aid workers starting out with the relatively small Irish NGOS – GOAL, Concern, Trocaire, etc. – but then, after working in the field with people in a UN-sponsored agency who though they may be just as idealistic as the volunteers, earn $3,000 a month more than they do. They graduate over to the International Red Cross, UNICEF or the UN.

There is a question as to whether much of what is done by these Agencies should not be done by the governments responsible. The Secretary General of the UN Kofi Annan, himself an African, delivered an unusually frank assessment of the quality of African leaderships:

> The quality of the leaders, the misery they have brought to their people and my inability to work with them to turn the situation around are very depressing. Unless we find a way of getting them to focus on resolving conflicts and turn to the key issues of economic and social development, the efforts that we are all making will be for nought.

In many countries, the wrong kind have made it to leadership. They seek power for the sake of power and for their own agrandisement rather than having a real understanding of the need to use power to improve their countries.[19]

Annan spoke on a week-end in April 2000 at almost the same time as two knowledgeable Irish commentators on Africa, Clare Short, the British Minister responsible for Overseas aid, and John O'Shea, Director of the Irish Aid Agency, GOAL, were, independently criticising the Ethiopian government for its handling of the current Ethiopian famine. Both experts pointed out that food was available but that Ethiopia's bureaucratic bottlenecks and its diversion of resources to the war with Eritrea was denying food to the starving. O'Shea said that Ethiopian bureaucracy had 'killed more people than anything else'.[20]

I debated the question of governmental responsibility with myself one morning in a shanty town outside Kampala, as I watched Ian Dolan of GOAL, an experienced field worker, standing in mud on a dull, drizzly morning negotiating with a headman to try to expedite a water project. When completed, the piped water would save the villagers having to walk downhill for two kilometres to an open stream which was often clogged with leaves amongst other less attractive detritus. It was unquestionably an excellent scheme. However, the occupants, mainly Rwandan refugees, were all squatters and no one knew the day nor the hour when some landlord could come along, throw everyone out on the road and turn the entire area into a housing project, bulldozing the piped water project out of existence in the process.

As I watched Dolan patiently explaining the need for more action to the headman, one of those rare moments of affirmation occurred. From one of the earth-floored huts an African man appeared. He was in his late twenties, wore a spotlessly clean shirt and tie, had immaculately pressed trousers and carried a stylish-looking jacket over his shoulder. He had a smart briefcase in his hand and, bestowing a bright friendly smile on the world, set off in the drizzle to work. Where in God's name he was going, or what he could hope to earn I don't know, but he epitomised the African qualities of both cleanliness and style, to say nothing of the incredible triumph of the human spirit over the myraid tribulations that beset the continent. To hell with what some landlord might do in the future. The young man's appearance was both a vote of confidence in the 'hug a leper' philosophy and the principle that it is better to light a candle than curse the dark.

AN EYE FOR AN EYE . . .

I subsequently went to the young African's homeland, Rwanda, one of the darkest and most accursed places on the continent. When I landed at Kigali Airport it was discovered that my Rwandan visa had already expired. Eventually, after some questioning, I was given a new temporary visa for $20, but the delay had given me plenty of time to examine the marks of gunfire on the airport's terrazzo floors. Some of the bullet holes were the size of dinner plates, obviously the result of a sustained burst of powerful automatic fire. One could only guess at the carnage wreaked upon those at whom the fire was directed.

I was met at the airport by Dominic McSorley, the Rwandan field director of Concern. McSorley, an impressive man from a respected North of Ireland medical family (his father, mother and four brothers are doctors, and two of his sisters are nurses), was a solicitor by training but had opted to place his talents at the disposal of Concern. I was given a briefing on the Rwandan genocide at a lunch with Dominic, the GOAL Director John Rynne and his African wife, a Trocaire representative John O'Brien who was an ex-priest, and our luncheon host Sean Cosgrave, also an aid worker, and his Korean/Finnish wife. As can be imagined in that company, in a pleasant villa, all was cheerfulness and good fellowship. Kigali (population approximately 300,000) itself also looked pleasant enough. There are few visible scars of war, and traffic and crowds all seem normal. Horror, however, is like learning to swim from a book: one has to experience the water to understand the reality.

The next morning I dived in.[21] I drove with Dominic, Roisin Boyd, an RTE reporter, and Rosemary, a new Concern volunteer, who was a young Irish nurse whom Dominic brought along to initiate into the backdrop of her future work.

At the height of the 1994 massacre, Niemata Church was situated in a compound with three other small buildings. People had crowded into the compound, packing the church and buildings to suffocation. Some say as many as 20,000 were involved, others as few as 3,000. Tutsis fleeing from Hutus, they had come in a vain hope of sanctuary.

When the Hutus surrounded the church the Tutsis locked the doors, but the Hutus blasted holes in the walls with grenades and slashed their way through with machetes. They systematically hacked to death the screaming terrified people inside, men, women and children. Previously I had thought that the worst record of man's barbarity contained in a church was the Basilica at Verdun, where the lowest floor of the Basilica is filled for the entire length of the huge church with human bones from unidentified bodies of the First Word War. At least they were adults, combatants. At Niemata debris, piles of clothing, children's toys were all mixed together with human bones, and there was still a smell, the unmistakable gagging, sickly sweet smell of death.[22] As we looked silently at this indictment of our species, Roisin Boyd gave a supreme example of professionalism. Her face had crumpled up and tears fell on to her tape recorder, but she kept her voice steady as she directed questions at Dominic. He, in turn, translated them into French for our Rwandan guide to the massacre site.

While the interview was being conducted I went on my own to inspect the smaller buildings. They were even worse: the human detritis was piled higher – to a depth of some feet – and because there were fewer windows than in the church, they were darker and literally more sepulchral. I leant against a tree and thought of Orpen's line, 'the friendless bodies of unburied men'. While I retched in the soothing sunshine, birds sang and butterflies flitted about me. The guide asked us to put our names and an inscription in the Visitors' Book. On an earlier page I noticed Angus Finucane, the founder of Concern, had replied to a similar invitation: 'God forgive us.' Underneath this a Rwandan had written: 'an eye for an eye . . .'

Further evidence as to why such a sentiment might be inscribed in such a book was to be had not far away, at a place called Kanzene, where another church had not been respected as a place of sanctuary. We drove to a school compound which had children playing in the yard. The first thing I noticed as we pushed open a door at the side of the church in the middle of the compound was what looked like a scattering of gold sovereigns on the floor. On inspection, the filigree of sovereigns turned out to be sunlight shining through the bullet holes in the galvanised roof. At first sight, however, nothing of particular horror caught the eye, although one's imagination filled in the background to the presence of machete slash marks on the seats.

I noticed in one case that a two-inch-thick mahogany kneeler had been slashed in two. What awful deed accompanied that expenditure of hate-filled energy, I wondered, but there was little else to indicate what had happened. There were a few bullet holes in the baptismal font and across the altar; a bluebottle buzzed disgustingly from a wall splashed with dried blood, but otherwise nothing – no teddy bears intermingled with smashed skulls. Then, as I stood at the altar looking down towards the back of the church, I saw a piled to roof height a mass of black plastic bags that encroached several yards across the floor of the church. Each was filled with human bones: Verdun, Rwandan style.

NTONCWE

The two churches were an essential preparation for one of the ugliest spectacles I have seen in my life. One of the functions of normality which was being delayed as a result of the genocide and a refugee exodus was the functioning of any sort of system of justice. The Rwandan authorities in Kigali had rounded up a number of Hutu prisoners, but, in the absence of a court system or properly compiled evidence, had not proceeded to try them. They were being detained in all sorts of holding areas in all sorts of conditions. After visiting Niemata and Kanzene, Dominic took us to one 'prison'. This time Rosalind, the young nurse and midwife from Naas, who had managed to maintain her composure at the two churches, found herself unable to control her feelings.

Ntoncwe 'prison' was reached by driving down what would be known in Ireland as a boithrin, for several miles after turning off a main road. The boithrin, a narrow dirt road, with trees arching overhead for most of the way, occasionally passed by villages whose inhabitants did not appear particularly friendly. At the end of it, we came to a small complex of buildings which originally housed a technical school. It now held 600 prisoners. In the case of the men, there were on average 100 prisoners in each smallish classroom. In one room, 8 x 30 metres, some 250 men and women were housed: the women in a smaller section of the classroom area were about twenty-four in number. The only times either group was let out during the day were once in the evening and once in the day to defaecate. The men were so crowded that they could only sit or lie down in relays, and the floors in both areas had been rendered odiferous and disgusting by human bodily fluids, which ran continuously in a foul steam out of the door. The latrines are about seventy-five yards from the furthest buildings. They consisted of poles placed across holes dug in the ground. The stench caused nausea at fifty paces and Dominic pronounced them the worst he had seen in his career. The prisoners are allowed approximately two minutes to get from their doors, at the run, defaecate and return. Diarrhoea and menstruation merely added to the foul flood seeping from the classrooms. One woman had a three-month-old baby which had been born in these conditions.

The following is a UN report on what these conditions led to in some cases:

During the night of 11–12 May . . . detainees began shouting and complaining about the lack of air and heat in the cell which was approximately 20 square metres (5 by four metres) and contained 94 detainees. Fighting subsequently broke out among the detainees . . .[Guards] refused to open the door for fear that detainees would escape. The panic in the cell continued until 4 a.m. The cell was reportedly opened between 6 a.m. and 7 a.m. Seventeen detainees were found to have died. In a second local detention centre, in the same area, 296 detainees were held in three cells . . . two detainees are reported to have died of suffocation on 11 May and three other detainees died of suffocation on 12 May . . .[23]

Readers may speculate for themselves as to the reasons why two separate detention centres should erupt on the same night. All I can say with certainty is that outside the prisons I visited, armed guards lolled about wearing jackets, dark glasses and carrying powerful automatic weapons, and told us frankly that they would enjoy shooting the prisoners if they attempted to escape.

The numbers in the classrooms were increasing all the time as the Tutsi authorities implemented an ID-card system to identify the Hutus. No family contact is allowed and the prisoners were being held indefinitely, until some attempt at processing their cases could be made.

Prior to the Irish becoming involved at Ntoncwe, the prisoners had received approximately half the nourishment required to sustain life, and this only because their families provided the food to the authorities. The Irish Department of Foreign Affairs then put up the money for a better diet, and Concern undertook the implementation of the scheme. The Irish dieticians had proposed a rice basis for the prisoners' diet, but this was prevented by the local residents. The villagers said that rice was a 'luxury food' which the prisoners did not deserve. In order to allow food, and the Concern volunteers, to pass safely down the long boithrin by which we reached the camp, Concern had had to agree to supply the villages we passed through with a measured plate of food for every plate that reached the prisoners. The food, at the time

I visited the camp, therefore consisted largely of maize and casava. Each prisoner received a plate heaped high with what to a Western eye appeared a fairly unappetising mess. Then the door was pushed shut on the classroom as the prisoners ate their mess standing up.

Another prison in the same area consists of one large room, again like a schoolroom, which contains 170 male prisoners. Off the main room was an ante-chamber with over a dozen women. There was no partition of any kind to separate the sexes and, not surprisingly, there were several babies in evidence. Whether AIDS would also manifest itself, apart from any other disease which the conditions appeared certain to breed, only time would tell. As we drove back to Kigali, rather more soberly than we had set out, I became aware that in Rwanda a high stone wall could be a kindly act. We passed a women's prison, around which the Irish Department of Foreign Affairs had erected a high wall at the Irish taxpayers' expense. Because of this, the women who were held there now had daily exercise in the fresh air. Prior to the wall being built, the authorities would not let the women exercise in the yard because the existing low perimeter fence had been deemed to create a security risk.

THE REFUGEE CAMPS

As a result of the genocide, refugees became a huge factor in the Rwandan problem. On either side of the country, in Zaire and in Tanzania, huge refugee camps were erected. In Goma in Zaire, just across the Rwandan border, Mobutu the Zairean dictator had allowed the creation of refugee camps containing well over a million of his Hutu allies. Another three-quarters of a million had gone into exile in Tanzania, and stayed there. Apart from understandable fears as to what might happen to them if they returned, they were also discouraged from doing so by the Hutu leadership within the camps.

No return to normality could even be contemplated within Rwanda while such a large proportion of its population remained outside its borders, sometimes actively fomenting unrest in Rwanda itself. As an Irishman, my immediate reaction was that it was as if the UN had connived at the removal of much of the nationalist population of the Six Counties into camps in the adjoining Republic. They would have provided a springboard for the IRA to operate at will into the Six.

After seeing the prisons and the genocide sites at Niemata, I drove to inspect the work of Concern, GOAL and a number of other Irish agencies in helping to run the refugee camps on the Tanzanian side of the border. All I had to do was to contend with a lot of boring formalities, which I would not have mastered were it not for my Muslim driver – although formalities can be worrying enough in a situation such as Rwanda. At the back of my mind, as we dealt with the delays and frustrations of the border checkpoint, I was thinking not of the possibilities of arrest or being turned back, but of what the Concern field director in Nairobi, Cleo O'Reilly, had told me about her memories of the crossing point. Neither the horrors of Rwanda, nor Irish involvement in them, ended at its borders.

We had been sitting in her bright, modern office enjoying a cup of tea and a sandwich, when suddenly her tea cup began to tremble in her hands, and her face reddened. She told me that while her companions were dealing with the customs formalities, she did as I did while my driver dealt with mine, crossed the road to view a waterfall spanned by a bridge that links Rwanda with Tanzania:

> I saw bodies pouring over the waterfall. It was horrible. After a few moments I moved away to get myself together, but that was the worst thing I could have done, because I came to a place in the river where the current had collected the arms and legs and the bits of bodies which had been smashed up by the rocks under the waterfall.

Like so much of Rwanda, the river can look either smilingly innocent or filled with menace when a cloud passes over. As I gazed down at the spot Cleo had described, an occasional log floated by and it was only too easy to recall what she had seen.

When I crossed into Tanzania one of her companions that day, Noel Moloney, who is in charge of the Concern section of the Tanzanian Refugee Camp, described to me how he and other concern workers had buried 12,000 bodies which had been carried into Lake Victoria by the river. Over the river's entire course he reckons there must have been at least another 12,000 bodies caught in roots and long grass. 'They used to put them in at night to avoid attention,' he said. 'You could put your hand through the bodies – often when you went to pick them up your hand went right through to the bone. I tried not to see their faces, by looking through them, at the earth, anything. They had screaming faces.'

When I first caught sight of the camps where Moloney worked, they seemed like cities spread out across the low hills of Tanzania. One of the problems posed by the refugee presence was that they were denuding the hills of trees, thus not only depriving the Tanzanians of badly needed firewood, but creating soil erosion. Altogether GOAL, Concern and the Irish aid community were responsible for what at home would have been a largish Irish town. Concern for example had 113,000 refugees in its section. The camp was well kept and its facilities included running water, a hospital and a TV station. An English doctor who worked at the hospital told me that in his opinion the Irish sections of the camp were the best run. They were certainly neater and cleaner than a Tanzanian town some miles away. Its hutments were not as new of course, nor were the roads as well kept, nor the open-air markets as well stocked.

At the time of my visit the debate as to the future of the camps was coming to a climax. I was actually present at a meeting when a UN official told the Hutus that they were going to have to prepare to go home. Both the Hutus and the Tutsis had a different version as to the camp's rationale. The Tutsis were saying that the Hutus did not have to be there; that they had deliberately fled, looting Tutsi possessions to enable them to do so; and were now either being intimidated into staying on, or using the camps to mount attacks on Rwanda. I was told there was evidence that the Hutus were killing off witnesses to the genocide and intimidating others to prevent them from going back. It was quite obvious that the pressure cooker was boiling up again. The Tanzanians did not want their meagre resources being devoured by a horde of refugees. From Uganda, President Museveni was assisting the Tutsi army, in Zaire, Mobutu was doing the same for the Hutus, and the international community was cutting back on aid. The Great Lakes area was receiving something less than a third of the expected UN support at the time of my visit.

Rwanda is one of the most inglorious chapters of the UN's history. There are well-documented accounts of UN soldiers, with armoured back-up, standing by as Hutus hacked Tutsi women and children to death in front of them. Then, after the genocide was over, donor countries, chiefly the US and the EU, gave £4 billion in aid – three billion to the refugees, the genocidalists; one billion to the Rwandan Government whose people had borne the brunt of the slaughter. I for one was not surprised when further slaughter and revenge-seeking took place a year later when the camps were broken up and the Hutus forcibly repatriated. However, at the time of my visit, the fiction was being maintained that neither the Rwandan authorities nor those of Uganda had anything to do with the continuing efforts to destabilise Zaire, with a view to overthrowing President Mobutu, and thus ending his support for the Hutus.

Rwanda's strong man, Paul Kagame, did not admit Rwandan involvement until the following year.[24] By then Tutsi complicity in the massacre of Hutus nominally under the protection of President Laurent Kabila's regime in Congo-Kinshasa had become known. The behaviour of Kabila's army was also the source of concern over human rights abuses in Rwanda itself where trouble continued between Hutus and Tutsis. Everything that happened in the year after my visit had been prophesied to a millimetre by McSorley, Moloney and the more senior Irish aid workers. No one was under any mis-apprehension that Irish intervention, or indeed that of most international aid, was going to prove the answer to the woes of either this part of Africa's inheritance or its own present policies and personalities.

THE MAN FROM THE MINISTRY

The aid community's problems were summed up by a little drama I witnessed at the Tanzanian camp. The Man From the Ministry had come to inform the Hutus that the Tanzanian authorities, in conjunction with the Office of the United Nations Commissioner for Refugees, were introducing a new regulation, aimed at identifying who was who in the camp. The regulation was, in effect, a first step in expediting a return to Rwanda. A young Concern representative sat beside the MFTM as he spoke. He had both to uphold the Irish interest and, at the same time, maintain good relations with the Tanzanian authorities – and, of course, take care not to get on the wrong side of the audience. As my eye travelled over the serried ranks of Hutus, I suddenly became aware that the young Concern worker and myself were the only two whites for a considerable distance.

Some of the stories from the days of the genocide began flitting through my consciousness like a rerun movie. 'Come back tomorrow and we'll kill you. We're too busy now,' was a frequently heard instruction to victims earmarked for slaughter who had obediently turned up at road blocks to be murdered, as instructed. Sometimes those people who were now sitting in front of me would have said to their Tutsi neighbours: 'Give us money, and we'll shoot you instead of using the machete.' Tutsis who had money were frequently glad enough to avail of this 'mercy'. Death from machete wounds often took twelve hours or more, and parents in particular sought to spare their children this suffering. Even Hutu nuns and priests took part in the genocide. Documented testimony exists for example of a nun who poured petrol over a victim and then set it alight, and of a priest who systematically pointed out his male parishioners for massacre and the women of the parish to be brought to him for other purposes.

The Man from the Ministry, however, created an atmosphere which could have existed in an Irish country co-op in the Gaelic-speaking districts of the west of Ireland. There were the same surroundings: the setting itself for the meeting was a large barn, with sacks of meal in evidence here and there. The young Concern volunteer might have been the local schoolteacher, forced to attend dutifully to the proceedings. The local dignitary who introduced the MFTM could have been an Irish TD (Member of Parliament). The MFTM could have been down from Dublin. He spoke, as such a figure would, in different tongues: at home it would have been Irish and English, but here it was in French and English and what I took to be occasional Swahili. The other difference was that the MFTM was Ethiopian.

He began by saying (in triplicate), 'I am not here to negotiate. I am not here to discuss. I am here to inform you of a decision taken by the authorities.' Then he launched into a long exposition of the decision. Just as would have happened in Ireland, he was given a polite hearing for some forty-five minutes, and then a seemingly innocent question was asked. Then another, and another. Time passed and we got to the 'and finally' stage. The young Concern worker was slumping lower in his chair. I was leaving my point of vantage at the barn door and taking air breaks, but still – speaking with great authority and conviction and humour evidently, because the audience laughed occasionally – the MFTM valiantly attempted to bring the meeting to a close. 'And finally,' he would begin, in triplicate, and another innocent question would be asked on the lines of 'How would this work in my case?' or some such.

The atmosphere in the barn grew hotter, the young Concern worker slumped lower and lower, but the meeting continued. Then, as if a miracle had occurred, a church bell was heard in the distance, sounding with singular sweetness over the rolling Tanzanian hills. The MFTM uttered what proved to be his last 'and finally'. And the meeting came to an end. The MFTM roared off in his chauffeured four-wheel drive, and the Hutus filed out, most of them smiling pleasantly at me as they went by. 'Why in God's name did you sit there all that time?' I asked the young volunteer. He shrugged: 'Ah sure somebody has to do it,' he said. 'The expect you to show a bit of interest.' I suppose they did, I reflected afterwards. He was young, and many of the Hutus who had smiled at me as they left had been listening to the first stages of a process that was going to return them across the Tanzanian border and into the arms of Tutsis waiting to kill them. A spot of water on a hot rock . . .

RUEBUN

And yet, seeds can grow out of such a spot, even on the hardest of rocks. At the Ruebun Development on the outskirts of Nairobi I met two more young Irish GOAL volunteers. Vanessa and Colman, both in their early twenties, had managed to provide a practical answer to the question: 'What do the Africans want?' The village, the sort of large shanty town settlement that one sees all over Africa, needed education. There was one school but it lost pupils when the fees were raised, microscopically to Western eyes, but for the villagers it presented a simple choice – fees or food? Initially, the children tried raising the money themselves, by collecting scrap and so on, but to little avail.

However, using the labyrinthine aid network of donor agencies, Vanessa and Colman succeeded in raising some money so that the parents' share of the fees was reduced. GOAL helped by buying schoolbooks. One of the most rudimentary, but important, innovations was the installation of a lavatory, so that the teachers and children 'did not have to answer a call' behind a bush. Another improvement came about as a result of more money becoming available for food: children no longer fell asleep in class from hunger. The young aid workers also managed to get a centralised building put up, albeit with a galvanised roof, no windows, earthen flooring and with desks of rough planks. Chickens scratched in the dusty soil outside the doorway, but inside there was singing and the repetition of lessons in eager childish voices. Perhaps Colman and Vanessa's greatest triumph was to arrange for the hiring of the headmistress, Betty.

Betty was married with two children, helping to support her family by selling maize, when the Ruebun job came up. Prior to the GOAL intervention, the dropout rate was high, but by the time I visited the school, children were attending regularly and were obviously clean and conducted themselves well. As the school took root, parents and the entire village co-operated to ensure that even out of school hours the children were well behaved, stayed out of trouble and did their homework.

The state did not pay for the development of such schools, but the ambition of Colman and Vanessa was to persuade the state to take it over as a going concern. This would put it on a permanent footing and guarantee teachers' salaries etc. Most education in Africa began with Ruebun-like projects, generally founded by missionaries, and Africa's crying need it still education.

The history of the continent means that the Africans have been left behind in the technological race. The irony is that, now that the era of colonialism and the Cold War is over, the international communities are losing the interest in Africa which the fig leaf of the 'civilising mission' once provided.

Accordingly, as the debate over aid versus development rages on, the contribution of Colman and Vanessa at Ruebun continues to demonstrate that sometimes it can help if you pour a spot of water on the rock.

A HOSPITAL IN UGANDA

Prior to the Irish Government becoming involved in aid and development projects in the 1990s, Ireland's main contribution to Uganda, certainly in education and health, was through the Medical Missionaries of Mary and the Franciscan Sisters. I visited a number of their foundations.

My first piece of research gave me an insight I had not expected. The Medical Missionaries of Mary nun was in her fifties, and therefore much younger than the other members of the congregation whom I had come to visit at Kitovu Hospital, over two hours' drive from Kampala. She was obviously concerned about being overheard. Having told me she wanted to ask me something, she then brought me out to an open space between some hospital buildings. Next we moved off the path and into the middle of a patch of grass. Then she looked around to ensure that no one could approach us unexpectedly. Finally, she put her face close to mine and, lowering her voice, asked in apprehensive urgency: 'It's not true about Father Cleary, is it?'

In that question, in the nun's age, in her intensity, in the setting, was encapsulated the entire clash of cultures between the old Ireland of 'the missions' – the collection box on the counters of shops bearing pictures of chubby African children, seeking 'a penny for the black babies – and the modern Ireland in which vocations had collapsed. I had to say to the nun as gently as I could, 'Yes I'm afraid it is true about Father Cleary.' It had just been revealed, after his death, that Cleary – 'the singing priest', one of the best-known clerics in Ireland and, apparently, one of the most conservative – had had a child by his long-term mistress. In fact, I had to tell the nun, he had had two children. Two days before I flew to Uganda, a second one had turned up on an Irish TV chat show. He had shown himself to be a composed, intelligent and humorous young man, but this was not of much comfort to the good sister. She told me that all in the convent were devastated by the news from Ireland, and were refusing to believe it.

We continued our walk and came to a small house surrounded by a garden in which someone was obviously trying, with a degree of success, to bring order to the lush chaos of Africa. There were flowers and vegetables in the midst of overhanging vegetation. As we commented on the flowers, the door opened and a pretty, stylish, red-haired young woman emerged to greet me. She had a very familiar look. I understood why when she said, 'My uncle Mick often spoke of you.' She was Father Cleary's niece, a pharmacist who was 'giving a couple of years of voluntary service to the sisters'. As with the vast majority of her age group, a career in the nuns was not for her, but in the midst of changing values, and a world of new insights, she still demonstrated the same impulse that had brought her uncle into the Church and the nuns to Kitovu.

The nun showed me a set of what looked like circular table tops standing against a wall. They were made of rough planking and had evidently just been scrubbed. The nun gave me a clue: 'They're the most important items in the hospital,' and asked me to guess what they were. I looked at the aged planking in incomprehension. 'Have another look,' the sister suggested, and then I saw that each set of 'table tops' had a hole in the middle. They were the latrine covers for the female lavatories. The covers set the tone for the rest of the hospital: simple, primitive almost, but highly efficient – efficient and enormously tragic. Parents sat at the bedsides of children dying from everything from malaria to meningitis. In the AIDS wards, most of the patients just lay apathetically on their beds, though one or two managed a smile as the sister introduced me. I'll never forget the look of terror in the face of a beautiful young woman in her early twenties who, though still able to dress herself and walk, was obviously in the last stages of what they call 'the thinning disease'. The AIDS pandemic means that: 'One out of every four people you bumped up against as you walked along the street coming here has AIDS.'

The hospital lies about two miles off the main road, reached by negotiating a rutted, dirt road that made me think wincingly of the agonies the pot holes must have caused seriously ill people in carts or ambulances. The hospital had survived both the ravages of the Idi Amin era and the even worse, though under-reported, hells of 'Obote II'. This was the period when the dictator whom Amin had initially overthrown was returned to power and set in train a period of genocide. This never received the same attention in the Western media as did the activities of the anti-British Amin. The only sign remaining of those terrible days when I visited Uganda was the unusually high number of Malibu storks. Theses horrible birds with their huge dagger-like beaks and their disgusting red wattles are to be seen all over Africa. In Uganda, as my driver explained simply, 'They came plentiful with the bodies in the fields.'

A VERY TRADITIONAL IRISH NUN?

Sister Miriam Duggan is an obstetrician turned war surgeon who became famous throughout Africa for her ability to know intuitively where a bullet would be found, no matter where the entrance wound. It is recorded that she sometimes saved lives by making incisions – often against the advice of her horrified assistants – two to three feet away from the bullet wound, and finding the projectile. She clearly loves the Africans and only speaks of her surgical exploits when pressed, and then in a detached matter-of-fact voice, as if she was speaking of someone else.

She remembered Amin's army as being quite disciplined in contrast to Obote's. During the war period her hospital in Kampala was full of casualties, as was the one at Kitovu. The embassies were advising the sisters to get out, but not one left the country. This endeared them to the Ugandans. Everyone else took flight, including the business community, and the American Peace Corps. As a result, Sister Miriam, like the other sisters, frequently found herself confronting armed soldiers demanding that they be allowed to shoot casualties from the other side.

One of the many stories I had heard about Miriam before our meeting was verified by her, reluctantly, after I brought it up. An army captain was brought in suffering from a head injury and in cardiac arrest. He was accompanied by twelve drunken soldiers. One of them put an automatic weapon to her head and told her that if the captain died she would be shot. She told him: 'Put that gun away. You think gun can save life.' The soldier put away his weapon. Miriam went on:

> God was very real to me in terms of protection. I operated on the captain with a heart pump in my hand and injected adrenalin into his heart. He survived. Two days later the soldiers came back. I sat them down and lectured them.

I'll bet she did.

> In those days they did operations you never saw done. You did things you'd say were crazy. When I look back and think of working around the clock in crowded spaces, no rest, dealing with psychotics who should be in a loony bin . . .
> I remember one night a group of drunken soldiers surrounded the hospital. They had shot a man who had refused them drink. I had an unconscious man on the operating table. If we began to operate on him, they might burst in and he would die. If I didn't operate, he would die anyway, so I told them to lay on the ether. My knees were knocking, but I prayed for courage, and prayed that God would change the soldiers' hearts. The next thing I knew, people burst in saying, 'They've gone.'
> War brings out the best and the worst in people. There were lives lost trying to hide people. We kept the hospital open and disguised some people, and hid others; 1985 was the worst year. There was very little food, no water, no electricity. We had some medical stores, but no milk, cheese, sugar. Pepsi was a great luxury.
> 'Why does she do it?'
> She answered, 'I suppose my main motivation is to help people to bring them up.

Sister Miriam in many ways is a very traditional Irish nun. She believed that the AIDS epidemic could be countered by abstinence, and introduced me to a group of beautiful young African catechists, men and women, who go around schools and youth organisations, lecturing on how to combat AIDS through prayer and self-control. When I suggest that condoms should be issued on a vast scale, she objected both on religious and practical grounds: 'Condoms! Sure they can't even get a decent pair of rubber gloves out here. They perish in the sun.' As with the Church generally in Uganda, Sister Miriam has now handed over to a Ugandan, a 'very dynamic' figure who specialises, as she did, in obstetrics and gynaecology as well as surgery. Whatever one's views about

Sister Miriam and her attitude to birth control, it has to be conceded that, leaving her heroism to one side, as a result of her daily work and those of her colleagues, at least a percentage of Ugandans who would otherwise have found it difficult to afford an aspirin are either alive and healthy or receiving first-class medical care.

STABILITY IS THREATENED

Another institution where Irish nuns stayed put throughout the bad years is a famous girls' school, Mount St Mary's at Namagunga, an hour or so's drive from Kampala. I visited the school on a beautiful May evening, and the African sun struck a gorgeous flash from the maroon uniforms of a group of girls gathered around their teacher in the shade of a huge tree. It reminded me of an Irish 'hedge school' in Penal days.[25] I later found that the penal motif was all too apposite. During the bad days of Obote II, soldiers often waited near the school gates where parents dropped off their children. The parents would be seized, taken around the corner, shot, and their cars would be returned to the school with the bodies in the boot. Mount St Mary's survived these atrocities as it did the upheavals of other evil days.

It has been educating the children of Ugandan leaders since the days of the Kabaka, as the former rulers of Baganda were known. Museveni's girls were pupils, and his Vice-president is a former St Mary's girl, Mrs Wandira Kazdewa, a doctor. When I visited the school the nuns were in the process of preparing to hand the school over to Ugandans. They had already gifted some fifty primary schools since 1942, when the Order first began its work in Uganda. It is said that when President Museveni heard that the head nun planned to return to Ireland he told her: 'Not until after my daughter does her exams!' When I mentioned to my driver that the nuns were leaving for Ireland he was visibly saddened and replied: 'Oh dear, the standards will fall so.' This could be an unduly pessimistic forecast. I met some of the teachers whom the Irish nuns had trained, and their calibre coupled with Museveni's reforms offer hope that St Mary's legacy will be a fruitful one.

It has to be recorded however, that as I concluded this chapter in the spring of 2000, some of the groups opposed to Museveni were engaged in bombings and other acts of urban terrorism which were threatening the brief stability which Museveni had introduced. He had made education his number one priority: had invited the Indian community, which Amin had expelled, back into the country to help get the economy restarted; had cracked down on crime, while at the same time showing a concern for human rights; and had confirmed his commitment to democracy by risking his power in a general election which he won fairly. It seemed almost up to 1999 that Uganda was about to become the shining light of Africa, with Museveni as the latter-day Mandela.

However, all this is now threatened. In the north of the country a group called The Lord's Resistance Army, led by Joseph Kony, steadily increased their attacks on the Kampala regime. Kony, a member of the Acholi tribe, was aggrieved because in Museveni's war against Obote, the Acholi tribe lost their cattle. Another quasi-religious sect opposed to Museveni is the Holy Spirit Movement, which derives its inspiration from a woman, Alice Lakwena, now in a Kenyan refugee camp; and in the mountainous west, the Allied Democratic Force, which invaded from Zaire, was both proving difficult to dislodge and claiming responsibility for the bombings which threatened Museveni's reforms. The ADF specialises in abducting young boys, and both abusing them and turning them into boy soldiers. As a result of these pressures, Uganda conducted a poll in June 2000 in which the government proposal not to proceed with multi-party democracy won an overwhelming majority. Foreign observers said the poll was not democratic. The March 2001 election was even less so. Amid such happenings the Irish AID programme amounts to far more than a spot of water on a hot rock.

BRIAN KAVANAGH

Brian Kavanagh was another Irish teacher who survived both Amin and Obote. He came to Kampala as apart of a group of teachers who were invited out by the British before Independence. In those days schools were generally run by missionaries: Catholic, Muslim or Protestant. After Independence, there were more Protestants in the Catholic schools than Catholics. With the exception of Amin, who was a Muslim, post-Independence Presidents tended to be Protestant, which led to a degree of religious warfare. Kavanagh thinks he survived these conflicts unscathed through being a bachelor – teachers with families found they had given hostages to an ill fortune. He became a headmaster in 1964, the year after Independence.

At the time, teachers and most employees of schools, apart from a few sweepers, were European, and initially standards were maintained, despite the difficulties posed by the introduction of a fast-track programme of Ugandanisation. However, the British began cutting grants to punish Amin for his various actions against British interests, and standards began to fall badly. Books disappeared and it became harder and harder to teach. Several teachers pulled out but Kavanagh stayed on. The only explanation he can give, apart from liking Ugandans, is that he:

> had a conscience about leaving. You had to be very careful about what you said. Amin had spies amongst the children in every classroom. There were roadblocks and the children's parents were picked up at these roadblocks and disappeared.

He taught the children as much classical literature as he could: *A Man For All Seasons*, *Animal Farm*. One day when he began discussing *Macbeth*, a pupil called out: 'That's Obote!' Somehow he just kept going. 'But,' he said, 'local people had tremendous courage. They were literally martyred in buses, on the streamers, on the lakes. I saw busloads of people being whipped.'

He hid a student in his home for much of Amin's reign. He never showed a light or went out, and they kept from going mad by playing Scrabble and dominoes together. Kavanagh is retired now, living in a bungalow in a pleasant suburb of Kampala, on a hill overlooking what seems like a huge expanse of flat grassland. It is in fact a section of Lake Victoria, which is becoming increasingly clogged – despite all efforts to remove it – by a fast-growing water hyacinth which seems to have escaped from some Europeans' ornamental ponds. A metaphor for Uganda?

TELEPHONES AND POP

As the era of the Irish religious reaches a watershed, the secular assistance moves on to a new plane. The Irish Government is making an attempt to assist Uganda's development through its Aid Programme, by targeting specific areas of the country for development. In the designated zones, Kabila, Kumi and Kiboya, infrastructure of all sorts was either improved or, in some cases, created. Roads, water, sanitation, primary schools, agricultural schools and adult training programmes were all originated under the Irish aid programme. Most of the expenditure on these projects was spent locally, thereby directly improving the standard of living of some 800,000 people, spread out over a region of nine thousand square kilometres. While I was in Uganda, technicians were busy giving the Kibali area an Irish telephone system. The dial telephones and Hitachi exchanges had become available because Ireland was upgrading and digitalising its own system. Given the state of the old Irish phone service, I was not immediately certain that this was an unmitigated boon for the Ugandans. However, the reality is that Ireland had to upgrade its system as its EU-fuelled, Western economy mushroomed; Uganda is trying to develop a Third World economy in the wake of a period of brutal warfare, both lengthier and more bloody than the thirty years of the Irish Troubles – better the old Irish phones than no phones at all. Using this approach the Irish Government was able to ensure that a practical form of assistance went to the people who needed it, not into the pockets of what are euphemistically termed 'entrepreneurs'.

There was one successful Irish innovation in operation in Uganda for which I do not propose to offer a defence. Every time a radio was turned on, I got the sense that I was listening to one of my pet hates, a particularly raucous (and popular) Irish pop station. Sounding uncannily like the mid-Atlantic voice I avoided in Dublin, there was a DJ who continually informed the world that his Kampala station boasted 'less talk, more music'. At a dinner, very kindly given for me by a group of Irish in Kampala's excellent Chateau restaurant, I met the man responsible. William Pike, who was the editor-in-chief of Museveni's newspaper, *New Visions*, and the man who had been the only Western journalist to cover the war against Obote with Museveni's army in the bush, was also the man behind the ghastly but successful pop station. A far nicer person than his station suggested he confirmed what I had half suspected: he got the idea from listening to the Dublin station.

Pike is of the Anglo-Irish missionary tradition, and personified the continuation of the Irish Protestant interest in Africa – his father had been an engineer in the old colonial days. Returning home to Ireland on a visit, William had been stressed out on the way to the airport by the condition of an appalling road which did not seem to have received any repairs for decades. Somehow he made the plane, and kept his appointment at Heathrow with his father. As they drove away from the airport, William began to tell his father about his ordeal on the awful road. The old man smiled gently and said: 'Yes, I know that road – I built it.'

A link of another sort was provided by one of the guests at the dinner, Aisling Stuart, a grand-daughter of the Irish novelist, Francis Stuart, who was a son-in-law of John McBride whom the British executed in 1916. She is married to Robert Law, an Irish lawyer who practices in Kampala. In another part of Africa, which I would shortly be visiting, a relation of Aisling's, Robert MacBride, was lucky to be still alive after his part in the ANC's military campaign against apartheid in South Africa.

The Irish in Kenya

While the contribution of the Irish to Uganda was, and is, obviously valuable, one would expect that numerically they would be less visible than the British. I was not surprised therefore to find that the attendance on the St Patrick's Day banquet was some 250 – respectable, but not overwhelming. However, in Kampala I ran into a group of musicians, some of them Irish, who had flown down from Nairobi to play at the British St George's Day celebration, which, I had been informed by a group of British expats, 'had been very well attended'. The musicians rated it differently: 'Only about a hundred and fifty turned up' (and two of these left in protest when the group played 'Flower of Scotland'). The musicians had a different yardstick to judge by in Kenya, where conditions had been more stable than those which obtained in Kampala, the Irish did not merely celebrate St Patrick's Day with a banquet in Nairobi, but with a week-long programme of events which included a race meeting!

The Irish Government has closed its embassy in Kenya, on grounds of economy during one of the credit squeezes of the eighties. But, by a coincidence, while I was researching this book, Art Agnew, the Irish Ambassador in Buenos Aires gave a dinner in my honour, at which he announced the purchase of an official residence by the Irish government in that lovely city, in which for the first time the dinner service taken from the Nairobi embassy was used again. So, though the credit squeeze has thankfully passed, the Irish diaspora continues to gain in strength.

It was certainly flourishing in Nairobi. One can find the Irish everywhere from shanty towns to the exclusive Muthaiga Country Club, shown in the film

Out of Africa. I was invited to dinner at the club by the Chairman of the Irish Society, Kevin Killian and his wife Patricia, to meet, amongst other members of the Kenyan Irish community, a legendary figure, St John Kelliher, the Kerry-born manager of the famous Mount Kenya Safari Club Hotel, of whom more anon. In general, however, one thinks of the Irish in Kenya, as in most other parts of Africa, not in relation to such exclusive establishments, but in terms of the caring tradition, serving in the field of either education, health or aid, either as missionaries or members of NGOs.

I saw the various strands of the community draw together at a GOAL function in the Karen Golf Club, on the outskirts of Nairobi. The club forms part of the old Karen von Blixen Estate, which also figured in the *Out of Africa* film. The dinner attracted professionals, aid workers, businessmen, teachers and religious. The attendance reminded me yet again of the scale of Irish emigration. If I kept bumping into people all around the globe who came from the tiny area on the east coast of Ireland where I grew up, what did this say about the numbers who must have emigrated over the years from the island as a whole? The guests at my table included Tony Gleeson and his wife, Maureen. Gleeson and I went to the same school and he now owns a flat on the road adjoining the one where I was born. Michael O'Leary, the EU Representative in Nairobi, has a home a few hundred yards from where I now live: Rena Hanrahan of the Irish Governmental Agency for Service Overseas (APSO) has a flat a couple of miles from us both, as indeed had Kevin Killian. Another guest, the top Kenyan jockey and trainer, turned out to be one Ken Coogan. His father and mine both came from the County Kilkenny.

There were divisions of opinion amongst the Irish community concerning the Kenyan Government. In general the professional and business class were more well disposed towards the Moi regime than were some sections of the clergy and the aid community. The former were conscious of Kenya's commercial advantages, and inclined to keep their heads under the parapet. The latter were more concerned at the rampant corruption and lack of attention to the rising social problems. Even without the corruption, the social problems would be grievous in their own right. Despite the ravages of AIDS, Kenya, like the rest of Africa, is suffering from a population explosion.

One of the ways in which the Irish Government attempts to assist Kenya is through Coillte, the Irish Forestry Organisation. Fertile Kenya with its huge game reserves should be a forester's paradise, but denudation and a brutal exploitation of natural resources for 'development' is counteracting much of the benefit of Coillte's presence. However, another area of Irish expertise had just scored a spectacular success prior to my arrival; Tony Gleeson had just won a major competition to design the new General Post Office for Nairobi's centre. Possibly the Kenyans recognised that the Irish had led the world in re-modelling GPOs in 1916!

Indeed I encountered echoes of 1916 and the colonialism of Mother England, at a chance meeting in Nairobi's Carnivore Restaurant. After a remarkable meal which included crocodile, zebra, eland, wildebeest, pork, lamb, beef, giraffe and God knows what else, I ran into a group of British soldiers. The huge restaurant modelled on the Brazilian custom of roasting meats over open fires could hardly have been more exotic in appearance, or remote from Belfast – but that's where the Swaddies had come from. Kenya is, of course, still an important British army training area. Even in that faraway locale, discussion on Ireland between myself and the soldiers, fundamentally decent working-class lads, provoked tensions. One much tattooed individual was obviously puzzled at the lack of receptivity from Catholics to whom he had tried to be 'understanding'. When I pointed out that, to the Nationalists, his bullets were just as hard, he replied: 'Ah, now you're bringing politics into it!' However, we had another chomp of wildebeest and poured a couple of beers on our argument. Would things could be settled as easily in Belfast.

Mini Sowetos

Throughout the nineties the Aid community and an increasing number of missionaries, particularly the nuns, were finding themselves on the opposite side of the fence to the Government on social issues. One could see at a glance why this was so. The GOAL field director, Noreen Prendeville, and her Swedish husband Goti, lived in a pleasant suburb of Nairobi. When they first came there, a few years earlier, the district was heavily forested and there were few houses. Soon after they arrived however, a shanty town began to form on a hillside in the middle of the elegant villas. It was known as 'mini Soweto' locally. As the months passed 'mini Soweto' kept growing. More and more villas were built and the forestation began to disappear. At the same time land values were increasing. One evening as Goti and Noreen drove home, they found 'mini Soweto' ablaze. Police had arrived, ordered the inhabitants out without warning, and set fire to the shacks. 'Without warning' means what it says. Not only did the slum dwellers often not have the chance to remove their meagre possessions such as cooking utensils, sometimes babies or young children were burned to death.

After the first burning, showing both the indomitable spirit of Africa and the desperation of not having anywhere else to go, the people, largely from rural areas, soon found their way back. The shanty town was rebuilt. It was subsequently burned down by the police on two more occasions; the developers obviously had influence with the Government.

Elsewhere in the city, something similar had happened on a grander scale the previous Christmas Eve, but the Irish Loreto nuns took a hand. Sister Nuala, who was particularly prominent in justice and peace issues, descended on the startled clergy in the city's cathedrals and demanded that they respond to what had happened. Accordingly, instead of cosy platitudes about the Christ Child's message at Christmas, the faithful got the benefit of Sister Nuala's wrath at the spectacle of 30,000 people being thrown out on the road 'like rubbish'. The phrase spoiled the Christmas dinners of many of the hearers, but the displaced persons were enormously gratified by the huge response to Sister Nuala's initiative. Nuala does not take prisoners. Shortly before I arrived in Nairobi a Gilded Personage (and an Irishman to boot) had arrived in Nairobi on behalf of the World Bank. Nuala arranged with a young aid worker to accost this Gilded Personage and speak unto him the word concerning the folly of certain of the Bank's lending policies in Kenya. However, the Great Man was surrounded by admirers and servitors throughout the night and Nuala's emissary could not penetrate his force field. She was outraged. 'What are you telling me? He had people with him! He went to the lavatory didn't he? Why didn't you follow him there?' However, the Moi regime are correspondingly angered at Nuala-type outbursts. Expressions of savage but honest indignation on the part of nuns or clergy have resulted in the outspoken ones being expelled from the country, and, as indicated at the beginning of this chapter, there have been some deaths.

SHARP DIVISIONS

Controversy was not confined to the Government alone. There was constant debate in missionary and NGO circles as between 'Aid' and 'Development'; and within the missionaries themselves there were sharp divisions between those who favoured working within the system and those who believed, like Sister Nuala, that reform could only be brought about by agitation and publicity. Certainly reform was and is badly needed. Daily, unbelievable stories of corruption appeared in the Kenya press, sections of which are remarkably free by African, or indeed any other, standards, probably because the Aga Khan is a leading press baron and too powerful to be interfered with. Of all the reports of land grabbing, embezzlement, murder and general skul-duggery, one that took my eye appeared on the front page of the *Nation*, with an accompanying photograph. This simply showed a bungalow. It was part of a development which some of Moi's hoodlum associates planned to erect on the grounds of the National Stadium. It was as though, through bribery, a group of carpet-baggers had managed to erect bungalows on the turf of Dublin's Croke Park or London's Wembley Stadium.

Some Irish clerics, particularly the older ones, tend to greet such outrages by sighing, 'That's Africa,' and getting on with their teaching. I took part in a discussion with a group of Holy Ghosts, about a controversy of the hour involving the outspoken Bishop Ndingi, a leading dissident and an out-standing member of the Kenyan hierarchy. He had publicly voiced his fears concerning the appearance of helicopters and strange men in his area which he thought might presage an onslaught on members of his diocese to drive them from their land. This has already happened elsewhere, accompanied by great brutality and loss of life. 'If Bishop Ndingi had evidence, he should have gone privately to the authorities in his area and had the matter dealt with' appeared to be a shared sentiment.

THE STREET CHILDREN

The Fathers were also inclined to question the concentration on street children, both by GOAL and a notable Irish nun, Sister Mary Killeen of the Irish Sisters of Mercy. Again they appeared to feel that the street children problem fell into the 'that's Africa' category.

The GOAL venture was in the hands of Maggie, a young Irishwoman who was setting up a drop-in centre for the children. GOAL had taken over an old house and a gang of workers were renovating this when I visited; Maggie was contending with the usual sexual innuendo and ostentatious lounging of loutish building workers anywhere, compounded by the fact that she was not a very robust white woman in a black situation. The idea was to provide hostel-type accommodation for both boys and girls. The AIDS pandemic means that street children are an ever-growing problem throughout Africa, as in the Third World generally. The homeless children sleep rough, join gangs, are pressed into prostitution or paedophile rings, and become prey to drugs, violence and sexually transmitted diseases of all sorts. As most of the kids, according to Maggie, are 'as high as kites', by the end of the day – on anything from alcohol or glue to hard drugs – road fatalities are also common in Nairobi's chaotic traffic. Maggie eventually succeeded, with the aid of donors, in creating her haven. The children now receive meals, some basic education, psychiatric counselling and, above all, security.

'Mother Theresa, move over', is how I have heard Sister Mary Killeen described. She showed me how she operates in one of Nairobi's mini Sowetos where sewage ran on the paths between the teeming shacks, and the unemployment and general deprivation was such that I doubt it would have been safe for me to venture into the area, even in daytime, without the protection of her presence. At one end of the cabin-type facility built by GOAL, which constitutes her centre, AIDS victims are beginning to take up more and more space. At the other end are the street children.

Sister Mary told me that as the AIDS epidemic spreads, a belief has taken hold that it is safer to have sex with the young, because they will not yet have been exposed to the diseases. Thus boys and girls are preyed upon by all levels of society, including both police and priests (although let it be said that amongst the former Sister Mary has found some of her best helpers). When I met her, Sister Mary was trying to get the Church authorities to take up complaints she had made against specific Catholic priests, but the hierarchy was displaying the all too familiar pass-the-parcel policy of the Church towards paedophilia. The Cardinal, an elderly African, had said he was too old to deal with such a complex issue and was leaving it for his successor. The Order, to which some of the men involved belonged, was also opposing Sister Mary's efforts, and, as I learnt at first hand, so were some members of her own congregation. Nevertheless, Sister Mary was prosecuting her enquiries undaunted either by criticism or worse possibilities.

I met her leading two light-skinned children by the hand. Neither was more than a year or two old and both had badly deformed feet. Sister Mary was bringing them to a wealthy American woman – who customarily took over not a suite, but the entire floor of the hotel she stayed in – in the hope that she could persuade the millionairess to pay for an operation to straighten their limbs. Their injuries had been caused by what was either intimidation or a murder attempt on their mother. Her bed was set on fire by a gang as she slept. The arsonists are alleged to have been attempting to dissuade her from giving evidence against a paedophile, who had fathered the children on her while she was under age. The man is a Catholic priest.

JOHN KELLIHER

By way of contrast to the conditions of the street children and the shanty towns, I drove from Nairobi with St John Kelliher to the Mount Kenya Safari Club Hotel, one of the most luxurious in Africa. Mount Kenya is both a sacred mountain – the bodies of climbers who die on the mountain are always removed, no matter at what risk, because no one is permitted to be buried on its slopes – and the centre of one of East Africa's most historic areas. It was the heartland of colonial exploitation, the legendary 'White Highlands' which figured in the film *White Mischief*. Its cool, fertile areas today produce many of the vegetables sold in the huge London supermarket chains. Seventeen hours after being taken from the fields, the vegetables have been washed, packaged, transported, and placed on the supermarket shelves. One wonders how much the workers involved have benefited from this miracle of modern marketing – I was told that some of them receive as little as 25 cents a day.

The drive from Nairobi with Kelliher was both a scenic and historical *tour d'horizon*. Mount Kenya was probably the strongest Mau Mau centre in the country. The green fertile countryside itself is a kaleidoscope of beauty, poverty, wealth, inefficiency, resignation, cheerfulness and corruption, all jumbled together. The shanty villages, the rutted roads, the land-grabbing opportunities can be seen as one drives. The state hospitals are so under-resourced and overcrowded that a stay in one for a European would be tantamount to a death sentence. Patients having to sleep three in a bed is a common situation. Nevertheless, the population explosion is outpacing the mortality rate.

The hotel itself is surrounded by game reserves. The spectacular snow-capped bulk of Mount Kenya looms above it and the hotel itself straddles the equator, which bisects one of the tennis courts exactly at the net. Multitudes of exotic birds walk the grounds, attracted both by artificial lakes and the fact that food is put out twice a day, and luxurious, log-fired bungalows dot the grounds around the hotel proper. The hotel's owners included the filmstars William Holden and Stephanie Powers.

Kelliher is an Irish music enthusiast, passionately interested in Irish history and culture. He took me with his wife and English father-in-law for a tour of a neighbouring game park. We drove almost as close to a herd of elephant as we would have to a herd of cattle in Ireland. In one corner of the park there is a tame hippo, a dwarf who only grew to weigh a ton or two because another hippo castrated him in a fight. We were able to feed him with branches broken off by armed guards with guns at the ready in case an angry hippo should turn up to finish off the dwarf.

Kelliher himself could easily have been finished off by this deceptively friendly environment. His home is situated in a compound some distance from the hotel, and not long after he was appointed manager, a raiding party came to the hotel seeking the keys to the safe. Though badly beaten, one of the staff members managed to direct the raiders out of the hotel and towards Kelliher's house, on the pretext that he had the keys. The man then managed to get to a phone to warn Kelliher that the raiders were coming. Kelliher in turn roused his wife and two daughters, and hid them in an attic – if not in safety, at least out of sight – by the time the raiders arrived at his door. Armed with a pump-action shotgun, he managed to keep them at bay, killing five of them in the process, until the Masai warriors who acted as the hotel's security staff eventually turned up. In the ensuing fight a further ten of the raiders were killed.

Kelliher then worked through the night with his staff, removing signs of the raiding party's attack from the hotel lobby and bars. There were spears and machetes embedded in the walls, as well as sundry breakages, to be taken care of. In the morning, none of the guests noticed anything amiss, but, despite all Kelliher's precautions, they discovered the whole thing via a CNN news item a couple of days later. The raid was apparently aimed at disrupting the Moi regime's plans for tourism in the region. It had no lasting effect on that front, but Kelliher's children were traumatised by the incident for several years afterwards.

The difference between his approach and that of some English expats was immediately observable. Friends of Kelliher's had invited me to a most hospitable lunch, and made me extremely welcome. Then the question of disturbances in nearby Eldoret came up. My hosts explained that the problem stemmed from 'a lot of agitators over there'. By then I knew enough to realise that the 'agitators included a number of Irish Kiltegan Fathers and Loreto nuns who were supporting the people against the predations of would-be land grabbers, documenting human rights abuses and publicising injustice. The attitude of the Kiltegans towards confronting the system may be gauged from the fact that the Moi regime has expelled four Kiltegans for every one Holy Ghost priest.

St Mary's

St Mary's Holy Ghost Boys' School, Nairobi, is one of the most prestigious in Africa. There was a 'Blackrock Rugby Festival' in progress as I arrived and St Mary's were playing against Strathmore, another élite college, run by Opus Dei. I felt as though I had stepped back in time to a Saturday afternoon during

AFRICA

my rugby-playing days at Blackrock College at Williamstown in County
Dublin – the smartly dressed girls on the touchline, admiring the good-
looking young footballers; the priests commenting knowledgeably on the
play; the open passing game; the rain falling; the tree-lined surroundings; all
exactly replicated the atmosphere of an early spring or autumn Blackrock
encounter. I had been at school with some of the priests on the touchline.
Others had taught my son. Like me they had known the famous President of
Blackrock and rugby coach of the senior team, Father Hamson, whose dictum
was: 'Remember boys, the two most important things in life are the Grace of
God – and the quick heel from the base of the scrum.' In terms of ambience
(and attitudes) we might have been meeting at a club rugby match in Dublin.

The only difference was that most of those present were black. A group of
expensively dressed young Africans were clustered around a red sports car
with a powerful radio. They were passing a champagne bottle between them.
I noticed a priest glaring at them and assumed that it was the champagne
which annoyed him, but no, it was the noise; he sent a boy over to the group
with a message to turn down the radio. The decibel level abated immediately,
but the noise of the spectators could still be heard as we walked to a neatly
kept graveyard a couple of hundred yards from the touchline.

Again, with the trees arching overhead and the Irish names on the
gravestones, one might have been in an Irish churchyard. The graveyard
holds the remains of two of the most famous figures in Irish missionary
history, Bishop Shanahan and Edel Quinn – or at least that's what one
would assume when one sees the two gravestones. In fact, Shanahan is not
buried there, although Quinn is. She was a notable member of the Legion of
Mary, regarded in the world church with an even greater veneration than
Alfie Lamb, whose grave I encountered on the far side of the world in
Argentina.

JOSEPH SHANAHAN

I very much doubt if a tiny fraction of those present at the match, other than
the priests, had ever heard of Shanahan.[26] However, his story is one of the
great poignancy and significance, both for the spread of the Church in Africa
and for what it says about the influence it exerted in Ireland, and for the
atmosphere of repressed sexuality which obtained before the era when Fr
Michael Cleary's humanity shattered the life-long illusions of a group of
simple pious women in Uganda. Joseph Shanahan came to Africa in 1906 and
was a legendary missioner in Nigeria. In that country he built up a vast
educational network, extending the Holy Ghost Order's foundations, and was
also directly responsible for the creation of an order of nuns, the Holy Rosary
Sisters of Killeshandra in County Cavan. Shanahan's school system became
the model for the missionary system throughout Africa. It was based on
rudimentary bush schools which taught religion, reading and writing. From
these beginnings the schools grew to provide every level of education.

537

How many plumbers, building contractors, rapacious war lords, condescending colonial administrators, unfeeling superiors, turbulent priests and lonely, tossing sweaty nights, did Shanahan confront in creating this massive achievement? What talents that could have made a statesman or a tycoon were invested? We don't know. What is certain is that by the time of his retirement, after a lifetime of labour in the exacting Nigerian climate, Shanahan was not in the best of health. He had planned to retire in Nigeria, which he loved even more than Ireland, but he had been a controversial figure in the Church. Some had opposed his policy on concentrating on school rather than missionary activity. It became apparent that his successor, Archbishop Heerey, whom he had consecrated, was not going to invite him to stay on, and he decided to return to Ireland.

He set his heart on living in a gate lodge in the Holy Rosary Sisters' Convent, to 'make his soul' and husband out his days in the company of the nuns amid the lakes and low hills of Cavan. So, when a nun who had worked closely with him, Mother Dominic, cracked up and had to return to Killeshandra, he decided to travel with her. What follows is told in the restrained words of Desmond Forrestal, a playwright and television documentary maker and, by way of illustrating the close-knit nature of the Irish diaspora, my local parish priest in Dalkey, County Dublin:

> On the ship as in Onitsha, he was kindness itself, attentive to her every need. By a sad chance, she misinterpreted his intentions and the signs of affection which were second nature to him. He thought nothing of putting his arms around a sister to comfort her, or letting her cry on his shoulder. He was their father, they were his daughters. What could be more natural?

However, Forrestal goes on, when Dominic got back to Killeshandra: 'She told Mother Xaviour that the Bishop was in love with her, with consequences that were to be little short of tragic.'

Mother Xaviour, who was in charge of the convent, was a product of her time:

> She knew that religious sisters must be trained in discipline and self control. In her direction of the Convent, she followed the time honoured traditions that instil a sense of discipline in innumerable small but significant ways. Sisters were taught to walk, not to run; to sit upright, not to slouch; to smile, not to laugh loudly. They moved in a quiet and restrained manner, they kept their hands folded and their eyes modestly downcast, they avoided unnecessary looks or gestures. They ate what was set before them at meals and avoided taking so much as a drink of water between meals. As celibates, they were particularly guarded in the presence of the opposite sex and even among themselves were careful to avoid any emotional friendships.

This was the sort of formation these unfortunate, brainwashed, brilliant, celibate women brought to Africa with them. However, when Shanahan took a group of nuns walking in the fields:

Their routine of Killeshandra was disrupted and the air of calm and decorum was disturbed. They came back to the convent giddy and excited, still spellbound by his magnetism, still flattered that a bishop could show them such attention and courtesy. Quite unconsciously, he could undo the work of patient weeks in a couple of hours.

Nuns were honed down by the system until they became denatured, sexless, disciplinarians, to whom humanity was a vice to be countered at every turn. Missionary Sisters in those days were commonly not allowed to return home for periods of from 15-20 years. This later broke down to intervals of from 5-3 years, but only in more recent years when falling vocations indicated to the Vatican that in the west nuns were becoming extinct. But in the 1940s, vocations were plentiful and Mother Xaviour was in the full infertile flowering of the ghastly, narrow-minded formation process which had moulded her. After hearing Mother Dominic's story, she lined up the sisters in the convent and addressed them as follows:

> You all know that Dr Shanahan is the one who started this congregation and that he is a very saintly bishop. It is to leave him in his sanctity and to safeguard your spiritual good and to safeguard your welfare that I am saying what I am going to say ... you all love him as your father and founder. You enjoy being with him in the parlour, listening to him. Now all this could become too human. You are all young and immature and have little experience of life. You could become attached to him in a merely human way. You would not know your place with other bishops and priests ...
>
> While he was away in Nigeria it was not so hard. Now that he has come to live in Ireland and would like to be with you all the time, the facts must be made clear ... Don't make things awkward for them [their superiors] by inviting Dr Shanahan to come and stay, or by making prolonged visits in the parlour. Respect him, pray for him, show him due reverence at all times, but be careful of all that is too human and too natural.

Unaware of this, Shanahan planned a visit to Killeshandra, and one of the community, a Sister Catherine, hearing of the visit, applied for permission to see him. When she was refused she burst into tears. Her Novice Mistress, asked why she was crying, and the young Sister replied: 'Because the Bishop is going to be so hurt.' The Novice Mistress summed up all the desolation of the psychology of the Irish nuns of the period in her response: 'It does not matter if you are hurt, or if he is hurt, or who is hurt. The important thing is, what does God want, and that we must do, no matter what it costs.'

And so Shanahan ended his days wandering between a room in a house in the grounds of Blackrock College and Kenya; Heerey never invited him back to Nigeria. He died in Nairobi on Christmas Day 1943, and was buried in the grave which I was shown. However, a movement grew up to have him returned to Nigeria. For a time it was resisted, but then Archbishop Heerey had a strange experience.

At the time, Nigerian independence was approaching and Heerey was embroiled in an acrimonious debate with his fellow bishops over whether or not the vast network of schools, which Shanahan had created, should be handed over to the civil authorities. Heerey wanted to hold on to the schools, but the bishops felt it would be good for Church/State relations to hand them over. One night, as Heerey was going to bed, he claims he saw Shanahan:

> as clear as ever he appeared during his life, standing looking down on me, in white satin, purple cincture, pectoral cross and all, as he was so well known to us. He had a surreal sympathetic look as if to convey to me that he understood the whole situation . . .There is no doubt that he came to sympathise and assure me.

Shortly after this apparition occurred, the Nigerians withdrew their demands to take over the school system.

The spirit of the builder, Shanahan, no longer had a political overtone. Heerey's guilt overcame him and he changed his mind about returning Shanahan's remains to Onitcha. The body was exhumed, and the coffin was flown first to South Africa where the Holy Rosary Nuns were able to honour their founder in death, as they had been prevented from doing in life, at a huge two-day ceremony. The remains were then flown to Nigeria. Again enormous crowds gathered in different parts of the country as the coffin was put on display before finally being interred in Onitcha Cathedral, following extraordinary scenes of mourning and respect.

Ironically, for all the envious, foetid caution about allowing Shanahan to retire to Nigeria, the entire Holy Ghost Order was subsequently expelled from the country, because some of the priests became involved with the Ibos on the losing side in the Nigerian civil war of the 1960s. But none of this is made known to a visitor to that quiet cemetery at the edge of the rugby field. Rugger, reality, and fashionable Catholicism are as un-comfortable with each-other in Africa as in Dublin Four.

As indicated The Holy Ghost Order has traditionally been associated with sport in particular, rugby, and has exported this British sport with great success to the Order's foundations throughout the English speaking world. It was the very appeal of what the early Sinn Fein movements termed the 'garrison games', rugby, soccer, cricket, and hockey, which led to their being proscribed for members of the GAA in the early days of the Sinn Fein struggle against British rule in Ireland. When, what became known as 'the GAA ban,' came into effect Vivion de Valera, the eldest son of President de Valera, was a student in Blackrock College. He told me that the day after the ban was enforced, he found that hurling sticks and sliothars, as the ribbed, hard-packed leather hurling balls are called, had vanished from the locker room. Hency forth the rugby ball became the college's sporting symbol. Mother church might be celibate but she knew how to evaluate the economic and political value of young men's balls.

BROTHER COLM'S ATHLETES

Watching the game at St Mary's, I was reminded that rugby is not the only sport which Irish religious have used to make an impact on Kenyan society. Brother Colm O'Connell, from County Cork, has helped to elevate the Kenyan's own natural prowess as runners to Olympic level, and has trained some of the world's most famous distance runners.[27] He is a Brother of the Patrician Order, and knew nothing about running when he arrived in Kenya in 1976 as a geography teacher at St Patrick's High School at Iten, in the Rift Valley. Since coming there, he has coached thirty Olympians: twenty from St Patrick's High School and ten from a nearby girls' school at Signore, where an Irish nun, Sister Christine, helps with the coaching. The runners he has trained include Kipkoech and Charles Cheruiyot, who are identical twins and broke junior world records for 1,500 metres and 5,000 metres. Not surprisingly, sports journalists have nick-named them Cheruiyots, of Fire. Also in O'Connell's stable are Peter Chumb, a double winner at Athens, Salina Chichir (who won a gold and a silver at Athens) and Peter Rono who also took a silver at Athens.

Brother Colm is dismissive about his own input into Kenya's running success. He attributes it all to the genes of the Kalenjin tribe. These elegant, nomadic pastoralists herd their cattle through the hills and high altitudes of the Rift Valley. Typically they have long thigh bones, high hips and are tall and lean. However, the Kenyan athletes themselves give him the credit. Peter Rono, the Olympic 1,500-metre medallist, has said that Brother Colm was the best coach in the world, and many of the world's top sports journalists attribute Kenya's resurgence in distance running to him.[28] For example, in the 1995 Commonwealth Games held in South Africa, Kenya had eleven star runners, and of these, Colm had trained eight. The Kenyans' eminence in world-class running has continued since.

Of the Kenyan women runners, 90 per cent come from Brother Colm and Sister Christine's coaching nursery. The girls had particular difficulties in breaking through in athletics. The traditional view in Africa of women being subsidiary, and the fact that, if married, they were expected to respect their husbands' wishes in the matter of child-bearing, stultified the growth of many a potential Olympic medallist. Nevertheless, the help of the two Irish coaches, and the general emancipation of women, has helped some women runners to hit the big time. Sister Christine, who came to Africa in 1986, has said about her pupils: 'When you see where they come from, you don't know how they can possibly scrape the money together.'[29] Primary school education is free in Kenya, but secondary school has to be paid for. The average wage of a family might be approximately $35 a year, but school fees could be around $250. Yet, somehow, the families and the communities scrape together the necessary money.

A naturally independently-minded thinker, Brother Colm is subject to the strictures of both Mother Church and African sensitivities. His philosophy is:

Keep your nose to the grindstone. Don't draw attention to yourself. Don't get too close to the Government and officials. It can work the other way. A lot of my reward comes from

541

the kids and from the athletes' attitudes. The children are wonderful. There's no such thing as trying to get them to work. They automatically get down to it and work. You have no problems with discipline. They're naturally still. If you compare them to a crowd of Irish kids in church say, the Irish kids would be skittin' and chattin'. The parents would have to check them. Not the African kids.

The athletes have the same approach. There is a stillness about them. They are like a wild animal. It shows no sign of tension, and then it suddenly explodes into activity. You'll see Kenyans with a smile on their face before the start of a race. All the rest will be tensed up. The Kenyans are lovely and simple in their approach.

One unlooked-for aspect of the diaspora came home to Colm at the 5,000 metres in Gothenborg in 1995. The winner was Sonia O'Sullivan from Ireland who beat three of his pupils! However, Sonia turned out to be particularly helpful, and as he and I were talking in Kenya a number of his girls were living with her in London and training together.

While Colm was cautious in expressing anything which might be termed an African opinion, he was quite outspoken about the future of the Church:

The Church will have to change its attitude on issues like celibacy, contraception and the position of women, married priests and so on, if it is to survive.

WOMEN IN THE CHURCH

In contrast to what one hears in Ireland, I constantly found that in Africa, as in America for example, Irish nuns were regarded as a force for what might be termed women's lib. Two of the pioneers were Mother Mary Martin who founded the Medical Missionaries of Mary, and Mother Kevin who founded the Franciscan Missionary Sisters of Africa. Both these women faced obstacles over and above African conditions: it took decades of lobbying and entreaty before, in 1936, the Vatican allowed women to be trained as doctors and midwives. The education and training in health matters which the Irish nuns initiated helped to raise the consciousness of African women, apart from saving their lives in a continent where infant mortality can be so high that sometimes as many as six out of seven children will die.

The Loreto nuns of the Irish province are to the forefront in the struggle for women's rights. As in Ireland, the Order is associated with the education of the elite. However as circumstances changed, so has the role of the nuns. Sister Columbiere came to Kenya in 1948. In those days, as in Ireland, most women were not educated, and the Loreto nuns educated only the élite of the country. Sister Columbiere, for example, numbered Jomo Kenyatta's daughter amongst her pupils.[30] However, her superior, a famous character in African Loreto history, Sister Joseph Teresa O'Sullivan, set out to change the system. She had been on the Republican side in the Irish Civil War and had served a sentence in Kilmainham jail. To the end of her days de Valera was her idol. Sister Columbiere told me:

It was one of the great blessings of my work to work with her. She was ex Cumann na mBan [the IRA's Women's Auxiliary] and she wasn't afraid of anything. She was a pioneer feminist. When she arrived here, girls weren't educated. The parents kept them at home. But Sister Teresa ran after them and brought them to school. She was a great mathematician and was very tough in insisting that all that mattered was girls' education. She was marvellous.

Sister Columbiere was dubious about the contemporary system of education. Although she dismissed suggestions that Africanisation meant a lowering of standards, she was concerned about 'the long-term effects of the fact that pupils now only spend four years in secondary school at A-level instead of six formerly'. When she criticised the system, Sister Columbiere was in fact blaming the population explosion: 'This was a lovely, beautiful, prosperous country when I came out – now look at it. Destroying the forests and the wild life. Nearly 50 per cent lived below the breadline.'

Two of Columbiere's younger colleagues, Sister Catriona Kelly, fifty-six, and Sister Nuala Branigan, forty-nine, discussed with me the challenges which these conditions posed for contemporary women religious. They saw seemingly trivial debates with the African hierarchy – for example, over issues such as the bishops' attempts to ensure that nuns wore veils – as being really battles over empowerment: 'Men's power over women.'

Nuala said: 'I'm not here to help or to give out aid. I'm here to gather the facts of what's happening in areas in injustice.' She cited a case where the Government had promoted tribal clashes, and then sent men in to grab the land and burn the shanty town. She described how one young mother had lost her baby in the flames. While Nuala could be expelled, she did not fear imprisonment or death, although she admitted neither could be ruled out. However, she calculates that: 'The Government is afraid to take on the Church because half the people are Catholic and the Church is a worldwide organisation. They would be afraid of the publicity.'

The nuns' spirit was impressive – for now – but what long-term prospect does a career in confrontation, depending on subscriptions from yuppie Dublin, offer the Order? Obviously the hope would be that the protests would cause the injustices to disappear, but as vocations fall in Ireland, what does the future hold for Irish religious such as themselves? The nuns stated ambition was to see their buildings and their Order completely taken over by Africans in a space of ten to fifteen years. In fact, this process is well under way. Unlike in the Western world, seminaries and convents in Africa are as full as they were in Ireland up to the dawning of the sixties. In their self-sacrificial view of the party-line vision of the future, the nuns' ambition is coming true. For instance, Catriona introduced me to one of the most beautiful women I have ever set eyes on.

'Isn't she a real Miss Kenya?' she asked. We were in a taxi, taking Immaculata, as the young woman was called, to the Institute where on that day she would enter the Loreto Order. In the fourteen years before she finishes her studies and is professed, Catriona and Nuala expect the Church to be completely Africanised.

Nuala and Catriona hoped that Africanisation would not be dogmatic, harsh or judgmental, that it would be a force for the development of a consciousness of being Kenyan, rather than the furtherance of tribalism. However, both nuns – Nuala especially, because she is concerned with justice and peace issues – were fearful about what the future would hold for Kenya after Moi. They accurately forecasted some of the tensions and protests against the Government which filled TV screens a year later. In a nutshell, this is the problem for Africa. Who comes after: the tyrant or the democrat? A Mobutu or a Mandela?

The continent still resembles one of those Imperial English Charters which, once bought, gave the recipient the right to extract as much as he could, as long as he could, from as many as he could, without sanction.

One of Nuala's most deeply felt concerns is about the custom of female circumcision. In Somalia, for example, they told me that it is not uncommon to lose up to a kilo and a half of flesh during this barbaric ritual. Sister Catriona, a formidable figure, who frequently interrupted our conversation to take calls on her mobile phone, summed up the nuns' position by saying:

> We have opted for the prophetic vision. Living with other races, being with them and their needs, rather than coming along with the mind set of standing for certain laws and observances.

DR MEYERHOLD

Catriona and her mobile phone probably saved my life. While I was interviewing her, she kept quizzing me on how I felt. She was taking a lot of calls at the time – she was in the process of handing over her role as head of the Order in Nairobi, prior to returning to Europe – and consequently I didn't realise that one of her calls concerned me. As we prepared to go to lunch, she pushed down the phone aerial firmly and said, 'Doctor Meyerhold will see you tomorrow.'

'Who is Doctor Meyerhold?' I not unreasonably enquired.

Meyerhold, an Austrian German Jew, turned out to be the Loreto nuns' doctor and top physician to Nairobi's expat community, and to make sure that I got there Catriona led me by the arm to his office. When Meyerhold took my blood pressure, he paled visibly and sat down. When he told me what the figures were, I sat down also. He then took me off the Lariam which I had been taking to ward off malaria and put a coach and four through my itinerary, placing me on different medication and grounding me in Nairobi for a month. Later on in my tour, in an area where the local hospital packed them in three to a bed, I obeyed Meyerhold's instruction to have a check-up. The local doctor was Indian. When I told him my Nairobi blood pressure levels, he did a creditable imitation of Peter Sellers and exclaimed: 'Oh my goodness!

Anything could happen. Please lie down immediately!' By then, however, Meyerhold's treatment had done its work. When my blood pressure was checked it was discovered that, though still high, it was no longer alarming.

Meyerhold talked with me about Africa and the Irish. He had been in the country for thirty years and seen the population grow from 6.5 million to its present level of a presumed 25 million. Most other areas of Africa show similar increases. Whem Meyerhold first came to Africa, Nairobi's Norfolk Hotel was known as the House of Lords because of the number of titled English folk who used to stay there. They could, and did, shoot deer, zebra, giraffe and game of all sorts from its windows, and Teddy Roosevelt had made the hotel the starting point for the largest game safari in Africa's history. I met a 38-year-old Scots woman who had grown up some miles outside Nairobi: as a girl she and her friends used to tether their ponies at the hotel and then 'walk across the fields until we came to Nairobi'. Today the Norfolk is engulfed by suburbs and Nairobi's fearsome traffic snarls past its verandas.

Meyerhold rated the population explosion as Africa's number one problem. 'At the moment,' he said, 'the only effective birth control agent is traffic accidents.' Unfortunately he was right. The traffic accidents are a horrific aspect of African life. One sees Hiace vans speeding along, with as many as fifty passengers, often driven with the rear doors open so that two passengers may be seen standing on each door. When one of them crashes, as they frequently do, the carnage is frightful. In Kampala they told me the record for horror was held by a van which hit a bus and then after spilling some of its passengers all over a busy road, where other vehicles drove into them, it careened into a deep ravine. In all sixty-five people died.

Unlike the population, the Irish, Meyerhold said, were 'shrinking, shrinking'. He accepted that the Africanisation of the Church would proceed apace, but added a rider: 'I see the Irish come to work and pray, but I think many Africans just come to pray.' This is a common comment about African men, but it is certainly not true of African women, be they religious or lay.

Meyerhold did, however, raise a key question for the continuation of the Irish presence. He cited a hospital run by Irish nuns and pointed out that they managed on an annual budget roughly equivalent to what the public laboratory at the main Nairobi hospital took in a day for tests. Like other religious-run hospitals throughout the continent, it was supported by donors who paid for plant and buildings – but what happens when the Sister Miriam-like figures retire? The hope is that in the short-term the increase in Irish governmental aid and NGO activity will fill the gap. In the long-term, of course, the best solution would be for the African economies to develop to the stage where they can fill their own gaps.

THE APPROACH FOR THE FUTURE

On the outskirts of a suburb of Nairobi, I visited a project that perhaps embodies the approach for the future. It had been co-funded by the Irish, the

545

British and the Belgians (there was criticism of the Belgians because of their unnatural custom of demanding receipts). Brian O'Sullivan, a Dublin architectural technician employed by APSO, was in charge – a similar scheme in Dublin would have employed a team of architects. He was building a Women's Development Centre which would include a nursery school, a technical school, hostel accommodation and a medical advice centre. Women were at work drawing water to mix concrete, and Stephen, a Kenyan Catholic and a mason who could read plans, was acting as Brian's liaison with the workforce. The site was filled with workers: one set of labourers were throwing the concrete up a storey to where a second gang shovelled it on to the next level and so on. The low wages explained the presence of such vast manpower. Stephen earned IR£1.30 a day, 30 per cent more than most labourers.

Brian introduced me to a little African nun (wearing a veil) who was bent double, whisking a clean space in front of an empty classroom. Also in front of the classroom was a large pile of concrete blocks. Brian told the nun: 'Don't worry Sister, I have spoken to the foreman, and he'll have them removed tomorrow. You'll be able to open on Monday all right.' The little nun flashed a beautiful smile at us and said in her lilting way: 'I'm not worrying. *I've* spoken to the foreman, and he'll have them removed in the next hour!' Some Irish Reverend Mother obviously had a hand in *that* formation.

Across a patch of waste ground we could see a huge green-roofed church. Had it been built in Ireland, it would have left little change out of £5 million sterling. Working in his spare time with Father Noel Sylvery, a Pallotine priest who had been educated in Ireland, Brian had overseen the building of the church for a total cost of £50,000. It was designed to house 2,000 people, but on the day it opened, a year before my visit, it was packed to suffocation. There were at least 3,000 people in the church, so one may safely deduce that Catholicism itself is in no danger of collapse in Kenya. What the missionaries sowed is flourishing.

Father Sylvery, according to Brian, had toured Ireland, raising the money for the church. Then, back in Kenya, he proved himself 'very good' at acquiring building materials either free, or at reduced rates. The very last project envisaged after the Women's Centre was completed was a house for the Pallotines, who were living in a tin shack.

I asked Father Sylvery how he would rate the pluses and minuses of the Irish presence. He replied:

> There are no minuses. Culture and sensitivity problems are a thing of the past. Young missionaries are very different. They don't come with the mentality 'to teach rather than to learn'. The priests learn the language. This is crucial. It's a two-way traffic. In the old days, the priest was also the Education Officer. But today it's recognised that the elders are very important, they are in on all decisions. It used to be that everything came from the priest. There would be no question about money.

He singled out education as the major Irish missionary contribution: 'The Irish-taught students were the best in the seminary.' He also made a point which I heard re-echoed right across Africa:

> The churches are in areas no one else goes, slums, remote areas. They constitute an unofficial opposition. Churches are indispensable windows to the people for aid organisations. People prefer the Church hospitals to the IMF-funded state hospitals. You go there and you'll find the doctors are selling the drugs in their own shops, prescribing the patients either to go to their shops or those of their friends.

At the risk of digression, I might observe that throughout Africa I encountered people telling me similar stories about IMF funding. The World Bank money seemed to have an uncanny knack of ending up in the wrong pockets. It fell victim to Africa's endemic corruption because it was paid over to Governments, rather than to accountable organisations and individuals.

CONTRACEPTION AND CELIBACY

On what Father Sylvery called the 'taboo subjects' of contraception and clerical celibacy, I found that in the former area he adopted a practice similar to that I had met elsewhere. 'A woman comes to me with nine children asking about contraception. Is it right? I tell her: "Do what you think right." We must be realistic,' he said, gesturing at a group of children jumping in and out of a nearby stream through which flowed raw sewage.

Before speaking to Father Sylvery, I had met an Irish nun who ran a family planning centre. She imported condoms but, because of the bishops' attitude – that of the Vatican – she could not advise on their use, or of course, dispense them. So she gave them to a neighbouring Muslim clinic, and told her women: 'I think you should go to the Muslims. They tell me that they might be able to help you . . .'!

How long the frankly hypocritical attitude of the official Church to sexual issues can be maintained is anybody's guess. Obviously the population explosion and the resultant upheavals are going to continue to present Africa, Ireland and the world with serious problems. The Women's Centre, for example, was being built for Rwandans who constitute a sizeable proportion of the populations of the shanty towns in the countries adjoining Rawnda and the almost equally troubled Burundi. Apart from the legacy of Belgian colonial policy's responsibility for the Rwandan situation, a principal cause of the trouble was, and is, population pressure. There was simply not enough room for the exploding Hutu and Tutsi populations.

On the other hand the geo-political Church is more than happy with a birthrate that fills its seminaries as they empty in the West. The hypocrisy of preaching clerical celibacy, when all through Africa sexual practice is such that even bishops are acknowledged to have families, is a small price to pay for such apparent success in the numbers game – but it's a cynical, cruel game which contributes to results like Noel Maloney and his young Irish volunteers having to pick 12,000 corpses out of Lake Victoria.

Individual Irish clerical voices have consistently been raised against Church policy on contraception. One of the best-loved priests in Africa is Father James Good, stationed in the Turkana desert region of Kenya where *homo erectus* first walked. He originally came to this beautiful, but harsh and extremely testing, area because of his opposition to the papal encyclical *Humanae Vitae*, which dashed the hopes raised amongst liberal Catholics during Vatican II by reaffirming the Church's position on contraception. Good was at the time a distinguished theologian in County Cork and his stand aroused national interest. It fell to his old friend 'Connie' Lucey, the Bishop of Cork, to enforce the Vatican line and, in effect, to silence Good, who subsequently moved to Kenya. Lucey was in many ways the archetypical, commentating conservative Irish bishop, who once replied to my question: 'But how is a poor man expected to raise ten children on a labourer's wages?' by saying: 'Ah sure, at the same time you never see a mother wanting to send them back.' Yet he was a kindly man, with a deep commitment to the poor. It was Lucey more than most who opened the Irish hierarchy's eyes to what was happening in Latin America, by sending priests from his diocese to Peru in the 1960s. One of these priests, Michael Murphy, succeeded him as Bishop of Cork when he retired, and helped to further the Irish Church's growing involvement with Latin America. After retiring, Lucey, then in his seventies, moved to the Turkana desert to serve under the local parish priest – James Good.

CORRUPTION AND CRIME

Beyond the population problem of course, there looms the impact of corruption and crime. Kenya is regarded as a major centre for drug distribution throughout Africa, for example, and though levels of crime are nothing compared to those of South Africa, the trend is bad. People talk fearfully of what will happen when Moi goes. He is universally spoken of as not being a bad man personally, but he has surrounded himself with some of the worst thugs in Africa. Everyone in the aid/missionary community wants to see the corruption ended and a stop put to the land grabbing and brutality, but they are fearful that the convulsions needed to achieve this may leave the last state worse than the first, a common occurrence in Africa.

In Kenya, as elsewhere, the poor get poorer, the rich richer. It is a common sight to see police on the road checking for 'traffic violations'. They don't stop whites, but the Africans have to pay on-the-spot fines for real, and frequently imaginary, flaws to their vehicles. Overall if they were affluent they would not buy, and rely on, such clapped-out vehicles, but, it's the policemen's way of making up for the inadequacy of their pay – and that of their superiors who send them out, confiscating a percentage of the takings. No one objects. It's only the poor who suffer.

This is how the system works. I took a taxi to a complex at the gates of which a police patrol was at work. My driver grew agitated and obviously fearful. 'They will fine me 100 shillings,' he said. The sum was well in excess of his day's income. The *modus operandi* was to let us into the complex unscathed, but to fine the driver when he re-emerged, without his European fare. I paid him off at the gate, gave him a large tip, and walked a considerable distance in the heat to my appointment. The episode did nothing for my blood pressure, in more ways than one, but it was a typical example of how life is lived in the Third World and why some Loreto nuns and Kiltegan fathers are thought of in Kenya as forming part of the unofficial opposition.

SOUTH AFRICA

One of the most interesting aspects of the Irish contribution to South Africa is the fact that the Irish made it possible for so many others to get there. The Harland & Wolff Shipbuilding Company in Belfast built many of the liners and mail ships which linked England with South Africa and produced a specially designed vessel, the G ship, to negotiate the harbours at Durban and East London. Though of course the Irish favoured America and Australia ahead of South Africa as an emigrant destination, nevertheless this was the part of Africa where the Irish settled in the greatest numbers. But this fact conceals a paradox. Unlike America or Australia, the settlers did not produce a second-generation Irish population, despite the encouragements offered by the diamond discoveries in 1860 and the finding of gold in 1886. The religious, political and military facts of life, underlined by the prevalance of signs readingl 'No Irish' in Cape Town boarding houses produced a head-under-the-parapet, pro-assimilation syndrome equalled only by that of England itself.

Writing at a time of a greatly increased consciousness of being Irish throughout the diaspora, 1921, the year in which the Irish Treaty was signed, after a period of guerilla warfare inspired in large measure by the South African experience, Thomas O'Culleanin bemoaned this assimilation in the Irish-South African paper *The Republic*:

> There are hundreds of young South Africans, men and women, Irish on both sides for generation, who are in no sense Irish. Their parents and grandparents might [as] well have come from Yorkshire or Devon. They have Irish names and Irish blood, but they are English of English. In no other country has there been such a complete loss of nationality.

The British did attempt an initiative, which had it succeeded might have increased the sense of Irishness, as it did in Australia. In the wake of the Young Irelander Uprising, an effort was made to establish a prison colony at Cape Town. However the colonists objected and after a lengthy sojourn aboard a prison ship (from September 1849 to February 1850) the ship sailed on for Van Diemen's Land with John Mitchell aboard. As in America, the bulk of the Irish emigrants tended to live in towns. In the early part of the 19th century, 88 per cent of the Irish settlers on the Cape were urban based, and it reckoned that some 19,000 Irish-born emigrants were to be found in the colonies.

This total placed the Irish fifth in the league table of emigrant groups living in South Africa, with three times the number of Dutch immigrants. The numbers swelled enormously of course during periods of warfare when Irish regiments were sent to the region. Though the Irish were numerically small, they made an impact whether they came from the Protestant or the Catholic tradition. Of the former, seven of the twenty Governors who held office between 1797 and 1910 were Irishmen. Irishmen were prominent in the professions, in politics, and in religion. Edward Carolin and Marcus O'Donovan developed huge diamond mines. Irish doctors, dentists and architects made a lasting contribution, as did teachers, sportsmen, and businessmen. Irish names like Rorke passed into history through episodes like the epic encounter at Rorke's Drift, but as in other parts of Africa, the ordinary business of living is commemorated to this day by the existence of farms bearing names like Murphy's Post, Rathmines, the Phoenix Park, the Curragh, and Home Rule.

The Orange tradition once flourished in South Africa, having been imported to the Cape by members of British regiments who served in Ireland during the 1798 rebellion. The first formal Orange Lodge was established in Cape Town in 1852 and, as we have seen in Canada, apart from its religious overtones, acted as a benevolent society for ex-service men and new emigrants. As in Canada at the time of writing, the Orange Order in South Africa has virtually died out.

The Ulster Unionists had a curiously ambivalent attitude towards the South Africans. They realised the implications of the similarities between their own policies towards the Nationalists and those of the South Africans. In 1960 the Unionists refused to allow the South African High Commissioner in London to open an exhibition in Belfast, celebrating the Commonwealth, because, in the words of the Unionist Minister, Brian Faulkner:

> . . . the word 'apartheid' had already been maliciously applied to conditions in Northern Ireland. Some sections of the national press might mischievously use the South African association with the Belfast Exhibition to make misleading and damaging comments.[31]

But when the South African Ambassador to the United Kingdom, Dr Denis Worrall, visited Northern Ireland in 1985, he was boycotted by nationalists and welcomed by the Unionists. The Unionists approved of the strong-arm methods being used by the South African Government against the ANC and wanted the British to adopt the same methods against the IRA!

For the Catholics, the names of Arthur Griffith, and of John MacBride, the Irish Brigade leader, may fairly be taken as representing the Green tradition. A turning point date in this tradition's contribution to South Africa is 14 April

1838, when Bishop Patrick Griffith from Limerick arrived at the Cape. He was the first resident Catholic bishop, and he and the priests who arrived with him made a marked impact on the Irish community. The Bishop suffered culture shock when he discovered the number of Irish emigrants living in concubinage, bringing their children up as Africans, but recovered to the extent that he seems to have succeeded in putting an end to many of these relationships in the best Irish clerical celibate tradition.

However in the wake of Griffith, there sprang up a powerful church which, while with the exception of outstanding individual figures like Archbishop Michael Hurley, cannot be said to have distinguished itself in universally outspoken condemnation of apartheid, did nevertheless make a notable contribution to the education of South African society. I had the privilege of meeting Nelson Mandela during a visit he paid to Ireland in April, 2000, both to receive an honorary degree from Trinity College, and to pay a visit to Tony O'Reilly, himself a notable example of the continuing Irish-South African links. Mandela, who seemed genuinely happy to be in Ireland, praised the contribution of the Irish to ending apartheid. He spoke with particular warmth of the Irish nuns and priests who had 'opened the doors of education to the black population.'

'They became human beings the day of the vote. I saw a woman with a wheelbarrow dancing in the street. It was a miracle. We couldn't believe it. We were singing as we stood in the queues to vote. There were whites queuing alongside blacks. For the first time they saw blacks as people.' The speaker was Sister Philomena, a Sister of Mercy originally from Counter Waterford, who had been sixty years in South Africa. With great pride she showed me the Oblate Fathers' Church, Regina Mundi, in Soweto: 'where all the ANC meetings were held. Archbishop Fitzgerald gave permission to politicise the church.'

In another part of Johannesburg another Irish religious described an outcome of the politicisation: 'We have sacrificed justice for truth and vengeance for reconciliation.' The speaker was Father Sean O'Leary, Co-ordinating Secretary of the Justice and Peace Department of the Southern African Bishops' Conference. He described the working of the Truth and Reconciliation Commission, which was holding hearings at the time, as follows:

> People just talk at the commission. They speak out, it's a cathartic process. People sit in a room, listening to men describe how they tortured and killed their loved ones. Children are learning for the first time what their parents were involved in. It's a wonderful thing.

The building where Father O'Leary and I talked, Khanya House in Pretoria, was a symbol of the reconciliation process. It was blown up by the police during the struggle. Now the rebuilt, bustling centre was filled with the hope of the new South Africa. The country does have terrible problems, problems of a magnitude which pose not only the question 'Do the Irish have a future in South Africa?' but 'Does South Africa itself have a future?' In 1996, the Government was forced to bring in fearsome austerity measures which added to an unemployment rate which was already fuelling a crime wave. The ANC administration was not responsible for the IMF-type squeeze (introduced before the IMF itself could force its introduction), but it had inherited a huge national debt from the white administration. This had been caused by extravagant expenditures on military interventions in South Africa itself, in its homelands and in Angola and Mozambique, all in a vain effort to prop up apartheid. Moreover, the once lucrative mining industry was not yielding the rewards of yore. The gold mines had been drilled so deep that further mining was uneconomic in the face of a slump in world gold prices. However, both O'Leary and the then Irish Ambassador to South Africa, Eamon O Tuathail, were optimistic. O Tuathil has served in the Sudan and Nigeria, and his verdict, which he confirmed to me again three years later was: 'They'll make it. Perhaps they won't make it as soon as the optimists hope, but it will be nothing like what the doom-sayers say either.'

THE DOOM-SAYERS AND THE OPTIMIST

It has to be conceded that the doom-sayers could point to some terrible evidence to bolster their case. For example, in Durban I spoke to an Irish consultant, a trauma specialist, who worked in a private clinic which had a large out-patients department. Because of this, the police frequently brought stabbing victims to the clinic as though it were a casualty ward. Of 600 such whom the doctor had inspected over the previous eighteen months, only one had been brought in alive, and he subsequently died. All had been stabbed to kill in the heart region: South African muggers do not believe in leaving witnesses.

In Johannesburg, the former financial district had become almost a no-go area. Certainly by night, a white would have to be contemplating suicide to venture out alone. At the time of my visit to the area, a luxury hotel, the Carlton, had just had ten floors closed and $70,000,000 written off its value. It was subsequently closed down. In the Hillbrow district, blocks of what were formerly luxury flats had mattresses and bedding hanging out of every window. Even the balconies were being sheeted in to provide further accommodation for letting at so much per day, per week or per mattress. People were pouring in from the bush, but there were no jobs, and so crime and prostitution became for some the only outlet.

Trapped by the falling rand, the older residents of the flats, mainly elderly whites, are now virtual prisoners in their apartments. There is no question of venturing out at night, and even by day it is hazardous to do so. Hearing my accent in a supermarket, where the prices were reasonable by Dublin standards, but high for anyone living on a falling-rand income, a nice old English lady came up to me and said: 'Oh I wish I could go back with you to Ireland. I am stuck here on my pension. My apartment is worth nothing and the crime terrible.'

Despite all this, Sean O'Leary not only shared O Tuathail's basic optimism for South Africa itself, but was confident about a continuation of the Irish presence:

> Here in South Africa, like the rest of Africa, you'll find Irish where you'll find no one else. In some God-forsaken swamp in Zambia, high up a mountain in Kenya, way out in the back of beyond, everywhere. Maybe the Irish haven't abolished poverty, but they've helped to reduce it, and suffering, wherever they've been. The Irish are very well thought of in South Africa because to the South Africans Ireland is a land of struggle. The IRA, Bobby Sands, his poetry, it all makes Northern Ireland well known here.
>
> I remember an incident at Orlando Stadium in Soweto, when Dick Spring [the former Irish Foreign Minster] was representing Ireland at a big Anniversary Commemoration for the ANC. The speaker gave a fiery address and then he said to the crowd, pointing at Spring, 'Do you want to be like that man's country?' 'No' roared back 50,000 people. The religious divisions arising from the sectarianism in Northern Ireland are the very kind of thing they are trying to get away from here.

So what is the role for the Irish in South Africa in future? O'Leary's prescription is:

> South Africa needs capacity training, political training of all sorts. That's a good field for the Irish. The Irish TDs [Teachtai Dali – members of the Dail, the Irish Parliament] who came out here were well liked by the South Africans. Sure we were all scandalised out here by the stories about the Irish paedophile priests and all the rest of it. But priest are human. We all live in the world. And South Africa has the biggest number of Irish missionaries in the world, something around 1,100. People judge us by what they have done and are doing.

Father O'Leary also had two concepts which he thought the Irish in Northern Ireland should learn from the South Africans, as opposed to the more normal proposition that it is the South Africans who should learn from the Irish! They were:

1. Eyeball contact. That is, whether one used the tactic of negotiating about negotiations, or whatever, the main thing to do is to sit down at a table and face one's adversary.

2. There should be no winners and no losers. Approach negotiations in a spirit of compromise.

It is worth noting that, because of their ANC contacts, the Sinn Fein negotiators actually used the South African techniques successfully during the negotiating of the Good Friday Agreement. Alas, the tactical formula was not designed to cover a situation in which, subsequent to the negotiations, one side, in this case the Unionists, did not implement what was agreed. In the case of South Africa, the Broederbond, the equivalent of the Orange Order in Ireland, had empowered de Klerk to do a deal. In the case of Ireland, the

Orange Order granted no such permission to the Unionist leader, David Trimble.

PESSIMISM

Apart from conflict resolution techniques, South Africa does have some fairly exact parallels with the Northern Ireland situation. The attitude of the Irish Nationalists and of the South African blacks to the police and to sections of the judiciary, is of 'them' and 'us' mistrust. In South Africa, in particular, the police are not well paid and their morale is low. The adjustment of an old police force into a new political order after a period of armed conflict is a live issue in both Johannesburg and Belfast, as is the crime which comes in its wake.

About eighty kilometres north of Pretoria, in a small bungalow in Langkloof, a mining township, I met a group of Irish Loreto nuns, with a lifetime in education behind them, but now engaged in what might be termed social work. They were Deirdre Hannon from Belfast, Marian Moriarty from Kerry, Linda Prest from Cape Town and Eileen Gallagher from Fermanagh/Tyrone. They spoke of positives as well as negatives – for example, the influence for reconciliation which the schools had been able to exert. Afrikaner women teachers had exhorted their community not to be fearful of blacks. It was possible to point to the fact that the supposedly congenitally stupid 'Kaffirs' were able to surpass white pupils if they got a decent chance of education. A white child, whose parents had been conditioned to notions of racial superiority, found it difficult to sustain them when the black boy sitting beside him got better marks than he did.

However, the negatives existed: 'The people are very poor and the poverty could very well kill us because people turn to crime.' They had just had a break-in in which armed robbers fired a shot. They managed to get out at the back and the raiders went off with a few rand and a pair of shoes. The violence is a constant lurking monster, and they cited a recent case in which a son had been forced to watch as petrol was poured down his father's throat and then ignited. The son was then deprived of his testicles and 'necklaced' (a tyre was placed around his neck and set on fire). In an adjoining street, shortly before I called, they had found a women in the process of being beaten to death because she had been accused of theft. She would have died had not the nuns intervened, but they knew that by doing so they were placing their own lives at risk.

At the Pretoria home of Marius Schoon,[32] a distinguished human rights activist (who died in 1999), an even more pessimistic note was struck by a former civil rights activist. Schoon's wife and daughter were murdered by the authorities while he was in exile in Angola. He had served time for bombing offences. During a spell in Ireland he was put in charge of the Irish Umbrella Group for NGOs, Comhair Lam. Schoon is now married to an Irish girl, Shirley Maclean, of APSO. Their friend Deno dropped in as we were talking. Deno, a poet and novelist, is a 'coloured' in the old apartheid nomenclature –

of Indian origin. He was a former ANC activist and he is now teaching in a
nearby township. He was depressed about the degree of anarchy in the
classroom and the street, and bore out the nuns' assessment. 'Family values
are breaking down.' The kids have no fathers, or role models. 'They are
virtually unteachable. You don't need a teacher in the classrooms, you need a
shrink.'

Speaking of the period of struggle which brought about the turbulent
period of transition which South Africa is now passing through, Schoon, who
could speak with unusual authority about Irish support, or lack of it, for the
anti-apartheid movement, judged that the Irish in South Africa were part of
the reaction, but the Irish Anti-Apartheid Movement in Ireland, and in
particular the Dunnes Stores strikers, were recognised and appreciated.[28]

THE DUNNES STORES STRIKE

The Dunnes Stores strike was an extraordinary little footnote to the overall
anti-apartheid struggle. The episode began in support of a call from the Irish
Distributive and Administrative Trade Union (IDATU) to its members to
refuse to handle South African produce. On 17 July 1984 Mary Manning, a
young shop assistant in an outlet of the Dunnes supermarket chain in Henry
Street, Dublin, refused to check out a purchase of Outspan oranges from
South Africa. She was immediately suspended and twelve fellow-workers
came out in sympathy with her. IDATU declared their action official and
picketed Dunnes.

The picket lasted for eighteen months and attracted attention from all over
the world. Bishop Tutu broadcast in support of the strikers and various
international bodies committed to the anti-apartheid struggle issued messages
backing them. Public interest in Ireland was heightened both by events in
South Africa itself, where the struggle was reaching a climax, and by the
holding of concerts and events at which the South African issue was
explained. The pro-strikers movement gained momentum as other groups of
workers refused to handle South African produce, and local government
bodies, such as County Councils, voted not to buy South African goods. The
strike probably cost the Dunnes supermarket chain 75 per cent of their Henry
Street business and bore extremely heavily on the strikers, whose action was
finally called off following prolonged efforts at arbitration by various
interested parties. It certainly served to increase the membership of the Irish
Anti-Apartheid Movement (IAAM).

THE IRISH ANTI-APARTHEID MOVEMENT

The founding Vice-chairman of the IAAM was Kadar Asmal, a law lecturer
in Trinity College Dublin, who had also been the first Honorary Treasurer of
the British Anti-Apartheid Movement. His Irish wife Louise became the
IAAM's Secretary. The Asmals were one of the most popular couples in

Dublin and when Kadar, a South African of Indian origin, was eventually appointed the Minister in Charge of Water in Mandela's first Cabinet, Dublin regarded the appointment as an honour for one of their own. In fact, Kadar told me that when he returned to Ireland, after being appointed a Minister, his taxi man's first words were: 'Welcome home Kadar.'[33] Asmal who became one of the most successful members of the Mandela Cabinet, dealing with Affairs and Forestry (at the time of writing he was appointed Minister for Education) would share something of Schoon's appreciation of the Irish position on apartheid. However, both his own experiences in Dublin, and his subsequent access to the Secret Service files of South Africa's former rulers gave him a unique insight into Irish attitudes which left him with a somewhat more kindly view than Schoon's.

He rightly pointed to the fact that the Church in South Africa was divided on the issue of apartheid, but that it was Irish religious, such as the Dominican nuns and Archbishop Hurley of Durban, who made major contributions to its fall. He cited the visit of Mary Robinson to South Africa as being of lasting impact in building bridges between the two countries. Asmal had worked with Robinson at Trinity where, apart from being a Professor of Law, she was also a staunch anti-apartheid campaigner. However, it has to be said that the visit of another notable Trinity graduate, Dr Conor Cruise O'Brien, to South Africa did not have benign consequences.

O'Brien, was one of those who resigned from the IAAM when Sinn Fein was allowed to affiliate with the movement. He broke the academic boycott of South Africa by accepting an invitation to give a series of lectures at the University of Cape Town in 1986. However, his lectures were broken up by students and O'Brien was forced to call off his tour.

O'Brien's behaviour was atypical. As one authority has pointed out:

> There is little doubt that the Irish anti-apartheid movement earned a special place in the international coalition against apartheid because of its persistent, imaginative and wide-ranging activities in support of liberation of Southern Africa. Thousands of Irishmen from all walks of life were successfully persuaded to take a more active interest in the affairs of the sub-continent and to direct their enthusiasm into constructive channels. The achievement was all the more remarkable in that Ireland was a small country with few trade relations with South Africa.[34]

ROOTS ARE GOING DOWN

In order to get a sense of what Irish relationships with South Africa were now, I went with Eamon O Tuathail to see a project which the Irish Government had helped to fund. The development was located on the side of a mountain 125 kilometres north of Johannesburg, amongst a community who had formed part of one of the 'townships' of the apartheid days. These townships were governed by one overriding philosophy: the blacks were to be placed so far from the whites that they could never threaten them. The townships were generally located a long way outside cities and did not have running water or electricity. The reasoning that the energy of the inhabitants would be drawn off in the fight for survival so that there would be none to spare for revolution. If a man has to be up at 3 am to get to work by eight – that is if he had any work – he would have little time or inclination for plotting the overthrow of government by the time he got home to a darkened, earthen-floored dwelling. So ran the theory.

Often the theory was applied in a planned but cruel fashion. O Tuathail told me of a case he knew about in which soldiers had forcibly removed what was knows as a 'black spot' – that is a black community inside an area legally designated for white habitation only. They rounded up the villagerrs, drove them several hundred kilometres out into the bush but inside a black 'homeland' and dropped them off. They had nothing in the way of habitation, save the material to make tin shacks. The members of the village who had livestock were left to drive them from the old location to the new, but as no water was provided, all the animals died. Then a few months later the army came and took away the tin shacks. The army later used the villagers' land, containing also the burial ground of their ancestors, for a shooting range. This took place at Lohatla in the Northern Cape. The South African army is still in possession.

The Irish project was based on an impressive brick-built hall. It forms a centre for democracy, and also provides a gathering place for concerts, dances, meetings and so forth. Everything of consequence that the village engages in can be thrashed out in that hall. Also, there were rooms provided and fitted for use as a modern clinic. This mean that sick people could get help without having to stand in the broiling sun for hours (or in the freezing winds in winter) before getting some rudimentary medical attention in a tin shack. Some assistance was also being provided for a nearby school which was still under completion. Nevertheless it had advanced to the stage where it could be used for a choir practice. The melodious African voices echoing across the mountain valleys were not only a joyous experience in themselves, but contained a paean of hope for the future. All the children were well dressed and healthy looking.

On the scale of the investment programme which South Africa so desperately needs, such projects might be dismissed as falling into the spot of water on the rock category. Nevertheless, through them, roots are being put down for the future. The school matriculation results were very good, even though as one of the teachers put it: 'After studying for the Matric, you find that the Matric won't get you a job.' Nevertheless, one got a feeling of growth, of things improving, despite the difficulties. For example, the reason for the choir practice was that the students were rehearsing for the gala official opening of the community centre some months later. It had been planned that every family would donate a chair – but a chair costs twenty-seven rand, far more than could be afforded, so sights were refixed at a realistic three rand.

Some 3,000–4,000 guests were expected for the opening, and everyone would be fed, but they would have to bring their own plates. To ensure that there would be something to go on the plates, the builder had donated 1,000 rand to buy an ox.

Like the telephones in Uganda, the significance of Irish involvement in such an enterprise has to be assessed in Third World terms rather than by developed countries' standards. The co-ordinator of the hall's event, a social worker cum Ms Fix-It of the area, was a Zulu woman with a warm Connemara personality and wonderful flashing eyes. I felt it was important that she made a point of telling me that she wrote short stories, inspired by Irish writers amongst whom James Joyce was her favourite.

BLACK OPTIMISM IN BLUE UNIFORMS

A more large-scale Irish contribution could be found in Moroko, Soweto. St Matthew's Secondary School, run by the Sisters of Mercy, contains some 1,500 pupils. I visited several classes and spoke to the pupils. In fact the nuns were so keen on ensuring that I met as many pupils as possible that I ended up missing my flight to Lesotho. They might not have extended such access to their charges had they heard my language on the way to the airport. However, I counted the missed connection well worthwhile. My abiding memory of the school was of black optimism in blue uniforms set in exactly the same atmosphere as that generated by exactly the same kind of nuns who had taught my daughters in Callan, County Kilkenny.

I was asked to say a few words, and made some remarks to the effect that education was the bread of the future; that, in general, the Irish were not in Africa as imperialists but were motivated, in the words of the Irish poet Tom Kettle, by 'A dream born in a herdsman's shed, and the secret scriptures of the poor'. The head teacher immediately began making arrangements with the art teacher to have my remarks inscribed on banners and hung up in the corridors! Sister, as they used to say of the products of the old Irish primary schools, where the children had to supply both the teacher's meagre stipend, and their own heating: 'The shilling and the sod of turf wasn't wasted on you.'

So far as Ireland was concerned, the senior pupils appeared interested and well informed. Some of them had heard a recent radio broadcast in which my book on the Irish Troubles had been reviewed. They wanted to know more and their questions were intelligent and to the point. A number of them wanted to become journalists and discussed the mechanics of writing in a thoughtful manner. They were courteous, but there was nothing obsequious or stuffy about them. When someone asked me was I a Catholic, I replied by suggesting that the nuns might want to cover their ears, because I was not a practising Catholic, but they might, if they wished, regard me as a 'cultural Catholic'. There was laughter and applause at what to a small degree, they regarded as a sally at the nuns' expense, but I also sensed that to a larger degree it struck a chord in their own attitude to religion.

When I asked them their views on the future, however, they revealed a shared attitude to that of the nuns. One girl summed up the feelings of the class: 'If you have a good background, you'll be optimistic.' She was referring not only to the school but to her family. They had all come from Soweto – formerly, as we saw on the TV screens, one of the twentieth century's trouble spots – but they were all intent on ensuring that trouble remained a thing of the past. They cited the work of the Truth Commission with approval. They were both shocked at what they had learned and determined to ensure that nothing like it would happen again. Most of them, in their bandbox fresh, bright blue tunics and sweaters, had stepped out of a shack that morning on to a dirt path, but perhaps Mary Catherine MacAuley had left a legacy which would help to pave their road ahead

UNCONSCIOUS SEGREGATION

While it is unsafe to generalise, particularly on the basis of a visit that only lasted a matter of weeks, I nevertheless formed the impression that as a class the Irish clergy empathised better with the South Africans than did many of the laity – that is the laity other than the aid workers and Irish governmental personnel, like O Tuathail who was obviously an outstanding Ambassador, or people who were on secondment from an Irish state agency. Such figures had obviously made a study of the country, both before and after they came to it.

I attended a mass celebrated by an Irish priest, Father John Cleary, in the poor district of Dobsonville, on the outskirts of Johannesburg. Cleary, a blond in his early forties from County Carlow, lived in a couple of shambolic rooms attached to his presbytery from which everything of worth had been stolen – generally in the course of an armed robbery. He had been minding two children all week in these surroundings. I saw him perform – and the word is used advisedly – the first of two masses which he celebrated every Sunday, each lasting for three hours. The masses leave him visibly drained. During the one I witnessed, he performed a marriage, received sixteen Cathectics into the Church and delivered a sermon. It was like a theatrical performance.

The church was packed to suffocation, people wandered in and out at will. The women outnumbered the men in a ration of roughly 3 to 2. The congregation included children and some whites, including a woman who brought her poodle. From time to time, Cleary invited anyone who wished to get up and make a few remarks and several of the Africans did take the opportunity of delivering mini sermons. The experience was fascinating but exhausting. I had to go outside for air several times, and even Father Cleary only kept going with the aid of a surreptitious cup of tea while the choir were performing. Enlivened by the tea, or perhaps the singing, which was an excellent combination of African chant and traditional Catholic hymns, he then got up and joined with some of his parishioners who were performing an African dance.

Afterwards, there was a huge, beautifully cooked, open-air meal, but most of the whites didn't eat anything. They abstained for the worthiest of motives – either in order to spare the food for those who needed it more than they, or because they were going back to their own lunches – but I felt it a pity. Despite the fact that the mass was celebrated by an Irish priest, I got very little sense of communication between the small Irish attendance and the blacks. One of the few white people I saw actually talking with the women who had made the meal was Tess Wade, the local GOAL director. There was no conscious racism on the part of the whites, although one man, an Irish businessman, told me he had very little hope for the future because: 'the African doesn't want to work'. Money and background had a great deal to do with the unconscious segregation. After the mass the Africans set off on foot to their cabin-sized homes – the whites got into their cars to return to fine residences set in their own gardens.

AT SCRUFFY MURPHY'S

Inevitably, some of them returned via an Irish pub. This was Scuffy Murphy's in the prosperous suburb of Sandton, run by two Irishmen, the Egan brothers, Kieran and Paul. It was the liveliest place I had been to in Africa. A local Irish group was playing, using instruments that included spoons, bones, bodhrans and a guitar. The place was full and children were obviously welcome, but the gaiety was in a sense deceptive. The party was for a young Irish couple who were going home to Ireland because of the violence in South Africa. With the exception of Father Cleary and the GOAL representative, most of those present were careerists. They had come out for employment or business opportunities and by and large had all done very well. The Egan brothers, for example, were planning to open a number of other establishments.

One tall athletic young man in his twenties turned out to be a quantity surveyor called Willie Duggan. He had come to South Africa for the World Rugby Cup Finals in Johannesburg – for which, incidentally, one of the principal commentators was the leading current affairs broadcaster, John Robbie, a Trinity graduate and former Irish rugby international. After the finals, Duggan decided to stay on. The only preparation he made before coming over was to place 'an interview suit' in his backpack along with a copy of his CV. 'But I just knew I'd get a job,' he said, and he did within two days. He had met several other lads who had also come out for a holiday but decided to stay on, and found jobs with no difficulty. They are now thinking of applying for permanent residence. This sort of optimism made a sharp contrast with the pessimism which underlay the reasons for the party.

In fact, there was a particular reason in the Egans' establishment to be concerned about violence. The previous owner had been Eoin Hand, a former manager of the Republic of Ireland soccer team. The pub had been as successful under him as it was with the Egans. Hand acted as a greeter for new members of the Irish community, and saw to it that they were put in touch with each other concerning job opportunities. A number of people remarked to me on what a fine person he was, and how benign his presence had been. However, one evening a customer, a girl, asked him the way to the toilet, and chatted briefly with him before moving from the bar. Her boyfriend, an Afrikaner, came up to Hand and, in the presence of several witnesses, asked him what the conversation was about and smashed a broken bottle into his face and eye. Hand subsequently sold the pub.

Shortly after hearing this story, I ran into an Afrikaner who displayed something of the same resentful pride and antagonism, though fortunately not the same aggression. He remarked of the GOAL agency's work: 'This isn't a bloody Third World country. We don't need aid and missionaries here.' He didn't object to the missionaries so much, but his attitude to the blacks was straight-up supremacist: 'You can't help these people.'

THE IRISH BRIGADE IN SOUTH AFRICA

However Donal McCracken, who could be taken as a more knowledgeable commentator, repudiated this attitude. McCracken is a member of a distinguished Irish academic family – his father, Emeritus Professor J. L. McCracken, a member of the British Council and the Royal Irish Academy, taught at colleges in Ulster, in Trinity College, Dublin and at the University of the Witwaterstrand, and his mother Eileen had been a distinguished botanist. Donal is a historian of both Irish and South African parliamentary procedure, and is also a well-known historical author, a professor of history and Dean of the Arts faculty at the University of Durban-Westville. He said when I interviewed him, 'I follow the example of the swallows; I spend my summers in Ireland and my winters in Africa, living with my sons.' In 1999, he published his book on the Irish Brigade's part in the Boer War which was to have a significant effect on subsequent Irish history: the youthful Michael Collins was impressed with the way in which the Boers became farmers by day and guerrillas by night and adapted their methods to fight the first successful urban guerrilla war of the twentieth century. The war, combined with the fact that the founder of Sinn Fein, Arthur Griffith, worked as journalist for a time in South Africa, played a part in the creation of friendly feelings towards South Africa in Ireland. Of course, a cynic of the school which holds that the more things change, the more they stay the same, might well point to the use which the Boers made of the freedom from the British which the Irish contingent fought to help them achieve. There is a certain wry symbolism in the fact that the monument to the Irish Brigade, which commands one of the best views of Johannesburg, on Brixton Ridge, was unveiled in 1975 by Betsie Verwoerd, widow of one of the principal architects of apartheid, Dr H. F. Verwoerd. Speaking at the unveiling Mrs Verwoerd said: 'I am here to pay back a little of the great debt the South African nation owes those brave Irishmen who gave their lives to our struggle for freedom and independence.'

Another more bizarre twist was added to the memorial's history after the chairmanship of the shared Irish and Afrikaner Committee, which had charge of the Irish Brigade Memorial Fund, passed into the control of the Afrikaner R. Van Tonder. Van Tonder, who shot himself in August 1999, was the founder of the fundamentalist Boerestaat Party which seeks to set up a state in which only Boers may become resident. (The party defines Boers as meaning the descendants of the Voortrekkers, or of those who fought in the Anglo-Boer Wars.) When the ANC leader Chris Hani was shot in 1993, Van Tonder's party announced that it would provide legal aid for those charged with the murder. While in Van Tonder's care the Monument began to fall into disrepair. Then he actually sold the site, claiming that it was impossible to maintain the memorial against vandalism because: 'Since the new dispensation hooligans have taken over in Johannesburg.'[35] But as the purchaser, Mr V. Scott, told the Northcliffe *Melville Times* (8 December 2000) that 'purely as a business matter' he intended to sell the site for office development, the monument's future seems uncertain.

This was not what the members of the Irish Brigade envisaged when they joined up in 1899. The idea of having an Irish Brigade in South Africa, as there had been elsewhere in the world, germinated in the commemoration services which were held to mark the anniversary of 1798. John McBride from Westport in County Mayo, who was working on the Witwatersrand as a mining surveyor, was convinced that war with England was inevitable and he led a group of like-minded Irishmen in setting up a committee to organise an Irish Brigade. At first President Paul Kruger turned down the Irishmen's suggestions out of concern for their safety; he feared that, as Ireland was under British rule, they would be executed as rebels. Then, as war neared, Kruger changed his mind and had a law passed in the Volkstaad which conferred Boer citizenship on the Irishmen.

As McBride had no military experience, command of the Brigade passed to another Irishman, John F. Blake, a graduate of West Point who had fought the Apaches before turning his hand to gold mining in South Africa. The Chicago branch of Clan na Gael sent an ambulance brigade, some of whose members joined the ranks of the combatants as soon as they arrived. However, Michael Davitt, who covered the war for America and French news agencies, has testified that the ambulance corps was one of the best of the war.[36] The Brigade was about 180 strong, and is remembered for having fought with great bravery, McBride always being in the thick of the fighting on his horse 'Fenian Boy'.

Amongst the Boer victories which the Irish took part in were those at Nicholsons Nek and Colenso, both on the Natal front. As usual the Irish were on both sides of the fighting. Indeed the sufferings of the Irish race as a whole under the flag of the military wing of the Two ColonialismSwas rarely better exemplified anywhere in the world than in South Africa. The peach orchard at Bronkhorstspruit, has already been mentioned at the beginning of this chapter, but during the second Anglo-Boer war there also occurred two battles, at Nicholson's Nek and Colenso, which stand out in military history as fatal monuments to the incompetences of British generalship and the skill and heroism of the Boers – and their Irish allies – who lost only one hundred men in the fighting. One brasshat, General Hart, deployed his men across open countryside losing fifty per cent of his Irish troops to Boer sharpshooters) and helping to give currency to the gibe: 'The Boers hid behind rocks and the British hid behind shamrocks'. On 11 December, 1999 a ceremony was held at Colenso to commemorate the centenary of the battle. Donal McCracken delivered a speech after which he wrote to me:[37]

> Up against the Dublin Fusiliers, Inniskillings and the Connaught Rangers were MacBride's Brigade. In Hart's 5th (Irish Brigade) there were 537 casualties that hot morning. Our ceremony yesterday was up at Colenso on the battleifield. Not much changed in a hundred years. I said it was time there was a memorial to the Irish who died in the war – upwards of 4,000 Irish casualties I reckon.There are more Irishmen buried in that Tugela valley than there are Irish living today in this province of KwaZulu-Natal.

A second Irish unit under Arthur Lynch fought with distinction in rearguard actions around Ladysmith and Glencoe, and was said to be the last unit to evacuate Johannesburg before the British entered. The Irish units were disbanded towards the end of 1900 as the Boers switched to guerrilla tactics which depended for their success on a knowledge of the veld which the Irish did not possess. As the Irish went out therefore, in a very real sense Michael Collins came in, and modern Ireland is the result.

It is evident from the testimonials paid to the Brigade at the time, that the Boers appreciated both the Irish assistance and their fighting qualities.[38] Contrasting qualities which were also appreciated, were those of a group of Irish Mercy nuns who ministered to the wounded of both sides during the siege of Mafeking. Sister Theresa Crowley and Sister Magdalene Dunne were each awarded the Victoria Cross after the fighting, and three postulants also received military decorations.

THE PROTESTANT CONTRIBUTION

Something of the same conflicting currents of loyalties were swirling around Durban at the time, of my visit. Apart from the legacy from the upheavals which preceded the ending of apartheid, there was continuing Inkatha-ANC tension arising from the strong Zulu presence in Durban and the surrounding area of Kwa-Zulu, Natal.

Donal McCracken's perspective was interesting because he is a Protestant, reared in Ireland of parents who both have a long association with South Africa. His mother had been a distinguished Botanist. In typically understated, self-effacing manner, the McCrackens mentioned in passing at dinner one evening that they had been at 'a little ceremony' that afternoon in the Botanic Gardens. The ceremony, which the authorities obviously felt important enough to go ahead with, although there was a students' strike in progress at the University and various pockets of actual or threatened disorder hanging in the air, was the unveiling of a plaque to commemorate Donal's mother, Dr Eileen McCracken who died in 1988. She too was a distinguished academic and the author of several definitive books on forest history and botanic gardening.

Donal and Patricia McCracken were reticent about discussing their very real contribution to the South African educational system. Of course the truth is that Donal McCracken's long list of publications on South Africa says all that needs to be said. However, I have noted with interest that he stirred into real exasperation when I asked him about the often-heard charge that Irish missionary education had tended to diminish local culture. He threw up his hands and burst out: 'Look! I'm tired of hearing that cant. I'm here at the sharp edge in the classroom and I can tell you within a day or two which of my new students have been educated by the Irish missionaries. They stand out. Don't mind that sort of trendy criticism.'

This tribute from a Protestant of good Co. Down stock at least bears recording, I felt!

However, it would be very wrong for me to give the impression that the Irish contribution to Africa was the product of nationalist and Catholic endeavour only. The Protestant Irish tradition supplied administrators, doctors, judges, soldiers and traders in great numbers.

Commenting on the Anglo-Irish contribution to Africa, Eamon O Tuathail the former Irish Ambassador to South Africa reflected on some judgements of my own which convey an idea both of the scale of that contribution and of the 'small world' syndrome which occurs so often throughout the diaspora:

There were many important and honorable Irish colonial Administrators in Africa: for instance the Irish-born Attorney General of Cape Colony, William Porter, who owed his appointment to Daniel O'Connell, drafted a constitution for the new Cape Parliament and strongly defended a universal franchise which would shut nothing out but 'vagrancy and crime'. The names MacCarthy, Moloney and Pope-Hennessy that still mark streets and squares in West African cities are testimony to the Irish colonial administrative involvement. There were Irish medical persons who researched tropical diseases in Africa, graduates of RCSI and TCD. One of the Stokes family is buried in Lagos where he went researching tropical fevers.

There are the Irish Protestant Scholars: I think of the great Arabist Lane-Pole and also the self-effacing Church of Ireland clergyman Higgs whose name is still inscribed on the outside of the Egyptian Museum in Cairo. As to the Irish explorers, there is my grandfather's cousin who stands outside Leinster House: Surgeon-Major Parke, a graduate of the RCSI who was medical officer to Stanley's Emin Pasha Relief Expedition. As to nationalism, there is Lady Gregory's defence of Ahmed Orabi, whom she met when she visited in Cairo in 1881 and George Bernard Shaw's intervention on behalf of the villagers implicated in the Denshawai affairs in Egypt in 1906.

I think also of important Irish Protestant initiatives such as the founding by Charlotte Pym of Monkstown in 1874 of the Mission to Lepers and of individuals like the Church Missionary Society medical missionary, Dr Harper from Kilkenny, who established a string of mission hospitals along the Nile from Omdurman to Old Cairo. We [The Irish

Government authors] have been funding equipment for one of those hospitals (Menouf in Egypt) which still survive. The hospital in Omdurman is still there also.

The fact is that Irish Methodists, Presbyterians Baptists (particularly in Malawi), Pentecostalists and, of course, the Church of Ireland have made a distinguished contribution to Africa, as they have, and are doing, in Asia and the Middle East. Nor should it be forgotten that, prior to the upheavals in Asia which accompanied the coming of Communism and Independence, Irish Protestant as well as Catholic missionaries once gave dedicated service in China and India. The Protestant missionaries function along less institutional lines than the Catholics. The Anglican missionary organisations, for example, do not have an official place in the structures of the Church and are mainly composed of lay people; probably only 10 per cent of the Anglican missionaries are clergy. And, of course, both clergy and lay missionaries can marry.

Unfortunately there is no room in this book to give to one African country the individual study of the impact of Irish Protestantism on its culture which it merits – Cameroon, where Ian Paisley regularly preaches. One hopes his influence will be more constructive than it has been in Ireland, and that his legacy will not be akin to that of Alice Lakwena in Uganda. Paisley apart, Protestant missionaries in Africa have experienced much the same culture shock problems as have Catholics. The teaching that the 'missionary position' was the form of copulation most pleasing in the sight of God formed part of the overall European 'civilising mission' approach to the 'dark continent'. Just as today's North of Ireland Protestant Orangemen wear bowler hats, because these were regarded in the nineteenth century as emblems of respectability, so did starched collars and black suits make their appearance on Africans taught by Protestant missionaries. The bowlers have a special significance in Ghana which is one of the more progressive African democracies, despite – or, who knows, possibly because of – having a flourishing branch of the Orange Order, a development which has led many North of Ireland Nationalists to comment that they are the only genuine 'black protestants'. In Uganda the influence of Protestant missionary ladies encouraged the Baganda women to wear the full-length Victorian-style dresses with mutton chop sleeves which, until recently, were their normal dress. Church of Ireland missionaries face the same debates as do Irish Catholic missionaries: should they be 'sending agencies', or 'funding agencies'? In other words, should they be sending people or money? Or should they be providing training? Just hugging a leper or helping them to help themselves?

Whatever its flaws, whatever may be the correct answer, the Irish Protestant missionary tradition has done a great deal to help. Beginning, like the Catholics, with a vision of spreading enlightenment and rescuing pagans from idolatry, the missionaries moved on to helping to provide basic African needs in education and health, and then on again to provide other forms of training, for example in animal care and crop growing.

Prior to Kenyan independence, the British colonial system did not allow Africans a direct say in their own affairs, and they were represented on the Legislative Council by a member of the CMS appointed by the Governor. One such was the Irish Archdeacon Owen who is commemorated in Kenya by a statue in Kisumu. He became famous for standing up for the Africans against unjust laws and practices such as forced labour and hut taxes.

In contemporary Kenya the Protestant missionaries have overseen developments such as setting up Maridadi Fabrics in Nairobi, a dyeing and hand-screen printing facility which is successfully providing employment for unmarried mothers. Also in Nairobi there is the Christian Industrial Training Centre (CITC) which has an impressive trace record in training boys for apprenticeships in industry.

THE DOCTOR'S DIFFICULTIES

One of the most remarkable people I interviewed in Africa was Ian Clarke, a Protestant doctor, who described himself as 'definitely middle class from Northern Ireland suburbs', whom I met in Kampala, Uganda. Clarke says he settled in Africa 'out of spiritual conviction'. Having come to Uganda on a preliminary trip he discovered that:

> Everything seemed bigger, more advanced and more virulent as far as medicine was concerned – the abscesses were bigger, the pneumonias were more severe. As a GP I was used to dealing with more minor complaints. Suddenly the medical conditions I was seeing were fulminant and there weren't enough doctors to deal with them . . . people with TB, diabetes, AIDS, cancer, pneumonia, peritonitis, hernias, gun-shot injury, typhoid, malaria, gastro-enteritis, all appeared in the out-patients department or were admitted to a ward.

He decided that he could no longer view the sufferings of the poor from a TV screen in his living room in Ireland, and opted to move to the heart of the Ugandan killing fields, the Luweero triangle, just as Yoweri Museveni with his tiny army (probably only 2,000 strong), which included many boy soldiers, took over Kampala. Clarke brought with him his wife Robbie and his three children: Michael, Sean and Lauren. His first reaction on driving into the area was:

> God, is this it? Is this the place to which we should come? There were hundreds of skulls and bones piled at the side of the road. During the war, it was commonplace for soldiers to stop people and demand money. If the person paid up, they were allowed to go. But if they had no money, they could be, and often were, shot dead. At Nakaseke, the soldiers introduced a new variant to murder – they used to throw people off the roof of the town's four-storey hotel.

This practice was popularised by General Idi Amin. In Kampala I was shown a skyscraper hotel where, after dinner, he would entertain his guests by having shrieking prisoners hurled off the roof. This was the milieu in which Ian Clarke came to work out of a sense of Christian duty, and when I interviewed him he made light of the various difficulties he and his family encountered. These included prolonged chemotherapy for a serious form of cancer: 'Yes I have cancer, but I'm over it – I think' was his reaction. He was more interested in talking about his plans for building a large modern hospital in Kampala. In the strange way that life works, he had just been given a sizeable piece of land on which to build his cherished hospital by the Stokes family. The Stokes are descended from one of the most colourful missionary figures ever to descend on Africa, Charlie Stokes. He originally came to Africa from Ireland as a CMS missionary, but he went native, married the daughter of a Wanyamwesi chief and became a drinker, ivory trader and gun runner. He was caught running German guns to the Congolese in 1895 and hanged on the orders of a Belgian officer, Captain Lothaire. The case became an international *cause célèbre*, but the incident occurred at the height of the scramble for Africa, and after a number of show trials, Lothaire was given a major administrative role in Belgium's exploitation of the Congo.

Clarke was so self-effacing that I had to go to his book *The Man With the Key is Gone* to get some insights into the kind of life he and Robbie led.[39] First of all he discovered that although he was Irish, he had had to come to Uganda to learn how 'Murphy's Law' really worked. As Ian says, 'Murphy's Law is a kind of fatalism based on the premise that anything that can go wrong, will go wrong.' In other words, he was encountering an attitude, commoner during my far off boyhood than in contemporary Ireland, that was a compound of a blissful ignorance of anything mechanical with a conviction that if things went wrong: 'Ah well, the case could be worse.' There was a belief in Uganda that life consisted of a series of unpleasant happenings which one put up with through the agency of as much humour and alcohol as one could deploy.

Initially, 'The Man With the Key is Gone syndrome' beset Clarke at every step of the way. A typical example was the day he found his staff locked out of the hospital laboratory because, literally in this case, The Man with the Key had gone. He bethought himself of the New Testament incident involving the man who, when he couldn't get in the front door to see Jesus, came through the roof. There was a key for the room next door to the laboratory, so Clark let himself in there, stood on a table, sawed a hole in the roof, moved through the roof space and sat on the edge of the trap door in the laboratory's ceiling, weighing up the benefits of jumping against the possibility of breaking his ankle. Just as he had made up his mind to jump, the door opened and the staff poured in – they had found another key.

With the aid of another remarkable Irish Protestant doctor, Donal Brownlee, Clarke eventually managed to build both a clinic and a hospital. Amongst the myraid dangers they faced was the ever-present risk of contracting AIDS through a nick from a needle or a scalpel. Both men got through an incredible case load, 500 children in a morning, by developing production line techniques. The syringes were preloaded. The children were lined up in rows, their teachers issuing the vaccination cards. Then the team of trained health workers went into operation: 'Hold arm, swab, inject, new needle; hold arm, swab, inject, new needle . . .'

However, even the production line technique was not proof against the placenta pit problem. This arose when an assistant accidentally dropped a filter essential for AIDS testing into the placenta pit along with a variety of dangerous hospital wastes. A morning was spent in the festering Ugandan sun in a fruitless effort to fish out the missing filter. It could be seen but not hooked. After a lunch break they came back to find that Murphy's Law was in full swing. While they were at lunch, someone had thrown another pile of waste on top. Eventually, one of the staff dressed himself 'like a spaceman' and climbed down into the pit to recover the filter, which along with its rescuer was then heavily disinfected and put back to work. Apart from the 'Man With the Key' syndrome Clarke also had to contend with other peculiarly African crises. In one, a black mamba, one of the world's deadliest snakes, invaded his surgery. He escaped the mamba, but in a second crisis was badly stung by a swarm of killer bees.

Whether one seeks to evaluate the Catholic or the Protestant contribution to the Irish caring tradition, the fact that people like Ian and Robbie Clarke work on through the horrors and the difficulties and devote their lives, and those of their children, to that tradition's continuation is an indication of its worth.

The contribution of both traditions deserves to be preserved. I will leave the last word to Patricia McCracken:

> As a journalist with 3 million mainly black readers I'm well aware that the dimming of the media spotlight on South Africa is now a good sign, but we owe it to the many Irish who have assisted in the struggle to establish (normality here to continue a new struggle to consolidate that. In the context of Irish-European or Irish-American relations, for instance, normality includes cultural and educational exchanges from the grassroots up. Given the fascination that I've found here with the Celtic pantheism and its resonance with traditional cultural beliefs here – as well as the natural identification of one fighting race with another – this could proke an exciting and unexpected range of synchronicities that would naturally enrich the relationship in exciIting and unexpected ways.
>
> I have no doubt that future Irish South African relationships will be good. But I think much will hang on what happens to the Irish population living permanently in South Africa, a group largely unknown in Ireland. There should be a special relationship between the two countries and not one where there are occasional exchanges. South Africa should be more to Ireland than a country which receives some of her overseas aid. The existence of an Irish population in South Africa is a force which should be harnessed to build that special relationship.

EIGHT

THE CARIBBEAN

'. . . their poems remained laments, their novels propaganda tracts, as if one general apology on behalf of the past would supplant imagination, would spare them the necessity of great art. Pastoralists of the African revival should know that what is needed is not new names for old things, or old names for old things, but the faith of using old names anew, so that mongrel as I am, something prickles in me when I see the word Ashanti as with the word Warwickshire, both separately intimating my grandfathers' roots, both baptising this neither proud nor ashamed bastard, this hybrid, this West Indian'

Derek Walcott

MONTSERRAT

MUCH OF WHAT WALCOTT WRITES about his West Indian colonial heritage in the foregoing quotation was applicable to the outpourings of the earlier Sinn Fein generation of Irish writers in the early 20th Century. On Montserrat I was to find that the introduction of the word Irish along with, or indeed before, that of Warwickshire, had added a particular dimension of prickliness to the roots issue.

Given the history of England and Ireland, there is a certain symbolism in the fact that Britain's most Irish colony in the Caribbean contains a live volcano. Initially there was little evidence of its activity when I visited Montserrat, known to the tourist brochures as 'The Emerald Isle of the Pacific'. The wrath came later. First the welcome: Cead mile failte, a hundred thousand welcomes, said the green-lettered banner across the airport building. Inside, my passport was stamped with a shamrock, and when I called at the Governor's mansion I found that it too was adorned not only with a carved shamrock, but with the figure of a woman, symbolising Ireland, holding a Celtic harp. St Patrick's Roman Catholic Church located appropriately enough at St Patrick's village, boasted a large statue of St Patrick and a shamrock altar. Throughout my stay on the island the Irish resonances continued. Indeed, after it, because whenever I phoned the island subsequently from Ireland it reminded me of what it used to be like phoning the Aran Islands. If you could not find whoever you were looking for, you simply phoned a neighbour, who would volunteer either your friend's whereabouts, or give you the number of someone who would know. If a

Montserratian renders you some kindness, probably at a place with a name like St Patrick's or Galway Estate, he is apt to respond to your thanks with: 'Not at all, at all.' You could well be in Galway, to judge from accent or estate name, but not from the colour, for Montserratians are of course generally black, the descendants of both Irish and Africans.

DIVERGENT ATTITUDES

Much of the Irish influence on the island owes its existence to an enforced transportation, in particular under Cromwell, but overall the Irish experience was preferable to that of the Africans, who were brought there unwillingly as slaves during the 1660s. The Irish proved difficult to control, and in any case, after Cromwell's reign ended, the supply of transportees from Ireland dwindled. Some Anglo-Irish did, however, go there voluntarily, becoming sugar planters, or even Governors.

A distinguished Monsterratian, the poet E. A. Markham, who during 1991 was writer-in-residence at the University of Ulster at Coleraine, said in an interview:

> In the 1630s the Irish came to Montserrat. It was your first and only colony. There is a certain symmetry in my coming to Ireland 300 years later. After all, the first foreign voices I heard were Irish, and there were towns with Irish names all over Montserrat. The African slaves took on their master's name, so most black people in Montserrat have Irish surnames, like Ryan or Harris.[1]

Markham found the Irish presence beneficial. He said:

> We had the sense that there were different sorts of whiteness, and that white power wasn't the unified monolithic power that it appears to most black people. It was discovered that you could play the English and the Irish off each other and if you were clever you could find an ally on one side or the other.[2]

Despite Markham's relatively benign attitude to the Irish heritage I found that, on Montserrat, the difference in the African and the Irish experience had resulted in two sharply divergent attitudes towards the celebration of St Patrick's Day, which is Montserrat's National Feast Day. In fact, until the Ontario Legislature decision in May 1998, the island was the only place outside Ireland where the holiday is regarded as an official national-day festival. A sizeable element of the population, probably a majority, were prepared, in Markham's terminology, to 'play off' the Irish connection so that they could benefit from Irish-American tourism. This section wanted to see the Irish festival celebrated as it is elsewhere in the world. However, there were some who felt that it should be regarded as a day of national mourning and that the lady with harp should be painted black.

The leading Monserratian mourner was Howard Fergus, a historian and

Speaker of the Montserrat Legislative Council. He once underlined his
position by replying to a St Patrick's Day invitation from the Governor, Sir
Frank Savage, to the effect that the day should be seen as one of mourning,
wearing black not celebrating the green. Savage had wanted him to meet a
group of Irish travel writers who were visiting Montserrat for St Patrick's Day
while this book was being compiled.[3] The sensitivities arising from questions
of Irish identity were further underlined while the Governor arranged a
souvenir photograph. One of the journalists was Gerry O'Hare, a former *Irish
Press* reporter and Belfast republican who, as a younger man, had edited the
IRA newspaper, *An Phoblacht* and served a prison sentence. O'Hare suddenly
realised that the picture was being taken under a Union Jack. 'Jasus!' he
exclaimed, 'Think of what the lads in Belfast would say if they got hold of the
picture for *An Phoblacht.*' He insisted that the group be reassembled out of
camera range of the offending flag.

THE HEROES OF ST PATRICK'S DAY, 1768

The paradox of St Patrick's Day, 1768, is that it was chosen by a group of
slaves as an opportune date on which to strike a blow for their freedom –
largely against the Anglo-Irish. A big St Patrick's Day celebration had been
planned for the Governor's mansion, which, on previous years' experience,
was expected to involve a lot of drinking. Most of the island's planters were
expected to attend, and the custom was for the men to hand in their swords
before the festivities began. The slaves planned to take advantage of this
temporary arms decommissioning by attacking the Governor's mansion
during the celebration. However, they were betrayed by a woman, a black
according to some, and brutally done to death.[4]

A poem by Howard Fergus, 'Dedication To Heroes of St Patrick's Day',
commemorates the slaves' memory and encapsulates the differing attitudes:

> To heroes
> Of St Patrick's Day
> In whose black breast
> The multicoloured pulse
> Of freedom
> Beat
> A bloody march
> To Bloody death
>
> To heroes
> Of a nighted thrall
> Whose livid lips
> Made Universal call
>
> To freedom
> Evoking

Stony silence
From St Patrick's
Whited gods

. . .

To heroes
Of the spirit
Proud Ebo rise to thee

BY WAY OF VIRGINIA AND ST KITTS

The 'whited gods' had been invoked in the Caribbean (called after the Carib
Indians whom the invading Europeans either enslaved or exterminated) more
than a century before that St Patrick's Day uprising. The Irish presence there
largely owed its existence, as it did elsewhere in the world, to British imperial
policy in Ireland, with its attendant ancestral conflict between Catholicism
and Protestantism. A British state paper of 1620 speaks of Ireland as having
been 'famous, or rather infamous, during so many years for continual
slaughters, attacks of towns, burning of houses, famine, fury, barbarity and
poverty'.[5]

Twenty-three years later, according to a Jesuit, Father Mathew
O'Hartegan, these conditions had caused 'twenty thousand Irishmen' to flee
to the West Indies to escape 'persecution and hardship'.[6] Father O'Hartegan
evidently overstated the numbers involved, because he wanted to be sent to
the Caribbean, specifically to St Christopher's Island, to minister to the exiles.
However, no contemporary source disputes the fact that during the
seventeenth century sizeable numbers of Irish either went, or were sent, to the
Caribbean.

The reason for the sending is contained in several documents of the time
(1620 *et seq*) which speak of the threat posed to the Protestant planters in
Ireland by the presence of 'an infinite number of young, idle people in all
countries [counties].[7] The danger was especially acute in areas like Wexford
'where the late plantations had been made'; the dispossessed Irish, being
'unprovided of means to live', were 'becoming discontented and eager after
altercation and rebellion . . . there might be murders committed upon some of
the inhabitants of the plantations'.

A solution for dealing with 'this kind of rabble, and many others of the
mere Irish' was suggested: '. . . if Virginia or some other of the newly
discovered Islands in the West were filled with them, it could not but serve and
raise the country much, and relieve and advance them withal'. When a group
of some two hundred dispossessed Wexford Irish came to Dublin seeking
justice, they were jailed and some of them were sent to Virginia. Others
followed in their footsteps. Virginia did not prove to be the answer, but it did
have a significant bearing on the presence in today's Montserrat telephone

book of names like Farrell, Fergus, Lynch, Moore, O'Garro, Ryan and, a very popular surname, Irish. Being heavily British and Protestant, Virginia was antipathetic to the Irish Catholics who found the atmosphere there little more congenial than at home. Eventually, therefore, a party sailed for the Caribbean, and the Virginian Irish arrived at Montserrat in 1633. Here they linked up with another group of Irish who had made their way from neighbouring St Kitts the previous year.

St Kitts had been the first island in the Caribbean to be colonised by the British (under Thomas Warner, in 1628), Columbus having given the Spanish a head start in the region almost one hundred and fifty years earlier. It was he who gave Montserrat its name, because it reminded him of Santa Maria de Monserrate, an abbey near Barcelona. After the English claimed Montserrat in the seventeenth century, it was, as was then the custom, handed over to a syndicate which, under patent, was entitled to exploit the land, having responsibility for all expenses incurred and control over any profits made. Although Warner had controlled Montserrat for some five years by the time the Irish contingent left his other colony on St Kitts, he had either been unable to make a profit from Montserrat or, more likely, to find the time to develop it as he worked to make a success of St Kitts. One of the problems which preoccupied Warner was the transplanted Catholic/Protestant tension that existed on St Kitts, and it was in an effort to get rid of this that he sent the Catholic Irish to Montserrat under the command of the Anglo-Irish Captain Anthony Brisket.

The link-up of the two Irish contingents on Montserrat seems to have achieved some success in their settlement very quickly because, in the New Year following the landing of the contingent from Virginia, a diarist noted:

Jan. 26,1634
    By noone we came before Montserat, where is a noble plantation of Irish Catholique, whome the Virginians would not suffer to live with them because of their religion.[8]

We know from the letters of a Jesuit missionary[9] that, by 1650, Irish emigration to the West Indies had reached a stage where there were about 3,000 Irish on Montserrat and as many more on St Kitts.

Over the succeeding centuries the Irish attempted, where possible, to 'not suffer' the British to live with them, and they sided with the Catholic French in the various wars that flared along the West Indies as British, Dutch, French and Spanish interests clashed. The numbers of Irish available to take part in such hostilities were greatly augmented by the policies of the Cromwellian era. Following the capture of the town of Drogheda, Cromwell himself wrote: 'When they submitted, their officers were knocked on the head; and every tenth man of the soldiers killed and the rest shipped for the Barbadoes.'[10] At the risk of digression I might observe here that these British foundations led to 'the Barbadoes' ultimately becoming the most British island in the Caribbean. Even today the place looks more like a slice of Cheltenham than an island in the tropics. On the outbreak of the Second World War, the Barbados Legislature sent a telegram to Whitehall saying: 'Carry on England. Barbados stands behind you!' Thus emboldened, the British duly took on the Nazi hordes with gladdened hearts.

To return to the Lord Protector. Apart from the survivors of the Drogheda massacre, Cromwell subsequently sent many more Irish to the Caribbean region, via Barbados. How many thousand is a matter of argument, but the term 'to Barbadoes' passed into the English language as a synonym for transportation. Part of the motivation was to find a dumping ground for 'undesirables', widows, orphans and the unemployed, and another emerges from an account of the period which speaks of a shipment from Galway of 1,000 men and boys and 1,000 women who were described as:

> a great benefit to the West Indian sugar planters who desired men and boys for their bondsmen and women and Irish girls in a country where they had only maroon women and Negresses to solace them.[11]

This sort of thinking, combined with the usual British impulse to get the Irish out of Ireland, may have resulted in as many as 40,000 Irish being sent to the Caribbean during the seventeenth century. By 1669 it was estimated that there were 8,000 Irish on Barbados and also large numbers on Jamaica which had been captured from Spain four years earlier.[12] However, the difference between Montserrat and the other Caribbean island lay in the fact that the Irish constituted the largest percentage of whites, seven out of ten of the population, and, to an extent unequalled elsewhere, the island was ruled by Irishmen. Between 1632 and 1687 six of the island's governors were Irish.

In 1678 the Governor, Edmond Stapleton, estimated the population as comprising: Irish 1,869; slaves 992; English 761; and Scotch 52. By comparison, on the other Leeward Islands,[13] the census showed the Irish to comprise 26 per cent of the population of Antigua, 22 per cent of Nevis and 10 per cent on St Kitts. When, in 1690, the British finally defeated the French who had taken over St Kitts, the remaining Irish on that island were shipped to Montserrat. Thus a solidly Irish gene pool was established. The Irish spread out elsewhere through the Caribbean, and marked traces of their influence, chiefly through the Church, can be found all over the archipelago, mostly in the eastern part as we shall see, but the Montserratian presence is of particular interest. It encapsulates the manner in which the Irish, either at home or abroad, continued to struggle for liberty and equality. Catholic emancipation (1892) and the Forty Shilling Franchise (freeholders whose property was worth forty shillings a year got the vote) were equally welcome to Patrick Murphy in Kinsale on Montserrat and Patrick Murphy in Kinsale in County Cork. The difference was that by now Patrick Murphy of Montserrat was probably black.

THE IRISH AND THE FRENCH

The main importance of the island was strategic, not economic. The intelligence provided by Irish Catholics helped the French to take control of the island on a number of occasions, the last in 1782 for a period of a year and a half.

Both the Irish and the African slave population were discriminated against, and one reason that the Irish aided the French was the fact that in 1749 the Montserratian Assembly had passed a law which effectively disenfranchised the Irish Catholics: it required all voters to pledge allegiance to the Church of England and the King.

EMANCIPATION

As sugar took over from tobacco as the island's dominant industry, slaves increasingly replaced Irish indentured labour and the treatment of them led to the savagely repressed attempt at rebellion on St Patrick's Day in 1768. The constant fears of a recurrence, coupled with the decline in the sugar industry, caused many of the English landowners to pull out. As in Ireland, their estates were inefficiently run by agents on behalf of the absentee landlords, and the result was that the soil became impoverished and the island virtually lost whatever attractions it had had as a magnet for white emigration. In 1832, when Catholic emancipation was extended to the island, the total number entitled to vote was 144 out of a population of 7,119.

The blacks were emancipated a few years later in 1838, but the economic conditions made for heavy emigration from the island, and in 1865 the Governor's report stated that the bulk of the members of the legislature could neither read nor write. The powers of this Parliament, like those of the other legislatures of the British-controlled Leeward Islands, were subsumed into a Leeward Islands legislative council. Such new Irish influences as there were on the island's subsequent development were exercised largely through individual priests, traders and planters.

IRISH RESONANCES

The principal effect of these combined influences falls on the visitor's ear as Howard Fergus chose to illustrate with a distinctly non-politically correct Irish joke:

> Montserrat had Irish colonists for its early settlers and the negroes to this day have the Connaught brogue curiously and ludicrously engrafted on the African jargon. It is said that a Connaught man on arriving at Montserrat, was, to his astonishment, hailed in vernacular Irish by a negro from one of the first boats that came alongside. 'Thunder and

turf,' exclaimed Pat, 'how long have you been here?' 'Three months, and so black already! T'anam a dhoul,' says Pat, thinking Quashie a countryman, 'I'll not stay among ye'; and in a few hours the Connaught man was on his return, with a white skin to the Emerald Isle.[14]

Certainly the local patois today bears strong Connemara, or indeed working-class Dublin overtones. For example: 'If awll me come li quicka, yuh wouldie got an me woulda get.' The International Centre for Montserratian Linguistics (the Bird's Nest pub) assured me that this translates as: 'If we had arrived sooner, both of us would have got on.' Who am I to question them. Another example is: 'A yo me born; a ya me rear', meaning, 'I was born and raised here.' The foregoing reminded me of the Dublin dialect encapsulated in Brendan Behan's anecdote about a friend of his who exclaimed on first seeing the Leaning Tower of Pisa: 'Looka! It's crooka!' And to anyone familiar with the history of Dublin's Abbey Theatre there are also similarities with the Kiltartan dialect of the Galway peasants that Lady Gregory used in her plays. To be fair, it would be hard to detect Irish resonances in the name Bam-Chicklay Chiga Foot Maya, the title of a form of Montserratian dance that appears to be linked to Irish step dancing, but the bodhran, a type of goatskin-covered tambourine, which is widely used in Irish music groups is common on Montserrat.

'Goat Water', made from goat meat, is the most distinctive island dish and is said to have been derived from an Irish recipe. The anthropologist, John Messinger, who has also worked on the Aran Islands off the Connemara coast says that: 'An identical recipe learned in her youth when goat often was eaten was given to my wife by the aged spouse of a Connemara farmer the week after we left Montserrat.'[15] Insofar as other Irish traditions on Montserrat are concerned, however, Messinger was not able to cite much more than 'the making and smuggling of liquor, alcoholism, violence, factionalism, coffee drinking, well digging' and the existence of 'long acres'. The long acres are the strips of grass between fence and roadway where the landless Irish traditionally grazed their cattle. He did establish, to his own satisfaction, a relationship between Montserratian and Irish fairy-tales. The equivalent of the Irish 'pookah', or fairy spirit, is the 'jumbie', much talked of on Montserrat, where one can encounter everything from a 'jumbie' wind to a 'jumbie' volcanic explosion. Messinger says that:

The pookah that we discovered is seen occasionally on moonlight nights on the road in front of the Catholic Church in St Patrick's village. It is a huge dog with a bushy tail, which can alter its size at will and appears and disappears instantaneously. This demon does no harm other than frighten people by its sudden materialisation, thus resembling the pookah of Aran, called the 'dog of the tumulus' ... which inhabits a Bronze Age burial mound.[16]

I must say Messinger has the advantage over me on both Aran and Montserrat. On neither island did I encounter any canine spirit other than that known as the hair of the dog. However, I did share with the American anthropologist a very strong sense of the emotion he and his wife experienced on discovering the:

> weed-covered grave of one of the thousands of Irish men and women who lived and died in this small island of the Caribbean between 1632 and the present day; and it aroused my wife and me emotionally when we contemplated the tragic exodus of countless Irish from their homeland to the far corners of the earth. How isolated and how different in climate and physiography was Montserrat compared to Ireland over 3,000 miles away . . .[17]

I thought of the mosquitoes, and of what they and the burning Caribbean sun must have done to the Irish rain-conditioned skins of the transportees, particularly the women press-ganged into concubinage with Cromwellian soldiers and sugar planters, in the days before fly-spray, contraception or sun block.

CALAMITIES IN PARADISE

Montserrat is tiny, only about twelve miles long by seven wide, rising at Chances Peak to 3,000 feet above sea level, but it boasts a remarkable variety of vegetation – Chances Peak itself is crowned by a cloud forest – which has attracted the attention of Lydia Mihelic Pulsipher, a professor of geography at the University of Tennessee, who has visited the island for a quarter of a century. She was responsible for preserving the 253-year-old ruins of the Galway Estate, a sugar plantation once owned by an Irishman, David Galway. Dr Pulsipher sums up the island as follows:

> The island is one of the most incredible microcosms you can ever hope to come across. That's true culturally: even as small as Montserrat is, the people speak at least three different dialects, depending on what part of the island they come from. And it's geographically diverse, too. There are ten different climate types and many forest complexes, from rain forests and elfin woodland to semi-evergreen and dry deciduous. It gives geographers a chance to study changes in terrain on a scale not accessible elsewhere.[18]

Montserrat's paradisal qualities led to its becoming a major recording centre for a brief period in the 1980s. The former Beatles producer, George Martin, founded Air Studios on the island in 1979 and recording stars such as Eric Clapton, Boy George and Paul McCartney recorded albums there.

Prophetically, Jimmy Buffet recorded the song 'Volcano' on Montserrat. It contains the lines:

> I don't know,
> I don't know where I am gonna go,
> When the volcano blow.

There was a major earth tremor in 1985, and Hurricane Hugo either destroyed or damaged some 98 per cent of the island's houses in 1989. Then, in 1995, the island was again hit by a hurricane, and more seriously by a series of large-scale volcanic eruptions which continued over a four-month period. These disasters caused considerable damage and loss of tourism revenue, and a 650-strong medical school which, somewhat improbably, had flourished on the island was removed to a safer location.

Father Larry Finnegan from Dublin, a Divine Word Missionary and parish priest of St Patrick's Roman Catholic Church, Plymouth, my hospitable host and guide on Montserrat, was deeply involved in the relief effort necessitated by these calamities. A year after they occurred, he drove me around the island, showing me its scars and its beauties. Most of the former's visible traces had healed by then – people were no longer sleeping on the floors of church halls and so on – but there was great unemployment, a fear of what would happen when the insurance money ran out, and, above all, an even greater fear as to what might happen if the volcano erupted again. Tragically, this last fear was shortly to be realised. In April 1996, volcanic eruptions became so dangerous that Plymouth had to be evacuated. Volcanic activity continued for more than a year, the worst eruption occurring on 25 June 1997, killing nineteen people.

Even during my visit the volcano was omnipresent. It dominated conversation and you learned to smell and fear it. There was a tang of sulphur, an occasional dusting of black ash on flat surfaces and a deceptively attractive white cloud, about three miles long, drifting from the crater. Yet, it was a background fear. Father Larry and I were able to confine our attentions to things like the Montserratian national flower, the heliconia, which an inspired American travel writer, Bob Morris, has described as a 'golden asparagus on steroids, garishly bursting loose among its spiky green leaves'. The helonicia has the additional advantage of being the home of the national bird, the black and orange oriole, found only on Montserrat and, perhaps symbolic of the Irish links also, in sadly diminishing numbers.

HEROES AND SCOUNDRELS

The island certainly had an Irish 'feel' to it. Despite the helonica and attendant vegetation, both Father Larry and I found the place redolent of the rural Ireland of our boyhood. Hens scratched in the middle of such traffic as there was in the main street of Plymouth, the island's biggest town. As we drove up a hill to visit the remains of the Galway Estate, our way was blocked by an old man, sitting side-saddle on a donkey trotting up the middle of the road. He was wearing a cap, smoking a pipe, and, apart from his black skin, might well have been a typical Irish cottier ascending a Connemara boreen.[19] As he eventually became aware of our presence – Father Larry would never dream of honking the horn – he pulled into the side to let us past. We thanked him. 'Not a tall a tall!' he beamed.

While we toured the ruins of the estate Father Larry talked of the Irish

578

heroes and scoundrels who had walked this ground before us. Amongst the heroes one would have to include Father Larry's first predecessor, a Limerick Jesuit, Father John Stritch, who came to the area in 1650, disguised as a lumber dealer, and managed to travel between St Kitts and Montserrat, ministering to the Irish. Amongst the scoundrels was one Roger Osborne, a member of a powerful Anglo-Irish family and the Governor of Montserrat in 1654. In order to secure some family property held by his brother-in-law, Samuel Waad, he had him judicially murdered.

Osborne first provoked Waad by arresting one of his guests on a fictitious charge. The furious Waad wrote to Osborne protesting about this and asking why Osborne had not prosecuted an 'Irish murderer' in his employment and why he allowed the 'barbarous Irish' to carry arms in the militia. Osborne, an Irishman, employed a colonial legal device well known in Irish legal history, the packed jury, to find Waad, an Englishman, guilty of mutiny at a court-martial. The unfortunate Waad was marched out of the courtroom and shot. Osborne then confiscated his estates and everyone and everything on them.

Apart from the land-based scoundrels, the Irish had their share of the sea-borne ones also. At the time of the early plantations the Caribbean swarmed with pirates; one of the most notorious was allegedly 'an Irishman, his name Plunkuet [the name is probably Plunkett and there is some dispute as to the pirate's nationality], a man bold enough; but had the character of being more merciless than became a valiant man'.[20]

SERVANTS AND SLAVES

A lack of mercy was not confined to pirates, however. The Irish administered the prevailing laws of slavery and of indenture on Montserrat. These laws and customs affected the lives of the men and women who had once worked the estate in which Father Larry and I conducted our conversation. The ruined walls and untilled fields we looked over once rang to the sound of the voices, and sometimes the screams, of both indentured servants and slaves. The Slavery Acts specified that 'any Negro who was found stealing . . . to the value of 12d. would suffer such death as the Governor and Council may decree'. For thefts of goods worth less than 12d. however, 'the offender would receive a severe whipping and have both ears cut off'. This was for a first offence only. A second would cause 'he or she' to be put to death 'in a manner prescribed by the Governor and Council'.

The Act which probably led to the St Patrick's Day rebellion was that of 1736 which prevented the slaves planting crops of their own or holding a Sunday market to sell them. This prevented the slaves from earning a little money with which perhaps to purchase their freedom. It also denied them a break, after a six-day week of dawn to dusk working, during which they could relax, and, most importantly exchange news and gossip – perhaps of a slave uprising on one of the other islands. The blacks were virtual prisoners on the plantations. If they left without permission the least punishment they could expect was a whipping.

Bad as all this was, the lot of the indentured servants was often worse. A contemporary account, by Arthur Ligon, states:

> The slaves and their posterity being subject to their masters for ever, are kept and preserved with greater care than the servants, who are there but for five years according to the law of the Island. For the time the servants have the worse lives, for they are put to very hard labour, ill lodging, and their diet very slight . . .[21]

The servants were normally given no meat. Their diet was potatoes, bonavist[22] and 'lob-lolly', which was made out of maize pounded in a mortar and then boiled. The blacks disliked this and were fed instead on plantain, when they could be grown, and water. Some masters treated their servants well, however. As the plantations became established and a better type of planter arrived, diet, clothing and accommodation all improved – but not in every case. Ligon writes:

> if the masters be cruel, the servants have very wearisome and miserable lives . . . I have seen such cruelty done to servants as I would not think one Christian could have done to another . . .[23]

THE SALEM MASS

Over the years Irish emigration fell off and master, slave, servant and adventurer all blended together. The names remained Irish – Allens, Cartys, Daleys, Farrells, Kirwans, etc – but the pigmentation became African. One of the changes which occurred was that the name Osborne ceased to be associated merely with a murderous Governor and came to be that of one of the most prominent business and political families on the island. After we had finished our tour, Father Larry introduced me to Cedric and Carole Osborne who run the island's biggest hotel, the Vue Pointe, a beach-side complex, one of whose many attractions is a scattering of romantic-looking, conical-shaped, thatched chalets. Cedric is a black Montserratian, Carole, a white former Bostonian descended from the O'Driscolls of West Cork. Their children are brown, beautiful and gifted. One boy, having gained his primary degree in the U.S., is now studying in Madrid. Another helps to run the hotel. Two others study in the U.S. and the fifth, a girl, is married there.

The Osbornes tried to keep up the Irish links by employing Irish staff where possible; I met a barman and a trainee manager from Ireland during my stay. Volcanic eruptions permitting, the Obsornes also made a notable effort to maintain the Irish tradition of hospitality. On Sunday evenings anyone visiting the island, whether a guest of Vue Pointe or not, was welcome to a generous reception held in their home. Thus, in the space of an hour or two, one easily became acquainted with both Montserratian society and the latest tourist arrivals.

They knew Ireland well, Cedric being especially fond of the Irish comedian, Hal Roche, whose jokes he used at his Chamber of Commerce lunches because they were 'very funny, very clean'. They told me that on a recent Irish visit, by pure chance, they had booked into Renvyle House Hotel in County Galway. Renvyle House, they discovered, was originally built, on Montserratian profits, by one of the early Irish sugar planters, Henry Blake. The Blake's Estate district of Montserrat is still named after a member of the family, one of the historic 'Ten Tribes of Galway', all of whom had representatives on Montserrat in the early plantation days.

Cedric is a devout Catholic and took a prominent part in the readings and greetings which are a feature of Father Larry's innovative liturgy. Mass on Montserrat was a particularly good occasion on which to observe the cross-fertilisation process. The fact that mass was celebrated at all was due to by-gone Irish priests, but the colour of many in the congregation, and the nature of the celebration, bespoke the influence of Africa.

Arriving on the island a few years earlier, Father Larry had discovered that his congregation had shrunken to a 'handful of ex-pats' but very few Montserratians. He set out rectifying this situation by celebrating mass as he would have in Dublin, making it short and snappy – but to no avail. Attendances remained low. Then one day an island woman explained why. 'Father,' she said, 'Sunday come and we get dressed up in our best clothes. We go to the Methodist preacher. He give us three and one half-hour service. The Baptist man he does even better. And The Seventh Day Adventist Man! He do seven and a half hours. But you only give us twenty-five minutes and we all dressed up!'

As I do not normally attend mass, and Father Larry told me the story as we drove across the island to one of his outlying churches, at Salem, where he was going to take one of his normal three Sunday masses, the anecdote filled me with forebodings of a Caribbean return to the old 'long gospel' Latin marathons of my boyhood. However, I worried needlessly; the liturgical mixture of black and green provided a most enjoyable ceremony. There was great lay participation with much singing and reading by members of the congregation, an excellent choir and Father Larry acted as much host as celebrant. He introduced me to the congregation and they responded by singing, 'We love you. We love you', to the air of 'She'll be coming round the mountain when she comes'! This made it particularly difficult for me to keep a straight face because the air is indelibly etched in my mind by a parody, the party piece of a lady on the Aran Islands which goes:

> Oh she has a lovely bottom
> Oh she has a lovely bottom when she comes
> Yes she has a lovely bottom when she comes . . .

However, the bright Caribbean sunlight, shining through the open door, suffused by the colours of the stain-glass windows; sea breeze that kept the church cool and airy; Father Larry resplendent in particularly vibrantly coloured vestment and blazing white surplice; all combined to make the ninety-minute challenge to the Baptists pass, not merely painlessly, but memorably. Afterwards, the congregation – fifty-two Africans and twenty-two ex-pats – chatted to each other outside the church.

Thanks to Larry's introduction, I met Tom Mitchell, his wife Marcia, and their charming friend Ann McKay from Dakota who was holidaying with them. Tom, who was of Irish parentage, was a former FBI agent who had gone into industry. He was also a 'snow-bird', that is, someone who escapes to a Montserrat home from a northern latitude winter. The Mitchell's home on Montserrat, Mango Falls Villa, was one of the loveliest I have ever seen. The many-windowed, single-storey, marble-floored structure perched on a cliff edge. Beside it a small waterfall cascaded down to the sea, alongside a flight of steps cut into the cliff which led to a swimming place – a scuba diver's or snorkeller's paradise.

HEIGHTENING THE IRISH CONNECTION

As the island's economy was in such a precarious condition it appeared to me to be self-evident that such paradisical attractions should be made known to the world's tourists, particularly the Irish-Americans who have both the money and the sense of Irish heritage to make a Montserratian holiday appear attractive. Some of the people we had met at the Salem mass (the juxtaposition of the words conjures up an interesting contrast in itself) were Irish-Americans attracted by a small clip of film about the island, featuring Father Larry, which had been shown on Boston TV a little earlier.

Not surprisingly preparations were in hand to make the forthcoming St Patrick's Day Parade an even bigger success than the previous year's. The man who led the parade, an English Protestant with a beard resembling that of St Patrick, had already made the customary arrangement whereby Father Larry would turn a blind eye while St Patrick's staff disappeared out of the hand of the blessed statue in his parish church, to reappear in the hand of the Saint leading the parade. Some four hundred tickets had already been sold for the annual St Patrick's Banquet at the Vue Pointe.

However, as I have indicated earlier, there are those on the island who disapprove of St Patrick's Day being used, as they see it, to heighten the Irish connection at the expense of the African one. Their leading figure, Howard Fergus, had written:

> This author had an occasion recently to warn against incipient distortion in the significance and celebration of the holiday. It was, in his view, beginning to resemble the style in which the Irish diaspora in the United States celebrate St Patrick's Day. The holiday was intended to honour our slave ancestors who bravely essayed to overthrow their oppressive European overlords – and these were English, Scottish and Irish.

I had not been aware of Dr Fergus's attitude to the Irish connection before coming to the island. However, because of his reputation as a historian, I had made arrangements for an interview with him, through his secretary, a black lady whose surname of Lynch indicates, as does Dr Fergus's own, some Irish origin. On arrival at the great man's office she made me welcome, assured me that I was expected, and that although delayed – at a ceremony for the opening of the courts – he would be along shortly. I waited for an hour and a half before I had to leave for another interview, but he still had not turned up. I left, explaining that I was staying with Father Larry, some two hundred and fifty yards away, and suggesting that we make another arrangement by phone to meet.

No phone call came, so I am not in a position to put the case of the anti-Irish lobby, as it were, more fully.

Moreover, fate also intervened to prevent me from keeping a promise I had made to the Governor, Sir Frank Savage, to play my part in rekindling Irish-Montserratian links. With a view to attracting Irish and Irish-American tourism Savage was keen to twin Kinsale on Montserrat with Kinsale in County Cork. As Kinsale was the site of the battle which, more than any other, broke the power of the old Gaelic order in Ireland, I felt there was a certain poetic justice in colluding with an Englishman to help restore Irish influence in the Caribbean. However, before my endeavours had time to bear any fruit the volcano erupted once more. The following extract from a letter of Marcia Mitchell tells what happened:

> I'm certain you heard the tragic news about Montserrat . . . Some villages were completely destroyed, with some of the areas now under as much as fifteen feet of hot ash. Ten lives were lost and a number of people are missing and presumed to be dead. About fifty were rescued by Dutch and French helicopters (the British had not yet arrived!) dropping harnesses as the surface was too hot for landings. One flow made it to the end of the airport runway, and the airport is unusable and closed. A ferry service was launched yesterday . . . subsequent eruptions have sent . . . the boiling flow . . . within hailing distance of the Vue Pointe Hotel.
>
> We are of course terribly worried not only about our own property but about the future of the entire island and its population. More people have left and there is concern now that the minimum level of 4,000 inhabitants considered necessary for maintenance of an island infrastructure is threatened.[24]

Initially the island population fell from 11,000 to only 3,000 people but by June 30th, 2000 had recovered to over 4,500 and was climbing slowly. The volcano was still quietly, but there was much re-building in progress, both by the natives and 'snow birds'. Tourists were returning. The Hotel 'Tropical Mansions' was back in business, and the Vue Pointe was on the verge of re-opening (although unscathed by lava, the volcanic ash had corroded metal fittings such as locks, window catches, stainless steel kitchen fittings and so on). The insurance companies had either reduced or ended their cover. But a combination of the islanders spirit and not ungenerous grants from London, administered by a hard-working team of officials in the Frank Savage mould – he and his wife Veronica have transferred to Tortilla, in the British Virgin Islands – hold out hope for a continuation of 'Ireland's only colony'.

Ironically the Irish connection gave rise to controversy in the wake of the volcano's eruption. The Labour Minister responsible for the island, the feisty Clare Short, became so exasperated at, what she considered to be the unreasonable demands of some of the island politicians, that she uttered a celebrated complaint that nothing would satisfy them except 'showers of golden elephants'. This caused another volcanic eruption. This time of indignation. At the time of writing, three visits by Prince Andrew had still not mollified the Monterratians and Clare herself had still to make one visit.

However, I am happy to record that one island controversy does appear to have reached détente. During the evacuations Dr. Howard Fergus and Fr Larry, who was awarded an honorary MBE for his exertions throughout the crisis, shared a house. Perhaps the experience helped to mellow Dr. Fergus's approach because, in a Pentecostal Church, he took part in the 1999 St. Patrick's Day celebrations! These honoured both the African and Irish traditions. There was a St. Patrick's Day feast and a slave feast and slave revolution commemoration. Dr. Fergus delivered a lecture on his tradition and the former Irish Minister for the Arts, Michael D. Higgins, spoke on the Irish one. Two feasts for one! An Irish solution to an African problem. Truly a fellow volcano doth make us wondrous kind.

TRINIDAD

Away from Montserrat, the very lack of physical traces of Irish presence in the Caribbean region resulted in my thinking again and again of the 'two colonialisms', the mental and physical imprint which both have left on the Irish psyche, and the extent to which both have drawn off reservoirs of energy and initiative which could have been of incalculable benefit both to Ireland and to the individuals concerned. Despite the history of transportation and its attendant ills, I was often more conscious of the mental, or religious, form of colonisation than I was of the physical, precisely because it was neither immediately observable, nor acknowledged.

Trinidad is one of the greatest of the Caribbean's melting pots, and has managed, despite occasional racial flare ups, to produce a multi-cultural, relatively tolerant society. Its 1,125,128 inhabitants are divided as follows: African 40.8 per cent, East Indian 40.7 per cent, Whites 0.6 per cent, Chinese and Syrian-Lebanese 0.3 per cent. Given the foregoing population break-down, it can be taken that when the remaining 18.4 per cent are described as 'Mixed', the census-takers really do mean mixed! The largest religious sect is Roman Catholic – 330,655, with Hindus coming next at 266,040. It was through Catholicism that the Irish, who of course only formed part of the tiny white percentage, came to exercise a considerable influence on Trinidadian society. Some knowledgeable observers, like the Irish Dominican Father Tiernan, an important figure in the Port of Spain diocese, would go so far as to say that, even apart from the discovery of oil, it was the education provided by the Irish which put Trinidad ahead of the other islands both socially and economically.

An invisible influence

However, for many Trinidadians this claim, for which valid evidence can be adduced, is not so much disputed as overlooked. For example, Eric Williams, the first Prime Minister of Independent Trinidad and Tobago, was one of the greatest political figures of twentieth-century Caribbean political history, and in 1962 he published his *History of the People of Trinidad and Tobago*. However, this Harvard and Oxford scholar made no mention of the contribution of Irish priests and nuns to the educational development of either island, beyond chronicling the rivalries which existed between the various Christian sects, Creoles and Indians.

Nor need one expect to find any such mention in the more popular type of work which the general visitor might be expected to read. For example, the excellent Insight Guides edition dealing with Trinidad and Tobago, having referred (accurately) to the whites in Trinidad and Tobago as being a 'privileged minority', makes only this passing reference to education:

> Some whites work in education, in religious orders which function as the old 'prestige' schools originally founded for white and mulatto children, and in the new private schools set up for the still predominantly light-skinned children of today's upper classes.[25]

Yet the extent of Irish influence on education was assessed in a report written as far back as 1869 in the following terms:

> The books which I found in use were chiefly the publications of the Irish National Board . . . no set of primary school books ever previously published in the English language could surpass or even equal them. But notwithstanding their recognised excellence and reputation, I should like to see them superseded by a set of books whose lessons would be racy of the Colony, descriptive of this history, of its resources, of its trade, of the national phenomena of its trees, plants, flowers, fruits, etc.[26]

The author found that the Trinidadian system lacked 'everything that gives character and tone to a well-worked school in Great Britain or Ireland'.[27]

Education in Trinidad

As indicated earlier, Ireland was Britain's premier colonial laboratory and it was therefore not surprising that the fruits of educational experiments carried out in Ireland should have been exported to other parts of the empire.

Moreover, as the main thrust of the Irish educational system was to provide the administrators and functionaries necessary to run the empire, it is equally unsurprising that the character of the education provided should have been pro-British and anti-revolutionary in tendency. At primary level for instance, Irish schoolchildren were taught to give thanks for the boon of being born a 'happy English child'. Similarly, in Trinidad, raising a sense of national consciousness in their first Crown Colony was far from being the objective of Britain's colonial educators in polyglot Port of Spain. What the planters required was sugar-cane fodder – workers, not citizens: hence the colourless, denatured character of the curriculum of which Keenan complained. Hence, too, the fact that, although Irish nuns, priests and brothers came to the Caribbean from a country with one of the world's longest records of resistance to colonialism, being white and travelling in the wake of the colonists, they inevitably fell victim to the general Africanist, Indian and Nationalist revulsion against colonialism.

In some cases one could hardly argue that this revulsion was unfairly earned. One John Black, a Protestant from Antrim, was a notorious slave trader in the last quarter of the eighteenth century. Amongst other infamies he is remembered for having once sold 'at exorbitant prices a parcel of forty diseased negroes, thirty-four of whom died within three days'.[28] There was also an understandable British reluctance to have its history in Ireland taught in Caribbean schools. Indeed, reluctance to have any education whatsoever was a feature of Trinidadian society until well into the twentieth century.

Philip Emmett Taafe O'Connor, a scion of one of Trinidad's most distinguished Irish families, has recorded his surprise when, as a boy at Clongowes Wood College in 1912, he first learned:

> the history of Ireland – that Sir Ralph Abercrombie had acted as a perfect gentleman in his conquest of Trinidad compared with his treatment of the Irish when he governed them, that the Irish peasant had been, and still was, far worse off than the working classes in Trinidad, that thousands had died of starvation during the potato famine while other thousands had emigrated to America under conditions comparable or worse to those experienced during the slave trade or East Indian immigration.[29]

THE IRISH REGIMENTS

The O'Connors owed their presence in Trinidad to the same agency which transported so many other Irishmen, and women, around the world – the British army. Emmett O'Connor's great grandfather, James Lynch O'Connor, arrived in Port of Spain as an army surgeon as far back as 1817. All that now remains of the presence of Irish regiments like the Connaught Rangers or the Inniskilling Fusiliers is a plaque here, a place name there. High on a hill overlooking Kingston, Jamaica there is an Irishtown. None of the locals today know how it came by the name, but if one searches through the archives it emerges that it was the district where the Irish regiments were once stationed.

Sometimes the reputation of a particularly colourful Irish soldier survives. John Fahey, who left Cappoquin, County Waterford in 1847 at the age of sixteen, during the height of the famine, is still remembered in Trinidad where he married an Alsatian woman. She bore him children in Bermuda, Burma and India. On being demobbed after a 25-year stint, he returned to Trinidad and worked for a further twenty-five years as a police clerk. The melting pot nature of Caribbean society may be gauged from the fact that: 'His daughters married into the Geollnicht, Nothnagel and Cadiz families, and his two sons wed a D'Azevedo and a Neil.'[30]

The Caribbean climate gives the use of the melting pot simile a sad appositeness, as a description of an Irish regiment in Demarra, Guyana during the 1830s indicates:

> There is an Irish regiment in garrison here which gives such a vast deal of trouble. They are a wild set, but nothing can exceed their piety when they are 'fuddled' and when they are in that state they seldom fail to pay His Reverence a visit [for Confession]. Their intemperance and the effect of the climate bring many of them 'up' to the Hospital and there has not been a night since my return that I have not had half a dozen sick to attend. Three hundred of the regiment died. I attended them all.[31]

All the waste, the loneliness, the unrequited lust, the wild heroism, of these men's lives came home to me as I stood before a memorial on the high peak of Morne Fortune, commanding Castries, the capital of the island of St Lucia. Its altitude provides one of the most breathtaking views in the entire Caribbean. How the heights could have been scaled in the teeth of hostile canon fire, by soldiers armed with musket and bayonet defies imagination. Yet, in large measure because such a successful assault had taken place, there was a British warship in the bay and a contingent from it had just laid a wreath on the memorial. It was from the officers and men of the Royal Irish Regiment, in commemoration of the 200th anniversary of the capture of this impossible vantage point.

The commemorative plaque on the memorial informs the visitor that, on 24 May 1796, the 27th Inniskilling Regiment had stormed Morne Fortune. As a mark of appreciation for the enormous courage involved in this feat, General Abercrombie had ordered the French to surrender to the 27th, and had the 27th's flag flown for an hour before hoisting the British flag. So, for the flap of a flag, in defence of colonialism, Irish Catholic lads had fought and died to defeat a Catholic force. After showing appreciation for the gallantry, their commanding officer had then sailed for Ireland to devastate their homeland in the wake of the 1798 Rebellion.

In his fine history of Trinidad, Father Verteuil writes of the Irish soldiers: 'They came and they died, unheralded and now unknown (how many of them it is almost impossible to estimate) and from the viewpoint of the social historian they had (officially) no permanent impact on the country.'[32] No they did not – but at least I can testify to the fact that I came to St Lucia to honour their passing, and fresh flowers are still being laid in some Irish soldiers' memories at Castries.

LAW ENFORCEMENT

Another memory which had not died out when I visited the Caribbean area was that of the Irish contribution to law enforcement. In the latter part of the nineteenth century Trinidadian policing was modelled on the lines of the Royal Irish Constabulary, to much the same extent as was the educational system based on the Irish model. The architect of this system was a famous Irish detective, one J. N. Brierly who, in the 1890s, travelled the island on horseback, setting up the force. The Irish were also active in the Barbados police force where, as in Trinidad, in addition to native-born Irishmen large numbers of 'redlegs', poor whites of Irish descent, served with distinction in police uniforms.

One of the few areas the British have never been accused of stinting on in Ireland is the provision of cause for riot. Perhaps therefore it is not surprising that Irish police acquired such an expertise in dealing with public disorder that to this day one will encounter tales of legendary police action by Irishmen, even up to the famous present-day Carnival riots of the 1980s. In those of 1881, the Irish are remembered for the manner in which eighty policeman subdued a stick-wielding, stone-and-bottle-throwing crowd of several thousands, and during the Hosay riots three years later fourteen policemen confronted 4,000 rioters. The authorities decided that even the Irish police needed an extra edge after the Arouca riots of 1891. Armed only with a switch a police officer called Fraser – one of a party of ten led against thousands of rioters by Brierly – was beaten to a pulp, and subsequently police on riot duty were issued with guns.

THE COMMON IRISH BOND

To return to the O'Connors. In Ireland, the family are one of the most ancient and respected clans, but in my ignorance I had been unaware of the equally well-respected Trinidadian branch until I was introduced to Emmett's son Peter, an architect. This occurred at a dinner given for me in Port of Spain by Kathleen Quill, a Dublin artist and former researcher with RTE's premier programme, *The Late Late Show*, who had married a Trinidadian architect and furniture designer, Allan Walker. Kathleen was making something of a reputation for herself as a portrait painter as this was being written. That reputation was considerably enlarged when she staged an exhibition on the theme of the fecundity of the tropics: the paintings included lilies which sprouted penises, and one of Adam inverting the Judaeo-Christian myth by seducing Eve – using, moreover, not an apple but a particularly suggestive banana.

Viewed from outside, the Walkers' dinner might have appeared to be merely a social gathering of expatriates and some of their Creole friends. However, when one enquired more closely into the guest list, the common Irish educational and cultural bond became apparent. All had been educated by Irish nuns or priests. One, an Irish banker working in Trinidad, had like P. E. O'Connor been educated at Clongowes. His wife and son ran an egg and citrus farm. Some of the Trinidadians had met their spouses while studying in Ireland. Ross Graham, from County Tyrone, was teaching linguistics at the University of the West Indies. Patricia Ismond was teaching English at the same institution and, amongst other Irish writers, her courses featured Beckett, Heaney, Joyce, Shaw and Yeats.

The talk flowed along beautifully on a candlelit Caribbean night, carried on a warm tide of Trinidadian and Irish good fellowship, until we suddenly hit a conversational reef. One of the guests silenced the company by observing musingly: 'You know, our generation saw the two most significant developments in society – the coming of marijuana and the coming of AIDS.' My Creole companion, Peter O'Connor, chose the moment of silence engendered by this profundity to inform me that he was descended from the High Kings of Ireland! It turned out that he was perfectly correct; he subsequently produced a copy of his family tree for me. It traced his lineage back to Roderic O'Connor, the last High King of England, via the clan O'Connor of Sligo, and has been verified as authentic by Trinidadian historians.

REDLEGS

Not all the Irish fared as well in the Caribbean as did the O'Connors through the professions, sugar plantations and oil. If one arrived in the West Indies as a professional man related to an Irish 'county' family, then one's self and one's descendants generally did far better than did families who owed their origins to indenture, transportation, or enlistment as a private in the British army. Of course, 'county' or not, the Irish came far lower in the pecking order than did the British who held the bulk of both power and property. The French, whom the British supplanted, also lived a life of privilege, caste and elegance, and both races lorded it over the African and Indian populations.

To this day, one can encounter 'redlegs' Irish. In fact these do not have red legs, they are partly descended from English and Scots, as well as the Irish from whom presumably they inherit their frequently met with red hair, and are now all black. They are mainly to be found in the Patna village district, not far from Port of Spain, and in their speech, as on Montserrat, one can detect Irish rhythms. Kelly Village, some twenty miles south of Port of Spain, also demonstrates an Irish heritage. The village was called after members of the 'barbadoed' Kelly family who, during the nineteenth century, eventually managed to lay hands on sufficient money to move from Barbados and buy land in the district that now bears their name.

THE IRISH MISSIONARY TEACHERS

The educational legacy of the Irish missionary teachers should be viewed in two ways: one, the geo-political perspective of Mother Colonial, as seen from Rome; and second that of the Irish priest, or nun, on the ground. In the case of the first it should be remembered that in the late nineteenth century the same educational debate that raged through Ireland about 'godless colleges' (state-founded universities over which the Irish hierarchy, and through it Rome, would not have the final say) also convulsed the Trinidadian Church. Moreover, the fact of Trinidad's being one of the principal English colonies in the Caribbean area meant that Rome also had an interest in overseeing the spread of its empire through the English language, even if this had to be at the expense of its loyal Francophone disciples in the area. Ilium was falling and Rome was intent on arising. The Congregation of the Holy Ghost, founded in France and with powerful roots in Ireland, presented a perfect vehicle for the advancement of Roman Catholicism.

It was, however, a dangerous vehicle for its occupants. Tuberculosis was rife in Ireland, and the enclosed life of the religious often served to spread the contagion, with the result that, as a contemporary Holy Ghost has noted:

> The reports from the superiors of the College to the Mother House at Paris often read like medical bulletins. William Lahiffe, for instance, came out to Trinidad in October 1866; he was too ill to teach the two English classes assigned to him, did what little he could, and in spite of vomiting blood, kept on his feet till August 4th, 1868 when he went to bed and died on the 6th of August after taking perpetual vows in the Congregation on the 5th.[33]

The College referred to is the famous St Mary's Holy Ghost College in Port of Spain, founded in 1863 at the suggestion of the Private Chamberlain to the Pope, Monsignor Talbot, to counter the influence of the recently opened Queen's Collegiate School.

In the same year the first Irish nun arrived to join the Sisters of Cluny Convent in Port of Spain. Thereafter, despite the ravages of typhus and yellow fever, which claimed several of the young Irish religious in the early stages of their arrival, Irish nuns spearheaded the growth of the Church in Trinidad and throughout the Caribbean by their use of English. The first Irish Cluny Superioress, the formidable Mother Mildburge Walton (1894–1919), was responsible for completely anglicising convent studies, in the face of considerable opposition from the *ancien régime* who regarded French as being synonymous with Catholicism.

These rivalries faded as the French Creoles came to realise that, in the English-dominated society, the Irish educators were conferring upward mobility on their sons and daughters. However, an indication of the hostilities generated at the time may be gleaned from a poem written by a French Creole, ostensibly to commemorate the arrival of a comet over Trinidadian skies. The poet speculates on the new era heralded by the comet's arrival, and on what changes it might cause:

> Then, the fat abbess, sons of green Erin,
> The salvation of souls will seek to win,
> Will leave right aside their rum and their gin.

The Dominican Order also provided a vehicle for the introduction of a sizeable Irish influence into Trinidad. To further its influence through the spread of English, Rome decreed in 1895 that this hitherto French-controlled order should henceforth replace retiring priests with either English or Irish priests. As the Dominicans were heavily engaged in parochial work, the flood of Irish vocations ensured that, within a couple of decades, a majority of parishes were being administered by Irish priests. Along with the Dominicans, the Irish diocesan colleges, particularly All Hallows, also sent priests to Trinidad and to the Caribbean generally.

The rigors of seminary life in Ireland, and then the loneliness and the hardships of Caribbean life took its toll on these young Irish diocesan clergy. For example All Hallows's records show that between 1843 and 1878 thirty-four Irish seminarians destined for Trinidad studied at the College. Of these six died or left before ordination and five more died within a year of arriving in the West Indies. The average life expectancy was indicated by the case of one Patrick Smith, ordained at the age of twenty-three and dying, as parish priest of Diego Martin, fourteen years later aged thirty-seven.

It is possible to make some sort of assessment of the lasting impact of all this heroic, adamantine dedication on Trinidad today, as it is of the Irish contribution elsewhere in the Caribbean. On the clerical side, one gets an indication of the Irish clout from the fact that of sixteen holders of the See of Port of Spain between 1828 and 1966, eight prelates were Irish. Where the laity were concerned, Irish educators enabled Caribbeans to move into the decision-taking echelons in great numbers, taking over from the old English and French élites. If one looks at the records of St Mary's – or indeed of the Cluny Nuns, Presentation Brothers, Holy Faith Sisters, or any of the Irish teaching orders for that matter – one can see at a glance why it is said, for example, that 58 per cent of Trinidad's doctors are Irish trained.

FINBAR

Speaking to Marion O'Callaghan and her husband Maurice, one soon realised how, along with the doctors, all those pictures of leading politicians, judges and administrators got into those annuals. Marion O'Callaghan, a Creole in her sixties, whose Irish ancestors were transported from Ireland by Cromwell, is a distinguished anthropologist, author and former Caribbean Director of UNESCO. Her father was Catholic, her mother Methodist. She carries an Irish passport and lives in a foliaged, shuttered, verandaed house, that could have come straight out of Enda Ferber's novel, *Saratoga Trunk*. She said of her delightful neighbourhood that it was a place for 'rising blacks and fallen wives'. Maurice, or Moss as Marion always referred to her husband, was an ex-Presentation Brother from Cork.

The Irish figure who made the greatest impact on their lives was 'Finbar, a Dominican Archbishop of Port of Spain, Finbar Ryan from Cork, who died in 1975. He occupied the same position of awe and exasperation in the eyes of his flock as did his famous Irish contemporary, the Archbishop of Dublin, John Charles McQuaid. Finbar's role in various Church controversies, his legendary strictness, his kindness and his energy were all retold as though he were still living and working in Port of Spain. One of Finbar's enduring legacies was the bringing to Trinidad of the Presentation Brothers; Moss was one of four whom he had brought out from Cork.

Having landed in blazing heat with no one to meet them, they discovered that their task, starting from scratch, was to rival and surpass the élite St Mary's. Finbar was still furthering the Church's policy of spreading its influence through the English language to as many souls as possible. 'It was very hard,' said Moss, 'we had to kill ourselves to bring them up to scholarship level from nothing.' However, by submitting themselves to a regime which was the contemporary Caribbean equivalent of slave labour, the Brothers achieved their goal. In six years their school was rivalling the St Mary's output of scholarship students. One of Moss's first students was a young Indian, Basedo Panday who, as we spoke, had just become Prime Minister of Trinidad. The leader of the opposition was also a former pupil of Moss's.

Finbar's influence enforced another breakthrough. From the outset the Brothers admitted black pupils to their classrooms, and the élite St Mary's was forced to do likewise, as were the exclusive girls' schools run by Irish nuns, the Sisters of Cluny, and the Holy Faith and Presentation converts. Marion remembered being the first black to stand on the stage of the Sisters of Cluny. In those days, in the late 1940s and early 1950s, miscegenation was considered immoral.

The dress code was as strict as the moral one. The girls were taught that: 'Our Lady would weep whenever a girl wore trousers.' Chaste girls were regarded as roses in Our Lady's garden, but an illegitimate child was a weed, not fit to be admitted to élite classrooms. Apart from the colour bar, this was practically the same cultural backdrop as would have been met with at that time in any convent school in Ireland – except that the history of Ireland was not taught. Marion learned that this was because 'the Irish would shoot each other'. Finbar was following the geo-political line laid down by his predecessors. Any republican tendency on the part of a teacher was stamped on instantly.

Mother Church grew by co-operating with the system, not by bucking it. St Patrick's Day was always a big occasion, but the big oil companies would not allow their Irish employees to sing revolutionary songs on that night. Today an indication of the Irish presence in Port of Spain may be gleaned from the fact that the St Patrick's Day dinner at the Hilton Hotel attracts an average of 400 diners, and one will inevitably find, as one does around the globe, individual Irish people in unexpected roles.

Dr Maura Imbert is a good example. She was born in Dublin and had the unusual distinction of founding the Trinidad and Tobago Astronomical Society. Because of her expertise in chemistry, Dr Imbert, an ethereal figure with a beautiful lilting voice that made me think of wind chimes, was chosen to meet Queen Elizabeth and Prince Philip when the royals visited the school she taught at in Guildford, Surrey. Unfortunately, as she was explaining an experiment to the Queen her apparatus malfunctioned. Suddenly the royal couple were enveloped in a cloud of choking, rotten-egg-smelling gas. This embarrassing incident was not however the reason Dr Maura came to Trinidad. She married a Trinidadian engineer, in the teeth of family opposition. An aunt of hers, the very model of prim respectability, had lived on Tobago in some comfort. However, it emerged after her marriage, to the horror of the family, that, as was frequently the case, a family friend had an 'outside family'. This dire prospect was held out for Maura also, but happily did not come to pass. She became a contented member of Port of Spain society, recognised both as an astronomer and a newspaper columnist.

Michael Camps, a doctor who lives mostly in St Lucia – a relatively short air trip away – where he specialises in the treatment of the sickle-cell disease, is a product both of the Irish Presentation Brothers and of the methods which were sometimes employed in fulfilling Finbar's targets. As a boy of twelve he was slow getting into 'the line' for roll call. He recalled: 'I remember the Brother coming towards me and I saw this right coming at me and that was it, I was unconscious.' Michael bears the Brother no malice for this muscular Irish Christianity. Later, when he was a boarder in the Presentation Brother's School in Bray, County Wicklow, he had an even more abrasive encounter with another member of the Irish diaspora – Tony O'Reilly. In a Leinster Schools Cup match, Michael, who is fit and wiry but slight and small sized, had to mark O'Reilly, who was fit and burly and large sized. O'Reilly's side won by a large margin and Camps ended up black and blue.

Neither experience of muscular Irish Christianity however dissuaded him from taking an Irish wife, Helen O'Malley Camps. Helen was to interact with another product of Irish education, the Nobel Laureate Derek Walcott, in one of the most significant experiments in Caribbean theatre history, the bringing of Carnival to the theatre. She used the images and characters of Carnival to tell stories or make political points on the stage.

CARNIVAL

To understand the importance of this departure one has to understand something of the importance of Carnival itself. Camps defines it thus:

Carnival touches the corelife/creative energy of a person. It fosters freedom, release and artistic expression in the body, voice, imagination and emotions, rooting everything in the physical. In Carnival a person is allowed to show off, to take centre stage and proclaim: 'I am here, look at me!' Carnival allows for the expression of the dark underside of a person – the part we like to pretend does not exist. By removing – through ritual – that which impedes our energy and creative fullness we can experience complete surrender to, and absorption in, a living process. Carnival is about inclusiveness and creative problem-solving.[34]

At its base, though not in appearance, Carnival's origins are similar to those of old Irish traditions which O'Malley Camps was aware of. These survive in Ireland today, but only in remote areas like the Aran Islands 'on Pookie night' – Hallowe'en. Pookie Night is evolving today, albeit on an infinitesimal scale, in the same manner as has Carnival, in the sense that it too involves using ever more lavish use of costume. Pookie night also traditionally involved the use of masks and devils, representing hidden emotions and unclean spirits. The Irish devils, like the Trinidadian ones, had a nasty habit of throwing stones at people, or lashing at them with whips. The Irish and Caribbean pookies or 'jab jabs' venture out at different times of the calendar: the Irish around All Souls Night and the coming of winter; the Trinidadians in spring, and at the approach of Lent, though fasting and mortification of the flesh are very far from the essence of Carnival.

Today's lush expression, in Caribbean terms, of the conflict between the sublime and the devilish, provides one of the fleshiest, most sumptuous spectacles on the globe. People go into training for months so as to be fit for the several days of the festival which now, because of sponsorship and tourism revenue, takes many forms. Some don beautiful costumes, but the devils, the 'jab jabs', smear their near-naked bodies with a coca solution, wear masks and carry rubber tridents. The hazard in dancing with some beautiful female 'jab jab' comes not from the tridents but from the coca dye. Then there is the extraordinary, all-night procession of the steel bands. The sound of this uniquely Caribbean musical form is literally amplified a hundred-fold by the fantastic sound systems mounted on the lorries which carry the bands through the streets, pushed, not driven, by the supporters of the various groups. The noise is so terrific that one can feel the sound reverberating in one's ribcage as the bands pass. The dancing in the wake of the trucks, and sometimes on them, is as erotic as it is energetic. At Carnival time anyone can dance or 'jump up' with anyone one chooses – the basis of a 'jump up' would appear to consist of having the female partner stand in front of the male with her buttocks pressed firmly against his genitalia while both dancers wave their hands in the air to the accompaniment of much pelvic undulation. The dancers also undulate against each other frontally in a manner which gives new life to the expression 'dirty dancing'. A former Trinidadian disc jockey, with a nostalgic glint in his eye, told me of one Carnival session in which he only realised that the dye on his blue jeans had run after uproar had broken out over the discovery that the entire membership of a white-trousered, all-girl, dancing troupe had somehow acquired large blue stains on their crotches.

Judging Day, when the participants in the Carnival parade before the judges in their finery, is one of the most spectacular human pageants on earth. Apart from the costumes which are of every hue in the rainbow, the parade embodies almost every epoch and race in man's history. There are Romans, Vikings, Indian and African warriors, Venetians and astronauts. The contestants include huge half-naked Africans, followed by binkinied, blonde Scandinavians, swarthy Indians in magnificent gold costumes from Indian mythology and Trinidadians descended from most races under the sun in blue, yellow, green and white marionette outfits. The beat, the heat and the booze also add a new dimension to the term 'Carnival atmosphere'. The coming of sponsorship and television has, however, put an end to the old Carnival riots which were reminiscent of the faction fighting which once occurred at Irish fairs.

While the parades attract some of the most fantastical costuming, and some of the most beautiful men and women in the world, from the four corners of the globe, there is still a serious heart to the display, the singing and the dancing. The calypso song form has traditionally been a vehicle for political comment, and the winning calypso at the Carnival I attended mirrored the political tensions of the moment. These centred on the fact that Basedo Panjay's Indian-controlled administration had just won power for the first time from the Africans.

The winning calypso, sung by the leading calypsonian Cro Cro, an African, was called 'The Boat' and dealt with the terrible boat trip which the slaves endured en route to the Caribbean. The papers and television were filled with controversy about Cro Cro's calypso and its racial implication. Happily however, the tensions were dissipated in a manner foreshadowed skilfully by a spectacular, and very Trinidadian Carnival tableau which I was lucky enough to witness. Night had fallen on an open-air 'jump up', which had been accompanied by much drinking and feasting on a variety of Caribbean dishes. As the moon rose the electric lighting dimmed, and suddenly the park was illuminated by the smoky glare from the same sort of lamp once used to illuminate the slave compounds. Traditional Indian Tasa drums were heard and then there appeared a group of brightly costumed African and Indian children, swaying on top of huge stilts. As they moved through the crowd to the accompaniment of both Tasa and calypso music there was a tremendous, spontaneous outpouring of applause. Point taken, it said, both cultures are of value and can co-exist.

THE CARNIVAL AND THE THEATRE

In the same spirit, for the first time in Caribbean theatrical history, Helen O'Malley Camps distilled the lush, conflicting themes of Carnival to the stage – but she used the Jabs Jabs, the Midnight Robber and other Carnival characters such as Pierrot Grenade, to make political points. She tackled themes like nuclear war and social injustice. This made her a highly controversial figure in conservative circles, and one of her productions, *King Jab Jab*, is credited with helping to bring down the government of the day.

She joined Walcott's Trinidad Workshop in 1967. Thus, though Irish, she was wholly trained in the Caribbean ethos. She created the role of Isabella, Duchess of Naples in Walcott's *Joker of Saville* and then set up the influential Little Carib Theatre where she produced the première productions of both Walcott's *Pantomine* and *Remembrance*. She also introduced the poets Joseph Brodsky and Mark Strahan to the Trinidadian public. In 1982 she founded the Tent Theatre company, using the satire and ritual of Carnival to bring theatre to the streets, schools and shopping malls: 'Where the people are, the same as Carnival itself,' she explains. Though now defunct, the theatre for a time was so successful that the company was invited to tour London, Berlin, Milan and Rome. During the late 1980s she turned her attention to psychotherapy, studying with distinction at Trinity College Dublin (in 1995 she won the Robert King Memorial Prize for the best dissertation), and is now engaged in using the techniques of theatre and Carnival in psychotherapy.

MARRIAGE

Sadly, an area which will afford much scope for her efforts is in the area of Irish-Trinidadian marriage. The divorce rate is high – colour and class differences make for strains on marriages contracted in Ireland between student Trinidadians and working-class Irish girls. The Irish girls find it difficult to adjust to the position of women in Hindu households for example, and when they bring brown babies back to their parents in Ireland, difficulties can ensue.

ST LUCIA

If one picks up the Catholic Directory for the Caribbean area, one will find it dotted with the names of institutes either run or founded by the Irish, but at the time of writing, the influence of the Irish is fading as numbers decline. However, the effects of the careers of 'Moss O'Callaghan'-like figures lingers on. One of the most successful of the European banana companies is the Irish-based Fyffes. 'I find it much easier to deal with the Irish than I did with the British, they have no imperial hang-ups and they treat you as an equal,' I was told by Calixte George, a politician and a spokesman for the banana industry which, along with tourism, is St Lucia's mainstay. Whether it remains the mainstay depends on the outcome of the effects of the trade war which the Americans successfully conducted against the Caribbean producers of bananas. The Lome Convention, which gave the old colonial powers in the Caribbean access to the European market, was perceived by the Americans as

THE CARIBBEAN

giving the Caribbean advantage over the banana republics of South America
which they controlled, and the World Trade Organisation ruled in favour of
their view.

THE BROTHERS AND THE SISTERS

George's affection for the Irish predated America's exercise of the right to
make the world safe for the American banana. He had been taught by the Irish
Presentation Brothers on St Lucia, for whom he had unstinted praise:
'Whatever I am they made me. They gave me my education. They are like my
family. They come to our birthdays, our weddings, our feasts.'

By way of illustrating his affection for the Brothers, he had brought with
him one of his most prized possessions – a photograph showing the pupils of
his school in which five white-robed Irish Brothers peered out from a sea of
black faces. By the time George showed me the picture most of the Brothers
had died, but a large number of the black faces were now middle-aged and
involved in the power structure of the island and its neighbours. Figures like
St Lucia's two Nobel Laureates, Sir Arthur Lewis (Economics) and Derek
Walcott (Literature), once peered out of such photographs. The Irish
influence on Walcott, apart from whatever the Presentation Brothers
conveyed, was a literary one. He is a friend of the Irish Nobel laureate, Seamus
Heaney and it is possible to see resonances of both Joyce and Synge in his
work. Like Joyce, Walcott resists the thrall of history while at the same time
trying to give new life to a bygone era, writing about a provincialism rather
than the industrialised landscape of modern society. Having declared a
ringing '*Non Serviam*' both Joyce and Walcott promptly burrow back through
the origins of their race. Just as Joyce sought to create a consciousness of what
the Irish were not conscious of, Walcott speaks of making 'an electric fusion
of the old and the new'.[35] Like Joyce, he talks of his people having 'awaited a
language', as he struggles to articulate what it is to make sense of 'the
contradiction of being white in mind, and black in body'. Joyce, for his part,
spurned the land from which he departed, but in reality never left, saying that
Ireland was his first and only love although Christ and Caesar were hand in
glove. Like Synge in *Riders of the Sea*, Walcott, in *Sea at Dauphin*, a work
which clearly shows the influence of Synge, highlights the hopeless struggle of
fishermen trying to live from the sea. Though Walcott's hero in *Dauphin* is
defiant, unlike the mother in the Synge play, who, looking at the last member
of her drowned family, exclaims 'the sea can do no more to me,' the spirit of
Dauphin echoes that ringing through Synge's rumbustious *Playboy of the
Western World*. The St Lucian equivalent of 'Moss' O'Callagan was Brother
de Lellis O'Sullivan. He was in his mid sixties – with a brother who is Garda
Superintendent in charge of my own district of Dalkey – and had the same
broad Cork accent he had when he first arrived on a banana boat in his clerical
black outfit almost half a century previously. He took me to see the Brothers'
huge thriving school overlooking Castries. Now locally administered, a mere

handful of Brothers walk the spacious corridors of the once populous living area. There were only two young Brothers, over from Cork and Boston, but the older men seemed just as cheerful and lively as they. Brother O'Sullivan showed me his garden where he relaxed: 'The garden helped me to keep going, after a day in the classroom. Coming towards the end of the afternoon, it was all I could do to keep awake.' I found the vignette of that sturdy little Corkman stoically working away in his lonely garden one of the more affecting images of the West Indies. There was a more obvious sense of decline when I visited the Convent of St Joseph of Cluny. This was actually brighter and better kept than the Brothers' establishment, but the parlour was a microcosm of the problem of vocation patterns worldwide. Many of the Sisters were in their late seventies and eighties. The youngest Irish Sister was fifty-eight. However, I was assured that young Caribbean women are joining the Order. Some of the Sisters went back to the days when leaving Ireland meant leaving for good. One nun had her first holiday after forty years. She found it painful: the only relative left in her family home had been a grand-nephew. Over the years, the holiday periods had come down first to every twelve years, then to ten, then to its present level of every three years. One of the sisters, Annunciata O'Sullivan, was a niece of Kitty Kiernan, Michael Collins's fiancée whom he did not live to marry.

Like the Brothers, the Sisters made an impact on St Lucian society and, as in America, proved to be a force for the emancipation of women. Until the 1950s, it was assumed that education was largely for boys and the island scholarships were for boys only. However, the nuns began preparing girls for scholarships for Oxford and Cambridge, and from 1954 there has been a steady alteration so that the girls now dominate in the scholarship stakes. The nuns talked to me with pride of former pupils like Dame Eugenia Charles, a former Prime Minister of Dominique, and Susie D'Aubergne, who before becoming the wife of the Prime Minister of St Lucia had been the island's only woman judge. As with the brothers, the nuns were able to take me on a Caribbean *tour de l'horizon* of achievement amongst former pupils. At one name there was a general expression of sadness and a shaking of heads: 'Poor Jackie, she was no Marxist.' They were talking about Jacqueline Bishop, the wife of the former ruler of Grenada. He was overthrown and murdered along with his wife during the American invasion of the island.

BUMPING INTO THE IRISH

St Lucia has the highest fertility rate in the Caribbean, and one of the highest unemployment rates, almost 17 per cent. Of its largely African and Roman Catholic population, 41 per cent fall into the 15 to 19-year-old bracket. Drugs are an increasing scourge. These facts would not lead one to expect much in the way of entrepreneurship, particularly Irish enterpreneurship, and yet I seemed to bump into Irish people wherever I went.

When I went to book a boat trip, I found that the catamaran service was owned by an Irishman, Mike Greene, whose parents once farmed in County Wicklow. A colourful character, the 41-year-old Greene was training for the Olympics in a Laser – the bucking bronco of small yachts – when I met him. Even though he has a pronounced English accent (he grew up in England), everyone knows him as an Irishman and he retains his Irish passport.

The manager of the newest hotel in Castries turned out to be another Irishman, John Parles – who had gone to school with me, and was born only a few hundred yards from where I live. In fact one of the largest hotel projects is the rebuilding of the famous Sandy Lane Hotel in Barbados. An Irish consortium including Dermot Desmond and J. P. Macmanus (owner of Istabrak, the Cheltenham hero) is investing millions on this. The owner of the best restaurant on the island was Mick Ashwort, 'happily divorced' and living with a St Lucian by whom he had little brown Eamonn. Ashwort looks like a burly version of Anthony Quinn. His father was a North of England Methodist, his mother a Wexford Catholic, and he was born in Belfast. He had a classical Irish combination of attraction/revulsion for his native race and place. He goes back to Ireland regularly and is delighted with its prosperity, but despaired of a solution being found to the Northern Ireland problem: 'There's too many hard heads on both sides, Catholic and Protestant. I'm a humanist. I think the phrase "thinking clergy" is an oxymoron.'

On the morning that I met Ashwort I thought for a moment that my own preoccupation with the Northern Ireland problem had brought on a hallucinatory condition like that of the hero of Evelyn Waugh's *The Ordeal of Gilbert Pinfold*. At six o'clock I had been drinking coffee and enjoying the sunbeams dancing on the water at the bottom of the Camps's lagoon-side garden, when I suddenly began to hear North of Ireland men's voices heatedly arguing about arms decommissioning. The shock made me spill my coffee. Then, through the French windows behind me, Michael Camps appeared and announced: 'I've just managed to get the BBC World Service for you.' And there on a Caribbean morn were Martin McGuinness of Sinn Fein and Ken Maginnis of the Unionist Party slugging it out. If I never did so before, I understood then how Joyce could never leave Ireland behind him.

JAMAICA

After Cuba, Jamaica is the most populated island in the Caribbean. With approximately the same land mass as Trinidad – roughly 4,500 square kilometres – it holds twice the population, about 2.5 million, of whom only some 95,000 are Roman Catholic. The bulk of the population is of African descent, with some pockets of Chinese, Indians and Syrians. The white population is less than one per cent. Is it not, therefore, one would think, a likely site to find traces of Irish influence. Yet, if one consults the Jamaican phone book, one will find several Murphys, Moores, O'Connors, O'Briens,

Burkes and O'Garros. The possessors of these very Irish names, like those on Montserrat, are almost invariably black. Most of the names owe their origins to the heyday of transportation, the British army and to emigrant schemes aimed at getting 'surplus' Irish out of Ireland.

IRISH ORIGINS

After the British captured the island from the Spanish in 1655, Cromwell saw an additional merit to the strategic and economic values of Jamaica – it 'now indeed served him as another Siberia' for disposing of unwanted Irish.[36] The ensuing centuries of raiding and trading brought more Irish to the West Indies, some in the service of the Church, but most in either the British army or navy, then, in the 1840s, Whitehall came up with an Irish emigrant scheme which was denounced by Daniel O'Connell as: 'a new wrong inflicted by the Saxon on the long-suffering Irish race'. Despite this denunciation, the scheme went ahead and on 7 March 1841: 'The first group of Irish emigrants arrived in Kingston, after a seven-week voyage on the SS *Robert Kerr*.'[37] The *Kingston Gleaner* noted that the emigrants landed in Kingston wearing their best clothes and temperance medals. They were taken to an immigration depot for processing, ultimately to blend unnoticed into the pages of Jamaican history – and pigmentation.

From 1855 to the time of writing, the Jesuits have controlled the Archdiocese of Kingston. Amongst them were several Irish Americans – including the Reverend Thomas Addis Emmet, a descendant of the executed Irish patriot, Robert Emmet – and one finds references to notable contributions by them to Jamaican welfare, in the Jesuits' archives in St George's College in Kingston. For example, there is Admiral Davis's thanks for their work during the Jamaica earthquake of 1907, or a reference by the great Jamaican radical poet, Claude McKay, to the Irish. McKay wrote in 1921, as the Black and Tan War was reaching its peak: 'I suffer with the Irish. I think I understand the Irish. My belonging to a subject race entitles me to some understanding of them.'[38]

It's fair to say that a reciprocal 'understanding' makes the way of the Irish in Jamaica, as in all the West Indies, a generally easy and welcoming one. Despite Jamaica's fearsome reputation for violence – an average year's violent deaths in the 1980s was around the 750 mark, more than the worst year of the North of Ireland troubles – the friendliness in the average bar is immediately apparent, particularly in rural Jamaica. The easy atmosphere, and the poverty, are redolent of the Ireland of a few decades ago.

However, Irish links have to be sought after, rather than become readily apparent. Symbolically, Tom Redcam Street, one of Kingston's principal thoroughfares, is named after an Irish campaigner against colonialism, Tom MacDermot – Redcam being a sort of backwards spelling of MacDermot. However, if one mentions Ireland to the average Jamaican male, the response is likely to be: 'Irish! Guinness, very good for the bamboo!'

WHAT OF THE FUTURE?

There is a saying in Jamaica that the reason that the hummingbird is Jamaica's national emblem is because it, like the Jamaican male, partakes of the nectar and then flits away. In colonial days, slaves were prohibited from having children and a reaction throughout the Caribbean has been for men to scatter their seed as widely as possible, in a sort of macho overcompensation for what was once denied. I got an insight into the hummingbird syndrome when I visited Father McLoughlin at St George's Jesuit College in Kingston. He was caring for one of the results of the scattering, a beautiful little three-year-old who looked like a hummingbird herself: 'It's the old story,' Father McLoughlin sighed, 'Babies having babies.' The child's mother was seventeen. She might have had two other children. But at least life was continuing, and so, one would add, was the caring tradition of Father McLoughlin and those like him at St George's, but the once thronged corridors of St George's were empty and room after room where classes were once held lay idle, gathering dust. Scholarly volumes in the library told of the origins of the Church in Jamaica. But what did the future hold for the Irish?

As with the Church anywhere in the world, there will always be a special niche of 'the good' Irish priest or nun. The legendary Father Bobby Gilmore had moved to Jamaica, via New York, and was ministering to the poor when I visited the island. Overall however, the Irish presence in Jamaica and the Caribbean in coming years is likely to be the sort of people I sat down to dinner with at a wonderful open-air Italian restaurant, as the sun went down over Kingston harbour: Denis McClean, a former *Irish Press* journalist, now the regional director of the Caribbean Red Cross; Peadar O'Sullivan, an engineer specialising in water technology, on secondment from Dublin Corporation to a Lome project which was building a huge reservoir in Ocho Rios; Rob Mullally an executive with the Jamaican Corporation; and Anthony Murphy a quantity surveyor. They, and their wives like the Jamaican people and they made a worthwhile contribution, but they would be moving on. The days of service either of the indentured variety, or in the ranks of the two colonialisms were over.

NINE

LATIN AMERICA

'It was a ghastly sight,' said Father O'Neill.[1] 'Blood splashed everywhere. The carpet was saturated. Seventy-three bullets were found. They were shot in the back, with silenced weapons, apparently kneeling. They were all identified first, because their personal documents were found on a table. The killers came in two cars. They waited outside for two hours, seemingly waiting for members of the Pallotine community to turn up. The death toll might have been higher but one was in Columbia, two on retreat and another was visiting his family.'

THE GHASTLY INCIDENT DESCRIBED ABOVE, to which we shall return, in a way epitomises the destiny of many of the Irish who came to Latin America. It was their karma to serve the conflicting claims of the Cross and the armed forces.

THE FIRST ARRIVALS

As indicated already, Irish monks may have been the first Europeans to come to the Americas. There have even been suggestions that St Brendan, who set off from Kerry, may have been the prototype for the Mexican god, Quetzalcoatl, because the deity is described as being tall, fair-skinned and bearded. However, it can be said with some certainty that the Irish came to Latin America principally in three ways: via the armed services of England and Spain – the fact that Britain and Spain were the two major opposing colonial powers in the region meant that Irishmen in South America, as in the North, were frequently to be found fighting on opposite sides – as missionaries or – mainly in the case of Argentina – as emigrants.

The first authenticated Irish arrivals were those of the Farrel brothers in Argentina in 1510. That they landed with the Pedro de Mendoza expeditionary force to the River Plate is recorded, but little else.[2] The first Irishman to leave an imprint on the continent was the Limerick Jesuit, Thomas Field, who landed in Brazil on New Year's Eve 1597. He moved to Paraguay some ten years later, surviving a brush with English pirates in the River Plate estuary: the pirates towed his vessel out to sea with only five barrels of water aboard. However, Field subsequently made it safely to Asunción with two other Jesuits from Portugal and Italy and the three set up a province of the Society which embraced modern Paraguay, Uruguay, most of Argentina and Bolivia.

It was Field who largely influenced the setting up of the Jesuit 'reductions' amongst the Guarani people. These missionary villages acquired an international fame recently through being featured in the film *The Mission*. For a time the settlements were safe havens for the Guarani against the depredations of Spanish and Portuguese slave traders. Although, as shown in the film, the villages were ultimately destroyed, the fact that remnants of Guarani culture still survive is attributed to the Jesuits. In the footsteps of Field, who is credited with being the first Irishman to say mass in the Americas, there followed, over the years, a number of other Irish Jesuits and religious people – and some not so religious.

IRISH SETTLEMENT

The first Irish settlement in Latin America is thought to have been along the Amazon, set up by the Anglo-Irish tobacco trader Philip Purcell in 1612. Purcell and a colourful character who followed him in 1620, Bernard O'Brien, appeared to have established good relationships with the Indians: the Irish defended their Amazonian holdings by assisting the Indians against the Portuguese. O'Brien may have had other methods. In his journal he writes of:

> A country where they saw no men but many women . . . 'Amazons'. These have very small right breasts like men, [treated] so that they do not grow, in order to shoot arrows, and the left breasts are as large as other women's. They armed [*sic*] like the Indians. Their Queen is called Cuna Muchu, which means great woman or lady.[3]

O'Brien's journal goes on to describe how he dressed the great woman in a: 'Dutch Linen Shirt, of which she was very proud', and at the end of a week, when he took his leave promising to return, 'she and her subjects signified that they were grieved by his departure'. However, the Portuguese had been grieved by the Irish arrivals, and in 1625 massacred an Irish and Dutch force at Mandiutuba, killing Phillip Purcell. News of Irish settlement in the region becomes uncertain for some centuries thereafter and Irish interest tended for a time to focus on the West Indies, particularly on the island of Montserrat.

THE O'HIGGINS INFLUENCE

Then a remarkable Irishman appeared on the scene, Ambrosio O'Higgins. O'Higgins was born in Sligo in 1721 and worked as an errand boy for Lady Bective in Dangan Castle in County Meath. His break came when an uncle sent him to Cadiz in Spain and he went on to become Spain's most important functionary in South America, the Viceroy of Peru. He is remembered as being a beacon light of liberalism in an encircling sea of tyranny and slavery. He abolished the 'encomienda' system whereby land and its people were handed over to Spanish adventurers to be ruthlessly exploited for their new owners' benefit. Instead he substituted 'inquilino' whereby free land and seed were given to a labourer to work as best he could.

O'Higgins died in 1801 and his death resulted in the return to Peru from England of his illegitimate son, Bernardo O'Higgins, to claim his estate. Bernardo demonstrated that he had inherited some of his father's philosophy of life by becoming the liberator of Chile. However, he encountered severe criticism for his authoritarian methods and had to flee to Peru, where he fought with Bolívar. Nevertheless, he is still so well thought of that in 1996 the Chilean Government presented the Irish people with a bust of Bernardo which stands in Dublin's Merrion Square.

FIGHTING FOR BOLÍVAR

It was Simón Bolívar who acted as the greatest magnet for Irish soldiers. He appealed for British volunteers for his campaigns in Venezuela and Columbia and the majority of those who responded were Irish, now jobless as a result of the ending of the Napoleonic Wars. These soldiers fought under an Irish commander, Arthur Sandez, from County Kerry.

In the Venezuelan War of Independence, they acquired a better reputation than another contingent which fought for Bolívar under John Devereux. These troops arrived in Latin America between September 1819 and May 1820, but no arrangements appeared to have been made for them with regard to food and pay. Moreover, many of them were killed in an attack at Rio Hacha, which led to widespread mutinies. The troops were subsequently shipped home via Jamaica, Bolívar commenting that he was 'pleased to be rid of these vile mercenaries who would do no killing until they had been paid for it'. This appears to have been an unduly harsh judgement on Devereux's troops because, at one stage at least, they contained a sufficient quotient of idealism to encourage the enlistment of Morgan O'Connell, a son of the Irish liberator, Daniel O'Connell.

The Irish also served with distinction in the Anglo-Irish legion and took part in the famous march across the Andes in 1819, and in several other battles crucial to Bolívar's success, notably that of Carabobo, in which an Irish legion of 350 men suffered over 150 casualties. The Irish fought so bravely that all the survivors were awarded the Order of the Liberator and the legion was renamed the Carabobo Battalion and still exists as a unit of the Venezuelan Army.

Bolívar favoured Irish aides de camp, correctly reckoning that they would prove both loyal and courageous. One of them, William Ferguson, was killed saving the Liberator from an assassin in Bogota in 1828, but the most famous aide was Daniel Florence O'Leary who was born in Cork in 1800, took part in the Andes march and acted as one of Bolívar's principal diplomats. He negotiated a truce with the Spanish in 1820 and attempted unsuccessfully to unite Peru, Bolivia and Grand Colombia (Venezuela, Colombia and Equador). O'Leary travelled to London, Paris and Madrid seeking diplomatic recognition for Venezuela, and was so well thought of by the British that they appointed him chargé d'affaires in Bogota. His writings on the Independence Wars are still studied in Latin America and one of Caracas's principal squares is called after him. Venezuela has also erected a plaque to his memory at his Cork birthplace.

THE MARITIME IRISH

The Irish played a particularly prominent role in Latin American maritime history. The outstanding figure is that of William Brown, the Mayo man who founded the Argentinian Navy; and the navy of Argentina's great rival, Brazil, also owes much to descendants of the Wild Geese like Diago Keating, his son, also Diago, Jorge Cowan and Diago O'Grady. They had been officers in the Portuguese Navy but sailed for Brazil with the Portuguese royal family when the king sought refuge there in 1808.

The Equadorian, Uruguayan and Chilean navies were also founded by Irishmen: by Thomas Wright of Drogheda, and of Uruguay by Peter Campbell from Tipperary. Wright's victory at the Battle of Callao was said to have made him 'the Architect of the final overthrow of Spanish power in South America.'[4] George O'Brien founded the Chilean Navy at the behest of Bernardo O'Higgins and died in a sea battle in which his force captured a number of Spanish vessels. As with O'Higgins, his reputation endures in modern Chile and ships are still named after him.

THE LYNCHES

A Chilean Irish naval hero with a more ambiguous reputation is Patricio Lynch. A technical genius who served in the British Navy in both the Opium War and the War of the Pacific, he is said to have pioneered concepts of naval warfare which were not fully developed until the Second World War. However, while military governor of Lima in 1880, he was guilty of several atrocities against the Peruvians. To the credit of the Irish, however, his conduct was denounced by another prominent Chilean-Irishman, the writer and politician Benjamin McKenna. Nevertheless, Lynch was rewarded for his prowess in taking Lima by being given Chile's top diplomatic post, Ambassador to Spain. There was another famous – or infamous – bearer of the name of Lynch. This was Elisa Alicia Lynch. She was born in Ireland, and at the age of fifteen, in the year 1850, she married a French army doctor whom she deserted three years later. Despite, or perhaps because of, subsequently acquiring a lurid reputation in Paris, she was introduced to Francisco Lopez, the heir to the dictator of Paraguay. Lopez took her with him to Asunción, where she bore him five children, and when he succeeded his father as President, in 1862, he defied the gossips and appointed his mistress as first lady. The couple enjoyed eight years of power, wealth and happiness. She was at the dictator's side during the war of the Triple Alliance (1865–70) and is credited with exerting a significant influence. However, she was also present when he was killed in 1870. She buried him with their eldest son and was deported at the end of the war, dying, poverty stricken and forgotten, in Jerusalem in 1886.

The most famous Lynch in Latin American history, however, is a man who discarded the name – Ernesto Guevara Lynch became simply Che Guevara. The Cuban revolutionary's ancestors were Irish emigrants to Argentina where they formed 'an important family of merchants in the middle of the 18th Century'.[5]

CUBA

Cuba had a fascination for Irish revolutionaries long before Guevara's time. The fact of its being an island, fighting for independence in the lee of a powerful colonial neighbour, had resonances for the Irish. This fascination is reciprocated in Cuba. Irish diplomats have confirmed to me that in private Fidel Castro has frequently been known to display admiration for Ireland's struggle for independence.

One of the classic accounts of the Cuban struggle was written by an Irish Fenian, J. J. O'Kelly, who had seen service with the French Foreign Legion in Algiers and Mexico, and became a correspondent for the *New York Herald*. In this capacity, in 1873, he managed to smuggle himself into an area of Cuba under the control of the famous Cuban General Carlos de Cespedes, much to the horror of the Spanish. When he recrossed the frontier between Cuban and Spanish-held territory he was sent to prison and there were fears that he was about to be executed. His case became a *cause célèbre* both in Cuba and the United States where sympathisers raised his plight with the White House. A temporary Republican take-over in Spain appears to have saved his life and he was shipped to a Madrid prison from which he was subsequently released. He made his way to Gibraltar and then back to America. Here, in 1874, he issued his *Herald* articles in book form: *The Mambi-Land, or Adventures of a Herald Correspondent in Cuba*.

'Mambi' was the term the insurgents applied to themselves. It comes from an African dialect and can mean either 'bandit' or 'rebel'. (There may be other, less obvious manifestations of Cuban appreciation of the 'rebel' connotations of 'Mambi'. I have heard it rumoured that wanted IRA men have found a safe haven in Cuba during the recent North of Ireland troubles.) The book had an enormous and continuous success when translated into Spanish. On the centenary of the war which O'Kelly had covered, Fidel Castro sanctioned the publication of a new edition of *Mambi*, containing an in-depth profile of the author. O'Kelly ultimately returned to Ireland where he became a member of the Irish Parliamentary Party, and a Parnellite. He died, appropriately enough, in a revolutionary year, 1916.

O'Kelly was luckier than another Irish supporter of the Cuban cause, his contemporary, Charles Ryan, who had Fenian sympathies. However, while on a Washington business visit, a chance meeting with a Cuban, General Goicouria, led him to take up arms for the Cubans rather than the Fenians. After a year on active service he had impressed the Cubans sufficiently to be sent back to Washington to recruit other volunteers. Unfortunately, he had also made a marked impression on the Spanish. They captured him before he could cross back into Cuban-held territory and he was executed in 1873, despite protests on his behalf organised in New York by Clan na nGael.

To this day Irish interest in Cuba continues, via sporting encounters (principally in boxing), through tourism and, where possible, in cautious but noticeable diplomatic support. Irish foreign policy has been to censure human rights abuses in Latin America generally, rather than to line up behind selective US condemnations of Cuban behaviour. In 1988 Ireland refused to support just such a US-sponsored United Nations resolution directed at Cuba, and, as this book was being written, at a time when Dublin was seeking and getting maximum support for the Irish Peace Process from the Clinton White House, Ireland refused to back the US in its sanctions policy against Havana. In 2000, Ireland and Cuba exchanged ambassadors on a non-residential basis.

COURAGEOUS STANDS

A good deal of the Irish interest in human rights issues in Latin America stems from the influence of, and the information provided by, the Irish missionaries and NGOs. The sort of repression and injustice which they lobbied against will be dealt with in more detail in the Argentinian context; suffice it to say here that as a result of its caring tradition, Ireland took a number of courageous stands at the United Nations. In 1981 the acting Minister for Foreign Affairs, James Dooge, went against the Washington line by declaring Irish support for a Franco-Mexican declaration in favour of Salvador's opposition party the FDR-FMLN. The following year, Noel Dorr, then Ireland's Ambassador to the UN, attempted, against Washington's wishes, to broker a deal between Nicaragua – which at the time was threatened with invasion by the US – and the Americans, who wanted the matter dealt with, not by the UN, but by its puppet the Organisation of American States. In a notable speech Dorr criticised the 'unjust and repressive Somoza regime', which of course America had supported. Dorr pointed out that:

> Small nations, whose real need is peace and development, have been torn apart in civil strife as the violence built into unjust social structures over many generations, takes a more open form, once these structures are challenged. Ruling elites react repressively in face of threats to their position and seek to maintain themselves against militant expressions of popular discontent. Death and injury have become commonplace, and almost casual – not to say banal . . .[6]

The most remarkable demonstration of the diaspora's power to influence

Irish domestic policy occurred during President Reagan's visit to Ireland in 1984. Irish opinion, particularly Irish American opinion, was startled to see TV pictures of an American flag being set on fire in Dublin. There were so many protests at Reagan's visit that his spin doctors felt it necessary for him to give an interview on RTE before the visit commenced. Reagan claimed that criticisms of his visit stemmed from a Red smear campaign orchestrated by the Cubans and the Russians. The Irish Catholic organisation, Trocaire, issued a statement refuting a long list of factual errors in the President's interview and the Catholic hierarchy boycotted the visit. When Reagan was given a state banquet in Dublin Castle, over 10,000 people encircled the castle in a candlelit protest. There were protests also when Galway University conferred an honorary doctorate on him and, most pointedly, during the demonstrations a group of four nuns carried a coffin bearing bouquets of flowers, each carrying the name of one of the four US religious women murdered by the military in El Salvador in 1980.

One of these women, Jean Donovan, had studied in Cork while on a break from the US. In Cork she had met one of the moving spirits behind the opening of a mission to Peru, Father Michael Crowley, and was so inspired that on her return to Cleveland she volunteered to go to El Salvador, with fatal results. Subsequent Irish and Latin American links have been strengthened by her memory. Each year since 1984 a Jean Donovan lecture has been given at Cork University by a visiting Latin American expert.

STRENGTHENING THE TIES

Dublin intends to strengthen Latin American ties. The pace of trade, tourism, and official visits is quickening; President MacAleese visited Mexico in 1999, and an Irish ambassador was appointed later in the year (Art Agnew was moved from Buenos Aires). Hitherto Ireland had been represented by one of the more colourful figures in the penumbra of Irish Consul Generalships, a product of the diaspora, Romulo O'Farill, who has extensive interests in television and the hotel business.

Ireland already has significant trade links with Mexico through large Irish corporations like the Kerry Group and the packaging giant, Smurfit. Irish tourism is also increasing. There is one Irish link which has become somewhat attenuated, however. The introduction of divorce to Ireland in 1997 has affected the custom whereby the better-off flew to Acapulco to obtain a Mexican divorce and a sun tan, not necessarily in that order.

Divorce apart, the potential for an expansion of Irish trade, not only in Mexico but throughout Latin America generally, is enormous. Brazil is next on the list for an Irish Embassy. One was scheduled to have been opened along with that in Mexico, but the cost of appointing Consul Generals to Scotland and Wales, combined with the expense involved in moving the Irish Embassy from Bonn to Berlin, caused a delay.

Martyrs in Mexico

Ireland's most renowned contributions to Mexican history are martyrs. William Lambert from Wexford, known to the Mexicans as Guillermo de Lampart was a notable forerunner of the many Irish figures who, in our day, took a more liberal line than that espoused by the Church, and paid dearly for it. Lambert was burned by the Inquisition in the Zocalo, Mexico City's main square during the 1660s. Probably the most famous set of martyrs are commemorated on a marble plaque erected in the San Angel district of Mexico City. It reads: 'In memory of the Irish soldiers of the heroic San Patricio Battalion, martyrs who gave their lives for the cause of Mexico during the unjust American invasion of 1847.' The plaque was created in 1959 by the Mexican sculptor, Lorenzo Rafael, who has an Irish wife, Stephanie Counihan. She came from the same county, Galway, as did the leader of the San Patricios, John Riley, sometimes referred to as O'Reilly. The plaque commemorates one of the few occasions in which Irishmen fought against, rather than for, the American Government.

Their action occurred during the Mexican American War of 1846–8, one of the least popular wars in American history. Lincoln described it as a war of 'the sheerest deception...and unconstitutional'. The writer Thoreau went to prison for refusing to pay his taxes and for calling on 'all good men to rise up'. The actual *casus belli* was the long-standing land dispute between the North European, and largely Protestant-led, colonialists who had settled America from the north and north-east, and the Catholic and Spanish colonialists of South America. The latter held what are now New Mexico, Arizona, Nevada, California and parts of Colorado and Texas. In 1846, US President Polk brought the dispute to a head by sending an American army, under the command of General Zachery Taylor, into Texas in furtherance of manifest destiny.

The Irish in that army, like the Mexicans, were Catholic. How much they were motivated (if at all) by feelings of hostility to the concept of an unjust invasion by news of the Famine, then ravaging Ireland, is not known. However, their inclination to regard Mexico as a victim of aggression, as Ireland had been, would certainly have been heightened by nativist sentiment in the north, directed in general at the ever-increasing tide of European emigration, and at the Catholic Irish in particular. The era of the 'Know-Nothings' was dawning. At the same time, Mexican Catholic priests were exhorting the Irish to leave the army, pointing out that Mexico was, like Ireland, a Catholic country. A pamphlet issued by the Mexican Government offered the Irish a variety of inducements to follow the priests' advice, including land, money and free passage to Europe at war's end. The pamphlet went on:

> Could Mexicans imagine that the sons of Ireland, that noble land of the religious and the brave, would be seen amongst their enemies? Sons of Ireland, have you forgotten that in any Spanish country it is sufficient to claim Ireland as your home to meet a friendly reception

from authorities as well as citizens? Is religion no longer the strongest of all bonds?

Irishmen, you are expected to be just because you are the countrymen of that truly great and eloquent man O'Connell, who has devoted his whole life to defend your rights, and finally, because you are said to be good and sincere Catholics. Why, then do you rank among our wicked enemies?[7]

Riley and his comrades apparently agreed with these sentiments. As indicated in Chapter One, the treatment of the Irish by the Spanish was traditionally extraordinarily generous. In the months leading up to the war, Riley, a former West Point drill sergeant, and his comrades formed part of the approximately 25 per cent of the US Army who had been born in Ireland. He and Patrick Dalton from Ballina, County Mayo, who became his second in command, were stationed in Texas under General Taylor. Watching the preparations for war build up, Riley decided to take the advice of former President Quincy Adams who urged 'all officers to resign and all soldiers to desert'. He and a group of followers crossed the Rio Grande and enlisted in the Mexican Army. Here Riley was given the job of organising a detachment of foreign-born, ex-US soldiers into a special unit. In all, some 50 per cent of the American Army at the time were born outside America, but the bulk of those who joined Riley's outfit were Irish, hence the name San Patricios.

Riley's unit, which in all seems to have involved some 500 men, gained a reputation for bravery in several encounters with the American-led forces, and suffered heavy casualties in the process. Their last stand came at Churubusco, outside Mexico City. It was a familiar situation for Irish rebels at home. They knew they fought without the status of belligerents and in the shadow of the noose. Accordingly, before they were overwhelmed, they displayed a desperate courage, several times tearing down white flags which the Mexicans hoisted in token of surrender. The fighting lasted some three hours and only ended when the San Patricios' ammunition ran out. The two companies of San Patricios, some 102 men each, had lost 60 per cent of their number to either death or capture, and most of those who escaped were later hunted down and captured.

Of the eighty-five Patricios captured at Churubusco, seventy were sentenced to death by hanging. However, the American rage at what they considered deserters was balanced by a Mexican admiration for the Patricios' courage. There was a public plea for clemency and some twenty were reprieved by order of General Winfield Scott. These included John Riley. However, he, like the other Patricios who had joined the Mexicans before fighting began, was sentenced to be flogged and branded on the face with the letter D for deserter. In addition, the men were forced to wear an eight-pound, three-pronged iron collar for so long as the American Army remained in Mexico. Then their heads were shaved and they were drummed out of the army. The officer in charge of the court-martial was also called Riley, but he showed hostility rather than affinity towards his compatriot namesake, ordering him to be branded on both cheeks. Not surprisingly, John Riley later found it hard to obtain employment and is said to have become a bandido.

Sixteen of the condemned men were hanged at San Angel on 10 September 1847; four, the next day at the village of Mixcoac; and the remaining thirty, also at Mixcoac, two days later. The last hangings were particularly barbaric. The officer in charge of the executions decided that the men should not be done to death until they saw the American flag hoisted over Chapultepec Castle where the final battle of the war was in progress. Accordingly the officer, a Colonel William Harney, who was also apparently an Irishman, forced the condemned men to wait on the gallows in the hot sun with nooses around their necks, from daybreak until approximately 9.30 am when the flag was raised. It is said that the San Patricios greeted the hoisting of the flag with loud cheers which only ceased when the ropes tightened. The manner in which the sentence was carried out has been described as follows:

> they strung thick ropes with heavy knots at intervals, stretched horizontally above nooses hanging vertically at each knot . . . The prisoners were lined along the nooses which were attached at one end to each other. They whipped the horse that drew the carts away from beneath them . . . [8]

Harney's blood lust was such that he included in the executions a Francis O'Connor from Cork, who had lost both legs in the battle of Churubusco. Harney only became aware of O'Connor's absence when the sun rose and the prisoners were counted. He immediately rode to the tent where O'Connor lay dying and ordered that he be brought to the gallows to await the fatal flag raising along with his companions.

O'Connor's and his luckless companions' esteem shows from the wording on the plaque to their memory in San Angel. It includes the following: 'They were not deserters! They were loyal to themselves and to the dream of being free which brought them to America.' Apart from the annual commemoration at San Angel, interest in the San Patricios has grown throughout America in recent decades. A play by the writer-director Chris Mathews, which was received with critical acclaim when it was first staged at the Celtic Arts Center on Hollywood Boulevard, Los Angeles, in 1989, is also being made into a movie. Like many other Irishmen of their type the San Patricios are finding a vindication beyond the grave.

Mother Church has created one tie with Mexico which has been the subject of some controversy. This is the presence in Ireland of the Legionnaires of Christ, a secretive, élite Catholic religious order which operates mainly amongst the rich, and has considerable influence in Mexico. Vincente Fox, who was elected President in 2000 and who is of Irish descent, has sent four of his children to study with the Legionnaires in Ireland.

The Legion's stated philosophy is to convert the rich to God's laws so that they will behave with kindness to the poor. Somehow this notion has become so attractive to the Legion's wealthy backers that the kind of funding available to the Legion allowed it, for example, to buy a 264-acre site in Mount Pleasant, New York, in 1997, for some $40 million. The Legion was founded by Father Macial Degollado, a friend of Pope John Paul II, in Mexico in 1941. Members are required to take a vow never to speak ill of the Legion, its founders or its superiors, and to report anyone discovered breaking the rule.

The Legionnaires own a sizeable property in the wealthy Foxrock district of Dublin. When they sold some 20 acres of their holding in May 1998, the Legionnaires benefited to the tune of some £25 million. The Legionnaires' routine includes flagellation and extreme fasting. Seminarians letters are apparently opened, anything negative has to be rewritten. Radio and television are not permitted. Not surprisingly, Irish vocations to the Legion are dropping. But it appears to make up the shortfall with entrants from Third World countries with a military background.

CONCANNON'S WHITE WINE

Another Galway man, who landed in Mexico some decades after John Riley, fared better than did the leader of the unfortunate San Patricios. He was James Concannon, of Inis Maan, the middle of the three Aran Islands which lie at the mouth of Galway Bay. Concannon was eighteen when he left in 1865. He spoke no English, but came of a gifted clan, probably one of those who, in earlier times had been given the choice of being sent 'to hell or Connacht'. Though the Concannons lost their lands, they evidently held on to their intelligence. James's brother Thomas helped to revive the Irish language, becoming a national organiser of the Gaelic League, and to this day the Concannons are noted on Inis Maan for producing educators, religious and craft workers of unusual ability.

As this is being written, Rory Concannon is famous for his skill as a fisherman and is regarded as the best currach builder on the island. Although his children have all joined the diaspora, he and his wife Mairin chose to remain on Inis Maan rather than heed the urgings of his brothers to join them in the building trade in America where he would undoubtedly have become a rich man.

James Concannon did become a rich man, but not from the building industry. He worked for a time in Boston for the Singer Sewing Corporation and later became in turn a hotel manager and a book salesman. His business activities took him to Mexico where he became well thought of and persuaded President Diaz to award him a franchise to clean the streets of Mexico City. He subsequently sold this, at a large profit, to a German consortium and moved to the San Francisco area in 1883.

According to family history he had intended to invest in the building trade. To further this ambition Concannon, who was a devout Catholic, and recited the family's daily Rosary in Irish, was invited to dinner by his friend, Archbishop Joseph Alemany. The Archbishop outlined for him the Church's plans for a huge building programme, including churches, schools and hospitals to cope with the influx of Irish Catholics then flooding into the city. It is said that, in moving a set of architectural drawings produced by the Archbishop, Concannon accidentally knocked over a glass of red wine, staining the white linen tablecloth.

The Archbishop jokingly commented that the real fortune to be made awaited the man who could develop a white wine. This would save the nuns the labour of laundering not only table cloths, but shirts, vestments and altar cloths used in the saying of mass. The Archbishop's chance remark is said to have ignited the same spark of originality which had impelled Concannon to seek wealth in Mexico City, rather than the North American metropolises favoured by his fellow countrymen. What is certain is that he began studying viticulture at the University of California at Berkeley and made a tour of French vineyards. He was highly gratified to discover that, given the correct climatic conditions, vines grew well on poor, gravelly soil. In other words on cheap, gravelly soil, of which, like the favourable climatic conditions, there was a plentiful supply in Northern California, particularly in the Livermore district where he founded the Concannon Winery. A French wine-grower, whom he persuaded to emigrate to Livermore, helped him to develop the famous Concannon white wine.

His friendship with Archbishop Alemany again proved fruitful when the Archbishop replicated Concannon's experience with President Diaz and gave him another franchise, this time to supply the Archdiocese of San Francisco with white wine. It was this contract which enabled Concannon to survive throughout the Prohibition era which killed off so many other wine producers. Concannon's descendants sold the firm in 1980, but the quality of Concannon's wine remained such that four years later – just over a century since James had had his fateful dinner with Archbishop Alemany – when President Reagan visited Ireland he toasted the President of Ireland, Patrick Hillery, in Concannon's white wine.

ARGENTINA

Although the ambience of Newfoundland and – to a lesser degree – the Caribbean island of Montserrat will remind an Irishman of his homeland at every hand's turn, Argentina is the one place in the world where the Ireland-that-was could still be revisited in the year 1997. When English was spoken, particularly amongst the older age groups, the accents transported one back to Longford, Westmeath and Wexford. I found it uncannily like the Ireland of the 1960s.

On the one hand there were the passionate, committed comments of the younger generation: 'This is a very bad thing to say, but except maybe for the Germans, the Argentinians are one of the nastiest peoples in the world.' Or: 'The curse of Argentina is the Three Damnations – Colonialism, Catholicism and Capitalism.' On the other hand, I could see Ireland symbolised by pictures of Round Towers, wolfhounds, Padraig Pearse and Eamon de Valera, and by the sight of an Irish Christian Brother stepping on to a stage at prestigious Newman College in Buenos Aires to sing Clancy Brothers songs to a huge and rapturous audience. The first comment I quoted was from an Irishman in his thirties who, in a typically Irish contradictory fashion, does not shake from his feet the dust of a society he so stigmatises, but lives a life of opposites. He combines being an international businessman with being an activist in Irish clubs and charities, many of whose members are of a backwards-looking, inward character which he detests. The second comment comes from the respected Irish-Argentinian intellectual who has made a study of Irish writers' contribution to Argentinian literature. The differing strands of opinion represented by the foregoing are bound together by a shared, albeit differently perceived, Irish and Catholic heritage.

There is one simple test one can apply, which helps in evaluating the differing opinions encountered amongst the Irish community, and how these fit in with the traditional friendliness of the Argentinians towards foreigners, which has much to do with the fact that there is an Irish community in Argentina today. The test consists of the following: make a suitably crafted, sympathetic reference to Argentina's recent troubled past and the response will tell you whether you are in the company of a liberal or a conservative. The liberal will shake his, or her, head over 'the disappearances'. The conservative, displaying an equal horror, will recall the activities of 'the guerrillas'.

THE BELGRANO MASSACRE

It was the application of this simple guideline in conversation with members of that centrally important corps in Irish-Argentinian life, the Roman Catholic clergy, which led me to the scene of the bloody event I described at the beginning of this chapter. The Belgrano massacre in 1976 epitomises only too well the dichotomy between 'liberal' and 'conservative'. It helps to explain how Irish Churchmen, and women, became involved between the differing viewpoints towards the junta that governed Argentina in the terror-filled years of both the 'disappearances' and the 'guerrillas'.

I visited this pleasant scene of horror on a fine April Sunday morning.[9] Nothing in the outward appearance of either church or presbytery gave any clue as to what had happened. Belgrano is a classic leafy suburb, one of the richest areas of Argentina. Preceded by a surpliced server, a grave and contemplative priest from Dungannon in County Tyrone passed through the front entrance of the church to say mass. A beggar sat numbly before them, too befuddled from the night before even to beg. Elderly nuns, in greater numbers than one would have seen in Ireland, helped each other up the steps of the church. Smiling, friendly mass-goers directed us to the presbytery around the corner. Smiles greeted us at the door, the same door that one of the victims of the massacre had unsuspectingly opened for his killers.

614

The parlour where the murders took place could have been situated in any one of a hundred religious houses I have visited around the world: black leather seats; cheerful, ordinary, spotlessly clean; furnished with an eye to economy rather than style; piles of newspapers, a liquor cabinet, a TV in one corner. In another corner was a crucifix, and beside it the only indication of what happened, a plaque giving the names of the murdered men.

It is generally assumed that the navy did the actual killings and that the police covered up for them. What was the purpose of the murders? Some say it was in reprisal for a bomb explosion in a police canteen a little earlier. The death toll in that atrocity may have gone as high as forty persons. This theory is fuelled by the fact that after the priests' shooting a message was found written on one of the presbytery doors: 'For our comrades, victims of the bombing of the Federal Security building.' Another message read: 'For twisting and indoctrinating virgin minds.' Other people say it was a warning to the Church to shut up. Father Kevin O'Neill recalled how one of the murdered men, Father Kelly, would generate publicity whenever a priest was arrested.

There is, however, another theory – that the murders occurred because some of those killed were guerrillas. I had not been aware of this rumour and was surprised to be made aware of it by an Irish priest while I was attending a gathering arranged by the Irish Ambassador. In a very Irish fashion the priest appeared to know more about my itinerary than I did, and was able to tell me that I would be visiting Belgrano shortly. 'But,' he said, 'they won't tell you the full story. And the full story is still interfering with my efforts to preach the gospel.' Decoded this meant that he was a conservative, working amongst conservatives and that the suspicion that Belgrano could have been involved in guerrilla activities was still provoking rifts.

How deep these rifts were I realised a few days later when I was passed some documents containing background information of the killings. Though unsigned, their content makes it clear that they were compiled by a knowledgeable member, or members, of the Pallotine Order. One is a long account, replete with classical allusion, of the situation within the community leading up to the slayings. It says:

> Regardless of their activities or possible imprudent groupal involvement, in no way did they deserve such a fate ... The reputations of the Belgrano group must be preserved intact, but let us always be truthful because 'the Truth shall set you free'. Let us not ascribe fictitious attributes to them as it would be disloyal to bequeath a partisan version of events to future generations knowing that Rome may wish to examine the writings of virtuous Fr. Kelly [with a view to possible canonisation as a martyr]. In fact, the months preceding the sad event were submerged in acute sorrow and dire incompatibility ...[10]

The sorrow and incompatibility arose out of the larger forces playing about the community and manifested themselves in a variety of disputes. One was the question of whether the Pallotines should have been living in the community at all or whether they should have been living with the poor. On top of this dispute, there was fear in the community: fear of the police by some, fear of the guerrillas by others. There was controversy over the display of a portrait of Che Guevara in the house, and it was eventually taken down. Father Kelly was out of the presbytery earlier on the night of the murders. According to the writer he was on a mission to seek help in expelling: 'a member from the parochial house because he feared for his life at the hands of that member's friends'. The writer of the document calls this situation 'the ultimate Pallotine disgrace'. The divisions in the community ran deep. An Irish priest was asked, 'What brought you here?' and told, 'Stay in your own country.' The document alleges that the divisions were so deep that after the Fiat chief, Dr Sallustro, was murdered a 'reliable eyewitness' said that:

> The reaction of one of the priests killed in the Belgrano massacre, in the presence of his seminarians was, 'Well done! There are more like him who deserve the same.'[11]

The document goes on to say that one of the victims of the massacre, a postulant, was 'an active member of the Montoneros' whose *nom de guerre* was 'Alberto' and concludes that the deaths occurred: 'because of the guerrilla activities of one of the victims which were being conducted from the presbytery'.

One of the most senior members of the Pallotine, and of the Irish-Argentine community – he was at the time of writing the editor of the *Southern Cross*, the organ of Irish-Argentine society – Father O'Neill denied this charge strongly. He said that he himself was 'more involved than the priest and postulant'. He had condemned disappearances and preached against military excesses. (I subsequently verified that Father O'Neill had indeed been so courageously outspoken that his friends continuously feared for his life.) He said the postulant was:

> An open and acknowledged nationalist. Very patriotic. Very Catholic. When told that he had to choose between violence and non-violence, he chose non-violence. He very definitely had made that choice.

The postulant Father O'Neill was talking about was a seminarian, Emilion Barletti. The other seminarian was Salvador Barbetio and the three priests were Alfredo Kelly, Alfredo Leaden and Pedro Duffau. All were Argentinian-born members of the Irish Province of the Pallotine Order. John Cleary, who was born in Ireland and whose life was spared because he was away in the Buenos Aires satellite town of Mercedes, subsequently left the Pallotines and now lives in Dublin. It was he who cleaned his colleagues' blood from the carpet on which the men were shot. This carpet now hangs in a little oratory in the presbytery and the women of the parish keep fresh flowers placed before it. Incredibly its bullet holes form the shape of a cross. Cleary was adamant that Father O'Neill's version of events was correct. He came to the scene as soon as word of the murders reached him. His first job was removing the blood-soaked carpet and a bullet-shattered television set, and filling in the bullet holes in the parquet floor. The killers put so many bullets into the murdered men that their bodies were almost ripped in half. They could not be dressed in their vestments and laid out in their coffins in the normal way. The vestments had to be simply tucked around them. In fact it was only the insistence of their families and some Church authorities that resulted in there being a funeral at all. The police came for the bodies, and initially refused to hand them back. The presumption is that the intention was to dispose of the bodies by dropping them over water from an aeroplane.

Cleary was visibly moved as he spoke to me, in Dublin some twenty years after the slaughter, when he recalled details like: 'The awful look of terror on their faces; I will never forget it'. He had often discussed the threat to all their lives with the dead priests, particularly Kelly who knew he was a marked man because of his outspoken sermons. Cleary recalled:

> He spoke English with a Westmeath accent and he was a very passionate man. The churches were always full, for his sermon. Poor Duffau liked nothing better than talking about football over a beer. He was just killed because they wanted to lay a marker on the Church. The Irish-Argentinian priests were very outspoken. It's coming out now that a lot of religious collaborated with the military, but the Irish never did. In fact, they took great risks. Father Federico Richards (a Passionist Father) used to stand up to them in the *Southern Cross*. He was the editor. Another good journalist was Bob Cox, the editor of the *Buenos Aires Herald*. He was brave too. His house was bombed and his kids threatened. Eventually he had to go back to England.
>
> Federico used to say things like, 'Our ancestors fought against repression and tyranny. We can do no less.' He used to cite Admiral Brown against the navy. He'd say things like 'The navy is a disgrace to the memory of the Irishman who founded it.' He was one of the very few journalists to speak out. Our men were murdered as part of the climate of the time. I was picked up myself and held for a few hours until the Irish Ambassador got me out. But I still got nasty phone calls at all hours of the day and night. A month after the Pallotines were murdered they murdered Bishop Angelli.
>
> He'd been a conservative originally but he had turned to supporting the poor. He had documents proving military involvement in the murder of nuns, and he had preached to the army the previous Sunday: 'Lay down your arms.' It was the climate that got them murdered. Kelly and Leaden were two good men but you still get rumours that they were involved. In fact – – – [another Irish priest] was vituperative after the murders; he blamed the dead priests for riling the military. That's the trouble with a police state. You are trained to feel guilty, that it is wrong to speak out against the Government.

THE SCHOOL OF THE AMERICAS

Describing how a police state came to Argentina, as it did to other countries in the region, the Latin American expert, Penny Lernoux, has described how Christ and Caesar worked hand in glove:

Because of its political and economic importance and its monopoly of education, the Catholic Church was the arbiter of Latin-American society. It taught the Indian and African slaves to embrace fatalism on the basis of a better hereafter. It planted the seeds of a machismo brought from Spain and Portugal. It encouraged a deep strain of cynicism among the upper classes, who learned that they might do anything, including slaughter innocent peasants, so long as they went to mass, contributed land and money to the Church's aggrandisement and baptised their children . . . Their descendants run the military regimes that today govern two-thirds of the area's people. Look behind a dictator; there stands a bishop.[12]

Ms Lernoux might well have continued: 'And behind both dictator and bishop there stood the US Government.' The shock to the system administered by Cuba's embrace of socialism, the Bay of Pigs disaster and the subsequent missile crisis, helped to deepen Washington's anti-Communist phobia in the region. Apart from covert CIA-type operations such as involvement in the destabilisation process that brought down Salvador Allende's democratic regime in Chile during 1973, American policy was exerted through the military School of the Americas in Panama. By the time it closed in 1984, an estimated 44,000 officers from the region had studied there and been inculcated with the Cold War virus. Many of Latin America's dictators learned their lessons of power in the School of the Americas. These lessons, which included the use of torture and counter-insurgency techniques that built on the examples of Nazi Germany, were subsequently applied only too enthusiastically by tyrants across the continent, ranging from Nicaragua's Anastasio Somoza to Leopoldo Galtieri of Argentina.

A CLASH OF IDEOLOGIES

In Argentina, bishops were paid by the state, at the same rate as judges. Yet, as Penny Lernoux points out, it was from this very Church that opposition to dictatorship and privilege began to emerge both in Argentina and throughout Latin America, in the wake of the Second Vatican Council, called by Pope John XXIII in the 1960s. The Council spoke of the Church as cherishing both rich and poor, comprising all 'The people of God', rather than being an authoritarian organisation catering largely for the rich. As part of the 'People of God', the Council argued that the poor too should have the option of peace and justice. This sounded very like Communism to the alumni of the School of the Americas – and particularly so when some priests' opposition took the form of embracing 'liberation theology'. Father O'Neill gave a thumbnail sketch of how this clash of ideologies affected the climate of debate:

The Argentinian Church is more conservative than that of Brazil. If you spoke out in favour of just plain justice and mentioned the poor, you could be labelled by the conservatives. In this climate the steps towards 'liberation theology' for some priests took the form of all legal and lawful methods, moral violence, fasts, strikes, etc, for a minority, actual violence, based on the grounds of Aquinas's 'just war', that it was legal to oppose a tyrant.[13]

Utilising the influence both of priests of the 'plain justice' school, like Father O'Neill, and those who preached (and practised) 'liberation theology', Christ's institutional force enabled His followers at least to make a significant protest to Caesar on behalf of there being 'an option for the poor' – but at a great cost. Throughout Latin America, in one twelve-year period alone, between 1968 and 1980: 'over 850 priests, nuns and bishops have been arrested, tortured, murdered or expelled, and thousands of Catholic laity have been jailed and killed'.[14] The repression was fiercest in Brazil, but, as we have seen, Argentina too had its martyrs.

JUAN AND EVA PERON

The immediate story of the road to martyrdom probably starts with the appearance of Juan Peron and his wife Eva on the Argentinian political stage. Peron emerged from the ranks of the army in which he was a colonel, to become the elected President of Argentina in 1946. The man he replaced was an Irish-Argentinian, General Edelmiro J. Farrell, who, for reasons we will examine later, is one of the comparatively few Irish names one will find in Argentinian political life, compared with the long list of outstanding figures in the history of the armed services, the civil service or the Church.

Peron ruled as dictator until 1955 when he was overthrown and went into exile. Eva, his actress wife, who had risen to the top in a society which upheld privilege, despite being born into poverty and illegitimacy, died in 1952 at the age of thirty-three. Though she had no official title, she had effectively ruled with Peron. He had her body embalmed in a bizarre process that took some six months and later led to the corpse being spirited out of the country by Peron's successors, to be buried, they vainly hoped, along with her legend. However, the legend proved so strong that her body was brought back to Argentina. The remains now rest in an honoured place in Buenos Aires Recoleta cemetery, where unknown admirers place fresh flowers at her mausoleum every day. (Here it might be remarked that flowers are also placed on the grave of an Irishman, Alfie Lamb, who died of cancer at the age of twenty-six. Lamb's canonisation is now being considered by the Vatican for his work in spreading the Legion of Mary through Argentina and Latin America.)

The Perons' legacy was a combination of a number of factors. His oratorical prowess, his nationalism, his seeming concern, initially at least, for the poor – 'the shirtless ones' – and the unions, enabled him to create a power base outside the Army. All this was mixed with a generally fascist-tinged, machismo blustering approach to making the trains (and the economy) run on time. Eva identified totally with the 'shirtless ones'. In their name she attacked the oligarchy which owned most of the wealth of the country. She wanted to arm the unions, and bought guns for the purpose. Her deathbed statement – that 'We must not pay too much attention to people who tell us to be prudent. We must be fanatical' – reached beyond the grave. Nothing like her posthumous popularity was seen in the world until the untimely death of Princess Diana, Princess of Wales. Amongst the Irish community one still encounters suggestions that she was Irish! Her maiden name, Duarte, is said to have been derived from Doherty.

A succession of eight presidents, six of them military figures, followed Peron, but prosperity did not accompany them. Argentina is potentially a wealthy country. The size of India, with a population currently standing at only some 30 million, it has cattle, grain, oil and mineral wealth. While this book was being written, it was giving some encouraging signs of realising this potential although Brazil's economic problems were having a retarding effect on the Argentinian economy. Indeed, much of its post Second World War history could be studied by students of political economy as a classic example of the correlation between the growth of inflation and the growth of systems of government which apply electrodes to the testicles of the governed. The decline in the value of the peso against the dollar gives some idea of the economic misery and chaos endured by Argentinians in that time. In 1947 the peso stood at five to the dollar. After two years of Peron it slumped to sixteen in 1949. However, under his various successors it fell to astounding depths: to 250 in 1966, to 400 in 1970 and to a nightmarish 1,100 in 1973, the year of Peron's return.

CHAOS

An older generation might have associated Peron with tyranny, torture, thievery and duplicity; the man who shifted a great deal of Argentina's reserves to his own accounts in Swiss banks; the man who diverted the guns which Eva bought for the unions to the police. Nevertheless, the desperation of the moment and the support of the young who knew the legend but not the reality, brought Peron back to power for a brief period. He died after less than a year in office and was succeeded by his widow, Isabella. She possessed neither Eva's personality, nor her political skills and was overthrown by a military coup in 1976. Military rule became the norm for Argentina until a bloodstained decade later when the outcome of the Falklands War resulted in the restoration of democracy under Raul Alfonsin. By that stage inflation was being computed in thousands of per cent per year.

There were other more serious costs, arising from the economic and political chaos. Prior to Peron's return, guerrilla activity had broken out. Some of it was Communist-inspired, some the work of a group called the Mononeros which, nominally at least, supported Peron and was a factor in his return. Initially the guerrillas had some idealistic and intellectual content. They derived inspiration from Che Guevara, the French student risings of 1968, and the example of Camillio Torres, the Columbian priest who died fighting with a guerrilla group in 1966. The guerrillas gave away free food in the slums – but the methods they used to get the money to buy the food included kidnapping and bank robbery. Murder, especially the killing of policemen, became commonplace. In the beginning the guerrillas' support was such that they could hold public parades in full battle dress, or collect tolls on highways. The pendulum of approval swung away from them towards a law-and-order military policy as their campaign intensified and a number of particularly high-profile assassinations took place. Dr Oberan Sallustro, head of Fiat-Concord, was kidnapped and murdered, although a seven-digit ransom had been paid for his release. Ex-President Aramburu was shot down on his doorstep by a man dressed as a priest. General Sanchez, the Commander of the Second Army Corps, who had a nasty reputation as a torturer, was ambushed and shot dead in the town of Rosario on the same April day in 1976 that the Sallustro murder occurred.

Blood called for blood, and, to the accompaniment of widespread, albeit short-lived public approval, the security forces answered the call. Peron began the crackdown. In exile he had supported the guerrillas, but, as soon as he had successfully accomplished his return, he rejected them. The country was divided up into three virtually autonomous regions between the army, the air force and the navy. While the guerrillas were the prime target, the Communists, the political parties, the student groupings and the unions were all banned, and their membership subjected to jailings and killings. The Congress disappeared, as did civil courts, the latter being replaced by military tribunals. Press censorship was introduced. Torture, always the unwritten subtext of Argentina's legal code, became the automatic accompaniment to arrest. Beatings and electric shocks were administered to both men and women, with particular emphasis on the genital areas.

A great number of the killings were caused by brutal stupidity – the military simply did not know who was a guerrilla, and who not – but according to Pat Rice, who spent seven years investigating this subject all over Latin America, 'disappearances' formed part of a definite policy. They were introduced as a method of breaking the guerrillas' cell system. He said: 'The picking up of people in illegal detention led to the "disappearances" of innocents, but it was an effective military tactic. People never knew whether people had talked or not. Some then talked because they thought their comrades or leaders had already given them away. No one knew when anyone might be picked up.'

Hilda Sabato, one of the most respected figures in the Irish-Argentinian community, corroborated Rice's statement. She recalled that, as a student, she never knew when some informer might denounce her as meriting 'disappearance'. Her field of interest lay not in revolution but in researching the methods by which the nineteenth-century Irish immigrants in Argentina developed new methods of sheep farming. This was of no consequence. She did not need to be a guerrilla. To be outstanding for any reason could result in torture and death – perhaps because she was seen talking to a fellow student, or teacher, who unknown to her had been denounced by someone else as being a guerrilla supporter, or simply because some fellow student had a grudge against her.

As in Nazi Germany, both students and teachers were expected to denounce each other. So too, of course, were people in all other walks of life. Thus the mangled bodies of the innocent came to be found, alongside those of guerrillas, on rubbish dumps or in burned-out cars. That is, those which were found – many never were. In all, some 20,000 to 30,000 people vanished.[15] The Navy handled 'disappearances', presumably because the possession of ships allows for the undetected disposal of bodies, but I discovered that there was a regular Wednesday 'death flight' from Buenos Aires. This took naked, usually drugged, victims to a high altitude over the River Plate. The disappearees were then thrown out at a point where their unidentified bodies would wash up on the Uruguayan shore of the huge river.

One of the reasons why Alfredo Astiz, the so called 'White Angel' (after Dr Mengele, the Nazi war criminal who was called 'the Angel of Death'), could not leave Argentina, though his life was constantly under threat from the families of disappearance victims, is because of French anger at his complicity in the aeroplane deaths of two French nationals, both nuns. The nuns were compiling information on disappearances when they were kidnapped and tortured by Astiz, and I have been told that they were alive when their time came to be thrown out of the 'Wednesday flight'. Astiz was arrested by the Alfonsin regime as this was being written.

PAT RICE

Jack-booted, black-leather-jacketed troops patrolled the streets, accompanied by Alsatian dogs. Unmarked Falcon cars appearing in a suburb heralded the arrival of death squads. The Nazi atmosphere was further heightened by touches such as the painting of huge red swastikas in jails to help in the intimidation of prisoners. One of the surest ways of becoming a prisoner was to show an interest in the poor. This was Pat Rice's crime.

A Cork man, he had originally come to Argentina from Ireland as a Divine Word Missionary, but he switched from this Order because: 'they put me in with Germans'.[16] Instead he joined the French worker priests group of Charles Foucauld, and he went to work in the Buenos Aires shanty town slum of Villa Soldati, which was built on the city dump. Here he earned a little money working as a carpenter and organised prayer meetings in the evenings and weekends. His friends feared for his safety. One priestly colleague (Father Kelly, who was later murdered at Belgrano) urged his mother to use her influence to get him out. His advice was so doom-laden that when news of Pat's arrest became known his family held a wake for him.

Pat's ordeal began on the night of 11 October 1976. He was then thirty-two and he had been six years in Argentina. As was customary, the shanty town was in pitch darkness. It was not a safe area, so he was escorting to her home a 21-year-old Argentinian woman, Fatima Cabrera. She was a part-time maid who earned five dollars a week, and had come to him for medicine for a seriously ill sister, whom she was supporting along with a younger brother. They were negotiating the piles of garbage on the streets near her home when they were stopped at gunpoint, bundled into a jeep and taken to a police station. Here Pat was told: 'You'll find out that the Romans were very civilised to the early Christians compared to what's going to happen to you.' His shirt was pulled up over his head and face and the beatings began. After some hours, he was hooded, placed in the boot of a car and taken to another barracks. Fatima was also driven there.

The hood he was wearing was apparently an improvised one made of rags. It was removed and a custom-made hood, fashioned from yellow canvas, was tied around his neck. Pat said that the man changing the hood told him: 'Don't look at me. If you do, you're dead.' He was beaten again. By this time, he says, 'I was in a bad state.' He was to be in worse: 'They started with water torture. My nose was held and water was poured in my mouth. You swallow a lot of water and it has a drowning effect.'

This treatment, alternating with beatings, continued at three- or four-hour intervals for the rest of that day (12 October). Sometime during the night they walked him to another room where they commenced giving him electric shock treatment. Electrodes were systematically applied to all the more sensitive parts of his body. The same thing was done to Fatima who was in the torture chamber with him. All day long (13 October) he could hear her screaming. 'It drove me crazy,' he said. To stop her screaming, after they had thrown water over her naked body to increase the shock, they applied electrodes to her mouth.

Once, he managed to lift his hood and view his surroundings. He was in a torture chamber in which seven other yellow-hooded prisoners were chained to a wall. In an adjoining chamber he could see two or three torturers at work. When it was realised that he had lifted the hood: 'They nearly lynched me with a cord around my neck.' Then, on 14 October, he was given a little water and, for the first time, allowed to go to the bathroom. He was told: 'You have been in detention for eight hours.' He was again placed in the boot of a car and driven to police headquarters (1550 Moreno Street, Buenos Aires) where he was given another beating. However, when he recovered, he was also given a meal and allowed to take a shower, during which he was horrified by the marks on his body. He was then told to say that these marks, his black eye, and badly cut foot had all been caused by falling down stairs. Any other explanation would cause him to 'be found in the river'.

What were the charges? Rice is not sure. He knows from the questions levelled at him during his interrogation that he was accused of putting up anti-army slogans in the shanty town – which he denies – and he was continually asked to give the names of people he knew in the Villa. This he refused to do, because he was afraid that they would be subjected to the same treatment. Eventually, he says, his torturers realised that he did not know anything and was innocent of any violence. One of his interrogators told him: 'I am also against violence and for that reason I won't kill you.' Fatima's crime appears to have been that she was with him when he was arrested. However, he was luckier than she. The Irish community and the Church rallied to his support, and the Irish Government, through its Ambassador, interceded for him. Fatima, however, had no such protection. She was kept in jail, subject to gross abuse of all kinds from the guards, for a further year and then released into house arrest.

On 18 October the Irish Ambassador, Wilfred Lennon, managed to get in to see Pat. Rice spoke to him in Irish, warning that the policemen in the room spoke English, and telling the Ambassador that it was best he did not comment on his condition. Rice was held for a further two months, probably to give the marks on his body time to disappear. Then he was given a paper to sign, promising that he would not speak about what had happened. However, on his release, he gave a press conference and spoke to American Representative Andrew Young at the UN.

Hitherto, the Irish-Argentinian community had been united behind him, but after the publicity the community split for and against his cause. This split, which was contained while he was in custody, had a good deal to do with the fact that Pat, and his Divine Word colleagues who had come from Ireland, were mission-oriented and identified with the workers. The Irish-Argentinian community, however, tended to be less liberal and to support the regime. There were some exceptions to this: a prominent member of the Irish-Argentinian community, Rodolfo Walsh, paid with his life for his outspokenness. Walsh, an author and journalist, published an open letter criticising the regime for its abuses. He was lured by a telephone call to a Buenos Aires backstreet and murdered. Michael MacCaughan, an Irish journalist, was writing a book about Walsh as this was being written.

Following a period of psychiatric treatment in a London hospital, Pat worked for the UN and helped to set up the Latin American Federation for the Investigation of Disappearances. 'It was heavy going,' he says. He visited concentration camps all over the continent – in Guatemala, Peru, etc – and came to the conclusion that in all there must have been in excess of 90,000 'disappeared'. On a break from an investigation in Venezuela he learned for the first time that Fatima was still alive. They met, fell in love, and decided to get married. They now live in a pleasant Buenos Aires suburb with their three children. Fatima became a teacher and Pat now works for the Ecumenical Movement for Human Rights, run jointly by the Catholic and Protestant Churches. He would go back to the priesthood, if the Church would accept him as a married priest, and sometimes he conducts services for the Methodists.

A LENGTHY LINEAGE

The involvement of Pat, and of Irishmen generally, in the cause of the oppressed of Argentina has a lengthy lineage. A British force which invaded Argentina in 1806, under the command of the Anglo-Irish General Beresford, contained a high proportion of Irish who had either been press-ganged or condemned by the courts to serve in the Army. So many of these deserted to the Argentinians after Beresford captured Buenos Aires that he had the Irish confined to barracks. In one engagement an Irish gunner, Michael Skennon, manned a cannon, firing on the British long after his Argentinian comrades had retreated. He was eventually captured by the British, strapped to a gun carriage and taken to Buenos Aires and shot.

When the Connaught Rangers landed a year later, British distrust for the Irish was so great that the Rangers were not given flints for their muskets. Hundreds of them were slaughtered when they were sent into battle defenceless. However, the Irish under Beresford who either deserted or, like the surviving Connacht Rangers, having been captured by the Argentinians, subsequently fought for them, are regarded as having played a significant role in the Argentinian War of Independence. Two Irish names stand out in this war, those of William Brown, the founder of the Argentinian Navy, and John Thomond O'Brien, the most important Irish military figure in the early Argentinian land forces.

Brown was born in Foxford, County Mayo, and by the time of the Revolution of 1810, was an experienced merchant captain, blockade running on the River Plate. His ship was captured by the Spaniards, but he in turn managed to capture one of the blockading ships and on bringing it safely to port was offered the command of the then infant Argentinian Navy. Of the myriad engagements, both successful and unsuccessful in which he subsequently became involved, one has a particularly Irish resonance. On 11 March 1814, Brown led an attack on the Spanish fleet in the Plate area. The Spanish Naval Commander, Romarte, easily repulsed the attack with the aid of a land battery stationed on the island of Martin Garcia commanding the estuary. Brown's badly damaged flagship was driven aground. It seemed that the rebels had taken a mauling from which they could not easily recover and Romarte made no effort to follow up his advantage. However, while the Spaniards slept, Brown rowed through the night to all the ships under his command, issuing pep talks and rallying his men. This was how Brown would later maintain the strict discipline he exerted in the Argentinian Navy, by leadership and example. He abolished flogging thirty years before the British did, at the instigation of another Irishman, Charles Stewart Parnell.

By dawn on 15 March, two days before St Patrick's Day, Brown had restored his men's morale sufficiently to mount another attack. It was a misty morning and, as he had hoped, the Spaniards concentrated on firing at his apparently suicide-bent ships. Meanwhile, Brown and his marines encircled Martin Garcia in rowing boats and successfully stormed the Spanish battery from its blind side. As Brown led his troops into battle he ordered his piper to play 'St Patrick's Day in the Morning', which to this day is the anthem of the Argentinian Navy in commemoration of the victory.

Thomond O'Brien, a Wicklow man, arrived in Argentina in 1814, where his qualities were recognised by San Martin, Argentina's liberator, who appointed him his aide de camp. O'Brien was at San Martin's side in all the major wars of the Independence struggle, not only in Argentina, but Chile and

Peru also. He and Brown maintained a keen interest in Ireland, gathering a group in Buenos Aires to assist Daniel O'Connell in furthering Catholic emancipation. O'Brien toured Ireland in 1827, seeking to get Irish emigrants for the Argentine as part of an agreement he had made with President Bernardo Rivadavia. He succeeded in bringing at least one group of 200 to work as sheep herders on the pampas. O'Brien's efforts were augmented by a default on the part of the Brazilian Government which had promised a group of Irish 'agriculturalists and soldiers' money, rations and, after five years, fifty acres of land, in return for military service.[17] The Brazilians did not keep their promises and imprisoned the Irish when they protested. Three hundred of them made their way to Argentina on their release in 1830.

A further spur to emigration came from three Irish merchants who had done well in Argentina: William Mooney, Patrick Bookey and Patrick Brown. Mooney and Bookey were from Westmeath, Brown from Wexford. They visited Ireland in Thomond O'Brien's wake and their efforts had a permanent effect on the character of Irish emigrants to Buenos Aires. To this day the bulk of Irish emigrants are from Wexford and Longford/Westmeath and their English is still spoken with the accents of those counties. One will meet what seems like a typical Irish farmer called Guilermo Power, Salvatore Rossiter or some such, and, were it not from his habit of conversing in Spanish with his companions, you could be forgiven for thinking you were speaking to one of the characters from Radio Telefis Eireann's most popular TV serial, a long-running soap on Irish rural life, called *Glenroe*.

WOOL

As the nineteenth century wore on, and famine loomed in Ireland, more and more emigrants followed in the footsteps of Thomond O'Brien, Bookey and Co. By 1895, when the last census of the century was conducted, the Irish-Argentinian population was 18,617 out of a total population of some 4 million. The Argentinian Government had a policy of encouraging emigration and the Irish, being Catholic and hard-working, were particularly welcomed. The vast open pampas, 'the Camp' as it was known, offered land to the Irish. On top of this the increasing concentration on sheep-rearing provided an excellent opportunity for profiting from the land. An Irishman named Peter Sheridan is credited with being a major force in improving the Argentinian herds through his purchase of 100 merino sheep in 1824.

It may be remarked in passing that it is ironic that the type of ranching which led to the clearances of Ireland and drove the Irishmen off their holdings was to be the source of their wealth in Argentina. Between 1822 and 1837, the production of wool shot up as, throughout Europe, the Industrial Revolution created a demand for woollen products. Buenos Aires exported 33,417 arobas (an aroba is about 25 pounds) of wool in 1822. In 1837 the figure was 164,706 arobas and the price had gone up from US$1 to US$2 each. By 1893, it is reckoned that 261 million pounds of sheep wool were being exported annually and the number of sheep was estimated at 69 million.[18] The Irish were at the heart of this expansion as the following quotation shows:

> On Saturday last sold by auction . . . about ¾ of a square league of land for the sum of $1,010,000 ... the largest price ever known in this country. It is unnecessary to state that the purchaser was an Irishman. Who can pay $1,010,000 for ¾ of a league except an Irishman? The fact is that Irishmen pay for lands what no one else can afford; and hence their becoming owners of the best lands of the province. There are whole counties in the north belonging exclusively to Irishmen. At this rate no one can compete with them. Persevering and laborious, their first aspiration, their leading passion is a flock of sheep and after that a piece of ground whereon to feed them. Thanks to this the Irishmen for 10 years back have been working an incredible revolution in the country. In the midst of wars, in spite of disturbances, drought and depreciation of produce, they have kept up the value of land, and gradually increased the figure to an amount which the most sanguine could never have expected . . . We hope they will continue to buy land by the million.[19]

Irish ranchers were responsible for almost half of Argentina's wool exports in the 1870s. By 1890 some 300 (out of 3,000) Irish families owned 1,508,335 acres in Buenos Aires province alone. The *Standard* newspaper estimated, appropriately enough on St Patrick's Day 1888, that the Irish owned 20 million sheep, from which they derived an income of £1.3 million a year. Generally these farms did not exceed some 6,000 acres which could sustain some 10,000 sheep and a family of seven in comfort, but on St Patrick's Day 1877 the paper carried a report describing the purchase of an estancia by an Irishman for £2.5 million.

The owners of these huge estates had arrived in Argentina penniless: men like Michael 'Big Mickey' Murray, who came to Chascomus in 1835 with little more than the clothes he stood up in. He died in 1868 owning two estancias, each a league (three miles) across, containing a total of 30,000 sheep, 500 cows and 150 horses. Not did the passage of time dissipate all this wealth. The Irish have remained a significant segment of Argentinian society. To this day, for example, the Duggan family is said to be one of the richest in the country. One member of the family told me that her great-grandfather: 'Gave more money than anyone else in the world to the IRB. He would not sell any milk or meat to the British and he owned more land than the total area of Ireland.' I believe her!

However, one does hear of the erosion of family fortunes through the influence of that other trefoil associated with the Irish: liquor, slow horses and fast women; and it is also true that there was a tendency of elderly and autocratic parents to delay in passing on their holdings to their heirs. They also failed to train them in the running of the estates. As a result, both energy and initiative were sapped by the time inheritance occurred, with harmful consequences.

Overall, however, the Irish helped to transform the region into one of the world's foremost food producing areas.[20] Hilda Sabato and Juan Korol point to some of the methods used, apart from sheer hard work.[21] The development of the Rambouillet sheep, which yield both high-quality meat and wool, helped to cushion producers against the vagaries of the wool market, and the Irish tended both to improve and expand their holdings by an intelligent use of wire fencing, irrigation and fertiliser, despite heavy expenditure on education, support for Catholic agencies, and the purchases of luxuries such as town houses. An Irishman, Michael Ballesty, introduced the first steam thresher in 1859.[22] The Irish also encouraged the spread of railways, and sometimes, on the larger estancias, opened railway stations on their own land. It's not surprising that Irish names still figure prominently in today's Argentinian land-owning aristocracy.

LONELINESS AND HOSTILITY

The Irish had a stronger inducement than most to overcome the pressures of life on the pampas. It was infinitely preferable to living at, or below, the starvation level in Ireland. A principal inducement was the system of 'halves'. The landlord gave the tenant Irishman a flock of say 2,000 sheep, which doubled over a period of three to four years. When these were sold, the Irishman got half the profit and generally used it either to buy more sheep or to acquire land, or both. As the century wore on, and competition for land grew more intense between the Irish and other emigrants, notably the Italians, the system of halves was modified: the herders' share became a third, a quarter, or simply wages. One lucrative form of income was the collection of majada, sheep manure.

Apart from the loneliness and hardships of pampas life, the Irish had to contend with the hostility of the indigenous people who, like their North American counterparts, objected to their traditional land being taken over. Bandits were also a threat, particularly as the Irish gained a reputation for having money. Several Irish farms were attacked and a number of people were murdered before a combination of Government action and the spread of the railways curtailed the bandits' freedom of manoeuvre.

The Government's most drastic actions were focused on the Indians, against whom a series of wars of extermination were mounted, the last of which occurred in 1877. The character of these wars of liquidation may be judged by one early experiment in germ warfare. Borrowing from an idea first introduced by the British in the American colonial wars, the Argentinians decided to get rid of the Indians and of a number of black troops in their ranks, by issuing the unfortunate blacks with blankets infested with the smallpox virus. Thus attackers and attacked were both wiped out.

EMIGRATION DECLINES

Irish emigration to Argentina on a large-scale basis ended in the 1890s. This was partly because of the attractions of North America; partly because the development of the pampas, and competition from other ethnic groups, had reduced opportunities for the Irish; and partly because of some hostility in Ireland itself to the idea of Argentinian emigration, largely fomented by shipping interests which wanted to concentrate on the lucrative North American trade. It was also a fact that the journey to the River Plate, either by sail (60 days) or by steam (30 days), was twice as long and two and a half times as expensive (£10) as the voyage to America.[23]

The *Dresden* affair had a particularly bad effect on the reputation of Argentina as an emigration destination. This had its origin in a decision by the Argentinian President, Julio Roca, to send Dean Patrick Dillon back to Ireland in 1881 in the hope of enticing Irish emigrants to the Argentine. Dillon encountered hostility from the shipping agents, but did something to encourage the flow of Irish to the Plate. Other emigration officials were sent in his wake in 1887, and information centres offering pre-paid passages were set up in Dublin and Cork. As a result the *City of Dresden* sailed from Cork to Buenos Aires in January 1889 with 1,800 passengers aboard, 1,100 of them Irish. Alas, when the ship docked in Buenos Aires on 17 February, they found no provision had been made for their arrival. A great public outcry ensued but it took months, and some deaths, before the *Dresden* emigrants were finally accommodated. As a result of the fiasco, the Archbishop of Dublin was asked to do what he could to restrict further emigration from his archdiocese, and the Cork emigration office was prevented from distributing pre-paid passages.

GOOD FATHER FAHEY

The flavour of pampas life has been described for posterity in the colourful, if somewhat rose-tinted, prose of the Irish-Argentinian journalist, William Bulfin. His son Eamon took part in the 1916 Rising, and his daughter Kit married Sean MacBride, the Nobel Peace Prize-winner whose father, John, was executed for his part in the Rising.

Bulfin wrote:

> God be with the old times when the boys, having established themselves fairly well in the camp, came into Buenos Aires to look for wives. Here again the good Father Fahey was their friend in need. He knew all the marriageable girls in the city, knew where they came from at home, knew the particular kind of a boy for whom each would make the best possible wife. And so the matches were made in Heaven as well as on earth.
>
> God be with the rough old honeymoon tour which began the morning after the marriage when the happy pair started for their distant home in the camp. Their chariot was a big covered-in bullock-cart. The axles were of wood and whistled wedding marches. The motive power was furnished by six oxen. A swarthy Basque armed with a twelve-foot driving spike [a cane wattle, which served as both rein and whip] took charge of the show, and that solemn procession tore through the country at the rate of ten or twelve miles per day, when the weather was fine. In the bullock-cart, besides the bridal pair, were stowed away some necessary articles of furniture for the new housekeeper, also a plentiful supply of shears, top-boots, clay pipes, cake tobacco, some bottles of strong water and many other sundries too numerous to mention. The expedition reached its destination in two or three or five weeks, according to the weather, and the hero and heroine lived happy for ever after.[24]

The 'good Father Fahey' whom Bulfin refers to was the greatest single influence on the Irish community in Argentina. Anthony D. Fahey (he favoured his name being spelt with an E, though most writers subsequently spell it Fahy) was a 39-year-old Irish Dominican when he was sent to Buenos Aires in 1843 as chaplain to the Irish. He quickly became not only a pastor but an adviser in matters temporal. Through his friendship with a Protestant banker, Thomas Armstrong, he arranged loans for the Irish, and developed an information system which informed them of the best places to sell crops or buy equipment. He also acquired a reputation as a marriage broker. The custom at the time was for the men to come in from the 'camp' twice a year to sell their wool. Fahey used to allow them two days on the spree and then the prospective bridegrooms were instructed to turn up at a dance which he organised. Here they would be introduced to their prospective spouses and, unless something untoward occurred, married the next day.

Father Fahey influenced the character of Irish emigration by constantly exhorting the Irish to keep out of the cities and make their futures on the pampas. Bob Santamaria would have approved! Fahey also encouraged the Irish to stick to what they were good at: farming, and in particular sheep rearing, as opposed to tillage. Fahey was thus largely responsible for much of the prosperity of the Irish, and for the fact that in Argentina, unlike other parts of the world, they did not create large urban ghettos.

They did, however, create ghettos of the mind, and Fahey's influence in building up an Irish presence on the pampas may have assisted in a process of cultural and political isolation which notably affected the Irish settlers, even long after he died. Though they were on the pampas, their mind-set was that of the ghetto. They tended not to have their children taught Spanish, but strove to maintain their Irish identity, as if they had never left the country. They kept in contact with Ireland, founded Irish Societies and married within the community. Fahey tried to encourage the learning of Spanish, particularly by the young Irish priests whom he helped to bring to Argentina. He made an arrangement whereby priests were trained at his expense at All Hallows in Dublin for Buenos Aires, and during the 1860s a dozen Irish priests found their way to the pampas this way. One of his creations is still flourishing, the Fahey Institute in Buenos Aires. This is a boys' boarding school which provided (albeit via a strict regime) education for many who otherwise would have remained untaught. It continues to flourish today, teaching boys and girls from both the Irish and Argentinian communities. Fahey also set up hospitals. It was he who was responsible for bringing the Sisters of Mercy from Ireland to establish a hospital in Buenos Aires and to care for orphans.

He was a legendary traveller. Even when he was advanced in years he managed to visit large numbers of his flock, travelling up to sixty miles a day on horseback, sometimes sleeping rough in the open. The early dwellings of the Irish settlers which Fahey visited have been described by Bulfin as follows:

The roof is of rushes or of long sedge ... the doors made of stout boards and can be strongly barred (against Indians and other marauders). A hole in the roof serves as a chimney, and holes here in the walls serve as windows ... an iron spike about 6ft from the ground [holds] the carcass of mutton for the maintenance of the family which consists of the squatter, his men and dogs ... the floor is of virgin earth ... with here and there a flea, and here and there a frog to give it a homely air. Now and then a snake drops in ...

[The dwelling consisted of] one apartment which cannot be much less than 12 x 8 ft. The bed which occupies one corner is an ordinary stretcher with a tough horse hide instead of canvas, a few woolly skins serve as mattress, a poncho takes the place of sheets and counterpane ... there are hanging on the wall a kettle, a pot, a frying pan, a drinking cup, a candle mould and a few spare objects of riding gear ... an empty packing case turned bottom upwards serves as a table. Under it are stored tea, sugar, rice and other provisions. When the black ants come along the box is surrounded by a fosse of four inches deep, which is filled with water ... an aged trunk in the other corner holds all the squatter's wardrobe and other valuables, chairs and stools there were none. The only seats were two or three skeleton skulls of cows ...

After a lifetime in which he made himself 'indispensable to his country-men',[25] Fahey's finest hour occurred during a succession of killer epidemics which struck Buenos Aires in 1867 and 1871. Fahey weathered the first epidemic, cholera, tending to the sick and dying no matter what their nationality, and raising money for the stricken. However, the yellow fever, which came along in 1877, carried off the indefatigable priest, along with between 180,000 and 200,000 other victims. Fahey's biographer claims with some justice that under Fahey: 'the Irish in Argentina had been transformed into an important, organised prosperous community'.[26]

LIFE ON THE PAMPAS

I was fortunate enough to be presented with copies of a set of diaries[27] preserved in the Savage family of Lujan, by Mr Diego Savage, who looked, and sounded, exactly like a contemporary farmer in Westmeath from which his family came. The diaries span the years 1875 to 1916 and although the entries generally amount to only one neatly written line each, they convey a picture of steadily increasing prosperity. The numbers of sheep, the references to land under cultivation all grow with the years, as do the varieties of the foods and fruit delivered to the estancia. Much of the diaries are taken up with the weather, generally simple references like 'rained all day' or 'a very dusty day'. The Savages were obviously charitable; people called for loans of money for themselves or for donations to the Church. The centrality of religion to the daily life of the Irish community is indicated by the frequent references to priests and nuns calling, mass being said in the house, or to attending special masses in Lujan. The combination of a preoccupation with both religion and the weather is summed up by an entry which says: 'The weather continues very dry. Camp's bad. A number of bishops are in Lujan now.'

The sheer ordinariness of the vast bulk of the entries – the garden is weeded, a new pair of boots is bought – indicates the humdrum nature of much of the quality of life. Very Irish methods of combating tedium occur; there are occasional notations such as 'Joe is a week in Lujan on a spree', or 'Willy Savage called, he not sober.' A hint of a dangerous subtext to pampas existence comes from a terse entry: 'Christobel Kiernan got a mortal wound of a knife by Tom Cod, Rioja.' The unfortunate Christobel is not the only fatality mentioned, and an indication of how the law looked on such matters may be gleaned from the fact that a subsequent entry says that Cod got 'six years and six months for the crime'.

The encapsulated nature of life on the 'Camp' is summed up by the fact that an entry for 1916 speaks of attending a mass celebrated in Lujan Cathedral 'for an end to the European war', but there is no reference to another event which preoccupied the Irish of the period, both at home and abroad, the 1916 Rising.

IRISH WOMEN IN ARGENTINA

Father Fahey had another lasting influence on the Irish community. He laid down a pattern whereby the Irish rendered unto Christ the things that were His and they paid Caesar the compliment of staying out of his affairs. Economically they were progressing, and their political needs could be met either through their own channels or those of their Church, by co-operating with rather than confronting the power structures. He set the tone for the relationship in a celebrated letter to the *Dublin Review*, in which he praised one of the bloodiest dictators in Argentinian history, Juan Manuel de Rosas, for his many fine qualities. Qualities let it be said which eluded most other observers. Fahey's fulsome praise for the dictator was largely motivated by the fear that he might turn on the Irish community generally the facet of his character that he showed in the tragic Camila O'Gorman affair.

In addition to the forces of the state, Camila may be said to have been crushed by the forces of her own family and the Church, truly a triple damnation. She was born in 1828 to one of the outstanding Irish families of the time. Her grandfather, Miguel O'Gorman, had been a famous doctor who had reorganised medical teaching and the building of hospitals. His nephew Thomas was a wealthy merchant who acted as a spy for the British and made possible the invasion of 1806 under General Beresford. Both of Camila's brothers were Establishment figures, one becoming a priest, the other a police chief. Camila was received at the Rosas mansion and was a friend of the dictator's daughter, Manuelita.

However, she fell in love with a scion of another prominent Argentinian family, Uladislao Gutierrez, a friend of her brother's and, like him, a priest. They eloped, to the horror of Argentinian society. Camila's father, Adolpho O'Gorman, writing to Rosas, described the elopement as 'the most atrocious and unheard of event in this country'.[28] Fearing that the couple's rebellion against the mores of the time might become a symbol of opposition to his regime, Rosas issued an order demanding that the fugitives be arrested to 'satisfy religion and the law and to prevent further cases of immorality and disorder'.[29]

For some months the couple eluded the tyrant, walking by rivers at night, avoiding civilisation, and sleeping in the open. They made their way to Goya in the province of Corrientes where they started a successful school. Its success and their popularity was their undoing. At a celebration in their honour they were recognised by a relation of Camila's, a Father Gannon. The priest gave them away, and they were arrested and condemned to death. Amongst those who concurred in the sentence was Camila's father and the great law maker, Dalmacio Velez Sarsfield, a relation of the Irish hero Patrick Sarsfield, the defender at the siege of Limerick (after whom one of today's leading Argentinian soccer teams is named). On the morning of 18 August 1848, Camila and Uladislao were executed by firing squad. Camila was almost nine months pregnant at the time.

Camila's tragedy at least had the merit of being unique. Other Irish women figure in Argentinian history for happier reasons. Cecilia Griarson became South America's first woman doctor in 1889, and was one of the pioneering movers in the teaching of braille to the blind. She founded the first nursing school in South America. In the main square of Buenos Aires, the Plaza St Martin, one can point to a notable feminist landmark, the Kavanagh building. It was erected by a business woman of Irish descent in the 1930s and, at thirty storeys, is the highest building in Argentina.

However, the overall pattern of Irish society in Argentina, until at least a decade or two before the time of writing, was male-dominated and clerically male-dominated at that. Evidences of the domination are still to be found. I met a cultured Irish-Argentinian lady in Buenos Aires who was agog to get hold of my books, so that she could read about the IRA and the Troubles. When I told her the name of my publishers she was amazed. 'But they're English!' she exclaimed. 'Brother X told me never to read a book on Irish history from an English publisher because they only print propaganda . . .'

FREE MASONRY

Free Masonry has a bogey-man image amongst the Catholic Irish, not merely because of its Protestantism, but because of its traditional Orange associations, particularly its character in Northern Ireland and its involvement in both the Royal Ulster Constabulary and the British police force. In Argentina, however, Masonry has a more honourable history, despite the fact that it was introduced to the country by Beresford to spread British influence. It played a role in the liberation of many countries in the region. San Martin, the Liberator of Argentina, was a mason, as were many other Latin American leaders, including Brown and Bolivar. The secrecy of the Masonic cells was partly enjoined for the same reason as that of the Irish Republican Brotherhood, to guard against spies, but the masons played a role in encouraging social reform in the eighteenth century. In our day, the Buenos Aires newspapers carry daily columns detailing Masonic events, and the Argentinian national colours of blue and white, which some think are those of the Blessed Virgin, are said by others to be Masonic-inspired.

After Father Fahey's death Dean Patrick Dillon succeeded him. He took a more political approach than had the purely pastorally motivated Fahey, and was a moving spirit behind the establishment of the Admiral Brown Club in 1879. The club became a forum for the pursuit of Irish interests. Dillon also founded Argentina's first weekly Catholic newspaper, the *Southern Cross*, in 1875. (There was another Irish-owned paper in existence at the time, the *Standard*, but it was geared towards the British community.) In 1874, in a circular which set out the policy of the proposed paper, Dillon said it would:

> Supply the want of an Irish and Catholic organ in the country, *The Southern Cross* will appear on the 1ˢᵗ of January. I hope the paper will be found on the table of every Irish and English house in the Argentine Confederation. I have already experienced the love you bear to your religion and the Land of your Fathers, and, consequently, count upon you for your support. The tone of the paper will be liberal (like the *Freeman* of Dublin). The paper will not adhere to any particular party in the country. The events of the week will be narrated with those comments which proceed from a strictly impartial pen ... I have already appointed correspondents in Dublin, Rome and New York.[30]

It may be safely assumed that the expense accounts of the three correspondents were not a source of envy to the other journalists of Rome, Dublin and New York.

The paper did, however, play an important role in Irish-Argentinian society. William Bulfin was its most notable editor in the early part of the century, but its most courageous journalist was undoubtedly Father Frederico Richards who was appointed editor in 1968. He not only stood up to the Junta throughout the years 1976–84, he also defied his own readership and Church. Both were conservative to the point of being reactionary. They objected to his condemnations of human rights abuses and to his publication of interviews with liberation theologians, like Dom Helder Camera. Although he lost circulation, Richards gained in reputation, particularly for his coverage of the Pallotine murders in Belgrano. This was completely at variance with the stance of the established Church whose attitude may be gauged from the behaviour of Cardinal Aramburo. The Cardinal attended the Requiem Mass for the dead priests, but neither preached, nor offered any word of sympathy to their families.

The Richards editorship may be viewed as having played a part in the Passionists' decision to sell their shares in the paper to the foundation which now runs it – the Pallotines control one-third of the shares, the Federation of Irish Argentinian Societies another third, and the remaining tranche is held by a troika of leading businessmen: Willy Patrick Ford, Luis Maria Flynn and John Edmund Rossiter, all of whom, like the editor Father O'Neill were most generous with their time in helping me to understand the Irish community.

LATIN AMERICA

The newspaper's offices are a marvellous amalgam of the past and present. On the walls are pictures of the founder of the Irish Christian Brothers 'Edmund Ignacio Rice', Padraig Pearse, Admiral Brown, General San Martin, Eamon de Valera, Mary Robinson, a St Bridget's Cross and a map of Ireland. The paper's layout reminded me of the *Irish Press* of the 1950s, and I was not surprised to be told that its policy was 'strongly Catholic and nationalistic. We used to be all for the IRA and de Valera, but not now.' Not now indeed. De Valera's *Irish Press*, which he had founded in 1931, with money subscribed by the diaspora towards the Irish independence movement, died because no foundation was set up to guide the paper through changing times. Edmund Rossiter told me that his father had been a member of the Irish Altar Society [these societies provide for the upkeep of altars, vestments, church furniture etc: Author] on the 50th anniversary year of the paper, and that he was a member on its 100th anniversary. The *Southern Cross*, on the other hand, despite its 'Round Tower and shamrocks' image, has lasted far longer than the *Press*, and seems certain to continue to play an influential role in the Irish community.

FLOATING THE SHAMROCK

Parallel to Father Dillon's efforts in founding the *Southern Cross*, there were other developments within the Church. The Passionist Order arrived in Buenos Aires in 1879, followed by the Pallotines in 1885. As we have seen, along with moving into the paper's editorial chair, the Pallotines were to make bloody history, but initially it was the Passionists who created controversy. The first Passionist, Father Martin Byrne from Dublin, had intended that the Argentinian house should be exclusively Irish, and the Irish community subscribed generously to this objective. However, ever political, Rome, with an eye on the numbers of Italians flocking into Buenos Aires, wanted Italian Passionists involved in the new foundation. Byrne resisted and was expelled in 1884. Until the issue was resolved in 1914, in favour of the Irish, the dispute remained: 'a benchmark in the tensions between Irish nationalists and pro-British elements of the Irish population'.[31]

The various educational and charitable organisations which grew up as the Irish became more prosperous, provided foci for the maintenance of both religious and national traditions. The Sisters of Mercy brought education to such sections of the Irish community as they could reach across the country's vast spaces. Like the Pallotines, they taught only in English. Spanish was taught only as an extra subject and the schools remained English-speaking and Irish until Peron enforced ethnic integration.

Horse racing and the celebration of St Patrick's Day maintained a sense of communal identity, and William Bulfin introduced hurling in 1884. The sport remained popular in Argentina until the outbreak of the Second World War made it difficult to obtain hurling sticks from Ireland. In Buenos Aires this identity tended to be maintained by floating the shamrock rather than drowning it as occurred in America and elsewhere. The Irish organised racing clubs throughout the province, which had circulating libraries as part of their attractions, and the Irish are credited with being partly responsible for the foundation of the Buenos Aires Jockey Club, which helped Argentina towards securing its position in the world as a bloodstock breeder. Towns sprang up bearing Irish names – Duggan, Gahan, Gaynor, Kenny and Murphy.

CLOSE LINKS WITH HOME

As the Irish kept in such close touch with their homelands, events in Ireland had an influence on the Irish community in Argentina. Associations both for Catholic Emancipation and for repeal of the Union with Great Britain were founded in the 1820s under Admiral Brown and General Thomond O'Brien. Father Fahey organised a relief fund for Famine victims. Some years later, in 1868, another Irish priest, Father John Leahy, founded a fund to help Fenians 'who had landed in British jails for their fight for Independence'.[32] Although the Irish in Argentina never had to undergo the antagonism from Protestant sectarianism which they encountered in America, Freemasonry had its effect and rioting inspired by the Masons caused the burning of a Jesuit college in Buenos Aires in 1879. Because of their contribution during the cholera and yellow fever epidemics, the Sisters of Mercy Convent was spared, but the anti-Catholic feeling was a factor in the nuns withdrawal from Argentina for a decade. They returned in 1890, possibly moved by the fact that Father Dillon had died in the interval, the sisters having preferred the Fahey to the Dillon era.

As the Land League and the Celtic Renaissance took off in Ireland, Irish Argentinians supported these departures also. A branch of the Gaelic League was established in 1899 and, along with the Irish Relief Fund, formed specifically with the aim of assisting the Land League, sent 'substantial support to Ireland'.[33] The close links between the Argentinian Irish and their homeland during this period caused me a pang of nostalgia a hundred years later – similar to that which I experienced in the offices of the *Southern Cross* – during a visit to the Cathedral of Lujan. This neo-Gothic edifice is probably the finest building in Argentina. Its spires are 106 metres high and the towering impact they make, rising sheer above the pampas, has to be experienced to be understood.

The Virgin of Lujan is celebrated throughout Argentina and there have been twinned pilgrimages between the Basilica at Knock in County Mayo and Lujan. Images of the Virgin have also been exchanged between Lujan and Mullingar in County Westmeath, where so many of the ancestors of today's Irish community hail from. In fact, the more pious will tell you that a set of miracles occurred during the exchange. As the pilgrims mounted the steps of Mullingar the statue toppled out of a glass case being carried on the shoulders of worshippers and fell hard on the concrete steps. Miraculously, it did not break. 'And then,' a participant in the pilgrimage told me solemnly, 'as they were going up the aisle, someone slipped and the statue fell again. Again it did not break. It was a miracle.' One wonders if the carrying party temporarily become infected with the falling sickness because, as they approached the altar, The Virgin Fell The Third Time. And, yet again, the plaster of Paris statue did not break: 'It *must* have been a miracle,' said my informant fervently. I did not argue. Who am I to cast aspersions on a promising development in the miracle industry. The Bouncing Virgin of Lujan may yet be found providing employment in Mullingar when all the multi-nationals have gone and the Celtic Tiger is licking its wounds. Currently some six million people a year visit the shrine of the Virgin of Lujan. And one miraculous happening may be inspected in its vicinity.

The former Viceroy's home is preserved as a museum and is reckoned to contain the most important collection of artefacts and jewellery in Latin America. The magnificence of some of the pearls and the finely worked silver ornaments and statuary defy description – but the place does not even have a burglar alarm.

One of the features of Lujan Cathedral, which contains many mementoes of the Irish in the form of stained-glass windows, plaques to donors, etc, is a lavishly adorned altar to St Patrick with statues of St Columbus, St Malachy, St Brendan, St Clara and Patrick himself. On the Sunday nearest to St Patrick's Day each year, the annual celebrations of the Irish Societies pack the Cathedral to suffocation. At the altar there is a green flag inscribed 'Eireann go bragh' and 'God Save Ireland', and near it is the source of my nostalgia: a plaque commemorating the first Irish pilgrimage to Lujan in 1901. The inscription, in Irish, was the motto chosen in 1931 at the foundation of the *Irish Press*. It said: De Cum Gloire De agus Onora na h-Eireann (For the glory of God and the honour of Ireland).

The help and sympathy shown by the Irish in Argentina to the Irish Independence movements was reflected in the fact that the first revolutionary Irish Parliament, illegal in the eyes of the British, set up an Irish diplomatic presence in Argentina. On 17 June 1919, the first Dail appointed Eamon Bulfin as its representative in Buenos Aires. This was a year before the Dail appointed representatives to either France, Germany, Spain or to a number of American cities.

The Dail then sent a special envoy to Buenos Aires on 25 July 1921, seeking recognition for the Irish Republic. This was Laurence Ginnell, a prominent Sinn Fein spokesperson during the Anglo-Irish War. He succeeded in having Requiem Masses said for 'Las Victimas de la Tirania Inglesa', but the outbreak of hostilities amongst the Irish themselves caused de Valera to recall Ginnell, his mission unfulfilled, after eight months.

The Civil War had a blighting effect on Irish-Latin American relationships, as it had on domestic Irish development. Thereafter, for several decades, the principal focus of the Irish-Argentinian community's concentration where Ireland was concerned was the Eucharistic Congress in 1932, to which the Argentinians sent a delegation. The process of arrest was added to by the outbreak of the Second World War. The following table gives an indication of the level of Irish contact in this period:

Period	Arrivals	Departures	Balance
1925–1930	938	259	679
1931–1940	1,006	157	849
1941–1946	80	10	70
TOTAL:	2,024	426	1,598

ISOLATION

The forties and fifties were stagnant years in Ireland, and there was little governmental enthusiasm for broadening diplomatic contact with Latin America. However, the first diplomatic mission was opened in 1947 and in 1958 Dublin appointed its first ambassador in Buenos Aires, Joseph Horan. Indeed, for the next thirty years it was to be Ireland's only Embassy in Latin America. By the time Horan arrived, Irish-Argentinian contact had dwindled. The Irish who did come were largely contracted professionals: business consultants, engineers, teachers, bank employees or priests. Horan concluded that Irish emigration had ended and that Argentina, unlike the Irish diaspora in Australia, Canada, America and the United Kingdom, was not receiving any fresh blood. This factor of course accentuated the isolation of the Irish community within Argentina.

One result was that Irish-Argentinian women were not trained for urban occupations. As early as 1912 an Irish-Argentinian paper, *Fianna*, criticised the prevailing attitude in the community towards female education:

> there is a wide demand at present in Buenos Aires for typists, shopgirls and governesses that can command two languages, and it would be criminal to condemn young girls of our race to the most slavish and worst-paid occupations like domestic service, who for a few dollars extra for their education, could easily be fitted for high positions in life, with easier work, and a brighter future and consequently more certainty of finding husbands and becoming mothers of educated and cultured families.

There may be some symbolism in the fact that after those comments (31 July 1912) the paper ceased publication! While elsewhere in the world women went to work in factories or offices, the influence of the Irish-Argentinian clergy was deployed against such occupations, lest they come in contact with the 'blacks' (Italians, Spanish and descendants of indigenous peoples).. The blacks were really browns, being descended from Indians, but this racist attitude resulted in large numbers of Irish girls being fitted only for work as domestic servants and child minders, few being educated well enough to become governesses. Indeed evidence could be given of priests taking to the pulpit to condemn marriages outside the community.[34] Such pressures of course encouraged the practice of intermarrying within the community. A rather gloomy report on the Irish-Argentinians judged that the isolationist policy, although begun under Fahey for the best of motives, had the unforeseen result of producing:

> A large population of landless serfs, an Irish rural proletariat, and thus had consequences which affect to this day the status of the Irish in Argentina. From the Irish colonisation in Argentina, no middle class developed.[35]

This picture has changed since the fifties but it is of course true that only a relatively small number of emigrants could own estancias and become part of the ruling oligarchy – far fewer than the numbers who worked on them. It is also true that a very high proportion of the Irish did not receive education. In the fifties Irish names were rarely met within the professions – but then very large numbers of Argentinians did not make it into the ranks of the middle class either, and back in Ireland, at the time of the report's compilation, large numbers of Irish also lacked education. However, along with the Fahey tradition of staying out of politics, lack of professional training was certainly a contributory factor in keeping the Irish out of politics.

TWO CASUALTIES

The Irish, or rather Ireland itself, did make a notable incursion into politics during the Falklands/Malvinas War, which temporarily boosted Irish popularity throughout the whole of Argentina. She invoked the unanimity rule and succeeded in forcing the EC to drop the sanctions policy initiated by the British. Following the sinking of the cruiser *Belgrano* by the British during the war, Ireland succeeded in getting EC sanctions removed from Argentina. For a time I was repeatedly told that the Irish Prime Minister responsible, Charles Haughey, 'was a hero'. The obverse side of this medal of popularity were two casualties amongst the Irish diaspora, one living, one already dead.

When the war broke out, Joseph Doherty, as mentioned earlier, had been fighting his extradition from the US to Belfast. His lawyer, the legendary Paul O'Dwyer, succeeded in coming to an agreement with the US Justice Department whereby Doherty could be released to a friendly third country – that is, one which did not have reciprocal extradition agreements, as for example did Ireland and the UK – if O'Dwyer could find one.[36] Eventually he did – Argentina. However, in a gush of gratitude after the Falklands conflict, the Argentinians concluded all sorts of agreements with the Irish, including one governing extradition. As a result, Doherty could not be sent to the Republic of Ireland and wound up back in Long Kesh.

The dead casualty was Padraig Pearse, the leader of the 1916 Rebellion. As part of the Irish-Argentinians' support for Irish Independence movements, a bust of Padraig Pearse was placed standing on a plinth in the Plaza Irlanda, located at the end of the Primera Junta Metro line beside the Irish-founded St

Brigid and Monsignor Dillon Colleges. However, during the anti-British fervour of the Falklands War, some patriots failed to pause long enough to read the inscription in Spanish which began 'docente, poeta y patriota Irlandes . . .' As a result, poor Pearse, whom the British had executed, was blown up as a British hero!

GENERATIONS OLD AND NEW

Like all pockets of Irishness in the world it is difficult to be certain of the exact size of the Irish community. The earlier emigration records gave the nationality of the Irish and English emigrants as British, but thanks mainly to the research of one man, Eduardo Coghlan, who extrapolated the Irish names, a clearer picture became possible. Coghlan's work is today the most consulted reference work in the Irish Embassy. On the basis of these and other figures, Guillermo McLoughlin – the Buenos Aires economist and historian who travels between Ireland and Argentina, and has researched the links more thoroughly than most – has concluded: 'Currently more than half a million people spread all around the country can claim Irish descent.'[37] Others, taking purely Irish surnames as their guide, reckon the number to be about 300,000. McLoughlin, however, points out that in the case of Irish women marrying, the Irish surnames disappeared.

With the growth of prosperity in both Ireland and Argentina, and the improvement in the availability of cheaper air fares, travel links between the two countries improved immeasurably throughout the decade 1987–1997. As elsewhere, the worldwide interest in Irish music has played its part. The popular Irish group, the Wolfetones, had a hit song in both Argentina and Ireland which managed to combine Admiral Brown and the Malvinas. An Argentinian group, the Shepherds, specialises in Celtic music, and Irish groups like U2 and the Chieftains are popular in their different ways. The pop group, Boyzone, had visited Argentina not long before me, and the colourful Irish academic and politician, Senator David Norris, was drawing packed houses for his one-man show on Joyce as this was being written. In sport Irish and Argentinian rugby teams frequently play each other, when the amateur Pumas usually restore a little humility to the hubristic Celtic Tigers by giving the professional Irish teams well deserved beatings.

The various Irish institutions one can visit around Buenos Aires offer glimpses of both the old and the newer generations. About fifty kilometres south of Buenos Aires, there is an old folks' home for the Irish, St Patrick's Home. A portrait of Daniel O'Connell hangs in an honoured place, inscribed in the Liberator's own handwriting, 'Your faithful servant Daniel O'Connell'. At St Patrick's, one can hear stories of toil, adventure and misadventure. One man had lost a farm of several thousand hectares through a freak flood. Now in his eighties, he had been a famous athlete in his day, who had played rugby, skied in the Andes, and had gone around the world in a yacht. 'Now I will stay here 'til God says come home,' he said.

Like all the other inmates he was spotlessly clean, his clothes neat and pressed and his fingernails clipped. Another had come over at the age of seventeen as a student missionary in 1925. He remembered the Anglo-Irish war – 'I saw the boys from the hill take over Clonmel barracks' – and told me wistfully: 'I wish I had never crossed that sea.' Another inmate had been a secretary in the Irish Embassy. She was quite cheerful and happy. The home is maintained by the Irish community through a variety of fund-raising activities but the building, a former flour mill, is old. Even if the money were plentiful, it is doubtful whether expenditure on the existing structure would be justified. Everything was spotlessly and highly polished, but the carpets were scuffed and the furniture was old. The home gets nothing from the Government. It is likely that in years to come it will close – the numbers have already dropped down from fifty to thirty-two – and people like the present inmates will move into homes in their local communities.

At the Hurling Club in the suburbs of the city, one encounters a large shamrock at the gates, and further evidence of Irishness in touches like having the goal posts padded in the colours of the Irish flag, green, white and orange. Irish gossipy humour and cheerful malice is inevitable also: 'Oh God yes, Belgrano was gay, everyone knows that, and San Martin had a 14-year-old girlfriend. They were all Freemasons, Brown too. He was a drunken corsair. Never learned to speak Spanish!' Then, after a few further words of demolition of the country's icons, the speaker, a member of the club, introduced me to a swarthy-looking Frenchman. 'He is our only black.'

The president of the club, Alex Quinn, an energetic young businessman, was a member of the club from the day he was born; his brother is the vice-president and their father before them a president. However, the Hurling Club now has only 900 members where formerly there were 3,000. Quinn reckoned that the fall-off was due to the multiplicity of other attractions available, but he was planning to utilise the club's extensive grounds to do a deal with a local military club which would yield enough funds both to enlarge the club and build a new school. The local English school was proving too expensive for the Irish community.

One of the existing Irish schools which is clearly flourishing is Newman College run by the Christian Brothers, some of whom live in the College but work in the barrios. 'It's all right when they get to know you, but the drugs and the unemployment make it dangerous otherwise,' I was told. No drugs are likely to be found at Newman. The buildings and grounds are impressive, and the Brothers, while obviously maintaining the Irish traditions, have branched out into Argentinian sports. A large glass case in the main entrance hall was filled with magnificent silver trophies won by the school's polo team.

I attended a mass and concert at the college. The church held at least 700 people for the service, during which the Irish flag and portraits of St Patrick and Brother Edmundo Ignacio Rice were displayed on the altar alongside the flag of Argentina. The congregation varied in age from babies in arms to nonagenarians. The crowd was even bigger in the concert hall – where the roof lifted when one of the community came on stage to sing Clancy Brothers songs – and there was standing room only at the bar. It was a cheerful occasion which clearly betokened a vibrant community. Father Fidelis, a Passionist in his eighties who acted as a sort of latterday Father Fahey and who died not long afterwards, was the moving spirit behind the event. He planned to hold similar functions in the four corners of the city, and reckoned that the crowds would be about the same, if not bigger. Despite the evidence of the declining old folks home, the number of children at the Newman College event would seem to augur well for the future of the Irish community.

I was invited to give lectures both at Lujan University and at St Brigid's College, which was founded by the Sisters of Mercy. In both venues there were large attendances – although at St Brigid's the girls were a captive one! They slipped me notes making derogatory remarks about their teachers. I needed the services of a translator at Lujan, but nevertheless, the questions showed an evident interest in Ireland generally and the Peace Process in particular. A day or two after my talk at St Brigid's, the efficient headmistress – the days of the nuns are over – brought some of the girls to attend a barbecue and display of Gaucho dancing, put on in my honour. One of the girls recited a poem of Seamus Heaney's which she had learned since hearing my talk.

Bookshops and book sales are a reliable indicator of a culture's intellectual and economic growth. It is not without significance that some of Argentina's, and indeed Latin America's, most important booksellers are Irish. Kathleen Duggan is the elegant, but deceptively efficient, member of a troika of sisters (the others are Maureen and Margaret) who, with the aid of Kathleen's daughters, Rosanna and Eileen, run the Kel bookshops. Kathleen told me that interest in Irish writing grows continuously. Kel is the largest English-speaking bookseller in Buenos Aires, and the large, airy, attractively appointed auditorium, which is a feature of its headquarters, will fill for an Irish reading or lecture. The Duggans hold Irish classes in their shop at Belgrano which are also well attended. They are a second-generation family, their father came from Tipperary.

THE FUTURE

Will there be more like them? What are the prospects for the future of this section of the Irish diaspora? Obviously it will depend on both contact with Ireland and on whether the leadership of the Irish community will continue to be taken over by the new generations. When I asked Father O'Neill what he thought of the prospects of the Irish community rejuvenating itself, he replied: 'I never saw any prospect of its dying out . . .'

I will leave the last word to Hugh O'Shaughnessy, the London-based author, journalist and broadcaster, who is regarded as a leading authority on both the Irish presence and Latin America generally:

In retrospect the Irish achieved much more in the region than their mere number would have led anyone to expect. An Irish viceroy and Irish soldiers, religious, architects and business people are woven into Latin America's history. What would Buenos Aires be without the Edificio Cavanagh? Or San Juan if Marshal Alejandro O'Reilly hadn't built its great Morro fortress? What would Chile have been without the martial dash of Liberator General Bernardo O'Higgins? Or Paraguay without the sophistication of Eliza Lynch?

Ireland poured a very special essence into the Latin American cocktail. You can taste it there still.[38]

You can indeed, and for my part I have to say that I found the Argentinian flavour particularly attractive.

TEN

JAPAN, RICE PADDIES AND AN ASIAN PERSPECTIVE

'How do you translate: "Ya thick bitch!" into Japanese?'

Japanese translator working on Roddy Doyle's film, *The Snapper*.

'I know a couple who sit together with great fruit. They claim that silent meditation, which is a kind of wordless dialogue, has opened up a whole new dimension in their relationship. And be prepared for shock!'

Fr William Johnston, S.J.

ONE DAY IN the mid-seventies, a veteran Irish American newspaper man, Jim McCoy from Cleveland, Ohio, came to my office at the *Irish Press*. He told me that one of his earliest memories as a journalist was of Eamon de Valera visiting McCoy's paper during the 1920s, while de Valera was soliciting the funds to set up the *Irish Press*. What had struck him was that de Valera's main interest lay in getting information, not about journalism, but about how one controlled a newspaper.

My main interest lay in his companion, a beautiful young family friend of McCoy's called Mary Jordan. She was studying at Trinity College Dublin, and had been chosen as an entrant in the Rose of Tralee competition by the Mayo community in Cleveland, Ohio. At that stage, Mary, who was taking a semester in Trinity, and working at night in Brian Loughney's Dublin pub, Kitty O'Shea's, had very little idea of what she was going to do after college. I suggested that she write an article for the *Irish Press* women's page. She did so. It began: 'Irishmen are like soda bread. Every Irish mother has her own special recipe . . .' On the strength of that I advised Mary to take up journalism, and she did.

Twenty years later, as I researched the Irish diaspora in Asia, I made my headquarters in Tokyo at the home of the *Washington Post*'s bureau chiefs – Mary Jordan, her husband Kevin Sullivan, and their two-year-old daughter Catherine. Yet again the diaspora was taking effect.

THE IRISH IN ASIA

Writing in the *Irish Times* (20 March 2000), Conor O'Clery, the paper's Asia

644

correspondent, remarked on the fact that everywhere he travelled: in Beijing, Tokyo, Kuala Lumpur, Manila, Hong Kong, Jakarta, Singapore, he came across 'interesting Irish people in a variety of occupations'. A few days earlier, he had attended the St Patrick's Ball in Singapore, at which he was told the typical Irish member of today's diaspora:

> aspires to membership of the exclusive Tanglin Club, drives a 5 series BMW, plays golf in Johor Baru, goes back to Ireland for GAA finals or rugby internationals, has the odd pint in Molly Malone's, Fr Flanagan's, or Muddy Murphy's, especially when they are showing a rugby international, and calls up the *Irish Times* every day to see how Eddie Jordan and Darren Clarke are doing.

Whether the members of the diaspora do indeed rely on the *Irish Times* as much as Conor O'Clery suggests, he is correct in saying that the Irish presence in Asia is significant and growing. It is a demonstrable fact that the St Patrick's Day Balls are the best attended expatriate social events in Asia. St Patrick's Day 2000 saw large attendances in a series of Asiatic capitals, and many thousands disappointed in their quest for tickets. In Kuala Lumpur, a thousand people attended the ball in the Shangri-La Hotel, five hundred at the Westin in Tokyo, six hundred and fifty at the one in the Sheraton Great Wall in Beijing, six hundred at the Furama in Hong Kong, and five hundred and sixty attended the festivities at the Mariott in Bangkok. Not all the attendance at these functions would be Irish of course. Nevertheless the growth of the Irish presence may be judged from the fact that the Irish now stage an annual Asian Gaelic Games. That scheduled for the year 2000 is to be held in Phuket, Thailand, and knowledgeable commentators reckoned that the final would be between Singapore, whose Gaels won the event in 1999, and Tokyo.

The Tokyo St Patrick's Day Emerald Ball is particularly significant as it is always attended by members of the Royal Family. Generally speaking, the Tokyo section of the Irish diaspora, like that of Asia generally, is a new one. The average Irishman or woman which makes it up is generally in his or her thirties, and is to be found, by and large, in the better paying jobs: banking, computers, electronics, multinational companies and so on. This newer diaspora is superimposed on the old clerical network, like the Columban Fathers in the Philippines, or those colonial administrators and professionals, who would mainly have been found in the Hong Kong of other days.

For, while currently the Irish in Japan, and particularly Tokyo, deserve to be known as the most significant concentration of 'Rice Paddies', historically the Irish are not strangers to Asia. Having fought the empire at home, they built it abroad. In the mid-1850s, returns show that of all the British regular army officers born in the British Isles, a quarter were Irish, mostly Protestant Irish. Similarly, the Indian Civil Service was one-quarter Irish-born between 1855 and 1863. Approximately a fifth of these were Catholics. Some remarkable men were to be found amongst the ranks of the Irish in this service

– for instance, James McNeill, a Commissioner of the Bombay Presidency, who subsequently became Governor General of the Irish Free State, and Sir Michael O'Dwyer, Lieutenant Governor of the Punjab, who has the dubious distinction of being remembered for recruiting half a million Indians for the Great War. At the risk of digression, it might be pointed out that these men, or at least their families, represented the point-counterpoint nature of the Irish political personality. James McNeill, a pillar of British colonial rectitude, was the brother of Eoin McNeill, the Chief of Staff of the Irish Volunteers, which staged the 1916 Rising. Although Eoin made an unsuccessful effort to call it off, the British imprisoned him. Two of Michael O'Dwyer's brothers were Jesuits. The truth of the matter is that the Irish were as prominent in the institutions of the Mother England form of colonialism – be they armies, police forces, churches, professional bodies or political parties – as they were in the services of Mother Church.

Tokyo is currently the most important centre for the Irish in the Pacific area, although there are of course pockets of Irish all over the continent, a growing one in Beijing, a falling one in Hong Kong, a presence in the Philippines – at whose centre lies the missionary tradition of the Irish Columban Fathers – and communities of some hundreds in places like Djakarta, Singapore and Seoul.

JAPANESE LINKS

Japanese investment in Ireland is considerable and is responsible for the employment of more than 3,500 people. In fact Ireland has the highest per capita Japanese manufacturing investment in Europe. There were 8.57 Japanese companies per million of population in Ireland in 1994; this compares with the British ratio of 3.45 or the Danish of 0.06. In comparison with the 'iffy' British attitude towards Europe, the wholehearted Irish membership of what was then the EEC offered the Japanese an opening to the European market. This is appropriate as it was an Irishman, Admiral Mathew C. Perry, whose mother came from County Down, who is famously remembered for having 'opened Japan to the West' by sailing his squadron of black ships into Tokyo Bay in 1852. With Perry's arrival Japan's decision-takers realised that the closed-door policy towards the West which had been in operation since the early seventeenth century was no longer viable. The restoration of the Meiji Emperor to act as a centralising influence on Japan's feudal fiefdoms followed, and American and European influences began to permeate Japan as part of a modernisation process whereby Japan in turn sent officials abroad to gain Western knowledge.

However, although in continuation of this policy Ireland and Japan have struck up a mutually advantageous relationship within Europe, Europe's presence in Japan is generally well below the Japanese level in Ireland. The number of Japanese in the EU, five times the number of Europeans in Japan, is closely related to levels of investment between the trading partners.

One of the key figures in the Irish-Japanese relationship is the banker and former Director General of RTE, Dr Tom Hardiman. He is a director of a number of Japanese companies in Ireland and along with his wife Rosaleen, made a point of learning Japanese. Hardiman points out an area in which Ireland can justifiably claim to have given a lead to Europe in improving EU Japanese links:

> A cross-cultural awareness has clearly been inadequate on the European side. We can claim with some justification that Ireland in recent years has given a useful lead in this area. The arrangement whereby some fifty or so graduates in engineering and the sciences are selected annually to work in industrial and business corporations in Japan for a two-year period has been successful in generating business and linguistic skills in the young graduate that will clearly have a beneficial long-term impact. The Irish experience, replicated proportionately in the largest EU Member States, could soon rectify the imbalances in the personnel ratio with significant benefit in the longer term for Europe and Japan.[1]

A STEADY FLOW

Joe Cashman is the father figure of the Irish investment drive in Tokyo; he opened the first office of the Irish Development Authority in 1973. Most of the early Japanese investment in Ireland, and the setting up of the necessary training programmes to enable the Irish to address the Asian market, can be traced to him. In the post Second World War days of the Irish effort to break into Asia, Tokyo was the bridgehead for not only Japan but Korea, Indonesia, Cambodia, Laos and Vietnam. By the 1970s, economic imperatives were replacing the spiritual ones of the Irish priests who had been the main representatives of the Irish (or of the Vatican) in Japan, as in Asia generally. Commenting on this Father Bill Johnston had remarked to me wistfully: 'It used to be all priests and nuns at the embassy parties. Now it's businessmen. Not a hooley atmosphere . . .'[2]

Cashman, who was originally a Columban priest, married a Filipino woman. The marriage was a success. This is by no means the norm for Irish marriages in Tokyo. Cashman summed up the culture shock both for the clergy and for matrimony as follows: 'Originally the Irish came to teach. We never taught them anything. We never learned. Irish women married Japanese men without understanding the society. It was a statistical disaster.'[3]

The experience of Irishmen in Japanese corporate society, however, is far from disastrous. Said Cashman:

> Every Japanese mother's dream is to see her son get into Mitsubishi, or one of the other big corporations. That's where the Irish guys start – after that it's on to Morgan Guaranty Trust, Citibank, wherever, these guys are lethal weapons in American business. What they could do for Ireland! You have to understand that Japanese personnel managers set unusual personality and problem solving tests. The results mean that they do get the brightest and best.[4]

Because of, not despite, these tests there is a growing concentration in Japanese studies in Ireland, particularly at Dublin City University and Limerick University. Also, as well as the developments noted by Hardiman, in recent years there has been a steady flow of Irish scholars, poets and writers who·have been lecturing and giving readings in Japan. In return Japanese scholars have been visiting Ireland, lecturing and translating Irish literature into Japanese. Given the vast cultural differences which exist between the two societies the quality of some of this activity is, not unexpectedly, uneven. Joseph O'Leary, a priest of the Cork diocese who teaches philosophy at Sophia University, summed up the difficulties for me: 'Look, can you imagine me teaching Shinto and Buddhism in Cork?'[5] Nevertheless, the important thing is that such activities exist and they are growing. Where there is growth there can be and, I would hazard a guess, will be progress and improvement.

THE INTERFACE

Another Irish cleric in Tokyo, Bill Johnston S.J, of Sophia University, who has spent forty-five years in Japan attempting to integrate the Christian gospel and the traditions of Western spirituality with Eastern mysticism, particularly Zen Buddhism, has written:

> Foreigners here talk, sometimes ruefully, about culture shock. On the surface Tokyo looks like New York or London; but underneath lies a different world, a different consciousness, a different mind-set. Japan has been moulded by centuries of Buddhism, Taoism, Confucianism, without losing its distinctively Japanese identity. Reactions are quite different from those of the West. Even businessmen need education on how to do business in Japan. So be prepared![6]

I like that 'even businessmen' – the dry reminder that though we live in a Celtic Tiger era of the spreadsheet, 'the corporate environment', and the company membership of the golf club, nevertheless certain verities persist. Father Bill, one of the most sophisticated and, at the same time, one of the most humble people I met on my travels, studied in St Malachy's College, Belfast with Brian Moore. 'I'm here forty-five years,'[7] he said, 'but my roots are in Belfast.' He went on to describe the contemporary North of Ireland situation in an up-to-date fashion that belied his near half-century of exile: 'Partition has worked. North of Ireland people are not really accepted in the South. When I meet my North of Ireland colleagues I resonate with them.'[8]

His principal example of the Irish-Japanese interface in recent years was a northern-based one, centring on the Belfast Nobel Peace Prize winner, Mairead Corrigan, who had visited Tokyo during the Gulf War with a group of Nobel Peace Prize winners. The group had uttered polite platitudes, but Mairead had made an apology for what Christians did in Hiroshima. She then went on to make an appeal that no soldiers be sent to the Gulf War. 'There were several other Nobel Peace Prize winners, but Mairead got the headlines.

It was very moving for the Japanese,' said Bill.

'How have the Irish influenced the Japanese?' I asked him. 'I don't think the Irish have influenced the Japanese as much as the Japanese have influenced the Irish,' he replied. 'You know they're teaching karate in Maynooth now!'

VISIBILITY

As is usual with the Irish in any part of the world, there are two sets of figures for the Irish presence: those supplied by the Embassy and those preferred by the emigrant community itself. It may well be that, as was suggested to me, there are five times the 850–1,000 whom the Embassy calculate are resident in Tokyo and elsewhere in Japan. Certainly the Irish are more visible than a mere 1,000-strong presence would suggest. This visibility is growing by the year, as Irish pubs spread through Japan's cities. Whether one takes the official or unofficial figure, what is certain is that already the Irish population is larger than that of any of the small European nations. This is remarkable when one thinks of the long trading associations which Japan has with Holland or Portugal, for example.

As noted earlier the annual Irish Embassy Emerald Ball is an increasingly important social event in Tokyo, but the growth of the St Patrick's Day parade is highly unusual because, apart from occasional right-wing demonstrations, the Japanese do not normally take part in marches. Accordingly, when the St Patrick's Day parade began in 1991, it was a very small affair. Approximately fifty Irish marched along the sidewalk in the Roppongi district of Tokyo. By 1999, however, the parade had moved to the more fashionable Omotersando district and some 5,000 people took part. The 'St Patrick's Day in Tokyo' T-shirts sold out and the marching numbers were swollen by Japanese wearing green wigs and doing Irish jigs. Amongst the banners that fluttered over the Irish-wolfhound-accompanied procession was one which said in Japanese: 'We're all Irish anyway.' At least that was what an Irish lad helping to carry it said he hoped it said. Many of the marchers wore fairly grotesque masks whose design appeared to owe more to the traditions of Hallowe'en and kabuki, than St Patrick. The Bewleys pub (called and designed after Bewleys coffee shops in Dublin) was jammed to suffocation inside, and outside some thousands milled around the steps bearing plaques commemorating Joyce, Synge, and Yeats. Inside Bewleys, the Japanese ate bacon and eggs and drank pints of Guinness at $8.50 a time (roughly three times the price in Dublin). Lager beer dyed green was also available. Irish music was provided by Isao and Masako Moriyasu, using the traditional Irish instruments: bodhran, accordian, concertina, flute and tin whistle. In Ireland the pair are better known on the Irish traditional music circuit, as Bridget and Paddy!

'Bridget and Paddy' are examples of the sort of quirky Japanese-Irish cultural links one encounters on every hand. For example, the Japanese academic, Nakoi Yanase, translated Joyce's *Finnegans Wake* into Japanese. It took him eight years. One encounters the usual critical disdain in some quarters as to the purity of the translation; nevertheless it must be regarded as a significant accomplishment, given the fact that there are those in Dublin who would tell you that the real priority for that formidable work is its translation into English.

IRISH WRITERS IN JAPAN

Arguably the best-known Irish figure in Japan, indeed one of the best-known foreigners of any race, is not Joyce but Lafcadio Hearn, better known by the name he took on adopting Japanese citizenship, Koizumi Yakumo. Hearn married the daughter of a Samurai family and wrote several books on Japan, becoming Professor of English at the Imperial University in Tokyo. Born to a Greek beauty and an Irish army surgeon in 1850, on the Ionian island of Lefkas, he was virtually abandonded by his father as a boy to be raised by his father's relatives in Ireland. He worked as a journalist in America and the West Indies, before travelling to Japan in 1890 on a journalistic assignment, as a result of the interest in Japan in the West stimulated by Perry's voyage.

Hearn was one of four distinguished English-language writers who lived in and wrote about Japan in the late nineteenth century. The others were Basil Chamberlain, Ernest Satow and William Aston. Aston, who was born in Northern Ireland and graduated from Queen's University, was, like Satow, a member of the British foreign service. Chamberlain was probably the most scholarly and widely travelled of this remarkable quartet, but Hearn achieved the greatest empathy with the Japanese. His Irish background enabled him to see the Japanese without adopting the patina of superiority which other English writers displayed. In describing the Japanese character to me, Tom Hardiman approvingly quoted Hearn's dictum: there are 'those who imagine the Japanese to be merely imitative ... As a fact they are assimilative and adoptive only and that to a degree of genius.'[9]

That's certainly how the Japanese like to see themselves! Hearn died in 1904, but today, almost a century later, his work is still regarded as giving one of the best insights into Japan's inner life for Westerners, particularly his book *Japan: An Attempt at Interpretation*. Unlike most Westerners of the time, he lived as the Japanese did, learned their language and also learned how to see the world through their eyes.

Irish ghost stories, which he listened to as a child, helped Hearn to an understanding of Japanese culture. The stories also gave him nightmares, as a result of which he developed a life-long fascination with the macabre. He wrote several horror stories of the calibre of Sheridan Le Fanu or Bram Stoker, both of whose families were related to him by marriage. His great-grandson Bon Koizumi has judged that one of Hearn's most famous works, *Kwaidan*, was inspired by 'Irish ghost stories and fairy tales. On this I think that he had the Irish spirit.'[10] Hearn himself once wrote: 'There is something ghostly in all great art.'

Thanks to the efforts of one of his biographers, the late Sean Ronan, a former Irish Ambassador to Japan, Hearn's portrait now hangs in the Dublin Writers Museum along with Swift and Joyce. It is a measure of Hearn's stature that two distinguished members of the Irish diplomatic corps were moved to write biographies of him. In addition to Ronan, Paul Murray, who once served in the Irish Embassy in Tokyo, and is now the Irish Ambassador to South Korea, has also written a well-received biography of the exotic Irishman turned Japanese.

THE JAPANESE INFLUENCE ON YEATS

The influence of the Japanese Noh form on Ireland's greatest poet, W. B. Yeats, was a crucial one in his development of mask, mime, dance, music and poetry in his mythological work. His play on the Cuchulain theme, *At the Hawk's Well*, dedicated to Ezra Pound, was first produced in the London home of Nancy Cunard, on 2 April 1916, a few weeks before the Easter rebellion in which Cuchulain's legendary warrior spirit was to descend so decisively on Dublin. The play featured the Japanese dancer Michio Ito. Later that year the Cuala Press, owned by Yeats's sister, Lily, published Fenollosa's Japanese plays, translated by Pound, with an essay on the drama by Yeats.

In 1920, Yeats undertook a lecture tour of America, 'one of the high points' of which was a meeting with Junzo Sato, then the Japanese Consul at Portland, Oregon.[11] Sato admired Yeats's work and had brought him a present wrapped in embroidered silk. Yeats said in a letter to Edmond Dulac, who had designed the sets for the *Hawk's Well* production in the Cunard drawing room, that Sato:[12]

> untied the silk cord that bound it and brought out a sword which had been for 500 years in his family. It had been made 550 years ago and he showed me the maker's name upon the hilt.

Yeats deeply appreciated the gift, the antiquity, the craftsmanship and, most importantly, the empathy. He placed the 'changeless sword' on a table near his pen and paper so that it would 'moralise' his 'days out of their aimlessness'. His poem, My Table, goes on:[13]

> Chaucer had not drawn breath
> When it was forged. In Sato's house,
> Curved like a new moon, moon-luminous
> It lay five hundred years.

As Professor Robert Welch comments: 'The affinity between Yeats's idea of unified intensity and the concept of total commitment without fear in Zen swordsmanship is striking.'[14]

CULTURAL INTERACTION

Welch is a County Cork Catholic and, significantly, holder of a Chair of Literature in Coleraine University in County Derry (written as Londonderry on the university's notepaper). The building of the university by the Unionists in a vain attempt to deny the surge of Celtic energy now engulfing the planter-controlled Six County University system, was one of the sparks which set off the Civil Rights movement, and the subsequent Troubles.[15] He is also one of the moving spirits in the International Association for the Study of Irish Literature (ISAIL), which has set up a flourishing branch in Japan. His summary of the interaction of Irish-Japanese culture indicates the underlying Celtic influence of the Irish contribution inasmuch as he takes as his starting point the authority of the German Celtologist, Kuno Meyer, whose influence has been indicated in Chapter 1. Welch says:[16]

> Kuno Meyer famously compared the delicacy and immediacy of Irish lyric poetry with Japanese understatement in the haiku and tanka forms There does seem to be at least some form of cultural similarity in the responsiveness of Japanese and Irish poetic traditions to the small details of nature: a bird singing, the moon in the water, a fall of rain, the sudden surge of delight while in the midst of natural things

One might take the cultural similarities further by noting that both the Irish and the Japanese are international in outlook, great travellers and traders, and, at the same time, literally deeply insular. Both the Japanese and the Irish are preoccupied with the minutiae, not only of nature, but of their families, their native places, their own distinctive sagas and their native sports, which generate a more passionate following than that even for soccer.

Yeats is not the only Irish poet to have been drawn to Japan, as Welch points out:[17] 'Derek Mahon has written a poem on Basho's 'Snow Party'; Michael Longley has written about Japanese–Irish friendship in pieces such as 'A Gift of a Box'; Paul Muldoon is everywhere alive to Japanese suggestion and subtlety; Friel, Murphy, and McGuinness are regularly performed in Japan.'

It has to be said that the brashness of contemporary Irish culture is beginning to overlay the Yeatsian stylism in Irish-Japanese cultural links. Seamus Hosey has recorded the difficulties experienced by his friend Roddy Doyle in securing adequate Japanese translations of his characters' north Dublin dialogue.[18] Japanese dictionaries were combed in vain during the construction of the subtitles for the film of Doyle's novel, *The Snapper*. Alas, there were no equivalents for such Dublinisms as: 'Ya thick bitch', and 'to throw a wobbler'. The subtitlers were particularly challenged by a scene in which Sharon is comforted by her friends with generous libations of vodka and tonic on discovering that she has become pregnant by a married man. One of Sharon's friends says: 'Sharon, I'm scarlet for you!' the subtitle reads: 'Sharon, I'm socially embarrassed at your predicament'! Similarly a major

Tokyo bookstore featured a window display of the novels of Maeve Binchy under a banner which translated her name as Mauve Binky.

The Japanese Theatre Director, Ukio Ninegawa, has made a more original attempt at translating Irish writers. He cast Beckett's *Waiting for Godot* with alternating all male and all female casts, and the play was set in a Zen garden of rock, water and a bare tree. Ninegawa used two kabuki actors as Vladimir and Estragon and, figure this one out, Lucky was played by a sumo wrestler.

Of contemporary Irish musical artists, Enya, Sinead O'Connor, the Chieftains, Van Morrison, Mary Black, James Galway, U2 and the other Irish rock bands are immensely popular. These singers and musicians form part of a tradition of Irish music that goes back to Tom Moore, though most Japanese have never heard of him. As the distinguished Japanese scholar, Ken'ichi Matsumura, has observed:

> Some melodies of Thomas Moore have been very popular in Japan, though people in general don't know they are Irish melodies, so, hidden contact. Everyone knows, for example, the melody of 'The last rose of summer', but the Japanese lyric is of such difference that they think it is a Japanese song.[19]

The contemporary Empress Michiko is known to be particularly fond of Moore's music. She is a graduate of the University of the Sacred Heart in Tokyo where Irish nuns taught. The Empress studied Irish history, literature and music, and has been described by Sister Ruth Sheehy as one of the convent's star pupils.[20] She is known to play the Irish harp, speaks Irish and, as her party piece, recites a poem by the executed 1916 leader, Thomas McDonagh: 'I see His Blood Upon The Rose'. She visibly enjoyed an official visit she paid to Ireland in 1984 when her husband, Emperor Akihito, was the Crown Prince.

A FORMATIVE FORCE

The Empress is an illustrious example of the influence of that formative, and formidable, force, already frequently met with in these pages: the Irish nun. However, she is by no means the only one. At a dinner which the Irish Ambassador to Japan, Declan O'Donovan, gave for me in Tokyo, one of that city's most distinguished academics, Professor Masako Saito, told me: 'I owe my education and my faith to Irish nuns.' She was educated by the Irish Sacred Heart Nuns in Washington and Tokyo.

Even though it is possible to encounter hostility to Christianity in Japan, it is also known that individuals from some of Japan's ruling, wealthy families who trace their lineage back to the Samurai have converted to Catholicism under the influence of Irish religious. In fact there were rumours that the Empress might have considered joining them. This seems a remote possibility. Such a conversion would create a Chernobyl-like fall-out in court circles. While the Empress is spoken of on all sides as a remarkable, warm, outgoing person, the 1,200 strong royal entourage is a combination of right-wing snobbery and conservatism that makes the British royal family set-up seem almost liberal by comparison.

HIDDEN CONTACT

Just as we have all found in our lives that a chance meeting, or suggestion, or opportunity has had a profound effect on our lives, so has a chance contact with Irish character and culture had a profound effect on different people I met in the course of compiling this book. Ken'ichi, now Professor, Matsumura, is but one. He was studying English literature at Waseda University in Tokyo when the late Professor Shotaro Moshima introduced him to Yeats, and, in his own words, 'that moment seems to have decided my whole course'.

He came to Ireland in the early eighties and, realising that he needed a knowledge of the Irish language if he was to fully appreciate Irish poetry, studied Old Irish at Trinity College, meeting Irish literary figures like Seamus Heaney and Brendan Kennelly. His interest in the concept of voyaging, the study of Irish poetry and the saga of the early Irish monks led him to publish *The Voyage of Bran* which might be regarded as the prototype of the better-known Irish classic *The Voyage of St Brendan*. For a Japanese this was probably an even more arcane project than the translation of *Finnegans Wake* into Japanese.

Professor Matsumura's comment 'hidden contact' is well taken. The average Japanese man or woman in the street would only know of Ireland from television clips of the Troubles, but they would all have heard of Jonathan Swift's *Gulliver's Travels* – which is published in Japanese in an abridged version – without realising who Swift was. Nor would there be a general awareness of the fact that the Irish made a significant contribution to the development of submarine warfare in Japan.

THE IRISH IN JAPANESE NAVAL HISTORY

John Philip Holland born in Liscannor, County Clare, in 1841, emigrated to New Jersey where he became a teacher and, as we have seen, designed the first ever submarine with the assistance of the Fenians.[21] As research by Sean Ronan has shown,[22] the Russo-Japanese War which broke out in 1904 provided a spur to Japanese interest in Holland's invention that predated the war.[20] Japanese dignitaries, including Counts Kosuke Kizaki and Takashi Sasaki, had both submerged in one of Holland's early designs during trials in New York harbour in 1898. Lieutenant Commander Ide of the Japanese Navy gave public lectures in which he urged the use of Holland's submarines, but Japanese governmental plans to buy any had gone on the back burner until war broke out. Then an order was placed with the Electric Boat Company for five of Holland's submarines to be built in the Fore River yard in Quincy,

Massachusetts. They were built, then dismantled and shipped to Japan where they were reassembled at Wokosuka, near Yokohama.

The submarines formed the first Japanese submarine force and were formally incorporated into the navy on 1 October 1905. The war ended before they could be used, although they did have a psychological effect on the Russians. They were subsequently used for training purposes for nearly fifteen years. Holland later designed two more, larger submarines, the first to be built in Japan. They were capable of doing a speed of 16 knots underwater.

Holland was presented with the Fourth Class Order of Merit Rising Sun Ribbon by the Japanese Ambassador to Washington. In their citation to the Emperor, urging that Holland be accorded the honour, the Minister for Foreign Affairs and the Navy, Count Kaoru Hayashi and Baron Saito said:[23]

> At the time of the Russo-Japanese war he [Holland] offered his plan of submarines to the Japanese Navy of his own will, which would be built at the Kawasaki Naval Dockyard. Holland dedicated himself to our country's benefit, sacrificing his own profit .. His achievement for our Navy is inestimable ... It is time to honour his distinguished services.

Ironically, although he originally developed the submarine to strike at England, Holland also believed as he told Thomas A. Edison in 1904, that submarines would serve to end naval warfare, because they were so deadly. Sean Ronan, however, quotes from a document which illustrates the reality that accompanied this fusion of Irish-Japanese ingenuity. It is the last, terrible log entry of the Holland submarine Dai-rokuh (sixth), which sank on manoeuvres in Hiroshima Bay in 1910 with the loss of all fifteen aboard. The entry is by Lieutenant Sakuma. While it is a classic encapsulation of the self-sacrificial heroism of the Japanese officer class, it also graphically illustrates the horror attendant on the development of Holland's invention:

> Words of apology fail me for having sunk His Majesty's submarine No.6. My subordinates are killed by my fault, but it is with pride that I inform you that the crew to a man have discharged their duties as sailors should with the utmost coolness until their dying moments. We now sacrifice our lives for the sake of our country, but my fear is that the disaster will affect the future development of submarines. It is therefore my hope that nothing will daunt your determination to study the submarine until it is a perfect machine, absolutely reliable. We can then die without regret ...
>
> The current submerged the electric generator, put out the light, and the electric wires were burned In a few minutes bad gas was generated, making it difficult for us to breathe.
>
> Surrounded by poisonous gas, the crew strove to pump out the water. As soon as the boat sank the water in the main tank was being pumped out. The electric light was extinguished and the gauge was invisible, but it seems the water in the main tank was completely pumped out. The electric current had become useless, gas cannot be generated, and the hand pump is our only hope. The vessel is in darkness, and I note this down by the light through the conning tower at 11.45 a.m. The crew are now wet and it is extremely cold. It is my opinion that men embarking in submarines must possess the qualities of coolness and nerve, and must be extremely painstaking; they must be brave and daring in their handling of the boat.

People may laugh at this opinion in view of my failure, but the statement is true . . . The crew of the submarine should be selected from the bravest, the coolest, or they will be of little use in time of crisis – in such as we are now. My brave men are doing their best. I always expect death when away from home. My will is therefore prepared and is in the locker. But this is of my private affairs. I hope Mr Taguchi will send it to my father. A word to His Majesty the Emperor. It is my earnest hope that Your Majesty will supply the means of living to the poor families of the crew This is my only desire, and I am so anxious to have it fulfilled. My respect and best regard to the following:

Admiral Saito, Minister of the Navy; Vice Admirals Shinamura and Fujii, Rear Admirals Nawa, Yamashita and Narita – the air pressure is so light that I feel as if my eardrums will be broken . . . Captain Funakehshi, it is now 12.30 p.m My breathing is so difficult and painful. I thought I could blow out gasoline, but I am intoxicated with it – Captain Nakano – it is now 12.40 p.m . . .

In all it took Lieutenant Sakuma two hours and forty minutes to die.

Apart from Holland, two other Irishmen also hold an honoured place in Japanese naval history, the brothers John and Cornelius Collins from Carrigaline, in County Cork. The twin brothers initially landed in Japan at the age of twenty-three in 1873, as ordinary seamen, part of a group of British naval personnel sent to help train the Japanese Navy. The brothers subsequently returned to Japan as naval instructors when the British tour of duty was over and their services were deemed to be so out of the ordinary that the Emperor, his Imperial Majesty Matso Hito, personally conferred on them the decoration of the Order of the Rising Sun. They were also awarded the Order of the Kir Ri.

During their stay, the Collins brothers had helped to transform the Japanese Navy from an inefficient sail-based navy to a modern steam-driven one whose power was shown in the havoc which the Japanese wreaked on the far larger Chinese fleet during hostilities in 1884. John Collins's notes on gunnery were translated into Japanese and used by the Navy. The war ended with the loss to China of the island of Formosa which is still a threat to world peace, being the subject of serious disagreement between China and the US. John Collins, by then a prosperous farmer in his native County Cork was asked by a reporter from the *Cork Examiner* if he were following the war. He replied in terms which could have been used by an Irish emigrant in Japan today looking at the Peace Process: 'I am following it with the same interest and anxiety that I followed the Parnell movement while we were in Japan.' As Mike Grey, the CBS correspondent in Tokyo, who left Ireland in 1965, told me, 'The longer you stay away the more Irish you get.'

The esteem in which the Collins brothers were held in Japan may be judged from an incident in 1902[24] when two Japanese warships called in to Cobh, County Cork, while on a European tour during which the ships were visited by royalty. The commanders of the vessels, including Admiral Goro Ishuuin, made sure the first courtesy call of their visit was on the Collins brothers at their home, Bellview, near the village of Douglas. Then during their subsequent official tour of Cork city, the Japanese officers were accompanied by the brothers. For such a hierarchical, caste-conscious society, only a few decades away from feudalism, this gesture of respect by Japanese noblemen for two men who had landed in Japan as ordinary British seamen was quite remarkable. As the Japanese Ambassador to Ireland Kiyosai Furukana said in August 1994 as he unveiled a memorial to the Collinses in Carrigaline: 'the story of the Collins brothers ... is a very important connection between Ireland and Japan'.

AN INCREASING INTEREST

While it is probably true that relatively few Japanese would have heard of either John Philip Holland or the Collins twins, one can certainly point to an increasing Japanese interest in Irish history. Arisa Mori teaches it, and visited Dublin to study the setting up of the then illegal Sinn Fein courts by the first Dail during the Anglo-Irish War, while she was preparing a thesis. She had an impressive number of students in Tokyo.[25] She taught at three university centres – at Gashuin (which the Emperor had attended and is remembered for his interest in things Irish), Chuo and Takasaki. Her classes numbered sixty, sixty-five and a hundred respectively. Arisa was wearing an Aran sweater when she came to see me, and talked wistfully about the smell of Irish turf fires. Two of her students were doing MAs: one on Roger Casement, the other on the Irish Poor Law Relief system of the Famine period. She finds that her students are drawn to such courses initially by the music and by the Troubles in Northern Ireland: 'They want to know why such terrible things happened.' Her boyfriend Makote, who was thirty-five and whom she subsequently married, ascribed his incredibly youthful appearance to the traditional Japanese diet of fish and seaweed, and said:[26] 'We don't have any background of religious warfare, nor of colonial guerrilla wars, and so we take an interest in Ireland and Iran – but they don't have Irish music in Iran!'

A MANY-FACETED SOCIETY

Japan's is an elusive, many-faceted society – and extremely elusive are the famous Yakusa, the gangsters whom the Americans reintroduced to Japan in 1945, to combat Communism, just as they had done earlier in the war with the Mafia in Italy. One could if one wished draw interesting parallels between the place of the Yakusa and that of the gangster in Irish American culture, or the secret society in Ireland. Like the IRA in Northern Ireland, the Yakusa are omnipresent but never seen. They traditionally recruit amongst policemen, and are reported to control, amongst other sources of revenue such as drugs and prostitution, the unbelievably lucrative Pachinko slot machine parlours which occupy so much of Japan's leisure time. The Yakusa have their own un-acknowledged fiefdoms and spheres of influence, which the authorities say are insignificant and Westerners say are all-powerful. 'They control everything – not just the Pachinko, the buses, everything,' one old Japanese hand told me.

I had approached him to find out about that other much denied but often-met-with character in Japanese society, 'The Man'.

He told me: 'Domestically the Japanese are the best people in the world, but when you go into their offices, behind the desk, you meet 'The Man'. 'The Man' is a product of a type of business and professional culture which means that encounters with bureaucrats, the police or, for instance, the Department of Education can be so unwelcoming that many foreigners speedily head for home. Japanese society is extremely controlled; people are trained not to show their feelings. Personalities are enclosed and suppressed. The feminine side of man's nature is virtually eradicated. As one observer put it for me:

> They spend their school years being harassed and brainwashed for the corporate world. Imagination is drummed out of them. That's why they've contributed nothing to world leadership, for all their wealth They went money mad after the Second World War. Then they enter the academic world for a number of years, during which there is little effort. They're programmed to be good at business and the technologies, but they're poor at the humanities. But they don't really do anything much at university normally Then they enter industry . . . wow! They spend the rest of their lives being harassed.[27]

It's a system which above all deprecates spontaneity. As the Irish are nothing if not spontaneous, particularly if there is a little Guinness and Irish music in the offing, it would appear that opposites attract. Yakusa and the Man notwithstanding (or perhaps because of them!), the Japanese like the Irish – one of the reasons the Japanese corporations locate in Ireland is because surveys show that there is less anti-Japanese sentiment than elsewhere in the European Community, particularly the UK. In my experience, Japanese diplomats make unusually large numbers of friends in Dublin, and when I looked up some of my own diplomatic friends in Tokyo I was given long lists of people in Ireland whom the outwardly remote ex-ambassadors remembered in the most affectionate and human terms.

DIFFICULTY

The only time the Irish as a race encountered any difficulty in Japan was during the Second World War, when they faced internment for being 'British'. Even in wartime, however, Irish ingenuity could sometimes cope with Japanese militarism. Father Aidan McGrath, a Columban missionary, tells a story of an incident which befell him in China during the 'Rape of Nanjing' as the Japanese invaded.[28] Some 1,500 women descended on Father McGrath, desperately seeking protection. They were followed by some 6,000 Japanese soldiers. Somehow, McGrath discovered that the officer in charge was a film buff and informed him that he was a personal friend of Loretta Young. According to McGrath the officer was:

Very excited to learn that I knew his love in Hollywood. He wrote something and sealed it and put it on the door. The soldiers all saluted and stayed away. The women stayed for six months – they dared not leave.[29]

Father McGrath survived the war and at the time of writing was happily based in Manila.

CONTACTS

For all the strange, unfamiliar aspects of Japanese society, when it came to the Irish diaspora itself I found Japan brought home to me the small-world syndrome more than most places I'd been. Apart from my earlier contact with Mary Jordan, I found on meeting a CBS correspondent, Irishman Mike Grey, that I had known both his father Tony and his uncle Ken in Dublin, where both were distinguished journalists. Sitting opposite a teacher of English, Seamus MacElwaine, at a dinner one evening, I discovered that he had been born in my father's native village of Castlecomer, County Kilkenny. However, Donal Doyle, a Jesuit priest, took the biscuit. His father turned out to have been our family doctor when I was a boy.

Father Doyle was formerly assistant to the President of Sofia University, and at the time of writing is Professor in the English Language Department. He has been living in Japan since 1958 and is regarded as one of the best-informed, and well-connected foreigners in Tokyo. Certainly, walking around the campus with him, it soon became obvious that he had established an extremely good rapport with his Japanese students. He brings parties of them on tours to Ireland and other European countries. Their favourite place in Europe – which, because of the tour dates, they visit in the howling month of February – is the Aran Islands. Such contacts have helped to integrate the Irish community into a close-knit Japanese society much more easily than other European nations – but then other countries don't have Arthur Guinness on their side.

Paddy Foley's Irish Bar is one of the most popular meeting places in all Tokyo. The Japanese come for the music, the Guinness and the craic. The young Irish business executives and computer experts one finds there with their Japanese friends will be an increasingly important resource for Ireland as their careers progress. Though the Japanese always retain ultimate control of their corporations, they do tend to promote the Irish, not only within their Japanese-based companies, but in their overseas holdings, which means that increasingly Irish executives are – or at least will be when the current Japanese recession ends – in a position to take decisions affecting both Japanese investment in Ireland and Irish business expansion in Japan.

The Japanese Exchange and Teaching programme (JET) which brings Irish teachers of language or sports to Japanese schools is annually increasing the level of contact between the two countries. Meanwhile, in Ireland, the Japanese have put down further roots by establishing a school for Japanese children at a particularly beautiful location in Newbridge, County Kildare. The Irish Industrial Development Authority reckons that these roots will produce shoots bearing fruit in the coming years. There is high praise in the IDA for Japanese standards of business honesty. The Japanese tendency to take a long view of investment, continuing to put money into their holdings even during recession, and making strenuous efforts to avoid lay-offs, is particularly appreciated. Although here have been some business failures because of the recession, notably the pottery company Noritake based in Arklow, County Wicklow, the overall Japanese approach contrasts favourably with that of American investors who, at the first whiff of recessionary grapeshot, pack up their equipment and head back to Fortress America.

RACING

There is a long-standing connection in the Irish public mind between Japan and the Irish racing industry, because a principal attraction of the Irish National Stud in Kildare is its Japanese Gardens. They were built by a specially imported gardener who lived happily in Ireland for several years, but he then destroyed himself during his return home to Japan with his family by losing all his money gambling in London. So, given the place of the horse in both Irish and Japanese society it was no great surprise to discover that one of Japan's top racehorse trainers is an Irishman, Harry Sweeney. Harry runs a vast stud farm in Hokaido, dominated by a huge castle equipped with space-age electronic gadgetry. Sweeney is a vet who was raised on a small farm in County Louth with eight brothers and sisters. He attributes his success to his parents and the Irish educational system:

> My father bought the farm through his own efforts. I don't know how they did it. But my father and mother worked themselves to the bone to make sure we all got to university. On top of that they'd be sending us off for things like music lessons. The other lads would be missing school doing potato picking and such like. We had to do our share of that stuff but the parents saw to it we got education as well.[30]

When I met Harry, he was off to see his boss about two matters. The first was his intention to spend some millions on buying European bloodstock – no big deal given the amounts involved in Japanese racing. The other was a little more delicate. He wanted to convince his employer that, on top of the ninety days a year he already spent travelling the world, he should be given an additional fifty days' leave so that he could get back to his farm in Ireland more often, and at the same time have his children educated at home. Sweeney's record as a trainer is such that the boss readily agreed: 'That is no problem. The manager of our New York operations lives in Frankfurt,' was the response. The Japanese are interested in the result, not the time spent in achieving it. The standing of the Irish in the Japanese bloodstock industry generally is such that, Japanese recession or no, during the 1999 Dublin Horse

Show the owner of an Irish staff recruitment agency made an appeal on RTE[31] to young Irish horse lovers to take up some of the jobs available to them in Japan.

FINALE

My last Japanese phone call was made from Narita Airport to Billy Kelly, Ted Turner's man in Japan. I had never met him but I had heard that he was hard to track down because he travelled a lot. Accordingly, as my schedule was a very full one, I had hesitated to invest time in the attempt. I rang as my flight was being called, merely out of courtesy, to tell his secretary that I had touched base. However, as I started to explain, she interrupted: 'Mr Coogan, oh yes, he was talking about you. Here he is . . .' The Irish grapevine! But there was more. As I started to explain that I was at the airport and what a pity it was that I hadn't known he was in Tokyo, he interrupted: 'Not to worry. We'll have a jar in Finnegans.' This is one of my favourite watering holes in Dalkey – it turned out that his Dublin home is up the road from me, a few hundred yards from where this is being written. Wherever green is worn . . .

EPILOGUE

I HAVE ATTEMPTED to chart the contours of the Irish from their origins through fame, fortune and disaster as they rose to their present plateau of success. As I said in the Introduction, this was something of a pioneering work. I leave it to others, perhaps better resourced, either to re-trace my steps so as to avoid the inevitable pit-falls, or to explore other facets of the subject. The innermost workings of heart and mind, of spirit, must delve beneath contour and require not merely the tools of description but those of the poet, novelist, or perhaps, the psychiatrist.

As I complete my odyssey I am reminded that in the Yeats poem from which the title of this book was taken, the poet's message was that the 1916 revolution had changed everything and that a terrible beauty had been born. Something of the same transformation has occurred for contemporary Ireland and its diaspora. Both contain beauties and terrors. In order to celebrate what has been achieved, and avoid repeating what has been committed, both have to be planned for.

The Irish must maintain a sense of proportion. The much vaunted Celtic Tiger, for example, seems more like the Mouse that Roared when one considers the scale of the Irish Republic. More people commute to work each day in either London or New York than live in the Irish State. But scale notwithstanding, the Irish economy is the fastest growing in Europe. True, the OECD warns us about the dangers of over-heating, labour shortages, inflation and the cost of housing, but as I write this, the airwaves resonate with claims for the Irish economy: 'Most US investment in any European country. Forty per cent of all software used in Europe manufactured in Ireland.'

In faraway Canada the former Canadian Prime Minister, Joe Clarke, in a speech delivered on May 8th 2000, said: 'In a little over a decade, the Irish economy has gone from proverbial basket case to boom. Today, it outperforms all other European economies, it has grown by over 50 per cent between 1992 and 1998 and is more competitive than Britain. In a population of 3.6 million people, the Irish have created a remarkable 400,000 jobs – this would be the equivalent of creating almost 3 million brand new jobs in Canada in the seven years of Liberal government.' Such are the common-places of commentators on the economic condition. But what of the human condition. How does it interact with the economic, and, in the short term at least, more importantly, with the political? One has to cast a wary eye on the six counties of North Eastern Ireland, which are in fact less northern than County Donegal, lying in the Irish Republic. One day, demographic forces, the sheer energy of the Celts, which we have observed in the preceding pages, will subsume the present Unionist majority.

But in the meantime, the long-term future of the Peace Process has to be commended to the gods of optimism rather than those of certainty It is to be hoped that the growing rapprochement between the two islands, which to some is symbolised by the close personal relationship of the Irish and British leaders, Bertie Ahern and Tony Blair, will continue. Nevertheless, while that friendship helped to sustain the Peace Process through the ill-advised suspension of the institutions that grew out of the Good Friday Agreement, it was not sufficient to induce the Secretary of State for Northern Ireland, Peter Mandelson, to desist from the suspension in the first place. Few tears were shed in Irish governmental circles at his fall from Blair's cabinet in January 2001.

The arbitrary and often incomprehensible manner in which London can oscillate between the policies of Mo Mowlam which made her a heroine in both Ireland and England, albeit a hate figure to the Unionists who, political outlook apart, detest women in politics anyhow, and those of Peter Mandelson, is a bad portent for the future. His sojourn in Belfast served to put a huge question mark over the future of the Good Friday Agreement. These swings in policy are not merely attributable to personality traits. Despite all the much-vaunted improvements in relationships between Dublin and London, and the frequently heard assertions of improvements in attitude towards the Irish in England, dark forces still stir under the surface, and have a knock-on effect on the Irish throughout the diaspora and at home.

What is it in the underbelly of British society that causes football hooligans during a soccer match, played in Belgium against Germany, with no obvious Irish associations, to make one of their principal chants as they rampage, 'no surrender to the IRA'? Writing on British attitudes towards the Irish, in the *Toronto Globe and Mail*, during the four-month period in which London effectively suspended the Good Friday Agreement, Mary Ambrose, a Canadian journalist living in London said: 'The love affair with things Irish continues around the world – unless you live in England . . . being Irish in England is still a liability.' Ambrose pointed out that most people in England blamed Sinn Fein and the IRA for the collapse of the Belfast parliament. But she also blamed 'the anti-Irish feeling that runs quietly through most of British society.' Most tellingly Ambrose pointed out that, incredible though it seemed, anti-Catholic feeling still existed in English society. She cited the 'widespread concern' which followed Blair's election victory, lest he turn Catholic (Britain has never had a Catholic Prime Minister); the facts that, though she had honoured him, the Queen 'snubbed the Catholic community' by not attending Cardinal Hume's funeral; and the prohibition against Prince Charles marrying a Catholic, as heir to the throne.

These disagreeable realities certainly exist. I have to confess that one of my abiding emotions on completing the research for this book was my sense of astonishment at the persistence of memories, and sometimes actualities of Protestant-Catholic hostilities around the globe. Resonances of the old British Protestant and Imperial project still persist, fainter now, but still distinct. The challenge for the Irish, both at home and abroad, will be to do everything in their power to combat such prejudices.

In aid of the proposition that it is likely that the Irish will do so, one might point to an example contained in an excellent hotel in the heart of London, Kensington's Tara Copthorne. It was once owned by Aer Lingus, and is now run by an international conglomerate. Its manager under Aer Lingus was Eoin Dillon, whose ancestor, Joseph Plunkett, was married in his cell ten minutes before he was executed for his part in the 1916 Rising. By an extraordinary coincidence he was succeeded by Desmond Kent whose ancestor Eamon Ceant (he used the Irish version of the name) was also an executed 1916 leader. Given reasonable luck, the professionalism of the Dillons, the Kents, the Murphys and the O'Flahertys can overcome the rancorous detritus of the Anglo-Irish relationship.

Mary Ambrose was unquestionably correct when she said that the love affair with all things Irish continues around the globe, and nowhere more noticeably than amongst the Irish themselves. From St Patrick's Day celebrations in Tokyo to those honouring James Joyce on Bloomsday in Toronto; from the growth of vibrant Irish-American newspapers and magazines, *The Irish Echo, Irish Voice, Irish-America, The Wonderful World of Hibernia, Eire Ireland, The Irish American Post*, and many others, to the *Irish Post* in London, or Val Noone's newly founded opinion journal, *Tain* in Australia. Globally, the citadels of music, literature, the stage have for so long been stormed and occupied by the Irish as to render further comment otiose.

A casual reader might not notice the significance of the changing advertisement patterns in the *Irish Post*, the newspaper of the Irish in England. But if he or she looks closely, they will see that ads for recruitment agencies are beginning to predominate over those concerning the attractions of Irish pubs. The Irish have not forsaken pubs, but they are returning home in droves, drawn by the siren purr of the Celtic Tiger.

I need not labour the significance of the turnaround in migration patterns, from emigration, to immigration. The fact of Rhodri Morgan standing in Holyhead through which so many frightened, shabby Irish emigrants shoaled to dead-end jobs in London and the Midlands, urging the Welsh to take jobs in Ireland, has already been alluded to. In the bars, check-out points, and garages of Dublin, one now encounters not Irish, but foreign workers. It is the significance of the change in migration patterns for Ireland itself that, along with the Peace Process, will present the greatest challenge for the future.

When, on a day in May 2000, the Irish Tanaiste, Mary Harney, stood up in Olympia to tell the 14,000 Irish emigrants who attended the job fair she opened, that Ireland planned to attract 200,000 workers from abroad to Ireland over the next five years, she was not merely making an optimistic forecast. She was throwing down a profound challenge for the future. The prestigious Irish think-tank, the Economic and Social Research Institute, had earlier issued a policy document urging that the Government slowed down its recruitment drive, and reduce economic growth so that inflationary pressures, such as the cost of housing, could be brought under control.

In rejecting the ERSI advice Harney was in fact echoing the words of the great Irish patriot, Charles Stewart Parnell, which are inscribed on his statue in O'Connell Street. With unconscious symbolism the sculptor has him pointing at the Rotunda maternity hospital, as he declaims: 'No man can set a boundary to the onward march of a Nation.'

It is Government policy to go for growth, not to set boundaries. But herein lies a challenge, not merely an economic one but a psychological and a moral challenge. The sufferers from the bad years of Irish emigration to the United Kingdom still live out their twilight lives in places like London's Arlington House. Young drop-outs still fall through the cracks in Ireland and present themselves in disturbing numbers to the Irish centres in London and throughout Britain. One in eleven of those sleeping rough in London are Irish. They must not be forgotten.

Growth has not benefited everyone and it has brought problems in its wake to Ireland, as it has everywhere else in the world. In February, 2001 the European Finance Ministers unanimously denounced Irish budgetary policies as 'inflationary', an unprecedented rebuke to a member state. The once 'good boys of the class' were now the bad boys. Drug-fuelled crime is rampant, murder is a weekly commonplace, and corruption reaching, and possibly exceeding, the scale achieved by the old Celtic bosses in America. The difference is that the contemporary Irish politicians are not stealing from the Wasps, they are robbing their own people, with disastrous consequences for public cynicism levels.

The huge wealth which is washing through the Irish coffers has produced an enshrinement of materialistic values. The numbers of child prostitutes and of people sleeping rough in Dublin, escalate it seems in direct ratio to the escalation of prices in the city's ever-proliferating hotels and restaurants.

Drugs spread, young male suicide increases, and, fuelled by a particularly wooden leadership-lacking Government, inertia on the asylum-seekers' problem, xenophobia and downright racism have reared their heads towards immigrants seeking a new life in Ireland. On one level this could be explained as part of the growing pains of multi-culturalism everywhere. But on the other one has to acknowledge a shocking attitude of historical ingratitude on the part of a nation that once scattered its children to the charity of the world. One thinks of those 'No Irish need apply' signs and winces. However, while these attitudes are as depressing as they are un-Christian, on a more positive note it is encouraging to be able to record that, as this is being written, voices are being raised against such callous attitudes.

The priest, Father Bobby Gilmore, mentioned earlier in these pages, is credited with being the inspiration behind a thoughtful statement by the Irish hierarchy calling on the Government to show a more humane face to the asylum-seekers. It was the most constructive statement to emanate from the hierarchy in decades, was correspondingly well-received, and may therefore filter into official policy. In some political circles, there is an acknowledgement both of Ireland's historic debt towards emigrants, and the finer feelings of what I still believe are the majority of the Irish public.

Like the horrific traffic congestion, and the soaring cost of housing – homes have increased in my area 12,000 per cent in the last 30 years – most of the rise taking place in the last decade, the asylum-seekers problem is one of success. The standing of the Irish in the world, including that of its diaspora, will be measured by their efforts to meet these challenges as they did those of adversity. It is simply not good enough to send the Irish to minister to the poor in Africa, and then spit on that poor when it turns up on the streets of Dublin seeking a better life. Nor can one go to far-off Newfoundland for some of the required 200,000 workers, and at the same time make a credible case for denying work to asylum seekers already in the country.

Thus, at home, in a post-clerical, though not yet post-Christian, society, now lies the challenge to those reservoirs of goodness, the intellect and of the imagination with which the Irish traditionally went forth into the world. St Brendan, the Navigator, who surfed the Atlantic in search of souls has given way to Laptop Man, who surfs the Net for profits. Can a synthesis be achieved between voyager and surfer? I believe it can. As I was concluding this book, the Munster rugby team won a famous victory over Toulouse in Bordeaux against all the odds. It was rugby's Fontenoy. Afterwards the team's trainer, Declan Kidney, spoke words which could be applied directly to Irish society at the start of the millennium:

'I do believe in Irish people. We are an unbelievably good nation. We turn out more good sports people in all codes than any other country in the world and instead of being harsh with one another, we just try and stress what is good about what we are doing.'

When the team subsequently went down to defeat gallantly in the final at Twickenham he reminded his players that it was only a game, that one could not truly savour the delights of the heights of victory unless one had experienced the lows of defeat, and told them to pick themselves up and get on with their lives.

England once believed that she won her battles on the playing-fields of Eton. Ireland never sought Imperial glory, but was forced too often in her history to swallow the bitter aloes of defeat. Today she can win her battles of the soul and of character by attending to the lessons of Munster on the sports field. Like Kidney, I too believe in the Irish people. Around the globe they have proved themselves to be 'an incredibly good nation'. My final wish for them is that, having conquered their demons at home, that their diaspora of the future may go forth only on an optional basis intent on upholding and building on the finest traditions of their race.

NOTES

INTRODUCTION

1. Gilley, Sheridan, *Journal of Ecclesiastical Studies,* vol. 35, 2, 1985.
2. Report by Gearoid O'Meachair, Federation of Irish Societies, February 1996.
3. *Dail Eireann,* 31 October 1951, vol. 127, 1, columns 3 and 4.
4. Commission on Emigration Report D/T S14249 A/2, NAI.

CHAPTER 1 EUROPE (PP 1 TO 108)

1. Lecture delivered by O'hAnnracháin at Cambrai, 21 June 1998. Copy in author's possession.
2. 24 June 1998.
3. The area inhabited by the Gauls could roughly be described in today's geographical terms as comprising Belgium, France, Germany, parts of Holland and Italy.
4. Considerable work has been done on the early Celts. It includes that of Dr Peter Beresford Ellis, *Celt & Greek,* Constable, 1997; Thomas Cahill, *How the Irish Saved Civilisation,* Septor, 1995; Ludwig Bieler, *Ireland, Harbinger of the Middle Ages,* Oxford University Press, 1963; and Frank Delaney, *The Celts,* HarperCollins, London, 1993 (which was based on the author's BBC TV series). These works draw on the writings of early scribes such as the Greeks, Diodorus Siculus and Strabo, or subsequently the Anglo-Saxon, the Venerable Bede. I have drawn on all of the foregoing.
5. Diodorus Siculus quoted by Beresford Ellis, op. cit. p. 39.
6. Cahill, op. cit. p. 135.
7. Joannon, Pierre, paper delivered at the Alliance Francaise, Dublin, 15 October 1998.
8. The God of the Sea, Mananaan, after whom the Isle of Man is named, is said to have ordered Bran to voyage across the seas until he came to a beauteous country.
9. Roughly corresponding to the ancient area of Gaul and West Germany.
10. The Irish diplomat, Charles Biggar, who was educated in Belgium, was taught the rhyme as a boy and translated it into English for me.
11. Bieler, op. cit. p. 97.
12. Lecture by Peter Beresford Ellis to the Desmond Graves Summer School, Dublin, 1998.

13. Between 1930 and 1932, Margaret C. Dobbs published a study which combined original text and translation in the *Revue Celtique*.
14. Cahill, op. cit.
15. John of Salisbury in 'Metalogicon', quoted by F. X. Martin, *A New History of Ireland*, Clarendon Press, Oxford, 1987, p. 57.
16. Bradshaw, Brendan, *Irish Historical Studies*, November 1989, vol. xxvi, no. 104.
17. Carter and Mears, *History of Britain*, Clarendon Press, Oxford, 1937, pp. 557–8.
18. Macaulay's *History of England* vol. 4, Macmillan, London 1914.
19. Bois, J-P, *Fontenoy, 1745*, Paris, 1996, p. 96
20. De Freine, Sean, *The Great Silence*, Mercier, Dublin and Cork, 1978.
21. Warren correspondence, E 1437, Morbihan Departmental Archives, Vannes. See also the *Irish Sword*, vol. xix, winter 1995, no. 78, p. 237 onwards for further Warren correspondence after Fontenoy.
22. *The Irish Augustinians*, ed. F. X. Martin OSA and Clare O'Reilly, St Patrick's Church, Rome, and the Augustinians, Ballyboden, Dublin, 1994, p. 21.
23. Griffin, William D., *The Book of Irish Americans*, Times Books, Random House, New York, 1990, p. 33.
24. Holohan, Renagh, 'The Bartons of Bordeaux,' *The World of Hibernia*, summer 1997.
25. Ibid.
26. McEnri, *The Paris Irish*, Ann t-Eirannach, Association Irlandaise, Paris, 1988.
27. There were a few pubs which specialised in Irish music and attracted Irish custom. For example Le Goblet d'Argent and Ti Jo's, a Breton establishment which is still a mecca for both British and Irish traditional music enthusiasts.
28. Interview with the author, Antibes, 11 June 1998.
29. Interview with the author, 18 June 1998.
30. Both historical and cultural contacts have been detailed by the German diplomat and scholar, Martin Elsasser, in *Germany and Ireland, 1000 years of shared history* (published in England and German), Brookside, Dublin, 1997.
31. 'The Kaiser's Irish Friends' is the title of a chapter in A. T. Q. Stewart, *The Ulster Crisis*, Faber, London, 1967. This is the standard work on the pre-First World War Home Rule controversy.
32. These links and the conduct of the Irish neutrality policy are described at length in the author's work: *The IRA*, HarperCollins, London, 1971.
33. Keogh, Dermot, *Jews in Twentieth-Century Ireland*, Cork University Press, 1998.
34. Interview with the author, 28 May 1998.
35. 29 May 1998.
36. The earliest version is credited to Owen Roe MacWard, who is thought

to have died sometime in the first half of the seventeenth century, possibly as early as the aftermath of the Flight of the Earls, that is, post-1607.

37. Quoted by Timothy O'Neill in *Merchants and Mariners,* Irish Academic Press, Dublin, 1986.

38. Father Luke Wadding, biographical and historical notes and documents by Gregory Cleary, OFM, Rome, 1925.

39. 15 June 1998.

40. He also made a series on the Irish wine traders of France, *The Wine Geese,* for RTE.

41. The Waxy's Dargle was an annual outing organised by tailors, cobblers, and other trades which used waxed threads.

42. 7 June 1998.

43. Enzo Farinella, ed., *Irish Italian Links* Guiseppe Bonanno Editore, and Dublin, 1997.

44. The original was preserved by the Irish Franciscans at Merchants Quay in Dublin.

45. Boyle, Leonard E. OP, *San Clemente Miscellany One*, Collegio San Clemente, Rome, 1977.

46. Quoted by F. X. Martin OSA in *The Irish Augustinians in Rome,* St Patrick's College, Rome, 1994.

47. Interview with the author, 27 May 1998.

48. Leersen, Joseph, 'Mere Irish and Fiorghael', *Remembrance and Imagination*, Cork University Press

49. Interview with the author, 26 May 1998.

50. Official Institute description document, copy in possession of author.

51. Interviews with the author, Gorajde, 3–5 June 1998.

52. Sabato Della Monica, Head of Unit, European Commission, European Community Humanitarian Office (ECHO) to Jose Pinto-Teixeira, 16 June 1997. Copy in possession of author.

53. Fax from Dr Mary McLoughlin to author, 4 October 1998.

CHAPTER 2 UNITED KINGDOM (PP 109 TO 252)

1. *Irish Studies in Britain*, spring/summer 1985.

2. *Developing a Community Response*, a survey on behalf of the Action Group for Irish Youth and the Federation of Irish Societies carried out with the co-operation of twenty-two of the leading advice and care centres amongst the Irish community in Britain, Ute Kowarzik, Charities Evaluation Services, London September 1994.

3. 27 May 1997, in London.

4. Hennigan, McEntee interviews, 6 May 1997.

5. The Irish and Policing in Islington 1891, A Report to Safer Cities, 1991; Report of the Islington Police and the Irish Community Consultative Group 1994; Policing the Streets – Stops and Search in London, 1994;

Jock Young, Centre for Criminology Middlesex University, 1994, and Islington Street Crime Survey, Middlesex University, 1995.

6. Quoted by Liz Curtis in *The Same Old Story*, Sasta, The Ashton Centre, Belfast, 1996, from a pamphlet by Thomas Churchyard, who accompanied Gilbert during his Irish campaigns.

7. Quoted by MacKay, Donald, *Fleeing from Famine*, Toronto and London, 1992.

8. Ibid.

9. Described by, amongst others, Woodham-Smith, Cecil, *The Great Hunger*, Ireland 1845–49, London, 1964.

10. MacKay, op. cit.

11. Woodham-Smith, op. cit.

12. Monteagle to Lord Gray, quoted by Christopher O'Mahony and Valerie Thompson, *Poverty to Promise*, 1994, Crossing Press, Darling Hurst, New South Wales, p. 9.

13. MacKay, op. cit.

14. MacKay, op. cit.

15. MacKay, op. cit.

16. *Racial Attacks and Harassment of Irish People*, Action Group for Irish Youth Survey by Joan O'Flynn, Dave Murphy and Martin Tucker, London, 1994.

17. Memoir supplied to the author by Frank Corrigan, 14 September 1998.

18. O'Connor, Kevin, *The Irish in Britain*, Torc Books, Dublin, 1974.

19. Ibid.

20. Pronounced Graw gal muh cree, the Irish words can be taken to mean: The shining love of my heart.

21. Edited by Dr Mary J. Hickman and Dr Bronwen Walter, CRE, Elliott House, London, June and October 1997.

22. The survey was carried out under the auspices of the increasingly well-organised Irish business community in London with the aid of Allied Irish Banks.

23. The name comes from the Irish expression 'Pogue mo tuin' – kiss my arse.

24. *Irish Post* Business '97.

25. *World of Hibernia*, summer 1995.

26. Ibid.

27. Interview with the author, 27 July 1997.

28. Interview by Anne Holohan in *Working Lives, The Irish in Britain*, The Irish Post Ltd, London, 1995.

29. Conducted at the Irish Chaplaincy premises, St Melitus, on 7, 8 and 29 May 1997, with the assistance of a team of workers from the Chaplaincy headed by Father Gerry French.

30. Hilliard, Paddy, *Suspect Community: People's experience of the Prevention of Terrorism Act in Britain*, Pluto Press, 1993. *Report of the Irish Commission for Prisoners Overseas and National Association of*

Probation Officers, February 1992, also analysed the workings of the Act.

31. Prisoners Commission/Probation Officers Report cited in Note 30.
32. Proposed Article 2 of Irish Constitution as defined in Annexe 2, Constitutional Issues, Good Friday Agreement, as arrived at in Multi-Party Talks, Belfast, 1998.
33. Reynolds, quoted in *Working Lives,* op. cit.
34. Source: 1991 Census and Cara Irish Housing Association.
35. Interview with Anne Holohan in *Working Lives*, op. cit.
36. Interviewed by the author, 8 May 1997.
37. O'Ciarain, Sean, *Farewell to Mayo*, Brookside, Dublin, 1991.
38. O'Meachair, Gearoid, *A Diplomatic Blind Eye, a Catalogue of Neglect*, London, February 1996.
39. On different occasions during May 1997, commencing on 8 May.
40. *Catholic Times,* 15 December 1996.
41. Coogan, T. P., *The Troubles,* Hutchinson, London, 1996.
42. Mansergh, Nicholas, *Britain and Ireland,* Longmans pamphlets on the British Commonwealth, London, 1942.
43. Bagley, Christopher, and Binitie, Ayo, Br. Journal, Addict, 1970, vol. 65, Pergamon, printed in Great Britain.
44. Haskey, John, Harding, S. and Balarian, R., *British Medical Journal,* vol. 132, June 1996.
45. Irish Support and Advice Centre Report, 1991.
46. Set up by the Bishops' Commission on Emigration in 1985.
47. *Irish Post,* 19 January 1999.
48. Interview with the author, 2 July 1997.
49. 2 May 1997
50. For a more extensive account of emigrant conditions and the Irish governmental response to the emigration crisis see T. P. Coogan, *Valera, Long Fellow, Long Shadow*, Hutchinson, London, 1993.
51. Quoted by T. P. Coogan in *De Valera*, op. cit., pp. 665–6.
52. The policy was actually a triple one involving Criminalisation, Normalisation and Ulsterisation, meaning that the IRA were to be criminalised; the war was to be 'Vietnamised' i.e. let the natives, the RUC, do the fighting; and the Six Counties made to appear 'normal' by spending vast sums on repairing bomb damage, and on leisure centres and cultural events. The story of the three policies is told in T. P. Coogan, *On the Blanket*, Rinehart, Colorado, 1998.
53. McLoughlin, Jim, *Ireland, The Emigrant Nursery and the World Economy,* Cork University Press, 1994.
54. *Nothing But The Same Old Story, The Roots Of Anti-Irish Racism*. There are several impressions of this work, first published in 1984, the most recent is that by Sasta, Belfast, reprinted 1998.
55. Busteed, M.A., and Hodgson, R. I., *A Geographical Journal,* vol. 162, part 2, July 1996.

56. Ibid.
57. Douglas, Roy, Harte, Liam, O'Hara, Jim, *Drawing Conclusions, A Cartoon History of Anglo-Irish Relations, 1798–1998*, Blackstaff Press, Belfast, 1998.
58. *Irish Historical Studies,* November 1989.
59. Davis, Graham, *The Irish in Britain, 1815–1914*, Gill & Macmillan, Dublin, 1991.
60. Quoted in Cecil Woodham-Smith, *The Great Hunger*, Penguin, 1991.
61. Kineally, Christine, *The Great Calamity, The Irish Famine, 1845–52*, Roberts Rinehart, Boulder, Colorado.
62. *Let's Talk* programme, BBC, 7 June 1999.
63. *Irish Studies in Britain*, eds Ivan Gibbons and Hilda McCafferty, Addison Press, 83, Frithville Gardens, London.
64. Interview with the author, 15 May 1997.
65. *Across the Water: Irish Women in Britain* by Mary Lennon, Marie Adams and Joanne O'Brien.
66. Correspondence with author, January 2001.
67. 23 July 1996.
68. *Observer,* 27 December 1998.
69. The presentation of a Famine Award, and unveiling of a memorial.
70. Bourke, Sister Mary Carmel RSM, *A Woman Sings of Mercy*, E. J. Dwyer, Sydney, Australia.
71. Ibid.
72. Interview with the author, Atlanta, 26 July 1997.
73. The most notable of these was a series by RTE, *States of Fear*, shown in late April/early May 1999.
74. Bruce, Stephen, *The Red Hand: Protestant Paramilitaries in Northern Ireland*, OUP, 1992.
75. Quoted by Frank Neil in *Sectarian Violence in Liverpool, 1819–1914*, Manchester University Press, 1988.
76. Rushton, Edward, p. 81.
77. Neal, op. cit.
78. Clare Short, interviewed by Anne Holohan, *Working Lives,* op. cit.
79. Rex, J., and Moore, B., *Race, Community and Conflict*, Oxford University Press, 1967.
80. Ibid.
81. *Economic Needs of the Irish Community in Birmingham*, by Iestyn Williams, Dr Mairead Dunne, and Professor Mairtin Mac an Ghaill, 1996.
82. Crilly, F. L., *The Manchester Martyrs*, The Irish Library series, John Ousley Ltd, London, 1908/9.
83. In 1819 a huge open-air meeting of workers, assembled at St Peter's Fields to hear 'Orator' Hunt speak on their grievances, was charged by sabre-wielding cavalry. Eleven people were killed and about five hundred injured. The derisory term 'Peterloo' was coined to compare the massacre with Waterloo.

84. Interview with the author, 15 May 1997.
85. Interview with the author, 12 May 1997.
86. Interview with the author, 13 May 1997.
87. 27 January 1999.
88. Price, Roger, *Little Ireland, Aspects of the Irish and Greenhill, Swansea*, Swansea City Council, 1992.
89. Menevia is perhaps better known nowadays as St David's in Pembrokeshire, a cathedral city called after the saint.
90. Sermon written by Dr Daniel Mullins, for the Famine Memorial Mass, St David's Cathedral, Cardiff, 19 December 1995, preached, in the Bishop's absence through illness, by Archbishop Aloysius Ward, OFM Cap.
91. Dr John Davies, *Planet*, 95, October–November 1992, Aberystwyth, reproduced in *The Green Dragon*, June 1997.
92. Professor O'Sullivan, for Angela Graham, during research for TV series on Irish/Welsh links.
93. Quoted in Carter and Mears, *History of Britain*, Clarendon Press, 1937.
94. Paper delivered at 'The Irish in Britain' Conference, Oxford, 26–29 September 1990.
95. John Leech, *Punch*, 1853, reproduced courtesy of the Glamorgan Records Office, *The Green Dragon*, Magazine of the Irish in Wales, 5, Winter 1997.
96. *Green Dragon*, 1, 1996.
97. Ibid.
98. Richard J. Finlay, 'Nationalism, Race, Religion and the Irish Question in Inter-war Scotland', *Innes Review*, spring 1991.
99. Salmond, Alex, *Peace in Ireland*, Humbert Bicentenary Papers, Humbert Publications, Dublin, 1998.
100. Quoted by John Cooney, Magill, February, 1999.
101. *Daily Record*, 13 January 1999.
102. *Scotsman*, 13 January 1999.
103. Ibid.
104. Handley, James Edmund, *The Irish in Modern Scotland*, Cork and Oxford University Presses, 1947.
105. 25 January 1947.
106. *The Green Dragon*, 1, January 1997.
107. Quoted in Handley, op. cit., p. 110.
108. McDermid, Jane, 'Catholic working-class girls' education in Lowland Scotland, 1872–1900', *Innes Review*, Spring 1996.
109. Cooney, John, *Scotland and the Papacy*, Harris, Edinburgh, 1982.
110. *Innes Review*, Spring 1996.
111. *The Historical Journal*, xv, 4, 1972.
112. 'The Catholic population of Scotland, 1878–1977', *Innes Review*.
113. Ibid.
114. Brown, Stewart J, *Innes Review*, Spring 1991.

115. *Glasgow Herald*
116. Billy Connolly to Martin Lewis, *Reflections on Success,* Leonard Publishing, Edinburgh 1997, reprinted *Daily Record,* 15 August 1997.
117. Handley, op. cit.
118. Interview with the author, 20 May 1997.
119. Those present included, apart from Cardinal Winning himself, Archbishop Keith O'Brien, Bishops Joe Devine, Maurice Taylor, John Mone and Vincent Logan, and Monsignor Michael Conway.
120. Father Noel Barry interview with the author, 20 May 1997.
121. *Sunday Herald,* Glasgow, 7 June 1999.
122. McNee, Gerald, *The Story of Celtic*, Stanley Paul, London, 1978.
123. McNee, op. cit.
124. *Sunday Herald,* 7 June 1999.

CHAPTER 3 AMERICA (PP 253 TO 368)

1. Emmet, Thomas Addis, MD, *Incidents of my Life,* New York, G. P. Putnam's Sons, 1911.
2. McCormack, who had researched the subject for the AOH, was kind enough to send me a copy of his writings inscribed: 'The Start of the Diaspora'!
3. Diary of Captain Ralph Lane, quoted by John A. Barnes in *Irish American Landmarks, A Traveller's Guide* Visible Ink. Press, Detroit and Washington, 1995.
4. Annie Moore entered Ellis Island on New Year's Day, January 1892. She was fifteen and accompanied by her two younger brothers. She married a Patrick O'Connell, descendant of Daniel O'Connell. They had eight children. Annie was killed in a train crash in Texas at the age of forty-six. The Ellis Island statue, a gift from The Irish American Cultural Institute Chairman, John S. Walsh, to the American people, was unveiled by the Irish President, Mary Robinson, on 18 May 1993.
5. McCaffrey, Lawrence, *Textures of Irish America,* Syracuse University Press, New York, 1992.
6. Leyburn, James G., *The Scotch Irish,* University of North Carolina Press, 1962.
7. Quoted in Leyburn, op. cit.
8. US Congressional Record, Washington, 5 March 1997.
9. Shannon, William V., *The American Irish*, Collier, 1974.
10. Shannon, James P., *Catholic Colonisation of the Western Frontier,* Newhaven, Yale University Press, 1957.
11. Interview with the author, 12 March 1997.
12. Harry Comstock, after whom the lode was named, was not its discoverer, but an adventurer who managed to talk himself into a share of the find, but not, ultimately to fortune. He, like the real finders, McLoughlin and O'Reilly, died penniless.

13. Interview with the author, 5 March 1997.
14. King, Joseph A, *Winter of Entrapresent*, K and K Publications, Lafayette, CA, 1988.
15. Interview with the author, 13 February 1997.
16. Conversation with the author, Irish Embassy, Washington, 17 March 1980.
17. Both Senator Ted Kennedy and his sister Jean Kennedy Smith, a former US Ambassador to Ireland, confirmed this to the author, as did a number of his aides.
18. It included academics, Bob Tracey and Tom Jordan; journalists Niall O'Dowd and Padraigin McGillicuidy; designer Eileen Callahan and the good wishes of one of the Bay area's legends, Warren Hinckle, who subsequently became Racing Editor of the journal.
19. Premier issue 3, winter 1981.
20. *Irish Echo*, 9 January 1988.
21. *Irish Echo*, 16 May 1987.
22. *Irish Echo*, 9 January 1988.
23. O'Dowd to author, 10 May 1999.
24. McNickle, Chris, in *The New York Irish*, eds Bayor, Ronald H., and Meagher, Timothy, J., Johns Hopkins, Baltimore and London.
25. Thomas Flemming, *Irish America* magazine, December 1988.
26. As with many other such gems I am indebted to the marvellous work of John A. Barnes in *Irish American Landmarks, A Traveller's Guide* Visible Ink Press, Detroit and New York, 1995 for this information.
27. Quoted by Alistair Cooke, America, 1973, in the book of the BBC's 1972 award-winning series, *America: A Personal History of the United States*.
28. Erie, Steven P., *Rainbow's End*, University of California Press, 1988.
29. Ibid.
30. Wendell Philips, quoted by Noel Ignatiev in *How the Irish became White*, Routledge, New York and London, 1995.
31. O'Donnell, L.A., *Irish Voice and Organised Labor in America*, Greenwood Press, Connecticut.
32. Ignatiev, Noel, Routledge, New York and London, 1995.
33. *New York Herald*, 24 October 1880.
34. Ignatiev, op. cit.
35. O'Connor, Thomas H., *South Boston, My Home Town*, North Eastern University Press, 1994.
36. Ibid.
37. Dolan, Jay P., *The Emigrant Church*, Johns Hopkins University Press, Baltimore and London, 1975.
38. Casey, Marion, *Seaport* magazine, spring 1996, New York.
39. Ibid.
40. The phenomenon of the American letter and what gave rise to it is examined by Paul Wagner in 'Letters Home', *World of Hibernia*, summer 1995, New York.

41. Dickens, Charles, *American Notes and 'Pictures from Italy'*, London, 1887.
42. Quoted in *The New York Irish*, eds Bayor, Ronald H. and Meagher, Timothy J., Johns Hopkins University Press, Baltimore and London, 1996.
43. Shannon, op. cit.
44. Shannon, op. cit.
45. 1 August 1986.
46. *Ireland on Sunday*, 6 June 1999.
47. Interview with the author, 7 March 1997.
48. McCaffrey, op. cit.
49. *Boston Globe*, 19 September 1988. Part of a four-part series, run by the *Globe* in September 1988.
50. Alan M. Dershowitz, *Boston Globe* magazine, February 1991.
51. Ibid.
52. *Boston Globe*, 21 September 1988.
53. Egan, Patrick, O'Donnell Lecture, University College, Galway, 14 June 1968.
54. Quoted by Dolan, op. cit.
55. Dolan, op. cit.
56. Quoted by Dolan op. cit.
57. Quoted by William V. Shannon in *The American Irish*, Collier, New York, 1963.
58. Ibid.
59. Interview with the author, 26 February 1997.
60. *Irish Voice*, 7–13 April 1999.
61. Bayor and Meagher, op. cit.
62. Mageean, Deirdre in *Peasant Maids, City Women*, ed. Christianne Harzig, Cornell University Press, 1987.
63. Ibid.
64. Ibid.
65. On 19 March 1997.
66. Mageean, op. cit.
67. Quoted by Howard Zinn in *A People's History of the United States*, Harper and Rowe, New York, 1980.
68. Quoted in O'Donnell, op. cit.
69. Speech by John J. Sweeney to the Irish American Labour Coalition, 23 January 1987.
70. Quoted by Mary Murphy in *Mining Cultures, Men, Women and Leisure in Butte, 1914–41*, University of Illinois Press, 1997.
71. O'Neill, Charles Edward, 'De Valera's visit to New Orleans in 1920', *Louisiana History XXXIV*, Summer 1993, Tulane U.
72. John J. Sweeney speech, ibid.
73. Miller, Kerby A., *Emigrants and Exiles*, Oxford University Press, New York and Oxford, 1985.

74. Fitzgerald and King, ibid.
75. Coleman, J. Walter, *The Molly Maguire Riots*, Garrett and Massey, Richmond, 1936.
76. Campbell, Patrick, *A Molly Maguire Story*, Princeton University Press/P.H. Campbell, New Jersey, 1992.
77. Quoted by David M. Emmons in *The Butte Irish*, University of Illinois Press, 1990.
78. In 1944 a Sergeant Frederick 'Fritz' Niland was recalled from service with the 101st Airborne Division in France after his three brothers were killed in action.
79. Quoted by Thomas Keneally in *The Great Shame*, Chatto & Windus, London, 1998.
80. Quoted by Constantia Maxwell in *Ireland under the Georges (1740–1838)*, London, 1936.
81. McWhiney, Grady, *Cracker Culture, Celtic Ways in the Old South*, University of Alabama Press, Alabama, 1988.
82. Barnes, John A., *Irish American Landmarks*, Visible Ink Press, Detroit, 1995.
83. The observations concerning the Irish in the Civil War are quoted by Thomas Keneally, op. cit.
84. Bruce Morrison to the author, 14 March 1997.
85. Ridge, John T., *Erin's Sons in America*, AOH 150th Anniversary Committee, New York.
86. All those involved with the Warrington case were released under the terms of the Good Friday Agreement.
87. Later Irish Ambassador to the US and currently Secretary General of the Irish Department of Foreign Affairs.
88. Statement to the author, 3 September 1997.
89. Greeley, Andrew M., *That Most Distressful Nation, The Taming of the American Irish*, Quadrangle Books, Chicago, 1972.
90. Elisabeth Shannon, who accompanied the author to lunch with Adele Dalsimer in Boston on 20 February 1997.
91. *The Times*, 11 October 1997.
92. 12 March 1997.
93. 28 March 1998.
94. 9 October 1996.
95. 17 October 1996.
96. Ibid.
97. 30 January 1997.
98. 24 January 1997.
99. O'Connor, Aine, *Leading Hollywood*, Wolfhound Press, Dublin, 1996.
100. *World of Hibernia*, autumn 1995.
101. Barnes, op. cit.
102. Fanning, Charles, *The Irish Voice in America, Irish American Fiction from the 1760s to the 1980s*, University Press of Kentucky, 1990.

103. Ossian returned on a visit to Ireland from Tir na nOg, The Land of Youth, but when he disobeyed his instructions, not to dismount from his horse, he became centuries old the moment his foot touched the ground.
104. In conversation with Peter Quinn, *The Recorder*, Winter 1985. New York.
105. Barnes, op. cit.
106. John Kernaghan, *Irish America*, November/December 1988.
107. Letter to the author, 27 August 1997.
108. Hamill, Pete, *The Irish in America* (book of PBS TV series), Hyperion, New York, 1997.
109. Account given to the author, 29 January 1999.
110. *World of Hibernia*, autumn 1995.

CHAPTER 4 CANADA (PAGE 369 TO 429)

1. Quoted by Donald MacKay in *Flight from Famine*, McClelland & Stewart, Toronto, 1992.
2. Mullan's book, *Eye-witness, Bloody Sunday,* published in 1997, amassed a wealth of new material and contained the evidence of hundreds of eye-witnesses to the events of Bloody Sunday, which the official British Governmental Inquiry into the shootings, conducted by Lord Widgery in 1972, had either not used or glossed over.
3. Fitzpatrick, David, 'Flight from Famine', in *The Great Irish Famine*, ed. Cathal Poirteir, Mercier, 1995.
4. Quoted by MacKay, op. cit.
5. Fitzgerald to his mother, quoted by Kildare Dobbs in *The Untold Story*, ed. Robert O'Driscoll and Lorna Reynolds, Celtic Arts of Canada, Toronto, 1988.
6. MacKay, op. cit.
7. Ibid.
8. St John, Common Council Committee Report, 27 October 1847, quoted by James M. Whalen in *The Untold Story: The Irish in Canada*, ed. Driscoll and Reynolds, Toronto, 1998.
9. Quoted by Whalen, op. cit.
10. Figures supplied courtesy of the Irish Embassy in Ottawa.
11. Official Programme, United Irish Societies, Irish Person of the Year Award Lunch, Toronto, 1997.
12. *Irish America*, January/February 1996. Also, in abridged form, in the Action Grosse Ile Commemorative Programme, 1977.
13. Ibid.
14. An Irish occasion of music and dance, meaning literally 'a Great Dance'.
15. Author's note of Marianna Gallagher's talk, Quebec, 17 July 1998.
16. First published in 1877 by McLear & Co., Toronto. This edition reprinted by the Irish University Press, Shannon, Ireland, 1969.
17. Grace, Robert J., *The Irish in Quebec*, IQRC, 1993.

18. Kildare Dobbs, op. cit.
19. Houston, Cecil J. and Smith, William J., *Irish Emigration and Canadian Settlement*, University of Toronto Press, 1990, published in Ireland and the UK by the Ulster Historical Foundation.
20. John Street, quoted by Donald Mackay, op. cit., p. 153.
21. Ibid.
22. Butler, William Francis, *The Great Lone Land*, Hurtig, 1968. I am also indebted for insights into this period to a lecture delivered by Denis Duffy: 'Mapping the Great Lone Land: How the Butlers Did It', delivered University College, Dublin, 16 April 1995.
23. Sean MacBride Address at 'Canada and the Celtic Consciousness' Festival, University of Toronto, February 1978.
24. Quoted by Robert Burns in 'Thomas D'Arcy Magee and the making of the Canadian Nation', in *The Untold Story: The Irish in Canada*.
25. Ibid.
26. Gowan's activities are described in the contemporary account of an insurgent leader, General Myles Byrne, who fled to Paris after 1798 where he became one of the Wild Geese. After his death, his widow published his memoirs in three volumes, and these were subsequently edited by the late Denys Gwynn, SJ.
27. For further details of Reil's Irish ancestry and career and of orangeism in Canada, see *The Untold Story*, particularly the excellent essay by Hereward Senior, 'The Orange, the Green and the Snow in-between'.
28. Cecil J. Houston and William J. Smith, op. cit., p. 182.
29. Stuart Rivans, quoting David Steele in MA dissertation: 'Irish Emigration in Glasgow and Philadelphia, 1845–1910', an interesting and insightful comparison of Irish success in two hostile citadels.
30. Davis, Richard, in *The Untold Story*, op. cit.
31. Letter to the author, 15 August 1999.
32. Quoted by James Reaney, who summarised the literature on the Donnellys and the story of the vendetta and its outcome in a fine essay in *The Untold Story*, op. cit.
33. Grace, Robert J., *The Irish in Quebec, An Introduction to the Historiography*, IGRC, Quebec, 1993.
34. Houston, Cecil J. and Smith, William J., op. cit.
35. Wilson letter to the author, 15 August 1999.
36. Hansard, Ontario Legislature, 14 May 1998.
37. Interview with author, 7 August 1999.
38. Published by Celtic Arts of Canada, Toronto, 1988.
39. Wilson to author, op. cit.
40. Telephone conversation with author, 27 August 1999.
41. Ibid.
42. The interviews for the Canadian section of this book were largely conducted between 15 August and 5 September 1997.
43. In the Tudor File, Newfoundland Historical Society, Colonial Building,

St John's.

44. Rowe, F. W., *History of Newfoundland and Labrador*, Toronto, 1980.
45. Published by the Historical Committee of the 200th Anniversary of the formal establishment of the Roman Catholic Church in Newfoundland, 1984, St John's.
46. Verse by Sheila Whelan, *Guide to Basilica of St John the Baptist*, St John's, Newfoundland, Roman Catholic Church, Newfoundland, 1984.
47. O'Flaherty, Patrick, *Growing Up Irish in a Newfoundland Outpost: The Untold Story*.
48. Ball, Vincent, *Buck Jones, Where Are You?*, Random House, Australia, 1996.
49. The statistics quoted in this paragraph were compiled by John J. Mannion, Professor of Geography at Memorial University.
50. Grimm, Gertrude E., *The Political History of Newfoundland, 1832-64*, University of Toronto Press, 1966.
51. Ibid.
52. Conversation with author, 25 August 1997.
53. Kelly to author, 12 July 1999.

CHAPTER 5 AUSTRALIA (PP 430 TO 486)

1. Hughes, Robert, *The Fatal Shore*, Pan, London, 1988.
2. Interview with the author, 30 September 1996.
3. Grassby, Al, *The Tyranny of Prejudice* A. E. Press, Melbourne, 1984.
4. Interview with the author, 26 September 1996.
5. Prior, Tom, *A Knockabout Priest,* Hargreen, Melbourne, 1985
6. 23 October 1996.
7. O'Farrell, a distinguished academic and historian, has produced definitive work on the Irish in Australia and on the Catholic Church, including *The Irish in Australia*, revised edition, NSW University Press, 1993.
8. Robert Hughes op. cit.
9. Campion, Edmund, *Australian Catholics*, Penguin, 1988.
10. Pakenham, Thomas, *The Year of Liberty*, The Literary Guild, London, 1969 (published by arrangement with Hodder and Stoughton).
11. Whitaker, Anne-Maree, *Unfinished Revolution*, Crossing Press, Sydney, 1994.
12. *Memoirs of Miles Byrne*, ed. Stephen Gwynn.
13. O'Farrell, *The Irish in Australia* (revised edition), NSW University Press, 1993.
14. Whitaker, op. cit., quoting from Holt mss. MLA 2024 p. 321. In 1838, T. Crofton Croker edited the Holt mss. to produce *Memoirs of Joseph Holt*, which was published by Henry Colburn of London. Croker suppressed the reference to the flogging of the women, but printed the reference to his horse being burned as the reason for his joining the rebels.

15. Quoted by Hughes, op. cit. and by Crofton Croker, in *Memoirs of Joseph Holt,* Colburn, London 1838.
16. Whitaker, op. cit., p. 196.
17. Val Noone, 'Disturbing the War', *Spectrum,* 1993, Victoria, p. 25
18. *Valiant Women, Letters from the Foundation Sisters of Mercy in Western Australia, 1845–1849,* ed. Geraldine Byrne, Polding Press, Melbourne, 1981, p. 50.
19. Quoted by Campion,op. cit.
20. Ibid.
21. Keneally, Thomas, *Homebush Boy, a Memoir,* Minerva, Melbourne, 1995.
22. Ibid. p. 55.
23. Speech at Waverley College Presentation, Opera House, Sydney, 18 November 1994.
24. Keneally, op. cit.
25. Ibid.
26. Campion, op. cit.
27. Sherington, Geoffrey, *Australia's Immigrants,* Allen & Unwin, Sydney, 1980, p. 70.
28. Quoted by O'Farrell, op. cit.
29. *The Irishman,* 4 June 1870.
30. O'Farrell, op. cit., p. 170.
31. Kiernan, T. J., *The Irish Exiles in Australia,* Clonmore & Reynolds, Dublin, 1954.
32. Kiernan, op. cit.
33. O'Mahony, Christopher and Thompson, Valerie, *Poverty to Promise, the Monteagle Emigrants, 1839–58,* Crossing Press, Darlinghurst, 1994, p. 12.
34. Trevelyan to Sir W. M. Somerville, 25 January, 1848, Pro. 364/368a.
35. Judy Collingwood in *The Irish Emigrant Experience in Australia,* ed. O'Brien & Travers, Poolbeg, Dublin, 1991, p. 49.
36. Ibid., p. 55.
37. Ibid.
38. McLoughlin, Trevor, '*Exploited and Abused', Irish Orphan Girls,* paper delivered at Irish Australian Conference, July 1993.
39. Dr Cross O'Brien delivered her observations in a paper delivered to a conference to commemorate the Great Irish Famine, in Macquarie University, Sydney, in September 1996, entitled 'Out of Ireland ... Reflections on a Living Past.'
40. Overlack, Peter, 'The Past Recaptured and Lost, Irish and German political romanticism compared', *Irish Australian Studies,* ed. Pelan, Quirke and Finnane, Crossing Press, Sydney, 1994.
41. Kelly, Paul, 'Address to the Sydney Institute,' reprinted *Quadrant,* November 1993.
42. Interview with the author, 17 October 1996.

43. An Australian term meaning people who have to battle with life from a disadvantaged economic and social position.
44. 28 September 1996.
45. *The Tribune*, 19 October 1922, quoted in T. P. Boland, *James Duhig*, University of Queensland Press, 1986.
46. Boland, op. cit., pp. 184–185.
47. Boland op. cit.
48. James Griffin, entry on Daniel Mannix, *Australian Dictionary of Biography*.
49. Ibid.
50. Sweetman, Rory, *Bishop in the Dock, the Sedition Trial of James Liston*, Auckland University Press, 1997, p. 254.
51. Calwell, Arthur, *Be Just and Fear Not*, Rigby in association with Lloyd O'Neill, Australia, 1978, p. 151.
52. Quoted in the Bombay Papers by Mary Elizabeth Calwell, paper delivered at St Francis's Pastoral Centre, Melbourne, 17 July 1994.
53. Campion, op. cit.
54. Campion, Edmund, *50 years of the Santamaria Movement, Eureka Street*, Paper 1, Jesuit Publications, 300 Victoria Street, Richmond, Victoria, 1992.
55. Interview with the author, 21 October 1996.
56. Paul Ormond, 'How Evatt scuppered Santamaria's Religious Vision', *Overland* magazine, Melbourne, 1995.
57. B. A. Santamaria to Archbishop Daniel Mannix, 11 December 1952, quoted by Gerard Henderson in a paper delivered 2 May 1992 at the State Library of New South Wales entitled '50 years of the Santamaria movement'.
58. Quoted by Ross McMullin in *The Light on the Hill, The Australian Labour Party 1881–1991*, OUP, Australia, 1992.
59. Campion, op. cit.
60. McMullin op. cit.
61. Calwell, op. cit.
62. Ibid. p. 131
63. Interview with the author, 21 October 1996.
64. Noone, op. cit., p. 151
65. Ian Turner, quoted in *The Winter Game*, Robert Pascoe, Mandarin, Port Melbourne, 1996, p. xi.
66. *Whatever It Takes* (with Jim Main), Celebrity Publishing, Australia, 1995.
67. Letter to the author, October 1996.
68. *The Irish Australian Review*, November 1996.
69. 'Still the Scapegoats after all these Years, Anti-Irish Prejudice Lingers on in Australia', unpublished paper by Barbara Walsh, copy in the author's possession.
70. Hayden, William, *Hayden*, HarperCollins, Australia, 1996, p. 18.

Chapter 6 New Zealand (pp 487 to 503)

1. Holt, Edgar, *The Strangest War*, Putnam, London, 1962, p. 13.
2. Tandem Press, Birkenhead, Auckland, 1990.
3. Davis, Richard P., *Irish Issues in New Zealand Politics*, Otago Press, Dunedin, 1974, p. 25.
4. Ibid.
5. Davis, op. cit.
6. The picture of the Black and Tans in operation in the film *Michael Collins* is based on the author's book of that name: *Michael Collins*, Hutchinson, London, 1990.
7. Rogers, Anna, *A Lucky Landing*, Random House, New Zealand, 1996, p. 83.
8. Ibid., p. 86.
9. Rogers, op. cit.
10. O'Farrell, Patrick, *Vanished Kingdoms, Irish in Australia and New Zealand* (contemporary photographs by Richard O'Farrell), New South Wales University Press, 1990.
11. Interview with Jim Sullivan in *Catholic Boys*, Penguin, 1996, p. 50.
12. Quoted by Sullivan, op. cit.

Chapter 7 Africa (page 504 to 568)

1. Hogan, Edmund M., *The Irish Missionary Movement*, Gill & Macmillan, Dublin 1990.
2. Ibid.
3. *Ireland on Sunday*, 10 January 1999.
4. Ibid.
5. 29 April 1996. Most of my African interviews and quotations may be taken as having occurred in or around two months of this date.
6. Fr Sean O'Leary. Copy in the author's possession.
7. Geoff Loane, Head of Regional Delegation, International Commission and Red Cross, interview with the author, 8 May 1996.
8. Doyle OFM, Father Francis Bernard, in *A History of Irish Catholicism* ed. Patrick J. Cornish, Gill & Macmillan, Dublin, 1971.
9. Tewodros spoke shortly before unsuccessfully engaging an invading British army in 1868. He then committed suicide.
10. Loane interview with the author.
11. *Challenges and Opportunities Abroad*, White Paper on Foreign Policy, Stationery Office, Dublin, 1996.
12. Professor Helen O'Neill, President of the European Association of Development Research and Training.
13. Loane interview with the author.
14. Davidson, Basil, *Let Freedom Come*, Little Brown, Boston, 1978.
15. Ibid.

16. Ibid.
17. Livingstone's last words inlaid on his tomb in Westminster Abbey, London.
18. Pakenham, Thomas, *The Scramble for Africa, 1876–1912,* Weidenfeld and Nicolson, London, 1991; Paperback Abacus, 1992–3.
19. *Sunday Times*, 10 April 1000.
20. *Irish Times*, 11 April 2000.
21. 20 May 1996.
22. I discussed this smell with a doctor who knows the area well and he was inclined to be suspicious as to the reasons why it should linger so long. 'By now, it should have gone away. They must be doing something.' By 'they', the doctor, and aid worker, meant the Rwandan authorities who are keen to utilise Niemata for PR purposes.
23. Parker, Ben, UN HFOR Status Report on deaths in Kivumu Commune, Kibue Prefecture, 16 May 1996.
24. Interview with Kagame, *New Africa*, 22 September 1997. See also *New Africa*, October 1997 and *The Economist*, 27 September 1997.
25. The hedge schools persisted beyond the Penal times, and were often the only source of education in the Irish countryside in the nineteenth century. Itinerant teachers, sometimes men of great scholarship, sometimes afflicted by drink, taught their charges in the open, often under hedges.
26. Shanahan's story is told in Desmond Forrestal, *The Second Burial of Bishop Shanahan*, Veritas, Dublin, 1990, which contains more detail than an earlier, rather more formal biography, *Bishop Shanahan of Southern Nigeria* by John Jordan, who was a Holy Ghost Priest and a friend and confidant of Shanahan.
27. Brother O'Connell very kindly drove 250 miles to meet me in Nairobi, 17 May 1997.
28. Peter Rono, *Evening Herald*, 28 November 1988.
29. Sister Christine, interviewed by Linda Villarosa, *Runners World*, August 1992.
30. Interview with the author 3 May 1996.
31. Follis, A. Bryan, 'Friend or Foe? Ulster Unionists and Afrikaner Nationalists, Ireland and South Africa', Donal P. McCracken, ed., University of Durban-Westville, Vol. 3, 1996.
32. Interview with Schoon 26 May 1996.
33. Interview with the author 8 July 1996.
34. Scher, D. M., *Ireland and South Africa*, ed. Donal P. McCracken, vol. 3, Southern African Irish Studies, Durban, 1996.
35. *Sunday Times*, 21 January 1995.
36. Davitt, Michael, *The Boer Fight for Freedom*, Funk and Wagnall, New York and London, 1902.
37. McCracken to author, 12 December 1999. Copy in author's possession.
38. McGrath, Walter, 'The Boer Irish Brigade', *Irish Sword*, Dublin,

autumn, 1967.
39. Clarke, Ian, *The Man With the Key is Gone*, New Wine Press, Chichester, 1993.

CHAPTER 8 CARIBBEAN (PAGE 569 TO 601)

1. Quoted in *Ireland and Latin America*, Trocaire and Gill & Macmillan Ltd., Dublin, 1992, p. 89.
2. Ibid.
3. Sir Frank Savage, interview with the author, 2 March 1997.
4. A document issued by the Government Information Unit, Plymouth, to mark St Patrick's Day, 1991 says 'local tales have painted her black'.
5. Calendar of State Papers (Ireland), 22 December 1620. Quoted by de Vere, *Studies*, 1929, Dublin.
6. Quoted by de Vere in *Studies*, op. cit.
7. These have been extensively quoted from by de Vere, and their provenance given in his *Studies* series.
8. Father Andrew White SJ quoted by Howard A. Fergus, *History of Alliougana, A short history of Montserrat*, p. 8.
9. Father John Stritch, quoted by Gwynne.
10. Cromwell to the Speaker of the Parliament of England, 17 September 1649. Quoted by Anthony de Verteuil CS Sp., *Silvester Devenish and the Irish in 19th Century Trinidad*, Paria, Port of Spain, p. 24.
11. Browne, MD, Patrick, *The Civil and Natural History of Jamaica*, London, 1756, quoted by William, Joseph, S J, in *Whence the Black Irish of Jamaica*, Dial Press, New York, 1932.
12. Figures quoted by Brian McGinn in *Irish Roots*, 1, Cork, 1994.
13. In the Caribbean context the Leeward Islands are those lying between Puerto Rico and Martinique – there are also Leeward Islands in the South Pacific – including Antigua, St Kitts, Nevis, Anguilla, Montserrat and the British Virgin Islands. The Caribbean Windward Islands are in the South Eastern West Indies and include Grenada, the Grenadines, Martinique, St Lucia and St Vincent's.
14. *British Colonial Library*, vol. 5. Quoted by Fergus, op. cit., p. 10.
15. Paper to the American Anthropological Association, 1996.
16. Ibid.
17. Ibid.
18. *Islands*, Magazine, March/April 1995.
19. A small laneway.
20. *Diary of Richard Ligon*, 'printed for Humphrey Mosley, at the Princes Armes in St Paul's Churchyard'. Quoted by Gwynne. op. cit.
21. Ligon, op. cit.
22. The hyacinth bean.
23. Ligon, op. cit.
24. Mitchell to author, 30 June 1997.

25. *Insight Guides, Trinidad and Tobago,* APA Productions (HK) Ltd, Singapore, 1987, p. 70.
26. Keenan, Patrick, *Report upon the State of Education in the Island of Trinidad,* Dublin, 1869.
27. Ibid.
28. De Verteuil, op. cit., p. 14.
29. O'Connor, P.E.T., p. 63, Some Trinidad Yesterdays, Imprint Caribbean Ltd., Port of Spain, 1978.
30. Verteuil, op. cit., p. 35.
31. *The Good News on the Wild Coast*, Bridges, S J, John, 1984.
32. De Verteuil, op. cit., p. 41.
33. De Verteuil, op. cit.
34. Camps to author. Our conversations, like the others mentioned in these chapters, took place in the weeks February 10–March 14, 1996.
35 Walcott, Derek, *Dream on Monkey Mountain and Other Plays,* Farrar, Straus & Giroux, New York,
36. Browne MD, op. cit.
37. *The Gleaner*, in a feature of 7 March 1996 detailing momentous events of the past, recorded the arrival of the Irish.
38. *Claude McKay, A Black Poet's Struggle for Identity* by Tyrone Tillery, University of Massachusetts Press, Amherst, 1946.

CHAPTER 9 LATIN AMERICA (PAGE 602 TO 643)

1. Interview with the author, 6 April 1997.
2. Barnwell, David, *19th Century Irish Emigration to Argentina*, Columbia University Studies Seminar, 15 April 1988.
3. Quoted by Peadar Kirby, *Ireland and Latin America,* Trocaire, Gill & Macmillan, Dublin, 1992 p. 85.
4. Ireland, John de Courcy, *Ireland and the Irish in Maritime History,* Glendale Press, Dublin, 1986, p. 230.
5. Barnwell, op. cit.
6. Quoted by Peadar Kirby, op. cit.
7. Quoted by Katherine Hatch, *Ireland of the Welcomes*, vol. 26. 1994.
8. Elgy Gillespie, *Irish Times,* 3 November 1997.
9. The visit occurred on 6 April 1997.
10. Document in the author's possession.
11. Ibid.
12. Lernoux, Penny, *Cry of the People*, Doubleday & Co., Inc., New York, 1980, p. 10.
13. Interview with the author, 6 April 1997.
14. Ibid.
15. Experts differ on this figure.
16. Interview with the author, 29 March 1997.
17. Kobel, W. H., *British Exploits in South America*, New York, 1917, p. 328.

18. Scobie, James, R., *A City and a Nation*, New York, 1964, p. 84.
19. *La Nacion Argentina*, September 1862, quoted in Irish diplomatic report 1958, copy in the author's possession.
20. I have found the following academic papers to be the most enlightening: *The Forgotten People. The Irish in Argentina and other South American countries*, by Guillermo MacLoughlin; *Irish Emigration to Argentina*, Korol, J. C. and Sabato, H.,; *Tango Shamrock, the Irish in Argentina*, Julianello, Maria Teresa and Vazquez, Maria Silvana; *19th Century Irish Emigration to Argentina*, David Barnwell, *The Development of the Irish Community in Argentina, 1840–1890* by Sullivan, Paul John.
21. Op. cit.
22. *Tango Shamrock*, op. cit.
23. *Standard*, 20 July 1871.
24. Quoted by Thomas Murray in *The Story of the Irish in Argentina*, Kennedy and Sons, New York, 1919.
25. Ussher, Mgr James M., *Father Fahy, a biography*, Buenos Aires, 1951.
26. Ibid.
27. The Diaries were probably the work of Maria Geoghegan de Savage, but it is possible that they were continued by Thomas Savage's second wife, Margareta Manny de Savage.
28. 'The Scarlet Trinity', paper by Maria Teresa Julianello and Maria Silvana Vazquez, compiled to accompany the screening of a film about Camila O'Gorman.
29. Rosas letter, 17 January, 1848, quoted by Julianello and Vazquez, op. cit.
30. *The English Language Press in Latin America*, Institute of Latin American Studies, London,. 1996, p. 13.
31. Barnwell, op. cit.
32. *Southern Cross*, 16 January 1975.
33. Quoted by O'Sullivan, op. cit.
34. Taken from an Irish diplomatic paper in the author's possession.
35. Diplomatic papers in the author's possession.
36. O'Dwyer interview with the author.
37. 'The Forgotten People, the Irish in Argentina and other South American countries', paper delivered at seminar on The Irish Diaspora, University College Cork, 24–27 September 1997.
38. Letter to the author, 26 July 1999.

CHAPTER 10 JAPAN, RICE PADDIES AND AN ASIAN PERSPECTIVE (PAGE 644 TO 661)

1. Hardiman to the author, 22 August 1999.
2. Father Johnston interview with the author, 4 November 1996.
3. Interview with the author, 5 November 1996.
4. Ibid.

5. Interview with the author, 2 November 1996.
6. William, Johnston S J, *Letters to Contemplatives*, Orbis Books, Maryknoll, New York, 1992.
7. Interview with the author, 4 November 1999.
8. Ibid.
9. Hardiman letter, op. cit.
10. *Irish Times*, 10 January 1999.
11. Jeffares, Norman A., *Yeats: a biography*, Hutchinson, London, 1988.
12. Quoted by Jeffares, op. cit.
13. From 'The Tower' sequence, 1928, quoted from The Norman A. Jeffares Collection, Macmillan, London, 1989.
14. Letter to the author, 19 August 1999.
15. Rather than enlarge the existing Magee College, in the Nationalist city of Derry, which was showing signs of having a largely Catholic enrolment, the Unionists decided to build Coleraine in what was then a heavily Protestant area, now overtaken by the Catholic birth rate.
16. Welch. Ibid.
17. Ibid.
18. *Irish Times*, 10 January 1997.
19. Letter to the author, 29 August 1998.
20. *Irish Times*, 10 January 1999.
21. Holland's Fenian connection has been extensively described in several publications, including my own book on the IRA, which of course does not treat of Holland's life in anything like the same detail as a work such as Richard Knowles Morris's, *John P. Holland, Inventor of the Modern Submarine*, Arno Press, New York, 1980. However the former Irish Ambassador to Japan, Sean Ronan, approached Holland's life from a Japanese perspective and his original researches from primary sources resulted in an important paper on Holland and his contribution to submarine development both in Japan and America, delivered to the Military History Society of Ireland on 12 March 1999 and due for publication in the Society's journal, *The Irish Sword*, in the spring edition, 2000. Ambassador Ronan kindly gave me permission to quote from his unpublished paper before his untimely death as this book was being written.
22. Op. cit.
23. Ibid.
24. The incident is described by Sean O'Mahony, a local historian, in his book *The History of Carrigaline*.
25. Arisa Mori interview with the author, Tokyo, 4 November 1996.
26. Ibid.
27. He asked to remain anonymous.
28. *Ireland on Sunday*, 10 January 1999.
29. Ibid.
30. Interview with the author, 4 November 1996.
31. Deirdre Purcell Show, 5 August 1999.

BIBLIOGRAPHY

Akwanya, A.N., *Semantics and Discourse,* Acena, Nigeria, 1996.

Allen, Tullos, *Habits of Industry,* University of North Carolina Press, 1989.

Amos, Keith, *The Fenians in Australia,* University of NSW, 1990.

Archdeacon, Thomas, *Becoming American,* The Free Press, New York, 1983.

Ardagh, John, *Ireland and the Irish,* Hamish Hamilton, London, 1994.

Ball, Vincent, *Buck Jones, Where are You?,* Random House Australia Pty Ltd., NSW, 1996.

Barnes, John A., *Irish American Landmarks,* Visible Ink Press, Detroit, 1995.

Barrett Brown, Michael, *Africa's Choices,* Penguin Group, Middlesex, 1995.

Bayor, Ronald H, and Meagher Timothy, *The New York Irish,* The John Hopkins University Press, Baltimore & London, 1996.

Beatty, Jack, *The Rascal King,* Addison-Wesley Publishing Co., USA 1992.

Behr, Mark, *The Smell of Apples,* Abacus, London, 1996.

Benson, Mary, *A Far Cry,* Rowan Press, South Africa, 1996.

Bernardin, Tom, *The Ellis Island Immigrant Cookbook,* Tom Bernardin Inc., New York, 1991.

Berry, Simon and Whyte, Hamish, *Glasgow Observed,* John Donald Publishers Ltd, Edinburgh, 1987.

Best Australian Sports Writing and Photography, *Carlton & United Breweries,* William Heinemann Australia, Victoria, 1996.

Bland, F.E., *How the Church Missionary Society Came to Ireland,* Church of Ireland Printing & Publishing Ltd, Dublin, 1935.

Blessing, Patrick J., *The Irish in America,* The Catholic University of American Press, Washington, 1992.

Boland, T.P., *James Duhig,* University of Queensland Press, Queensland, 1986.

Bourke, Sister Mary Carmel, *A Woman Sings of Mercy,* E.J. Dwyer (Australia) Pty Ltd., NSW, 1991.

Brannan, Sam, *Builder of San Francisco,* James Stevenson Publisher, California, 1996.

Broderick, John, *London Irish,* Barrie & Jenkins Ltd., 1979.

Brown, Richard Howard, *I am of Ireland,* Roberts Rinehart Publishers, Dublin, 1995.

Brown, Thomas N., *Irish American Nationalism,* J.P. Lippincott Co., New York, 1996.

Bruce, Steve, *The Edge of the Union,* Oxford University Press, Oxford, 1994.

———, *The Red Hand,* Oxford University Press, Oxford 1992.

Burchell, R.A., *The San Francisco Irish 1848–1880,* Manchester University Press, 1979.

Burke, A.J., *Gunyah, Grit & Gantry*, Bell Bird Books, Brisbane, 1985.

Burns-Bisogno, Louisa, *Censoring Irish Nationalism*, McFarland & Co. Inc., 1997.

Byrne, Geraldine, *Valiant Women*, 1981.

Cahill, Thomas, *How the Irish Saved Civilization*, Hodder & Stoughton, London 1995.

Calwell, A.A., *Be Just and Fear Not*, Rigby Ltd, Australia, 1978.

Camps, Helen C., *Iron in her Soul, E.G. Flynn*, Washington State University Press, Washington, 1995.

Campbell, Patrick, *A Molly Maguire Story*, P.H. Campbell, Jersey City, NJ, 1992.

Campion, Edmund, *Australian Catholics*, Penguin Books Australia Ltd, Victoria, 1988.

——, *Rockchoppers*, Penguin Books Australia Ltd, Victoria, 1982.

Carroll, Francis M., *American Opinion and the Irish Question 1910–23*, Gill & Macmillan, Dublin, and St Martin's Press, 1978.

Carter, E.H. and Mears, R.A.F., *A History of Britain*, Oxford University Press, London, 1937.

Carter, Michael, *Broken Noses & Metempsychoses*, Fly by Night Press, 1996.

Clark Hunter R., *Justice Brennan*, 1995.

Clarke, Dr Ian, *The Man with the Key has Gone!*, New Wine Press, West Sussex, 1993.

Coffey Michael, and Golway Terry, *The Irish in America*, Hyperion, New York, 1997.

Cohen, Barry, *Life with Gough*, Allen & Unwin Pty Ltd., NSW, 1996.

Collins, Peter, *Nationalism and Unionism*, Institute of Irish Studies, The Queen's University of Belfast, 1994.

Coogan, Tim Pat, *Eamon de Valera*, Hutchinson, London, 1993.

——, *Ireland and the Arts*, Namara Press, London, N.D.

——, *Ireland since the Rising*, Pall Mall Press Ltd., London, 1966.

——, *On the Blanket*, Ward River Press Ltd., Dublin, 1980.

——, *The IRA*, HarperCollins, London, 2000.

——, *The Irish – A Personal View*, Phaidon Press Ltd., London, 1975.

——, *The Troubles*, Hutchinson, London, 1995.

Cooke, Alistair, *Alistair Cooke's America*, Book Club Associates, United Kingdom, 1976.

Coombes, David, *Ireland and the European Communities*, Gill & Macmillan, Dublin, 1983.

Cooney, John and McGarry, Tony, *Place in Ireland*, Humbert Publications, Dublin, 1999.

Cooney, John, *Scotland and the Papacy*, Paul Harris Publishing, Edinburgh, 1982.

Curtis Liz, *Nothing but the Same Old Story*, Sasta, Belfast, 1996.

——, *Ireland the Propaganda Wars*, Sasta, 1998.

Davidson, Basil, *Let Freedom Come,* Little, Brown & Company, Boston, Toronto, London, 1978.

Davis, Graham, *The Irish in Britain 1815–1914,* Gill & Macmillan Ltd., Dublin, 1991.

Davis, Richard, P, *Irish Issues in New Zealand Politics 1868–1922*, University of Otago Press, Dunedin, 1974.

De Courcy Ireland, John, *The Admiral from Mayo,* Edmund Burke Publisher, Dublin, 1995.

De Freine, Sean, *The Great Silence,* The Mercier Press, 1965.

De Laroque, Lucinda, *Paradise Found,* Camerapix Publishers Int., Kenya, 1992.

De Verteuil, Anthony, C.S.Sp., *Sylvester Devenish and the Irish in 19th Century Trinidad,* Paria, Trinidad, 1986.

Dept of Foreign Affairs, *Challenges & Opportunities Abroad, White Paper of Foreign Policy,* Government of Ireland, 1996.

Dickson, R.J., *Ulster Emigration to Colonial America,* Ulster Historical Foundation, Belfast, 1988.

Doherty & Hickey, *A Chronology of Irish History since 1500,* Gill & Macmillan Ltd., Dublin 1989.

Dolan, Jay P., *The Immigrant Church,* The Johns Hopkins University Press, Baltimore, 1975.

Douglas, Ray, Harte, Liam, and O'Hara, Jim, *Drawing Conclusions,* Blackstaff Press Ltd., Belfast 1998.

Doyle, David Noel, *Ireland, Irishmen and Rev. America,* Mercier Press, 1981.

Durack, Mary, *Kings in Grass Castles,* Constable & Co. Ltd., Great Britain, 1959.

Edward, Mary, *Who Belongs to Glasgow,* Glasgow City Libraries Publications Board, Glasgow, 1993.

Emmons, David M., *The Butte Irish,* University of Illinois Press, Urbana & Chicago, 1997.

Erie, Steven, *Rainbow's End,* University of California Press, California, 1988.

Fanning, Charles, *The Irish Voice in America,* The University Press of Kentucky, 1990.

Fanning, Ronan, Kennedy, Michael, Keogh, Dermot, O'Halpin, Eunan, *Documents on Irish Foreign Policy,* Royal Irish Academy, Dublin, 1998.

Farragher, Sean, P., CS.Sp., *Blackrock College 1860–1995,* Paraclete Press, Dublin, 1995.

Fischer, David Hackett, *Albion's Seed,* Oxford University Press, New York, Oxford, 1989.

Fitzgerald, Margaret E. and King Joseph A., *The Uncounted Irish in Canada and the United States,* P.D. Meany Publishers, Toronto, 1991.

Fitzpatrick, David, *Oceans of Consolation,* Cornell University Press, 1994.

Flannery, James W., *Dear Harp of my Country,* J.J. Sanders & Co., 1997.

Flood, Nicholas Davin, *The Irishman in Canada,* Irish University Press, Shannon, 1969.

Forrestal, Desmond, *The Christian Heritage,* Veritas Publications, Dublin, 1976.

——, *The Second Burial of Bishop Shanahan*, Veritas Publications, Dublin, 1990.

Gallagher, Thomas, *Paddy's Lament*, Harcourt Brace Jovanovich, New York & London, 1982.

Garrison, Jim, *The Trail of the Assassins,* Penguin Books Ltd., London, 1988.

Genealogical Society of Queensland, *Memorial to the Irish in Queensland,* Irish Group and the Queensland Irish Association, 1988.

Grace, Robert J., *The Irish in Quebec, Institut Quebecois de Recherche sur la Culture* Quebec, N.D.

Grassby, A.L. and Hill, Marji, *Six Australian Battlefields*, Angus & Robertson Publishers, NSW, Australia, 1988.

Grassby, Al, *The Australian Republic*, Pluto Press Australia Ltd., NSW, 1993

——, *The Morning After,* Judicator Publications, Canberra, 1979.

——, *The Tyranny of Prejudice*, Australasian Educational Press Pty, Ltd., Victoria, 1984.

Gray, Marie, *Irish in the Blood*, Hodder Moa Beckett Publishers Ltd., 1997.

Greeley, Andrew, *That Most Distressful Nation*, Quadrangle Books Inc., Chicago, 1972.

Griffin, Mullans D., *Book of Irish Americans,* Times Books, New York, 1990.

Handley, James Edmund, *The Irish in Modern Scotland,* Cork University Press, Oxford, 1947.

Hanson, A.H., and Walles, Malcolm, *Governing Britain*, Fontana Paperbacks, Great Britain, 1970.

Harman, Donald Akenson, *Half the World from Home*, Victoria University Press, Wellington, 1990.

Harzig, Christiane, *Peasant Maids, City Women,* Cornell University Press, New York, 1997.

Hayden, Tom, *Irish Hunger*, Wolfhound Press Dublin, 1997.

Henderson, Anne, *Mary MacKillop's Sisters*, HarperCollins Publishers, NSW, 1997.

Hickman, Dr Mary J, and Walter, Dr Bronwen, *Discrimination and the Irish Community in Britain,* Commission for Racial Equality, London, 1997.

Higham, John, *Strangers in the Land,* Rutgers University Press, 1955.

Hillyard, Paddy, *Suspect Community*, Pluto Press, London, 1993.

Hodgins, Jack, *Sister Island,* CMS, Ireland, 1994.

Hogan, Edmund M., *The Irish Missionary Movement,* Gill & Macmillan, Dublin, 1990.

Hogan, Michael, *The Irish Soldiers of Mexico,* Fonto Editorial Universitario, 1997.

Holohan Anne, *Working Lives, The Irish Post*, Middlesex, 1995.

Houston, Cecil J, and Smyth William J, *Irish Emigration and Canadian Settlement,* University of Toronto Press, 1990.

Hughes, Robert, *The Fatal Shore,* Pan Books, London 1988.

Ireland, Land of Love and Flowers, in co-operation with the Embassy of Ireland in Japan, NTT Mediascope Inc., 1995.

——, *Irish Convicts,* Ireland, 1989.

Ignatiev, Noel, *How the Irish became White,* Routledge, New York, 1995.

Jeffares, A. Norman, *Yeats' Poems,* Gill & Macmillan, 1989.

——, *W.B. Yeats, Man and Poet,* Routledge and Kegan Paul, 1949.

Joannon, Pierre, *Michael Collins,* La Table Ronde, Paris, 1996.

Johnston, Patricia Condon, *Minnesota's Irish,* Johnston Publishing Inc., Afton, Minnesota, 1984.

Johnston, William, *Letters to Contemplatives,* Orbis Books, 1991.

Jones, Ian, *Ned Kelly.,* Thomas C. Hollision, Victoria, 1995.

Keane, Frank, & Lavin Patrick, *Thank You Ireland,* Garryowen Inc., British Columbia, 1994.

Kearney, Richard, *Migrations – The Irish at Home & Abroad,* Wolfhound Press, Dublin, 1990.

Keneally, Thomas, *A Family Madness,* Sceptre, A Divison of Hodder & Stoughton, 1986.

——, *Homebush Boy – A Memoir,* Minerva, Reed Books Australia, Victoria, 1995.

——, *Gossip from the Forest,* Sceptre, Hodder & Stoughton, Ltd., Great Britain, 1988.

——, *The Great Shame,* Chatto & Windus, London 1998.

Keogh, Dermot, *Jews in 20th Century Ireland,* Cork University Press, Cork, 1998.

Kiernan, T.J., *The Irish Exiles in Australia,* Clonmore & Reynolds Ltd., Republic of Ireland, 1954.

Kimel, Eduardo, *La Masacre de San Patricio,* Lohle-Lumen, Buenos Aires, 1995

King, Joseph, *Winter of Entrapment,* K & K Publications, 1992.

Kirby, Peadar, *Ireland & Latin America,* Trocaire & Gill Macmillan, 1992.

Kurmansky, Mark, *Cod, a Biography of the Fish that changed the World,* Jonathan Cape, London, 1998.

Larkin, Emmet, *Alexis de Tocqueville's Journey in Ireland,* Wolfhound Press, Dublin, 1990.

Lawton Collins, General J., *Lightning Joe,* Presidio Press, California, 1979.

Laxton, Edward, *The Famine Ships,* Bloomsbury, 1996.

Lee, Steere Ernest Henry, *Be Fair and Fear Not, An Autobiography,* Success Printy, N.D.,

——, *Lesotho's Long Journey,* Gechaba Consultants, 1995.

Leyburn, James G., *The Scotch-Irish,* The University of North Carolina Press, 1962.

Luna, Felix, *A Brief History of Argentina,* Editorial Planeta, Argentina 1996.

MacGill, Patrick, *Children of the Dead End,* Caliban Books, London, 1985.

——, *The Rat Pit,* Caliban Books, London, 1993.

Mackay, Donald, *Flight from Famine*, McClelland & Stewart Inc., Toronto, 1992.

Madden Deirdre, *Hidden Symptoms*, The Atlantic Monthly Press, Boston & New York, 1986.

Malcolm, Elizabeth, *Elderly Return Migration from Britain to Ireland – A Preliminary Study*, National Council for the Elderly, Dublin, 1996.

Malouf, David, *Remembering Babylon*, Vintage, London, 1994.

Mansergh, Nicholas, *Britain & Ireland*, Longman, London, 1942.

————, *Nationalism & Independence*, Cork University Press, 1977.

Marks, Lara, *Working Wives and Working Mothers*, PNL Press, Ireland, 1990.

Martin, Augustine, *W.B. Yeats*, Gill & Macmillan, 1983.

Martinez, Tomas Eloy, *Santa Evita*, Transworld Publishers Ltd., London, 1995.

McCaffrey, Lawrence J., *The Irish Diaspora in America*, Indiana University Press, London, 1976.

————, *Textures of Irish America*, Syracuse University Press, New York, 1992.

McCourt, Frank, *Angela's Ashes*, Scribner, New York, 1996.

McCracken, Donal P., *Ireland and South Africa in Modern Times – Volume 3*, University of Durban, Westville, 1996.

————, *The Irish in Southern Africa (ed) – Volume 2, 1796–1910*, University of Durban, Westville, 1992.

McGill, David, *The Lion and the Wolfhound*, Grantham House Publishing, N.D.

McMahon, Martin, *I Cry for my People*, Martin McMahon, Sandgate, Queensland, 1996.

McMullin, Ross, *The Light on the Hill*, Oxford University Press, Melbourne, 1992.

McNee, Gerald, *The Story of Celtic, An Official History*, Stanley Paul & Co. Ltd., 1978.

McWhiney, Grady, *Cracker Culture*, The University of Albama Press, Tuscaloosa, Alabama, 1988.

Miller, A. Kerby, *Emigrants and Exiles*, Oxford University Press, New York, 1985.

Molohan, Cathy, *Germany & Ireland 1945–1955, Two Nations' Friendship*, Irish Academic Press, 1999.

Murphy, Lionel, *A Radical Judge*, McColloch, Victoria, 1987.

Murphy, Mary, *Mining Cultures*, University of Illinois Press, Urbana & Chicago 1997.

Murphy, William M, *Family Secrets*, Syracuse University Press, 1994.

Neal, Frank, *Sectarian Violence, The Liverpool Experience 1819–1914*, Manchester University Press, 1988.

Neary, Bernard, *Irish Lives – The Irish in Western Australia*, New Zealand, 1990.

————, *The Irish in Australia, NSW,* 1987.

Noble, Christina, *Bridge Across My Sorrows,* John Murray Ltd, London, 1994.

Noone, Val, *Disturbing the War,* Spectrum Publications Pty Ltd., Victoria, 1993.

O'Brien, John & Travers, Pauric, *The Irish Emigrant Experience in Australia,* Poolbeg Press Ltd, Dublin, 1991

O'Clery, Conor, *The Greening of the White House,* Gill & Macmillan Ltd, 1996.

O'Connor, Aine, *Leading Hollywood,* Wolfhound Press, Dublin, 1996

O'Connor, Kevin, *The Irish in Britain,* Gill & Macmillan Ltd, 1972

O'Connor, P.E.T., *Some Trinidad Yesterdays,* Imprint Caribbean Ltd, Trinidad, 1978

O'Connor, Thomas H., *South Boston – My Home Town,* Quinlan Press, USA, 1988

————, *The Boston Irish,* North Eastern University Press, Boston, 1995.

O'Doherty, Michael Kevin, *My Parents and other Rebels,* Errigal Press, 1999.

O'Donnell, L.A., *Irish Voice and organised Labour in America,* Greenwood Press, Connecticut, 1997.

O'Dowd, Anne, *Spalpeens & Tattie Hokers,* Irish Academic Press, 1991.

O'Driscoll, Robert & Reynolds Lorna, *Vols 1 and 2, The Untold Story: The Irish in Canada,* Celtic Arts of Canada, Ontario, 1988.

O'Faolain, Sean, *The Irish,* Penguin Books Ltd, Middlesex, 1947.

O'Farrell, Patrick, *The Irish in Australia,* NSW University Press

————, *The Catholic Church in Australia: A Short History, 1788–1967,*

————, *Documents in Australian Catholic History, 1788–1968.*

————, *Ireland's English Question: Anglo-Irish Relations, 1534–1970.*

————, *Letters from Irish Australia 1825–1929.*

————, *Through Irish Eyes.* Aurora Books in association with David Lovell Publishing, Victoria, 1994.

————, *Vanished Kingdoms, Irish in Australia – A Personal Excursion,* NSW University Press, NSW, 1990.

O'Laughlin, Michael C., *Irish Settlers on the American Frontier,* Irish Genealogical Foundation, Missouri, 1984.

O'Mahony, Christopher, & Thompson, Valerie, *Poverty to Promise,* Crossing Press, NSW, 1994.

O'Neill, Kevin, *Apuntes Historicos Palatines,* Editora Palletti, Santa Maria, 1994.

O'Reilly, John Boyle, *Selected Poems, Speeches, Dedications and Letters of John Boyle O'Reilly,* The National Gaelic Publications (Western Australia), 1994.

Ormonde, Paul, *The Movement,* Thomas Nelson (Australia) Ltd., Melbourne, 1972.

Pakenham, Thomas, *The Scramble for Africa,* Abacus, London, 1992.

Pascoe, Prof. Robert, *The Winter Game,* Mandarin, Victoria, 1995.

Patrick, Ross and Heather, *Exiles Undaunted,* University of Queensland Press, Queensland, 1989.

Pelan, Rebecca, asst. by Quirke, Noel and Finnane, Mark, *Irish Australian Studies,* Crossing Press, NSW, 1994.

Philips, Jock, *New Worlds? The Comparative History of New Zealand and the USA,* Platform Publishing, 1989.

Prior, Tom, *A Knockabout Priest,* Hargreen Publishing Company, Victoria, 1988.

Quinn, Brother Charles B., *Iona College,* Scholarship Vision Service, N.D.

Reece, Bob, *Exiles from Erin,* Macmillan Academic & Professional Ltd., London, 1991.

————, *Irish Convict Lives,* Crossing Press, NSW, 1993.

Ridge, John T., *Erin's Sons in America,* AOH Publications, New York, 1986

Robinson, Philip, *The Plantation of Ulster,* Gill & Macmillan Ltd., Dublin 1984

Rogers, Anna, *A Lucky Landing,* Random House New Zealand Ltd., 1996.

Ryan, Dennis P., *Beyond the Ballot Box,* The University of Massachusetts Press, Amherst, 1989.

Sabato, Hilda, *Agrarian Capitalism and the World Market,* University of New Mexico Press, Albuquerque, 1990.

Santamaria, B.A. *Daniel Mannix,* Melbourne University Press, Victoria, 1985

Schmitz, Nancy, *Irish for a Day,* Carraig Books, Quebec, 1991.

Senior, Hereward, *The Fenians & Canada,* Macmillan of Canada, 1978.

Shannon, William, V., *The American Irish,* Collier Books, New York, 1974.

Sherington, Geoffrey, *Australia's Immigrants,* George Allen & Unwin, Australia Pty Ltd., NSW, 1980

Stalker John, *Stalker,* Harrap Ltd, London, 1988.

Steel, Edward. Jr., *The Court Martial of Mother Jones,* University Press of Kentucky, 1995.

Stynes, Jim, *Whatever it Takes,* Celebrity Publishing, Australia, 1996.

Sullivan, Jim, *Catholic Boys,* Penguin Books (New Zealand) Ltd, Auckland, 1996.

Sweetman, Rory, *Bishop in the Dark,* Auckland University Press, Auckland, 1997.

Swift, Roger & Gillery, Sheridan, *The Irish in Britain 1815–1939,* Pinter Publishers 1989.

Talese, Nan A., *A River Town,* Bantam Doubleday Dell Publishing Group Inc., New York, 1995.

Tansill, Charles Callan, *America and the Fight for Irish Freedom 1866–1922,* Devin-Adair Company, New York, 1957.

The Western Australian Memorial Doors and Sculpture, The W.B. Yeats Society of Western Australia, 1988.

Tourigny, Yves W.F., *So Abundant a Harvest,* Darton Longman & Todd Ltd., London, 1979.

Trioli, Virginia, *Generation F*, Minerva, Victoria, University Press of NSW, 1996

Urquhart, Jane, *Away*, McClelland & Stewart Inc., Toronto, 1993.

Walker, Doris, edited by Malone, Myrtle D., *Orange Country – A Centennial Celebration*, Pioneer Publications Inc., Houston, Texas, N.D.

Wall, Rita, *Leading Lives, Irish Women in Britain*, Attic Press Dublin, 1991.

Walsh, Packard Kathleen, *Fling Old Glory, The Story of Patrick Walsh*, Gateway Press, 1992.

Wannan Bill, *The Wearing of Green*, NEL Books, London 1969

West, Rebecca, *The Meaning of Treason*, Virago Press, 1982

Whitaker, Anne-Maree, *Unfinished Revolution*, Crossing Press, NSW, 1994

White, de Vere, Terence, *Tom Moore*, Hamish Hamilton, London, 1977.

Williams, William H.A., *'Twas only an Irishman's Dream*, University of Illinois Press, Urbana and Chicago, 1996.

Wilson, Andrew J., *Irish America & the Ulster Conflict*, Catholic University of America Press 1996.

Wooding, Jonathan M., *Old Myths, New Lights*, Queensland Irish Association, Brisbane, 1991

Woodward, Otway, *Divided Island*, Heinemann Educational Books, Auckland, 1976.

Yeats, W. B., *The Collected Plays of W.B. Yeats*, Macmillan, 1934.

DIRECTORIES

Caribbean Catholic Directory 1994, Published by Most Rev. Donald Reece DD.

Catholic Missions, *Official Organ of the Society for the Propagation of the Faith*, 1942

Catholic Province of Cardiff, *Wales & Herefordshire Directory & Yearbook 1999*, Authority of the Bishops of Wales.

Cooper, Brian, E., Managing Editor, *The Irish American Almanac and Green Pages*, GSQ Irish Group, *Memorials to the Irish in Queensland*, Saft, Elizabeth.

Insight Guides – Trinidad and Tobago, APA Productions (HK) Ltd., Singapore, 1987.

ARTICLES AND PAMPHLETS

A non-alphabetical selection of some of the papers that I have also consulted in preparing this work.

McDermid, Jane, 'Catholic working class girls, education in lowland Scotland, 1872–1900', *The Innes Review*, Vol. 47, No. 1, Spring 1966.

Aspinwall, Bernard, 'Scots and Irish Clergy ministering to Emigrants, 1830–1878', *The Innes Review*, Vol. 47, No. 1, Spring 1966.

McCaffrey, John F., *The Innes Review*, Vol. XXXIX No. 1, Spring 1988.

Massie, Allan, 'Catholics go cool on love affair with Labour', *Sunday Times*, August 30th, 1988.

Harrington, Aine, 'Irish are an economic success story in Scotland', *Glasgow Herald*, February 28th, 1998.

McColm, 'Historian to plunge into Scotland's great divide', *Scotsman*, November 17th, 1997.

Cooney, John, 'The Irish Republican brotherhood in Scotland', Paper in author's possession.

Ross, John, and Silver, David, 'Minister's attack on Catholics condemned', *Scotsman*, 10.9.97.

Finlay, Richard J., 'Nationalism, Race, Religion and the Irish question in inter-war Scotland', *The Innes Review*, Vol. XLII No. 1, Spring 1991.

In September 1997, a groundbreaking Conference on Irish emigration, the Scattering conference, was held at University College Cork, through the initiative of Piaras McHenry. I am indebted to the organisers and participants who allowed me to peruse the papers, which although I did not quote from them, provided extremely useful background material, particularly those of Shannon, Catherine B., 'Linking the old and the new Irish in Boston, 1845-1997', and Corcoran, Mary, 'Voting with their feet: Returning Irish Emigrants in the 1990s'.

Fitzpatrick, David, 'The Scattering: Ireland and the Empire, 1801–1921.

Fraser, Lyndon, 'The Ties that Bind, Irish Catholic Testamentory evidence of Christ Church, 1876–1915', *The New Zealand Journal of History*, April, 1995.

Campbell, Malcolm, 'Irish Nationalism and Immigrant Assimilation: Comparing the United States and Australia, *The Australasian Journal of American Studies*, December 1996.

Rifkind, Malcolm, 'Scotland and Europe: A new United Kingdom for a new Century', *Scottish Affairs*, No. 25, Autumn 1998. Also Browne, Alice, 'Re-Defining Relationships, North-South and East-West Links in Ireland and Britain in the new Millennium'. Round Table meeting, Newman House, Dublin, January 8th, 1999.

Edmondson, Richard, 'Has the Sport of Kings been making dopes of us all?', *The Independent*, January 28th, 1998.

Darragh, James, 'The Catholic Population of Scotland 1878–1977', *The Innes Review*, op. cit.

Brown, Stuart J., 'Outside the Covenant, Presbyterianism and Irish Immigration', *The Innes Review*, Vol. XLII, No. 1, Spring 1991.

Donovan, Robert Kent, 'Voices of Distrust, Anti-Catholic Feeling in Scotland, 1778–1781', *The Innes Review*.

Wall, Vincent, 'Racing Uncertainty, The Irish Bloodstock Industry', *Business & Finance*, March 18th, 1999.

Congressional Record, Senate, Washington, March 5th, 1997, 'The Contributions of the Scots/Irish in America'.

O'Neill, Charles Edwards, 'De Valera's visit to New Orleans, 1920', *Journal of Louisiana History*, Summer 1993.

McElrath, Karen, 'Unsafe Haven, The United States, the IRA and Political Prisoners', PhD Thesis, Queen's University, Belfast.

Gallagher, Tom, 'Soccer, the real Opium of the People', *The Innes Review*. Op. cit.

Cooney, John, 'Aherne wants close links with Scottish Parliament', *Glasgow Herald*, May 11th 1998.

Cooney, John, 'Scots toast of Albert a sign of the times', *Sunday Tribune*, 8.12.96.

Greeley, Andrew, 'An Irish National Identity', Paper in author's possession.

Lambert, Eric, 'General O'Leary and South America', *The Irish Sword*, Vol. 11, No. 43, 15.7.77.

Lambert, Eric, 'Irish Soldiers in South America, 1818–1830, *Studies* Winter 1969.

Patmore, 'A Navvy Gang of 1851', *The Journal of Transport History*.

Karsten, Peter, 'Irish Soldiers in the British Army 1792–1922', *Journal of Social History*, Vol. 17, No. 1, 1983.

White, Robert W., 'From Peaceful Protest to Guerrilla War, Micro-Mobilisation of the Provisional Republican Army', *American Journal of Sociology*, Vol. 94, No. 6, May 1989. Lawton, R.,'Irish Emigration to England and Wales in the mid-19th Century', *Irish Geography*, Vol. 4, No. 1, 1959.

Nelson, Colonel J.E., 'Irish Soldiers in the Great War', *The Irish Sword*, Vol. 11.

Neal, Frank, Liverpool, The Irish Steamship Companies and the Famine Irish', *Immigrants and Minorities*, Vol. 5, No. 1, March 1986.

Inglis, Joan, 'The Irish in Britain, A question of identity', *Irish Studies in Britain*, No. 3, Spring/Summer 1982.

Williams, Rory, 'Britain's Regional Mortality: A legacy from disaster in the Celtic periphery', *Society of Scientific Medicine*, Vol. 39. No. 2, 1994.

Alexander, Jane, 'The Irish amongst us, how they feel now', *Inside London*, No. 1, 1973.

Snell, Janet, 'Joke Over', *Nursing Times*, March 1997, Vol. 93, No. 11.

Neal, Frank, 'A criminal profile of the Liverpool Irish', *Transactions of the Historical Society of Lancashire and Cheshire for the year 1990*, Vol. 140.

Yearley, Stephen, Colonial Science and Dependent Development; the case of the Irish experience', *Sociological Review*, Vol. 37, 1989.

Walsh, Brendan M., 'A perspective on Irish population patterns, Eire-Ireland', *Irish American Cultural Institute*, 1996.

Scally, Robert, 'Liverpool ships and Irish emigrants in the age of sail', *Journal of Social History*, Vol. 17, No. 1, 1983.

O'Connell, Bernard, 'Irish Nationalism in Liverpool, 1873–1923', *Eire-Ireland*, Vol. 10, No. 1, 1975.

O'Higgins, Rachel, 'Irish Influence in the Chartist Movement,' *Past and Present*, No. 20, 1961.

Ullah, Philip, 'Rhetoric and Ideology in Social Identification: the case of second-generation Irish youths', *Discourse & Society*, Vol. 1, 1990.

Walsh, T.A., 'Emigration to the Republic of Ireland, 1946–71', *Irish Geography*, Vol. 12, 1979.

'Outbreak against the Irish in Cardiff', *The Tablet*, 18.11.48.

Walsh, Dermot, 'Alcohol and Ireland', *British Journal of Addiction*, No. 82, 1987.

Treble, J.H., 'Irish Navvies in the North of England, 1830–50', *Transport History*, Vol. 6, No. 3, 1973.

Gribben, 'A Tribute to Irish Ingenuity', *The Irish Post*, January 18th, 1997.

Neal, Frank, 'English/Irish Conflict in the North-East of England, Irish in Britain, Labour History': Conference Proceedings in Irish Studies, No. 1, Ed. Patrick Buckland and John Belcham, 1992.

Maynes, Paddy, 'Mental Health: Counselling Irish Women in Britain', *Women's Health Newsletter 25*, February 1995.

Mullen, Kenneth, Williams Rory, and Hunt Kate, 'Irish Descent, Religion, and Alcohol and Tobacco Use', Research Report, Vol. 91, Journal of Addiction, 1996.

Schofield, Carey, 'The Kilburn Irish', *Kilburn Times*, N.D.

Bennett, Ronan, 'An Irish Answer', *Guardian Weekend*, July 16th 1994.

'The Irish in Cardiff', *The Green Dragon* No. 1, December 1966.

O'Kane, Paul, 'Business People at breakfast reflect Irish success in Britain', *Sunday Tribune*, 11.5.97.

Cochrane, Raymond, and Stopes Roe, Mary, 'Psychological Disturbance in Ireland, in England and in Irish emigrants in England: a comparative study', *Economical & Social Review*, Vol. 10, No. 4, July 1979.

Bagley, Christopher, and Binitie, 'Alcoholism and Schizophrenia in Irish men in London', *British Journal of Addiction*, 1970, Vol. 65.

Connolly, Gerard, '"No law would be granted us": Institutional Protestantism and the problem of Catholic Poverty in England, 1839–42', *Studies in Church History*, Vol. 21, 1984.

Connolly, Gerard, 'Little Brother, be at peace: The priest as holy man in the 19th century ghetto', *Studies in Church History*, Vol. 19, 1982.

Culhane, Robert, 'Irish Catholics in Britain', *The Furrow*, Vol. 1, No. 8, 1950.

Darcy, Fergus, 'The Irish in 19th-century Britain: Reflections on their role and experience', *Irish History Workshop 1*, 1981.

'The Irish Abroad', *Edinburgh Review*, Vol. 27, April 1868.

Haskey, John, 'Mortality among second-generation Irish in England and Wales', *British Medical Journal*, Vol. 312, June 1st 1996, also: Harding, S., and Balarian, R., 'Patterns of Mortality in second-generation Irish living in England and Wales: a Longitudinal Study'.

Crichton, Torcuil, 'Most Scots hate sectarianism, so why does it poison our lives?' *Glasoow Sunday Herald*, June 6th 1999.

Hamilton, Celia, 'Irish Catholics of New South Wales and the Labour Party 1890–1910', *Historical Studies*, Australia and New Zealand, Vol. 8, November 1957–May 1959.

Collins, Brenda, and O'Ferrall, Fergus, Thesis abstracts, 'Aspects of Irish Emigration into two Scottish towns, and the growth of political consciousness in Ireland 1824–1848', *Irish Economic and Social History*, Vol. 6, 1979.

'The Story of the Irish Society in London', *The Irish Society*, London, 1913.

Boyle, Kevin, 'The Irish Immigrant in Britain', *Northern Ireland Legal Quarterly*, Vol. 19, No. 4, December 1968.

Parsons, Brian, 'The Historical Roots of Anti-Irish Racism', *Multi Ethnic Education Review*, Winter–Spring 1985.

Divine, T.M., and Dixon, David, 'In pursuit of comparative aspects of Irish and Scottish developments: A review of the Symposium', John Donald, Edinburgh, 1983.

Irish Studies Centre Occasional Paper Series:

Bennett, Christopher, 'The Housing of the Irish in London: Updated and revised edition.'

Bradley, Joseph M., 'Football, Religion and Ethnicity: Irish Identity in Scotland.'

Harris, Mary, 'Education, Revolution and Partition'.

Hazelkorn, Ellen, 'Irish Immigrants Today: A socio-economic profile of contemporary Irish emigrants and immigrants in the UK'

Hickman,, Mary J., 'The Irish Community in Britain, Myth or Reality?'

Kells, Mary, 'Ethnic Identity amongst Young Irish Middle Class Migrants in London.'

Lloyd, Cathie, 'The Irish Community in Britain, Discrimination, Disadvantage and Racism: an Annotated Bibliography.'

Marks, Lara, 'Working Wives and Working Mothers: A comparative study of Irish and Eastern European Jewish married women's work and motherhood in East London, 1870–1914.'

MacLaughlin, Jim, 'Historical and Recent Irish Emigration: A Critique of Coreperiphery and Behavioural Models.'

Moore, Jonathan, 'Ulster Unionism and the British Conservative Party. A Study of a Failed Marriage.'

Sharkey, Sabina, 'Ireland and the Iconography of Rape: Colonisation Constraint and Gender.'

'Franciscan Missions among the Colliers and Ironworkers of Monmouthshire', a record of Franciscan labours prepared for Cardinal Edward, Archbishop of Westminster, Burns & Oates, London, 1876.

Campbell, John L., 'The MacNeills of Barra and the Irish Franciscans', *The*

Innes Review, also, Stevenson, David, 'Irish Franciscan Mission to Scotland: the Irish Rebellion of 1641'.

Callahan, Bob, *Callahan's Irish Quarterly*, Premier Issue, Winter 1981, San Francisco.

Gwynn, Aubrey, S.J., 'Some notes on the history of the Irish and Scottish Benedictine Monasteries in Germany.'

Eagleton, T. 'Ireland's obdurate nationalisms', *New Left Review*, No. 215, September–October 1995.

Miller, Kerby A., with Bruce Boling and David N. Doyle, 'Emigrants and Exiles: Irish Cultures and Irish emigration to North America, 1790–1922', *Irish Historical Studies*, September 1980.

McCaffrey, Laurence J., ed., 'Irish Nationalism and the American Contribution', Arno Press, New York, 1976.

De Breffney, Brian, ed., *The Irish World, History and Cultural Achievements of the Irish People*, Thames & Hudson, N.D.

Le Fevour, Virginia McHugh, 'No Irish need apply – never applied', Chicago's 26th annual St Patrick's Day Parade programme.

Walter, Bronwen, 'The Geography of Irish Migration to Britain since 1939 with special reference to Luton and Bolton', *Irish Economic and Social History*, Vol. 8, 1981.

O'Leary, Paul, 'Accommodation and Resistance: A comparison of cultural identities in Ireland and Wales, c.1880–1914', 'Kingdoms United?' S.J. Connolly, ed.,Four Courts Press.

Cooney, John, 'Risky Galore', Magill, January 1999.

Price, R.G.G., 'Punch and the Near West', *Punch*, January 6th 1971.

Reaney, Bernard, Saothar 10, 1984.

O'Connell, Noel, 'Irish Studies in the 80s, A Signpost', *Irish Studies in Britain* No. 2, Autumn/Winter 1981.

Gilley, Sheridan, 'The Roman Catholic Church and the 19th Century Irish Diaspora', *Journal of Ecclesiastical History*, Vol 35, No. 2, April 1984.

Barber, Sarah, 'Irish Migrant Labourers in 19th-Century Lincolnshire', Saothar 8, 1982.

Brooke, D., 'Railway Navvies on the Pennines, 1841–71', *Journal of Transport History*, Vol. 3, No. 1, 1975.

Harrison, Paul, 'Cultural Migration, The Irish/English', *New Society*, 20th September, 1973.

Hornsby-Smith, Michael P., and Dale, Angela, University of Surrey, 'The assimilation of Irish emigrants in England', *The British Journal of Sociology*, Vol. XXXIX, No. 4.

Coughlan, Patricia, 'Cheap and Common Animals: The English Anatomy of Ireland in the 17th Century', Cambridge University Press, 1990.

Raftery, James, Jones, David, Rosato, Michael, 'The Mortality of First and Second Generation Irish Emigrants in the UK', *Journal of Social Medicine*, Vol. 31, No. 5, 1990.

Smith, Dai, 'A Welsh Fighting Class, Sport and the Working Class in Modern

Britain'. Ed. Richard Holt, Manchester University Press, 1990.

Aspinwall, Bernard, Review of 'The Uneasy Peace, an Edinburgh divided', both by Tom Gallagher, *The Innes Review*, Vol. XL, No. 1, Spring 1989, also Furgol, E.J., reviewing *Celtic Warfare*, by James Michael Hill.

Holland, Mary, 'The New Wave in the Bronx', *Observer Magazine*, October 30th, 1988.

Connolly, Jerome, 'The Irish Churches and Foreign Policy', *Studies*, Spring 1988.

Molloy, Darina, 'Drug Abuse concern about new arrivals', *Irish Voice*, May 26th 1999, New York.

INDEX

Abbey Theatre, Dublin 71, 178
Abercromby, General Sir Ralph 436, 586, 587
Aberdeen 248
abortion 91, 159, 247, 303, 460
Acheson, Dean 287
Achill Island, County Mayo 54, 240
Acholi tribe 527
ACIS *see* American Committee for Irish Studies
Act of Union (1800) 116, 168, 374, 445
Action Grosse Ile Committee 378, 379, 380, 407
Action Group for Irish Youth 121, 155
Active Service Units (ASUs) 183, 337
Acton, London 160
Adair, Sean 243
Adams, Gerry 83, 84, 165, 253, 254, 269-72, 323, 332, 333, 334, 484
Adams, Quincy 610
Adelaide 442
Admiral Brown Club 634
Adrian IV, Pope (Nicholas Breakspear) xi, 26, 35
Aer Lingus 4, 6, 140, 265, 340, 663
Aer Lingus Hurling Club 2
AFL/CIO (American Federation of Labor and Congress of Industrial Organizations) 270, 314, 318-19, 331, 335
Africa 75, 76, 107, 504-68, 665
African National Congress (ANC) 530, 550, 551, 553
Africanisation of the Church 543, 545
Aga Khan 533
Agnew, Art 530, 608
Agnew, Paddy 73
Ahern, Bertie 272, 480, 662
AIDS 137, 142, 147-8, 303, 519, 525, 526, 534, 566, 567, 568, 589

Aiken, Frank 473
Air Studios 577
Akihito, Emperor 653
Al-Anon 137
Albania 59
Albany 260, 276, 288, 315
Albericus, Bishop of Cambrai 9
Albert, King of Belgium 94
Albright, General Charles 321, 323
Alcala de Henares University 38
Alcatraz 293
Alcoa 258
alcoholism 156-9, 162, 358
Alcott, Chauncey (John Chancellor) 355
Alemanni 20
Alemany, Archbishop Joseph 613
Alexander, General 393
Alfonso, Raoul 620
Alford, David 100
Alfred, Prince, Duke of Edinburgh 449, 491
Algiers 66
Alitalia 73
All Blacks rugby team 487, 498, 500
All Hallows College, Dublin 237, 239, 591, 630
All Hallows secondary school, Queensland 441
All-Party Irish in Britain Parliamentary Group 133
Allan, Sarah 208
Allende, Salvador 618
Alliance High School, Kenya 509
Allied Democratic Force 528
Allied Irish Banks 176
Alva, Duchess of 66
Ambrose, Mary 663, 664
Ambrosian Order 85
Amergin (Amheirgin) 61
America 120, 142, 143, 245, 253-368

Breuil Abbey 21
Bridgend 216
Bridgewater State College 347
Bridgewater Three 165
Brierly, J.N. 588
Brighton bombing 113
Brighton Pavilion 45
Brigid, Sister 310
Brigid, St 17
Brisbane 442, 458
Brisbane, Governor 448
Brisket, Captain Anthony 573
Bristol 161
British and Irish Association 176
British Army 7, 13, 37, 48, 166, 169, 179,
    187, 215, 243
British Association for Irish Studies
    (BAIS) 176, 177
British Board of Film Censors (BBFC) 350
British Columbia 391
British Council 231
British Council Library, Madrid 70
British Empire xiii, 183, 187, 309, 393, 421,
    511
British Medical Journal 156
British Midland 140
British Oxygen 130
British-Irish Council 231
Brittan, Leon 95
Brittany xii, 21
Broadcasting Act 171, 343
Brodsky, Joseph 596
Broederbond 553
Brolly, Nodlaig 2, 3, 11
Bronx, New York 262, 289, 314
Brookborough raid (1956) 217
Brooklyn 260, 366
Brooklyn Archdiocesan Catholic
    Migration Office 305
Brookside (television programme) 170
Brophy, John 318
Brophy, Nial 500
Brosnan, Father John 432-4, 471
Brosnan, Pierce 351
Brotherhood of Carpenters 280
Brown, Dave 476
Brown, Gordon 249
Brown, Max 626
Brown, Patrick 626
Brown, Stewart 244
Brown, Tommy 341
Brown, Admiral William 324, 605, 617,
    625, 626, 632, 635, 636, 640, 641
Browne, Field Marshal 34
Browne, Dr Michael 468
Browne, Father Pat 161, 162
Brownlee, Donal 567

Brownson, Orestes 296-7, 298
Bruce, Steve 188
Brussels 13, 90, 93-9
Bruton, John 95, 428
Buchanan, James 260
Buckland, Patrick 183
Buckley, Christopher 275
Buenos Aires 602, 608, 622-7, 629-38, 640,
    643
Buenos Aires Herald 617
Buenos Aires Jockey Club 636
Buffalo 260, 315
Buffet, Jimmy 577
building industry 55-6, 127-8, 138, 304,
    314-16
Bulfin, Eamon 629, 637
Bulfin, William 629-31, 634
Bulger, Bill 272-5, 291-5
Bulger, Brendan 274
Bulger, James 'Whitey' 274, 291, 293-5
Bulger, Mary 293
Bulkelly (Irish Brigade commander) 31
Bulwark 235
Burke, Patrick 4
Burke, Richard 317
Burke, Ronald 317
Burke, Vincent 499
Burns, Julia 226-7
Burns, Lizzy 50
Burns, Mary 50
Burns, Robert 248-9
Burns collection 344-5
Burundi 509, 547
Bush, George 269, 271, 291, 333, 344
Business '97, the influential Irish in Britain
    127
Busteed, Mervyn 167, 168, 174-5, 202
Bute Ironworks, Rhymni valley 220
Butler, 'Black Tom', Earl of Ormond
    64
Butler, Lieutenant General William 389
Butt, Isaac 228
Butte, Montana 323-4
Byrne, Alfie 161
Byrne, Gabriel 351
Byrne, Jane 367-8
Byrne, Father Martin 635
Byrne, Mary 161
Byrne, General Miles 38, 436-7
Bytown, Canada 402-3, 406

Cabot family 420
Cabrera, Fatima (later Rice) 622-3, 624
Caesar, Julius 13, 16
Cagney, James 351, 352, 363
Cahil, Devin 311, 312
Cahill, Thomas xvii, 15, 24, 356

Clarke, Darren 645
Clarke, Dennis 285, 288
Clarke, Gerard 500
Clarke, Ian 566-8
Clarke, Michael 566
Clarke, Robbie 566, 567, 568
Clarke, Sean 566
Clashmalcolm Cave 338
Claudius, Emperor 85
Cleary, Father John 559
Cleary, John 602, 616-17
Cleary, Father John 559
Cleary, Father Michael 75, 524, 537
Cleborne, Pat 328
Clement, Pope St 85
Clery, Philip, of Raphoe 82
Cleveland, Grover 260
Clifden, County Galway 78
Clinton, Bill 253, 254, 269, 270, 271, 323,
    331-4, 344, 380, 607
Clinton, Hillary (née Rodham) 269
Clissmann, Helmut 52
Clonfert 17, 24
Clongowes Wood College, Trinidad 586,
    589
Clonliffe seminary 76
Clonmacnoise 17, 24, 25
Clontarf, Battle of 24, 154-5
Clovis II of Neustria 22
Clune, Archbishop Joseph 468
Clwyd 212
CNN 383, 511, 536
Coatbridge 236
Cobh, County Cork 228, 256, 656
Cod, Tom 632
Cody, Buffalo Bill 455
Cody, Cardinal John Patrick 301-2
Coghlan, Eduardo 640
Cognac region 39
Cohan, George M. 351-2
Cohan, Gerry 352
Cohan, Josephine 352
Cohan, Nelly 352
Coillte (Irish Forestry Organisation) 531
Colenso, South Africa 562, 563
Coll, 'Mad Dog' 360
College de Montigu, Paris 45
College des Irlandais, Paris 44
College des Lombards, Paris 45
College of Cardinals 76
College of New Jersey 259
Collingridge, Bishop 216
Collingwood FC, Melbourne 477
Collins, Cornelius 656-7
Collins, Airforce Colonel Eileen Marie
    331
Collins, John 656-7

Collins, Martin 150
Collins, Michael x, 8, 42, 147, 179, 203,
    223, 243, 331, 339, 351, 417, 561, 563,
    598
Collins, Michael (grand-nephew) 147
Collins, Peter 443, 444, 485
Colman, St 23
Cologne 23
Cologne University 38
Colorado 312, 609
Columba, St (St Columcille; the Dove of
    Derry) 20-1, 33
Columban Fathers 645, 646
Columbanus, St 20, 21, 24, 33
Columbia 602, 604, 605
Columbiere, Sister 542-3
Columbus, Christopher 62, 573
Columbus, St 637
Comaskey, Sean 90, 91
Comerford, Judge James 335
Comhair Lam (Irish Umbrella Group for
    NGOs) 554
Comhaltas Ceoltoiri Eireann 2, 203, 204,
    205, 213
Commission for Racial Equality (CRE)
    124, 145, 169, 178, 195
Commitments 356
Committee for Industrial Organisation
    (CIO) 318
Common Agricultural Policy (CAP) 97,
    165
Community Futures Conference (London)
    133
Compagnie Irlandaise 38
Company of Santa Barbara 67
Compton, Betty 286
Comstock Lode 263, 320, 323
Conall Clan 20
Concannon, James 612-13
Concannon, Mairin 612
Concannon, Rory 612
Concannon, Thomas 612
Concannon Winery 613
Concern 514, 515-16, 518-22
Concordia, Mother 444
Concordia University, Montreal 413
Congo 504
Congregationalists 259
Conn, Billy 362
Connaill, Clan 15
Connaught Rangers 504, 563, 625
Connell, Sister Eileen 505
Connemara 138, 147, 417, 576
Connery, Sean 323
Connolly, Brother Austin 78
Connolly, Billy 245
Connolly, James 122, 190, 314

INDEX

O'Dwyer, William 286-7
O'Farrell, Patrick 430, 431, 435, 450, 496
O'Farril, General 37
O'Farrill, Romulo 608
Office of Strategic Services (OSS) 330
O'Fiaich, Cardinal Tom 160
O'Flaherty, Brian 421
O'Flaherty, chieftain 62
O'Flaherty, Monsignor Hugh 77
O'Flaherty, Liam 360
O'Flaherty, Patrick 424, 425
O'Flanagan, Father Michael 465
O'Gara, chieftain, of Sligo 94
O'Gara, General 34
Ogham inscriptions 214, 254-5, 421
O'Gorman, Adolpho 633
O'Gorman, Camila 633
O'Gorman, Miguel 633
O'Gorman, Richard 448
O'Grady, Brendan 414
O'Grady, Desmond 88
O'Grady, Diago 605
O'Halloran, Michael 123
O'hAnnracháin, Eoghan 1, 2, 3, 10
O'Hara, Bishop of Scranton 321
O'Hara, Charles 326
O'Hara, Jim 181-2
O'Hara, John 359
O'Hara, Maureen 351, 353
O'Hare, Edward 331
O'Hare, Gerry 571
O'Hare International Airport, Chicago 331
O'Hartegan, Father Mathew 572
O'Higgins, Ambrosio 603-4
O'Higgins, General Bernardo 604, 605, 643
O'Higgins, Kevin xiii
Ohio 315
O'Kane, Maggie 103
O'Keeffe, Tim 146-7
O'Kelly, Colonel Antonio 67
O'Kelly, J.J. 606-7
O'Kelly, J.J. (Sceilig) 465
Okinawa 330
O'Laighin, Padraig 380
Olcott, Sydney 350
O'Leary, Daniel Florence 605
O'Leary, Dave 127
O'Leary, Denis 95, 98
O'Leary, Joseph 648
O'Leary, Michael 531
O'Leary, Paul 220, 221
O'Leary, Father Sean 551, 552-3
Olongapo, near Manila, Philippines 507
Olympia exhibition centre, 209
Omagh bombing 170

O'Mahoney, General 34
O'Mahoney, John 390, 391
O'Mahony, Ambassador 34
O'Malley, chieftain 62
O'Meachair, Gearoid xiii, 149, 156, 160
O'Neill, Arturo 66
O'Neill, Billy 224
O'Neill, Brendan 127
O'Neill, Eugene 358
O'Neill, Father 602
O'Neill, Felix 66
O'Neill, General 34
O'Neill, Hugh 61, 65, 67, 74, 84, 87
O'Neill, Colonel John 392
O'Neill, Father Kevin 615, 616, 618-19, 635, 642
O'Neill, Martin 127
O'Neill, General Owen Roe 81
O'Neill, Shane 63
O'Neill, Captain Terence 259
O'Neill, Terence 175
O'Neill, Tip 265-6, 463
Onitcha Cathedral 540
Ono, Yoko 19
Onslow township, Canada 396
Ontario 370, 373, 387, 391, 394, 399, 406, 408, 412
Operation Understanding 301
Orabi, Ahmed 564
Orange Order/Orangeism xiii, 138, 183, 184, 187-90, 202, 231, 396-401, 498, 499, 550, 553
Orange Riots (1870, 1871) 285
Orangemen 28, 61, 138, 139, 140, 176, 187, 244, 248, 335, 385, 394, 426, 493, 503-4, 565
Order of Poor Servants of God 44
Order of the Star Spangled Banner 280
Oregon trail 261
O'Reilly, Marshal Alejandro 643
O'Reilly, Count Alexander 66
O'Reilly, Art 363
O'Reilly, Bill (Tiger) 476
O'Reilly, Cameron 481
O'Reilly, Cleo 519-20
O'Reilly, General 34
O'Reilly, John 52-3
O'Reilly, John Boyle 268, 278, 293, 329, 345, 449
O'Reilly, Peter 263
O'Reilly, P.J. 485
O'Reilly, Tony 131, 132, 176, 363, 481, 483, 500, 501, 551, 593
Organisation of African Unity 513
Organization for Economic Cooperation and Development (OECD) xv, 43, 44, 662

O'Riordan, Conor 210, 211
Ormond, Paul 471, 479
O'Rourke, Jim 213
Orpen, Sir William 344-5, 516
Orr, Sir David 176
Orr, John Sayers ('Angel Gabriel') 234, 235-6
Osborne, Carole 580-1
Osborne, Cedric 580-1
Osborne, Roger 579
Osborne, Walter 344
Oscar Wilde pub, Berlin 56
O'Shannon, Cathal 70
O'Shaughnessy, Hugh 642-3
O'Shea, Conor 181
O'Shea, Dan 455
O'Shea, Jerome 181
O'Shea, John 104, 106, 512
O'Shea, Kitty 47
Osian 361
Ossory 46
O'Sullevan, Peter 127
O'Sullivan, Annunciata 598
O'Sullivan, Brian 545, 546
O'Sullivan, chieftain 62
O'Sullivan, Brother de Lellis 597, 598
O'Sullivan, Fergal 473
O'Sullivan, Humphrey 120
O'Sullivan (Irish writer) 69
O'Sullivan, Jean Baptiste 37
O'Sullivan, Colonel Sir John 32
O'Sullivan, Sister Joseph Teresa 542
O'Sullivan, Mary Kenny 313
O'Sullivan, Sonia 542
O'Sullivan, Timothy 386
O'Sullivan, Tyrone 212
O'Sullivan Beare 66, 70
O'Toole, John 408
Ottawa 393, 396, 406, 428
Ottawa Lumber Association 403
Ottawa River 370, 402, 405
Ottawa Valley 372, 374, 401, 429
Oudenade 31
Ouray, Colorado 320
Out of Africa (film) 530, 531
Overlack, Peter 458
Owen, Archdeacon 565
Oxfam 514
Oxford English Dictionary 109
Oxford University 38, 175

Packenham, Thomas 436
Packer, Asa 321, 323
Paddy Foley's Irish Bar, Tokyo 659
Padua 24
Paisley 234, 236
Paisley, Reverend Ian Kyle 188, 191, 231,

232, 234, 235, 397, 565
Paisleyism 189
Pakenham, Thomas 513
Pakistan 506
Palatines 401
Pale, The 27, 62, 174, 285
Palladio, Andrea 78
Pallotine Order 546, 602, 615, 616, 617, 634, 635, 636
Palmerston, Lord 376
Panama 618
Panday, Basedo 592, 595
Paola, Queen of Belgium 94
Papen, Franz von 48
Paradise 341, 343
Paraguay 603, 606, 643
Paramatta 437
Paramount 350
Paris 40, 41, 43-5
  Irish College 38, 44
Paris Revolution (1848) 40
Paris, Treaty of (1763) 386
Parish, Charles 321, 323
Parke, Surgeon-Major 564
Parkes, Gerard 411
Parkes, Henry 449
Parkhead, Glasgow 252
Parkin, Graham 433
Parles, John 599
Parma, Duchy of 77
Parnell, Charles Stewart 47, 168, 219, 228, 313, 338, 423, 625, 656, 664
Parnellism 237
Partnership for Peace 98
Partridge Island 373, 376
Passionate Fathers 617, 635, 642
Pataki, George A. 348, 349, 350
Paterson, Andrew Barton 448
Patrician Order 540
Patrick, St 13, 15, 16, 22, 40, 66, 69, 114, 215, 247, 306, 408, 582, 637, 641
Patrick, Vincent 359
Patterson, Lindsay 248
Paul, Father 57
Paul VI, Pope 302
Paul O'Dwyer Peace and Justice Award 271
Paul of Tarsus 14
Peace Process xiii, xvi, xvii, 5, 18, 46, 84, 99, 110, 113, 114, 125, 131, 135, 177, 209, 247, 249, 251, 271, 303, 323, 331, 344, 379, 431, 464, 478, 485, 498, 607, 642, 656, 662-3, 664
Peace Tower, Peace Park, Mesen (Messines) 94
Pearse, Padraig 51, 219, 223, 635, 640
Pearson, Drew 287

Peel, Sir Robert 118, 119
'Peep O Day Boys' 183
Pemisapan, King of the Indians 255
Peninsular campaign 327
Penn, Sean 351
Pennsylvania 259, 260, 320, 321, 323, 327
Pennsylvania Packet 253
Pentecostalists 564
Pentridge prison, Victoria 432
Performing Rights Society 92
Peron, Eva 619-20
Peron, Isabella 620
Peron, Juan 619, 620
Peronne 22
Perry, Admiral Mathew C. 325, 646, 650
Perry, Oliver 325
Perth 449
Perth Arts Festival 481
Peru/Peruvians 538, 604, 605, 624, 626
Peterborough district, Lake Ontario 374
Peterloo massacre 202
Peto, Brassey and Betts 382
Petrov, Vladimir 472
Phelan, Francis M.C. 388
Phibbs, Sir Charles 219
Philadelphia 221, 255, 259, 260, 279, 280,
  281, 288-9, 312, 315
Philadelphia Athletics 364
Philadelphia Folk Festival 355
Philip, HRH The Duke of Edinburgh 593
Philip II, King of Spain 61, 63
Philip III, King of Spain 63, 66, 80, 94
Philip IV, King of Spain 63
Philip V, King of Spain 34
Philippines 330, 504, 506-7, 645, 646
Philomena, Sister 551
Phoenix Park, Dublin 57
Phuket, Thailand 645
Picardy 4, 21, 22
Piccadilly Advice Centre 132
Pickett, General George Edward 329
Pigeon, Don 381
Pike, William 529-30
Pilger, John 480
Pillars of Hercules 18
Pillon, Eoin 663
Pinkerton, Allan 323
Pinkerton Detective Agency 322
Pinto-Teixeira, José 107
Pittsburg 260, 315, 318
Pittsburgh Catholic 317
Pittsburgh Steelers 363
Pittsburgh Symphony Orchestra 355
Pittsburgh Three Rivers Festival 355
Pius IX, Pope 86, 445, 527
Pius V, Pope 64
Plaid Cymru 225

Plant Mari (film) 216
Plas Gwynfryn 219
Plate River 602, 603, 622, 629
Plunkett, Joseph 51, 663
Plunkett, Oliver, Archbishop of Armagh
  64, 82, 84
Plunkitt, George Washington 276-7, 278
Plymouth, Montserrat 578
Poe, Edgar Allan 260
Poepping, Hilde 52
Pogues 41, 127, 130
Point St Charles 381
Polding, Bishop John Bede 440
Polk, James 260
Pondicherry 35
Pookie Night 594
Poor Laws 120, 657
Port Glasgow 235
Port of Spain, Trinidad 585, 586, 590, 591,
  592, 593
Port Talbot 213
Portadown, County Armagh 183, 188
Portarlington 28
Porter, William 564
Portillo, Michael 124
Portlaoise jail 337
Portrush 42
Portsmouth 160
Portugal xii, 603, 605
Positively Irish Action on AIDS 147
Post Office Tower bombing 124
Potawatomi Indians 363
Pound, Ezra 651
Powderly, Terence 298, 314, 318
Power, Billy 150
Power, Bishop Michael 381, 426-7
Power, Tyrone 355
Power, Vince 129-30
Powers, Stephanie 535
Prague 38-9
Prendergast, Jim 276
Prendergast, Thomas 'T. J.' 278
Prendergast, Tom 276
Prendeville, Noreen 532
Presbyterian Baptists 564
Presbyterianism xi, xii, 168, 187, 229, 244-
  7, 254, 504
Presentation Order 185, 591-2, 593, 597
President's Commission on Organised
  Crime 291
Press Complaints Commission 194
Press Council 170
Prest, Linda 554
Preston, General Thomas 81
Pretoria 554
Prevention of Terrorism Act 110-13, 126,
  135-6, 141, 150-2, 154, 165, 177, 198,

Sweeney, Sean 46
Swift, John 89, 90
Swift, Jonathan 651, 654
Switzerland 13
Sydney 437, 440, 458, 477, 485-6
Sydney Harbour 435, 447, 463
Sydney Morning Herald 463, 481
Sykes, Sir Christopher 13
Sylvery, Father Noel 546-7
Synge, John Millington 40, 71, 178, 356, 361, 597, 649
Synnott, Richard 80

Taaffe, Father Joe 160, 200
Tain journal 664
Talbot, Monsignor 590
Talbot de Malahide, Colonel 489-90
Tallaght 25
Tamborini, Pietro 82
Tammany Hall 275-8, 281, 285, 286, 287
Tammany Society 277
Tanzania 511, 519, 520
Tanzanian Refugee Camp 520, 521-3
Tara Copthorne hotel, Kensington 663
Tara mine, County Meath 413
Tara Television Company 179
Tarian y Gweithiwr (The Workman's Shield) 222
Tarrant, Liam 161
Taschereau, Dr 298
Tasman, Abel 489
Tasmania (previously Van Diemens Land) 448, 458, 461, 549
Taylor, George 259
Taylor, Kevin 202
Taylor, Lorette 358
Taylor, Peter 169
Taylor, General Zachery 609, 610
Teatro de la Comedia, Madrid 71
Temm, Peter 499
Templeman's fish company 415
Tennant, Reverend William 259
Termonfeckin, County Louth 264
Terror, the (France) 38, 44
Terry (wine producer) 68
Tetuan, Dukes of 67, 68, 71
Tewodros II, Emperor 509
Texas 408, 626
Texas Rangers 261
Thatcher, Margaret, Baroness 113, 124, 134, 174, 210, 266, 348
Thayer, Father Karl 292
Theresa, Sister 126
Theresa of Calcutta, Mother 534
Therry, Father John Joseph 440
Theuderic II, King 21
Thiepval 6

Thiery, Father 383
Third Reich 52
Thirty Years War 28, 81
Thomas di Hibernia 9
Thompson, John 251, 252
Thoreau, Henry 609
Thornton, Matthew 259
Thurnysen, Rudolph 51
Tiernan, Father 585
Timaru, New Zealand 493
Times, The 189, 285, 348
Timmoney, John 288
Timmons, Father Larry 505
Tin-pan Alley 354
Tinney, Martin 211
Tipperary 403, 409, 417
TMA (Tony Meehan Associates) 247
Toal, Martin 80-1, 470
Toal, Timothy 470
Tobin, Brian 68, 409, 428
Tobin, Father 216
Tocqueville, Alexis de 40
Today programme 177
Toibin, Colm 479
Tokyo 18, 453, 644-9, 653, 657, 664
Tokyo St Patrick's Day Emerald Ball 645, 649
Tom, Brother 102
Tone, Theobald Wolfe 37, 48, 313, 400
Tonquin 513
Toowong 465
Topajovic, Slavko 107
Toronto 372, 378, 379, 380, 394, 398, 401, 407, 410, 411, 664
  Ireland Fund 379
  Irish Centre 379
Toronto Globe 392
Toronto Globe and Mail 411, 663
Toronto Life 410
Torres, Camillio 620
Torrione vineyard episode 86
Torvill, Jayne 102
Totnan, St 23
Tottenham, Charles 36
Toulouse rugby team 666
Tour de France 40
Tournai 38
Tower of Hercules, La Corona 61
Tower Mine Project 212
Tracey, Spencer 359
Tradeston Gasworks 243
Tralee, County Kerry 429
Tramore racecourse 130
Transport and General Workers Union 192
Transport Workers' Union 319
Travers, Mary 411